Lecture Notes in Artificial Intelligence 2070

Subseries of Lecture Notes in Computer Science
Edited by J. G. Carbonell and J. Siekmann

Lecture Notes in Computer Science
Edited by G. Goos, J. Hartmanis and J. van Leeuwen

Springer
Berlin
Heidelberg
New York
Barcelona
Hong Kong
London
Milan
Paris
Singapore
Tokyo

László Monostori József Váncza
Moonis Ali (Eds.)

Engineering of Intelligent Systems

14th International Conference on Industrial
and Engineering Applications of
Artificial Intelligence and Expert Systems, IEA/AIE 2001
Budapest, Hungary, June 4-7, 2001
Proceedings

Springer

Series Editors

Jaime G. Carbonell,Carnegie Mellon University, Pittsburgh, PA, USA
Jörg Siekmann, University of Saarland, Saarbrücken, Germany

Volume Editors

László Monostori
József Váncza
Intelligent Manufacturing and Business Processes
Computer and Automation Research Institute
Hungarian Academy of Sciences
Kende utca 13-17, 1111 Budapest, Hungary
E-mail:{laszlo.monostori/vancza}@sztaki.hu

Moonis Ali
Southwest Texas State University
Department of Computer Science
601 University Drive, San Marcos, TX 78666-4616, USA
E-mail: ma04@swt.edu

Cataloging-in-Publication Data applied for

Die Deutsche Bibliothek - CIP-Einheitsaufnahme

Engineering of intelligent systems : proceedings / 14th International Conference on Industrial and Engineering Applications of Artificial Intelligence and Expert Systems, IEA/AIE 2001, Budapest, Hungary, June 4 - 7, 2001. László Monostori ... (ed.). - Berlin ; Heidelberg ; New York ; Barcelona ; Hong Kong ; London ; Milan ; Paris ; Singapore ; Tokyo : Springer, 2001

(Lecture notes in computer science ; Vol. 2070 : Lecture notes in artificial intelligence)
ISBN 3-540-42219-6

CR Subject Classification (1998): I.2, F.1, F.2, I.5, F.4.1, D.2

ISBN 3-540-42219-6 Springer-Verlag Berlin Heidelberg New York

Springer-Verlag Berlin Heidelberg New York
a member of BertelsmannSpringer Science+Business Media GmbH

http://www.springer.de

Typesetting: Camera-ready by author, data conversion by PTP Berlin, Stefan Sossna
Printed on acid-free paper SPIN 10781682 06/3142 5 4 3 2 1 0

Preface

"What I cannot create I do not understand."
Richard P. Feynman

The success of engineering work depends on the recognition and use of several synergic factors. While the analytic approach is the key to solving some well-defined subproblems, creativity helps us to free ourselves of prejudices and to find useful analogies. Moreover, critical thinking opens up the way to argumentation with inexact premises and rules. While engineering is based on such complex mental features, it is perhaps more transparent than some other human activities: its world is that of man-made artifacts that should be useful in a broad sense of the word.

This leads us to our belief that in consideration of the advancements in *Engineering of Intelligent Systems* one may have a proper view of the state of research in the whole of Artificial Intelligence (AI). Knowledge gleaned here is valid not only in this particular application area but provides valuable hints to all perspectives of AI theory and its potential for solving other problems as well.

Having recognized the above features of engineering problem solving, the *International Society of Applied Intelligence (ISAI)*, more than a decade ago, initiated a series of conferences named *Industrial & Engineering Applications of Artificial Intelligence & Expert Systems (IEA/AIE)*. The Hungarian AI community was honored by the invitation of the ISAI to organize and host the IEA/AIE 2001 conference (June 4–7, 2001, Budapest, Hungary), which is the 14th in the series.

The Call for Papers announcement attracted many researchers and engineers from all over the world. A total of 140 papers was submitted and 104 – representing all continents – were selected for presentation at this conference and are included in these proceedings. Main areas of the AI research and different application domains are represented in the papers that are arranged in conference sections / book chapters as follows: Search, Knowledge Representation, Model-Based Reasoning, Machine Learning, Data Mining, Soft Computing, Evolutionary Algorithms, Distributed Problem Solving, Expert Systems, Pattern and Speech Recognition, Vision, Language Processing, Planning and Scheduling, Robotics, Autonomous Agents, Design, Control, Manufacturing Systems, Finance and Business, Software Engineering, and Tutoring.

In addition to ISAI, the main sponsor of the conference, our special thanks are due to the American Association for Artificial Intelligence (AAAI); the Association for Computing Machinery (ACM/SIGART); the Canadian Society for Computational Studies of Intelligence (CSCSI); the European Coordinating Committee for Artificial Intelligence (ECCAI); the European Research Consortium for Informatics and Mathematics (ERCIM); the Hungarian Academy of Sciences (HAS); the Institution of Electrical Engineers (IEE); the International Neural

Network Society (INNS); the Japanese Society of Artificial Intelligence (JSAI); the Ministry of Education, Hungary (OM); and the Southwest Texas State University (SWT) who all supported the 14th IEA/AIE conference.

We wish to thank the members of the International Program Committee, especially those who played specific roles: Soundar Kumara (Program Co-chair), Khosrow Kaikhah (Publicity Chair) and Gusztáv Hencsey (Local Organization Chair). We would also like to thank all the authors and referees for their contribution and efforts which made IEA/AIE 2001 possible.

Last but not least, we would like to express our gratitude to Mrs. Mariann Kindl, Congress Secretary, and Mrs. Cheryl Morriss (SWT) for their enthusiastic and unflagging contributions.

March 2001

László Monostori
József Váncza
Moonis Ali

Organization

The IEA/AIE 2001 conference was organized by the Computer and Automation Research Institute of the Hungarian Academy of Sciences in cooperation with AAAI, ACM/SIGART, CSCSI, ECCAI, ERCIM, HAS, IEE, INNS, JSAI, SWT.

Chairs

General Chair:	Moonis Ali (USA)
Program Chair:	László Monostori (Hungary)
Program Co-chair:	Soundar Kumara (USA)
Local Chair:	József Váncza (Hungary)
Publicity Chair:	Khosrow Kaikhah (USA)
Local Organization Chair:	Gusztáv Hencsey (Hungary)

Program Committee

F. Anger (USA)
D. Barschdorff (Germany)
F. Belli (Germany)
I. Bratko (Slovenia)
P. Brezillon (France)
B.G. Buchanan (USA)
K.H. Chang (USA)
P.W.H. Chung (United Kingdom)
L. Cser (Hungary)
A.P. del Pobil (Spain)
G. Dini (Italy)
T. Dobrowiecki (Hungary)
R. Engels (Germany)
R. Fenton (Canada)
G.F. Forsyth (Australia)
I. Futó (Hungary)
L. Giles (USA)
P. Groumpos (Greece)
H.W. Guesgen (New Zealand)
M.T. Harandi (USA)
J.P. Haton (France)
G. Horváth (Hungary)
I. Inasaki (Japan)
L. Kóczy (Hungary)
A. Kusiak (USA)
S.R.T. Kumara (USA)
S. Linnainmaa (Finland)
R.L. Loganantharaj (USA)
A. Márkus (Hungary)
M.M. Matthews (USA)
D. Mitra (USA)
Y.L. Murphey (USA)
V. Prabhu (USA)
H. Prade (France)
F. Sebastiani (Italy)
M. Shpitalni (Israel)
R. Teti (Italy)
S. Tzafestas (Greece)
P. Valckenaers (Belgium)
T. Vámos (Hungary)
H. Van Brussel (Belgium)
F.J.A.M. Van Houten (The Netherlands)
G. Widmer (Austria)

Auxiliary Reviewers

A. Ekárt (Hungary)
J. Fürnkranz (Austria)
L. Gulyás (Hungary)
U. Loerch (New Zealand)
R. Rodrigues (USA)
C. Schittenkopf (Austria)
U. Straccia (Italy)
P. Szolgay (Hungary)

Sponsoring Institutions

International Society of Applied Intelligence (ISAI)

European Research Consortium for Informatics and Mathematics (ERCIM)
Hungarian Academy of Sciences
Ministry of Education, Hungary

Table of Contents

Search

Knowledge Representation

Model-Based Reasoning

Machine Learning

Data Mining

Soft Computing

Evolutionary Algorithms

Distributed Problem Solving

Expert Systems

Pattern and Speech Recognition, Vision

Language Processing

Planning and Scheduling

Robotics

Autonomous Agents

Design

Control

Manufacturing Systems

Finance and Business

Software Engineering

Tutoring

Solving Network Synthesis Problems Using Ant Colony Optimisation

Marcus Randall[1] and Elliot Tonkes[2]

[1] School of Information Technology
Bond University, QLD 4229
[2] Department of Mathematics
University of Queensland, QLD 4067

Abstract. Ant colony optimisation is a relatively new meta-heuristic search technique for solving optimisation problems. To date, much research has concentrated on solving standard benchmark problems such as the travelling salesman problem, quadratic assignment problem and the job sequencing problem. In this paper, we investigate the application of ant colony optimisation to practical telecommunication design and synthesis problems having real-world constraints. We consider a modelling approach suitable for ant colony optimisation implementation and compare the results to the simulated annealing meta-heuristic.

Keywords: Ant colony optimisation, autonomous agents, heuristic search and telecommunications

1 Introduction

The Ant Colony Optimisation (ACO) [10] paradigm has been successfully applied to standard benchmark problems such as the travelling salesman problem (TSP) and quadratic assignment problem (QAP) with varying degrees of effectiveness [10]. Many practical optimisation problems have constraints that are difficult for ACO algorithms to process. New methods and extensions of ACO therefore have great importance in the development of this meta-heuristic technique. We examine Ant Colony System (ACS) [9] as a representative ACO technique. Our findings are generalisable to other members of the ACO family.

In this paper, we introduce a network synthesis problem that has application in the design of telecommunications networks [2,3]. It is a highly constrained problem for which it can be difficult to even find feasible solutions [16]. We investigate a modelling approach for this problem that is suitable for processing by ACO. In addition, we explore the more general issues of how ACO can be adapted to solve difficult problems. According to Schoonderwoerd, Holland, Bruten and Rothcrantz [20], "Extending ant-like algorithms to situations like telecommunication networks which are not found in nature will also increase our understanding of the abstract and general abilities of such algorithms over and above those applications found in nature".

L. Monostori, J. Váncza, and M. Ali (Eds.): IEA/AIE 2001, LNAI 2070, pp. 1–10, 2001.

This paper is organised as follows. Sect. 2 describes the ACS algorithm while Sect. 3 outlines the network synthesis problem. Sect. 4 defines the ACS modelling approach and the strategy that we will use to solve the problem. From this, we present the results in Sect. 5 and the conclusions in Sect. 6.

2 ACS

ACS is a constructive population based meta-heuristic search technique for optimisation problems. It is designed to simulate the ability of ant colonies to determine shortest paths to food. Although individual ants possess few capabilities, their operation as a colony is capable of complex behaviour. Ant system techniques expand upon existing paradigms which simulate natural behaviour such as neural networks, simulated annealing (SA) and genetic algorithms.

Within each step of an ACO process, each ant adds an *element* to its solution until some *termination condition* is satisfied. In terms of the TSP [14], the QAP [5] and the job sequencing problem (JSP) [12], "element" and "condition" are outlined in Table 1.

Table 1. "Elements" and "Condition" for the TSP, QAP, JSP.

Problem	*Element*	*Condition*
TSP	an edge	until a Hamiltonian tour is constructed
QAP	a facility	until all the facilities have been placed
JSP	a job	until all jobs have been assigned an order

Using this general terminology, the basic operations of ACS can be described thus. In discrete time steps, allow each ant to add one element to its solution until the termination condition is satisfied. After adding an element, the amount of *pheromone* on that element is modified. Pheromone is a scalar quantity that allows ants to communicate with one another about the utility of an element. The accumulated strength of pheromone on element i is denoted by $\tau(i)$.

At the commencement of each time step, (1) is used to select the next element s to add to the solution. The elements that are still legal to add to the solution (i.e. those that won't break constraints) by ant k at step r are indexed by $J_k(r)$. $\eta(s)$ is the measure of how good element s would be for the solution, in other words an incremental cost measure. In terms of the TSP, this would correspond to the distance between two cities.

Equation (1a) is a highly greedy selection technique favouring the best combination of pheromone level and cost. In order to ensure that other elements are incorporated into an ant's solution, (2) selects elements probabilistically. This is essential to avoid premature convergence to a small group of elite solutions. The use of each equation is governed by the q_0 parameter. q is a uniform random number.

$$s = \begin{cases} \arg\max_{s \in J_k(r)} \left\{\tau(s)[\eta(s)]^{\beta}\right\} \text{ if } q \leq q_0 & \text{(a)} \\ \text{Equation 2} & \text{otherwise} \end{cases} \tag{1}$$

$$p_k(r,s) = \begin{cases} \frac{\tau(s)[\eta(s)]^{\beta}}{\sum_{u \in J_k(r)} \tau(u)[\eta(u)]^{\beta}} & \text{if } s \in J_k(r) \\ 0 & \text{otherwise} \end{cases} \tag{2}$$

For minimisation (maximisation) problems, the parameter β is negative (positive) so that smaller (larger) costs of each s are favoured. The pheromone level of the selected element is updated according to the local updating rule (3).

$$\tau(s) \leftarrow (1-\rho) \cdot \tau(s) + \rho \cdot \tau_0 \tag{3}$$

Where:

ρ is the local pheromone decay parameter. $0 < \rho < 1$.
τ_0 is the initial amount of pheromone deposited on each of the elements.

Upon conclusion of an iteration (i.e. all ants have constructed a feasible solution), elements that compose the best solution are rewarded with an increase in their pheromone level. Mathematically, (4) relates the new pheromone level to the old.

$$\tau(s) \leftarrow (1-\gamma) \cdot \tau(s) + \gamma \cdot \Delta\tau(s) \tag{4}$$

Where:

$\Delta\tau(s)$ is used to reinforce the pheromone level of the elements that compose the best solution found (see (5)). L is the cost of the best solution[1] and Q is a constant that is usually set to 100 [8].
γ is the global pheromone decay parameter, $0 < \gamma < 1$ and

$$\Delta\tau(s) = \begin{cases} \frac{Q}{L} & \text{if } s \in \text{ solution by the best ant} \\ 0 & \text{otherwise} \end{cases} \tag{5}$$

2.1 ACO and Difficult Problems

Much ACO research has focused on problems such as the TSP and QAP that do not have difficult constraints. This is mainly due to the fact that this meta-heuristic is relatively new and research has therefore been directed at defining and exploring the technique. However, ACO is increasingly being used to solve more difficult problems. This section provides an overview of ACO for telecommunication related problems.

Schoonderwoerd et al. [20] use a highly abstracted ant system for solving problems involving the routing of telephone calls between origin and destination nodes using a switched network. The networks they study are not capable

[1] The best solution can either be defined as the *global-best* (the best solution found in all iterations) or the *iteration-best* (the best solution found in the current iteration).

of connecting all calls at a given time so the objective becomes a system that minimises the number of lost calls. In their ant based solution, ants operate independently of the calls. Each ant travels between an origin and a random destination node based on a function of pheromone, distance and node congestion. Calls are routed according the pheromone level on each neighbouring node. The link with the maximum pheromone is always chosen. This new approach compares favourably with existing mobile agent methods of British Telecom [20].

Di Caro and Dorigo [7] have designed an ACS to build forwarding tables for packet routing problems (such as those that occur on the Internet). The authors have shown that their system compares favourably with existing routing algorithms. Similar work has also been performed by White, Pagurek and Oppacher [23] except that separate ant colonies are used to determine the routes, allocate traffic to the routes and deallocate routes. No comparison to other algorithms was provided in this paper. In addition, preliminary work has also been carried out on routing with fiber optic cables [22].

3 The Network Synthesis Problem

The problem of network synthesis is common in the design of efficient telecommunications networks. The aim of the problem is to satisfy all traffic requirements at minimum cost between a set of nodes. For the network synthesis problem having n nodes, there are $2^{\frac{n(n-1)}{2}}$ possible topologies, i.e. trillions of possibilities for a network as small as 10 nodes. The information required to formulate the problem is the traffic demand between each origin and destination (O-D) pairs, and the cost function for carrying traffic on each (possible) link between nodes i and j.

Recent interest in the problem has been in the application of Genetic Algorithms (GAs). Work by Berry, Murtagh, Sugden and McMahon [2,3] has demonstrated this approach in which a GA is used to synthesise the network while a linear programme (LP) is used to allocate the traffic amongst the routes of the network. However, this approach has the potential to be inefficient due to the typically large LP component (though no empirical investigation was undertaken in Berry et al. [2,3]). A new approach by Randall, McMahon and Sugden [16] has used SA to solve the problem as a modified knapsack problem with very encouraging results. In this work, routes are precomputed and selected (using SA) to form the network. Other solution techniques have been described in Balakrishnan, Magnanti, Shulman and Wong [1], Gavish [11], Kershenbaum and Peng [13], Minoux [15] and Sharma, Mistra and Bhattacharji [21].

The network synthesis problem can be formulated mathematically using linear programming [2,3]. Let $\mathbf{G}$ be the set of all undirected graphs on n nodes with G a member of this set. We represent G by its upper triangular node-node adjacency matrix B with elements b_{ij}. The problem is to find a member G^* which minimises the cost of transporting required origin-destination (O-D) flows subject to specified link, node capacity, node degree and chain hop-limit constraints. The total bandwidth (flow) requirement on virtual path connections between O-D pair $p-q$ is given by F^{pq} (without loss of generality represented as an element of an upper triangular matrix). The partial flow along the rth route between node p and node q is denoted by h_r^{pq} and C_r^{pq} is the cost per unit flow on this route.

$$\underset{G \in \mathbf{G}}{\text{Minimise}} \sum_{p=1}^{n} \sum_{q>p} \sum_{r} C_r^{pq} h_r^{pq} \tag{6}$$

s.t.

$$f_{ij} = \sum_{p=1}^{n} \sum_{q>p} \sum_{r} a_{ij,r}^{pq} h_r^{pq} \qquad \forall i,j \tag{7}$$

$$\sum_{r} h_r^{pq} = F^{pq} \qquad \forall p,q \tag{8}$$

$$\frac{1}{2}\left[\sum_{p=1}^{n}(F^{pi} + F^{ip}) + \sum_{j \neq i} f_{ij}\right] \leq u_i^{max} \tag{9}$$

$$0 \leq f_{ij} \leq f_{ij}^{max} \qquad \forall i,j \tag{10}$$

$$\sum_{(i,j)} a_{ij,r}^{pq} \leq H^{max} \qquad \forall p,q,r \tag{11}$$

$$\sum_{j=1}^{n}(b_{ij} + b_{ji}) \leq d_i^{max} \qquad \forall i \tag{12}$$

$$0 \leq h_r^{pq} \qquad \forall p,q,r \tag{13}$$

Where:

n is the number of nodes.
C_r^{pq} is the cost per unit flow on route r between O-D pair $p-q$.
F^{pq} is the total bandwidth (flow) requirement between O-D pair $p-q$.
$a_{ij,r}^{pq}$ is 1 if the link $p-q$ exists on route r between nodes i,j, 0 otherwise.
f_{ij}^{max} is the upper bound on the available capacity (total flow) on the link (i,j).
u_i^{max} is the upper bound on total flow at node i. This flow comprises traffic originating at, terminating at and traversing node i.
H^{max} is the upper bound imposed on the number of links in a route (the hop limit).
h_r^{pq} is the amount of traffic routed between p and q on route r.

Equations (6) to (13) represent the model of the network synthesis problem. Equation (6) is the objective function in which the traffic costs along the routes are minimised. Equation (7) is used to calculate the total flow on each link. Constraint (8) ensures that the bandwidth is distributed amongst the appropriate routes. Constraint (9) ensures that the node capacities are not exceeded while (10) ensures that the link capacities are not exceeded. The hop-limit is preserved in (11) and the constraints that ensure that the nodes meet the node degree constraints are modeled in (12).

4 Application of ACS to Network Synthesis

We apply the idea that a set of traffic routes can be pre-computed before the application of an optimisation technique. This was first proposed in Randall et al. [16]. A route is a sequence of nodes between an origin and destination node and has a length not greater than the hop-limit. Fig. 1 shows a simple seven node network that has four routes. The set of possible routes can be large for moderately size problems, therefore techniques have been developed to reduce the size of the set.

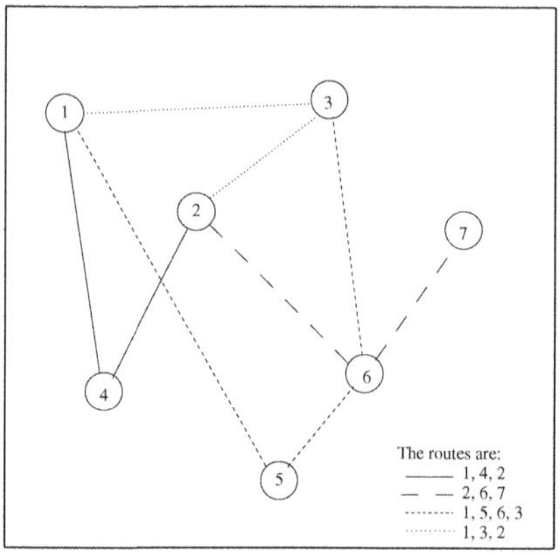

Fig. 1. An example network.

The pre-computed routes approach has several distinct advantages which are: hop limits are automatically satisfied and routes are feasible (i.e. there are no circuits or repeated nodes in the routes). The problem becomes one of progressively building up a set of routes until the requirements (constraints (7) - (13)) are met. In terms of the ant strategy, at each step of an iteration, each ant adds a new route (from the precomputed route set) to its network. The set $J_k(r)$ excludes the routes already present in the solution of ant k and those routes that would make the solution infeasible. This follows a *feasibility maintenance* approach that has been found to be successful in other meta-heuristics [17].

It can be more difficult to apply a feasibility maintenance approach to a constructive heuristic (such as ACO) than an iterative heuristic (such as SA and tabu search (TS)). This is because some constraints cannot be satisfied at each step/iteration of the algorithm. Consider the case where a constraint of the form $\sum_{i=1}^{N} C(x_i) > D$ is present in the problem model. Clearly in the beginning stages of the construction, the length of the solution vector is small and it is unlikely that this constraint will be satisfied. Hence, these types of constraints must be treated as special in the design and construction of ACO solvers. Only once these types of constraints have been satisfied can the algorithm consider the termination of element augmentation of a particular ant's solution. For the network synthesis problem, this type of constraint is the requirement that demand between a set of O-D pairs be satisfied (i.e. during the construction of a solution, not all O-D pairs will be satisfied). Other problem classes will require different and possibly creative approaches to dealing with these types of constraints. How this can be done in a generic manner is an open question.

For the network synthesis problem each ant terminates once it has constructed a network that satisfies the O-D requirements as well as the other constraints of the problem. Similarly ants are terminated (killed) if at any step of the algorithm, a feasible route cannot be added and the O-D requirements have not been met. This notion of termination of ants at various steps within an iteration of the algorithm (some of which return a feasible solution and some will not) is necessary for complex problems.

As there may be more than one route in a solution that services a particular O-D pair, methods need to be introduced for splitting the traffic amongst the routes. We have adopted the greedy approach outlined in Randall et al. [16]. This technique allocates traffic to routes based on the cost of the routes and runs in $O(p)$ time, where p is the size of the route set. The algorithm will allocate proportionally more traffic to cheaper routes.

The full set of routes for a practical size problem can be extremely large. Therefore we limit the size of the route sets according to a parameter that specifies a percentage of routes to form the pre-computed route set. These routes are chosen according to their cost (i.e. the cost of including the route if it was fully loaded with communication traffic). For instance, if 10% is specified, only 10% of the best routes for each O-D pair would be included in the route set. This corresponds to a simple candidate set approach [9] as the set of elements (routes) available for selection is reduced in order to make the search process more efficient.

5 Computational Experience

A set of problem instances have been generated with which to test the ACS solver (see Table 2). These are a subset of the problems that have been used in Randall et al. [17]. These problem instances have demand matrices that are 90% dense. This means that 90% of the O-D pairs have non-zero traffic requirements. Subsequently this should make it difficult to find good quality solutions to these problems. The problems used here (as well as a problem generator) are available at `http://www.it.bond.edu.au/randall/tele.exe`.

The size of the pre-computed route set for each problem is also varied in order to determine whether this factor has an effect on solution quality and runtime efficiency for the ACS. We use route subsets of 10%, 50% and 100% of the total number of routes available for each problem instance. The hop limit has been set to 3.

The computer platform used to perform the experiments is a Sun SPARC-station 4 running at 110 MHz. Each problem instance is run across 10 random

Table 2. Problem instances used in this study.

Name	Size(Nodes)	Best Known Cost [16]
tele5-1	5	1082
tele5-2	5	656
tele10-1	10	2982
tele10-2	10	1712

seeds. We use the following parameter settings: $\beta = 2$, $\gamma = 0.1$, $\rho = 0.1$, $m = 5$ (for $n = 5$) 10 otherwise, $q_0 = 0.9$ and iterations=2500.

The results are given in Table 3. The minimum (**Min**), average (μ), maximum (**Max**) and standard deviation (σ) measures are used to summarise the results.

Table 3. Results of running ACS on the test problems. CNS denotes "Could Not Solve" and means that the ACS could not construct a solution given the routes in the route set.

Problem	Route Size	Cost Min	μ	Max	σ
tele5-1	10%	CNS			
	50%	CNS			
	100%	1035	1035.6	1041	1.9
tele5-2	10%	902	902	902	0
	50%	902	902	902	0
	100%	656	656	656	0
tele10-1	10%	CNS			
	50%	3917	3970	4004	458.1
	100%	2822	2830.67	2843	10.97
tele10-2	10%	CNS			
	50%	1676	1701.5	1724	17.92
	100%	1541	1545.33	1548	3.8

Improved solutions are produced for three out of the four tested problem instances over the SA code given in Randall et al. [16]. SA and ACS give the same solutions for the problem tele5-2. For problem instance tele10-2, ACS consistently finds better solutions using a smaller route set (50%) than SA using a larger route set (100%). These performances suggest that ant based techniques have application to complex optimisation problems. However, the runtimes required to reach these solutions are significantly longer than for the SA implementation. Whereas SA produces very reasonable solutions to the 10 node problem within a few minutes, the ACS engine requires approximately a day.

6 Conclusions

This paper has presented an effective application of the ACO paradigm to a difficult network synthesis problem. In particular, we have shown that constraints can be processed by using a feasibility maintenance approach in which only elements that do not cause constraint violation are considered.

The ACS meta-heuristic described herein is capable of finding improved solutions to nearly all of the problems over the SA implementation described in Randall et al. [16]. The main disadvantage is the computational time required by ACS. The ACS implementation is significantly slower than the SA code running on the same computer architecture. To overcome efficiency problems, our research is now focusing on candidate set strategies [18] and parallel implementations [19].

The network synthesis problem has a low problem size (n) to search space size ratio. This means that for relatively small values of n, the search space is very large. The use of meta-heuristic approaches that examine various alternative elements at each step/iteration (such as ACO and TS) can lead to substantial performance degradation. To overcome this problem, appropriate candidate set strategies need to be devised. The candidate set strategy described within this paper is very simple. More effective sets need to be devised which limit the number of elements examined at any one step while not sacrificing quality. This is essential to effectively solve the network synthesis problem in computational time comparable to other heuristics.

References

1. Balakrishnan, A., Magnanti, T., Shulman, A. and Wong, R. (1991)"Models for Planning Capacity Expansion in Local Access Telecommunication Networks", Annals of Operations Research, vol. 33, pp. 239-284.
2. Berry, L., Murtagh, B., Sugden, S. and McMahon, G. (1995) "Application of a Genetic-based Algorithm for Optimal Design of Tree-structured Communications Networks", Proceedings of the Regional Teletraffic Engineering Conference of the International Teletraffic Congress, South Africa, pp. 361-370.
3. Berry, L., Murtagh, B., Sugden, S. and McMahon, G. (1997) "An Integrated GA-LP Approach to Communication Network Design," Proceedings of the 2nd IFIP Workshop on Traffic Management and Synthesis of ATM Networks, Canada.
4. Berry, L, Murtagh, B, McMahon, G. Randall, M. and Sugden, S. (1999) "Network Design with a Genetic Algorithm", **TR99-12** School of Information Technology, Bond University.
5. Burkard, R. (1984) "Quadratic Assignment Problems", *European Journal of Operational Research*, 15, pp. 283-289.
6. Colorni, A., Dorigo, M and Maniezzo, V., (1991) "Distributed Optimization by Ant Colonies", Proceedings of ECAL91, Elsevier, pp. 134-142.
7. Di Caro, G. and Dorigo, M. (1998) "Mobile Agents for Adaptive Routing", Proceedings of the 31st Hawaii International Conference on Systems Science, pp. 74-83.
8. Dorigo, M., Maniezzo, V. and Colorni, A. (1996) "The Ant System: Optimization by a Colony of Cooperating Agents", IEEE Transactions on Systems, Man and Cybernetics, 26, pp. 29-41.

9. Dorigo, M. and Gambardella, L. (1997) "Ant Colony System: A Cooperative Learning Approach to the Traveling Salesman Problem", IEEE Transactions on Evolutionary Computation, 1, pp. 53-66.
10. Dorigo, M and Di Caro, G. (1999) "The Ant Colony Optimization Meta-Heuristic", in Corne, D., Dorigo, M. and Glover, F. (eds), New Ideas in Optimization, McGraw-Hill, pp. 11-32.
11. Gavish, B. (1985) "Augmented Lagrangian based Algorithms for Centralised Network Design", IEEE Transactions on Communications, 33, pp. 1247-1257.
12. Glover, F. and Laguna, M. (1997) *Tabu Search*, Kluwer Academic Publishers, Boston, 402 pages.
13. Kershenbaum, A. and Peng, S. (1986) "Neighbor Finding Algorithms for CMST Customer Calculations," IEEE INFOCOM, Miami, Florida.
14. Lawler, E., Lenstra, J., Rinnoy Kan, A. and Shmoys, D. (1985) *The Traveling Salesman Problem: A Guided Tour of Combinatorial Optimization*, Wiley, Chichester, 465 pages.
15. Minoux, M. (1989) "Network Synthesis and Optimum Network Design Problem: Models, Solution Methods and Applications", Networks, 19, pp. 313-360.
16. Randall, M., McMahon, G. and Sugden, S. (1999) "A Simulated Annealing Approach to Communication Network Design", Journal of Combinatorial Optimization (to appear).
17. Randall, M. and Abramson, D. (2000) "A General Meta-heuristic based Solver for Combinatorial Optimisation Problems", Journal of Computational Optimization and Applications (to appear).
18. Randall, M. and Montgomery, J. (2001) "Candidate Set Strategies for Ant Colony Optimisation", Working paper
19. Randall, M. and Lewis, A (2000) "A Parallel Implementation of Ant Colony Optimisation", Submitted to the Journal of Parallel and Distributed Computing.
20. Schoonderwoerd, R., Holland, O., Bruten, J. and Rothcrantz, L. (1996) "Ant-based Load Balancing in Telecommunication Networks", Adaptive Behavior, 5, pp. 169-207.
21. Sharma, U., Mistra, K. and Bhattacharji, A. (1991) "Applications of an Efficient Search Techniques for Optimal Design of Computer Communication Networks", Micro Electronics and Reliability, 31, pp. 337-341.
22. Varela, G. and Sinclair, M. (1999) "Ant Colony Optimisation for Virtual-Wavelength-Path Routing and Wavelength Allocation", Proceedings of the Congress on Evolutionary Computation, Washington DC.
23. White, T., Pagurek, B. and Oppacher, F. (1998) "Connection Management by Ants: An Application of Mobile Agents in Network management", Proceedings of Combinatorial Optimization, Brussels.

A Combined Swarm Differential Evolution Algorithm for Optimization Problems

Tim Hendtlass

Center for Intelligent Systems and Complex Processes,
Swinburne University of Technology,
P.O. Box 218 Hawthorn AUSTRALIA 3122.
{thendtlass@swin.edu.au}

Abstract. An algorithm that is a combination of the particle swarm and differential evolution algorithms is introduced. The results of testing this on a graduated set of trial problems is given. It is shown that the combined algorithm out performs both of the component algorithms under most conditions, in both absolute and computational load weighted terms.

Introduction

Problems involving the minimization of real valued multi-model objective functions are common throughout science and industry. The aim of any algorithm used to achieve this objective is to find the absolute minimum as fast as possible with the lowest likelihood of prematurely converging to a local, but sub-optimal, minimum. It is also ideal for the algorithm to require few parameters and the values of those that it does use should ideally be problem independent.

All such algorithms require the value of the objective function to be determined for a collection of points in problem space. If this fitness evaluation is complex and time consuming it is advantageous to require as few points to be evaluated as possible.

Probably the best known algorithm for finding the optimum of such multi-model functions is the evolutionary algorithm (often called the genetic algorithm) [Holland 1975]. This algorithm, while very powerful, can exhibit slow convergence with many generations passing (and objective function evaluations done) without improvement. Two more recent algorithms are differential evolution [Storn and Price 96, Storn and Price 97] and particle swarm [Kennedy and Eberhart 1995].

Differential Evolution

Differential evolution is a population-based algorithm that creates new individuals one at a time. It is a greedy algorithm in which the new individual replaces the poorest performing population member provided the new individual outperforms it.
Combining three existing population members (M1, M2 and M3) drawn from the total population of Q creates new individuals. Let each individual have D dimensions (M_{xi} being the ith dimension of the xth individual in the population). Two parameters are

L. Monostori, J. Váncza, and M. Ali (Eds.): IEA/AIE 2001, LNAI 2070, pp. 11-18, 2001.

required for the algorithm, a fraction F (0-1, typically ~0.8) and a probability P (0-1 typically 0.5). Each of the dimensions of the new individual N are created separately, the ith dimension being created as:

$$\begin{aligned} Ni &= M_{1i} + F(M_{2i} - M_{3i}) \quad && \textit{if random}() <= P \qquad \textbf{(1)} \\ &= M_{1i} && \textit{otherwise} \end{aligned}$$

where *random()* is a random number in the range from 0 to 1.

With Q individuals there are Q^3 possible new individuals if the probability P = 1. Only some of these will have a better fitness than the current worst performing individual and be accepted into the population. As the worst fitness increases with each successive replacement, the proportion of acceptable new individuals would be expected to drop. This effect will be exacerbated as population diversity decreases and duplicate population members occur. The increased probability of duplicate individuals coupled with the reducing number of possible viable new individuals leads to a rapid decrease in diversity and may result in convergence to a sub optimal position.

If P is less than one then the number of unique offspring increases to $2^D Q^3$ as the effect of only varying some of the D dimensions is to also have a probability of exploring the 2^D-1 points around each of the points explored when all dimensions are modified. Using the common value for P of 0.5 all of these points are equally likely. As there is no *a priori* information on which to decide which points should be explored with a higher probability, there seems little point in varying P.

The algorithm has some obvious limitations. Firstly, it only explores discrete points being limited to those points that may result from the combination of any three of the current population members. Secondly, the algorithm suffers from the effect of winnowing. When a child is produced that is identical to an existing population member it may still be accepted into the population. Only modifying some of N1's dimension values will decrease the probability of this happening, but it will still happen. Once it has happened it will be more probable that one of the individuals at this common position will be chosen than an individual at any other position, which will reduce the range of possible offspring positions. If multiple individuals exist at each of two positions, the degree of commonality between their offspring will increase, this tending to produce more individuals at common positions. As the number of common positions increases so does this tendency to group, rapidly leading to a decrease in diversity. Hence this algorithm rapidly converges to one or a small number of points.

The Swarm Algorithm

The Swarm algorithm is also a population-based algorithm but is not a greedy algorithm as no individual is ever replaced. Rather, the individuals move through the problem space with a velocity that is updated with every step. The updated velocity is a combination of the previous velocity (V_T), a component towards the best position (B) found by any individual in the swarm so far, and a component towards a position (S) derived from comparing the relative performance of this individual with the performances of a number of other swarm members.

The new velocity (V_{T+t}) is:

$$V_{T+t} = MV_T + (1-M)(G(\frac{X-B}{t}) + (1-G)(\frac{X-S}{t})) \quad (2)$$

where M is the momentum, X is the current position of the individual and G sets the relative attention to be placed on the positions B and S. Both M and G are bounded to the range from 0 to 1. If M is large, the B and S positions have little effect; if G is large B has more influence than S. The parameter *t* is the time between updates and is required for dimensional consistency. It is usually taken to be unity.

Without the component towards S, the swarm tends to rush towards the first minimum found. An appropriately chosen S will cause the swarm to spread out and explore large areas of the problem space more thoroughly. Many ways of deriving S have been proposed. (See, for example, [Eberhart et al 1996]).

Mostly these involve an attraction to the position of the currently best performing of the *C* closest neighbours of this individual, where *C* can be any number from 1 to the swarm size. In the former case, the social interaction between the swarm members is limited to a knowledge of the single best position found so far, with the tendency for each individual to return to the best place it has found so far acting as a limited counter against premature convergence. If *C* is the number of members in the swarm, the last term in the equation above becomes but a scaled version of the previous term. Practically, *C* should not be at either extreme of the range (for further discussion, see [Kennedy and Eberhart 1999]). A value of *C* between the extremes requires that the appropriate swarm population members be identified, which can add to the computational cost.

In the work described in this paper the position S is derived in an effective, but computationally modest, way developed by this author. All other swarm members influence all other individuals but the magnitude of the influence decreases with both fitness and distance for a minimization problem. (For a maximization problem it would increase with fitness but decrease with distance.) Individuals within a nominated threshold distance are considered to be exploring the same region of space and make no contribution. An individual *j* is attracted to the position S_j whose components S_{ji} are calculated from D_{ni}, the distance along the ith axis from this individual to some other individual *n* in the swarm together with F_n, the fitness of individual *n*. The position S for individual *j* is defined by:

$$S_{ji} = \sum_{n=1}^{N} W_{ji} \quad where\ W_{ji} = \frac{1}{D_{ni}^2(1+F_n)}\ if\ D_{ni} \geq threshold,\ 0\ otherwise \quad (3)$$

In general, each particle will have a unique position S to which it is attracted giving the swarm good spreading characteristics. In the swarm algorithm individuals continuously search the problem space under the influence of both the entire swarm's current performance and prior history. The momentum component ensures that individuals are less likely to get trapped in a local minimum. In time, all swarm individuals will circle around one or a few points in problem space.

The Combined Algorithm (SDEA)

Individuals following the swarm algorithm search continuously with their exact path being influenced by both the current collective performances of the swarm members as well as the best point found so far. It is quite compatible with the differential evolution algorithm that moves individuals to discrete points each better than the last. In the SDEA algorithm each individual obeys the conventional swarm algorithm, but from time to time the differential evolution algorithm is run which may move one individual from a poorer area to a better area to continue the search. The individual moved retains its velocity.

Obviously, the ratio of the number of times the differential evolution algorithm is run compared to the number of runs of the swarm algorithm (T) will affect the overall performance. If T is very small, it is highly probable that only the swarm algorithm will be making any significant contribution. If T is large the disruptive effect of frequent spontaneous movement of individuals will effectively remove the swarm algorithms collective behaviour. The only significant contribution will, in all probability, come from the differential evolution algorithm – except at the end when few, if any, individuals will be moved by the DE algorithm owing to the high average performance of the population.

In the results given T is expressed as a percentage, the relative probability of running the DE algorithm cf. the swarm algorithm that is always run.

The Test Problems

A set of four problems has been used to test each individual and the combined algorithms. The two dimensional problem surfaces are shown in the figure below.

These functions are graduated in difficulty. The first two, the Goldstein-Price Function and the six hump camel back function, are taken from the De Jong set [De Jong 1975] and are reasonably simple to solve. The second two have been developed to test the ability of an algorithm to operate in regions with similar local minima. The Timbo2 function [Copland and Hendtlass 1998] has a series of narrow minima with only a slight advantage to the global minimum. It has proved a good problem for testing an algorithm's tendency to premature convergence. The final problem has a similar aim, with the global minimum being in a narrow region outside the wide basin of attraction formed by the combination of the other two local minima. It has the advantage of being able to be specified in any number of dimensions and thus can be used to test the dimensional sensitivity of an algorithm.

Results

The results of a number of tests using each of the four functions are shown in the table above. In all cases the swarm parameters used were M= 0.6 and G = 0.33; the DE parameters used were F = 0.8 and P = 0.5. The threshold distance was set, somewhat arbitrarily, at 0.1. All results reported come from 1000 repeats with initial random starting positions.

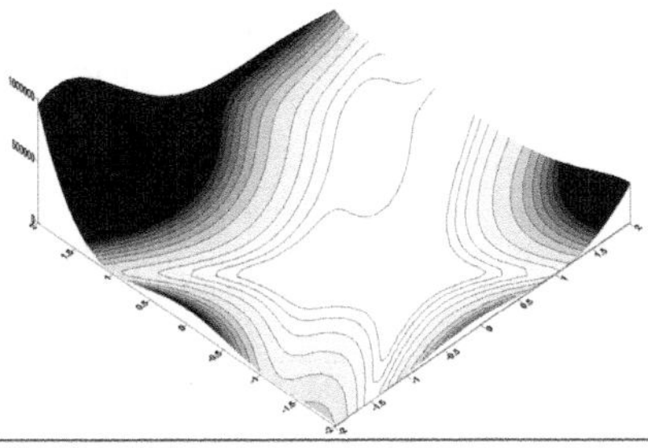

The Goldstein-Price Function

$1+(X_1+X_2+1)^{2*}$
$(19-14\ (X_1+X_2)+3(X_1+X_2)^2))*$
$(30+(2X_1-3X_2)^{2*}$
$(18-32X_1+12X_1^2+48X_2-36X_1X_2+27X_2^2)$

This function has a single minimum with a value of 0 at (-1,3). For this problem all individuals were initialised with each co-ordinate set to a value between –2 and 2.

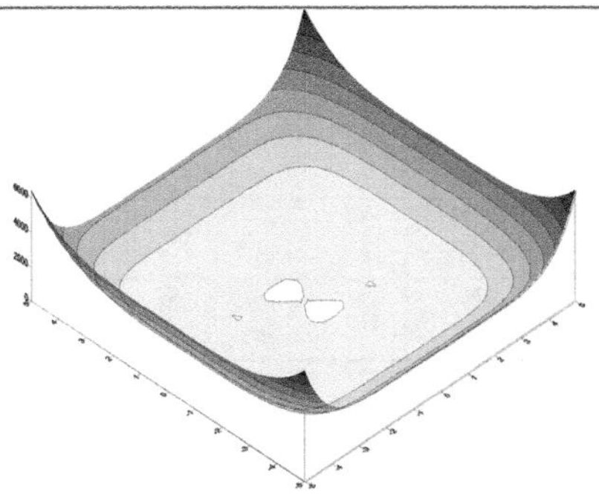

The six hump camel back function

$4X_1^2-4X_2^2+4X_2^4-2.1X_1^4+X_1^6/3+X_1X_2$

This function has two symmetrical minima with a value of –1.0316285 at (0.08983, -0.7126) and at (-0.08983, 0.7126).- For this problem all individuals were initialised with each co-ordinate set to a value between 5 and –5.

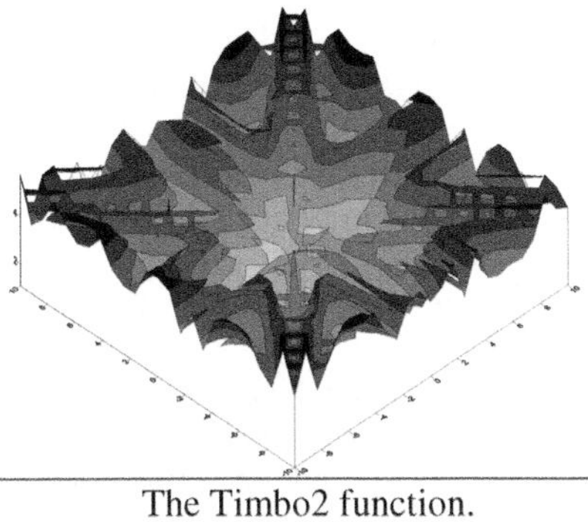

The Timbo2 function.

$1+((X_1-0.2)^2+(X_2-0.1)^2)^{0.25}-\cos(5\pi((X_1-0.2)^2+(X_2-0.1)^2)^{0.5}$

This function has a single minimum with a value of 0 at (0.2,0.1). For this problem all individuals were initialised with each co-ordinate set to a value between –10 and +10.

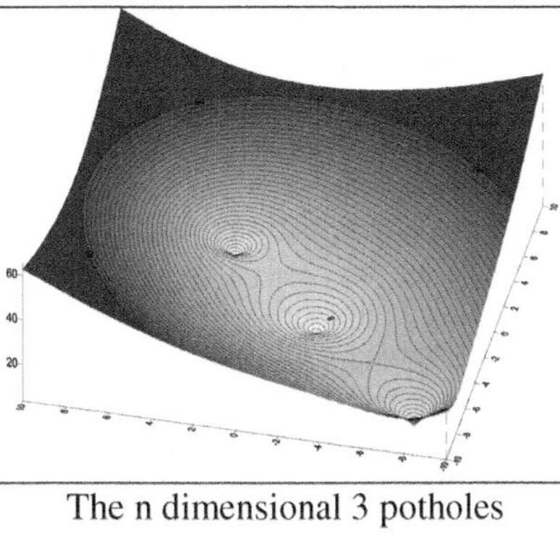

The n dimensional 3 potholes function.

$$\sqrt{\sqrt{\sum_{i=1}^{n}(X_i+8)^2}+0.1*\sqrt{\sum_{i=1}^{n}(X_i+2)^2}+0.2*\sqrt{\sum_{i=1}^{n}(X_1-3)^2}}$$

The surface above is for n = 2. Irrespective of n this function has a single minimum with a value of zero when each value of X = 3. For this problem all individuals were initialised with each co-ordinate set to a value between –10 and +10.

The four test problems used.

Problem (population)	Swarm only	DE only	Swarm + DE (T=0.25)	Swarm + DE (T=0.5)
Goldstein-Price (10)	999/57.6 /1.72	864/11.92 /1.10	1000/26.62 /3.01	1000/23.33 /2.86
Goldstein-Price (20)	-	994/9.14/4.11	-	-
Camel back (10)	998/93.53 /1.06	49/15.04 /0.01	981/114.7 /0.64	1000/55.96 /1.19
Camel back (20)	-	110/38.4 /0.01	-	-
Timbo2 (10)	145/255.5 /0.03	0/- /0	975/104.5 /0.68	1000/61.13 /1.09
Timbo2 (20)	-	64/74 /0.01	-	-
2D potholes (10)	999/16.62 /5.84	43/32.91 /0.01	1000/12.03 /6.65	1000/11.79 /5.65
2D potholes (40)	-	452/37.76 /0.04	-	-
4D potholes (10)	955/103.4 /0.79	0/- /0	982/78.29 /0.91	995/65.97 /0.97
4D potholes (80)	-	5/231 /0	-	-
6D potholes (10)	886/167.8 /0.43	0/- /0	900/158.9 /0.37	923/156.5 /0.34
6D potholes (120)	-	1/96 /0	-	-

Two performance measures were used. The first is the number of times the known minimum was found in the 1000 trials. It is the relevant performance measure if execution time and the number of evaluations are not of importance. The second performance measure is designed to reflect both the number of correct solutions and the number of evaluations taken. It is calculated as the number of successes divided by the average cycles (successes and failures). The higher the figure the better the performance, although the figures are only really directly comparable for different attempts at the same problem.

Except for the potholes function, each run was terminated when any individual had a fitness within 0.05 (Goldstein-Price) or 0.01 (Camel back and Timbo2) of the optimum fitness or 500 evaluation cycles had passed. The potholes functions were considered solved when any individual was within 0.1(2D), 0.3 (4D) or 0.5 (6D) of the optimum position or 500 evaluation cycles had passed. The choice of 500 evaluations for the cut off point was made after observation that, by that stage, it was almost certain that convergence had occurred for all populations and problems.

One cycle was one application of the swarm algorithm and/or DE to each member of the population. The three figures given for each run (e.g. 999/57.6/1.72) are the number of times the function was solved out of 1000 (the first performance measure described above), the average number of cycles to a solution (when solved) and the second performance measure. The differential evolution algorithm was run with two populations, the first the same as the population used for all other runs, the second with a population that met the guidelines for using DE [Price 99].

The Goldstein-Price function is a fairly simple function and the optimum could be found readily by all five approaches used here. The performance of differential evolution improved noticeably with the larger population. The average number of cycles for a successful attempt was far smaller for DE than for either swarm alone or swarm plus DE.

The Camel back function is a somewhat more difficult function and was a problem for the DE algorithm, even with the larger population. The combined algorithm slightly outperformed swarm alone for one of the T values used but was somewhat poorer for the other.

The Timbo2 function was designed to be hard due to the presence of many local minima that differ only slightly in value from the global minimum. Neither swarm nor the DE algorithms were very successful at this. The combination of the two algorithms dramatically improved the search performance.

The Timbo2 function may be considered too fractured to be able to reflect practical real life problems. The pothole function was developed to reflect real life problems with a gentle gradient of improving performance leading to three minima. The minimum at $x_i = -2$ is wider and will often trap any algorithm with a tendency to lose diversity rapidly when a minimum is found. The global minimum, however, is in the narrower region at $x_i=3$. The pothole function may be expressed in any number of integer dimensions and can be used to test the sensitivity of algorithms to the dimensionality of the problem space. Differential evolution did not perform well on this problem, especially when the number of dimensions exceeded two. The combined algorithm outperformed the swarm algorithm alone on the first performance measure, especially for four and six dimensions. However, the increased number of evaluations resulted in the swarm algorithm having the best results on the second performance measure.

Conclusions

An algorithm has been introduced that is a simple combination of two established algorithms and its performance tested on four optimization problems. Although the combined algorithm has one extra parameter (*T*) over the combined parameters of the two component algorithms, the improved performance seems to warrant this. While the optimum value for this new parameter is undoubtedly problem specific (as are the optimum values of all the other parameters), the value does not seem to be highly critical. Experience has shown that a value between 0.25 ands 0.5 seems to work well for all problems tried so far.

The new algorithm does increase the number of fitness evaluations required and as such, for problems with computationally demanding fitness evaluations it may be advantageous to stay with one of the component algorithms alone, in particular the swarm algorithm.

References

Copland and Hendtlass 1998. *An Evolutionary Algorithm with a Genetic Encoding Scheme.* Copland, H. C. and Hendtlass, T. Lecture Notes in Artificial Intelligence Vol. 1415 pp.632-639 Springer-Verlag Berlin. ISBN 3-540-64582-9

De Jong 1975. *Analysis of the Behavior of a Class of Genetic Adaptive Systems.* De Jong, K. A. Ph.D. Dissertation, Department of Computer and Communication Sciences, University of Michigan, Ann Arbor, MI, USA.

Eberhart et al 1996. Eberhart. R. C., Dobbins, P., Simpson, P. *Computational Intelligence PC Tools,* Academic Press, Boston.

Holland 1975. *Adaption in Natural and Artificial Systems.* Holland J.H. University of Michigan Press, Ann Arbor 1975.

Kennedy and Eberhart 1995. *Particle Swarm Optimization.* Kennedy, J and Eberhart. R.C, Proc. IEEE International Conference on Neural Networks, Perth Australia, IEEE Service Centre, Piscataway NJ USA IV:1942-1948

Kennedy and Eberhart 1999. *The Particle Swarm: Social Adaptation in Information-Processing Systems.* Chapter 25 in *New Ideas in Optimization.* David Corne, Marco Dorigo and Fred Glover Editors, McGraw-Hill Publishing Company, England 1999. ISBN 007 709506 5

Price, Kenneth. 1999. *An Introduction to Differential Evolution* Chapter 6 in *New Ideas in Optimization.* David Corne, Marco Dorigo and Fred Glover Editors, McGraw-Hill Publishing Company, England 1999. ISBN 007 709506 5

Storn, Rainer and Price, Kenneth 1996. *Minimizing the real functions of the ICEC'96 contest by Differential Evolution.* IEEE International Conference on Evolutionary Computation, Japan pp.842-844. IEEE press, New York 1996.

Storn, Rainer and Price, Kenneth (1997). *Differential Evolution – a Simple and Efficient Heuristic for Global Optimization over Continuous Spaces.* Journal of Global Optimization, 11(4) pp.341-359, December 1997. Kluwer Academic Publishers.

An Evolutionary Optimum Searching Tool

Zoltán Tóth[1] and Gabriella Kókai[2]

[1] Department of Informatics, University of Szeged
Árpád tér 2, H-6720 Szeged, Hungary
znt oth@inf.u-szeged.hu
Now visiting: Department of Computer Science, Programming Languages
Friedrich-Alexander University of Erlangen-Nürnberg

[2] Department of Computer Science, Programming Languages
Friedrich-Alexander University of Erlangen-Nürnberg
Martensstr. 3, D-91058 Erlangen, Germany
kokai@informatik.uni-erlangen.de

Abstract. This paper is an introduction to the *Generic Evolutionary Algorithms Programming Library (GEA)* system. The purpose of the *GEA* system is to provide researchers with an easy-to-use and extendable programming library which can solve optimization problems by means of evolutionary algorithms. *GEA* is implemented in the `ANSI C++` programming language and is designed in a way that enables users to integrate new methods and individual representation forms easily.[1]

Keywords: Evolutionary algorithms, programming library

Introduction

Engineering applications provide a wide range of optimization problems for people working in this area. In most cases, the different tasks require different programming environments to achieve the best results.

The purpose of *Generic Evolutionary Algorithms Programming Library* system is to provide researchers with an easy-to-use, widely applicable and extendable programming library which solves these tasks by means of evolutionary algorithms [3][5][9].

Evolutionary algorithms are general purpose function optimization methods which search for optima by making potential solutions compete for survival in a population. The better a potential solution is, the better chance it has to survive. The search space is explored by modifying these potential solutions by genetic operators observed in nature: generally mutation and recombination [10].

Evolutionary algorithms have (among others) the following two advantages over other optimization methods: first, in most cases they converge to global optima, and second, the usage of the black-box principle (which only requires knowledge about a function's input and output to perform optimisation on it)

[1] This work is supported by the Bayerisches Habilitationsförderpreis, the Deutscher Akademischer Austausch Dienst (DAAD) and Siemens

L. Monostori, J. Váncza, and M. Ali (Eds.): IEA/AIE 2001, LNAI 2070, pp. 19–24, 2001.

makes them easily applicable to functions whose behaviour is too complex to handle with other methods.

The *GEA* system contains algorithms for various evolutionary methods, implemented genetic operators for the most common representation forms for individuals, various selection methods, and examples on how to use and expand the library.

The implemented genetic operators, selection methods and evolutionary algorithms make the system easy-to-use even for beginners: If the user wants to solve a problem with *GEA* and the search space consists of, say, bit-strings or real vectors, then he/she only has to implement the problem-specific fitness function, set the parameters of the algorithm and start searching for the solution.

GEA is implemented in the `ANSI C++` programming language and the class hierarchy is designed in a way that enables users of the system to easily add new selection methods, representation forms for individuals or even evolutionary algorithms (e.g. evolutionary programming, steady-state GAs). The development and integration of new evolutionary algorithms will be soon supported by the *Evolution Algorithm Editor.*

One must admit that there exist a nice amount of programming libraries that deal with the problem of kinds of evolutionary algorithms [1][2][7][14]. *GEA* tries to be the 'alloy' of these libraries in a manner that it contains several methods and representation forms, so it can be used to solve a large amount of problems. Although there are functions in *GEA* (such as algorithms for ESs, the so-called meta-ES and the adaptation of the probability of the genetic operators [4]) which are supported only by a few other libraries.

In the following, Section 1 contains details of the *GEA* system: The class hierarchy and the purpose of the classes. Section 2 describes *GREDEA*, an application of *GEA*. Finally in Section 3 a summary of present and future work is given.

1 The GEA System

This section describes the *GEA* system in detail. It is explained how the idea of creating such a programming library came up. Then the implemented representation forms, their genetic operators and the evolutionary algorithms of the latest version are presented.

The first aim of the *GEA* system was to provide a basis for the evolution of *Lindenmayer systems* (*L-systems* for short) [6]. These structures are capable of describing fractal structures such as trees (see the *Tevol* program, [12]) or even the blood vessels of the human retina (the *GREDEA* project, [13]). These two projects required the evolution of the rewriting rules of the *L-systems* as well as the parameters of them. The rewriting rules can be evolved with genetic algorithms, and the parameter vectors with evolutionary strategies. A suitable `C++` programming library which dealt with GAs and ESs at the same time could not be found, so the design and implementation of *GEA* has begun. Since the system is implemented in the *ANSI C++* language, in principle it can be used under any 32 bit operating system. So far the library has been tested on Linux, SunOS, DOS and Win32 platforms.

The class hierarchy of *GEA* is quite simple but still powerful. The `Evolvable` abstract class is the superclass of all evolvable objects. The classes `SelectionMethod` and `NextGenMethod` are the abstract classes defining interfaces for selection methods and evolutionary algorithms. These enable the user of the system to easily integrate new methods into *GEA*. The integration of new elements can be done without recompiling or relinking the binaries, for all possibly external objects and functions are loaded at running time by the recently strongly propagated *plug-in* technique.

Class `GenParams` holds all the parameters that an evolutionary algorithm can have in the *GEA* system. The latest version uses the general `e_params` data structure which can be used to hold parameters of arbitrary systems; it is easy to define the types and restrictions of parameters, and even relations between them. The parameter values can be set using a graphical user interface and are stored in easily readable and modifiable text files. The *GEA* system is designed in a way that the evolutionary parameters can be modified even during an already started evolutionary process, too.

Class `Evolvable` is the abstract superclass of all evolvable classes: It declares all the functions a class has to have in order to become an evolvable class. The standard *GEA* system contains two individual representations: `Evolvable-BitString` and `EvolvabeRealVector` are classes which implement the genetic operators of these two individual representations. If the possible solutions of a problem can be represented by bitstrings or real valued vectors, then only the fitness function has to be implemented and passed to the constructor of the selected class as a callback function.

The genetic operators are implemented according to the representation form. The system can optionally adapt the probability of the genetic operators, that is, it can observe their effectiveness and change the probabilities according to the result. This feature can be useful to set up the appropriate operator probabilities.

Class `Population` represents a population (a community of individuals) in the *GEA* system. The pointers to the individuals are stored in an array and are sorted by decreasing fitness values. The class has some functions supporting certain special selection methods.

Being a subclass of `Evolvable`, populations of populations can be created, thus populations can be evolved, too. This makes *meta-ES* available in the system. The fitness value of a population can be either its best individual's fitness value or the mean of all individuals' fitness values.

Class `EA` represents an evolution process in the *GEA* system. It has all methods that are necessary to handle a population and create new generations from it. It has to know the parameters of the evolutionary algorithms and the representation type of the individuals. After creating an `EA` object, only its `NextGen` function has to be called to run the evolution process. Eventual errors are handled with a general error handling data structure.

The *GEA* system was compared with other freely available evolutionary programming libraries with respect to speed and performance [1][2][7][14]. As this would exceed the space available for the paper, the results of this comparison cannot be presented here. In short, the test functions were chosen so that they differ in their modality, separability and regularity. With respect to execution times, in most cases the unoptimized *GEA* performed somewhat worse than the overall fastest system (*GENESIS*). The best solutions were found by *GEA* for four out of six test functions. The exact results of the comparison can be found in [11].

2 GREDEA: Description of the Human Retina

This section describes a real application of *GEA*: The *GREDEA* system. It applies combined evolutionary algorithms to evolve *L-systems* which describe the blood vessels of the human retina and is a very interesting medical application.

The main idea behind the *GREDEA* (**G**rammatical **Re**tina **D**escription with **E**volutionary **A**lgorithms) system is to develop patient-specific monitoring programs for examining the blood circulation of the human retina. The system can be used on patients with diabetes who need to be monitored over long periods. It is essential to check the eyesight of patients with this disease, because the deterioration of the vascular tree caused by diabetes has a direct effect on the vision quality.

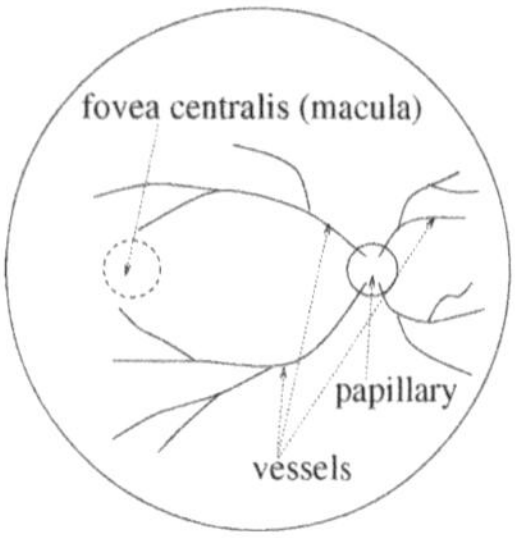

Fig. 1. The structure of the retina

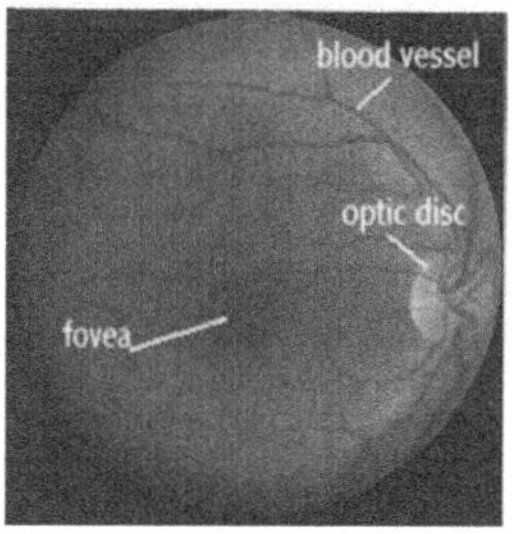

Fig. 2. Fundus image of the retina

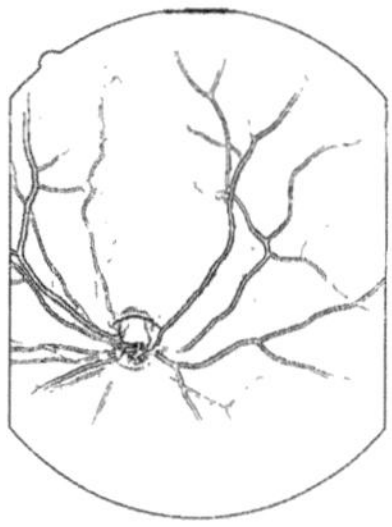

Fig. 3. A preprocessed retina image

In *GREDEA*, an individual description of the blood circulation of the human retina is created for each patient. To obtain the description, the process starts from fundus images taken with fundus cameras. They are then preprocessed (Figures 2 and 3). Then a parametric *Lindenmayer system* is developed which creates the pattern closest to the vascular tree of the patient. This *L-system* can be stored and used later to make comparisons.

L-systems are special kinds of descriptive grammars introduced by A. Lindenmayer in order to describe natural development processes [6]. These are called Lindenmayer grammars or *Lindenmayer systems*. The most important characteristic of them compared to Chomsky grammars is *parallel rewriting*. In Lindenmayer systems rewriting rules are applied in parallel and all instances of the left hand side of a chosen rewriting rule in a given word are simultaneously replaced.

Different *L-system* classes are introduced, such as deterministic or nondeterministic, context free or context sensitive L-systems. The definition of these classes are similar to the definition of Chomsky language classes. In the application described here, parametric L-systems are evolved, which introduce parallel rewriting to parametric words. The evolution of parametric *L-systems* requires two kinds of evolutionary algorithms: GAs are used to evolve the rewriting rules of the evolved *L-system*, and ESs are applied on the parameters of the *L-systems*.

Because the shape of the generated image depends both on the rewriting rules and on the parameters, the representation can be divided into two important parts. The right sides of the rules are represented as strings while the parameters are described as vectors of real values. *L-systems* with the same rules are considered an *L-system group*. In an *L-system group* the rules are constant, but the parameters can vary. To find the best parameters ESs are used inside the *L-system group*. Therefore an *L-system group* works as a *subpopulation*. A subpopulation can be represented by rewriting rules. Because the number of the rules and left sides are constant, an *L-system group* can be represented by an array of strings. To find the rewriting rules, GA is applied on the string arrays representing an *L-system group*.

For a detailed description of the *GREDEA* system, see [13].

3 Summary and Future Work

In this document the *GEA* (**G**eneric **E**volutionary **A**lgorithms) system, an evolutionary algorithms programming library written in the ANSI C++ programming language is presented.

The design and implementation of *GEA* was started with projects that evolve *parametric Lindenmayer systems* to describe branching structures. These evolution processes required the use of *evolutionary strategies*, and at that time there were no programming libraries that provided them.

The *GEA* system in its present phase contains implementations of genetic algorithms and evolutionary strategies, several types of selection methods, and genetic operators for bitstring and real-vector individual representation. The examples and the applications contain the implementation of genetic operators for permutations and parametric L-systems as well. The library is designed to be modular, so it can be easily expanded by subclassing certain classes.

The comparison of the *GEA* system with other libraries with a similar goal has brought very interesting and useful results for the future development: In most cases, the speed of the system is quite good, but the more important observation was that *GEA* does not perform very well on a few test functions. These points will be investigated and will be improved in the future. Furthermore, the following modifications and improvements are planned to be performed on the system:

- Coevolution [8] will be made available by letting the individuals know about their mates in the population. This is not implemented in any of the libraries found so far.

- A graphical user interface is under development for *GEA* which will enable the user to set the genetic parameters easily, to observe the performance of an EA run, and to display the individuals graphically. The *GTK GUI Toolkit*[2] is used in the implementation.
- A utility will be designed and implemented which will help the user to design evolutionary algorithms by the drag-and-drop technique.

It can be seen that the *GEA* system in its present state is a widely applicable and easy-to-use library. As many research projects, of course it is constantly under development. The above mentioned improvements will be implemented in the foreseeable future. Other modifications will be carried out as further reports and comments arrive from the researchers and users of the field.

References

1. D. Goldberg. Simple GA code (C translation of the code from Goldberg, D. E. ftp://ftp-illigal.ge.uiuc.edu/pub/src/simpleGA/C/.
2. J. J. Grefenstette. The GENEtic Search Implementation System (GENESIS Version 5.0). gref@aic.nrl.navy.mil.
3. J. H. Holland. *Adaption of Natural and Artificial Systems.* University of Michigan Press, Ann Arbor, Michigan, 1975.
4. C. Jacob. *Principia Evolvica - Simulierte Evolution mit Mathematica.* Dpunkt Verlag, 1997.
5. J. R. Koza. *Genetic Programming: On the Programming of Computers by Means of Natural Selection.* MIT Press, Cambridge, Massachusetts, 1992.
6. A. Lindenmayer. Mathematical models for cellular interaction in development. *Journal of Theoretical Biology*, 18:280-315, 1968.
7. J. J. Merelo. EO Evolutionary Computation Framework. http://geneura.ugr.es/~jmerelo/EO.html.
8. J. Paredis. *The Handbook of Evolutionary Computation, 1st supplement*, chapter Coevolu-tionary algorithms. Oxford University Press, 1998.
9. I. Rechenberg. *Evolutionsstrategien: Optimierung Technischer Systeme nach Prinzipen der Biologischen Evolution.* Fromman-Holzboog, Stuttgart, 1973.
10. W. M. Spears, K. De Jong, T. Bäck, D. B. Fogel, and H. de Garis. An overview of evolution-ary computation. In *European Conference on Machine Learning*, 1993.
11. Z. Tóth. The *Generic Evolutionary Algorithms Programming Library.* Master's thesis, Uni-versity of Szeged, Szeged, Hungary, 2000.
12. Z. Tóth, G. Kókai, and R. Ványi. Interactive visual tree evolution. In EIS2000 *Second International ICSC Symposium on Engineering of Intelligent Systems, June 27 - 30, 2000 at the University of Paisley, Scotland*, U.K., 2000.
13. R. Ványi, G. Kókai, Z. Tóth, and T. Petö. Grammatical retina description with enhanced methods. In R. Poli, W. Banzhaf, W. B. Langdon, J. F. Miller, P. Nordin, and T. C. Fogarty, editors, *Genetic Programming, Proceedings of EuroGP'2000*, volume 1802 of LNCS, pages 193-208, Edinburgh, 15-16 Apr. 2000. Springer-Verlag.
14. M. Wall. GAlib - A C++ Library of Genetic Algorithm Components. http://lancet.mit.edu/ga/.

[2] http://www.gtk.org

Value Prediction in Engineering Applications

G. Ziegler[1], Z. Palotai[2], T. Cinkler[1], P. Arató[2], and A. Lőrincz[3]

[1] Budapest University of Technology and Economics,
Department of Telecommunication and Telematics
High Speed Networks Laboratory, `http://hsnlab.ttt.bme.hu`
`mailto:ziegler@ttt.bme.hu`
[2] Budapest University of Technology and Economics,
Department of Control Engineering and Information Technology
`http://www.iit.bme.hu/nwelcome.html`
[3] Eötvös Loránd University, Department of Information Systems,
Neural Information Processing Group, `http://valerie.inf.elte.hu/~lorincz/`
Budapest, Hungary

Abstract. In engineering application heuristics are widely used for discrete optimization tasks. We report two cases (in Dense Wavelength Division Multiplexing and High Level Synthesis), where a recent "intelligent" heuristic (STAGE) performs excellently by *learning* a value-function of the states. We have found that if a global structure of local minima is found by the function approximator then search time may not have to scale with the dimension of the problem in the exponent, but it may become a polynomial function of the dimension.

1 Introduction

One of the most fundamental activities in an engineer's life is to find good, probably the best (i.e., *optimal*) choice of different alternatives in situations offering many alternatives while respecting certain limitations. Given a *problem* one usually *evaluates* the *possibilities* according to some *strategy* and finally selects one, which seems optimal for him. In engineering the problem of finding the best possible answer from a large space of possible answers is called *global optimization.* Formally speaking a global optimization task consists of the following tuples: a *state space* X together with a scalar *objective function* $Obj : X \to \mathbb{R}$ used for assessing the states. Our goal is to find the "best" state $x^* \in X$, which minimizes[1] Obj, that is, $Obj(x^*) \leq Obj(x)\ \forall x \in X$.

If the state space is small, then x^* can be trivially obtained by exhaustive search, otherwise special knowledge or some heuristics have to be utilized for performing effective partial search [1]. Many practical *combinatorial optimization problems* in engineering where X is finite, but enormous in size fall into the class of *NP-Hard* problems [2], to which no efficient exact solution algorithm is known.

One possibly adapts the solution algorithm according to his best knowledge in order to incorporate his special "insights" regarding the problem. The main

[1] In the followings when we speak about optimization, we will always assume minimization, unless explicitly noted.

L. Monostori, J. Váncza, and M. Ali (Eds.): IEA/AIE 2001, LNAI 2070, pp. 25–34, 2001.

problem comes from the fact that the true nature of the problem can be very well hidden behind the objective function, therefore searching only by objective function can be very inefficient.

In the theory of Reinforcement Learning [3] the fundamental instrument in decision making is the so called evaluation function, or shortly *value function.* It maps *features* of a given state to a single scalar value that gives us the "promise of the state" with respect to the solution to the problem. [4]. Obtaining this mapping is not a straightforward task. The good news is that evaluation functions can be *learnt* automatically [3], [4].

In the subsequent section we shortly overview the details of a recent algorithm called STAGE. In the main part of our paper we will report our experience that value prediction can indeed help to find either better results, or similar results but faster and more reliably than the widely used original heuristics.

2 Global Optimization with Value Prediction: STAGE

As we discussed in Section 1, if exhaustive search is not feasible one can resort to local search (LS). There is a big number of heuristics used for improving the chance of the LS to find global optimum, the interested reader is kindly referred to [1].

Performing local search requires the definition of the *neighborhood structure* N, which gives a set of states that is considered to be reachable directly (i.e., *locally*) from current state x. The definition of N can strongly influence the effectiveness of LS.

STAGE [4] falls into the class of multiple-restart heuristics and exploits the fact that the result of a LS might be strongly dependent on the start point of the search. The "value" of a state equals to the likely outcome of the LS starting from that state. Using this promise as an evaluation function STAGE performs "intelligent" restarts by searching the state with the most promising value. The values of the states are produced by a *function approximator* (FAPP) via a user-defined scalar "feature" vector $\mathcal{F}$ that should grasp the main attributes of the problem.

STAGE works cyclically, it repeatedly performs two LS-s consecutively. Firstly the LS π_{loc} defined by the user is run. It should produce a finite trajectory used for retraining the FAPP. Secondly STAGE starts another LS independent from the one that was used for searching by Obj to find the state $\widehat{x}^*$ with the best value estimate, i.e., $\widehat{V}(\widehat{x}^*) \leq \widehat{V}(x)\ \forall x \in X$. It uses $\widehat{x}^*$ as the re-start point for its next cycle.

STAGE highly benefits from using this approach. On one hand it allows the user to freely replace the input with a few selected feature. On the other hand, using FAPP opens the door before generalization (inter- and extrapolation). If there is a trend toward the global optimum among local optima then this trend can be learnt by the FAPP dramatically boosting the efficiency of STAGE. The precise details of STAGE is beyond the length-limits of this paper, it can be found in [4].

3 Joint Multilayer Configuration of GMPLS Networks

3.1 Problem Overview

In DWDM (Dense Wavelength Division Multiplexing) optical telecommunication networks [5] an end-to-end optical channel routed over several network nodes can be established. This is referred to as WR (Wavelength Routing). Unfortunately, for networks consisting of N nodes $N(N-1)$ unidirectional light-paths are needed ($N(N-1)/2$ pairs), which number depends on the square of N. Wavelength conversion does not help much. For this reason Multi-hop WR is used, i.e., two or more traffic streams can be carried jointly, over a single light-path by multiplexing and demultiplexing of these traffic streams in time division manner (it is called "grooming"). Therefore, electrical (de-)multiplexer devices are needed.

Recently introduced GMPLS (Generalized Multi-Protocol Label Switching) networks use packet switching over WR-DWDM networks handling several network layers jointly over a single control plane[2] [6]. Although GMPLS signalling will allow configuring all the layers on demand, at the moment it seems to be most reasonable to re-configure the layers rarely.

Following this approach here we propose a novel model for joint configuration of the GMPLS layers. This model allows use of heuristic optimization methods like STAGE and other techniques.

To make the presentation easier, the result on an example network is depicted in Fig. 1. The drawing shows the given six-node (N1-N6) network. The nodes are interconnected by seven physical links (L1-L7). In this example we assume three different wavelengths WL1, WL2 and WL3 and we assume that all node-pairs wish to communicate. There are 15 traffic streams between the node-pairs and 25 so-called *Basic Building Units* (BBUs 1-25). A BBU defines the assigned wavelength of a given stream on a given link. With the given physical topology we obtain 15 initial light-paths using 15 hops where opto-electrical and electro-optical conversions were needed. Seven of length one (4;8;10;12;14;18;22) six of length two (2-9;3-7;5-11;13-21;15-24;19-23) and two of length three (1-6-16;17-25-20). The minimal necessary four hops remained after optimization are denoted by small circles in Fig. 1.

We first route the traffic demands over the physical network then we search for an optimal wavelength assignment for each traffic demands over each physical links. We cut the paths between node-pairs into sequences and merge the sequences into so called λ-links, assigning them the same wavelength across consecutive physical links along the path. The problem size grows rapidly with the number of nodes and the number of available wavelengths. This problem very likely belongs to the class of NP-hard problems, because the subproblem of it, the Static Light-path Establishment (SLE) has been shown to be NP-complete [7].

Already in the example given in Fig. 1 with six nodes, three available wavelengths and 25 BBUs the state space consists of 3^{25} different states. The problem

[2] Packet Switching Layer, Time-Division Multiplexing Layer, Lambda(Wavelength)-Switching Layer and Fiber-Switching Layer

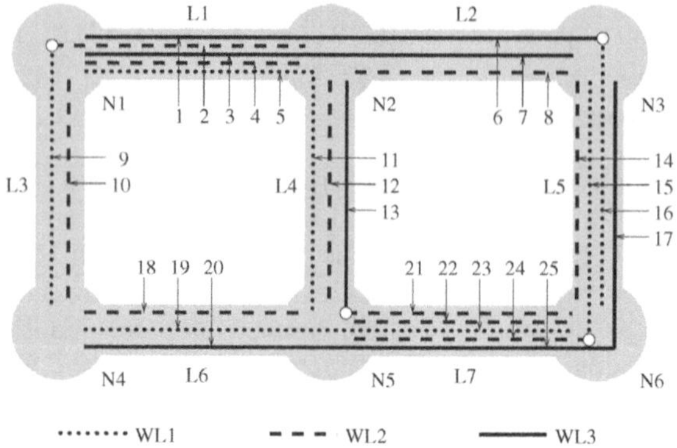

Fig. 1. The optimal configuration of the example

will be significantly reduced if the state space is tightened by starting with assigning one and the same wavelength to all traffic streams between adjacent nodes (i.e., of length one).

3.2 Reformulating the Problem for STAGE

For solving the GMPLS configuration problem with STAGE we have to define the building blocks of the STAGE algorithm. Beyond π_{loc} we need a second LS algorithm to find the extremum of the estimated values over the feature-space. We follow the suggestion of [4] and we use quadratic regression as FAPP, and Stochastic Hill-Climber to search in the feature space. The X problem space is defined by the possible allocations of wavelengths to BBU-s. The Obj to be minimized is the number of electro-optical conversions, that is, the sum of the number of wavelength-conversion and the number of multiplexing and de-multiplexing of different traffics to–from the same wavelength at some node. The neighborhood structure N is defined by the allowed configuration actions: changing the wavelength of one BBU. As for features several metrics can be defined. STAGE can automatically select from the features. The effect of irrelevant features will be simply noise and they will be integrated out by the FAPP. From the tried features finally the most successful ones have been chosen, namely the loads of the individual wavelengths (how many traffic demands have been carried over a particular wavelength) and the distribution factor of loads over all wavelengths. This experience is in correlation with the statement of [4] that using only a few, coarse feature of the problem is usually the most efficient solution.

3.3 Performance of STAGE on the GMPLS Problem

We have tested the following local searches [8]: Hill-Climber with equi-cost moves (HC) and Simulated Annealing (SA), each with and without smart restarts (SR). The networks have been the 6-node one of Figure 1 using 3 wavelengths (problem 'A'), and a bigger 10-node one using 3 and 5 wavelengths (problems 'B' and 'C', respectively), see Table 1.

Table 1. Comparison of GMPLS optimization results w. and w/o. SR

Problem	SR	Heur	Best Obj	Length of trajectory	# best	#best / #visited	Obj gain
A	--	HC	4	800	55071	75,4%	0%
	SR	HC	4	80	33405	45,8%	
B	--	HC	60	6400	2631	3,6%	0%
	SR	HC	60	80	26160	35,8%	
	SR	HC	57	80	240	0,3%	5%
C	--	HC	46	6400	1727	2,4%	0%
	SR	HC	46	640	12405	17,0%	
	SR	HC	44	80	240	0,3%	4%
A	--	SA	4	800	47428	65,0%	0%
	SR	SA	4	10	35008	48,0%	
B	--	SA	61	6400	67	0,1%	0%
	SR	SA	61	640	38043	52,1%	
	SR	SA	55	640	622	0,9%	10%
C	--	SA	43	6400	1516	2,1%	0%
	SR	SA	43	640	1440	2,0%	
	SR	SA	42	640	533	0,7%	2%

SR—Smart Restart, HC—Hill–Climb., SA—Sim.Anneal., BestObj—best Obj., #best—no. of visited states with BestObj, #visited—tot. no. of visited states, Obj gain—BestObj gain of SR over non-SR

Firstly the non-SR algorithms were run. We have tried different settings to determine the upper limit of trajectory length where no further significant improvement was probable. Experience has shown that the FAPP usually stabilized after ten retrain cycles, so in the SR mode we have cut-back the permitted trajectory length of π_{loc} to one tenth. It has resulted in having the same total number of visited states for both SR and non-SR modes (around 73000).

We have found that for smaller problems the STAGE approach has not improved significantly the obtained results. However, as the problem size has grown STAGE has begun to excel in robustness[3].

Note the table rows separated by dashed lines in Table 1. Each these dual rows contains data for SR runs of the same problem. Rows immediately above dashed lines contain the number of occurrences of those states where the *Obj* is at least as good as the best one in the non-SR runs of the same problem instance.

SR runs have yielded appr. the same quality results with the same number of visited states as the non-SR runs, but with a robustness usually better by more than one order of magnitude. In the following section we will turn to another engineering problem instance, where the SR approach has also helped to get better results than earlier algorithms.

[3] We call robustness the number of visited states with the best Obj versus the total number of states visited.

4 High Level Synthesis Design Problem

Our design problem is a high–level synthesis (HLS) problem: register transfer level (RTL) hardware description is to be given from a task formulated at a higher level [9], [10]. We compare the performance of STAGE with graph–coloring heuristics see, e.g.,[2] and with the state–of–the–art heuristics, DECIP [11]. Our methodology allows the joint optimization of software and hardware components. In general, the first step of any kind of design is to determine the components that will not be decomposed any further. We shall call such components extended elementary components, or *extended elementary operations* (EO-s, see [12]). The word 'extended' is added to emphasize that the algorithms we utilize are not limited to addition, subtraction, and multiplication, but higher order units, such as FFT, ciphering, etc. units can be considered as EO-s. Restrictions on the properties of EO-s define the type of design under consideration.

Combinatorial explosion of the design phase deprives the direct translation of HLS description into layout at more complex design tasks. Therefore, we rely on using elements that can perform different operations, called Intellectual Property (IP, see [13], [14]). The method described here can be extended to pipelined operations. The HLS problem has been formulated for this novel class. In turn, the method can deal with pipelining IP-s as sub–units [15].

We are interested in the so called "allocation problem", which determines which EO will be executed by which IP. One should try to schedule the EO-s as early as possible (potentially requiring parallel, or pipe-lined operation of several IP-s). On the other we have to allocate processors (IP-s) for each EO using as few IP as possible. The optimization problem is known to be NP–complete (see, e.g., [9] and references therein).

We will show that allocation can be transcribed into a generalized "satisfiability" problem of CNF formulae. Assigning cost to each clause of the CNF, the sum of the individual costs of unsatisfied clauses constitutes the total cost of the CNF, which is to be minimized. The novelty of our approach is in the "transcription". Our transcription allows the incorporation of any solution derived by heuristics, a major advantage for future steps. Our method is general enough to take into account constraints (inequalities), biases (cost components), and heuristics (suboptimal policies) in the global search procedure.

4.1 Allocation as a Weighted CNF Problem

We have reformulated the above mentioned allocation problem as a special *binary satisfiability* problem. The set of EO-s that the ith IP is capable of executing ('compatible') is denoted by R_i, $i = 1, \ldots, n$. The so-called *maximum compatibility classes* are formed by those EO-s that can be safely allocated to one IP (for formal details please refer to [9]) are denoted by M_k, $k = 1, \ldots, \kappa$. The CNF reformulation starts with *creating variables*. Let us denote the set $\{R_i \bigcap M_k \mid 0 \leq i \leq n, 1 \leq k \leq \kappa\}$ by $m_{i,k}$ and call these sets *allocation sets*. To each set $m_{i,k}$ there belongs a binary variable $t_{i,k}$. The variable can take values 'true' and 'false'. The value of the $t_{i,k}$ variable is 'true' provided that the EO-s belonging to set $m_{i,k}$ are allocated to the ith IP, Π_i.

Next we create the so called *unused clauses* (UC-s). The negated values of the variables will be included into our CNF. These are trivial clauses. This type of clause is called 'unused compatibility clause' or shortly, UC clause. The name denotes that a 'true' UC clause means that the compatibility class of the clause is not used. Later cost will be rendered to the UC clauses.

Finally we create the so called *EO clauses.* EO clauses express the conditions that each EO should be allocated. The number of EO clauses is equal to the number of EO-s. In each EO clause the possible allocations of that EO are listed with 'OR' relations in between. An allocation in allocation set $m_{i,\kappa}$ is possible if the set contains the EO under consideration. If an EO clause is true then the EO is allocated. Our listing concerns only compatible allocations. In turn, if every EO clause is true then every EO is allocated.

The CNF expression is created by making the disjunctions of the conjunctions. In turn, the allocation problem is transformed into a CNF expression.

4.2 Turning CNF into a Minimization Problem for STAGE

We note, that in our formulation a solution of the design problem is 'found' if all of the variables are set to value 'true'. This solution, however, can be very expensive. This is so, because we are using every UC clause instead of using as few as necessary. In what follows we will derail from traditional solutions to CNF-s. Costs will be assigned to each clause. The task will be the minimization of the cumulated costs. This formulation fits the philosophy of the STAGE algorithm. We shall make restrictions on the costs in order to force the algorithm to find solutions.

The state space X is trivial: the boolean variables $T_{i,k}$. Two CNF states are considered neighbors (N) if they differ in the value of a single variable. We use WalkSat [16], a highly efficient search algorithm as the local policy of STAGE. The change of the value of a variable is possible provided that the cost of the CNF is decreasing. If this is not the case but at least one state with identical cost is found then one of these states is selected with predefined probability. The design of the cost structure is of crucial importance. In our design we have included variables and clauses and fabricated the cost of those to ensure that any local search provides a solution. Such solutions can be, however, very costly. The underlying structure of the cost, however, can be discovered by STAGE. Details of the cost structure can be found elsewhere [15]. A quadratic approximator served as a FAPP (see Section 2). Features were chosen as follows: (i) $Obj(x)$, (ii) the number of clauses that can be satisfied by a single variable, (iii) the number of clauses that can be satisfied by two variables, (iv) the number of variables that make a clause of the actual CNF 'false' if inverted and, (v) the number of 'spurious' variables. (A variable is called 'spurious' if the number of its normal occurrences in the CNF is larger than the number of its negated occurrences.)

4.3 Computational Results

Allocation problems were tested on several realistic problems. To any design problem these parameters, e.g., the cost of the IP, or the time of execution can

Table 2. Overview of results for different problems

Problem Name	Number of EO-s	Number of types of IP-s	Restart time	Number of compatibility sets	Number of variables in the CNF formulae	Cost of the problem: Graph Coloring	DECIP	STAGE
Cosine equation	8	14	10	8	56	58	58	58
			30	11	54	58	50	50
Sine expansion	16	6	31	24	56	80	76	72
			49	52	103	56	48	40
			64	93	174	36	40	32
12 point FFT	36	6	14	180	302	180	180	180
			34	941	832	120	108	96

be chosen according to the designers data. Tests were started by running PIPE with its internal graph-coloring procedure. Compatibility classes were generated at this step. Compatibility classes were used in DECIP. The same compatibility classes were used for STAGE. Time requirements of the computer runs are illustrative; different computer languages were used for the different algorithms — depending on the flexibility and time requirements of the different sub–problems. Communication between optimization routines was automated when it was desired.

Parameters of STAGE were 'tweaked' experimentally on small problems [15]. Tested examples included cosine theorem; a 5 term Taylor–expansion of sine function and a 12 point Fast Fourier Transformation with different scheduling parameters (restart times). The dimension of the search space (the 'size') of the individual problems and the computational results are summarized in Table 2. Local search times are shown in the inset diagram of Fig. 2 with respect to problem size (which equals to 'No. of EO-s' * 'No. of IP-s' * 'No. of compatibility classes'.

DECIP has three parameters that weight relative costs. One cycle of DECIP corresponds to one choice of parameter vectors. DECIP was computed for an exhaustive search of 125 parameter combinations. This exhaustive search for DECIP was made for the sake of safety in the comparison. According to our computer simulations STAGE with FAPP-s are ideal to speed–up the search in the parameter space of DECIP too. In the case of STAGE one cycle consists of a local search and the search for intelligent restart. Graph-coloring is not shown in these figures. Graph coloring was much faster than the two other algorithms, however, it has produced relatively poor results.

5 Closing Remarks

We have found that function approximator based estimation of the value function is advantageous in two engineering applications, in Dense Wavelength Division Multiplexing and in High Level Synthesis. It is important that if global structure is found by the function approximator then search time may not have to scale with the dimension of the problem in the exponent, but it may become a polynomial function of the dimension. We underline this point by a comparison

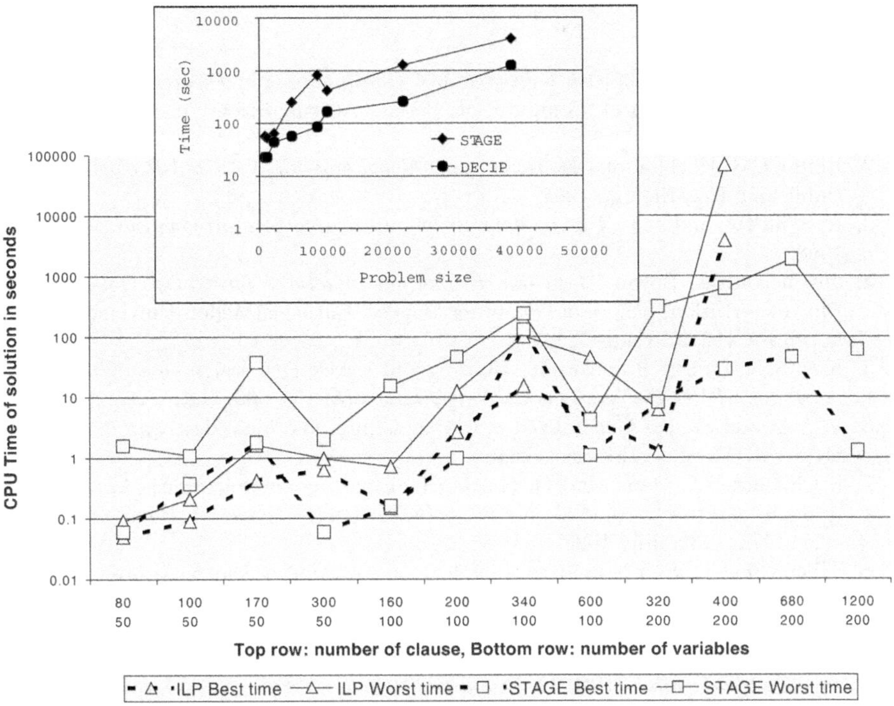

Fig. 2. Inset diagram: Experienced running time versus problem size, **main diagram**: Comparison of CPLEX and Stage

between CPLEX (a commercially available ILP solver) and STAGE. Comparisons between running times for different CNF-s are shown in the main diagram of Fig. 2. A trend can observed that 'intelligent restart' can be, indeed, intelligent. This is the reason that the relative performance of STAGE is improving by problem complexity. (CPU strength was was better by about a factor of five for CPLEX.)

Finally we note that there is no known algorithm for designing features. This problem is left for the designer and requires experience. It is an intriguing question whether the design of features can be automated. From the theoretical point of view, the question is to find higher order descriptors or non-linear transformations for a given problem that diminish the number of local maxima stopping local search procedures. Transcription of this sentence to reward, e.g., by considering the distance traveled by the local search procedure and the improvement of the cost achieved allows one to formulate the search problem for features that could make use of function approximators. This point, however, remains to be seen.

References

1. D. P. Bertsekas. *Network Optimization: Continuous and Discrete Models.* Optimization and Neural Computation Series. Athena Scientific, Belmont, Massachusetts, 1998.
2. Editor D.S. Hochbaum. *Approximation Algorithms for NP-Hard Problems.* PWS Publishing Co., Boston, 1995.
3. R. S. Sutton and A. G. Barto. *Reinforcement learning: An introduction.* MIT Pess, 1998.
4. Justin Andrew Boyan. *Learning Evaluation Functions for Global Optimization.* PhD dissertation, School of Computer Science, Carnegie Mellon University, Pittsburgh PA 15213, August 1998.
5. K.N. Sivarajan R. Ramaswami. Routing and wavelength assignment in all-optical networks. *IEEE Transactions on Networking*, 3(5):489–500, Oct. 1995.
6. P. Ashwood-Smith. Generalized mpls - signalling functional description. http://www.ietf.org/internet-drafts/.
7. I. Chlamtac, A. Ganz, and G. Karmi. Lightpath communications: An approach to high bandwidth optical WANs. *IEEE Transactions on Communications*, 40(7):1171–1182, July 1992.
8. Tibor Cinkler. Heuristic algorithms for configuration of the ATM-layer over optical networks. In *Proceedings of the ICC'97, IEEE International Conference on Communications, Montréal*, pages 1164–1168, June 1997.
9. P. Arató, I. Jankovits, S. Szigeti, and T. Visegrády. *High-level Synthesis of Pipelined Datapaths.* PANEM, Budapest, 1999.
10. R. Camposano and W. Rosenstiel. Synthetizing circuits from behavioural descriptions. *IEEE Transactions on Computer Aided Design*, pages 171–180, 1989.
11. P. Arató, T. Kandár, Z. Mohr, and T. Visegrády. An algorithm for decomposition into predefined IP-s. Technical report, Technical University of Budapest, 2000.
12. G. DeMicheli. *Synthesis and Optimization of Digital Circuits.* McGraw Hill, 1994.
13. J. Staunstrup and W. Wolf (eds). *Hardware/Software Codesign: Principles and Practice.* Kluwer Academic Publisher, 1997.
14. Rolf Ernst. *Embedded System Architectures, System Level Synthesis*, volume 357 of *Nato Science Series.* Kluwer Academic Publisher, 1999. Edited by A.A. Jerraya and J. Mermet.
15. Z. Palotai and A. Lőrincz. Joint optimization of scheduling and allocation of IPs. manuscript in preparation.
16. B. Selman, H. A. Kautz, and B. Cohen. Local search strategies for satisfiability testing. *Second DIMACS Challenge on Cliques, Coloring and Satisfiability*, pages 44, 95–96, 1996.

Scatter Search with Random Walk Strategy for SAT and MAX-W-SAT Problems

Habiba Drias and Mohamed Khabzaoui

USTHB, Electrical and Computer Engineering Faculty,
Computer Science Department,
BP 32 El-Alia Bab-Ezzouar, 16111 Alger, Algeria
Drias@wissal.dz

Abstract. The recent evolutionary approach called scatter search is studied for solving the satisfiability problem designated by SAT and its weighted version MAX-W-SAT. It is a population-based meta-heuristic founded on a formulation proposed two decades ago by Fred Glover. It uses linear combination on a population subset to create new solutions while other evolutionary approaches like genetic algorithms resort to randomization.
First we propose a scatter search algorithm for SAT and MAX-W-SAT, namely SS-SAT. We present a procedure to generate good scattered initial solutions, a combination operator and a technique for improving the solutions quality. The method is tested and various experimental results show that SS-SAT performs better than or as well as GRASP for most benchmark problems.
Secondly, we augment scatter search with the random walk strategy and compare its performance to the standard version. It appears that the added strategy does not lead to increased performance.

Keywords. heuristic search, genetic algorithm, evolutionary approach, scatter search, Weighted maximum satisfiability problem, optimization problem

1 Introduction

The satisfiability of a logical formula is a classical problem of the computational complexity theory. The studies of the conjunctive canonical form, by a great number of researchers have not yet revealed all the mysteries of this problem. Its wide applications in the domain of AI, in mathematical logic, and in computational theory, motivate the huge interest of the researchers for this problem. Its decision version, namely SAT, which consists in verifying that the conjunction of clauses is satisfied by at least one variables interpretation, has been shown to be the first NP-complete problem. SAT and its variants play also an important role in the characterization of approximation classes like APX and PTAS.
The optimization version of SAT, the maximum satisfiability problem or MAX-SAT is a partial constraint satisfaction problem, where the aim is to maximize the number of satisfied clauses. By associating a weight to each clause, the maximum weighted satisfiability problem or MAX-W-SAT is defined and the objective function becomes the weights sum of the satisfied clauses.
Among the applications of MAX-SAT is an important practical problem in expert systems, where information is expressed by a set of clauses. The problem is to check

L. Monostori, J. Váncza, and M. Ali (Eds.): IEA/AIE 2001, LNAI 2070, pp. 35-44, 2001.

the consistency of the knowledge base after updating by adding and deleting some of the rules. If the knowledge base is not consistent, it is desirable to find the smallest set of rules which should be deleted in order to restore consistency. Such a set can be obtained by solving MAX-SAT for the clauses corresponding to all rules in the knowledge base. An identical problem exists in deductive databases.

The decision problem SAT has been widely studied, relatively to MAX-W-SAT. Heuristics methods for solving these problems include Simulated Annealing [14], Taboo Search [16], Genetic Algorithms [4, 6, 13] and Guided Local Search [17] among others.

The evolutionary population based approach, the scatter search is introduced recently as a meta-heuristic for solving complex optimization problems [11, 15]. It is based on a formulation for integer programming developed in 1977 by Fred Glover [7] and uses linear combination of a population subset to create new solutions. It could be viewed as a bridge between taboo search and genetic algorithms [9]. It has been recently applied to a number of combinatorial optimization problems, for instance, the quadratic assignment problem [3] and the linear ordering problem [2].

In this paper, Scatter Search is used for the first time to solve the problems SAT and MAX-W-SAT. The purpose of this study is to accomplish extensive experiments in order to compare the solutions quality with those obtained by GRASP, another meta-heuristic applied recently to MAX-W-SAT [18]. We present hereafter this approach and the general algorithm. We describe the issues of the method in the general context. Then, we propose an implementation of its main ingredients for MAX-W-SAT. A procedure to generate good initial scattered solutions as well as an operator to combine solutions and a classical technique to improve the quality of solutions are presented. We compare our empirical results with those obtained by GRASP as they are published in [18].

In a second step, the scatter search algorithm is augmented by the random walk strategy, which has been tested on other heuristics like GSAT [19] and taboo search[4]. Numerous experiments have been performed on this hybrid version and results are compared with those of the standard algorithm.

1.1 SAT and MAX-W-SAT Problems

Let consider the following elements of propositional logic:

- A set of n logical variables $\{x_1, x_2, \ldots x_n\}$
- A set of m clauses $\{C_1, C_2, \ldots, C_m\}$, each of which is a disjunction of a set of literals (a variable or it's negation). For example $x_1 \vee -x_2 \vee x_3$ is a clause of 3 literals where $-x_i$ denotes the negation of x_i, $1 <= i <= 3$.
- Each clause has a weight w_j $1 <= j <= m$, associated with it.

The problem SAT consists in determining whether there exists a valuation for variables that satisfies all clauses. The goal of the weighted MAX-W-SAT problem is to find an assignment of values to variables, if one exists, that satisfies all clauses and if none exists, an assignment which maximizes the weights sum of satisfied clauses.

2 A General Overview of the Scatter Search

Basically, the scatter search method starts with a population of good and scattered solutions. At each step, some of the best solutions are extracted from the collection to be combined and included in a set called the reference set. A new solution is then obtained as a result of applying a linear combination on the extracted solutions. The quality of the new solution is then enhanced by an improvement technique such as a local search. The final solution will be included in the reference set if it presents interesting characteristics with regards to the solution quality and dispersion.
Although it belongs to the population-based procedures family, scatter search differs mainly from genetic algorithms by its dynamic aspect that does not involve randomization at all.

Scatter search allows the combination of more than two solutions, it gets thus at each step more information. By combining a large number of solutions, different sub-regions of the search space are implicated to build a solution. Besides, the reference set is modified each time a good solution is encountered and not at the combination process termination. Furthermore, since this process considers at least all pairs of solutions in the reference set, there is a practical need for keeping the cardinality of the set small (<=20). The scatter search can be summarized in a concise manner as follows:

Generate an initial population P
while not Stop-Condition **do**
- Initialize the reference set with the solutions selected to be combined
- Generate new solutions by applying the combination process
- Improve new solutions quality
- Insert new solutions in population with respect to quality and dispersion criteria

end while

The procedure stops as in many meta-heuristics, when during a small number of iterations no improvement in solutions quality is recorded or when we reach a certain number of iterations limited by physical constraints.

2.1 The Reference Set

The utility of the reference set *RefSet* consists in maintaining the b best solutions found in terms of quality and diversity, where b is an empirical parameter. *RefSet* is partitioned into $RefSet_1$ and $RefSet_2$, where $RefSet_1$ contains the b_1 best solutions and $RefSet_2$ contains the b_2 solutions chosen to augment the diversity. The distance between two solutions is defined to measure the solutions diversity. We compute the solution that is not currently in the reference set and that maximizes the distance to all the solutions currently in this set. Note that *RefSet* creates a compromise between the best solutions and the scattered solutions.

2.2 The Subset Generation Method

Scatter search generates new solutions by combining solutions of *RefSet*. A new solution replaces the worst one in $RefSet_1$ if its quality is better. In the negative, the distances between the new solution and the solutions in *RefSet* are computed. If diversification is improved, the new solution replaces the element of $RefSet_2$ that has the smallest distance. Otherwise, it is discarded.
The solution combination procedure starts by constituting subsets from the reference set that have useful properties, while avoiding the duplication of subsets previously generated. The approach for doing this, consists in constructing four different collections of subsets, with the following characteristics:
Subset-Type = 1 : all 2-element subsets.
Subset-Type = 2 : all 3-element subsets derived from the 2-element subsets by augmenting each 2-element subset to include the best solution not in this subset.
Subset-Type = 3 : all 4-element subsets derived from the 3-element subsets by augmenting each 3-element subset to include the best solution not in this subset.
Subset-Type = 4 : the subsets consisting of the best i elements, for i=5 to b.

2.3 The Solutions Combination

Scatter search generates new solutions by combining those in the reference set. Specifically, the design of a combination method considers the solutions to combine and the objective function. A newly generated solution is compared with the worst solution in *RefSet*. It replaces the worst solution if its objective value is better than the fitness value of the worst solution in *RefSet*.

3 Scatter Search for SAT and MAX-W-SAT

First, note that the scatter search algorithm is the same for either SAT and MAX-W-SAT. The only difference lies in the fitness function, for SAT it consists in determining the number of satisfied clauses, whereas in MAX-W-SAT, it consists in evaluating the sum of weights of satisfied clauses. The implementation of the meta-heuristic requires the design of the following components ; the initial population, the improvement method, the diversification generator and the solution combination method .

The initial population. The generation of scattered solutions depends only on the search space. An appropriate generator is described as follows. We choose a parameter h <=n-1, where n is the number of variables and the initial solution is (0,0,…,0). For each value smaller than h, two solutions are generated. The first one is obtained using the following formula:
$x'_1 = 1 - x_1$
$x'_{1+h*k} = 1 - x_{1+h*k}$ (k=1,…, n/h)
The second solution is the complement of the first one. This process is repeated until we obtain *p-size* solutions where *p-size* is the cardinality of the population.

The improvement method. Many solutions improvement methods exist in the literature and have been used in meta-heuristics like taboo search and GSAT[19] for instance. The improvement method is context-dependent and is applied to the initial solutions and the generated solutions to enhance their quality. Our improvement method consists in choosing the best solution in the neighborhood of the current solution. The neighborhood is obtained by flipping the bit, which evaluates the best value for the objective function. This operation is repeated until no improvement in the evaluation function is observed. Another technique consists in crossing the bits of the solution and inverting those that improve the objective function value.

The diversification generator. The reference set *RefSet* is a subset of the population P, which includes both the best solutions and the scattered solutions. A function distance d(x,y) between two solutions x and y is calculated to measure the solutions diversity. For MAX-W-SAT, we define this distance to be the sum of the absolute values of the differences between the corresponding bits of the solutions. For example, let us consider an instance of SAT of six variables and two instantiations x_1 and x_2 given as follows :

$x_1 = (010110)$
$x_2 = (100010)$
then $d(x_1,x_2) = 1+1+0+1+0+0= 3$

The combination method. Combining two or more solutions consists in determining for each variable, a value that takes into account the corresponding solutions values and of course the fitness function. It is easy to see that for MAX-W-SAT, the value to attribute to a variable is that one of the solution that maximizes the weights sum of the satisfied clauses. In case of conflict, that is when for a same variable, the opposite values (0 and 1) yield the same result for

the objective function, an arbitrary choice is made between both values. To illustrate the combination method, let us consider the following example of an instance of 3 clauses built over 5 variables with respective weights:

x_1	$-x_3$	x_4	3
x_3	$-x_4$	$-x_5$	4
$-x_2$	x_3	$-x_5$	2

and the following three solutions to combine : (01001), (01101) and (01010). Then the result of the combination is 01100. If we consider the variable x_3 for instance, the weights sum of the clauses satisfied by $x_3=1$ is equal to 6 whereas the weights sum of the clauses satisfied by $x_3=0$ is equal to 3. The appropriate value is then equal to 1.

The overall procedure. The scatter search procedure or SS-SAT can be summarized as follows:

```
Procedure SS-SAT(var seed: solution);
Begin
    For (Iter = 1 To maxIter) do
    begin
        P = div-gen(seed, pop-size); { generate a diversified population }
        RefSet(P,b1,b2); { construct the reference set }
        NewElements = TRUE;
        While (NewElements) do
        Begin   NewElements = FALSE
                Generate-subsets(RefSet);
                Suppress all the subsets that do not contain at least one element;
                { apply combination operators }
                Combine_type1(x1,x2) for all (x1,x2) ∈ Type1;
                Combine_type2(x1,x2,x3) for all (x1,x2) ∈ Type2;
                Combine_type3(x1,x2, x3,x4) for all (x1,x2, x3,x4) ∈ Type3;
                Combine_type4(x1, ...,xi) for all i=5 to b;
                For all obtained solution xs do
                Begin
                  xs* = improve(xs);
                  If (xs* ∉ RefSet and ∃x∈ RefSet1 / OV(xs*) > OV(x))
                        { OV represents the evaluation function }
                        then    begin   replace x by xs*;
                                        NewElements = TRUE;
                                End
                  Else if (xs* ∉ RefSet and ∃x∈ RefSet2 / dmin(xs*)>dmin(x)) then
                                Begin   replace x by xs* { dmin(x) is the smaller };
                                        NewElements = TRUE;
                                End
                End
        End;
        If (iter < MaxIter) then { maxIter is the maximum number of iterations }
                Seed = the best solution of RefSet1;
    End;
End;
```

4 Scatter Search with Random Walk Strategy

Scatter search does not involve randomized instructions except for the generation of the seed for creating the initial population. In this section, we try to incorporate a randomized strategy called the random walk in order to see whether increased performance can be achieved. If such improvement is settled by experiments, it will be mainly caused by the diversification in the search space provided by the strategy. Speed in the search may also be observed.

The random walk strategy consists in introducing a noise in the search in order to deviate it from its usual rules. Technically, it consists in inverting at random a bit of the current solution that increases the number of satisfied clauses when a generated random number is smaller than the noise probability and in running the scatter search in the contrary. The scatter search with random walk called RWSS-SAT is presented as follows:

```
Procedure RWSS-SAT;
    begin
    S = seed; { generated randomly }
    For (Iter = 1 To maxIter) do
    begin
        RN = random(0..1); { generate a random number between 0 and 1 }
        If   RN < p        then SS-SAT(S);
                           Else  invert a bit of S that increases the number of
                                               satisfied clauses;
        S = x*;  {  x* being the new solution }
     End;
   End;
```

The probability p is an empirical parameter as well as maxIter. We now turn our attention to the computational experiments used to assess the merit of our scatter search implementation.

5 Numerical Results

The procedure SS-SAT has been implemented in C on a personal Pentium computer and numerical tests were performed on benchmark instances available on a web site given below. In the following figures we compare the performance of SS-SAT with a sequential version of GRASP [18].

Preliminary tests were carried out in order to set the key parameters of the scatter search algorithm. After extensive experiments, the following values yield solutions of high quality: P-size =150, b_1=5, b_2=5 and Maxiter=5 for SS-SAT and : P-size =150, b_1=5, b_2=5, Maxiter=30 and p = 0.5 for RWSS-SAT.

The numerical results which are more expressive than a curve or a histogram, are reported in table 1 and show for each problem, the optimal solution, the best solution found by GRASP and those obtained by SS-SAT. This table shows that SS-SAT outperforms sequential GRASP for most instances of problems.

Table 2 shows the result of applying the random walk strategy to scatter search for MAX-W-SAT instances. Here, no improvement is observed when adding such strategy.

---

http://www.research.att.com/~mgcr/data/index.html

Table 1. Experimental results comparing SS-SAT and sequential GRASP

instance	Optimal solution	GRASP		SS-SAT	
		solution	time	solution	time
Jnh01	420925	420632	1525.2	420892	203.99
Jnh10	420840	420463	964.4	420479	901.47
Jnh11	420753	420398	1330.1	420141	439.82
Jhn12	420925	420518	564.1	420701	250.65
Jnh13	420816	420592	567.0	420716	930.12
Jhn14	420824	420491	982.6	420491	298.22
Jhn15	420719	420429	899.2	420632	624.63
Jhn16	420919	420809	18.7	420889	716.51
Jhn17	420925	420712	1062.8	420794	401.95
Jhn18	420795	420289	560.5	420404	129.64
Jhn19	420759	420307	287.3	420330	403.10
Jnh201	394238	394154	1099.6	394238	161.72
Jnh202	394170	393680	261.2	393924	269.99
Jnh203	393881	393446	1352.3	393875	294.10
Jnh205	394063	393890	1163.5	394060	203.37
Jnh207	394238	394030	41.8	394228	313.58
Jnh208	394159	393859	890.1	393771	137.19
Jnh209	394238	393959	1740.0	394238	463.31
Jnh210	394238	393950	219.3	394067	394.46
Jhn211	393979	393529	281.8	393742	408.04
Jhn212	394238	394011	171.5	394082	758.00
Jhn214	394163	393737	1272.2	394152	1159.15
Jhn215	394150	393818	350.8	393942	202.51
Jhn216	394226	394042	1215.7	393806	181.43
Jhn217	394238	394232	438.8	394238	799.40
Jhn218	394238	394009	825.2	394189	166.47
Jhn219	394156	393792	1308.3	393800	530.35
Jhn220	394238	393951	1055.1	393985	597.70
Jhn301	444854	444612	347.6	444842	1267.63
Jhn302	444459	443906	46.6	443895	698.77
Jhn303	444503	444063	1046.7	444223	437.91
Jhn304	444533	444310	142.5	444533	1175.98
Jhn305	444112	444112	1465.8	443594	463.33
Jhn306	444838	444603	1003.0	444515	604.53
Jhn307	444314	443836	972.3	443662	288.14
Jhn308	444724	444215	607.9	444250	768.57
Jhn309	444578	444273	564.6	444483	662.58
Jhn310	444391	444010	1290.4	444313	240.01

6 Conclusion

Our study shows that a careful scatter search implementation can be quite effective and rival the best procedures in the literature. Through this first experimental results, SS-SAT on MAX-W-SAT outperforms the sequential version of GRASP, which has been shown very efficient. The robustness of scatter search relies on the design of the initial scattered population, the solution combination operator and the solution improvement method. The initial population is created according to a diversification generator. The combination operator in our case does not deal with complicated arithmetic formulas as in the knapsack problem for instance, it is derived straightly from the Boolean feature interpretation of the fitness function. The solution improvement technique is used in many heuristics like GSAT and taboo search. With these settings, the sequential version of the scatter search has shown yet very interesting results. However the random walk strategy incorporated in the heuristic has not been of any interest according to the experiments.

Table 2. Experimental results comparing SS-SAT and RWSS-SAT

instance	Optimal solution	RWSS-SAT		SS-SAT	
		solution	time	solution	time
Jnh01	420925	420892	766.91	420892	203.99
Jnh10	420840	420132	1393.5	420479	901.47
Jnh11	420753	420141	450.33	420141	439.82
Jhn12	420925	420701	604.35	420701	250.65
Jnh13	420816	420412	618.93	420716	930.12
Jhn14	420824	420475	821.42	420491	298.22
Jhn15	420719	420180	433.03	420632	624.63
Jhn16	420919	420889	411.94	420889	716.51
Jhn17	420925	420689	414.66	420794	401.95
Jhn18	420795	420404	226.36	420404	129.64
Jhn19	420759	420409	969.00	420330	403.10
Jnh201	394238	394238	364.82	394238	161.72
Jnh202	394170	393752	210.2	393924	269.99
Jnh203	393881	393548	907.67	393875	294.10
Jnh205	394063	393975	389.13	394060	203.37
Jnh207	394238	394022	553.60	394228	313.58
Jnh208	394159	393560	593.40	393771	137.19
Jnh209	394238	393776	608.29	394238	463.31
Jnh210	394238	393473	275.71	394067	394.46
Jhn211	393979	393731	472.30	393742	408.04
Jhn212	394238	394020	427.31	394082	758.00
Jhn214	394163	393277	153.95	394152	1159.15
Jhn215	394150	393957	758.36	393942	202.51
Jhn216	394226	393933	486.56	393806	181.43
Jhn217	394238	394233	703.67	394238	799.40
Jhn218	394238	394189	327.71	394189	166.47

References

1. Battiti R. , Protasi M. : Solving MAX-SAT with non Oblivious Functions and History based Heuristics, Dimacs Workshop on Satisfiability problems : Theory and Applications, Rutgers University , (1996)
2. Campos V., Glover F., Laguna M., Marti R.: An Experimental Evaluation of a Scatter Search for the Linear Ordering Problem, (1999)
3. Cung V.D., Mautor T., Michelon P. , Tavares A.:A Scatter Search based Approach for the Quadratic Assignment Problem, research Report N° 96/037 Versailles university, (1996)
4. Drias H.: Randomness in Heuristics : an Experimental Investigation for the Maximum Satisfiability Problem, LNCS 1606 proceeding of IWANN'99, Alicante Spain, (1999) 700-708
5. Drias H. , Azi N.: Scatter search for SAT and MAX-W-SAT problems, to appear in the proceedings of the IEEE SSST, Ohio, USA, (2001)

6. Frank J. : A Study of genetic algorithms to find Approximate Solutions to Hard 3CNF Problems, in Golden West International Conference on Artificial Intelligence, (1994)
7. Glover F.: Heuristics for Integer Programminig Using Surrogate Constraints, Decision Sciences, vol 8, N° 1, (1977) 156-166
8. Glover F.: Taboo Search for non linear and parametric optimization with links to genetic algorithms, Disc Appl Math 49, (1994) 231-255
9. Glover F., Kelly J.P., Laguna M.: Genetic Algorithms and Taboo Search : Hybrids for Optimization, Computers and Operation Reseach vol 22 1,(1995) 111-134
10. Glover F., Laguna M., R. Marti: scatter search, 2000.
11. Glover F., Laguna M., Marti R.: fundamentals of scatter search and path relinking, 2000
12. Goldberg D.E.: Algorithmes Génétiques : Exploration, Exploitation et Apprentissage Automatique, Addison Wesley France 1994
13. Gottlieb J., Voss N.: Representations, fitness functions and genetic operators for the satisfiability problem, Springer Verlag Heidelberg (1998)
14. Hansen P., Jaumard B.: Algorithms for the Maximum Satisfiability , computing 44, (1990) . 279-303
15. Laguna M.: Scatter Search, document internet, (1999)
16. Mazure B., Sais L., Grégoire E.: Taboo Search for SAT, in proceedings of AAAI, (1997)
17. Mills P., Tsang E.: Solving the MAX-SAT problem using Guided Local Search, Rapport technique CSM-327, (1999)
18. Resende M.G., Pitsoulis L.S., Pardalos P.M.: Approximate Solution of Weighted MAX-SAT Problems using GRASP, in Dimacs series on discrete mathematics and theoretical computer Science vol 35, (1997) 393-405
19. Selman B., Kautz H.A., Cohen B.: Local Search Strategies for Satisfiability Testing, in cliques, coloring and satisfiability: second DIMACS implementation challenge, vol 26, D.S. Johnson and M.A. Tricks eds., (1996) 521-531

Move Ordering Using Neural Networks

Levente Kocsis, Jos Uiterwijk, and Jaap van den Herik

Department of Computer Science, Institute for Knowledge and Agent Technology,
Universiteit Maastricht, P.O. Box 616, 6200 MD Maastricht, The Netherlands
{l.kocsis,uiterwijk,herik}@cs.unimaas.nl

Abstract. The efficiency of alpha-beta search algorithms heavily depends on the order in which the moves are examined. This paper focuses on using neural networks to estimate the likelihood of a move being the best in a certain position. The moves considered more likely to be the best are examined first. We selected Lines of Action as a testing ground. We investigated several schemes to encode the moves in a neural network. In the experiments, the best performance was obtained by using one output unit for each possible move of the game. The results indicate that our move-ordering approach can speed up the search with 20 to 50 percent compared with one of the best current alternatives, the history heuristic.

1 Introduction

Most game-playing programs nowadays use the alpha-beta algorithm. The efficiency of alpha-beta is closely related to the size of the expanded search tree and depends mainly on the order in which the moves are considered. If good moves are inspected first, the likelihood of cut-offs is increased, decreasing the size of the search tree.

For move ordering, the existing programs frequently rely on information gained from previous phases of the search. Major examples are a transposition table and the history heuristic [4]. Additionally, the original move-ordering techniques which are independent of the search process are still valid. In chess, for example, checking moves, captures and promotions are considered before 'silent' moves. However, the resultant move ordering only based on the latter group is somewhat poor, mainly because of the small number of move classes and the incidental relation with the board position.

It is a challenging idea to use learning methods to obtain a better search-independent move ordering. To achieve this, we trained a neural network to estimate the likelihood of a move being the best in a certain position. Subsequently, the estimated quality of the moves was used for move ordering.

A similar approach to ours is the chessmaps heuristic [1]. This heuristic is pattern based and uses a neural network to learn a relation between the control of the squares and the influence of a move. There are two main differences with our approach. First, in the chessmaps heuristic the neural network is trained to evaluate classes of moves, while our neural-network approach is tuned to

L. Monostori, J. Váncza, and M. Ali (Eds.): IEA/AIE 2001, LNAI 2070, pp. 45–50, 2001.

distinguish individual moves. Second, in our approach the target information for a neural network is the likelihood of the move being the best in a certain position, whereas in the chessmaps heuristic the target vector is the influence of the move on the squares of the board.

We use as test domain Lines of Action (LOA), a game suitable for pattern-recognition techniques [5]. LOA is one of the games played at the Mind Sports Olympiads and the last Computer Olympiad.

The article is organised as follows. Three move-encoding schemes are investigated in section 2. The experimental set-up for evaluating the efficiency of the move-encoding schemes and the resulting move ordering is described in section 3. The experimental results are given in section 4. Finally, section 5 presents the conclusions and some ideas for future research.

2 Three Move-Encoding Schemes

The evaluation functions involved in our experiments used a feed-forward neural network with a hidden layer consisting of 40 neurons. Both the output and the hidden neurons used a sigmoidal activation function. A board position was encoded by 65 input units. Each square was associated to a neuron (+1 for a black piece, −1 for a white one, 0 for an empty square) with an additional neuron indicating the side to move. The output neuron represents the minimax estimation of the position. The evaluation functions were trained using temporal difference learning. More details about the set of evaluation functions are described in [2].

The neural network used for move ordering has to be provided with the current board position and the legal moves in the position. The board position can be encoded in the input of the neural network in an identical way as described for evaluation functions. However, the method of how to encode the moves leads to a difficult choice. In the following we investigate three schemes of encoding the moves, and analyse the potential strengths and weaknesses of each of them.

The most natural move-encoding scheme is to use the input vector. The move is then additional to the board position. A move in LOA has two components: a 'from' part (denoting the stone to be moved) and a 'to' part (the destination of the move). For instance, we may assign 8 input units to the file and 8 to the rank of the 'from' part, and similarly 8 input units to the file and 8 to the rank of the 'to' part. For every move, four units corresponding to the 'from-file', 'from-rank', 'to-file' and 'to-rank' of the move are set to 1, the rest of the units are set to 0. Consequently, the size of the input layer is 97 (65 units for the board and 32 units for the move). In the output layer one single unit representing the estimated quality of the move under discussion can be used.

The time necessary to propagate the input vector through the neural network is similar to the time used by our evaluation functions. The neural network, when used for move ordering, has to inspect all legal moves in all internal nodes of the search tree, while the neural network for the evaluation function (the most time-consuming component so far) has to inspect only all leaf nodes. Since the ratio between the number of leaf nodes and the number of internal nodes is significantly less than the branching factor (approximately 7 compared to 30), the gain from a better move ordering with this encoding scheme will most likely be lost by the overhead produced.

A second move-encoding scheme results from an analysis of the first one. The main problem with the previous encoding scheme is that with one activation of the neural network we estimate the quality of one move only. To make it faster, we should estimate the quality of all moves in a certain position simultaneously. However, encoding of all moves at once in the input vector of the neural network is not feasible. An alternative is to have separate output units for all possible moves, an output vector with 4096 (64x64) units. At first glance, the activation time is huge. However, we only have to compute the outputs corresponding to the legal moves of the input position. Consequently, the 'effective' size of the output vector is only the branching factor of the game. If we compare the number of effective weights for this encoding scheme with the number of weights of the evaluation function, we can observe that with the same hidden-layer size, the time necessary for move ordering in an internal node is not more than 1.5 times the time used by the evaluation function. Considering that the number of internal nodes is 7 times fewer than the number of leaf nodes, with identical hidden-layer sizes, the time overhead of this move ordering will be approximately 20%. If the size of the hidden layer is somewhat smaller, the overhead will be insignificant (<10%). A potential problem with this move-encoding scheme is that, since the number of 'real' weights is high, the generalisation during the learning phase is likely to be weak.

A third move-encoding scheme was designed to overcome the weakness of generalisation. This encoding scheme is similar to the second one, except that we now have one output unit for every 'from' square and one output unit for every 'to' square ($64 + 64 = 128$ units) instead of one output unit for every move. The estimation of a move will be the mean of the activation value of the output unit corresponding to its 'from' part and that of the output unit corresponding to its 'to' part. So, the training information for a certain move is generalised to the moves with the same origin or destination. To reduce the 'effective' size of the output layer, the same technique can be applied as in the previous case. Now we have to compute the activation in the 'from' half of the output vector corresponding to the stones of the player to move (approximately 10 units) and the activation in the 'to' part of the legal moves. If we compare this move-encoding scheme to the previous one, we observe that the 'real' size of the output is reduced from 4096 to 128 (enforcing some generalisation between the moves) and that the 'effective' size is increased from approximately 30 to approximately 40 (avoiding a significant increase of the overhead).

Summarising the analysis of the three move-encoding schemes, we expect that the first one has a significant time overhead, and the second one a poor generalisation. The third encoding scheme is expected to generalise better than the second one, but it is somewhat slower. Since the analysis do not lead to a clear conclusion, we investigated all three move-encoding schemes in our experiments.

3 Experimental Set-Up

We performed two experiments: (1) the neural networks are trained to estimate the quality of the moves, and (2) the efficiency of the move ordering based on the neural networks is evaluated.

During the first experiment the neural networks were trained to recognise whether a certain move is found to be the best by a search algorithm using the evaluation functions mentioned in section 2. Three types of pattern sets were generated: a *learning set* used to modify the weights of the neural networks, a *validation set* used for training-stopping criteria, and a *test set* used to evaluate the move-ordering performance in this experiment. A pattern in these sets consisted of a board position, the moves which are legal in the position, and the move found to be the best by the search algorithm within a certain depth. The learning set and validation set were generated using 2- and 3-ply deep searches, while the test set used 4- and 5-ply deep searches. The reason for a shallower search for the learning set was to be able to generate large sets. The validation set and the test set contained approximately 5000 board positions each. Moreover, these positions did not appear in the learning set. The size of the learning set varied.

As learning algorithm we used RPROP [3], known for its good generalisation. Like most of the supervised-learning algorithms for neural networks, RPROP also minimises the mean square of the error (i.e., the difference between the target value and the output value). In RPROP, however, the update of the weights uses only the sign of the derivatives, and not their size. The algorithm uses an individual adaptive learning rate for each weight, which makes the algorithm more robust with respect to initial learning rates.

During learning, the target value for moves 'known' to be the best was 1, otherwise 0. The error measure for evaluation and stopping criteria was the rate of not having the highest output activation value for the 'best' move. In each epoch the whole learning set was presented to the neural network updating the weights after each epoch. The error on the validation set was tested after each update. The training was stopped if the error on the validation set did not decrease after 100 epochs. For the three move-encoding schemes of section 2, the size of the hidden layer and the size of the learning set varied. Other parameters than these seemed to have less influence on the final performance.

In the second experiment the efficiency of the move ordering was evaluated using the neural networks that resulted from the first experiment. We compared the size of the search tree expanded by the move ordering described above with the size expanded using the history-heuristic move ordering. The size of the search trees is averaged over approximately 600 positions covering complete game sequences.

4 Experimental Results

In the first experiment, using the three types of pattern sets of section 3, we trained the neural networks with the three move-encoding schemes, varying the

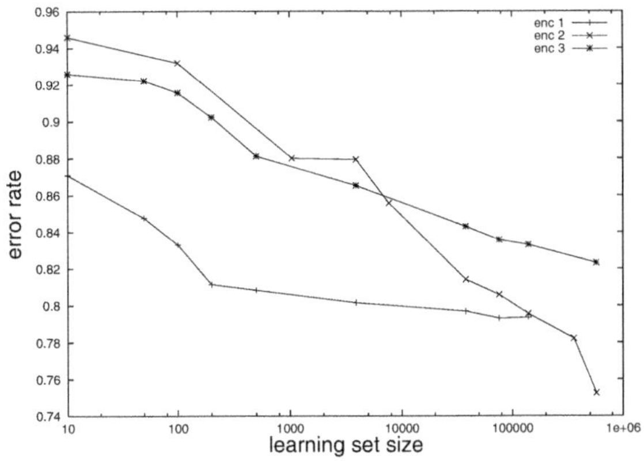

Fig. 1. The error rate on the test set as function of the size of the learning set.

size of the hidden layer and the size of the learning set. The increase of the hidden layer had only a clear influence on the first encoding scheme, namely, when large learning sets were used. Unfortunately, for this scheme the required time was already high with a small hidden layer. The remaining experiments, for each move-encoding scheme, were performed with a hidden layer consisting of 10 units and direct connections from the input to the output units. The dependency between the error rate on the test set and the size of the learning set is plotted in Figure 1. For smaller learning sets (up to 5000 board positions), the second encoding scheme had the worst results out of the three encoding schemes. However, this scheme gains the most from an increasing size of the learning set, clearly obtaining the lowest error rate for the largest training set. For smaller sets, the weak performance of the second encoding scheme was likely due to the poor generalisation (as predicted in section 2). For very large sets the available freedom of this scheme became more important than its generalisation. The first encoding scheme continuously outperformed the third one.

For the second experiment, we selected for each encoding scheme the neural network which had the smallest error rate in the first experiment. The three neural networks, corresponding to the three move-encoding schemes, were compared in terms of expanded search-tree size. The sizes of the search trees were normalised by dividing them by the sizes of the search trees expanded using the history heuristic for move ordering. The results are plotted in Figure 2. The node-count reduction can be interpreted as the reduction of the tree size if the history heuristic is replaced by the neural networks. The first and second move-encoding schemes seem to lead to similar results, and perform significantly better than the third scheme. Since the time used by the first encoding scheme to compute the estimated quality of the moves in a position is significantly higher than the time used by the other two, the second scheme can be considered as the best choice. Comparing the results obtained by the history heuristic, we observe a saving between 20 and 50 percent.

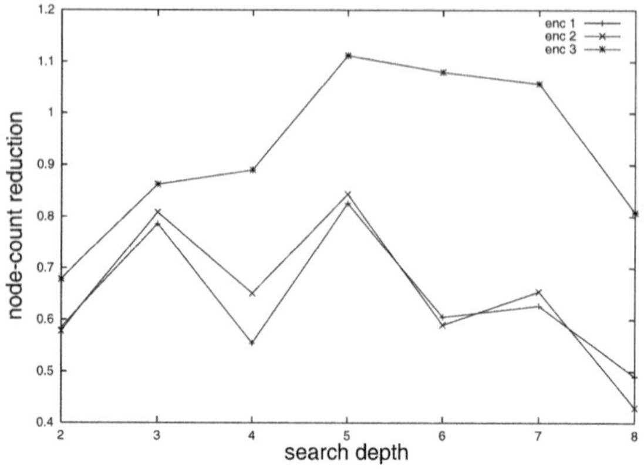

Fig. 2. The size of the search trees expanded using the best neural network for each encoding scheme as a function of search depth.

5 Conclusions and Future Research

This paper presents a new approach to move ordering, using neural networks to estimate the likelihood of a move being the best in a certain position. The move-ordering algorithm was tested for the game of LOA. From the experiments we conclude that the best choice is to use one output unit for each possible move of the game. The results from game-tree searches indicate that this approach to move ordering can speed up the search process with 20 to 50 percent compared with one of the best current alternatives, the history heuristic.

In practice, most search enhancements are not used in isolation. A major test for the move ordering presented is how it can be combined with other search enhancements or move-ordering techniques. Early results suggest that our move ordering works well in cooperation with a transposition table. An interesting issue is whether the neural networks obtained can be used in tree search for other purposes than move ordering. A challenging task is to develop selective-search techniques, which can exploit the strength of these neural networks.

References

1. Greer, K.: Computer Chess Move-Ordering Schemes using Move Influence. *Artificial Intelligence* **120** (2000) 235–250
2. Kocsis, L., Uiterwijk, J.W.H.M., Herik, H.J. van den: Learning Time Allocation using Neural Networks. *Working Notes of the Second International Conference on Computers and Games* (2000) 297–314
3. Riedmiller, M., Braun, H.: A Direct Adaptive Method for Faster Backpropagation Learning: The RPROP Algorithm. *Proceedings of the IEEE International Conference on Neural Networks 1993 (ICNN 93)* (1993) 586–591
4. Schaeffer, J.: The History Heuristic. *ICCA Journal* **6**(3) (1983) 16–19
5. Winands, M.H.M.: Analysis and Implementation of Lines of Action. MSc thesis CS 00-03, Department of Computer Science, Universiteit Maastricht (2000)

Why Use a Unified Knowledge Representation?

John Debenham

Faculty of IT, University of Technology, Sydney, PO Box 123, NSW 2007, Australia
debenham@it.uts.edu.au

Abstract. In a unified knowledge representation, data, information and knowledge are all represented in a single formalism. A unified knowledge representation based on "items" is described. Items contain two classes of constraints that apply equally to knowledge and to data. Items are compared to an if-then, or rule-based, knowledge representation. Simple chunks of knowledge that can only be represented by a number of rules are represented as single items. Rule-based formalisms are prone to the introduction of potential maintenance hazards caused by one rule being hidden within another. A single operation for items enables some of these hidden relationships to be removed. Items make it difficult to analyse the structure of a whole application. To make the inherent structure of items clear, 'objects' are introduced as item building operators. The use of objects to build items enables the hidden links in the knowledge to be identified. A single operation for objects enables all of these hidden links to be removed from the conceptual model thus simplifying maintenance.

1. Introduction

A *knowledge representation* is a formalism for representing at least the data, information and knowledge things in an application. The *data* things in an application are the fundamental, indivisible things. Data things can be represented as simple constants or variables. If an association between things *cannot* be defined as a succinct, computable rule then it is an *implicit* association. Otherwise it is an *explicit* association. An *information* thing in an application is an implicit association between data things. Information things can be represented as tuples or relations. A *knowledge* thing in an application is an explicit association between information and/or data things. Knowledge can be represented either as programs in an imperative language or as rules in a declarative language. A *rule* is a chunk of knowledge in an if-then form.

A knowledge representation is *unified* if there is no formal distinction between the representation of data, information and knowledge things [1]. A unified knowledge representation for conceptual modelling is described in [2]. A *conceptual model* is a representation of an application using a particular knowledge representation. The unified knowledge representation in [2] is expressed in terms of "items" and "objects"; objects are item-building operators. The key to this unified formalism is the way in which the "meaning" of an item, called its "semantics", is specified. A single rule of decomposition is specified for items [2]. Items are *either* represented

L. Monostori, J. Váncza, and M. Ali (Eds.): IEA/AIE 2001, LNAI 2070, pp. 51-60, 2001.

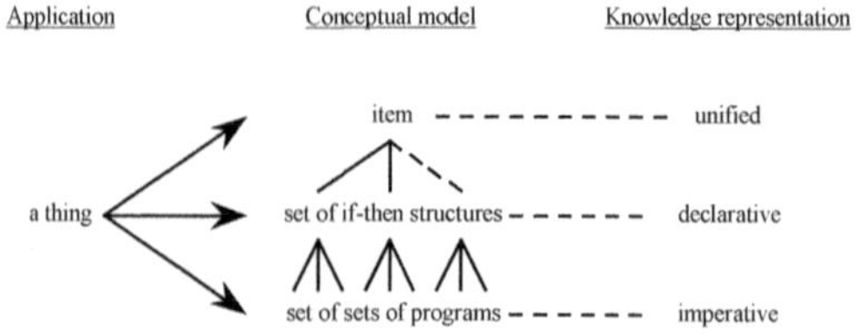

Fig. 1. A thing and its representation in the unified representation, a declarative representation and an imperative interpretation.

informally as "i-schema" *or* formally as λ-calculus expressions [3]. The i-schema notation is used in applications.

A rule of inference, called item (and object) "join" is defined [4]. A single rule for "knowledge decomposition" is defined in terms of join. Knowledge decomposition may be applied to simplify the maintenance of the conceptual model and its implementation [5]. Classical database normalisation [6] is a special case of the application of that single rule. The notion of an item and the resulting conceptual model reported in [2] is extended here to fuzzy measures of knowledge integrity. This is achieved by introducing fuzzy functions to describe a graduated region of varying degrees of integrity. These fuzzy functions are generalisations of the knowledge constraints described in [3].

The expressive power of a knowledge representation must be able to describe *at least* the data, information and knowledge things. In the unified representation items also contain two classes of constraints that apply equally to knowledge and to data. In [3] these constraints are generalised to fuzzy acceptability measures of knowledge base integrity. Item and object join has been extended to apply to those measures [4].

Why use a unified knowledge representation? In the 1980s there was considerable interest in building expert systems. At that time declarative formalisms, in particular if-then formalisms such as logic programming, provided one way of computing with knowledge that was far easier to use than imperative formalisms. The comparative ease of use of if-then formalisms was responsible for the misapprehension that knowledge could be thought of as "if-then stuff". In a sense this is true. If a chunk of knowledge has a number of if-then interpretations then it is unlikely that more than one of those interpretations will be useful at any particular time. One consequence of this misapprehension is that changes in the validity of one if-then interpretation that is not even represented may have subtle and serious implications for the validity of a number of parts of the knowledge base that are implemented. Approaches to modelling expert systems applications were based on other than declarative; for example, on frame-based systems but these are not considered here. During the 'age of expert systems' it was not uncommon to hear knowledge engineers observe "I took considerable trouble to build the knowledge base well but now I find that a simple change in the application can lead to an extensive maintenance task". One reason for such an observation is that apparently useless links in the raw knowledge have been ignored. So a knowledge representation with the property that a single chunk of knowledge, which may have a number of if-then interpretations, can be represented as a single entity could be a superior practical formalism for knowledge base design. The unified knowledge representation has this property. The unified representation is at a level of abstraction that is far closer to 'reality' than traditional declarative formalisms. There is a hierarchy: a real chunk of knowledge is represented as a single "item" in the unified representation. Each item has a number of interpretations as if-then forms. Each if-then form has a number of interpretations as imperative programs. This is illustrated in Fig. 1.

Further, the unified knowledge representation treats data, information and knowledge in the same way and so links between these three classes of things may also be represented. The majority of knowledge representation formalisms treat these three classes quite differently and so such links have no natural representation.

Items are compared to an if-then, or rule-based, knowledge representation. Simple chunks of knowledge that can only be represented by a number of rules are represented as single items. Rule-based formalisms are prone to the introduction of potential maintenance hazards caused by one rule being hidden within another. A single operation for items ensures that all of these hidden relationships can be removed. Items make it difficult to analyse the structure of a whole application. To make the inherent structure of items clear, 'objects' are introduced as item building operators. The use of objects to build items enables the hidden links in the knowledge to be identified. A single operation for objects enables these hidden links to be removed from the knowledge thussimplifying maintenance.

2. Two Difficulties with Declarative Formalisms

In a *declarative formalism* an if-then interpretation of a knowledge thing is represented in some "if-then" form. Two difficulties with declarative formalisms are illustrated using Horn clause logic as the representation formalism [7]. Logic is chosen because it is a widely understood notation, and *not* for any practical reason.

Consider the chunk of knowledge: [K1] "The sale price of a part is the cost price of that part marked up by the markup rate for that part". This single chunk is a simple statement of fact: it is *not* in an if-then form. Under a reasonable understanding of the meaning of chunk [K1] it admits three different if-then interpretations:

part/sale-price(x, y) ← part/cost-price(x, z),
  part/mark-up(x, w), y = (z × w) [C1.1]
part/cost-price(x, z) ← part/sale-price(x, y),
  part/mark-up(x, w), y = (z × w) [C1.2]
part/mark-up(x, w) ← part/sale-price(x, y),
  part/cost-price(x, z), y = (z × w) [C1.3]

For the third of these if-then interpretations—with "part/mark-up" as its head—there is a possibility of round-off error. The three clauses [C1.1]—[C1.3] are a rather inconvenient representation of the single chunk [K1] because *one* statement of fact has been represented as *three* logical statements. Consider another chunk of knowledge: [K2] "The profit on a part is the difference between the sale price of that part and the cost price of that part." As for [K1], the chunk [K2] is not in an if-then form. Under a reasonable understanding of its meaning, it also admits three if-then interpretations:

part/profit(x, y) ← part/sale-price(x, z),
  part/cost-price(x, w), y = z – w [C2.1]
part/sale-price(x, z) ← part/profit(x, y),
  part/cost-price(x, w), y = z – w [C2.2]

part/cost-price(x, w) ← part/sale-price(x, z),
  part/profit(x, y), y = z – w [C2.3]

The six Horn clauses [C1.1]—[C2.3] may be combined using resolution to give some potentially useful clauses:

part/profit(x, y) ← part/cost-price(x, w),
  part/mark-up(x, u), z = (w × u), y = z – w [C3.1]
part/profit(x, y) ← part/sale-price(x, z),
  part/mark-up(x, u), z = (w × u), y = z – w [C3.2]
part/mark-up(x, w) ← part/sale-price(x, y),
  part/profit(x, u), u = y – z, y = (z × w) [C3.3]

as well as some rather useless clauses:

part/sale-price(x, y) ← part/sale-price(x, v), part/profit(x, u), u = v – z,
  part/mark-up(x, w), y = (z × w) [C3.4]

A danger with all of [C3.1]—[C3.4] is that they are assembled from particular if-then interpretations of two chunks of knowledge, namely [K1] and [K2]. If the meaning of either of those two chunks should change then [C3.1]—[C3.4] may all have to be changed as well. This is not a problem if the relationships between [C3.1]—[C3.4] and both [K1] and [K2] are represented. But in the declarative representation, it is not clear that the meanings of [K1] and [K2] are buried in the four clauses [C3.1]—[C3.4]. So [C3.1]—[C3.4] and any other clauses derived from the original six clauses above, are potential maintenance hazards [10]. Given the six original clauses [C1.1]—[C2.3] there is no reason to combine them as illustrated in [C3.1]—[C3.4]. But clauses such as [C3.1]—[C3.4] are valid and could have been constructed by a knowledge engineer as part of a knowledge base. If they form part of a knowledge-based system then they may constitute a maintenance hazard [8].

Two problems with declarative formalisms have been identified. First, they have insufficient expressive power to represent all that a single chunk of knowledge has to say. Second there is no mechanism to prevent rules from being constructed that are a potential maintenance hazard [9].

part/sale-price		*part/cost-price*		*part/mark-up*	
1234	1.44	1234	1.20	1234	1.2
2468	2.99	2468	2.30	2468	1.3
3579	4.14	3579	3.45	3579	1.2
1357	10.35	1357	4.50	1357	2.3
9753	12.06	9753	6.70	9753	1.8
8642	12.78	8642	8.52	8642	1.5
4321	5.67	4321	2.70	4321	2.1

Fig. 2. Value set for a knowledge item.

3. The Unified Representation: Items

Consider again the chunk of knowledge [K1]. Suppose that that chunk is represented in a formalism—which we will call an *item*—with the name *[part/sale-price, part/cost-price, part/mark-up]*. The data associated with this item may be presented as a rather messy relation; such a relation is called the *value set* of the item, a possible value set is shown in Fig. 2. An *item* consists of: an item name, item components, item semantics, item value constraints, and item set constraints. The *item name* is usually written in italics, *A*. The *item components* is a set of the names of items which this item represents some association between. The *item semantics* is an expression which recognises the members of the value set of this item, S_A. The *item value constraints* is an expression which must be satisfied by all members of the value set of this item, V_A. The *item set constraints* are constraints on the structure of this item's value set, C_A. If two items have the property that the semantics of one logically implies the semantics of the other then the first item is a *sub-item* of the second. If two items have the property that they are both sub-items of each other then those two items are said to be *equivalent*.

For example, in an application there are 'parts'represented by the *part* data item. Each 'part' is identified by a 'part-number'. The value constraint for *part* requires that part numbers should lie in the range (1000, 9999). The set constraint for *part* requires that there are less than 100 different part numbers. Further there are 'costs' represented by the *cost-price* data item. Each *part* is associated with a *cost-price*. This association is represented by the information item *part/cost-price*. That item is subject to the "value constraint" that parts whose part-number is less that 1 999 will be associated with a cost price of no more than $300. That item is subject to the "set constraints" that every part must be in this association, and that each part is associated with a unique cost-price. The *part/cost-price* item is:

$$part/cost\text{-}price[\ \lambda xy\bullet[\ S_{part}(x) \wedge S_{cost\text{-}price}(y) \wedge \text{costs}(x, y)\ ]\bullet,$$
$$\lambda xy\bullet[\ V_{part}(x) \wedge V_{cost\text{-}price}(y) \wedge ((x < 1\,999) \rightarrow (y \leq 300))\ ]\bullet,$$
$$C_{part} \wedge C_{cost\text{-}price} \wedge (\text{Uni}(part) \wedge \text{Can}(cost\text{-}price, \{part\})_{part/cost\text{-}price}\ ]$$

where "Uni" specifies a *universal constraint* which requires that all members of the value set of *part* must be in the value set of *part/cost-price*. "Can" specifies a *candidate constraint* which requires that members of the value set of *part* functionally determine the members of the value set of *cost-price* in this item—in traditional database jargon, part is a potential key of the part/cost-price relation. Candidate constraints for a knowledge item identify potential if-then interpretations of that item.

Items are a universal formalism in that they can describe knowledge just as naturally as information (ie relations) or data. For example, consider the chunk of knowledge [K1]. [K1] is represented as the knowledge item *[part/sale-price, part/cost-price, part/mark-up]*:

$$[part/sale\text{-}price, part/cost\text{-}price, part/mark\text{-}up][$$
$$\lambda x_1x_2y_1y_2z_1z_2\bullet[\ S_{part/sale\text{-}price}(x_1,x_2) \wedge S_{part/cost\text{-}price}(y_1,y_2)$$
$$\wedge\ S_{part/mark\text{-}up}(z_1,z_2) \wedge ((x_1 = y_1 = z_1) \rightarrow (x_2 = z_2 \times y_2))\ ]\bullet,$$

$$\lambda x_1 x_2 y_1 y_2 z_1 z_2 \bullet [\, V_{part/sale\text{-}price}(x_1, x_2) \wedge V_{part/cost\text{-}price}(y_1, y_2) \wedge V_{part/mark\text{-}up}(z_1, z_2) \wedge ((x_1 = y_1 = z_1) \rightarrow (x_2 > y_2))\,]\bullet,$$

(Uni(*part/sale-price*) ∧ Uni(*part/cost-price*)
∧ Can(*part/sale-price*, {*part/cost-price*, *mark-up*})
∧ Can(*part/cost-price*, {*part/sale-price*, *mark-up*})
∧ Can(*mark-up*, {*part/sale-price*, *part/cost-price*})
)*[part/sale-price, part/cost-price, mark-up]*
∧ $C_{part/sale\text{-}price} \wedge C_{part/cost\text{-}price} \wedge C_{part/mark\text{-}up}$]

Its candidate constraints identify the three if-then interpretations represented above as the clauses [C1.1]—[C1.3]. So this item represents *all* that the chunk of knowledge [K1] says. Items appear to have resolved the first difficulty with rules identified above. Items are more than a convenient way of representing a set of rules; they can be manipulated, combined and decomposed. Computing with a collection of items amounts to computing with the set of rules represented within those items so items present no greater level of computational complexity than rule-based formalisms.

4. An Algebra of Items

Item join is an operation that may be applied to two items *A* and *B* that share a set of common components E to construct a third item called the *join* of *A* and *B* on E, and denoted by: $A \otimes_E B$. Item join is defined formally in [2]. The following is an example of the use of the join operator:

[part/profit, part/sale-price, part/cost-price, part/mark-up] =
[part/sale-price, part/cost-price, part/mark-up] $\otimes_{\{part/sale\text{-}price,\ part/cost\text{-}price\}}$
[part/profit, part/sale-price, part/cost-price]

Using the rule of composition ⊗, knowledge items, information items and data items may be joined with one another regardless of type [11]. For example, the knowledge item:

[cost-price, tax] [$\lambda xy \bullet [x = y \times 0.05]\bullet$, $\lambda xy \bullet [x < y]\bullet$,
(Uni(*cost-price*) ∧ Can(*tax*, {*cost-price*}))*[cost-price, tax]*]

can be joined with the information item *part/cost-price* on the set {*cost-price*} to give the information item *part/cost-price/tax*. In other words:

[cost-price, tax] $\otimes_{\{cost\text{-}price\}}$ *part/cost-price* =
part/cost-price/tax[$\lambda xyz \bullet [\text{costs}(x, y) \wedge z = y \times 0.05]\bullet$,
$\lambda xyz \bullet [((1000 < x < 1999) \rightarrow (0 < y \leq 300)) \wedge (z < y)]\bullet$,
(Uni(*part*) ∧
Can(*cost-price*, {*part*}) ∧ Can(*tax*, {*cost-price*}))*part/cost-price/tax*]

In this way items may be joined together to form more complex items [12]. Alternatively, the ⊗ operator may form the basis of a theory of decomposition in which each item may be replaced by a set of simpler items. An item I is *decomposable* into the set of items $D = \{I_1, I_2, ..., I_n\}$ if:

- I_i has non-trivial semantics for all i,
- $I = I_1 \otimes I_2 \otimes ... \otimes I_n$, where
- each join is *monotonic*; that is, each term in this composition contributes at least one component to I.

If item I is decomposable then it will not necessarily have a unique decomposition. So items can be combined using the ⊗ operator. The ⊗ operator also forms the basis of a theory of decomposition that removes hidden relationships from the represented knowledge. So items overcome the second difficulty described above for rules.

Items are a universal formalism for knowledge representation but make it difficult to analyse the structure of the whole application. For example, two chunks of knowledge that share the same basic wisdom may be expressed in terms of quite different components; this could obscure their common wisdom [13]. To make the inherent structure of items clear 'objects' are introduced as item building operators [4].

5. The Unified Representation: Objects

The introduction of objects enables the structure of the conceptual model to be analysed. In [4] it is shown that objects support a formal structure which may be used to manage maintenance. Objects are item building operators which have four important properties: objects have a uniform format no matter whether they represent data, information or knowledge things; objects incorporate powerful classes of constraints; objects enable items to be built in such a way as to reveal their inherent structure, and a single rule of 'decomposition' can be specified for objects such that if a 'decomposed' set of object operators is applied to a 'decomposed' set of 'base' items then the resulting conceptual model will contain only 'decomposed' items and will thus be maintainable. As for items, objects may either be represented informally as "o-schema" or formally as λ-calculus expressions. Object names are written in bold italic script. For example, suppose that ***costs*** is an operator that generates the information item *part/cost-price* from its components *part* and *cost-price*; that is:
part/cost-price = ***costs***(*part, cost-price*)

Further, suppose that the object ***mark-up-chunk*** is an operator which generates the knowledge item *[part/sale-price, part/cost-price, part/mark-up]* from its components; that is:

[part/sale-price, part/cost-price, part/mark-up] =
 mark-up-chunk(*part/sale-price, part/cost-price, part/mark-up*)

In general, an n-adic object is an operator which maps n given items into another item for some value of n. Further, the specification of each object will presume that the set of items to which that object may be applied are of a specific "type". The *type* of an m-adic item is determined both by whether it is a data item, an information item or a knowledge item and by the value of m. The type is denoted respectively by $\mathbf{D}^m$, $\mathbf{I}^m$ and $\mathbf{K}^m$; unspecified, or free, type which is denoted by $\mathbf{X}^m$ is also permitted. The definition of an object is similar to that of an item. An *object* consists of: an object name, argument types, object semantics, object value constraints, and object set constraints. The *object name* is usually written in bold italics. The *argument types* are a set of types of items to which that object operator may be applied. The *object semantics* is an expression which recognises the members of the value set of any item generated by the object. The *object value constraints* is an expression which must be satisfied by all members of the value set of any item generated by the object. The *object set constraints* are constraints on the structure of the value set of any item generated by the object. If two objects have the property that the semantics of one logically implies the semantics of the other then the first object is a *sub-object* of the second. If two objects have the property that they are each sub-objects of each other then those two objects are said to be *equivalent.*

For example, the ***mark-up-chunk*** object is:

$$\textbf{\textit{mark-up-chunk}}[\lambda P{:}\mathbf{X}^2 Q{:}\mathbf{X}^2 R{:}\mathbf{X}^2\bullet\lambda x_1x_2y_1y_2z_1z_2\bullet[\ S_P(x_1,x_2) \wedge S_Q(y_1,y_2) \wedge S_R(z_1,z_2) \wedge ((\ x_1 = y_1 = z_1\ ) \rightarrow (x_2 = z_2 \times y_2))\ ]\bullet\bullet,$$
$$\lambda P{:}\mathbf{X}^2 Q{:}\mathbf{X}^2 R{:}\mathbf{X}^2\bullet\lambda x_1x_2y_1y_2z_1z_2\bullet[\ V_P(x_1,x_2) \wedge V_Q(y_1,y_2) \wedge V_R(z) \wedge ((\ x_1 = y_1 = z_1\ ) \rightarrow (\ x_2 > y_2\ ))\ ]\bullet\bullet,$$
$$\lambda P{:}\mathbf{X}^2 Q{:}\mathbf{X}^2 R{:}\mathbf{X}^2\bullet[C_P \wedge C_Q \wedge C_R \wedge (\mathrm{Uni}(P) \wedge \mathrm{Uni}(Q) \wedge \mathrm{Can}(P,\{Q,R\}) \wedge \mathrm{Can}(Q,\{P,R\}) \wedge \mathrm{Can}(R,\{P,Q\}))_{v(\textbf{\textit{mark-up-chunk}},P,Q,R)}\ ]\bullet\ ]$$

The ***mark-up-chunk*** knowledge object represents the essence of the knowledgewithin the knowledge chunk [K1] without any reference to the components of that chunk. Objects represent abstract knowledge. Objects also represent value constraints and set constraints in a uniform way. A "join" operation for objects is defined in a similar way [4] to the join operation for items described above. If a set of objects have been decomposed using the object join operator then items generated by those objects will also be in a decomposed form.

There are a number of different senses in which two objects can be considered to be "equal". Three of these senses of "object equality" are described now. Given two n-adic objects of identical argument type $(X^{m_1}, X^{m_2},\ldots, X^{m_n})$ where each X is a type such as **X**, **K**, **I** or **D** (standing respectively for "free", "knowledge", "information" or "data"): $\boldsymbol{A}[\ E_{\boldsymbol{A}}, F_{\boldsymbol{A}}, G_{\boldsymbol{A}}\ ]$ and $\boldsymbol{B}[\ E_{\boldsymbol{B}}, F_{\boldsymbol{B}}, G_{\boldsymbol{B}}\ ]$.

A and ***B*** are *identical* written $\boldsymbol{A} \equiv \boldsymbol{B}$, if:

$$(\forall Q_1,Q_2,\ldots,Q_j)[E_{\boldsymbol{A}}(Q_1,Q_2,\ldots,Q_j) \leftrightarrow E_{\boldsymbol{B}}(Q_1,Q_2,\ldots,Q_j)]$$
$$(\forall Q_1,Q_2,\ldots,Q_j)[F_{\boldsymbol{A}}(Q_1,Q_2,\ldots,Q_j) \leftrightarrow F_{\boldsymbol{B}}(Q_1,Q_2,\ldots,Q_j)]$$
$$(\forall Q_1,Q_2,\ldots,Q_j)[G_{\boldsymbol{A}}(Q_1,Q_2,\ldots,Q_j) \leftrightarrow G_{\boldsymbol{B}}(Q_1,Q_2,\ldots,Q_j)]$$

A and ***B*** are *equal* written $\boldsymbol{A} = \boldsymbol{B}$, if:

$$(\forall Q_1,Q_2,\ldots,Q_j)[E_{\boldsymbol{A}}(Q_1,Q_2,\ldots,Q_j) \leftrightarrow E_{\boldsymbol{B}}(Q_1,Q_2,\ldots,Q_j)]$$

If two objects are either identical or equal then they will not necessarily have the same name.

A and ***B*** are *equivalent* written ***A*** $\simeq$ ***B***, if they are both of the same argument type and there exists a permutation π such that:

$$(\forall Q_1,Q_2,...,Q_j)[E_{\boldsymbol{A}}(Q_1,Q_2,...,Q_j) \leftrightarrow E_{\boldsymbol{B}}(\pi\,(Q_1,Q_2,...,Q_j))]$$
$$(\forall Q_1,Q_2,...,Q_j)[F_{\boldsymbol{A}}(Q_1,Q_2,...,Q_j) \leftrightarrow F_{\boldsymbol{B}}(\pi\,(Q_1,Q_2,...,Q_j))]$$
$$(\forall Q_1,Q_2,...,Q_j)[G_{\boldsymbol{A}}(Q_1,Q_2,...,Q_j) \leftrightarrow G_{\boldsymbol{B}}(\pi\,(Q_1,Q_2,...,Q_j))]$$

Data objects provide a representation of sub-typing. Knowledge is quite clumsy when represented as items; objects are a more compact representation. For example, consider the *[part/sale-price, part/cost-price, part/mark-up]* knowledge item which represents the chunk of knowledge [K1]. This item can be built by applying a knowledge object ***mark-up-chunk*** of argument type $(\mathbf{I}^2, \mathbf{I}^2, \mathbf{I}^2)$ to the items *part/sale-price*, *part/cost-price* and *part/mark-up*.

6. Conclusion

A unified knowledge representation has been described. That representation is based on "items". Items contain two classes of constraints that apply equally to knowledge and to data. Items overcome two difficulties with rule-based knowledge representations. Simple chunks of knowledge that can only be represented by a number of rules are represented as single items. Potential maintenance hazards caused by one chunk of knowledge being hidden within another that plague rule-based formalisms may be removed from the unified representation by a singleoperation. Items make it difficult to analyse the structure of a whole application. To make the inherent structure of items clear, 'objects' are introduced as item building operators. Objects are an abstraction representing the structure of knowledge.The use of objects to build items enables the hidden links in the knowledge to be identified. A single operation for objects enables these hidden links to be removed from the knowledge thus simplifying maintenance.

References

1. Barr, V. (1999). "Applying Reliability Engineering to Expert Systems" in *proceedings 12th International FLAIRS Conference*, Florida, May 1999, pp494-498.
2. Debenham, J.K. "*Knowledge Engineering*", Springer-Verlag, 1998.
3. Debenham, J.K. "The Degradation of Knowledge Base Integrity", in *proceedings 13th International FLAIRS Conference FLAIRS-2000*, Orlando, Florida, May 2000, pp113-117.
4. Debenham, J.K. (1999). "Knowledge Object Decomposition" in *proceedings 12th International FLAIRS Conference*, Florida, May 1999, pp203-207.
5. Debenham, J.K. "Representing Knowledge Normalisation", *in proceedings Tenth International Conference on Software Engineering and Knowledge Engineering SEKE'98*, San Francisco, US, June 1998.

6. Date, C.J., "*An Introduction to Database Systems*" (4th edition) Addison-Wesley, 1986.
7. Mayol, E. and Teniente, E. (1999). "Addressing Efficiency Issues During the Process of Integrity Maintenance" i*n proceedings Tenth International Conference DEXA99*, Florence, September 1999, pp270-281.
8. Ramirez, J. and de Antonio, A. (2000). "Semantic Verification of Rule-Based Systems with Arithmetic Constraints" in *proceedings 11th International Conference DEXA2000*, London, September 2000, pp437-446.
9. Katsuno, H. and Mendelzon, A.O., "On the Difference between Updating a Knowledge Base and Revising It", in *proceedings Second International Conference on Principles of Knowledge Representation and Reasoning, KR'91*, Morgan Kaufmann, 1991.
10. Johnson, G. and Santos, E. (2000). "Generalizing Knowledge Representation Rules for Acquiring and Validating Uncertain Knowledge" in *proceedings 13th International FLAIRS Conference*, Florida, May 2000, pp186-2191.
11. Werner, E. "Logical Foundations of Distributed Arttificial Intelliegence" in O'Hare, G.M.P. & Jennings, N.R. (Eds) "*Foundations of Distributed Artificial Intelligenece*", pp57-118, Wiley, 1996.
12. Darwiche, A. (1999). "Compiling Knowledge into Decomposable Negation Normal Form" in *proceedings International Joint Conference on Artificial Intelligence, IJCAI'99*, Stockholm, Sweden, August 1999, pp 284-289.
13. Jantke, K.P. and Herrmann, J. (1999). "Lattices of Knowledge in Intelligent Systems Validation" in *proceedings 12th International FLAIRS Conference*, Florida, May 1999, pp499-505.

Lazy Knowledge Base Update

Witold Łukaszewicz and Ewa Madalińska-Bugaj*

Institute of Informatics, Warsaw University
Warsaw, Poland

Abstract. Knowledge base update has been given much attention in the AI literature. The best-known solution to this problem is Winslett's PMA formalism. In this paper we propose different intuitions standing behind knowledge base update. Roughly speaking, we consider an update formula α not as an effect of an action to be performed, but rather as an observation about dynamically changing world made by an agent. This observation, if it is consistent with the knowledge base, is assumed to be just a new piece of information about the world. Otherwise, it is assumed that a *single* action has been performed and α is its, usually partial, effect.
We formalize our approach using Dijkstra's semantics. We also examine the properties of our update operator with respect to Katsuno and Mendelzon's postulates.

1 Introduction

There are two kinds of modifications of a knowledge base that have been given much attention in the AI literature: *knowledge base revision* and *knowledge base update.*

Knowledge base revision, (*KBR*, for short) [2,13] is formulated as follows. We are given a knowledge base KB, representing a static world, and a formula α representing new information. Our task is to determine the resulting knowledge base, $KB * \alpha$. The crucial point is that KB can contain incorrect information, so that α may be inconsistent with KB[1]. The theoretical foundations of *KBR* have been formulated in [2] by means of *rationality postulates*, referred as the AGM postulates.

Knowledge base update (*KBU* for short) [14,15,11,9,3,10] is similar to *KBR* with the exception that KB represents dynamic world and α represents the effect of an action to be performed. It is worth noting that under this interpretation *KBU* is nothing else but a very restricted form of reasoning about action. The formal basis for *KBU* has been proposed by Katsuno and Mendelzon [11] in the form of eight postulates, referred as the KM postulates. The best-known solution to *KBU* satisfying the KM postulates is Winslett's PMA [14].

* The authors were partially supported by the Wallenberg Foundation and by KBN grant T 11C 009 19.

[1] In this case, it is assumed that α is more reliable than KB.

L. Monostori, J. Váncza, and M. Ali (Eds.): IEA/AIE 2001, LNAI 2070, pp. 61–70, 2001.

A number of researchers have observed [3,9] that the KM postulates in the context of classical formulation of *KBU* can give rise to unintuitive results. The example frequently given is this. Suppose that $KB = p$ and $\alpha = p \vee q$. Since $KB \models \alpha$, then by postulate 2, we receive $KB * \alpha = p$. This result is clearly problematic. For instance, if α is the effect of tossing a coin, where p is *tails* and q is *heads*, we obviously do not want to conclude that our world does not change after the action.

In recent years, a few *KBU* formalisms trying to eliminate unintuitive results have been proposed [7]. All of them violate some of the KM postulates.

In this paper we propose different intuitions standing behind knowledge base update. We assume that the knowledge about the world is generally incomplete and that this world can change dynamically as the result of performing actions. Roughly speaking, we consider the update formula α not as an effect of an action to be performed, but rather as an observation about world made by an agent. If this observation is consistent with the knowledge base, there is no reason to conclude that an action has been performed. Accordingly, in this case α is assumed to be just a new piece of information about the world. Otherwise, we conclude that a *single* action has been performed and α is its, usually partial, effect. An example will help to illustrate this.

Suppose I have a neighbour living in Warsaw. Assume first that I have no information about where my neighbour is and where his car is. If I observe the neighbour's car behind his house, I treat this observation as a new piece of information increasing my knowledge about the world. Assume now that I know that yesterday my neighbour went by his car outside. Today, I observed that the car is parked behind his house. The presence of the car clearly suggests that the action of coming back to Warsaw has been performed by the neighbour. It is worth noting that the observation, i.e. the presence of the car, is only a part of the action's effect. Obviously, we should be able to infer more, namely that the neighbour is in Warsaw as well. Note that to make this inference, we must know the full specification of all admissible actions.

The paper is organized as follows. In section 2 we provide a general formalization of the problem and define our update operator referred to as *lazy knowledge base update operator* (*LKBU*, for short). In section 3 we represent *LKBU* in terms of Dijkstra's semantics. In section 4, we illustrate our update operator with a few examples. Section 5 is devoted to formal properties of *LKBU* operator. Finally, section 6 contains concluding remarks.

2 Formalization of the Problem

We are given a knowledge base *KB* and an observation α. If α is consistent with *KB*, we treat it as new information about the world, so the new *KB* is just the old one augmented with α. Otherwise, we conclude that the world has been changed as the result of performing an action. In this case, our task is the following: (1) To identify the action that has been performed; (2) To describe the new knowledge base representing the world.

To resolve the above task, we have to know all admissible actions. Suppose that these are $A_1, \ldots, A_n$. Assume further that $\circ$ is an operator that, for a given *KB* and an action *A*, returns the new knowledge base representing the world after executing the action[2]. Note that under these assumptions:

1. If the performed action is A_i, the new knowledge base *KB'* is $KB \circ A_i$.
2. Since α has been observed after executing the action *A* then *KB'* should be restricted to $(KB \circ A_i) \wedge \alpha$.
3. If we do not know which action has been performed, all we can conclude is that the new knowledge base is

$$\bigvee_{i=1}^{n} ((KB \circ A_i) \wedge \alpha). \tag{1}$$

   It is easy to see that the disjuncts of (1) that are not equivalent to false, specify all possible performed actions.

In conclusion, our update operator, called lazy knowledge base update and abbreviated to *LKBU* is defined by

$$KB * \alpha = \begin{cases} KB \wedge \alpha & \text{if } KB \wedge \alpha \text{ is satisfiable} \\ \bigvee_{i=1}^{n}((KB \circ A_i) \wedge \alpha) & \text{otherwise} \end{cases}$$

3 *LKBU* in Terms of Dijkstra's Semantics

In this paper we assume that *KB* and α are based on classical propositional language, (with boolean constants $\top$ and $\bot$ standing for truth and falsity, respectively) and actions are represented in terms of Dijkstra's semantics, originally developed to reason about programs [6].

In [6] we are provided with a very simple programming language whose semantics is specified in terms of formula transformers. More specifically, with each command *S* there are associated three formula transformers, called the *weakest precondition*, the *weakest liberal precondition* and the *strongest postcondition*, denoted by *wp*, *wlp* and *sp*, respectively. In this paper we ignore the first two transformers, because they will not be used in the sequel. Before providing the meaning of the *sp* transformer, two remarks are in order.

Firstly, we assume here that the programming language under consideration contains one type of variables only, namely Boolean variables. To be in accord with our earlier terminology, Boolean variables will be referred to as *atoms*. Secondly, in Programming Languages terminology, interpretations are usually referred to as *states*. We shall use this latter term here because it seems to be more appropriate in dynamic settings.

If α is a formula, x is a variable and β is a boolean expression, then $\alpha[x \leftarrow \beta]$ denotes a formula obtained from α by replacing all free occurrences of x by β.

[2] The technical details concerning both the representation of actions and the specification of $\circ$ will be presented later.

Let p be an atom and suppose that α is a formula. By $\exists p.\alpha$ we denote the formula $\alpha[p \leftarrow \top] \vee \alpha[p \leftarrow \bot]$.

The *sp* transformer is to be understood as follows. For each command S and each formula α: $sp(S, \alpha)$ is the formula whose models are precisely all states such that each of them can be reached by starting execution of S in some state satisfying α.

3.1 SDPL: A Simple Dijkstra Programming Language

The considered programming language consists of *skip* command, *assignment* command, *sequential composition* of commands and *alternative* command. Semantics of these commands is specified in terms of *sp* transformer as follows.

1. **The *skip* command.** This is the "empty" command.
$$sp(skip, \alpha) = \alpha.$$
2. **The *assignment* command.** This command is of the form $x := e$, where x is a (Boolean) variable and e is a (Boolean) expression.
$$sp(x := e, \alpha) = \exists y.((x \equiv e[x \leftarrow y]) \wedge \alpha[x \leftarrow y]),$$
where y is a fresh variable. If the variable x does not occur in the expression e, the above equation can be simplified to
$$sp(x := e, \alpha) = (x \equiv e) \wedge \exists x.\alpha \tag{2}$$
3. **The *sequential composition* command.** This command is of the form $S_1; S_2$, where S_1 and S_2 are any commands.
$$sp(S_1; S_2, \alpha) = sp(S_2, sp(S_1, \alpha)).$$
4. **The *alternative* command.** This command is of the form
$$\textbf{if } B_1 \rightarrow S_1 \parallel B_2 \rightarrow S_2 \parallel \cdots \parallel B_n \rightarrow S_n \textbf{ fi} \tag{3}$$
where $B_1, \ldots, B_n$ are Boolean expressions and $S_1, \ldots, S_n$ are any commands. $B_1, \ldots, B_n$ are called *guards* and expressions of the form $B_i \rightarrow S_i$ are called *guarded commands.* In the sequel, we refer to the general command (3) as IF. The command is executed as follows. If none of the guards is true, then the execution is equivalent to skip command. Otherwise, one guarded command $B_i \rightarrow S_i$ with true B_i is *randomly* selected and S_i is executed.[3]
$$sp(\text{IF}, \alpha) = \bigvee_{i=1}^{n}(sp(S_i, B_i \wedge \alpha)) \vee (\bigwedge_{i=1}^{n} \neg B_i) \wedge \alpha.$$

In the sequel we shall use the following two properties of the *sp* transformer: For any command S and any formulae α and β

$$sp(S, \bot) = \bot \tag{4}$$
$$sp(S, \alpha \vee \beta) \equiv sp(S, \alpha) \vee sp(S, \beta). \tag{5}$$

[3] Note that when more than one guard is true, the selection of a guarded command is nondeterministic.

3.2 Computing Eliminants

Recall that by $\exists p.\alpha$ we denote the formula $\alpha[p \leftarrow \top] \vee \alpha[p \leftarrow \bot]$. A formula of the form $\exists p.\alpha$ is called an *eliminant of* p *in* α.[4] Computing eliminants is crucial in computing the *sp* transformer. In the literature (see [4]), eliminants are computed by first transforming α into its disjunctive normal form. Since transforming a knowledge base into its disjunctive normal form is very expensive, we provide a new algorithm to compute eliminants. This algorithm is based on a DLS algorithm, originally developed to reduce second-order formulae into their first-order equivalents (see [8]). The DLS algorithm is based on Ackermann's lemma [1].

The algorithm consists of three phases.

Phase 1. Preprocessing
The purpose of this phase is to transform the formula $\exists p.A$ into the form

$$\exists p.[(A_1(p) \wedge B_1(p)) \vee \cdots \vee (A_n(p) \wedge B_n(p))] \tag{6}$$

where $A_i(p)$ contains positive and B_i negative ocurrences of the atom p.

1. Eliminate $\Rightarrow$ and $\Leftrightarrow$ and move $\neg$ to the right.
2. Distribute all top-level conjunctions over the disjunctions containing both possitive and negative occurrences of p. For this purpose, apply the equivalences $A \wedge (B \vee C) \equiv (A \wedge B) \vee (A \wedge C)$ and $(A \vee B) \wedge C \equiv (A \wedge C) \vee (B \wedge C)$ only if $B \vee C(A \vee B)$ have both positive and negative occurrences of p until the resulting formula is in the form (6).
3. Replace (6) by its equivalent given by

$$\exists p.(A_1(p) \wedge B_1(p)) \vee \cdots \vee \exists p.(A_n(p) \wedge B_n(p)) \tag{7}$$

Phase 2. Preparation to Ackermann's lemma
Repeat this step for each $1 \leq i \leq n$

1. Transform $A_i(p)$ to the form $(p \vee C_i) \wedge D_i$ or $B_i(p)$ to the form $(\neg p \vee C_i) \wedge D_i$, where C_i, D_i do not contain p. This transformation is always possible using thec equivalences $(A \wedge B) \vee C \equiv (A \vee C) \wedge (B \vee C)$ and $A \vee (B \wedge C) \equiv (A \vee B) \wedge (A \vee C)$.

Phase 3. Application of Ackermann's lemma
Use Lemma 4.1 (Ackermann's Lemma) from [8].
Repeat this step for each $1 \leq i \leq n$

1. Replace $\exists p(p \vee C_i) \wedge B'_i(p \leftarrow \neg p)$ by $B'_i(p \leftarrow \alpha)$ or $\exists p(\neg p \vee C_i) \wedge A'_i(p)$ by $A'_i(p \leftarrow \alpha)$. ■

---

[4] Intuitively, such an eliminant can be viewed as a formula representing the same knowledge as α about all atoms except p and providing no information about the atom p. The reader interested in a detailed theory of eliminants should consult [4].

4 Examples

In this section we illustrate our update operator with a few examples.

Example 1
There are two fluents, n and c, standing for *my neighbour is in Warsaw* and *his car is in Warsaw*, respectively, and four actions: *leave(Warsaw)-by-car*, *leave(Warsaw)-by-train*, *come-back(to Warsaw)-by-car* and *come-back(to Warsaw)-by train*, specified as follows:

A_1 : *leave-by-car*: **if** $c \wedge n \rightarrow c := \bot; n := \bot \| \neg c \vee \neg n \rightarrow skip$ **fi**
A_2 : *leave-by-train*: **if** $n \rightarrow n := \bot \| \neg n \rightarrow skip$ **fi**
A_3 : *come-back-by-car*: **if** $\neg c \wedge \neg n \rightarrow c := \top; n := \top \| c \vee n \rightarrow skip$ **fi**
A_4 : *come-back-by-train*: **if** $\neg n \rightarrow n := \top \| n \rightarrow skip$ **fi**.

Assume first that $KB = \neg n \wedge \neg c$ and our observation α is n. Since $KB \wedge \alpha$ is unsatisfiable, $KB * \alpha = \bigvee_{i=1}^{4} sp(A_i, KB) \wedge \alpha \equiv [sp(A_3, KB) \wedge \alpha] \vee [sp(A_4, KB) \wedge \alpha]$[5] $\equiv (c \wedge n) \vee (\neg c \wedge n) \equiv n$.

Note that it is impossible to determine how my heighbour came back to Warsaw without an additional observation concerning his car.

Suppose now that KB is as before but α is c. Again $KB \wedge \alpha$ is unsatisfiable, so $KB * \alpha = \bigvee_{i=1}^{4} sp(A_i, KB) \wedge \alpha \equiv sp(A_3, KB) \wedge \alpha \equiv c \wedge n$.

Note that now we can conclude additional information, namely that my neighbour is in Warsaw. ■

The next example shows that it is sometimes possible to infer new information that is not an effect of a performed action.

Example 2
There are two fluents km, standing for *my son knows undergraduate maths*, and pm, standing for *my son passed undergraduate maths exam.* Suppose that there is one action se (*my son stand to undergraduate maths exam*), defined as

if $km \rightarrow pm := \top \| \neg km \rightarrow pm := \bot$ **fi**.

Assume further that KB is $\neg pm$ and α is pm. Since $KB \wedge \alpha$ is unsatisfiable, we infer that the action se has been performed and new KB is $sp(se, KB) \wedge \alpha \equiv (pm \wedge km \vee \neg pm \wedge \neg km) \equiv pm \wedge km$. ■

Example 3
There are three fluents denoting a colour of the wall: *blue*, *green*, *red* and three actions: *paint-blue*, *paint-green*, *paint-red* defined as:

paint-blue: $blue := \top; green := \bot; red := \bot$
paint-green: $blue := \bot; green := \top; red := \bot$
paint-red: $blue := \bot; green := \bot; red := \top$

[5] Remaining disjuncts are reduced to false.

Assume first that $KB = blue \wedge \neg green \wedge \neg red$ and $\alpha = blue \vee green$. Since $KB \wedge \alpha$ is satisfiable, $KB * \alpha = KB \wedge \alpha \equiv KB$.

It is worth noting that the disjunctive formula α is not treated here as an effect of a non-deterministic action but rather as an uncertain observation (possibly due to noisy sensors).

Assume now that KB is as before and α is $green \vee red$. Since $KB \wedge \alpha$ is unsatisfiable, we conclude that an action has been performed.

$$\begin{aligned} KB * \alpha = &\ sp(paint\text{-}blue, KB) \wedge (green \vee red) \\ &\vee sp(paint\text{-}green, KB) \wedge (green \vee red) \\ &\vee sp(paint\text{-}red, KB) \wedge (green \vee red) \\ &\equiv \neg blue \wedge (green \wedge \neg red \vee \neg green \wedge red). \ \blacksquare \end{aligned}$$

5 Formal Properties of the *LKBU* Operator

As we remarked earlier, Katsuno & Mendelzon [11] proposed a number of postulates (the KM postulates) that they claim every update operator should satisfy. In this section, we check these postulates with respect to *LKBU* operator.

Below, KB is a knowledge base, α is an update formula and $A_1, \ldots, A_n$ is the set of all admissible actions. We assume that this set is *complete* in the following sense: if $KB \wedge \alpha$ is unsatisfiable for satisfiable KB, then there exists at least one action A_i such that $sp(A_i, KB) \wedge \alpha$ is satisfiable. This intuitively means that each observation that is inconsistent with the current world can be explained by at least one action. The KM postulates are the following:

(U1) $KB \star \alpha$ implies α.
(U2) If KB implies α, then $KB \star \alpha$ is equivalent to KB.
(U3) If both KB and α are satisfiable, then $KB \star \alpha$ is also satisfiable.
(U4) If $KB_1 \equiv KB_2$ and $\alpha_1 \equiv \alpha_2$, then $KB_1 \star \alpha_1 \equiv KB_2 \star \alpha_2$.
(U5) $(KB \star \alpha_1) \wedge \alpha_2$ implies $KB \star (\alpha_1 \wedge \alpha_2)$.
(U6) If $KB \star \alpha_1$ implies α_2 and $KB \star \alpha_2$ implies α_1, then $KB \star \alpha_1 \equiv KB \star \alpha_2$.
(U7) If KB is complete, i.e. has at most one model, then $(KB \star \alpha_1) \wedge (KB \star \alpha_2)$ implies $KB \star (\alpha_1 \vee \alpha_2)$.
(U8) $(KB_1 \vee KB_2) \star \alpha \equiv (KB_1 \star \alpha) \vee (KB_2 \star \alpha)$.

Theorem 1
The *LKBU* operator satisfies the postulates (U1) – (U7).
Proof: We start with the following

Lemma 1.
If KB is unsatisfiable, then $KB * \alpha$ is equivalent to $\perp$, for any α.
Proof of the lemma: Follows immediately from (4). ■

In view of Lemma 1, it is obvious that the postulates (U1) – (U7) hold if KB is unsatisfiable. We can, therefore, assume that KB is satisfiable.

(U1) and (U4) are straightforward.

(U2) Since KB implies α, KB and $KB \wedge \alpha$ are equivalent, and thus, since KB is satisfiable, $KB \wedge \alpha$ is satisfiable. In conclusion, $KB * \alpha$ is $KB \wedge \alpha$, and so, $KB * \alpha$ is equivalent to KB.

(U3) If $KB \wedge \alpha$ is satisfiable, the postulate obviously holds. Assume therefore, that $KB \wedge \alpha$ is unsatisfiable. Then $KB * \alpha = \bigvee_{i=1}^{n} sp(A_i, KB) \wedge \alpha$, and so, $KB * \alpha_1$ is satisfiable by the assumption that the set $A_1, \ldots, A_n$ is complete.

(U5) If $KB \wedge \alpha_1$ is satisfiable, the postulate clearly holds. Assume, therefore, that $KB \wedge \alpha_1$ is unsatisfiable. Then $KB * \alpha_1 = \bigvee_{i=1}^{n} sp(A_i, KB) \wedge \alpha_1$, and so, $(KB * \alpha_1) \wedge \alpha_2 = [\bigvee_{i=1}^{n} sp(A_i, KB) \wedge \alpha_1] \wedge \alpha_2 = \bigvee_{i=1}^{n} [sp(A_i, KB) \wedge \alpha_1 \wedge \alpha_2]$. On the other hand, since $KB \wedge \alpha_1$ is unsatisfiable, $KB \wedge \alpha_1 \wedge \alpha_2$ is also unsatisfiable, and hence, $KB * (\alpha_1 \wedge \alpha_2) = \bigvee_{i=1}^{n} [sp(A_i, KB) \wedge \alpha_1 \wedge \alpha_2]$.

(U6) Assume first that $KB \wedge \alpha_1$ is satisfiable. Then, $KB * \alpha_1$ is $KB \wedge \alpha_1$. Hence, since $KB * \alpha_1$ implies α_2, $KB \wedge \alpha_2$ is also satisfiable, and so, $KB * \alpha_2$ is $KB \wedge \alpha_2$. Thus, we know that $KB \wedge \alpha_1$ implies α_2 and $KB \wedge \alpha_2$ implies α_1, what immediately implies that $KB \wedge \alpha_1$ and $KB \wedge \alpha_2$, and so $KB * \alpha_1$ and $KB * \alpha_2$, are equivalent. Assume now that $KB \wedge \alpha_1$ is unsatisfiable. Then, by a similar argument as before, we conclude that $KB \wedge \alpha_2$ is also unsatisfiable. Thus, we infer that $\bigvee_{i=1}^{n} sp(A_i, KB) \wedge \alpha_1$ implies α_2 and $\bigvee_{i=1}^{n} sp(A_i, KB) \wedge \alpha_2$ implies α_1. Hence, by propositional logic alone, we conclude that $\bigvee_{i=1}^{n} sp(A_i, KB) \wedge \alpha_1$ and $\bigvee_{i=1}^{n} sp(A_i, KB) \wedge \alpha_2$, and so, $KB * \alpha_1$ and $KB * \alpha_2$, are equivalent.

(U7) If at least one of $KB \wedge \alpha_1$, $KB \wedge \alpha_2$ is satisfiable, the postulate clearly holds. (Note that in this case $KB \wedge (\alpha_1 \vee \alpha_2)$ is also satisfiable.) Assume, therefore, that $KB \wedge \alpha_1$ and $KB \wedge \alpha_2$ are both unsatisfiable, what implies that $KB \wedge (\alpha_1 \vee \alpha_2)$ is also unsatisfiable. Then $KB * \alpha_1 \wedge KB * \alpha_2$ is equivalent to (*) $\bigvee_{i=1}^{n} sp(A_i, KB) \wedge \alpha_1 \wedge \alpha_2$ and $KB * (\alpha_1 \vee \alpha_2)$ is equivalent to (**) $\bigvee_{i=1}^{n} sp(A_i, KB) \wedge (\alpha_1 \vee \alpha_2)$. Obviously, (*) implies (**). Note that we did not use the assumption that KB is complete. ■

It should be stressed that postulate (U8) need not to hold for the *LKBU* operator. To see this, assume that KB_1 is $\neg p \wedge q$, KB_2 is $p \wedge \neg q$ and α is p. Suppose further that there is one action, A, given by $p{:=}\top$. Then $(KB_1 \vee KB_2) * \alpha$ is equivalent to (*) $p \wedge \neg q$, whereas $(KB_1 * \alpha) \vee (KB_2 * \alpha)$ is equivalent to (**) p. Obviously, (*) and (**) are not equivalent.

The *LKBU* operator behaves similarly like belief revision operator of [2] if α is consistent with KB. Accordingly, one may suspect that the *LKBU* operator satisfies some of the AGM postulates that do not hold for the classical update operator. The next theorem, whose proof is straightforward, shows that this is indeed the case.

Theorem 2
The *LKBU* operator satisfies the following postulates:

(U9) If $KB \wedge \alpha$ is satisfiable, then $KB * \alpha \equiv KB \wedge \alpha$.

(U10) If $(KB * \alpha_1) \wedge \alpha_2$ is satisfiable, then $KB * (\alpha_1 \wedge \alpha_2)$ implies $(KB * \alpha_1) \wedge \alpha_2$.

6 Conclusions

In this paper, we have proposed a new approach to knowledge base update, called *LKBU*. The main difference between *LKBU* and other formalisms directed at knowledge base update is that an update formula, if consistent with a knowledge base, is regarded not as an effect of an action but rather as a piece of new information about the considered world.

We have formalized *LKBU* using Dijkstra's semantics, originally developed to reason about programs. Also, we have examined formal properties of our formalism with respect to update postulates of Katsuno and Mendelzon.

In this paper we do not consider integrity constraints. However this extension can be easily incorporated by using a technique proposed in [12].

As we observed (Examples 1, 3), in general, an update formula α do not allow to extract a single performed action. Instead, we receive a number of actions corresponding to α. An interesting topic to consider is to specify a minimal set of additional observations which could eliminate some of these actions. For instance, in Example 1 (first part) the new observation that the car is in Warsaw would eliminate the action *come-back-by-train*. We plan to work on this problem in the future.

References

[1] W. Ackermann. Uutersuchungen über das Eliminantionsproblem der mathematischen Logik. *Mathematische Annalen*, 110, 390-413, 1935.

[2] C. E. Alchourrón, P. Gärdenfors, D. Makinson. On the Logic of Theory Change: Partial Meet Contraction and Revision Functions. *Journal of Symbolic Logic*, 50, 1985, 510-530.

[3] G. Brewka, J. Hertzberg. How to Do Things with Worlds: on Formalizing Actions and Plans. *Journal of Logic and Computation.* Vol. 3, No. 5, 1993, 517-532.

[4] F. M. Brown. *Boolean Reasoning.* Kluwer Academic Publishers, 1990.

[5] M-O. Cordier, P. Siegel. A Temporal Revision Model for Reasoning about World Change. In *Int'l. Conference on Principles of Knowledge Representation and Reasoning*, 732-739, Morgan Kaufmann, 1992.

[6] E. W. Dijkstra, C. S. Scholten. *Predicate Calculus and Program Semantics.* Springer-Verlag, 1990.

[7] P. Doherty, W. Łukaszewicz, E. Madalińska-Bugaj. The PMA and Relativizing Minimal Change for Action Update. *Fundamenta Informaticae* **44** (2000) 95-131.

[8] P. Doherty, W. Łukaszewicz, A. Szałas. Computing Circumscription Revisited: A Reduction Algorithm. *Journal of Automatic Reasoning*, **18**, 1997, 297-336.

[9] A. Herzig. The PMA Revisited. In: *Proc. of the 5th Int'l. Conference on Principles of Knowledge Representation and Reasoning*, Morgan Kaufmann, 1996, 40-50.

[10] G. Grahne. Updates and Counterfactuals. In *Proc. of the 2nd Int'l. Conference on Principles of Knowledge Representation and Reasoning*, Morgan Kaufmann, 1991, 269-276.

[11] H. Katsuno, A. O. Mendelzon. On the Difference between Updating a knowledge base and revising it. In: *Proc. of the 2nd Int'l. Conference on Principles of Knowledge Representation and Reasoning*, KR'91, Morgan Kaufmann, 1991, 387-395.

[12] Madalińska-Bugaj, E. (1997) How to Solve Qualification and Ramification Using Dijkstra's Semantics for Programming Languages, in: *AI*IA-97: Advances in Artificial Intelligence, Proceedings of 5th Congress of the Italian Association for Artificial Intelligence*, Springer-Verlag, Lecture Notes in Artificial Intelligence, **1321**, 381-392, 1997.

[13] B. Nebel. A Knowledge Level Analysis of Belief Revision. In: *Proceedings of the 5th International Conference on Principles of Knowledge Representation and Reasoning*, 1989, 301-311.

[14] M. Winslett. *Updating Logical Databases.* Cambridge Tracks in Theoretical Computer Science. Cambridge University Press, 1990.

[15] M. Winslett. Updating Logical Databases. In: D. Gabbay, A. Galton, J. A. Robinson (eds.). *Handbook of Logic in Artificial Intelligence and Logic Programming.* Vol. 4 (Epistemic and Temporal Reasoning), 1995, Oxford University Press, 133-174.

On the Computational Aspect of Rule Based Database Updates

Yun Bai and Yan Zhang

School of Computing & Information Technology
University of Western Sydney
Locked Bag 1797, Penrith South DC NSW 1797, Australia
{ybai,yan}@cit.uws.edu.au

Abstract. We develop a general framework of rule based database update on the basis of prioritized logic programs. This approach has advantages in representing and handling information conflict in updates. We then focus on the computational aspect of this approach. We show that under our framework, the model checking in an update is co-NP-complete, while the associated inference problem is Π_2^P-complete. From a practical viewpoint, we propose two strategies to simplify an update specification so that under some conditions, solving an update problem can be based on solving some smaller components of the original problem. Our experimental result shows that these strategies indeed significantly reduce the time cost of evaluating an update specification.

Keywords: knowledge representation, intelligent databases, automated problem solving

1 Introduction

The rule based database update addresses the following problem: given a database and a set of update rules, what is the resulting database after updating this database with the set of update rules? For example, consider a domain of specifying user access rights to a computer system. Given an access policy base including facts that *Peter* can access file F and he is in group G, if the computer system officer wants to update the policy base in terms of a rule saying that if a user belongs to group G, then the user is no longer allowed to access file F, then after updating this policy base with the rule, we would expect that *Peter* cannot access file F any more. Although different syntax and semantics issues related to this update problem have been investigated by researchers recently, e.g. [4], no detailed study on computational and implementational aspects of rule based updates has been reported in the literature.

In this paper, we develop a general framework of rule based database update on the basis prioritized logic programs. This approach has advantages in representing and handling information conflict in updates. We then investigate the computational complexity of this approach. From a practical viewpoint, we also propose two strategies to simplify an update specification so that under some

L. Monostori, J. Váncza, and M. Ali (Eds.): IEA/AIE 2001, LNAI 2070, pp. 71–81, 2001.

conditions, solving an update problem can be based on solving some smaller components of the original problem. Our experimental result shows that these strategies indeed significantly reduce the time cost of evaluating an update specification.

The paper is organized as follows. The next section presents a general framework of rule based update. Section 3 addresses the issue of computational complexity of our approach. Section 4 proposes two strategies to simplify an update specification. Section 5 then illustrates our experimental results to show how these two strategies improve update evaluations in practice. Finally, section 6 concludes the paper with some remarks.

2 A Framework of Rule Based Updates

2.1 PLPs - An Overview

To begin with, we first briefly review prioritized logic programs (PLPs) proposed by the authors recently [8]. To define PLPs, we need to introduce the extended logic program and its answer set semantics developed by Gelfond and Lifschitz [1]. A language $\mathcal{L}$ of extended logic programs is determined by its object constants, function constants and predicates constants. *Terms* are built as in the corresponding first order language; *atoms* have the form $P(t_1, \cdots, t_n)$, where t_i $(1 \leq i \leq n)$ is a term and P is a predicate symbol of arity n; a *literal* is either an atom $P(t_1, \cdots, t_n)$ or a negative atom $\neg P(t_1, \cdots, t_n)$. A *rule* is an expression of the form:

$$L_0 \leftarrow L_1, \cdots, L_m, notL_{m+1}, \cdots, notL_n, \qquad (1)$$

where each L_i $(0 \leq i \leq n)$ is a literal. L_0 is called the *head* of the rule, while $L_1, \cdots, L_m$,*not* $L_{m+1}, \cdots$, *not* L_n is called the *body* of the rule. Obviously, the body of a rule could be empty. A term, atom, literal, or rule is *ground* if no variable occurs in it. An *extended logic program* Π is a collection of rules.

To evaluate a extended logic program, Gelfond and Lifschitz proposed the answer set semantics for extended logic programs. For simplicity, we treat a rule r in Π with variables as the set of all ground instances of r formed from the set of ground literals of the language of Π. In the rest of paper, we will not explicitly declare this assumption whenever there is no ambiguity in our discussion. Let Π be an extended logic program not containing *not* and *Lit* the set of all ground literals in the language of Π. The *answer set* of Π, denoted as $Ans(\Pi)$, is the smallest subset S of *Lit* such that (i) for any rule $L_0 \leftarrow L_1, \cdots, L_m$ from Π, if $L_1, \cdots, L_m \in S$, then $L_0 \in S$; and (ii) if S contains a pair of complementary literals, then $S = Lit$. Now let Π be an extended logic program. For any subset S of *Lit*, let Π^S be the logic program obtained from Π by deleting (i) each rule that has a formula *not* L in its body with $L \in S$, and (ii) all formulas of the form *not* L in the bodies of the remaining rules[1]. We define that S is an *answer set* of Π, denoted $Ans(\Pi)$, iff S is an answer set of Π^S, i.e. $S = Ans(\Pi^S)$.

[1] We also call Π^S is the Gelfond-Lifschitz transformation of Π in terms of S.

It is easy to see that an extended logic program may have one, more than one, or no answer set at all. A rule with the form (1) is *satisfied* in a set of ground literals S if and only if the fact that $L_1, \cdots, L_m$ are in S and $L_{m+1}, \cdots$, and L_n are not in S implies the fact that L_0 is in S. Clearly, each rule of an extended logic program Π is satisfied in every answer set of Π.

The language $\mathcal{L}^P$ of PLPs is a language $\mathcal{L}$ of extended logic programs with the following augments:
- *Names:* $N, N_1, N_2, \cdots$.
- A strict partial ordering $<$ on names.
- A naming function $\mathcal{N}$, which maps a rule to a name.

A *prioritized logic program* (PLP) $\mathcal{P}$ is a triple $(\Pi, \mathcal{N}, <)$, where Π is an extended logic program, $\mathcal{N}$ is a naming function mapping each rule in Π to a name, and $<$ is a strict partial ordering on names. The partial ordering $<$ in $\mathcal{P}$ plays an essential role in the evaluation of $\mathcal{P}$. Intuitively $<$ represents a preference of applying rules during the evaluation of the program. In particular, if $\mathcal{N}(r) < \mathcal{N}(r')$ holds in $\mathcal{P}$, rule r would be preferred to apply over rule r' during the evaluation of $\mathcal{P}$ (i.e. rule r is more preferred than rule r'). Consider the following classical example represented in our formalism:

$\mathcal{P}_1$:
$N_1 : Fly(x) \leftarrow Bird(x),\ not\ \neg Fly(x),$
$N_2 : \neg Fly(x) \leftarrow Penguin(x),\ not\ Fly(x),$
$N_3 : Bird(Tweety) \leftarrow,$
$N_4 : Penguin(Tweety) \leftarrow,$
$N_2 < N_1.$

Obviously, rules N_1 and N_2 conflict with each other as their heads are complementary literals, and applying N_1 will defeat N_2 and *vice versa*. However, as $N_2 < N_1$, we would expect that rule N_2 is preferred to apply first and then defeat rule N_1 after applying N_2 so that the desired solution $\neg Fly(Tweety)$ can be derived. This idea is formalized by following definitions.

Definition 1. Let Π be an extended logic program and r a rule with the form $L_0 \leftarrow L_1, \cdots, L_m$, not $L_{m+1}, \cdots$, not L_n (r does not necessarily belong to Π). Rule r is *defeated* by Π iff Π has answer set(s) and for every answer set $Ans(\Pi)$ of Π, there exists some $L_i \in Ans(\Pi)$, where $m+1 \leq i \leq n$.

Definition 2. Let $\mathcal{P} = (\Pi, \mathcal{N}, <)$ be a PLP and $\mathcal{P}(<)$ denote the set of $<$-relations of $\mathcal{P}$. $\mathcal{P}^<$ is a *reduct* of $\mathcal{P}$ with respect to $<$ iff there exists a sequence of sets Π_i $(i = 0, 1, \cdots)$ such that:

1. $\Pi_0 = \Pi$;
2. $\Pi_i = \Pi_{i-1} - \{r_1, \cdots, r_k \mid$ (a) there exists $r \in \Pi_{i-1}$ such that $\mathcal{N}(r) < \mathcal{N}(r_i) \in \mathcal{P}(<)$ $(i = 1, \cdots, k)$ and $r_1, \cdots, r_k$ are defeated by $\Pi_{i-1} - \{r_1, \cdots, r_k\}$, and (b) there does not exist a rule $r' \in \Pi_{i-1}$ such that $\mathcal{N}(r_j) < \mathcal{N}(r')$ for some j $(j = 1, \cdots, k)$ and r' is defeated by $\Pi_{i-1} - \{r'\}\}$;
3. $\mathcal{P}^< = \bigcap_{i=0}^{\infty} \Pi_i$.

Clearly $\mathcal{P}^<$ is an extended logic program obtained from Π by eliminating some rules from Π. In particular, if $\mathcal{N}(r) < \mathcal{N}(r')$ and $\Pi - \{r'\}$ defeats r', rule r' is eliminated from Π if no *less preferred rule* can be eliminated (i.e. conditions (a) and (b) in (ii)). This procedure is continued until a fixed point is reached. Note that due to the transitivity of $<$, we need to consider each $\mathcal{N}(r) < \mathcal{N}(r')$ in the $<$-closure of $\mathcal{P}$. It should be also noted that the reduct of a PLP may not be unique generally [8]. Now it is quite straightforward to define the answer set for a prioritized logic program.

Definition 3. Let $\mathcal{P} = (\Pi, \mathcal{N}, <)$ be a PLP and Lit the set of all ground literals in the language of $\mathcal{P}$. For any subset S of Lit, S is an *answer set* of $\mathcal{P}$, denoted as $Ans^P(\mathcal{P})$, iff $S = Ans(\mathcal{P}^<)$, where $Ans(\mathcal{P}^<)$ is an answer set of extended logic program $\mathcal{P}^<$. A ground literal L is *entailed* from a PLP $\mathcal{P}$, denoted as $\mathcal{P} \models L$, iff $\mathcal{P}$ has answer set(s) and L belongs to every answer set of $\mathcal{P}$.

Example 1. Using Definition 1 and 2, it is not difficult to conclude that $\mathcal{P}_1$ has a unique reduct: $\mathcal{P}_1^< = \{\neg Fly(x) \leftarrow Penguin(x), not\ Fly(x), Bird(Tweety) \leftarrow, Penguin(Tweety) \leftarrow\}$, and then from Definition 3, it has a unique answer set $Ans^P(\mathcal{P}_1) = \{Bird(Tweety), Penguin(Tweety), \neg Fly(Tweety)\}$.

2.2 Rule Based Database Update

Consider a language $\mathcal{L}$ of extended logic programs as described in section 2. We specify that a *database* $\mathcal{B}$ is a *consistent* set of ground literals of $\mathcal{L}$ and an *update program* Π is a set of rules of $\mathcal{L}$ of form (1) that are called *update rules.* Note that we allow a database to be *incomplete.* That is, a literal not in a database is treated as *unknown.*

We will use a prioritized logic program to specify an update of $\mathcal{B}$ by Π, where Π is an extended logic program. For this purpose, we first need to extend language $\mathcal{L}^P$ by the following way. We specify $\mathcal{L}^P_{new}$ to be a language of PLPs based on $\mathcal{L}^P$ with one more augment: For each predicate symbol P in $\mathcal{L}^P$, there is a corresponding predicate symbol $New\text{-}P$ in $\mathcal{L}^P_{new}$ with the same arity of P.

To simplifying our presentation, in $\mathcal{L}^P_{new}$ we use notation $New\text{-}L$ to denote the corresponding literal L in $\mathcal{L}$. For instance, if a literal L in $\mathcal{L}$ is $\neg P(x)$, then notation $New\text{-}L$ simply means $\neg New\text{-}P(x)$. We use Lit_{new} to denote the set of all ground literals of $\mathcal{L}^P_{new}$. Clearly, $Lit_{new} = Lit \cup \{New\text{-}L \mid L \in Lit\}$. Now we are ready to formalize our generalized rule-based update.

Definition 4. The *specification of updating $\mathcal{B}$ with Π* is defined as a PLP of $\mathcal{L}^P_{new}$, denoted as $Update(\mathcal{B}, \Pi) = (\Pi^*, \mathcal{N}, <)$, as follows:

1. Π^* consists of following rules:
   Initial fact rules: for each L in $\mathcal{B}$, there is a
   rule $L \leftarrow$;
   Inertia rules: for each predicate symbol P in $\mathcal{L}$,
   there are two rules:

$New\text{-}P(x) \leftarrow P(x)$, not $\neg New\text{-}P(x)$, and
$\neg New\text{-}P(x) \leftarrow \neg P(x)$, not $New\text{-}P(x)$,

Update rules: for each rule $L_0 \leftarrow L_1, \cdots, L_m$, not $L_{m+1}, \cdots$, not L_n in Π, there is a rule
$New\text{-}L_0 \leftarrow New\text{-}L_1, \cdots, New\text{-}L_m,$
not $New\text{-}L_{m+1}, \cdots$, not $New\text{-}L_n$;

2. Naming function $\mathcal{N}$ assigns a unique name N for each rule in Π^*;
3. For any inertia rule r and update rule r', we specify $\mathcal{N}(r) < \mathcal{N}(r')$.

An update specification $Update(\mathcal{B}, \Pi)$ is *well defined* if it has a consistent answer set.

It should be noted that in the above definition, we specify inertia rules to be *more preferred* than update rules in $Update(\mathcal{B}, \Pi)$. The intuitive idea behind this is that a preference ordering between an inertia rule and an update rule in $Update(\mathcal{B}, \Pi)$ will affect the evaluation of $Update(\mathcal{B}, \Pi)$ *only if* these two rules conflict with each other, eg. applying one rule causes the other inapplicable. On the other hand, a fact in the initial database $\mathcal{B}$ is always preferred to persist during an update whenever there is no violation of update rules[2]. Therefore, when conflicts occur between inertia and update rules, inertia rules should defeat the corresponding update rules. If no conflict occurs between inertia and update rules, the preference ordering then does not play any role in the evaluation of $Update(\mathcal{B}, \Pi)$.

Finally, on the basis of Definition 4, we can formally define a database $\mathcal{B}'$ resulting from updating $\mathcal{B}$ with Π in a straightforward way.

Definition 5. Let $Update(\mathcal{B}, \Pi)$ be a specification of updating $\mathcal{B}$ with Π as defined in Definition 4. A set of ground literals of $\mathcal{L}$, $\mathcal{B}'$, is called a *possible resulting database* with respect to the update specification $Update(\mathcal{B}, \Pi)$, iff $\mathcal{B}'$ satisfies the following conditions:

1. if $Update(\mathcal{B}, \Pi)$ has a consistent answer set, say $Ans^P(Update(\mathcal{B}, \Pi))$, then $\mathcal{B}' = \{L \mid New\text{-}L \in Ans^P(Update(\mathcal{B}, \Pi))\}$.
2. if $Update(\mathcal{B}, \Pi)$ is not well defined, then $\mathcal{B}' = \mathcal{B}$.

Example 2. Let $\mathcal{B} = \{\neg A, B, C\}$ and $\Pi = \{\neg B \leftarrow not\ B,\ A \leftarrow C\}$. From Definition 4, the specification of updating $\mathcal{B}$ by Π, $Update(\mathcal{B}, \Pi)$, is as follows:

Initial fact rules:
$N_1 : \neg A \leftarrow,$
$N_2 : B \leftarrow,$
$N_3 : C \leftarrow,$
Inertia rules:
$N_4 : New\text{-}A \leftarrow A, not\ \neg New\text{-}A,$

[2] Note that an update rule in $Update(\mathcal{B}, \Pi)$ is defeasible if it contains a weak negation *not* in the body.

$N_5 : New\text{-}B \leftarrow B, not\ \neg New\text{-}B,$
$N_6 : New\text{-}C \leftarrow C, not\ \neg New\text{-}C,$
$N_7 : \neg New\text{-}A \leftarrow \neg A, not\ New\text{-}A,$
$N_8 : \neg New\text{-}B \leftarrow \neg B, not\ New\text{-}B,$
$N_9 : \neg New\text{-}C \leftarrow \neg C, not\ New\text{-}C,$

Update rules:

$N_{10} : \neg New\text{-}B \leftarrow not\ New\text{-}B,$
$N_{11} : New\text{-}A \leftarrow New\text{-}C,$

$<$:

$N_4 < N_{10}, N_5 < N_{10}, N_6 < N_{10},$
$N_7 < N_{10}, N_8 < N_{10}, N_9 < N_{10},$
$N_4 < N_{11}, N_5 < N_{11}, N_6 < N_{11},$
$N_7 < N_{11}, N_8 < N_{11}, N_9 < N_{11}.$

Now from Definitions 2 and 3, it is not difficult to see that $Update(\mathcal{B}, \Pi)$ has a unique answer set: $\{\neg A, B, C, New\text{-}A, New\text{-}B, New\text{-}C\}$. Note that in $Update(\mathcal{B}, \Pi)$, only $N_5 < N_{10}$ is used in $Update(\mathcal{B}, \Pi)$'s evaluation, while other $<$-relations are useless (see Definition 2). Hence, from Definition 5, the only resulting database $\mathcal{B}'$ after updating $\mathcal{B}$ with Π is: $\{A, B, C\}$

3 Complexity Analysis

Now we analyze the computational complexity of rule based database update. For this purpose, we first present a result which shows that the update specification $Update(\mathcal{B}, \Pi)$ in language $\mathcal{L}^P_{new}$ defined in Definition 5 can be simplified to a PLP in language $\mathcal{L}^P$.

Lemma 1. *Let $Update(\mathcal{B}, \Pi)$ be a well defined update specification as defined in Definition 5 and $\mathcal{B}'$ a resulting database with respec to $Update(\mathcal{B}, \Pi)$ if and only if $\mathcal{B}'$ is an answer set of prioritized logic program $\mathcal{P} = (\Pi \cup \{L \leftarrow not\overline{L} \mid L \in \mathcal{B}\}, \mathcal{N}, <)$, where for each rule $r : L \leftarrow not\overline{L}$ with $L \in \mathcal{B}$, and each rule r' in Π, $\mathcal{N}(r) < \mathcal{N}(r')$*[3]*.*

Given a database $\mathcal{B}$ and an extended logic program Π, the update of $\mathcal{B}$ with Π is specified as an update specification $Update(\mathcal{B}, \Pi)$ which is a PLP as defined in Definition 5. From Lemma 6 stated above, we know that any set $\mathcal{B}'$ is a resulting database with respect to $Update(\mathcal{B}, \Pi)$ if and only if $\mathcal{B}'$ is an answer set of a PLP $\mathcal{P} = (\Pi \cup \{L \leftarrow not\overline{L} \mid L \in \mathcal{B}\}, \mathcal{N}, <)$, where for each $r : L \leftarrow not\overline{L}$ with $L \in \mathcal{B}$ and each $r' \in \Pi$, $\mathcal{N}(r) < \mathcal{N}(r')$. So we call this $\mathcal{P}$ the *equivalent PLP* of update specification $Update(\mathcal{B}, \Pi)$. From this result, it is clear that to evaluate a resulting database with respect to $Update(\mathcal{B}, \Pi)$, we only need to compute the answer set of $\mathcal{P}$. So the computational complexity of evaluating an update specification $Update(\mathcal{B}, \Pi)$ is equivalent to the the computational complexity of computing the answer set of $\mathcal{P}$.

[3] $\overline{L}$ stands for the complement of literal L.

Theorem 1. (Complexity of model checking in update) *Let $\mathcal{P}$ be the equivalent PLP of an rule based update specification, and S a set of ground literals. Deciding whether S is an answer set of $\mathcal{P}$ is co-NP-complete.*

Theorem 2. (Complexity of inference in update) *Let $\mathcal{P}$ be the equivalent PLP of an rule based update specification. For a given ground literal L, deciding whether $\mathcal{P} \models L$ is Π_2^P-complete.*

4 Two Strategies of Simplifying an Update Specification

Since the computation of the rule based database update under our framework is intractable as showed earlier, in practice we usually believe that no polynomial algorithm is available to implement this approach. Therefore, from an implementation consideration, it becomes a crucial issue to find possible methods to simplify the underlying reasoning procedure during an update.

Specifically, we consider two simplification strategies. Given an update specification $Update(\mathcal{B}, \Pi)$, we would like to investigate under what conditions the database $\mathcal{B}$ can be split into two disjoint parts as $\mathcal{B} = \mathcal{B}_1 \cup \mathcal{B}_2$ such that the evaluation of $Update(\mathcal{B}, \Pi)$ can be based on the evaluation of $Update(\mathcal{B}_1, \Pi)$ or $Update(\mathcal{B}_2, \Pi)$. Note that if such a split is non-trivial (i.e. none of $\mathcal{B}_1$ and $\mathcal{B}_2$ is empty), the size of $\mathcal{B}_1$ or $\mathcal{B}_2$ is smaller than $\mathcal{B}$. Hence the cost of evaluating $Update(\mathcal{B}_1, \Pi)$ or $Update(\mathcal{B}_2, \Pi)$ should be cheaper than that of evaluating $Update(\mathcal{B}, \Pi)$. Similarly, we also want to know under what conditions the update program Π can be split as $\Pi = \Pi_1 \cup \Pi_2$ such that the evaluation of $Update(\mathcal{B}, \Pi)$ can be based on the evaluations of $Update(\mathcal{B}, \Pi_1)$ or $Update(\mathcal{B}, \Pi_2)$.

Before we present our formal results, we need to introduce some useful notations. Let r be a rule in Π:

$$L_0 \leftarrow L_1, \cdots, L_m, \; not \; L_{m+1}, \cdots, \; not \; L_n.$$

We use $pos(r)$ to denote the set of literals in the body of r without negation as failure $\{L_1, \cdots,$
$L_m\}$ in r, and $neg(r)$ the set of literals in the body of r with negation as failure $\{L_{m+1}, \cdots, L_n\}$ in r. We specify $body(r)$ to be $pos(r) \cup neg(r)$. We also use $head(r)$ to denote the head of r: $\{L_0\}$. Then we use $lit(r)$ to denote $head(r) \cup body(r)$. By extending these notations, we use $pos(\Pi)$, $neg(\Pi)$, $body(\Pi)$, $head(\Pi)$, and $lit(\Pi)$ to denote the unions of corresponding components of all rules in Π, e.g. $body(\Pi) = \bigcup_{r \in \Pi} body(r)$. Given a set of literals $\mathcal{B}$, we also use $\overline{\mathcal{B}}$ to denote the set of complement literals of $\mathcal{B}$ with respect to classical negation sign $\neg$.

Theorem 3. *Given a well defined $Update(\mathcal{B}, \Pi)$. If $\mathcal{B} = \mathcal{B}_1 \cup \mathcal{B}_2$ and $body(\Pi) \cap \mathcal{B}_2 = \emptyset$, then every resulting database $\mathcal{B}'$ with respect to $Update(\mathcal{B}, \Pi)$ can represented as $\mathcal{B}' = \mathcal{B}'_1 \cup \{L \mid L \in \mathcal{B}_2 \text{ and } \overline{L} \notin \mathcal{B}'_1\}$, while $\mathcal{B}'_1$ is a resulting database with respect to $Update(\mathcal{B}_1, \Pi)$.*

Theorem 4. *Given a well defined Update*$(\mathcal{B}, \Pi)$*. If* $\Pi = \Pi_1 \cup \Pi_2$ *and* $head(\Pi_2) \cap (\overline{\mathcal{B}} \cup body(\Pi_1)) = \emptyset$*, then every resulting database* $\mathcal{B}'$ *with respect to* $Update(\mathcal{B}, \Pi)$ *is an answer set of program* $\{L \leftarrow \mid L \in \mathcal{B}'_1\} \cup \Pi_2$*, where* $\mathcal{B}'_1$ *is resulting database with respect to* $Update(\mathcal{B}, \Pi_1)$*.*

The above two theorems actually provide two simplification strategies to evaluate an update specification. In general, for a given $Update(\mathcal{B}, \Pi)$, we can apply the above two theorems sequentially and alternatively to split both $\mathcal{B}$ and Π into parts such that the evaluation of $Update(\mathcal{B}, \Pi)$ can be maximally simplified. The following example illustrates this application.

Example 3. Let $\mathcal{B} = \{\neg A, B, C\}$ and Π be a program consisting of the following rules:

$\neg B \leftarrow not\ B,$

$A \leftarrow C.$

Consider the update of $\mathcal{B}$ with Π. Firstly, since $body(\Pi) \cap \{\neg A\} = \emptyset$, according to Theorem 9, we can split $\mathcal{B}$ into $\mathcal{B}_1 = \{B, C\}$ and $\mathcal{B}_2 = \{\neg A\}$, and the resulting database $\mathcal{B}'$ with respect to $Update(\mathcal{B}, \Pi)$ is then represented as

$$\mathcal{B}' = \mathcal{B}'_1 \cup \{\neg A \mid \text{ if } A \notin \mathcal{B}'_1\}, \tag{2}$$

where $\mathcal{B}'_1$ is a resulting database with respect to $Update(\{B, C\}, \Pi)$. Therefore, the evaluation of $Update(\mathcal{B}, \Pi)$ is reduced to the evaluation of $Update(\{B, C\}, \Pi)$.

It is then observed that $head(A \leftarrow C) \cap \{\neg B, \neg C, B\} = \emptyset$, according to Theorem 10, Π can be split into $\Pi_1 = \{\neg B \leftarrow not\ B\}$ and $\Pi_2 = \{A \leftarrow C\}$, and $\mathcal{B}'_1$ is then represented as an answer set of the following program:

$$\mathcal{B}'_1 = Ans(\{L \mid L \in \mathcal{B}'_2\} \cup \{A \leftarrow C\}), \tag{3}$$

where $\mathcal{B}'_2$ is a resulting database with respect to $Update(\{B, C\}, \{\neg B \leftarrow not\ B\})$.

Since $body(\neg B \leftarrow not\ B) \cap \{C\} = \emptyset$, from Theorem 9 again, $Update(\{B, C\}, \{\neg B \leftarrow not\ B\})$ can be further simplified. That is, $\mathcal{B}'_2$ can be represented as

$$\mathcal{B}'_2 = \mathcal{B}''_2 \cup \{C \mid \text{ if } \neg C \notin \mathcal{B}''_2\}, \tag{4}$$

where $\mathcal{B}''_2$ is the resulting database with respect to $Update(\{B\}, \{\neg B \leftarrow not\ B\})$. Now it is easy to see that the unique result of $\mathcal{B}''_2$ is $\{B\}$. Then from (4), (3) and (2), we have

$\mathcal{B}'_2 = \{B, C\}, \quad \mathcal{B}'_1 = \{A, B, C\}, \quad \text{and} \quad \mathcal{B}' = \{A, B, C\}$

respectively. From the above reduction, we can see that the evaluation of $Update(\mathcal{B}, \Pi)$ is finally reduced to the evaluation of $Update(\{B\}, \{\neg B \leftarrow not\ B\})$, where the sizes of database and update program from initially three facts and two rules reduced to one fact and one rule.

5 Experimental Results

Since our rule based database update is based on the prioritized logic program, to implement this approach, we first should have a prioritized logic programming system. In fact, the second author and his student Cheng-Min Wu have implemented a propositional prioritized logic programming system (named PLPS) on the digital AlphaStation. The PLPS system is based on Niemelä and Simon's implementaitons of stable model semantics of logic program, i.e. smodel [5]. Details of the system implementation and performance have been reported in our another paper [7]. Based on the system PLPS, we have recently implemented a rule based database update system (named RuleUpdate) which follows the update framework described in this paper. In the following, we will show experimental results under the system RuleUpdate to justify our simplification strategies on update proposed previously.

Given an update specification $Update(\mathcal{B}, \Pi)$, we use a pair (x, y) to measure the size of $Update(\mathcal{B}, \Pi)$, where x is the number of literals in $\mathcal{B}$ and y is the number of rules in Π. Our experiment consists of four parts: (1) evaluating $Update(\mathcal{B}, \Pi)$ without any simplifications; (2) evaluating $Update(\mathcal{B}, \Pi)$ after splitting $\mathcal{B}$ into two parts; (3) evaluating $Update(\mathcal{B}, \Pi)$ after splitting Π into two parts; and (4) evaluating $Update(\mathcal{B}, \Pi)$ after maximally splitting both $\mathcal{B}$ and Π into parts. In the following tables, the time cost (in seconds) is for computing all possible resulting databases with respect to $Update(\mathcal{B}, \Pi)$. Note that the two simplification strategies have implemented in system RuleUpdate. So in Tables 2, 3, and 4, the extra cost of simplifying $Update(\mathcal{B}, \Pi)$, e.g. verifying conditions in theorems 3 and 4, etc. is counted in our tests.

Table 1. Evaluating $Update(\mathcal{B}, \Pi)$ without simplification.

$(\mathcal{B}, \Pi)$	time cost (sec) without simplification
(30, 10)	0.81
(100, 50)	1.79
(500, 100)	11.24
(1000, 500)	34.78

Table 2. Evaluating $Update(\mathcal{B}, \Pi)$ - splitting $\mathcal{B}$ only.

$(\mathcal{B}, \Pi)$	time cost (sec) after simplification
(30, 10)	0.37
(100, 50)	0.86
(500, 100)	6.04
(1000, 500)	19.23

Table 3. Evaluating *Update*($\mathcal{B}, \Pi$) - splitting Π only.

$(\mathcal{B}, \Pi)$	time cost (sec) after simplification
(30, 10)	0.51
(100, 50)	0.92
(500, 100)	4.89
(1000, 500)	18.41

Table 4. Evaluating *Update*($\mathcal{B}, \Pi$) - splitting bothe $\mathcal{B}$ and Π.

$(\mathcal{B}, \Pi)$	time cost (sec) after simplification
(30, 10)	0.18
(100, 50)	0.67
(500, 100)	3.54
(1000, 500)	13.96

From the above tables, it is quite clear that whenever splitting is possible for a update specification, the effects of two simplification strategies are quite significant. On the other hand, From Tables 2 and 3, it is observed that splitting $\mathcal{B}$ is not necessarily always better than splitting Π, and *vice versa*. However, Table 4 confirms that in any case, whenever $Update(\mathcal{B}, \Pi)$ can be maximally simplified, the effect is always better than that of only splitting $\mathcal{B}$ or Π.

6 Conclusion

We have proposed a general framework of rule based update and investigated its computational issue. A specific feature of our approach is that our rule based update framework is based on the prioritized logic program which provides a flexible and explicit mechanism to represent and handle possible information conflict in updates. It is worth to mention that the intractable complexity of our approach is inherited from the well-known computational property of the answer set (stable model) semantics of logic programs [6]. It is the fact that all rule based database updates approaches based on answer set (stable model) semantics, like those we mentioned in this paper, are computationally intractable. Within this computational limit, our work, nevertheless, provides an applicable idea to achieve better implementation results under some conditions.

References

1. M. Gelfond and V. Lifschitz, Classical negation in logic programs and disjunctive databases. *New Generation Computing*, **9**, pp365-386, 1991.
2. V. Lifschitz and H. Turner, Splitting a logic program. In *Proceedings of Eleventh International Conference on Logic Programming*, pp23-37, 1994.
3. J.J. Alferes and *et al*, Dynamic logic programming. In *Proceedings of KR-98*, pp98-109, 1998.

4. V. Marek and I. Pivkina and M. Truszcyński, Annotated revision programs. In *Proceedings of LPNMR'99*, pp49-62, 1999.
5. I. Niemelä and P. Simons, Efficient implementation of the well-founded and stable model semantics. In *Proceedings of IJCSLP'96*, pp 289-303, 1996.
6. V.W. Marek and M. Truszczyński, Autoepistemic logic. *Journal of the Association Machinery*, **38(3)**, pp588-619, 1991.
7. C.-M. Wu and Y. Zhang, Implementing prioritized logic programming. In *Proceedings of ISMIS'99*, pp 85-93, 1999.
8. Y. Zhang and N.Y. Foo, Answer sets for prioritized logic programs. In *Proceedings of the 1997 International Logic Programming Symposium (ILPS'97)*, pp69-83, 1997.

Building an Information and Knowledge Fusion System

Tamás Mészáros, Zsolt Barczikay, Ferenc Bodon,
Tadeusz P. Dobrowiecki, and György Strausz

Department of Measurement and Information Systems,
Budapest University of Technology and Economics (BUTE),
Műgyetem rkp. 9., Budapest, Hungary, H-1521
{meszaros, barczy, bodon, dobrowiecki, strausz}@mit.bme.hu

Abstract. In this paper authors present a system for information and knowledge fusion that provides an integrated management of information in a particular task domain. The proposed system uses structured (database and XML-based) and unstructured (information retrieval) data acquisition techniques, various knowledge representation schemes to integrate retrieved information, and customisable reports generated based on profiles supplied by the end user. This paper concentrates on modelling the problem domain, information and knowledge fusion methods, and technology fields used in the proposed system.

Introduction

Efficient knowledge retrieval is being investigated within the framework of the Information and Knowledge Fusion EUREKA Applied Research Project[1]. Our main goal is to analyse, design and implement a new Intelligent Knowledge Warehousing environment, which would allow advanced knowledge management in various application domains (e.g. banking, revenue service, insurance, legal information, training & education, health care, etc.) [1].

Conventional information sources in such application areas provide only limited and frequently unreliable information. It is also hard to evaluate such data in an optimal way. Despite the fact that nowadays quite a variety of information sources provide data for applications in these domains, the human evaluation is still needed to select the relevant information. This method has limited depth, scope and reliability. Only very few sources are considered for gathering information and the human resources are in all respects limited.

Successful applications of automatic extraction of information from data sources for the computer-based or human-based decision support show that even without considering the meaning of the stored data, useful information, e.g. trends or anomalies, can be determined. *Data mining* deals just with such extraction of implicit, previously unknown, and potentially useful information and with using it for crucial business decisions [2]. It uses machine learning, statistics and visualisation techniques for knowledge discovery and presentation in a form that is easily comprehensible to the humans. Data mining deals primarily with structured and well-defined data sources, especially with large relational databases.

---

[1] This research was also supported by the Hungarian NSF (OTKA) Grant Nr. F-030763.

L. Monostori, J. Váncza, and M. Ali (Eds.): IEA/AIE 2001, LNAI 2070, pp. 82-91, 2001.

Information retrieval means collecting information from unstructured text documents (like books, papers, and electronic documents) [3]. In the 90s the easiness experienced in the Internet publishing resulted in a greatly increased volume of documents stored in global computer networks. To find the right piece of information in this rapidly growing and unstructured data storage, new kinds of systems were developed, like e.g. Internet catalogues and search systems. Automatic indexing systems attempt to cope with vast amount of data and to build structured index schemes. Internet search engines use them then to find the required information.

In the today's information retrieval and data mining the meaning of the information, which is looked for, is not used. Any related knowledge, however, can vastly increase the effectiveness of the retrieval process.

The project formulated a number of objectives, namely:

(1) to determine suitable methods for describing semantic information, that can be used to enhance the retrieval efficiency in information retrieval;

(2) to evaluate the state of the art of knowledge representation and reasoning methods, and to integrate these techniques into the retrieval process; and

(3) to build knowledge-based information retrieval system.

Such system can be used as an electronic alternative to the conventional data collection and analysis tools. It can provide new services, greater depth of the analysis, and higher reliability in the data acquisition process. In particular it can **continuously monitor information sources**, and automatically update the related knowledge, and it can **select the relevant data and provide reliability information** as well.

Modelling the Problem Domain

At an abstracted level all of the applications mentioned before can be modelled as a formation and a purposeful interaction of three *information environments. Target Environment* is a fragment of the real world, where the targeted (monitored) objects (corporations, bank clients, business processes, etc.) do exist. *Information Cumulating Environment* comprises all forms and media, which cumulate information about the targets. In our case it is Internet, various Intranet resources, corporation databases, published resources, financial experts, etc. *Information Utilising Environment* represents the users of information (e.g. the staff of a bank), at various level of management. In the following, when convenient, we will address these three environments as the "Client", the "Web", and the "Bank" respectively, according to the financial application example.

Target Environment (TE, "Client") is the physical source of knowledge. It comprises objects, phenomena, relations, etc., whose particular properties (parameters, relations, and state variables) are of interest for both Information Cumulating ("Web") and Information Utilising Environments ("Bank"). Target objects are usually interrelated, i.e. part of the knowledge is common to whole subsets or structures of domain objects.

Information Cumulating Environment (ICE, "Web") is coupled to the Target Environment by knowledge acquisition process of various sorts. Knowledge embedded in the "Web" is thus to an extent a veritable model of the "Client". It is however important to note that such knowledge is heavily distributed within the

"Web" and that the application (i.e. "Bank") has no control over the whole extent and timeliness of the acquisition process. Consequently the "Bank" has no control over what knowledge is stored and where.

Information Utilising Environment (IUE, "Bank") represents active and possibly intelligent entities that require particular knowledge about the objects from within the "Client" to achieve their specific goals within the "Bank". An interesting feature adding to the complexity is that the "Web" and the "Bank" can be related, even overlapping. This will be true if e.g. the "Web" involves knowledge cumulated in human (expert) resources.

Knowledge Retrieval and Fusion

Our primary problem to face is that the knowledge acquisition between "Client" and "Web", and its storage in the "Web" are not specific to the goals found in the "Bank". The character of the knowledge acquisition reflects rather the physical and technological possibilities of the "Web" or some unrelated goals pending within that environment. Consequently, the form, the quality, and the validity of information are questionable from the users' point of view.

Specific goals require more condensed information than that available in the "Web's" sources. On the other hand when the user goals vary, so does the character of the requested information, even about the same "Client's" objects. In consequence the "Web" and the "Bank" must be interfaced by a mediating system embedded in both, which can accept as input the "Bank's" goals and which to provide answers should be familiar with the "Web's" possibilities and limitations, see Fig. 1.

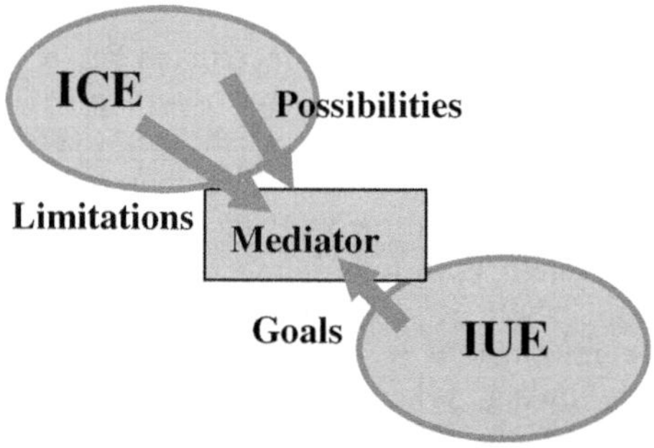

Fig. 1. Mediating system.

The components of the required mediating system follow logically from its function. Such system must help to find the information essential for the "Bank's" goals, however, for typically recurrent and related goals producing the information by the repeated request to the "Web" would mean an unjustified and badly organised spending of system resources. Consequently a **Knowledge Repository (KR)** is needed, which reflects a portion of the "Client" and would puffer the information to avoid spending too much of the system resources on extracting from the "Web" knowledge needed for recurrent and related retrieval requests.

This repository must be up-dated with intensity and agility defined by the "hunger" for the information in the "Bank" and with the information accumulated in the meantime in the "Web". The question is therefore where from and in what form seek the information? To handle this problem an **Information Retrieval Subsystem (IRS)** is required, which will perform knowledge sensitive and knowledge intensive information retrieval. The IRS should know models of the "Client" (essentially the structure of the KR), should know the model of the "Web", and should perform search for information.

Similarly to the IRS a **Knowledge Fusion Subsystem (KFS)** interacts with the KR and the "Bank". The Repository stores more information than the particular needs of the particular users in order to serve the diversified goals of the whole "Bank". Therefore, the KFS component must be told what to fetch in the KR and in what form to present it to the ordering entity in the "Bank".

Managing the System

In the following let us shortly review various support functions provided by the system. From the design point of view the "Bank" is composed from end-users and managers. End-users ask simple queries and accept data. Managers, in addition, shape the overall flow of information.

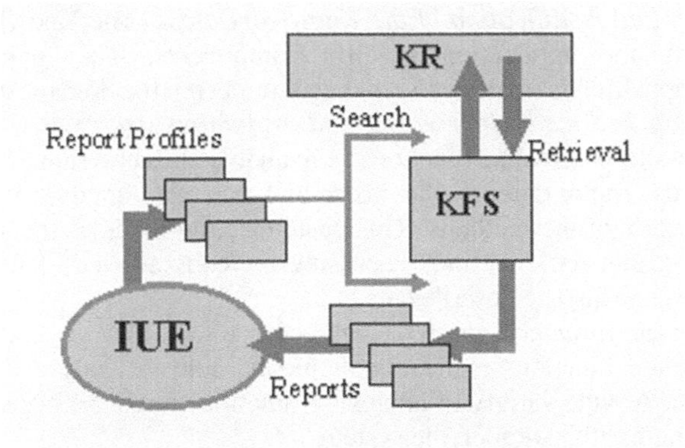

Fig. 2. Information flow related to the Knowledge Fusion Subsystem.

The information flow at the end-user level (i.e. the level of the individual goals in the "Bank") is governed by the Report Profile - a concise representation of the user's goals - stating which objects, parameters, etc. should be fetched from the KR and transformed into actual personalised reports (Fig. 2). The KFS finds the required information (continuously up-dated by the IRS), and reports it to the users in the "Bank" with automatically generated periodic and one-shoot summaries. The KFS works with a number of report profiles.

Similarly to the user defined Report Profiles managers must define suitable Search Profiles describing what, how, and where to search. Search Profiles modify the searching strategy within the "Web" and the up-dating strategy within the KR (Fig. 3). Managers can also add Report Profiles to define reports to be distributed all over the "Bank" (e.g. corporation news, daily or hourly exchange rates, etc.).

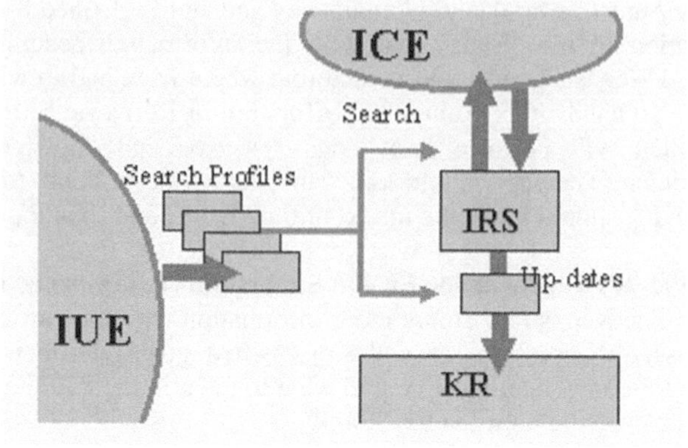

Fig. 3. Information flow related to the Information Retrieval Subsystem.

The key part of the system is the internal **Knowledge Base (KB)** that models the application area and in particular the application task. The model building process is difficult and requires expertise in both the internal structure of the IKF system and in the specific application field. Therefore only managers can use its development and management services. These tools are hidden at the user level.

Main tasks of the management services are the followings:

(1) *Design and modification of the Knowledge Base.* The Knowledge Base contains general and application specific components. The main purpose of this decomposition is to allow the manager to design the domain specific information.

(2) *Defining and modifying search and evaluation strategies.* A set of information search and processing functions is available in the system. Managers can select methods appropriate to the tasks and can also modify them by setting the parameters of the methods. This customisation includes the specification of data sources, and retrieval and processing methods as well. The reliability of these sources can also be described.

(3) *System performance analysis.* In order to be able to accomplish the above mentioned functions managers should be able to analyse the behaviour of the system. A wide variety of analysing functions might be necessary to accomplish the general utilisation on the system.

(4) *Monitoring, and supervising.* Monitoring and supervising is necessary in every complex system, but this task is especially critical for systems with adaptive nature.

(5) *Input form specification.* One of the important tasks of manager is to create application specific input forms for the user. Designing input forms means not only generating fields to fill-in, but also describing the relations between the fields and the internal representation.

(6) *Output report structure definition.* Manager can determine what part of the information should be recallable from the Knowledge Base. Manager can also define what part of the Knowledge Base is reachable for the end-users and what part should remain hidden for them. Pre-defined report forms can also be created and customised. The user can select these forms during the report creation.

User level services provide the interface for the end-users to define their requests and to read the results. The basic strategy applied here is that the end-user has only limited access to the system services. End-users can only reach information relevant to their working topics and are offered basically three types of services:

(1) *Generating queries using pre-defined input forms.* End-users can input information into the Knowledge Base and also pose queries to the system through pre-defined forms. End-users have limited possibility to configure the forms from the list of entities defined earlier by the manager.

(2) *Generating output reports by using and customising pre-defined report forms.* Users have similar possibilities for defining output report forms like in case of the input forms. This way end-users can produce dense reports on a given topic.

(3) *Asking for the information about the results of a query.* An important service is to provide explanation about the output data and also how the output data was generated.

Technologies in the IKF System

It is obvious that this system requires a wide variety of information acquisition, storage and access tools.

The "Web" contains a very diverse set of information repositories starting from relation databases, Internet resources up to the interfaces to various human data resources. In order to gather all these data the IRS should be equipped with several kinds of properly customised retrieval methods. We can categorise them into two main groups:

(1) *Structured retrieval.* **Data retrieval (DR)** from structured and well-defined data sources (like databases). It can also involve an automated **data mining (DM)** approach to exhaustively explore and determine complex relationships in very large databases.

(2) *Retrieving unstructured data.* **Information retrieval (IR)** deals with the retrieval process from unstructured data sources, e.g. the Internet resources.

We expect that many methods developed in data mining and information retrieval will be applicable to solve the knowledge acquisition problem.

Data Mining

Data mining investigates knowledge discovery techniques that obtain predefined structured knowledge solely from huge databases. Some data mining problems (like e.g. clustering [4] [5]) had already been known for a long time, and had been studied by many researchers in other fields of science (like statistics, machine learning, and visualization). Promising, possibly optimal, results were obtained (like K-L transform for dimensionality reducing), the size of databases, however, made it impossible to implement them in practice. The newly posed requirement, i.e. that the time and the memory demands of any algorithm in this field have to be linear in the size of the database, initiated further research.

There are several data mining approaches and application areas. *Association rules* try to find association between set of items in a given database of e.g. sales transactions (or market baskets), where each transaction contains some product [4] [6]. *Clustering* finds classes of closely related (similar) objects within a database of pattern vectors using a distance (similarity) function [5]. *Sequence matching* searches a database of event sequences, and it tries to find the closest to a query sequence [7]. In *Episode finding* a database about a long sequence of events with timestamps is given, and the task is to find those serial episodes that are present in at least a certain fraction of all windows [8]. *Classification* uses a database of training records with class labels for each, and it tries to build a concise model (generally a decision tree) to decide the classification for future, unlabeled records [9] [10]. *Web mining* is a data retrieval form in a linked environment that considers similar page/plagiarism finding, sophisticated query answering, page ranking etc [11].

Information Retrieval

Information retrieval is becoming a more and more important research topic as the publicly available information sources grow very fast. The World Wide Web, as an example, is a fast growing source of information. It introduced a set of technologies that allow the easy publication of electronic documents. However, its document formats, storage and access scheme do not help in finding the relevant information the user is looking for.

Information retrieval (IR), born as part of the library science in the 50's, deals with systems for indexing, searching, and recalling data, particularly text and other unstructured forms. With the growing amount of electronic data sources, IR received wide support from research organizations as well as from commercial companies in the 90's. Web indexing and search sites (like Altavista, Google, or Yahoo), text indexing and search options in databases (like Intelligent Miner for Text in DB2 from IBM, or Oracle interMedia), and client-based text indexing software (e.g. Autonomy's Kenjin) are examples of this.

Despite this growing activity in developing new IR methods and tools, the performance of these methods and tools is still far behind the similar tools for structured data retrieval. Web search engines overload their users with a waste amount of search hits (or they do not return any result at all). The basic problem behind this poor performance is that most systems are based on statistical indexing methods, and these methods cannot provide relevant results without understanding the meaning of the query and texts. Other systems based on natural language processing methods (where the aim is to "understand" the text and the query) have even worse performance due to missing proper techniques for automatically building semantic models from the text.

The Role of XML

The Extensible Markup Language (XML, standardized by the World Wide Web Consortium, W3C) defines text-based document in a structured way [12]. After successful attempts to standardise on the hardware and software, XML is an attempt to standardise on the information format, to make efficient search, storage and retrieval possible. XML is a so called mark-up language, i.e. a set of mark-up conventions to encode the meaning of the text. XML is extensible and various concrete languages can be created for particular domains.

XML is also a basis for many internationally accepted recommendations for electronic data exchange protocols. From the IKF point of view the most interesting developments are: XML-Based Ontology Exchange Language [13], Financial Products Mark-up Language [14], Artificial Intelligence Mark-up Language [15], DARPA Agent Mark-up Language [16], Extensible Financial Reporting Mark-up Language, Trading Partner Agreement Mark-up Language [17], Extensible Business Reporting Language, and the like [18].

Multi-agent System Architecture

The distributed nature of the problem suggests a generic multi-agent architecture, where the main components, and the parts of those are described as individual agents that co-operate or compete to fulfil their goals and thus overall system aims.

An intelligent agent is a software system that operates autonomously to fulfil locally specified goals [19]. The main characteristics of these systems are reactivity (it senses its environments and makes actions based on the perceptions), proactivity (it works to fulfil its goals), social ability (it is able to communicate with other agents and humans), and persistency (it continuously maintains an internal state). Other secondary characteristics may include being veritable, adaptive, robust, rational, and mobile.

There are emerging standards in this field, like the ARPA Knowledge Sharing Effort (KSE), the OMG Mobile Agent Facility (MAF), and the Foundation for Intelligent Physical Agents (FIPA) [20]. Multi-agent systems (MAS) contain autonomous agents that communicate with each other to solve common tasks. This requires a formalised communication language that can be implemented by the creators of the individual agents. The KQML (Knowledge Query and Manipulating Language) is and example of such a language [21].

Different agents can be designed and customised for different information sources. The multi-agent architecture can also be used to increase the reliability of the collected data. Co-operating agents will deal with the different information sources, and competing agents can be utilised to enhance the retrieval effectiveness. The agent methodology can be also applied during the interaction with the user. The complexity of the IKF system and the problem domain can be hidden from the user using specialised agents. Simple interface agents have tasks like helping the user in filling-in forms, or automatically correcting errors in user inputs. More sophisticated agents can be used as application helpers, explaining and teaching the usage of the system.

Knowledge Repository

Regarding the details of the Knowledge Repository two leading concepts are the knowledge organised around the suitable domain ontology and the XML-based document retrieval, mapping and storage. An ontology is an explicit (possibly formal) specification of the names for referring to the objects in the application and the (logical) statements that describe what these objects are, and how they are related or not to each other [22] [23].

Ontology therefore provides a vocabulary for representing and communicating knowledge that can exist for an agent or a community of agents, for the purpose of enabling knowledge sharing and reuse. The so-called ontological commitment means an agreement to use a vocabulary (i.e. for queries) in a way that is consistent with the theory. Research in ontology is one of the most far-reaching issues in the now-a-days artificial intelligence.

The crucial role of well-defined ontology has already been recognised. IEEE Computer Society pioneered a Standard Ontology Study Group [24]. A strong research group related to the IKF project is tackling the question of the meta-organisation of the ontological hierarchies [25], finally fairly recently a number of ontology based enterprise models has been developed [26] [27]. All these developments serve as a basis for the development of the suitable Hungarian enterprise ontology and knowledge base.

Summary

The collection of information forms a vast number of information sources available through the global computer networks and a knowledge intensive processing (reduction) of such information with the purpose to back up management decisions and evaluations opens new dimension in several applications fields.

Designing information systems that provide such support is already possible, if a number of emerging software, information processing, and system integrating technologies is used and further developed to meet the needs of the application. Designed approaches, tools and methods are portable to numerous domains, where the abundance of information and difficulty of making decisions made the introduction of the automated information system questionable until now.

In the framework of the Hungarian IKF project the authors have described a functional system architecture that integrates information acquisition, knowledge building, and profile-based report generation techniques to provide support for financial applications. In the current phase of the project technologies and software tools are investigated in the field of automated information retrieval, XML-based document processing, and data mining.

References

1. EUREKA PROJECT “IKF - Information and Knowledge Fusion”, March 2000.
2. U. M. Fayyad, G. Piatetsky-Shapiro, P. Smyth, R. Uthurusamy (Eds), “Advances in Knowledge Discovery and Data Mining”, Mit Press, 1996
3. Korfhage, R., “Information storage and retrieval”, Wiley Computer Publishing, 1997
4. R. Agrawal, T. Imielinski, A. Swami: "Mining Associations between Sets of Items in Massive Databases," Proc. of the ACM SIGMOD Int'l Conference on Management of Data, Washington D.C., May 1993, pp. 207-216.
5. S. Guha, R. Rastogi, and K. Shim, “CURE: An Efficient Clustering Algorithm for Large Databases,” SIGMOD 1998.
6. H. Toivonen, “Sampling Large Databases for Association Rules,” VLDB 1996, pp. 134-145.

7. C. Faloutsos, M. Ranganathan and Y. Manolopoulos, "Fast subsequence matching in time-series databases," SIGMOD, 1994, pp. 419-429.
8. H. Mannila, H. Toivonen, and A. I. Verkamo, "Discovering Frequent Episodes in Sequences," In U. M. Fayyad and R. Uthurusamy, eds, Proc. of the 1st Int'l Conf. on Knowledge Discovery and Data Mining (KDD-95), Montreal, Canada, Aug. 1995.
9. J.C. Shafer, R. Agrawal, M. Mehta, "SPRINT: A Scalable Parallel Classifier for Data Mining," VLDB 1996, pp.544-555
10. J.E. Gehrke, V. Ganti, R. Ramakrishnan, and Wei-Yin Loh, "BOAT -- Optimistic Decision Tree Construction," In Proceedings of the 1999 SIGMOD Conference, Philadelphia, Pennsylvania, 1999.
11. S. Chakrabarti, et.al., "Mining the Web's Link Structure," IEEE Computer 32: 60-67 (1999)
12. P. Prescod and Ch. F. Goldfarb, "The XML Handbook - 2nd Edition", Prentice Hall, 1999
13. XML-Based Ontology Exchange Language (XOL), http://www.oasis-open.org/cover/xol.html
14. Financial Products Mark-up Language (FpML), http://www.oasis-open.org/cover/fpml.html
15. Artificial Intelligence Mark-up Language (ALICE), http://www.oasis-open.org/cover/aiml-ALICE.html
16. DARPA Agent Mark-up Language (DAML), http://www.oasis-open.org/cover/daml.html
17. Trading Partner Agreement Markup Language (tpaML), http://www.oasis-open.org/cover/tpa.html
18. XML: Proposed Applications and Industry Initiatives, http://www.oasis-open.org/cover/ xml.html#applications
19. J. M. Broadshaw, "Software Agents", The MIT Press, 1997
20. Y. Labrou, T. Finin, and Yun Peng, "Agent Communication Languages: The Current Landscape", IEEE Intelligent Systems, March/April 1999, pp. 45-52
21. UMBC KQML Web, http://www.cs.umbc.edu/kqml/
22. John Sowa's web site devoted to knowlege representation and related topics of logic, ontology, and computer systems, http://www.bestweb.net/~sowa/direct/index.htm
23. N. Guarino and Ch. Welty, "Towards a methodology for ontology-based model engineering", in Proc. of the ECOOP-2000 Workshop on Model Engineering. June, 2000.
24. Standard Upper Ontology, IEEE Study Group, IEEE Computer Society, Standards Activity Board, June 2000, wysiwyg://634/http://ltsc.ieee.org/suo/index.html
25. N. Guarino and Ch. Welty, "A Formal Ontology of Properties", LADSEB/CNR Technical Report 01/2000, http://www.ladseb.pd.cnr.it/infor/ontology/Papers/OntologyPapers.html
26. M.S. Fox, J.F. Chionglo, and F.G. Fadel, "A Common-Sense Model of the Enterprise", Proceedings of the 2nd Industrial Engineering Research Conference, 1993, pp. 425-429, Norcross GA: Institute for Industrial Engineers
27. US Taxonomies, US GAAP C&I Taxonomy 00-04-04, http://http://www.xbrl.org/US/default.htm

Hierarchical Approach for Engineering Skills Acquisition

Mark S. Levin

Dept. of Mechanical Engineering
Ben-Gurion University, Beer-Sheva, 84105, Israel
marksh@bgumail.bgu.ac.il

Abstract. The article addresses the use of hierarchical morphological design framework for engineering skills acquisition. The hierarchical approach is the best way for structuring some complex design skills in the field of composite systems. Applications of the hierarchical morphological approach involve hierarchical description, design and analysis of composite systems, and an analysis of system evolution. Our material describes the following: (i) some hierarchical structures and combinatorial operations, (ii) hierarchical information, (iii) hierarchical processes (e.g., AHP, hierarchical decision making), (iv) our hierarchical morphological approach (HMA), (v) many applications of hierarchical morphological approach, (vi) some strategies for acquisition of engineering skills, and (vii) usefulness for engineering education and extension / structuring of engineering skills.

1 Introduction

In recent years, issues of skill / knowledge acquisition have been played a central role in many domains (e.g., cognitive modeling, information technology, problem solving, knowledge based systems, system design, engineering design, systems engineering, process systems engineering, team distributed design processes) ([2], [3], [10], [11], [16], [40], [46], [44], etc.). Let us point out some other important research directions closed to the above-mentioned domain: (a) cognitive modeling of design processes [1], [2], [3], etc.); (b) relation between cognitive processes and operations research [19]; (c) organization and management of engineering information on complex products / systems and their reengineering ([4], [24], [39], [48], etc.); (d) studying and developing the knowledge and skills of specialists ([10], [11], etc.); and (e) cognitive modeling for conceptual design ([24], [33], etc.).

This article focuses an experience in acquisition of systems engineering / system design skills. In our opinion, the significance of the direction is increasing because engineering of many complex systems is based on domain expert knowledge. The following human operations for information processing have been considered as basic ones [35], etc.): *1.* accumulation of knowledge; *2.* generalization of knowledge; *3.* revelation of problems; *4.* usage of judgment for problem solving; *5.* explanation of judgment; *6.* joint work with other specialists and, as a

L. Monostori, J. Váncza, and M. Ali (Eds.): IEA/AIE 2001, LNAI 2070, pp. 92–100, 2001.

result; accumulation of new knowledge; *7.* restructuring of knowledge; *8.* usage of exceptions; and *9.* understanding a situation that a problem is connected with a certain expert domain.

In this paper, a hierarchical morphological framework is examined which is an useful organizational basis for a systems engineering process: to execute operations for the description, design, analysis and improvement of composite systems. Hierarchical approach allows to combine the above-mentioned operations at various hierarchical levels, and decompose a global problem into more simple problem domains. Note we consider, at the same time, declarative hierarchical information on a system and procedure hierarchical information (mainly, system description, selection and composing of alternatives, revelation of bottlenecks) on the analysis, design and transformation of the system. Usually the systems engineering process has to integrate cooperative works of many domain experts. As a result, the organizational workflow problem is the following: (a) to divide an initial system problem into subproblems, (b) to solve the subproblems, and (c) to integrate local decisions for subproblems above into a global decision of the initial system problem. This workflow is a *cascade-like* one.

Conclin has pointed out that a hierarchical representation of information is more natural for users with an engineering background [9]. Thus the hierarchical approach is the best way for structuring some complex design skills in the field of composite systems. In this paper, our way is the following:

(i) some hierarchical structures and combinatorial operations,

(ii) hierarchical information,

(iii) hierarchical processes (e.g., AHP, hierarchical decision making),

(iv) our hierarchical morphological approach (HMA),

(v) applications of hierarchical morphological approach,

(vi) some strategies for acquisition of engineering skills, and

(vii) usefulness for engineering education and extension / structuring of engineering skills.

Note construction of a generalization space some domain knowledge is a contemporary approach in the field of conceptual structuring ([6], [7], etc.). Minsky has pointed out the following architecture of representations ([37] and [38]): (1) stories written in natural language; (2) story-like scripts; (3) transframes; (4) frame-arrays and picture-frames; (5) semantic nets; (6) K-lines; (7) neural nets; and (8) micronemes.

HMA is a hierarchical combination of several types of the above-mentioned representations including the following:

(a) description of goals, system components, criteria, etc (stories and story-like scripts);

(b) frame arrays, picture-frames and their graph-like modeling (e.g., system structure, interconnection between system parts and components, alternatives and relations on them, criteria and preference relations on them);

(c) semantics nets (e.g., for system improvement process, modeling the system evolution as a network of system generations).

Our hierarchical system model is a special generalized space for modeling many composite systems and their generations ([24] and [29]).

2 Hierarchical Information Systems

2.1 Hierarchical Structures and Operations

Shenhar has described three kinds (levels) of complex systems (assembly, system, array) [45]. Thus it is necessary to apply various kinds of hierarchical structures for the description of systems ([5], [9], [24], [42], [48], etc.), for example: (a) tree; (b) forest; (c) hierarchy of various kinds, e.g., organic hierarchy [8]); and (d) pyramid. Here the following requirement have to be taken into account: (i) correspondence (adequacy) to the described system; (ii) correspondence to an experience / background of domain expert(s) (usefulness for human); and (iii) usefulness from viewpoint of data processing (simpleness for computer processing).

At the same time, it is reasonable to take into account main life cycle stages for a structure as design and support (search, coordination, improvement, merging / integration, transformation). Well-known operations are the following ([15], [17], [24], [42], [47], etc.):

I. Traditional operations: input of data, correction, search (retrieval).

II. Structural processing: (1) comparison; (2) revelation of substructure of a certain kind; (3) analysis of interconnection between some substructures; (4) analysis of some properties (e.g., balance) (4) integration of structures; (5) approximation of structures by some structures of a certain kind (e.g., by tree-like ones); and (6) transformation.

For each operation above, we can use well-known and some new kinds of mathematical models (e.g., various types of metrics or proximity; models of matching; models of integration; models of approximation or covering) ([5], [15], [21], [24], etc.).

2.2 Some Hierarchical Information Systems

Main functional operations for the design, utilization, and maintenance of design information systems are the following ([12], [22], and [41]): (1) acquisition of new data and knowledge; (2) structuring, modeling; (3) representation; (4) learning; (5) access, control; (6) analysis, evaluation, correction; and (7) maintenance. Support information systems may be oriented to various components of a systems engineering (system design) process. Also, it is reasonable to list reference examples of some information systems:

(1) Information Design Model (EDM) for engineering design [13];

(2) hierarchical hypertext system (HHS) involving components of different kinds and their criterial descriptions for various problem domains ([21] and [22];

(3) Designer's Electronic Guidebook for mechanical engineering in Cambridge Engineering Center [14]; and

(4) An Information Model for Cooperative Product Development SHARED [48].

3 Hierarchical Morphological Approach

Hierarchical processes and problem solving techniques on the basis of decomposition (problem partitioning) are well-known ones, for example: (a) dynamic programming ([15], etc.); (b) Analytic Hierarchy Process AHP [43]; and (c) Branch-And-Bound method in combinatorial optimization ([15], etc.).

In this section, we briefly describe our hierarchical morphological approach HMA which integrates the following methodologies:

1. design frameworks (generalized hierarchical design approach to the description, analysis and synthesis of the designed and / or redesigned composite system;

2. multicriteria decision making (e.g., for ranking some design alternatives, for analysis of composite decisions);

3. morphological analysis (for composition of composite alternatives);

4. combinatorial optimization (e.g., morphological clique model to combine local decision into a resultant composite one); and

5. knowledge based methodology and knowledge engineering (e.g., techniques for acquisition of ordinal expert knowledge on design alternatives and their compatibility).

Note an explanation of our approach and the above-mentioned components (methodologies) to an domain expert / specialist is an essential part of each application project.

3.1 Description

Our basic framework or hierarchical morphological multicriteria design HMMD [24] consists of the following:

I. Design of hierarchical model and description for a system: *1.1.* design of hierarchical model for a system; *1.2.* design of multicriteria (multifactor) hierarchical description of the model nodes (system parts, components) including ordinal scales for each criterion; and *1.3.* design of multi-factor description for compatibility between design alternatives of different system parts.

II. System Synthesis: *2.1.* generation of design alternatives (DA's) for the system parts / components; *2.2.* evaluation of DA's upon criteria; *2.3.* evaluation of compatibility between DA's; and *2.4.* step-by-step synthesis of DA's to obtain composite DA's for a higher level of the model hierarchy.

III. Analysis of composite DA's to reveal bottlenecks (by DA's, by Ins).

IV. Design of improvement actions for the system: *4.1.* generation / selection of a set of some possible improvement actions; *4.2.* selection / composition of the best subset of the improvement actions under taking into account certain design and technological situations; and *4.3.* scheduling of the improvement actions.

HMMD uses hierarchical tree-like structure (organic hierarchy) of a designed system as a basic hierarchy. The representation of this hierarchy is easy. Many of researches apply similar approach ([13], [18], [20], [34], etc.).

HMMD implements "cascade-like" strategy of organizational process:

1. Divergent stage: "Top-Down" Hierarchical description of the system.

2. Convergent stage: "Bottom-Up" system design (generation of alternatives, their selection and composition)

Basic information components are the following (information support is pointed out in brackets):

1. Hierarchical system model.

2. Design module:

2.1 Requirements: 2.1.1 criteria (standard criteria); 2.1.2 compatibility factors (standard factors); and 2.1.3 restrictions (standard restrictions).

2.2 Design alternatives DA's: 2.2.1 set of DA's (standard design alternatives); 2.2.2 estimates; and 2.2.3 priorities.

2.3 Interconnection Ins (standard interconnection): 2.3.1 estimates on factors; and 2.3.2 resultant estimates.

3. Composite solutions (standard constraints):

4. Improvement as a set of improvement actions and schedule (basic examples, strategies of improvement).

5. Systems versions (basic examples of systems versions, tendencies for various problem domains).

3.2 Examples of Hierarchical Morphological Approach

Realistic system design examples illustrate our framework (domain, domain expert, complexity of a problem by scale [1...5], existence of a basic example, level of structural thinking of expert by scale [1...5] and type of strategy, reference):

1. Information technology; M.Sh. Levin & L.S. Levinsky; 5; Yes; 5,d; [24].

2. Composite software system; M.Sh. Levin; 3; Yes; 5,p; [24].

3. User interface; M.Sh. Levin; 5; No; 5,d; [24].

4. Team design; M.Sh. Levin; 3; Yes; 5,d; [24].

5. Allocation of personnel; M.Sh. Levin; 4; Yes; 5,d; [24].

6. Design of curriculum; M.Sh. Levin; 4; Yes; 5,d; [24].

7. Design of problem solving strategy; M.Sh. Levin; 3; No; 5,p; [24].

8. Geological exploration; V.I. Poroskoon; 3; No; 5,d; [24].

9. Concrete technology; M.L. Nisnevich; 3; No; 3,d; [32].

10. Redesign of buildings; M.A. Danieli; 3; Yes; 2,d; [28].

11. Vibration conveyor; Yu.T. Kaganov; 5; No; 2,d; [24].

12. Product marketing trajectories; M.Sh. Levin et al.; 3; Yes; 4,p; [26].

13. Design of product life cycle; M.Sh. Levin et al.; 3; Yes; 4,p; [27].

14. Medical treatment; L. Sokolova; 4; No; 4,p; [31].

15. System evolution: example for software; M.Sh. Levin; 4; No; 5,d; [24].

16. System evolution: example for signal processing; B.J. Feldman & M.Sh. Levin; 5; [29].

17. Immunoassay technology; M. Firer; 5; No; 5,d; [30].

3.3 Strategies for Skill Acquisition

Now let us point out some basic strategies as follows:

1. Direct strategy (step-by-step execution of HMA) ("d" in section 3.2).

2. Prototype strategy ("p" in section 3.2): (a) preparation of a simple example (prototype); for the system description of an design; and (b) analysis of the example with the expert(s); (c) correction / improvement / extension of the example.

Evidently, the second strategy is more useful for experts who has no experience in problem structuring. In this case, we can often to organize our dialogue with expert on the level of a language (system description) of his / her problem domain. At the same time, it is impossible to use the prototype strategy for new domain. Thus it was very difficult to design a system description for vibration conveyor. An additional useful stage consists in a preliminary explanation of the HMA for the expert including an analysis of examples.

Note the most hard stages of HMA are the following: (a) start of the work with expert(s); (b) explanation for expert the main problems and work strategy (e.g., knowledge-based system methodology); (c) generation of design alternatives; (d) analysis and evaluation of compatibility between design alternatives, and (e) analysis of results.

It is necessary to point out that domain specialists often are not ready to understand HMA and its components. In this case, it is reasonable to conduct an application project and after that to explain HMA on the basis of the joint work.

4 Ethics Issues of Expert Procedure Support

A procedure of engineering skill acquisition involves two main sides (roles): (a) domain expert (E), (b) "knowledge engineer" who is an organizer of the procedure (O). It is reasonable to consider a set of principles (that are close to the Hippocratic oath) for the organizer, for example ([23], etc.):

1. Honesty.

2. Orientation to global goals.

3. To tell "No" , "It is impossible".

4. To take into account properties of the expert (background, experience, mentality, style of thinking).

5. To support the collaboration by special instrumental (tables, software, etc.) and organizational (useful time, style, etc.) efforts.

6. To apply various approaches.

7. To learn the expert (e.g., decision making technology, required models).

5 Structuring / Extension of Skills and Engineering Education

In fact, HMA combines all basic learning operations [36]: (i) direct indications; (ii) explanations; (iii) observation of examples; and (iv) discovery. Thus we can usually decompose faced engineering problems and decrease their intellectual levels. Note basic system analysis / design procedures are the same ones: (a) hierarchical design and description of system model; (b) selection of alternatives; and (c) synthesis of composite decisions. Expert experience in the above-mentioned basic procedures is a fundamental to increase a level of expert thinking and to extend expert skills. Thus HMA can be used as an organizational basis for structuring and extension of the engineering skills including team work modes. Note some issues of engineering education on the basis of HMA are considered in ([23] and [25]).

6 Conclusion

We have described our experience in the use of HMA for engineering skills acquisition. Our results are preliminary one, and it is reasonable to investigate the following:

1. examination of additional real engineering examples including systems engineering problems and strategic design problems;

2. analysis of negative results of the applications from various viewpoints (e.g., organizational, psychological, educational);

3. significance of expert classification (type of thinking, design styles, etc.);

4. usage of our approach for engineering skills acquisition in maintenance of complex industrial systems (e.g., diagnosis, planning, information allocation and personnel management);

5. realization of the hierarchical morphological approach in engineering education (e.g., course on systems engineering, course on design methods, continues education course); and

6. development of special support educational computer tools (computer environment).

References

1. B. Adelson, "Cognitive Research; Uncovering How Designers Design; Cognitive Modeling: Explaining and Predicting How Designers Design", *Research in Engineering Design*, **1** (1), 1989, 35–42.
2. J.R. Anderson, *The Architecture of Cognition*, Harvard Univ. Press, Cambridge, MA, 1983.
3. J.R. Anderson, "Skill Acquisition: Compilation of Weak-method Problem Solutions", *Psychological Review*, **94**, 1987, 192–210.
4. R.A. Baldwin, and M.J. Chung, "Managing Engineering Data for Complex Products", *Research in Engineering Design*, **7** (4), 1995, 215–231.
5. R.A. Botafogo, E. Rivlin, and B. Shneiderman, "Structural Analysis of Hypertext: Identifying Hierarchies and Useful Metrics", *ACM Trans. on Information Systems*, **10** (2), 1992, 83–110.
6. I. Bournaud, and J.-G. Ganascia, "Conceptual Clustering of Complex Objects: A Generalization Space Based Approach", *Proc. of the Third Intl. Conf. on Conceptual Structures*, LNAI **954**, Springer-Verlag, Berlin, 1995, 173–187.

7. I. Bournaud, and J.-G. Ganascia, "Accounting for Domain Knowledge in the Construction of a Generalization Space", *Conceptual Structures: Fulfilling Peirce's Dream*, D. Lukose, H. Delugach, M. Kecler, L. Searle, J. Sowa, (Eds.), LNAI **1257**, Springer-Verlag, Berlin, 1997, 446–459.
8. R.C. Conant, "Information Flows in Hierarchical Systems", *Intl. J. of General Systems*, **1** (1), 1974, 9–18.
9. J. Conklin, "Hypertext: An Introduction and Survey", *IEEE Computer*, **20** (9), 1987, 17–41.
10. R. Cordero, "Developing The Knowledge and Skills of R & D Professionals to Achieve Process Outcomes in Cross-Functional Teams", *The J. of High Technology Management Research*, **10** (1), 1999, 61-78.
11. N. Cross, "Skills of Expertise in Engineering Designers", *Research in Engineering Design,* **10** (3), 1998, 141–149.
12. G.H. Demes, et al., "The Engineering Design Research Center of Carnegie Mellon University", *Proc. of the IEEE*, **81** (1), 1993, 10–23.
13. C.M. Eastman, A.H. Bond, and S.C. Chase, "Application and Evaluation of an Engineering Data Model", *Research in Engineering Design*, **2** (4), 1991, 185–207.
14. K.L. Edwards, "Improved Design through Guidelines Support", *Engineering Designer*, **19** (5), 1993, 22–23.
15. M.R. Garey, and D.S. Johnson, *Computers and Intractability. The Guide to the Theory of NP-Completeness*, W.H. Freeman and Company, San Francisco, 1979.
16. I.E. Grossmann, and A.W. Westerberg, "Research Challenges in Process Systems Engineering", *AIChE Journal*, **46** (9), 2000, 1700–1703.
17. F. Harary, R.Z. Norman, and D. Carthwright, *Structural Models: An Introduction to the Theory of Directed Graphs*, J. Wiley & Sons, New York, 1965.
18. S.Z. Kamal, H.M. Karandikar, F. Mistree, and D. Muster, "Knowledge Representation for Discipline-Independent Decision Making", *Expert Systems in Computer-Aided Design*, J.S. Gero (ed.), Elsevier, Amsterdam, 1987, 289–318.
19. J.H. Klein, "Cognitive Processes and Operations Research: A Human Information Processing Perspective", *J. of Operational Research Society*, **45** (8), 1994, 855–866.
20. M. Klein, "Capturing Design Rationale in Concurrent Engineering Teams", *Computer,* 1993, 39–47.
21. M.Sh. Levin, "A Hierarchical Hypertext System", *Aut. Doc. and Math. Linguistics,* **23** (3), 1989, 52–59.
22. M.Sh. Levin, "Hierarchical Components of Human-Computer Systems", *Human Computer Interaction*, LNCS **753**, Springer-Verlag, Berlin, 1993, 37–52.
23. M.Sh. Levin, "The Third Literacy", *Aut. Doc. and Math. Linguistics*, **29** (3), 1995, 66–81.
24. M.Sh. Levin, *Combinatorial Engineering of Decomposable Systems*, Kluwer, Dordrecht, 1998.
25. M.Sh. Levin, "Towards Systems Engineering Education", *Proc. of Eur. Meeting on Cybernetics and Systems Research*, **1**, 2000, 257–262.
26. M.Sh. Levin, R. Shraga, H. Zamir, A. Shiff, and S. Inon, "Multicriteria Design of Product Trajectory: Example", Presentation, *Israeli National Conf. on Operations Research ORSIS'2000,* Eilat, Israel, 2000.
27. M.Sh. Levin, E. Ben-Ezri, Y. Blonder, K. Hershkovits, N. Lev, and A. Shem-Tov, "Multicriteria Design of Life Cycle: Example", Presentation, *Intl. Conference MCDM'2000,* Ankara, Turkey, 2000.
28. M.Sh. Levin, and M. Danieli, "Framework for Evaluation and Improvement of Buildings", *Proc. of Intl. Conf. CoDesigning2000*, **2**, Univ. of Coventry, 2000, 209–214.

29. M.Sh. Levin, and B.J. Feldman, "System Evolution: Example for Signal Processing", *Proc. of Intl. Conf. on Systems Engineering*, Univ. of Coventry, 2000, 377–380.
30. M.Sh. Levin, and M. Firer, "Hierarchical Morphological Design of Immunoassay Technology", Manuscript (under submission).
31. M.Sh. Levin, and L. Sokolova, "Hierarchical Example of Medical Treatment", Manuscript.
32. M.Sh. Levin, and M. Nisnevich, "Combinatorial Scheme for Management of Life Cycle: Example for Concrete Macrotechnology", *J. of Intelligent Manufacturing*, (in press), 2001.
33. S.I. Madanshetty, "Cognitive Basis for Conceptual Design", *Research in Engineering Design,* **7** (4), 1995, 234–240.
34. M.L. Maher, "Engineering Design Synthesis: A Domain Independent Representation", *AI EDAM,* **1** (3), 1987, 207–213.
35. R.H. Michaelson, D. Michie, and A. Bonlander, "The Technology of Expert Systems", *BYTE,* **4**, 1985, 303–312.
36. J. Nilsson, *Problem Solving Methods in Artificial Intelligence*, MacGraw Hill, New York, NY, 1971.
37. M. Minsky, "Commonsense-Based Interfaces", *Comm. of the ACM,* **43** (8), 2000, 67–73.
38. M. Minsky, The Emotion Machine. Pantheon, available in 2001, corresponding presentation: *Eur. Meeting on Cybernetics and Systems Research*, Univ. of Vienna, 2000.
39. M.E. Nissen, "Knowledge-based Knowledge Management in the Reengineering Domain", *Decision Support Systems*, **27** (1-2), 1999, 47-65.
40. D.A. Norman, "Design Principles for Cognitive Artifacts", *Research in Engineering Design*, **4** (1), 1992, 43–50.
41. C.V. Ramamoorthy, and B.W. Wah, "Knowledge and Data Engineering", *IEEE Trans. on Knowledge and Data Engineering*, **1** (1), 1989, 9–16.
42. F.R. Roberts. *Discrete Mathematical Models with Applications to Social, Biological and Environmental Problems*, Prentice Hall, Englewood Cliffs, NJ, 1976.
43. T.L. Saaty, *The Analytic Hierarchy Process*, MacGraw-Hill, New York, NY, 1988.
44. A.C. Scott, and J.E. Clayton. *A Practical Guide to Knowledge Acquisition*, Addison-Wesley, New York, NY, 1991.
45. A.J. Shenhar, "From Theory to Practice: Toward a Typology of Project Management Styles", *IEEE Trans. on Eng. Manag.*, **45** (1), 1998, 33–48.
46. Ch. Tong, and D. Sriram, (Eds.). *Artificial Intelligence in Engineering Design: Knowledge Acquisition, Commercial Systems, and Integrated Environments*, Academic Press, New York, NY, 1992.
47. R.J. Waller, "The Synthesis of Hierarchical Structures: Techniques and Applications", *Decision Sciences,* **7**, 1976, 659–674.
48. A. Wong, and D. Sriram, "SHARED: An Information Model for Cooperative Product Development", *Research in Engineering Design*, **5** (1), 1993, 21–39.

Dealing with Information in the Different Styles Together – Skill Inheritance and Integration of Information

Setuo Ohsuga and Naoto Ueda

Department of Information and Computer Science, Waseda University
3-4-1 Ohkubo Shinjyuku - ku Tokyo 169-8555, Japan
Phone ; +81 3 5286 3342
ohsuga@ohsuga.info.waseda.ac.jp

Abstract. Method of dealing with information processing in the different styles together is discussed. Skill inheritance and integration of different styles of information processing are paid attentions as the typical examples. A relation between symbolic processing and non-symbolic processing is first analysed. There is the substantial difference between them. An intermediate form to represent both of them in the same framework is introduced. It enables us to make clear the difference between symbolic and on-symbolic representations and to discuss the possibility of skill inheritance and integration of information.

1. Introduction

Today, various styles of information processing are used such as those based on procedural language, declarative language, non-symbolic information processing, etc. Every style has its own processing objective and processing object to which the processing style is best suited. It also has its own problem representation scheme and processing method. A specific information-processing unit (IPU in the sequel) has been implemented in each style in computers based on its representation scheme and processing method. A computer program for a specific problem, for example, is an IPU of the procedural processing style. A specific neural network as a non-symbolic system is another type IPU. Human skill is also a non-symbolic IPU between sensory organs (sensors) and motor organs (actuators). Actually it is difficult to represent it formally like this but a communication aspect of skill inheritance is paid attention in this paper and it is assumed that the sensor-and-actuator relation can be represented explicitly.

Each IPU is used separately and independently from each other. An IPU is defined as a triple of (I, O, M) in which I and O represent the scope of input and of output respectively in the world and M is the mapping from I to O. In reality a pair (I, M) is enough for the purpose of discriminating the IPUs from the others. A scope of problems that an IPU can deal with is limited. It is desirable that these different IPUs can be integrated easily in order to expand the scope and to achieve a function beyond that of each single IPU. However it has been considered uneasy to integrate different IPU of the different styles and it has to be done manually by persons in an ad hoc way for a pair of specific IPUs.

L. Monostori, J. Váncza, and M. Ali (Eds.): IEA/AIE 2001, LNAI 2070, pp. 101-106, 2001.

It seems that skill inheritance is similar to integrating different information-processing methods. If a skill could be translated into a symbolic language, then its inheritance becomes possible. In reality these are very different. What is the difference between them and what is the difference between non-symbolic and symbolic representations? This paper discusses these issues.

2. Relation between Symbolic and Non-symbolic Processing

Skill might be represented formally as a transformation from a set of sensor inputs to another set of actuator outputs. Let there be sensors S1, S2,--, Sm and actuators A1, A2, --, An with the inputs x1, x2, --, xm and outputs y1, y2, --, yn respectively. It is assumed that the input variables are continuous. Then the skill is a function from an input vector **X** = (x1, x2, --, xm) to an output vector **Y** = (y1, y2, --, yn). Usually it is a complex relation and is difficult to represent it in a mathematical form.

On the other hand, a symbolic language is a system of finite symbols. Everything is represented as a combination of these symbols.

It seems that skill inheritance and integration are similar. In reality there is a big difference between them. Skill inheritance is a process of translations from non-symbolic to symbolic representations for the purpose of communication and again back to non-symbolic representations for practice. It needs the faithful translation between different representation styles. It requires the same expressive power for these styles. But there is a big gap between them. It is necessary first to study this gap. In order to compare directly the characteristics of symbolic and non-symbolic systems, a common expression for both of these is made. An intermediate form between symbolic and non-symbolic processing is introduced in order to clarify the difference between these two.

A non-symbolic processing is defined by the specific functions between continuous input and continuous/discrete output variables. For example, a neural network has a function as a compound of linear transformation followed by a non-linear (Sigmoid) function. But a simplest linear form is considered here such as $yi = \Sigma_j wij \times xj$, i = 1,2,--, n, or in the form $\mathbf{Y} = \mathbf{X} \times W$ where **X** and **Y** are the vectors to represent the multi-dimensional input and output variables respectively. W is a matrix $| wij |$.

Predicate logic on the other hand is used as a typical symbolic representation. An implicative formula $(\forall x/D)[F(x) \rightarrow G(x)]$ is considered. Here D is a set of elements, D = (a,b,c,--z), and x/D means D ∋ x. Let the predicates F (and G) be interpreted as a property of x in D, that is, `F(x) ; an element x in D has a property F'.

First a state of D is defined as a combination of F(x) for all x/D. For example, `F(a) :True`, `F(b):False`, `F(c):False`,--, `F(z):True` forms a state, say SF_I, of D with respect to F. Namely, SF_I = (F(a), -F(b), -F(c), --, F(z)). There is $N=2^n$ different states. Let `F(x):True` and `F(x):False` be represented by 1 and 0 respectively. Then SF_I as above is represented (1, 0,0,--,1). Let the sequence be identified by a binary number I = 100---1 formed by concatenating 0 or 1 in the order of arrangement. Let SF_I be I-th state in N states. By arranging all states in the increasing order of I, a state vector **Sf** = (SF_0,SF_1,--,SF_{N-1}) is defined. Among them, the ordinary predicate can represent only $\mathbf{Sf}_\forall$ = {(1,1,--,1)} = $(\forall x/D)F(x)$ and $\mathbf{Sf}_\exists$={**Sf**-(0,0,--0)}= $(\exists x/D)F(x)$.

If truth or false of one of the elements in D changes, then the state of D changes accordingly. Let the change occurs probabilistically. Then a state probability Pf_I is defined to a state SF_I and a probability vector **Pf** are also defined. **Pf** = (Pf_0, Pf_1,--, Pf_{N-1}) where 'Pf_I; probability of D being in the state SF_I '.

Then it is shown that a logical inference $F \wedge [F \rightarrow G] \Rightarrow G$ can be represented in the similar form as a stochastic process, **Pg** = **Pf** × T, if a transition matrix T=$| t_{IJ} |$ satisfies a special condition. Since $F \rightarrow G = - F \vee G$, by definition, if `F(x);True` for some x in D, then G(x) for corresponding x must be true. That is, there is no transition from a state SF_I including `F(x);True` to a state SG_J of D in regard to G including `G(x); False` and t_{IJ} for this pair is put zero. Thus, many elements in this matrix are zero [4].

The computation $Pg_J = \Sigma_I Pf_I \times t_{IJ}$ or **Pg** = **Pf** × T is formally the same as that included in a non-symbolic system. The input and output vectors, **X** and **Y**, correspond to **Pf** and **Pg** respectively.

A transition matrix for representing predicate logic has many restrictions comparing with a matrix to represent a non-symbolic system. In order for a matrix to represent logical implication, it has many zeros as shown above while the matrix to represent non-symbolic system is free from such a restriction. A non-symbolic system can represent an object at the very fine level. In other words, granularity of representation is very fine in the framework of non-symbolic system. But the framework is rigid and to expand its scope is difficult.

There is another approach to merge symbol and non-symbol processing. It is to represent a neural network by means of special intuitive logic. Some attempts have been made so far and some kinds of intuitive logic have been proved equivalent to neural network [3]. But these approaches lose some advantages of classic logic such as expandability and completeness of inference. As the consequence these systems cannot have such large usability as the classic logic system.

3. Extending Syntax of Logical Expression

Some attempts have been made for extending the syntax of logical expression. One is to introduce some quantitative values into predicate logic. For example an occurrence probability is given to every proposition, say `(a);True'. But there is a substantial difference between non-symbolic and symbolic processing other than quantitative measure. The former includes cross-coupling terms in the processing of inputs. That is, i-th input's element affects the j-th output's element. In predicate logic on the other hand, every element is independent to each other. This characteristic is kept strictly in the inference operation. Because of this independence of elements many zero's appeared in the transition matrix to represent logical inference. It causes representation of predicate logic very course. But in compensation for this loss of expressive power in the fine level it acquires a flexibility of accepting new elements and also new predicate formula without affecting any operation in the old system. It brings a large capability of extending scope to predicate logic. An attempt of extending predicate logic in order to let it closer to non-symbolic processing is discussed in [5]. Because of lack of space it is abbreviated.

4. Characteristic of Symbolic Representation

There are different symbolic systems. Some has a fixed universe of discourse. An example is procedural language for computers. It cannot accept new elements and algorithms without affecting operations so far. Therefore it cannot extends the scope automatically. Declarative language has a variable table for mapping between symbols and university of discourses and the same language can adapt to the different universes by changing the tables. A typical example is seen in predicate logic. Thanks to this flexibility and its modularity a declarative IPU has a capability to accept new elements without disturbing the main part of the IPU. Therefore its scope can expand. It is the characteristic of predicate logic but is not seen in any other IPU. In addition, predicate logic has a capability to find unknown relation between objects by using existing rules using logical inference. With these characteristics predicate logic has a large potentiality of integrating various IPUs [OHS00c]. It does not mean that the translation between predicate logic and non-symbolic systems is possible. It is difficult because of the constraint for attaining modularity and the lack of granularity of expressions of predicate logic.

5. Skill Inheritance and Integration of Different IPUs

Skill inheritance is to copy the non-symbolic IPU made by a skilled person to non-skilled people. There are many difficulties in achieving this goal. It is not easy to represent this non-symbolic IPU explicitly. Even if the issue is limited to the communication problem, it is difficult to represent a skill by any symbolic language as has been discussed so far. As a conclusion it is difficult to define a formal method of inheritance of technical skill.

Integration on the other hand is to merge two or more IPUs into an IPU with a larger scope. A special transformation is necessary between different representation schemes. Manual integration of specific IPUs has been achieved so far [1,2]. The objective of this paper is to discuss automatic integration. It is discussed hereafter in two steps.

In the first step integration is defined as an operation of an IPU to take in the other IPU(s) in order to expand the scope or to use the function of the latter and to realise a new function as a whole. The former is called the master IPU and the latter is the slave IPU. In order to take in the slave IPU, the master IPU must be able to represent the characteristics of the slave IPU with its own representation scheme. The master is also required the format transformation of input/output between master and slaves in such a way that the master IPU can take in the slave any time when necessary and exchange data. These methods are added to the master IPU for the purpose of integration. Thus the master IPU has to be able to expand its scope accepting this additional information without disturbing its own processing. The expanded master IPU can decide the way to evoke the slave and translate the data to send to the slave. Receiving its output and translating it into the master scheme, the master IPU can continue the operation.

Among number of styles of information processing only some declarative processing, i.e. predicate logic or its equivalent systems, can meet this condition and integrate various IPUs of the different styles. A description of a slave is created when the slave IPU is first defined and added to master's knowledge base. The internal mechanism of the slave could be a black box to the master. Only the external definition of the operation of slave is described.

Then it is generalized. Let two IPUs, say (Ia, Ma) and (Ib, Mb) of styles Sa and Sb respectively, be to be merged. If at least one of them is a declarative IPU, then the integration as discussed above is possible by letting this IPU the master. If both IPUa and IPUb are non-declarative ones, a third IPU is introduced as a master to both IPUa and IPUb. It must be a declarative IPU. Thus non-declarative IPUs can be integrated indirectly via the third declarative IPU. It is possible to prepare such a declarative IPU for the purpose of integrating arbitrary IPUs. At integration it is assumed that a master IPU receives input from outside. When a slave IPU accept it directly, the system is changed so that a master accepts it first and passes it to the slave from the master.

This capability of integration depends on the flexibility of a master IPU to expand its scope of information processing as well as its expressive power to describe the slave IPU. Both depend on representation method. Thus, from the integration point of view, a style with a representation method that has the largest expandability as well as the enough expressive power should be selected as a central scheme of information processing. Among all styles used today, only declarative representation scheme has such expandability. A typical example is predicate logic. Therefore classic first order logic is considered as such a central scheme in the following.

Example; As a simple example, assume that IPU1(x1, y1) and IPU2(x2, y2), are to be integrated. These are developed in order to achieve the specific activities, primitiveActivity1(x1, y1) and primitiveActivity2 (x2, y2) respectively. The inputs x1 and x2 come from sensor1 and sensor2 respectively. On the other hand, the master IPU is defined to perform some operation on the results of these primitive activities. For example, it is an operation on the difference of the results of the primitive activities, i.e. z = y1 – y2. But the master IPU is not provided with any function for executing the primitive activities. Therefore it takes in IPU1 and IPU2 for the purpose of using their functions. The sensor signals are first accepted by a master IPU and send to the IPU1 and IPU2. The format of the sensor signals accepted by the master IPU and of the inputs to the IPU1 / IPU2 can be different.

Let an activity(u1, u2, w) be an operation of the master IPU to generate w as a function of the sensor inputs. The following predicate is provided to the master IPU as the required activity.

activity(u1, u2, w):- sensor1(u1), sensor2(u2), primitiveActivity1(u1, v1),
primitiveActivity2(u2, v2), subtract(v1, v2, z), function(z, w).

For the purpose of integration the following definitions of IPU1 and IPU2 are added to the master IPU. The symbol # denotes that a calling procedure including the conversions of inputs and outputs are necessary in the master IPU because of the difference of the formats.

primitiveActivity1(x1, y1):-#IPU1(x1, y1),
primitiveActivity1(x2, y2):-#IPU1(x2, y2),

These rules are executed through the rule of activity(u1, u2, w). The obtained result, w, can be used in whatever the ways in the master IPU. In this example the function(z, w) is assumed defined in the master IPU. It can be still the other processor, IPU3. In this case, IPU1, IPU2 and IPU3 are integrated via the master IPU.

6. Conclusion

An issue of dealing with information processing in the different styles together has been discussed. Skill inheritance and integration of different information processing mechanisms are paid attentions as the typical examples. A relation between symbolic processing and non-symbolic processing was first analysed. Predicate logic and a simple non-symbolic system were selected for the purpose. An intermediate form was introduced to represent both of them in the same framework. Using the result of this analysis the difference between symbolic and non-symbolic representations has been made clear. There is a substantial difference between them. It is possible to introduce quantitative measures in classical predicate logic in order to expand the framework of predicate logic and to make the granularity finer while preserving its advantages of modularity. But it was not enough for bridging the gap between them because the difference is not only the matter of quantitative measure but also in the structure of information processing. As the conclusion, the skill inheritance that needs translation between symbolic and non-symbolic representation to the detail cannot be achieved by means of representation method today. On the other hand, integration problem is easier than that because it does not need such translation. By the use of expandable representation method as the master IPU, integration of the different processing methods is possible.

References

[1] V. Honavar and L. Uhr (eds.) ; Artificial Intelligence and Neural Networks, Steps toward Principled Integration, Academic press, 1994.

[2] L. Monostori, Cs. Egresits, and B. Kadar ; Hybrid AI Solution and their Application in Manufacturing, Proc.Ninth International Conference on Industrial and Engineering Applications of Artificial Intelligence and Expert Systems, Gordon and Breach Publishers, 1996.

[3] Hiroshi Tsukimoto; Symbol pattern integration using multi-linear functions, Deep Fusion of Computational and Symbolic Processing, T. Furuhashi, S.Tano, and H.A.Jacobsen eds., Springer-Verlag, 2000

[4] S. Ohsuga; Symbol Processing by Non-Symbol Processor, Proc. Pacific Rim International Conference on Artificial Intelligence (PRICAI-1996), 1996

[5] S. Ohsuga; The Gap between Symbol and Non-Symbol Processing -An Attempt to Represent a Database by Predicate Formulae-, Proc. Pacific Rim International Conference on Artificial Intelligence (PRICAI-2000), 2000

Knowledge Modelling in Support of Knowledge Management

Robert Kende

Dept. of Cybernetics and Artificial Intelligence
University of Technology in Kosice, Letna 9, 041 20 Kosice, Slovakia
kende@tuke.sk

Abstract. In this paper KnowWeb – European Commission funded research project is briefly introduced. The project aims at the development of tools as well as methodology to support knowledge management especially in small and medium sized enterprises (SME). We build our approach on top of conceptual modelling of company specific problem domain. Such a conceptual domain model may serve as a shared vocabulary to express context of various documents published within the company. Also it may be used for a sophisticated retrieval of documents as a reference.

1 Introduction

A considerable amount of knowledge is scattered throughout various documents within organisations. It is quite often that this knowledge is stored somewhere without possibility of being retrieved and reused any more. As a result of this, most knowledge is not shared and is forgotten in relatively short time after it has been invented or discovered. Therefore, it has become very important for "learning organisations" to make the best use of information gathered from various document sources inside the organisations and from external sources like the Internet. Organisations are concerned with preserving knowledge within an organisational setting. There are three stages in the information life cycle: finding (acquisition), organising and sharing. Many technologies have been developed for the finding stage. On the other hand, there is a lack of efficient technologies focused on organising and sharing of existing knowledge. One possibility is to utilise an organisation memory mechanism aiming at storing knowledge and making it retrievable. At a macro-level, organisational memory corresponds to organisational knowledge with persistence. At a micro-level, information seeking by some organisational member within an organisational context can be considered as the process of finding the right 'piece' of organisational memory [1]. The KnowWeb project aims at providing support for knowledge management (including capture, update and retrieval of knowledge) within an organisation, fostering efficient communication and supporting distributed groups to share knowledge and exchange information efficiently. Two distinct levels of representing knowledge in an organisation can be distinguished. There is a repository of physical documents (reports, tables, etc.) on one side. These documents can be retrieved using

L. Monostori, J. Váncza, and M. Ali (Eds.): IEA/AIE 2001, LNAI 2070, pp. 107–112, 2001.

existing search facilities of a file system. On the other side, background knowledge is attached to each document. It defines the document's context, its relation to other documents, and its relation to organisation's activities. Thus, this background knowledge interprets documents and gives them a deeper meaning within the context of a particular organisation, because originally such knowledge is not explicit but tacit [8]. KnowWeb aims at making at least a part of this knowledge explicit and usable for the retrieval and sharing. One type of background knowledge can have the form of well-structured 'common vocabulary'. Such vocabulary is known as ontology [2], [4]. We assume that there is a conceptual description of an application domain in the form of a domain model.

2 DOMAIN MODELLING

Theoretical foundations for the research of domain modelling can be found in the works of Chandrasekaran [3], Gruber [4], Wielinga [9], and others on ontologies and knowledge modelling. Ontology is a term borrowed from philosophy where it stands for a systematic theory of entities what exist. In context of knowledge modelling, Gruber introduced the term ontology as a set of definitions of content-specific knowledge representation primitives consisting of domain-dependent classes, relations, functions, and object constants. The ontology represents formal terms with which knowledge can be represented and individual problems within a particular domain can be described. Ontology in this sense determines what can 'exist' in a knowledge base. Chandrasekaran understands ontology as a representation vocabulary typically specialised to some domain. He suggests basically two purposes for which ontologies may be used:

- to define most commonly used terms in a specific domain, thus building a skeleton,
- to enable knowledge sharing and re-using both spatially and temporally [6].

Ontology with syntax and semantic rules provides the 'language' by which KnowWeb(-like) systems can interact at the *knowledge level* [7]. Ontology allows a group of people to agree on the meaning of few basic terms, from which many different individual instantiations, assertions and queries may be constructed. Common understanding of the meaning of notions used in a given domain (the understanding may be domain-specific) results in the definition of *concepts*. Concepts are more or less abstract constructs on which a relevant part of the world is built, or better, which can be used to describe this relevant part of the world. Since concepts can differ in their character, several types of concepts, namely *classes*, *relations*, *functions* or *procedures*, *objects*, *variables* or *constants*, can be distinguished. These primitive constructs can be represented differently in different applications but they have the same meaning in all applications – i.e. when someone wants to communicate with somebody else, he/she can do it using constructs from the ontology of shared concepts.

3 BASIC KNOWWEB SYSTEM FUNCTIONALITY

The KnowWeb system enables to store knowledge in the form of documents with attached concepts from ontologies – documents with their conceptual descriptions. The main purpose of using ontology is to define concepts that are useful to express knowledge about a particular document in domain specific terms. Subsequently, the concepts can be also used for search and retrieval of relevant documents. In such case the domain model serves as a 'reference vocabulary' of company-specific terms [9]. Such approach supports searching not only in the physical document discourse but also in the document context. It also supports 'soft' techniques where a search engine can utilise the domain model to find out related concepts to those specified by the user.

3.1 Enriching documents

Documents are hierarchically structured from the syntactic point of view. They are divided into chapters (sections); and further into subchapters (subsections), these into paragraphs, and paragraphs into sentences. Sentences consist of words – the smallest syntactic units. Syntactic units (in general document fragments) are addressable – the result of some operation over a document (e.g. retrieval) will refer to a specific syntactic unit (or more units) within the document. Conceptual descriptions will consist of references to the knowledge context contained in the particular document in the future and will make this knowledge accessible in an easy and efficient way. The authors can select a text fragment and link it to the domain model. The linking can be done directly to ontology concepts or to a template representing a particular subset of ontology concepts. This type of links to concepts is of many-to-many type. It means that it is legal to link a document fragment to several concepts and vice-versa, a single concept to several fragments of one or more documents. When a document with its description is available for storage and publishing (after manual or semi-automatic linking within the KnowWeb system), it can be incorporated into the organisational memory represented by a KnowWeb server. The document and its conceptual description are stored in the KnowWeb server data repository.

3.2 Document retrieval

The aim of storing documents in the organisational memory is to access the right knowledge in the right time and/or situation. In order to express requirements on documents, which should be retrieved from the organisational memory, the users will formulate search queries. When formulating queries they can take advantage of use of the existing concepts (or their attributes) from the domain model. Therefore, a query for knowledge retrieval is given in company-specific conceptual terms instead of traditional keywords. The queries can be composed of more complex structures using various logical operators and/or various available options that are supported in the KnowWeb toolkit. In general, the concepts used in the query together with the concepts that are related to them in a domain model will be used to search conceptual descriptions of documents. The level determining how many 'neighbouring' concepts should be added to the query will be given as an option in users' queries.

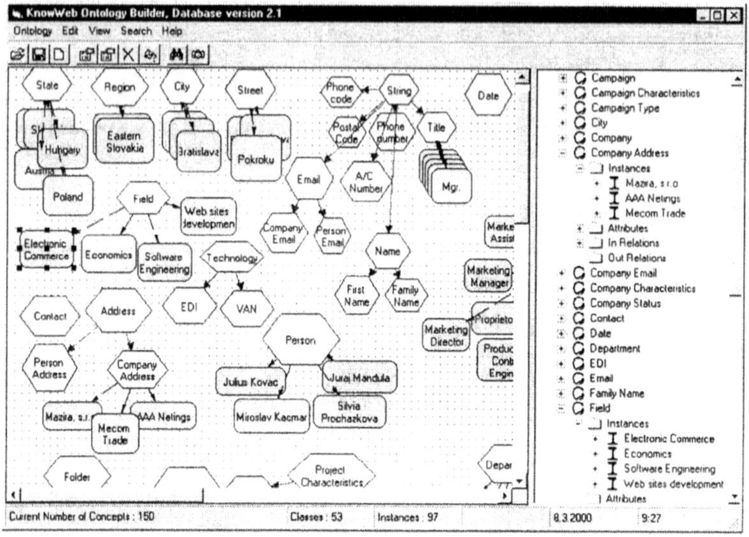

Fig. 1. Sample of a domain model

The Retrieval function enables to retrieve document(s) that are contextually relevant to a given query. Another issue addressed by the KnowWeb system is the simplification of the post-processing phase after document retrieval – document viewing and browsing. The focus is on the retrieval of relevant knowledge chunks from a document repository. With traditional search engines users have troubles to find relevant information in a retrieved document especially if the document is extensive or the information is not explicit but hidden 'between lines'.

4 SYSTEM STRUCTURE

Within the project a conceptual framework and a generic architecture for computational support of organisational memory have been developed. The organisational memory enables to store documents together with their context knowledge and to access them in a user-friendly way. The organisational memory will be accompanied by a set of tools for: preparing the documents to be stored, defining, viewing, browsing, and editing domain model, enriching documents by association links with relevant knowledge concepts, defining a context attached to the stored documents, storing and retrieving documents, browsing stored knowledge, etc. All these tools together with an organisational memory constitute the KnowWeb system.

From the practical point of view, the system is implemented using client-server architecture.

4.1 KnowWeb server

The server represents the heart of the KnowWeb system – it is a unit responsible for storing, maintaining, and accessing knowledge. The server consists of the following main modules (see Fig. 2.):

1 Document store – where physical documents are stored,
2 Association file management system – for maintenance of background knowledge, document contexts (e.g. association links from a document or its parts to the concepts within the domain model),
3 Domain model – a core of the system,
4 Server interface – for an efficient and user-friendly communication with KnowWeb clients.

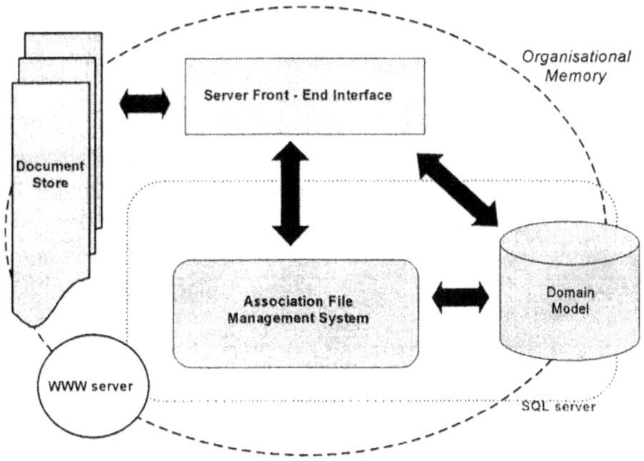

Fig. 2. **KnowWeb server structure**

5 CONCLUSIONS

The aim of the KnowWeb system is to help organisations to manage the knowledge they currently possess, and to focus their operations towards knowledge-centred and knowledge-intensive business practices. To fulfil this goal a specific architecture dedicated to support knowledge management within organisations (including capture, update and retrieval of knowledge) has been designed and implemented. Priority application areas of the implemented system are those organisations which require large volumes of data to be processed during the decision-making processes in a satisfactory way. The focus is on the storage of knowledge in so-called organisational memory and retrieval of relevant knowledge chunks within documents. The KnowWeb system supports attachment of the contextual knowledge to the documents. A query to the implemented system is supposed to be defined in company-specific conceptual terms instead of traditional keywords. The employed knowledge-based approach enables searching not only in the physical document discourse but also in the document context space. The system enables users to find those particular documents (or those particular parts of these documents) that are most relevant to their current needs without the need of browsing large volumes of retrieved data.

6 ACKNOWLEDGEMENTS

This work is supported by the European Commission within the ESPRIT 29065 project "Web in Support of Knowledge Management in Company (KnowWeb)".

REFERENCES

1. Ackerman, M.S. Augmenting the Organizational Memory: A Field Study of Answer Garden. In: Proceedings of the ACM Conference on Computer Supported Cooperative Work, 1994, pp 243-252.
2. Chandrasekaran, B., Josephson, J.R., Benjamins, V.R. Ontology of Tasks and Methods. In: Proceedings of the 11th Knowledge Acquisition for KBS Workshop, Banff, Canada, April 1998.
3. Chandrasekaran, B., Josephson, J.R., Benjamins, V.R. What Are Ontologies and Why Do We Need Them. IEEE Intelligent Systems, 14 (1), 1999, pp 20-26.
4. Gruber, T.R. A Translation approach to Portable Ontology Specifications. Knowledge Acquisition, 5 (2), 1993.
5. Malhotra, Y. Knowledge Management in Inquiring Organisations. In: Proceedings of the 3rd Americas Conference on Information Systems, 1997, pp 293-295.
6. Motta, E., Zdrahal, Z. A principled approach to the construction of a task-specific library of problem solving components. In: Proceedings of the 11th Knowledge Acquisition for KBS Workshop, Banff, Canada, April 1998.
7. Newell, A. The Knowledge Level. Artificial Intelligence, 18 (1), 1982, pp 87-127.
8. Sveiby, K.E. Tacit Knowledge. [WWW page]. Available at <http://www.sveiby.com.au/Polanyi.html> [referenced 7/4/1999].
9. van Heijst, G., Schreiber, A.T., Wielinga, B.J. Using explicit ontologies in KBS development. International Journal of Human-Computer Studies, 46 (2/3), 1997, pp 183-292.

A New Approach in Object-Based Knowledge Representation: The AROM System

Michel Page[1,2], Jérôme Gensel[1,2], Cécile Capponi[4], Christophe Bruley[1], Philippe Genoud[1,3], Danielle Ziébelin[1,3], Daniel Bardou[1,2], and Véronique Dupierris[1]

[1]Action Romans, INRIA Rhône-Alpes, ZIRST, 655, av. de l'Europe, Montbonnot
38334 Saint Ismier Cedex - France
[2]Université Pierre Mendès-France, BP 47,
38040 Grenoble Cedex 9, France
[3]Université Joseph Fourier, Grenoble, BP 53,
38041 Grenoble Cedex 9, France
[4]Labo. d'Informatique de Marseille, Univ. de Provence, 163 av. de Luminy,
13288 Marseille Cedex 9, France
arom@inrialpes.fr

Abstract. This paper presents AROM, a new object-based knowledge representation system. AROM is original in two ways. Firstly, in addition to classes, knowledge representation in AROM uses associations for describing links between classes instances. Secondly, AROM integrates an algebraic modeling language (AML) for describing operational knowledge (equations, constraints and queries) in a declarative way. AROM comes as a platform for knowledge representation and manipulation. It includes an interactive modeling environment, a Java API, an AML interpreter for processing queries and solving sets of equations, and a tool for consulting and editing knowledge bases on the Web.

1 Introduction

Most object knowledge representation systems fall into two categories: description logics (DL) and object-based knowledge representation systems (OBKRS). DL systems like KL-ONE [1] represent concepts using formal syntax and semantics; emphasize is put on complexity study of both subsumption and concept classification, which is the main inference mechanism of these systems. OBKRS (KRL [2], KEE [3], for instance) are declarative systems for describing, organizing and processing large amounts of knowledge; they offer various inference mechanisms such as classification, procedural attachment, default values, filters, etc.

In this paper, we present AROM (Associating Relations and Objects for Modeling), a new OBKRS which departs from existing systems in two ways. Firstly, in addition to classes which are usually found in existing OBKRS, AROM uses *associations* similar to those found in UML [4] for organizing links between objects having common structure and semantics. Secondly, in addition to classical inference mecha-

L. Monostori, J. Váncza, and M. Ali (Eds.): IEA/AIE 2001, LNAI 2070, pp. 113-118, 2001.

nisms found in other OKBRS, AROM integrates an algebraic modeling language (AML) for expressing operational knowledge in a declarative manner. This language allows one to write constraints, queries, numerical and symbolic equations between the various elements composing a knowledge base (KB).

AROM comes as a platform with a Java API, an interactive graphical environment for designing and manipulating KBs, an AML interpreter for processing queries and solving sets of equations, and tools for consulting and editing KBs on the Web.

The paper is organized as follows. Knowledge representation in AROM is presented in section 2 along with an example. The AROM platform is detailed in section 3. Related work and conclusion are presented is section 4.

2 Knowledge Representation in AROM

Many data and knowledge engineering methods involve two notions for modeling a domain: entity and relation. In object-oriented models like UML, three kinds of relation are considered: specialization/generalization, association and aggregation (a particular case of the latter being composition). An association denotes a group of similar links between instances of two or more, distinct or not, classes.

Most OBKRS handle specialization, and sometimes aggregation (and/or composition). Associations usually have no specific representation; they are implemented either by *link-attributes* or by reification of associations as classes.

A link-attribute is a slot typed by a class and its value references one (or several) instance(s) of this class. Several OBKRS like SMECI [5], implement binary associations with two inverse link-attributes, and integrate mechanisms for maintaining their consistency. This technique has two problems. It works fine only for binary associations [6], and it does not easily take into account attributes of associations (*i.e.* properties attached to links; for instance, the wedding date of two married persons).

Using reification, associations are considered as classes whose attributes correspond either to links between objects or to specific properties. This enables associations with an arity greater than two to be described. However, since no distinction is made between classes and associations, operations or mechanisms specific to either of them cannot be defined.

Neither link-attributes nor reification is thus satisfactory for representing associations. Furthermore, using both techniques within a KB can only lead to inconsistencies and lack of extensibility. This has led us to promote associations as first-class entities for knowledge representation, on equal ground with classes.

2.1 Knowledge Representation in AROM Using Classes and Associations

Classes and objects. A class in AROM describes a set of objects sharing common properties and constraints. Classes are descriptive: they provide a set of necessary yet not sufficient conditions for membership. Each class is characterized by a set of properties called variables and by a set of constraints.

A variable denotes a property whose type is *not* a class of the KB. In AROM, no variable can reference object(s), but associations are used for this purpose. AROM includes an extensible set of basic types for mono- and multi-valued variables. Each variable is characterized by a set of facets, which can be divided in the three categories: domain restriction facets, inference facets, and documentation facets.

Constraints are necessary conditions expressed in the AML for an object to belong to the class. They bind together variables of – or reachable from – the class.

The generalization/specialization relation is a partial order organizing classes in a hierarchy supported by a simple inheritance mechanism. Specialization of a class involves the following operations: addition or refinement of a facet, addition of a new variable, addition of a constraint. Unless redefined, a class inherits all the variables (including facets) as well as all the constraints of its super-class.

An AROM object represents a distinguishable entity of the modeled domain. Each object is attached to exactly one class at any moment. The term "attached", used with the same acceptation as in the TROEPS system [7], enlightens the dynamic aspect of class membership: an object may move from a class to another whenever additional information about it becomes available.

Object identity is ensured by the use of unique identifiers, provided either by the user, or by the system.

Associations and tuples. In AROM, associations are similar to those found in UML: an association represents a set of similar links between n ($n \geq 2$) classes, being distinct or not. A link contains objects of the classes (one for each class) connected by the association. An association thus defines a subset of the Cartesian product of the classes it connects.

An association is described by means of roles, variables and constraints. A role r corresponds to the connection between an association and one of the classes it connects, called the *corresponding class* of the role and noted as $C(r)$. Each n-ary association has thus n roles and the value of each role r_i ($1 \leq i \leq n$) is an instance of $C(r_i)$. Each role has a multiplicity, whose meaning is the same as in UML.

A variable of an association denotes a property associated with a link and has the same set of facets as the one available for a class variable. We call *tuple* of an n-ary association having m variables v_i ($1 \leq i \leq m$), the (n+m)-uple made up of the n objects of the link and of the m values of the variables of the association. A tuple can then be seen as an "instance" of an association. Its identity relies on the identities of the instances of its link. This ensures that two tuples can *not* share the same link. As for classes, constraints involving variables or roles belonging to or reachable from an association can be written in the AML, and must be satisfied by every tuple of the association.

Associations are organized in specialization hierarchies. As for classes, association inheritance is simple and relies on set-based inclusion. Specializing an association A involves the following operations: specializing the corresponding class of a role of A, restricting or adding a facet to a variable or to a role of A, adding a constraint to a variable or to a role of A, adding a constraint to A, and adding a variable to A. Note that specialization of an association can *not* involve the addition of a role.

2.2 Algebraic Modeling of Operational Knowledge

First introduced in Operations Research, algebraic modeling languages (AMLs) make it possible to write systems of equations and/or of constraints, in a formalism close to mathematical notations. They support the use of indexed variables and expressions, quantifiers and iterated operators like $\sum$ (sum) and $\prod$ (product), in order to build expressions such as $\forall i \in I, x_i = \sum_{j \in J} x_j$. AMLs have been used for linear and non-linear [8], for discrete-time simulation [9], and recently for constraint programming [10].

In AROM, the AML is used for writing both equations, constraints, and queries. AML expressions are built from the following elements: constants, indices and indexed expressions, operators and functions, iterated operators, quantified expressions, variables belonging to classes and associations, and expressions that allow to access to the tuples of an association. In AROM, an AML interpreter solves systems of (non-simultaneous) equations and processes queries. A constraint satisfaction mechanism is currently under development.

2.3 Example

Fig. 1 and 2 present an excerpt of an AROM KB involving three hierarchies of classes: Teaching, Training, Course, and two hierarchies of associations: Manages and Teaches. Association ManagesPostGraduate specializes association Manages by refining the type of its roles and by adding a new variable.

```
knowledge-base: Teaching

class: Teacher
 variables:
  variable: socSecNumber
    type: string
  variable: service
    type: float
    definition: service =
      sum(t in this!Teaches: t.hourlyVolume * t.course.coeff)
  ...
association: Teaches
 roles:
  role: teacher
    type: Teacher
    multiplicity: min:0  max:1
  role: course
    type: Course
    multiplicity: min:0  max:*
  role: training
    type: Teaching
    multiplicity: min:0  max: *
 variables:
  variable: HourlyVolume
    type: integer

association: Manages
 roles:
  role: manager
    type: Permanent
    multiplicity: min:1   max:1
  role: training
    type: Teaching
    multiplicity: min:0  max:1

association: ManagesPostGraduate
 super-association: Manages
 roles:
  role: manager
    type: Prof
  role: training
    type: PostGraduateTraining
 variables:
  variable: bonus
    type: float
```

Fig. 1. Excerpt of an AROM KB. The AML definition (definition: facet) of service in class Teacher allows the computation of this variable as the sum, for each tuple t in this!Teaches – the set of tuples of Teaches in which this (the current Teacher) appears as teacher – of the product of the hourly volume of t and of the coefficient of the course associated with this tuple.

3 The AROM Platform

Written in Java 1.2, AROM is available[1] as a platform for knowledge representation and exploitation. It comprises an interactive modeling environment (see Fig. 2), which allows one to create, consult, and modify an AROM KB; a Java API, for developing applications based on AROM, an interpreter for processing queries and solving sets of (non-simultaneous) equations written in AML, and tools for consulting and editing knowledge bases through a Web browser.

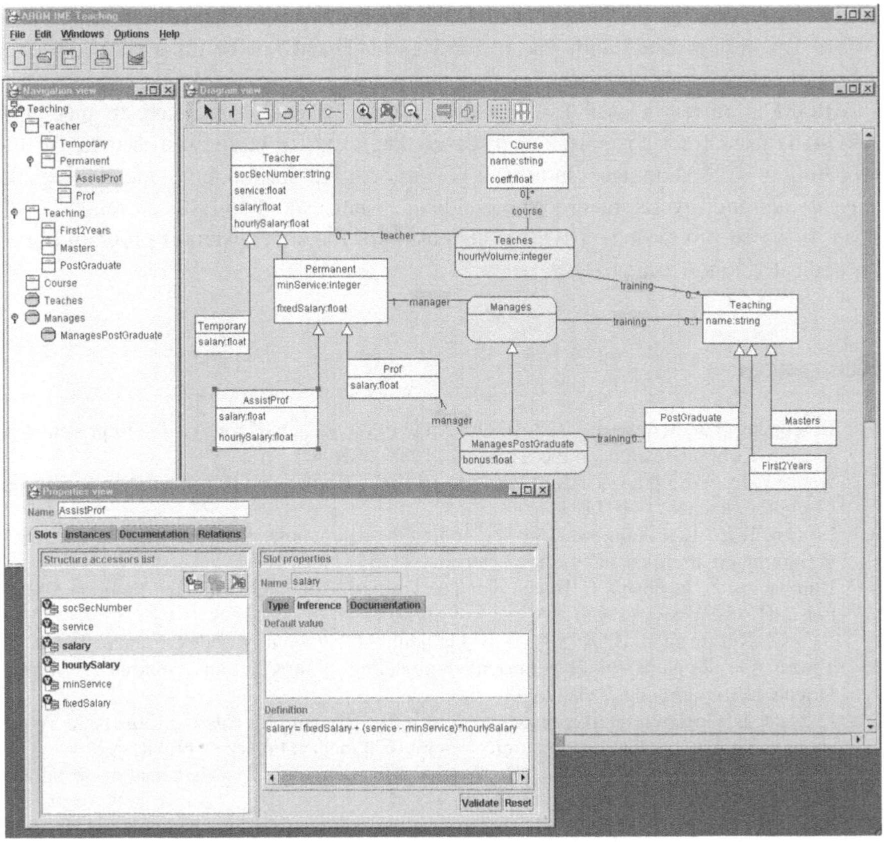

Fig. 2. Screenshot of the interactive modeling environment of AROM, using the example KB. Graphical notations are similar to those of UML except for associations, which are represented by gray rectangles with rounded corners.

[1] http://www.inrialpes.fr/romans/arom. In this site are also presented some formal aspects of knowledge representation in AROM, in particular its denotational semantics.

4 Discussion and Conclusion

In this paper, AROM, a new knowledge representation system has been presented. The first originality of this system is to propose two complementary entities for representing knowledge: classes and associations. The second originality is the presence of an algebraic modeling language allowing one to write equations, constraints and queries in a declarative manner.

AROM shares some similarities about the representation of associations in Description Logics (DL) using roles. However, roles as defined in DL systems are generally binary, described within concepts, and are not organized by subsumption. Only few of DL systems deal with role hierarchies [11], and few of others studied *n*-ary roles (DLR [12]).

AROM is currently used for developing KBs in several domains. In medicine, AROM is used for neuromuscular diseases diagnosis. In biology, it is used for the modeling of several domains in human genomic. A KB for modeling metabolic pathways containing several hundred thousands of instances and tuples is currently developed. In signal processing, AROM is also used for the supervision of program libraries dedicated to spectral analysis.

References

1. Brachman, R.J., Schmolze, J.G.: An Overview of the KL-ONE Knowledge Representation System. Communications of the ACM, 31 (1988) 382–401
2. Bobrow, D., Winograd, T.: An Overview of KRL, Knowledge Representation Language. Cognitive Science, 1 (1977) 3–46
3. Filman, R.E.: Reasoning with worlds and truth maintenance in a knowledge-based programming environment, Cognitive Science, 9 (1985) 171–216
4. Rumbaugh, J., Jacobson, I., Booch, G.: The Unified Modeling Language Reference Manual. Addison-Wesley (1999)
5. SMECI: Ref. manual. ILOG S.A., 2 av. Galliéni, 94253 Gentilly Cédex, France (1991)
6. Tanzer, C.: Remarks on object-oriented modeling of associations. Journal of Object-Oriented Programming, 7 (1995) 43–46.
7. Euzenat, J.: On a purely taxonomic and descriptive meaning for classes, 13th IJCAI Workshop on Object-Based Representation Systems, Chambéry, France (1993) 81–92
8. Fourer, R., Gay, D., Kernighan, B.: A Modeling Language for Mathematical Programming. Management Science, 36 (1990) 519–554
9. Page, M., Gensel, J., Boudis, M.: AMIA: An environment for knowledge-based discrete-time simulation. 2nd IMACS Int. Conf. on Computational Engineering in Systems Applications, Hammamet,Tunisia (1998) 56–61
10. van Hentenryck, P.: The OPL Optimization Programming Language. MIT Press (1999)
11. Horrocks, I., Sattler, U.: A Description Logic with Transitive and Inverse Roles and Role Hierarchies. International Workshop on Description Logics, Trento, Italy (1998)
12. Calvanese, D., de Giacomo, G., Lenzerini, M.: Conjunctive Query Containment in Description Logics with *n*-ary Relations. Int. Workshop on Description Logics, Paris (1997) 5–9

Ontology Integration Tasks in Business-to-Business E-Commerce

Borys Omelayenko

Division of Mathematics and Computer Science, Vrije Universiteit, De Boelelaan 1081a, 1081 hv, Amsterdam, The Netherlands
borys@cs.vu.nl

Abstract. In this paper we discuss the problem of document integration for business-to-business e-commerce. We present the infrastructure of the business documentation from the integration perspective and identify the integration subtasks. For each subtask we discuss the arising problems, and available technologies able to solve them.

1 Introduction

Nowadays e-business includes thousands of companies which provide tremendous number of products for electronic markets. Unlike the traditional markets, the electronic markets allow the participants to easily compare the offers and perform business negotiation faster due to electronic document interchange between the market participants. The product catalogs and other documents have a complicated structure and require knowledge-intensive ontological integration.

In this paper we discuss the integration scenario used in the Business-to-Business (B2B) area and the ways in which it enforces the ontology integration. In Section 2 we discuss the document infrastructure for B2B document interchange, followed by the document (Section 3) and content integration (Section 4). The paper ends with the technology overview in Section 5 and conclusions.

2 The B2B Document Infrastructure

The bunch of business documents (purchase orders, contracts, delivery requests and responses, product catalogs, etc.) are connected in the following way:

- The product catalogs describe the products, their prices, and available quantity in stock. They are linked to the content standards which specify the place of the product in the hierarchy of products, where each category provides a set of attributes used to specify the product. Besides these sets, the catalogs may introduce additional product attributes. The catalogs also introduce the internal company's identification codes for the products used in the further negotiation documents.

L. Monostori, J. Váncza, and M. Ali (Eds.): IEA/AIE 2001, LNAI 2070, pp. 119-124, 2001.

- Other documents, which do not contain the descriptions of the trade items, are linked only to the internal product codes and document numbers (e.g. delivery confirmations) or they are not linked at all (e.g. company information requests).
- The content standards described in Section 4 are linked one to each other. The horizontal content standards are mapped to other horizontal standards and to the vertical standards, and the latter are also linked together.

Because of the separation of the document and content standards we have two different types of ontologies: *document ontologies* (e.g. the ontology of a purchase order) and *product ontologies* used in the content standards. In the next two subsections we discuss the problems which occur in their integration.

3 The Document Standards

The B2B area operates with a large number of different business documents. For example, CommerceOne[1] offers the XML Common Business Library (xCBL)[2] standard with about 600 different document types for B2B interactions. Ariba[3] offers the Commerce XML (cXML)[4] standard with a smaller number of document types. Both standards provide the DTDs for the documents and assume that all of the documents are represented in XML. Hence, B2B document integration shifts to the XML document integration.

There are several non-XML document standards already accepted and widely used by the industries. First is the well-known EDIFACT format, approved by the United Nations Economic Commission for Europe[5]. An EDIFACT document is presented with complicated formatted text, non-understandable for a non-specialist. Several text wrappers able to translate an EDIFACT catalog into XML are available now, for example the XML-EDIFACT[6] wrapper that transfers EDIFACT documents into their XML representation and vise versa. Another non-XML standard is ISO 10303 [8] (also known as STEP) that is an International Standard for the computer-interoperable representation and exchange of product data. It contains a rich set of modeling primitives that allows building hierarchical product specifications. ISO has developed an XML syntax for STEP, that is now being standardized as part 28 of the ISO 10303 specification.

For both non-XML standards their XML representations have been already developed and are now in the process of approval by the community. Hence, we expect the problem of non-XML document integration not to be in the focus of the e-commerce research in the future.

The document standards provide only the structure for the document instances, and not the document ontologies themselves. The structures are represented in documents' DTDs that contain only part-of relation. Hence, the ontologies must be

---

[1] http://www.commerceone.com/solutions/business/content.html

[2] http://www.xcbl.org

[3] http://www.ariba.com/

[4] http://www.cxml.org

[5] http://www.unece.org/trade/untdid/welcome.htm

[6] http://www.xml-edifact.org/

induced from the instances prior to integration. The fragments of the document structures are represented in Fig. 1 for (a) xCBL and (b) cXML standards. The tags in the figure represent the elements of the structure and roughly correspond to the XML tags, which describe the instance documents. The values of the tags are given in the italic font as an example to illustrate the intended meaning of the tags. Graphical tags nesting represent the part-of relation. We see that the structures provide slightly different representations for very similar content. Both standards introduce internal product IDs, import the manufacturers' product IDs and names; they contain pricing information, product descriptions and a reference to a certain content standard. We expect the document ontologies to concord in general, because they appeared as a result of many years of natural standardization of business documentation.

```
CatalogSchema
  SchemaVersion> 1.0
  SchemaStandard> UNSPSC
  SchemaCategory
    CategoryID> C43171801
    ParentCategoryRef> C43170000
    CategoryName> Computers
    CategoryAttribute
      AttributeName> Processor Speed
CatalogData
  Product
    SchemaCategoryRef> C43171801
    ProductID> 140141-002
    Manufacturer> Compaq
    CountryOfOrigin> US
    ShortDescription> Armada M700 PIII 500
    LongDescription> This light, ...
      ObjectAttribute
        AttributeID> Processor Speed
        AttributeValue> 500MHZ
    ProductVendorData
      PartnerRef> Acme_Laptops
      VendorPartNumber> 12345
      ProductPrice
        Amount> 1000
        Currency> USD
```

(a) xCBL

```
PunchOutOrderMessage
  BuyerCookie> 342342ADF
  ItemIn
    quantity> 1
      ItemID
    SupplierPartID> 1234
    SupplierPartAuxiliaryID> 854374263
  ItemDetail
    UnitPrice
      Money
        currency> USD
        Money> 10.23
      Description> Learn ASP in a Week!
        UnitOfMeasure> EA
        Classification
          domain> SPSC
          Classification> 12345
        ManufacturerPartID> ISBN-23455634
        ManufacturerName> O'Reilly
```

(b) cXML

Fig. 1. A fragment of the xCBL and cXML formats

The same time the structures from Fig. 1 indicate the following problems:

- The ontologies have different names for semantically equivalent attributes.
- Some attributes are missing in the ontologies.
- The ontologies have different granularity levels.

A synergy of the web technology and the knowledge engineering technology is required for the integration, as discussed in Section 5.

4 The Content Standards

The catalogs presented in Fig. 1 contain the references to a certain content standard, and define additional attributes for the products, as in the xCBL case.

There exists a number of content standard, which may be classified into 'horizontal' standards and 'vertical' standards. The horizontal standards provide a high-level classification of *all* products in many domains. They provide an extensive but shallow hierarchy of product categories, but normally contain no product attributes. For example, the UN/SPSC[7] standard contains more than 12,000 categories, the NAICS[8] standard – more than 3,000 categories; both standards have five levels in their classification trees and provide no attributes.

The vertical standards provide deep and narrow classifications of a certain limited domain; they expand several bottom-level categories of the horizontal standard. The vertical standards provide the attributes for the categories. For example, RosettaNet[9] contains a catalog of IT products and expands 136 UN/SPSC elements with 445 categories and 2,660 attributes. Another standard, eCl@ss[10] uses more than 12,700 categories to describe the industrial domain of machines and materials and also expands a limited number of UN/SPSC elements.

From the knowledge engineering perspective the hierarchy of product categories with their attributes can be viewed as the product ontology. The B2B document interchange requires mapping of these ontologies, e.g. when the supplier uses UN/SPSC and the buyer searches for the products with NAICS. The ontologies have a two-level hierarchical composition: the general ontology (which corresponds to the horizontal standard) links to a number of domain-specific ontologies (the vertical standards).

We need three types of mappings to integrate the ontologies: the mappings between the horizontal standards, between the horizontal and vertical standards, and between the vertical standards.

Mapping of the horizontal standards has the following properties:

- The standards differ significantly in their classifications because of the absence of a consensus classification scheme.
- The standards differ in the level of granularity of the classifications.
- The equivalence is not evident from the category descriptions, e.g. the NAICS' code [39] 'Miscellaneous Manufacturing Industries' is equal to the UN/SPSC code [73] 'Industrial Production and Manufacturing Services'.

Mapping of the vertical standards has the following properties, in addition to the problems mentioned for the horizontal mapping:

- It requires mapping of attribute names, and attribute types (including mapping of the attribute value lists used for enumerating types).
- It requires transformations between different value formats and unit scales.

---

[7] www.unspsc.org
[8] www.naics.com
[9] www.rosettanet.org
[10] www.eclass.de

- The attribute domains must be mapped, i.e. in the source standard the attribute may apply to a set of categories, some of them may have no equivalent set in the target standard.
- Each catalog document can introduce its own set of attributes to be mapped.

Linking between the vertical and horizontal standards requires:

- Mapping of a relatively small number of top-level vertical concepts to more general concepts from the horizontal standard.
- Mapping of the concepts, which lay outside the focus of the vertical standard to the correspondent concepts of the horizontal standard. In this case the detail level of the horizontal standard may be higher than the level of the vertical standard.

These problems are very hot and important in the B2B area, but they are not new in the database, knowledge engineering, and information modeling areas, which provide a number of relevant and potentially useful technologies.

5 The Technology Overview

The integration can be done on three natural layers: the ontology layer, the data models layer, and the catalog layer [11].

The Catalog layer corresponds to the actual product catalogs in the XML format. The integration on this layer must be naturally based on the XML low-level integration architecture provided by the W3C[11] consortium with the XSLT [4] and XPath [5] languages. An attempt [10] to apply it directly showed a number of drawbacks, which must be solved in the multi-layer scheme.

The Data Models layer serves as a bridge between the catalog layer and the ontology layer. On this layer the representations are abstracted from the encoding peculiarities and the documents are represented with the object-attribute-value triples. For this layer W3C provides RDF [9], a standard for describing machine-processable semantics of data, which is also based on the object-attribute-value triples. Another possible candidate for this layer is SOAP[12] (see [7] for the comparison to RDF). This layer is connected with the catalog layer [10] and the ontology layer (cf. [2] for possible solutions).

The Ontology layer corresponds to the document and product ontologies. The ontologies are now intensively applied in e-commerce (cf. [6]) and they remain a hot topic in the knowledge engineering research. A number of integration technologies are applicable on this layer: model-based integration [1], Lisp-like ontology integration languages [3], and a tool support with Protégé[13] and Chimaera[14].

---

[11] www.w3c.org

[12] www.w3.org/TR/SOAP/

[13] http://protege.stanford.edu

[14] http://ksl.stanford.edu/software/chimaera/

6 Conclusions

The document integration problems are very important and moderately new for the area of B2B e-commerce. The paper presents the initial partitioning between the two separate integration tasks: document integration and product integration. This separates the integration of the document ontologies from the product ontologies. A special set of technologies must be selected from the bunch of potentially relevant techniques and standards listed in the paper, and adopted for each task.

Acknowledgement. The author would like to thank Dieter Fensel for helpful discussions and comments.

References

[1] Bowers, S., Delcambre, L.: Representing and Transforming Model-Based Information. In: Proceedings of the Workshop on the Semantic Web at ECDL-00, Lisbon, Portugal, 21 September (2000)
[2] Broekstra, J., Klein, M., Decker, S., Fensel, D., Horrocks, I.: Adding formal semantics to the Web building on top of RDF Schema. In: Proceedings of the Workshop on the Semantic Web at ECDL-00, Lisbon, Portugal, 21 September (2000)
[3] Chalupsky, H.: OntoMorph: A Translation System for Symbolic Knowledge. In: Proceedings of the 17-th International Conference on Knowledge Representation KR-00, Morgan Kaufmann Publishers, San Francisco, CA (2000)
[4] Clark, J.: XSL Transformations (XSLT), W3C Recommendation, November (1999); available online at http://www.w3.org/TR/xslt/
[5] Clark, J., DeRose, S.: XML Path Language (XPath), version 1.0, W3C Recommendation, 16 November (1999); available online at: http://www.w3.org/TR/xpath
[6] Fensel, D.: Ontologies: Silver Bullet for Knowledge Management and Electronic Commerce. Springer-Verlag, Berlin (2001)
[7] Haustein, S.: Semantic Web Languages: RDF vs. SOAP Serialization, In: Proceedings of the Workshop on the Semantic Web at WWW-10, Hong Kong, 1 May (2001)
[8] Integrated generic resource: Fundamentals of product description and support, International Standard ISO 10303-41, Second Edition (2000)
[9] Lassila, O., Swick, R.: Resource Description Framework (RDF). Model and Syntax Specification, W3C Recommendation, February (1999); available online at http://www.w3.org/TR/REC-rdf-syntax/
[10] Omelayenko, B., Fensel, D.: An Analysis of the Integration Problems of XML-Based Catalogues for B2B Electronic Commerce. In: Proceedings of 9th IFIP 2.6 Working Conference on Database Semantics, Hong Kong, 25-28 April (2001)
[11] Omelayenko, B., Fensel, D.: A Two-Layered Integration Approach for Product Catalogs in B2B E-commerce, submitted; available online at: http://www.cs.vu.nl/~borys/papers/

Using Multiple Models for Debugging VHDL Designs*

Franz Wotawa

Technische Universität Wien, Institut für Informationssysteme,
Database and Artificial Intelligence Group,
Favoritenstraße 9–11, A-1040 Vienna, Austria
wotawa@dbai.tuwien.ac.at

Abstract. Debugging is a time-consuming task especially for larger programs written by a group of people. In this paper we describe the use of multiple models for debugging VHDL designs, and presents some practical results. The models are derived from a general value-based model representing different fault situations that should be handled by a debugger. We propose the use of a probability-based selection strategy for selecting the most appropriate model in a given situation. For example large programs should be debugged using a model only distinguishing concurrent VHDL statements and not sequential statements. As a result of multi-model reasoning in this domain we expect performance gains allowing to debug larger designs in a reasonable time, and more expressive diagnosis results.

1 Introduction

Program debugging, i.e., locating and fixing a bug in a piece of software, is a difficult and time-consuming task. This holds especially for large programs written by a group of programmers. Because time to market is a major factor, tools for assisting a programmer in debugging are required. Traditional debuggers only allow to go step by step through a program and therefore require heavy user interaction. To avoid this problem several approaches for automating debugging has been proposed so far (see for example [15, 17,18,12,3,4,11]). These approaches are more or less generally applicable, use different aspects of programs, e.g., dependencies between variables or fault probabilities, for debugging, and introduce their own algorithms. In contrast more recently it has been recognized that model-based diagnosis (MBD) can be adapted for software debugging [6, 1,2,8,16]. In [6] the authors claim that MBD reduces the required user interaction when compared to [15]. The approach described in this paper makes use of previous MBD research in the software domain.

As in [8,21,20,19] we concentrate on programs written in the hardware description language VHDL. VHDL is an ADA-like programming language and an IEEE standard [9]. A VHDL program consists of an entity declaration that describes the interface, and an architecture declaration that describes the behavior of the design of an digital circuit. The architecture declaration comprises processes which are working in parallel. Each process comprises sequential statements, e.g., assignments and conditionals. The communication between processes is handled using signals. Variables are only allowed in processes. For more details about VHDL have a look at [13]. Figure 1 shows a

* The work described in this paper was partially supported by the Austrian Science Fund project P12344-INF and project N Z29-INF.

L. Monostori, J. Váncza, and M. Ali (Eds.): IEA/AIE 2001, LNAI 2070, pp. 125–134, 2001.

```
entity DECODER is
end DECODER;

architecture BEHAV of DECODER is
  signal ADDR, O, OI : BIT ;
  signal I1, I2 : BIT ;
begin
  ...   -- Here should be VHDL code for test case
           stimulating signals ADDR, I1, I2
  work: process (ADDR) -- DECODER behavior
  begin
    if (ADDR = '0') then
      O <= I1;
      OI <= not(I1);
    end if;
    if (ADDR = '1') then
      O <= I2;
      OI <= not(I2);
    end if;
  end process work;
end BEHAV;
```

Fig. 1. VHDL DECODER(BEHAV) program

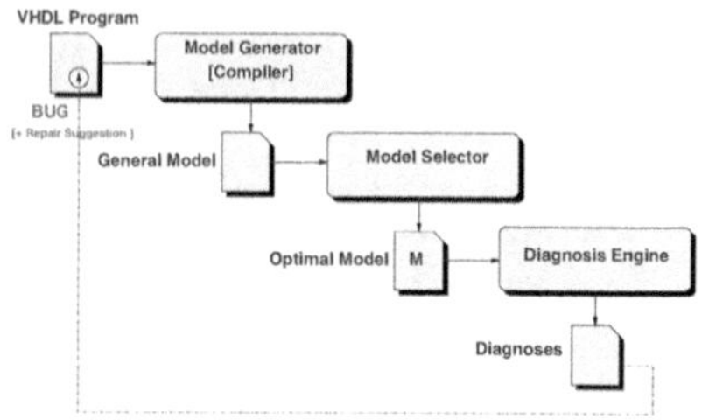

Fig. 2. Structure of an intelligent debugger

small VHDL program implementing a decoder. VHDL is a general language, allowing to specify (possible recursive) functions and data types. However, most programs are element of the register transfer level (RTL) subset where some syntactically restrictions apply. The reason for using this subset is that RTL programs can be (semi-)automatically compiled into a gate level representation from which there is only a small step to real hardware. Several syntactical restrictions apply to RTL programs, e.g., loop statements are only allowed if the number of loops is known at compile time, delay times must not be specified, and others. More informations about the RTL subset can be found in [10].

The basic idea about the application of MBD in software debugging is to translate a program into its logical representation, and use this representations together with a diagnosis engine [14,7] to compute diagnoses. The resulting diagnoses can be mapped back to their associated program fragments afterwards. In [8] and [21] VHDL concurrent statements, i.e., processes, are considered as diagnosis components, and signals as connections between components. This representation allows to state that a process may has a bug or not. The models introduced in [20,19] ensure more detailed results. This is done by mapping (sequential) statements and expressions to components and signals (and variables) to their connections. Although, this model is similar to the one we describe in this paper, it is not as general as ours and causes problems in some situations because of the underlying assumptions, e.g., structural correctness of the model.

Our approach of debugging RTL programs introduces a general model for VHDL programs with the capability of locating all functional faults. We define functional faults as faults occurring in a compilable program causing an unexpected behavior for at least one test case. Functional faults can be corrected by replacing expressions, adding or removing lines of code, or by changing variables or signals. The potential search space for locating and correcting functional faults is infinite. Therefore, we assume that the corrected program is a small variant of the original one. Although, this assumption restricts the search space, debugging is still time consuming especially for large programs, leading to a system description SD, i.e., a model, comprising a large amount of diagnosis components $COMP$. Using MBD for computing all single diagnosis has a worst case time complexity $O(|COMP|^2)$ assuming that SD is a propositional horn clause formula. Since, our extended model has more components as the previous model from [20, 19], debugging time increases. To avoid this problem we derive smaller models from the general one. A debugger then selects an appropriate derived model using knowledge about the current situation, e.g., source code size, type of the misbehavior, and others. In the next step this derived model is used for debugging instead of the general one.

The introduced debugger concept depicted in Figure 2 consists of a compiler, a model selector, and a diagnosis engine. The compiler transforms a VHDL program into a general model. The model selector takes the general model and uses additional knowledge, e.g., probability distributions or file size, to derive the diagnosis model. This is used (together with the expected behavior) by the diagnosis engine to compute diagnoses, which are mapped back to the source code. An advantage of this concept is that the used model is adapted to the current situation and overall diagnosis time is reduced. Note, that the situation can change during debugging, because of additional knowledge, e.g., expected values of signals provided by the user. Hence, the diagnosis model may change during debugging. However, in the worst case the overall diagnosis time is of the same order as the diagnosis time of the general model, but we expect a better performance in the average case.

The paper is organized as follows. In the next section we give a short overview of MBD and introduce the model. Afterwards, we show how smaller models can be derived, and how a debugger can handle multiple models. Some preliminary results obtained by using such a derived model are given, indicating that MBD substantially help finding bugs in hardware designs. Finally, we conclude the paper and discuss future research issues.

2 The General Model

Model-based diagnosis [14,7] is characterized by using a model SD, that describes the structure and the behavior of a system, and a set of observations OBS to determine a set of diagnoses, i.e., components from $COMP$ responsible for a misbehavior. Formally, a diagnosis problem is a triple $(SD, COMP, OBS)$. A component set $\Delta \subseteq COMP$ is a diagnosis iff $SD \cup OBS \cup \{\neg AB(C) | C \in COMP \setminus \Delta\} \cup \{AB(C) | C \in \Delta\}$ is consistent. A diagnosis is minimal if no proper subset is a diagnosis. The predicate $AB(C)$ ($\neg AB(C)$) denotes that component C behaves wrong (correct). This basic definition can be extended to handle fault modes, i.e., component modes associated with a specific behavior, e.g., stuck-at-0 in the digital domain. For our purposes we assume that each component C has modes $\Gamma(C)$, denoted by symbols starting with an upper-case letter, e.g., S0 for stuck-at-0, whereas the mode AB denotes the situation where the faulty behavior is not known. In the extended diagnosis definition a diagnosis is an assignment of modes to components leading to a consistent theory. Important to MBD is the existence of a component-oriented model. Such a model exists for systems from technical domains and the software domain.

The general VHDL model M_G of a program Π reflects the semantics of VHDL and the syntactical properties of Π. As stated previously M_G is automatically generated from Π. This transformation maps statements and expressions to diagnosis components and signals (and variables) to connections. A VHDL program Π is converted by successively converting the processes declared by the VHDL architecture declaration. Signals used in an expression or the sensitivity list of a process, e.g., signal *ADDR* from process *work* in Figure 1, are inputs, and signals used as target of an assignment statement, are outputs of the process and its associated diagnosis component. Note, that it is possible that several processes have the same signal as an output. In this case VHDL introduces a resolution function that allows to compute a single value for the signal. For the general model M_G in this case a diagnosis component representing the resolution function is used.

The conversion of a single process is done by introducing a diagnosis component for the process and successively converting each sequential statement starting from the first and going to the last. Again, each signal or variable used in an expression occurring in a sequential statement is an input, and each statement or variable used as target of an assignment are outputs of the statement. In order to reflect the semantics of VHDL there is a difference between connections representing variables and signals. For every output variable a new connection is created, that is connected with an input of a statement converted later. Instead, every input signal for a statement is connected using the same connection. The connection created for every signal is unique. The different handling of variables and signals used in an expression correctly represents the VHDL semantics. In VHDL the signal value is changed only after leaving a process. More details and a formal definition of the conversion process (returning a more simplified model) can be found in [20,19]. Note, that resulting structural model may contain cycles. They must be eliminated by introducing additional connections associated with signals (see [20, 19]). This procedure is similar to the conversion of sequential circuits to combinational circuits [5]. During the rest of this paper, we assume that the model M_G is acyclic. In the following we describe the created diagnosis components for each considered statement.

- **Processes**: According to the VHDL semantics processes must be executed if at least one signal S from the sensitivity list has changed its value. In this case the implicit available signal $S'EVENT$ is true. To represent this behavior correctly, we introduce a new diagnosis component $PROC(C)$ for each process. This component has a port $sens$ for every signal S from the sensitivity list, and ports ex_S, nex_S, and out_S for every output signal of the process. The ex_S ports are connected to the last signal connection for S obtained during converting the sequential statements. nex_S is connected to the original signal connection. This connection represent the state of S before executing a process. The output out_S represents the state of S after considering the process. The $sens$ ports are connected to the $S'EVENT$ connections. The behavior of a process is simple. If at least one $sens$ port has the value true, then the value of ex_S must be equal to the value of out_S. Otherwise, the value of nex_S is equal to out_S.
  $\neg AB(C) \Rightarrow (\exists_S sens_S(C) = true \rightarrow \forall_X ex_X(C) = out_X(C)$
  $\neg AB(C) \Rightarrow (\forall_S sens_S(C) = false \rightarrow \forall_X nex_X(C) = out_X(C)$
  The diagnosis components for processes have only two modes $\{\neg AB, AB\}$.
- **Signal assignments** are mapped to a diagnosis component $SA(C)$ having a port in and a port out. If the assignment is correct, i.e., use the correct target signal and expression, the input port has the same value as the output port.
  $\neg AB(C) \Rightarrow (in(C) = out(C))$
- **Conditionals** are mapped to a diagnosis component $COND(C)$ with a port $cond$ connected with the converted conditional expression, and ports $then_S$, $else_S$, and out_S connected with every connection associated with a signal or variable S used as target in an assignment statement either in the then-branch or the else-branch of the conditional. The behavior is defined as follows:
  $\neg AB(C) \Rightarrow (cond(C) = true \rightarrow \forall_S then_S(C) = out_S(C))$
  $\neg AB(C) \Rightarrow (cond(C) = false \rightarrow \forall_S else_S(C) = out_S(C))$

In addition we introduce the fault mode $WCOND$ that indicates a bug in the conditional expression.
$WCO(C) \Rightarrow (cond(C) = false \rightarrow \forall_S thens_S(C) = out_S(C))$
$WCO(C) \Rightarrow (cond(C) = true \rightarrow \forall_S elses_S(C) = out_S(C))$
Hence, a conditional has three modes $\{\neg AB, AB, WCOND\}$. Note that the considered VHDL subset allows neither to define a general loop nor a recursive function. Therefore, the $WCOND$ mode never causes an infinite loop (which can be the case if the restrictions do not apply).

- **Expressions** consists out of signal or variable accesses, constants, and functions. For each category we use a different mapping.
  - **Signal access** are mapped to a diagnosis component $SAC(C)$, with one output out, and a port in_S for every signal S declared in the program. The accessed signal T is stored in a predicate $sig(C,T)$. The correct behavior of the diagnosis component is as follows:
    $\neg AB(C) \Rightarrow (sig(C,T) \rightarrow out(C) = in_T(C))$
    In addition for every signal $S \neq T$ we add the known misbehavior:
    $WSIG_S(C) \Rightarrow (out(C) = in_S(C))$
    to the system description. This part of the model allows the diagnosis engine to switch between available signals and to explain a wrong signal access.
  - **Constants** are mapped to a diagnosis component $CONS(C)$ with one output out delivering the constants value stored in the predicate $const(C,V)$.
    $\neg AB(C) \Rightarrow (const(C,V) \rightarrow out(C) = V)$
    Additionally, we introduce fault modes delivering other constant values depending on the type of the constant. For boolean constants for example we add the following rule:
    $WCON(C) \Rightarrow (const(C,V) \rightarrow out(C) = \neg V)$
    For other domains similar rules can be formalized. However, for describing digital circuits the considered domains must be finite.
  - **Functions** $f \in \{and, or, not, \ldots\}$ are mapped to corresponding diagnosis components $f(C)$, e.g., for an **and** function we have a component $AND(C)$ with ports $in1, in2, out$ and the following behavior:
    $\neg AB(C) \Rightarrow (out(C) = in1(C) \wedge in2(C))$
    In addition we assume fault models that represent repair suggestions, e.g., a wrong **and** function that should be repaired by replacing it with an **or** function.
    $WFUN_{or}(C) \Rightarrow (out(C) = in1(C) \vee in2(C))$
    $WFUN_{nand}(C) \Rightarrow (out(C) = \neg(in1(C) \wedge in2(C)))$
    ...

For space reasons the rules for converting variables used in assignments or expressions is not included. They are similar to the one given for signals, with a slightly different handling of connections accordingly to the semantical differences between variables and signals in VHDL. Moreover, the computed model is not intended to handle faults related to wrong target signals. Handling this kind of faults would makes the resulting model more complicated but would has no influence on further contributions of this paper, i.e., the derivation of less general models and the handling of multiple models for optimizing the debugging process using MBD. Using the above conversion our running example from figure 1 is converted to a model depicted in Figure 3. The model comprises 19 diagnosis components: $\{S1, S2, S3, S4, S5, S6\}$ (Signal access), $\{A1, A2, A3, A4\}$ (Assignments), $\{N1, N2\}$ (Negations), $\{E1, E2\}$ (Equivalence functions), $\{C1, C2\}$ (Constants), $\{CS1, CS2\}$ (Conditionals), and $\{PS1\}$ (Process *work*).

The general model M_G of a program Π consists of a system description SD_G and a set of components $COMP_G$. SD_G can be divided into a structural part SD_{GS} and a

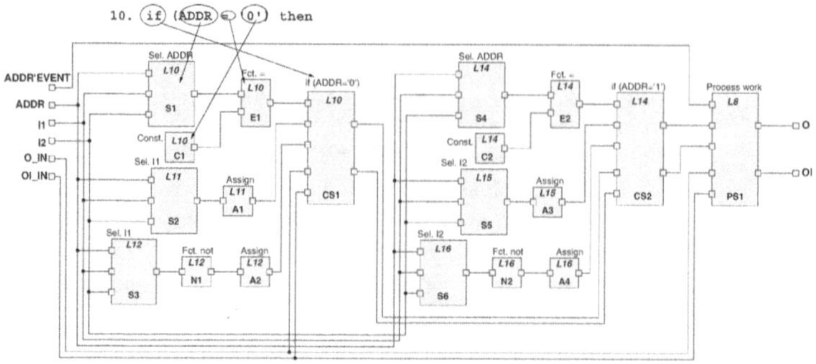

Fig. 3. A model of the DECODER(BEHAV) program

behavioral part SD_{GB}. The structural part comprises knowledge about the interconnection an corresponds with the syntactical structure of Π while SD_{GB} is only defined once for a programming language and used in all general models. Only some instantiation informations, e.g., $const('1', C2)$ in our example, which is assumed to be part of SD_{GB} has to be added to get the final model.

3 Deriving Models

With the introduced general model M_G we can handle almost all fault situations, including the wrong use of signals or variables, wrong functions, wrong conditions, and others. Therefore, in some cases we get too many different diagnoses. Moreover, they are difficult to handle by a programmer. Consider for example that the diagnosis engine delivers a diagnosis corresponding to a structural bug[1] and another (different) diagnosis corresponding to a wrong function. Without further guidance it is difficult (1) to see the different nature of the bugs, and (2) to distinguish between the diagnoses. Therefore, we suggest the use of different models handling different kind of bugs, e.g., structural bugs and wrong functions. Another argument motivating the use of multiple models is the performance of diagnosis. A sub-model of M_G with less diagnosis components reduces the time for computing all diagnoses in the average. In order to allow MBD for debugging larger designs, it is an requirement to use the most appropriate model for computing bug locations in a reasonable time.

For our purposes we distinguish two types of sub-models for $M_G = (SD_G, COMP_G)$:

- **Partial models** are models derived from a general model M_G, where the system description is extended using correctness assumptions for the non-empty set of components $CO \subseteq COMP$, and the set of components is reduced to $COMP = COMP_G \setminus CO$. Formally, a partial model is a tuple $(SD \cup COA, COMP)$ with $COMP = COMP_G \setminus CO$, and COA set of assumptions about the state of the components in CO, e.g., correctness of a component $\neg AB(PS1)$.

[1] A structural bug is due to a wrong use of a signal or variable while a functional bug is due to a wrong use of a function or operator.

- **Hierarchical models** are models derived from M_G where new components representing a set of components from $COMP_G$ are introduced, together with rules specifying the correct behavior of the new components. $(SD \cup MAP, COMP)$ with $COMP \cap COMP_G = \emptyset$, and MAP is a set of rules defining the correct behavior of a component $C \in COMP$ using modes of components $C' \in COMP_G$, e.g., $\neg AB(work) \rightarrow (\neg AB(PS1) \wedge \neg AB(CS1) \wedge \ldots)$.

Because of the definition both sub-models have less components than the original model M_G. The size of the system description slightly increases but should have almost no effect on the overall run-time. Hence, if it is possible to select the right sub-model for debugging, we expect substantial savings of the overall diagnosis time.

The following propositions follows directly from the definition of model-based diagnosis and partial models.

Lemma 1. *A diagnosis for a partial model* $M = (SD \cup COA, COMP)$ *and observations* OBS *derived from a general model* M_G *exists iff* $SD \cup COA \cup OBS$ *is consistent.*

Hence, a minimal requirement for partial model is that $SD \cup COA$ is consistent. For the VHDL debugging domain we distinguish the following models:

- *Correct structure* M_{COR} For this partial model we assume that the structure is correct, i.e., we set all signal access components and process components to the correct state. In our running example we have $CO = \{S1, S2, S3, S4, S5, S6, PS1\}$. This assumptions allows us to use multiple test cases and filter criteria as described in [19, 16].
- *Structural faults* M_{SF} In the structural fault model we assume that only signal access components can be faulty, i.e., all other components are assumed to behave correct. For our running example we get $CO = \{E1, E2, A1, A2, A3, A3, N1, N2, CS1, CS2, PS1\}$ and only the statements $S1, S2, S3, S4, S5, S6$ remain as diagnosis components.
- *Wrong condition* M_{WCOND} This partial model is used to locate faults in the condition part of a conditional statement. It is required that the observations include the expected value of the condition expression. All components are set to the correct mode except the component associated with the conditional statement having a bug in the condition, i.e., the conditional is set to WCO. The set of diagnosis components for M_{WCOND} comprises all components that are associated with the condition expression (and its sub-expressions). M_{WCOND} should only be used if a wrong condition has been located using another model, e.g., M_{COR}.
- *Concurrent statements* M_{CONC} This model is a hierarchical model considering processes as single diagnosis components. In our running example all components are mapped to a single diagnosis component representing the process. M_{CONC} is intended to be used for larger programs in order to reduce the number of diagnosis components and therefore to reduce the overall diagnosis time.

This four derived models represent different aspects of debugging VHDL programs. Similar models are expected to be useful for debugging programs written in other programming languages. In order to reduce the overall debugging time the selection of the best model in a current situation is a crucial requirement. We define the best model informally as the model that lead to the localization of a bug in a minimum number of required questions about values at specific points in the program and in the shortest time. For example if the program is large, then the hierarchical model should be used. After identifying one process a more detailed model can be used for further discrimination. A more detailed view on the model selection process has been left for future research. But we expect that a probability-based technique similar to [3,4] would be a good choice in this context.

4 Results

In this section we give first results for model M_{COR} using multiple test cases [16] and filtering as described in [19]. We show that both techniques significantly reduce the number of computed candidates. The empirical results based on three different VHDL designs with several faulty variants. The faulty designs where derived from the correct programs by introducing bugs like changing constant values or functions. Table 1 gives the programs together with the number of different architectures and the range of computed diagnosis components for each designs. Design COUNTER1 implements a simple digital counter. COUNTER2 implements a counter with a 1 from 4 output. The ENCODER1 and ENCODER2 program implement two variants of a BCD to 7-segment LCD display decoder.

The results of diagnosis using our prototype implementation are given in Table 2. In this Table the column $DIAG$ gives the number of candidates obtained by building the union of all diagnoses computed for all test cases without applying the filtering rules, i.e., $DIAG = |\cup_{\Delta \in DIAGNOSES_i} \Delta|$. $DIAG\_MT$ gives the number of diagnosis for the multiple test case diagnosis where the intersection of diagnoses is used, again without filtering. In column $DIAG\_MTF$ the resulting number of diagnoses after applying multiple test case diagnosis and filtering is given. Column EXP is true, whenever the expected diagnosis remains after multiple test case diagnosis and filtering was applied. Note, that the expected diagnosis was always computed whenever neither filtering nor multiple test case diagnosis was applied. It is worth noting that $DIAG$ gives an upper-bound of the number of minimal diagnoses while $DIAG\_MTF$ can be viewed as lower-bound.

The obtained result indicates the use of multiple test cases together with the application of filter rules indeed drastically reduces the number of computed diagnoses. In 11 out of 17 cases, where the expected result was computed, our approach delivers only 1 diagnosis. In the other cases at most 6 candidates remain. However, there are cases, where our approach computes wrong diagnoses. This happens only when structural faults causes the wrong behavior. Since, M_{COR} together with multiple test case diagnosis is not allowed to be used in case of structural faults, the result is the expected one.

5 Conclusion

This paper describes how multiple models help to decrease debugging time of VHDL designs. The multiple models are derived from a general model handling almost all fault situations. We propose the selection of a most probable model in the given situation. A situation is characterized by propositions. For example the proposition *large program*

Table 2. Results of the multiple test case diagnosis

Design	DIAG	DIAG_MT	DIAG_MTF	EXP
COUNTER1(BEHAV1)	12	6	1	yes
COUNTER1(BEHAV2)	6	4	1	yes
COUNTER1(BEHAV3)	11	7	1	yes
COUNTER1(BEHAV4)	13	11	3	yes
COUNTER1(BEHAV5)	14	7	1	yes
COUNTER1(BEHAV6)	14	9	2	yes
COUNTER1(BEHAV7)	8	5	5	no
COUNTER1(BEHAV8)	16	11	3	no
COUNTER1(BEHAV9)	17	2	2	no
COUNTER1(BEHAV10)	8	6	5	no
COUNTER2(BEHAV1)	5	1	1	yes
COUNTER2(BEHAV2)	2	0	0	no
COUNTER2(BEHAV3)	4	3	2	no
COUNTER2(BEHAV4)	11	3	1	yes
COUNTER2(BEHAV5)	10	7	3	yes
ENCODER1(BEHAV1)	79	3	1	yes
ENCODER1(BEHAV2)	85	8	5	yes
ENCODER1(BEHAV3)	60	59	2	yes
ENCODER1(BEHAV4)	15	15	1	yes
ENCODER2(BEHAV1)	65	3	1	yes
ENCODER2(BEHAV2)	67	9	6	yes
ENCODER2(BEHAV3)	55	55	1	yes
ENCODER2(BEHAV4)	63	24	1	yes

Table 1. VHDL Designs

Entity	Num. Arch.	Diag. Components
COUNTER1	11	23...24
COUNTER2	6	41...42
ENCODER1	5	440
ENCODER2	5	440

is valid if the program exceeds a specific size, say 10 k-Byte.In this case a hierarchical modeling approach is expected to be used in order to allow for computing diagnoses in a short time. Future research should focus on the model selection process. Probabilities of models with respect to a given situation should be computed. To do this a concise analysis of the probability of bugs and their effects is needed. In addition to the analysis of the model selection process, models for a greater subset of VHDL (or better full VHDL) are of interest. However, the contributions of this paper, i.e., the general model, the computation of derived models, and the view of debugging as multi-model reasoning process proved a good foundation for future research in the domain of intelligent debugging.

References

1. G. W. Bond and B. Pagurek. A Critical Analysis of "Model-Based Diagnosis Meets Error Diagnosis in Logic Programs". Technical Report SCE-94-15, Carleton University, Dept. of Systems and Computer Engineering, Ottawa, Canada, 1994.
2. Gregory W. Bond. *Logic Programs for Consistency-Based Diagnosis.* PhD thesis, Carleton University, Faculty of Engineering, Ottawa, Canada, 1994.
3. Lisa Burnell and Eric Horvitz. A Synthesis of Logical and Probabilistic Reasoning for Program Understanding and Debugging. In *Proceedings of the International Conference on Uncertainty in Artificial Intelligence*, pages 285 –291, 1993.
4. Lisa Burnell and Eric Horvitz. Structure and Chance: Melding Logic and Probability for Software Debugging. *Communications of the ACM*, pages 31 – 41, 1995.
5. Kwang-Ting Cheng and Angela Krstic. Current Directions in Automatic Test-Pattern Generation. *IEEE-Computer*, 32(11), November 1999.
6. Luca Console, Gerhard Friedrich, and Daniele Theseider Dupré. Model-based diagnosis meets error diagnosis in logic programs. In *Proceedings* 13th *International Joint Conf. on Artificial Intelligence*, Chambery, August 1993.

7. Johan de Kleer and Brian C. Williams. Diagnosing multiple faults. *Artificial Intelligence*, 32(1):97–130, 1987.
8. Gerhard Friedrich, Markus Stumptner, and Franz Wotawa. Model-based diagnosis of hardware designs. *Artificial Intelligence*, 111(2):3–39, July 1999.
9. IEEE. IEEE Standard VHDL Language Reference Manual LRM Std 1076-1987, 1988. Institute of Electrical and Electronics Engineers, Inc. IEEE.
10. IEEE. IEEE P1076.6/D1.12 Draft Standard For VHDL Register Transfer Level Synthesis, 1998. Institute of Electrical and Electronics Engineers, Inc. IEEE.
11. Daniel Jackson. Aspect: Detecting Bugs with Abstract Dependences. *ACM Transactions on Software Engineering and Methodology*, 4(2):109–145, April 1995.
12. Bogdan Korel. PELAS–Program Error-Locating Assistant System. *IEEE Transactions on Software Engineering*, 14(9):1253–1260, 1988.
13. Zainalabedin Navabi. *VHDL Analysis and Modeling of Digital Systems*. McGraw-Hill, 1993.
14. R. Reiter. A theory of diagnosis from first principles. *Artificial Intelligence*, 32(1), 1987.
15. Ehud Shapiro. *Algorithmic Program Debugging*. MIT Press, Cambridge, MA, 1983.
16. Markus Stumptner and Franz Wotawa. Debugging Functional Programs. In *Proceedings* 16th *International Joint Conf. on Artificial Intelligence*, Stockholm, Sweden, August 1999.
17. Mark Weiser. Programmers use slices when debugging. *Communications of the ACM*, 25(7):446–452, July 1982.
18. Mark Weiser. Program slicing. *IEEE Transactions on Software Engineering*, 10(4):352–357, July 1984.
19. Franz Wotawa. Debugging synthesizeable VHDL Programs. In *Proceedings of the Tenth International Workshop on Principles of Diagnosis*, 1999.
20. Franz Wotawa. New Directions in Debugging Hardware Designs. In *Proceedings of the International Conference on Industrial and Engineering Applications of Artificial Intelligence and Expert Systems*, 1999. Springer, Lecture Notes in Artificial Intelligence 462 (LNAI 462).
21. Franz Wotawa. Debugging VHDL Designs using Model-Based Reasoning. *Artificial Intelligence in Engineering*, 14(4):331–351, 2000.

Lessons Learned from Diagnosing Dynamic Systems Using Possible Conflicts and Quantitative Models

Belarmino Pulido[1], Carlos Alonso[1], and Felipe Acebes[2]

[1] Dpto. de Informática
[2] Centro de Tecnología Azucarera
Universidad de Valladolid. Edificio de Nuevas Tecnologías.
Camino del cementerio s/n. E-47011. Valladolid (Spain)
{belar,calonso}@infor.uva.es, felipe@cta.uva.es

Abstract. For more than ten years different techniques have been proposed to perform model-based diagnosis of dynamic systems. Nevertheless, there is no general framework yet. Main part of the research effort has been devoted to modeling issues. Most approaches have relied upon qualitative models due to the lack of accuracy, certainty and precision in quantitative models. Hence, one question arises, is still possible to use quantitative models in the Artificial Intelligence approach to model-based diagnosis? Despite of mentioned drawbacks, quantitative models offer some advantages. If combined with pre-compiled dependency-recording, these systems avoid one of the traditional problems in the qualitative modeling approach, the feedback loop problem. These are the bases of MORDRED, a model-based diagnosis system that combines quantitative models and the possible conflict concept. This work presents results obtained in MORDRED verification and validation processes. Moreover, it analyses drawbacks found, proposed solutions, and lessons learned during the whole design and implementation cycle.

1 Introduction

Since the late 80's the AI community have been working in model-based diagnosis of dynamic systems. Nevertheless, there is no accepted general framework yet [11,9]. Nowadays, a lot of research effort is still devoted to this area[5,7, 15] due to the inherent complexity of the task. The GDE (see [11]), which is the classic paradigm in consistency-based diagnosis, was initially extended with temporal reasoning capabilities (see references to XDE, CATS or SIDIA in [11]). Afterwards, different approaches, mostly based on qualitative models, have been proposed to perform model-based diagnosis of dynamic systems [7,3,14,18]. As a consequence, there is a small number of references to quantitative approaches [5]. When quantitative models are used, it is obvious that it is not straightforward to perform consistency-based diagnosis of dynamic systems, due to the inherent complexity of dynamic behaviour modeling and simulation. Moreover, a main drawback when consistency-based diagnosis is applied to dynamic systems is on-line dependency-recording. This can cause the so called feedback loop problem

L. Monostori, J. Váncza, and M. Ali (Eds.): IEA/AIE 2001, LNAI 2070, pp. 135–144, 2001.

[8], which produces estimations dependent upon the majority of the constraints in the model in few integration steps [5]. Few years ago, pre-compilation of dependencies has emerged as a suitable alternative to on-line dependency-recording. Pre-compilation takes advantage of behavioural information, implicit in system description, and identifies, off-line, behavioural and/or functional dependencies among components or variables [13,12,10,6].

These techniques are specially useful in the field of industrial continuous processes, where sensor placement seldom changes. MORDRED, a diagnosis system relying upon off-line dependency recording and quantitative models, takes advantage of that feature and organises the diagnosis process around the *possible conflict* concept [17]. This work analyses results obtained by MORDRED when it was used to diagnose a laboratory plant.

This paper is organised as follows. In the next section we review the possible conflict concept and its integration in the consistency-based diagnosis cycle. Afterwards we analyse problems found during the verification phase of the approach. Next section presents results obtained when the approach was validated on a real system. Last section is devoted to discussion.

2 Consistency-Based Diagnosis of Dynamic Systems Using Possible Conflicts

The main idea behind the possible conflict concept is that the set of subsystems capable to become a conflict can be identified off-line, disregarding observations, and with no model evaluation. Initially, MORDRED analyses an abstract representation of system description looking for subsystems containing analytical redundancy, which are essential for model-based diagnosis. These subsystems are called *minimal evaluable chains*. Afterwards, it takes advantage of an abstraction of constraints imposed by behavioural restrictions to build a model for each minimal evaluable chain, if possible. These models, called *minimal evaluable models*, can predict the behaviour of parts of the system. If there is a discrepancy between predictions and observations, the set of constraints in the minimal evaluable model responsible for the prediction is confirmed as a conflict. Afterwards, diagnosis candidates are obtained from conflicts following Reiter's theory[11].

To diagnose dynamic systems MORDRED makes difference of two kinds of constraints: *instantaneous*, which estimate static behaviour, and *differential*, which predict system evolution over time. It is assumed that only instantaneous relations contain useful information for diagnosis purposes. Moreover, MORDRED should be classified as an integration method since differential constraints can be used *only* to estimate the value of a variable through the integration step:

$$v_i(t) = \int_{t-1}^{t} \frac{dv_i}{dt} \cdot dt + v_i(t-1)$$

Summarizing, every possible conflict can be pre-computed off-line because no observation is needed. Since conflicts will arise only when models are evaluated with available observations, the set of constraints in a minimal evaluable model is called a *possible conflict*, for short pc.

Therefore, MORDRED does interpret classical consistency-based diagnosis in the following way:

1. the system must be analysed looking for any minimal evaluable chain;
2. those minimal evaluable chains with no evaluable model must be rejected,
3. exactly one minimal evaluable model associated to a minimal evaluable chain must be selected,
4. build the model of the possible conflict pc_i, SD_{pc_i}, from the description of the minimal evaluable model,
5. *repeat*
   a) simulate SD_{pc_i} using OBS_{pc_i} and producing $PRED_{pc_i}$,
   b) *if* $\| PRED_{pc_i} - OBS'_{pc_i} \| > \delta_{pc_i}$ *then* confirm pc_i,
   c) *if* a new pc_i is confirmed, *then* compute the new set of candidates

   until there is no pc_i to be simulated

Where OBS_{pc_i} denotes the set of input observations available in SD_{pc_i}, $PRED_{pc_i}$ represents the set of predictions obtained from SD_{pc_i}, OBS'_{pc_i} denotes the set of output observations in SD_{pc_i}, and δ_{pc_i} is the maximum value allowed as the difference between OBS'_{pc_i} and $PRED_{pc_i}$.

As it was mentioned above, dynamic behaviour prediction is not a trivial task. To do simulation over time, MORDRED assumes that the initial state of the system is completely known. Therefore, the whole simulation process in MORDRED can be summarized as:

while $t < t_{max}$ *do*
  use instantaneous constraints, the current state, and observations to estimate $v_i(t)$;
  estimate the next state using $v_i(t)$ and the set of differential constraints;
  t := t + 1;
end

Moreover, dealing with real data makes more difficult the verification and validation processes of any approach. We have decided to verify MORDRED using a simulated model of a laboratory plant and, afterwards, to validate the approach with data from the real plant. Next section is devoted to discuss the verification phase, and specially to the implementation of steps 5.(a) and 5.(b).

3 Verification

A laboratory plant was selected to verify MORDRED. This plant, completely described in [16], is made up of typical components in any industrial continuous process, such as tanks, pumps, valves or controllers. In figure 1 is shown the scheme of this plant. In this system, MORDRED has found four possible conflicts[1]:

$$PC_1 = \{tr1_1, tr1_2, tr1_3, tr1_4, t2_1, t2_2, t2_3, t2_4, t2_5, p2_1, p2_2, p2_3\}$$

[1] MORDRED assumed that the model of a generic component is made up of more than one constraint. Hence, it makes difference of components –represented by means of capital letters–, and of model constraints –represented by small letters–. Moreover, different constraints within the same model will exhibit different indices.

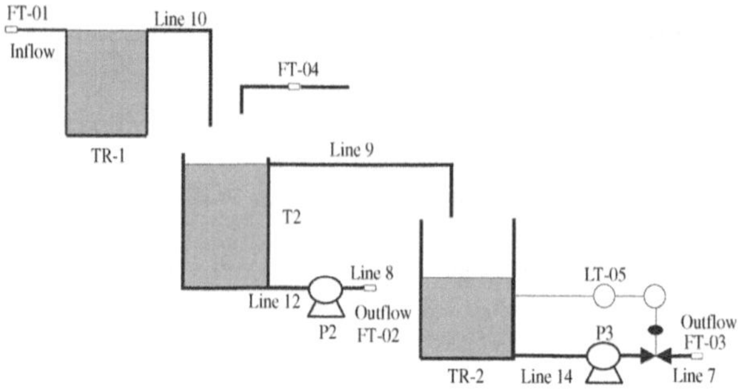

Fig. 1. Scheme of the system to be diagnosed. Measured variables are flows $FT01$, $FT02$, $FT03$, and $FT04$; level of tank $LT05$, and the value of the control action in $TR2$.

$$PC_2 = \{tr2_1, tr2_3, p3_1, p3_2, p3_3, v2_1, v2_2\}$$
$$PC_3 = \{t2_2, t2_4, p2_1, p2_2, tr2_4, tr2_5, tr2_6, p3_3, v2_1\}$$
$$PC_4 = \{tr1_1, tr1_2, tr1_3, tr1_4, t2_1, t2_2, t2_3, t2_5, p2_3, tr2_4, tr2_5, tr2_6, p3_3, v2_1\}$$

Each possible conflict is able to predict the evolution of a measured variable: PC_1 estimates the evolution of outflow $FT02$ based on $FT01$ and $FT04$; PC_2 predicts the value of $FT03$ given the level of tank $TR2$ and the value of the control action; PC_3 estimates the evolution of $LT05$ from the values of $FT02$ and $FT03$; and PC_4 predicts the evolution of $LT05$ based on $FT01$, $FT03$ and $FT04$. The reader should notice that MORDRED works on the basis of minimality w.r.t. sets of constraints instead of minimality w.r.t. sets of components. This assumption enables MORDRED to make use of any constraint in system description. A component-oriented diagnosis framework would miss information about PC_4 since it is not minimal w.r.t. sets of components.

Once the case study has been presented, we focus on MORDRED's verification. In this process we have found two problems inherent to continuous systems diagnosis:

- the model of the whole plant, and the models of the possible conflicts, must deal with noisy measurements and parameter uncertainty,
- usually, discrepancy detection requires a more elaborated method than a point to point comparison.

Quantitative simulation must analyse main characteristics of the models and main features of the simulator. We have considered the proposal by Chantler et al.[4] to do this analysis; therefore, we have studied precision, accuracy and certainty in available measurements and in the predictor engine.

MORDRED have relied upon SIMPD[1],which is able to build executable ACSL[2] models from topological, functional and phenomenological descriptions of the system. SIMPD was used to build the model of the entire plant, and

[2] ACSL is a registered trademark by MGA Software.

this model was the basis for the construction of the possible conflicts models. Executable models have neither accuracy nor precision limitations. However, they should deal with uncertainty. There were two sources of uncertainty. First one came from model parameters. Second one came from noisy measurements. To solve the first drawback we relied in an optimisation tool in the design phase. To deal with the second problem we decided to filter both input and output data following the scheme depicted in figure 2.

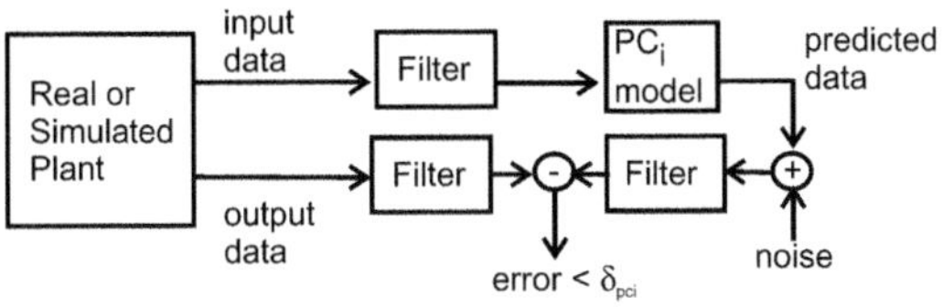

Fig. 2. Low pass filter is applied to data introduced in the models. At the same time, noise is introduced in predicted data from the models to emulate real noise conditions. Output data from the plant and the models of possible conflicts are filtered before comparison.

First lesson learned came from the application of this scheme. We concluded that MORDRED could not use the model of PC_3. Although the model was able to produce accurate results in simulation without noise, one of the constraints in the possible conflict model proved to be highly sensitive to noise. Therefore, MORDRED could not use this possible conflict with real data.

Finally, despite of the optimisation phase and the filtering process, some parameter uncertainty remained in the models. This uncertainty would manifest in the predictor output, and it could cause wrong detections. To reduce the number of wrong detections, additional considerations should be done.

Discrepancy check in consistency-based diagnosis is straightforward only when measurements are certain, precise and accurate[4]. This is not the case in our system due to the presence of noise and uncertainty. And this is not the case in most diagnosis systems. For this reason, most approaches have relied upon a comparison of the discrepancy between predicted and observed values against a threshold. This threshold can be fixed or variable. Whenever the discrepancy does surpass the threshold for a given period of time, a fault is detected.

MORDRED will use a slighty different approach. It will not do a point to point comparison. It will estimate the trajectory of certain variables –the output of the possible conflict models– for a given period of time. We have selected this period of time based on the criticity of the faults in the plant. And we will compare estimated and observed trajectories for the same variable. If the difference between both trajectories surpasses a fixed threshold, a detection is done. The difference between both trajectories will be the disimilarity value returned by the Dynamic Time Warpping algorithm, DTW. This algorithm solves the variational problem of finding an optimal alignment function between two patterns applying the Bellman's optimality principle[2]. DTW has been succesfully used in off-line diagnosis and in time-domain pattern-recognition problems.

DTW has a set of parameters that must be customized. Two of them are of special interest for diagnosis purposes:

- the local distance, between each pair of points,
- N, the size of the series to be compared.

We have tested different values for N –10, 20, 30, and 45–, and several local distances –euclidean, cuadratic, and exponential–. We have chosen N=45 and euclidean local distance based on:

- symptom dynamics and criticality considerations,
- the amount of time required to simulate three ACSL models for large and small N values,
- the size of N makes influence in the speed of the detection, and
- euclidean and cuadratic distances were less sensitive to noise.

The last issue in the verification phase is how to determine the threshold. We have proceeded in the following way:

1. We have selected 10 different normal behaviours: nominal, above and below nominal, with and without perturbations.
2. We have chosen 16 single fault modes and two double fault modes[3].
3. We have analysed which fault can be detected by each possible conflict[4].
4. We have computed the maximum disimilarity values returned by DTW for non faulty modes, and the required minimum disimilarity value to detect a faulty mode.
5. We have established the threshold δ_{pc_i} between the maximum and the minimum disimilarity values.

Once this analysis was performed, we obtained the following values for the thresholds:

	PC1	**PC2**	**PC4**
δ_{pc_i}	0.025	0.05	0.075

Verification results, which are shown in table 1, indicate that the consistency-based approach based on qualitative models and possible conflicts is suitable for continuous systems diagnosis.

The reader should notice that as a result of consistency requirements, the diagnostician is able not only to perform fault detection but fault localisation. MORDRED finds the set of constraints which could be blamed for the fault. However, since consistency-based diagnosis only allows correct behaviour models, fault identification is not possible.

[3] Underlying assumption in most approaches are that multiple simultaneous faults seldom happen. Moreover, a key advantage of consistency-based diagnosis is that it can deal automatically with multiple faults without further assumptions.

[4] Since a possible conflict contains information of parts of the system, it will be able only to detect some faults in these subsystems.

Table 1. Results of the verification phase. Abbreviations used are: PC, possible conflict; FMND, Fault modes which should Not be Detected by possible conflict; FMD, Fault modes which should be Detected by possible conflict; CD: Correct Detections.

	FMND	FMD	CD	%
PC1	22	6	6	100
PC2	22	6	6	100
PC4	19	9	9	100

4 Validation

In the validation phase we did not study double faults in the real plant. And we could not produce three of the faulty behaviours due to security reasons. Hence, only 13 single faults were studied. In this phase, where real data from the plant were used, uncertainty in model parameters caused new threshold determination. Again, we have followed the same scheme described above. We have found out some drawbacks in the model of pump $P3$. While building the model it was necessary to obtain *tablePQ* for pump $P3$ from scratch, because there were no design specifications. This caused that the model does not accurately resemble $P3$ behaviour far from the nominal working point. This situation, $FT03_{real} \gg FT03_{nominal}$ also appeared if pump $P2$ was partially or completely blocked. In such a case,

$$FT03_{faulty} = FT03_{nominal} + (FT02_{nominal} - FT02_{faulty})$$

Therefore, we decided to select thresholds to reduce the number of missing detections. Final values of the thresholds were:

	PC1	PC2	PC4
δ_{pc_i}	0.05	0.155	0.08

Validation results for 10 normal modes and 13 faulty modes are shown in table 2. In the case of $PC2$ and $PC4$ all three incorrect detections correspond to correct or faulty behaviour where $FT03_{faulty} \gg FT03_{nominal}$.

In figure 3 it is shown the evolution of significative plant measurements and the estimations done by possible conflicts $PC1$, $PC2$, and $PC4$. In this case only $PC4$ is confirmed. And figure 4 shows MORDRED's output when the possible conflict was confirmed.

Table 2. Results of the validation phase. Percentage applies to the number of incorrect or false detections, since the number of correct detections is 100%. Abbreviations used are: PC, possible conflict; FMND, Fault modes which should Not be Detected by possible conflict; FMD, Fault modes which should be Detected by possible conflict; CD: Correct Detections; ID, Incorrect detections.

	FMND	FMD	CD	ID	%
PC1	20	3	3	0	0
PC2	20	3	3	3	15
PC4	15	8	8	3	20

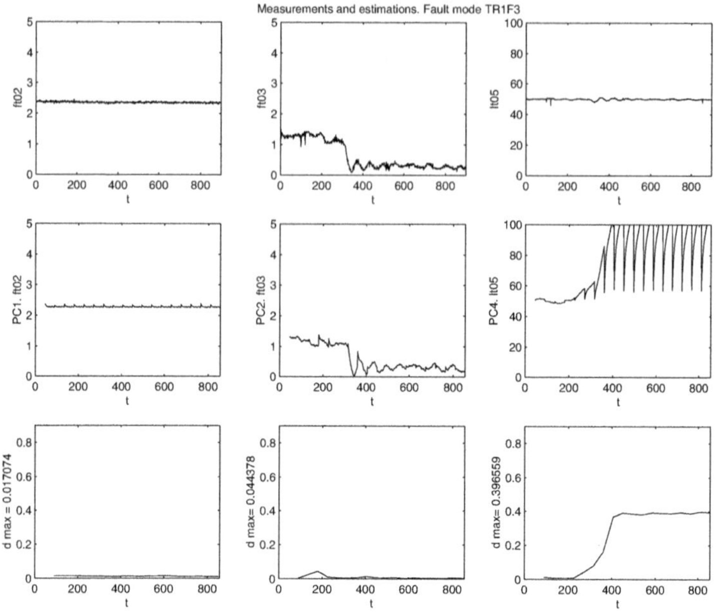

Fig. 3. In the first row, evolution of plant measurements when pipe number 10 becomes clogged. In the second row, estimation of the possible conflicts $PC1$, $PC2$, and $PC4$ is shown. Third row presents disimilarity values returned by the DTW algorithm when observations and estimations were compared.

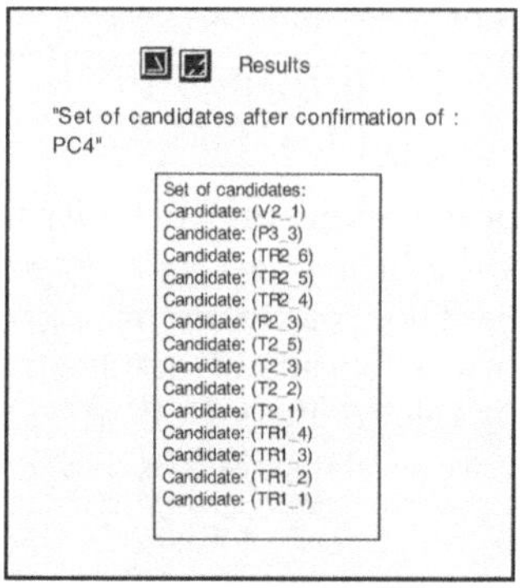

Fig. 4. Sets of constraints which could be responsible for a fault when only $PC4$ is confirmed.

5 Discussion

In this paper we have presented the verification and validation process of MORDRED, a new model-based diagnosis system that relies upon quantitative models and off-line dependency recording. Its results were considered as promising because: the technique has proven to be suitable for dynamic systems diagnosis, the system was able to correctly detect faults when it was supplied with real data, and incorrect detections were due to modeling issues. This last result can be explained because there was no design information for the model building process, and because it is hard to obtain accurate models for non-linear systems which should resemble real behaviour in different and distant nominal working points.

From the analysis of these results we have concluded that it is still possible to perform model-based diagnosis using quantitative models and AI methodology. Nevertheless, as Davis and Hamscher pointed out in 1988 (in [11]), model-based diagnosis is as good as the model is. Hence, it is necessary to improve pure quantitative models through better parameter estimation and/or semi-quantitative models.

As further research we are concerned in improving current parameter estimation technique, testing MORDRED with semi-quantitative models, using different models in distinct nominal working points, and extending MORDRED capabilities to deal with fault models.

Acknowledgments. This work was financially supported by the Spanish Ministry of Education and Culture (CICYT TAP 1999-0344). We also want to thanks Centro de Tecnología Azucarera for its financial and technical support.

References

[1] L.F. Acebes and C. de Prada. SIMPD: An intelligent modelling tool for dynamic processes. In *Proceedings of the Ninth European Simulation Symposium and Exhibition*, pages 177–181, Germany, 1997.

[2] R.E. Bellman. *Dynamic Programming.* Cambridge Studies in Speech Science and Communication. Princeton University Press, Princeton, 1957.

[3] K. Bousson, J.-P. Steyer, L. Trave-Massuyes, and B. Dahhou. From a heuristic-based to a model-based approach for monitoring and diagnosis of biological processes. *Engineering Applications of Artificial Intelligence*, 11:447–493, 1998.

[4] M.J. Chantler, G.M. Coghill, Q. Shen, and R.R. Leitch. Selecting tools and techniques for model-based diagnosis. *Artificial Intelligence in Engineering*, 12:81–98, 1998.

[5] M.J. Chantler, T. Daus, S. Vikatos, and G.M. Coghill. The use of quantitative dynamic models and dependency recording engines. In *Proceedings of the Seventh International Workshop on Principles of Diagnosis (DX-96)*, pages 59–68, Val Morin, Quebec, Canada, 1996.

[6] M.O. Cordier, P. Dague, M. Dumas, F. Levy, J. Montmain, M. Staroswiecki, and L. Trave-Massuyes. AI and automatic control approaches of model-based diagnosis: links and underlying hypotheses. Internal report 00185, LAAS, Toulouse, France, 2000.

[7] O. Dressler. On-line diagnosis and monitoring of dynamic systems based on qualitative models and dependency-recording diagnosis engines. In *Proceedings of the Twelfth European Conference on Artificial Intelligence (ECAI-96)*, pages 461–465, 1996.

[8] O. Dressler and P. Struss. Model-based diagnosis with the Default-based Diagnosis Engine: effective control strategies that work in practice. In *Proceedings of the Eleventh European Conference on Artificial Intelligence (ECAI-94)*, pages 677–681, 1994.
[9] O. Dressler and P. Struss. The consistency-based approach to automated diagnosis of devices. In Gerhard Brewka, editor, *Principles of Knowledge Representation*, pages 269–314. CSLI Publications, Standford, 1996.
[10] P. Froelich and W. Nejdl. A static model-based engine for model-based reasoning. In *Proceedings of the Fifteenth International Joint Conference on Artifical Intelligence (IJCAI-97)*, pages 446–471, Nagoya, Japan, 1997.
[11] W.C. Hamscher, L. Console, and J. de Kleer (Eds.). *Readings in Model based Diagnosis.* Morgan-Kaufmann Pub., San Mateo, 1992.
[12] E. Loiez. *Contribution au diagnostic de systemes analogiques. Modelisation par des bandes temporelles.* Phd thesis, L'Universite des Sciences et Technologies de Lille, Lille, France, Marzo 1997.
[13] J. Lunze and F. Schiller. Logic-based process diagnosis utilising the causal structure of dynamical systems. In *Proceedings of the Artificial Intelligence in Real-Time Control (IFAC/IFIP/IMACS)*, pages 649–654, Delft, Holland, 1992.
[14] P.J. Mosterman. *Hybrid dynamic systems: a hybrid bond graph modeling paradigm and its applications in diagnosis.* Phd thesis, Vanderbilt University, Nashville, Tennessee, USA, May 1997.
[15] P.J. Mosterman, E.J. Manders, and G. Biswas. Qualitative dynamic behaviour of physical system models with algebraic loops. In *Proceedings of the Eleventh International Workshop on Principles of Diagnosis (DX-00)*, Morelia, Mexico, 2000.
[16] B. Pulido and C. Alonso. Possible conflicts instead of conflicts to diagnose continuous dynamic systems. In *Proceedings of the Tenth International Workshop on Principles of Diagnosis (DX-99)*, pages 234–241, Loch Awe, Scotland (UK), 1999.
[17] B. Pulido and C. Alonso. An alternative approach to dependency-recording engines in consistency-based diagnosis. In *Artificial Intelligence: Methodology, Systems, and Applications. Ninth International Conference (AIMSA-00)*, Lecture Notes in Artificial Intelligence. Subseries of Lecture Notes in Computer Science, pages 111–120. Springer Verlag, Berlin, Germany, 2000.
[18] P. Struss. Fundamentals of model-based diagnosis of dynamic systems. In *Proceedings of the Fifteenth International Joint Conference on Artifical Intelligence (IJCAI-97)*, pages 480–485, Nagoya, Japan, 1997.

Intelligent Assumption Retrieval from Process Models by Model-Based Reasoning

R. Lakner[1] and K.M. Hangos[1,2]

[1] Dept. of Computer Science, University of Veszprém, Veszprém, Hungary
[2] Systems and Control Laboratory, Computer and Automation Research Institute HAS, Budapest, Hungary

Abstract. Process models can be seen as structured knowledge base elements with syntax and semantics dictated by the underlying physical and chemical laws. The effect of model simplification assumptions is then determined by forward reasoning in order to take into account all of their implications. A bidirectional reasoning method for the retrieval of modelling assumptions from two related process models is proposed. An intelligent model editor is constructed to perform and test the model-based reasoning methods related to the assumption retrieval.

1 Introduction

Process modelling is one of the most important areas in process systems engineering and process control. Models should not be regarded as simply equation sets but incorporate such facets as the underlying modelling assumptions, the limitations of the models and the record of all decision leading to the model. Moreover, there is a need for supporting the reuse and subsequent modification of existing models.

There are a number of Computer Aided Process Modelling (CAPM) tools available in the literature for automated model construction, verification, validation and analysis [10] which fall into two main categories. There are *general modelling languages*, such as *ASCEND* [3], and *Modelica* [9] where the user writes models in a structured language. *Modelling environments or toolkits* (e.g. [5], [6]) are also available which offer pre-fabricated model elements, as well as model construction and analysis tools providing an advanced graphical user interface.

Modelling assumptions have been found to be an artifact of process modelling. An assumption-driven process modelling methodology [1] and an intelligent model editor based thereon [2] has been proposed for process model simplification. The inverse task of model simplification is the assumption retrieval from two related process models. The result of assumption retrieval can be and should be applied when we want to reuse or further develop an already existing process model to avoid inconsistencies and to retrieve the record of decisions leading to the model.

Model-based reasoning is applied for the solution taking into account the syntax and semantics of process models as structured knowledge collections. The proposed bidirectional algorithm is implemented as a new module in our intelligent model editor.

L. Monostori, J. Váncza, and M. Ali (Eds.): IEA/AIE 2001, LNAI 2070, pp. 145–154, 2001.

2 Model-Based Reasoning

2.1 Process Model as a Structured Knowledge Collection

Lumped process models are the most important and widespread class of process models for control and diagnostic applications. The majority of CAPM tools and dynamic process simulators deal only with lumped process models. Therefore we also restrict ourselves to this case.

Process models originate from the conservation of mass, component masses and energy described by ordinary differential equations in a lumped system [4]. These are called conservation *balance equations*, and are equipped by suitable algebraic *constitutive equations*. Constitutive equations describe the underlying static relationships between model variables dictated by the physics and chemistry. The process model is then a set of ordinary differential and algebraic equations (DAEs) where there are underlying semantical relationships between various variables, equations and equation terms in the model.

Therefore this DAE set can be seen as a stuctured knowledge collection constructed form the following main knowledge elements:

- *balance volumes* for which conservation balance equations are set up,
- *extensive quantities* for each balance volume, such as mass, component masses and energy,
- *balance equations* for each extensive quantity,
- *transport mechanisms* for each balance equation, such as convection, transfer, reaction etc.,
- *constitutive equations* describing property relations, extensive-intensive relationships, transfer and reaction rate relations, equipment and control relations and balance volume relations.

Also, we need mathematical elements, like variables and equations of the following type:

- *differential equations* originating from the conservation balance equations,
- *algebraic equations*,
- *differential variables* with their first time derivative present in the differential equations,
- *algebraic variables* including *constants and specified (design) variables.*

Finally there are other auxiliary elements such as surfaces for constructing a process model.

The syntactical and semantical relationships between the above knowledge elements are depicted in Fig. 1. in an object-oriented way. Each element is described as an instance of a class denoted by a rectangle. Multiple instances of the same class are frequently present. There are encapsulating relationships between the elements and also syntactical and semantical dependencies shown by arrows.

It is important to note that algebraic transformations may change the mathematical form of a model, but an algebraically transformed model is the same from the process engineering point of view. Such algebraically equivalent models form a *model class*. It is then useful to define and use a *canonical form* of process models and represent each class with the member, which is in canonical form. The above structured knowledge collection defines a canonical form with engineering meaning [1].

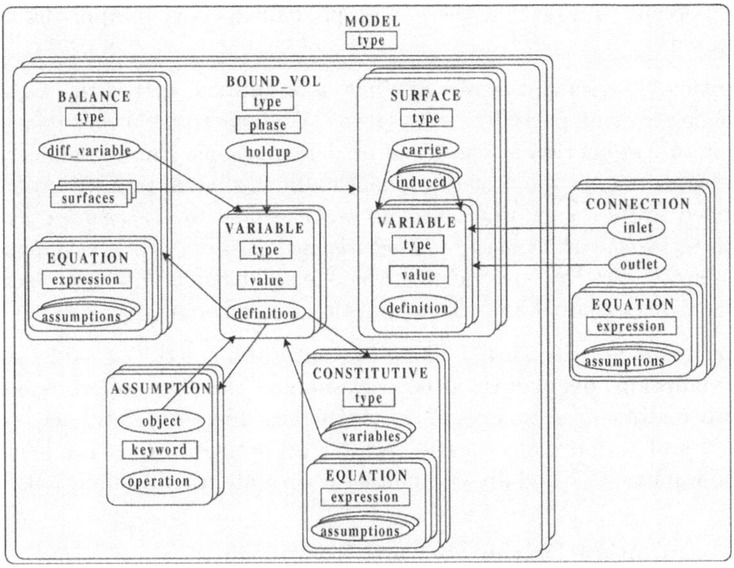

Fig. 1. The structure of a process model

2.2 Assumptions as Knowledge Elements

If we want to describe the evolution of a process model then we need additional knowledge elements describing the modelling actions, which led from the original model to the present one. The modelling actions are described by *modelling assumptions*, which act as modelling transformations on a process model. These can also be seen as additional mathematical relationships to a process model. Modelling assumptions can be simplification and enrichment assumptions depending on whether we constrain or extend the elements in the model.

Syntax. A modelling assumption is a conjunction of elementary modelling assumptions which are in the form of a triplet:

model_element_name **relation** *argument*

where *model_element_name* is the identifier of a knowledge element in the model, **relation** is a relation identifier and *argument* is either another *model_element_name* or a *constant.* Simple examples are:

tank_temperature = *0*
tank_reaction **is** *nil*
tank_heat_transfer **is** *negligible*

The set of possible assumptions. The possible assumptions for process models can be classified according to the model element to which they refer as follows:

- assumptions on the balance volumes,
- assumptions on the differential variables,
- assumptions on the transport mechanisms,
- assumptions on the algebraic variables.

It is important to note that there is no predefined order in applying modelling assumptions.

Semantics. The semantics of modelling assumptions, that is the way they act on a model, is given partially by its syntax. We have to add every relation in the assumption conjunction to the set of model equations. But the underlying syntax and semantics of the process model should also be taken into account, which is encoded in its structure. *Rules can be generated to describe the syntax and semantics, which can be used for model-based reasoning* [7]. The *implications* of an assumption are the consequences (new model elements) which we can derive from the process model and the assumption by reasoning.

Hierarchy of assumptions. There is a natural hierarchy of model simplification assumptions depending on how widespread the effect of an assumption is on a process model. Assumptions in the highest hierarchy level act on balance volumes, and assumptions on the lowest level acting only on a model element have no implications and are commutative with all other assumptions.

2.3 Assumption-Driven Forward Reasoning

We associate a suitable transformation to each model simplification assumption, which formally defines the effect of the assumption on a process model. Unlike algebraic transformations which do not lead out from a given model class, *model simplification transformations* are projections in mathematical sense, and generate a member of another model class. A model simplification transformation can be elementary corresponding to an elementary modelling assumption or composite. Composite transformations are performed as a composition of their elementary transformations of which they are composed.

Quite often, but not always, an elementary simplification transformation is performed in two substeps:

1. Add the equality describing the assumption to the already existing set of model equations and perform algebraic transformations (for example substitutions) to get a more simple form.
2. Adjust the set of differential, algebraic and design variables to satisfy the degree of freedom requirement.

It is important to note that not every simplification transformation is applicable to a particular process model. Moreover, a transformation may influence only part of a process model and then this effect propagates through the relationships between the model elements. Therefore *forward reasoning is applied to find all of the implications* of a simplification transformation. The effect of a composite transformation is then computed by generating a sequence of simplified process models starting from the original one with the goal being the final model.

Properties of model simplification transformations. Composite, i.e. non-elementary simplification transformations have unusual algebraic properties. If one performs a sequence of model simplification transformations, the resultant model may be different if the order of the assumptions is changed. The reason is that model *simplification transformations may be related and non-commutative* [1]. Another important property of model simplification transformations is that they do not always have an inverse that is, they are *in general not reversible.*

2.4 Assumption Retrieval as Bidirectional Reasoning

Assumption retrieval aims at finding the sequence of model simplification assumptions from a detailed and a simplified model through which they are related. As model simplification transformations are projections in mathematical sense, it is not possible in general to retrieve fully the original model from the simplified one and from the simplification transformations. Because of this, the *result of an assumption retrieval from the original and the simplified models may not be and in general will not be unique.* Our aim is then to find *all of the possible assumption sequences* leading from one model to a simpler one. Note that both models should be in canonical from.

Assumption retrieval can be seen as the inverse task of model simplification, therefore a *model-based backward reasoning using two process models* as structured knowledge collections would solve the problem. In order to reduce the search space of the reasoning, we propose a bidirectional reasoning method consisting of two phases.

1. The *backward reasoning phase* starts form the less detailed model to find unambiguous and reversible assumption transformations by comparing the two models. This way a "middle detailed" or partially retrieved model is constructed.
2. Then a list of possible assumptions is constructed on the basis of the differences of the two models. Using this list we use *forward reasoning with iterative deepening search* starting from the detailed model to compute all the possible implications of all the possible assumptions for finding the partially retrieved model as the goal. Because of practical (engineering) reasons the maximum depth of the searching tree is limited by the user.

3 A Model-Based Reasoning Environment: An Intelligent Model Editor

The model editor itself consists of three well-separated main parts: the model builder, the model simplifier and the assumption retrieval module. To demonstrate the operation of the model editor a simple single component phase equilibrium system with two (vapour and liquid) phases has been examined.

3.1 Phase Equilibrium Example

This process example is shown in Fig. 2. Vapour (denoted by variable ending "*v*") and liquid ("*l*") are taken from the vessel with mass flow rate V and L, whilst energy is supplied via a heater. Inside the vessel we have two phases with respective holdups Mv, Ml and temperatures Tv, Tl. A feed with mass flow rate F comes into the system. In this model we consider two distinct balance volumes for the two phases. The model equations are shown in the left-hand side window of Fig. 3.

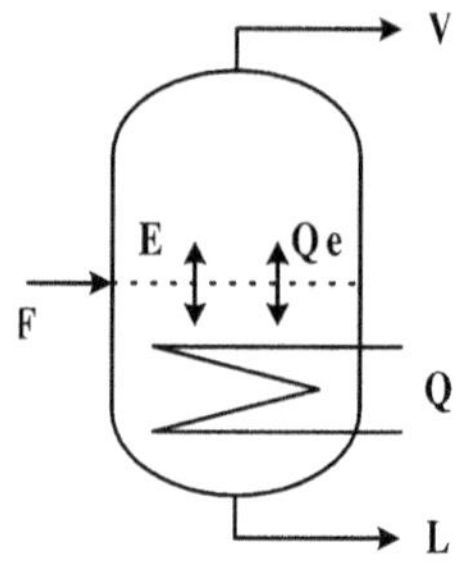

Fig. 2. Simple phase equilibrium process

3.2 Model Builder

The model builder is implemented in the form of an interactive and intelligent interface asking for the knowledge elements specified in section 2.1. The main steps of the modelling procedure are as follows:

1. specification of the balance volumes
2. specification of the conserved extensive quantities for each balance volume
3. specification of the basic transport terms in each balance volume and generation of the balance equations in an automatic way
4. specification of the constitutive (algebraic) equations for all of the algebraic variables appearing in the balance equations and in the constitutive equations

The canonical form of the process model is the result of the model builder where the consistency is ensured by construction. More about the model builder is found in [2].

3.3 Model Simplifier

The model simplifier accepts simplifying assumptions as additional mathematical relationships and derives the effect of the accepted assumptions on the set of model equations constructed by the model builder. The main steps of the simplification procedure are as follows:

1. *collection of possible assumptions* which can be applied for the simplification of the given process model
2. *selection of an assumption by the user*
3. *forward reasoning to find the effects of the selected assumption on the model equations*
   This reasoning step consists of two main substeps, namely the implication of the modelling assumptions on the model equations using syntactical and semantical rules, and the rearrangement of the resulted equations making use of formal algebraic transformations.
4. *examination of the resulted simplified model*
   When the user is not satisfied with resulted model the procedure backtracks to step 2. (Naturally the last assumption and its implications are canceled.) When the simplified model is acceptable and the user does not want to enter more, then stop and return with the selected assumption list and the resulted model.
5. *the effect of the selected assumption on the possible assumption list*
   The assumptions which contradict to the already selected assumptions and which therefore become useless are removed from the possible assumption list.
6. return to step 2.

The result of the model simplification is a set of simplified model equations in canonical form together with the set of selected assumptions.

The effect of model simplification assumptions on process models as well as the model simplifier module in our intelligent model editor is reported in [2].

3.4 Assumption Retrieval

The assumption retrieval module is used for the construction all of the assumption sequences which lead from a detailed model to a simplified one. Search is needed for the solution, where the nodes of the searching tree are process models in their canonical forms and the actions are the possible simplifying assumptions. As a process model is a large structured knowledge collection stored in a database and there are several possible simplifying assumptions applicable to a process model, it is worth to generate all of the examined nodes immediately from the root with systematic testing of assumptions and assumption sequences, and to keep only the initial, the goal and an actual node.
The proposed assumption retrieval algorithm consists of three main phases:

1. *clumsy comparison of the two process models*
   Comparison of the number and type of variables and equations in order to examine whether the models are in the same model hierarchy and both are in canonical form. When the comparison is not succeed, fail.

2. *backward reasoning*
   Determination of the unambiguous and reversible (i.e. low level) transformations by comparing the two models to find better starting points for the next forward reasoning retrieval step. The result of this deterministic step is a (or in case of non-commutative assumptions several) partially retrieved process model(s) and the used assumption sequence(s). When the partially retrieved model is same as the detailed model, stop and return with the assumption sequence (in reversed order).
3. *forward reasoning*
   Further retrieval by forward search starting from the detailed model toward the (or a) partially retrieved model with the following substeps:
   a) Collect the list of possible assumptions on the basis of the differences of the two models.
   b) Execute an iterative deepening search by transforming the detailed model using the list of possible assumptions, and by comparing the resulted simplified models with the partially retrieved model. The branching factor of every node is restricted in a heuristic way with the elimination of useless and contradictory assumptions from the assumption list. Because of practical and safety reasons the maximum depth of the searching tree is bounded by the user.
      The final result is the assumption sequence lead from the detailed model to the partially retrieved one completed with the assumption sequence from step 2. when the partially retrieved model is reached.
   c) Continue with step 3. until all partially retrieved models are examined.

The result of the assumption retrieval is one or more assumption sequences.

An assumption retrieval result of the phase equilibrium system is seen in Fig. 3. Both the free and the simplified (transformed) model equations are shown in separate windows together with some of the assumption sequences found by the assumption retrieval algorithm.

3.5 The Implementation and the Software Structure of the Intelligent Model Editor

We have implemented the algorithms of the model editor in Visual Prolog 5.0 (except the oldest model builder module, which is implemented in PDC Prolog 3.3) [8]. The main parts of the presented modeling system and their connections are shown in Fig. 4.

The *knowledge base* consists of two main parts:

- The *models* and *assumptions* are stored as knowledge base *facts*, where the model equations are coded in form of binary trees and the modelling assumptions as sentence like database elements.
- The model builder, the model simplifier and the assumption retrieval *rules* are coded as *Prolog rules*.

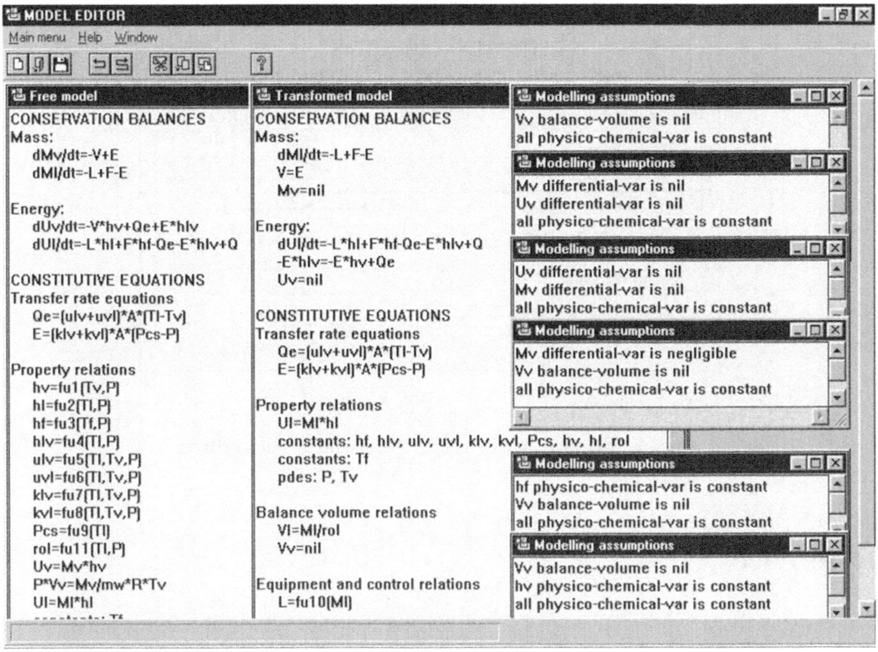

Fig. 3. The result of assumption retrieval

The knowledge base facts can be used and modified by the Prolog built-in reasoning mechanism (as inference engine) applying the knowledge base rules and the Prolog rules can be modified by the developer with the help of Prolog developer interface.

4 Conclusion

An intelligent model editor serves as a framework for model-based reasoning methods for constructing, simplifying and comparing process models. The syntax and semantics of process models give rise to the model-based reasoning rules which are different but related for the purposes of model construction, model simplification and assumption retrieval from two related process models.

A novel bidirectional assumption retrieval algorithm has been proposed using forward and backward model-based reasoning in an iterative deepening manner. The resulted non-unique assumption sequences have been analyzed to improve the retrieval algorithm. The algorithm has been found effective on process models with medium complexity.

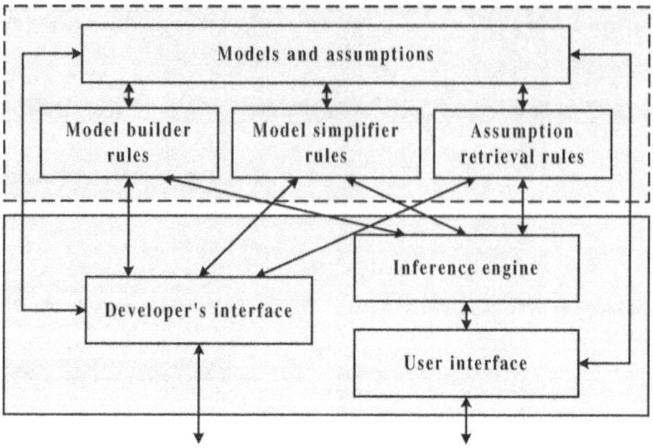

Fig. 4. The software structure of the model editor

References

1. Hangos, K.M. and Cameron, I.T.: A formal representation of assumptions in process modelling. Comput. Chem. Engng. in print (2001)
2. Lakner, R., Hangos, K.M. and Cameron, I.T.: An assumption-driven case sensitive model editor. Comput. Chem. Engng. (Supplement), **23** (1999) S695-S698.
3. Piela, P.C., Epperly, T. G., Westerberg, K. M. and Westerberg, A.W.: ASCEND: An object oriented computer environment for modeling and analysis: The modeling language. Comput. Chem. Engng., **15** (1991) 53.
4. Hangos, K.M. and Cameron, I.T.: Process modelling and model analysis. Academic Press. (2001)
5. Bogusch, R., Lohmann, B. and W. Marquardt: Computer aided process modelling with ModKit, Computers Europe III, Frankfurt, Germany (1996)
6. G. Stephanopoulos, G. Henning and H. Leone: MODEL.LA a modeling language for process engineering - the formal framework. Comput. Chem. Engng. **8** (1990) 813-846.
7. S. Russell and P. Norvig: Artificial intelligence, A modern approach, Prentice-Hall (1995)
8. Visual Prolog, Language Tutorial, Prolog Development Center, (1986-1997)
9. P. E. V. Fritson and J. Gunnarson: An integrated modelica environment for modelling, documentation and simulation. Proc. 1998 Summer Computer Simulation Conference SCSC98, Reno, Nevada, July 19-22. (1998)
10. W. Marquardt: Trends in computer-aided modelling. Comput. Chem. Engng., **20** (1996) 591-609.

A Knowledge Model for Automatic Configuration of Traffic Messages

Martín Molina[1] and Mónica Robledo[2]

[1]Department of Artificial Intelligence, Technical University of Madrid
Campus de Montegancedo s/n, 28660 Boadilla del Monte (Madrid), Spain
mmolina@fi.upm.es
[2]Artificial Intelligence Group, E.S.C.E.T, University Rey Juan Carlos
C/Tulipan s/n, 28993 Mostoles (Madrid), Spain
mrobledo@escet.urjc.es

Abstract. This paper describes a knowledge model for a configuration problem in the domain of traffic control. The goal of this model is to help traffic engineers in the dynamic selection of a set of messages to be presented to drivers on variable message signals. This selection is done in a real-time context using data recorded by traffic detectors on motorways. The system follows an advanced knowledge-based solution that implements two abstract problem solving methods according to a model-based approach recently proposed in the knowledge engineering field. Finally, the paper presents a discussion about the advantages and drawbacks found for this problem as a consequence of the applied knowledge modeling approach.

1 Introduction

In the past 15 years, researchers within the knowledge engineering field have paid special attention in knowledge share and reuse in order to decrease the effort in building large and complex knowledge based applications. One important conclusion of this research is that, to build a knowledge-based system, it is appropriate to follow a modeling approach to emulate how a human expert solves problems in a particular professional area. For this purpose, it is useful to describe such a model in a cognitive level (called *knowledge level* [1]) by using certain description entities closer to human thinking than computer processing.

These results carried out an interesting proposal about how to reuse problem-solving knowledge. Authors proposed the concept of *problem solving method* (PSM), an abstract cognitive structure specialized in classes of problems, derived from original proposals of different authors such a J. McDermott [2], B. Chandrasekaran [3] and J. Clancey [4]. Each PSM defines a knowledge intensive architecture together with the reasoning process to solve certain class of problems, such as parametric design, classification, diagnosis, etc. Since then, some initial PSMs were identified as standard typical intuitive reasoning processes followed by human experts in certain kind of

L. Monostori, J. Váncza, and M. Ali (Eds.): IEA/AIE 2001, LNAI 2070, pp. 155-164, 2001.

problems [5]. For example, a diagnostic task can be solved by the cover-and-differentiate PSM or a classification task can be solved by the establish-and-refine PSM.

Thus, presently, there is a new generation of useful techniques in the knowledge engineering community to help in the development of complex and large knowledge-based systems. To mature and extend this new and emergent technology, it is required experimentation with real-world problems, whose results complement the dissemination of theoretical approaches and contribute to identify open issues that require further research. This paper contributes in this direction by presenting a real-world knowledge modeling experience in the domain of traffic control. The paper presents a knowledge model for automatic configuration of a set of traffic messages for a set of variable message signals, according to the current state of a road network.

The paper presents, first, the characteristics of the traffic problem. Then, the knowledge model is described, following a model-based approach to structure and organize the set of knowledge bases together with the strategies of inference. Then, the implementation for the city of Madrid is presented. Finally a discussion is included about the utility of the knowledge modeling approach for this problem.

2 Real-Time Traffic Management

Control centers for traffic management are usually connected on-line to devices such as detectors on roads, cameras, traffic lights, etc., in such a way that operators can supervise the state of the road by consulting data bases with recent information from detectors and can modify the state of control devices. The effective use of these traffic monitoring and management facilities requires sophisticated support tools for on-line operators, to help them in dealing with the information complexity and the diversity of sensors and control devices. In the last decade, expert systems for decision support have been successfully introduced in this field [6], [7], [8], [9].

Figure 1 shows a typical infrastructure for real-time traffic control that can be found in different cities. There are detectors on major roads recording several traffic measures such as speed (Km/h), flow (vehicle/h or vehicle/min) and occupancy (percentage of time the sensor is occupied by a vehicle). The distance between successive sensors on a freeway is usually about 500 meters. The information arrives periodically to the control center (e.g., every minute). The control center receives also information about the current state of control devices.

Control devices include traffic signals at intersections, traffic signals at on-ramps, variable message signs (VMS) that can present different messages to drivers (e.g., warning about an existing congestion or alternative path recommendation), radio advisory systems to broadcast messages to drivers, and reversible lanes (i.e., freeway lanes whose direction can be selected according to the current and expected traffic demand). In the control center, operators interpret sensor data and detect the presence of problems and their possible causes. Problems are congested areas at certain locations caused by lack of capacity due to accidents, excess of demand (like rush hours), etc. In addition, operators determine control actions to solve or reduce the severity of existing problems. For instance, they can increase the duration of a phase (e.g., green time) at a traffic signal, or they may decide to show certain messages on some VMSs to divert traffic.

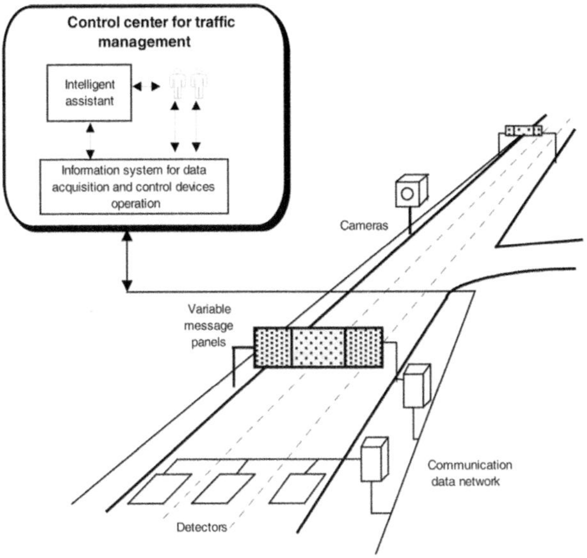

Fig. 1. Typical information infrastructure for real-time traffic management

3 A Knowledge Model for Message Configuration

In order to help operators in this problem of traffic management, a computer system has been conceived as an intelligent assistant. The concept of *intelligent assistant* [10] emphasizes the fact that the role of the computer system is to help the user in decision-making but the final responsibility is taken by the user. To develop such a system, we followed a *model-based* approach in which the goal was to formulate a formal abstraction of the knowledge that we ascribe to operators for real-time traffic management. The operational version of this model is used to automatically reproduce by simulation part of the decision-making reasoning. For this purpose, we followed advanced knowledge modeling techniques (similar to the CommonKads approach [11]) that use a conceptual level for expertise description, with specific formal intuitive entities.

According to this, figure 2 shows a global view of the knowledge model that we designed for the traffic problem. This figure shows a hierarchy of tasks (circles) and methods (squares) with types of knowledge bases (at the bottom). The main task of the system is to recommend every moment an appropriate state of control devices. The top-level node corresponds to this global task called *configure traffic messages*. This is a configuration task where, from an initial situation (the traffic state at different locations), a complete design must be determined as a set of states for control devices (e.g., messages for each VMS panel). In this process, two general requirements have to be considered: (1) each traffic message must be consistent with the traffic state, and (2) each traffic message must be consistent with the rest of traffic messages. The qualitative nature of messages together with specific criteria (area-dependent) based on a heuristic knowledge of the area for certain panels makes difficult the use of generic algorithmic solutions for this problem.

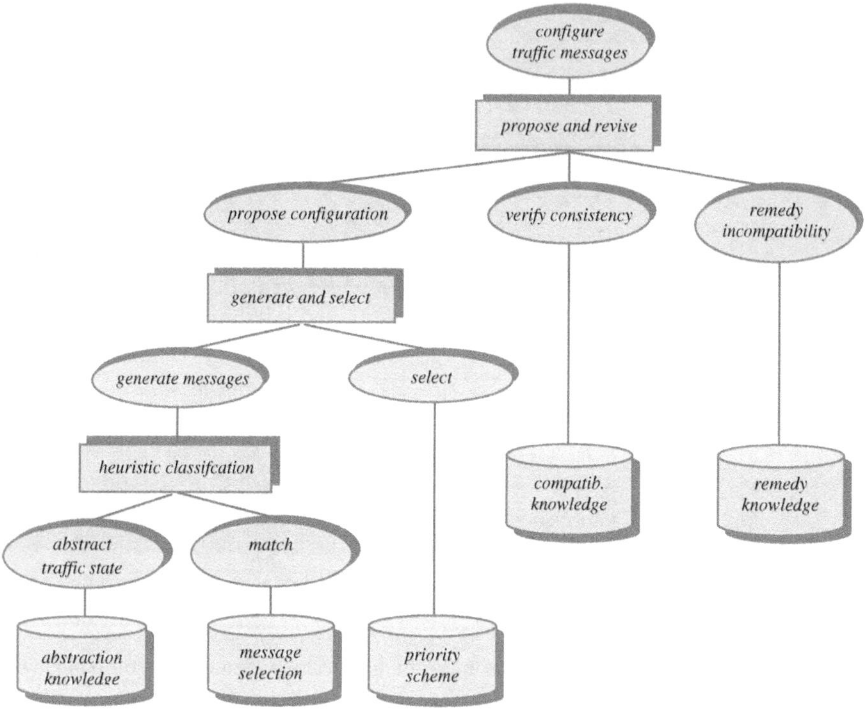

Fig. 2. Knowledge model for the traffic problem

The usual way of reasoning in this problem follows a tentative search supported by specialized knowledge. Thus, in a first step, a set of messages is proposed based on the current state of the traffic. Then, the proposal is analyzed to check whether this proposal violates some constraints about coherence of messages (e.g., it is not acceptable to present too many messages about the same problem in consecutive panels). If so, a remedy is applied based on heuristic knowledge to modify the original proposal. This process is repeated until, if possible, a satisfactory configuration is found. This type of reasoning has been already identified and typified as a problem-solving method in the knowledge engineering literature and receives the name of *propose-and-revise* [12].

In particular, the abstract structure of this method assumes the existence of three kinds of knowledge: (1) *derivation knowledge*, that includes specific criteria to deduce a design from initial specifications, (2) *compatibility knowledge*, to verify a proposed design and includes a set of criteria to identify incompatible cases, and (3) *remedy knowledge* that includes a set of criteria about how to solve a violation detected in the design. According to this knowledge organization, the method decomposes the global configuration task into three sub-tasks: propose configuration, verify consistency and remedy incompatibility (see figure 2).

In its turn, the first sub-task is carried out by a specific method defined for this purpose that, first, generates proposals of messages (several messages for each panel) and, then, one of them is selected based on a priority scheme. To carry out the first step (generate messages) row data recorded by sensors need to be abstracted and related to candidate traffic messages. For this purpose, given the qualitative nature of the problem, the heuristic classification PSM [4] can be used. This method receives a set of observables (e.g., sensor data) and produces a set of solutions (e.g., proposals of traffic messages). The general version of this method includes three types of knowledge: (1) *abstraction knowledge*, to abstract the row data, (2) *heuristic match knowledge*, to classify abstracted data into classes of solutions and (3) *refinement knowledge*, to refine the classes of solutions into specific solutions. However, the particular version of the heuristic classification method for the traffic problem requires only two subtasks: abstract traffic state and match.

At the bottom level, figure 2 shows the set of knowledge types included in the model. There are a total of five specific types of knowledge bases that give support to the respective five subtasks. The general inference procedure makes use of the previous knowledge bases following three main steps:

1. *Propose configuration*. From the current traffic state, a set of potential messages is generated for each panel by using the *abstraction knowledge* and the *message selection knowledge*. For each panel, one message is selected by using the *priority scheme*.
2. *Verify consistency*. From the set of candidate messages and using the *compatibility knowledge*, the proposal is verified to check whether it satisfies the coherence criteria. If the proposal is coherent, the proposal is accepted as a final result. Otherwise, step 3 is performed.
3. *Remedy incompatibility*. From the detected incompatibilities, and using the *remedy knowledge*, a new set of candidate messages is proposed. For each incompatibility, the panel that must change the proposal is selected. Then, the loop starts again from step 1 selecting alternative messages and verifying the consistency.

This model can be considered as a global pattern that serves as a guide to acquire, organize and implement the specific knowledge of the system. The model divides the whole knowledge of the system in different categories (control knowledge, domain knowledge) according to the generic reused problem-solving strategies.

3.1 Symbolic Knowledge Representation

The previous model needs to be complemented with the specific symbolic representation used for each type of knowledge base. The availability of each knowledge base gives the required level of generality to apply this model for different traffic networks, by providing the specific control strategies for each case.

First of all, the model includes a conceptual vocabulary to establish the basic traffic terminology used by the knowledge bases. This vocabulary includes, among others, the following main concepts: (1) *VMS panel* V_i, to identify the set of VMS panels on the road, (2) *message* M_i, i.e., a particular message to be written on a particular panel, (3) *road section* S_i, that identifies a section of the road corresponding to a point where a detector is located, and (4) *path* P_i, that defines a path as sequence of road sections.

The purpose of the first knowledge base, *abstraction* knowledge, is to deduce traffic characteristics of higher level of abstraction through data interpretation of information recorded by sensors. This knowledge base can be considered as logic implications to deduce values for attributes of sections or paths with a formulation like the following($\langle C,A,V\rangle$ means that the attribute A of the concept C takes the value V):

$$\langle S_i, Observable, X_i\rangle, \ldots, \langle S_j, Observable, X_j\rangle, \ldots \rightarrow \langle S_n, Abstraction, X_n\rangle$$
$$\langle S_i, Abstraction, X_i\rangle, \ldots, \langle S_j, Abstraction, X_j\rangle, \ldots \rightarrow \langle P_k, Abstraction, X_k\rangle$$

This format can include elaborated relations such as the following (for instance, to compute a particular travel time using a specific function f):

$$\langle S_i, speeed, X_i\rangle, \ldots, \langle S_j, speed, X_j\rangle, \ldots, f(X_i, \ldots, X_j, \ldots) = X_k \rightarrow \langle P_k, travel\ time, X_k\rangle$$

The knowledge base for *message selection* is used to deduce one or several proposals of messages for each VMS panel according to the measures recorded by traffic detectors. This knowledge can be represented with the following type of sentences:

$$\langle S_i, Attribute_i, X_i\rangle, \ldots, \langle P_j, Attribute_j, X_j\rangle, \ldots \rightarrow \langle V_k, message, M_k\rangle$$
$$\langle V_i, message, M_i\rangle, \ldots, \langle V_j, message, M_j\rangle, \ldots \rightarrow \langle V_k, message, M_k\rangle$$

The previous knowledge relates the traffic state and the signal state and it must be formulated with the important requirement that the relations do not have to include loops to avoid circular calculation, according to the propose and revise strategy. This symbolic representation provides the required flexibility to write specific cases corresponding to each type of message (congestion, incident, travel time, etc.). Together with this, it is necessary to have criteria to select one message within a set of candidate messages. For this purpose the *priority scheme*, is defined as follows:

type-of-message(M1, type-X)	*priority-level(type-X, level-1)*
type-of-message(M2, type-Y)	*priority-level(type-Y, level-2)*
...	...
type-of-message(Mn, type-Z)	*priority-level(type-Z, level-k)*

For instance the most prioritary level can be assigned for the messages of the type incident, the second level to the traffic jam warning type, third level for destination travel time, and so on.

The *compatibility* knowledge base includes conditions that establish unacceptable combinations of messages in order to avoid inconsistency between messages. This knowledge is formulated with constraints as following:

$$constraint_k\!: \langle V_i, message, M_i\rangle, \ldots, \langle V_j, message, M_j\rangle, \ldots, \langle traffic\ conditions\rangle$$

The constraint includes a set of messages for panels together with a logic expression (that optionally can include values about the traffic state) to define an incompatible message combination. This representation is flexible enough to include both general and particular conditions about compatibility according to the requirements of each traffic network. For instance, it is useful to formulate that it is not acceptable to present the same message on two specific panels.

Finally, the *remedy* knowledge base includes the criteria with which the detected inconsistencies are solved by modifying a proposed configuration. In this case, this means to select which panel is required to change the message in order to avoid the inconsistency. This is represented by:

constraint$_k$, *<traffic conditions>* → *panel* V_j

which means that, to solve the violation represented by *constraint*$_k$ panel V_j should change its message (when certain traffic conditions are present).

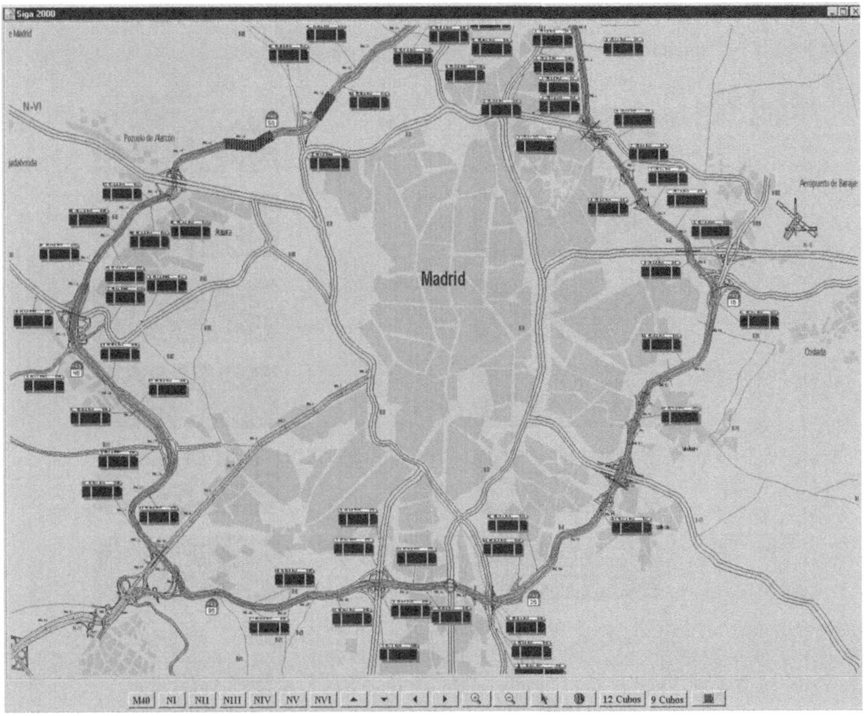

Fig. 3. The M-40 motorway of Madrid with variable message panels

4 Experience and Example

Following this general model, a system was developed for the city of Madrid, to control part of the M-40 Urban Ring (figure 3). This road is a motorway of around 60 Km in both ways that includes a total of 63 panels to present messages to drivers. The road includes the typical information infrastructure for real-time traffic management and operators must decide on real-time the set of messages to be presented in those panels according to the behavior of the road (traffic jams, incidents, etc.).

Figure 4 presents an example of the output produced by the system. It corresponds to an example where the system receives input data like the following:

<detector D41, speed, 45>
<detector D41, occupancy, 25>
<detector D41, flow, 38>
<detector D44, speed, 25>
<detector D44, occupancy, 40>
...

<detector D42, speed, 30>
<detector D42, occupancy, 37>
<detector D42, flow, 82>
<detector A32, occupancy, 25>
<detector A32, flow, 41>
...

According to this input data, a problem is detected between road detectors D41 and D44 given that a decrease of the speed is observed, and due to that the travel time to the road M-607 is a high travel time compared with a normal state of the traffic. The high measure of the detector A32 (corresponding to an off-ramp) is used to deduce that there is a traffic jam at N-V Exit.

VMS	Message	VMS	Message
Panel P4401	Traffic Jam at N-V Exit	Panel P1511	To M-503 2 Min To N-VI 9 Min To M-607 20 Min
Panel P3401	To N-V 4 Min To M-503 12 Min To N-VI 19 Min	Panel P27	To M-503 2 Min To N-VI 9 Min To M-607 20 Min
Panel P2401	To N-V 3 Min To M-503 11 Min To N-VI 18 Min	Panel P29	To M-503 1 Min To N-VI 8 Min To M-607 19 Min
Panel P1401	Traffic Jam at N-V Exit	Panel P1513	To N-VI 5 Min To M-607 16 Min
Panel P23	Traffic Jam at N-V Exit	Panel P3503	To N-VI 5 Min To M-607 16 Min
Panel P26	To M-503 4 Min To N-VI 11 Min To M-607 22 Min	Panel P2503	To N-VI 5 Min To M-607 16 Min
...	...	...	...

Fig. 4. Example of outputs produced by the system (English version)

This system was implemented by using a knowledge modeling software tool, called KSM (Knowledge Structure Manager) developed by our own group [13] and it was integrated with the rest of the information system to run on-line at the Traffic Control Center of the city of Madrid. The specific software was designed following an object oriented design, and was implemented in C++. There were about 3000 lines of code C++ specific for the system and about 70000 lines of reused code C++, corresponding to the KSM tool for knowledge representation.

5 Discussion and Conclusions

In summary, the qualitative nature of traffic messages together with specific criteria area-dependent, corresponding to heuristic knowledge of the area for specific traffic panels, makes difficult a solution based on general algorithms. Thus, an approach from the field knowledge-based systems, in particular problem-solving methods for configuration design problems, has been useful to solve this problem.

To analyze the problem, it was very useful to reuse generic problem-solving methods according to a model-based knowledge acquisition process. However, for design and implementation it was necessary to provide additional solutions. This was performed by using our own knowledge-modeling tool, KSM, that incorporates some of the recent advances about knowledge modeling and provides reusable software components.

As a difficulty, the model-based approach for knowledge engineering requires to revise and know a set of potential problem-solving methods that are defined using a particular level of abstraction. To understand totally such a descriptions, it is required additional work using diverse information sources. To decrease this, it is still necessary to make an effort in the knowledge engineering community to bring together and standardize all this technology as a continuation of initiatives such as [Breuker, Van de Velde, 94].

The proposed model is open. It allows developers to define particular control strategies for traffic message configuration, thanks to the availability of a set of knowledge bases with a declarative representation. At the same time, instead of having a unique global knowledge base, the knowledge is distributed in different specialized bases, according to intuitive problem-solving methods, that makes easier the total comprehension of the systems and contributes to keep the consistency.

On the other side, the applied method presents some similarities with the idea of Truth Maintenance Systems TMS. In general, a TMS ([14], [15]) keeps a predefined set of declarations in terms of consistency, i.e. if in a given state the set of assumed TMS nodes is inconsistent the TMS identifies the assumed nodes responsible for the inconsistency and modifies the assumptions to keep the compatibility. However, the specific model presented here is a solution that is defined at a lower level of abstraction closer to the design problem, which make easier its application, and it proposes an explicit representation for heuristic knowledge to remedy violations, which can make easier its application for the traffic control problem.

Finally, the model presented in this paper can be considered an innovative development within the field of transport that takes advantage of the recent advanced proposals in the domain of knowledge engineering. The solution makes available on real time strategic knowledge to help operators in selecting the most appropriate state of control devices, taking care every moment the compatibility between the road state and the signal state. This development was carried out for the M-40 urban ring for the city of Madrid and it was installed on-line at the Traffic Control Center of the city.

Acknowledgments. The authors would like to thank the *Dirección General de Tráfico* of Spain who provided financial support for the development of this system. The INDRA company provided technical support for real-time operation in the traffic control center of Madrid.

References

1. Newell A.: "The Knowledge Level" In Artificial Intelligence Vol 18 pp. 87-127, 1982.
2. McDermott J.: "Preliminary Steps Toward a Taxonomy of Problem Solving Methods". In "Automating Knowledge Acquisition for Expert Systems", S.Marcus ed., Kluwer Academic, Boston, 1988.
3. Chandrasekaran B., Johnson T.R, Smith J.W.: "Task Structure Analysis for Knowledge Modeling", Communications of the ACM, 35 (9), 124-137. 1992.
4. Clancey W.: "Heuristic Classification". Artificial Intelligence 27, 1985.
5. Breuker J., Van de Velde W.: "CommonKADS Library for Expertise Modelling: Reusable Problem Solving Components". IOS Press. 1994.
6. Cuena J., Ambrosino G., Boero M.: "A general Knowledge-based architecture for traffic control: the KITS approach". Proceeding of the International Conference Artificial Intelligence in Transportation Engineering. San Buenaventura, California.
7. Deeter D.L., Ritchie S.G.: "A prototype real-time expert system for surface street traffic management and control". ASCE, Third International Conference on Applications of Advanced Technologies in Transportation Engineering. Seattle, Washington, USA, 1993.
8. Molina M., Logi F., Ritchie S., Cuena J. : "An architecture integrating symbolic and connectionist models for traffic management decision support". Proceedings of the VI International Conference on Applications of Advanced Technologies in Transportation Engineering.
9. Molina M., Hernández J., Cuena J.: "A Structure of Problem-solving Methods for Real-time Decision Support in Traffic Control". Interational Journal of Human and Computer Studies (Academic Press) N.49, 577-600, 1998.
10. Boy, G., Gruber T.R.: "Intelligent Assistant Systems: Support for Integrated Human-Machine Systems" Technical Report KSL 90-61, Knowledge Systems Laboratory, Computer Science Department, Stanford University, 1990. Also in the proceedings of 1990 AAAI Spring Symposium on *Knowledge-Based Human-Computer Communication*, March 1990, Stanford University.
11. Schreiber G., Akkermans H., Anjewierden A., de Hoog R., Shadbolt N., Van de Velde W., Wielinga B.: "Knowledge Engineering and Management. The CommonKADS Methodology" MIT Press, 2000.
12. Marcus S., McDermott J.: "SALT: A Knowledge Acquisition Language for Propose-and-Revise Systems". Artificial Intelligence, Vol 39, No.1, 1989.
13. Cuena J., Molina M.: "The Role of Knowledge Modeling Techniques in Software Development: A General Approach based on a Knowledge Management Tool". International Journal of Human and Computer Studies. No.52. pp 385-421. Academic Press, 2000.
14. Mc. Allester: "An Outlook to Truth Maintenance" AI Memo 551 MIT Cambridge Mass, 1980.
15. Doyle: "A Truth Maintenance System" Artificial Intelligence 12. Elsevier Science Publishers B.V. (North Holland) 1979.

Information Extraction from HTML: Combining XML and Standard Techniques for IE from the Web

Luo Xiao, Dieter Wissmann

Siemens AG, CT SE 5 Erlangen, Germany
(Luo.Xiao, Dieter.Wissmann)@erls.siemens.de
Michael Brown

Interprice Technologies GmbH. Berlin, Germany
Mike@Interprice.com
Stefan Jablonski

Dept. of Computer Sciences VI (IMMD VI) University of Erlangen-Nuremberg, Germany
Stefan.Jablonski@informatik.uni-erlangen.de

Abstract. This paper describes Information Extraction for applications concerning the automated filling of templates from an input of HTML documents. We developed a complete system to extract information from Web sites. The system is able to use a number of algorithms to learn the document structure, rules and keywords to locate specific information and spatial relations between different information items. Experiments with well known data set show a substantial performance improvement over standard *wrapper* systems.

1. Introduction

The World Wide Web, with its explosive growth, is swiftly becoming the main knowledge resource for many areas. Web pages are primarily designed for human browsing. Mechanically extracting their contents is in general a rather difficult task. Most software systems that extract information from web pages do so on the basis of hand-coded or automatically learned wrappers [MUSL98,FREI98].
Wrappers can extract content from Web sites by exploiting the structural (tag) information, but they are unable to find content without tag. Other systems are designed for extracting information from normal free text or semi-structured documents. Such systems use different techniques for Information Extraction from (plain text) documents. One common method is using hand-crafted or learned rules. Another approach is to use NLP analyse or learning to generate extraction patterns [CALI97,RILO94,COHE99]. However, such systems are not always optimal for Web sites because they do not use the helpful tag information. A better approach would be to integrate the advantages of wrappers and traditional IE techniques.

L. Monostori, J. Váncza, and M. Ali (Eds.): IEA/AIE 2001, LNAI 2070, pp. 165–174, 2001.

Another consideration is how to best exploit the rich tag information used to define the structure of Web pages. Emerging standards such as XML will simplify the extraction of structured information from heterogeneous sources [KUSH00]. Another observation is, that wrapper induction algorithms may be able to use XML as a source of supervised training data [KNOB98]. We considerate that we can use the (implicit) structured information in HTML sites with help of an XML-Parser and thus exploit the structural properties of the contents.
With these observations in mind, we have developed a complete system to extract information from Web sites. This system uses both structured information defined by HTML-tags and classical IE methodologies for normal documents. The system is able to use different algorithms to learn the document structure, rules, keywords and spatial relations between contents.

2. System Architecture

We partition the system into three components. The system architecture is showed in Figure 1. The pre-processing component converts HTML sites to XML-style documents. The NE-Agents [CUNN99] extract the contents from the pre-processed documents using structured information and classical IE methods. The extracted contents can be inserted into the predefined template by using TE-Agent [CUNN99].

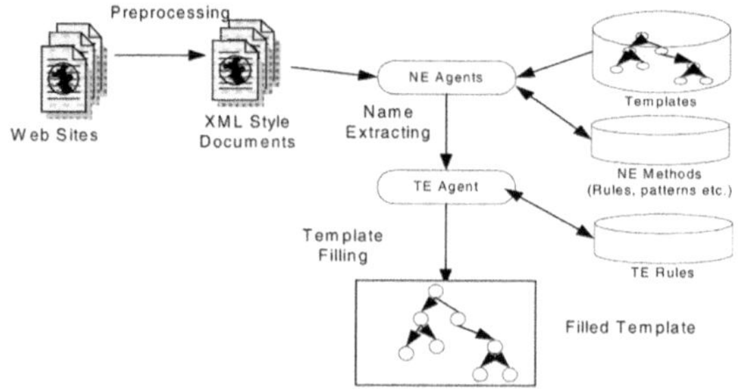

Fig. 1. System Architecture

2.1 Pre-processing

Although the tags of a HTML document imply its structure, we can not use this information reliably, because we can not follow the structure exactly. By contrast, XML documents have a complete hierarchical structure specified by start tags and end tags. To analyze the structure we need to convert HTML sites to well formed XML-style documents. HTML documents are not well formed because, for example, some start tags exist that do not have end. Hence, normally a HTML site can not be parsed by an XML-parser. We use TIDY provided by W3C to automate the conversion. One limitation of TIDY is that it does not convert special characters such as "&", which can cause parser error. To work around this problem, we replace all "&" by legitimate XML description.

2.2 NE-Agent

Here NE-Agents extract the contents using various IE methodologies. Figure 2. Presents the construction of the NE-Agent.

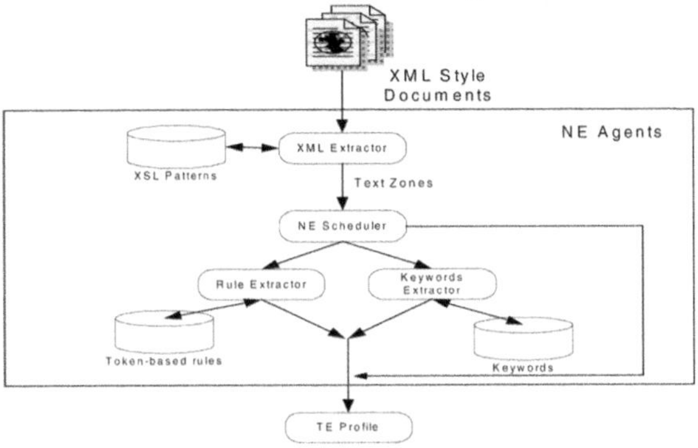

Fig. 2. Construction of NE-Agent

At first we use structure information to find the text zone of the content. The structure information is described by XSL-patterns[W3C]. Each content can have one or more XSL-pattern(s). With the help of patterns we can locate the text zones of the contents. As soon as the text zones are recognized, the traditional IE components can extract the exact information within these text zones. The system uses two distinct IE methods: one is named Rule Extractor and the other is Keywords Extractor. The first extractor uses token-based rules for extracting information, which can be described, by rules such as number, date, speed etc. (The initial version of token-based Rule Extractor is provided by The German Research Center for Artificial Intelligence) [XIAO00].
The second extractor is designed for more open texts where rule-based extraction is difficult (e.g., description about a product). This extractor uses keywords, which are relevant to the contents. A list of keywords with relevance weights can be generated automatically in the training phase. They are evaluated in the extraction phase, text zones are extracted when the overall match exceeds some predefined threshold.
In general there can be multiple Extractors acting as NE-Agents. Each provides solution for a definite problem. The In this sense, the NE-Agents part of the system is a multi-Agents system itself. A NE-Scheduler is therefore necessary to identify the various problems and to distribute them to the suitable Extractor.

2.3 TE-Agent

Many information extraction systems do not have a TE-component to aid in filling the values into the template. The template filling is achieved only with NE-Agents. We observed that a TE-Agent that takes into account global constraints between different template slots could greatly improve extraction accuracy [XIAO00]. We developed the TE-Agent to improve the total performance of template filling. In the learning phase, the TE-Agent uses statistical data to analyse spatial relations between template elements. In the extraction phase, the TE-Agent uses a *greedy voting* algorithm to select the best suitable value for the template element. When the TE-Agent detected multi-instance, the template will be duplicated automatically and be filled with right values. The details of the TE-Agent are not discussed further here.

3. Learning from examples

Hand-coding patterns and rules is time consuming and error-prone. The system provides various learning algorithms to generate XSL-patterns, token-based rules, keywords and TE spatial rules automatically. In the training phase, the input is a number of manually filled template examples. We use a GUI tool to create the examples interactively. The examples are defined by maintaining the references to value positions in the original document(s). Training the NE-Agents and TE-Agent proceeds stepwise. The NE-Agent for each slot of a template is trained separately. For each slot the system gathers all corresponding examples and generates patterns and rules. For the TE-Agent, the learning performs statistical analysis across all slots. After the training the results are saved into an empty template, referred to as the profile, which can be used in the extracting phase.

3.1 Learning XML-Pattern

At first we use the standard XML parser to recognize XML text nodes specified by examples. Because the examples are given by positions, we have to index all XML text nodes with position information. For each found XML node an XSL pattern can be generated. The generation of an XSL pattern is processed bottom-up: from the actual XML text node we go to the parent nodes until the root is reached. An XSL pattern is then generated as the path of node names with their attributes. Once we get all XSL patterns, we can use a supervised learning algorithm to induce the patterns. The algorithm is shown in figure 3.

WHILE Example Set is not empty
    Get an example and generate XSL pattern for this example as input pattern
    FOR each trained XSL pattern in Training
        Get a trained pattern P_i
        New Pattern = GetOverlappingPattern (trained pattern, input pattern)
        Calculate the error rate E_i *for New Pattern*
    IF all E_i > *Threshold*
        Add the input pattern in Training
    ELSE
        Add new Pattern with the lowest E_i *in Training*
    Reorganize the Training and delete example from Example Set

Fig. 3. Algorithm for learning XSL Patterns

The system induces rules bottom-up. For each iteration, an overlapping XSL pattern of the input and trained pattern is created that covers all contents extracted by the two patterns. For example, the overlapping pattern of *html/body/table/td/tr* and *html/body/table/td/font* is assigned as *html/body/table/td/**. The metric used to accept the overlapping pattern is the error rate predicted for the pattern, given by the following formula, where n is the number of extractions made on the training set and e is the number of error among those extraction:

$$\text{Error rate} = (e + 1)/(n+1) \quad (1)$$

If the error rate is lower than a given threshold, the overlapping pattern will be set to be the trained pattern with the lowest error rate. Otherwise, the input pattern is added as itself to the set of trained pattern. Subsequently, the trained pattern set is reorganized to make sure that it contains only disjunctive patterns.

In following we give an example in figure 4 to illustrate how XSL patterns are inductive generated. To simplify the examples, all attributes of the nodes are not shown in the example patterns. However, the attributes play sometimes an important role to distinguish the XML nodes in the real evaluation.

Given are 4 examples, the XSL patterns (without attributes) for each example are:
P1: html/body/tr/td/table/tr/td/b *P2: html/body/tr/td/table/tr/td/font*
P3: html/body/tr/td/table/tr/font *P4: html/body/tr/td/table/tr/p/font*
Iteration 1: Examples: (P1, P2, P3, P4), Training: (Empty), Input pattern: P1
Add P1 as T1 into Training, remove P1 from Examples
Iteration 2: Examples: (P2, P3, P4), Training: (T1), Input pattern: P2
Overlapping O1 (P2, T1): html/body/tr/td/table/tr/td/, Error rate: calculated as 0.1,*
Pattern accepted, Add in O1 as T2 into Training, remove P2 from Example
Reorganize Training, in Training (T2)
Iteration 3: Examples: (P3, P4), Training: (T2), Input pattern: P3
Overlapping O1 (P3, T2): empty Add in P3 as T3 into Training, remove P3
Reorganize Training, in Training (T2, T3)
Iteration 4: Examples: (P4), Training: (T2, T3), Input pattern: P4
Overlapping O2 (P4, T2): html/body/tr/td/table/tr//*, Error rate: calculated as 0.6,*
Pattern not accepted
Overlapping O3 (P4, T3): empty, Add in P4 as T4 into Training, remove P4
Reorganize Training, in Training (T2, T3, T4)
Training result: (T2, T3, T4)

Fig. 4. Example for learning XSL-Patterns

3.2 Learning IE rules and Keywords

Before the training, the system has to decide which training algorithm is to be use for the content. The system described here has only two Extractors: rules for fine information and keywords for plain text description. The algorithm for recognizing and scheduling is therefore, for this restrict problem, simple. The decision is made as

following: the number of words in the content is counted, if the count is less than a threshold (e.g. 5), the Rule Trainer is applied, otherwise the Keywords Trainer. In general the recognition and scheduling in a multi-agents NE-System should be more complicated and sophisticated (see future work).
The Rule Trainer indexes document before training. Characters in content are typed as number, alphabetic string and tokens specified by special characters. The Trainer uses an inductive supervised training algorithm. The output of training is a set of token-based rules with relevance. Figure 5 shows a simple example of learning token-based rules. While the float at the beginning of a rule gives the relevance of the rule:

Given are 4 examples, the XSL patterns (without attributes) for each example are:
1) Speed: 20 km/h 2) Speed: 14.5 km/h 3) Speed: 2000 m/h 4) ....
The training results may be:
0.8 Speed {c <int> c}km/h; 0.5 Speed {c <int> . <int> c}km/h; 0.6 Speed {c <int> c}m/h ...

Fig. 5. Example for Token-based rule learning

The Keywords Trainer first eliminates stop words from the examples and then analyses statistical information about the words. Keywords are generated if the occurrence frequencies are greater than a threshold. The output of training is a set of keywords with relevance. For example a keyword based query can be defined as *{{0.40, "travel"}, {0.37, "accommodation"}, {...}}*.

3.3 Learning TE-Agent

For the class of document that is of interest here (structured or semi-structured documents), significant spatial relationships are expected between the individual contents of a given template – in other words, the order in which the feature instances occur is not completely random. Furthermore, the capture of these spatial relationships is a task that can be automated and achieved in a non-intrusive manner – i.e. based on observing the actions of a user carrying out the task of manually transferring information from text into the template [XIAO00].

4. Extracting and template filling

In the extraction phase a trained profile is loaded. The system drives correspondent extractors stepwise. Each output of an extractor is automatically set as input of other extractors.

4.1 Extracting in NE-Agents

Extracting with XSL pattern is achieved by using a standard XML parser provided by Microsoft. Because the parser extracts only XML nodes, which are defined by an XSL pattern, the position information of contents is not available, which is necessary for other extractors and TE-Agent. A match from the XML nodes to a concrete position in the document has to be processed and the resulting text zone positions forwarded to other extractors. The Rule Extractor interprets the given token-based rules and matches pattern within defined text zone. As soon as the matching is successful, the Extractor outputs result with position information and relevance value. The Keywords Extractor evaluates defined keywords within text zones. Relevance value R is given by following formula, where r_i is relevance of keywords found in content, N is total number of keywords. If the relevance is larger than a defined threshold, the total text zone is output as a result with position and relevance information.

$$R = \sum r_i / N \tag{2}$$

After extraction, all position and relevance information of all elements in the template is forwarded to the TE-Agent.

4.2 Template filling in TE-Agent

The TE-Agent detects conflicts between extracted NE-results. Conflicts can be resolved by eliminating one of the conflicting feature instances, using a *greedy voting* algorithm. This is achieved by allowing all feature instances outside of the conflict to vote for each of the conflicting instances. The content instance that receives least votes is eliminated from all conflicts. The eliminating is processed so long, until all conflicts have been solved [XIAO00].

5. Experiment Description

We tested our system with two text genres: structured and semi-structured text [SODE99]. Structured text will be presented by CNN weather forecast web pages. The CNN Weather Forecast domain consists of Web sites for various domestic and international cities with four-day weather forecast. The second genre is semi-structured text. Experiments are reported from two domains of semi-structured Text: the Rental Ads and Last Minute Holidays. The Rental Ads domain was collected from the Seattle Times online-classified ads. We downloaded the test set from RISE Repository (http://www.isi.edu/~muslea/RISE/repository.html). To make comparison we used template defined by WHISK [SODE99]. The template consists of three contents: information about neighborhoods, about price and about bedrooms. The Last Minute Holidays Services is collected from the Web sites in lastminute.com (http://www.lastminute.com). To extract are names of ranges, a range of price, a short description about the range, information about award minutes per item, information about tickets, additional information to children and infants.

For CNN Weather Forecast, we used 10 examples for training and 100 examples for testing. As for WHISK [SODE99] we used a training set of 400 examples and a test set of a further 400 examples. For Last Minute Holidays the training set has 40

examples, while the testing set has 100 samples. All these examples were made manually in a GUI tool.
Table 1 shows the results of the experiments. With two examples the system gets 100% recall and 100% precision for CNN Weather Forecast domain. In Rental Ads the recall and precision are improved with more examples. Recall begins at 88% from 50 examples and climbs to 95% when 400 examples. Precision starts at 87% from 50 examples and reaches to 98% when 400 examples. For Last Minute Holidays the recall is 91% and precision is 98% with 20 examples. With 40 examples the recall is improved to 97%, but the precision goes down to 96%.

Example Name	Examples	Precision	Recall
CNN Weather	2	100%	100%
Rental Ads	50	87%	88%
	400	98%	95%
Last Minute Holiday	20	98%	91%
	40	96%	97%

Table 1. Experiment result

6. Analysis and Discussion

In this section we will discuss some interesting points about three different test domains. We found that in different situations some single agents are especially important. In CNN Weather Forecast, training with one example can already lead to perfect results. As the values of contents are exact the texts of XML nodes, Rule Extractor and Keyword Extractor are then unnecessary. In this case, the TE-Agent plays a very important role. Some slots, such as temperature for the coming four days, have the same XSL pattern. However, they are ordered in a strict sequence. Here we observed a common problem occurs also in *Wrapper Induction*: with *Wrapper* or XSL patterns alone we can not perform an exact filling in the template if the contents have same *wrapper* description or XSL pattern but different spatial locations. With the help of the TE-Agent the system is able to select the right value for one each of a set of potentially confused slots.
In Rental Ads the XSL patterns do not improve performance of the result because all information is in one XML node. Actually the Rule Extractor and TE-Agent alone are sufficient to carry out the IE task. In this case the extracting is somewhat similar as IE from normal (not HTML-coded) documents. As same as WHISK, the TE-Agent performs template filling with multi-instances.
More interesting is Last Minute Holidays domain. Some contents are extracted exactly after XSL pattern extracting (such as range title and range price), because they have unique XSL patterns. Some content can be distinguished by the NE-Agents alone (such as short description and includes information) using different keywords. Further content only can be extracted exactly after the TE-Agent processing (such as

additional information about children and infants), because they have same XSL patterns, same keywords but different spatial location.
Generally, good recall and poor precision is achieved by the NE-Agent processing. After the TE-Agent the precision is improved considerably with a slightly loss of recall. For example, in Rental Ads the system reaches 85% precision and 96% recall after NE-agent processing with 250 training examples. After the TE-Agent, we get 95% precision and 95% recall. Table 2 shows the overall precision and recall after each extracting step (The Precision and Recall after XSL pattern are calculated for the text zones whether cover the to be extracted contents).

Example Name	Examples	After XSL Patterns		After IE-Agents		After TE-Agent	
		P	R	P	R	P	R
CNN	2	30%	100%	30%	100%	100%	100%
Rental Ads	250	33%	100%	85%	96%	95%	95%
Last Minute	40	44%	100%	89%	98%	96%	97%

Table 2. Precision and Recall for each processing step

Related Work

In comparison to other *wrapper* systems our system uses not only tag information but also classical IE algorithms. The Wrapper Induction system [KUSH00] works only on rigidly structured text. STALKER [MUSL98], SVR [FREI98] and RAPIER [CALI97] extend information extraction to semi-structured text, but these systems extract only isolated slots. All these systems do not take into account the spatial dependencies between the various features of the template. WHISK [SODE99] performs multi-slot extraction and considers the orders of the template elements. We compare our system with WHISK with the same sample set Rental Ads. WHISK achieves 98% precision and 94% recall, while our system reaches 98% precision and 95% recall with same amount of examples. A considerable difference is that WHISK uses background knowledge before extracting, so called *semantic class*. They are defined by user and as part of WHISK's input. Our system does not use handcrafted background knowledge and learns all rules and patterns merely from given examples.
Another advantage of our system is the Keywords Extractor. All the other systems try to extract some fine-grained pieces of information but they are not able to extract text parts in documents. Actually the Keywords Extractor does a primitive Information Retrieval task and treats the text zones as some mini-documents to be classified.

7. Conclusion and Future Work

In this paper we introduced a new methodology for extracting information from Web pages. In our system we showed how different evidence in Web pages could be

seamlessly combined to perform high quality information extraction. The implies structure information defined by tags can be used to recognise text zones of the content of a document. A classical IE Rule Extractor can extract exact fine information within text zones. The Keywords Extractor can be used to extract a whole text area. The TE-Agent can filter values to improve overall precision. It can also provide automatic duplication for multi-slot documents. Our system provides full automatic learning from examples without background knowledge. Various machine leaning algorithms are used to learn different patterns, rules and keywords.
A major area for improvement lies in investigating an incremented learning process so that the learning performance can be improved. Another possible improvement to the XSL pattern may be to include learning the pre- and post XSL patterns. In some cases there are very strong constraints before and after an XML text node. Introducing the XSL patterns as constraints can generally improve the precision of the text zones. An improved inductive learning algorithm should be developed to extract this complicate XSL pattern chain w.r.t. extracting performance.
Currently two extraction techniques are used as NE-Agents. In the future we will try to use further Extractors to deal with more difficult IE-tasks, such as Extractors with NLP to parse free text sentence, Extractors with CBR for some content with only weak syntactic structure, etc. A more complicated and sophisticated NE-Scheduler should be investigated to provide an automatic distribution of various problems to suitable NE-Agents. Furthermore, Agents should work not only autonomously but also co-operatively. Multi-Agents NE-System should therefore be developed.
With the introduction of our system, and other IE systems like it, we can begin to address the larger problem of designing artificially intelligent agents for information extracting from Web pages.

References

[CALI97] Relational Learning of Pattern-Match Rules for Information Extraction, M E Califf and R J Mooney, Proceedings ACL-97: Workshop on Natural Language Learning, 1997
[COHE99] A Simple, Fast, and Effective Rule Learner, W Cohen, AAAI-99 Proceeding, 1999
[CUNN99] Information Extraction a User Guide , H Cunningham, CS-99-07, 1999
[FREI98] Information Extraction from HTML: Application of a General Machine Learning Approch, D Freitag, AAAI-98 Proceeding, 1998
[KNOB98] Trends and controversies: Information Integration, A Levy, C Knoblock, S Minton, W Cohen, IEEE Intelligent Systems 13 (5), 1998
[KUSH00] Wrapper induction: Efficiency and expressiveness, N Kushmeric, Artificial Intelligence 118, 15-68, 2000
[MUSL98] STALKER: Learning Extraction Rules for Semistructured, Web-based Information Sources – Muslea I, Minton S, AAAI'98 Workshop "AI and Information Integration"
[RILO94] Information Extraction as a Basis for High-Precision Text Classification, E Riloff and W Lehnert, ACM Transactions on Information Systems vol. 12 no. 3 1994.
[SODE99] Learning Information Extraction Rules for Semi-Structured and Free Text, S Sonderland, Machine Learning 34, 233-272, 1999
[XIAO00] Where to Position the Precision in Knowledge Extraction from Text, L Xiao, 2000

Flexible Similarity Assessment for XML Documents Based on XQL and Java Reflection

Dieter Bühler and Wolfgang Küchlin

University of Tübingen, Department of Computer Science
Symbolic Computation Group, http://www-sr.informatik.uni-tuebingen.de
Sand 13, D-72076 Tübingen, Germany
{buehler, kuechlin}@informatik.uni-tuebingen.de

Abstract. In this paper we present a flexible similarity assessment framework for *XML* documents and describe its usage on the example of *XML*-based fault diagnosis for remote fieldbus automation systems. Our approach combines the expressive power of both *XQL* and Java to overcome the limitations of standard *XML* query languages and to provide a convenient platform for rapid definition of distance functions for any kind of *XML* structured data. The presented framework allows the extraction of fragments from *XML* documents, the wrapping of these fragments in any desired Java objects, the dynamic invocation of Java methods with the created objects as parameters and the computation of a scalar overall result from the partial results which can be interpreted as a distance value. The actual mapping of *XML* fragments to Java instances assessing their similarity is specified by an *XML to Java Mapping Language* (*XJML*) *XML* document in a formal and flexible way. The framework consists of the *XML* to Java mapping concept, the *XJML* DTD, and various Java packages to evaluate an *XJML*-based nearest neighbor search on local documents or on *XQL* query result sets of (remote) *XML* database systems.

1 Introduction and Motivation

XML provides a means of representing structured data of any kind in a standardized, platform and (programming) language independent way. The data becomes available to a wide variety of free general purpose *XML* tools and programming environments which in turn provide a platform for the rapid development of dedicated *XML* applications and tools for special purposes. Today, the use of *XML* as a generic data format becomes more and more common in many fields of information technology like eCommerce, software system configuration, multimedia databases and monitoring systems. Recently, *XML* also emerged in the field of fieldbus-based industrial automation systems (e.g. [16][11][3]).

Efficient data retrieval in large hierarchical *XML* data repositories is a subject of current research. Different query languages (e.g. *XQL* [12], *XML*-QL [8], *XML* Query [10], *XML*-GL [6]) are under construction or are already standardized.

These query languages basically allow the selection of specific parts of *XML* documents by specifying one ore more paths through the *XML* document structure while evaluating predicates which correspond (to some extent) to the

L. Monostori, J. Váncza, and M. Ali (Eds.): IEA/AIE 2001, LNAI 2070, pp. 175–186, 2001.

WHERE clauses in *SQL*. This functionality is not sufficient for a more sophisticated data mining like a nearest neighbor search (cf. [13]) for instance.

The CANINSIGHT [4] remote fieldbus management and maintenance system for example monitors the system state of automation systems by generating and archiving *XML* documents. The current system state is encoded by a corresponding *XML* document which contains the current parameter values. A nearest neighbor search in such an *XML* process data repository can perform a fuzzy system state assessment and can result, for example, in a diagnosis proposal for a yet unknown error state of the (remote) automation system. This scenario will be further outlined in Section 6.

The framework which we are presenting in this paper features concepts and tools to specify and evaluate flexible distance functions which can be used to measure the degree of similarity of two *XML* documents. In most cases, the two documents will in fact share the same *XML Document Type Definition* (DTD) which ensures a certain inherent structural similarity of the documents but a shared DTD is not a prerequisite. Furthermore a nearest neighbor search for a given *XML* document and an *XML* document repository can be evaluated. The *XML* repository can consist of an *XQL* query result on a TAMINO *XML* database (cf. www.tamino.com) or a filtered directory of a file system.

The specification of the distance functions is based on our *XML* to Java mapping concept which is a crucial part of our system. It allows the extraction of fragments from *XML* documents, the wrapping of these fragments in any desired Java objects, the dynamic invocation of any desired Java methods with the created objects as parameters and the computation of a scalar overall result which can be interpreted as a distance value.

As depicted in Fig. 3, the framework consists of the *XML to Java Mapping Language* (*XJML*) which allows the specification of *XML* to Java mappings, the *XJML_Eval* Java evaluation tool together with its auxiliary Java class library, and the *XML* database system which is optional.

The following section will introduce the overall approach and the system overview will be given in Section 3. The succeeding Section 4 will focus on *XJML* and *XJML*-based definition of distance functions and the evaluation procedure. Section 5 will present the *XJML_Eval* tool which is based on Java Reflection. The practical usage of the system will be outlined in Section 6 on the example of similarity assessment within the CANINSIGHT system. The paper will conclude with a summary and an outlook.

2 The Overall Approach

Our similarity assessment fulfills the following task:

> Let $\mathbb{D}$ be the set of well-formed *XML* documents and $\mathbb{O}$ the set of generic Java instances of type *java.lang.Object*. Given
> (i) an *XML* document d',
> (ii) a vector $D = (d_1, ..., d_u)$ of *XML* (sub-) documents,
> (iii) a vector $M = (m_1, ..., m_w)$ of *XML* to Java mappings with $m : \mathbb{D} \times \mathbb{D} \rightarrow \mathbb{O}$

(iv) and a function $E : \mathbb{O} \times ... \times \mathbb{O} \rightarrow \mathbb{O}$ which evaluates the mapping results,

do compute $nearestNeighbor(d', D, M, E) = n \in \mathbb{N}$,
such that $E(m_1(d_n, d'), ..., m_w(d_n, d')) \leq E(m_1(d_i, d'), ..., m_w(d_i, d'))$,
$\forall\, 1 \leq i \leq u$

The Document d'. The *XML* document d' is the document for which we want to compute the most similar *XML* document of D.

The Vector of Documents D. D is an ordered set of *XML* (sub-) documents which may be contained in one or more *XML* documents of the local file system or an *XML* database query result. The (sub-) documents are extracted from the documents by specifying their root element tag name. This fragmentation feature has proven useful in practice.

The Vector of *XJML* Mappings M. The *XML* to Java mapping concept is a crucial part of our system. An *XML* to Java mapping $m : \mathbb{D} \times \mathbb{D} \rightarrow \mathbb{O}$ provides for example[1] a distance information of two *XML* documents with respect to a specific distance property.

An individual mapping m is specified by one or more so-called *Selections* and a *Target* specification (cf. Fig. 1 b). Each *Selection* is defined by a further *Target* specification and an *XQL* statement which is evaluated on both documents resulting in two specific fragments of the two documents.

In order to be able to perform a typed Java comparison of these fragments, they are wrapped in Java objects. This is achieved by passing the document fragments as *java.lang.String* values to the constructors of the Java classes that are referenced by the corresponding *Target* information. There are no restrictions on the type of the referenced Java classes (except that they must provide a constructor which takes one single *String* value) nor on the actual location on the Internet from where they are to be downloaded. The dynamically created Java instances are then passed as parameters to a method of a Java class as referenced by the *Target* information of m. Again there are no restrictions on the class type nor on the actual location or the return type of the referenced Java class and method. It is clear that the dynamically instantiated parameter objects must match a signature of the referenced Java method, otherwise the result of m would be undefined.

Thus, an *XJML* mapping is a three step procedure (cf. Fig. 2) starting with the *selection phase*: *XQL* statements are used to extract specific parts from existing documents which are transformed to Java string values. These extracted parts may be well-formed *XML* subdocuments or any other kind of document fragment like an attribute value for instance. The *XQL* statements are evaluated on both documents, so that n selections result in $2 \cdot n$ string values.

[1] The *XML* to Java mapping concept may be used as well for a lot of other purposes not concerned with similarity assessment.

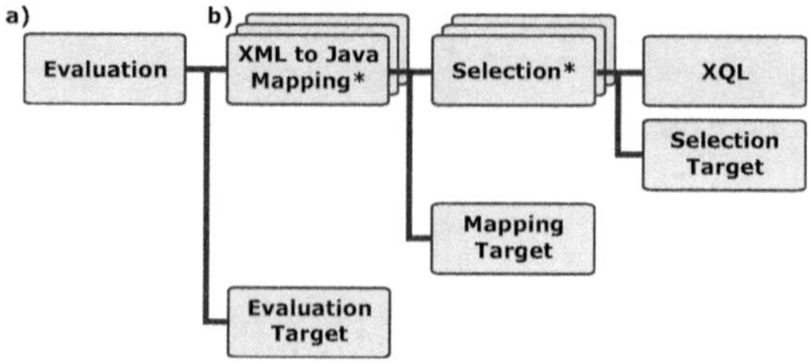

Fig. 1. a) The evaluation structure b) The *XML* to Java mapping structure

These Java strings are wrapped into Java objects during the *wrapping phase*: The extracted document fragments are used to parameterize the invocation of a constructor of a wrapping Java class referenced by the corresponding *Target* information. This wrapping can be used to transfer the string representation of the data into a typed Java object. For example, the string value "127" can be transformed to a simple core Java object like a *java.lang.Integer* object or into a user defined Java object with specific properties and behaviour like the *CANopenNodeState* class (cf. Section 4) for instance.

The created Java objects are used as parameters to invoke a static (distance) method of a further Java class in the *invocation phase*: the Java objects created from text fragments of both documents are passed to the referenced method in alternating order (cf. Fig. 2). The return type of this method may be of any core or user defined Java type.

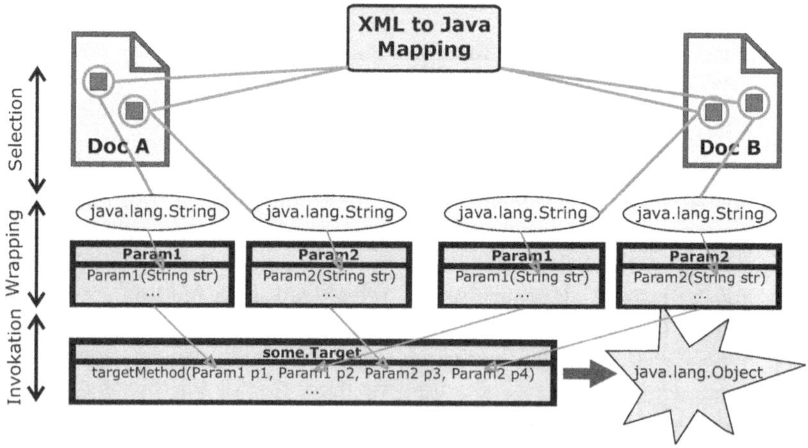

Fig. 2. The *XML* to Java mapping procedure: selection, wrapping, invocation

The Evaluation Function *E*. Since M may consist of more than one mapping (cf. Fig. 1 a), the evaluation function E is required to compute the overall distance of the two documents from the partial results provided by the specified *XJML* mappings. The method is referenced in the same way like it is done in the invocation phase of the *XJML* mapping procedure.

The *nearestNeighbor()* Function. As we saw in the previous paragraph, E can provide a single distance value for two *XML* documents. Since we want to find the most similar document to d' in D we have to apply E on all possible document pairs (d_i, d') and retrieve the index of the document resulting in a minimal E value. Table 1 summarizes the properties[2] of the mapping target entities.

Table 1. *XJML* mapping targets

	Mapped instance	Purpose	Restriction	Return type
Selection Target	Java class	*XML* parameter wrapping	String constructor	no
Mapping Target	Java method	Distance evaluation with respect to a specific distance property	Static	any
Evaluation Target	Java method	Distance evaluation with respect to all distance results	Static	Double

3 System Overview

Fig. 3 gives an overview of the system which mainly consists of *XJML*, the *XJML_Eval* tool, and the optional *XML* database back-end.

The entities D, M, and E are specified or referenced by a single *XJML* document (cf. Section 4). The *XJML_Eval* tool (cf. Section 5) features the *nearestNeighbor()* method. It reads an *XJML* document, creates the *XML* data structures, downloads all necessary Java classes, wraps the *XML* document fragments, invokes the specified distance functions and retrieves the document with the lowest overall distance to document d'. The system also provides Java classes and interfaces to encapsulate different kinds of *XML* data repositories. The Java class *de.uni_tuebingen.xjml.XmlDataRepository* provides convenient access to *XML* documents of the local file system or an *XQL* query result of a TAMINO native *XML* database system. All necessary data cursoring on large result sets is managed transparently by this class.

[2] The return type *Double* of the Evaluation Target is only required if the Evaluation will be further processed by the *nearestNeighbor()* method.

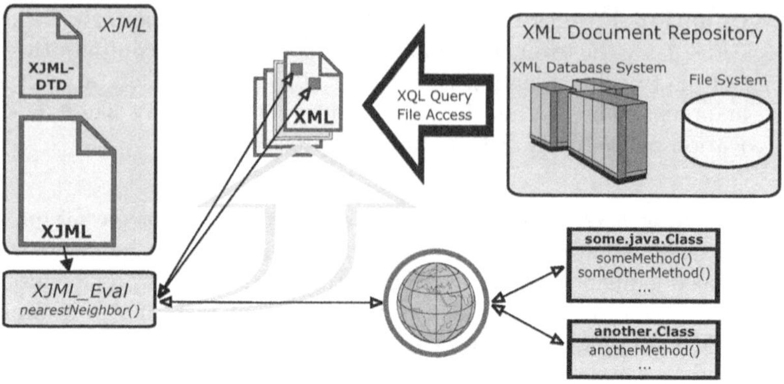

Fig. 3. Similarity assessment system overview

4 The *XML* to Java Mapping Language (*XJML*)

XJML provides the syntactical means to specify and identify the introduced entities D, M and E. The language is a so-called *XML* application and is defined by the *XJML* DTD which is listed in Fig. 4.

```
<!-- http://www-sr.informatik.uni-tuebingen.de/CanInsight/XJML.dtd -->
<!ELEMENT XJML ( Statement+ )>
<!ELEMENT Statement ( XMLDataRepository, ( Mapping* ), Evaluation )>
<!ELEMENT XMLDataRepository ( FileSystem | URL | Database )>
<!ATTLIST XMLDataRepository RootElement CDATA #IMPLIED>
<!ELEMENT FileSystem EMPTY>
<!ATTLIST FileSystem Directory CDATA #REQUIRED
                     Suffix CDATA #IMPLIED>
<!ELEMENT URL EMPTY>
<!ATTLIST URL Name CDATA #REQUIRED>
<!ELEMENT Database EMPTY>
<!ATTLIST Database Location CDATA #IMPLIED
                   Name CDATA #IMPLIED
                   Query CDATA #REQUIRED>
<!ELEMENT Mapping ( Selection, Target )>
<!ELEMENT Selection ( XqlQuery | Fixed )+>
<!ELEMENT XqlQuery ( Target )>
<!ATTLIST XqlQuery Xql CDATA #REQUIRED>
<!ELEMENT Fixed ( Target )>
<!ATTLIST Fixed Value CDATA #REQUIRED>
<!ELEMENT Target ( JavaRef )>
<!ELEMENT JavaRef EMPTY>
<!ATTLIST JavaRef Codebase CDATA #IMPLIED
                  Class CDATA #REQUIRED
                  Method CDATA #IMPLIED>
<!ELEMENT Evaluation (Target)>
```

Fig. 4. The *XML* to Java Mapping Language DTD

The vector D defining the search space is defined by the `XMLDataRepository` element which contains a `FileSystem`, `URL` or `Database` sub-element depending on the type of the document source. These sub-elements provide all information necessary to instantiate the previously mentioned *XmlDataRepository* Java class which provides the abstract concept of an *XML* document repository featuring methods like *getNextDoc()* for example. The example document depicted in Fig. 5 references a database data source by giving an *XQL* query to a TAMINO system. The query is encoded in an URL expression which holds additional information about the location of the database on the Internet and the name of the database.

```
<?xml version="1.0" encoding="UTF-8"?>
<!DOCTYPE XJML SYSTEM 'http://www-sr.informatik.uni-tuebingen.de/CanInsight/XJML.dtd' [
  <!ENTITY dieter "http://dieter.informatik.uni-tuebingen.de/classes">
  <!ENTITY base "de.uni_tuebingen.xjml">
 ]>
<XJML>
 <Statement>
  <XMLDataRepository RootElement="StateInformation">
   <Database Query="http://mfb.informatik.uni-tuebingen.de/tamino/CoML?_xql=CoML/StateInformation"/>
  </XMLDataRepository>
  <Mapping>
   <Selection>
    <XqlQuery Xql="Device[@ModuleId='10']/LogEntry[@Index='6000' $and$ @Subindex='1']/@Value">
     <Target><JavaRef Codebase="&dieter;" Class="&base;.IntegerHex"/></Target>
    </XqlQuery>
    <Fixed Value="255">
     <Target><JavaRef Class="java.lang.Integer"/></Target>
    </Fixed>
   </Selection>
   <Target><JavaRef Codebase="&dieter;" Class="&base;.eval.Methods" Method="integerDistance"/></Target>
  </Mapping>
  <Mapping>
   <Selection>
    <XqlQuery Xql="Device[@ModuleId='10']/LogEntry[@Index='1002' $and$ @Subindex='0']/@Value">
     <Target><JavaRef Class="de.uni_tuebingen.can.CanProtocol.CANopenNodeState"/></Target>
    </XqlQuery>
   </Selection>
   <Target>
    <JavaRef Codebase="&dieter;" Class="&base;.eval.Methods" Method="CANopenNodeStateDistance"/>
   </Target>
  </Mapping>
  <Evaluation>
   <Target><JavaRef Codebase="&dieter;" Class="&base;.eval.Methods" Method="doubleAverage"/></Target>
  </Evaluation>
 </Statement>
</XJML>
```

Fig. 5. An example *XJML* document for industrial process data

The vector M defining the individual distance properties is defined by a sequence of `Mapping` elements. Each `Mapping` element contains one `Selection` and one `Target` element. The Selection may contain any sequence of `XqlQuery` elements representing *XQL* queries and `Fixed` elements. The `Fixed` elements can be used to parameterize target methods with fixed values. At the moment the `Target` element only allows a `JavaRef` sub-element which uniquely references a Java class or method in the local class path or on the Internet. At this point, the framework could be extended to integrate further programming languages like C# for instance.

The example document maps specific parameter values identified by attributes `ModuleId`, `Index` and `Subindex` to the user defined class *HexInteger* which interprets the selected string values as hexadecimal representations of integer values. These parameters together with a fixed *Integer* value of 255 (indicating the maximum distance of two values) are used to invoke the static *integerDistance()* method of the *Methods* class. The second mapping computes the CANopen protocol specific distance of the bus states of two CANopen devices (cf. Section 6).

The sequence of `Mapping` elements must be terminated by an `Evaluation` element which just contains a further `Target` element, referencing the overall evaluation method.

5 The *XJML_Eval* Tool

XJML_Eval is a Java application which evaluates a single *XJML* document for a given *XML* document d'. In order to evaluate the *nearestNeighbor()* method, it reads an *XJML* document, creates the *XML* data structures and the *XmlDataRepository* object, downloads all necessary Java classes, wraps the *XML* document fragments, invokes the specified Java distance functions and retrieves the document with the lowest overall distance to document d'. Extensive code documentation is available online[3].

The *XQL* support is provided by the *GMD-IPSI XQL engine* (http://xml.-darmstadt.gmd.de/xql/) which is free for non-commercial use. To dynamically download and instantiate the specified Java classes while the evaluation is running, *XJML_Eval* uses its custom Java class loader to download Java byte code from any desired URL or from the local class path. In fact, the method *createNewInstance()* of the *Projection* class (cf. Table 2) just takes a `JavaRef` DOM [17] node (cf. Section 4) parameter to transparently create the Java instance. The `JavaRef` node holds all necessary information for the custom class loader to instantiate the corresponding class (cf. Fig. 4 and 5). The dynamic object instantiation is possible due to Java's reflection facilities [1], which allow for example to retrieve the constructor of the loaded class that takes exactly one *java.lang.String* parameter and to invoke this previously unknown constructor at runtime. In a similar way, the *Projection* class features the *invokeMethod()* method which invokes the method specified in a `JavaRef` node on a corresponding newly created Java object.

XJML_Eval is based on the free *Java API for XML Processing* (*JAXP*) library [15] and does not use any proprietary libraries.

6 Similarity Assessment within the CanInsight System

CanInsight [4] was developed to create a device and platform independent fieldbus management and maintenance system for highly distributed manufac-

[3] http://www-sr.-informatik.uni-tuebingen.de/CanInsight/doc/

Table 2. The *Projection* class (extract)

Result	Method	Signature
Object	createNewInstance	(ElementNode javaRefNode, String initValue)
Object	invokeMethod	(ElementNode javaRefNode, Object[] params)

turing enterprises. System data are represented as *XML* documents which are instances of the CANopen Markup Language (*CoML*) [2]. *CoML* is an *XML* application for Controller Area Network (CAN) [9] and CANopen [5] fieldbus device profiles, setup information, and process data. The system uses a *CoML*-based Java client/server architecture to access CANopen fieldbus systems via the Internet.

The CANINSIGHT system monitors the system state of CANopen automation systems by generating and archiving *XML* documents. The current system state is encoded by a corresponding *CoML* document which contains the current parameter values as specified by a further monitoring configuration *CoML* document (cf. Fig. 6). An enterprise is now able to maintain a database of past error states, encoded as *CoML* documents. A nearest neighbor search for an unknown error state in such a database results in a diagnosis proposal for the error state without the requirement for further expertise.

The database may also offer a set of predefined *XJML* documents specifying distance functions for special purposes. For example, there may be special *XJML* documents for wear out errors. Furthermore, the distance functions can be tuned and adjusted without having to recompile the generic *XJML_Eval* evaluation tool or even to create dedicated evaluation tools from scratch.

Since the CANINSIGHT system is completely transparent with respect to the actual locations of the automation system, the database and the engineer, the use of *XML* and *XJML* support a flexible error diagnosis on remote automation systems based on data collected within the whole distributed enterprise.

7 Summary

The presented framework allows the extraction of fragments from *XML* documents, the wrapping of these fragments in any desired Java objects, the invocation of methods with the created objects as parameters and the computation of a scalar overall result from the partial results. This is a true improvement over the currently available *XML* query languages. As we showed in this paper, the results can be used for a similarity assessment of *XML* documents and to evaluate a nearest neighbor search on a set of *XML* documents.

The actual mapping is defined in a corresponding *XJML* document containing *XQL* statements and Java references. There are no restrictions on the Java classes (except for the few requirements stated in Table 2) concerning their type or the URL of where their byte code data resides. Thus, our system combines the syntactic power of *XML* to specify structure and references with the semantic

a)
```
<?xml version="1.0" encoding="UTF-8"?>
<!DOCTYPE CoML SYSTEM 'http://www-sr.informatik.uni-tuebingen.de/CanInsight/CoML.dtd'>
<CoML>
 <CanSetup>
  <MetaInformation>
   <SetupDescription>CANopen setup featuring three CANopen I/O modules ... </SetupDescription>
   <!-- ... -->
  </MetaInformation>
  <Module ModuleId="10">
   <!-- ... -->
   <ObjectDictionary>
    <!-- ... -->
    <MandatoryObjects>
     <Object Index="1000" Subindex="0" DataType="7" ObjectType="7" AccessType="ro" PDOMapping="0">
      <ParameterName>Device Type</ParameterName>
      <DefaultValue>0x30191</DefaultValue>
     </Object>
     <!-- ... -->
```
b)
```
<?xml version="1.0" encoding="UTF-8"?>
<!DOCTYPE CoML SYSTEM 'http://www-sr.informatik.uni-tuebingen.de/CanInsight/CoML.dtd'>
<CoML>
 <StateInformation StartOfQuery="973689545541" EndOfQuery="973689546302" LocationId="WSISand13"
                   CanSetupCreationTime="2000-07-27 15:48:38.253">
  <Device ModuleId="10">
   <LogEntry Index="1000" Subindex="0" Value="30191" />
   <LogEntry Index="1001" Subindex="0" Value="0" />
   <LogEntry Index="1002" Subindex="0" Value="7f0000" />
   <!-- ... -->
```

Fig. 6. *CoML* examples: a) A monitoring configuration document b) *CoML* process data

power of the Java programming language. The result is an extremely flexible formalism to specify relationships and similarity between *XML* documents.

The flexibility of our approach results from the separation of distance function specification in *XJML* from their actual implementation in Java. Thus, the distance function can be tuned and adjusted without having to recompile the generic evaluation tool. Furthermore, specialized and adapted distance function specifications can be stored in a database as *XJML* documents. Sophisticated distance function implementations, for example pattern matching algorithms for graphical data, could be provided by third parties and may reside on any location on the Internet. This flexibility is especially valuable in the field of data mining where the distance function often becomes a parameter which has to be adjusted for a given task.

We further successfully implemented the *XJML_Eval* tool to evaluate such *XJML* specifications.

8 Outlook

If the overall distance function defined by an *XJML* document is a metric distance function (especially with respect to the triangle inequality), the *XML* document repository could be enhanced with an index structure (cf. e.g. [7][18]) to improve retrieval efficiency.

We are further planning to extend the *XML*-based distributed software system monitoring middleware presented in [14] with an *XJML*-based nearest neighbor search facility to automatically detect and identify malfunctions in distributed software systems. Since the parameterizations are defined by a single small *XJML* document we are also currently discussing a mobile agent approach for a fast state similarity assessment in distributed systems.

Acknowledgement. This paper is partially based upon work funded by the *Ministerium für Wissenschaft, Forschung und Kunst* of the German state of Baden-Württemberg within the research initiative "*Virtuelle Hochschule*".

References

1. K. Arnold, J. Gosling, and D. Holmes. *The Java Programming Language.* Addison-Wesley, Reading, Massachusetts, third edition, 2000.
2. Dieter Bühler. The CANopen Markup Language – Representing fieldbus data with XML. In *Proc. of the 26th IEEE International Conference on Industrial Electronics, Control and Instrumentation (IECON 2000)*, Nagoya, Japan, October 2000. IEEE.
3. Dieter Bühler and Gruhler Gerhard. XML-based representation and monitoring of CAN devices. In *Proc. of the 7th International CAN Conference (ICC 2000)*, Amsterdam, The Netherlands, October 2000. CAN in Automation (www.can-cia.com).
4. Dieter Bühler and Wolfgang Küchlin. Remote fieldbus system management with Java and XML. In *Proc. of the IEEE International Symposium on Industrial Electronics (ISIE 2000)*, Puebla, Mexico, December 2000. IEEE Computer Society Press (to appear).
5. Can In Automation (CiA) e.V., Erlangen, Germany. *CANopen Communication Profile for Industrial Systems, Based on CAL*, 1996. CiA Draft Standard 301.
6. S. Ceri, S. Comai, E. Damiani, P. Fraternali, S. Paraboschi, and L. Tanca. XML-GL: A graphical language for querying and restructuring XML documents. In *Proc. of the 8th International World Wide Web Conference (WWW8)*, Totonto, Canada, May 1999. Elsevier Science.
7. K. L. Clarkson. Nearest neighbor queries in metric spaces. In *Proc. of the 29th ACM Symposium on Theory of Computing (STOC 97)*, El Paso, TX USA, May 1997.
8. D. Deutsch, M. Fernandez, D. Florescu, A. Levy, and D. Suciu. *XML-QL: A Query Language for XML.* World Wide Web Consortium (W3C), http://www.w3c.org/-TR/NOTE-xml-ql/, 1998.
9. ISO. *ISO 11898 – Road Vehicles, Interchange of Digital Information - Controller Area Network (CAN) for High-Speed Communication*, 1993.
10. M. Marchiori and M. Fernandez. *XML Query.* World Wide Web Consortium (W3C), http://www.w3.org/2000/Talks/www9-xmlquery/, 2000.
11. OPC Foundation. OPC and Microsoft start XML initiative. *OPC Quarterly*, 2(4), Dec 1999.
12. Jonathan Robie, Joe Lapp, and David Schach. *XML Query Language (XQL).* World Wide Web Consortium (W3C), http://www.w3c.org/TandS/QL/QL98/-pp/xql.html, 1998.

13. N. Roussopoulos, S. Kelley, and F. Vincent. Nearest neighbor queries. In *Proc. of the ACM International Conference on Management of Data (SIGMOD 95)*, San Jose, CA USA, May 1995.
14. Ralf-Dieter Schimkat, Matthias Häußer, Wolfgang Küchlin, and Rainer Krautter. Web application middleware to support XML-based monitoring in distributed systems. In *Proc. of the ISCA 13th International Conference on Computer Applications in Industry and Engineering (CAINE-2000)*, Honolulu, Hawaii USA, November 2000.
15. Sun Microsystems, http://java.sun.com/xml/download.html. *Java API for XML Processing.*
16. Martin Wollschlaeger. CANopen Device Descriptions using general purpose modeling languages. In *Proc. of the 6th International CAN Conference (ICC 99)*, Torino, Italy, November 1999. CAN in Automation (www.can-cia.com).
17. World Wide Web Consortium (W3C), http://www.w3c.org/TR/REC-DOM-Level-1/. *Document Object Model (DOM) Level 1 Specification*, 1998.
18. P. N. Yianilos. Data structures and algorithms for nearest neighbor search in general metric spaces. In *Proc. of the ACM-SIAM Symposium on Discrete Algorithms*, Austin, TX USA, January 1993.

Where to Position the Precision in Knowledge Extraction from Text

Luo Xiao, Dieter Wissmann

Siemens AG, CT SE 5 Erlangen, Germany
(Luo.Xiao, Dieter.Wissmann)@erls.siemens.de
Michael Brown

Interprice Technologies GmbH. Berlin, Germany
Mike@Interprice.com
Stefan Jablonski

Dept. of Computer Sciences VI (IMMD VI) University of Erlangen-Nuremberg, Germany
Stefan.Jablonski@informatik.uni-erlangen.de

Abstract. This paper concerns knowledge extraction for applications concerning the automated filling of templates from an input of semi-structured textual documents. The template filling task can be viewed as a collaboration between a number of agents, including NE-Agents that are specialised to detect occurrences of specific features in the text and TE-Agents that specialise at combining the results from multiple NE-Agents in order to create a template instance. This paper presents an automated learning approach for the generation of a TE-Agent that extracts spatial relationships between the various features of a template. It is shown that this TE-Agent can compensate for imprecise performance on the part of the NE-Agents.

1. Introduction

This paper addresses the problem of extracting knowledge from textual documents. This problem generally involves the transformation of information in an informal (i.e. non-machine-readable) format into a formal format. This conversion is a necessary pre-condition for the automated management of knowledge within a modern organisation. The information contained in a disparate body of textual documents can be gathered together into a central knowledge resource. Once the information owned by a corporation is made explicit, a wide range of automated facilities are enabled, such as; document generation and summarisation [RAJM98], automatic filtering and analysis of WWW pages [MUSL98,SODE99] etc.

The work described in this paper is focussed on the more limited problem of template-filling for knowledge extraction; that is, given a predefined description of a concept as a list of salient features, find all instances of the concept within a textual document and for each instance extract the value(s) for each of its features. The underlying

L. Monostori, J. Váncza, and M. Ali (Eds.): IEA/AIE 2001, LNAI 2070, pp. 187–196, 2001.

premise is that the same information (i.e. the same concept with the same set of features) is repeatedly instantiated in many textual documents. Specifically, for the template filling task, at least two separate modules/agents can be identified:

- The pattern matchers that are specialised for the extraction of individual feature values (e.g. dates, company names, etc.). This task is referred to as the Named Entity (NE) recognition [CUNN99] and has been tackled with many different technologies such as statistical [RAJM98], or AI technologies [MUSL98,RILO94,SODE99]. This type of agent is referred to here as a NE-Agent.
- The module that combines the information provided by the set of NE-Agents. This task is typically referred to as Template Element (TE) construction [CUNN99] and the corresponding module will be referred to here as a TE-Agent.

For template filling within this class of document, this paper presents a new technique for the automated construction of a TE-Agent (3). The method is tested for well known knowledge extraction tasks, namely the automated analysis of job adverts for computer programmers [CALI97], and Rental Ads. The results of an experimental investigation of the qualitative role of the NE/TE-Agents on the overall knowledge extraction performance will be presented and discussed (4). Finally, the implications for the general design of knowledge extraction applications will be discussed (5)

2. System Architecture

We partition the system into two components. The system architecture is showed in Figure 1. As a first step, the NE-Agents [CUNN99] extract the contents from the documents using classical IE methods. The extracted contents can then be gathered together and inserted into the predefined template by using a TE-Agent [CUNN99].

The task of NE-Agent is to find the individual feature values of the template elements. NE-Agent can use various IE methodologies to extract the contents. The possible methodologies are for example full text searching with keywords; keywords searching with similarity, regular expression pattern matching, token-based rule extracting or combination of some methodologies [XIAO00].

Many systems neglect the use of a TE-agent and rely on the NE-Agents writing directly to the template. However, we have observed that the TE-Agent is important for dealing with a number of global issues concerning the filling of a template:

1. In the structured or semi-structured documents [SODE99], a number of relations between different parts of the content can be identified and made use of, for example, the spatial relation. Such information can be used to improve the performance (accuracy) of IE.
2. If NE-Agents may find multiple values for a template element, in which one is the right value and the others are false. A TE-Agent has to find out the right one.
3. Some documents have multi-instances. That means, there are more than one template instance contained in the document. The system must be able to duplicate the template and to distinguish between the slot values of different instances.

4. Automatically generated high-performance NE-Agents typically rely on a set of localized syntactic rules. The rules have typically a high precision performance. The problem is then that the set of automatically generated NE-Agents filter too strongly – i.e. by enforcing early-on a high precision rate, the overall recall of the information extraction system is impaired.

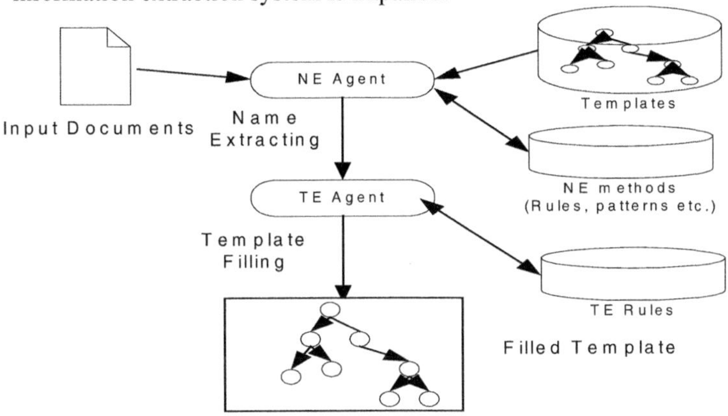

Fig. 1. System Architecture

With these observations, we have developed a type of TE-Agent to improve the total performance of template filling by tolerating and filtering the results generated by imprecise NE-Agents. In the learning phase, the TE-Agent uses statistical data to analyse spatial relations between template elements. In the extraction phase, the TE-Agent uses a greedy voting algorithm to select the best suitable value for the template element and perform an automatically duplicating if multiple instances are detected.

3. A New Approach to Template Instantiation

This section describes a new approach for the automated extraction of a TE-Profile through the exploitation of spatial relationships between the features of a template.

3.1 Automatically Generating the TE Profile = Spatial Model

For the class of document that is of interest here, significant spatial relationships are expected between the individual features of a given template– in other words, the order in which the feature instances occur is not completely random. Furthermore, the capture of these spatial relationships is a task that can be automated and achieved in a non-intrusive manner – i.e. based on observing the actions of a user carrying out the task of manually transferring information from text into the template.

The model of the spatial relationships between the feature instances corresponds to the profile of our TE-Agent. Note that the user who, in effect, trains the TE-Agent need

not be an expert user with respect to the knowledge extraction technology; they merely must be capable of reliably carrying out the template filling task manually.
Four types of possible special relationship are captured here (examples):

- DirectBefore(A,B) – i.e. an instance of feature B comes directly before feature A
- DirectAfter(A,B) – i.e. an instance of feature B comes directly before feature A
- Before(A,B) – i.e. an instance of feature B comes somewhere before feature A
- After(A,B) – i.e. an instance of feature B comes somewhere before feature A

These relationships are created based on the statistical analysis of multiple manually filled templates. The relationships are further sub-divided into:

- Constraints – i.e. spatial relationships that cannot be invalidated (they were observed always to hold)
- (Weighted) Preferences – relationships that are not always valid but have a statistically significant frequency. These relationships are typically represented as a numeric weight < 1.0.

An example of part of the TE-profile for one of the experimental tests is displayed below. Note that the After / Before relationships generally result in constraints where as the more specific Direct Before / Direct After relationships generally result in weighted preferences: this reflects a persistent overall structure for the description of each template instance although the detailed ordering of individual feature instances is less well defined. This observation justifies our classification of the document type as being semi-structured.

After Title: Salary; After City: State; ....
Direct After Title: Salary: 0.33, Req_Exp_Year: 0.26; Direct After City: State: 0.82...
Direct Before Req_Exp_Year: Title: 0.35

3.2 Applying the spatial model to filter NE-Agent results

The TE-Profile, described above can be used in order to filter the results communicated from a collection of NE-Agents – i.e. it is to be used to rule-out falsely identified feature instances while preserving the correctly identified feature instances. There are a number of possible ways in which the statistically derived information could be exploited (see future work). The algorithm tested here resolves conflicting feature instances based on a greedy voting algorithm.
The first stage is to identify conflicts. For example, for our TE-Agents, three types of conflict are possible (based on the assumption concerning document structure):

- Multiple instances for a given feature have been found, although it is known in the template that the feature has cardinality 1
- The instances of two different features occur in an order that is contradictory with respect to known constraints of the TE Profile.
- A given part of the text is used as the basis for the value of more than one template feature.

As an example, assume the following tupple reflects the order in which feature instances for a given template instance occur within the document (as communicated by the NE agents):

(Salary_1, Title_1, Reg_Exp_Year_1, City_1, Salary_2)

The conflicts that are generated w.r.t. the previously given example TE-Profile are:

Conflict1(Salary_1, Title_1) -> Salary feature must come after Title feature instance

Conflict2(Salary_1, Salary_2) -> Multiple instances of same feature

Conflicts can be resolved by eliminating one of the conflicting feature instances. This is achieved by allowing all feature instances outside of the conflict to vote for each of the conflicting instances. Namely:

$$Votes(F_{conf,i}) = \Sigma\, Vote(F_{conf,i}, F_j), \text{ where } F_j \text{ is a feature instance not in the current conflict.} \quad (1)$$

The values for Vote($F_{conf,i}$, F_j) are as follows:

- -1 if the relationship between $F_{conf,i}$ and F_j violates a known constraint
- +1 if the relationship between $F_{conf,i}$ and F_j conforms to a known constraint
- -w if the relationship between $F_{conf,i}$ and F_j violates a known Preference of weight W
- +w if the relationship between $F_{conf,i}$ and F_j conforms to a known Preference of weight w
- else 0.

For example, for Conflict1

Votes(Salary_1) = Vote (Salary_1, Reg_Exp_Year_1)+ Vote (Salary_1, City_1)+ Vote (Salary_1, Salary_2) = (0.0) + (0.0) + (0.0) = 0.0

Votes(Title_1)= Vote (Title_1, Reg_Exp_Year_1) + Vote (Title_1, City_1) + Vote (Title_1, Salary_2) = (0.26 + 0.35) + (0.0) + (1.0 – 0.33) = 1.28

The feature instance that receives least votes is eliminated from all conflicts. In other words, Salary_1 would be eliminated on the strength of Conflict1. As this also resolves Conflict2, no further action need be taken, i.e. the resultant feature instance set after the filtering by our TE-agent would be:

(Title_1, Reg_Exp_Year_1, City_1, Salary_2)

As shown in the above example, the elimination of a feature instance as a result of resolving one conflict is propagated to other conflicts. This means that the performance of the TE-Agent is sensitive to the order in which conflicts are resolved. This problem is partly solved by randomly selecting the conflict to be resolved, but there is still a significant danger of reaching a locally optimal solution. That is to say, the feature instance eliminated by resolving the first conflict is not necessarily the best feature instance to be eliminated from other untried conflicts. In this sense, we are applying a greedy optimisation algorithm. Future work will address this problem and provide a more globally optimal solution at the cost of increased computational effort.

4. Experiment Description

In this section, the performance of the TE-Agent created by the above method is tested on two standard data sets: Job advertisements and Rental Ads. Both data sets are downloaded from Repository (http://www.isi.edu/~muslea/RISE/repository.html).

4.1 Job Advertisements

The data set for the experimentation is a set of 300 job advertisements (see [CALI97] for details). Each job advert is sent as a separate email. Each template comprises 17 features such as Title, State, City, etc. Typically, the value for a feature occurs exactly once in the text, although for any given email some values may be missing.
The data set is divided into three parts of 100 job adverts. The performance was evaluated using a cross-validation approach; i.e. each experiment was repeated three times, training on each of the 100 jobs and the evaluation on the remaining jobs.
For the first experiment, the TE-Agent is trained automatically. The user manually performs the template filling task on the examples and the resulting filled templates are given to the previously described learning algorithm in order to create a TE-Profile representing the spatial dependencies between the different features. The low quality NE-Profiles are derived automatically – i.e. from all examples of the text used to fill a given slot in the template, the set of keywords is extracted and used as the basis for an NE-Profile. These low quality NE-Agents typically yields a high degree of recall but poor precision. The results of the experiment are summarised in the following table. The results of two other systems LearningPinocchio [CIRA99] and RAPIER [CALI97] are shown also in the table. The performance (precision and recall) is measured by first determining the total precision and recall for each feature independently and then taking the mean across all features.

System	Precision	Recall
Our system	86.9%	93.7%
RAPIER	65%	89%
LearningPinocchio	86%	82%

For a deep analysis the precision / recall results are measured both immediately after the NE-Agents have been applied and again after the TE-Agent has operated on the results of the NE-Agents.

	Precision	Recall
Experiment (Low Quality NE) – After NE-Agents	76.6%	94.7%
Experiment (Low Quality NE) – After TE-Agent	86.9%	93.7%

Here we can see that the automatically generated TE-Agent improves the overall precision at a minimal cost to the overall recall.
A more detailed analysis of the above results reveals that a majority of the feature values were extracted with near 100% precision / recall and that the sub-optimal performance can be attributed to the following 4 features:

	Precision	**Recall**
State (After TE_Agent)	72.2%	93.8%
City (After TE_Agent)	74.8%	94.0%
Title (After TE_Agent)	51.5%	91.2%
Des_Year (After TE_Agent)	34.0%	100.0%

This opens up a third possibility whereby the hand-crafted NE-Agents are used for these problematic features and the automatically generated NE-Agents are relied on for extracting the other features. With this third configuration for the experiments, the following set of results was achieved:

	Precision	Recall
Low Quality NE + 4 High Quality NE: After NE-Agents	89.6%	93.4%
Low Quality NE + 4 High Quality NE: After TE-Agent	96.6%	92.6%

In both experiments above, the automatically generated TE-Agent significantly improves the precision of the overall system without significantly damaging the recall.

4.2 Rental Ads

The Rental Ads domain was collected from the Seattle Times online-classified ads. To make comparison we used the same template as defined by WHISK [SODE99]. The template consists of three contents: information about neighborhoods, about price and about the number of bedrooms.

For this experiment, both the NE-Agent(s) and TE-Agent are trained automatically. We used a token-based Rule Extractor to train and extract the NE values. The token-based rules are similar to regular expressions. The token-based rules consist of three parts: precore, core and postcore. While the core describes the underlying content, the pre- and postcore define information before and after the content. The rule distinguishes number, alphabetic string and tokens. Tokens are white space and special characters (such as ",", "!", "&" etc.). Number and string are separated by tokens. For example, the rule *sf [1] {c <int> c} bed* extracts a number (between "*{c*" and "*c}*" is the underlying core), which has a string before and after it. One of the two strings "*sf*" must occur before and "*bed*" after the core. There can (but must not) be another string (specified by *[1]*) between "*sf*" and core. Rules are generated with an inductive supervised learning algorithm [XIAO00].

As for WHISK [SODE99] we used a training set of 400 examples and a test set of a further 400 examples. In this experiment the recall and precision are improved with more examples. Recall begins at 88.5% from 50 examples and climbs to 95.0% when 400 examples. Precision starts at 87.0% from 50 examples and reaches to 97.7% when 400 examples. The results are show in comparison with WHISK as following:

	Examples	**Precision**	**Recall**
WHISK	50	94%	73%
	400	98%	94%
Our system	50	87.0%	88.4%
	400	97.7%	95.0%

As for the first experiment, there is already good recall and poor precision after NE-Agent processing. However, after applying the TE-Agent the precision is improved considerable with only a slightly loss of recall. For example, in Rental Ads the system reaches 85.4% precision and 95.8% recall after NE-agent processing with 250 training examples. After applying the TE-Agent, we get 95.1% precision and 94.7% recall. Figure 2 shows the total learning curve for the Rental Ad domain.

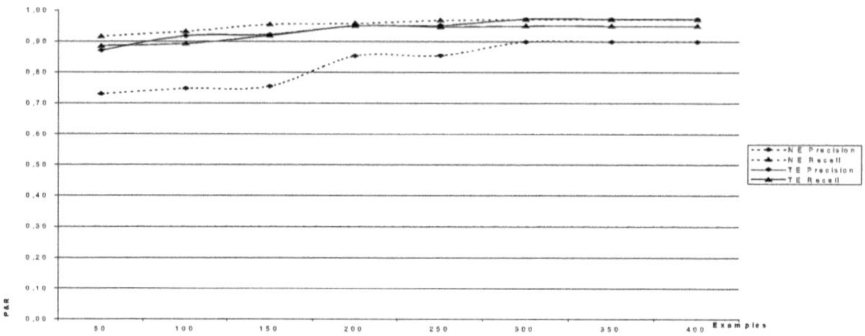

Fig. 2. Learning curve for the Rental Ad domain

5. Analysis and Discussion

The title of this paper poses the question "Where to Position the Precision in Knowledge Extraction from Text?". Within the scope of our agent-based model for the template filling task we have investigated the two possibilities of either positioning the precision early (i.e. in the NE-Agents) or late (i.e. in the TE-Agent(s)). However, our investigation has led to the interesting observation that, for an optimal performance at minimal cost knowledge extraction system, a combination is required. Moreover, the determining in which NE-Agents it is worthwhile investing the most development effort in can be guided by first testing the TE-Agent with crude, automatically generated NE-Agents.

These leads to a proposed methodology for the construction of a knowledge extraction system, at least for the sub-class of problems that involve template filling from semi-structured documents:

1. A non-expert manually performs the template filling task on a number of example documents
    1.1) An automatic learning technique is used to construct a TE-Profile (e.g. 0)
    1.2) A set of primitive NE-Agents are constructed based on the known values of template slots
2. The initial knowledge extraction system is applied to a further set of test documents
    2.1) The performance w.r.t. each feature / NE-Agent is evaluated
    2.2) The dependencies between different features in the TE-Profile is evaluated
3. An expert user manually trains NE-Agents only for the selected critical features

A weakness of the TE-Agent is that the greedy voting algorithm selects merely the "best" candidate. The algorithm is not able to decide whether all candidates are false. In such cases, the current TE-Agent will assign one of the false candidates as the "best" result and filled into template. This is a reason why the system can not reach 100% precision in a situation where some values are only optional. The main reason why we use the local optimization method (such as greedy voting) is that the system must perform a real time extracting to ensure that the user does not have to wait for a long time to get the result. Note, this consideration is less critical for an application of the system in an off-line (batch mode) IE scenario.

6. Related Work

The equivalent application problem was previously tackled by a number of IE systems, including LearningPinocchio [CIRA99] and RAPIER [CALI97]. RAPIER is an attempt to fully automated the Information Extraction task. The only input to the system is a set of manually filled templates. RAPIER creates a set of pattern matching rules for each template slot based on an inductive learning approach. While full-automation may seem a desired goal. Difference between RAPIER and our system is that RAPIER does not take into account the spatial dependencies between the various features of the template – indeed RAPIER effectively has no TE-Agent. The learning algorithm for generating rules typically requires each rule to have a high precision and recall performance so only strong rules are generated. This leads to the problem that the set of automatically generated NE-Agents filter too strongly – i.e. by enforcing early-on a high precision rate, the overall recall of the IE system is impaired.

WHISK [SODE99] performs multi-slot extraction and considers the orders of the template elements. We compare our system with WHISK with the same sample set Rental Ads. WHISK achieves 98% precision and 94% recall with 400 examples, while our system reaches 98% precision and 95% recall with same number of examples. A considerable difference is that WHISK uses background knowledge before extracting, so called *semantic class*. Such *semantic classes* are defined by user and as part of WHISK's input. This is the reason why the precision in WHISK is nearly flat regardless of the number of examples are trained. Our system does not use any predefined handcrafted background knowledge and learns all rules and patterns merely from given examples.

7. Conclusion and Future Work

This paper has provided technical ideas on the problem of template filling (knowledge extraction) from semi-structured documents. A new approach for automatically generating a TE-Agent, based on the results of a set of manually filled templates, has been detailed. The approach is based on finding spatial relationships between the features of the template w.r.t. the document positions of the values of those features. It

has been shown that this approach can significantly improve the precision of the overall system in the case where low-precision high-recall NE-Agents are first used.
The results achieved on the example applications are extremely encouraging. However, it must be noted that this data set is relatively simple; for example it may be that the example job adverts are artificially well structured in terms of the ordering of their information content.
In terms of improving the algorithm for applying a TE-Profile, the main weakness until now probably lies with the greedy approach taken to resolving the conflict set. The application of a more gradual relaxation-based technique to determining the optimal combination of feature values of the TE-Profile should be investigated.
Another major area for improvement lies in increasing the sophistication of the spatial model that comprises the TE-Profile. For many practical applications, some features will have multiple values per template instance. It is an open issue whether sufficiently strong spatial constraints can be automatically learnt and applied to eliminate false occurrences of optional and/or multi-value features. Another possible improvement to the model may be to include some other spatial relations. Examples are: a measure of distance in text , containment, table structure etc.
The practical consequence of successively improving the filtering power of the TE-Agent is to successively reduce the development burden in terms of reducing the precision requirements of the NE-Agents.

References

[CALI97]- Relational Learning of Pattern-Match Rules for Information Extraction, M E Califf and R J Mooney, Proceedings ACL-97: Workshop on Natural Language Learning

[CIRA99]- LearningPinocchio, Ciravegnd F, http://ecate.itc.it:1025/cirave/LEARNING/JOBS/home.html

[CUNN99]- Information Extraction a User Guide , H Cunningham, CS-99-07, Dept. Of Comp Sci., Uni. Of Sheffield, 1999

[MUSL98]- STALKER: Learning Extraction Rules for Semistructured, Web-based Information Sources – Muslea I, Minton S, Knoblock C, AAAI'98 Workshop "AI and Information Integration"

[RAJM98]- Text Mining – Knowledge extraction from unstructured textual data, M Rajman and Besançon - 6th Conf. of International Federation of Classification Societies

[RILO94]- Information Extraction as a Basis for High-Precision Text Classification, E Riloff and W Lehnert, ACM Transactions on Information Systems vol. 12 no. 3 1994.

[SODE99]- Learning Information Extraction Rules for Semi-Structured and Free Text, S Sonderland, Machine Learning 34, 233-272, 1999

[XIAO00]- Information Extraction from HTML: Combining XML and standard Techniques for IE from the Web, L Xiao, 2000

Generation of Similarity Measures from Different Sources

Benno Stein and Oliver Niggemann

Dept. of Mathematics and Computer Science—Knowledge-Based Systems,
University of Paderborn, D–33095 Paderborn, Germany
{stein,murray}@uni-paderborn.de

Abstract. Knowledge that quantifies the similarity between complex objects forms a vital part of problem-solving expertise within several knowledge-intensive tasks. This paper shows how implicit knowledge about object similarities is made explicit in the form of a similarity measure.
The development of a similarity measure is highly domain-dependent. We will use the domain of fluidic engineering as a complex and realistic platform to present our ideas. The evaluation of the similarity between two fluidic circuits is needed for several tasks: (*i*) Design problems can be supported by retrieving an existing circuit which resembles an (incomplete) circuit description. (*ii*) The problem of visualizing technical documents can be reduced to the problem of arranging similar documents with respect to their similarity.
The paper in hand presents new approaches for the construction of a similarity function: Based on knowledge sources that allow for an expert-friendly knowledge acquisition, machine learning is used to compute an explicit similarity function from the acquainted knowledge.
Keywords. Machine Learning, Knowledge Acquisition, Case-Based Reasoning

1 Introduction

This paper addresses a key aspect within various knowledge-based analysis and synthesis tasks: The construction of a measure that adequately models the similarity between two problem instances. This may be the similarity between two documents within a document retrieval task, the similarity between two cases within a case-based reasoning task, or a similarity assessment between two points in a graph when working on a visualization task.

When given two problem instances, a domain expert is in a position to assess the similarity between these instances with respect to a problem solving task in hand. It is a question of high importance, and it is the central question of this paper how this part of an expert's problem-solving expertise can be elicited and made explicit.

In its general form, a set of objects (problem instances), O, is given, where each object is described by a set of features $x_1, \ldots x_n$. The similarity between two objects x and y is taken to assess the usability of a solution of instance x as a solution for instance y. Usability can be stated a-posteriori only while the similarity between two objects can be stated immediately [14]. The quantification of the concept usability by means of the similarity between two feature vectors shows the crucial importance that comes up to the computation of the features.

In the following, the similarity between two objects x and y is designated by a relation "sim" where $sim(x, y)$ determines a value from the interval $[0; 1]$. The larger is the value of sim the more similar are x and y to each other.

L. Monostori, J. Váncza, and M. Ali (Eds.): IEA/AIE 2001, LNAI 2070, pp. 197–206, 2001.

1.1 Where Similarity Measures Come from

A similarity measure establishes a particular form of knowledge, which—using AI terminology—can be acquainted from some source. An often applied concept to elicit similarity knowledge is the interview of domain experts: "Are these two problem instances, x and y, similar?" "What are the significant features that make x and y similar?" "To which extent are x and y similar?"

These sample questions make problems of the concept "knowledge acquisition by questioning" obvious. On the one hand, it is hard for the domain expert to give quantifiable answers, while on the other hand, it is hard for the knowledge engineer to access the quality of these answers.

Note that a similarity measure can also be constructed from other knowledge sources; for instance from the knowledge that is encoded within an existing object classification [21]. Obviously, each classification implies knowledge about feature relevance and feature similarity with respect to the classified objects. Given such a knowledge source, methods from the field of machine learning can be used to transform implicit knowledge on object similarities into an explicit similarity measure.

In Section 4, we will concentrate on three different knowledge sources where classification knowledge can appear in:

1. *Partial Similarity Quantification.* Similarity assessments are known for only a subset of $O \times O$, which is called the learning set here.
2. *Partitioning of O.* The knowledge on object similarity is encoded through the division of (a subset of) O into equivalence classes respecting particular similarity aspects.
3. *Graphical Similarity Specification.* The knowledge on object similarity is encoded within geometric distances of a 2-dimensional plot.

The development of a similarity measure is highly domain dependent. Hence we will introduce a particular domain from which the object set O is drawn and which will serve as realistic example throughout the paper. This domain is the domain of fluidic engineering.

2 Using Similarity Measures in Fluidic Engineering

Similarity measures can be used for those tasks in fluidic engineering that are not treated at a deep, physical level of behavior but at the much more abstract level of function. At this level, the complex physics of a fluidic circuit is reduced to a set of features which characterizes the circuit's usability to fulfill a desired function. The following list outlines tasks that are solved at an abstract functional level.

- *Functional Analysis.* Check whether two fluidic systems are similar with respect to their intended operation [22].
- *Fluidic System Design.* Construct a new fluidic system by coupling together already designed units (fluidic axes) from different systems [20,9].
- *Document Retrieval.* Query a database for diagrams of fluidic systems that are similar with respect to a given set of demands.

The model of fluidic function as specified in Definition 1 establishes the knowledge level at which the mentioned tasks are solved. Subsection 3.2 shows in which way this functional model is encoded as a feature vector for fluidic circuit objects.

Taken an engineer's point of view, the gist of a model of fluidic function consists of a set of state variables, F_X, along with the discrete state prescription function, Δ. Each state variable in F_X represents a subfunction of a fluidic axis; Δ characterizes the behavior of the fluidic axes by means of the working phases of the output units, which are cylinders in most cases.

Definition 1 (Model of Fluidic Function). *Let S be a fluidic system. A model of fluidic function of S is a discrete event model* $\langle F_X, F_Y, \mathcal{X}, \mathcal{Y}, \Delta, \Lambda\rangle$ *whose elements are defined as follows.*

1. F_X *is the set of state variables. Each state variable corresponds one-to-one to a fluidic axis in S and defines the phases that can be adopted by this axis. Hence,* $|F_X|$ *is the total number of axes in S.* F_Y *is the set of output variables, defining the positions, the velocities, and the pressures at the working elements within the fluidic axes.*
2. *The sets* X_f *and* Y_f *designate the domains of the variables f in* F_X *and* F_Y *respectively. Likewise,* $\mathcal{X}$ *designate the Cartesian product of the state variable domains, and* $\mathcal{Y}$ *designate the Cartesian product of the output variable domains.*
3. $\Delta : \mathbf{R}^+ \to \mathcal{X}$ *is the discrete state prescription function and specifies the phase transitions of a model of fluidic function. Given a point in time,* $t \in \mathbf{R}^+$, Δ *determines a vector of phases.*
4. $\Lambda : \mathcal{X} \times \mathbf{R}^+ \to \mathcal{Y}$ *is the output function. Given a vector of phases,* $\mathbf{x} \in \mathcal{X}$, *and a point in time,* $t \in \mathbf{R}^+$, Λ *determines an output vector,* $\mathbf{y} \in \mathcal{Y}$.

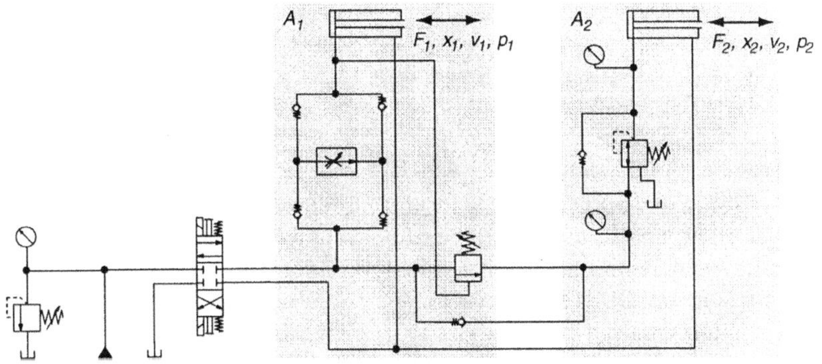

Fig. 1. Hydraulic circuit with two axes A_1, A_2. $F_1, F_2, x_1, x_2, v_1, v_2, p_1$, and p_2 designate the forces, positions, velocities, and pressures respectively that are necessary to define a functional model of the circuit.

Example. The example specifies the functional model of the fluidic system in Figure 1. The shown circuit contains two axes each of which having three states, say, phases.

1. *Variables.* $F_X = \{P_1, P_2\}$, $F_Y = \{x_1, x_2, v_1, v_2, p_1, p_2\}$, $F = F_X \cup F_Y$.

2. *Domains.* $X_{P_1} = X_{P_2} = \{$*constant-drive-in, constant-drive-out, fast-drive, null-phase, hold-pressure*$\}$, $Y_f = \mathbf{R}^+$, $f \in \{x_1, x_2, p_1, p_2\}$, $Y_{v_1} = Y_{v_2} = \mathbf{R}$.
3. *State Prescription.* $\Delta : \mathbf{R}^+ \to X_{P_1} \times X_{P_2}$. Given an absolute point in time t, the function Δ is given in Table 1 (left-hand side).

Table 1. State prescription (left-hand side) and output function (position-time diagrams, right-hand side) of the hydraulic axes, A_1, A_2.

t	P_1	P_2
[0; 1.6)	*constant-drive-out*	*null-phase*
[1.6; 3.2)	*constant-drive-in*	*hold-pressure*
[3.2; 4.0)	*null-phase*	*fast-drive*
≥ 4.0	*null-phase*	*null-phase*

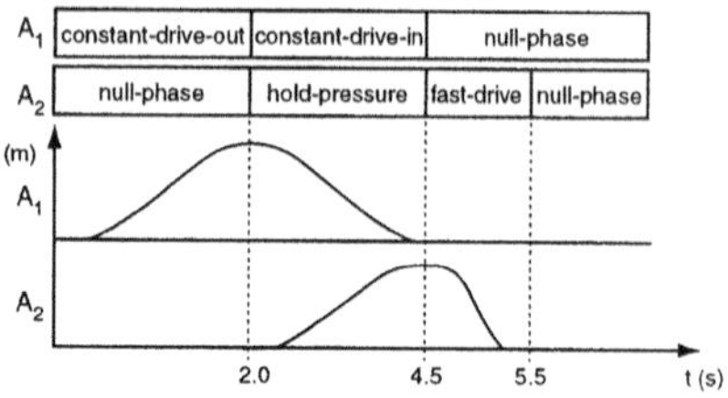

4. *Output Function.* Typically, the output function is represented by means of different graphs which show the courses of the positions, velocities, or pressures at the working elements for a particular input. The right-hand side of Table 1 shows the phase transitions and position-time diagrams for a particular input.

Remarks. The abstraction from a physical behavior model, which is grounded on continuous time, towards a functional model, which is event-based, can be done automatically. For this, the state prescription function of the continuous time model is simulated and investigated with respect to intervals of stationary velocity. However, the development of such an abstraction is not discussed in this place.

3 Learning Similarity Measures

Since any automatic comparison between fluidic drawings themself is hardly possible, an abstract circuit description has to be found. The functional model developed in Section 2 captures the abstract aspects of fluidic drawings that are also used by an expert to assess circuit similarities.

The subject of this section is the application of learning methods to the construction of similarity measures. These algorithms bridge the gap between implicit expert knowledge about circuit similarities and explicit similarity functions.

In order to apply machine learning, the functional model has to be encoded into a so-called feature vector. A feature vector is a list of values describing an system. For instance, ⟨Smith, James, 1967, 85 kg⟩ is a feature vector describing a person.

3.1 On Similarity Measures in General

Much work has been done in the last decades on similarity measures; good overviews can be found in [16,7,12,23,15]. A common similarity measure is the simple weighted linear similarity function. Let $(f_1^{(1)}, \ldots, f_p^{(1)}), (f_1^{(2)}, \ldots, f_p^{(2)}), p \in \mathbf{N}$ be two feature vectors. Then the simple weighted linear similarity measure is defined as:

$$\sum_{1 \le i \le p} w_i \cdot (f_i^{(1)} \ominus f_i^{(2)}), w_i \in \mathbf{R}$$

The definition of the operator $\ominus$ depends on the feature's type:

- *Cardinal.* We call a features cardinal if and only if all values of the feature are real numbers. Typical cardinal features are height, temperature, or distances. Values of cardinal features can be added, subtracted, multiplied, and divided and the result is still a reasonable value for the feature. For cardinal features, $x \ominus y$ is normally defined as $|x - y|$, i. e. the simple weighted linear similarity measure can be rewritten as $\sum_{1 \le i \le p} w_i \cdot |f_i^{(1)} - f_i^{(2)}|, w_i \in \mathbf{R}$.
- *Nominal.* Nominal values can only be compared with respect to equality. Name or profession of a person are nominal features. If a nominal feature has only two possible values (e. g. gender of a person), it is called a binary feature. For nominal features, x, y, the following definition is often used [24]:

$$x \ominus y = \begin{cases} 0, \text{ if } x = y \\ 1, \text{ otherwise} \end{cases}$$

Note that learning such functions means finding values for the parameters w_i. More complex distance functions have been examined by the authors in [21].

3.2 A Similarity Measure for Fluidic Systems

As described in Section 2, each fluidic system S can be reduced to a functional model. In accordance with [9,22], the similarity between two hydraulic systems, S_1, S_2, is defined using the similarities between individual axes in the respective circuits:

$$sim(S_1, S_2) = \sum_{A_1 \in \mathcal{A}_1} \max\{sim_{axes}(A_1, A_2) \mid A_2 \in \mathcal{A}_2\}$$

where $\mathcal{A}_1$ denotes the axes of S_1, $\mathcal{A}_2$ denotes the axes of S_2, sim_{axes} denotes a function measuring the similarity between two axes, and $|\mathcal{A}_1| \le |\mathcal{A}_2|$ holds.

For two axes, A_1, A_2, the similarity function $sim_{axes}(A_1, A_2)$ is defined by the function $sim(\boldsymbol{f}(A_1), \boldsymbol{f}(A_2))$ where $\boldsymbol{f}(A_i)$ denotes a vector of cardinal features describing A_i, i. e. $\boldsymbol{f}(A_i) \in \mathbf{R}^m, i = 1, 2$. In the following text, the simple weighted linear similarity function $sim(\boldsymbol{f}(A_1), \boldsymbol{f}(A_2)) = \sum_{i=1}^{m} w_i \cdot |f_i^1 - f_i^2|$ is used.

The feature vector of fluidic axes, $\boldsymbol{f}(A)$, which is necessary to compute the similarity between two fluidic circuits, S_1, S_2, can directly be extracted from the functional models of S_1 and S_2. Each axis is described by two types of features: (*i*) phase descriptions and (*ii*) phase orders. These groups of features are defined as follows.

(*i*) *Phase Descriptions.* Phases are classified into the categories *constant-drive, position-drive, hold-position, accelerate, fast-drive, hold-pressure*, and *press*; each category in turn is characterized by 6 features:

1. How many phases of the specific category exist in the respective axis?
2. How long (in seconds) is the duration of the phase ?
3. Which distance (in mm) is covered by the working element?
4. Which force (in Newton) is applied to the working element?
5. How precisely must the axis work? This is a value from [0; 1] that defines the acceptable deviations from the duration, the distance, and the force.

(*ii*) *Phase Orders.* These 49 features $f^{\text{ord}}_{i,j}$, $1 \leq i, j \leq 7$ capture the order of the phases. For example, $f^{\text{ord}}_{1,2}$ is the number of times a phase of category 1 (*constant-drive*) is directly followed by a phase of category 2 (*position-drive*).

Together, the feature vector $\boldsymbol{f}(A)$ for an axis A is of the following form:

$$f(A) = \big(\ (\text{phase description } \textit{constant-drive}),\ (\text{phase description } \textit{position-drive}),\\ (\text{phase description } \textit{hold-position}),\ (\text{phase description } \textit{accelerate}),\\ (\text{phase description } \textit{fast-drive}),\ (\text{phase description } \textit{hold-pressure}),\\ (\text{phase description } \textit{press}),\ (\text{phase orders})\ \big)^T$$

Related to the example from Page 3, the feature vectors for the axes A_1 and A_2 are given as follows.

$$f(A_1) = \big(\ \underbrace{(2, 1.6, 500, 300, 0.8), (), (), (), (), (), ()}_{\text{phase descriptions}}, \underbrace{(1, 0, \ldots, 0)}_{\text{phase orders}}\ \big)^T$$

$$f(A_2) = \big(\ \overbrace{(), (), (), (), (1, 0.8, 500, 0, 0.6), (1, 1.6, 500, 2000, 0.8), ()},\\ \underbrace{(0, \ldots, 0, 1, 0, 0, 0, 0, 0, 0, 0, 0, 0)}_{\text{phase orders}}\ \big)^T$$

3.3 Methods for Constructing Similarity Measures

Existing methods for constructing similarity measures can be divided into two main classes: (*i*) Methods that employ reinforcement-learning and (*ii*) algorithms that rely on statistical analysis for the main part.

Reinforcement-learning methods predict a similarity value and ask the user or a different system to rate the prediction. Based on this rating the weights w_i are adjusted. Statistical methods analyze given examples and deduce appropriate weights. Table 2 lists representatives of well known methods; more examples can be found in [4,1,19].

Table 2. Selected existing methods for the construction of similarity measures.

Name	Type	Remarks	Literature
EACH	reinforcement-learning	extra parameters needed	[17]
RELIEF	reinforcement-learning	binary weights	[13]
CCF	statistical	only binary features	[6]
GM-CDW	statistical		[11]

These methods have in common that the knowledge acquisition step (how to obtain the necessary knowledge from an expert) and the learning step (finding appropriate values for the weights w_i) are not treated separately. Our approach, which is described in the next section, differentiates between these two steps.

Combining the knowledge acquisition step and the learning step entails several problems:

- Since the expert is integrated into such methods in a predefined manner, no flexibility is granted in the way the knowledge is obtained. Hence additional knowledge sources cannot be tapped.

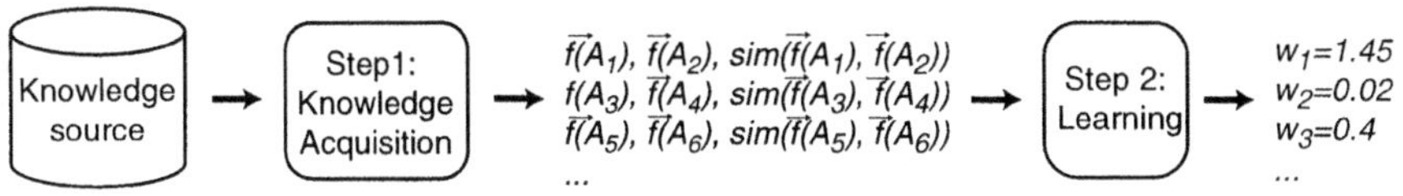

Fig. 2. The general framework for the construction of similarity measures.

- Although the methods mentioned in Table 2 rely on standard learning paradigms such as reinforcement learning, they do not apply standard learning algorithms such as regression or neural networks but employ proprietary algorithms. While for standard learning algorithms advantages and disadvantages have been examined, almost nothing is known about the proprietary algorithms.
- Verifying a combined method is difficult since learning problems cannot be distinguished from knowledge acquisition problems.

3.4 A General Framework

Figure 2 shows the general framework for constructing similarity measures used in this paper: Two main steps are identified, a knowledge acquisition step and a learning step. This separation allows for the usage of both different acquisition methods and different learning methods to obtain the necessary information from an expert. The first step always results in a set of feature-vector-pairs whose similarity is known (see Figure 2), e. g. $\{(\boldsymbol{A}_1, \boldsymbol{A}_2, sim(\boldsymbol{f}(A_1), \boldsymbol{f}(A_2))), (\boldsymbol{A}_3, \boldsymbol{A}_4, sim(\boldsymbol{f}(A_3), \boldsymbol{f}(A_4))), \ldots\}$

The second step uses the rated vector pairs and applies a supervised learning strategy to find values for the weights w_i. For our applications both regression and neural networks have been used. Note that only a small but typical set of objects, the learning set, is used for learning purposes.

4 Knowledge Acquisition

In Section 3, the definition of similarities between fluidic circuit has been reduced to the problem of finding similarities between fluidic axes. Finding such similarities poses a knowledge acquisition problem, because experts have the necessary knowledge only implicitly. When asked to express their knowledge about axes similarities explicitly as a mathematical function, most experts are overstrained.

Below, three methods that tackle the knowledge acquisition problem are presented. The methods differ from each other in the explicitness of the underlying knowledge source.

4.1 Knowledge Source 1: Partial Similarity Quantification

This technique is quite simple: The expert assesses the similarity of m axes pairs which are presented to him, e. g. on a scale from 0 to 10. These assessments are used to learn a similarity measure which then is used to compute the similarity between n, $n \gg m$, pairs of axes.

Exploiting this knowledge source has disadvantages:

- If m axes are used to build the measure, the expert has to rate $\frac{m^2}{2} - m$ object pairs.
- The similarities have to be comparable; i. e., the expert has to decide whether object A is more similar to object B then object C to D. Such decisions turn out to be quite difficult.

In the field of statistics, the problem of assessing object similarity is well known. Most methods,[1] such as ranking, free sorting, or anchor stimulus, rely on a user who defines all object similarities. Hence, no learning or abstraction mechanisms are applied.

4.2 Knowledge Source 2: Partitioning the Set of Objects

For this method the expert has to classify the axes. Two axes are similar if and only if they belong to the same class. Let $\mathcal{A} = \{A_1, \ldots, A_n\}$ be the set of axes and let $c : \mathcal{A} \rightarrow \mathcal{C}$ be the classification function, where $\mathcal{C}$ comprises the set of possible classes. The classification function c is specified by the domain expert. Then the similarity sim is defined as follows.

$$\forall_{A_1, A_2, \in \mathcal{A}} : \; sim(\boldsymbol{f}(A_1), \boldsymbol{f}(A_2)) = \begin{cases} 1, \text{ if } c(A_1) = c(A_2) \\ 0, \text{ otherwise} \end{cases}$$

Reasonable classes, for example, are $\mathcal{C} = \{$*manipulation, press, hold*$\}$ or $\mathcal{C} = \{$*high-pressure, low-pressure, fast-drive*$\}$.

The main disadvantage bound up with this knowledge source is that a partitioning, say, a disjunctive classification, is sometimes difficult to be stated. The advantages of this knowledge source are:

- n classifications define $\frac{n^2}{2}$ similarities.
- Domain experts have few problems in classifying fluidic axes.

Although in the learning set only the similarity values 0 and 1 are given, learning algorithms like regression result in similarity measures that can yield any similarity value from the interval $[0; 1]$. This is because the given data is abstracted by the learning algorithms.

4.3 Knowledge Source 3: Graphical Similarity Specification

The method presented now demands a minimum of explicit knowledge. The expert is asked for an exemplary visualization of his understanding of the similarity between objects. By means of a computer, this visualization is abstracted towards a graph, from which a similarity measure is computed. No additional knowledge is demanded from the expert, i. e., this method can always be applied.

Again let $\mathcal{A} = \{A_1, \ldots, A_n\}$ be the set of axes. The expert manually defines a layout by specifying a function $\rho : \mathcal{A} \rightarrow \mathbf{N} \times \mathbf{N}$, which defines a two-dimensional position for each axis. The similarity of two axes A_1, A_2 is defined by:

$$sim(\boldsymbol{f}(A_1), \boldsymbol{f}(A_2)) = -||A_1, A_2||_2$$

where $||x, y||_2$ denotes the Euclidean distance between the positions of x and y.

[1] Good overviews can be found in [2,5].

The following points distinguish this knowledge source from the previous one:

- The graphical definition of similarities is closer to the mental model of the user than is the definition of a classification function c.
- By placing n objects, $\frac{n^2}{2}$ similarities are defined.

A difficulty of the graphical similarity specification is that by placing one axis, the distances to $n - 1$ other objects must be taken into account. To simplify this layout problem, only object distances up to certain maximum distance are considered. For this, the layout is clustered in a first step, say, groups of closely related objects are identified.

5 Learning and Results

Input for the learning step (cf. Figure 2) was a set of rated axes pairs $\{(\boldsymbol{A}_1, \boldsymbol{A}_2, sim(\boldsymbol{f}(A_1), \boldsymbol{f}(A_2))), (\boldsymbol{A}_3, \boldsymbol{A}_4, sim(\boldsymbol{f}(A_3), \boldsymbol{f}(A_4))), \ldots\}$, which was used to find values for the weights w_i of the similarity function $sim(\boldsymbol{f}(A_1), \boldsymbol{f}(A_2)) = \sum_{i=1}^{m} w_i \cdot |f_i^1 - f_i^2|$. Learning was done by applying least-square regression and by means of neural networks. Details can be found in [3,18,25,10].

The acquisition methods described in Subsection 4.2 (knowledge source 2) and 4.3 (knowledge source 3) have been implemented and applied to the learning of similarity measures for fluidic axes.

- *Knowledge Source 2.* 67 fluidic axes were classified into 9 classes by a domain expert. Using the method described on Page 8, a similarity measure was constructed. The error rate was defined as the percentage of axes pairs whose similarity was assessed incorrectly by the learned measure. The error rate on the learning set[2] was 12%, while the error rate on a test set[3] was 16%. Obviously, a good similarity measure has been constructed.
- *Knowledge Source 3.* A graphical arrangement of circuit documents, which has been proposed by the domain expert, was analyzed and similarity measures were constructed. To evaluate the quality of the learned measures the Mean Square Error (MSE) was used:

$$\sqrt{\sum_{A_i, A_j} (sim^t(A_i, A_j) - sim^e(A_i, A_j))^2},$$

  A_i and A_j denote fluidic axes, sim^t denotes the similarity as predicted by the learned similarity measure, and sim^e denotes the empirical similarity measure defined by the manual layout. On a test set, an MSE of 0.22 has been achieved. All similarity values are from the interval $[0, 1]$, hence the MSE defines an average variation from the correct similarity. I. e., also with this knowledge source a good similarity measure could be constructed.

[2] The learning set comprised axes pairs used for the learning process.

[3] The axes pairs in the test set have not been used for the learning process.

References

1. D. Aha. Tolerating noisy, irrelevant, and novel attributes in instance-based learning algorithms. *International Journal of Man-Machine Studies*, 1992.
2. K. Backhaus, B. Erichson, W. Plinke, and R. Weber. *Multiv. Anaylsem.*. Springer, 1996.
3. R. Beale and T. Jackson. *Neural Computing*. Inst. of Physics, Bristol, Phil., 1994.
4. A. Bonzano, P. Cunningham, and B. Smyth. Using introspective learning to improve retrieval in cbr: A case study in air traffic control. In *Second ICCBR Conf.*, 1997.
5. I. Borg and P. Groenen. *Modern Multidimensional Scaling*. Springer, 1997.
6. R. H. Creecy, B. M. Masand, S. Smith, and D. Waltz. Trading mips and memory for knowledge engineering. *Communications of the ACM*, 35, 1992.
7. B. S. Everitt. Cluster analysis. Eward Arnolds, New York, Toronto, 1993.
8. F. Hayes-Roth, D. Waterman, and D. Lenat. *Building Expert Systems*. Addison Wesley Publishing Company, London, 1983.
9. M. Hoffmann. *Zur Automatisierung des Designprozesses fluidischer Systeme*. Diss., Univ. of Paderborn, Dept. of Mathematics and Computer Science, 1999.
10. D. W. Hosmer and S. Lemeshow. *Applied Logistic Regression*. Wiley & Sons, NY, 1989.
11. N. Howe and C. Cardie. Examining locally varying weights for nearest neighbor algorithms. In *Proceedings of the Eleventh ICML*. Morgan Kaufmann, 1997.
12. M. Jambu. *Explorative Datenanalyse*. Gustav Fischer Verlag, 1992.
13. K. Kira and L. Rendell. A practical approach to feature selection. In *Proceedings of the Ninth International Conference on Machine Learning*, 1992.
14. B. Nebel. Plan Modification versus Plan Generation. In A. Horz, editor, *7. Workshop "Planen und Konfigurieren", Hamburg*, number 723 in Arbeitspapiere der GMD, 1993.
15. A. Reckmann. Ähnlichkeitsmaße und deren Parametrisierung für die fallbasierte Diagnose am Beispiel einer medizinischen Anwendung. Master's thesis, Univ. of Paderborn, 1999.
16. M. M. Richter. Introduction to CBR. In M. Lenz, B. Bartsch-Spörl, H.-D. Burkhard, and S. Weß, editors, *Case-Based Reasoning Technology. From Foundations to Applications*, Lecture Notes in Artificial Intelligence 1400, pages 1–15. Berlin: Springer-Verlag, 1998.
17. S. L. Salzberg. A nearest hyperrectangle learning method. *Machine Learning*, 1991.
18. W. S. Sarle. Neural Networks and Statistical Models. In *9th Annual SAS Users Group Intl. Conf.*, 1994. SAS Instit. Inc.
19. C. Stanfill and D. Waltz. Toward memory-based learning. *Communications of the ACM*, 29:1213–1228, 1986.
20. B. Stein. Optimized Design of Fluidic Drives—Objectives and Concepts. Techn. Rep. tr-ri-97-189, Uni. of Paderborn, Depart. of Mathematics and Computer Science, 1996.
21. B. Stein, O. Niggemann, and U. Husemeier. Learning Complex Similarity Measures. In *Jahrestagung der Gesellschaft für Klassifikation*, Bielefeld, Germany, 1999.
22. E. Vier. *Automatisierter Entwurf geregelter Hydrostatischer Systeme*, volume 795 of *Fortschritt-Berichte VDI. Reihe 8*. VDI, Düsseldorf, 1999.
23. S. Wess. Fallbasiertes Problemlösen in wissensbasierten Systemen zur Entscheidungsunterstützung und Diagnostik: Grundlagen, Systeme und Anwendungen. Technical report, Sankt Augustin: Infix, 1996.
24. D. Wilson and T. Martinez. Improved Heterogeneous Distance Functions. *Journal of Artificial Intelligence Research*, 6, 1997.
25. T. Wonnacott and R. Wonnacott. Regression: a second course in statistics. John Wiley & Sons, New York, Chichester/Brisbane/Toronto, 1981.

SNN: A Supervised Clustering Algorithm

Jesús S. Aguilar, Roberto Ruiz, José C. Riquelme, and Raúl Giráldez

Department of Computer Science. University of Sevilla
Avda. Reina Mercedes s/n. 41011 Sevilla. Spain.
aguilar@lsi.us.es

Abstract. In this paper, we present a new algorithm based on the nearest neighbours method, for discovering groups and identifying interesting distributions in the underlying data in the labelled databases. We introduces the theory of nearest neighbours sets in order to base the algorithm S-NN (Similar Nearest Neighbours). Traditional clustering algorithms are very sensitive to the user-defined parameters and an expert knowledge is required to choose the values. Frequently, these algorithms are fragile in the presence of outliers and any adjust well to spherical shapes. Experiments have shown that S-NN is accurate discovering arbitrary shapes and density clusters, since it takes into account the internal features of each cluster, and it does not depend on a user-supplied static model. S-NN achieve this by collecting the nearest neighbours with the same label until the enemy is found (it has not the same label). The determinism and the results offered to the researcher turn it into a valuable tool for the representation of the inherent knowledge to the labelled databases.

Keywords: clustering, supervised learning, nearest neighbours.

1. Introduction

In the area of the supervised learning there are several techniques to classify a new example from the labelled database from which the inherent knowledge has been obtained. The form in which it estates the knowledge is dependent on the technique (decision rules, decision trees, association rules, etc.); however, some methods do not provide that knowledge limiting themselves to carry out the classification (neuronal networks, Bayesian model, nearest neighbours, etc.).

From the works of [3], [5], [9], [6], [7], [4], [10], [11], or more recently [12], [8], and [1] the research has been mainly focused on the convergence of the method, the search of prototypes or surfaces of separation, the techniques of editing and condensing and in the acceleration of algorithm. However, there has not been any interest on providing to the technique of the nearest neighbours a form to represent the inherent knowledge to the information.

Clustering, in Data Mining, is a useful technique for grouping data points such that points in a single cluster have similar characteristics (or are close to each other). Traditional clustering algorithms are applied in the area of the learning non-supervised.

S-NN employs a novel hierarchical clustering algorithm based on the nearest neighbour techniques. S-NN stars with each input as a separate cluster and at each successive step merges the clusters with identical neighbours. We collect all the

L. Monostori, J. Váncza, and M. Ali (Eds.): IEA/AIE 2001, LNAI 2070, pp. 207-216, 2001.

neighbours that their distances are shorter than the first enemy, that is to say, with not the same label.

The remainder of the paper in organised as follows. In section 2 and 3, we survey basis contents of the theory of the nearest neighbours' sets. These hard definitions allow us apply the supervised clustering algorithm. The step involved en clustering using S-NN are described in Section 4. In Section 5, we present the results of our experiments. Section 6 concludes and presents our ideas for future work.

2. Basic Concepts

Before beginning to describe the near set theory, we have to mention the concepts of the classic theory of sets that are necessary for the development of that theory. We will use the operations known on sets: $\in$, $\cup$, $\cap$ and # (cardinal of a set). Also we will use the logic operations on the set *{F, T}* (false and true): $\wedge$, $\vee$, and $\neg$; and the following generalisations: $\forall$ (universal quantifier) and $\exists$ (existential quantifier), where

$$z = \forall i : D(\bar{x}).E \equiv E(x_1) \wedge E(x_2) \wedge ...E(x_n)\,) \qquad \textbf{(1)}$$
$$z = \exists i : D(\bar{x})\cdot E \equiv E(x_1) \vee E(x_2) \vee \ldots \vee E(x_n)$$

and z is T if all the expressions (if some of the expressions) $E(x_i)$ are T in the domain D for $\bar{x} = (x_1,...,x_n)$, if we consider the universal quantifier (existential quantifier).

Definition 1 (Sequence): a sequence is a finite or infinite collection of elements with an inherent order of access (sequential). It is always begun by first and to accede to any element *i*, it will be necessary to pass through *i-1* previous. Since its definition is inherited of sets, it also inherits the operations associated to these $\in$, $\cup$, $\cap$, - and #.

Likewise, we defined the following operations for sequence *S* of elements of *T* type: *<>:* $\rightarrow S$ (empty sequence); *_+_:S×T* $\rightarrow S$ (insertion of an element in the end of the sequence); *[_]:S×N* $\rightarrow T$ (access to *i*th element of the sequence, with $i \in \{1... \#S\}$); and $+$i:D·E (generalised concatenation of sequences), where

$$+\, i : \{1..k\}\cdot s(i) = \mathrm{s(1) + s(2) + ... + s(k)} \qquad \textbf{(2)}$$

with *s(i)* sequences. By convenience, it will be written as $\overset{k}{\underset{i=1}{+}} s(i)$.

Definition 2 (Ordered Sequence): a sequence *s*, of size *#s* is ordered if it satisfies:

$$\forall i : \{1..(\# s) - 1\}\cdot s[i] \leq_T s[i+1] \qquad \textbf{(3)}$$

where $\leq_T$ is an established relation of total order between the elements of *T* type of the sequence.

3. Definitions

Definition 3 (Attribute): attribute *A* is defined by a set of values. The attribute can be continuous or discrete. If the attribute is continuous, the set of values will be limited by the extreme values of an interval, forming therefore the rank of values for the attribute. If the attribute is discrete, the set of values of this one will appear like an enumeration of the possible values of the attribute. We will name *C* the set of values that can adopt the label.
Definition 4 (Example): an example E is one row formed by the Cartesian product of the attributes of condition and decision. Likewise, we defined the following operations to get to the attributes of condition or their label.

$$\mathrm{atr}: \mathrm{E} \times \mathrm{N} \rightarrow \mathrm{A} \quad \mathrm{etiq}: \mathrm{E} \rightarrow \mathrm{C} \qquad (4)$$

Definition 5 (Universe): the universe *U* is a sequence of examples. We will say that a database with *n* examples, each one of them with *m* attributes (the last one is denominated label), will form the particular universe from this moment. Then *U=<u[1]...,u[n]>*.

Since we will model the database with a sequence, the access for an example of the database will be made by means of the access to the sequence, that is to say, the sequence is *s*, then *s[i]* represents the example *i*th of the database. To accede to *j*th attribute of the example, since we have modelled to this one with one row, one will become *atr(s[i],j)*, and to know its label, *etiq(s[i])*.
Definition 6 (Distance): the distance between two examples is a function that fulfils the properties of a metric space, that is to say,

$$d: E \times E \rightarrow \Re^{+} \cup \{0\} \qquad (5)$$

with the following properties: reflective, defined nonnegative, symmetrical and transitive.

Since the examples belong to a sequence, we can redefine the distance basing on the position that these examples occupy in the sequence, therefore, compute the range between two examples e_i and e_j, we will do *d(i,j)*.
Definition 7 (Sequence of Distances): sequence *SD(i)* formed by the distances of an example *i* to all the others, and is defined by

$$SD(i) = \mathop{+}_{j=1}^{\#s} (j, d(i,j)) \qquad (6)$$

In the universe *U*, the sequence associated for the first example will be: *SD(1)=<(1,d(1,1)),(2,d(1,2)),(3,d(1,3))>* and each element of the sequence are a pair formed by the position of the example for which it is wanted to compute the range and the value of the distance. Hence, in the expression *(j,d(i,j))* the first coordinate is the index of an example and the second coordinate is the distance of an example *i* for the example whose index is indicated in the first coordinate. In order to access to each one of the two coordinates easily we defined two operations on the pair:

$$\mathrm{ind}: \mathrm{N} \times \Re \rightarrow \mathrm{N} \quad \mathrm{dist}: \mathrm{N} \times \Re \rightarrow \Re \qquad (7)$$

Definition 8 (Ordered Sequence of Distances): as of a sequence *P* of pairs (index, distance), we can obtain a sequence *Q* ordered by the distance if this one fulfils the following property:

$$\forall j:\{1..\#Q-1\}\cdot dist(Q[j]) \le dist(Q[j+1]) \wedge \forall j:\{1..\#Q\}\cdot \exists k:\{1..\#P\}\cdot ind(P[k]) = ind(Q[j]) \quad \textbf{(8)}$$

that we can be resumed like *ordered(Q,P)*. A ordered sequence *OSD(i)* of distances fulfils *ordered(OSD(i), SD(i))*.

Definition 9 (Relation of Neighbourhood): two examples whose positions in the ordered sequence are *i* and *j* are neighbours to a third *k* if in the ordered sequence of distances of example *k*, *OSD(k)*, any example between *i* and *j* does not exist (or between *j* and *i*) whose label is different from which they have *i* and *j*. Therefore, if examples *i* and *j* do not have the same label, are not neighbours. The relation can be defined of the following way:

$$R_k=\{(u[ind(OSD(k)[i])],u[ind(OSD(k)[j])])\in U^2 \mid \forall h:\{min(i,j)+1..max(i,j)-1\}) \cdot(etiq(u[ind(OSD(k)[i])])=etiq(u[ind\ (OSD(k)[j])])=etiq(u[ind(OSD(k)[h])])\} \quad \textbf{(9)}$$

For example, it is *OSD(1)=<(1,0),(4,1),(5,2),(34,3),(3,4)>*, we will say that examples 4 and 3 are neighbours of 1 if examples 4 and 3 have the same label and all the examples that are between these (5 and 34) have the same label that those too.

Definition 10 (Class of Neighbours of an Example i respect to another Example k): class of neighbours of an example *i* is defined respect to another *k* like all those that in the ordered sequence of distances of *k* can be grouped around *i* in a region of examples of the same class. The class is defined from the neighbourhood relation as it follows: $[\,i]_k=\{j\in N \mid u[i\,]\ R_k\ u[j]\}$

This class of neighbours can also be understood like a sequence, because intrinsically an order relative to the distance exists [2].

Definition 11 (Ordered Subsequence of Order k respect to an Example i): given to the relation of neighbourhood and the definition of class of neighbours, we can construct the ordered sequence of distances of an example *i* from the concatenation of ordered subsequences, that is to say,

$$OSD(i)=OSD(i)_1+OSD(i)_2+\ldots +OSD(i)_k+\ldots +OSD(i)_z \quad \textbf{(10)}$$

where every subsequence $OSD(i)_k$ is constructed from the classes of separates examples in relation to *i*. This way, each $OSD(i)_k$ is a class of examples whose attribute of decision is the same one, but that differs from the decision attribute of the classes $OSD(i)_{k-1}$ and $OSD(i)_{k+1}$. Therefore, we could represent the database (together with the information relative to the distances) of the following way:

$$\begin{array}{l} OSD(1)=OSD(1)_1+OSD(1)_2+\ldots +OSD(1)_{k1} \\ OSD(2)=OSD(2)_1+OSD(2)_2+\ldots +OSD(2)_{k2} \\ \ldots\ldots\ldots\ldots\ldots\ldots\ldots\ldots\ldots\ldots \\ OSD(n)=OSD(n)_1+OSD(n)_2+\ldots +OSD(n)_{kn} \end{array} \quad \textbf{(11)}$$

where $K_i \in \{1..n\}$; however, if some K_i were 1, all the examples would belong to the same class, and the more it approaches *n*, in principle, the more homogeneously distributed will be the examples of the same class in the database.

Since the sequence *OSD* has got associated with each element an example and the distance to it, we are going to do without the distance now to associate for each example of the database a sequence of classes, where the concatenation of all of them will group the total of examples of the database. Hence we will have associated for each example (preceding to the symbol ≈) an indefinite number of classes in a specific order that implicitly contains the information about the "proximity" of these for the example of the beginning. Then,

$$\begin{aligned} [1] &\approx [1]_1 + [1]_2 + \ldots + [1]_{k1} \\ [2] &\approx [2]_1 + [2]_2 + \ldots + [2]_{k2} \\ &\ldots\ldots \\ [n] &\approx [n]_1 + [n]_2 + \ldots + [n]_{kn} \end{aligned} \quad \textbf{(12)}$$

it indicates that example *k* has a class of neighbouring examples $[k]_1$ whose labels are the same ones that the one of *k*. Afterwards, there is another class of neighbouring examples $[k]_2$ whose labels are different that those of the previous class $[k]_1$ and the later class $[k]_3$. And so on. To these classes, $[i]_j$, we will denominate classes *j*-neighbours of an example *i*.

From a mathematical point of view, we have obtained the joint quotient according to the relation of neighbourhood *R* for each example of the universe:

$$\forall i : \{1..\#U\} \cdot [i] = {}^{OSD(i)}\!/_{R} \quad \textbf{(13)}$$

For example, if *OSD(1)=<(1,0),(4,1),(5,2),(34,3),(3,4)> + <(73,5),(2,6),(31,7)>+* ... we are indicating that examples 1, 4, 5, 34 and 3 have the same label (values 0, 1, 2, 3 and 4 would be the distance of each example for example 1), that in addition differs from the one to examples 73, 2 and 31. From this we can here construct the class [1] of the following form: *[1]≈[1,4, 5, 34,3]+[73, 2, 31]+*....The class 1-neighbour of 1 is [1, 4, 5, 34,3]; the class 2-neighbour of 1 is [73, 2, 31]; and so on.

Definition 12 (Class of Order k j-Neighbour of an Example i): the class of order 0 is defined 1-neighbour of an example *i*, $[i]_1^0$, like the class of neighbours of an example *i* respect to itself. That is to say, since in the ordered sequence of distances of an example *i*, *OSD(i)*, the first example always will be the own *i*, since the distance to itself is 0, the class of order 0 1-neighbour of example *i* will be the set of neighbouring examples of this one whose label is the same one, or of another form, they will be those that belong to $OSD(i)_1$.

On the other hand, the class of order 0 *j*-neighbour of an example *i* will be $[i]_j^0$. We are specially interested on the classes of order *k* 1-neighbours. We define then the order class 1 1-neighbour like:

$$[i]_1^1 = [i]_1^0 \cup \left\langle j \,\middle|\, j \in \bigcup_{k \in [i]_1^0} [k]_1^0 \right\rangle \quad \textbf{(14)}$$

The interpretation of this expression is the following one: since *i* contains all the examples with the same label than *i* that is nearer to it (including it) until finding another example of different label, the class $[i]_1^1$ has to those contained in $[i]_1^0$ plus the 1-neighbours of them. For example, in Fig. 1 we have $[i]_1^0$=*<i,1,2,3,4,5>* (the 6 does not belong to it, it has another label).

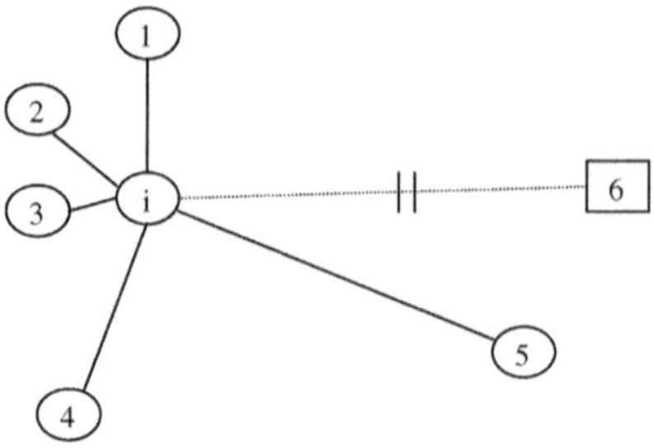

Fig. 1.

In general, the class of order k 1-neighbour of an example i is defined as:

$$[i]_1^k = \bigcup_{0 \le j < k} [i]_1^j \qquad \textbf{(15)}$$

And, therefore, the class of order k j-neighbour of an example i is defined as:

$$[i]_j^k = \bigcup_{0 \le h < k} [i]_j^h \qquad \textbf{(16)}$$

By convenience, we will speak of k-class instead of class of order k, and therefore, k-class j-neighbour, instead of class of order k j-neighbour. In particular, we are interested on the k-classes 1-neighbours, and when we will speak about them we omit subscript 1, that is to say, instead of $[i]_1^k$ we will write $[i]^k$. Only when the neighbourhood order is different from 1 we will express this order.

Definition 13 (Equality of Classes): two classes are equal when both contain exactly the same examples, although in different order. Formally,

$$[i] = [j] \Leftrightarrow (\forall e \in [i] \Rightarrow e \in [j] \wedge \forall e \in [j] \Rightarrow e \in [i]) \qquad \textbf{(17)}$$

Definition 14 (Set of k-Classes 1-Neighbours): we define the set of k-classes 1-neighbour like the set formed by the k-classes 1-neighbour for each example. Also, by convenience, k-set of neighbouring classes will be named, instead of set of k-classes 1-neighbour, and it will written like SN^k where

$$SN^k = \{[1]^k, [2]^k, \ldots, [n]^k\} \qquad \textbf{(18)}$$

Definition 15 (Reduced k-Set of Neighbouring Classes): we define k-set reduced of neighbouring classes as the set of k-classes 1-neighbours where there are not two equal classes. Formally,

$$RSN^k = \{[i]^k \in SN^k \mid \forall [j]^k \in SN^K \cdot i \neq j \Rightarrow [i]^k \neq [j]^k\} \qquad \textbf{(19)}$$

We will identify the reduced sets of neighbouring classes with the examples that have been reduced so that we do not lose information, that is to say, if the class [i] and the class [j] are equal, since their neighbours are the same $[w_1,\ldots,w_k]$, then [i, j] has as neighbours to $[w_1,\ldots,w_k]$.

4. Algorithm "Similar Nearest Neighbour" (S-NN)

Once seen all the necessary definitions that support the theory that we present in this work, we describe the details of our algorithm in figure 2.

```
S-NN (U: Database) ret (RSN: Set of Classes)
        i ← 0
        SN_1^i ← { }
        For each example j de U
          SN_1^i ← SN_1^i ∪ {[j]_1^i}
        RSN_1^{i-1} ← { } (by convenience RSN_1^{-1})
        While SN_1^i ≠ RSN_1^{i-1}
          RSN_1^i ← reduction(SN_1^i)
          SN_1^{i+1} ← { }
          For each [j]_1^i ∈ RSN_1^i
            For each k ∈ [j]_1^i
              [j]_1^{i+1} ← [j]_1^i ∪ [k]_1^i
            SN_1^{i+1} ← SN_1^{i+1} ∪ {[j]_1^{i+1}}
          i ← i+1
```

Fig. 2. Algorithm

The Input parameters are the U database, containing n examples with m attributes. As we mentioned earlier, starting with the individual points as individual clusters, at each successive step the clusters with identical neighbours are merged. The process is repeated until we can not simplify the set of clusters.

S-NN treats each input point as a separate cluster, in each iteration of the while-loop, until we can not simplify the set of clusters, we compute the neighbours of each cluster member.

```
reduction (C:Set of Classes) ret (RSN:Set of Classes)
        RSN ← C
        For each (x,y) con x, y ∈ C
          If [x] ≡ [y]          ( [x] ≡ [x] ∪ [y] - [x] ∩ [y] )
            RSN ← RSN - {y}
            x ← x ∪ y
```

Fig. 3. Reduction

The expression $\mathrm{RSN}_1^i \leftarrow \mathrm{reduction}\,(\mathrm{SN}_1^i)$ invokes to the following algorithm shown in figure 3, whose assignment is to simplify the set of classes by means of the elimination of those classes that have exactly the same neighbours. If there are two classes x and y and they have the same neighbours, then the examples of y are added to those of x, which both, will have exactly the same neighbours.

5. Results

5.1. Iris

We have used the database Iris to illustrate the complete results of the method because they are possible to be included in the article. However, we regret not to be able to include, by lack of space, the intermediate results (set SN and RSN for each order of iterations).

The next table contains two types of rows:

- odd rows: [class, examples of the class, neighbours of the examples of the class]. The first value refers to the class or labels; the second indicates how many examples belong to the class that has the mentioned label; and the third value corresponds with the number of neighbours that have got that class.
- even rows: the example of the class are placed on the left column, whose cardinal corresponds with the second number of the previous row; and in the right column the neighbours of the examples of the class are placed, of the left column, and has got as cardinal the third value of the previous row.

[A,50,50]	
1, 6, 10, 18, 26, 31, 36, 37, 40, 42, 44, 47, 50, 51, 53, 54, 55, 58, 59, 60, 63, 64, 67, 68, 71, 72, 78, 79, 87, 88, 91, 95, 96, 100, 101, 106, 107, 112, 115, 124, 125, 134, 135, 138, 139, 143, 144, 145, 149, 136	1, 95, 106, 55, 36, 64, 125, 88, 107, 112,145, 134, 72, 67, 63, 37, 100, 31, 54, 135, 50, 47, 68, 6, 18, 101, 144, 78, 42, 143, 149, 139, 53, 51, 26, 115, 40, 10, 44, 96, 60, 124, 91, 58, 79, 138, 87, 59, 136, 71
[C, 47, 48]	
2, 4, 17, 21, 23, 24, 39, 41, 45, 73, 80, 89, 102, 110, 126, 7, 13, 15, 20, 35, 27, 49, 104, 56, 57, 74, 148, 77, 81, 83, 111, 122, 123, 127, 131, 132, 146, 16, 75, 32, 34, 46, 52, 62, 82, 108, 137	2, 57, 122, 83, 131, 4, 15, 132, 13, 35, 81, 27, 41, 111, 123, 74, 17, 102, 23, 20, 127, 148, 34, 7, 80, 146, 46, 32, 75, 16, 5, 56, 49, 77, 126, 52, 104, 110, 73, 24, 62, 45, 108, 137, 82, 39, 21, 89
[B, 47, 49]	
3, 28, 113, 8, 11, 14, 76, 85, 86, 116, 109, 121, 129, 19, 29, 30, 43, 66, 70, 99, 33, 98, 48, 133, 38, 61, 119, 65, 69, 84, 150, 93, 92, 94, 97, 103, 105, 114, 141, 118, 120, 140, 128, 130, 142, 22, 147	3, 92, 141, 113, 142, 119, 61, 29, 128, 11, 117, 103, 130, 28, 118, 147, 22, 69, 30, 105, 114, 76, 86, 66, 94, 19, 121, 43, 99, 116, 85, 65, 8, 109, 14, 33, 140, 98, 133, 70, 48, 129, 93, 38, 9, 150, 97, 84, 120
[C, 1, 1]	
5	5
[B, 1, 1]	
9	9
[B, 1, 1]	
12	12
[C, 1, 1]	
25	25
[C, 1, 1]	
90	90
[B, 1, 1]	
117	117

For the database Iris 4 iterations have been needed, in each one of which the cardinal one of set RSN has been: 98, 62, 19 and last the 9 that is in the table.

The method offers a very valuable information because it provides:

- The number of regions: 9.
- If the examples of the class agree with the neighbours (fact that happens for the class A) then the region is clearly separable of the rest.
- Which are the examples that make difficult the classification (5, 9, 12, 25, 90 and 117), therefore, we could extract them from the database for a later classification.
- An estimation of the error rate on the training file (let us take into account that if we keep the three first regions we would be around 96%, that is approximately what they provide other good sort keys).

5.2. Breast Cancer

For this database (with the 683 examples without noise), and needing 5 iterations we have obtained 44 regions. The regions calculated in each iteration are: 440, 308, 142, 45 and 44. The two first are stops A (427 examples) and for B (210 examples), which means that only with these two we would be around the 93,26% of the information.

Regarding the computational cost of the algorithm, the executions have been made in a PC Pentium 550 MHz and for the database Iris it uses less than 1 second; for the breast cancer database it uses 2 minutes.

6. Conclusions

The definitions presented in this article base the theory that it supports on algorithm S-NN. The algorithm, besides does not need parameters is determinist. As for the information that it provides, in the example Iris it is demonstrated that it is able to obtain: a geometric idea of the distribution of examples of the database; an estimation of the number of regions (possible rules); an estimation of the difficulty of classification of the database; and which are the examples that make difficult the learning of the database, with a view to eliminate them in the phase of learning.

On the other hand, algorithm S-NN allows some interesting directions, which we are studying, as far as the reduction criterion is concerned (it see point 2,1 of the reduction algorithm). Three criteria of reduction exist: a restrictive criterion (the one that at the moment is applied, that is to say, they will be reduction if the two classes are exactly equal); a moderate criterion (there will be reduction if one of the classes is included in the other); and, finally, a relaxed criterion (there will be reduction if the intersection of the classes is not empty). These criteria provide different solutions, as much more numerous as for regions, as restrictive is the reduction criterion. The characteristics of the contributed solutions as well as their differences, both analytical and geometrically, will be object of next works. In the same way, another interesting line is the use of the set of classes of neighbours like sort key.

Acknowledgements. This work has been supported by the Spanish Research Agency CICYT under grant TIC99-0351.

References

1. Aha, D. W. A (1990). Study of Instance-Based Algorithms for Supervised Learning Tasks: Mathematical, Empirical, and psychological Evaluations. Ph. D. Dissertation. UCI.
2. Codrington, C. W. y Brodley, C. E. (1997). On the Qualitative Behavior of Impurity-Based Splitting Rules I: The Minima-Free Property. Technical Report, Purdue University.
3. Cover, T. M. y Hart, P. E. (1967). Nearest Neighbor Pattern Classification. NN-Pattern Classification Techniques. IEEE.
4. Chang, C. L. (1974). Finding Prototypes for Nearest Neighbor Classifiers. IEEE Transactions on Computers.
5. Hart, P.E. (1968). The condensed nearest neighbor rule. IEEE Transactions on Information Theory, IT-14.
6. Hellman, M. E. (1970). The Nearest Neighbor Classification Rule with a Reject Option. NN-Pattern Classification Techniques. IEEE.
7. Jarvis, R. A. y Patrick, E. A. (1973). Clustering using a Similarity Measure Based on Shared Near Neighbors. IEEE Transactions on Computers.
8. Joussellin, A. y Dubuisson, B. (1987). A Link Between k-Nearest Neighbor Rules and Knowledge Based Systems by Sequence Analysis. Pattern Recognition Letters.
9. Patrick, E. A. y Fischer, F. P. (1970). A Generalized k-Nearest Neighbor Rule. NN-Pattern Classification Techniques. IEEE.
10. Ritter, G. L., Woodruff, H.B., Lowry, S.R. y Isenhour, T.L. (1975). An algorithm for a Selective Nearest Neighbor Decision Rule. IEEE Transactions on Information Theory, 21.
11. Tomek, I. (1976). An Experiment with the Edited Nearest-Neighbor Rule. IEEE Transactions on Systems, Man, an Cybernetics SMC-6.
12. Wilson, D. (1972). Asymptotic Properties of Nearest Neighbor Rules using Edited Data. IEEE Transactions on Systems, Man and Cybernetics 2.
13. D. Fisher. (1995). Optimization and Simplification of Hierarchical Clusters. Proceedings of the International Conference on Knowledge Discovery and Data Mining.
14. S. Guha, (1998). CURE: An Efficient Clustering Algorithm for Large Databases. Proceedings of the 1998 ACM SIGMOD Conference.

An Eager Regression Method Based on Best Feature Projections

Tolga Aydın and H. Altay Güvenir

Department of Computer Engineering
Bilkent University
Ankara, 06533, TURKEY

Abstract. This paper describes a machine learning method, called *Regression by Selecting Best Feature Projections* (RSBFP). In the training phase, RSBFP projects the training data on each feature dimension and aims to find the predictive power of each feature attribute by constructing simple linear regression lines, one per each continuous feature and number of categories per each categorical feature. Because, although the predictive power of a continuous feature is constant, it varies for each distinct value of categorical features. Then the simple linear regression lines are sorted according to their predictive power. In the querying phase of learning, the best linear regression line and thus the best feature projection are selected to make predictions.

Keywords: Prediction, Feature Projection, Regression.

1 Introduction

Prediction has been one of the most common problems researched in data mining and machine learning. Predicting the values of categorical features is known as classification, whereas predicting the values of continuous features is known as regression. From this point of view, classification can be considered as a subcategory of regression. In machine learning, much research has been performed for classification. But, recently the focus of researchers has moved towards regression, since many of the real-life problems can be modeled as regression problems.

There are two different approaches for regression in machine learning community: Eager and lazy learning. Eager regression methods construct rigorous models by using the training data, and the prediction task is based on these models. The advantage of eager regression methods is not only the ability to obtain the interpretation of the underlying data, but also the reduced query time. On the other hand, the main disadvantage is their long train time requirement. Lazy regression methods, on the other hand, do not construct models by using the training data. Instead, they delay all processing to prediction phase. The most important disadvantage of lazy regression methods is the fact that, they do not provide an interpretable model of the training data, because the model is usually the training data itself. It is not a compact description of the training data, when compared to the models constructed by eager regression methods, such as regression trees and rule based regression.

In the literature, many eager and lazy regression methods exist. Among eager regression methods, CART [1], RETIS [7], M5 [5], DART [2], and Stacked

L. Monostori, J. Váncza, and M. Ali (Eds.): IEA/AIE 2001, LNAI 2070, pp. 217-226, 2001.

Regressions [9] induce regression trees, FORS [6] uses inductive logic programming for regression, RULE [3] induces regression rules, and MARS [8] constructs mathematical models. Among lazy regression methods, *k*NN [4, 10, 15] is the most popular nonparametric instance-based approach.

In this paper, we describe an eager learning method, namely *Regression by Selecting Best Feature Projections* (RSBFP) [13, 14]. This method makes use of the linear least squares regression.

A preprocessing phase is required to increase the predictive power of the method. According to the Chebyshev's result [12], for any positive number k, at least $(1 - 1/k^2) * 100\%$ of the values in any population of numbers are within k standard deviations of the mean. We find the standard deviation of the target values of the training data, and discard the training data whose target value is not within k standard deviations of the mean target. Empiricaly, we reach the best prediction by taking k as $\sqrt{2}$.

In the first phase, RSBFP constructs projections of the training data on each feature, and this phase continues by constructing simple linear regression lines, one per each continuous feature and number of categories per each categorical feature. Then, these simple linear regression lines are sorted according to their prediction ability. In the querying phase of learning, the target value of a query instance is predicted using the simple linear regression line having the minimum relative error, i.e. having the maximum predictive power. If this linear regression line is not suitable for our query instance, we keep searching for the best linear regression line among the ordered list of simple linear regression lines.

In this paper, RSBFP is compared with three eager (RULE, MARS, DART) and one lazy method (*k*NN) in terms of predictive power and computational complexity. RSBFP is better not only in terms of predictive power but also in terms of computational complexity, when compared to these well-known methods. For most data mining or knowledge discovery applications, where very large databases are in concern, this is thought of a solution because of low computational complexity. Again RSBFP is noted to be powerful in the presence missing feature values, target noise and irrelevant features.

In Section 2, we review the *k*NN, RULE, MARS and DART methods for regression. Section 3 gives a detailed description of the RSBFP. Section 4 is devoted to the empirical evaluation of RSBFP and its comparison with other methods. Finally, in Section 5, conclusions are presented.

2 Regression Overview

*k*NN is the most commonly used lazy method for both classification and regression problems. The underlying idea behind the *k*NN method is that the closest instances to the query point have similar target values to the query. Hence, the *k*NN method first finds the closest instances to the query point in the instance space according to a distance measure. Generally, the Euclidean distance metric is used to measure the similarity between two points in the instance space. Therefore, by using Euclidean distance metric as our distance measure, k closest instances to the query point are found. Then *k*NN outputs the distance-weighted average of the target values of those closest instances as the prediction for that query instance.

In machine learning, inducing rules from a given train data is also popular. Weiss and Indurkhya adapted the rule-based classification algorithm [11], Swap-1, for regression. Swap-1 learns decision rules in Disjunctive Normal Form (DNF). Since Swap-1 is designed for the prediction of categorical features, using a preprocessing procedure, the numeric feature in regression to be predicted is transformed to a nominal one. For this transformation, the P-class algorithm is used [3]. If we let $\{y\}$ be a set of output values, this transformation can be regarded as a one-dimensional clustering of training instances on response variable y, in order to form classes. The purpose is to make y values within one class similar, and across classes dissimilar. The assignment of these values to classes is done in such a way that the distance between each y_i and its class mean must be minimum. After formation of pseudo-classes and the application of Swap-1, a pruning and optimization procedure can be applied to construct an optimum set of regression rules.

MARS [8] method partitions the training set into regions by splitting the features recursively into two regions, by constructing a binary regression tree. MARS is continuous at the borders of the partitioned regions. It is an eager, partitioning, interpretable and an adaptive method.

DART, also an eager method, is the latest regression tree induction program developed by Friedman [2]. It avoids limitations of disjoint partitioning, used for other tree-based regression methods, by constructing overlapping regions with increased training cost.

3 Regression by Selecting Best Feature Projections (RSBFP)

RSBFP method tries to determine the feature projection that achieves the highest prediction accuracy. The next subsection describes the training phase for RSBFP, then we describe the querying phase.

3.1 Training

Training in RSBFP begins simply by storing the training data set as projections to each feature separately. A copy of the target values is associated with each projection and the training data set is sorted for each feature dimension according to their feature values. If a training instance includes missing values, it is not simply ignored as in many regression algorithms. Instead, that training instance is stored for the features on which its value is given. The next step involves constructing the simple linear regression lines for each feature. This step differs for categorical and continuous features. In the case of continuous features, exactly one simple linear regression line per feature is constructed. On the other hand, the number of simple linear regression lines per each categorical feature is the number of distinct feature values at the feature of concern. For any categorical feature, the parametric form of any simple regression line is constant, and it is equal to the average target value of the training instances whose corresponding feature value is equal to that categorical value. The training phase continues by sorting these regression lines according to their predictive power. The training phase can be illustrated through an example.

Let our example domain consist of four features, f_1, f_2, f_3 and f_4, where f_1, f_2 are continuous and f_3, f_4 are categorical. For continuous features, we define *minvalue*[*f*] and *maxvalue*[*f*] to denote the minimum and maximum value of feature *f*, respectively. For categorical features, *No_categories* [*f*] is defined to give the number of distinct categories of feature *f*. In our example domain, let the following values be observed:

$minvalue[f_1] = 4,\ maxvalue[f_1] = 10$
$minvalue[f_2] = 2,\ maxvalue[f_2] = 8$
$No\_categories\ [f_3] = 2$ (values: A, B)
$No\_categories\ [f_4] = 3$ (values: X, Y, Z)

For this example domain, 7 simple linear regression lines are constructed: 1 for f_1, 1 for f_2, 2 for f_3, and finally 3 for f_4. Let the following be the parametric form of the simple linear regression lines:

Simple linear regression line for f_1: target = $2f_1$ - 5
Simple linear regression line for f_2: target = $-4f_2 + 7$
Simple linear regression line for A category of f_3: target = 6
Simple linear regression line for B category of f_3: target = -5
Simple linear regression line for X category of f_4: target = 10
Simple linear regression line for Y category of f_4: target = 1
Simple linear regression line for Z category of f_4: target = 12

The training phase is completed by sorting these simple linear regression lines according to their predictive accuracy. The relative error (RE) of the regression lines is used as the indicator of predictive power: the smaller the RE, the stronger the predictive power. The RE of a simple linear regression line is computed by the following formula:

$$RE = \frac{MAD}{\frac{1}{Q}\sum_{i=1}^{Q} |t(q_i) - \bar{t}|}$$

where Q is the number of training instances used to construct the simple linear regression line, $\bar{t}$ is the median of the target values of Q training instances, $t(q_i)$ is the actual target value of the ith training instance. The MAD (Mean Absolute Distance) is defined as follows:

$$MAD = \frac{1}{Q}\sum_{i=1}^{Q} |t(q_i) - \hat{t}(q_i)|$$

Here, $\hat{t}$ (q_i) denotes the predicted target value of the ith training instance according to the induced simple linear regression line.

We had 7 simple linear regression lines, and let's suppose that they are sorted in the following order, from the best predictive to the worst one:

f_3=A > f_4=X > f_2 > f_1 > f_4=Y > f_4=Z > f_3=B

This shows that any categorical feature's predictive power may vary among its categories. For the above sorting schema, categorical feature f_3 's predictions are reliable among its category A, although it is very poor among category B.

3.2 Querying

In order to predict the target value of a query instance t_i, the RSBFP method uses exactly one linear regression line. This line may not always be the best one. The reason for this situation is explained via an example. Let the feature values of the query instance t_i be as the following:

$$f_1(t_i) = 5, \quad f_2(t_i) = 10, \quad f_3(t_i) = \text{B}, \quad f_4(t_i) = \text{missing}$$

Although the best linear regression line is f_3=A, this line can not be used for our t_i, since $f_3(t_i) \neq$ A. The next best linear regression line, which is worse than only f_3=A, is f_4=X. This line is also inappropriate for our t_i. No prediction can be made for missing feature values ($f_4(t_i)$ = missing). Therefore, the search for the best linear regression line continues. The line constructed by f_2 comes next. It is again not possible to benefit from this simple linear regression line. Because $f_2(t_i) = 10$, and it is not in the range of f_2, (2,8). Fortunately, we find an appropriate regression line in the fourth trial. Our $f_1(t_i)$, which is 5, is in the range of f_1, (4,10). So the prediction made for target value of t_i is $(2 * f_1(t_i) - 5) = (2 * 5 - 5) = 5$. Once the appropriate linear regression line is found, remaining linear regression lines need not be dealed anymore.

4 Empirical Evaluation

RSBFP method was compared with the other well-known methods mentioned above, in terms of predictive accuracy and time complexity. We have used a repository consisting of 26 data files in our experiments. The characteristics of the data files are summarized in Table1. Most of these data files are used for the experimental analysis of function approximation techniques and for training and demonstration by machine learning and statistics community.

10 fold cross-validation technique was employed in the experiments. For lazy regression method k parameter was taken as 10, where k denotes the number of nearest neighbors considered around the query instance.

In terms of predictive accuracy, RSBFP performed the best on 9 data files among the 26, and obtained the lowest mean relative error (Table 2).

In terms of time complexity, RSBFP performed the best in the total (training + querying) execution time, and became the fastest method (Table 3, 4).

In machine learning, it is very important for an algorithm to still perform well when noise, missing feature value and irrelevant features are added to the system. Experimental results showed that RSBFP was again the best method whenever we added 20% target noise, 20% missing feature value and 30 irrelevant features to the system, by having the lowest mean relative errors. RSBFP performed the best on 7 data files in the presence of 20% missing feature value, the best on 21 data files in the presence of 20% target noise and the best on 10 data files in the presence of 30 irrelevant features (Table 5, 6, 7).

5 Conclusions

In this paper, we have presented an eager regression method based on selecting best feature projections. RSBFP is better than other well-known eager and lazy regression methods in terms of prediction accuracy and computational complexity. It also enables the interpretation of the training data. That is, the method clearly states the best feature projections that are powerful enough to determine the value of the target feature.

The robustness of any regression method can be determined by analyzing the predictive power of that method in the presence of target noise, irrelevant features and missing feature values. These three factors heavily exist in real life databases, and it is important for a learning algorithm to give promising results in the presence of those factors. Empirical results indicate that RSBFP is also a robust method.

Table 1. Characteristics of the data files used in the empirical evaluations, C: Continuous, N: Nominal

Dataset	Original Name	Instances	Features (C+N)	Missing Values
AB	Abalone	4177	8 (7 + 1)	None
AP	Airport	135	4 (4 + 0)	None
AU	Auto-mpg	398	7 (6 + 1)	6
BA	Baseball	337	16 (16 + 0)	None
BU	Buying	100	39 (39 + 0)	27
CH	Cpu	209	7 (6 + 1)	None
CN	Country	122	20 (20 + 0)	34
ED	Education	1500	43 (43 + 0)	2918
EL	Electric	240	12 (10 + 2)	58
FA	Fat	252	17 (17 + 0)	None
FC	Fishcatch	158	7 (6 + 1)	87
FF	Fruitfly	125	4 (3 + 1)	None
HO	Housing	506	13 (12 + 1)	None
HR	Home Run Race	163	19 (19 + 0)	None
NE	Northridge	2929	10 (10 + 0)	None
NT	Normal Temp.	130	2 (2 + 0)	None
PL	Plastic	1650	2 (2 + 0)	None
PV	Poverty	97	6 (5 + 1)	6
RE	Read	681	25 (24 + 1)	1097
S2	Solar Flare	1066	10 (0 + 10)	None
SC	Schools	62	19 (19 + 0)	1
SE	Servo	167	4 (0 + 4)	None
SP	Stock Prices	950	9 (9 + 0)	None
TV	Televisions	40	4 (4 + 0)	None
US	Usnews Coll.	1269	31 (31 + 0)	7624
VL	Villages	766	32 (29 + 3)	3986

Table 2. Relative errors (REs) of algorithms. Best REs are shown in bold font

Dataset	RSBFP	KNN	RULE	MARS	DART
AB	0.729	**0.661**	0.899	0.683	0.678
AP	0.550	0.612	0.744	0.720	**0.546**
AU	0.489	**0.321**	0.451	0.333	0.346
BA	0.768	**0.443**	0.666	0.493	0.508
BU	**0.678**	0.961	0.946	0.947	0.896
CH	0.781	0.944	0.678	0.735	**0.510**
CN	**1.429**	1.642	6.307	5.110	1.695
ED	0.668	0.654	**0.218**	0.359	0.410
EL	**1.003**	1.194	1.528	1.066	1.118
FA	0.725	0.785	0.820	**0.305**	0.638
FC	0.578	0.697	0.355	**0.214**	0.415
FF	1.016	1.201	1.558	**1.012**	1.077
HO	0.698	0.600	0.641	0.526	**0.522**
HR	0.890	0.907	0.890	**0.769**	0.986
NE	0.969	1.034	1.217	0.928	**0.873**
NT	**0.976**	1.232	1.250	1.012	1.112
PL	0.887	0.475	0.477	**0.404**	0.432
PV	0.921	0.796	0.916	1.251	**0.691**
RE	**0.997**	1.062	1.352	1.045	1.189
S2	**1.434**	2.307	1.792	1.556	1.695
SC	0.376	0.388	0.341	**0.223**	0.352
SE	0.868	0.619	**0.229**	0.432	0.337
SP	1.416	**0.599**	0.906	0.781	0.754
TV	**1.176**	1.895	4.195	7.203	2.690
US	**0.402**	0.480	0.550	0.412	0.623
VL	**0.940**	1.017	1.267	1.138	1.355
Mean	**0.860**	0.905	1.200	1.140	0.864

Table 3. Train time of algorithms in milliseconds. Best results are shown in bold font

Dataset	RSBFP	KNN	RULE	MARS	DART
AB	148	**8.9**	3219	10270	477775
AP	1.1	**0**	90.8	159.2	62
AU	8.9	**0.6**	248.9	570.5	1890.1
BA	19	**0**	181.8	915.1	3171.1
BU	10.5	**0**	67.1	761.7	794.4
CH	4.1	**0**	52.7	575.3	286
CN	8	**0.1**	108.6	475.3	481
ED	278.2	**13.5**	862.8	10143.9	27266
EL	8.1	**0.2**	69.5	407.5	1017
FA	15.8	**0**	161.1	985	1773.9
FC	2.1	**0**	47.8	240.2	201.4
FF	1.1	**0**	34.1	99.5	45.9
HO	21.2	**1**	264.9	1413.9	8119.7
HR	8.2	**0**	57.5	616.3	893.9
NE	130.5	**7.4**	3493	5709.9	87815
NT	**0**	**0**	30.6	69.3	18.9
PL	10	**0.2**	175.3	824.8	10024.4
PV	1	**0**	40.9	127.3	44
RE	52	**3**	196	2744.6	33044.6
S2	36.1	**3.5**	108.8	667.2	971.4
SC	3	**0**	45.3	260.8	84.4
SE	1.8	**0**	37	116.4	83.4
SP	28.5	**1.4**	365.1	2281.4	17346.4
TV	**0**	**0**	30.9	31.1	3.1
US	136.4	**7.4**	2547.1	8435.2	168169
VL	74.6	**4.4**	513.6	3597.8	23405
Mean	38.777	**1.985**	501.93	2019.2	33261

Table 4. Query time of algorithms in milliseconds. Best results are shown in bold font

Dataset	RSBFP	KNN	RULE	MARS	DART
AB	23.3	6547	14433.1	7.9	**6.1**
AP	1	3.4	141.7	**0**	**0**
AU	3	64.5	462.2	**0**	**0**
BA	2.1	54.6	244.8	**0**	**0**
BU	**0**	11.6	32.1	**0**	**0**
CH	1	11.6	87.3	**0**	**0**
CN	1	8.4	98.4	**0**	0.1
ED	9	2699.7	312.3	2.7	**1.7**
EL	1.6	21	117.5	**0**	**0**
FA	2	33.1	96.4	**0**	**0**
FC	1.1	7.9	48.8	**0**	**0**
FF	0.9	2	45.4	**0**	**0**
HO	3.2	107.8	410.5	**0**	**0**
HR	0.6	13.3	43	**0**	**0**
NE	14	3399.4	11326.8	4.7	**1.75**
NT	1	1.9	30.8	**0**	**0**
PL	16.7	571.9	2192.7	**0.2**	1.2
PV	**0**	2.2	37.1	**0**	**0**
RE	3	265.6	627.2	**0**	1
S2	4	407.8	223.6	0.4	**0**
SC	**0**	2	27.8	3.7	**0**
SE	0.1	4.2	49.1	**0**	**0**
SP	6.2	303.2	1090.9	0.1	**0**
TV	**0**	**0**	24	**0**	**0**
US	8	1383.2	1877.3	7	**2**
VL	6	439	1118.2	0.3	**0**
Mean	4.184	629.47	1353.8	1.038	**0.533**

Table 5. REs of algorithms, where 20% missing feature value are added. Best Res are shown in bold font (* Means result isn't available due to singular variance/covariance matrix)

Dataset	RSBFP	KNN	RULE	MARS	DART
AB	0.729	0.750	0.961	0.748	**0.688**
AP	0.562	0.726	0.676	0.798	**0.546**
AU	0.500	0.414	0.526	0.414	**0.363**
BA	0.785	**0.553**	0.833	0.637	0.576
BU	**0.785**	0.951	0.878	0.862	1.026
CH	0.746	0.922	0.832	0.747	**0.608**
CN	**1.480**	1.856	3.698	3.733	2.377
ED	0.685	0.743	**0.497**	0.595	0.536
EL	**1.005**	1.097	1.537	1.073	1.191
FA	0.749	0.849	0.948	**0.731**	0.735
FC	0.570	0.675	0.543	0.537	**0.401**
FF	1.019	1.711	1.557	**1.012**	1.347
HO	0.718	0.761	0.748	0.649	**0.590**
HR	0.899	0.910	1.040	**0.836**	0.974
NE	0.974	1.072	1.272	**0.972**	*
NT	1.020	1.229	1.363	**0.989**	1.222
PL	0.903	0.733	0.686	0.679	**0.420**
PV	0.920	0.976	1.189	1.026	**0.792**
RE	**0.996**	1.059	1.364	1.048	1.229
S2	1.429	1.851	1.751	1.557	**1.421**
SC	0.409	0.449	0.500	**0.303**	0.370
SE	0.879	0.921	0.849	0.746	**0.495**
SP	1.430	0.744	0.904	0.930	**0.707**
TV	**1.272**	4.398	3.645	16.50	2.512
US	**0.460**	0.558	0.620	0.497	0.844
VL	**0.949**	1.056	1.410	1.090	*
Mean	**0.880**	1.086	1.186	1.527	0.920

Table 6. REs of algorithms, where 20% target noise are added. Best REs are shown in bold font

Dataset	RSBFP	KNN	RULE	MARS	DART
AB	**0.819**	7.592	9.301	7.602	6.603
AP	0.952	0.807	1.122	0.856	**0.785**
AU	**0.488**	1.832	2.531	2.107	1.981
BA	0.813	**0.457**	0.712	0.537	0.556
BU	**0.597**	12.66	12.92	13.30	10.67
CH	0.815	0.930	0.782	0.745	**0.636**
CN	**1.516**	1.676	3.102	5.874	2.040
ED	**0.653**	2.166	2.384	2.164	2.276
EL	**0.978**	1.465	1.899	1.148	1.431
FA	**0.684**	2.525	3.208	2.447	2.058
FC	0.544	0.710	0.528	0.501	**0.387**
FF	**1.030**	2.394	3.247	1.710	2.089
HO	**0.865**	2.801	3.635	2.893	2.611
HR	**0.863**	7.853	11.53	10.29	6.115
NE	**0.986**	38.84	42.32	37.66	31.54
NT	**0.951**	1.403	2.220	1.037	1.196
PL	**0.852**	5.492	5.777	4.921	5.107
PV	**0.829**	9.429	9.456	4.213	6.038
RE	**0.952**	6.597	10.33	6.759	7.108
S2	**2.366**	73.89	77.21	70.90	71.40
SC	**0.538**	0.583	0.968	0.700	0.627
SE	**0.697**	21.29	27.77	22.01	21.72
SP	**1.183**	1.921	3.887	1.966	1.871
TV	**1.468**	2.087	4.569	7.267	2.671
US	0.643	0.636	0.865	**0.541**	0.764
VL	**0.973**	1.030	1.513	0.977	1.518
Mean	**0.925**	8.041	9.377	8.120	7.378

Table 7. REs of algorithms, where 30 irrelevant features are added. Best Res are shown in bold font (* Means result isn't available due to singular variance/covariance matrix)

Dataset	RSBFP	KNN	RULE	MARS	DART
AB	0.728	0.873	0.934	**0.682**	*
AP	**0.555**	1.514	0.723	0.682	0.657
AU	0.488	0.538	0.491	**0.368**	0.511
BA	0.768	0.568	0.574	**0.536**	0.628
BU	**0.678**	0.968	1.073	0.877	0.969
CH	0.781	1.107	0.753	**0.613**	0.668
CN	**1.425**	2.854	1.794	4.126	1.662
ED	0.668	0.802	**0.268**	0.404	0.573
EL	**1.006**	1.037	1.367	1.134	1.236
FA	0.725	1.026	1.039	**0.249**	0.877
FC	0.578	0.917	0.456	**0.247**	0.420
FF	**1.030**	1.063	1.513	1.777	1.430
HO	0.698	0.920	0.701	**0.521**	0.653
HR	0.890	0.932	1.049	**0.847**	1.165
NE	0.969	1.076	1.284	**0.916**	*
NT	**1.000**	1.079	1.484	1.370	1.156
PL	0.887	0.961	0.575	**0.407**	0.734
PV	0.966	**0.855**	0.934	1.005	1.013
RE	**0.998**	1.045	1.380	1.042	1.311
S2	**1.433**	1.454	1.765	1.629	1.490
SC	0.376	0.582	0.386	**0.305**	0.391
SE	0.926	0.835	**0.471**	0.798	0.641
SP	1.416	1.188	0.914	0.817	**0.756**
TV	**1.220**	3.241	5.572	5.614	2.709
US	0.402	0.757	0.557	**0.394**	0.906
VL	**0.939**	1.050	1.454	1.257	1.307
Mean	**0.867**	1.124	1.135	1.100	1.000

References

[1] Breiman, L, Friedman, J H, Olshen, R A and Stone, C J *'Classification and Regression Trees'* Wadsworth, Belmont, California (1984)
[2] Friedman, J H 'Local Learning Based on Recursive Covering' Department of Statistics, Stanford University (1996)
[3] Weiss, S and Indurkhya, N ' Rule-based Machine Learning Methods for Functional Prediction' *Journal of Artificial Intelligence Research* Vol 3 (1995) pp 383-403
[4] Aha, D, Kibler, D and Albert, M 'Instance-based Learning Algorithms' *Machine Learning* Vol 6 (1991) pp 37 – 66
[5] Quinlan, J R 'Learning with Continuous Classes' *Proceedings AI'92* Adams and Sterling (Eds) Singapore (1992) pp 343-348
[6] Bratko, I and Karalic A 'First Order Regression' *Machine Learning* Vol 26 (1997) pp 147-176
[7] Karalic, A 'Employing Linear Regression in Regression Tree Leaves' *Proceedings of ECAI'92* Vienna, Austria, Bernd Newmann (Ed.) (1992) pp 440-441
[8] Friedman, J H 'Multivariate Adaptive Regression Splines' *The Annals of Statistics* Vol 19 No 1 (1991) pp 1-141
[9] Breiman, L 'Stacked Regressions' *Machine Learning* Vol 24 (1996) pp 49-64
[10] Kibler, D, Aha D W and Albert, M K 'Instance-based Prediction of Real-valued Attributes' *Comput. Intell.* Vol 5 (1989) pp 51-57
[11] Weiss, S and Indurkhya, N 'Optimized Rule Induction' *IEEE Expert* Vol 8 No 6 (1993) pp 61-69
[12] Graybill, F, Iyer, H and Burdick, R 'Applied Statistics' Upper Saddle River, NJ (1998)
[13] Aydın, T 'Regression by Selecting Best Feature(s)' *M.S.Thesis*, Computer Engineering, Bilkent University, September, (2000)
[14] Aydın, T and Güvenir, H A 'Regression by Selecting Appropriate Features' *Proceedings of TAINN'2000*, Izmir, June 21-23, (2000), pp 73-82
[15] Uysal, İ and Güvenir, H A 'Regression on Feature Projections' *Knowledge-Based Systems*, Vol.13, No:4, (2000), pp 207-214

On the Relationship between Learning Capability and the Boltzmann-Formula

Péter Stefán and László Monostori

Computer and Automation Research Institute, Hungarian Academy of Sciences, Kende u. 13-17, H-1111 Budapest, Hungary, Phone: (36-1) 4666 644, Fax: 4667 503
{stefan, laszlo.monostori}@sztaki.hu

Abstract. In this paper a combined use of reinforcement learning and simulated annealing is treated. Most of the simulated annealing methods suggest using heuristic temperature bounds as the basis of annealing. Here a theoretically established approach tailored to reinforcement learning following Softmax action selection policy will be shown. An application example of agent-based routing will also be illustrated.

1 Introduction

Agent-based solutions for certain kinds of problems have become quite popular nowadays. The main advantage of all of these approaches is that an agent system is created to be able to cope with dynamically changing environment. Most of the agents capable of learning, apply reinforcement learning (RL). RL approaches maintain preference values or, simply, values (state values, action-state values) which are some estimations of environment's possible future honor or dishonor. Action selection policy can be defined over these preferences, i.e. what action the agent should choose in order to maximize the long-run reward given by the environment. In order to set up preferences, the agent must gain as much experience from interacting with its environment as possible. This behavior is called exploration. When the agent uses its knowledge it does exploitation. However, balancing between exploration and exploitation is fundamentally a difficult task and in the literature [10] only heuristic solutions have been suggested for solving it.

In this article some theoretical considerations of combining action selection policy with simulated annealing will be provided. It will be shown that the exploration as well as the exploitation properties can be approached with any small error and finite temperature values can be assigned to the two extreme behaviors marking a possible cooling (or in this context, balancing) domain.

2 The Problem

Suppose that there is a decision-making agent (either a human being, or a computational agent), having n action choices denoted by $a_1, a_2, \dots, a_n$ in a certain situation. To each action a finite preference value is assigned, which represents the "goodness" of that choice. The higher this number, the higher the preference. Preferences are denoted by $Q_1, Q_2, \dots, Q_n$. and $Q_1 \le Q_2 \le \dots \le Q_n$. Suppose that the agent follows Boltzmann

L. Monostori, J. Váncza, and M. Ali (Eds.): IEA/AIE 2001, LNAI 2070, pp. 227-236, 2001.

action selection policy, i.e. defines a probability distribution on the full action set, assigning probabilities to actions according to the formula as follows:

$$p_i = \frac{e^{\frac{Q_i}{T}}}{\sum_{j=1}^{n} e^{\frac{Q_j}{T}}} \text{ , } i = 1,2,\ldots,n \text{ .} \tag{1}$$

In the formula above, a non-negative real-valued parameter *T*, which is called temperature, controls the action selection policy. (Note that in statistical mechanics the exponential of both the numerator and the denominator was $-\frac{E_i}{kT}$ where E_i is the potential energy, *k* is Boltzmann's constant.)

3 Convergence of Boltzmann-Formula

Theorem 1: *If T temperature approaches to infinity, the action selection probability of all of the actions approaches to the uniform distribution; if T goes to zero the probability of selecting the strictly highest Q-valued action goes to 1, while the selection probability of others' goes to 0. If there are k numbers of maximal equally preferred actions, the probability of making selections from among these actions goes to* $\frac{1}{k}$ *as T goes to zero*[1]. ■

Let us prove the above principles. First a transformation of the Boltzmann-formula is required serving as the starting point of all proofs through the rest of the paper.

$$p_i = \frac{e^{\frac{Q_i}{T}}}{\sum_{j=1}^{n} e^{\frac{Q_j}{T}}} = \frac{1}{\frac{\sum_{j=1}^{n} e^{\frac{Q_j}{T}}}{e^{\frac{Q_i}{T}}}} = \frac{1}{\sum_{j=1}^{n} \frac{e^{\frac{Q_j}{T}}}{e^{\frac{Qi}{T}}}} = \frac{1}{\sum_{j=1}^{n} e^{\frac{Q_j}{T} - \frac{Qi}{T}}} = \frac{1}{\sum_{j=1}^{n} e^{\frac{Q_j - Q_i}{T}}} \tag{2}$$

The parameters' domain is set to

$$Q_i \in [Q_{\min}, Q_{\max}] \subset \mathrm{Z} \text{ , } i = 1,2,\ldots,n \text{ ,}$$

$$p_i \in [0,1] \subset \mathrm{R} \text{ , } i = 1,2,\ldots,n \text{ .}$$

Here Z denotes the set of integers and R denotes the set of real numbers.

---

[1] Note that T may never reach 0. Also note that if T goes to 0, the action selection becomes more deterministic.

Since, $|Q_j - Q_i|$ is finite $\forall i, j$, and $\lim_{T\to\infty} \frac{Q_j - Q_i}{T} = 0$,

$$\lim_{T\to\infty} p_i = \lim_{T\to\infty} \frac{1}{\sum_{j=1}^{n} e^{\frac{Q_j-Q_i}{T}}} = \frac{1}{\lim_{T\to\infty} \sum_{j=1}^{n} e^{\frac{Q_j-Q_i}{T}}} = \frac{1}{\sum_{j=1}^{n} \lim_{T\to\infty} e^{\frac{Q_j-Q_i}{T}}} = \frac{1}{\sum_{j=1}^{n} e^{\lim_{T\to\infty}\frac{Q_j-Q_i}{T}}} = \frac{1}{n}.$$

The case of temperature approaching infinity has, therefore, been proven.

In the second case, when temperature approaches to zero, there are two sub-cases: the first one is when there is only one maximal preference value, and the second one is when there are k equal and maximal preference values.

Before deriving the limes expressions, equation (2) should be further transformed. Since j runs from 1 to n, it is necessary that $j = i$ be satisfied at least once. Thus,

$$\frac{1}{\sum_{j=1}^{n} e^{\frac{Q_j-Q_i}{T}}} = \frac{1}{1+\sum_{\substack{i=1 \\ j\neq i}}^{n} e^{\frac{Q_j-Q_i}{T}}}. \tag{3}$$

If $Q_i > Q_j$, for $j = 1,2,\ldots,n,\ j \neq i$, then $\lim_{T\to 0} \frac{Q_j - Q_i}{T} = -\infty$, and $\lim_{T\to 0} e^{\frac{Q_j-Q_i}{T}} = 0$, and hence

$$\lim_{T\to 0} \frac{1}{1+\sum_{\substack{j=1 \\ j\neq i}}^{n} e^{\frac{Q_j-Q_i}{T}}} = 1.$$

If $\exists j$, for which $Q_j > Q_i$, then $\lim_{T\to 0} \frac{Q_j - Q_i}{T} = \infty$, and $\lim_{T\to 0} e^{\frac{Q_j-Q_i}{T}} = \infty$, and therefore

$$\lim_{T\to 0} \frac{1}{1+\sum_{\substack{j-1 \\ j\neq i}}^{n} e^{\frac{Q_j-Q_i}{T}}} = 0.$$

If $Q_{i_1} = Q_{i_2} = \ldots = Q_{i_k} > Q_j$, for $j = 1,2,\ldots,n$, $j \neq i_l$, $l = 1,2,\ldots,k$, then the formula (3) becomes

$$\frac{1}{\sum_{j=1}^{n} e^{\frac{Q_j - Q_i}{T}}} = \frac{1}{k + \sum_{\substack{i=1 \\ j \neq i_l, l=1,2,\dots,k}}^{n} e^{\frac{Q_j - Q_{il}}{T}}} .$$

For the rest of Q_js $\lim_{T \to 0} e^{\frac{Q_j - Q_{i_l}}{T}} = 0$, and therefore

$$\lim_{T \to 0} \frac{1}{k + \sum_{\substack{j=1 \\ j \neq i, l=1,2..,k}}^{n} e^{\frac{Q_j - Q_{il}}{T}}} = \frac{1}{k} . \blacksquare$$

4 Accuracy of the Approach

It has been proven that Boltzmann's formula converges to uniform distribution as T goes to infinity and to the greedy distribution[2] as T goes to 0. It is also an interesting question that in case the Q-values are let constant, to what degree the formula approaches the extremities when the T parameter changes. The question can also be posed in the following way: can a maximal temperature be found so that the p_i probabilities approach uniform distribution with any small error, say ε, and also can a minimal temperature be determined from below reaching the greedy distribution is also guaranteed with a small error. The answer to both questions is positive, and the following theorem provides the values of these temperature bounds.

Theorem 2: *Given an $\varepsilon > 0$, small positive number, and an upper and a lower limit of Q-values, Q_{max} and Q_{min}. The following inequalities are held under these circumstances:*

(a) $\left| p_i - \frac{1}{n} \right| < \varepsilon$ if $T > \dfrac{Q_{\max} - Q_{\min}}{\ln \min\{\frac{1}{1-n\varepsilon}, 1+\varepsilon n\}}$, for $i = 1,2,\dots,n$ and

(b) $\left| 1 - p_i \right| < \varepsilon$ if $T < \dfrac{-\delta}{\ln \frac{\varepsilon}{(1-\varepsilon)(n-1)}}$, where $Q_i > Q_j$, $j \neq i$, $\delta = \min_{\substack{j=1,\dots,n \\ j \neq i}} \left| Q_i - Q_j \right|$.

(Note that δ is the minimal difference between the highest and second highest Q-value, and due to the discrete nature of Qs, this difference is minimally 1. Also note that more than one maximal and equal Q-values are excluded from this examination.

---

[2] Greedy distribution is used as a synonym for a distribution in which the probability of one action is 1 and of the others are 0.

Also note that the minimal T for which the inequality (a) is satisfied will be referred to as T_{max} (or exploration temperature) and the maximal T for which inequality (b) is satisfied will be referred to as T_{min} (or exploitation temperature) throughout the rest of the paper.) ■

It is a simpler task to establish (a), since the upper bound of temperature comes from the limitation of Q-values. The goal is as follows:

$$\left| p_i - \frac{1}{n} \right| < \varepsilon ,$$

$$\frac{1}{n} - \varepsilon < p_i < \frac{1}{n} + \varepsilon ,$$

$$\frac{1}{n} - \varepsilon < \frac{1}{\sum_{j=1}^{n} e^{\frac{Q_j - Q_i}{T}}} < \frac{1}{n} + \varepsilon . \tag{4}$$

It comes from the preconditions that $Q_i, Q_j \in [Q_{\min}, Q_{\max}]$, which can be written as $Q_{\min} \le Q_i, Q_j \le Q_{\max}$, for $\forall i, j$. So it is easy to see that

$$\frac{1}{\sum_{j=1}^{n} e^{\frac{Q_j - Q_{\min}}{T}}} \le \frac{1}{\sum_{j=1}^{n} e^{\frac{Q_j - Q_i}{T}}} , \tag{5}$$

since $e^{\frac{Q_j - Q_i}{T}} \le e^{\frac{Q_j - Q_{\min}}{T}}$, and $\frac{Q_j - Q_i}{T} \le \frac{Q_j - Q_{\min}}{T}$, and $Q_i \ge Q_{\min}$ are always true.

And it is also true that

$$\frac{1}{\sum_{j=1}^{n} e^{\frac{Q_{\max} - Q_{\min}}{T}}} \le \frac{1}{\sum_{j=1}^{n} e^{\frac{Q_j - Q_{\min}}{T}}} , \tag{6}$$

since $e^{\frac{Q_j - Q_{\min}}{T}} \le e^{\frac{Q_{\max} - Q_{\min}}{T}}$, and $\frac{Q_j - Q_{\min}}{T} \le \frac{Q_{\max} - Q_{\min}}{T}$, and $Q_j \le Q_{\max}$.

Putting inequalities (5) and (6) together, a lower bound on p_i is received. Following similar calculations, also an upper bound can be determined, and the two bounds for p_i can be written as

$$\frac{1}{ne^{\frac{Q_{\max}-Q_{\min}}{T}}}=\frac{1}{\sum_{j=1}^{n}e^{\frac{Q_{\max}-Q_{\min}}{T}}}\le\frac{1}{\sum_{j=1}^{n}e^{\frac{Q_j-Q_i}{T}}}\le\frac{1}{\sum_{j=1}^{n}e^{\frac{Q_{\min}-Q_{\max}}{T}}}=\frac{e^{\frac{Q_{\max}-Q_{\min}}{T}}}{n}. \tag{7}$$

ε value must be found for which the bounds of equation (4) could be held to the bounds of equation (7) as well. Hence, a stricter property is formulated as

$$\frac{1}{n}-\varepsilon<\frac{1}{ne^{\frac{Q_{\max}-Q_{\min}}{T}}}, \tag{8a}$$

$$\frac{e^{\frac{Q_{\max}-Q_{\min}}{T}}}{n}<\frac{1}{n}+\varepsilon. \tag{8b}$$

Denoting the term $e^{\frac{Q_{\max}-Q_{\min}}{T}}$ by x, formulae (8a) and (8b) take the form of

$$\frac{1}{n}-\varepsilon<\frac{1}{nx},$$

$$\frac{x}{n}<\frac{1}{n}+\varepsilon.$$

Arranging these formulae to x, the lower limit of x is given as

$$x<\min\{\frac{1}{1-n\varepsilon},1+n\varepsilon\}.$$

Replacing x with the original exponential phrase,

$$e^{\frac{Q_{\max}-Q_{\min}}{T}}<\min\{\frac{1}{1-n\varepsilon},1+n\varepsilon\},$$

$$\frac{Q_{\max}-Q_{\min}}{T}<\ln\min\{\frac{1}{1-n\varepsilon},1+n\varepsilon\},$$

$$T>\frac{Q_{\max}-Q_{\min}}{\ln\min\{\frac{1}{1-n\varepsilon},1+\varepsilon n\}}.$$

As for part (b) of Theorem 2, the theoretical lower bound of the temperature is naturally 0, but using zero temperature causes division by zero error during numerical computations. So, in practical applications the lower limit of the temperature must be slightly higher than zero, even high enough to avoid floating point errors, but small enough to guarantee greedy probability distribution on a certain error level.

Since the probability p_i can never be larger than 1, instead of equation $|1-p_i|<\varepsilon$, equation $1-p_i<\varepsilon$ is considered. It was clear in part (a) that bounds on p_i values must be found, but in this special case only the lower bound of p_i is to be examined. Taking the form of equation (3) of the Boltzmann-formula, the lower bound can be set as

$$\frac{1}{1+\sum_{\substack{j=1\\ j\neq i}}^{n} e^{\frac{-\delta}{T}}} < \frac{1}{1+\sum_{\substack{i=1\\ j\neq i}}^{n} e^{\frac{Q_j-Q_i}{T}}} \tag{9}$$

for some δ Getting denominators disappeared, the previous inequality is held if $e^{\frac{Q_j-Q_i}{T}} < e^{\frac{-\delta}{T}}$, $j=1,2,\dots,n$, $j\neq i$, which yields $Q_j-Q_i<-\delta$, thus $Q_i-Q_j>\delta$. In the preconditions of the theorem it was stated that Q_i is the highest among all Q-values, therefore,

$$\delta = \min_{\substack{j=1,\dots,n\\ j\neq i}} |Q_i-Q_j| . \tag{10}$$

Returning to $1-p_i<\varepsilon$, the inequality must also be held, if the value p_i is replaced by a stronger constraint, by the left-hand side part of inequality (9). So,

$$1-\frac{1}{1+\sum_{\substack{j=1\\ j\neq i}}^{n} e^{\frac{-\delta}{T}}} < \varepsilon ,$$

$$1-\varepsilon < \frac{1}{1+\sum_{\substack{j=1\\ j\neq i}}^{n} e^{\frac{-\delta}{T}}} = \frac{1}{1+(n-1)e^{\frac{-\delta}{T}}} ,$$

$$(1-\varepsilon)(1+(n-1)e^{\frac{-\delta}{T}}) < 1 ,$$

$$e^{\frac{-\delta}{T}} < \frac{\frac{1}{1-\varepsilon}-1}{n-1} = \frac{\varepsilon}{(1-\varepsilon)(n-1)} ,$$

$$\frac{-\delta}{T} < \ln \frac{\varepsilon}{(1-\varepsilon)(n-1)} .$$

Property 1: *Since ε is a small positive error, it is reasonable to suppose that $\varepsilon < 0.5$, in which case the argument of the logarithmic expression falls between 0 and 1, yielding the whole logarithmic expression to be negative.*

Due to the division by a negative number, the relational signal turns over, and the lower temperature bound is expressed as

$$T < \frac{-\delta}{\ln \frac{\varepsilon}{(1-\varepsilon)(n-1)}} .$$

Notice that, due to the negative sign of the numerator and also to Property 1 (negative sign of the denominator), the temperature will be positive. ■

5 Implementation Experiences of Temperature Bounds

The use of temperature bounds emerges when the preferences are changing in time and there is a balance problem between exploitation of agent's current knowledge and exploration of new, supposedly better actions. If the preference values change in time, the agent should raise its temperature up to T_{max} in order to let actions be selected with equal probability. Then, cooling to T_{min} is required according to some cooling function [6].

It is easy to see that the theoretical values of T_{max} and T_{min} are useful. In practice, however, it is also satisfactory letting "exploration temperature" (i.e. T_{max}) slightly below and "exploitation temperature" slightly above the theoretical values.

A concrete implementation of the temperature bounds' theorem is carried out in agent-based Internet packet routing protocol assignment. In this example a network of routers is represented by a directed graph and the task is to transfer data packet from a source node to a sink node, on the shortest possible path in time [1][8]. Each agent maintains a routing table, which is defined as a preference table with rows indicating possible next-hop routers, and columns stating the known destinations, and table slots maintaining the preference values. The routing decision is about to assign a next-hop machine to each incoming data packet provided that its destination is known. (This type of routing is referred to as destination-based routing in networking technology.) A router must make its decision locally. Two extreme behaviors of router agents are distinguished: the router tries to find new routes and wishes to deliver data via known routes. The temperature parameter is used to balance the agent between the two extreme behaviors and temperature bounds are used to mark the possible domain of balancing. By implementing temperature-based models it is also possible that each agent has its own temperature value and, therefore, its own capability of finding new routes. This feature is particularly important when the network is large, and re-calculating routes for the whole network, due to some change in the environment, would be infeasible.

A routing simulator has been implemented in Java, and a network-level temperature model has been created. An automatic cooling and re-cooling algorithm was used based on the theoretical temperature bounds, which provided good results in the sense of dynamic behavior on a large variety of test-topologies.

Conclusions

In the paper reinforcement learning algorithm that uses Boltzmann's action selection policy has been shown. A crucial question of all reinforcement learning approaches is how exploration and exploitation can be balanced. The paper has given theoretical limits of the balancing domain by using temperature parameter and bounds familiar from simulated annealing.

An application example of re-learning shortest paths on large-scaled networks was also mentioned.

Acknowledgements. The authors would like to express their appreciation to József Váncza, András Márkus, Anikó Ekárt, László Dudás for their thorough help and inspiration. This work was partially supported by the National Research Foundation, Hungary, Grant number T026486 and T034632.

References

1. Ahuja, R., Magnanti, T.L., Orlin, J.B.: Network flows, Prentice Hall, ISBN 013617549-X, 1993
2. Crites, P.H., Barto, A.: Improving elevator performance using reinforcement learning, Advances in Neural Information Processing Systems, Vol. 8, MIT, 1996
3. Kaelbling L.P., Littman, M., Moore A.J.: Reinforcement learning: a survey, Journal of Artificial Intelligence Research, Vol. 4, 1996, pp. 237-285
4. Monostori, L., Márkus, A., Van Brussel, H., Westkämper, E.: Machine learning approaches to manufacturing, CIRP Annals, Vol. 45, No. 2, 1996, pp. 675-712.
5. Monostori, L., Kádár, B.; Viharos, Zs.J., Stefán, P.: AI and machine learning techniques combined with simulation for designing and controlling manufacturing processes and systems, Preprints of the IFAC Symposium on Manufacturing, Modeling, Management and Supervision, MIM 2000, 2000, Patras, Greece, pp. 167-172
6. Stefán, P., Monostori, L., Pupp, Z.: Reinforcement learning methods in information engineering, MicroCAD'2000 International Computer Science Conference, February 22-24, 2000, University of Miskolc
7. Sutton, R., Barto, A.: Reinforcement Learning (An Introduction), 1998
8. Tanenbaum, A.: Computer networks, Panem Press, ISBN 963 545 213 6, 1996

9. Viharos, Zs. J.: Application capabilities of a general, ANN based cutting model in different phases of manufacturing through automatic determination of its input-output configuration; Journal of Periodica Politechnica - Mechanical Engineering, Vol. 43, No. 2, 1999, pp. 189-196
10. Numerical recipes in C: The art of scientific computing, Cambridge University Press, ISBN 0-521-43108-5, http://www.nr.com

A View Selection Tool for Multidimensional Databases

Hasan M. Jamil and Giovanni A. Modica

Mississippi State University, Department of Computer Science
Mississippi State MS 39762, USA
{jamil,gmodica}@cs.msstate.edu

Abstract. Materialized views speed up query response time at the cost of view maintenance and data duplication. However, for some systems, the use of materialized views is restricted by factors like space availability and query response time. Not all possible views for a multidimensional cube can be materialized because the number of views grows exponential to the number of cube dimensions. The system must decide which subset of materialized views produce the maximum benefit in terms of some constraints. There are many algorithms in the literature that address this problem, BPUS and PBS algorithms address the problem of view selection in multidimensional database using a benefit metric based on space availability. This paper presents a design and implementation of a tool for view selection for multidimensional databases.

1 Introduction

Queries on OLAP systems need a great amount of aggregation (i.e. summation, average, count, etc.) on the fact table for all the possible combinations of dimensions. Aggregations in databases take a lot of computational time and people using OLAP systems for decision support can't afford that. If these aggregations are precalculated an stored in the database as materialized views, the query response time decreases since the system doesn't need to recalculate all the aggregations every time a query is asked to the OLAP system. However, depending on the data configuration, the number of possible materialized views grows exponentially with the number of dimensions of the cube, making impossible to materialize all possible views due to system (or user) restrictions.

In general, a cube with n dimensions has 2^n possible views. System restrictions like space availability make impossible to store and maintain so many views. However, this is not an all-or-nothing problem. Only a subset of the views can be materialized and the rest of the views can be calculated using a rewritten expression based on the materialized ones. But one question arises: What subset to materialize? The answer is the views that produce the best benefit given some system/user restrictions. For 256 views, the number of possible subsets is 2^{256}. So it's impossible to try to attempt an exhaustive search for the best subset, it's just impracticable.

L. Monostori, J. Váncza, and M. Ali (Eds.): IEA/AIE 2001, LNAI 2070, pp. 237–246, 2001.

The problem of view materialization can also be seen as a search problem (like search problems in artificial intelligence) where the search space is all the possible subsets of views and the goal state is the subset that maximizes/minimizes the restriction. As in all search problems in AI, the search process must use some kind of heuristic to boost the speed and performance of the search. This is why most of the algorithms in the literature for view materialization selection use some kind of heuristics (depending on the restriction) to drive the search. These algorithms don't produce the best subset but instead a subset that achieves some degree of performance (63% in the case of the PBS algorithm). A general framework for view selection problems is detailed in [1]. The framework identifies the view selection problem as the problem of selecting views to materialize based on the satisfaction of different design goals. Goals can be a minimization of a cost function (e.g. query evaluation cost, view maintenance cost, operational cost, etc.) or system/user constraints (e.g. space available, query response time, etc.).

This paper uses as a design goal a benefit metric defined in [2] that can be catalogued according to [1] as a system constraint: space availability. The subset of views to be materialized has to produce the maximum benefit to the system [2]. The trade-off between available space for materialized views and query response time is explained in detail in [2] and [3]. Different algorithms have been proposed to address the problem of view selection on multidimensional databases. Some of them, like the BPUS [5], the PBS [2] and the Modified PBS [4], are based on a benefit metric that the algorithm has to maximize in order to select the subset of views with better query response time vs. space availability.

This paper presents the design and initial implementation of a general tool for view selection problems in multidimensional databases. It is organized as follows. The tool functionality is presented first, describing all the features implemented in this version of the tool. Then, the tool architecture and modules are described in section 3. Section 4 introduces some implementation details like algorithms and data structures. Section 5 introduces the user interface. Finally, conclusions and future work oriented to the enhancement of the tool for the next version is discussed in section 6.

2 Tool Functionality

The tool has a modular design where every module can be replaced as needed. For example, the module responsible of the view benefit calculation, which by defaults, is based on the PBS [2] algorithm, can be replaced for a different module implementing any other benefit based algorithm like BPUS [5] or Modified PBS [4], in the case of space availability, or any other algorithm that uses different goals as view selection conditions. The input to the tool is metadata describing a star/snowflake schema. The metadata includes: description of the fact table, dimensions, aggregation operations against the fact table, and statistics about the data. Statistics about the data include cardinality of the dimensions domain, number of tuples in the fact table as well as expected number of tuples for each view in the multidimensional cube. This metadata can be entered to the system in three ways: (1) the user can specify an input data file containing the required metadata following a specific XML format, (2) the user can interactively specify the metadata using a graphical user interface for that purpose, or (3) the user can use one of the integration modules to obtain the metadata from data dictionaries on databases like Oracle and MSSQL Server OLAP Server.

Once the tool analyzes the metadata, the user is provided with important information, like for example: total number of possible views to materialize, total space required in case all views are materialized, and any other relevant information that can be derived about the fact table and dimensions attributes. Also, a graphical implementation of a lattice for the views and the star/snowflake schema is presented to help the user visualize the problem. The system explains to the user why the subset chosen is the best subset using different criteria like time required vs. space used or number of tuples to scan saved. The system presents to the user a selection interface where the user can interactively modify and expand/contract the view selection conditions. For example, in the case of space availability, the user can increase/decrease the amount of space available while the system calculates the views to select in real time.

The system also provides the functionality that, given a set of views to materialize indicated by the user, it calculates the benefit of that set compared with the optimal solution as calculated by the view selection algorithm. The details about this feature are explained in the implementation details in section 4. Finally, the system must explain what assumptions, if any, where considered to obtain the results.

3 System Architecture

The system architecture for the view selection tool is presented in figure 1. The main two modules for the tool are the Metadata Analyzer Module and the Calculation Module.

The job of the Integration Module is to retrieve the metadata about the fact table and dimensions, as well as statistics about dimension cardinality and number of tuples. As explained in section 2, metadata can be retrieved from input data files, interactively using a GUI or from database data dictionaries. In order to accommodate for heterogeneous database systems, wrappers must be defined for each DB. For the specific implementation of the tool, Java JDBC is used as a universal wrapper. JDBC has a wide range of interoperability with the most common databases, so it's not needed to implement new wrappers. For further information about wrappers refer to [3]. The Integration Module is also responsible to pass the metadata information in the proper format to the Metadata Analyzer Module. This module is responsible of the metadata interpretation. It also creates an abstraction level between the format used as data input and the format required by the calculation algorithm residing in the Calculation Module. Using this approach is easy to replace the calculation

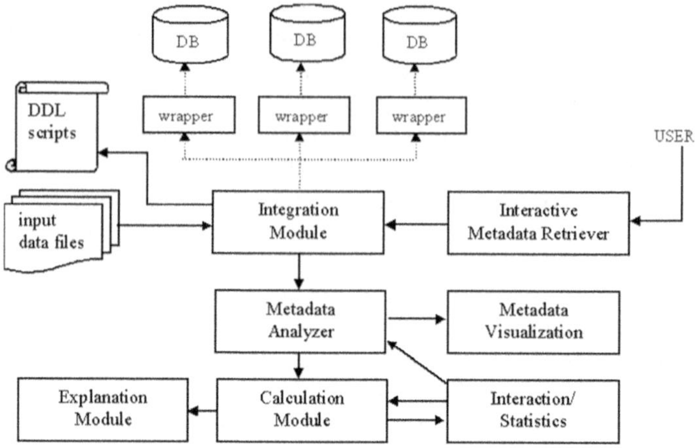

Fig. 1. System Architecture for the view selection tool

algorithm without affecting the front end of the tool. The metadata analyzer also serves information to the Metadata Visualization Module.

The job of the Metadata Visualization Module is to provide to the user a graphical representation of the metadata, currently represented as a lattice and the star/snowflake schema representation of the fact table and dimensions. The Explanation Module is responsible of presenting the technical justification of the set of views chosen by the tool to the user. Every algorithm plugged in the tool needs to provide different "explanation" sets, like for example, an explanation of the selection goal used by the algorithm, an explanation of the metrics used to accomplish the goal, set of statistics used, etc. The job of the Interactive/Statistics Module is to manage statistics calculation for the representation, like for example, in the case of an algorithm that uses space constraints, a graph of space vs. query response time [2]. It also allows the user to manipulate this statistics and the result set of views to see differences in view selection criteria.

Finally, the most important module, the Calculation Module is responsible of the calculation of the optimal set of views that maximize the benefit. Although the current algorithm used for this module is the PBS algorithm of [2], this module can host multiple algorithms that can be applied to the same metadata to see differences in algorithm response time and result set. As explained before, to allow for the implementation of multiple algorithms, this module retrieves the data from the Metadata Analyzer Module.

4 Implementation Details

4.1 View Selection Algorithm

The most important requirement for this tool is to allow working with any kind of view selection algorithm. Using Java interface declaration, an interface for a generic algorithm is defined which every algorithm plugged in the tool must implement. The following is a subset of the methods declared by the interface: `getAdvantageMeasure()`, `getBenefitTable()`, `findOptimalViews()`, `getBenefitExplanation()`, `getAdvantageMeasureExplanation()`.

The `Algorithm` interface defines the signature required by algorithms to be plugged in to the tool. The `findOptimalViews` method is used to calculate the set of views to materialize using a benefit table (in case the algorithm uses some kind of benefit metric to satisfy the condition, like in the case of the PBS algorithm [2]). The `getBenefitTable` method returns a table representation of the benefit table to be displayed in the statistical module of the tool. The `getBenefitExplanation` method returns a string that represents an explanation of the benefit function used by the algorithm to calculate the subset of views to materialize, this method is used by the explanation module to display explanation information to the user. Finally, the `findOptimalViews` method is the principal and most important method in the interface. It encapsulates the implementation of the algorithm to calculate the optimal set of views to be materialized. The `findOptimalViews` method can use information encapsulated in a `Lattice` and `Database` structure to calculate the set of views. It can also make use of the benefit table in case the algorithm requires it.

The `getAdvantageMeasure` method is used when a performance comparison between the views selected by the algorithm and the views selected by the user is necessary. For the case of the PBS Algorithm the advantage measure represents the number of rows saved to scan for a particular set of materialized views. The advantage measure can represent different comparisons values depending on the algorithm used in the implementation. With the use of the method `getAdvantageMeasureExplanation`, is possible to present to the user an explanation (either quantitative or qualitative) of the advantage measure. For the PBS Algorithm the advantage measure is calculated as follows:

$$advantage = \sum_{i \in lattice} f(i), \text{ where } f(i) = \begin{cases} tuples(i) & \text{if } i \text{ is selected} \\ tuples(j) & \text{if } i \text{ is not selected} \end{cases} \tag{1}$$

In the formula above, $tuples(i)$ is the number of tuples that the element i has in the lattice. The element i is selected if it belongs to the set of materialized views selected by the algorithm or selected interactively by the user. The j represents the parent of the element i that is selected and has the minimum number of tuples among the parents. If the element i has no selected parent then the parent is the upper most element in the lattice.

The tool allows the dynamic load and unload of different algorithms, however only one algorithm can be active at any given time. Future work will be focused on the implementation of and MDI (Multi Document Interface) so the user can have multiple instances of the same problem and apply different algorithms and measures to each instance. Algorithms are loaded/unloaded using the concept of a plug-in. Plug-ins are added to the tool in a dynamic fashion using a Plug-in Manager. A plug-in is basically a `.class` compiled Java file that implements the algorithm interface described earlier. When a plug-in is loaded, the file name (without the `.class` extension) is used as the plug-in name. Every time an algorithm needs to be executed the system checks for the current selected plug-in. In order to dynamically create class instances at run time, the `createInstance` method in the `Class.forName(<plug-in>)` class is executed. Using this method, the tool is not tied to a particular algorithm.

The benefit table is a table identifying the benefit metric as given by the specific algorithm and obtained from view materialization per every possible materialization combination. For the PBS Algorithm, the benefit for each element is given by [2]:

$$benefit = (tp - te) * (sb + 1)/te \tag{2}$$

where tp is the number of tuples in the upper most element of the lattice, te is the number of tuples for the current element, and sb us the number of subsets of the current element.

Most of the methods in the interface use an implementation of a lattice structure that contains the set of all possible views to materialize. The lattice structure defines methods to traverse the lattice, to obtain the top element of the lattice, to select or deselect a lattice element, and methods required by the visualization model to display a graphical representation of the lattice.

The tool implements the PBS Algorithm defined in [2] for which pseudo-code for the main method in the interface is given below:

```
findOptimalViews(Lattice lattice,double space)
  LatticeElement e=lattice.topElement();
  e.setSelection(true);
  Iterator i=benefitTable.iterator();
  while(space > 0 && i.hasNext())
     smallest=i.next();
     if((space - smallest.tuples) >= 0)
        space-=smallest.tuples;
        e=lattice.findLatticeElement(smallest);
        e.setSelection(true);
     else space=0;
```

Note that the specific implementation of the PBS algorithm for this tool always selects the top view (the view that includes all the dimensions) to be part of the optimal set of materialized views. This is because any other view in the lattice can be represented as a rewritten expression of the top view. The space constraint represents the total number of tuples available for materialization of views excluding the top view, e.g., if the space is n tuples, then the total number of tuples in the set of materialized views cannot exceed n tuples. Although the algorithm defined in [2] uses number of tuples as the space metric, the tool modifies the algorithm to consider a most realistic metric representation for the space constraint: the actual physical storage space (in bytes) of a view in the RDBMS. The tool can retrieve this information from RDBMS statistics since every data dictionary contains the type and size in bytes for every column in the fact table and the dimensions attributes.

With this metric, the benefit table presented earlier adds a fourth column that represents the size in bytes of the materialized view. The size in bytes is given by the following formula:

$$N_b = \left(\sum_{i \in dimension} size(d_1) + \sum_{i \in fact} size(f_i) \right) * tuples \tag{3}$$

where N_b is the size in bytes of the materialized view, $size(x)$ is the size in bytes of an attribute in a DB, and *fact* and *dimensions* correspond to the set of attributes in the fact table and dimensions of the fact table. Currently the number of tuples for each materialized view is estimated and given as input, however, future work is oriented in the calculation of this approximation using statistics obtained from the DB like the cardinality of the attributes.

4.2 Data Structures

Most of the methods implemented by the algorithm interface use a special implementation of a lattice and database structure. A lattice is generated given a set of dimensions used in the view materialization algorithm. Figure 2 presents the lattice representation of an example view selection problem. Every element in the lattice is represented by a `LatticeElement` structure, which defines a set of methods and attributes to allow the manipulation and display of the lattice element. The most important attributes of a lattice element are: the set (which defines the subset of the dimension represented by the element, e.g. `{storeID, quarter}`), the tuples (the number of tuples in the materialization of the view represented by the lattice element), the size in bytes of the materialization, and the selected attribute (which indicates if a lattice element was selected by the view selection algorithm).

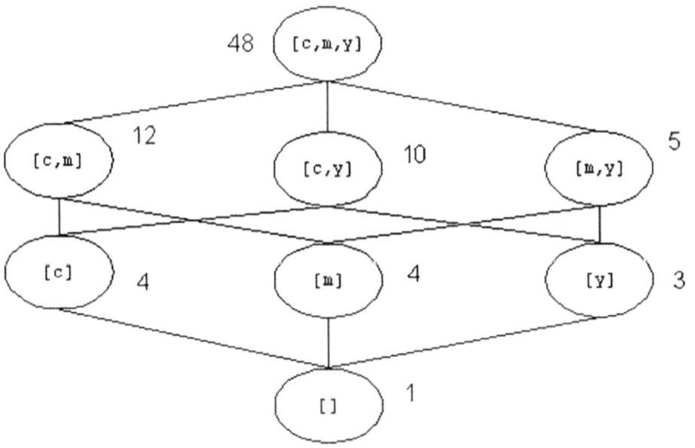

Fig. 2. A lattice representation of a view problem

Every lattice element is represented as a binary string of the size of the dimensions. Using this binary format, a 1 in position i indicates the presence of the attribute i in the lattice element, while a 0 represents the absence of the attribute. For example, and reusing the lattice of figure 2, the size of the binary string is 3 since there are only three dimensions and the order of the attributes is `cmy`. With this attribute order, the string `111` represents the top most view and the string `000` represents the lower most view. Other elements in the lattice are, `cy`, represented by `101`, and `m` represented by `010`. This binary representation of a lattice element speeds up operation in the view calculation algorithm, like for example: calculate if a specific view is "child" of another view. Particularly a view is a child of another if the following condition is true:

$$V_a \subseteq V_b \Longleftrightarrow B(V_a) \otimes B(V_b) \leq B(V_a) \tag{4}$$

where V_i represents the i view and $B(x)$ is the binary representation of view x. The $\otimes$ operator is the binary `AND` operator. The binary representation is then transformed to its integer value and compared with the "child" view.

Using a binary representation of a lattice element is easy to know in what level in the lattice the element resides (which is useful to construct the level index explained later). Calculating the level of the element in the lattice is just counting the number of 1s in the binary representation of the element.

The lattice structure also uses two index structures to store the lattice. The first structure is an array of views indexed by the binary representation of the view. Figure 3 shows an example of the index for the lattice in figure 2. The other index structure represents the levels of the lattice; it stores the integer representation of the binary string for every materialized view. Even if the level of an element in the lattice can be calculated as explained before, the precalculation of this information stored in an index improves the speed of certain operations (specially graphical operations). This second structure is used mostly for graphical purposes even if it is also available to the algorithm interface methods in case the algorithm needs to have access to the levels of the lattice. Using the second index can improve calculation time in case of lattice with a high number

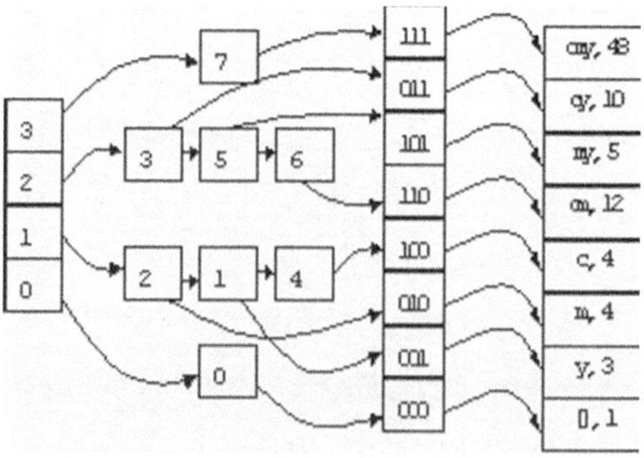

Fig. 3. Index structure for a lattice

of dimensions, since the algorithms don't need to calculate the hierarchy of the lattice. Both index structures are calculated the first time the lattice is loaded and don't need to be maintained by the algorithms for view selection calculation.

Another data structure used by the tool is the `Database` structure. This structure is created by the integration module and it constitutes the middle interface between the calculation module and the RDBMSs. The database structure is designed to accommodate any type of RDBMS. This is basically a hierarchical structure where all the metadata information about a database is stored. This structure allows storing the information about only one server at a time; if the bases/dimensions tables reside in more than two servers then two database structures are required. When the tool connects to a RDBMS the user needs to specify which table constitutes the fact table and which table(s) constitute(s) the dimension table(s). Future work is oriented to adopt a broader specification for the database structure allowing different fact tables and fact table attributes as dimensions (e.g. `Time` dimension).

5 User Interface

The interface was entirely created using the Java Swing UI library. Figure 4 presents the interface of the View Selection Tool. The figure is a snapshot of the tool after the PBS Algorithm is applied to an example lattice retrieved from a database. Note how the PBS Algorithm chooses the views marked in red in the lattice displayed on the visualization panel. Note also how the explanation panel

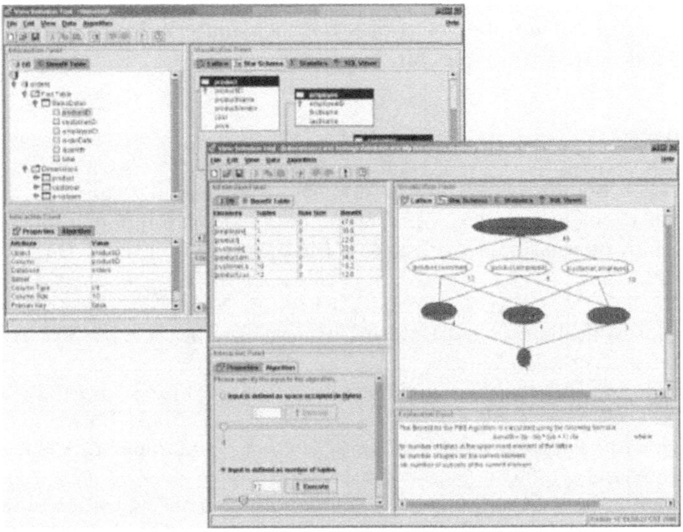

Fig. 4. A snapshot of the View Selection Tool after the PBS algorithm is applied

and the statistical panel are updated with the relevant information returned by the implementation of the PBS Algorithm. The messages displayed in these areas will vary with every implementation of a view selection algorithm plugged into the tool.

Different panels comprise the tool. Panels like the lattice panel, star schema panel, statistics panel and SQL views of the materialized views selected present different alternatives to the database administrator to work with the view selection problem.

6 Conclusion

This paper presents an implementation for a view selection tool. The modular design of the architecture and the implementation of the algorithm interface allow for the use of multiple view selection algorithms using different goals and metrics for the view selection problem. Even though the algorithm used by the tool is the PBS algorithm, other algorithms like the BPUS and Modified PBS can be used as well.

Future work is directed to the implementation of additional features proposed in this paper. This includes the implementation of different view selection algorithms to be plugged into the tool as well as the comparison module to allow statistical and metric comparison between different algorithms in the same category or different categories. Future versions will also focus on the problem of view selection for object oriented or object-relational oriented databases. More work will be oriented to enhance the DB interoperability between the tool and the JDBC interface to the different databases. Although most of the metadata is retrieved automatically from the database connection, the user still needs to specify some information in order to be able to run the algorithms in the tool. Data, like expected number of tuples for each materialized view, will be automatically calculated from the database.

References

1. Dimitry Theodoratos, Mokrane Bouzeghoub. A General Framework for the View Selection Problem for Data Warehouse Design and Evolution. Proceedings of the ACM Third International Workshop on Data Warehousing and OLAP, 1-8. McLean, VA, 2000.
2. Amit Shulka, Prasad M. Deshpande, Jeffrey F. Naughton. Materialized View Selection for Multidimensional Datasets. Proceedings of the 24th VLDB Conference, 488-99. New York, USA, 1998.
3. Ashish Gupta, Inderpal S. Mumick (Editors): Materialized Views: Techniques, Implementations, and Applications. First Edition, MIT Press, 1999.
4. Xingquan Lu. Fast Aggregates of Data Cube by Materializing Views. Mississippi State University, 1999.
5. V. Harinataran, A. Rajaraman, J.D. Ullman. Implementing Data Cubes Efficiently. Proceedings. ACM SIGMOD International Conference On Management Data, 205-227, 1996.

Inductive learning of a knowledge dictionary for a text mining system

Shigeaki Sakurai, Yumi Ichimura, Akihiro Suyama, and Ryohei Orihara

Corporate Research & Development Center, TOSHIBA Corporation
1, Komukai Toshiba-cho, Saiwai-ku, Kawasaki, Kanagawa, 212-8582, Japan

Abstract. A text mining system using domain-dependent dictionaries efficiently analyzes text data. The dictionaries store not only important words for the domains, but also rules composed of some important words. The paper proposes a method that automatically acquires the rules from the text data and their classes by using a fuzzy inductive learning method. Also, in order to infer a class corresponding to new text data, the paper proposes an inference method based on the acquired fuzzy decision tree. Moreover, the efficiency of the methods is verified through numerical experiments using more than 1,000 daily business reports concerning retailing.

1 Introduction

Recently text mining techniques[1][2][3] that process directly reports have attracted attention. One of the techniques[2] classifies daily business reports by using two kinds of knowledge dictionaries and shows only the reports included in a class of interest to us. In the case of this technique, the knowledge dictionaries are important and have a great influence on classification results. However, since the dictionaries are created through trial and error, it is difficult to apply the technique to numerous problems. In this paper, section 2 introduces the text mining system in [2], section 3 proposes a learning method and an inference method of a knowledge dictionary, section 4 shows numerical experiments using daily business reports, and section 5 shows summary and future works.

2 Text mining system

The text mining method in [2] classifies daily business reports by using two kinds of knowledge dictionaries. One is called the key concept dictionary. The dictionary is composed of three layers. The first layer is called the concept class and shows a set of concepts that have a common feature. The second layer is called the key concept and shows a set of expressions that have the same meaning. The third layer is called the expression and shows important phrases and words concerning a target problem. In this layer, the phrases and the words are described in consideration with the inflection. For example, Figure 1(a) shows a key concept dictionary in retailing. On the other hand, the other is called the

L. Monostori, J. Váncza, and M. Ali (Eds.): IEA/AIE 2001, LNAI 2070, pp. 247–252, 2001.

concept relation dictionary. The dictionary is composed of condition part that is a conjunction of key concepts and result part that is a text class. The text class shows a viewpoint that classifies reports concerning a target problem. For example, Figure 1(b) shows a relation described in a concept relation dictionary in retailing.

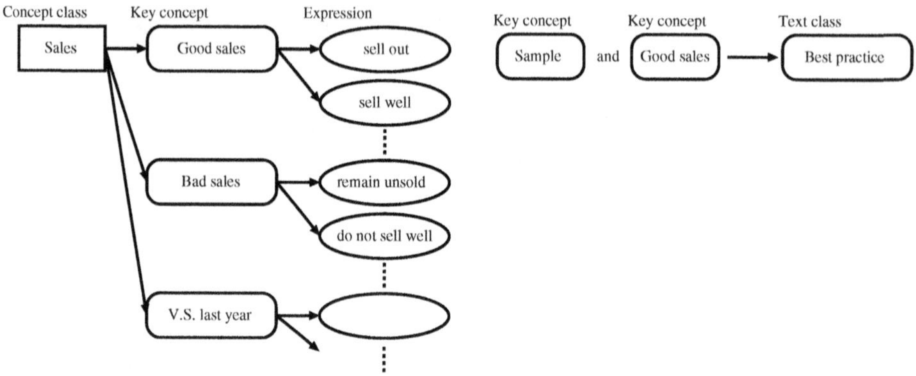

(a)Key concept dictionary (b)Concept relation dictionary

Fig. 1. Knowledge dictionary

The method decomposes the reports to words by lexical analysis. Each word is checked as to whether it is registered in the key concept dictionary. If the word is registered in it, the key concept corresponding to the word is assigned to the report. The method also puts reports that have a concept relation into a group; the relation is registered in the concept relation dictionary and is composed of some key concepts and a text class. A reader reads the reports classified in classes where each class represents her/his interests and looks through the trend of the key concepts for all reports. Therefore, he/she efficiently utilizes the information.

3 Automatic acquisition of a knowledge dictionary

3.1 Learning method

A relation stored in a concept relation dictionary shows a meaning that occurs by combining key concepts and is regarded as a kind of rule. On the other hand, if it allows us to regard key concepts extracted by lexical analysis of a daily business report as attribute values, their concept classes as attributes, and a text class given by a human as a class of a training example, the example is generated from the report. Thus, an inductive learning method[4][5] acquires the relation from examples. It is necessary for the method to deal with the examples that consist of attribute values with fuzziness and have some classes, because the report usually includes fuzzy descriptions and the human may allocate some classes to the report. So, the IDTF shown in Table 1 is adapted as the method, because it solves these problems based on the fuzzy set theory.

Table 1. IDTF algorithm.

---

1. Allocate a training example set to a new node and stack up the node.
2. Pick out a node from the stack. This algorithm is over, when you cannot do it.
3. Evaluate whether classes with degree of certainty should be allocated to the node. Return to the step 2, when it is decided that the classes should be done.
4. (a) Create such fuzzy sets that represent an attribute for each attribute A_i, where the sets are called by fuzzy class items.
   (b) Calculate evaluation values of the attributes according to their items and the training example subset allocated to the node.
   (c) Select an attribute with the best evaluation value and allocate the attribute to the node.
   (d) Decompose the training example subset into new subsets according to its items and allocate each subset to a new node.
   (e) Create such branches that connect the original node to each new node and allocate each item to its corresponding branch.
   (f) Stack up the new nodes and return to the step 2.

The IDTF acquires rules, described by a fuzzy decision tree shown in the left of Figure 2, from the examples. In this figure, each intermediate node described by a shaded circle stores an attribute, each terminal node described by a highlighted circle stores classes with degree of certainty, each branch described by a line between nodes stores a fuzzy class item, and a course from the top intermediate node to a terminal node shows a rule. That is, the tree has three rules shown in the right of Figure 2.

3.2 Inference method

A fuzzy decision tree utilizes such an inference method that does not take into consideration the fuzziness and such an inference method that do it. In the former method, a class of an evaluation report is regarded as impossibility or default class, when an attribute value of it is not equal to any fuzzy class items on lower branches corresponding to a node. On the other hand, in such case, the latter method transfers the report with degree of certainty to nodes immediately below the node, evaluates both their degree and the degree of certainty of the text classes in terminal nodes, and decides a text class corresponding to it by total of results of the evaluations. The latter method utilizes attribute values of the report more efficiently than the former one.

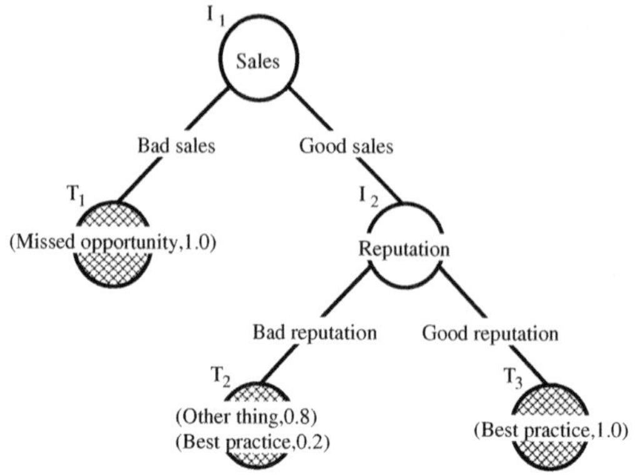

(1)If "Sales" is "Bad Sales", then the class is "Missed opportunity" with 1.0.
(2)If "Sales" is "Good Sales" and "Reputation" is "Bad reputation", then the class is "Other thing" with 0.8 and the class is "Best practice" with 0.2.
(3)If "Sales" is "Good Sales" and "Reputation" is "Good reputation", then the class is "Best practice" with 1.0.

Fig. 2. Fuzzy decision tree

4 Numerical experiments

4.1 Training examples

The text mining system[2] classifies daily business reports concerning retailing into three text classes: "Best practice", "Missed opportunity", and "Other thing". The system has a key concept dictionary composed of 13 concept classes and a concept relation dictionary composed of 349 rules. In this experiments, 142 attributes are generated by structurizing the classes to keep their independence. Also, reports with some key concepts belonging to the same attribute are deleted, because the reports contain contradictions. Thus, 780 training examples are generated from 1,044 daily business reports, where the number of "Best practice", "Missed opportunity", and "Other thing" are 47, 50, and 683.

4.2 Evaluation examples

Using the knowledge dictionaries and random numbers generates evaluation examples. That is, at first, an attribute value corresponding to each attribute is decided by selecting either "nothing" or a key concept included into the attribute based on the random numbers. Next, a class corresponding to a generated attribute value set is decided by evaluating the concept relation dictionary. Thus, an evaluation example is composed of a pair of the value set and the class. In this experiments, 10,000 evaluation examples are utilized.

4.3 Evaluation method

In this experiments, it allows us to generate a concept relation dictionary from training examples, infer classes of evaluation examples based on the generated dictionary, and evaluate whether a class based on the dictionary given by a human and a class based on the generated dictionary are equal. Here, the decomposition ratio changes 0%, 10%, and 20%, and the prune ratio changes 85%, 90%, 95%, and 100%. These parameters are parameters of the IDTF which control size of a fuzzy decision tree, the former parameter shows the minimum ratio of training examples included in a terminal node for all training, and the latter parameter shows the minimum ratio occupied by the maximum class in a terminal node. On the other hand, the inference methods are changed in an intermediate node and a terminal node. That is, the method in the intermediate node is performed both in a case in which fuzziness is taken into consideration and in one in which fuzziness is not taken into consideration. Also, the method in the terminal node is performed both in a case in which priority is accorded to the classes "Best practice" and "Missed opportunity" and in one in which priority is not accorded to the classes.

4.4 Experimental results

Table 2 shows accuracy in the case that the prune ratio is 100%, the decomposition ratio changes 0%, 10%, and 20%, and four inference methods are used. In this table, "Deco. ratio = 0", "10", and "20" show results in the case that the decomposition ratio is 0%, 10%, and 20%, "Propagation" and "Non-propagation" show results in a case in which fuzziness is taken into consideration in an intermediate node and in one in which fuzziness is not taken into consideration, and "Priority" and "Non-priority" show results in a case in which priority is accorded to the classes "Best practice" and "Missed opportunity" and in one in which priority is not accorded to the classes.

Table 2. Accuracy for daily business reports

	Deco. ratio=0	Deco. ratio=10	Deco. ratio=20
Non-priority/Non-propagation	85.34	88.65	75.03
Non-priority/propagation	100.00	99.61	75.03
Priority/Non-propagation	85.34	86.04	100.00
Priority/Propagation	100.00	100.00	100.00

4.5 Considerations

This section shows that the proposed methods are efficient in terms of size of fuzzy decision trees, accuracy, and selected attributes.

(1)Size of fuzzy decision trees: The maximum size of fuzzy decision trees is 90 and is composed of 37 intermediate nodes and 53 terminal nodes. The number of rules included in the tree is 53. The number of the rules is much smaller than the 349 rules given by a human. Thus, we consider the learning method acquires a compact concept relation dictionary.

(2)Accuracy: In the case of "Propagation" and "Priority", each fuzzy decision tree infers the appropriate class regardless of the decomposition ratios. The tree also does so regardless of the prune ratios, however we do not show the table in this paper. Thus, we consider that the learning method acquires fuzzy decision trees with high accuracy and the inference method infers a class for an evaluation example appropriately. Here, one reason is that "Propagation" has an effect such that makes good the loss of training examples and the other reason is that "Priority" has an effect such that makes good the loss of rules for "Other thing".

(3)Selected attributes: The learning method selects "Sales" as the top attribute in all cases. The result corresponds to the intuition that "Best practice" and "Missed opportunity" have a strong relation with "Sales". Thus, we consider that the method acquires a concept relation dictionary coinciding with human intuition.

We consider that the methods acquire a compact and accurate concept relation dictionary and infer an appropriate class for each evaluation example by these considerations.

5 Summary and future works

The paper proposed the learning method that acquires a concept relation dictionary for a text mining system and the inference method using the dictionary. The paper also verified the efficiency of the methods through numerical experiments based on daily business reports concerning retailing.

In future works, we intend to try to acquire a key concept dictionary, because it is time-consuming for a human to create it. Also, we intend to try to analyze a questionnaire. The analysis is more difficult than the one concerning retailing, because a questionnaire includes a lot of contents and is described with many kinds of forms.

References

1. R. Feldman, "Exploiting background information in knowledge discovery from text", Journal of Intelligent Information Systems, 9, 83-97(1997).
2. Y. Ichimura, Y. Nakayama, T. Akahane, M. Miyoshi, T. Sekiguchi, and Y. Fujiwara, "Text mining for sales person's daily reports -extraction of best practice and missed opportunity-", Proceedings of the 14th annual conference of JSAI, 532-534(2000) (*in Japanese*).
3. P. Losiewicz, D. W. Oard, and R. N. Kostoff, "Textual data mining to support science and technology management", Journal of Intelligent Information Systems 15, 2, 99-119(2000).
4. J.R. Quinlan, "C4.5: Programs for machine learning", Morgan Kaufmann (1992).
5. S. Sakurai, and D. Araki, "The improvement of fuzzy inductive learning algorithm", T. IEE Japan, 116, 9, 1057-1063 (1996) (*in Japanese*).

Combining Symbolic and Numeric Techniques for DL Contents Classification and Analysis

Yannick Toussaint and Jean-Charles Lamirel

LORIA,
BP 239,
54506 Vandœuvre Cedex, France
Yannick.Toussaint@loria.fr, lamirel@loria.fr

Abstract. The goal of this article is to prove that the mixture of different classification and mining techniques coming from so different areas such as the numeric and the symbolic worlds can combine their mutual advantages in order to produce a significant enhancement of the overall classification and retrieval performance in a Data Mining or Information Retrieval context.

1 Introduction

The goal of this article is to prove that the mixture of different classification and mining techniques coming from so different areas such as the numeric and the symbolic worlds can combine their mutual advantages in order to produce a significant enhancement of the overall classification and retrieval performance in a Data Mining or Information Retrieval context. We will first present the models. Then we describe three different heuristics to combine them. We end with the definition of criteria to evaluate the quality of the different results.

2 The Models

The numerical model used in our experiment is the MicroNOMAD multiSOM 4 model, which represents itself a significant extension of the classical Kohonen SOM topographic map model 3. Conversely to the original Kohonen model, the MicroNOMAD multiSOM model is abble to manage the communication between several topographic maps. In the following section we will nevertheless not focus on the MicroNOMAD multiSOM specific capabilities but rather on its direct exploitation of the classical SOM principles. The SOM approach considers that a data classification can be viewed as a non linear mapping on a 2D neuron grid in which neurons establish predefined neighborhood relation. After the classification process, each neuron of the map will then play the role of a data class representative.

The symbolic approach to Database Content Analysis is based upon a Galois lattice1. An element in the lattice will be call **formal concept** to distinguish it from the notion of Kohonen class previously introduced. The analysis which

L. Monostori, J. Váncza, and M. Ali (Eds.): IEA/AIE 2001, LNAI 2070, pp. 253–258, 2001.

results from the overall symbolic process is composed both of a set of formal concepts structured in a hierarchy (the Galois lattice) and of a set of association rules.We will focus, in this article, on the hierarchical structure of the lattice.

3 The Complementarity of the Two Approaches

Each approach has its own strength and weakness that we underline in this section. The results of topographical classification methods such as MicroNOMAD results lead to interpretation problems due to the fact that the profile of the obtained classes are mostly complex weighted combination indexes extracted from the documents. The main characteristics of the classes are therefore difficult to highlight to the user and could cause shortcomings or mistakes in the interpretation of the database content.

The usually high number of classes of a lattice, its hierarchical structure and the lack of any topological structure makes of course harder its visualization and decrease the global readability of the analysis. Even if building a lattice is a time-consuming process with a high complexity, their interests in information retrieval and in text mining activities relies on their incrementality, the possible extraction of association rules and the possible integration of background knowledge.

4 The Experiment

The core experiment consists in building both the Kohonen topography and the lattice using the same initial data set. It has been carried out on the iconographic database of the "Art Nouveau" period managed by the BIBAN server. BIBAN is a research prototype for iconographic Digital Libraries. The BIBAN database contains approximately 300 images related to the various artistic works of the Art Nouveau School. The images are associated to a bibliographic description containing a title, keywords and author information. Each image constitutes an individual and each of its keywords is considered as a property.

4.1 The Methodology

To study the complementarity of the numerical and symbolic models, we will adopt a three-level approach:

1. **projection:** we first project each Kohonen class onto one or more formal concept of the lattice. "Projection" designates either the process of calculation or, for a given Kohonen class, the formal concept(s) it has been projected on. We aims at defining criteria to evaluate the quality of the pairs (kc, fc) where kc is a Kohonen class and fc its projection.
2. **grouping:** grouping is not a process but uses the structure provided by the projection process. Instead of evaluating the pairs (kc, fc) we will study the pairs $(\bigcup_{i=1}^{n} \mathtt{kc_i}), fc)$ where $\mathtt{kc_i}$ are the different classes projected onto $\mathtt{fc}$.

3. **agglomerating:** the agglomeration algorithm associates to the formal concept fc_2 the set of Kohonen classes associated to his sons by projection or by agglomeration. Agglomeration is supposed to answer the question "how could we group Kohonen classes into areas, and areas into bigger ones?".

The definition of the heuristics to project a Kohonen class onto a formal concept and the quality of this projection is of course crucial for further observations. We tested three of them :

The subsumption: The subsumption is the first heuristics coming to mind to projet a Kohonen class onto a formal concept in the lattice. It is in complete accordance with the lattice building principle. The major problem comes from the fact that a Kohonen class is characterized by a number of properties – sometimes with a very low weight – much higher than the formal concepts in the lattice. Carpineto 2 kept the `k` first properties, `k` being the average of the properties in the numeric method. We adopted the notion of treshold and tested four different ones: 0.0 – keeping all the properties of the Kohonen class, 0.1 keeping properties which value is under 0.1, then 0.2 and 0.3. Using subsumption, a Kohonen class is generally projected onto more than one formal concept.

The definition of a distance: In order to prune the structure obtained by the subsumption projection and to obtain an easier-to-read hierarchical structure with less formal concepts, another heuristics for the projection is based upon the definition of a distance between a Kohonen class and a formal concept. The Kohonen class is then projected onto only one formal concept, the closest one.As the weights of the profile of the individuals have been normed in the Kohonen model, the cosine distance C has been choosen for the comparison :

$$C = \frac{T.K}{\|T\| * \|K\|}$$

where K and T represent respectively the weighted vector of the Kohonen class and of the formal concept. N is the length of these vectors.

Combining subsumption and distance: This method searches for all the subsumants to the Kohonen class and then choose the closest one following the distance.

Heuristics for agglomeration: Starting from the Kohonen map, groups define a first level of areas. Then, these areas are agglomerated into larger ones until all the map is grouped into a single vaste area. The hierarchical structure of the lattice seems a good structure to build these areas. The first heuristics for agglomeration is the most immediate. Each formal concept fc_i groups one or more Kohonen classes. Agglomeration propagates this set of classes to the immediate fathers of fc_i. And so on, until being at the top of the lattice which is though associated to the whole set of Kohonen classes. However, because of multiple inheritance in the lattice, this heuristics "activates" a great number of nodes. The second heuristics uses the same principle except that we only keep one father among all the fathers in the lattice. We keep the closest one to fc_i

using the cosine distance. That is the heuristics we will use in the rest of the paper.This heuristic leads to a tree structure. In this case, a only partial inheritance from top to leaves of the tree is preserved as the partial order is not preserved.

4.2 Comparative Analysis of the Results of the Different Heuristics and Distances

We present in this section a comparative analysis of the experiments depending on the heuristics for the projection and for the agglomeration. We choose two criteria to evaluate the final structure obtained. The first uses the well known recall-precision measure issued from Information Retrieval, completed by elementary measures for evaluating the quality of the projections. The second one, more subjective, is concerned by how Kohonen classes are grouped together and agglomerated. It relies on the mesure of the connexity of Kohonen classes (how closely related are these classes). Both aims at defining which final hierarchical structure is better-suited for a user to analyse the content of the data set. We have explored six types of projection : subsumption with a treshold at 0.0, 0.1, 0.2 and 0.3, cosine and, finally, subsumption at 0.0 combined with cosine.

The initial set of data is composed of 162 individuals characterized by 191 properties. The lattice built upon these data has 307 formal concepts; the Kohonen map has 100 classes. The lattice has 11 level including top (level 0) to bottom (level 10). The level for a formal concept is defined as being the shorter way from the top to itself.

Recall and precision. In Information Retrieval, recall (R) is the proportion of relevant materials retrieved and precision (P) is the proportion of retrieved materials which are relevant. We will use these two indicators to evaluate each projection of a Kohonen class onto a formal concept as well as to evaluate the groups and agglomerations of Kohonen classes onto a formal concept. R and P are calculated upon extensions: $P = \frac{|K \cap T|}{|T|}$, $R = \frac{|K \cap T|}{|K|}$, where K and T represent (resp.) the extension of the Kohonen class and of the formal concept.

Two other kinds of measure can be used with benefit to measure the quality of the projection.The average projection level (APL) in the lattice give an information that is complementary to the precision for measuring the accuracy of

Table 1. Indicators for projection

	Subsp0.0	Subsp0.1	Subsp0.2	Subsp0.3	Cos.	Subsp-Cos
Nb of fc involved in a projection (InvP)	180	108	20	9	44	41
Nb of selected pairs (kc,fc) (Nbp)	360	75	20	31	29	29
Average projection level (APL)	3.83	3.26	1.5	1.33	4.20	4.51
Average Recall (AR)	0.05	0.28	0.87	0.99	0.52	0.25
Average Precision (AP)	0.26	0.59	0.35	0.17	0.81	0.86
Average Group Recall (AGR)	0.06	0.28	0.75	0.99	0.49	0.35
Average Group Precision (AGP)	0.73	0.63	0.70	0.61	0.82	0.94
Average Agglomeration Recall (AAR)	0.15	0.40	0.78	0.99	0.61	0.54
Average Agglomeration Precision (AAP)	0.88	0.72	0.84	0.69	0.83	0.88

the projection and also its generalization sharpness. The discriminating power of a projection can be directly estimated by comparing the number of Kohonen classes to be projected with the number of formal concept involved in the projection (InvP).

Recall and Precision on the extension of the groups of Kohonen classes. Let $\mathtt{K_i}$ for i=1,n be the n Kohonen classes projected over one formal concept of the lattice C. Group Recall (GR for group recall) and Group precision (GP) are defined as follows:

$$GP = \frac{|\bigcup_{i=1}^{n}\{\mathtt{K_i}\} \cap T|}{|T|}, GR = \frac{|\bigcup_{i=1}^{n}\{\mathtt{K_i}\} \cap T|}{|\bigcup_{i=1}^{n}\{\mathtt{K_i}\}|}$$

Recall and Precision for agglomerations. Agglomeration recall AggR and precision AggP are calculated upon the same basis as GR and GP but for each formal concept which is associated to Kohonen classes when coming back up to the top of the hierarchy.

Recall and Precision: conclusions. Cosine and Subsumption-cosine are stable on projection, grouping and agglomerating (up in the lattice) with good values for R and P. Subsumption 0.2 and 0.3 has lower values for projection but higher for groups or agglomeration. However, recall and precision measures should be considered as unperfect measures for estimating the intrisic quality of a projection method. Indeed, they do not permit to explicitly highlight which is the nature of the properties of the Kohonen classes that are dropped out by the projection process, either important ones or marginal ones. It appears clearly that the risk of eliminating important properties during the projection process is minimized by the cosine method as compared to the pure subsumption methods. The former one is indeed the only one that takes directly into account the property weights in the projection process.

Connexity and agglomerations. The hierarchical structure obtained by agglomeration can be evaluated through its global characterics like its number of nodes, the number of different levels, the balance between the levels. Another important criteria is the connexity : how closely related are the Kohonen classes which are grouped or agglomerated onto the same formal concept. The idea is that if agglomeration enables us to relate Kohonen classes which are topologically close, then we suppose that it will be easier for an expert to comment the hierarchical structure. In the same way, if the connexity is verified through all the agglomeration process, the property of the formal concepts belonging to the agglomeration could then be automatically used to generate explanation of different order of magnitude on the Kohonen maps.

The analysis the table 2 leads to the conclusions that the cosine-based measures give the best results: the hierarchy corresponding these measures is well balanced and the three formal concepts which do not correspond to closely related Kohonen classes are distributed on two level.

Table 2. Connexity among the different step of agglomeration. The bold values represent the number of connexe classes for each projection method and for each level of agglomeration

heuristics	Subsp 0.0	Subsp 0.1	Subsp 0.2	Subsp 0.3	Cos	Subsp-Cos
level 0	**126**/138	**76**/80	**14**/14	**6**/6	**36**/36	**38**/39
level 1	**33**/41	**22**/27	**5**/5	**2**/2	**11**/12	**8**/11
level 2	**17**/21	**7**/10	**1**/1	**1**/1	**5**/7	**2**/4
level 3	**9**/11	**4**/5	-	-	**3**/3	**3**/3
level 4	**4**/6	**1**/1	-	-	**1**/1	**1**/1
level 5	**1**/1	**1**/1	-	-	-	-
level 6	**0**/1	**1**/1	-	-	-	-
level 7	**1**/1	**1**/1	-	-	-	-

5 Conclusion

Cosine seems to be the best criteria to project the Kohonen classes onto formal concepts of the lattice. The agglomeration process coming back up to the top of the lattice enable us to simplify the hierarchy and to obtain a well-balanced hierarchical structure.

Combining both numerical and symbolic approaches can be sucessfully applied to Digital Librairies. It provides the user with an intelligent way of analyzing, of visualizing the data set including some generalisation operations. It also brings some new elements that each method could not separately provide. The first results of our experiment tends to prove that our techniques can be used with strong benefits to highlight properties from the most specific to the most general ones which can be derived from larger area of the Kohonen map. This can be performed considering the conservation of the topographic coherence of the merged classes when coming back up to the top of the lattice.

References

Bordat J.P. : Calcul pratique du treillis de galois d'une correspondance. Maths. Sci. Hum. **96** (1986) 31–47

Carpineto C., Romano G. : Order-theoritical ranking. JASIS. **51** (2000)

Kohohen T. : Self Organization and Associative Memory. Springer Verlag (1994)

Lamirel J.C., Crehange M.: Application of a symbolico-connectionnist approach for the design of a higly interactive documentary database interrogation system with on-line learning capabilities. Proc. of ACM/CIKM, (1994)

Neural Learning from Unbalanced Data Using Noise Modeling

Hong Guo and Yi L. Murphey

Department of Electrical and Computer Engineering
University of Michigan-Dearborn
Dearborn, Michigan 48128-1491, U.S.A.
yilu@umich.edu

Abstract. This paper describes the result of our study on neural learning to solve the classification problems in which data is unbalanced and noisy. We use multidimensional Gaussian distribution to analyze the separation of different class samples in a training data set, and then generate artificial noise samples in the training set using a noise modeling algorithm. The noise analysis allows us to identify special densities in the feature space that are prone to prediction error. We argue that by properly generate extra training data samples around the noise densities, we can train a neural network to have stronger capability of generalization and control the classification error of the trained neural network. In particular, we focus on the problems that require a neural network to make favorable classification to a particular class. The noise modeling algorithm has been implemented to solve a classification problem of good(pass) and bad(fail) vehicles in test sites of automobile assembly plants and a multi-layered Back Propagation neural network has been used in our experiments. The experimental results showed that the noise modeling algorithm was very effective in generate extra data samples that can be used to train a neural network to make favorable decisions to a minority class and to have increased generalization capability.

1 Introduction

Neural networks have been applied to various problems including engineering diagnosis, pattern classification, intelligent manufacturing and control problems [1, 2, 3]. There has been much progress in developing methods for training complex configurations of these networks, but little was known about the general learning properties of neural networks [4]. Our research is focused on the following three major issues within the problem scope of pattern classification: neural learning from unbalanced data samples, neural learning from noise data, and making intentional biased decisions. In many application problems, the training data for each class is extremely unbalanced. One example is to classify defect products at the end of manufacturing lines such as automobile assembly plants. One thing in common in manufacturing environment is that most products

L. Monostori, J. Váncza, and M. Ali (Eds.): IEA/AIE 2001, LNAI 2070, pp. 259-268, 2001.

are good and only a few are defects. If we further divide the defect products into classes of different defect types, we will have far more data samples from the "good" class than any one of the defective classes for neural learning. This problem has been referred to as classification under unbalanced training data. Lu et al showed in [1] that different neural networks have different degree of abilities in learning from unbalanced data. If the training methods are not proper, the features representing the classes that have small number of samples in the training set may likely be ignored by the neural networks. This problem is caused by the overwhelming number of learning samples in one class input to the learning system that partially undo the training effect on the small learning samples of a different class. This problem is more serious when data set has high level of noise. Data noise in classification problems can be generally described as data samples of different classes inseparable in the feature space. In another word, if a data set is considered noisy, the class boundary to separate different class samples in the feature space is almost impossible to draw. Noise in training and test data rises from a number of sources, the set of features used for classification is not sufficient to draw class boundaries, data samples are miss labeled, poor data acquisition processes, etc. These problems are inevitable in many engineering applications. In particular in cases where the data samples in each class are unbalanced, the classification features of the minority classes are often ignored during neural learning [1].

In this paper, we present a noise modeling algorithm that uses the multidimensional Gaussian distribution to analyze the separation of difference class samples in a training data set. Based on the analysis it generates artificial noise samples to add in to the training set in order to train a neural network that can make more favorable classification decision to a particular class and, more important, a neural network that can generalize. Our approach is based on the following hypothesis: in supervised learning, the noise model or distribution in the unknown test data set is not grossly different from the training data and the ability of generalization of neural networks is very much depending on the data noise along the class boundaries. We applied the noise modeling algorithm to a multi-layered neural network with Back Propagation. The performance of the neural network trained using the data generated by the noise model algorithm is presented and compared with the networks trained with conventional methods.

2 Noise Estimation and Modeling

The problem under the study is two-class pattern classification. For a given data sample s_i in a given class, if we assume the noise is in the Gaussian distribution, data samples of opposite class distributed around s_i can be modeled as random vectors Z that have the density function:

$$f_z(Z \mid s_i) = (2\pi)^{-\frac{M}{2}} |\Sigma_i|^{-\frac{1}{2}} \exp\left(-\frac{(Z - s_i)^T (Z - s_i)}{2|\Sigma_i|} \right) \quad (1)$$

where M is the dimension of each data sample and Σ is the covariance matrix of s^i and its M nearest neighbors. We can further decompose Σ as

$$\Sigma = Q\Lambda Q^T \tag{2}$$

where the diagonal entries of Λ and the column vectors of Q are the eigenvalues and eigenvectors of Σ respectively. Since Σ is symmetric, all eigenvalues and eigenvectors are real. According to [5], if covariance matrix Σ is positive definite and symmetric, there exists a unique lower triangular matrix C such that such that $\Sigma = CC^T$ .The random vector Z can be represented as:

$$Z = CY + s_i \tag{3}$$

where $Y=(y_1,y_2,\ldots y_M)$ is a random vector generated by a Gaussian function with zero mean and identity covariance matrix. The *jth* column vector of Q, q_j, j = 1, 2,…, M, is computed recursively using the following formulas:

$$q_j = \frac{b_j}{\|b_j\|}, \text{ and } b_j = (a_j - s_i) - \sum_{k=1}^{j-1} b_k^T (a_j - s_i) b_k \tag{4}$$

The initial vector is computed using $b_1 = a_1 - s_i$, where a_1 is the nearest neighbor of the opposite class of s_i. The successive column vectors can be computed recursively. The eigenvalues of Λ can be obtained by

$$\lambda_j = \frac{1}{4r^2}\|b_j\|^2 \tag{5}$$

for j = 1, 2,…, M, where r is the radius of a hypersphere that the probability of the hypersphere enclose the local density is v. Musavi et al showed that for a given v, there is a fixed function relation between r and M, and the values of r for M = 1, …, 10 can be found in [6].

The eigenvectors of Q are the principal axes of the ellipsoid of the constant potential surface (CPS) of the Gaussian distribution function, and the square roots of the neural networks the eigenvalues define the lengths of the principal axes of the ellipsoid. The M nearest neighbors of the opposite class are all on the surface of the hyper-rectangle round s_i. We use Figure 1 to illustrate the CPS and its relationship to class boundary in the 2D space. In the figure, A is a sample data from one class, B and C are its two nearest neighbors of the opposite class. B and C are on the boundary of larger rectangular bounded by $2\|b_j\|$, for j = 1, 2. The classification boundary between the two classes can be drawn by the smaller rectangle, which is bounded by $\|b_j\|$ and encloses the CPS ellipse. The new random vectors Z_j generated use formula above are mostly located within the ellipse shown in green "x"s. In our implementation, we chose v = 0.9545, with M = 2, r^2 = 6.18 according to [6].

The shape of the hyper-ellipsoid is controlled by the distribution of the M nearest neighbors of the opposite class of the sample data s_i. We use Fig. 1 and the three examples in Fig. 2 to analyze the relationship between the distribution of the data samples in the feature space and the Gaussian CPS. In each example in Fig. 2, we have one sample data illustrated in blue color, and its two nearest neighbors of opposite class marked as neighbor 1 and neighbor 2 illustrated in

RED. One hundred new data samples were generated by the procedure described above and are represented by green "x"'s in all examples.

It is clear that the newly generated data samples form an ellipse centered at the selected data sample. The principal axes are proportional to the two eigenvalues. In both Fig. 2(a) and (b), the two nearest neighbors of the are located in the same direction, and the resulting ellipse is long and narrow. In both Figure 1 and Fig. 2(c), the two nearest neighbors of each data sample are located in different directions in the feature space, more than 90° apart, the resulting ellipses are more like a circle, which means that the two eigenvalues in each example have very close values. Table 1 illustrates the eigenvalues, eigenvectors and the Euclidean distances between every sample data to its nearest neighbors. The characteristics of the eigenvalues and eigenvectors of the CPS are summarized as follows.

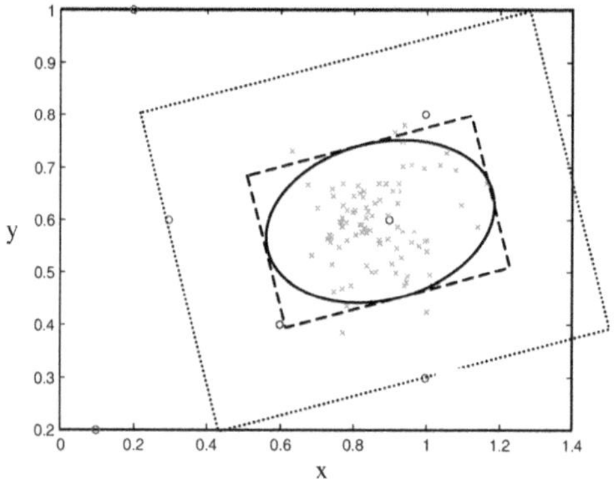

Fig. 1. Illustration of Gaussian local density. A is a data sample from one class, B and C are its two nearest neighbors of the opposite class. The generated random vectors are green "x"'s

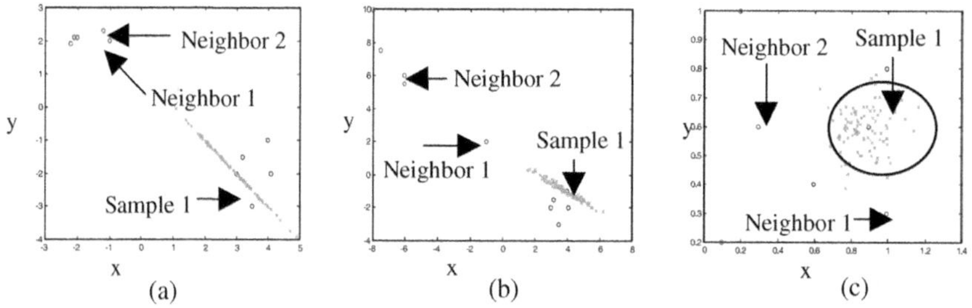

Fig. 2. Three examples of different Gaussian CPS generated by different distributions of sample points

1. According to its definition, the first eigenvalue λ_0 is a monotonically increasing function of the distance between sample data and its nearest neighbor of the opposite class. This is verified by our experiment result shown in Table 1.

2. If the nearest neighbors are located in the same orientation with respect to the sample point, the CPS ellipsoid is long in the principal axis but narrow at the others, and the new data samples have high density in the ellipse. In Fig. 2 (a), the two nearest neighbors are close and at the same direction with respect to the sample data, and in (b), the two nearest neighbors are in the same direction but quite apart. However the two CPS's in Fig. 2(a) and (b) are similar in shape, and the new data samples have high density in the both ellipses.
3. If the neighboring samples are far away from one another in terms of direction with respect to the sample data, the corresponding principal axes in the Gaussian CPS should be similar in lengths and the CPS is more like a circle. Both Fig. 1 and Fig. 2(c) along with Table 1 show this property of CPS. Quantitatively, this property can be measured by the ratio of λ_i i =0, 1. The difference between eigenvalues can help us to understand the distribution of the samples of the opposite class. For example, if λ_i is much larger than all of the other eigenvalues λ_i (I=1,2,...M-1), most of the data samples of the opposite class concentrate in the direction of the eigenvector corresponding to λ_0. If all of the M eigenvalues are very close to each other, the samples of the opposite class distribute evenly (to some extent) in a hyper-sphere around the sample.

These properties of eigenvalues and the corresponding CPS ellipsoid are used to guide our training of neural networks.

Table 1. The Euclidean distances d_i, eigenvectors, q_i, eigenvalues, λ_i for i = 0, 1 of the examples shown in Fig. 1 and 2

	Fig. 1	Fig. 2(a)	Fig. 2(b)	Fig. 2(c)
d_0	0.1211	0.9727	0.224	0.26
λ_0	0.0049	0.0393	0.00906	0.0105
E_0	$[0.2873, -0.9578]^T$	$[-0.6438, 0.7652]^T$	$[-0.873, 0.488]^T$	$[-0.1961, -0.9806]^T$
d_1	0.3600	1.10269	0.933	0.6678
λ_1	0.01336	0.000059	0.000045	0.0228
E_1	$[-0.9578, -0.2873]^T$	$[0.7652, 0.6438]^T$	$[0.488, 0.873]^T$	$[-0.9806, 0.1961]^T$

3 Neural Learning from Unbalanced Training Data

This section describes the neural learning method that utilizes the Gaussian CPS distribution described in the last section. We attempt to train a neural network to learn the classification features from the data samples of a minority class in the training set and to make more favorable decisions to the minority class. For the convenience of description, we referred to the two classes of data as minority and majority classes respectively. In many applications, if error is inevitable, a neural network is expected to err on one particular class rather than the other. For example, in the classification of good/defect products in a manufacturing line, if a product is classified as a defect, it will be checked and repaired if necessary. Therefore, it is better to misclassify good products as defect rather than the other opposite type of error. Lu et al[1] showed that in the case of unbalanced, noisy training data samples, multi-layered backpropagation network(BP), Radial-Basis Function(RBF) and FUZZY ARTMAP all ignore the minority class, namely minority data samples are often misclassified. The algorithm we investigated was to generate new minority data samples near the classification boundary using the Gaussian CPS and add these new data samples to the training data. The neural networks trained on this set should make more favorable decision to the minority class with the minimization of misclassification of the majority class and have increased generalization capability.

For every data sample *s* of the minority class in the training set, we attempt to generate *p* new data samples around *s* subject to its local Gaussian distribution of the opposite class. Let us assume the input vector is *M* dimensional. The noise modeling algorithm first finds the *M* data samples of the majority class that are closest to *s*, t_1, t_2, ..., t_M, from which we construct the *MxM* covariance matrix of the Gaussian probability density function described in the last section., and obtain *M* eigenvalues of the covariance matrix λ_0, λ_1, .. λ_{M-1}.

We need to be cautious about generating new noise samples. If we generate unnecessary ones, we may weaken the classification capability of the neural network on the majority class. For example, if λ_0 is large, it implies that *s* is quite apart from the majority class, and a neural network may easily learn the classification boundary around *s*. If we artificially generate more minority samples, we may force the trained neural network to make more classification error on the majority class than necessary. The noise modeling algorithm generates new data samples only at the locations where it is difficult to differentiate minority data samples from the majority samples, and adding noisy random vectors does not affect too many majority samples.

Based on the properties of Gaussian CPS, we developed the following rules. Let ρ_1 and ρ_2, the number of majority and minority samples falling within the hyper bounding box R of sample data *s* and *s*, t_1, t_2, ..., t_M respectively. Specifically, R is equal to $||s-t_1||x||s-t_2||x...||s-t_M||$.

Rule1: If ρ_1, the density of majority class samples around *s*, is large, do not generate noisy data around *s*.

Rule2: If ρ_2, the density of minority class samples around *s*, is small, do not generate noisy data around *s*.

Rule3: If λ_0, the 1st eigenvalue of Gaussian covariance matrix, is large, do not generate noisy data around *s*.

For a minority data sample *s*, only if s does not satisfy any of the three rules, the noise modeling algorithm will generate *p* new data samples around *s*. The value *p* can be determined based on the ratio of the number of data samples in the majority and the minority class.

Another important issue is to limit the noise random vectors in the hyper bounding box R. As we discussed in the last section that the random vectors fall within the CPS ellipsoid with the probability of *v*. However with the probability of 1-v, the new random vectors may fall outside the Gaussian CPS. Furthermore, the CPS ellipsoid may exceed the hyper bounding box R due to the symmetry of Gaussian distribution. Since we have no knowledge of what beyond these data samples, the noise modeling algorithm discard the new noise data samples generated beyond the hyper bounding box(see Fig. 3). Therefore, the noise modeling algorithm accepts a random vector as a noise data sample only it belongs to the conjuncture of the rectangular and the ellipse(see Fig. 3, where the rectangular is the bounding box equal to $||s-t_1||x||s-t_2||$.)

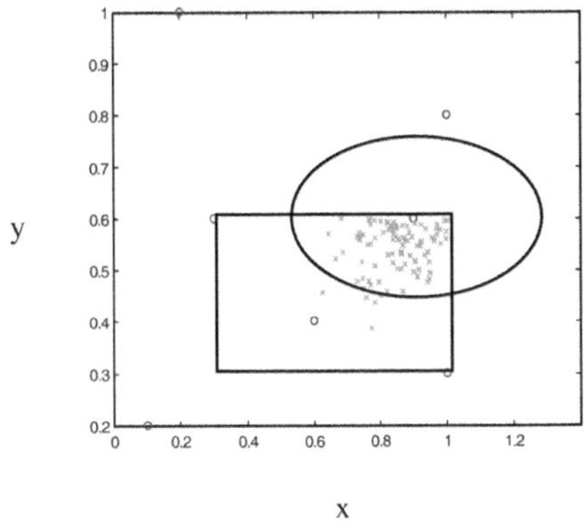

Fig. 3. Only the data samples that are within the conjuncture of the bounding box and the ellipse are accepted as new training data samples

4 Experiments and Performances

In this study, we conducted neural training using the noise modeling algorithm on a BP neural network[7] of three layers and a FUZZY ARTMAP neural network. The BP neural network has nodes 5-4-4-1, Momentum =0.90, Tanh function, and epoch size=16. A FUZZY ARTMAP network consists of two interconnected layers of neurons, F1 and F2. The input leads to activity in the feature detector neurons in F1, which is also called short-term memory activity. The short-term activity passes through connections to the neurons in F2. Each F2 neuron adds together its input from all the F1 neurons and generates an output. A measure will be taken over all the neurons in F2 and the output of one neuron will be selected as the system output, i.e. Winner-take-all. A major characteristic of a FUZZY ARTMAP network is that it allows a top-down feedback from F2 to reinforce the activity in F1. A learning algorithm of an FUZZY ARTMAP network is to determine w_{ij}, the top-down weight from winning node j in the F2 layer to a node i in the F1 layer, and z_{ij}, the corresponding bottom-up weight. The detail of the learning algorithm can be found in[8, 1].

The data used in the experiments are the vehicle test data acquired at the end-of-assembly lines in the Ford Motor Company. The two neural networks are trained to classify whether a given vehicle is "good" or "bad" using input vectors in five dimensions. Since new vehicles manufactured by Ford Motor Company are mostly in the "good" class, the data samples in both the training set and test set are unevenly distributed. The data sets used in our study were downloaded directly from assembly plants in the Ford Motor Company. To illustrate the algorithm, we particularly chose the data samples from one particular vehicle model that contains high level of noise. We randomly separate the entire data samples into training and test with the ratio of 2:1.

One way to estimate the noise level in a data set is to count the number of the opposite class samples within the hyper-bounding box of a given class. In the training set, we have total 727 good vehicle samples and 136 bad vehicle samples. We found that 96% good data samples are inside the hyper bounding box of bad vehicle class, and 88% of bad data samples are within the hyper bounding box of good vehicle class. In the test set, we have 356 good vehicle samples and 121 bad vehicle samples. We found that 93.3% of good vehicle samples are within the bad vehicle hyper bounding box and 85.7% bad vehicle samples are within the good vehicle hyper-bounding box. It can be interpreted as follows. In the training set, if we want to classify bad vehicles 100% correctly, we may be able to classify correctly only 4% of good vehicles; if we want to classify good vehicles 100% correctly, we may be able to classify correctly only 12% of bad vehicles. Similarly in the test set, if we want to classify bad vehicles 100% correctly, we may be able to classify correctly only 6.7% of good vehicles; if we want to classify good vehicles 100% correctly, we may classify correctly only 14.3% of bad vehicles. These figures can be used as the performance metrics for a classifier: a neural network must give better performance than these figures.

The experiment results of the two neural networks are shown in Table 2. The first experiment was conducted on the original training and test set. As we see from the first entry in Table 2 that the BP neural network was not at all capable of learning the features of the minority class from the training set, and as a result, the BP network fail to classify any bad vehicles in either the training nor the test set. The FUZZY ARTMAP was better than the BP at learning the minority class features. It has achieved much better performance than the BP network on the minority class in both the training and the test data. The second experiment was conducted on the new training set obtained by duplicating every bad vehicle sample in the original training set 10 times and adding the newly generated ones to the training set. The BP network was able to classified a few of the minority class samples with the price of misclassifying a large number of good vehicle samples. FUZZY ARTMAP did not learn more about the minority class on this set of training data. Instead its performance on the minority class in the test set has dropped from the first experiment, even though its performance on the training data was very good. The third experiment was conducted on the new training data set generated using the noise modeling algorithm described in this paper. In the implementation, if the Gaussian CPS of each selected bad samples contained less than three good vehicle samples and more than one bad vehicle samples, then the noise modeling algorithm would generate ten random data samples around each of the selected bad vehicles were generated and added to the training set. The result of this experiment showed that both the BP network and the FUZZY ARTMAP network were able to learn from this new set of training data the classification feature of the minority class, and both gave much better classification capability on the minority class. The improvement of classification performance of the BP network is particularly interesting. While trained on the original training set, the BP network fail to classify any bad vehicles. After the training on the new training data, the BP network was able to classify more than 66% of bad vehicles on the training data and more than 45% on the test set, which is comparable to the FUZZY ARTMAP network. The FUZZY ARTMAP has in general better capability of learning the minority class features than the BP network as shown in the first two experiments. When the FUZZY ARTMAP network was trained on the new data set generated by the noise modeling algorithm, it gave better performance not only on the minority class but also on the majority class.

Table 2. Experiment results of BP and FUZZY ARTMAP

Data sets	BP network: correctly classification rate		FUZZY ARTMAP: correctly classification rate	
	Training set	Test set	Training set	Test set
Original Training set	GV: 100% BV: 0%	GV: 100% BV: 0%	GV: 87.3% BV: 91.91%	GV: 69.66% BV: 45.45%
Duplicate 10	GV: 45.94% BV: 28.67%,	GV: 48.31% BV: 32.47%	GV: 90.51% BV: 94.12%	GV: 75.28% BV: 41.56%
Training data generated by the Constrained Gaussian CPS algorithm	GV: 48.56% BV: 66.77%	GV: 48.88% BV: 45.45%	GV: 88.72% BV: 94.25%	GV: 71.91% BV: 48.05%

GV: Good Vehicles; BV: Bad Vehicles.

5 Conclusion

We have presented an algorithm, noise modeling algorithm, for training a neural network to learn the classification features from unbalanced data samples. The algorithm was developed based on the Gaussian CPS theory to generate random noise over the classification boundary for a given training set with the aim of increasing classification features of a given class and the capability of generalization for the neural networks. We showed through experimental results that the noise modeling algorithm is effective in the training of both BP and FUZZY ARTMAP neural networks. We speculate that the algorithm can be extrapolated to the general classification problem of P classes within which the p classes are to be emphasized, where $p < P$. By generating noise data samples along the classification boundaries for these p classes using the noise modeling algorithm, the trained neural network would have increased classification capability and generalization ability over the p classes.

Acknowledgments. This work is supported in part by a Grant from NSF DMII.

References

1. Lu, Y., Guo, H., Feldkamp, L.: Robust Neural Learning from Unbalanced Data Samples, IEEE IJCNN (1998)
2. Dali, C. (ed.): Artificial Neural Networks for Intelligent Manufacturing (1992)
3. Kosko, B.: Neural Networks and Fuzzy Systems: A Dynamical Systems Approach to Machine Intelligence, Prentice-Hall (1992)
4. Mackay, D.: Bayesian Methods for Adaptive Models, Ph.D thesis, CIT (1991)
5. Rubinstein, R.: Simulation and the Monte Carlo Method, John Wiley & Sons (1981)
6. Musavi, M., Chan, K., Hummels, D., Kalantri, K.: On the Generalization Ability of Neural Network Classifiers, IEEE Trans. On PAMI-16, No. 6 (1994) 659–663
7. Rummelhart, D., McClelland, J.: Parallel Distributed Processing: Explorations in the Microstructure of Cognition, Vol. 1: Foundations , MIT press, Cambridage, MA (1986)
8. Carpenter, G., Grossberg, S., Markuzon, N., et al: Fuzzy ARTMAP: An adaptive Resonance Architecture for Incremental Learning of Ananlog Maps, IJCNN (1992) 309–314

Neural Modeling of an Industrial Process with Noisy Data

P. Berényi, J. Valyon, and G. Horváth

Budapest University of Technology and Economics,
Dept. of Measurement and Information Systems
Budapest, Műegyetem rkp. 9. Hungary

Abstract. In industry there are many complex modeling tasks where the most of the available information is in the form of input-output data. In such cases only black box modeling can be used, where the model can be built using learning methods. In black-box modeling one of the most important tasks is to obtain good training data. However, in most real world problems the available data are imprecise, contain noise or some distortion. This paper discusses some problems of neural model building based on noisy training data. Two methods - the errors-in-variables training method (EIV) and the support vector machines (SVM)- are introduced and compared to the performance of the traditional neural network solution. The performance of the SVM method is also tested on a real industrial problem, namely on the modeling of a Linz-Donawitz steel converter.

1 Introduction

In industry many complex modeling tasks can be found where the main knowledge which can be used to build a model is experimental – measured – data. If other information cannot be obtained only input-output models (black-box models) can be constructed. For black-box modeling neural networks are good means as they are universal approximators, however to obtain an accurate model, first of all a reliable database must be formed.

In forming a proper database the following main problems have to be considered:

- the problem of dimensionality,
- the problem of uneven distribution of data,
- the problem of noisy and imprecise data,
- the problem of missing data,
- the effects of the correlation between consecutive data.

This paper discusses only the questions arising because of using noisy data. For obtaining accurate models based on noisy data, the applied methods must be able to compensate the effects of the noise somehow. Some of these methods may utilise some kind of preprocessing of the data (e.g. filtering) or they may use certain model

L. Monostori, J. Váncza, and M. Ali (Eds.): IEA/AIE 2001, LNAI 2070, pp. 269-280, 2001.

building approaches which take the main features (e.g. distribution, or at least the most important statistical parameters) of the noise into consideration.

In this paper two different approaches will be examined. The first one, the errors in variables (EIV) training method is a general way to handle noisy data. It was proposed many years ago for noisy linear systems and it has received considerable interest in system identification [1]. Recently it was reconsidered as a possible way for neural modeling using noisy training data [2].

The second one - the support vector machine (SVM) approach - is an entirely new approach to learn from data and it is based on statistical learning theory. Both statistical learning theory and the construction of support vector machines were suggested and mainly developed by Vapnik [3].

The paper presents the results of an extensive experimental study of these two approaches in model building with noisy data. First the two approaches will be shortly introduced, than in a simple nonlinear approximation problem the effects of noisy data will be shown. The results of these two approaches will be compared to the results of the classical neural network-based black box model building. After concluding some general consequences from these experiments the SVM approach will be applied for a real complex industrial modeling problem. The results will also be compared to that of a previously developed modeling system, which applies hybrid-neural approach.

2 Noisy Data

Before the description of the Errors In Variables method let us take a short look at the analysis of noise effects on the training of neural networks.

Output noise - The samples, $\{(\mathbf{x}, \mathbf{y})_i\}$ (i=1, ..., N), used for the training neural networks are generated in optimal case by the $\mathbf{y}=f(\mathbf{x})$ formula, where $\mathbf{x}$ is the input vector, $\mathbf{y}$ the output vector and $f(.)$ is the function to be approximated. If the samples contain noise this expression changes to $\mathbf{y}=f(\mathbf{x})+\eta$, the available set of data contains $(\mathbf{x},\mathbf{y}+\eta)$ input -output samples, where η is the noise, generally with not known distribution, but independent from the input and output. (In many cases η can be considered as a zero mean Gaussian or uniformly distributed noise. The error function of the training with noiseless samples has the following form:

$$C = \frac{1}{N}\sum_{k=1}^{N}(\mathbf{y}_k - f_{NN}(\mathbf{w},\mathbf{x}_k))^2 , \tag{1}$$

where $f_{NN}(.)$ denotes the mapping of a neural network, the function realised by a network with $\mathbf{w}$ weight vector.

The cost function - if noisy output data are used in the training - will be:

$$C_\varepsilon = \frac{1}{N}\sum_{k=1}^{N}(\mathbf{y}_k + \boldsymbol{\eta}_k - f_{NN}(\mathbf{w},\mathbf{x}_k))^2 . \tag{2}$$

Taking the expected value of the cost function

$$E[C_\varepsilon] = \frac{1}{N}\sum_{k=1}^{N}[(\mathbf{y}_k - f_{NN}(\mathbf{w},\mathbf{x}_k))^2 + E[(\boldsymbol{\eta}_k)^2]], \tag{3}$$

because the expected value of the noise is zero, $E[\eta_k(\mathbf{y}_k\text{-}f_{NN}(.))]=0$. Here $E[(\eta_k)^2]$ is the variance of the noise. Therefore the two cost function differ only in a constant term which is the variance of the output noise. So training with noisy output samples leads to the same solution as the training with noiseless samples.

Input noise - It may happen that the output data are noiseless but the input data are noisy. In this case the samples are the $(\mathbf{x}+\eta, \mathbf{y})$ pairs, where $\mathbf{y}=f(\mathbf{x})$ as before and the η is again the noise with zero mean value. In our study it is also assumed that the noise is independent from the input and output data.

This case must be considered more exactly, because this happens if one uses the often-proposed method of adding jitter to generate new samples for having more training data. [5] According to this method, if only a small number of original samples are available, new samples are generated by slightly changing the input while supposing that the output does not change too much.

All studies in this area have reached the conclusion that the input noise in the training samples leads to a different performance than training without noise. A weight-dependent term modifies the original cost function. However, there are different views of this modification. It can be viewed as a measure of the sensitivity of the network output for small changes in the input [4], [5]. So the resultant network will be less sensitive to the small changes in the input and the possibility of overfitting will be smaller. In case of noisy inputs the cost function will have the following form:

$$C_\varepsilon = \frac{1}{N}\sum_{k=1}^{N}(\mathbf{y}_k - f_{NN}(\mathbf{w},\mathbf{x}_k + \boldsymbol{\eta}_k))^2 , \tag{4}$$

and by using the Taylor expansion of the neural network function

$$f_{NN}(\mathbf{w},\mathbf{x}_k + \boldsymbol{\eta}_k) = f_{NN}(\mathbf{w},\mathbf{x}_k) + \sum_{i=1}^{\infty}\frac{(\boldsymbol{\eta}_k)^i}{i!}\cdot\frac{\partial^i f_{NN}(\mathbf{w},\mathbf{x}_k)}{(\partial\mathbf{x}_k)^i}, \tag{5}$$

it can be written in the form:

$$C_\varepsilon = \frac{1}{N}\sum_{k=1}^{N}(\mathbf{y}_k - f_{NN}(\mathbf{w},\mathbf{x}_k) - \sum_{i=1}^{\infty}\frac{(\boldsymbol{\eta}_k)^i}{i!}\cdot\frac{\partial^i f_{NN}(\mathbf{w},\mathbf{x}_k)}{(\partial\mathbf{x}_k)^i})^2 . \tag{6}$$

It can be seen that in comparison to the original function some new, higher order derivatives of the neural network function appear. At this point one could say that this new term is a penalty, which has the effect that the realised function of the network will be less changing. A better analysis can be done if we bring the formula to the following form:

$$C_{\varepsilon} = \frac{1}{N}\sum_{k=1}^{N}\Bigg[(\mathbf{y}_k - f_{NN}(\mathbf{w},\mathbf{x}_k))^2 - 2\cdot(\mathbf{y}_k - f_{NN}(\mathbf{w},\mathbf{x}_k))\cdot\sum_{i=1}^{\infty}\frac{(\boldsymbol{\eta}_k)^i}{i!}\cdot\frac{\partial^i f_{NN}(\mathbf{w},\mathbf{x}_k)}{(\partial\mathbf{x}_k)^i} + \left(\sum_{i=1}^{\infty}\frac{(\boldsymbol{\eta}_k)^i}{i!}\cdot\frac{\partial^i f_{NN}(\mathbf{w},\mathbf{x}_k)}{(\partial\mathbf{x}_k)^i}\right)^2\Bigg] \quad (7)$$

where the first part is the original cost function, the second and the third parts are the terms with the derivatives. Because the output error has zero mean value the effect of the second term is smaller than that of the third one and this way a smoothing effect appears.

An other possibility to interpret the input noise is to transform it to the output of the network by the following way:

- Let $\mathbf{y}=f(\mathbf{x})$ again and the training samples let be given in $(\mathbf{x}+\eta, \mathbf{y})$ pairs
- Let $\nu=f(\mathbf{x}+\eta)-\mathbf{y}$, so the training samples can be written as $(\mathbf{x}, \mathbf{y}+\nu)$, where ν is an output noise.

This way it is easy to see, that ν is no more an additive noise term with zero expected value and that it is not independent from the input any more. This can easily be followed on the next figure (Fig.1).

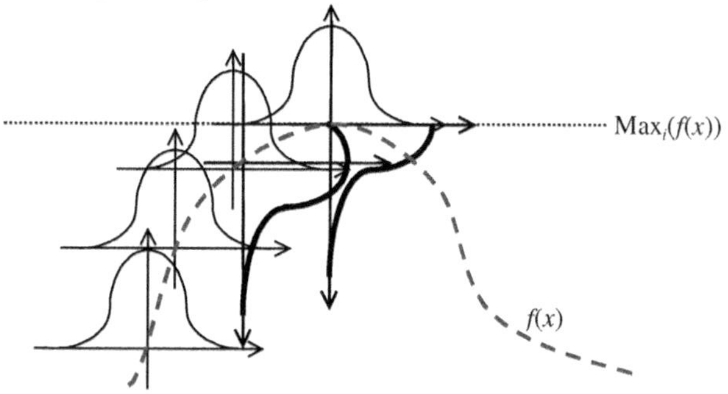

Fig. 1. Transforming the input noise to the output

On the figure the dashed, thick (grey) line represents an original function ($f(x)$), the thin black functions represent the distribution of the input noise and the thick black lines represent the distribution of the transformed output noise. The expected value of the function - that is modified with this output-noise - is smoother than the original one. As it can be seen the density functions of the transformed noise are chopped off by the local extreme values of the original function, so the expected value of this noise is not zero. Therefore the modified function can change only in a smaller interval than the original - the expected value of the noisy function will be below the original one in the maximum points and over the original one in minimum points -, but it has the same number of extreme points, so we get the smoothing effect.

3 The Errors in Variables Training Method

The Errors In Variables training method was introduced to reduce the negative effects originating from the errors in the training samples [2]. The goal of the method is to reach the best possible approximation of the original, not noisy – and naturally not known – function. The idea behind the method is that knowing some properties of the error, the training process can be modified to compensate the error effects. The new cost function of the method is the following:

$$C_{EIV} = \frac{1}{N} \cdot \sum_{k=1}^{N} \left[\frac{(\hat{\mathbf{y}}_k - f_{NN}(\mathbf{w}, \mathbf{x}_k))^2}{\sigma_{y,k}^2} + \frac{(\hat{\mathbf{x}}_k - \mathbf{x}_k)}{\sigma_{x,k}^2} \right], \tag{8}$$

where $\sigma_{y,k}^2$ and $\sigma_{x,k}^2$ are the variances of the input and output noise respectively, and where the original, noiseless and naturally not known inputs ($\mathbf{x}_k$) are also used.

Because these values in a real world problem are generally not known these must be estimated during the optimisation process. The weight modification and the approximation is done through the following formulas [2]:

$$\Delta \mathbf{w}_j = -\mu \frac{1}{N} \cdot \sum_{k=1}^{N} \frac{\mathbf{e}_{y,k}}{\sigma_{y,k}^2} \cdot \frac{\partial f_{NN}(\mathbf{w}, \mathbf{x}_k)}{\partial \mathbf{w}_j}, \text{ and} \tag{9}$$

$$\Delta \mathbf{x}_k = -\mu \left[\frac{\mathbf{e}_{y,k}}{\sigma_{y,k}^2} \cdot \frac{\partial f_{NN}(\mathbf{w}, \mathbf{x}_k)}{\partial \mathbf{x}_k} - \frac{\mathbf{e}_{x,k}}{\sigma_{x,k}^2} \right], \tag{10}$$

where $\mathbf{e}_{y,k} = \hat{\mathbf{y}}_k - f_{NN}(\mathbf{w}, \mathbf{x}_k)$, $\mathbf{e}_{x,k} = \hat{\mathbf{x}}_k - \mathbf{x}_k$, μ is the learning factor and $\mathbf{w}_j$ is a weight vector.

In general it can be stated that the EIV training results in a slightly better approximation than the standard backpropagation, however to reach this better result good approximation of the noise properties is important. An other problem with the EIV training is, that it is more prone to overfitting, than the standard backpropagation method [2]. This side effect can be avoided using some early stopping method during the training, however some extra care must be taken when early stopping is used in EIV training. As the validation set is built in the same way as the training set, the validation set consists of similarly noisy samples. The performance on the noisy test samples is the best, when the network approximates the expected value of the samples, and the goal of the EIV method is to reach an approximation - different from the expected value. To get reliable validation results the true input values ($\mathbf{x}_k$) must be estimated prior to the evaluation of the cost function, which needs an extra learning process each time a validation is performed.

4 Overview of Support Vector Machines

In this section a brief introduction to Support Vector Machines (SVM) is given. In the case of noisy learning data, the use of traditional neural networks (NN) raises the problem of poor generalisation, as a result of its learning method that may result in overfitting and lead to a deformed system model. Support Vector Machines incorporate some useful features that make them favourable in the above-described situations. While a traditional neural network minimises the error rate on the training points, the SVM minimises the upper bound on the 'generalisation error'. To learn a classification or regression problem, the NN adapts the parameters of a predefined, fixed structure. The SVM 'automatically' designs both the structure and parameters of the network. This can result in a quite large model, but with better generalisation capabilities. The construction of an SVM incorporates the idea of Structural Risk Minimisation (SRM). According to the SRM principle, the generalisation error rate (error rate on test data, which was never seen before) is upper bounded by an expression depending on the Vapnik–Chervonenkis (VC) dimension. By minimising this, an SVM may provide better, or at least more predictable generalisation results then the classical NN systems [6], [7].

Support Vector Machines can be used for both *classification* and *regression* problems. The classification approach is easier to understand, and more historic, but our problem concerns regression, therefore we discuss briefly only this in the sequel. A detailed description can be found e.g. in [6], [7], [8]. We are given the $\{(\mathbf{x}_1, d_1),\ldots,(\mathbf{x}_N, d_N)\}$ training data set, where $\mathbf{x}_i \in \mathbf{R}^p$ represents a p dimensional input vector and $d \in \mathbf{R}$ is the scalar target output. Due to the noisy inputs and output our data represent a relation like: $d = f(\mathbf{x}+\eta_i) + \eta_o$, where η_i and η_o stands for the input and output noise respectively. A *loss function* must also be defined, which for every $\mathbf{x}_i$ input, represents the cost of the deviation from the target output d_i. We are using the ε–Insensitive loss function (L_ε):

$$L_\varepsilon = \begin{cases} 0 & for \quad |f(\mathbf{x}) - d| < \varepsilon \\ |f(\mathbf{x}) - d| = \varepsilon & otherwise \end{cases} \tag{11}$$

In this case approximation errors smaller than ε are ignored, while the larger ones are punished in a linear way. Other (e.g. non–linear) loss functions, can be found in [3] and [6]. Our goal is to give an $y = f(\mathbf{x})$ function, that captures the dependence of the output d from the input $\mathbf{x}$. Let's define the form of this function as formulated below:

$$y = \sum_{j=0}^{m_1} w_j \varphi_j(\mathbf{x}) = \mathbf{w}^{\mathrm{T}} \varphi(\mathbf{x}), \text{ where } \mathbf{w} = [w_0, w_1, \ldots, w_{m_1}]^T \text{ and}$$
$$\varphi = [\varphi_0(\mathbf{x}), \varphi_1(\mathbf{x}), \ldots, \varphi_{m_1}(\mathbf{x})]\,. \tag{12}$$

The $\varphi_0(\mathbf{x})$ basis function is assumed to be 1, therefore w_0 represents the bias b. In our experiments $\varphi(\mathbf{x})$ is a Gaussian function; therefore this definition is equivalent to the classical RBF (Radial Basis Function network) structure.

Under certain conditions, defined in [6], [7] the risk may be defined by an *empirical risk functional*: $R_{emp}[f]=\frac{1}{N}\sum_{i=1}^{N}L_{\varepsilon}(f(\mathbf{x}_i,d_i))$. This empirical risk functional should be minimised subject to the constraint of $\|\mathbf{w}\|^2 \le c_0$ to keep **w** as small as possible (c_0 is a constant). To deal with training points outside the ε boundary, the $\{\xi_i\}_{i=1}^{N}$ and $\{\xi_i'\}_{i=1}^{N}$ slack variables are introduced:

$$\begin{aligned} d_i - \mathbf{w}^T\varphi(\mathbf{x}_i) &\le \varepsilon + \xi_i, \quad \xi_i \ge 0, \\ \mathbf{w}^T\varphi(\mathbf{x}_i) - d_i &\le \varepsilon + \xi_i', \quad \xi_i' \ge 0, \end{aligned} \qquad i = 1,2,\ldots,N \tag{13}$$

The slack variables describe the penalty for the training points lying outside the ε boundary. The measure of this cost is determined by the loss function. This constrained optimisation can be solved by minimising the

$$F(\mathbf{w},\xi,\xi') = \frac{1}{2}\mathbf{w}^T\mathbf{w} + C\left(\sum_{i=1}^{N}(\xi_i + \xi_i')\right) \tag{14}$$

cost function, subject to the four inequality constraints described above. The first term stands for the minimisation of $\|\mathbf{w}\|^2$, while the C constant is the trade–off parameter between this and the minimisation of training data errors. The user defined parameters C and ε, controls the VC dimension of the resulting function. One must also choose the parameters of $\varphi(\mathbf{x})$. In our RBF structure it means the selection of a suitable σ for the Gaussian function.

In practice, it is very hard to determine the optimal values for these three parameters, because there is no universal approach so far. Another problem is that SVM learning is very slow, especially for large problems [9]. There are several solutions to speed up this process [9], [10]. In our experiments we used the method described in [10] along with the SVM software provided to it. The training of an SVM requires the solving of a constrained quadratic optimisation. When it comes to large dimensional inputs along with a large number of sample points, the usual solution techniques become highly memory and time consuming. In [9] this problem is solved by decomposing the optimisation to smaller tasks. The result is an iterative training algorithm, where each iteration solves a smaller optimisation problem.

5 The Comparison of the EIV and SVM Methods

This section gives some results of an extensive experimental comparison of the EIV and the SVM approaches for regressional problems. In this experimental study more function approximation problems were solved using both methods where in all cases the approximations are based on noisy samples. These experimental tasks were chosen in such a way, that functions with different characteristic properties (with different smoothness) were approximated. Here only the results of the *sinc* function approximation will be presented, however, similar consequences can be obtained solving other problems. The EIV method was used with an MLP network of 1 input, 6 hidden neurons and 1 output – this network size seemed the best fitting from several other configurations. The shown results are also the best from some different learning procedures. The results were also compared to that of a same size network trained with standard backpropagation algorithm. (In this case also many different NN structures were trained and this structure was also among the best ones.)

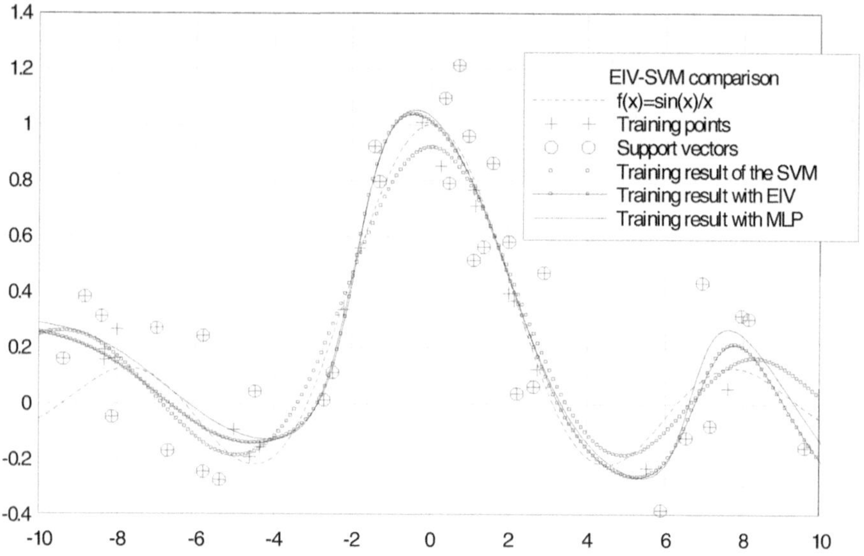

Fig. 2. Comparison of the neural, EIV and SVM approximation of the simple noisy *sin(x)/x*

Figure 3. presents that all three methods provide a reasonably good approximation, in spite of the low number and the poor quality of the training data. None of the generated functions are perfect, but the results produced by the methods have different characteristics. It can be seen, that the SVM is less sensitive to the misleading data points, i.e. points with large noise, therefore as expected, SVM also shows the best generalisation characteristics. In other words, it means, that the approximation seems to behave better on areas, where only a few and extremely erroneous data points are available. In such places the function provided by the SVM stays *"flat"*. This flatness is mainly controlled by the C parameter. To visualise the effects of parameters σ, C and ε to the result, the mean error is plotted as a function of σ and C (for a fixed ε=0.1). It can be seen, that if σ and C are chosen properly, then the changes of these parameters don't have significant effects on the performance. This means that the error surface is quite smooth. Similar behaviour could be observed in other artificially created function approximation test (e.g. *sin*, two–dimensional *sinc*, etc.).

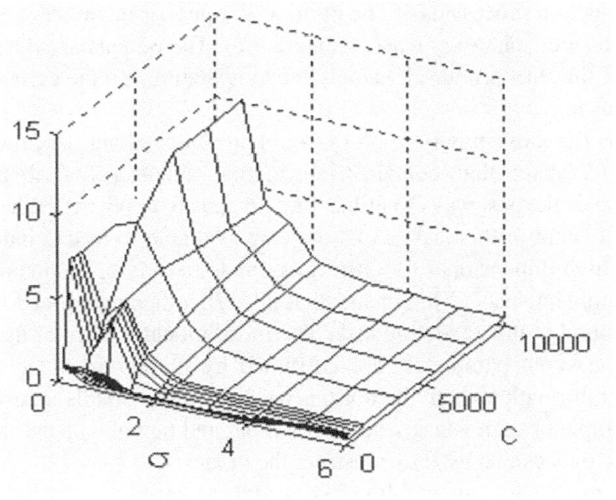

Fig. 3. The mean error plotted as a function of σ and C, for the *sinc* function

6 Experiments with an Industrial Problem

Based on the experimental study presented in the previous parts the SVM approach was applied for a complex industrial problem, where the task is to build reliable model for a Linz-Donawitz steel converter. Linz-Donawitz converter steel making. (Basic Oxygen Steelmaking, BOS) is one of the most important production process of steel, where to build a reliable and high accuracy model is crucial for efficient control of the production.

Description of the process - Steelmaking with an LD converter (Linz-Donawitz steel converter) is a complex physico-chemical process where many variables have influences on the quality of the resulted steel. The complexity of the whole process and the fact that there are many effects that cannot be taken into consideration make this task highly difficult. The main features of the process are the followings: a large (~150-ton) converter is filled with recycled steel scrap (~30 tons), molten pig iron (~ 110 tons) and many additives, then this fluid compound is blasted through with pure oxygen to oxidise the unwanted contamination (e.g. silicon, most of the carbon, etc.). [12], [13]

The blasting with pure oxygen is the main part of the whole process. At the end of the oxygen blowing the quality of the steel is tested and its temperature is measured. If the main parameters are within the acceptable and rather narrow range, the whole process is finished, the steel and the slag is tapped off for further processing.

The quality of the steel are influenced by many parameters, however the amount of oxygen used during blasting is the main parameter that can be controlled to obtain predetermined quality steel. To determine the necessary amount of oxygen, a model of the steel production process has to be built. The inputs of the model are formed by all available, measured data (e.g. mass, temperature). The outputs are the most important parameters of the steel produced, namely the temperature and the carbon content at the end of the blasting.

In our case the most important part of the knowledge about the process is the relatively large database that contains information about a few thousand previous blastings. One of the best ways to utilise these data is to apply neural networks.

The main feature of this task is that the data available from this industrial problem is relatively high-dimensional (30-50), noisy and sparsely and nonuniformly distributed in the problem space. This means that all difficulties mentioned in the introduction can be found in this modeling task. The most critical feature of the data available is that the measured parameters are corrupted by measurement noise, where even approximate information about the noise is hard to obtain. So this industrial problem is a typical example of such a task where both input and output data are noisy and where relatively few data can be used to construct the model.

This means that for our real-life task it makes sense to apply the EIV and SVM methods and compare the results with those obtained from a large project using classical neural approach [13], [14], [15].

There are many practical difficulties to use EIV method for this LD modeling problem. The most important one is that EIV is rather sensitive to the exact values of the noise variances, and in this task only a very rough estimation of the noise parameters can be obtained. Thus only the SVM approach has been studied.

Application of SVM for modeling the industrial problem. Although the parameters of the SVM method also depend on the noise level, and since there is no algorithm to determine the optimal, or even the near optimal parameters, our only alternative was to take a rough guess, and then try to fine-tune these parameters by a cross–validation method. This is of course very time-consuming, since it requires several test runs, i.e. teach and test cycles. In the sequel we will show some results we got for our data set. To get a rough approximation for the C, ε and σ parameters test runs where done. To increase speed, smaller training sets were used in these test runs. The exact parameters were then fine-tuned, with the use of the whole data set. Experiments show that once the correct parameters are found, the small changes in these do not have a large effect on the performance. To validate the model a performance measure can be determined. This performance measure depends on the temperature error at the output of the model if the predicted oxygen is applied. For the temperature error a relatively narrow interval is defined as a tolerance interval, and if the real error is within this interval than the prediction can be accepted otherwise cannot. The performance measure is the ratio of the accepted cases and all cases.

The results of this experiment are shown in the next table. Two different data sets where used, which differ both in the number of data points (A~3000,B~4500) and noisiness (the seemingly misleading data points where filtered out in the first case). The model has 53 inputs and 1 output.

Table 1. The results of the SVM on two different industrial data sample

		Parameters			Number of points relative to the tolerance interval			Percentage of good results
#		ε	σ	C	Above	Under	Inside	Hit (%)
A	1	0.01	1	1000	94	58	450	74.75
	2	**0.01**	**1.2**	**1000**	**95**	**56**	**451**	**74.92**
	3	0.01	1.4	1000	96	59	447	74.25
B	1	0.01	1.2	1000	203	241	653	59.53
	2	**0.01**	**1.4**	**1000**	**204**	**239**	**654**	**59.62**
	3	0.01	1.5	1000	202	242	653	59.53

The best result was obtained by the use of parameters shown in line A-2 and B-2. From this table it can be seen that the parameters have effect on the performance of the model, however once these parameters are in the right domain, this effect is not too significant. These results can be compared to that of a classical MLP-based neural model, where two-hidden-layer networks were trained with 12 and 10 hidden neurons respectively. This architecture was chosen as a result of an extensive study where many different size networks were trained and tested with different but similar data bases. For comparison the best MLP was trained and tested with the same database as the SVM and 70.18% and 57,5 % hit rate could be achieved for the case A and B respectively.

7 Conclusions

The paper presents the problem of noisy data in neural system modeling. This problem is common in many complex industrial black-box identification tasks. To reduce the effect of noise two different approaches are considered, the EIV and the SVM approach. Both methods can result in slightly better solutions than the classical NN; however, both methods have parameters, which have to be chosen according to the variance of the noise of the data. While in most cases this variance is not known, the parameters of the methods can only be chosen using an estimate of the noise variance. Based on an experimental study it seems, that the EIV method is more sensitive to this estimate, so only the SVM method is used in the industrial modeling task. The first results in this steel converter modeling problem with SVM are rather encouraging, however to reach a final conclusion more experiments with much more data must be done.

All three of the discussed (SVM, EIV, and NN) solutions have generalisation, and certain noise reducing properties, but the EIV method, that theoretically gives better results, is quite prone to overfitting, and to realise some early stopping further optimisations are needed. The use of a classical NN raises the problem of determining the optimal structure. The SVM method solves this problem, but it still requires some parameters to be defined. Fortunately it seems that these choices are not to critical once the right domain is found. Another disadvantage is the slow learning process, but this drawback is not too significant in case of slowly changing industrial processes.

8 References

1. Andersson, B.D.O.: "Identification of scalar errors in variables models with dynamics" Automatica, Vol. 21. No. 6. pp. 709-716., 1985
2. Van Gorp, J., Schoukens, J. and Pintelon, R.: "Learning neural networks with noisy inputs using the errors-in-variables approach" IEEE Trans. on Neural Networks, Vol. 11. No. 2 pp. 402-414. 2000.
3. Vapnik, V.N. "Statistical Learning Theory", John Wiley, 1998.
4. Wang, Ch. and Principe, J.C. "Training neural networks with additive noise in the desired signal" IEEE Trans. on Neural Networks, Vol. 10. No. 6., pp. 1511-1517. 1999.
5. An, G. "The effect of adding noise during backpropagation training on the generalization performance" Neural Computation, Vol. 8, pp. 643-674. 1996.
6. Gunn, S.: "Support Vector Machines for Classification and Regression", ISIS Technical Report, 14 May 1998.
7. Haykin, S.: "Neural Networks, A Comprehensive Foundation" Prentice Hall, New Jersey, 1999.
8. Smola, A. and Schölkopf, B.: "A Tutorial on Support Vector Regression" NeuroCOLT2 Technical Report Series NC2–TR–1998–030, October, 1998
9. Joachims, T.: "Making large-Scale SVM Learning Practical. Advances in Kernel Methods - Support Vector Learning", in Schölkopf, B., Burges, C. and Smola, A. (eds.), MIT-Press, 1999
10. Platt, J.C.: "Sequential Minimal Optimization: Fast Algorithm for Training Support Vector Machines" Microsoft Research Technical Report MSR–TR–98–14, April 21, 1998
11. Polkovnyikov, A.: "Possibilities of Modeling of an LD Converter", Inner report (In Hungarian) Dunaújváros, 1996.
12. Kaptay, Gy. and Benkő, M.: "The Physical-chemical Background of Modeling of an LD Converter", Inner report, (In Hungarian) Miskolc University, Miskolc, 1999.
13. Horváth, G., Pataki, B. and Strausz Gy.: "Black-box Modeling of a Complex Industrial Process", Proc. of the 1999 IEEE Conference and Workshop on Engineering of Computer Based Systems, Nashville, TN, USA. 1999. pp. 60-66
14. Pataki, B., Horváth, G., Strausz, Gy. and Talata, Zs. "Inverse Neural Modeling of a Linz-Donawitz Steel Converter" e & i Elektrotechnik und Informationstechnik, Vol. 117. No. 1.. pp. 13-17. 2000.
15. Horváth, G., Pataki, B. and Strausz Gy.: "Research Report of the Hybrid-neural Modeling of an LD Steel-Converter" Budapest University of Technology and Economics, Dept. of Measurement and Information Systems, (In Hungarian) Budapest, 2000.

Enhanced Artificial Neurons for Network Applications

Gerard Murray and Tim Hendtlass

Centre for Intelligent Systems and Complex Processes,
School of Biophysical Science and Electrical Engineering,
Swinburne University of Technology,
P.O. Box 218 Hawthorn AUSTRALIA 3122.
gmurray@swin.edu.au, thendtlass@swin.edu.au

Abstract. It is hypothesised that conventional back propagation networks have limitations arising at least, from the simplicity of the artificial neuron model that is used. A more complex neuron, called a micronet, to distinguish it from the conventional neuron, is introduced. The architecture and heuristic of the micronet are described. Visual examples of the complex decision surfaces that can be produced by a single micronet in response to a range of problems are presented.

1 Introduction

Biology interposes a synapse between the axon of one neuron and the dendrite of another. The synapse is the chemical conduit of signal conduction between the neurons [11] and the site of parallel modes of non-linear neurotransmission.

The artificial neural network analogue of the synapse is the weight. This configuration has worked well in multi-layered architectures as the conduit of signal conduction. However, such networks have definite performance limits and the authors contend that this is, in part, due to the over simplistic artificial neurons that are used. It is widely accepted that conventional MLP's are universal approximators. The authors suggest that more complex synaptic analogues between artificial neurons are desirable and that this increased architectural complexity may lead to neurons and therefore networks capable of better approximation over far more complex feature spaces.

In extending his seminal ideas on artificial neurons, McCulloch developed neurons capable of satisfying the XOR proposition twelve years before Minsky and Papert [14]. This was accomplished by incorporating second order product terms into the input activations to overcome the limitations of the linear discriminants observed in traditional McCulloch-Pitts or Rosenblatt neurons.

The simplest way to implement product terms into conventional multi-layer architectures is to place two conventional weights in series in such a way that they cannot be mathematically decomposed to a single weight entity. This condition will not be realised if both the weights are conventional. In a micronet, a conventional weight is placed in series with a control element. Product terms are introduced that yield a non-linear discriminant suitable for difficult classification.

Control elements have properties that render them distinct and separate from conventional weights. To fully appreciate this, an explanation of their biological inspiration is needed. Although the neural metaphor is liberally disseminated in this

L. Monostori, J. Váncza, and M. Ali (Eds.): IEA/AIE 2001, LNAI 2070, pp. 281-289, 2001.

field as the source of artificial neural computation, consideration of some of the other components of the synaptic neuropil are paid little attention.

Cells such as astrocytes in the cortical grey matter are examples of glia. Although glial processes are not fully understood, it is believed that they form an intimate and necessary co-existence with neurons [1]. Glial membranes interpose or sheathe synapses in the mammalian central nervous system. Once thought to be the cellular support of neurons and devoid of signal transfer, glia are now thought to be capable of signaling through complex, intracellular calcium dynamics [8].

To attempt an artificial neural architecture which includes artificial glia would be over ambitious without a more complete understanding of the structure and function of the biological congener. However, an artificial scheme that uses the output of a single node, or network of nodes, to generate control elements is possible. These secondary structures, biologically inspired if not fully biologically plausible, can differ from the output neurons by their architecture, learning rates and transfer functions. This heterogeneity may also be extended to the heuristic used to train these structures.

Control elements, in series with conventional weights, can form a number of parallel independent channels that combine to be the path from an input to the output neuron. Under differing conditions these channels behave like an ensemble of domain experts, each knowledgeable over a subset of input space [7].

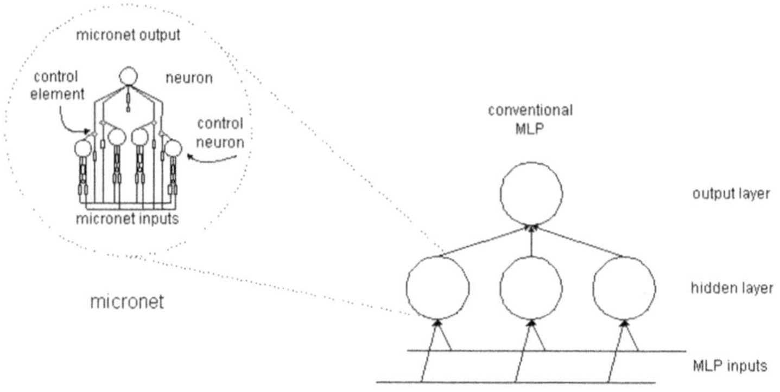

Fig. 1. The substitution of a micronet into MLP architecture is possible at the neuronal level

2 Duality in Utilisation of Micronet Architecture

Figure 1, above, shows the familiar representation of a conventional MLP (on the right). This network has two inputs, a single hidden layer containing three neurons and an output layer, containing a single neuron. All the neurons are conventional, McCulloch-Pitts neurons. The network is maximally connected.

A micronet is depicted encircled by the dotted line. The micronet has two inputs and a single conventional, McCulloch-Pitts, output neuron. Two separate channels, each consisting of a conventional weight and a control element connect an input to the output neuron.

The control neuron, receives activation from both inputs and a bias. All three activations are summed and transformed through a sigmoid transfer function. The resultant output is the value of the control element. The control element ensures that the weight values from channels on the same input cannot be mathematically combined.

The product of the weight and the control element provide a single activation to the output neuron. In this example there are four input activations and a bias supplied to the output neuron. All five activations are summed and transformed through a tanh transfer function. The resultant output is the micronet output. The micronet output can be used to calculate a global error, which can be backpropagated. In this way this micronet can be trained.

The micronet depicted can be substituted for any or all of the conventional neurons in the hidden layer of the MLP. This because the micronet has the same input requirements as the conventional neuron and similarly, provides a single output. The advantage being the non-linearity introduced by incorporating micronet architecture into the MLP. As long as there is a global error, with some minor modifications, credit assignment by backpropagation should train the hybrid MLP.

3 Channels of Control Elements and Weights in Micronets

A typical input activation in a conventional artificial neural network connects an input, $\boldsymbol{i}$, to a neuron through a weight, $\boldsymbol{w}$. Let $\boldsymbol{e}_{(ia)}$ be the error in the internal activation and η be the learning rate of the neuron. By Hebbian learning the weight change, $\Delta \boldsymbol{w}$, to be made to weight $\boldsymbol{w}$ will be,

$$\Delta w = i\eta e_{(ia)} \tag{1}$$

Micronet architecture defines the effective value of the channel as the product of a conventional weight, $\boldsymbol{w}$, and a control element, $\boldsymbol{c}$. Figure 2 is a simple channel in which the value of the control element is set by the output of a single control neuron, connected to all inputs and a bias.

A more complex channel may have the value of the control element set by the output of a complete subservient control network. The control neuron or network has conventional weights.

Training of a channel ensemble requires a cascaded or 'trickle through' approach. The steps involved are. For the first example calculate the output of the control neuron (or network.)

$$c_{(r,s)} = Sigmoid\left[\left(\sum_{r=1}^{R}\left(i_{(r)} w_{c(r)}\right)\right) + w_{c(bi)}\right] \tag{2}$$

$$o_{(\alpha)} = Tanh\left[\left(\sum_{r=1}^{R}\left(\sum_{s=1}^{S}\left(i_{(r)} w_{p(r,s)} c_{(r,s)}\right)\right)\right) + w_{o(bi)}\right] \tag{3}$$

Let $\boldsymbol{o}_{(\alpha)}$ be the actual output of the network and $\boldsymbol{o}_{(\delta)}$the desired output of the network. The output error of the network for this example is therefore

$$\boldsymbol{e}_o = \boldsymbol{o}_{(\delta)} - \boldsymbol{o}_{(\alpha)} \tag{4}$$

The error, $\boldsymbol{e}_{o(ia)}$, in the internal activation of the output neuron is calculated as:

$$\boldsymbol{e}_{o(ia)} = \boldsymbol{e}_o \left(\boldsymbol{f}' \left(\boldsymbol{o}_{(\alpha)} \right) \right) \tag{5}$$

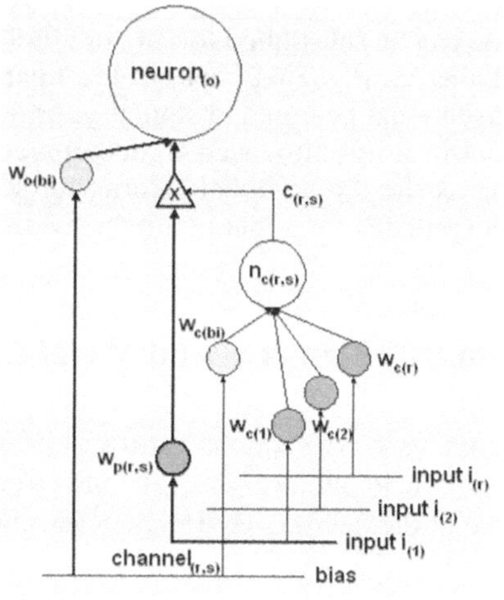

Fig. 2. A single channel, 's' in a micronet with 'r' inputs. In this instance input (1) has a single channel but multiple channel configurations are possible for this path

The error, $\Delta\boldsymbol{c}$, in control element, $\boldsymbol{c}$. is estimated to be:

$$\Delta\boldsymbol{c}_{(r,s)} = \boldsymbol{e}_{o(ia)} \eta_{(o)} \boldsymbol{i}_{(r)} \boldsymbol{w}_{p(r,s)} \tag{6}$$

The error, $\boldsymbol{e}_{c(ia)}$, in the internal activation of the control neuron is therefore:

$$\boldsymbol{e}_{c(ia)} = \Delta\boldsymbol{c}_{(r,s)} \left(\boldsymbol{f}' \left(\boldsymbol{c}_{(r,s)} \right) \right) \tag{7}$$

Thus far, training has followed the back propagation heuristic exactly with the estimate of the error in the control element being that predicted by basic Hebbian learning. However, the neuron that sets the control element has an associated learning rate that effectively attenuates the error, $\boldsymbol{e}_{c(ia)}$. As a result the actual change that is made will only be a fraction of that required to reduce the output error by the amount required. A forward pass through the control neuron (or network) is now made, using the same inputs, to set the value of the control element to the new value $\boldsymbol{c}'_{(r,s)}$.

The error in the path weight $\Delta\boldsymbol{w}_p$, is estimated, since it contains the value $\boldsymbol{c}'_{(r,s)}$. Thus, it too has been attenuated, and written to reflect this as the partial error, $\partial\boldsymbol{w}_{p(r,s)}$. This change is made to the weight $\boldsymbol{w}_p$.

$$\partial w_{p(r,s)} = e_{o(ia)} \eta_{(o)} c'_{(r,s)} \, i_{(r)} \tag{8}$$

The bias weight associated with the output neuron is updated conventionally by

$$\Delta w_{o(bi)} = e_{o(ia)} \eta_{(o)} i_{(bias)} \tag{9}$$

This completes the training process for this example, the next input vector can now be applied and the process repeated until satisfactory convergence is realised.

4 Results

The results presented were obtained by randomly initialising a single micronet and training. In the case of the rings, two spirals and four shapes, training continued until a desired tolerance was achieved across all the members in the training set.

Table 1. Two concentric rings. The training data is shown on the left with the micronet output surface on the right

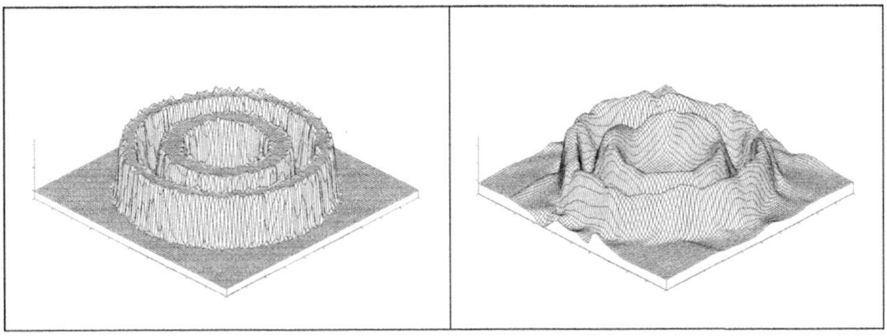

Table 2. Twin spirals. The microonet output surface is on the right

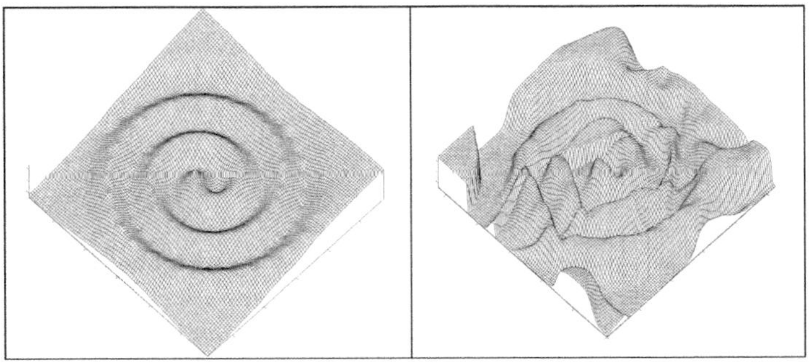

Table 3. Four shapes. The micronet output surface is on the right

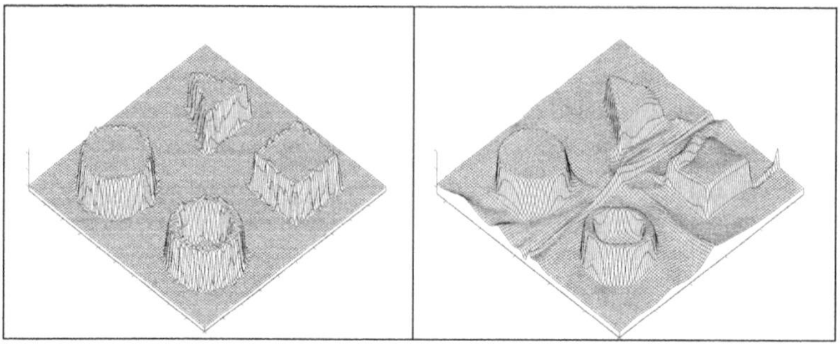

The mouse is a qualitative demonstration of the complex feature space a single micronet can learn.

Table 4. A complex feature space. The micronet output surface is on the right

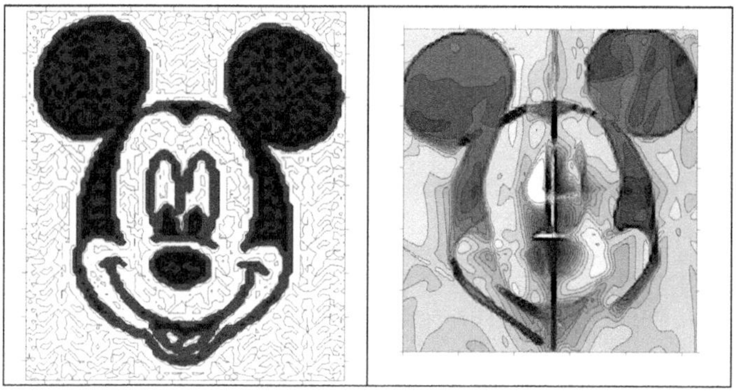

5 Discussion

Non-linear approaches to classification problems are not new [2, 9, 12,]. Digital classification problems with bounded regions were chosen to demonstrate the ability of a micro-net to generate non-linear discriminators. To visually represent this phenomenon the problem sets have a two-dimensional input space. This allows their output space to be mapped and sampled as the micronet learns.

The four problems whose results are shown in this paper form a set that, amongst other things, tests for sensitivity of the micronet to symmetry. The two concentric rings (Table 1) is a complex problem but symmetrical, the two spirals problem (Table 2) has a high degree of symmetry. The four shapes set (Table 3) has high local symmetry for each shape but is asymmetric in total. Finally the image of a well-known mouse (Table 4) has high symmetry about the vertical axis, but no symmetry about the horizontal axis.

All but the two spirals data set have been learned successfully by modular neural network ensembles [13]. This provides the micronet with a direct comparator to gauge learning efficiency and generalising capability.

As these problems are all but impossible for single backpropagation networks to solve, it can be inferred that any solution found by a micronet is found purely as a result of the architectural enhancements.

A conventional neuron can only produce open decision boundaries, albeit curved. By adding multiple paths whose relative importance varies as a result of the data input, these open decision boundaries may be combined to form closed decision boundaries of almost arbitrary complexity. This can be seen in the results where very good approximations to both circular and straight-line edges can be generated. In the contour plot of the mouse (Table 4), complex closed regions are quite reasonably reproduced, although the fine detail of the eye area has proved too much for the network architecture used.

Table 5. A comparison of resources. (n.a. - not available)

	Ensemble network results				Micronet results		
	networks	Largest hidden layer	Smallest hidden layer	weights	Channels	Control nodes	weights
Two rings	25	7	1	293	10	3	281
Twin spirals	-	-	-	-	12	12	1201
Four shapes	39	13	1	539	12	10	1009
Mouse	208	n.a.	n.a.	n.a.	12	12	1201

Table 5 illustrates the efficiency of learning with respect to the weight resource. The micronet and the ensemble approach are comparable in the instance of the 2 rings data set. The 4 shapes data set required a micronet with almost double the number of weights an ensemble required. An ensemble starts with a single network and learns what it can. If error reduction is not observed a second network is initialised and begins to learn what the first network could not. In this manor, each network becomes knowledgeable over a region of the input space. A micronet attempts much the same thing. The difference is that the ensemble has an adaptable topology where the micronet topology is essentially fixed. The result may reflect a micronet that is over resourced. In the case of the 4 shapes a micronet with more compact control networks may have been just as effective.

In the instance of the 2 spirals, a number of neural network approaches have been tried [3, 4, 5, 10, 15], but because of the differences in architecture, these results are not directly comparable to the micronet. Backpropagation can learn the shape but fails to recognise the spatial relationship between the spirals [6]. The micronet has demonstrated that its enhanced architecture can recognise the curvature of the shape as well as the spatial relationship between the two spirals.

The results for the mouse data set are included in Table 5. Again comparisons between the micronet and ensemble networks are only qualitative. This is because the ensemble consisted of neural networks and evolved polynomials. 208 networks were required in the ensemble because of the curved features prevalent in the feature space. A micronet with the same resources as the one that learned 4 shapes has made considerable progress.

6 Further Study

The true value of micronet architecture will be realised when it is incorporated into conventional networks. It is possible to replace all neurons in a multi-layered perceptron with micronets, alternately a mixture of conventional neurons and micronets can be assembled. Control networks within a micronet can themselves be assembled from micronets or combinations of micronets and conventional neurons.

This research was aimed at developing viable architectures and a robust training heuristic. The task of optimisation is yet to be fully addressed. A single micronet yields numerous possibilities of adaptation. The sensitivity of the system to initial conditions, the addition and pruning of channels, the adaptation of learning rates, deciding on the size of the control networks and the nature of the transfer functions employed will all effect the quality of solution. All of these issues must be evaluated before the possibility of an adaptive topology can even be considered.

7 Conclusion

The product terms introduced by the unique architecture of the micronet have yielded non-linear discriminators that are capable of learning complex data with a two dimensional input vector. Continuing investigation into the generalising ability of the micronet is continuing.

Acknowledgments. The authors gratefully acknowledge the visualisation software provided by Clinton Woodward and the many helpful discussions with colleagues at The Centre for Intelligent Systems and Complex Processes.

References

1. Dani, J.W., Chernjavsky, A. and Smith, S.J.: Neuronal Activity Triggers Calcium Waves in Hippocampal Astrocyte Networks. Neuron, 8, pp 429-440 (1992).
2. Duda, R. and Hart, P.: Pattern Classification and Scene Analysis, Wiley, New York, (1973).
3. Carpenter, G.A., Grossberg, S., Markuzon, N., Reynolds, J.H. and Rosen, D.B.: Fuzzy Artmap: A Neural Network Architecture for Incremental Supervised Learning of Analog Multi-dimensional Maps. IEEE Transactions on Neural Networks, 3, pp 698-713 (1992).
4. Fahlman, S.E.: Faster-Learning Variations on Backpropagation, Proceedings of the Connectionist Models Summer School, Morgan Kaufmann, San Mateo, (1988).
5. Fahlman, S.E. and Lebiere, C.: The Cascade Correlation Learning Architecture, Advances in Neural Information Processing Systems II, Morgan Kaufmann, San Mateo, (1990).

6. Garavaglia, S.B.: IEEE Proceedings of the International Joint Conference on Neural Networks, 1, pp1158-1163, (1999).
7. Jordan, J.M. and Jacobs, R.A.: Hierarchical Mixtures of Experts and the EM Algorithm. Neural Computation, 6, pp 181-214 (1993).
8. Keener, J. and Sneyd, J.: Mathematical Physiology, Springer-Verlag, New York, (1998).
9. Klassen, M. and Pao, Y.: Characteristics of the Functional-Link Net: A Higher Order Delta Rule Net, IEEE Proceedings of the 2nd. Annual International Conference on Neural Networks, San Diego, California, (1988).
10. Lang, K.J. and Witbrock, M.J.: Learning to Tell Two Spirals Apart, Proceedings of the Connectionist Models Summer School, Morgan Kaufmann, (1988).
11. Lundberg, J.M. and Hokfelt, T.: Neurtransmitters in Action. Elsevier Biomedical Press, New York, pp 113 (1985).
12. Nilsson, N.: The Mathematical Foundations of Learning Machines, Morgan Kaufman Publishers, San Mateo, California, (1990).
13. Philpot, D.N. Growing Modular Ensembles of Neural Networks, Doctoral Thesis, Swinburne University, Melbourne, (1998).
14. Scott, R.J.: McCulloch's Neurons Revisited. Proceedings of the International Workshop on Artificial Neural Networks '93. Springer-Verlag, Berlin, pp.63 (1993).
15. Weenink, D.: Category ART: A Variation on Adaptive Resonance Theory Neural Networks, 21 st. Proceedings of the Institute of Phonetic Sciences, University of Amsterdam, pp117-129 (1997).

Time Delay Neural Networks Designed Using Genetic Algorithms for Short Term Inter-City Traffic Forecasting

Pawan Lingras and Paul Mountford

Department of Mathematics and Computing Science
Saint Mary's University, Halifax
Nova Scotia, Canada, B3H 3C1
pawan@cs.stmarys.cs

Abstract. Estimation of short-term traffic volumes is an important issue in the development of intelligent transportation systems (ITS). This paper uses genetic algorithms to maximize statistical correlation for selecting connections between input and hidden layers of a time delay neural network for inter-city traffic volume estimations. The predictions for high traffic volume hours using proposed approach reflect a high degree of accuracy.

1. Introduction

Neural networks have proven to be useful in developing models for non-linear systems. A variant of neural networks called the time-delay neural network (TDNN) has proved especially useful for modeling time series. Hansen, *et al.* (1999) showed that the TDNNs designed using genetic algorithms can provide better time series predictions than conventional statistical time series techniques for non-linear time series. Hansen *et al.*'s approach is not computationally feasible for a large time series model such as the one used in this study. The present study applies a variation of Hansen, *et al.*'s approach for inter-city traffic forecasting. The approach proposed in this study combines a statistical measure with evolutionary and neural computing. The proposed approach is computationally less intensive than Hansen, *et al.*'s approach.

Advancements in computer and communications technologies are making it possible to address several challenges in transportation, such as safety, productivity, and mobility. One of the ways of alleviating the congestion problems is to redistribute the traffic over the highway network. This redistribution can be spatial as well as temporal. If travelers have advance information about the traffic conditions, they can reschedule or reroute their trips. One of the important issues in an Advance Traveler Information System (ATIS) is accurate forecasting of traffic conditions in the short-term future.

Most of the earlier research on short-term traffic volume forecasting compared the results of models developed based on traditional statistical models with advanced techniques like neural networks. Smith and Demetsky (1997) developed historical average, time-series, neural network, and non-parametric regression models for Northern Virginia's Capital Beltway. Hua and Faghri (1994) concluded that neural

L. Monostori, J. Váncza, and M. Ali (Eds.): IEA/AIE 2001, LNAI 2070, pp. 290-299, 2001.

networks provide most techniques needed in some ITS implementation domains such as real time traffic forecasting, neural networks are found to be superior to conventional techniques. Zhang and Ritchie (1997) developed a multi-layer feed-forward artificial neural network to model the freeway traffic system. Park *et al.* (1998) applied radial basis function (RBF) neural network for time-series forecasting. Cheu (1998) developed multilayer feedforward neural networks to predict freeway conditions at I-880 Freeway in the San Francisco Bay Area.

Many of the above studies illustrated the advantages of using neural networks. Some studies favored statistical models (Smith and Demetsky, 1997). This study deals with neural network models. Neural networks are considered clever and intuitive, because they learn by example rather than by following programmed rules. They are good at pattern recognition. They learn the trends from the data and develop the ability to categorize, imitate, and generalize. Their other characteristics are adaptability, plasticity, self-organization, dynamic stability, convergence, fault tolerance, and normalization. These properties can be applied to most types of artificial neural networks.

Even though the majority of previous studies are restricted to urban highway networks, some of the researchers have conducted experiments with other categories of highways (Dougherty and Cobbett, 1997). Highway agencies, such as Minnesota Department of Transportation, have clearly stated their intentions of extending ATIS to other categories of highways over the next few years. Dougherty and Cobbett (1997) studied the use of backpropagation neural networks for short term traffic forecasts of inter-urban traffic in Netherlands. They identified the vast number of possible input parameters as one of the major problems. Dougherty and Cobbett used stepwise reduction to reduce the size of the network. This paper proposes the use of genetic algorithms to address a similar problem, namely the design of connections from the input layer to hidden layer in a time-delay neural networks for modeling an inter-urban traffic volume time series in Alberta, Canada. The results are compared with other models that were developed based on intuitive understanding of the time series.

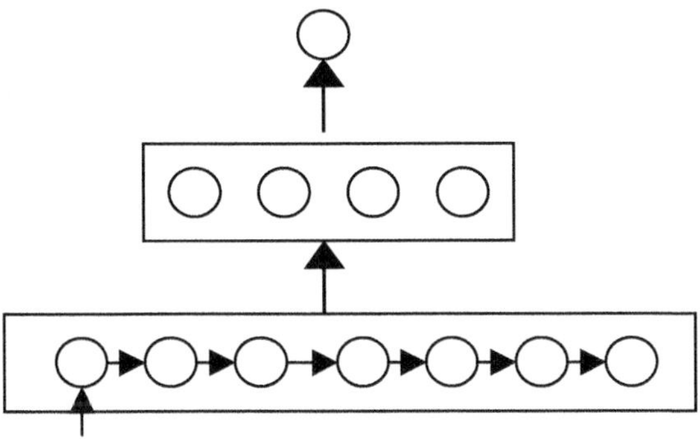

Fig. 1. Time Delay Neural Network Design

2. Time-Delay Neural Networks

The network used in this study consists of three layers: input, hidden, and output. Figure 1 shows the network used in this study. The input layer receives data from the outside world. The variant of neural network used in this study is called Time-Delay Neural Network (TDNN) (Hecht-Nielsen, 1990). Figure 1 shows an example of a TDNN, which are particularly useful for time series analysis. The neurons in a given layer can receive delayed input from other neurons in the same layer. For example, the network in figure 1 receives a single input from the external environment. The remaining nodes in the input layer get their input from the neuron on the left delayed by one time interval. The input layer at any time will hold a part of the time series. Such delays can also be incorporated in other layers.

The input layer neurons send information to the hidden layer neurons. The hidden neurons are all the neurons between the input and output layers. They are part of the internal abstract pattern, which represents the neural network's solution to the problem. The hidden layer neurons feed their output to the output layer neurons, which provide the neural network's response to the input data.

Neurons process input and produce output. Each neuron takes in the output from many other neurons. Actual output from a neuron is calculated using a transfer function. In this study, a sigmoid transfer function is chosen because it produces a continuous value in the range [0,1]. It is necessary to train a neural network model on a set of examples called the training set so that it adapts to the system it is trying to simulate. Supervised learning is the most common form of adaptation. In supervised learning, the correct output for the output layer is known. Output neurons are told what the ideal response to input signals should be. In the training phase, the network constructs an internal representation that captures the regularities of the data in a distributed and generalized way. The network attempts to adjust the weights of connections between neurons to produce the desired output. The backpropagation method is used to adjust the weights, in which errors from the output is feedback through the network, altering weights as it goes, to prevent the repetition of the error.

3. Genetic Algorithms

The origin of Genetic Algorithms (GAs) is attributed to Holland's (1975) work on cellular automata. There has been significant interest in GAs over the last two decades. The range of applications of GAs includes such diverse areas as: job shop scheduling, training neural nets, image feature extraction, and image feature identification. This section gives a brief overview of GAs.

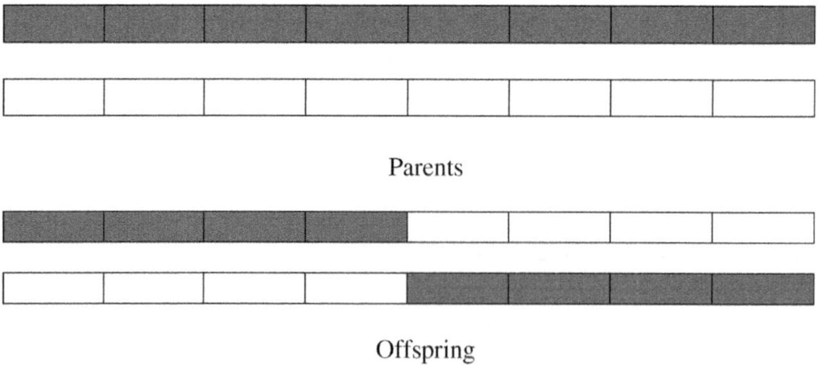

Fig. 2. Crossover operation

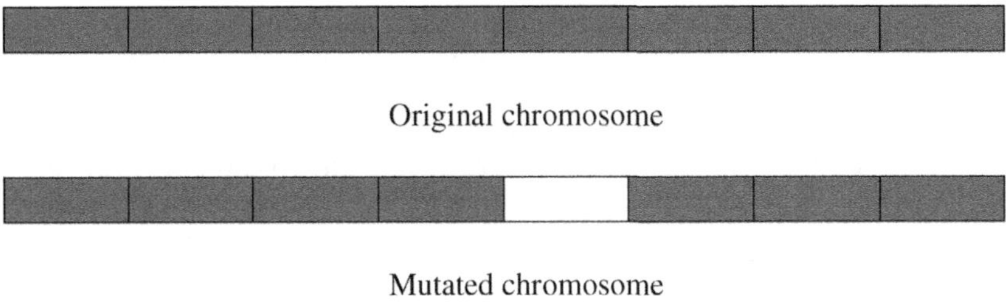

Fig. 3. Mutation operation

GAs follow the principles of evolution through natural selection. The domain knowledge is represented using a candidate solution called an *organism.* In most cases an organism is a single chromosome represented by a vector of length n: $c = (c_i \mid 1 \le i \le n)$, where c_i is called a *gene.*

A group of organisms is called a *population.* Successive populations are called *generations.* A GA starts from an initial generation $G(0)$, and for each generation $G(t)$ generates a new generation $G(t + 1)$.

The genetic algorithm is based on two fundamental evolutionary concepts:

1) the Darwinian notion of *fitness*, which describes an organism's ability to survive; and
2) *genetic* operators, which determine the next generation's genetic makeup based upon the current generation.

Conventionally, (2) consists of *crossover* and *mutation* operators. The crossover operator creates new organisms called *offspring* by recombining the genetic material of two existing organisms, the *parents.* Parents are chosen to „pass on" their genes to the next generation based on their fitness. Such crossovers ensure the exploitation of successful subspaces of the solution space. Figure 2 depicts a crossover operation. As shown in the figure, the offspring contain some of the genes from one parent and the rest of the genes from the other parent. The mutation operator randomly alters one or more genes in an organism. Mutations add genetic diversity to the population. Figure 3 shows the mutation operation, where the value of a randomly chosen gene is altered. Through mutation, GAs search previously unexplored sections of the solution space, consequently ensuring that the entire search space remains connected. Through the combination of crossovers and mutations, GAs are able to simultaneously explore new subspaces and exploit successful ones.

3.1 Genetic Algorithms for Designing Neural Networks

Many researchers have used GAs to determine neural network architectures. Harp, *et al.* (1989) and Miller, *et al.* (1989) used GAs to determine the best connections among network units. Montana and Davis (1989) used GAs for training the neural networks. Chalmers (1991) developed learning rules for neural networks using GAs.

Hansen, *et al.*(1999) used GAs to design time-delay neural networks (TDNNs), which included determination of important features such as number of inputs, number of hidden layers, and number of hidden neurons in each hidden layer.

Hansen, *et al.*(1999) applied their networks for modeling chemical process concentration, chemical process temperatures, as well as Wolfer sunspot numbers. Their results clearly showed advantages of using TDNNs configured using GAs over other techniques including conventional Autoregressive integrated moving average (ARIMA) methodology as described in Box and Jenkins (1970).

Hansen *et al.*'s approach consisted of building neural networks based on the architectures indicated by the fittest chromosome. The objective of the evolution was to minimize the training error. Such an approach is computationally expensive.

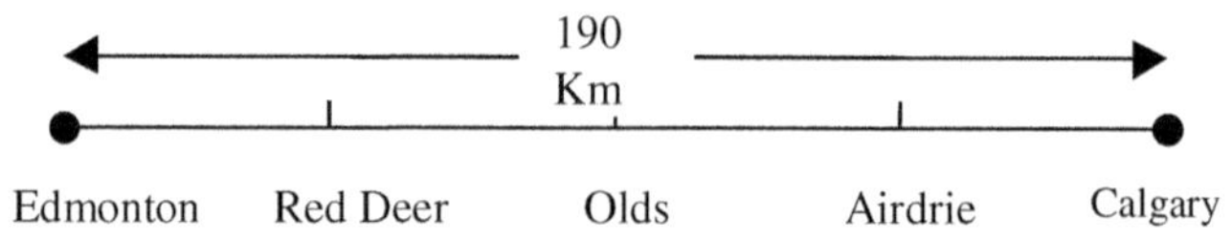

Fig. 4. Highway No. 2 (Between Calgary and Edmonton)

Another possibility that is used in this study is to choose the architecture of the input layer using genetic algorithms.

4. Study Data and Design of Experiments

The rural primary highways in Alberta experienced increased traffic volumes in the past years (Gopalkrishnan, 2000). During 1997, they experienced an increase in traffic volume of 7.1% over 1996 levels and in 1998 increase in traffic volume amounted to 3.9% over 1997 levels. This increase is primarily resulting from the growing economy leading to increased movements of goods by truck as well as increased tourism. Highway No. 2 between Calgary and Edmonton is one of the strategically located primary highway in Alberta. Traffic along this section has increased considerably over the years. This highway also forms part of the Canada-America-Mexico (CANAMEX) Project under consideration.

The study focuses on the development of short-term traffic prediction models along Highway No. 2 between Calgary and Edmonton. Figure 4 gives a schematic sketch of the four main counters between Calgary and Edmonton. The counters are identified based on the importance of their location with respect to Highway No. 2 and their access roads. They are also identified based on their traffic volumes, i.e. Annual Average Daily Traffic (AADT). The data used for this study are from years 1996 and 1997. The data are available in three files for each counter. Two of the files contain volume for each direction of travel and the third file contains the traffic volume for both directions.

The analysis (Gopalkrishnan, 2000) of traffic data clearly showed that except for the counter at Airdrie, three other locations experience a steady traffic flow throughout the day. The location at Airdrie clearly indicated a presence of commuter traffic in the form of distinct morning and evening peaks. For all the locations, the traffic volume variation remained very similar on all days except on Fridays, where the volume registered is a little higher than other days. Like other provincial highways in Canada, the summer months of June, July and August recorded higher traffic volumes.

4.1 Models

The objective of the study was to test the feasibility of using genetic algorithms for selecting connections from the input layer to the hidden layer of a TDNN. The inter-urban traffic from Edmonton to Calgary was the focus of the study. The assumption was that previous traffic volumes from all the four locations would influence the prediction of nth hourly traffic volume. Previous studies have used manual pattern analysis to decide the appropriate neural network design (Gopalkrishnan, 2000). This study uses genetic algorithms for designing the connections between input and hidden layers.

Figure 5 shows the model used in this study. To test the effectiveness of the proposed technique it was decided to predict the hourly traffic volumes at Airdrie, which has the highest traffic volumes among the four counters. Four time series from the four counters are used to form the time-delayed input layer. Each time-series is delayed 168 times corresponding to one-week worth of history. This results in $168 \times 4 = 672$ input neurons. If all of the neurons were connected to the hidden layer, it will result in an unwieldy neural network. Such a large neural network will take extremely long training time. Moreover, large number of connections can also result in deterioration in the learning ability of a network.

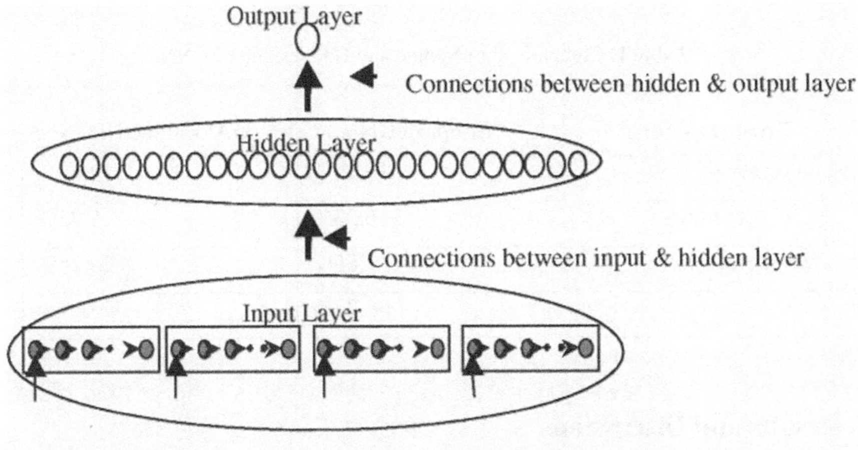

Figure 5. TDNN for Forecasting Short-Term Traffic

The data from 1996 and 1997 was used for creating the pattern files for each hour. A total of 17,112 observations comprised the training set. As mentioned before, Hansen, *et al.* (1999), used the training performance of neural networks as an objective of search for the best neural network architecture. However, given the size of present training set, such an objective is computationally infeasible. It was decided to use the maximization of linear correlation between the input layer variables and the output layer variable as the objective of the search for appropriate connections between input layer and hidden layer neurons. Note that all the 672 neurons will still have to be part of the input layer as they are used for the delay links. The genetic selection will be used to determine which input layer neurons will feed their input to the hidden layer. A careful design of neural network can be used to make sure that keeping all the 672 neurons in the hidden layers does not cause additional overhead in the neural computations.

Genetic algorithms were used to identify 50 variables from input layer that have highest linear correlation with the output variable. Each chromosome consisted of 50 genes. The input variables were labeled from 1 to 672 depending upon their position in the input layer as shown in figure 5. Each gene was allowed to take a value from 1 to 672. The chromosomes with higher values of linear correlation were selected for creating the next generation. The population size was set to 110, meaning that for each generation the genetic algorithm would retain the top 110 solutions. The genetic algorithms were allowed to evolve for 1000 generations. The crossover rate was set at 90%, and the probability of mutation was set to 1%. The best chromosome from 1 to 1000 generations was used as the final solution of the search. The connections selected by the genetic algorithm were used to design and implement a neural network.

The results from the GA designed neural network were compared with a simple TDNN that used connections from a total of last 50 hourly traffic volumes from the four counters. That means the simple model used last 13 hours from the counters at Leduc and Red Deer, and last 12 hours traffic from counters at Olds and Airdrie. Both the neural networks used twenty-five hidden layer neurons.

Table 1. Comparison of Simple and GA designed TDNNs

Error measure	Simple TDNN	GA designed TDNN
Average	15.29%	12.63%
50th percentile	6.53%	5.92%
85th percentile	33.85%	20.25%
95th percentile	66.27%	47.67%

5. Results and Discussions

The genetic algorithms attempted to maximize the linear correlation between the output variable and 50 of the 672 input layer variables. Figure 6 shows the distribution of the 50 selected input variables according to the counters. Two upstream counters at Olds and Red Deer seemed to have the most influence on traffic at Airdrie. The historical traffic at Airdrie contributed to the next most populous set of input variables. The farthest highway section at Leduc contributed smallest number of variables.

The predictions from the simple and GA designed TDNNs were compared using absolute percentage error calculated as:

$$error = \frac{|actual\ volume - estimated\ volume|}{actual\ volume} \times 100 \quad (2)$$

The key evaluation parameters used for comparison consisted of average, and 50th, 85th, and 95th percentile errors. Table 1 shows the comparisons of these four measures

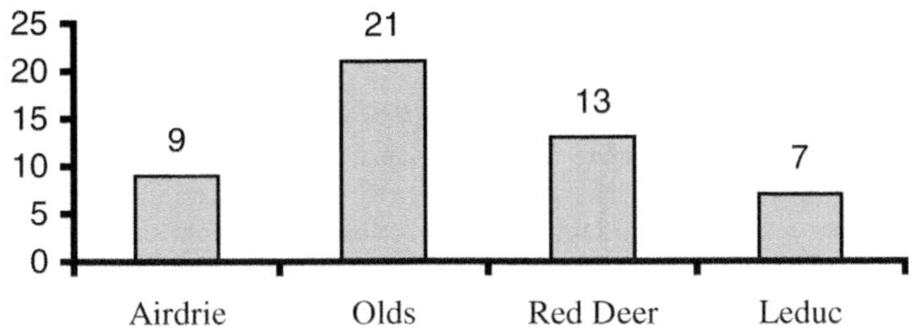

Figure 6. GA Assigned variables

for the simple and GA designed TDNN. As can be seen from table 1, the GA designed neural network has lower errors than the simple TDNN. The average error for GA designed TDNN is 2.5% lower than the simple TDNN, while the median (50th percentile) error is reduced from 6.53% to 5.92%. The difference between these two networks becomes more pronounced for 85th and 95th percentile errors. The 95th percentile error is reduced from 66% to 48% by adopting GA designed architecture.

Even though the average error of 12.6% for the GA designed TDNN seemed rather high, the median (50th percentile) error of 5.9% was significantly lower than the average error. This anomaly seemed to indicate that there are a few hours, which are contributing large percentage errors. It was hypothesized that these hours may typically be the low-volume or *silent* hours from late night to early morning. Typically, these low traffic volume hours have unstable traffic patterns. Moreover, even small variations in these low numbers can result in large percentage errors. A more detailed study of actual and estimated traffic volumes confirmed the hypothesis. A summary of the investigations appears in table 2.

The highest hourly traffic volume was 2754. The data set was analyzed using three types of hours. The first category consisted of hours with traffic volumes greater than 1377 (or 50% of the highest volume). These hours have some of the highest congestion found at that highway section. Accurate predictions of hours from this type is an important issue. There were a total of 2223 hours belonging to this category. The average error for this important first category was only 3.7%. The second category subsumes the first category and includes hours with traffic volumes greater than 689 (or 25% of the highest volume). In addition to the 2223 hours with high interest, this category may include an additional 7554 hours that may be less interesting to a road user. The average error for such an expanded category was also relatively low at 4.7%. On the other hand, 7335 hours had traffic volumes less than 689. The predictions for these hours are not critical, due to smooth traffic flow. The percentage errors for these hours were higher with an average of 22.9%. Such a high error still doesn't result in high absolute error for low traffic volumes. For example,

Table 2. Average errors for different types of hours using GA designed TDNNs

Type of hours	Number of hours	Average error
Traffic volume > 1377 (Greater than 50% of the highest traffic volume)	2223	3.73%
Traffic volume ≥ 689 (Greater than 25% of the highest traffic volume)	9777	4.68%
Traffic volume < 689 (Less than 25% of the highest traffic volume)	7335	22.86%

percentage error of 23% for a traffic volume of 689 will result in an absolute error of 158 vehicles per hour. The traffic conditions are likely to be similar for traffic volumes of 689 or 847.

In summary, it can be said that the average errors for high traffic volume errors are in 3-4% range. These errors are comparable or smaller than previous elaborate models developed for the same data (Gopalkrishnan, 2000). Gopalkrishnan (2000) used a detailed manual analysis of traffic patterns and developed neural network and regression models for the daytime hours. He found that developing different models for each hour increased the accuracy of predictions. The model developed in this study is universally applicable for any hour. Further refinement that excludes silent late night hours may improve the efficiency. One of the disadvantages of using a universal model is that the weights from the hidden layer have to adjust to different types of traffic hours. Using different hidden layer for different times of the day can further improve the accuracy of predictions. Such refinements will require an extensive set of experiments. Results of these experiments will be presented in a future publication.

6. Summary and Conclusions

This paper proposes a computationally feasible approach for designing large time delay neural networks. The study used four time series from different traffic counters on highway 2 to predict inter-urban traffic near Calgary, Alberta, Canada. The connections from time delayed input layer were chosen using genetic algorithms. The objective of the genetic algorithms was to maximize the linear correlation between output variable and fifty of the 672 variables from the input layer. The average prediction errors for important high traffic volume hours were found to be in the 3-4% range. Further experiments will be carried out to develop models that take into account the time of day to further improve the accuracy. The technique will also be tested for other locations on the same highway.

Acknowledgments. The authors would like to thank NSERC, Canada for their financial support and Alberta Infrastructure for the data used in this study.

References

1. Box, G. and Jenkins, J. (1970). *Time Series Analysis: Forecasting and Control.* Holden-Day, San Francisco.

2. Chalmers, D. (1991). The evolution of learning: An experiment in genetic connectionism. *In Connectionist Models: Proceedings of the 1990 Summer School.* Edited by D. Touretzky, J. Elman, and G. Hinton, Morgan Kaufmann, San Mateo, CA.
3. Cheu , R.L. (1998). Freeway Traffic Prediction Using Neural Networks. *Proceedings of 5th ASCE International Conference on Applications of Advanced Technologies in Transportation.* ASCE, April 26-29, pp. 247-254.
4. Davis, G.A., Nihan, N.L., Hamed, and M.M., Jacobson. L.N. (1990). Adaptive Forecasting of Freeway Traffic Congestion. *Transportation Research Record*, Transportation Research Board, Washington D.C., 1287, pp. 29-33.
5. Dougherty, M.S. and Cobbett, M.R. (1997). Short-Term Inter-Urban Traffic Forecasts using Neural Networks. *International Journal of Forecasting*, 13, pp.21-31.
6. Gopalkrishnan, S. (2000). Prediction of Short-Term Traffic Volume for Applications in Intelligent Transportation Systems, *unpublished M.A.Sc. thesis*, Faculty of Engineering, University of Regina, Regina, Saskatchewan, Canada.
7. Hansen, J. V., McDonald, J. B., and Nelson, R. D. (1999). Time Series Prediction with Genetic Algorithm Designed Neural Networks: An Experimental Comparison with Modern Statistical Models. Computational Intelligence, Vol. 15(3), pp. 171-184.
8. Harp, S.. Samad, T., and Guha, A. (1989). Towards the Genetic Synthesis of neural networks. *In Proceedings of the Third International Conference on Genetic Algorithms.* Edited by D. Shaffer, Morgan Kaufmann, San Mateo, CA.
9. Hecht-Nielsen, R. (1990). *Neurocomputing*. Addison-Wesley Pub. Co, Don Mills, Ontario.
10. Holland, J.H. (1975). *Adaptation in Natural and Artificial Systems.* University of Michigan Press, Ann Arbor.
11. Hua, J., and Faghri, A., (1994). Applications of Artificial Neural Networks to Intelligent Vehicle- Highway Systems. *Transportation Research Record*, Transportation Research Board, Washington D.C., 1453, pp. 83-90.
12. Miller, G., Todd, P., and Hedge, S. (1989). Designing neural networks using genetic algorithms, *In Proceedings of the Third International Conference on Genetic Algorithms.* Edited by D. Shaffer, Morgan Kaufmann, San Mateo, CA.
13. Montana, D. and Davis, L. (1989). Training feedforward networks using genetic algorithms. *In Eleventh International Joint Conference on Artificial Intelligence*, Detroit. Edited by N. Sridhara. pp. 762-767.
14. Park, B., Messer, C.J., and Urbanik, T. (1998). Short-Term Freeway Traffic Volume Forecasting Using Radial Basis Function Neural Network. *Transportation Research Record*, Transportation Research Board, Washington D.C., 1651, pp. 39-47.
15. Smith, B.L. and Demetsky, M.J. (1997). Traffic Flow Forecasting: Comparison of Modeling Approaches. *Journal of Transportation Engineering*, 123(4), July/August, pp. 261-266.
16. Zhang, H., Ritchie, S.G., and Lo, Z.P. (1997). Macroscopic Modeling of Freeway Traffic Using an Artificial Neural Network. *Transportation Research Record*, Transportation Research Board, Washington D.C., 1588, pp. 110-119.

An Efficient Hardware Implementation of Feed-Forward Neural Networks*

Tamás Szabó and Gábor Horváth

Technical University of Budapest,
Department of Measurement and Information Systems,
H-1521. Budapest, Műegyetem rkp. 9, Bldg. R. I./113. Hungary,
[szabo, horvath]@mit.bme.hu

Abstract. This paper proposes a new way of digital hardware implementation of nonlinear activation functions in feed-forward neural networks. The basic idea of this new realization is that the nonlinear functions can be implemented using a matrix-vector multiplication. Recently a new approach was proposed for the realization of matrix-vector multiplications which approach can also be applied for implementing the nonlinear functions if the nonlinear functions are approximated by simple basis functions. The paper proposes to use B-spline basis functions to the approximate nonlinear sigmoidal functions, it shows that this approximation fulfills the general requirements on the activation functions, presents the details of the proposed hardware implementation, and gives a summary of an extensive study about the effects of B-spline nonlinear function realization on the size and the trainability of feed-forward neural networks.

1 Introduction and Motivations

Many modeling, control, pattern recognition, etc. tasks can be solved using neural networks. The motivations behind this general applicability are the universal capabilities and adaptive nature of neural networks. Feed-forward neural networks (FFNNs) are universal approximators and classifiers [1], which means that a properly constructed FFNN can approximate any continuous function with arbitrary accuracy or can solve any classification task. On the other hand neural networks are parallel distributed systems and as a consequence rather high speed operation can be achieved if they are implemented in parallel hardware form. A relatively large segment of the possible applications needs this high-speed operation. Real-time recognition of different patterns (e.g. printed or handwritten characters), certain control tasks, etc. [2], [3] require embedded solutions, where relatively small-size, high-speed implementation can be applied only. This paper deals with a new digital hardware implementation, which is

* This work was supported by the Hungarian Fund for Scientific Research (OTKA) under contract T023868

L. Monostori, J. Váncza, and M. Ali (Eds.): IEA/AIE 2001, LNAI 2070, pp. 300–313, 2001.

based on a recently suggested efficient matrix-vector multiplier architecture [4] , [5]. The main advantage of this multiplier architecture is that - if at least one of the multiplicands is constant - it can be built into the architecture and a bit-level optimization process can be performed which results in a more simple hardware structure.

Feed-forward neural networks implement nonlinear mappings between input and output data:

$$\mathbf{y} = \mathbf{W}_2 f(\mathbf{W}_1 \mathbf{x}) \tag{1}$$

where $\mathbf{W}_1$ and $\mathbf{W}_2$ are the weight matrices of the hidden and the output layer, respectively.

From the viewpoint of hardware realization the critical operations of the neural mapping are the multiplications required in the calculation of linear combinations, (e.g. $\mathbf{Wx}$) and the elementary nonlinear mappings denoted by $f(.)$ in Eq. 1. The recently proposed multiplier architecture is a partly parallel partly serial structure. Using this architecture all required multiplications can be calculated in parallel, while every multiplier implements bit-serial operation [4], [5].

The second critical operation in a feed-forward neural network is the elementary nonlinear mapping that is realized by the activation function in an MLP. The activation functions, which must fulfill certain conditions to obtain universal approximator neural networks, are usually implemented by look up tables [6]. This paper proposes a new solution that is also based on the efficient hardware multiplier architecture. In this solution the activation functions - usually logistic or hyperbolic tangent functions - are approximated by B-spline basis functions and these B-spline based activation functions are realized using the proposed multiplier structure. The application of this multiplier structure for implementing both critical operations, the multiplications and the elementary nonlinear mappings makes it possible to get efficient hardware implementation of FFNNs using field programmable gate arrays (FPGAs) or ASICs. FPGA-based neural realizations are ideal solutions for relatively low-cost, medium/high-speed embedded systems, especially if a prototype or a small series of the product is needed.

The paper gives a short review of the general requirements of the activation functions, shows that the B-spline based solution fulfill these requirements and details the proposed hardware architecture. The general requirements on an activation function to get the universal approximating capability are rather weak. However, these requirements usually do not deal with the question of the size of the neural network (the number of the hidden neurons) and with the relation between the activation function and the size of the neural network. Moreover, from practical point of view a further important question if a neural network with the required approximating capability can be reached using standard gradient based error back-propagation training. Whether a selected activation function let the network efficiently trainable or not cannot be determined easily. Also, to determine the optimal size of the network using a selected activation function is a hard task that theoretically has not been solved so far. The paper - in addition to the new way of implementation - gives the results of an extended experimental study for determining the effects of the implemented activation function on the size and the trainability of the network.

2 Requirements against the Activation Function

Several theorems and different approaches exist in the literature, which prove the universal approximation capability of single hidden layer MLP. Good surveys can be found for example in [7] and [8]. These results are different in more points:

- They use different conditions and constrains for the activation function and/or they use different error measures.
- The proof of a theorem can be constructive or non-constructive. A proof is constructive if it gives an algorithm for computing the appropriate weight set (or it is proved that the weight set is computable on a Turing machine). Unfortunately, even if an algorithm exists it is not sure that the widely used gradient learning algorithms find the solution.
- They do not give practically useful results about the optimal size of the network (at most they can give a - usually too pessimistic - upper limit).

Now just the most important theorems are cited from the literature which prove that the presented implementation method is suitable for FFNNs and a network with such activation function has the universal approximation capability.

Theorem 1 ([9]). *Let $\sigma(.) : \mathbb{R} \to \mathbb{R}$ be any function. Denote $\Sigma^3_{\sigma,d}$ the functions, which can be realized by the three layered d dimension FFNN with $\sigma(.)$ activation function. Then $\Sigma^3_{\sigma,1}$ is dense in $C(\mathbb{R})$ if and only if $\Sigma^3_{\sigma,d}$ is dense in $C(\mathbb{R}^d)$ for every positive integer d.*

This theorem is important, because it states that the results, which are achieved for a one-dimensional network can be generalized to higher-dimensional networks. However, the theorem is not constructive.

Theorem 2 ([10]). *Let $\sigma(.) : \mathbb{R} \to \mathbb{R}$ be a locally bounded piecewise continuous function. Then $\Sigma^3_{\sigma,d}$ is dense in $C([0,1]^d)$ for all positive integers d if and only if $\sigma(.)$ is not an algebraic polynomial.*

Theorem 2 is a comprehensive interpretation of Leshno et al.'s theorem by Kůrková in [8]. It proves the universal approximation capability of the three layered FFNNs under very weak conditions on the activation function. Similar results, or ones with even weaker conditions can be found in [11] using different error norms. It is clear that the key property of the activation function is the non-polynomiality.

3 B-Spline Based Hardware Implementation of the Activation Function

3.1 Implementation Technique

Our main goal is to find an efficient way for implementing the activation functions. It will be shown in the sequel that an efficient implementation can be obtained if the nonlinear mappings of the activation functions can be expressed as matrix-vector multiplications. In the proposed solution a special spline approximation of the activation functions will be used. In the rest of the paper the approximated activation function will be called spline activation function. A spline function which is a piecewise polynomial function is formed as a linear combination of B-spline basis functions. The univariate B-spline basis functions can be defined by different ways [12]. A simple definition can be obtained using a recurrence relationship. Denoting the j-th univariate basis function of order k by $b_j^k(.)$, it is defined by:

$$b_j^k(x) = \left(\frac{x-\lambda_{j-k}}{\lambda_{j-1}-\lambda_{j-k}}\right) b_{j-1}^{k-1}(x) + \left(\frac{\lambda_j - x}{\lambda_j - \lambda_{j-k+1}}\right) b_j^{k-1}(x) \tag{2}$$

$$b_j^1(x) = \begin{cases} 1 & \text{if } x \in I_j \\ 0 & \text{otherwise} \end{cases} \tag{3}$$

where the $\lambda(i)$ $i = 1, 2...$ form the so called knot sequence which partitions the x axis, and $I_j = [\lambda(j-1), \lambda(j))$ is the j-th interval of the partitioned x axis.

On each interval the basis function is a polynomial of order k, and at the knots the polynomials are joined smoothly. The basis functions become smoother as the order increases. B-splines are good candidates for implementing the activation functions as:

- The B-spline-based construction fully fulfill the requirements detailed in section 2, so a FFNN with spline activation function can approximate any continuous functions with arbitrary accuracy under some very weak conditions.
- B-spline is a smooth function, so any function composed of B-splines is also a smooth function. If the order of the spline is k the first $k-1$ derivatives of the spline exist and under a certain condition (spline has only knots with multiplicity one) the derivatives are continuous. This makes it possible to use gradient learning rules in the training of the network.
- B-splines are basis functions with final support. If the knot (breakpoint) sequence is equidistant all basis functions are similar. This feature is important from the viewpoint of efficient hardware implementation.

The properties of the realized sigmoidal function are determined by the knot sequence, the order of the polynomials and the way the spline coefficients are computed. The more segments are used the better approximation can be achieved, however, as it will be shown later efficient hardware implementation can be obtained if not too many segments are used. Next the spline approximation of the activation function will be presented.

The basic concept of the proposed activation implementation method applies equidistant knot sequence. If equidistant knot sequence is used the B-spline basis functions will be similar disregarding their displacements. The basis functions have finite supports, which means that for a given x input a finite number - exactly k - basis functions will be activated, and that for any input value the approximated activation function will be composed of this k basis functions. On the other hand the support of a basis function contains exactly $k+1$ grid points which partitions the basis functions into k segments. This segmentation will be found in the approximated activation function too. This means that the activation function to be approximated will also be partitioned into segments. As all segments of the activation function will be formed as the weighted sum of all basis function segments, first these basis function segments must be calculated, than the weighted sums have to be computed with the predetermined weight values. To compute the basis function segments an alternative expression of the B-splines have to be used. Instead of using the recurrence relationship given in Eq. 3. every segment of a B-spline basis function can be written as a polynomial. The polynomial expressions depend on the order of the B-spline basis function and the knot sequence. For cubic splines (the order of the spline k is 4, which means that 3rd degree polynomials are used) with equidistant knot sequence the equations are as follows:

$$b_0^4(x) = \begin{cases} \frac{x^3}{6} & 0 \le x \le 1 \\ \frac{-3x^3+12x^2-12x+4}{6} & 1 \le x \le 2 \\ \frac{3x^3-24x^2+60x-44}{6} & 2 \le x \le 3 \\ \frac{-x^3+12x^2-48x+64}{6} & 3 \le x \le 4 \end{cases} \tag{4}$$

As these segments will be used in the activation function approximation, efficient implementation of the segments is also important. For this implementation a slightly modified version of the previous segments will be used. The modification will shift all segments into the first interval (into the [0, 1] interval). These modified segments - which we call standard segments - are shown in Fig. 1 b). The modified segments can also be computed as a result of a matrix vector multiplication where a vector of properly chosen powers of the input variable is multiplied by a matrix. The elements of this matrix can be calculated from Eq. 4 if we take into consideration that all segments are shifted into the [0, 1] interval.

$$\begin{bmatrix} b_I^4(\breve{x}_l) \\ b_{II}^4(\breve{x}_l) \\ b_{III}^4(\breve{x}_l) \\ b_{IV}^4(\breve{x}_l) \end{bmatrix} = \mathbf{B} \begin{bmatrix} (\breve{x}_l)^0 \\ (\breve{x}_l)^1 \\ (\breve{x}_l)^2 \\ (\breve{x}_l)^3 \end{bmatrix} = \frac{1}{6} \begin{bmatrix} 1 & -3 & 3 & -1 \\ 4 & 0 & -6 & 3 \\ 1 & 3 & 3 & -3 \\ 0 & 0 & 0 & 1 \end{bmatrix} \begin{bmatrix} 1 \\ (\breve{x}_l)^1 \\ (\breve{x}_l)^2 \\ (\breve{x}_l)^3 \end{bmatrix} \tag{5}$$

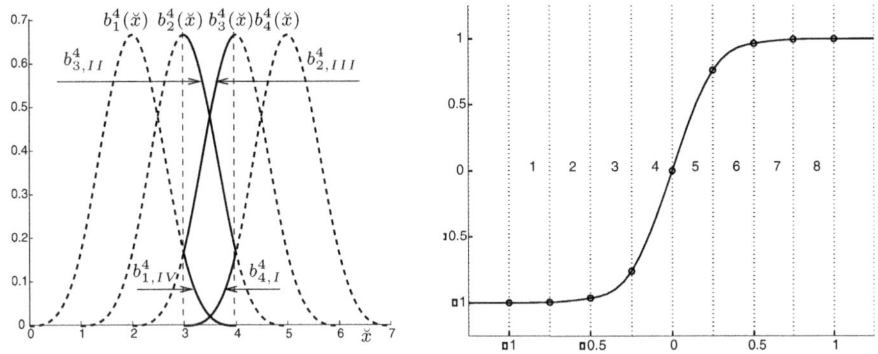

Fig. 1. a) Activated basis functions; b) Piecewise polynomial activation function; Knots are denoted by circles

Now as all standard segments are computed the approximation of the activation function can also be determined. As it was mentioned the activation function will also be partitioned into segments. To determine the value of the approximated activation function for a given input value first the proper segment must be selected then this segment must be evaluated according to the relative position of the input value within this segment. This means that the input values will be separated into two parts: one for the segment selection and the remaining part for determining the relative position within the selected segment. Assuming that B_x-bit binary representation form is used, the first several (B_{xh}) MSB bits will be used for segment selection and the remaining number of bits (B_{xl}) are used as a relative coordinate of the basis function. Certainly, $B_x = B_{xh} + B_{xl}$.

In order to work with unsigned digits we will apply a simple displacement transformation: $\breve{x} = x + 1$. Thus,

$$y = f(\breve{x}) = \frac{1-e^{-8\breve{x}+8}}{1+e^{-8\breve{x}+8}} \; ; \breve{x} \in [0,\ 2] \tag{6}$$

is the function to be approximated.

To follow the activation function construction let see an example. Let $B_{xh} = 3$ and thus $B_{xh} = 5$. This means, that $2^{B_{xh}} = 8$ segments will be used. See Fig. 1 a). Every segment will be formed as a weighted sum of the previously implemented B-spline basis function segments.

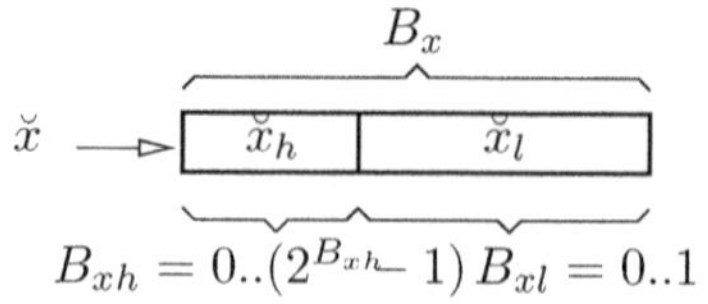

Fig. 2. Arranging the bits of x

$$\hat{y} = \hat{f}(\breve{x}) = \sum_{\forall i:\ \breve{x} \in supp(b_i^k)} v_i b_i^k(\breve{x}_l) \tag{7}$$

v_i denotes the weight, and $supp(b_i)$ the support of the corresponding basis function.

The weights of the basis functions can be selected from a table according to the active interval using $\breve{x}_h$ as an address. This is a solution of the problem and the block diagram of the necessary hardware is discussed in 3.2. However, we can go a step further and compute all the output values parallel:

$$\hat{y} = \mathbf{V} \begin{bmatrix} b_{IV}^4(\breve{x}_l) \\ b_{III}^4(\breve{x}_l) \\ b_{II}^4(\breve{x}_l) \\ b_I^4(\breve{x}_l) \end{bmatrix} = \begin{bmatrix} v_1 & v_2 & v_3 & v_4 \\ v_2 & v_3 & v_4 & v_5 \\ v_3 & v_4 & v_5 & v_6 \\ \vdots & \vdots & \vdots & \vdots \\ v_{2^{B_{xh}}} & v_{2^{B_{xh}}+1} & v_{2^{B_{xh}}+2} & v_{2^{B_{xh}}+3} \end{bmatrix} \begin{bmatrix} b_{IV}^4(\breve{x}_l) \\ b_{III}^4(\breve{x}_l) \\ b_{II}^4(\breve{x}_l) \\ b_I^4(\breve{x}_l) \end{bmatrix} \tag{8}$$

This Eq. 8 and the previous Eq. 5 can be combined as

$$\hat{y} = \mathbf{VB} \begin{bmatrix} 1 \\ (\breve{x}_l)^1 \\ (\breve{x}_l)^2 \\ (\breve{x}_l)^3 \end{bmatrix} = \mathbf{V_B} \begin{bmatrix} 1 \\ (\breve{x}_l)^1 \\ (\breve{x}_l)^2 \\ (\breve{x}_l)^3 \end{bmatrix} \tag{9}$$

One can see that both the $\mathbf{V}$ and $\mathbf{B}$ are constant matrices, thus their multiplication ($\mathbf{V_B} = \mathbf{VB}$) can be computed in advance. In the final step, the "real" output can be chosen based on $\breve{x}_h$. As it was mentioned, a cost effective matrix-vector multiplier architecture had been developed earlier which can also be used herewith providing an efficient implementation for the non-linear activation function. It is discussed in the next section.

3.2 The Hardware

The previous section depicted an implementation idea for activation functions using B-splines computed in a form of matrix-vector multiplication. The elements of the matrix are constant, while the vector is composed from the different powers of the input. The upper part of the input word is used as an address, which selects the active spline piece and puts its value to the output. As one can see, if a k-order B-spline is used the first $k-1$ powers have to be computed. Fortunately, these powers must be computed for $\breve{x}_l$ which is formed from just the several lower bits of the input signal $\breve{x}$. After all, two possible block schemes are presented depending on whether

1. the whole $\mathbf{V_B \breve{x}_l}$ matrix product is computed, where the result will be a vector and the output is the properly selected element of this vector(Fig. 3), or
2. only the necessary vector-vector (inner) product is computed (the fix coefficients are selected). This way directly results in the required activation function value, however in this case non-constant vectors must be multiplied (Fig. 4).

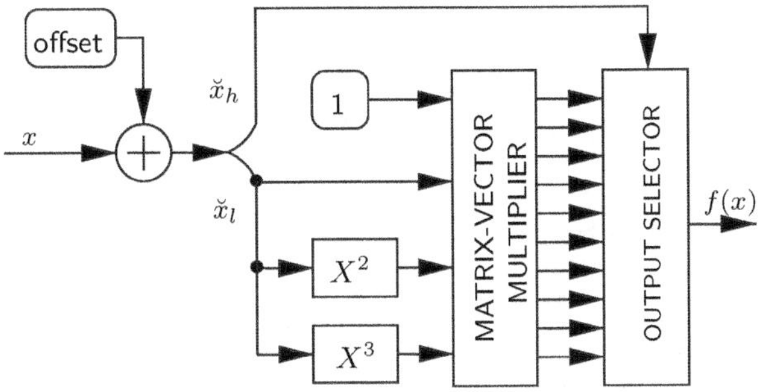

Fig. 3. Implementation using dedicated matrix-vector multiplier

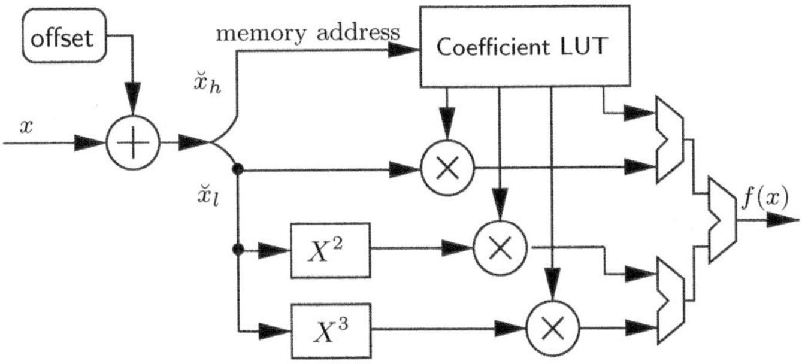

Fig. 4. Implementation using coefficient look-up table

The implementation with look-up table requires complex variable-variable multipliers and a memory, which can provide k coefficients in the same time and stores $k2^{B_{xh}}$ values. The optimized matrix-vector multiplier depending on the size of the matrix can efficiently replace them.

In the implementation a further question may arise: what type of arithmetic should be used in the realization, as so far no bindings were taken on the arithmetics. Either bit-serial, bit-parallel or digit-serial arithmetics can be used. The decision depends on the required speed, the accessible amount of hardware and the number of B-spline basis functions. If we have more basis functions,

- the B-spline approximation gives more accurate result,
- this may allow in some cases to decrease the order of the spline (k),
- which results in simpler hardware, because only lower powers of the input variable have to be computed,
- less bits remain for $\breve{x}_l$, that is the computation of its powers is simpler,
- more coefficients have to be stored (in the look-up table, or to built into the special matrix-vector multiplier)

In practice higher order ($k > 4$) splines are rarely applied, because the accuracy of the spline approximation does not increase rapidly for larger orders (see the spline literature, e.g. [12], [13]). Above these qualitative deliberations it is very hard to set up more accurate guidelines. Some empirical experiences should be made in order to choose the good setup respecting the required output accuracy.

4 Effect of the Application of Spline Activation Functions

Theorems presented in section 2 show (necessary and) sufficient conditions for the universal approximation capability of a feed-forward neural network. These theorems do not ensure that a gradient type learning algorithm, like back-propagation - finds the appropriate weight set. Moreover, they are usually existence theorems, that is they usually do not provide any point regarding how large the hidden layer should be constructed in order to reach a given approximation error. At most, there are upper bounds (or order of magnitude) for the number of hidden neurons for special cases. The two most important properties the activation function must have from the viewpoint of gradient learning rules are the existence of the first derivative and the monotony. There is no problem with the derivatives, as B-splines have $k-1$ derivatives. However, monotony is not automatically ensured. According to the knowledge of the authors there is no result in the literature, which proves that monotony of the activation function is necessary for gradient type learning algorithms. Nevertheless, a simple example can be considered: if the first derivative of the activation function changes its sign, the correction term in the learning algorithm goes to wrong direction. We can accept that such disturbances make the error surface more complex with more and more local minima. One knows well, that the convergence of the learning process can stuck at in such local minima or at least they slow the learning procedure. This is an experimental result, which warns us to beware of using non-monotone activation function.

Our implementation method does not tell anything about the derivation of the weights for the spline basis functions. General methods (for interpolating and least-squares splines) can be found in the basic spline literatures ([12], [13]). Unfortunately, these methods do not yield necessarily monotone splines. Due to the page limit (and while this does not influence the implementation method) we do not pay attention on the computation of monotone spline coefficients, the necessary results can be found in (e.g. [14], [15], [16], [17]). Hereafter simple interpolating splines are used, which may have just tiny non-monotony.

The other problem is the optimal number of hidden neurons. In order to clarify the picture the main results of an extensive simulation are presented. for this simulation experiments the teacher-student concept is used [18]. Simulations are done with the following conditions:

- Single input, single output teacher net using 5 hyperbolic tangent neurons in the hidden layer is applied. Theorem 1 makes it possible to examine only one dimensional cases and generalize to higher dimensions. However, this theorem does not tell anything about the number of hidden units. Nevertheless, here just the one-dimensional case is discussed, our further task to prove the results for higher dimensional nets.
- There were 200 training and 2000 test points selected randomly from a Gaussian distribution. Standard back-propagation training was used with $\lambda = 0.1$ learning rate using the SNNSv4.2 neurosimulator ([19]).
- Activation functions are built up using interpolating splines. The splines approximate the hyperbolic tangent function in the $[-4,\ 4]$ interval, the approximated activation function is constant outside this interval (zero first derivative). The splines have equidistant knot sequences without knot multiplicity using three different number of pieces: 4, 8 and 16. The order of the splines is in the range of $k = 2..4$. The use of the interpolating spline approximation results in that the activation function will be slightly non-monotonic close to the saturated region. However, this non-monotonous behavior is small -it is in the range of the LSB.
- While all of our spline activation functions approximate the hyperbolic tangent activation function the derivatives were computed according to $f^{'}(x) = 1 - (f(x))^2$ as if the activation function would be the original hyperbolic tangent function. This makes sense, because its computation is very easy and this approximate derivative hides the tiny non-monotonous behavior of the spline activation function.
- Number of the hidden neurons is selected as 5,7,9,...15. For each cases we have 10 trial runs.

4.1 Simulation Results

Figure 5/a shows the performance of the student network. The lower curve always means the average mean squared error (MSE) in the 200 training points, while the upper curve is for the 2000 test points. All the MSEs are normalized by the number of points as it is provided by the SNNSv4.2 simulator [19]. 10 runs correspond to a given network size. A fare stage denotes the variance of the 10 runs, the upper and lower ends are for the worst and best errors respectively. The limits of the box are at the 2nd worst and best runs, while the horizontal

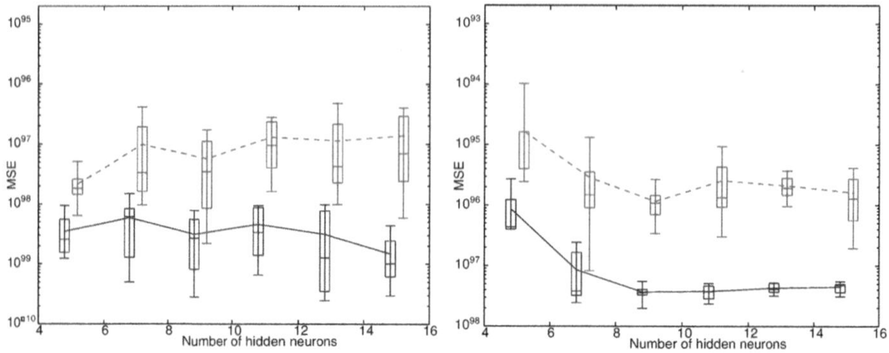

a) Original tangent hyperbolic b) Cubic spline, $i = 8$ pieces

Fig. 5. Using conventional tangent hyperbolic function a) and cubic B-spline b)

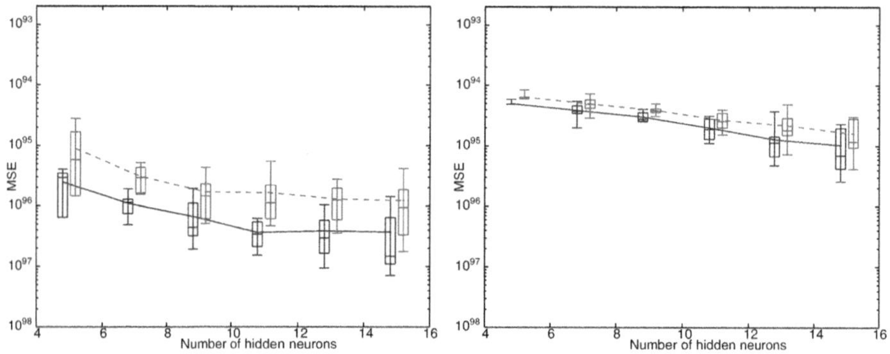

a) $k = 3$ order spline, $i = 8$ pieces b) $k = 2$ order spline, $i = 8$ pieces

Fig. 6. Using B-spline activation functions I

line in the box is at the middle between the 5th and 6th elements of the ordered errors. A line joints the points in the boxes, which represent the mean values of each 10 runs. We can say that the limit of the precision of the simulation is around $< 10^{-8}$ in term of MSE at training points and $< 5*10^{-6}$ in term of MSE at test points. This performance limit is mainly due to the applied precision at the representation of the input and desired output point pairs in the simulator or more exactly at the import and export of these points to and from the simulator.

The following experiments can be seen from the simulation results on Fig. 5 . . 7:

Concluding remark 1. *Nets with B-spline activation functions have poorer performance at the same network size, but increasing the complexity of the network we can decrease the error. This means that more neurons can compensate for the less "nice"activation function.*

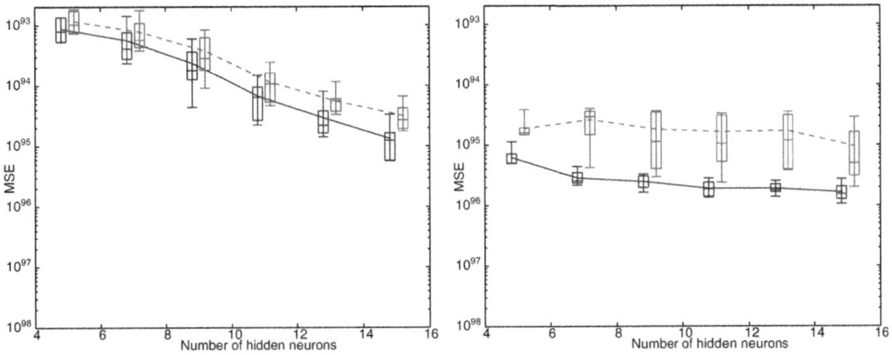

a) $k = 2$ order spline, $i = 4$ pieces   b) $k = 2$ order spline, $i = 16$ pieces

Fig. 7. Using B-spline activation functions II

Concluding remark 2. *The higher order the B-spline is the better error performance can be obtained at the given network size.*

Concluding remark 3. *The more pieces in the activation function the better error performance can be obtained at the given network size.*

Concluding remarks 1 and 2 are straightforward. Let we assume a piecewise linear activation function built up from 3 pieces including constant ones. The number of the neurons determines the number of pieces in the approximation provided by the whole net. If there are more neurons this means more pieces for the approximation provided by the whole net. However, this is not so plausible for the remark 3, because if the number of the basis functions is increased in the construction of the B-spline activation function, the number of the independent pieces does not increase regarding the function approximated by the network. This is why the "slope", the position and the "active region" of a neuron (the influence of its activation function) can be controlled by the weights and we have no more free parameters if just the number of basis functions for the B-spline activation function is increased. Let we see for instance piecewise linear activation functions. The function represented by the network is also piecewise linear one. The input weights of the neuron in the hidden layer determines the distance between two breakpoints at the output of the net which are originally correspond to the breakpoints of the B-spline activation function. Let we choose the ith neuron in the hidden layer. Let the input weight value for this neuron is 10 and its bias is -1 while the output weight value is -2. This means that the effect of this neuron at the output of the net is in the interval $x \in [-0.3,\ 0.5]$ outside it gives a constant -2 or $+2$. This ith neuron provides breakpoints in this $x \in [-0.3,\ 0.5]$ interval equidistantly, that is the linear pieces due to the piecewise polynomial activation function of the ith neuron have always the same length and well determined slope. Nevertheless, the shape which has more pieces is closer to a smooth arch and this arch can be controlled by the weights but keeping the pieces of the arch equidistant and correlated. Correlation means here that the ratio of the derivatives of these pieces are fixed (by the B-spline constants).

Conclusion

This paper suggests a new and efficient neural network implementation method. A recently suggested efficient matrix-vector multiplier architecture is cited as the basic building block of the NNs. Here it is proved that the nonlinear activation function can also be realized in the form of a matrix-vector multiplication using the B-spline function approximation method. The application of these architectures for both critical operations, the multiplications and the nonlinear mappings results in an efficient dedicated hardware implementation of NNs. Theoretical background of the usage of B-spline activation functions is also discussed and an empirical study was made on the effect of B-spline activation functions to test the performance of the neural networks.

References

1. M.H. Hassoun, *Fundamentals of artificial neural networks*, MIT Press, 1995.
2. T.G. Clarkson and Y. Ding, *RAM-Based Neural Networks*, chapter Extracting directional information for the recognition of fingerprints by pRAM networks, pp. 174–185, World Scientific, 1998.
3. "White blood cell classification & counting with the ZISC," http://www.fr.ibm.com/france/cdlab/zblcell.htm, 2000.
4. Tamás Szabó, Béla Fehér, and Gábor Horváth, "Neural network implementation using distributed arithmetic," in *Proceedings of the International Conference on Knowledge-based Electronic Systems*, Adelaide, Australia, 1998, vol. 3, pp. 511–520.
5. Tamás Szabó, Lőrinc Antoni, Gábor Horváth, and Béla Fehér, "An efficient implementation for a matrix-vector multiplier structure," in *Proceedings of IEEE International Joint Conference on Neural Networtks, IJCNN2000*, 2000, vol. II, pp. 49–54.
6. Manferd Glesner and Werner Pöchmüller, *Neurocomputers, an overview of neural networks in VLSI*, Neural Computing. Chapman & Hall, 1994.
7. Franco Scarselli and Ah Chung Tsoi, "Universal approximation using feedforward neural networks: A survey of some existing methods, and some new results," *Neural Networks*, vol. 11, no. 1, pp. 15–37, 1998.
8. Věra Kůrková, "Approximation of functions by neural networks," in *Proceedings of NC'98*, 1998, pp. 29–36.
9. M. B. Stinchcombe and H. White, "Approximating and learning unknown mappings using multilayer networks with bounded weights," in *Proc. of Int. Joint Conference on Neural Networks, IJCNN'90*. 1990, vol. III, pp. 7–16, IEEE Press.
10. Moshe Leshno, Vladimir Ya. Lin, Allan Pinkus, and Shimon Schocken, "Multilayer feedforward networks with a nonpolynomial activation function can approximate any function," *Neural Networks*, vol. 6, pp. 861–867, 1993.

11. Kurt Hornik, "Some new results on neural network approximatiom," *Neural Networks*, vol. 6, pp. 1069–1072, 1993.
12. Carl de Boor, *A practical guide to Splines*, Springer-Verlag, 1978.
13. Larry L. Schumaker, *Spline functions, Basic Theory*, Wiley & Sons, 1981.
14. James T. Lewis, "Computation of best monotone approximations," *Mathematics of Computation*, vol. 26, no. 119, pp. 737–747, 1972.
15. Ronald A. De Vore, "Monotone approximation by splines," *SIAM J. Math. Anal.*, vol. 8, no. 5, pp. 891–905, October 1977.
16. Eli Passow and John A. Roulier, "Monotone and convex spline interpolation," *SIAM J. Numer. Anal*, vol. 14, no. 5, pp. 904–909, October 1977.
17. X. M. Yu and S. P. Zhou, "On monotone spline approximation," *SIAM J. Math. Anal.*, vol. 25, no. 4, pp. 1227–1239, July 1994.
18. D. Saal and S. Solla, "Learning from corrupted examples in multilayer perceptrons," Tech. Rep., Aston University, UK, 1996.
19. University of Stuttgart, Institute of Parallel and Distributed High-Performance Systems (IPVR), http://www.informatik.uni-stuttgart.de/ipvr/bv/projekte/snns/snns.html, *Stuttgart Neural Network Simulator, User Manual 4.2*, 2000.

MAPS: A Method for Identifying and Predicting Aberrant Behavior in Time Series

Evangelos Kotsakis[1] and Antoni Wolski[2]

[1] Joint Research Center (CCR), Space Application Institute, Via Enrico Fermi 1, TP 261, I-21020 Ispra (VA), Italy.
kotsakis@acm.org

[2] SOLID Applied Research Center, Merimiehenkatu 36 D, FIN-00150 Helsinki, Finland.
a.wolski@acm.org

Abstract. We present a method for inducing a set of rules from time series data, which is originated from a monitored process. The proposed method is called MAPS (Mining Aberrant Patterns in Sequences) and it may be used in decision support or in control to identify faulty system states. It consists of four parts: training, identification, event mining and prediction. In order to improve the flexibility of the event identification, we employ fuzzy sets and propose a method that extracts membership functions from statistical measures of the time series. The proposed approach integrates fuzzy logic and event mining in a seamless way. Some of the existing event mining algorithms have been modified to accommodate the need of discovering fuzzy event patterns.

1 Introduction

An industrial process is a series of operations performed in manufacturing or some other industrial activities. Monitoring is used in time dependent industrial processes in order to ensure that the process is effective. Monitoring is particularly important in aligning the process with other processes and ensuring that the process operates according to the specifications. Many variables are measured during monitoring. Such variables may include pressure, temperature, humidity etc., and are called process attributes here. Measurements are made on some constituent parts of the industrial process, which are considered critical for the operation and stability of the process. Those attributes participating in monitoring are chosen carefully, so that the monitoring is effective in identifying important aspects of the process. The monitoring is accomplished by frequently sampling the values of the temporal attributes. The frequency of sampling is user defined and it can range from a few milliseconds to many days. Suppose we are given such a process P with n temporal attributes $a_1, a_2, ..., a_n$,

---

[1] This research was done while the author was visiting VTT Information Technology, Finland from March to November 2000 and it was supported by the VTT and by the fellowship program of the European Research Consortium for Informatics and Mathematics (ERCIM).

[2] The work was performed when the author was with VTT Information Technology, Finland.

L. Monostori, J. Váncza, and M. Ali (Eds.): IEA/AIE 2001, LNAI 2070, pp. 314-325, 2001.

each of which is sampled every τ time units (one time granule) at time points t_1, t_2, ..., t_j, ..., where $t_j=j\tau$. Then, the observation data may be viewed as time series. Each attribute observation constitutes a single time series. A data element $d(i,j)$ indicates the value of the attribute a_i at time point t_j.

One of the challenges is to discover important events hidden in this time series data. Consequently the question becomes: how is it possible to utilise this time series data in such a way that we are able (1) to identify abnormal events in a process and (2) to describe or predict the behaviour of a sequence of such abnormal events that may lead to failures? Therefore, the main goal focuses on the development of a systematic way to identify and predict abnormal events and event patterns in time sequences. We are, in particular, interested in methods that require no a priori knowledge and allow us to obtain the above goal by studying monitoring information acquired by measuring time varying attributes. This paper describes a method (named MAPS - Mining Aberrant Patterns in Sequences) that determines the necessary steps, we need to perform, in order to develop a knowledge-based system, which is able to identify abnormal events and deduce rules for describing or predicting the behaviour of such abnormalities. The knowledge is acquired from observed (aberrant) behaviour during the lifetime of the industrial process. No a priori knowledge is required. The proposed method provides fully adaptable mechanisms that allow the knowledge base to be enriched during the lifetime of the process. Our main goal focuses on discovering knowledge concerning abnormal behaviour. Towards this goal, we start directly with data sequences, which represent measurements of various attributes of the monitored process. The MAPS method employs a fuzzy set technique to identify aberrant events and generate event sequences. An event sequence is then mined for interesting patterns and rules are extracted from these patterns. Prediction is obtained by matching the most recent events of the sequence with the antecedent part of such rules.

The rest of the paper is organised as follows: in Section 2, we present an outline of the MAPS method and discuss briefly its constituent components. Section 3 contains discussion of related work. In section 4, we present how regular behaviour is captured in time series by employing fuzzy sets; and then how these fuzzy sets are utilised for identifying abnormal events. In Section 5, we introduce the event mining technique we use to discover frequent fuzzy event patterns as well as the method for extracting rules that involve event patterns. In Section 6, a method for predicting aberrant events is presented. We conclude in section 7 by summarising the contributions and pointing out some further work to be done.

2 Outline of the Method

The proposed method employs fuzzy sets for identifying aberrant events and event mining techniques for extracting rules from the event sequences. The method is divided into four steps. Each step constitutes a separate unit. The outline of the MAPS method is shown in Fig. 1. The four units are as follows:

Training unit: It collects statistical information from measurements. Based on this information, the training module defines the membership functions of the fuzzy sets that describe the regularity of the attribute values. The membership functions of the fuzzy set are stored in the database of the training unit.

Identification unit: The membership functions of the fuzzy sets in the training unit are used to identify abnormal values that may cause aberrant events. Each aberrant event is identified by its type, its occurrence time and its intensity. An aberrant event is a fuzzy event whose intensity specifies the level of abnormality. Sequences of such fuzzy events are stored in the database of the identification unit.

Event mining unit: This unit has two constituent parts; the first one identifies frequent event patterns in the event sequences stored in the identification unit and the second one extracts rules from the set of frequent patterns. Once the most frequent patterns are known, they are used to obtain rules that associate closely related event patterns. The rules are stored in the rule base of the event-mining unit.

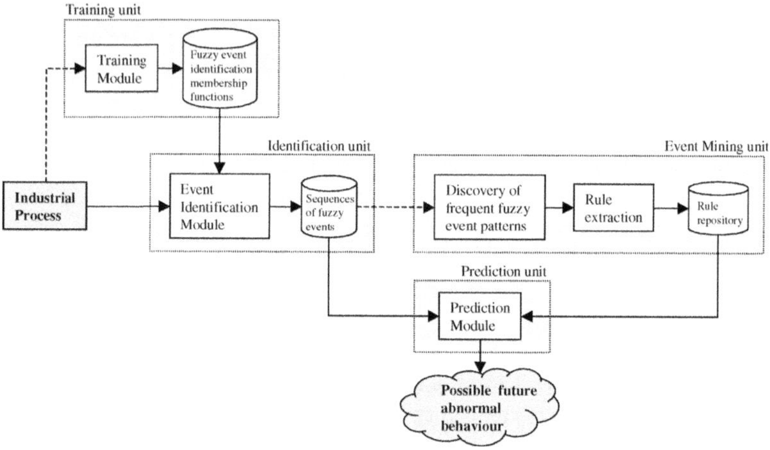

Fig. 1. Layout of the MAPS method.

Prediction unit: It predicts a possible future event pattern by studying the occurrence of the event patterns during the last few observation windows. That is, if an event pattern occurs in one of the most recent windows, then the predicting module checks whether such a pattern matches the premise of a rule in the rule repository; and if so, it suggests the conclusion of the matched rule as a possible future behaviour.

The arrows in Fig. 1 represent data or information flows. The dotted arrows depict temporal flows, which are active only when the receiving module needs data for accomplishing its task. Information does not continuously run over dotted flows. For example, the flow connecting the industrial process and the training unit is active only during a training session when measurement data is used for determining the membership functions of the fuzzy sets. Upon completion of the training, this flow becomes inactive. The data flow from the identification unit to the event-mining unit is active when further mining in event sequences is necessary to update or refine the rule repository. Solid arrows depict continuous flow of data between connected modules.

3 Related Work

A lot of work has been done in the area of Artificial Intelligence for discovering patterns in sequential data (see for example [3, 6]). In the context of databases, the problem has been studied in a number of recent papers [1, 8, 2]. Our work with respect to mining event sequence is more related to [8] where event sequences are searched for frequent patterns. We use the same concept of windows for estimating the frequency of the patterns. However, we have extended the notion of pattern occurrence by introducing the concept of fuzzy events and fuzzy patterns. In order to deal with fuzzy patterns, we have introduced a new definition of pattern frequency. Our algorithms for finding the set of the most frequent patterns are based on those in [8]. However, the algorithms have been adapted to deal with fuzzy events and fuzzy patterns. In [1] the problem of discovering sequential patterns is considered over a customer transaction database. The strategy in [1] is similar to that in [8] and it starts with simple sub-patterns and incrementally builds longer sequence candidates for the discovery process. In [2] the discovery process considers more complex patterns where events may be in terms of different granularities and patterns may include temporal distances.

In the context of event identification, there has been recently an effort in Knowledge Discovery and Data mining (KDD) research area, which aims at generating such event sequences [4, 5, 7]. In [4], the problem of activity monitoring is discussed and a framework for evaluating activity monitoring is proposed for applications such as cellular phone fraud detection. However, in [4] the focus is on defining the functions used for scoring false alarms. The proposed approach in [5] focuses on how to detect events from phenomena with dynamic behaviour. This seems to be close to our goal, however, in [5], the authors investigate the potential to identify the time points at which the behaviour changes (change-point detection). Towards this, they suggest that there is a need to determine the number of change points and then to find the functions that match the behaviour between two successive change-points. In our approach change points are identified automatically by using the minimum, maximum and statistical mean values of an attribute, which are obtained during a training session. The idea of using fuzzy sets for mining association rules and frequent episodes is also discussed in [7]. However, the approach in [7] is based on attributing the events in a similar way as a customer transaction is attributed by items. In that sense, an event is not atomic, as it is in our approach, but rather a vector quantity whose elements are assigned a membership degree. This approach is close to detecting abnormal behaviour (fraud or intrusion) over a customer transaction database. Our approach considers the incoming data as time series data and assigns event types to each time series. Then, an abnormal event is generated by the occurrence of an abnormal value of a single attribute. This helps to quickly identify the abnormality in the industrial process by studying the type of the event occurred, and it may be used to suggest possible future abnormal events that might be caused by abnormal values of the corresponding attributes.

4 Fuzzy Identification of Abnormal Behaviour

The identification of abnormal events is obtained by way of training the system using measurement data. The result of a training session is a group of fuzzy sets used to identify abnormal values. The membership functions of the fuzzy sets are particularly employed for identifying these abnormal values, which consequently yield the occurrence of aberrant fuzzy events whose membership values determines the level of abnormality.

4.1 Training the System for Event Identification

The aim of training is to extract fuzzy sets from observation data collected during the normal operation of an industrial process. Each fuzzy set describes the normal behaviour of an attribute of the process. The method described in this section constitutes the main procedure of the training module in Fig. 1. The observation data of each attribute is viewed as a time series. The duration of the training period is M time granules and it is called *training session*. During the training session every single value of each attribute is observed and registered in a time sequence. Fig. 2 shows the time series obtained by observing the attribute a_i during a training session of M time granules. For each attribute a_i, three values are maintained at the end of the training session. These are the *minimum* value (a_i^{min}), the *maximum* value (a_i^{max}) and the *mean* value (a_i^{mean}) of the attribute a_i, which are defined as follows:

$$a_i^{\min} = Min_{j=1}^{M}\{a_i(j\tau)\} \quad (1)$$

$$a_i^{\max} = Max_{j=1}^{M}\{a_i(j\tau)\} \quad (2)$$

$$a_i^{mean} = \sum_{j=1}^{M} \frac{a_i(j\tau)}{M} \quad (3)$$

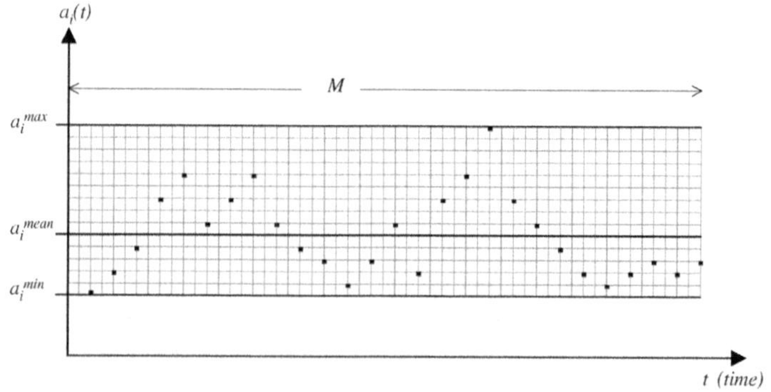

Fig. 2. Observation of the attribute a_i during a training session of M time granules.

These values form an indicator that is used to identify acceptable values of an attribute. In some industrial processes we encounter cases where some exceptional values occur beyond the maximum or below the minimum value. These exceptional values are called outliers and they are treated as noise in our case. A pre-processing is needed to remove this noise during the training session. The set of values $\{a_i^{min}, a_i^{max}, a_i^{mean}\}$ of an attribute a_i is called the *index* of a_i. Each attribute index is stored as an entry in a relation in the database of the training unit (see Fig. 1). The schema of this relation is: *AIndex(a, a^{min}, a^{max}, a^{mean}).*

The index of the attribute a_i is used to describe acceptable values of a_i. For example, values of a_i, which are within the interval $[a_i^{min}, a_i^{max}]$, are considered perfectly normal, while other values of a_i are considered abnormal. The level of abnormality is expressed by a fuzzy membership function, which assigns a number between 0 and 1 to such an abnormal value of a_i. The more distant the value of a_i is from the interval $[a_i^{min}, a_i^{max}]$, the more abnormal the value of a_i is. The generation of such a membership function is performed as follows:

First, a fuzzy set that describes the normal behaviour of the attribute a_i is defined by using the index of the attribute a_i and a threshold $0 \leq \vartheta \leq 1$. The threshold ϑ determines how the intensity that characterises abnormal values changes with respect to a_i. Knowing the index of an attribute a_i (i.e. a_i^{min}, a_i^{max}, a_i^{mean}) and the threshold ϑ, one can form a fuzzy set A_i, which describes the regularity of the values of the attribute a_i. Fig. 3 shows a triangular membership function of the fuzzy set A_i. In fact, the membership function of the fuzzy set A_i may be any unimodal function like trapezoidal or bell typed. For the sake of clarity we employ only triangular membership functions in this paper. The triangle A_i is formed by considering the following points: (a_i^{min}, ϑ), $(a_i^{mean}, 1)$ and (a_i^{max}, ϑ).

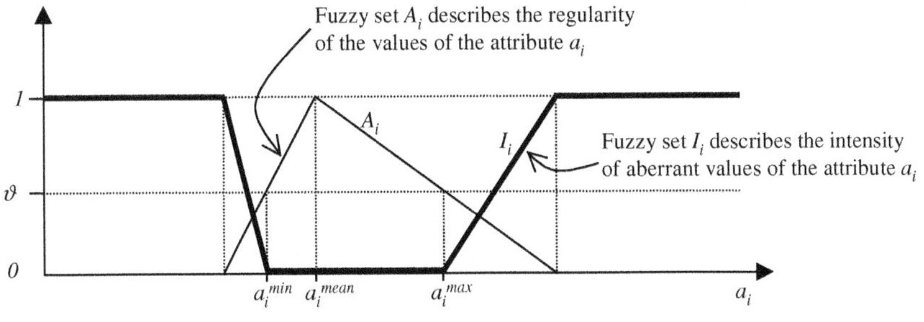

Fig. 3. Fuzzy sets A_i and I_i when $0< \vartheta < 1$. I_i is used to identify abnormal values of the attribute a_i. The majority of regular values of a_i is between a_i^{min} and a_i^{max}. The more distant a value of a_i is from the interval $[a_i^{min}, a_i^{max}]$, the more intense the aberrant event is.

Then, a second fuzzy set I_i that describes the intensity of an abnormal value of a_i is defined by using the following membership function:

$$I_i(a_i(t)) = \begin{cases} 0 & \text{if } A_i(a_i(t)) \geq \vartheta \\ 1 - \dfrac{A_i(a_i(t))}{\vartheta} & \text{if } A_i(a_i(t)) < \vartheta \end{cases} \qquad 0 < \vartheta \leq 1 \qquad (4)$$

$$I_i(a_i(t)) = \begin{cases} 0 & \text{if } A_i(a_i(t)) > 0 \\ 1 & \text{if } A_i(a_i(t)) = 0 \end{cases} \qquad \vartheta = 0 \qquad (5)$$

Where, $a_i(t)$ is the value of the attribute a_i at time t, $I_i(a_i(t))$ is the membership value that expresses the level of abnormality of $a_i(t)$, and $A_i(a_i(t))$ is the membership value that expresses the level of regularity of $a_i(t)$.

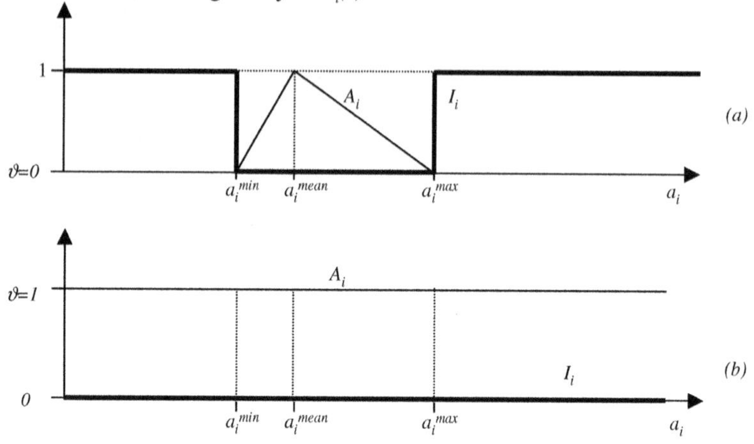

Fig. 4. Fuzzy sets A_i and I_i when (a) $\vartheta=0$ and (b) $\vartheta=1$.

Fig. 4-*a* shows the membership functions of A_i and I_i when $\vartheta=0$. In this particular case, I_i fuzzy set converges into a crisp set, which identifies all the values of a_i, which are outside of the interval $[a_i^{min}, a_i^{max}]$ as fully abnormal (with membership value equal to 1). If $\vartheta=1$, then constantly, for all t, $A_i(a_i(t))=1$ and consequently $I_i(a_i(t))=0$ (see Fig. 4-*b*). This means that none of the values of a_i is abnormal when $\vartheta=1$. The parameter ϑ specifies the sensitivity of the system in identifying abnormal values. When $\vartheta=1$ the system is fully indifferent; none of the values is identified as abnormal, no matter how far away from the normal level the value is. When $\vartheta=0$ the system is fully sensitive, which means that if a value of the attribute a_i appears to be outside the interval $[a_i^{min}, a_i^{max}]$, no matter how far away, then the value of a_i is considered abnormal with maximum intensity (i.e. 1). The value of ϑ usually is between 0 and 1 excluding the end points.

As we have previously mentioned, the aim of the training module is to observe the attribute time sequences for a given time period (training session) and then derive the attribute indices at the end of the training session. The threshold ϑ and the attribute indices are then used to define the membership functions of the fuzzy sets A_i and I_i $(1 \le i \le n)$. The fuzzy set I_i is then used to identify the intensity of abnormal events associated with the attribute a_i. The following section discuses how this identification is performed.

4.2 Event Identification

Let's assume that the industrial process can be observed by monitoring a set of n temporal attributes $A=\{a_1, a_2, ..., a_n\}$. At the end of the training session, we are able to specify a set of membership functions $I=\{I_1, I_2, ..., I_n\}$, where I_i $(1 \le i \le n)$ describes the extent to which a value of a_i is abnormal. Let $E=\{e_1, e_2, ..., e_m\}$ be a set of event types, which represent distinct kinds of abnormal behaviour. We may define a mapping f from A to E that assigns one or more attributes to one or more events. For example, if $f=\{(a_1, e_3), (a_1, e_4), (a_2, e_3), (a_3, e_2), ...\}$, it means that an abnormal value of a_1 causes a concurrent occurrence of the events e_3, e_4 and the event e_3 may occur due to an abnormal value of either a_1 or a_2. A fuzzy event is identified by using the following criterion:

> A value $a_i(t)$ of the attribute a_i causes the occurrence of an event e_j if only if $(a_i, e_j) \in f$ and $I_i(a_i(t))>\omega$ where $0 \leq \omega \leq 1$.

The threshold ω indicates the minimum intensity that an abnormal value must have in order to cause the occurrence of an event. This has been introduced to disallow the occurrence of events of a very low intensity. However, if we want to allow the occurrence of events of any intensity level, then we may define $\omega=0$. Upon the occurrence of an event, the system registers the data relevant to the event in a database in the identification unit (see Fig. 1). The event record includes the following data: (a_i, e_j, t, I_e), where a_i is the attribute whose abnormal value causes the occurrence of the event of type e_j (i.e. $e_j=f(a_i)$), t is the time of occurrence, which may be an integer indicating the time granule at which the event occurred and $I_e= I_i(a_i(t))$ is the event intensity. It suffices to represent such a fuzzy event as a triple (e_j, t, I_e). The database in the identification unit stores all the event occurrences forming in that way sequences of fuzzy events. Each event in a sequence has occurred due to abnormal attribute measurements of the industrial process.

The next step is to examine this sequence of events and extract useful knowledge from it by identifying frequent event patterns. This is discussed in the following section.

5 Event Mining Unit

The event-mining unit concerns itself with the discovering of rules that associate fuzzy event patterns. It is divided into two parts; the first one deals with the discovering of the most frequent fuzzy event patterns and the second one deals with the extraction of rules that associate closely related fuzzy event patterns.

5.1 Discovering Frequent Event Patterns

A fuzzy event is a triple $(e_j, t, I(e_j))$, where $e_j \in E$ is an event type, such that $e_j=f(a_i)$, t is the time at which the event occurs and $I(e_j)=I_i(a_i(t))$ is the intensity of the event. An event sequence is a triple (s, T_s, T_e), where s is an ordered set of events whose first event occurs at T_s and the last event occurs at T_e $(T_e \geq T_s)$. An event pattern p is a partial order $(B,<)$, where $B \subseteq E$. A pattern p matches a sequence s, if all of the events in p occur in s in an order respecting the partial order. The event sequence (s_1, T_{s1}, T_{e1}) is contained in the sequence (s_2, T_{s2}, T_{e2}) if only if $T_{s1} \geq T_{s2}$ $T_{e1} \leq T_{e2}$ and $s_1 \subseteq s_2$. Two typical sequences of such events are shown in Fig. 5.

The algorithms used to identify frequent event patterns in an event sequence are based on the *sliding window* algorithms [8]. However, we use a different definition of the frequency of the event patterns. Our definition takes in to account the intensity of the fuzzy events. In [8], the events are crisp (there is no indication of the event intensity, an event is fully present if it occurs) and consequently the frequency of an event pattern (episode) is defined as the fraction of the windows in which the pattern occurs. Our definition aims at estimating the uncertainty introduced by the occurrence of the fuzzy events. In our case, the events are not crisp, but they occur with an intensity, which is a measure of the abnormality of the attribute value. So, consecutive events appearing in two different patterns may have different effects if they occur with different intensities. It is obvious that the definition of the pattern frequency as the fraction of the windows in which the pattern occurs, does not suffices in the case of patterns consisting of fuzzy events. Therefore, we propose a new definition of pattern frequency, which is based on the intensity of the fuzzy events. Given a window of width l, the frequency of a pattern p in a sequence of fuzzy events s is defined as follows:

$$fr_p(s,l) = \frac{\sum_{w_i} I_p(w_i)}{|W(s,l)|} \tag{6}$$

Where w_i is the *i-th* window in s, $I_p(w_i)$ is the intensity of the pattern in the *i-th* window and $|W(s,l)|$ is the total number of windows on the sequence s. The width l of the window is an integer specifying the number of time granules The intensity of a pattern p is given by

$$I_p(w_i) = \underset{(e_j \in p) \wedge (e_j \in w_i)}{Min} \{I(e_j)\} \tag{7}$$

Where $I(e_j)$ is the intensity of the event e_j in the pattern p in the window w_i. This means that the intensity of a pattern, which occurs in a window w_i is equal to the minimum intensity of the events, which occur in the pattern of this window. In the case where the fuzzy events are crisp (i.e. $\vartheta=0$), then the above definition converges to the one given in [8], since the numerator converges to the number of the windows where the pattern occurs. In this sense, the above definition is viewed as a more general one that extends the notion of pattern occurrence in order to deal with uncertainty, which is expressed through the pattern intensity.

An event pattern p is considered frequent if its frequency fr_p is greater than or equal to a threshold σ, which is known as the *minimal support*. The identification of frequent event patterns is based on the principle that if an event pattern p is frequent, then all of its sub-patterns are frequent as well with a frequency, which is greater than or equal to that of the pattern p. For example, if the frequency of the pattern in Fig. 5-*b* is $f_b \geq \sigma$, then the pattern in Fig. 5-*a* is also frequent and its frequency $f_a \geq f_b \geq \sigma$. This principle is used to prune out non-frequent event patterns. The following algorithm is used to extract the set of frequent event patterns from a sequence of fuzzy events.

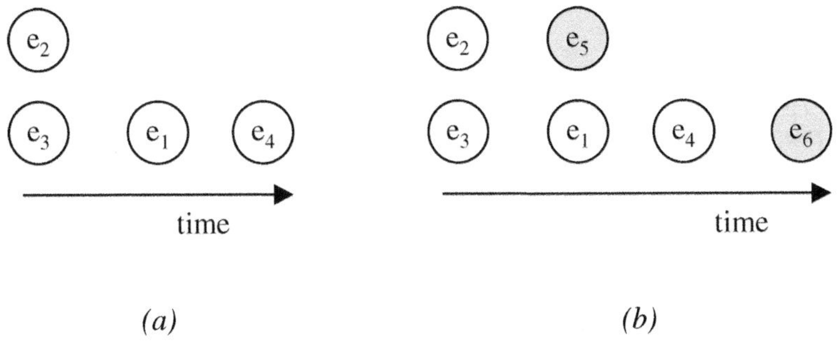

Fig. 5. Two event sequences. Sequence (b) contains sequence (a).

Algorithm 1. Extraction of frequent patterns

Input: An event sequence S
Output: The set F containing all frequent fuzzy event patterns in S
Method:

Let T be a temporary set of fuzzy event patterns. Let C_i be the candidate set of fuzzy event patterns containing i fuzzy events. First i=1 and C_1 is the set containing singleton fuzzy event patterns. Each of such a singleton fuzzy event patterns contains an event type occurring in the sequence S.

```
While Ci ≠∅ do
   T=∅
   for all x∈Ci do
        compute frx in S and if frx≥σ  then
             find all the patterns that extend x by a single
             event and add these patterns in T.
   Ci=T
```

The set of frequent patterns is used to obtain rules. The following section discusses how a rule base may be constructed by a set of frequent patterns.

5.2 Rule Extraction

Once the frequent patterns are known, they are used to obtain rules. A rule associates two closely related event patterns where one contains the other. Let F be the set of frequent event patterns. The frequency of a pattern $p \in F$ is greater than or equal to the minimal support σ. Let A and B be two frequent event patterns, $A \in F$ and $B \in F$, such that A is contained in B (i.e. $A \subseteq B$). Then the confidence of the rule $A \rightarrow B$ is given by the fraction $c_{A \rightarrow B} = \frac{fr_B}{fr_A}$. Literally, $c_{A \rightarrow B}$ is the strength of the rule and it is an estimate of the conditional probability of occurrence of B in a window, given that A occurs in this window. The rule is considered valid and it is added to the rule base if its confidence is greater than or equal to a confidence threshold ε, which is known as the *minimal confidence*. The following algorithm is used to extract rules from the set of frequent event patterns F.

Algorithm 2. Rule extraction

Input: set of frequent patterns *F*
Output: set of rules *R* (rule base)
Method:

```
R=∅
for all p∈F and q∈F such that p⊆q do
   c_{p→q} =fr_q/fr_p
   if c_{p→q} ≥ε then
      add the rule p→q to the set R with membership value
      equal to the confidence c_{p→q}
od
```

The set of rules *R* is stored in the rule repository in the event mining unit (see Fig. 1). The prediction unit guesses future events by using the rules of this repository. The prediction of future events is discussed in the following section.

6 Predicting Aberrant Events

Given a set of rules and a recent event sequence of *k* windows width, the goal is to guess future possible event patterns and to form a fuzzy set whose membership function assigns a likelihood value to each of the possible future event patterns. Let's denote *antecedent*(r_j) the premise of the rule r_i, *consequence*(r_j) the conclusion of r_j and $c(r_j)$ the confidence of the rule r_j. The algorithm for predicting event patterns is the following:

Algorithm 3. Prediction of event patterns

Input: the most recent *k* windows in the sequence
Output: the fuzzy set G of event patterns, which are likely to occur in the future
Method:

```
for all the most recent windows w_i do
  for all rules r_j in the rule base do
    if the antecedent(r_j) is present in the window w_i then
       add the pattern consequence(r_j) to G with membership
       value equal to the confidence c(r_j).
```

The members of the fuzzy set G are the event patterns guessed whose membership values represent the likelihood that the event pattern will occur.

7 Conclusions

Given a time series originated from an industrial monitoring process, MAPS method is able to identify marginal cases in the sequential data and automatically extract the fuzzy sets that describe the regularity of data. These fuzzy sets are then used to identify aberrant behaviour and generate relevant events. Such events are registered and they usually form event sequences. Event mining is then used over these sequences to discover frequent fuzzy event patterns and deduce rules that associate closely related frequent fuzzy event patterns. The antecedent part of such rules is used as a knowledge pattern that may match current event sequences. In case of a matching, we are able to predict future sequences of aberrant events that may affect the industrial process. The MAPS method employs fuzzy sets and seamlessly integrates fuzzy logic and event mining providing a more flexible way for identifying and predicting abnormal events. The contributions of this paper are summarised as follows:

- It introduces fuzzy logic for identifying abnormal events in observation data.
- It provides a new definition for frequent event patterns, which is based on the intensity of the event patterns. The intensity of events is defined as a membership value of the fuzzy set that describes the abnormal behaviour.
- It points out the way to define fuzzy membership functions in terms of some statistical measures (minimum, maximum and mean) of the sequential data.
- It modifies existing event pattern mining algorithms in order to accommodate the fuzzy metrics.
- It shows how prediction may be applied by utilising a rule base and the most recent event patterns in the sequence.
- It seamlessly integrates event identification, event pattern mining and event pattern prediction into a single system.

In this paper, we have utilised some statistical measures to construct fuzzy sets that describe the regularity of a sequence. However, other statistical measures such as standard deviation and variance may be also used in shaping the membership functions. Another important issue that may be considered in extracting such fuzzy sets is the utilisation of higher order metrics of the sequence (first derivative etc.). In rapidly changing time sequences, we may need to take into account such metrics in order to capture more accurately the regular behaviour of the sequence.

References

1. Rakesh Agrawal, Ramakrishnan Srikant: Mining Sequential Patterns. In *Proceedings of the Eleventh IEEE International Conference on Data Engineering (ICDE'95),* pp. 3-14, March 6-10, 1995, Taipei, Taiwan.
2. Claudio Bettini, Xiaoyang Sean Wang, Sushil Jajodia, Jia-Ling Lin: Discovering Frequent Event Patterns with Multiple Granularities in Time Sequences. *IEEE Transactions on Knowledge and Data Engineering (TKDE)* **10**(2): 222-237 (1998)
3. Thomas G. Dietterich and Ryszard S. Michalski: Discovering Patterns in Sequences of Events. *Artificial Intelligence* **25**(2): 187-232 (1985).
4. Tom Fawcett, Foster J. Provost: Activity Monitoring: Noticing Interesting Changes in Behavior. In *Proceedings of the Fifth ACM SIGKDD International Conference on Knowledge Discovery and Data Mining (KDD'99)*, pp. 53-62, August 15-18, 1999, San Diego, CA, USA.
5. Valery Guralnik, Jaideep Srivastava: Event Detection from Time Series Data. In *Proceedings of the Fifth ACM SIGKDD International Conference on Knowledge Discovery and Data Mining (KDD'99)*, pp. 33-42, August 15-18, 1999, San Diego, CA, USA.
6. Philip Laird: Identifying and Using Patterns in Sequential Data. In *Proceedings of the Fourth International Workshop on Algorithmic Learning Theory (ALT'93)*, LNCS 744, pp. 1-18, Tokyo, Japan, November 8-10, 1993.
7. Jianxiong Luo, Susan M. Bridges: Mining fuzzy association rules and fuzzy frequency episodes for intrusion detection. *International Journal of Intelligent Systems (IJIS)*, **15**(8): 687-703 (2000).
8. Heikki Mannila, Hannu Toivonen, A. Inkeri Verkamo: Discovery of Frequent Episodes in Event Sequences. *Data Mining and Knowledge Discovery* **1**(3): 259-289 (1997)

Comparisons of QP and LP Based Learning from Empirical Data

Vojislav Kecman and Tiru Arthanari

Department of Mechanical Engineering, University of Auckland,
Private Bag 92019, Auckland, New Zealand
http://www.support-vector.ws
v.kecman@auckland.ac.nz

Abstract. The quadratic programming (QP) and the linear programming (LP) based method are recently the most popular learning methods from empirical data. Support vector machines (SVMs) are the newest models based on QP algorithm in solving the nonlinear regression and classification problems. The LP based learning also controls both the number of basis functions in a neural network (i.e., support vector machine) and the accuracy of learning machine. Both methods result in a parsimonious network. This results in data compression. Two different methods are compared in terms of number of SVs (possible compression achieved) and in generalization capability (i.e., error on unseen data).

Keywords: support vector machines, neural networks, linear programming, quadratic programming, learning from experimental data

1. Introduction

Support Vector Machine (SVM) is a new type of learning machine that keeps the training error fixed (i.e., within given boundaries), and minimizes the confidence interval, i.e., it matches the machine capacity to data complexity. SVM that uses *quadratic programming* (QP) in calculating support vectors has very sound theoretical basis and it works almost perfectly for not too large data sets. When the number of points is large (say more then 2000), the QP problem becomes extremely difficult to solve with standard methods and program solvers. Recently, a lot of work was done on implementing an LP approach in support vectors selection. Kecman (1999) suggested optimal subset selection by using LP in solving regression tasks by minimizing the L_1 norm of the output layer weight vector **w**. Hadzic and Kecman (1999) implemented such an LP approach to classification problems. Zhang and Fuchs (1999) proposed an LP based method for selecting the hidden neurons at the initialization stage of the multilayer perceptron network. The LP approaches in solving regression problems have been implemented since 1950ties (see Charnes, Cooper and Ferguson 1955, Cheney and Goldstein 1958a, Stiefel 1960, Kelley 1957, Rice 1964). These results follow from minimizing L_1 norm of an error. (Interestingly, the first results on the L_1 norm estimators were given as early as 1757 by Yugoslav scientist Boskovic, see

L. Monostori, J. Váncza, and M. Ali (Eds.): IEA/AIE 2001, LNAI 2070, pp. 326-332, 2001.

Eisenhart, 1962). The summary and very good presentations of mathematical programming application in statistics were given by Arthanari and Dodge (1993). An early work on LP based classification algorithms dates back to the middle of 1960s (see Mangasarian 1965). Recently, a lot of work has been done on implementing LP approach in support vectors selection (Smola et all 1998, Bennett 1999, Weston et all 1999, and Graepel et all 1999, Kecman and Hadzic 2000). All these papers originate from the same stream of ideas clustered around controlling the (maximal) margin. Hence, they are close to the SVM constructive algorithms.
We state the LP based approach by using the regression example and we compare the results obtained by approximating function by LP and QP based learning. The slight difference between the two methods mentioned is that instead minimizing L_2 norm $\|\mathbf{w}\|_2$ (QP approach in the standard SVM learning) of the weight vector $\mathbf{w}$, we minimize L_1 norm $\|\mathbf{w}\|_1$ in an LP approach. In Section 2, we state the method for solving regression problems by LP (Kecman, 2001). In Section 3, the LP and the QP approaches are compared and some conclusions are drawn in Section 4.

2. Linear Programming in Regression

Minimization of the L_2 norm equals minimizing $\mathbf{w}^{\mathrm{T}}\mathbf{w} = \sum_{i=1}^{n} w_i^2 = w_1^2 + w_2^2 + \cdots + w_n^2$ and this results in the QP type of problem that leads to a maximization of a margin M (Vapnik, 1995). Here, instead minimizing an L_2 norm of the weight vector $\mathbf{w}$ we will minimize its L_1 norm. The geometrical meaning of the L_1 norm is not clear yet but the application of the LP approach for a subset (support vectors, basis functions) selection results in a very good performance of NN and/or SVM. At the same time there is no theoretical evidence either that, the minimization of the L_1 norm or L_2 norm of the weight vector $\mathbf{w}$ produces superior generalization.

Regression tasks could be formulated in many different ways. Here we show one approach. More can be seen in (Kecman and Hadzic, 2000). Our problem is to design a parsimonious NN containing less neurons than data points. Such a sparseness of an NN or SVM results from minimizing L_1 norm of the weight vector $\mathbf{w}$. At the same time, we want to solve $\mathbf{y} = \mathbf{G}\mathbf{w}$ such that $\| \mathbf{G}\mathbf{w} - \mathbf{y} \|$ is small for some chosen norm. In order to perform such a task we formulate the regression problem as follows - find a weight vector

$$\mathbf{w} = \arg\min\|\mathbf{w}\|_1, \text{ subject to}, \qquad | \mathbf{G}\mathbf{w} - \mathbf{y} \|_\infty \le \varepsilon, \tag{1}$$

where ε defines the *maximally* allowed error (that is why we used L_∞ norm) and corresponds to the ε-insensitivity zone in an SVM learning. This constrained optimization problem can easily be transformed into a standard linear programming form. First, recall that $\min\|\mathbf{w}\|_1 = \min\sum_{p=1}^{P} | w_p |$, and this is not an LP problem formulation where we typically minimize $\mathbf{c}^T\mathbf{w} = \sum_{p=1}^{P} c_p w_p$ and $\mathbf{c}$ is some known coefficient vector. (P denotes the number of training data). Thus, in order to apply the LP algorithm we use the standard trick by replacing w_p and $| w_p |$ as follows

$$w_p = w_p^+ - w_p^- \quad \text{2a)} \qquad |w_p| = w_p^+ + w_p^- \quad \text{(2b)}$$

where w_p^+ and w_p^- are the two non-negative variables, i.e., $w_p^+ \geq 0$, $w_p^- \geq 0$. Note, that the substitutions done in (2) are unique, i.e., for a given w_p there is only one pair (w_p^+, w_p^-) which fulfills both equations. Furthermore, both variables can not be bigger than zero at the same time. In fact there are only three possible solutions for a pair of variables (w_p^+, w_p^-), namely, (0, 0), (w_p^+, 0) or (0, w_p^-). Second, the constraint in (1) is not in a standard formulation either and it should also be reformulated as follows. Note that $\| \mathbf{Gw} - \mathbf{y} \|_\infty \leq \varepsilon$ in (1) defines an ε-tube inside which should our approximating function reside. Such a constraint can be rewritten as

$$\mathbf{y} - \varepsilon \mathbf{1} \leq \mathbf{Gw} \leq \mathbf{y} + \varepsilon \mathbf{1} \tag{3}$$

where $\mathbf{1}$ is a $(P, 1)$ column vector filled with ones. Equation (3) represents a standard set of linear constraints and our LP problem to solve is now the following. Find a pair

$$(\mathbf{w}^+, \mathbf{w}^-) = \arg\min \sum_{p=1}^{P} (w_p^+ + w_p^-), \text{ subject to, } \mathbf{y} - \varepsilon\, \mathbf{1} \leq \mathbf{G}(\mathbf{w}^+ - \mathbf{w}^-) \leq \mathbf{y} + \varepsilon\, \mathbf{1}, \text{ (4a)}, \ \mathbf{w}^+ \geq \mathbf{0}, \text{ (4b)},$$

$$\mathbf{w}^- \geq \mathbf{0}, \tag{4c}$$

where $\mathbf{w}^+ = [\, w_1^+, w_2^+, \cdots, w_P^+ \,]^T$ and $\mathbf{w}^- = [\, w_1^- \ \ w_2^- \ \ \ldots \ \ w_P^- \,]^T$. LP problem (4) can be presented in a matrix-vector formulation suitable for an LP solver as follows:
$\min_{\mathbf{w}} \mathbf{c}^T\mathbf{w}$, i.e.,

$$\min_{\mathbf{w}} \Big[\underbrace{1 \ \ 1 \ \ldots \ 1}_{P \ columns} \quad \underbrace{1 \ \ 1 \ \ldots \ 1}_{P \ columns} \Big] \Big[w_1^+ \ w_2^+ \ \cdots w_P^+ \ w_1^- \ w_2^- \cdots w_P^- \Big]^T \quad \text{subject to,}$$

$$\begin{bmatrix} \mathbf{G} & -\mathbf{G} \\ -\mathbf{G} & \mathbf{G} \end{bmatrix} \begin{bmatrix} \mathbf{w}^+ \\ \mathbf{w}^- \end{bmatrix} \leq \begin{bmatrix} \mathbf{y} + \varepsilon\mathbf{1} \\ -\mathbf{y} + \varepsilon\mathbf{1} \end{bmatrix}, \tag{5}$$

$$\mathbf{w}^+ \geq 0, \ \ \mathbf{w}^- \geq 0, \qquad \text{(6), (7)}$$

where both $\mathbf{w}$ and $\mathbf{c}$ are the $(2P, 1)$-dimensional vectors. $\mathbf{c} = \mathbf{1}(2P, 1)$, and $\mathbf{w} = [\mathbf{w}^{+T} \ \mathbf{w}^{-T}]^T$.

The QP based method which is the learning method in SVMs design is well known and it can be found in (Vapnik, 1995, 199) and (Kecman, 2001).

The basic crucial design constraints in a QP approach is that we must use exactly *P* basis functions placed at the training data. In the case when we use Gaussian kernels this means placing each Gaussian basis (kernel) function at each data in input space.

Unlike in QP, the greatest advantage in applying the LP base learning is that there is no constraint in terms of the number of basis functions placed at each training data (or elsewhere). In this case the constraint matrix on the left hand side of (5) will be rectangular having more columns than rows. However, this does not increases the complexity of the calculation (or, the computing time), because the constraining factor in an LP solver is the number of rows of the constraints matrix in the first place.

3. Simulation Example

NONLINEAR REGRESSION

We first comment the basic differences between the QP and LP approach in solving regression problems while placing one Gaussian kernel at each data point in both approaches. We investigated *sinus function* polluted with 20% noise. In a QP solution, an insensitivity zone was chosen to be $e = 0.1$, $C = 20{\cdot}10^6$ and the Gaussian bells parameter $\sigma = 3\Delta c$, (i.e., $k_S = 3$). Simulations were repeated on randomly selected data set one hundred times. Comparison of QP and LP based training algorithms shows that as number of training data increases computational time becomes significantly smaller for LP then for QP and that the number of chosen support vectors for LP is almost half their number for QP. At the same time, however, accuracy is slightly better for QP based algorithms.

The next modeled function was the Hermitian one shown in Fig 1 (LP method). However, the more interesting case is to exploit the full capacity of an LP based method. By 'full capacity', we mean the above-mentioned possibility to use more Gaussian basis functions than data available having various shapes. In this case, as it will be shown below, the LP approach shows stronger capabilities in modeling variously changing function above the input domain. We use the 1D Hermitian function here because it varies heavily along the input *x*, having at the same time both the smooth and the'hairy' portions. (See results in Fig 1).

In Fig 1, the SVs selection based on an LP learning algorithm (5) is shown for a Hermitian function $f(x) = 1.1(1 - x + 2x^2)exp(-0.5x^2) + 5$. The training set contained 41 training data pairs and the LP algorithm (out-of-820 basis functions offered) has selected 7 data points as the SVs shown as encircled crosses. Basis functions are Gaussians $G(x_i, c_j = x_j) = \exp(-0.5\| x_i - c_j\|^2/(\sigma)^2)$ where $\sigma = k_S\Delta c$ where Δc denotes the average distance between the adjacent centers of the basis functions. k_S varied between 2 and 15 for the LP algorithm, and it was fixed as 5 for the QP method. Table 1 shows the basic differences between the LP and QP methods:

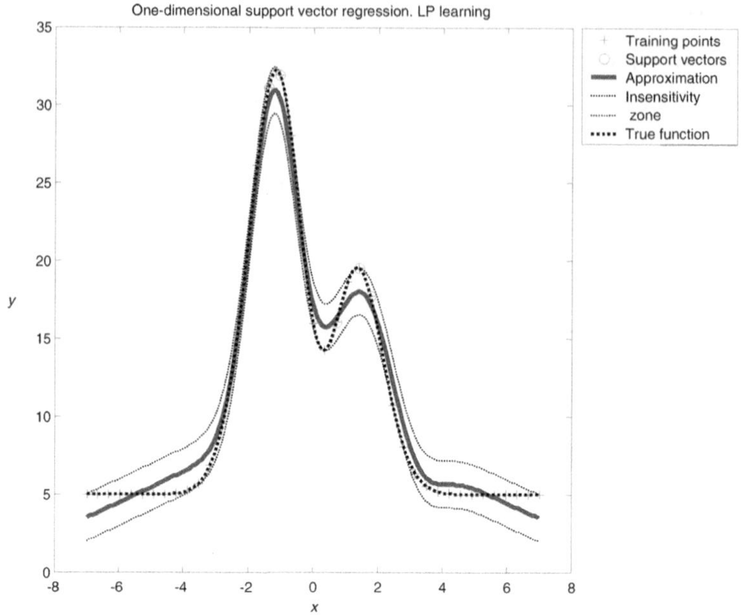

Fig. 1. Nonlinear regression: The SVs selection based on an LP algorithm (5). Hermitian function $f(x) = 1.1(1 - x + 2x^2)\exp(-0.5x^2) + 5$ (dashed). So obtained training set contains 41 training data points (crosses). An LP algorithm has selected 7 SVs shown as encircled data points and the QP one has chosen 10 SVs. Resulting approximation curve (solid). Insensitivity zone is bounded by dotted curves.

Table 1. Comparison between the LP and QP function approximation.

	Number of SVs	Maximal/minimal weights |w|	Error
LP	7	12.1 / 1.9	0.087 or 8.7%
QP	12	3902 / 40	0.101 or 10.1%

The results in Table 1 are the best ones obtained after a dozen simulation runs for each method. The LP method outperformed the QP one due to the fact that during the learning, a set of 820 Gaussians bells was 'offered' to model the data. (In fact, 20 Gaussians per data points have been placed having variable width factor i.e., standard deviation σ). After the learning the following *sigmas* have been chosen:

$$\sigma = [0.7216 \quad 0.7104 \quad 5.0818 \quad 5.2054 \quad 0.9671 \quad 0.8646 \quad 0.7293]$$

This means that the width factor i.e., standard deviation σ of the first Gaussians was 0.7216, of the second one 0.7104, and so on. The QP method is much more rigid and all 12 Gaussians chosen (or, all 12 SVs selected) have the same width factor i.e., standard deviation σ = 1.7500.

4. Conclusions

In this paper, we present an LP approach for solving *nonlinear* regression tasks and we compare it with the QP method. The approach and results show that an LP based learning (that resulted from the minimization of the L_1 norm of the weight vector $\mathbf{w}$) produces sparse networks. This may be of particular interest in modern days applications while processing a huge amount of data (say several dozens of thousands) that can not be processed by the contemporary QP solvers. The basic advantage of the LP based learning is that we can use much more kernel functions than the number of the experimental data. The results presented here are inconclusive in the sense that much more investigations and comparisons with a QP based SVs selection on both real and 'artificial' data sets should be done. Despite the lack of such an analysis yet, our first simulational results show that the LP subset selection may be more than a good alternative to the QP based algorithms when faced with a huge training data sets. Saying that we primarily refer to the following possible benefits of applying LP based learning: *a*) LP algorithms are faster and more robust than QP ones, *b*) they tend to minimize number of weights (meaning SV) chosen, and *c*) they naturally incorporate the use of kernels for creation of nonlinear separation and regression hypersurfaces in pattern recognition and function approximation problems respectively and *c*) they can use more kernel function having variable shapes. In this way, the selection of the basis function is data driven resulting in better performance (less SVs chosen and better generalization capacity).

References

1. Arthanari, T. S., Y. Dodge, 1993. Mathematical Programming in Statistics, J. Wiley & Sons., New York, NY
2. Bennett, K., 1999. Combining support vector and mathematical programming methods for induction. In B. Schölkopf, C. Burges, and A. Smola, Editors, *Advances in Kernel Methods - SV Learning*, pp 307–326, MIT Press, Cambridge, MA Charnes, A., W. W. Cooper, R. O. Ferguson, 1955. Optimal Estimation of Executive Compensation by Linear Programming, Manage. Sci., 1, 138
3. Cheney, E. W., A. A. Goldstein, 1958. Note on a paper by Zuhovickii concerning the Chebyshev problem for linear equations. J. Soc. Indust. Appl. Math., Volume 6, pp. 233-239
4. Eisenhart, C., 1962. Roger Joseph Boscovich and the Combination of Observationes, Actes International Symposium on R. J. Boskovic, pp. 19-25, Belgrade-Zagreb-Ljubljana, YU
5. Graepel, T., R. Herbrich, B. Schölkopf, A. Smola, P. Bartlett, K.–R. Müller, K. Obermayer, R. Williamson, 1999. Classification on proximity data with LP–machines, Proc. of the 9th Intl. Conf. on Artificial NN, ICANN 99, Edinburgh,7-10 Sept.

6. Hadzic, I., 1999. Learning from Experimental Data by Linear Programming Selected Support Vectors, PhD Thesis, (work in progress), The University of Auckland, Auckland, NZ
7. Hadzic, I., V. Kecman, 1999. Learning from Data by Linear Programming, NZ Postgraduate Conference Proceedings, Auckland, Dec. 15-16
8. Kecman, V., 2001. Learning and Soft Computing, SVM, NN, and FLS, The MIT Press, Cambridge, MA
9. Kecman V., Hadzic I., 2000. Support Vectors Selection by Linear Programming, Proceedings of the International Joint Conference on Neural Networks (IJCNN 2000), Vol. 5, pp. 193-199, Como, Italy,
10. Kelley E. J. jr., 1958. An application of linear programming to curve fitting (received by editors October 11, 1957), J. Soc. Indust. Appl. Math., Volume 6, pp. 15-22
11. Mangasarian, O. L., 1965. Linear and Nonlinear Separation of Patterns by Linear Programming, Operations Research 13, pp. 444-452.
12. Poggio, T., F. Girosi, 1993. Learning, Approximation and Networks, Lectures and Lectures' Handouts - Course 9.520, MIT, Cambridge, MA,
13. Rice R. J., 1964. The Approximation of Functions, Addison - Wesley Publishing Company, Reading, Massachusetts, Palo Alto, London
14. Smola A., T. T. Friess, B. Schölkopf, 1998. Semiparametric Support Vector and Linear Programming Machines, NeuroCOLT2 Technical Report Series, NC2-TR-1998-024
15. Smola, A., B. Schölkopf, G. Rätsch, 1999. Linear Programs for Automatic Accuracy Control in Regression, submitted to ICANN'99
16. Stiefel, E., 1960. Note on Jordan Elimination, Linear Programming and Chebyshev Approximation, Numer. Math., 2, 1.
17. Vapnik, V. N., 1995. The Nature of Statistical Learning Theory, Springer Verlag Inc, New York, NY
18. Weston, J., A. Gammerman, M. O. Stitson, V. Vapnik, V. Vovk, C. Watkins, 1999. Support Vector Density Estimation, In B. Schölkopf, C. Burges, and A. Smola, Editors, *Advances in Kernel Methods - SV Learning*, p.p. 307–326, MIT Press, Cambridge, MA
19. Zhang, Q. H., J.-J. Fuchs, 1999. Building neural networks through linear programming, Proceedings of 14th IFAC Triennial World Congress, Vol. K, pp. 127-132, Pergamon Press

A Fuzzy Cognitive Map Based on the Random Neural Model

Jose Aguilar

CEMISID, Dpto. de Computación, Facultad de Ingeniería, Av. Tulio Febres. Universidad de los Andes, Mérida 5101, Venezuela
aguilar@ing.ula.ve

Abstract. A fuzzy cognitive map is a graphical means of representing arbitrarily complex models of interrelations between concepts. The purpose of this paper is to describe a fuzzy cognitive map based on the random neural network model called the random fuzzy cognitive map, and to illustrate its application in the modeling of process. This model is based on the probability of activation of the neurons/concepts in the network. Our model carries out inferences via numerical calculation instead of symbolic deduction.

1 Introduction

Fuzzy Cognitive Maps (FCM) was proposed by Kosko to represent the causal relationship between concepts and analyze inference patterns [5], [6]. FCM is a hybrid method that lies in some sense between fuzzy systems and neural networks. So FCM represent knowledge in a symbolic manner and relates states, processes, policies, events, values and inputs in an analogous manner. FCM have gained considerable research interest and have been applied to many areas [3], [6], [7], [8], [9]. The Random Neural Network (RNN) has been proposed by Gelenbe in 1989 [4]. This model calculates the probability of activation of the neurons in the network. The RNN has been used to solve optimization and pattern recognition problems [1], [2]. The problem addressed in this paper concerns the proposition of a FCM, using the RNN. We describe the Random Fuzzy Cognitive Map (RFCM) and illustrate its application in the modeling of process. We shall use each neuron to model a concept. In our model, each concept is defined by a probability of activation, the relationships between the concepts are defined by positive or negative interrelation probabilities, and the procedure of how the cause takes effect is modeled by a dynamic system. This work is organized as follows, in section 2 the theoretical bases of the RNN and of the FCM are presented. Section 3 presents our RFCM. In section 4, we present applications. Remarks concerning conclusions are provided in section 5.

L. Monostori, J. Váncza, and M. Ali (Eds.): IEA/AIE 2001, LNAI 2070, pp. 333-338, 2001.

2 Theoretical Aspects

2.1. The Random Neural Network Model

The RNN model consists of a network of n neurons in which positive and negative signals circulate [4]. Each neuron i accumulates signals as they arrive, and can fire according to an exponential distribution of constant rate r(i) if its total signal count at a given instant of time is positive. Positive and negative signals have different roles in the network. A negative signal reduces by 1 the potential of the neuron to which it arrives or has no effect on the signal potential if it is already zero; while an arriving positive signal adds 1 to the neuron potential. Signals can either arrive to a neuron from the outside of the network or from other neurons. A signal which leaves neuron i heads for neuron j with probability $p^+(i,j)$ as a positive signal (excitation), or as negative signal with probability $p^-(i,j)$ (inhibition), or it departs from the network with probability d(i). Positive signals arrive to the ith neuron according to a Poisson process of rate $\Lambda(i)$. Negative signals arrive to the ith neuron according to a Poisson process of rate $\lambda(i)$. The main property of this model is the excitation probability of a neuron i, q(i), which satisfy the non-linear equation:

$$q(i) = \lambda^+(i)/(r(i)+\lambda^-(i)) \tag{1}$$

where, $\lambda^+(i) = \Sigma^n_{j=1}\, q(j)r(j)p^+(j,i)+\Lambda(i)$

$\lambda^-(i) = \Sigma^n_{j=1}\, q(j)r(j)p^-(j,i)+\lambda(i)$

The synaptic weights for positive ($w^+(i,j)$) and negative ($w^-(i,j)$) signals are: $w^+(i,j) = r(i)p^+(i,j)$ and $w^-(i,j) = r(i)p^-(i,j)$. Finally, $r(i) = \Sigma^n_{j=1}\, [w^+(i,j) + w^-(i,j)]$

2.2 Fuzzy Cognitive Maps

FCMs combine the robust properties of fuzzy logic and neural networks. FCM was proposed by Kosko [6], [7]. A FCM describes the behavior of a system in terms of concepts, each concept represents a state or a characteristic of the system. Particularly, a FCM is a fuzzy signed oriented graph with feedback that model the worlds as a collection of concepts and causal relations between concepts. Variable concepts are represented by nodes. The graph's edges are the casual influences between the concepts. The causal relationships are expressed by either positive or negative signs and different weights. The value of a node reflects the degree to which the concept is active in the system at a particular time. This value is a function of the sum of all incoming edges multiplied and the value of the originating concept at the immediately preceding state. In general, a FCM functions like associative neural networks. A FCM describes a system in a one-layer network which is used in unsupervised mode, whose neurons are assigned concept meanings and the interconnection weights represent relationships between these concepts. The fuzzy indicates that FCMs are often comprised of concepts that can be represented as fuzzy sets and the causal relations between the concepts can be fuzzy implications, conditional probabilities, etc. A directed edge E_{ij} from concept C_i to concept C_j measures how much C_i causes C_j. In general, the edges E_{ij} can take values in the fuzzy causal interval [-1, 1] allowing degrees of causality to be represented: a) $E_{jk}>0$ indicates direct (positive) causality between concepts C_j and C_k; b) $E_{jk}<0$ indicates inverse (negative) causality between concepts C_j and C_k; c) $E_{jk}=0$ indicates no relationship between C_j and C_k.

In FCM nomenclature, model implications are revealed by clamping variables and using an iterative vector-matrix multiplication procedure to assess the effects of these perturbations on the state of a model. A model implication converges to a global stability. During the inference process, the sequence of patterns reveals the inference model. The development of a FCM often occurs within an expert group. Each expert provides its individual FCM matrix, which is then synthesized into a group FCM matrix. The group matrix (E^G) could be computed as:

$$E_{ji}^{G} = \max_{t}\left\{E_{ji}^{t}\right\} \tag{2}$$

Where E_{ji}^{t} is the opinion of the expert t about the relationship among C_j and C_i.

3 Our Random Fuzzy Cognitive Maps (RFCM)

Our RFCM improves the conventional FCM by quantifying the probability of activation of the concepts and introducing a nonlinear dynamic function to the inference process. The value of W_{ij} indicates how strongly concept C_i influences concept C_j. $W^+_{ij}>0$ and $W^-_{ij}=0$ if the relationship between the concepts C_i and C_j is direct, $W^-_{ij}>0$ and $W^+_{ij}=0$ if the relationship is inverse, or $W^+_{ij}=W^-_{ij}=0$ if doesn't exist a relationship among them. To calculate the state of a neuron on the RFCM (the probability of activation of a given concept C_j), the following expression is used:

$$q(j) = \min\{\lambda^{+}(j), \max\{r(j), \lambda^{-}(j)\}\} \tag{3}$$

where
$$\lambda^{+}(j) = \max_{i=1,n}\{\min\{q(i), W^{+}(i,j)\}\}$$
$$\lambda^{-}(j) = \max_{i=1,n}\{\min\{q(i), W^{-}(i,j)\}\}$$

Such as, $\Lambda(j)=\lambda(i)=0$. In addition, the fire rate is:

$$r(j) = \max_{i=1,n}\{W^{+}(i,j), W^{-}(i,j)\} \tag{4}$$

The general procedure of the RFCM is the following:

1. Design the configuration of the FCM. Experts determine the concepts and causality.
2. Initialize the number of neurons (concepts).
3. Call the Learning phase
4. Call the Simulation phase.

3.1 The Learning Procedure

In this phase we must define the weights. The weights are defined and/or update as:

- *Based on expert's opinion:* each expert defines its FCM and the global FCM is determined according to the equation (2). The next algorithm determines the weight from a group of experts: a) If i≠j and if $E_{ij}>0$, then $W_{ij}^{+} = \max_{t=1,NE}\{E_{ij}^{t}\}$ and $W_{ij}^{-}=0$, b) If i≠j and if $E_{ij}<0$, then $W_{ij}^{-} = \max_{t=1,NE}\{E_{ij}^{t}\}$ and $W_{ij}^{+}=0$; c) If i=j or if $E_{ij}=0$, then $W_{ij}^{+}=W_{ij}^{-}=0$. The causal relationship (E_{ij}) is caught from each expert using the next set: E= {no relationship=>0, Slight=>0.2, Low=>0.4, Somehow=>0.6, Much=> 0.8, Direct=> 1}.
- *Based on measured data:* In this case we have a set of measures about the system. This information is the input pattern: $M=\{D_1, \ldots, D_m\} = \{[d_1^1, d_1^2, \ldots, d_1^n], \ldots, [d_m^1, d_m^2, \ldots, d_m^n]\}$, where d_j^t is the value of the concept C_j measured at time *t*. In this case, our learning algorithm follows the next mechanism:

$$W_{ji}^{t} = W_{ji}^{t-1} + \eta\left(\Delta d_j^t \Delta d_i^t \Big/ \Delta^+ d_i^t \Delta^+ d_j^t \right)$$

where $\Delta d_j^t = d_j^t - d_j^{t-1}$ $\qquad \Delta d_i^t = d_i^t - d_i^{t-1}$

$\Delta^+ d_j^t = d_j^t + d_j^{t-1}$ $\qquad \Delta^+ d_i^t = d_i^t + d_i^{t-1}$

η is the learning rate.

3.2 The Simulation Phase

Once constructed the RFCM of a specific system, we can perform qualitative simulations of the system. The RFCM can be used like an auto-associative memory. In this way, when we present a pattern to the network, the network will iterate until generate an output close to the information keeps. This phase consists on the iteration of the system until the system convergence. The input is an initial state $S_0= \{s_1, \ldots, s_n\}$, such as $q^0(1)=s_1, \ldots, q^0(n)=s_l$ and $s_i \in [0, 1]$ (set of initial values of the concepts ($S_0=Q^0$)). The output $Q^m=\{q^m(1), \ldots, q^m(n)\}$is the prediction of the RFCM such as *m* is the number of the iteration when the system converge. The algorithm of this phase is:

1. Read input state Q^0

2. Calculate the fire rate r(i)
3. Until system convergence
    3.1 Calculate q(i)

4 Experiments

In this section we illustrate the RFCM application. A discrete time simulation is performed by iteratively applying the equation (4) to the state vector of the graph. At the beginning, we must define an initial vector of concept states, and the simulation halts if an equilibrium state is reached. In our experiment, we discuss a simple model to determine the risk of a crisis in a country. The operative concepts are: a) Foreign inversion (C_1): the presence of a strong foreign inversion; b) Employ rate (C_2): The level of employ on the country; c) Laws (C_3): the presence or absence of laws; d) Social problems (C_4): the presence or absence of social conflict on the country; e) Government stability (C_5): a good relationship between the congress, the president, etc. The edge connection matrix (E) for this map is given in table 1.

Table 1. The edge connection matrix for the first experiment.

	C_1	C_2	C_3	C_4	C_5
C_1	0	0.8	0	0	0
C_2	0	0	0	-06	0.8
C_3	0.4	0	0	-0.8	0
C_4	0	0	0	0	-0.8
C_5	0.6	0	0	0	0

The table 2 presents the results for different initial states. Clamping two antithetical concepts allows to test the implications of one or more competing concepts. To illustrate, we begin by clamping C_1 and C_4 (S_0=(1 0 0 1 0)) – a strong foreign inversion can generate more employment. Despite of the foreign inversion, we have an unstable government due to the social problems (the system reaches an equilibrium state of (1 1 0 0 1)). With S_0=(1 0 1 1 0) foreign inversion and social problems remain clamped, but we also clamp the ability to have a good law system. The system reaches an equilibrium state of 1 1 1 0 0 – A peaceful country at the social level but one unstable government. Next, we test for S_0=(1 1 1 1 0). In our model, the inference process is: S_1 = (0.8 .0.6 0 1 0.8), S_2 = (0.8 .0.6 0 0.8 0.4), and S_3 = (0.8 .0.6 0.8 0.6 0). In this example, we could take advantage of the ability to study the inference process during execution of the simulation. This example suggests the social problem is the main factor to have an unstable government. Obviously, our goal in analyzing this model was not to determine policy choices for a country. Rather, we tried to illustrate the advantages of the RFCM to this sort of analysis. Our results indicate that RFCMs quickly come to an equilibrium regardless of the complexity of the model.

Table 2. The results for the first experiment.

Input	Kosko FCM	RFCM	Iteration
1 0 0 1 0	1 1 0 1 0	0.8 0.6 0.2 0.2 0.8	1
	1 1 0 0 1		2
1 0 1 1 0	1 1 1 1 0	0.8 .0.6 0.8 0 0	1
	1 1 1 0 0		2
1 1 1 1 0	1 1 1 1 0	0.8 .0.6 0 1 0.8	1
		0.8 .0.6 0 0.8 0.4	2
		0.8 .0.6 0.8 0.6 0	3

5 Conclusions

In this paper, we have proposed a FCM based on the Random Neural Model, the RFCM. We have shown that this model can efficiently work as associative memory. Our RFCM exhibit a number of desirable properties that make it attractive: a) Provide qualitative information about the inferences in complex social dynamic models; b) Can represent an unlimited number of reciprocal relationships; c) Facility the modeling of dynamic, time-evolving phenomena and process. Another important characteristic is its simplicity, the result of each RFCM's cycles is computed from the equation (4). Further on, we will study the utilization of the RFCM in modeling the behavior of distributed systems and dynamic systems. In addition, we will test our unsupervised learning approach.

References

1. Aguilar, J. Definition of an Energy Function for the Random Neural to solve Optimization Problems, Neural Networks, Vol. 11, Pergamo, (1998) 731-738.
2. Aguilar, J. Learning Algorithm and Retrieval Process for the Multiple Classes Random Neural Network Model. Neural Processing Letters, Vol. 13, Kluwer Academic Publishers, to appear, (2001).
3. Craiger J., Goodman D., Wiss R., Butler B. Modeling Organizational Behavior with Fuzzy Cognitive Maps. Intl. Journal of Computational Intelligence and Organizations, Vol. 1, (1996) 120-123.
4. Gelenbe E. Random neural networks with positive and negative signals and product form solution, Neural Computation, Vol. 1, (1989). 502-511.
5. Kosko B. Fuzzy Cognitive Maps, Int. Journal of Man-Machine Studies, Vol. 24, (1986) 65-75.
6. Kosko B. Fuzzy Engineering, Prentice-Hall, New Jersey (1997).
7. Miao Y., Liu C. On causal inference in Fuzzy Cognitive Map, IEEE Transaction on Fuzzy Systems, Vol. 8, (2000) 107-120.
8. Pelaez C., Bowles J. Using fuzzy cognitive maps as a system model for failure models and effects analysis, Information Sciences, Vol. 88, (1996) 177-199.
9. Stylios C., Georgopoulos V., Groumpos P. Applying Fuzzy Cognitive Maps in Supervisory Control Systems, Proc. of European Symposium on Intelligent Techniques, (1997) 131-135.

Synthetic Damage Assessment for RC Structure Based on Fuzzy Logic

Chung-Huei Tsai [1] and Deh-Shiu Hsu [2]

[1] Assistant researcher, Center for General Education, National Chung Cheng University
Chiayi, Taiwan 70101, R.O.C.
admcht@ccunix.ccu.edu.tw

[2] Professor, Department of Civil Engineering, National Cheng Kung University
Tainan, Taiwan 70101, R.O.C.
dshsu@ncku.edu.tw

Abstract. A fuzzy logic base synthetic damage assessment method which attempts to perform an objective and synthetic conclusion for various damage diagnostic results, subject to each test RC beam from the neural networks (NNs) is developed in this paper. Various damage diagnostic results are resulted from a feasible diagnostic model for the RC test beam through the ANN technique, based on four kinds structural response, i.e., acceleration time history (ATH), displacement time history (DTH), natural frequencies (NF), and static displacement (SD), are separately serve as the input characteristics of the NN in the diagnostic model. Fuzzy logic is then applied to reduce differences between situations and linguistically state the final diagnostic results. Therefore, this paper successfully fabricates a synthetic damage assessment method, which will be needed for real world damage assessment applications.

1 Introduction

Concrete has been widespread in structural engineering during a long time period. However, several defects in RC structures include the formation of honeycombs, cracking, scaling, corrosion, fatigue and lower than criteria material strength, all of which are induced by improper construction and maintenance. Improper treatment of these defects might cause loss of human life and property in the event of a natural disaster. Therefore, civil engineers must promptly diagnose and repair these defects to prolong structural life span and prevent collapse of RC structures following disasters.

The artificial intelligence (AI) diagnostic model as proposed by the author in the series study of this diagnostic work focuses mainly on developing a damage assessment technique based on a back-propagation network (BPN) and then performs it by applying it to a simply-supported RC beam, with a span of 4 meters and a rectangular cross section. Training and testing numerical examples then comprise variously assumed damage conditions and several different structural responses i.e., ATH.DTH.NF.and SD of the defected beams, respectively. Two stages of diagnostic procedure are then used for the NN application to identify the relevant structural damage. So, initially, in the so-called category identification, the NN is used to identify which category the damage belongs to (damage to steel member or concrete only, or damage to both steel and concrete). The NN is then used to thoroughly identify the damage matching condition in each category.

L. Monostori, J. Váncza, and M. Ali (Eds.): IEA/AIE 2001, LNAI 2070, pp. 339-348, 2001.

Moreover, to demonstrate that the proposed damage diagnostic model can be effectively applied to real RC structures, ten sets of test beams with assumed damage and the same sectional area of the numerical examples are also constructed on a full-scale. The ten sets of test beams are used to diagnose the damage scenario separately by the well-trained NN according to the structural responses. Finally, the degree of different or contradictory phenomena within the NN's damage diagnostic results and real situation of the test beam will be reduced by fuzzy logic. The ambiguous situations between four kinds of damage diagnostic results of NN will become a natural linguistic statement clarifying the damage case subject to each test beam or the damage level subject to a certain location in the test RC beams, respectively. Herein, a feasible and efficient AI damage diagnostic model is established for the RC structures.

Details of main tasks, numerical and experimental test results, and stages of diagnostic procedure within the ANN base diagnostic model, has been presented in the relative proceedings [1,2], journals [3] and dissertation [4] as listed in the reference, respectively. Therefore, this paper only focus mainly on recommending the part of synthetic damage assessment via the fuzzy logic for the RC structure as shown in the following section.

2 Applications of Fuzzy Logic

Fuzzy logic technique is based on the mathematical model of fuzzy sets, which can be applied not only to practical problems involving ambiguity, confusion, vagueness, and uncertainty, but also to conventional mathematical models can not be solved efficiently. Owing to its inherent characteristics of high nonlinear processing and fault tolerance ability, fuzzy logic resembles the artificial neural network (ANN) technique. Among the extensive applications of fuzzy logic include pattern classification, automatic control, decision making, optimization, and diagnosis in diverse areas such as engineering, financial management, and medical science. Notably, many researchers concentrated on developing automatic engineering in the control area via the fuzzy logic technique and obtained numerous significant performances and advanced commercial products over the past decade. In civil engineering, fuzzy logic is mainly applied to pattern recognition, prediction, diagnosis, and structural control. However, of these several tasks, diagnosis is by far the most popular application of the fuzzy technique. For instance, Ross et al. [6] developed a damage assessment code, formed as a rule-based expert system based on fuzzy set theory, to assess the structural integrity of a buried concrete box structure. Meanwhile, Chao and Cheng [7] provided a diagnostic model based on cause-and-effect diagramming and fuzzy pattern recognition to examine the effectiveness of the model in diagnosing crack formations in RC structures. Moreover, Chen et al. [8] proposed the approach to effectively handle uncertainty in the conventional SPT-based liquefaction evaluation of the soil by using the fuzzy numbers model.

This investigation presents an ANN base damage diagnostic model to detect damage in RC structures. Some of the assumptions or parameters used in this model consist of the ambiguity and uncertainty that might accompany each process. However, owing to ANN having a high fault tolerance ability in nature, the complicated damage diagnostic problem can then be feasibly solved by ANN techniques. In this investigation, using several approaches must results from different final damage results. These results are represented by the damage index and may be identical or different, even having serious contradictions. The best synthetic damage assessment can not be subjectively recognized or analyzed and obtained using the conventional mathematical method. Thus, efficiently integrating these results into an objective synthetic damage assessment, and must coincide with the principles commonly used to classify the degree of experience subject to a certain human event. Therefore, this paper attempts to apply fuzzy logic techniques which are also robust and fault tolerant to solve this problem, as mentioned before. In doing so, a meaningful solution can hopefully be obtained for practical implementation.

3 Method of Synthetic Damage Assessment

This section recommends methods of synthetic damage assessment based on the fuzzy logic technique. The underlying concepts of this method are based on Mau's [9] proposal for a quick post-earthquake building damage assessment method using recorded data. Furthermore, some fuzzy concepts and methodology used herein, such as relation matrix, fuzzy term, and fuzzy logic operation and so on, were also suggested and developed by Zadeh [10-12]. Details of five major tasks within the method are introduced separately as follows. Further details and how to yield the object of these tasks will be demonstrated and expressed in the example, as presented in the next section.

- Determine the fuzzy relation matrix $\boldsymbol{R}$ of the damage state depending on each damage state associated with its membership function.
- Define the fuzzy term "probability" by its membership function.
- Establish the fuzzy rules (multi criterion rules).
- Denote the probability state vector for the damage states by $\boldsymbol{P}$, and complete the final probability membership function $\boldsymbol{F}$ according to Eqs.(1).

$$\{\boldsymbol{F}\} = \{\boldsymbol{P}\}[\boldsymbol{R}] \tag{1}$$

- Defuzzify the final probability membership function and obtain a more definite concluding statement.

4 Example for the Case which Identifies the Category to which Damage Belongs

Example for the test beam related to first diagnostic classifiers that are used to examine the performance of the method proposed herein. Test beams that will identify the category to which the damage belongs (i.e., purpose of first classifier), include a61, a62, a63, b61, b62, b63, c81, c82, c83, B2. A portion of Table 1 summarizes the identification results of these test beams using four structural responses with the ANN technique. The major aim of the method of synthetic damage assessment is reduce vague or even seemingly conflicting damage state situations, founded as shown in Table 1. For example, an a61 test beam was adopted herein to illustrate the effectiveness of the proposed method. The real state of this test beam is the case of damage only occurring in concrete, then the damage index is 1 in concrete and 0 in steel. However, during ANN base damage, diagnostic approaches used different structural responses to classify whether damage belongs to concrete or steel, and to obtain the initial diagnostic result. According to Table 1, the damage index is 1 in concrete and 1 in steel for the ATH approach, 0.995 in concrete and 0.069 in steel for DTH, 0.999 in concrete and 0.114 in steel for NF, and 0.931 in concrete and 0.322 in steel for SD. Clearly, these data contain ambiguities. Therefore, the proposed the fuzzy logic base method was adopted to attempt to transform ambiguous situations into clearer damage state expressions.

Table 1. Summary of diagnostic results based on ANN techniques and fuzzy synthetic assessment for first classifier

Damage diagnostic approach		Material and damage state	Test beam									
			a61	a62	a63	b61	b62	b63	c81	c82	c83	B2
Real state		Concrete	1	1	1	0	0	0	1	1	1	0
		Steel	0	0	0	1	1	1	1	1	1	0
ANN base damage diagnostic results	ATH	Concrete	1	1	1	0.002	0.002	0.031	1	1	1	0.007
		Steel	1	0.065	0.000	1	1	0.831	0.998	0.998	0.997	0.010
	DTH	Concrete	0.995	0.999	0.999	0.001	0.000	0.007	1	0.999	1	0.999
		Steel	0.068	0.116	0.275	0.979	0.971	0.070	0.895	0.570	0.939	0.4
	NF	Concrete	0.999	0.999	0.999	0.953	0.999	0.995	0.908	0.996	0.999	0.999
		Steel	0.114	0.023	0.028	1	0.027	1	1	1	0.994	0.024
	SD	Concrete	0.931	0.932	0.930	0.93	0.67	0.915	0.93	0.933	0.929	0.003
		Steel	0.322	0.525	0.177	0.178	0.82	0.439	0.178	0.529	0.073	0.988
Synthetic assessment		**No damage** occurred in **concrete**.	Un-likely	Un-likely	Un-likely	Not Like-ly	Like-ly	Not Like-ly	Un-likely	Un-likely	Un-likely	Not Like-ly
		Have damage occurred in **concrete**	Like-ly	Like-ly	Like-ly	Not Like-ly	Not Like-ly	Not Like-ly	Like-ly	Like-ly	Like-ly	Not Like-ly
		No damage occurred in **steel**.	Like-ly	Very Like-ly	Like-ly	Not Like-ly	Not Like-ly	Not Like-ly	Not Like-ly	Not Like-ly	Not Like-ly	Like-ly
		Have damage occurred in **steel**	Not Like-ly	Not Like-ly	Not Like-ly	Like-ly	Like-ly	Like-ly	Like-ly	Like-ly	Like-ly	Not Like-ly

On the other hand, other test beams utilized the same process and membership functions of the damage state and multi criterion rule used in this example to obtain final synthetic damage state assessments, and are listed at the bottom of Table 1.

- Determine the fuzzy relation matrix $\boldsymbol{R}$ of the damage state.

  Since this example identifies the category the damage belongs to, the universal set "damage state" only includes two fuzzy set, i.e., "No damage occurred in this material"(first state) and "Damage has occurred in this material" (second state). Then, Fig. 1 illustrates the membership functions of these two fuzzy sets. The elements of these two fuzzy sets are discrete variables ranging from 0 to 1 with increments of 0.1. From this figure, the overlapping area can reflect the characteristic of this problem, i.e., a portion of these damage indexes represents whether the damage states are identical or different, or even whether severe contradictory phenomenon exist. Thus, the element of relation matrix of these two damage state $\boldsymbol{R}_{2\times2}$ can be defined according to the conditional probability and sigma count [11]as shown in eqs(2)

$$P\{X \text{ is } A \mid X \text{ is } B\} = \frac{P\{A \cap B\}}{P\{B\}} = \frac{\sum Count(A \cap B)}{\sum Count(B)} \tag{2}$$

Where

$$\sum Count(A) = \sum \mu_A$$

For instance, R_{12} denotes the probability of the first state occurring when the second state has occurred, and can be calculated as follows.

$$R_{12} = P\{\textit{Damage state} \text{ is } "\textit{No damge occurred in this material}" \mid \textit{Damage state} \text{ is } "\textit{Have dmage occured in this material}"\}$$

$$= \frac{\sum Count(\textit{No damage}...... \cap \textit{Have damage}.....)}{\sum Count(\textit{Have damage}.....)}$$

$$= \frac{0.5}{0.1 + 0.2 + 0.3 + 0.4 + 0.5 + 0.6 + 0.7 + 0.8 + 0.9 + 1}$$

$$= 0.091$$

The other elements in matrix $\boldsymbol{R}_{2\times2}$ are given depending on the method as mentioned above, therefore

$$[\mathrm{R}]_{2\times2} = \begin{bmatrix} 1 & 0.091 \\ 0.091 & 1 \end{bmatrix}$$

- Define the fuzzy term "probability" by its membership function. A fuzzy term "probability" that includes "Unlikely", "Not Likely", "Likely", and "Very Likely" is proposed by Zadeh [10] and is combine with the damage state to form the probably damage statement. The membership function of these four fuzzy terms is illustrated in Fig. 2. Some of their mapping relationships are defined in Eqs. (3) and (4).

$$\mu_{Likely} = 1 - \mu_{Not\ Likely} \tag{3}$$

$$\mu_{Very\ Likely} = (\mu_{Likely})^2 \tag{4}$$

- Establish the fuzzy rules. As mentioned earlier, ANN outputs four kinds of damage index (due to four kinds of structural response) that are displayed by discrete value, ranging from 0 to 1, to demonstrate the diagnostic results which classify damage belongs to. Then, fuzzy rules used in this example are extended from typical fuzzy rules as "IF ***antecedent*** THEN ***conclusion***" and can be fabricated as follows.

  IF $\boldsymbol{I_l > 0.75}$
  THEN *It is* ***Very Likely*** *that there is* ***Have Damage Occurred in This Material***
  AND *It is* ***Unlikely*** *that there is* ***No Damage Occurred in This Material***
  IF $\boldsymbol{0.5 \leq I_l \leq 0.75}$
  THEN *It is* ***Likely*** *that there is* ***Have Damage Occurred in This Material***
  AND *It is* ***Not Likely*** *that there is* ***No Damage Occurred in This Material***
  IF $\boldsymbol{0.25 \leq I_l \leq 0.5}$
  THEN *It is* ***Not Likely*** *that there is* ***Have Damage Occurred in This Material***
  AND *It is* ***Likely*** *that there is* ***No Damage Occurred in This Material***
  IF $\boldsymbol{I_l < 0.25}$
  THEN *It is* ***Unlikely*** *that there is* ***Have Damage Occurred in This Material***
  AND *It is* ***Very Likely*** *that there is* ***No Damage Occurred in This Material***

  Where $\boldsymbol{I_l}$ is a damage index that represents the damage statement and these indexes are outputted from four kinds of approach. The principle of setting boundary values in each rule is based on the quantitative method. Sixteen fuzzy rules can be obtained in this example. According to these rules and damage index in Table 1, the damage state of a61 test beam can be concluded as displayed in Table 2.

- Perform the probability state vector for the damage states by $\boldsymbol{P}_{1\times2}$ as indicated in Eqs.(5) and complete the final probability membership function $\boldsymbol{F}_{1\times2}$ as indicated in Eqs.(6). Herein, the weighed methodology is utilized to achieve the probability membership function combination illustrated below.

$$\{\ \mathbf{P}\ \}_{1\times2} = \{\ P_{No}\ \ P_{Have}\ \} \tag{5}$$

$$\{\ \mathbf{F}\ \}_{1\times2} = \{\ F_{No}\ \ F_{Have}\ \} \tag{6}$$

Where subscript "No" and "Have" in Eqs.(5) and (6) represent "No damage occurred in this material" and "Have damage occurred in this material", respectively.

For concrete material,

$$P_{No} = 4\times\frac{1}{4}(\boldsymbol{Unlikely}) = \frac{1}{0+0.1}+\frac{0.9}{0.2}+\frac{0.7}{0.3}+\frac{0.5}{0.4}+\frac{0}{0.5+...+1}$$

$$P_{Have} = 4\times\frac{1}{4}(\boldsymbol{Very\ Likely}) = \frac{0}{0+...+0.5}+\frac{0.3}{0.6}+\frac{0.5}{0.7}+\frac{0.8}{0.8}+\frac{1}{0.9+1}$$

For steel material,

$$P_{No} = \frac{1}{4}(\boldsymbol{Unlikely})+\frac{1}{4}(\boldsymbol{Likely})+2\times\frac{1}{4}(\boldsymbol{Very\ Likely}) = \frac{0.3}{0+0.1}+\frac{0.2}{0.2+0.3}+\frac{0.1}{0.4}+\frac{0}{0.5}+\frac{0.1}{0.6}+\frac{0.2}{0.7}+\frac{0.4}{0.8}+\frac{0.5}{0.9+1}$$

$$P_{Have} = 2\times\frac{1}{4}(\boldsymbol{Unlikely})+\frac{1}{4}(\boldsymbol{Not\ Likely})+\frac{1}{4}(\boldsymbol{Very\ Likely}) = \frac{0.5}{0+0.1+0.2}+\frac{0.4}{0.3}+\frac{0.3}{0.4+0.5}+\frac{0.1}{0.6+0.7}+\frac{0.2}{0.8}+\frac{0.3}{0.9+1}$$

Thus, final membership function $\boldsymbol{F}_{1\times 2}$ can be carried out as below via Eqs. (1).
For concrete material,

$$F_{No} = 1\times(P_{No})+0.091\times(P_{Have}) = \frac{0.3}{0+0.1}+\frac{0.2}{0.2+0.3}+\frac{0.1}{0.4}+\frac{0}{0.5}+\frac{0.1}{0.6}+\frac{0.2}{0.7}+\frac{0.4}{0.8}+\frac{0.5}{0.9+1}$$

$$F_{Have} = 0.091\times(P_{No})+1\times(P_{Have}) = \frac{0.1}{0+0.1+0.2+0.3}+\frac{0}{0.4+0.5}+\frac{0.3}{0.6}+\frac{0.5}{0.7}+\frac{0.8}{0.8}+\frac{1}{0.9+1}$$

For steel material,

$$F_{No} = 1\times(P_{No})+0.091\times(P_{Have}) = \frac{1}{0+0.1}+\frac{0.9}{0.2}+\frac{0.7}{0.3}+\frac{0.5}{0.4}+\frac{0}{0.5+0.6+0.7}+\frac{0.1}{0.8+0.9+1}$$

$$F_{Have} = 0.091\times(P_{No})+1\times(P_{Have}) = \frac{0.5}{0+0.1+0.2}+\frac{0.4}{0.3}+\frac{0.3}{0.4+0.5}+\frac{0.1}{0.6+0.7}+\frac{0.2}{0.8}+\frac{0.3}{0.9+1}$$

Table 2. Summary of damage assessment results of damage state with sixteen fuzzy rules

Damage state in concrete and steel		ANN base diagnostic approaches			
		ATH	DTH	NFs	SD
Concrete	No damage occurred in this material	Unlikely	Unlikely	Unlikely	Unlikely
	Have damage occurred in this material	Very Likely	Very Likely	Very Likely	Very Likely
Steel	No damage occurred in this material	Unlikely	Very Likely	Very Likely	Likely
	Have damage occurred in this material	Very Likely	Unlikely	Unlikely	Not Likely

- Defuzzify the final probability membership function. Figures 3~4 and 5~6 display the shape of final membership function $\boldsymbol{F}_{1\times 2}$ as obtained from the last step for the concrete and steel material, respectively. To obtain the best performance, the ordinary defuzzification method, namely, the center of gravity (CG) method, is used to defuzzify the final membership function herein. Then based on the principle of minimum distance between the CG of the final membership function and each CG of the probability membership function as indicated in these figures, the fuzzy base final damage statement which classifies the damage to the a61 test beam can be determined as below.

  The **a61** test beam is ***Unlikely*** that there is ***No Damage Occurred in Concrete Material***
  And it is ***Likely*** that there is ***Have Damage Occurred in Concrete Material.***
  The **a61** test beam is ***Likely*** that there is ***No Damage Occurred in Steel Material***
  And it is ***Not Likely*** that there is ***Have Damage Occurred in Steel Material.***

5 Conclusion

This paper demonstrates the effectiveness of the synthetic damage assessment method for the RC beam structure based on fuzzy logic for the case, which identifies the category to which damage belongs. Obviously, four kinds of ANN output diagnostic results within each test beam may be identical or different, even containing severely contradictory phenomenon, that can be efficiently integrated to produce an objective synthetic assessment and actually reflect the real state of the test beam via the proposed method. Therefore, the synthetic damage assessment method as proposed in this paper, which will be needed for damage assessment applications in the real world.

Acknowledgment. The author would like to thank the National Science Council of the Republic of China for financially supporting this research under Contract No.NSC88-2211-E006-019.

References

1. Tsai, C. H., Hsu, D. S.: Reinforced Concrete Structural Damage Diagnosis by Using Artificial Neural Network. Proceedings of Intelligent Information System. Dec. Bahamas (1997) 149-155
2. Tsai, C. H., Hsu, D. S.: Damage Diagnosis of Existing Reinforced Concrete Structures. Proceedings of The Fifth International Conference on The Application of Artificial Intelligence to Civil and Structural Engineering. Edinburgh (1999) 85-92
3. Tsai, C. H., Hsu, D. S.: Damage Assessment of RC Structures by Artificial Neural Network. J. of the Chinese Institute of Civil and Hydraulic Engineering, Vol.10 . (1998) 31-38
4. Tsai, C. H.: Diagnosis of Damage in RC Structure Based on Structural Responses Via the AI Technique. Ph. D. dissertation. National Cheng Kung University. Taiwan ROC. (2000)
5. Zadeh, L. A.: Fuzzy sets. Information and Control. Vol. 8. (1965) 338-353
6. Ross, T. J., Sorensen, H. C., Savage, S. J., Carson, J. M.: DAPS: Expert system for structural damage assessment. J. of Computing in Civil Engineering. Vol. 4. (1990) 327-348
7. Chao, C. J., Cheng, F. P.: A fuzzy diagnostic model for diagnosing cracks in reinforced concrete structures. Microcomputers in Civil Engineering. Vol.11. (1996)115-122
8. Chen, J. W., Chen, C. Y.: A fuzzy methodology for evaluation of the liquefaction potential. Microcomputers in Civil Engineering. Vol. 12. (1997) 193-204
9. Mau, S.T.: A quick post-earthquake building damage assessment method using recorded data. Proceedings of Asia-Pacific Workshop on Seismic Design & Retrofit of Structures. (1998) 440-451
10. Zadeh, L. A.: The concept of a linguistic variable and its application to approximate reasoning-II. Information Science. Vol. 8. (1975) 301-357
11. Zadeh, L. A.: A theory of commonsense knowledge. In: Skala, Termini, and Trillas. (1984)
12. Zadeh, L. A.: The role of fuzzy logic in the management of uncertainty in expert systems. Approximate Reasoning in Expert systems, Edited by Gutpa, M. M., Kandel, A., Bander, W., and Kiszka, J. B., North-Holland Publishing. (1985) 3-31

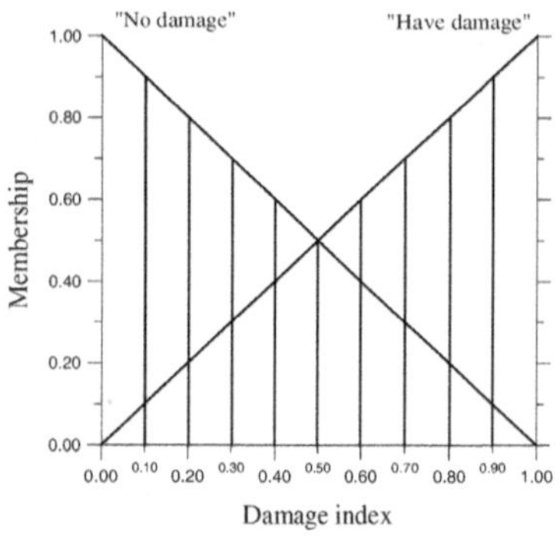

Fig. 1. Membership function of the two fuzzy sets from the damage state

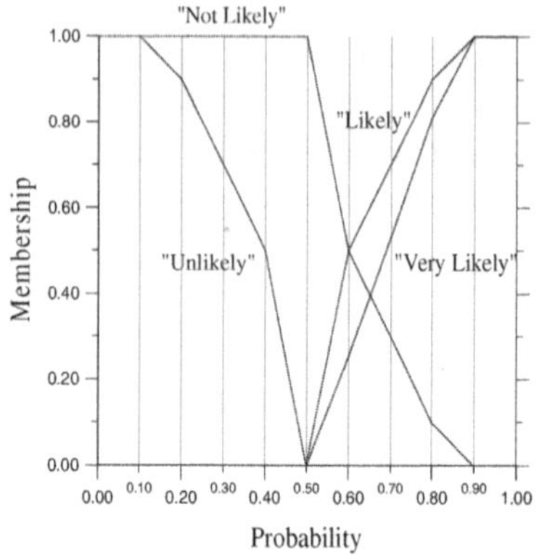

Fig. 2. Membership function of the four fuzzy sets from the probability

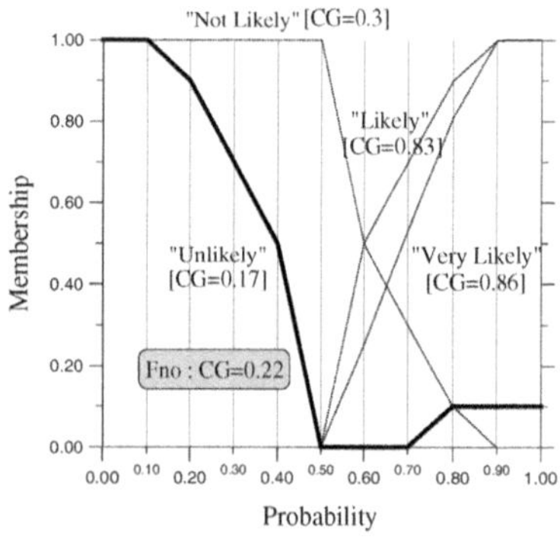

Fig. 3. Membership function of F_{No} in concrete material

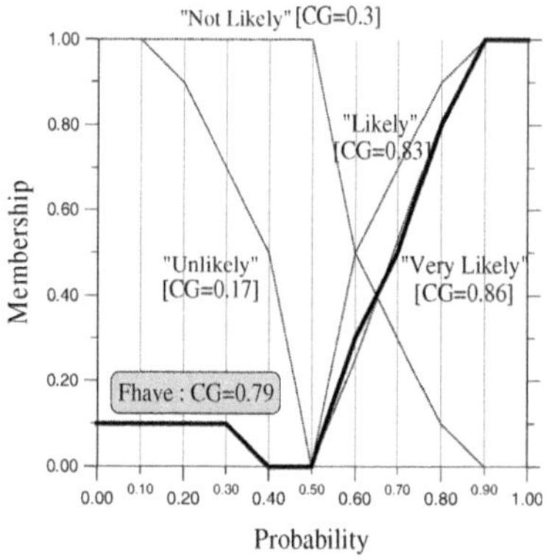

Fig. 4. Membership function of F_{Have} in concrete material

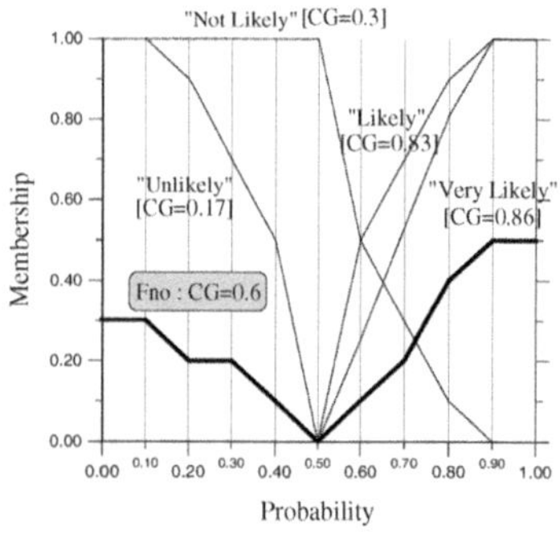

Fig. 5. Membership function of F_{No} in steel member

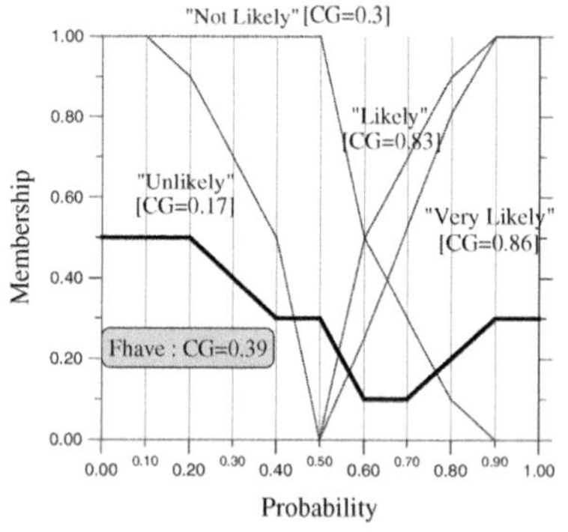

Fig. 6. Membership function of F_{Have} in steel member

Genetic Algorithm for Fuzzy Logical Equations Solving in Diagnostic Expert Systems

Alexander Rotshtein[1] and Hanna Rakytyanska[2]

[1] Jerusalem College of Technology – Machon Lev, Havvaad Haleumi St., 21, 91160, Jerusalem, Israel
rot@mail.jct.ac.il

[2] Vinnitsa State Technical University, Khmelnitske Sh., 95, 21021, Vinnitsa, Ukraine
anna@press.org.ua

Abstract. Application of the inverse logical inference in the expert systems of diagnosis is considered. The inverse logical inference allows to restore the causes by observed consequences using fuzzy relational matrix. Diagnosis decision finding requires fuzzy logical equations system solution. The genetic algorithm of optimization based on crossover, mutation and selection of the initial set of chromosomes is proposed for fuzzy logical equations system solving. Computer simulation illustrates the algorithm efficiency. The suggested genetic algorithm can find application in expert systems of technical and medical diagnosis and quality control.

1 Introduction

Fuzzy sets theory is a handy tool for expert information formalization while simulating cause-effect connections in technical and medical diagnostic problems [1]. The model of a diagnostic object, as a rule, is built on the basis of compositional Zadeh rule of inference which connects input and output variables of an object (causes and effects) using fuzzy relational matrix [2]. The problem of diagnosis can be formulated in the form of the direct and inverse fuzzy logical inference. The direct logical inference suggests finding diagnoses (output variables or effects) according to observable internal parameters of the object state (input variables or causes). In the case of the inverse logical inference some renewal of causes takes place (of the object state parameters) according to observable effects (symptoms).

In the majority of fuzzy logic applications to the diagnosis problems the direct logical inference is used [3-6]. At the same time the inverse logical inference is used insufficiently what is stipulated through the lack of effective algorithms solving fuzzy logical equations systems [4]. In this article we suggest some procedures of numerical solution of the fuzzy logical equations systems using genetic algorithm. The suggested procedures envisage growing of the optimal solution from a set of primary variants by way of using genetic cross-over, mutation and selection operations [7]. To serve the illustration of the procedures and genetic algorithm effectiveness study we present an example of the car engine faults diagnosis.

L. Monostori, J. Váncza, and M. Ali (Eds.): IEA/AIE 2001, LNAI 2070, pp. 349-358, 2001.

2 Fuzzy Logical Equations

The diagnosis object is treated as the black box with n inputs and m outputs:

$X=(x_1,x_2,...,x_n)$ - set of inputs;

$Y=(y_1,y_2,...,y_m)$ - set of outputs.

Simulation of the cause-effect "input-output" connections is done by way of interpreting the compositional Zadeh's rule of inference [2]

$$B = A \circ R, \tag{1}$$

where A and B are fuzzy sets given on the universal sets X and Y:

$$A=\left(\frac{a_1}{x_1},\frac{a_2}{x_2},...,\frac{a_n}{x_n}\right), \quad B=\left(\frac{b_1}{y_1},\frac{b_2}{y_2},...,\frac{b_m}{y_m}\right).$$

Here $a_i\,(i=\overline{1,n})$ and $b_j\ (j=\overline{1,m})$ are degrees of membership, that is of the numbers in the diapason from 0 to 1 interpreted as some measures of x_i causes and y_j effects significances;

R is the fuzzy relational matrix with elements r_{ij}, $i=\overline{1,n}$, $j=\overline{1,m}$, where r_{ij} is the number in the range of [0,1] characterizing the degree of the cause x_i influence upon the rise of the effect y_j;

$\circ$ is the operation of max-min composition [2].

The diagnostic problem is set in the following way. According to the known matrix R and fuzzy set B it is necessary to find some fuzzy set A. It is suggested that matrix R and fuzzy set B are formed on the basis of expert assessments, for example, by way of Saaty's paired comparisons [8].

Finding of fuzzy set A amounts to the solution of the fuzzy logical equations system:

$$\begin{aligned} b_1 &= (a_1 \wedge r_{11}) \vee (a_2 \wedge r_{21}) ... \vee (a_n \wedge r_{n1}) \\ b_2 &= (a_1 \wedge r_{12}) \vee (a_2 \wedge r_{22}) ... \vee (a_n \wedge r_{n2}) \\ &\dots \qquad \dots \qquad \dots \qquad \dots \\ b_m &= (a_1 \wedge r_{1m}) \vee (a_2 \wedge r_{2m}) ... \vee (a_n \wedge r_{nm}), \end{aligned} \tag{2}$$

which is derived from relation (1). Taking into account the fact that operations $\vee$ and $\wedge$ are replaced by max and min in fuzzy sets theory [2], system (2) is rewritten in this form

$$b_j = \max_{i=\overline{1,n}} \left(\min \left(a_i, r_{ij} \right) \right), \quad j=\overline{1,m}. \tag{3}$$

3 Optimization Problem

The problem of fuzzy logical equations system solution (3) is formulated in this way. Vector $\boldsymbol{a} = (a_1, a_2, ..., a_n)$ should be found which satisfies limitations of

$$a_i \in [0,1], \quad i = \overline{1,n},$$

and provides the least distance between expert and analytical measures of effects significances, that is between the left and the right parts of each system equation (3):

$$F(\boldsymbol{a}) = \sum_{j=1}^{m} \left[b_j - \max_{i=\overline{1,n}} \left(\min \left(a_i, r_{ij} \right) \right) \right]^2 = \min_{\boldsymbol{a}} . \qquad (4)$$

In general case system (3) can have no solitary solution but a set of them. Therefore, according to [4] we find the fuzzy logical equations system solution (3) in the form of intervals

$$a_i = \left[\underline{a}_i, \overline{a}_i \right] \subset [0,1], \quad i = \overline{1,n}, \qquad (5)$$

where $\underline{a}_i$ ($\overline{a}_i$) is the low (upper) boundary of cause x_i significance measure.

Formation of intervals (5) is done by way of multiple optimization problem solution (4) and it begins with the search for the null solution of it. The null solution of optimization problem (4) we designate in this way $\boldsymbol{a}^{(0)} = (a_1^{(0)}, a_2^{(0)}, ..., a_n^{(0)})$, where $a_i^{(0)} \in [\underline{a}_i, \overline{a}_i]$, $i = \overline{1,n}$. The upper boundary ($\overline{a}_i$) is found in range [$a_i^{(0)}$,1], and the low one ($\underline{a}_i$) - in range [$0, a_i^{(0)}$]. It is shown on the Fig.1 where the arrows correspond to direction of the search.

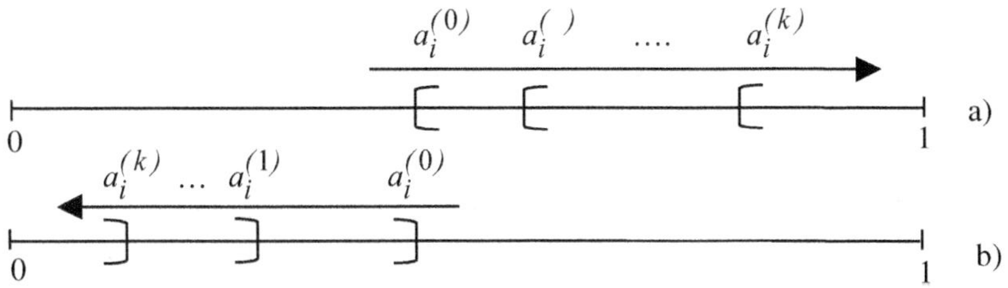

Fig. 1. Search for upper (a) and low (b) boundary of the interval

Let $\boldsymbol{a}^{(k)} = (a_1^{(k)}, a_2^{(k)}, ..., a_n^{(k)})$ be some k-th solution of optimization problem (4), that is $F(\boldsymbol{a}^{(k)}) = F(\boldsymbol{a}^{(0)})$ because for the all values of parameter a_i in the range [$\underline{a}_i$, $\overline{a}_i$] we have the same criteria (4). While searching for upper boundaries

($\bar{a}_i$) it is suggested that $a_i^{(k)} \geq a_i^{(k-1)}$, and while searching for low boundaries ($\underline{a}_i$) it is suggested that $a_i^{(k)} \leq a_i^{(k-1)}$. The definition of the upper (low) boundaries is done according to the rule: if $\boldsymbol{a}^{(k)} \neq \boldsymbol{a}^{(k-1)}$, then $\bar{a}_i(\underline{a}_i) = a_i^{(k)}$, $i = \overline{1,n}$. If $\boldsymbol{a}^{(k)} = \boldsymbol{a}^{(k-1)}$ then the search is stopped.

4 Genetic Algorithm

To realize the genetic algorithm of optimization problem solution (4) it is necessary to define the following main notions and operations [6,7]: chromosome - coded solution variant; gene - solution element; population - original set of solution variants; fitness function - criterion of variants selection; cross over - operation of providing variants-offsprings from variants-parents; mutation - random change of chromosome elements.

Let *P(t)* be chromosomes-parents, and *C(t)* – chromosomes-offsprings of the *t*-th iteration. The general structure of the genetic algorithm will have this form:

begin
t:=0;
To set the initial set *P(t)*;
To assess *P(t)* using fitness function;
while (no condition of completion) **do**
To generate *C(t)* by way of crossing over *P(t)*;
To perform mutation *C(t)*;
To assess *C(t)* using fitness function;
To select *P(t+1)* from *P(t)* and *C(t)*;
t:=*t*+1;
end;
end.

We define the chromosome as the vector-line of binary solution codes a_i, $i = \overline{1,n}$. Number of bits g_i for variable a_i coding is defined according to formula

$$2^{g_i - 1} < \left(\bar{d}_i - \underline{d}_i\right) \cdot 10^q \leq 2^{g_i} - 1,$$

where $[\underline{d}_i, \bar{d}_i]$ is the range of variable a_i change, q – required precision, that is the number of digits after decimal point in a_i solution.

The chromosomes of the initial population will be defined in the following way:

$$a_i = RANDOM([0,1]),\ i = \overline{1,n},$$

where $RANDOM([0,1])$ denotes the operation of random number finding, evenly distributed within the interval [0,1].

We choose criterion (4) taken with sign minus as the fitness function:

$$f(v) = -F(v), \tag{6}$$

that is the higher the degree of adaptability of the chromosome to perform the criterion of optimization the greater is the fitness function.

Let p_c be some cross-over factor, that is the share of the offsprings of each iteration performed, and K is the population dimension. Then it is necessary to select $\frac{K \cdot p_c}{2}$ pairs of chromosomes-parents of each iteration.

Selection of chromosomes-parents for cross-over operation should not be performed randomly. The greater the fitness function of some chromosome the greater is the probability for the given chromosome to yield offsprings. The probability of selection p_k, corresponding to each chromosome v_k, $k = \overline{1,K}$, is calculated according to formula [7]:

$$p_k = \frac{f(v_k) - \min\limits_{j=1,K}[f(v_j)]}{\sum\limits_{k=1}^{K}\left(f(v_k) - \min\limits_{j=1,K}[f(v_j)]\right)}, \quad \sum_{k=1}^{K} p_k = 1. \tag{7}$$

Using thus found probabilities we define chromosomes-parents in the following way. Let us mark row p_k on the horizontal axis (Fig.2).

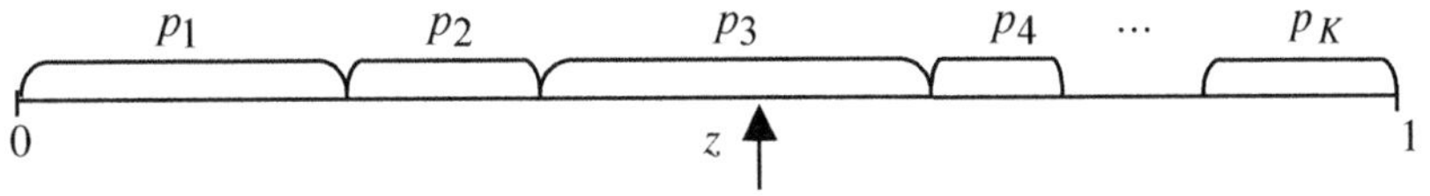

Fig. 2. Selection of chromosome-parent

We generate random number z, subordinate to the law of even distribution within interval [0,1]. We select chromosome v_k as the parent, this chromosome corresponding to subinterval p_k, within which number z finds itself. For example, in Fig.2 generated number z defines chromosome v_3 as the parent. Selection of the second chromosome-parent is carried out in similar way.

Operation of cross-over is defined in Fig.3. It is carried out by way of genes exchange inside each variable a_i, $i = \overline{1,n}$. The points of cross-over shown in dotted lines are selected randomly.

Mutation operation (Mu) implies random change (with some probability p_m) of chromosome elements $Mu(a_i) = RANDOM\left(\left[\underline{d}_i, \overline{d}_i\right]\right)$. So as this solution is coded by binary line then the mutation is reduced to inversion of some separate bits.

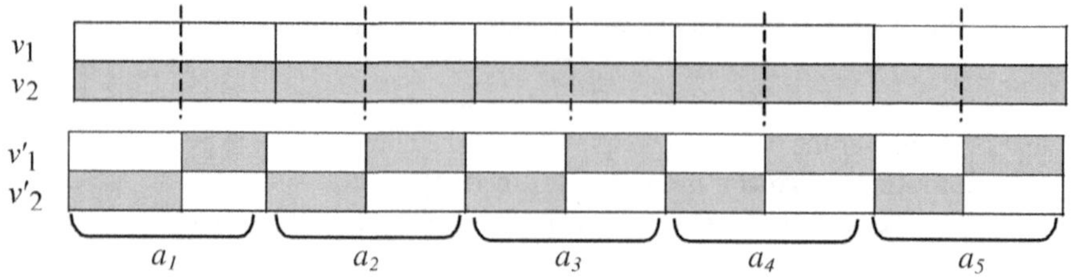

Fig. 3. Example of cross-over operation performance with n=5

While performing genetic algorithm the dimension of the population stays constant and equal to K. That is why after cross-over and mutation operations it is necessary to remove $K \cdot p_c$ chromosomes having the fitness function of the worst significance from the obtained population.

5 Example

Let us consider the algorithm performance having the recourse to the example of the car engine faults causes diagnosis.

Engine fault criteria are: y_1 - engine power insufficiency; y_2 - difficulties with engine starting; y_3 – smoky exhaust; y_4 - oil pressure too low.

Fault causes to be identified: x_1 - wear out of crank gear; x_2 - valve timing gear wear out; x_3 - carburettor fault; x_4 - battery fault; x_5 - oil pump fault.

Let expert matrix of fuzzy relations has this form:

R =

	y_1	y_2	y_3	y_4
x_1	0.8	0.4	0.8	0.3
x_2	0.7	0.3	0.6	0.1
x_3	0.9	0.7	0.3	0.1
x_4	0.1	0.9	0.1	0.1
x_5	0.5	0.6	0.4	0.9

As the result of the examination the expert defined the following measures of significance for the engine fault criteria:

$$b_1 = 0.8, \quad b_2 = 0.6, \quad b_3 = 0.2, \quad b_4 = 0.1.$$

It means that engine power insufficiency and difficulties in starting the engine with the smoky exhaust and oil pressure being normal were identified.

The system of fuzzy logical equations in this case will appear in this form:

$$\begin{aligned} b_1 &= (a_1 \wedge 0.8) \vee (a_2 \wedge 0.7) \vee (a_3 \wedge 0.9) \vee (a_4 \wedge 0.1) \vee (a_5 \wedge 0.5) \\ b_2 &= (a_1 \wedge 0.4) \vee (a_2 \wedge 0.3) \vee (a_3 \wedge 0.7) \vee (a_4 \wedge 0.9) \vee (a_5 \wedge 0.6) \\ b_3 &= (a_1 \wedge 0.8) \vee (a_2 \wedge 0.6) \vee (a_3 \wedge 0.3) \vee (a_4 \wedge 0.1) \vee (a_5 \wedge 0.4) \\ b_4 &= (a_1 \wedge 0.3) \vee (a_2 \wedge 0.1) \vee (a_3 \wedge 0.1) \vee (a_4 \wedge 0.1) \vee (a_5 \wedge 0.9) \ . \end{aligned} \quad \textbf{(8)}$$

To realize the genetic algorithm the initial population was formed as consisting of seven solutions:

v_1=(0.343, 0.257, 0.489, 0.136, 0.967); v_2=(0.345, 0.415, 0.848, 0.724, 0.261);

v_3=(0.536, 0.134, 0.677, 0.869, 0.880); v_4=(0.791, 0.010, 0.411, 0.245, 0.279);

v_5=(0.665, 0.315, 0.631, 0.199, 0.456); v_6=(0.400, 0.652, 0.943, 0.673, 0.551);

v_7=(0.622, 0.284, 0.992, 0.933, 0.072).

Fitness functions of these solutions found using formula (6) made up this representation:

$f(v_1) = -0.770$; $f(v_2) = -0.104$; $f(v_3) = -0.809$; $f(v_4) = -0.425$;
$f(v_5) = -0.362$; $f(v_6) = -0.383$; $f(v_7) = -0.318$.

Let cross-over probability be p_c=0.3. So as $\frac{K \cdot p_c}{2} = \frac{7 \cdot 0.3}{2} \approx 1$, then one pair of chromosomes must be selected to realize cross-over operation. On the basis of formula (7) the probability of each chromosome selection will make up this representation

p_1=0.016; p_2=0.283; p_3=0; p_4=0.154; p_5=0.179; p_6=0.171; p_7=0.197.

Let us assume that for the chromosomes-parents two random numbers z_1=0.183 and z_2=0.508 were generated. Then according to the algorithm of chromosomes-parents selection, chromosomes v_2 and v_5 must be subjected to the cross-over.

To realize cross-over operation we used 5 points of exchange which were generated randomly in range [1,10] what corresponds to solutions a_i representation using 10 digits. These random numbers made up 4, 3, 5, 4, 1 and defined points of chromosome exchange shown in Fig.4, where v_2, v_5 are chromosomes-parents, v'_2, v'_5 are chromosomes-offsprings. Same Fig. depicts mutation operation which implied inversion of the 49-th gene of v'_5 chromosome-offspring.

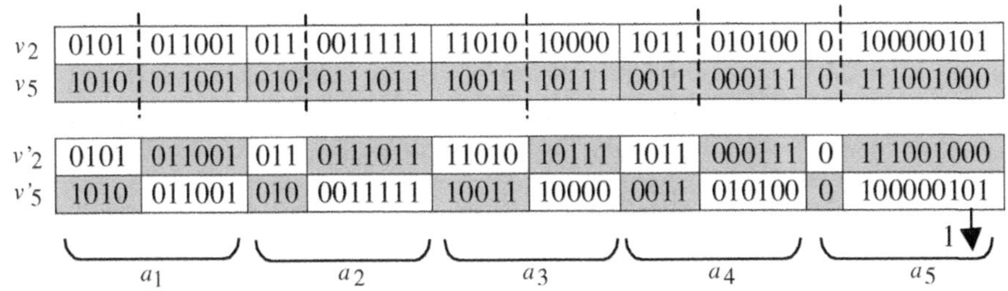

Fig. 4. Cross-over and mutation operations performance

Fitness function of chromosomes-offsprings

v'_2=(0.345, 0.443, 0.855, 0.711, 0.456), v'_5=(0.665, 0.287, 0.624, 0.212, 0.263)

made up this representation:

$f(v'_2) = -0.201$, $f(v'_5) = -0.275$.

To maintain the number of the population let us exempt 2 chromosomes with the worst fitness functions, that is v_1 and v_3. Then the new population will include also chromosomes: v_2, v_4, v_5, v_6, v_7, v'_2, v'_5. This operation completes one iteration of the genetic algorithm.

Sequential application of genetic cross-over, mutation and selection operations to the initial set of variants provides for the growth of the fitness function of the solutions being obtained. The dynamics of change of the optimization criterion (*F*) relative to the iteration number (*N*) are shown in Fig.5. Table 1 shows the list of chromosomes which were the best in carrying out some definite iterations of the genetic algorithm.

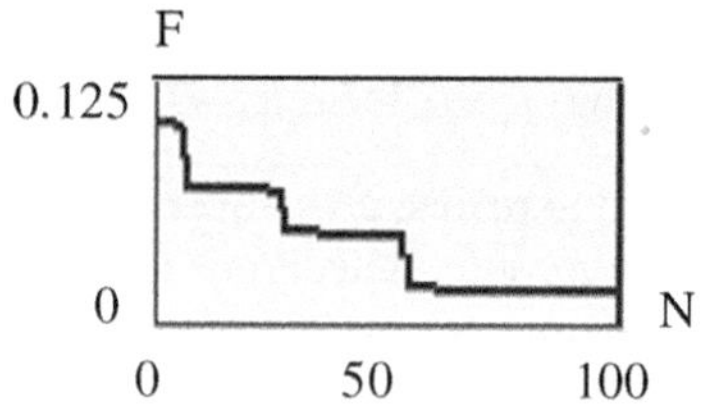

Fig. 5. Dependence of optimization criterion (*F*) on iteration number (*N*)

Table 1. The best solutions of various iterations of the genetic algorithm

Iteration Number	Solution	Optimization criterion
1	(0.345, 0.415, 0.848, 0.724, 0.261)	0.10390
4	(0.345, 0.415, 0.848, 0.660, 0.261)	0.09853
6	(0.320, 0.031, 0.784, 0.724, 0.256)	0.07003
7	(0.320, 0.031, 0.785, 0.724, 0.256)	0.07000
24	(0.320, 0.287, 0.789, 0.724, 0.256)	0.06990
27	(0.256, 0.287, 0.789, 0.724, 0.256)	0.04983
35	(0.256, 0.287, 0.789, 0.708, 0.256)	0.04612
43	(0.256, 0.279, 0.797, 0.708, 0.256)	0.04601
54	(0.075, 0.162, 0.808, 0.256, 0.024)	0.02006
61	(0.075, 0.162, 0.800, 0.256, 0.024)	0.02000

Fig.5 shows that after the 61-st iteration the solution doesn't improve. Therefore, we choose vector (0.075, 0.162, 0.800, 0.256, 0.024), to which goal function 0.02000 corresponds as the optimal solution. We obtain null solution

$$\boldsymbol{a}^{(0)} = (a_1^{(0)} = 0.075, a_2^{(0)} = 0.162, a_3^{(0)} = 0.800, a_4^{(0)} = 0.256, a_5^{(0)} = 0.024)$$

allowing us to arrange for the genetic search for a_i variables significances intervals. Search dynamics of upper and low solutions boundaries is depicted in Table 2.

Table 2. Genetic search for low and upper boundaries of intervals

N	$\underline{a}_1$	$\overline{a}_1$	$\underline{a}_2$	$\overline{a}_2$	$\underline{a}_3$	$\overline{a}_3$	$\underline{a}_4$	$\overline{a}_4$	$\underline{a}_5$	$\overline{a}_5$
1	0.075	0.075	0.162	0.162	0.800	0.800	0.256	0.256	0.024	0.024
10	0.039	0.084	0.151	0.178	0.800	0.800	0.173	0.359	0.010	0.054
20	0.022	0.088	0.085	0.251	0.800	0.800	0.159	0.420	0.004	0.078
30	0.017	0.095	0.043	0.275	0.800	0.800	0.084	0.573	0.001	0.095
40	0.011	0.098	0.028	0.287	0.800	0.800	0.047	0.585	0.000	0.100
50	0.005	0.099	0.016	0.298	0.800	0.800	0.038	0.640	0.000	0.100
60	0.001	0.100	0.008	0.299	0.800	0.800	0.020	0.688	0.000	0.100
70	0.000	0.100	0.003	0.300	0.800	0.800	0.007	0.695	0.000	0.100
80	0.000	0.100	0.000	0.300	0.800	0.800	0.002	0.699	0.000	0.100
90	0.000	0.100	0.000	0.300	0.800	0.800	0.000	0.700	0.000	0.100
100	0.000	0.100	0.000	0.300	0.800	0.800	0.000	0.700	0.000	0.100

Table 2 shows that fuzzy logical equations system solution can be represented in the form of intervals:

$$a_1 \in [0,0.1];\quad a_2 \in [0,0.3];\quad a_3 = 0.8;\quad a_4 \in [0,0.7];\quad a_5 \in [0,0.1].$$

Thus obtained solution allows to make the following conclusions. The cause of the observed engine state should be located and identified as the carburetor fault (x_3), so as the measure of significance of this fault is maximal. In addition, the observed state can be the effect of the battery fault (x_4), so as significance measure of this cause is sufficiently high. Insufficient wear-out of the valve timing gear (x_2) can also tell on engine proper functioning, the significance measure of which is indicative of the cause. Crank gear (x_1) and oil pump (x_5) function properly and practically have no influence on engine fault, so as significance measure of the given causes are small.

6 Assessment of Genetic Algorithm Effectiveness

Dependence of the number of iterations, necessary to obtain optimal solution, on the population volume (*K*), frequency of cross-over (p_c) and mutation (p_m) was studied in the course of computer experiment. Dependence of optimization criterion (*F*) on iteration number (*N*) under conditions of various parameters of the genetic algorithm is shown in Fig.6. It was determined that population volume of K=7 is sufficient for the system (8) solution. To exclude hitting the local minimum the experiment was carried out for large values of p_c and p_m. Fig.6,a shows that under conditions of $p_c = 0.6$ and $p_m = 0.02$ about 100 iterations were required to grow optimal solution. To cut time losses in unpromising fields studies some parameters of the main genetic operations were experimentally selected. Fig.6,b shows that setting of cross-over frequency at the level of 0.3 allowed to cut iteration number on the average to 75. Reduction of the mutation number to 0.01 allowed to cut iteration number to 50 (Fig.6,c).

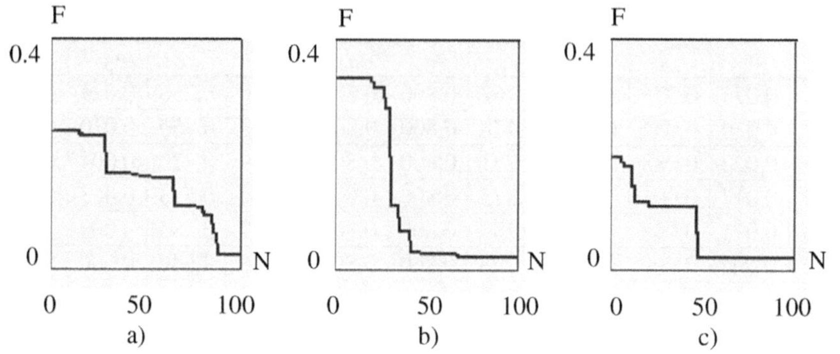

Fig. 6. Dependence of optimization criterion (*F*) on iteration number (*N*) under conditions of various parameters of genetic algorithm a) $p_c = 0.6$, $p_m = 0.02$; b) $p_c = 0.3$, $p_m = 0.02$; c) $p_c = 0.3$, $p_m = 0.01$

7 Conclusion

Application of fuzzy relations expert matrix to restore and identify the causes by observed effects requires fuzzy logical equations system solution. In this study the search for equations system solution amounts to optimization problem. Optimization algorithm is based on solution amounts coding and on the application of genetic operations of cross-over, mutation and selection to them. The suggested here genetic algorithm can find application in expert systems of diagnosis and quality control.

References

1. Zimmermann, H.-J.: Fuzzy Set Theory and Its Applications. Kluwer, Dordrecht (1991)
2. Zadeh, L.: The Concept of Linguistic Variable ant It Application to Approximate Decision Making. M.: Mir (1976) (in Russian)
3. Rotshtein, A.P.: Medical Diagnostics on Fuzzy Logic. Vinnitsa: Kontinent-Prim (1996) (in Russian)
4. Asai, K., Sugano, M., Tarano, T.: Applied Fuzzy Systems. M.: Mir (1993) (in Russian)
5. Rotshtein, A.: Design and Tuning of Fuzzy Rule-Based Systems for Medical Diagnostics. In: N.-H. Teodorescu A. Kandel (ed): Fuzzy and Neuro-Fuzzy Systems in Medicine. CRC Press (1998) 243-289
6. Rotshtein, A.P.: Intellectual Technologies of Identification: Fuzzy Sets, Genetic Algorithms, Neural Nets. Vinnitsa: «UNIVERSUM» (1999) (in Russian)
7. Gen, M., Cheng, R.: Genetic Algorithms and Engineering Design. John Wiley & Sons (1997)
8. Rotshtein, A.: Modification of Saaty Method for the Construction of Fuzzy Set Membership Functions. In: FUZZY'97 – International Conference «Fuzzy Logic and Its Applications». Zichron, Israel (1997) 125-130

Diagnosis Based on Genetic Algorithms and Fuzzy Logic in NPPs

Yangping Zhou, Xiang Fang, and Bingquan Zhao

Institute of Nuclear Energy Technology, Tsinghua University, Beijing 100084, People's Republic China
bingquan@inet.tsinghua.edu.cn

Abstract. There is an increasing trend toward introducing artificial intelligence into the fault diagnosis of nuclear power plants. However, processing imperfect information and uncertainty is the art of the fault diagnosis. This paper describes a fault diagnosis method based on genetic algorithms and fuzzy logic. This method utilizes the strings in genetic algorithms to simulate the various possible assemblies of results and updates the results with the evaluation. A new evaluation method in genetic algorithms is adopted. When calculating the fitness of strings, fuzzy logic is used to process the multi-knowledge: expert knowledge, mini-knowledge tree model and standard signals. Experiments on simulator show the advantages of this method in processing illusive and real-time signals, imperfect diagnosis knowledge and other instances.

1 Introduction

It is very important that the operators in the control room of nuclear power plants (NPPs) quickly and correctly judge the real fault cause of the abnormality and take the correct actions in time to reduce its consequence. There is an increasing trend toward introducing artificial intelligence into the fault diagnosis of NPPs [1,2].

The Genetic Algorithm (GA) described by Holland [3], aims to increase the average fitness of the individuals over a number of generations. Because of its effectiveness in solving a wide variety of complex problems [4], it has been quite successfully applied to optimal control [5], classification [6], fault diagnosis [7].

The theory of fuzzy logic formulated by Zadeh has been considered as an appropriate presentation method for uncertainty, imprecision and incompleteness. Fuzzy systems have been successfully used in many applications including recognition of handwriting [8], diagnosis [9], and other instances. The genetic-fuzzy approach is successfully used in mobile robot navigation [10], model and control system [11].

Based on Genetic Algorithms and Fuzzy Logic, A method of fault diagnosis that is processing related, uncertainty and fuzzy is introduced in the presented paper. This method utilizes the strings in GA to simulate the various possible assemblies of result. Restricted by the variational signals, the strings changed with the process of mutation, crossover and selection.

L. Monostori, J. Váncza, and M. Ali (Eds.): IEA/AIE 2001, LNAI 2070, pp. 359-366, 2001.

This method of fault diagnosis offers some advantage over other classical diagnostic methods, e.g. processing imperfect knowledge over rule-based systems and model-based systems. In addition, it is a more effective method to integrate multi-knowledge than that of normal method. Furthermore, it is easy to add other model-based knowledge to this method because of use of Fuzzy Logic.

2 Introduction of Method

This method is applied in the fault diagnosis on the simulator of Beijing NPPs simulation training center. The flow chart of the diagnosis process is shown in Fig.1. The entire process consists of seven parts: initializing strings, database, calculating fitness, evolution process (crossover, mutation and selection), termination, and getting result.

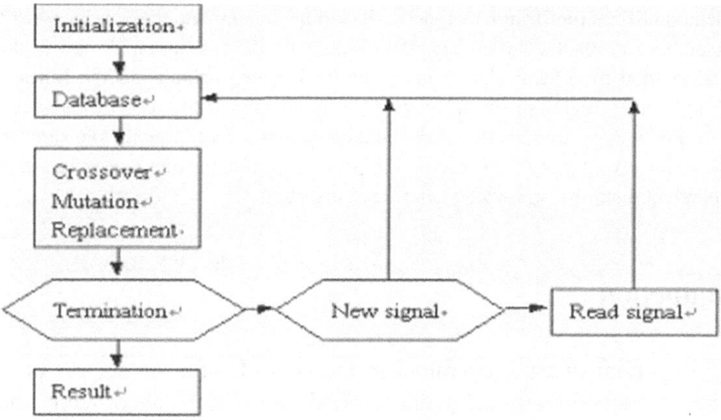

Fig. 1. The flow chart of diagnosis process

2.1 Initializing Strings

In fault diagnosis, we use the bit value of a string to denote one fault happens or not. For example, the value 1 or 0 of a bit denotes the corresponding fault takes place or not. Suppose the total number of the system faults is n, hence the string whose length is n bits can denote the state of the system. Usually only one or several faults will happen at the same time and we suppose that the max number is m, so the state of the system has C_n^m different instances. C_n^m is a big number when n is large. If one string denotes only one possible instance, then a lot of strings denoting the various result of fault diagnosis must be needed. A new method to initialize the strings is proposed: some (suppose the number is d) bits are set to be 1. In this method the possible result instances, which a string can denote, are C_n^d / C_n^m .

2.2 Database

The database consists of the expert knowledge, the mini-knowledge model knowledge [1] and the normal signals produced by the simulator. The structure of the database is shown in Fig. 2. The knowledge base can be divided into four parts: signal table, event table, knowledge base of initial events, and knowledge base of non-initial events.

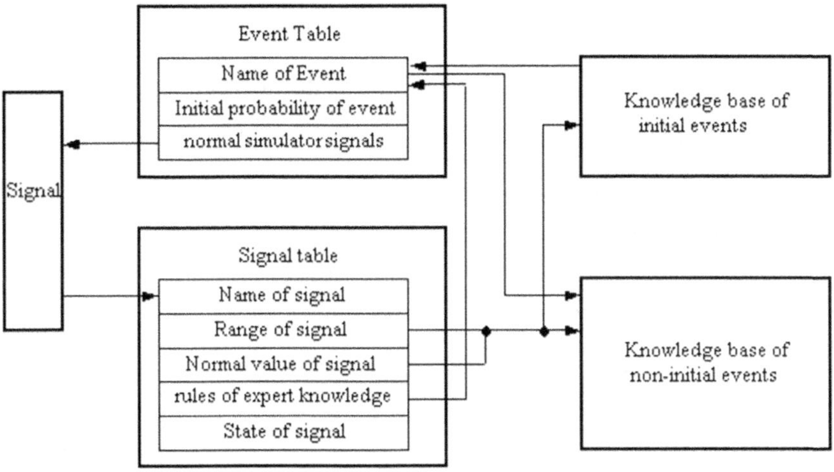

Fig. 2. The structure of the database

The signal table includes signal's name, range, normal value, normal state range and direct corresponding event. The event table consists of event's name, initial probability and feedback to signals. The knowledge base of the initial events is used to describe the various possible reasons of an initial abnormal signal. It consists of some text files. The content of the files is the name and the probability of the faults. The knowledge base of the non-initial events is used to describe the various possible reasons of an abnormal signal, which is not accord with the expected signals.

2.3 Calculating Fitness

We use fuzzy integrated evaluation to calculate the fitness based on a four factors (I, N, S, A) model. The fitness function is:

$$A_j = [I_j \; N_j \; S_j \; A_j^*] \times \begin{bmatrix} a_1 \\ a_2 \\ a_3 \\ a_4 \end{bmatrix}. \tag{1}$$

a_1, a_2, a_3, and a_4 are importance measure of each factor.

$$\sum_{i=1}^{4} a_i = 1 \qquad a_i \geq 0 . \tag{2}$$

I_j is the effect of the initial event in the jth string. The effect of the initial event consists of the expert knowledge and the initial event base of the mini-knowledge tree model.

$$I_j = \sum_{i=1}^{n}((\sum_{k=1}^{m} I_{ik}) \cdot \delta_i + (1-\delta_i) \cdot | \lg P_i |) \tag{3}$$

δ_i is the bit value of a string's i^{th} bit; I_{ik} is the probability that the kth signal connects to the ith fault in initial knowledge base; P_i is the initial probability of the ith fault (here P_i is about 10^{-n} $(2<n<7)$); m is the serial of the signal and *n* is the serial of the fault in the system.

S_j is the feedback that the faults give to the signals in the jth string. S_j is obtained from the normal signals in the simulator.

$$S_j = \sum_{i=1}^{n}(\delta_i \cdot \sum_{k=1}^{m} s_k) . \tag{4}$$

Here, s_k is the feedback value which i^{th} fault gives to k^{th} signal. If the kth expected signal of the ith fault coincides with the kth actual signal, s_k is positive, otherwise it is negative. s_k is different according to the degree which they are coincident or not.

N_j is the effect, which the non-initial event gives to the fitness of jth string. N_j can be obtained from the non-initial event base of the mini-knowledge tree model.

$$N_j = \sum_{l}\sum_{p}((\delta_l \cdot \delta_p) \cdot N_{lp}) . \tag{5}$$

δ_l is the bit value of a string's l^{th} bit and δ_p is the bit value of a string's p^{th} bit. N_{lp} denotes the non-initial probability of the lth fault (initial event) and the pth fault (non-initial event) in non-initial knowledge base.

A_j^* is an adjustment to the fitness of the jth string.

2.4 Evolution Process

Crossover, mutation and selection are three basic processes in GA. The process of crossover, mutation, and selection, which is restricted by the signals and the database, changes the strings to march the fault.

When processing the replacement scheme, we use a new method named direct compare replacement. This method puts the new strings and the old strings together and selects the better bit directly according to the fitness of every two bit. After the replacement scheme, there are 400 strings in the new population. The process of the GA is shown in Fig. 3.

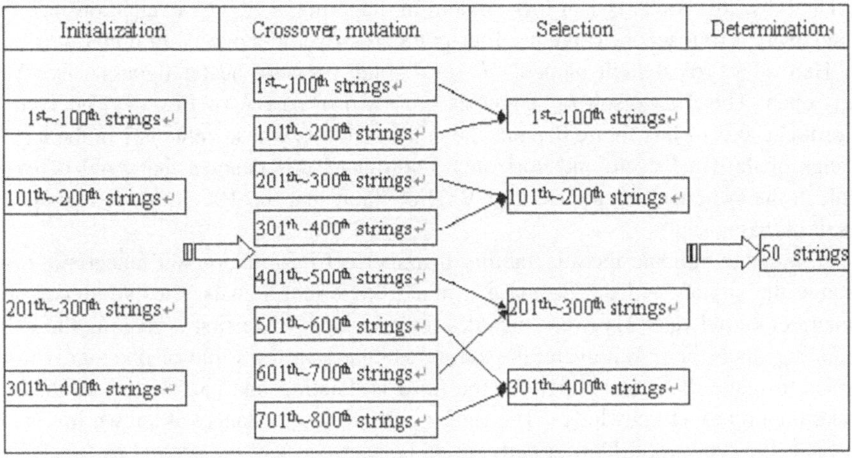

Fig. 3. The process of GA in this method

The direct compare replacement has the following advantages. Firstly, the time that the direct compare replacement costs is much less than that of the normal replacement. It will accelerate the process of fault diagnosis. Second, because the occurrence of the signals is not instant but progressive, the direct compare replacement can prevent the strings, which do not include the fault, getting predominate when the number of abnormal signals is not enough to diagnosis fault.

2.5 Terminations and Getting Result

Fault diagnosis in NPPs is very different from traditional optimization problems in termination. In typical optimization problems we can terminate the GA process when one string fits for the condition. In fault diagnosis, we cannot get this string because of the special initialization. When determining the fault diagnosis finish or not, we count the number of every bit whose value is 1 in the 50 strings gotten through the direct compare replacement. There are two cases: (1) the number of one bit whose value is 1 gets predominance in continuous several cycles; (2) the number of several bits whose values are 1 get predominance in continuous several cycles. In the first case, the fault that the bit denotes is the result; in the second case, the several faults that the several bits denote are the result.

3 Application of Method

Experimentation of fault diagnosis is carried out in the secondary loop of the 950MW full size simulator in Beijing NPPs simulation training center. The simulator produces signals every four seconds. There are 128 supposable faults in the second loop of the simulator. The length of each string is 128 bits and the number of the initial strings is 400. In each string there are 40 bits whose values are 1, and 88 bits whose values are 0. The bit whose value is 1 or 0 is random in the string. Two GA evaluations are finished every 4 four seconds. We use four-point crossover and one-point mutation.

Here is a typical fault named "V31FO": high pressure heater bypass valve V31 fails open. The final result of diagnosis is shown in part A of Fig. 4[1]. The vertical coordinate axis of this figure denotes the number of bits whose value is 1 in the last 50 strings of the final cycle and horizontal coordinate axis denotes the serial of every fault in the system. We can see the "V31FO" fault that the 108th fault denotes is the result of diagnosis.

In order to validate the adaptability to imperfect information and uncertainty, we change the signals and the database to make imperfect signals, illusive signals and imperfect knowledge. The work includes three instances: the first is making the value of all signals to be 0 in a cycle; the second is changing the value of one signal in all cycles to make the illusive signals; the third is deleting one part of the database to make the imperfect knowledge. The final result of these instances is shown in Fig. 4[1]: part B is the process of the first part; part C is the process of the second part; part D is the process of the third part. We can find the 108th fault is the right result from the final result of GA.

In addition we change some parameters of GA to see the variation of the process and the result in diagnosis. The result is shown in Table 1 when the strings' number is changed. Table 2 is the result when the evaluation number of each cycle is changed. The result is gotten as Table 3 when we change the strings' number that we get result from.

Table 1. Result changing strings number

Num. Strings	200	400	800
Get right result	×	v	v
Fulfil time require	v	v	×

Table 2. Result changing evaluation number in every cycle

Num. Evaluation	1	2	4	Much more
Get right result	×	v	v	×
Fulfil time require	v	v	v	×

Table 3. Result when changing string number which get result from

Num. Strings	25	50	100	400
Get right result	×	v	v	×
Fulfil time require	v	v	v	v

Table 4. The best parameter in GA

Num. Strings	Num. Evaluation	Num. Strings get result
400	2	50

We find the evaluation usually goes to local optimum due to the large evaluation numbers when the abnormal signals is not enough to diagnosis. Because the signals of the simulator change every 4 seconds, we must finish the whole GA process in the same time. According to these tables we get the best parameters in Table 4. From this table, we can see the speed of GA is twice every 4 seconds.

[1] Fig. 4 is shown in Appendx.

4 Conclusion and Further Work

- This method improves the GA according to the actual problem. There is no additional restriction when GA is used to resolve the problem. We can choose the concrete mode of fitness calculation, selection, termination, and other instances.
- This method has preferable ability to deal with the non-numerical problem and has some good characteristic in ANN. After the process of the GA, all strings are used to get the result. This utilizes the information in the strings efficiently and improves the ability to deal with the problem.
- Integrate the GA and Fuzzy Logic, this method can deal with the signals changed with time, uncertainty and fuzzy in the fault diagnosis of NPPs.
- Because how to use the strings to model the state of the system determines the efficiency and speed that the method resolves the problem, it will be discussed furthermore.
- The 0/1-encoded method is adopted in this paper. Different encoded method will be discussed in future work.

References

1. Qin, Zhang., Xuegao, An., Jin, Gu., Bingquan, Zhao., Dazhi, Xu., Shuren, Xi.: Application of FBOLES--Prototype Expert System for Fault Diagnosis in Nuclear Power Plants. Reliability Engineering and System Safety, Vol. 44. (1994) 225-235
2. Uhrig, Robert E., Tsoukalas, Lefteri H.: Soft Computing Technologies Nuclear Engineering Applications. Process in Nuclear Energy, Vol. 34(1). (1999) 13-75
3. HOLLAND, J. H.: Genetic Algorithms. Scientific America, Vol. 267. (1992) 66-72
4. K,F, Man., K,S, Tang., S, Kwong.: Genetic algorithms: concepts and designs. Springer, London; New York (1999)
5. Dipankar, D.: Evolving Neuro-Controllers for a Dynamic System Using Structured Genetic Algorithms. Applied Intelligence, Vol. 8. (1998) 113-121
6. Peter, K. S., Robin, P. G.: Efficient GA Based Techniques for Classification. Applied Intelligence, Vol. 11. (1999) 277-284
7. Fushuan, Wen., Zhenxiang, Han.: Fault section estimation in power systems using genetic algorithm. Electric Power Systems Research, Vol. 34(3). (1995) 165-172
8. Lee, H.M., Sheu, C.C., Chen, J.M.: Handwritten Chinese character recognition based on primitive and fuzzy features via the SEART neural net model. Applied Intelligence, Vol. 8. (1998) 269-285
9. Yi, L., Tie, Q. C.: A Fuzzy Diagnostic Model and Its Application in Automotive Engineering Diagnosis. Applied Intelligence, Vol. 9. (1998) 231-243
10. Dilip, K. P., Kalyanmoy, D., Amitabha, G., A genetic-fuzzy approach for mobile robot navigation among moving obstacles. International Journal of Approximate Reasoning, Vol. 20. (1999)
11. Wael A. Farag., Victor H. Quintana., Germano Lambert-Torres.: A Genetic-Based Neuro-Fuzzy Approach for Modeling and Control of Dynamical Systems. IEEE Transaction on Neural Network, Vol. 9(5). (1998) 756-767

Appendix: Fig. 4.

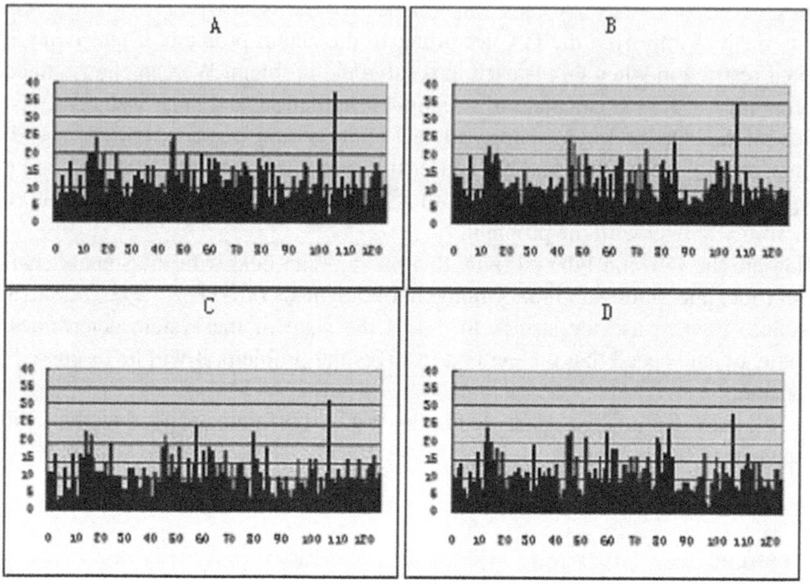

Fig. 4. The final result of GA in various instances

Vagueness in Spatial Data: Rough Set and Egg-Yolk Approaches

Theresa Beaubouef [1] and Frederick Petry [2]

[1]Computer Science Department, Southeastern La. University, Hammond, LA 70402 USA
tbeaubouef@selu.edu
[2]Elect. Eng. and Computer Science Dept., Tulane University, New Orleans, LA 70118 USA

Abstract. Uncertainty management is necessary for real world applications, especially spatial data and geographic information systems. The egg-yolk method has proven useful for representing vague regions in spatial data. Rough sets have been shown to be an effective tool for data mining and uncertainty management in databases. In this initial work, we apply rough set definitions for topological relationships previously defined for the egg-yolk method for continuous space. We show that rough sets can be used to express and improve on topological relationships and concepts defined with the egg-yolk model, and extend it to work for discrete space through the use of rough set indiscernibility.

1 Introduction

A spatial database is a collection of data concerning objects located in some reference space in the real world, which abounds in uncertainty. Any attempt to model aspects of the world should include some mechanism for incorporating uncertainty. There may be uncertainty in the understanding of the enterprise, in the data, or in the model, which leads to uncertainty in entities or the attributes describing them. At a higher level, there may be uncertainty about the level of uncertainty prevalent in the various aspects of the database.

In relational databases we have shown that uncertainty may be managed via rough set techniques by incorporating rough sets into the underlying data model [1] and through rough querying of crisp data [2]. In a previous work [3], we pointed out those areas of spatial databases and GIS [4] that are in need of uncertainty management, and suggested ways in which rough sets may be used to alleviate problems, resulting in a better overall system. In this paper we focus on the problem of uncertainty in topological structures in spatial data, and in particular, to spatial regions with uncertain boundaries. We investigate the application of rough sets [5] for improving the egg-yolk model [6,7], and extending it from continuous to discrete space via rough set indiscernibility.

2 Background: Rough Sets, Data, and Granularity

Rough set theory, introduced by Pawlak [5] and discussed in greater detail in [8,9], is a technique for dealing with uncertainty and for identifying cause-effect relationships in

L. Monostori, J. Váncza, and M. Ali (Eds.): IEA/AIE 2001, LNAI 2070, pp. 367-373, 2001.

databases as a form of database learning [10]. It has also been used for improved information retrieval [11] and for uncertainty management in relational databases [1,2].

Rough sets involve the following:

> *U* is the *universe*, which cannot be empty,
> *R* is the *indiscernibility relation*, or equivalence relation,
> $A = (U,R)$, an ordered pair, is called an *approximation space*,
> $[x]_R$ denotes the equivalence class of *R* containing *x*, for any element *x* of *U*,
> *elementary sets* in A - the equivalence classes of R,
> *definable set* in A - any finite union of elementary sets in A.

An approximation space defined on universe U with equivalence relation R partitions U into equivalence classes called elementary sets that may be used to define other sets in A. Given that $X \subseteq U$, X can be defined in terms of the definable sets in A by the following:

> *lower approximation of X in A* is the set $\underline{R}X = \{x \in U \mid [x]_R \subseteq X\}$
>
> *upper approximation of X in A* is the set $\overline{R}X = \{x \in U \mid [x]_R \cap X \neq \emptyset\}$.

Another way to describe the set approximations is as follows. Given the upper and lower approximations $\overline{R}X$ and $\underline{R}X$, of X a subset of U, the R-positive region of X is $POS_R(X) = \underline{R}X$, the R-negative region of X is $NEG_R(X) = U - \overline{R}X$, and the boundary or R-borderline region of X is $BN_R(X) = \overline{R}X - \underline{R}X$. X is called R-definable if and only if $\underline{R}X = \overline{R}X$. Otherwise, $\underline{R}X \neq \overline{R}X$ and X is rough with respect to R. In Figure 1 the universe U is partitioned into equivalence classes denoted by the rectangles. Those elements in the lower approximation of X, $POS_R(X)$, are denoted with the letter P and elements in the R-negative region by the letter N. All other classes belong to the boundary region of the upper approximation.

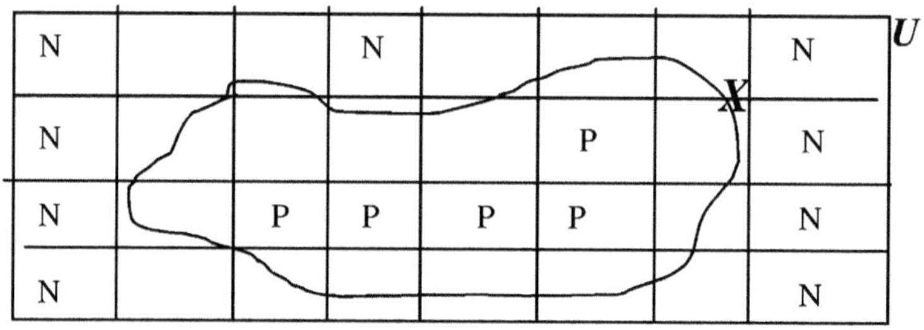

Fig. 1. Example of a rough set X

The indiscernibility relation partitions domains into equivalence classes and the lower and upper approximation regions allow the distinction between certain and possible, or partial, inclusion in a rough set. The indiscernibility relation allows grouping of items based on some definition of 'equivalence' as it relates to the application domain. We may use this partitioning to increase or decrease the granularity of a domain, to group items considered indiscernible for a given purpose, or to "bin" ordered domains into ranges.

In order to allow *possible* results, in addition to the typical results of querying, we may employ the use of the boundary region information in addition to that of the positive region. The results in the positive region are certain, and correspond to exact matches. The boundary region contains those results that are possible, but not certain.

Uncertainty prevails in all types of databases systems. Spatial databases and GIS contain descriptive as well as positional data. The various forms of uncertainty may occur in both types of data, so many of the issues discussed below apply to ordinary databases as well [1,2]. These same techniques, including integration of data from multiple sources, time-variant data, uncertain data, imprecision in measurement, inconsistent wording of descriptive data, and the "binning" or grouping of data into fixed categories, may also be employed for spatial contexts [3].

Often spatial data is associated with a particular grid. The positions are set up in a regular matrix-like structure and data is affiliated with point locations on the grid. There is a tradeoff between the resolution or scale of the grid and the amount of system resources necessary to store and process the data. Higher resolutions provide more information, but at a cost of memory space and execution time.

If we approach the data from a rough set point of view, we can see that there is indiscernibility inherent in the process of gridding or rasterizing data. A data item at a particular grid point in essence may represent data near the point as well. This is due to the fact that often point data must be mapped to the grid using techniques such as nearest-neighbor, averaging, or statistics. We may set up our rough set indiscernibility relation so that the entire spatial area is partitioned into equivalence classes where each point on the grid belongs to a class. If we change the resolution of the grid, we change the granularity of the partitioning, resulting in fewer, but larger classes.

The approximation regions of rough sets come into play when information concerning sizes, lengths, and other areal properties of spatial data features are calculated or displayed. This uncertainty maps naturally to the use of the approximation regions of the rough set theory, where the lower approximation region represents certain data and the boundary region represents uncertain data.

If we force a finer granulation of the partitioning (increase grid resolution) a smaller boundary region results. As the partitioning becomes finer, eventually a point is reached where the boundary region is non-existent. In this case, the upper and lower approximation regions are the same—there is no uncertainty in the spatial data.

The egg-yolk method [6] for vague regions in spatial data also uses two levels for outlining the vague boundary. These regions, called the yolk and the egg, basically correspond to the lower and upper approximation regions, respectively, of the rough set theory. The egg-yolk method, however, has no facility for partitioning the domain into equivalence classes, as does the rough sets indiscernibility relation. In fact, Roy and Stell [12] discuss the shortcomings of the egg-yolk method if it is to be applied to discrete rather than continuous space. They suggest that the egg-yolk method can be used in a multi-resolution context for a finite level of precision and that an extension to the framework may be appropriate. The idea that rough sets can, in fact, improve on this framework is the motivation behind this research.

3 Topological Uncertainty in Spatial Data

In GIS or spatial databases, it is often the case that we need information concerning the relative distances of objects. Is object A *adjacent to* object B? Or, is object A *near* object B? The first question appears to be fairly straightforward. The system must simply check all the edges of both objects to see if any parts of them are coincident. This gives the *certain* results. However, often in GIS, data is input either automatically via scanners or digitized by humans, and in both cases it is easy for error in position of data objects to occur. Therefore, we may also want to have the system check to see if object B is very near object A, to derive the *possible* result. If so, the user could be informed that "it is not certain, but it is possible, that A is adjacent to B." Assume we want to know whether a cliff is next to the sea. If the system returns the results that it is possible, but not certain, that the cliff is adjacent to the sea, we may be led to investigate the influence of the tides in the area to determine whether low beaches alongside the cliffs are exposed at low tide.

The concepts of connection and overlap can likewise be managed by rough sets. Connection is similar to adjacency, but related to line type objects instead of area objects. Overlap can be defined in a manner similar to that of nearness with the user deciding how much overlap is required for the lower approximation. Coincidence of a single point may constitute *possible* overlap, as can very close proximity of two objects, if there is a high degree of positional error involved in the data.

Inclusion is also related to overlap. If an object A is completely surrounded by some object B, we may conclude certainly that A is included in B, lacking additional information. If A and B overlap, then it is possible that one object includes the other. Approximation regions can be defined to reflect these concepts as well.

Both rough set and egg-yolk approaches are useful for managing topological uncertainty and vagueness such as nearness, contiguity, connection, orientation, inclusion, and overlap of spatial entities. We consider next some of the topological relationships associated with vague regions and how they relate to each other.

4 Egg-Yolk Approach

If we are only concerned about the vagueness of boundaries, we may be inclined to use the egg-yolk approach. In this approach concentric subregions make up a vague region, with inner subregions having the property that they are 'crisper' than outer subregions. These regions indicate a type of membership in the vague region. The simplest case, is that of two subregions. In this most common case, the center region is known as the yolk, the outer region surrounding the yolk is known as the white, and the entire region, as the egg.

The yolk and egg correspond to the boundary regions of rough set theory, which has only two approximation regions, unlike the possible numerous subregions that may make up a vague region in the egg-yolk method. However, because of the rough set indiscernibility relation, one can vary the partitioning to increase or decrease the level of uncertainty present, which results in changes to the approximation regions.

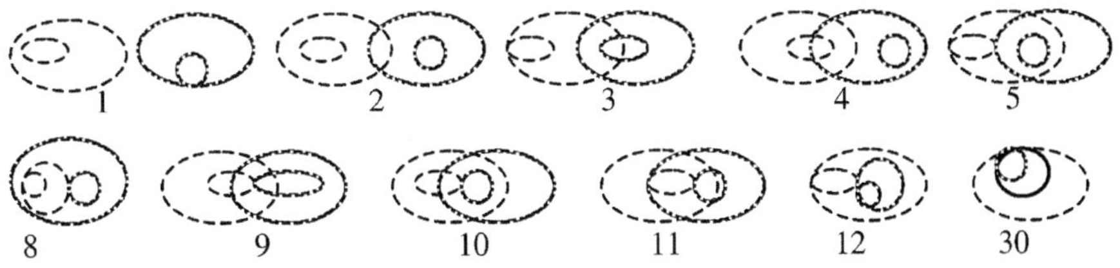

Fig. 2. A sample of the 46 possible relationships between regions X (dashed line) and Y (dotted line). See [7] for the complete listing.

Consider specifically the results of [7]. They delineate 46 possible egg-yolk pairs (see Fig. 2), showing all of the possible relationships between two vague regions. They then relate the egg-yolk configurations to dyadic relations of the type C(x,y), meaning "C connects x with y", of their RCC-5 theory of spatial regions. The RCC-5 relations include DR (Distinct Regions with no overlap), EQ (Equal: the regions are the same), PO (the regions Partially Overlap), PP (Proper Part: the first region is entirely contained within the second), and PPI (Proper Part Inverse: the first region entirely contains the second). For egg-yolk pairs a yolk is a PP of its own egg.

The 46 configurations of egg-yolk pairs were then clustered into 13 groups based on RCC-5 relations between complete crispings (Fig. 3). A configuration of a cluster can be crisped to the cluster pointed to by the arrow via one of the relationships.

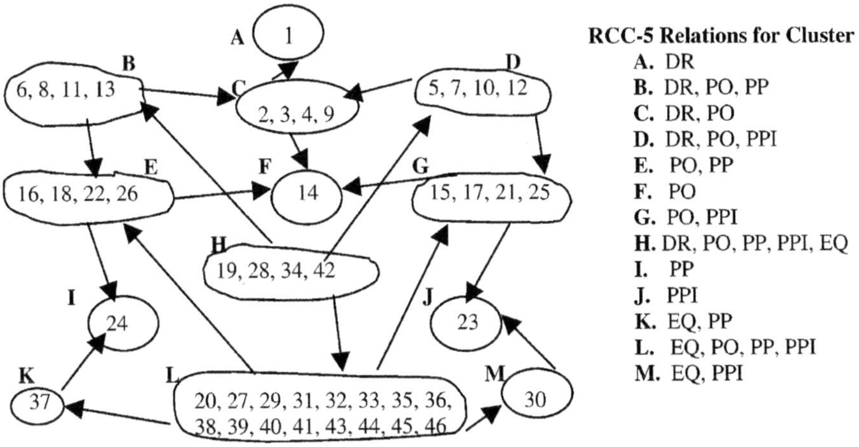

Fig. 3. Clustering of the 46 relations [7] using RCC-5 relations between complete crispings of the configurations. No hierarchy or order within the clusters is shown here for simplification

5 Rough Set Approach to Egg-Yolk Clustering

We now re-examine the clustering of egg-yolk pairs, noting the relationships for each cluster based on principles from rough sets. Recall that "crisping" from the egg-yolk theory can be related to forcing a finer partitioning on the domain for rough sets. We first review some rough set definitions that will be used in categorizing the clusters:

Two rough sets X and Y are equal, $X = Y$, if $\underline{R}X = \underline{R}Y$ and $\overline{R}X = \overline{R}Y$.

The intersection of two rough sets is defined by the approximation regions as follows: $\underline{R}(X \cap Y) = \underline{R}X \cap \underline{R}Y$, and $\overline{R}(X \cap Y) = \overline{R}X \cap \overline{R}Y$.

The subset relationship, $X \subset Y$ implies that $\underline{R}X \subset \underline{R}Y$ and $\overline{R}X \subset \overline{R}Y$.

Now look again at Fig. 3, but this time approach the clusters in terms of rough sets. Let X denote the first egg (dashed line) and Y denote the second egg (dotted line) in each egg pair. We see that the following hold for the clusters:

A. $X \cap Y = \emptyset$. **B.** $\underline{R}X \cap \underline{R}Y = \emptyset$; $\overline{R}X \cap \overline{R}Y \neq \emptyset$; $\underline{R}X \subset \overline{R}Y$.

C. $\underline{R}X \cap \underline{R}Y = \emptyset$; $\overline{R}X \cap \overline{R}Y \neq \emptyset$. **D.** $\underline{R}X \cap \underline{R}Y = \emptyset$; $\overline{R}X \cap \overline{R}Y \neq \emptyset$; $\underline{R}Y \subset \overline{R}X$.

E. $\underline{R}X \cap \underline{R}Y \neq \emptyset$; $\overline{R}X \cap \overline{R}Y \neq \emptyset$; $\underline{R}X \cap \overline{R}Y \neq \emptyset$; $\overline{R}X \cap \underline{R}Y \neq \emptyset$; $\underline{R}X \subset \overline{R}Y$.

F. $X \cap Y \neq \emptyset$; $X \neq Y$.

G. $\underline{R}X \cap \underline{R}Y \neq \emptyset$; $\overline{R}X \cap \overline{R}Y \neq \emptyset$; $\underline{R}X \cap \overline{R}Y \neq \emptyset$; $\overline{R}X \cap \underline{R}Y \neq \emptyset$; $\underline{R}Y \subset \overline{R}X$.

H. $\underline{R}X \subset \overline{R}X \cap \overline{R}Y$; $\underline{R}Y \subset \overline{R}X \cap \overline{R}Y$. **I.** $\overline{R}X \subset \underline{R}Y$. **J.** $\overline{R}Y \subset \underline{R}X$. **K.** $\overline{R}X = \underline{R}Y$.

L. $\underline{R}X \cap \underline{R}Y \neq \emptyset$; $\underline{R}X \subset \overline{R}Y$; $\underline{R}Y \subset \overline{R}X$; $\overline{R}X \cap \overline{R}Y \neq \emptyset$. **M.** $\overline{R}Y = \underline{R}X$.

A comparison of the rough set relationships expressed for each cluster with the RCC relationships denoted for the clusters in Figure 3 reveals similar properties.

6 Conclusion

Spatial information systems will continue to play an ever-increasing role in spatial data applications. Uncertainty management is necessary for any of these applications, and both rough sets and egg-yolk methods are appropriate for the representation of vague regions in spatial data. Rough sets, however, can also model indiscernibility and allow for the change of granularity of the partitioning through its indiscernibility relation, which has an effect on the boundaries of the vague regions, and also allows the extension of egg-yolk regions from continuous to discrete space.

We have shown how the clustering of egg-yolk pairs by RCC-5 relations can be expressed in terms of operations using rough sets. We believe that rough set techniques can further enhance the egg-yolk approach and are investigating the interrelationships between rough set, egg-yolk, and RCC models.

References

1. Beaubouef, T., Petry, F., Buckles, B., "Extension of the Relational Database and its Algebra with Rough Set Techniques," *Comp.Intelligence*, Vol. 11, No. 2 (May 1995) 233-245
2. Beaubouef, T., Petry, F., "Rough Querying of Crisp Data in Relational Databases," *Third Int. Workshop on Rough Sets and Soft Computing (RSSC'94)*, San Jose (1994)

3. Beaubouef, T., Petry, F., Breckenridge, J.,"Rough Set Based Uncertainty Management for Spatial Databases and Geographical Information Systems," in *Soft Computing in Industrial Applications* (ed. Y. Suzuki), Springer-Verlag, London (2000)
4. Laurini, R., Thompson, D., *Fundamentals of Spatial Information Systems*, Academic Press, London (1992)
5. Pawlak, Z., "Rough Sets," *Int. J. of Man-Machine Studies*, vol. 21 (1984) 127-134
6. Lehmann, F., Cohn, A. "The EGG/YOLK reliability hierarchy: Semantic data integration using sorts with prototypes," *Proc. 3rd Int. Conf. on Information and Knowledge Management*, Gaithersburg, MD (1994) 272-279
7. Cohn, A., Gotts, N., "The 'Egg-Yolk' Representation of Regions with Indeterminate Boundaries," in *Geographic Objects with Indeterminate Boundaries* (ed. P. Burrough and A. Frank), GISDATA II, European Science Foundation, chapter 12 (1996)
8. Pawlak, Z., *Rough Sets: Theoretical Aspects of Reasoning about Data*, Kluwer Academic Publishers, Norwell, MA (1991)
9. Komorowski, J., Pawlak, Z., Polkowski, L., et. al., "Rough Sets: A Tutorial," in *Rough Fuzzy Hybridization: A New Trend in Decision-Making* (ed. S. K. Pal and A. Skowron), Springer-Verlag, Singapore, (1999) 3-98
10. Slowinski, R., "A Generalization of the Indiscernibility Relation for Rough Sets Analysis of Quantitative Information," *First Int. Workshop on Rough Sets*, Poland (1992)
11. Srinivasan, P., "The importance of rough approximations for information retrieval," *International Journal of Man-Machine Studies*, 34, (1991) 657-671
12. Roy, A. Stell, J., "Spatial Relations Between Indeterminate Regions," (submitted for publication), http://www.keele.ac.uk/depts/cs/gis, (March, 2000)

Dynamic Trait Expression for Multiploid Individuals of Evolutionary Algorithms

Clinton Woodward and Tim Hendtlass

Centre for Intelligent Systems and Complex Processes
School of Biophysical Science and Electrical Engineering
Swinburne University of Technology
Victoria 3122 Australia
Fax: +61 3 9819 6443
{cjw,thendtlass}@swin.edu.au

Abstract. The use of multiploid structures for individuals in evolutionary algorithms has been shown to have the advantage of including redundant information, increasing population diversity and in some cases improving non-stationary function optimisation performance. These advantages can translate into improved avoidance of premature convergence and an ability to cope with complex problems. However, as multiple information for the same trait is available, a method of gene selection or activation is required. This paper describes a dynamic decision method for gene selection, presents proof of concept results for this type of structure and outlines proposed benefits and applications.

1. Introduction

Evolutionary algorithms (EA), of which genetic algorithms (GA) are a form, are used for many search and optimisation applications [7]. However, one of the problems of many applications is the occurrence of premature convergence to sub-optimal solutions, particularly for deceptive problems or high dimensional problem spaces [13], [23]. There are many EA/GA modifications that have been suggested and implemented to improve performance and avoidance of premature convergence [10]. For example, transformation of fitness functions by scaling and sharing [13], more effective selection mechanisms like generation gaps [8], ranking [1], island (sub) populations and distributed equlibria [3], [9], [28], and maintenance of diversity [23].

Multiploid representation (of which diploid is a multiploid structure of two chromosomes), along with the concepts of dominant and recessive genes, have been applied to artificial evolutionary algorithms before. See [13].

More recently, two main areas of work have been based around the avoidance of premature convergence [3], [15], [29], and applications to non-stationary fitness functions [14], [22], [24]. Other areas of multiploid applications include global optimisations [11], multi-criteria optimisation [26], modularity and neural networks [2] and spatial reasoning [25].

L. Monostori, J. Váncza, and M. Ali (Eds.): IEA/AIE 2001, LNAI 2070, pp. 374-382, 2001.

There are encouraging indicators from evolutionary biology and genetics that dynamic gene (trait) expression is an important and useful mechanism for rapid adaptation and robustness of biological systems. Investigations have presented evidence for gene regulatory mechanisms [17], and that the nature of gene expression can be represented as gene regulatory networks [19], Boolean systems and adaptive automata [20].

This paper is structured as follows. Section 2 contains an explanation of the dynamic expression method currently being used. Section 3 presents initial results from the implementation of this model, followed by a discussion (section 4) and concluding remarks (section 5).

2. Method

2.1 Explanation of the Model

The population of the evolutionary algorithm contains individuals that have multiple chromosomes. Multiple *trait types* are encoded along a single chromosome (eg weight, colour, shape). Each *trait instance* has two components; its *trait value* (eg red) and a *trait expression mechanism* (EM) (see figure 1). The trait expression mechanism used for the results presented here is a feed forward artificial neural network. However, the internal nature of the EM could be changed for different problems and be uniform or varied for each trait type or chromosome.

The network's number of hidden nodes and path weight values are evolved concurrently with the expressible trait values. For simplicity, each network's architecture is mostly fixed with a preset number of inputs, outputs and an upper limit for the number of hidden layer nodes.

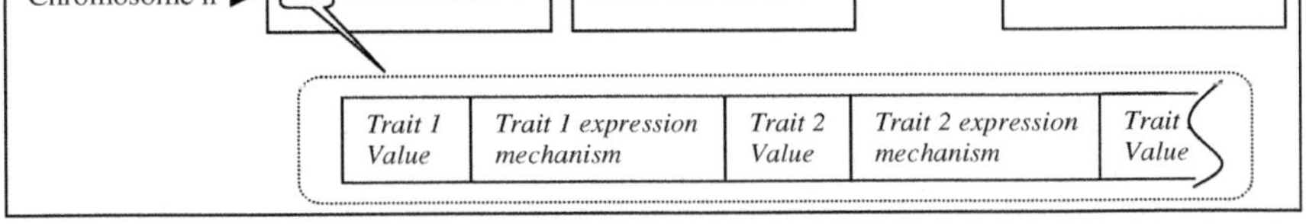

Fig. 1. Shows a population of N individuals, each with n chromosomes. Trait Values and Expression Mechanisms are encoded along each chromosome.

The structure of the finally expressed individual consists of a series of traits, each one chosen from the multiple values available for that trait type. One value for each trait type together with its EM, is stored on each chromosome of the individual. A method of trait value selection is therefore required to choose which trait value to express. This trait value selection process can also be referred to as trait dominance, with non-selected values considered recessive.

An exclusive selection method is used in this implementation. All EM instances of the same trait type contest with each other for the exclusive right to have their associated trait value expressed. Each EM generates an output based on the current input vector. The expression mechanism with the largest output of all expression mechanisms of that trait type 'wins', and its corresponding trait value is expressed.

Note that, in the work described here, an expression mechanism is only competing with expression mechanisms of the same trait type (eg. 'Colour' traits don't compete with 'height' traits), but inter-trait type interaction is a possible extension in future work. In a generalised sense, the expression mechanism can respond to any input from its environment, be it problem space input or alternatives like population fitness parameters (as in dominance change EA methods) or other currently expressed trait values.

2.2 Evolutionary Operators

When using multiploid structures most operators remain the same as those used for typical evolutionary algorithms. However, some operators need to be modified to work and some can be enhanced to make use of multiploid properties.

Population dynamics, that is the probabilistic selection of parents based on fitness or rank, the allocation of elites and steriles, and the replacement or generational addition of new individuals, are implemented as for typical evolutionary algorithms.

Selection pressure could be modified to take advantage of qualities other than fitness score, such as effective trait utilisation, to bias breeding probabilities. Strategies to encourage diversity (if desired) can be based on parent genotype diversity or recessive trait information (at computation expense).

Mutation effects can be hidden by the recessive properties of traits. How this modifies the effect of algorithm parameters such as mutation probability and mutation implementation varies dependent on the multiploid implementation used.

Reproduction and breeding operators are inherently non-standard for multiploid individuals. The crossover operator is a typical EA/GA method of recombining parent information to form children. This simplified analogy from biological systems does not include many of the processes necessary or possible for multiploid individuals.

Many multiploid biological species use a process of gametogenesis and fusion to generate children. Algorithmically, this is not necessary for an EA or GA breeding process. Children can be formed by a process of recombination that will 'pick and choose' genes from any parent and any chromosome. One point, two point, uniform crossover etc., can be emulated between any number of parents with multiple chromosomes.

However, given the nature of the implementation of traits, and that units of genes can posses a functional significance, it would seem prudent to investigate methods that can promote the reorganisation and recombination of these gene units. As an example, uniform crossover could cause a highly disruptive recombination of genes.

This may be very good for diversity, but possibly highly destructive to convergence performance.

The biologically inspired alternative to typical EA crossover is the generation of gametes through a process of artificial meiosis called gametogenesis. Each parent can generate multiple unique gametes, and each gamete, in a simple form, is an individual with a reduced number of chromosomes from its parent. For a two-parent scenario, a gamete will contain half the number of parent chromosomes. It is during the process of gametogenesis that biological crossover can occur, and thus is also possible in the artificial case.

In our artificial implementation, where we can use any number of parents in breeding, each gamete needs to contain an appropriately adjusted number of chromosomes. This requires special treatment in cases of odd numbers of parent chromosomes / breeding parent group combinations.

When gametes are combined through a process called fusion, the total number of chromosomes is that of a normal individual. Artificially, it is also possible to perform crossover at fusion instead of, or as well as, crossover during gametogenesis. Crossover during fusion would reorganise genes without altering gene frequencies. Work with artificial gametes or 'pseudo meiosis' has been investigated as part of diploid strategies to improve population diversity [29].

3. Proof of Concept Results

A population of multiploid individuals with dynamic trait expression mechanisms has been tested on various problems. These problems are of classification type, and of a visual nature to allow simple verification and analysis of results, however individuals are easily adapted for application to n-dimensional problem spaces.

The resultant information is presented as three columns of figures, each figure using the x and y-axes to represent input variables. Data sets are presented in the first column, the second column contains the output map of the best individual based on x and y input parameters and the third column shows trait instance usage (selection) where each region indicates a different trait instance.

Data Set Output Map Trait Usage Map

Fig. 2. The 9 point 'cross' problem.

Data Set Output Map Trait Usage Map

Fig. 3. The 9 point 'Y' problem.

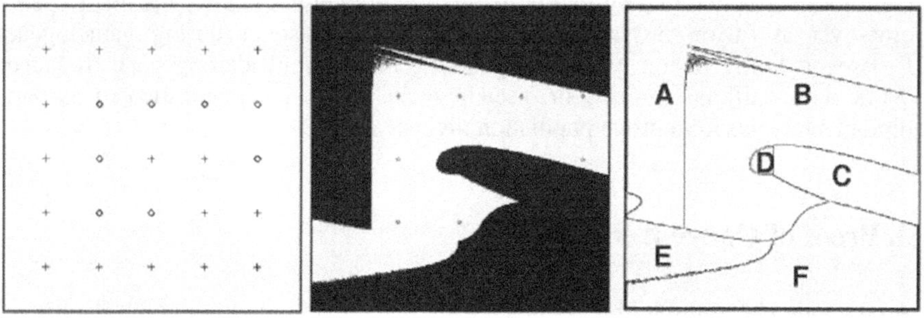

Data Set Output Map Trait Usage Map

Fig. 4. The 25 point 'hook' problem.

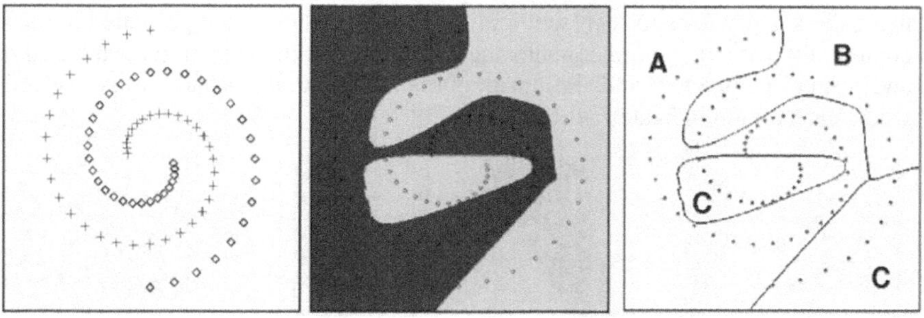

Data Set Output Map Trait Usage Map

Fig. 5. The reduced two spirals problem.

These results show trait decision maps containing straight line segments (fig 2), curved line segments (fig 4 & 5) and combinations of straight and curved lines that can result in the formation of simple and complex patterns (fig 4 & 5).

Some decision maps also display regions of bifurcation ('zig-zagged' or speckled regions) caused by accuracy quantisation (fig 4 & 5) of similar competing expression mechanisms.

From the trait maps we can see large regions intersected by small incursions of different trait types (fig 3). This would be an excellent situation for a modular decomposition of a problem where large generalised areas of similarity are divided by small exception rules.

4. Discussion

Multiploid individuals can have multiple trait values for the same trait type. A method of gene selection or activation is therefore required. The EM system described in this work has been shown as a novel and effective means of selecting trait values in multiploid individuals. Also, because of the nature of the EM's, this method can be used for the selection of traits in a dynamic fashion.

The fitness of an individual is based on its ability to express suitable trait values in response to the input vectors of the test data set. In the above cases, only one trait value (the colour in the output map) needs to be expressed for each input vector. To show the generalised expression of traits for an individual, sampling generates the "output map" and the "trait usage map" across the region of vector space. Each different area of the trait usage map represents a trait instance on a chromosome

Previous work using multiploid individuals in an EA have used simpler methods of determining trait expression and these expression mechanisms have typically been static. Work into changing dominance, or 'dynamic expression' as we refer to it, has been done with respect to a generation perspective - that is, dominance rules or methods may change between each generation [22], [24]. Our work has employed dynamic expression within the fitness performance of the individual. In this regard, individuals are similar to those in ALife research where each individual 'lives' in an environment.

Evolutionary selection pressure encourages the use of suitable trait values and the cooperation of trait expression mechanisms. In this regard the system is coevolving co-dependent aspects of the problem space.

The ability of the algorithm to created individuals with decision maps composed of many expression mechanism units is a very flexible method of solution formation. We believe the potential benefits of this type of algorithm are its good population diversity and avoidance of premature convergence, the inherent modular nature of solutions and the decomposition of problem spaces and the simultaneous evolution of trait values and trait decision surfaces.

With some local heuristic improvement, such as back-propagation and adjustment of estimated network error or directed random search adjustment of trait values, a hybrid system could improve solution convergence while the evolutionary properties of the system generate a diverse supply of new individuals.

Experiments show the application of individuals with dynamic trait expression to data set classification and the modular decomposition of problem spaces. The authors believe that these solutions could be used for rule extraction or generalisation of data sets. There are many problems that are modular in nature, including control systems, schedule allocations and genetic programming. In general, possible applications are problems that may be enhanced by a solution that is modular in nature.

As there is an inherent additional operator cost for the multiploid dynamic expression model, it is reasonable to expect that the application of this method is not suitable as a general search or optimisation tool. It is more likely to expect that this method will have a specific advantage for a particular type of application, as the No Free Lunch (NFL) theorem postulates [27]. However, through further investigation and adaptation it should be possible to improve the robustness of this method to make it more applicable for a wider range of problem types.

The ability of this evolutionary algorithm to find solutions, and the nature of those solutions, appears to closely depend on the amount of resources available. Specifically, resources are population size and diversity, the number of chromosomes per individual, and the number of genes per chromosome. An increase in resources allows the algorithm to develop more unique solutions. However, this also directly increases the algorithm operational overheads such as breeding operations and fitness evaluations.

Solutions can develop that show excessive use of complexity by comparison to the problem. This is an understandable phenomenon as there is currently no implemented mechanism for encouraging minimal use of resources. Future investigation may look at evolving the number of chromosomes for individuals, with incentive for minimal resources to be used so that appropriate numbers are allocated for problems.

The species information can be specified in one of two ways for multiploid individuals; genotype (gene information) or phenotype (expressed solution appearance). We believe that genotype speciation is an essential part of solution evolution with this method of trait expression.

It is the combination of trait expression mechanisms that produces the final 'decision map' of trait values for an individual. Two similar phenotype individuals may be vastly different at the genotype level. In order to refine a particular genotype species (to converge to optima) reproduction amongst similar genotypes should be advantageous. As a result speciation convergence methods may be used such as island population models [16], [28] or ecological environment models [6].

It is interesting to note that the use and combination of expression mechanism units is reminiscent of other work. For example, hybrid systems, co-evolving species (sympathetic and parasitic) [18] and evolved hierarchal structures such as the Messy Genetic Model [12], Genetic Programming [21] and the Structured Genetic Algorithm [5]. Application and adaptation of this dynamic expression model with respect to work of similar nature is being investigated.

5. Conclusions

The dynamic trait expression model presented here is a viable method of dominance selection for multiploid individuals.

It is the nature of the dynamically expressed solutions that is the expected performance benefit of this type of algorithm, not the computational costs which can be more expensive than simpler multiploid EA/GA's implementations.

The multiploid nature of individuals allows for modified evolutionary operators that can influence algorithm performance, in particular, the implementation of artificial gametogenesis and gamete fusion as evolutionary operators.

From the discussion, parallels can be drawn from the model presented here to other adaptive systems such as hybrid algorithms, co-evolving algorithms or genetic programming, and it is with application in mind of these fields that future work will be directed.

Acknowledgments. The authors gratefully acknowledge the assistance of and valuable discussion with Dr Howard Copland and colleagues of the Centre for Intelligent Systems and Complex Processes.

References

1. Baker, J. E. 1985. Adaptive selection methods for genetic algorithms. *Proceedings of First International Conference on Genetic Algorithms and their Applications*, editor J. J. Grefenstette, 101-11, Bittsburgh: Carnegie-Mellon University.
2. Calabretta, R., R. Galbiati, S. Nolfi, and D. Parisi. 1996. *Haploid and Diploid Genotypes for Neural Networks*, Technical Report NSAL-96005. Institute of Psychology, C.N.R., Rome.
3. Cohoon, J P, Hegde S U, Martin W N, and Richards D S. 1991. Distributed genetic algorithms for the floorplan design problem. *IEEE Transactions Computer-Aided Design,* CAD-10: 483-92.
4. Corne, David, Emma Collingwood, and Peter Ross. 1996. Investigating Multiploidy's Niche. In *Proceedings of AISB Workshop on Evolutionary Computation*.
5. Dasgupta, Dipankar, and Douglas R. McGregor. 1992. Designing Application-Specific Neural Networks using the Structured Genetic Algorithm. In *Proceedings of COGANN-92 (International Workshop on Combinations of genetic Algorithms and Neural Networks),* Editors L. D. Whitley, and J. D. Schaffer, 87-96, IEEE Computer Society Press.
6. Davidor, Yuval. 1994. Free the Spirit of Evolutionary Computing: The Ecological Genetic Algorithm Paradigm. *Computing With Biological Metaphors.* Editor Ray Paton, 311-22. London, UK: Chapman and Hall.
7. Davis, Lawrence, ed. 1991. *Handbook of Genetic Algorithms*. first ed. New York: Von Nostrand Reinhold.
8. DeJong, K. A. 1975. "Analysis of the behavior of a class of genetic adaptive systems." PhD thesis, University of Michigan.
9. Eldredge, N, and S J Gould. 1972. Punctuated Equlibria: an alternative to phyletic gradualism. In *Models of Palaeobiology*, editor T J M Schopf, 82-115, San Francisco, CA: Freeman, Cooper.
10. Eshelman, L. J., and J. D. Schaffer. 1991. Preventing premature convergence in genetic algorithms by preventing incest. Proceedings of the *Fourth International Conference on Genetic Algorithms*, 115-22, Morgan Kaufmann.
11. Fonteix, C., F. Bicking, E. Perrin, and I. Marc. 1995. Haploid and Diploid Algorithms, a New Approach for Global Optimization: Compared Performances. *Int. J. of Systems Science* 26, no. 10: 1919-33.
12. Goldberg, D. E., B. Korb, and K. Deb. 1990. Messy genetic algorithms: Motivation, analysis and first results. *Complex Systems* 3: 493-530.
13. Goldberg, David E. 1989. *Genetic Algorithms in Search, Optimization, and Machine Learning*. Addison-Wesley.
14. Goldberg, David E., and R. E. Smith. 1987. Nonstationary function optimization using genetic algorithms with dominance and diploidy. In *Proceedings of the Second International Conference on Genetic Algorithms and their Applications*, editor J. J. Grefenstette, 59-68, Morgan Kaufmann.
15. Greene, F. 1996. A new approach to diploid/dominance and its effects on stationary genetic search. In *Proceedings of the Fifth Annual Conference on Evolutionary Programming*, (Ed.) D. Fogel MIT Press.
16. Grosso, P. 1985. "Computer Simulation of Genetic Adaptation: Parallel Subcomponent Interation in a Multilocus Model." PhD thesis, University of Michigan.

17. Jacob, F., and J. Monod. 1961. Genetic Regulatory Mechanism in the Synthesis of Proteins. *Journal of Molecular Biology* 3, no. 3: 318-56.
18. Juillé, Hugues, and Jordan B. Pollack. 1996. Co-evolving Intertwined Spirals. In *Proceedings of the Fifth Annual Conference on Evolutionary Programming*, 461-68MIT Press.
19. Kauffman, S. 1971. Gene regulatory networks: A theory for their global structure and behavior. *Current Topics in Developmental Biology* 6: 145-54.
20. ———. 1986. Boolean systems, adaptive automata, evolution. in *Disordered Systems and Biological Organization.* eds E. Beinenstock, F. Fogelman-Soulie, and G. Weisbuch, New York: Springer.
21. Koza, J. 1992. *Genetic Programming.* Cambridge, MA: MIT Press.
22. Lewis, Jonathan, Emma Hart, and Graeme Ritchie. 1998. A comparison of Dominance Mechanisms and Simple Mutation on Non-Stationary Problems. In *Parallel Problem Solving from Nature - PPSN V*, Ed. Agoston E. Eiben, Thomas Bäck, Marc Schoenauer, and Hans-Paul Schwefel, 139-48.
23. Mauldin, M. L. 1984. Maintaining diversity in genetic search. In *Proceedings of the National Conference on Artificial Intelligence*, 247-50.
24. Ng, Khim Peow, and Kok Cheong Wong. 1995. A new diploid scheme and dominance change mechanism for non-stationary function optimisation. In *Proceedings of the Sixth International Conference on Genetic Algorithms.*
25. Schnier, T., and J. S. Gero. 1997. Dominant and Recessive genes in evolutionary systems applied to spatial reasoning. in *Advanced Topics in Artificial Intelligence.* Sattar A. (ed.) , 127-36. Heidelberg: Springer.
26. Viennet, R., C. Fonteix, and Marc I. 1995. New Multicriteria Optimization Method based on the Use of a Diploid Genetic Algorithm: Example of an Industrial Problem. *Lecture Notes on Computer Science. Artificial Evolution: European Conference, AE 95*, 120-127, Springer-Verlag Ed.
27. Wolpert, D. H., and W. G. Macready. 1995. No Free Lunch Theorems for Search. *Technical Report SFI-TR-95-02-010 Santa Fe Institute.*
28. Wright, S. 1964. Stochastic processes in evolution. ed J Gurland, 199-241, Madison, WI: University of Wisconsin Press.
29. Yoshida, Yukiko, and Nobue Adachi. 1994. A diploid genetic algorithm for preserving population diversity - pseudo-meiosis GA. In *the Third Conference on Parallel Problem Solving from Nature --PPSN III*, editors Yuval Davidor, Hans-Paul Schwefel, and Reinhard Manner, 36-45, Springer-Verlag.

A Genetic and Evolutionary Programming Environment with Spatially Structured Populations and Built-In Parallelism

Miguel Rocha, Filipe Pereira, Sónia Afonso, and José Neves

Departamento de Informática
Universidade do Minho
Braga
PORTUGAL
mrocha@di.uminho.pt, jneves@di.uminho.pt

Abstract. The recent development of the *Genetic and Evolutionary Computation* field lead to a kaleidoscope of approaches to problem solving, which are based on a common background. These shared principles are used in order to develop a programming environment that enhances modularity, in terms of software design and implementation. The system's core encapsulates the main features of the *Genetic and Evolutionary Algorithms*, by identifying the entities at stake and implementing them as hierarchies of software modules. This architecture is enriched with the parallelization of the algorithms, based on spatially structured populations, following coarse-grained (*Island Model*) and fine-grained (*Neighborhood Model*) strategies. A distributed physical implementation, under the *PVM* environment, running in a local network, is described.

Keywords: (Parallel) Genetic and Evolutionary Algorithms, Spatially Structured Populations.

1 Introduction

The unfolding of the *Genetic and Evolutionary Computation (GEC)* arena has been remarkable in the last few years. The success of the applications in scientific and engineering domains is, in fact, an undeniable fact. However, in the processes of software development and analysis, the success has not been of a similar nature, being still common that the elaboration of a *Genetic and Evolutionary Algorithm (GEA)* may imply the programming of an application from scratch. The motivation for this work stems from these facts, leading one to foresee programming environments that will enable programmers to adjust software modules to be reused.

In order to achieve the proposed aim, the major features of the object-oriented programming paradigm are used, namely its capabilities to divide and conquer, reutilization or modularity. Indeed, under the present framework, the entities that make the building blocks of the the different approaches to *GEC*

L. Monostori, J. Váncza, and M. Ali (Eds.): IEA/AIE 2001, LNAI 2070, pp. 383–392, 2001.

are identified, in terms of their common background. Each conceptual entity is, on the other hand, viewed in terms of an hierarchy of abstraction spaces, augmenting the programmer's degree of freedom.

The programming environment allows for several kinds of users, depending on the task's complexity and on the user's skills and knowledge. It provides both a tool for the rapid development of an application, taking advantage on existent knowledge, and for the possibility of redefining data structures or operators, at different abstraction levels, thus making room to the advent of more complex program's features.

The earlier work in the development of the proposed system contemplated panmictic *GEAs*; i.e., with a single evolving population [9]. The system has been used, both for academic purposes, being the basis for several projects executed by undergraduate students, and for practical applications, namely in the *Combinatorial Optimization (CO)* field, where it was applied to tasks such as the *Job Shop Scheduling Problem* [11], the *Traveling Salesman Problem*, the *0/1 Knapsacking Problem* or the *Graph Coloring* one [12]. It was also object of a process of fusion with an implementation of *Artificial Neural Networks*, developed under a similar methodology, giving rise to some interesting problem solving techniques, namely in the *Machine Learning* arena [10].

More recently, new features have been added to the system, namely considering different computational models for its parallelization, in terms of the population's spatial structure. So, new hierarchy levels were added to the environment, following two basic models: the *Neighborhood Model* and the *Island Model* [3]. In the former, a fine-grained strategy is followed, with a spatial structure being fed to the populations, by considering coordinates for each of its individuals in a n dimensional space. In the latter, a coarse-grained approach is considered, with different sub-populations evolving simultaneously and exchanging individuals at regular intervals. Both models have been implemented, in a sequential way, considering a single CPU.

Furthermore, a distributed implementation of the latter model is presented, built under the *Parallel Virtual Machine (PVM)* [1] environment. This system allows for the definition of several populations, evolving in different machines, and exchanging information through a local network infrastructure.

The paper is organized as follows: firstly, an overview of the basic framework developed for panmictic *GEAs* is presented; then, the two parallel *GEAs* models are defined and their implementation is described; next, the parallel implementation of the *Island Model* is uncovered; finally, some conclusions are drawn and prospective future work is presented.

2 Panmictic Genetic and Evolutionary Algorithms

The term *Genetic and Evolutionary Algorithms (GEA)* is used to name a family of computational procedures where a number of potential solutions to a problem makes the way to an evolving population. Each individual codes a solution into a string (*chromosome*) of symbols (*genes*), being assigned a numerical value (*fitness*), that stands for a solution's quality measure. New solutions are created through the application of genetic operators (typically *crossover* or *mutation*). The whole process evolves via a process of stochastic selection biased to favor individuals with higher fitnesses. Under this scenario, panmictic *GEAs* are defined as those that allow for any individual to reproduce with any other; i.e., there is no isolation by a spatial structure.

The architecture of the *GEA's* model is built upon three conceptual levels, that encapsulate the features and behaviors of the main entities involved: the *individuals*, the *populations* and the *GEA* itself [9]. Each of these abstraction levels is materialized by an hierarchy of classes, whose root defines the set of common data structures and methods, as well as a set of default definitions. Specific structures and methods are defined when one descends from the root into the leafs of the hierarchy.

As an example, consider the individual's hierarchy of classes depicted in Figure 1. The root class, *Indiv*, is an abstract one; its role is to define a set of common procedures and interfaces, to be implemented in its sub-classes. This class has a template field, that can be assigned, *a posteriori*, with the respective type. This field is used to keep the genetic information of an individual, a sequence of genes of a given type. Thus, it is possible to consider different types of representation alphabets. In Figure 1 some of the built-in representations are shown, but this set can be augmented, when the need arises.

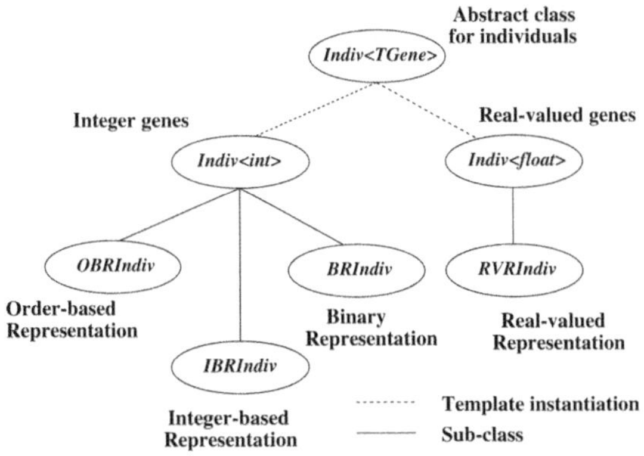

Fig. 1. The *individuals* hierarchy's class

Similar strategies are used at the *population's* and the *GEA's* abstraction levels. In the former, the selection and the re-insertion procedures are defined, as well as the methods for creating the initial population. In the latter, the overall structure of the algorithm is created, being provided a default one, namely those depicted in Figure 2, to can be used by the programmer or redefined.

```
BEGIN
  Initialize time (t = 0).
  Generate and evaluate the individuals in the initial population (P0).
  WHILE NOT (termination criteria) DO
    Select from Pt a number of individuals for reproduction.
    Apply to those individuals the genetic operators to breed the offspring.
    Evaluate the offspring.
    Select the offspring to insert into the next population (Pt+1).
    Select the survivors from Pt to be reinserted into Pt+1.
    Increase current time (t = t + 1).
  END WHILE
END
```

Fig. 2. Structure of a *GEA*

The last bit of the system's architecture is the *Evaluation Module*, whose function is to encapsulate the problem's dependent *decodification* and *evaluation* processes. This is achieved by an abstract class defining the syntax for the evaluation procedure. This class is instantiated whenever a different problem is to solved by a *GEA* (the corresponding fitness function is defined at this stage).

One interesting feature of the system under consideration relies on the genetic's operator handling flexibility. In fact, the user can specify, for a particular problem, the set of operators he/she may find more adequate, and also state their frequency of application. The concept of genetic operator was generalized to endorse both the traditional operators, such as *crossover* and *mutation*, and any kind of operator that may be considered of interest (since it can be stated as a function that takes n individuals and returns m different ones).

It is also provided a set of classes to configure the *GEA*, that can be used to set the values for the parameters in the *selection* and the *re-insertion* procedures, as well as the termination criteria, the population size or other parameters that control the process of evolution and the system's interfaces with the outside world.

One of the major system's requisites relies in its capability to define hybrid approaches; i.e., those that take the information of a problem's instance, and use it in the design of the genetic operators. The generalization of the genetic operator concept, and the hierarchy of classes at the individual's level, that allows the definition of specific operators and general purpose ones, not only makes possible to bring such operators into life.

3 The Neighborhood Model

In the *Neighborhood Model*, each individual in a population is given an unique location in a n-dimensional space, according to a predefined *topology*. The position of a given individual is given, in this case, by a set of n coordinates, being required that each possible location is inhabited by one individual [7]. Under this scheme, the neighbors of a specific individual can be identified, in terms of a *distance function* between each pair of individuals, and a threshold one that defines the size of the neighborhood. This will be used in order to identify an individual's *deme*; i.e., its possibilities to find reproduction mates.

For instance, consider the case where the population's topology is that of a two-dimensional *torus*. The *distance* between two individuals can, therefore, be set, i according to Von-Newmann, as the set of separate consecutive movements in the progression towards a final location, from a predefined one; i.e., the *d-neighborhood* of an individual may be now understood as being the set of individuals that are located at a distance smaller or equal to d (Figure 3).

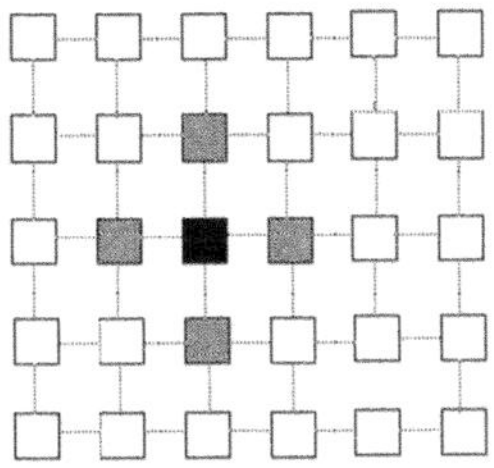

Fig. 3. An individual's 1-neighborhood in a 2D-torus

In terms of implementation, this model implies some major changes on the abstraction levels described in the previous section, namely on the *population's* and on the *GEAs* levels, making use of the original *individuals* classes.

To achieve a spatial structure in the population two new classes have been created, namely the *Space* and *Position* ones. The former enables the definition of different topologies, while the latter handles the individual's spatial distribution within the given topology. The topologies of a *ring* and of a *torus*, 2 or 3-dimensional, are handled by the system; other geometries are possible, if needed.

This approach differs from the one that makes use of panmictic *GEAs*, not only on the spatial distribution of the individuals, but also on the execution flow of the algorithms considered, which relies on a individual based engine; i.e., each individual can be thought to control its own evolution process. Therefore, the major structure of the algorithm is changed, being shown in Figure 4. In each generation, every individual in the population collects its neighborhood, selects from this pool its reproduction mates, applies the genetic operator and creates offspring. At this stage, an individual must decide on its own replacing offspring, and if such operation is or is not advantageous.

There are some considerations that must be taken into account when using this model. The tasks of collecting and selecting among neighbors, as well as the application of the genetic operators, repeated several times (per iteration) lead to an increased computational demand on the part of the *GEA*. So, one is lead

```
BEGIN
  Initialize time (t = 0).
  Generate the individuals of the initial population (P0).
  Assign a spatial position and evaluate each individual in P0.
  WHILE NOT (termination criteria) DO
    FOR EACH individual DO
      Select the genetic operator to be applied.
      IF (number of incoming individuals in the operator is more than one)
        Collect neighbors.
        Select individual(s) from the neighborhood for reproduction.
      END IF
      Apply the genetic operator, breeding the offspring.
      Select individual from the offspring to replace current individual.
      Decide if new individual replaces its parent.
    END FOR
    Increase current time (t = t + 1).
  END WHILE
END
```

Fig. 4. Structure of a *Neighborhood Model GEA*

to the necessity of simplifying the selection procedures in order to maintain an acceptable computational behavior. A good alternative to this task may rely on the use of the *tournament based* selection procedures [2].

Since this model has specific properties that differ from the ones observed when using the panmictic *GEA* approach, there is an increase in complexity, brought in by the use of additional parameters. These include the topology used, the distance that defines the neighborhood, the method used to select the offspring or the decision procedure that rules the parent's replacement by its offspring or its maintenance in the population. Two options were considered, namely that of always replacing the old individual by the offspring, or proceed with the replacement's operation if it is the case that the offspring presents a better fitness value.

Due to the use of the object-oriented paradigm, the implementation took advantage of numerous features of the *GEA*'s implementation, namely the selection procedures, the evaluation module, the genetic representations and the genetic operators.

4 The Island Model

The *Island Model* considers several sub-populations, evolving independently and exchanging individuals (*migrants*). The islands are connected by *channels*, through which individuals may move from one island to another. The *topology* defines the connection architecture of the system; i.e., which sub-populations can exchange individuals. The topology is defined by the programmer, which has the option of selecting an existing one, such as those of a ring or a fully connected scheme, or to create a new one.

Each island is home to one panmictic *GEA*, although the setup of the different *GEAs* is independent, being possible to have heterogeneous populations evolving simultaneously (e.g., *GEAs* with different genetic operators). The overall structure of the *Island Model GEA* is depicted in Figure 5.

A class, called *server*, was implemented in order not only to control the islander's evolution, but also to manage the migration, to collect the local statistics, and finally to generate the global ones.

```
BEGIN
  Initialize time (t = 0).
  FOR (each island)
    Generate and evaluate the individuals on the initial population.
  END FOR
  WHILE NOT (termination criteria) DO
    FOR (each island)
      Run GEA for mi generations.
    END FOR
    Exchange individuals between islands using channels.
    Collect statistics from each island and generate global statistics.
    Increase current time (t = t + mi).
  END WHILE
END
```

Fig. 5. Structure of an *Island Model GEA*

The exchange of individuals (migrations) occurs at fixed intervals, every mi generations, when a certain number of individuals goes through the existing channels in the topology. The *migration interval* and the exact number of individuals that migrates, through each channel are user defined parameter.

It is believed that exchanging individuals often and in large quantities accelerates the overall convergence of the *GEA* On the other hand, it contributes to a greater risk of being stuck in a local optimum. The opposite limits the speed of convergence and degrades the system's performance. So, a tradeoff must be achieved in order to find an equilibrium.

Two different ways of exchanging genetic material are allowed: *migration* and *pollination*. In *migration*, the individuals are moved from one island to another, while in *pollination* the information is simply copied and the individual is maintained in its original population. The user can decide what kind of exchange is more suitable to a specific problem. The programmer may also define how to select which individuals are the *migrants*, using one of the selection procedures inherited from the panmictic *GEAs* (e.g. *Roulette-Wheel*, *Tournament*, etc.).

5 A Distributed Implementation of the Island Model

Each of the two models here presented of *GEAs* with a spatial structure can be carried out either on a sequential or on a distributed architecture. In this work, and apart from the sequential implementation of both models, a distributed view of the *Island Model* was developed. It assumes different *islands*, that may reside in different computers, that cooperate in the search of the best solution to a given problem, by exchanging information (i.e., individuals) through the network. The environment includes a number of workstations and personal computers, with *Linux* or *Windows-95/98* operating systems, connected through an *Ethernet* local network with a bandwidth of 10 Mbit/s.

This implementation uses the *Parallel Virtual Machine (PVM)* [1] technology, which reduces the difficulty of implementing a distributed processing system, while having a reliable communication's infrastructure. It simulates a single virtual space in which several processes are executing, possibly in different machines (Figure 6), providing an ordered, asynchronous and reliable exchange of messages among them, in a anycast way. It is possible to have processes in different machines with different operating systems exchanging messages.

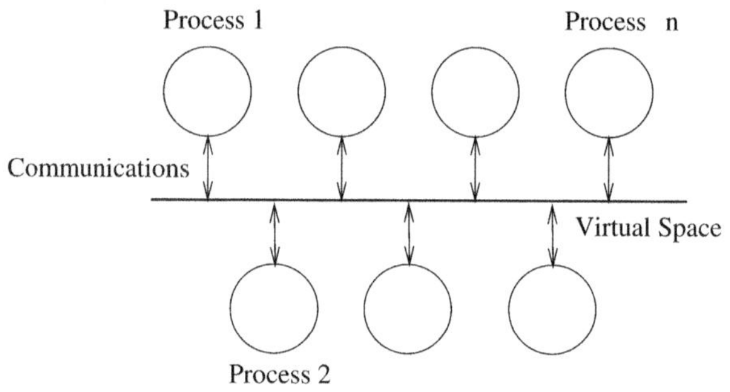

Fig. 6. A scheme of the *PVM* environment

The distributed implementation comprises two new classes, namely the *Server* and the *Island* ones. The former controls the whole process, by instructing the islands to proceed with their evolution a given amount of time (or generations), collecting local results, calculating global statistics and handling error situations. The latter implements the clients, by providing the interface between the *GEA*, that makes its core, and the virtual space, handling the communication with other islands and with the server (Figure 7).

The physical location of the islands and server processes is transparent, allowing the execution of the server in one computer, and of one or more islands in each computer situated in the local network. Thus, the use of the available resources can be maximized.

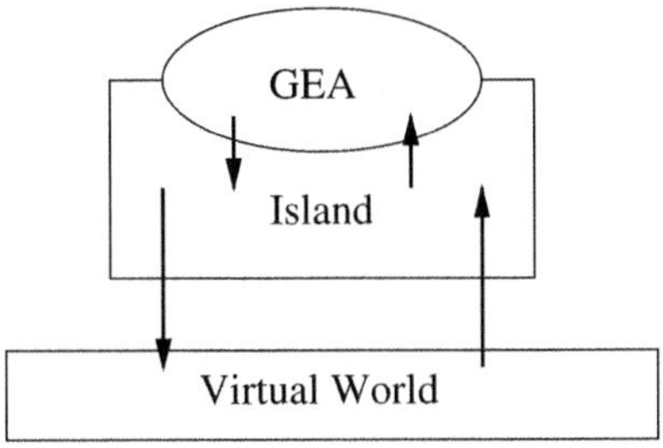

Fig. 7. A representation of an *Island* object

The configuration of the system follows what was said for the *Island Model* referred to above. The ultimate purpose is to achieve the same, or better, results when compared to those of the panmictic *GEA*, while greatly reducing the computational time.

6 Conclusions and Future Work

The proposed genetic and evolutionary programming environment, in its first release, shows itself as a powerful programming tool that makes easier the development of *GEAs* based applications. Furthermore, the system provided high connectivity, both with the problem's data structures making possible the development of hybrid approaches, and with other problem solving used in the intelligent system's design. An example of such endeavor is found in the combination achieved between *GEAs* and *ANNs*, both for *Machine Learning* tasks [10] and for *Time Series Forecasting* [5].

With the introduction of spatially structured populations, a new path towards better performances was revealed, allowing both for the better handling of the diversity in the populations and for the equation of models for the physical parallelization of *GEAs*, thus increasing their computational efficiency.

The implementation of the whole system followed the same methodology, giving a special attention to modularity, incremental development and reutilization, but never forgetting computational efficiency. The user with few knowledge in the area was remembered as well as the expert researcher, and the system fits the needs of both equally well. Therefore, the environment makes a very powerful tool for the programming of robust and efficient *GEAs*.

In the future one intends to extend the physical implementation in order to consider ways of dynamic load balancing, i.e., by assigning more work to the more powerful and more available computation nodes. Furthermore, one intends to study in detail the migration parameters [4] and the configuration of the *GEAs* in each *islands*, taking advantage on the flexibility of the implementation to achieve a better performance. The idea of developing a system that makes the migrations depend on each island's diversity, measured by the fitness standard deviation, is also a topic under study [8], as well as the behavior of heterogenous *islands*, enhanced for exploration or for exploitation of the search space by using different genetic operators [6]. Finally, the fact that the framework is highly integrated makes easy to design hybrid parallel systems, that mix both models. The idea would is to consider an *Island Model* at a top level, where each island would be a *Neighborhood Model GEA*.

References

1. A.Geist, A.Beguelin, J.Dongarra, W.Jiang, R.Manchek, and V.Sunderam. *PVM: Parallel Virtual Machine: A User's Guide and Tutorial for Networked Parallel Computing.* MIT Press, 1994.
2. J.E. Baker. Reducing Bias and Inefficiency in the Selection Algorithm. In J.Grenfenstette, editor, *Proceedings of the Second International Conference on Genetic Algorithms and their Applications.* Lawrence Erlbaum Associates, 1987.
3. E. Cantu-Paz. A survey of parallel genetic algorithms. IlliGAL Report 97003, University of Ilinois at Urbana-Champaign, Urbana, IL, may 1997.
4. E. Cantu-Paz. Migration policies, selection pressure, and parallel genetic algorithms. IlliGAL Report 99015, University of Ilinois at Urbana-Champaign, Urbana, IL, jun 1999.
5. P. Cortez, M. Rocha, J. Machado, and J. Neves. An evolutionary and connectionist approach for time series forecasting. In *Proceedings of Thirteenth International Conference on i Systems Engineering - ICSE 99*, Las Vegas, USA, aug 1999.
6. Francisco Herrera and Manuel Lozano. Gradual distributed real-coded genetic algorithms. *IEEE Transactions on Evolutionary Computation*, 4(1):43–63, apr 2000.
7. H. Mühlenbein. Evolution in time and space - the parallel genetic algorithm. In G. Rawlins, editor, *Foundations of Genetic Algorithms*, pages 316–337. Morgan-Kaufman, 1991.
8. Masaharu Munetomo, Yoshiaki Takai, and Yoshiharu Sato. An efficient migration scheme for subpopulation-based asynchronously parallel genetic algorithms. Technical Report HIER-IS-9301, Hokkaido University, 1993.
9. J. Neves, M. Rocha, H. Rodrigues, M. Biscaia, and J. Alves. Adaptive Strategies and the Design of Evolutionary Applications. In *Proceedings of the Genetic and Evolutionary Computation Conference (GECCO99)*, Orlando, Florida, USA, 1999.
10. M. Rocha, P. Cortez, and J. Neves. The relationship between learning and evolution in static and in dynamic environments. In C. Fyfe, editor, *Proceedings of the 2nd ICSC Symposium on Engineering of Intelligent Systems (EIS'2000)*, pages 377–383. ICSC Academic Press, 2000.
11. M. Rocha, C. Vilela, P. Cortez, and J. Neves. Viewing scheduling problems through genetic and evolutionary algorithms. In *Proceedings of the BioSP3 workshop*, 2000.
12. M. Rocha, C. Vilela, and J. Neves. A study of order based genetic and evolutionary algorithms in combinatorial optimization problems. In R. Loganantharaj, G. Palm, and M. Ali, editors, *Proceedings of the 13th IEA/AIE'2000.* Springer, 2000.

Genetic and Evolutionary Algorithms for Time Series Forecasting

Paulo Cortez, Miguel Rocha, and José Neves

Departamento de Informática Universidade do Minho
Braga - PORTUGAL
pcortez@di.uminho.pt, mrocha@di.uminho.pt, jneves@di.uminho.pt

Abstract. Nowadays, the ability to forecast the future, based only on past data, leads to strategic advantages, which may be the key to success in organizations. *Time Series Forecasting* allows the modeling of complex systems as black-boxes, being a focus of attention in several research arenas such as *Operational Research*, *Statistics* or *Computer Science*. On the other hand, *Genetic and Evolutionary Algorithms (GEAs)* are a novel technique increasingly used in *Optimization* and *Machine Learning* tasks. The present work reports on the forecast of several *Time Series*, by *GEA* based approaches, where *Feature Analysis*, based on statistical measures is used for dimensionality reduction. The handicap of the evolutionary approach is compared with conventional forecasting methods, being competitive.

Keywords: Genetic and Evolutionary Algorithms, Time Series Forecasting, Time Series Analysis, ARMA models.

1 Introduction

Time Series Forecasting (TSF), the forecast of a time ordered variable, turns on into a decisive tool in problem solving, since it allows one to model complex systems where the goal is to predict the system's behavior and not how the system works. Indeed, in the last few decades an increasing focus as been put over this field. Contributions from the arenas of *Operational Research*, *Statistics*, and *Computer Science* as lead to solid *TSF* methods (e.g., *Exponential Smoothing* or *Regression*) that replaced the old fashioned ones, which were primarily based on intuition.

An alternative approach for *TSF* arises from the *Artificial Intelligence (AI)* field, where one has observed a trend to look at *Nature* for inspiration, when building problem solving models. In particular, studies on the biological evolution influenced the loom of powerful artifacts, such as *Genetic and Evolutionary Algorithms (GEAs)*, that enriched the potential use of *AI* in a broad set of scientific and engineering problems, such as the ones of *Combinatorial* and *Numerical Optimization* [9].

L. Monostori, J. Váncza, and M. Ali (Eds.): IEA/AIE 2001, LNAI 2070, pp. 393–402, 2001.

GEAs are suited for combinatorial optimization problems, where the exhaustion of all possible solutions require enormous computational power, heuristically finding solutions where other methods seem to fail. The use of *GEAs* in *TSF* is expected to increase in importance, motivated by advantages such as explicit model representation and adaptive evolutionary search, which escapes from unsatisfactory local minima.

The present work aims at testing several *TSF* models, inspired on evolutionary strategies, over a broad range of real *TSs*. The paper is organized as follows: firstly, the basic concepts for *TS* analysis, and *GEAs* are defined; then, a description of the different models and experiments is given; finally, the results obtained are presented and compared with other conventional *TSF* methods.

2 Time Series Analysis

A *Time Series (TS)* is a collection of chronologically ordered observations x_t, each one being recorded at a specific time t (period). *TSs* can uprise in a wide set of domains such as *Finance*, *Production* or *Control*, just to name a few. A *TS* model ($\widehat{x}_t$), assumes that past patterns will recur in the near future. The *error* of a forecast is given by the difference between actual values and what was predicted:

$$e_t = x_t - \widehat{x}_t \tag{1}$$

The overall performance of a forecasting model is evaluated by an accuracy measure, namely the *Sum Squared Error (SSE)*, *Root Mean Squared (RMSE)*, and *Normalized Mean Square Error (NMSE)*, which are given in the form:

$$\begin{aligned} SSE &= \textstyle\sum_{i=1}^{l} e_i^2 \\ RMSE &= \sqrt{\tfrac{SSE}{l}} \\ NMSE &= \frac{SSE}{\sum_{i=1}^{l} (x_t - \overline{x})^2} \end{aligned} \tag{2}$$

where l denotes the number of forecasts and $\overline{x}$ the mean of the *TS*.

A common statistical instrument for *TS* analysis is the *autocorrelation* coefficient, defined by:

$$r_k = \frac{\sum_{t=1}^{s-k} (x_t - \overline{x})(x_{t+k} - \overline{x})}{\sum_{t=1}^{s} (x_t - \overline{x})} \tag{3}$$

in terms of the k's lag, where s denotes the *TS*' size. Autocorrelations can be useful for decomposition of the *TS* main components (*trend* and *seasonal* effects) (Figure 2).

One quite successful *TSF* method is *Exponential Smoothing (ES)*, which is based on some underlying patterns (e.g., *trend* and *seasonal* ones) that are distinguished from random noise by averaging the historical values. Its popularity is due to advantages such as the simplicity of use, the reduced computational demand and the accuracy of the forecasts, specially with seasonal *TSs*. The general model, also known as *Holt-Winters*, is defined by the basic equations [10]:

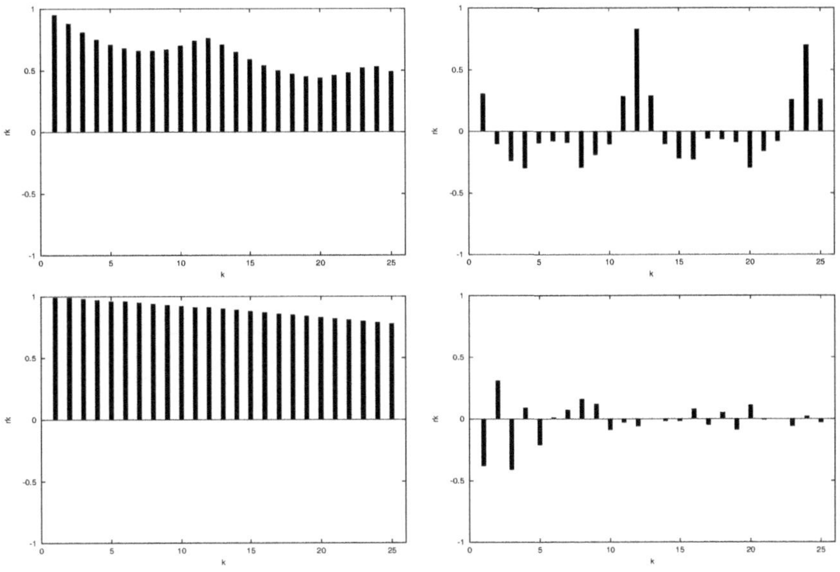

Fig. 1. Autocorrelation coefficients of typical *Seasonal and Trended*, *Seasonal*, *Trended* and *Non-Trended TS*

$$\begin{array}{l} F_t = \alpha \frac{x_t}{S_{t-K}} + (1-\alpha)(F_{t-1} + T_{t-1}) \\ T_t = \beta(F_t - F_{t-1}) + (1-\beta)T_{t-1} \\ S_t = \gamma \frac{x_t}{F_t} + (1-\gamma)S_{t-K} \\ \widehat{x}_t = (Fx_{t-1} + T_{t-1}) \times S_{t-K} \end{array} \quad (4)$$

where F_t, T_t and S_t stand for the smoothing, trend and seasonal estimates, K for the seasonal period, and α, β and γ for the model parameters.

The *AutoRegressive Integrated Moving-Average (ARIMA)* is another important *TSF* methodology, going over model identification, parameter estimation, and model validation [3]. The main advantage of this method relies on the accuracy over a wider domain of *TSs*, despite being more complex, in terms of usability and computational effort, than *ES*. The global model is based on a linear combination of past values (*AR* components) and errors (*MA* components) This model can be postulated as an $ARMA(P, Q)$ one, given in the form:

$$\widehat{x}_t = \mu + \sum_{i=1}^{P} A_i x_{t-i} + \sum_{j=1}^{Q} M_j e_{t-j}$$

where P and Q denote the AR and MA orders, A_i and M_j the AR and MA coefficients, being μ a constant value. Both the constant and the coefficients of the model are estimated using statistical approaches (e.g., least squares methods). Trended *TSs* require a differencing of the original values and seasonal *TSs* involve a transformation of the model. The methodology also contemplates the possibility of some kind of transformation in the original data (e.g., logarithmic).

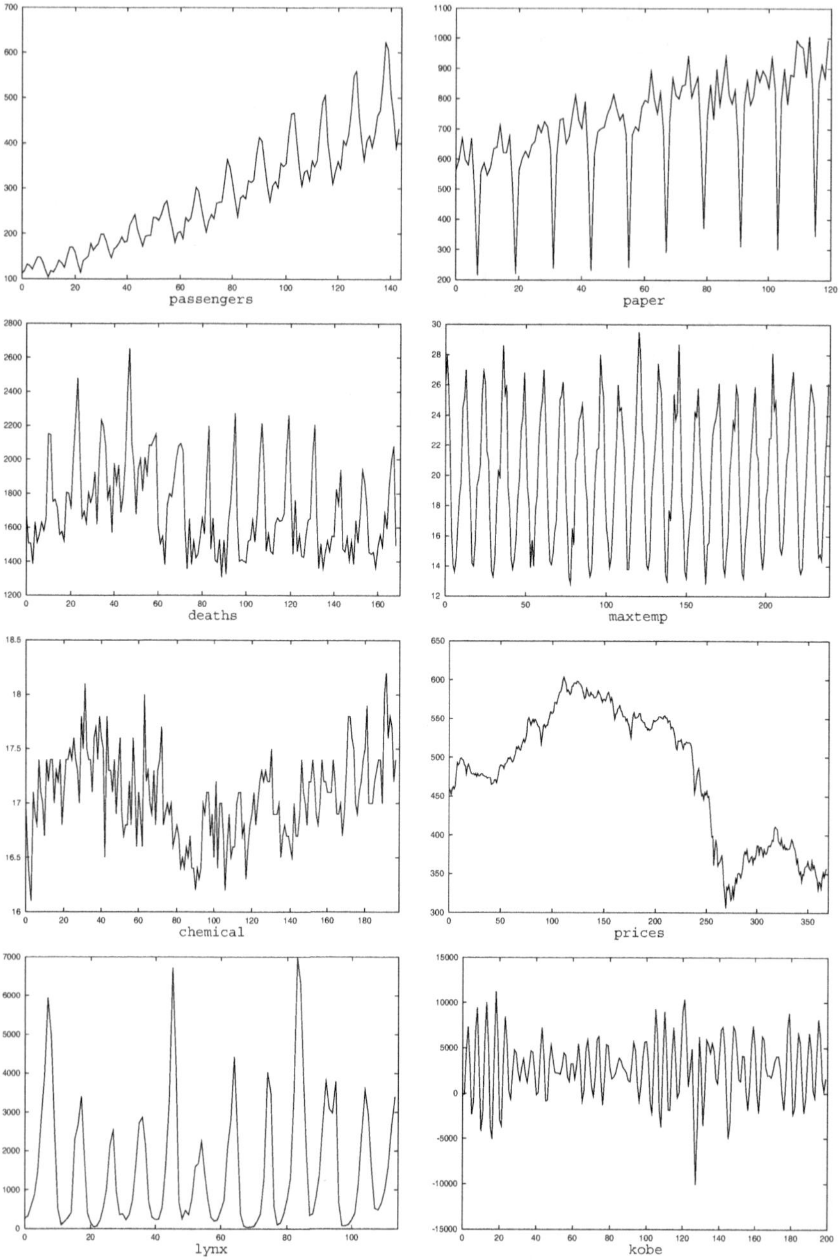

Fig. 2. The series of Table 1

Table 1. *Time Series* data

Series	Type	Domain	Description
passengers	*Seasonal*	Tourism	Monthly international airline passengers
paper	*& Trended*	Sales	Monthly sales of French paper
deaths	*Seasonal*	Traffic	Monthly deaths & injuries in UK roads
maxtemp		Meteorology	Maximum temperature in Melbourne
chemical	*Trended*	Chemical	Chemical concentration readings
prices		Economy	Daily *IBM* common stock closing prices
lynx	*Nonlinear*	Ecology	Annual number of lynx
kobe		Geology	Seismograph of the Kobe earthquake

For the experiments presented in this work, a set of eight *TSs* were selected (Table 1), taken from different origins, the majority of which are related with real problems, from different domains, ranging from the financial markets to natural processes [3][10][8] (Figure 2). All *TSs* were classified into four main categories that are expected to encompass all major *TS* types, namely: *Seasonal and Trended*, *Seasonal*, *Trended*, and *Nonlinear*.

3 Genetic and Evolutionary Algorithms

The term *Genetic and Evolutionary Algorithm (GEA)* is used to name a family of computational procedures where a number of potential solutions to a problem makes the way to an evolving population. Each individual codes a solution in a string (*chromosome*) of symbols (*genes*), being assigned a numerical value (*fitness*), that stands for a solution's quality measure. New solutions are created through the application of genetic operators (typically *crossover* or *mutation*). The whole process evolves via a process of stochastic selection biased to favor individuals with higher fitnesses.

The first *GEAs* [6], and most of the ones developed so far, make use of a binary representation; i.e., the solutions to a given problem are coded into a $\{0,1\}$ alphabet. However, some authors have argued that when one is faced with problems where the parameters are given by real values, the best strategy is to represent them directly into the chromosome, thus using a *Real-Valued Representation (RVR)*, which allows the definition of richer genetic operators [11]. In this work, two genetic operators were adopted. Its picture is given below:

Arithmetical Crossover - each gene in the offspring is a linear combination of the values in the ancestors' chromosomes in the same positions [11]. If a_i and b_i are the offspring's genes, and z_i and w_i the ancestors' ones, at the position i, then $a_i = \lambda \cdot z_i + (1-\lambda) \cdot w_i$ and $b_i = \lambda \cdot w_i + (1-\lambda) \cdot z_i$, where λ is a random number in the range $[0;1]$.

Gaussian Perturbation - this is a *mutation* operator that adds, to a given gene, a value taken from a Gaussian distribution, with zero mean.

4 Evolutionary Forecasting Models

In spite of its youth, in the *Evolutionary Computation* arena, a stream of new models and techniques for problem solving are coming into life, being particularly useful for numerical or combinatorial optimization processes. It is surprising to realize that the work in applying these techniques to forecasting is so scarce. In fact, although there are some publications in this area, these are not numerous nor noticeable. The existent work focuses mainly in some kind of parameter optimization, under a conventional model such as *Holt-Winters* [1] or *ARIMA* [7][4]. Recent developments such as *Genetic Programming (GP)* [2] and *GEAs* with *RVRs* [11], are expected to improve the performances of these approaches.

In this work, two approaches to forecasting, both based on *GEAs* with *RVRs*, were followed. In the former one, the forecasting model is a linear combination of previous values. Under this scenario, the genes in the chromosome code for the weights by which previous values are multiplied. With the latter, both previous values and errors are taken into account, following a strategy inspired on the *ARMA* models, where the genes code for the coefficients.

Both models make use of a *Sliding Time Window (STW)* that defines the set of time lags used to build a forecast, also defining the number of the model inputs. A *STW* will be denoted by the sequence $STW = < k_1, k_2, ..., k_n >$, for a model with n inputs and k_i time lags. The choice of a given *STW* is crucial to set the performance of a given model. A large sliding window can increase the system entropy, diminishing the learning capacity of the model, while small windows may contain insufficient information. The selection of the relevant time lags can improve forecasting (e.g., *ARIMA* models often use the $1, 12$ and 13 lags for monthly seasonal trended series).

An empirical approach to the problem is to use information based on the *TS* analysis. Four heuristic strategies will be used for *STW* selection, based on the autocorrelation values, and stated as follows:

A - a full *STW* with all time lags from 1 to a given maximum m: $STW = < 1, 2, ..., m >$ (m was set to 13, a value that was considered sufficient to encompass monthly seasonal and trended effects);

B - a *STW* with all lags with autocorrelation values above a given threshold (set to 0.2);

C - a *STW* with the four lags with highest autocorrelations (in the case of the seasonal trended series, these were taken after differencing, since trend effects may prevail over seasonal ones); and

D - the use of decomposable information; i.e.,
  - $STW = < 1, K, K+1 >$ if the series is seasonal (period K) and trended;
  - $STW = < 1, K >$ if the series is seasonal; and
  - $STW = < 1 >$ and $STW = < 1, 2 >$ if the series is trended.

The two models considered in this work are given, in terms of a predefined *STW*, by:

G1 - linear combination based *GEA*; i.e.,

$$\widehat{x}_t = g_0 + \sum_{i \in \{1,\ldots,n\}} g_i x_{t-k_i}$$

where g_i stands for the i-th gene of the individuals' chromosome, and n for the *STW* size.

G2 - ARMA based *GEA*; i.e.,

$$\widehat{x}_t = g_0 + \sum_{i \in \{1,\ldots,n\}} (g_i x_{t-k_i} + g_{i+n} e_{t-k_i})$$

A model is said to overfit when it correctly handles the training data but fails to generalize. The usual statistical approach to overfitting is *model selection*, where different candidate models are evaluated according to a generalization estimate. Several complex estimators have been developed (e.g., Bootstrapping), which are computationally burdensome [12]. A reasonable alternative is the use of simple statistics that adds a penalty that is a function of model complexity, such as the *Bayesian Information Criterion (BIC)* [13]:

$$BIC = N \cdot ln(\tfrac{SSE}{N}) + p \cdot ln(N) \qquad (5)$$

where N denotes the number of training examples and p the number of parameters (in this case $p_{G1} = 1 + n$ and $p_{G2} = 1 + 2n$).

5 Experiments and Results

The given models (**G1** and **G2**) were tested on the set of *TSs* from Table 1, using all the sliding window heuristics, when applicable. Thirty independent runs were performed in every case to insure statistical significance, being the results presented in terms of the mean and 95% confidence intervals. The *TSs* are divided into a training set, containing the first 90% values and a test set, with the last 10%. Only the training set is used for model selection and parameter optimization. The test set is used to compare the proposed approach with other methods.

In terms of the *GEA's* setup, the initial populations' genes were randomly assigned values within the range $[-1, 1]$. The population size was set to 100. The fitness of each chromosome was measured by the forecasting error (*RMSE*) over all the training patterns. The selection procedure is done by converting the fitness value into its ranking in the population and then applying a roulette wheel scheme. In each generation, 40% of the individuals are kept from the previous generation, and 60% are generated by the application of the genetic operators described in Section 3. The *crossover* operator is responsible for breeding $\frac{2}{3}$ of the offspring and the *mutation* one is accountable for the remaining ones. Finally, the *GEA* is stopped after 2000 epochs.

For each *TS* both models (*G1* and *G2*) were applied, considering all possible *STWs*. Therefore, each *TS* has several forecasting candidates. In order to select

Table 2. Results of the *GEA's* approach to the **prices** series

Model	Sliding Window	Training RMSE	BIC	Forecasting RMSE
G1	A=B	12.13	1673	10.72±0.69
	C	9.18	1443	8.24±0.32
	$D_{1,2}$	8.35	1372	7.49±0.05
	D_1	7.68	**1312**	**7.48**±0.00
G2	A=B	8.70	1536	8.78±0.33
	C	7.73	1357	7.68±0.10
	$D_{1,2}$	**7.63**	1325	7.65±0.02
	D_1	7.68	1318	7.49±0.00

the best one, the *BIC* criterium was used. As an example, the used methodology will be explained in detail for the **prices** series (Table 2). The results of the last three columns are given in terms of the mean of the thirty runs. The 95% confidence intervals are also shown for the short term forecasting errors [5]. The best training *RMSE* is achieved for the window $< 1, 2 >$ and model *G2*. The *BIC* criterium works better, selecting the model that provides the best forecast. This behavior occurred consistently in all the *TSs*.

Table 3. The selected *GEAs* forecasting models (with lower *BIC*)

Series	Model	Sliding Window	Forecasting RMSE
passengers	G1	D=$< 1, 12, 13 >$	20.9±0.7
paper	G1	D=$< 1, 12, 13 >$	56.3±0.9
deaths	G1	D=$< 1, 12, 13 >$	134±1
maxtemp	G1	C=$< 1, 11, 12, 13 >$	0.915±0.008
chemical	G1	B=$< 1, 2, 3, 7 >$	0.343±0.003
prices	G1	D=$< 1 >$	7.48±0.00
lynx	G2	C=$< 1, 9, 10, 11 >$	262±6
kobe	G2	A=$< 1, 2, ..., 13 >$	524±16

Table 3 shows the best *GEA* models, when adopting the *BIC* criterium for model selection. This criterium, which penalizes complexity, selects the *G*1 models for the linear series and the *G*2 for the nonlinear ones, which is a logical outcome.

A comparison throughout evolutionary and conventional models is given in Table 4. The error values over the test set are given in terms of two measures, namely the *RMSE* and the *NMSE* ones (in brackets). This last measure is included since it makes easier the comparison among the different series and methods considered. The *ES* parameters (α, β and γ) were optimized using a 0.01 grid search for the best *RMSE*, while the *ARIMA* models were achieved using a forecasting package (*FORECAST PRO*).

Table 4. Comparison between different *TSF* approaches

Series	ES	ARIMA	GEA
passengers	**16.7** (0.71%)	17.8 (0.81%)	20.9 (1.12%)
paper	**41.0** (3.1%)	61.0 (6.8%)	56.3 (5.8%)
deaths	145 (43%)	144 (42%)	**134** (37%)
maxtemp	0.917 (4.1%)	1.068 (5.6%)	**0.915** (4.1%)
chemical	0.354 (51%)	0.361 (53%)	**0.343** (48%)
prices	7.50 (0.39%)	7.72 (0.41%)	**7.48** (0.38%)
lynx	876 (57%)	504 (19%)	**262** (5%)
kobe	3199 (105%)	582 (4%)	**524** (3%)

The results of the evolutionary approach are very interesting, with the best forecasting handicaps in 6 of the 8 *TSs*. In terms of the different types of *TSs* considered the proposed method seems to have its weakness in the seasonal and trended series, where the *ES* prevails. In all other kinds of series the results are very good, specially in the non-linear *TSs*.

6 Conclusions

The results of the application of *GEAs* to the *TSF* field are, at least, encouraging. In fact, the methodology proposed presents better results than the traditional methods used in the majority of the *TSs* considered. Furthermore, the *BIC* criterium showed a good performance in model selection, making the approach easier to automate. In fact, the proposed system does not require complicated statistical pre-processing, being easy to use by a beginner in the field.

In the future, it is intended to pursue on the automation of the model selection stage, namely on the process of selecting the best *STW*. An alternative is to enlarge the number of different *STWs* attempted and to find, within this search space, the best alternative. Since this is an optimization task, the use of a *GEA* could be advantageous, thus creating a two-level architecture. Another area of interest may rely in the enrichment of the forecasting models, by considering the integration of nonlinear functions (e.g., logarithmic or trigonometric).

Acknowledgements. The work of Paulo Cortez was supported by the portuguese *Foundation of Science & Technology* through the PRAXIS XXI/BD/13793/97 grant. The work of José Neves was supported by the PRAXIS' project PRAXIS/P/EEI/13096/98.

References

1. Adriana Agapie and Alexandru Agapie. Forecasting the Economic Cycles Based on an Extension of the Holt-Winters Model. A Genetic Algorithms Approach. In *Proceedings of the IEEE Computational Intelligence for Financial Forecasting Engineering*, pages 96–99, 1997.

2. W. Banzhaf, P. Nordin, R. Keller, and F. Francone. *Genetic Programming, An Introduction.* Morgan Kaufmann Publishers, Inc, USA, 1998.
3. G. Box and G. Jenkins. *Time Series Analysis: Forecasting and Control.* Holden Day, San Francisco, USA, 1976.
4. C. Chai, C. Chuek, M. DP, and T. Huat. Time Series Modelling and Forecasting using Genetic Algorithms. In *Proceedings of the First International Conference on Knowledge-Based Intelligent Electronic Systems*, volume 1, pages 260–268, Adelaide, Australia, 1995.
5. A. Flexer. Statistical evaluation of neural networks experiments: Minimum requirements and current practice. In *Proceedings of the 13th European Meeting on Cybernetics and Systems Research*, volume 2, pages 1005–1008, Vienna, Austria, 1996.
6. John Holland. *Adaptation in Natural and Artificial Systems.* PhD thesis, University of Michigan, Ann Arbor, 1975.
7. C. Huang and H. Yang. A Time Series Approach To Short Term Load Forecasting Through Evolutionary Programming Structures. In *Proceedings of the EMPD'95 Internacional Conference*, pages 583–588, 1995.
8. R. Hyndman. *Time Series Data Library.* (http://www-personal.buseco.monash.edu.au/~hyndman/TSDL/), 2000.
9. G. Luger and W. Stubblefield. *Artificial Intelligence, Structures and Strategies for Complex Problem Solving.* Addison Wesley Longman, Inc., USA, 1998.
10. S. Makridakis and S. Wheelwright. *Forecasting Methods for Management.* John Wiley & Sons, New York, fifth edition, 1989.
11. Z. Michalewicz. *Genetic Algorithms + Data Structures = Evolution Programs.* Springer-Verlag, USA, third edition, 1996.
12. W. Sarle. Stopped Training and Other Remedies for Overfitting. In *Proceedings of the 27th Symposium on the Interface of Computer Science and Statistics*, pages 352–360, 1995.
13. G. Schwarz. Estimating the Dimension of a Model. *The Annals of Statistics*, 6:461–4, 1978.

Layout of Two Dimensional Irregular Shapes Using Genetic Algorithms

Rym M'hallah[1], Ahlem Bouziri[2], and Walid Jilani[2]

[1] Department of Quantitative Methods, Institut Supérieur de Gestion de Sousse, BP 763 Sousse 4000, Tunisia.
Rym.Mhallah@irsit.rnrt.tn

[2] Institution de Recherche en Sciences Informatiques et des Télécommunications BP 212 Cité Mahrajène, Tunis 1082, Tunisia
{Ahlem.Bouziri, Walid.Jilani}@irsit.rnrt.tn

Abstract. The two-dimensional layout optimization problem consists of finding the minimal length layout of a set of irregular two dimensional shapes on a stock sheet of finite width but infinite length. The layout should not contain any overlaps. The present paper solves this problem using a novice heuristic based on GA. The proposed heuristic uses a simple codification scheme, and a new placement strategy. The application of this heuristic yields, in reduced computational times, satisfactory results, that are comparable to those obtained by human markers.

1 Introduction

The two-dimensional layout problem consists of finding the best layout of a set of pieces on a stock sheet of finite width and infinite length, subject to a set of constraints. The garment industry requires the non overlapping of pieces with the added difficulty that the shapes can be oriented only in certain directions on the cloth. In this industry, the best layout is one that minimizes the overall length of used material.

Minimizing overall length and subsequently waste results in sizeable gains as the cost of cloth is a large proportion of the production cost. It is customary, for cutting efficiency, to position the layout on a spread fabric with various numbers of layers or plies. Thus, a minimal length layout in the placement is translated into every ply of the spread, yielding important savings. For example, in pants manufacturing, sixty is a typical number of plies, and an improvement of 1% per placement represents an average gain of $25. A pants manufacturing plant reports that an average improvement of 0.1% yields yearly savings of $2 million [11].

The layout problem is commonly solved by a human expert, called marker. The use of computer generated layouts is rare as the layouts generated by the markers are consistently better than those generated automatically. However, initiating and training a human expert is a long time process requiring an average 6 to 12 months of training.

The layout problem is NP hard [12]. Exponential time searches can be carried out only for a trivially small number of shapes. The problem becomes more complex as

L. Monostori, J. Váncza, and M. Ali (Eds.): IEA/AIE 2001, LNAI 2070, pp. 403-411, 2001.

the number of pieces and / or the number of vertices per piece become large. The search is made more difficult by a large number of invalid layouts that arise from the overlap of pieces. Thus, to solve realistic versions of this problem, efficient heuristic approaches must be used. Most of the so far proposed approaches, reviewed in [7, 3, 6], impose restrictions on the pieces (rectangular, convex, fixed orientation, etc.) [10, 1] or use indirect methods based on shape approximations [5].

Genetic Algorithms (GA) are known for their efficient exploration of the solution space and their effectiveness in combining solutions. GA based heuristics offer a large diversity of the solution space making them potentially suited for layout problems. So far, GA based heuristics adopt representations that can yield invalid (overlapping) configurations [13, 8, 2, 4]. This generally leads to extensive computation and forces the search to make trade offs between minimizing enclosure area and minimizing overlap. Since the solution space grows exponentially with the number of shapes, the search becomes inefficient when the number of shapes to be nested becomes large. In addition, the lack of a close mapping to the physical problem domain tends to make modification operators such as crossover less meaningful. An approach eliminating the problem of overlap computation and using the cross over operator in a meaningful manner is proposed. This approach assembles parts in a manner that avoids the creation of invalid layouts. This GA based placement of two-dimensional irregular pieces, a direct method minimizing total waste, is the object of this paper.

This paper is organized as follows. In Sect. 2, the sequential placement heuristic is introduced. In Sect. 3, the GA based approach is proposed. In Sect. 4, the application of the GA heuristic is illustrated and the results are discussed. A summary and perspectives are provided in conclusion.

2 Sequential Placement

The proposed sequential placement method follows closely the behavior of the marker in his/her ordering criterion, and placement strategy. Analyzing his/her strategy, it is fair to say that every piece is placed at the leftmost of the layout while maximizing the overall utilization of the width. Each placement minimizes the surface of any generated holes; taking advantage of perfect fits whenever possible. Certain placements are temporarily postponed in an attempt to better use existing holes. The marker considers the pieces according to "size". He/she starts by placing the larger pieces, and tempts to squeeze the smaller ones into any created holes. As the proposed sequential placement will be used in conjunction with GA, we will herein focus on the placement strategy.

Imitating the human marker, the pieces are placed successively starting with the first piece at the bottom left part of the material. The second piece is placed on top of this first one if the width constraint is not violated. The second piece is therefore removed from the list of unplaced pieces and the following piece is considered. If such a placement is not possible, the following pieces in the list of unplaced pieces are considered one at a time for such a position (top left of the first piece). Once a piece is suitable for this position, it is placed and removed form the list. A return to the top of the list is undertaken and the procedure is repeated. If however, no piece is eligible for a left top placement, the piece on top of the list of unplaced pieces is considered again. It is positioned to the bottom right of one of the pieces marking the right border of the layout or in a hole created by already placed pieces.

The positioning of a piece with respect to an already placed one is done such that the two pieces are in contact without superposition. In fact, the polygon is translated in the vertical and horizontal directions until it comes in contact with a placed piece. The translation distance is computed using projections of the left and bottom parts of the piece to be placed on the right and upper parts of the pieces already positioned.

To illustrate the sequential placement method, the layout of Fig. 1 has been constructed using the length as the ordering criterion of the pieces. The example corresponds to irregular geometric shapes forming a perfect puzzle. The layout was built in less than a second.

The proposed sequential method is very fast and gives excellent results when a good ordering of the pieces is at hand. The length, width, and area ordering provide in several instances the optimal placement. However, this is not always the case. Ideally, an exhaustive enumeration of all the possible permutations is needed to identify the global optimum. As this is impossible in a polynomial time, a selective guided search through these permutations could yield good results. Such a search is guaranteed by GA.

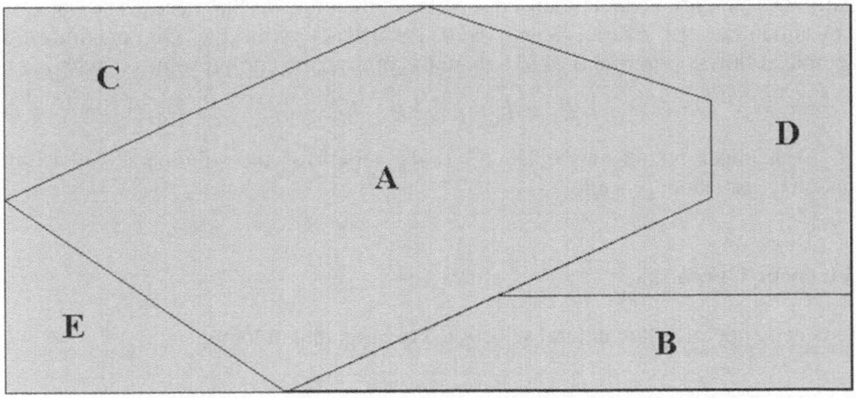

Fig. 1. Sequential placement of a perfect puzzle using the length criterion

3 Genetic Algorithms

The performance of GA depends on the adopted coding, evaluation function, and genetic operators.

3.1 Coding

The adopted Coding takes into consideration the notion of a piece and of a placement. A piece is represented with a gene, which corresponds to an alphabetic letter. A chromosome is subsequently the ordered set of unplaced pieces. The corresponding layout is obtained by sequentially packing each successive piece following the list from left to right. The order of a gene in the chromosome is simply its order of placement on the layout. For example, chromosome ABCDE corresponds to the placement of Fig. 1, obtained by applying the sequential placement of Sect. 2 to the ordered set {A, B, C, D, E}. A chromosome is therefore purely symbolic, and defines the layout uniquely.

3.2 Evaluation Function

The pieces are to be cut from a roll of constant width. The width constraint is commonly accounted for using a penalty term for its violation. The difficulties associated with this practice are avoided herein by generating valid layouts only. That is, the quality of the solution, assessed using L_c, the length of the layout generated by positioning the chromosome, depends solely on the order of the pieces. The objective is to minimize the overall length. For consistency with the GA maximization principle, a fitness criterion is used, where the fitness of a chromosome is given in (1).

$$F_c = L_{max} - L_{c}.\ L_{max} \tag{1}$$

L_{max}, an upper bound of the length, is the length of the solution issued by the sequential placement procedure.

3.3 Genetic Operators

The genetic operators are natural selection, crossing, and mutation.

3.3.1 Selection

The adopted selection strategy is simple GA with roulette selection and an elitist model. This selection allows the retention of the fittest parents for reproduction. A parent is selected with a probability P_s.

3.3.2 Crossing

The order crossover avoids the redundancy problem, caused by classical crossover, while exchanging pieces of information between the chromosomes. It is a two step operator. First, two crossover points are randomly chosen along the length of the chromosome creating a subsequence in the parents' chromosomes. The genes of the subsequence of each parent are carried into the offspring. The subsequence part of parent *i*, *i=1,2*, is copied directly into child *i* (i.e., assigned in the same positions to the child.)

The empty positions of the first child are successively filled with the genes of the second parent according to a simple rule. If the gene already appears in the child chromosome, it is rejected and the following gene is considered. Even tough obtaining the order from the second parent has little geometric interpretation (more of a random shuffling of the part of the chromosome than a combination), this operator is similar in spirit to finding a neighboring solution in simulated annealing and tabu search. The roles of the parents are then inverted to produce the second child.

For example, consider the two parents ABCDEFG and FDECABG. If positions 2 and 5 are chosen randomly, then the first child will automatically have BCDE fixed in positions 2 to 5 while the second child will have DECA in the same positions. The remaining positions of the first child will then be filled successively with F in the first position, A in the sixth position -after rejecting D, E, and C-, and G in the last one -after rejecting B-. D, E, C, and B are rejected because they already appear in the chromosome of the first child. Analogously, the empty positions of the second child will be filled with B, F, and G. The resultant children are therefore: FBCDEAG and BDECAFG.

The crossover operator maintains a part of each parent instead of recombining complementary parts from both parents. Preserving the subsequence of the chromosome is important as it represents a meaningful part of the chromosome. It is equally important not to consider a single point crossover yielding the retransmission of the left part of the chromosome through generations as this will limit the diversity of the population especially that layouts are highly dependent on the initial pieces that are placed. Any point in the chromosome divides the layout into two geometrically distinct regions. During the process of packing polygons, the polygons packed earlier (those on the left side of the chromosome) affect the packing of those packed later (those on the right), but not vice versa.

3.3.3 Mutation

Since the crossover maintains parts of the chromosome of each parent, the substrings are likely to be similar to those in the initial population. The mutation operator offsets any bias created by the initial population and guarantees the diversity of the population. It chooses two pieces at random and swaps their locations. For instance, the mutation of chromosome ABCDE in positions two and four yields the chromosome ADCBE.

3.4 Initial Population

The initial population is constructed using fit individuals. The sequential placement procedure of Sect. 3 is used to generate the first member of the population. This member is subject to mutation with probability P_m in order to generate N new individuals, subject to crossover with probability P_c.

3.5 Genetic Parameters

A judicious choice of the genetic parameters (N, number of generations, P_s, P_c, and P_m) guarantees a better exploration of the solution space and a quicker convergence towards the optimal solution. A good balance between crossover, which allows the exploration of a wider neighborhood of solutions, and mutation, which allows the diversification of the population, is needed. Similarly, a good tradeoff between the size of the population and the number of generations is necessary to guarantee good quality solutions in short run times.

A judicious choice of the genetic parameters (N, number of generations, P_s, P_c, and P_m) guarantees a better exploration of the solution space and a quicker convergence towards the optimal solution. A good balance between crossover, which allows the exploration of a wider neighborhood of solutions, and mutation, which allows the diversification of the population, is needed. Similarly, a good tradeoff between the size of the population and the number of generations is necessary to guarantee good quality solutions in short run times.

4 Computational Results

To evaluate the performance of the proposed heuristic, three examples are considered. For each example, the GA based solution l^* is compared to the length of the layout of the initial solution l_0 to assess the improvement due to GA, and to the best available solution l to assess its effectiveness.

The first example is a perfect puzzle that could not be restored via the sequential placement heuristic using the usual ordering criteria: length, area, and width. This puzzle is restored, as illustrated in Fig. 2, in less than 8 seconds, resulting in a length reduction of 10 units.

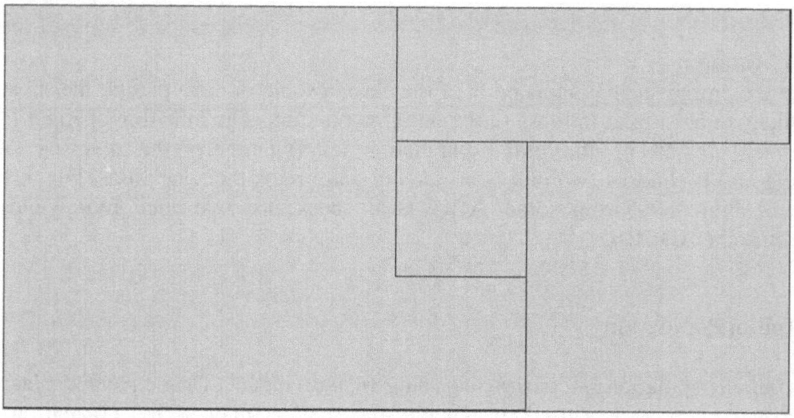

Fig. 2. Reconstruction of the perfect puzzle using GA

The second example, extracted from [9], corresponds to the pattern of a single size woman's dress with a total of 8 pieces to be displayed on a 59 in wide cloth. The length of the layout, displayed in Fig. 3, is 13.8 in shorter than the layout obtained in [9]. It is noteworthy that the sequential placement already yields a better solution than that of [9].

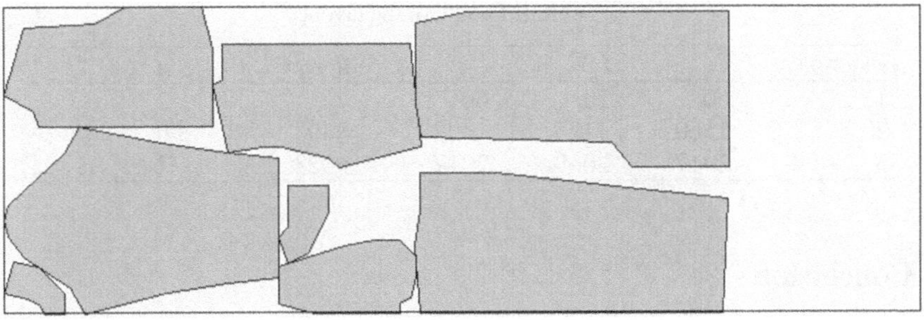

Fig. 3. Optimal layout of example 2 using GA

The third and last example, a real pattern obtained from a local industry, has a total of 21 pieces corresponding to two different sizes of a woman's jacket. The pieces are irregular, heterogeneous, and contain concavities. The width of the layout is 1300 mm, as constrained by the width of the cloth used. The length of the yielded layout, illustrated in Fig. 4, is 2017 mm which coincides with the length of the layout obtained by an expert marker.

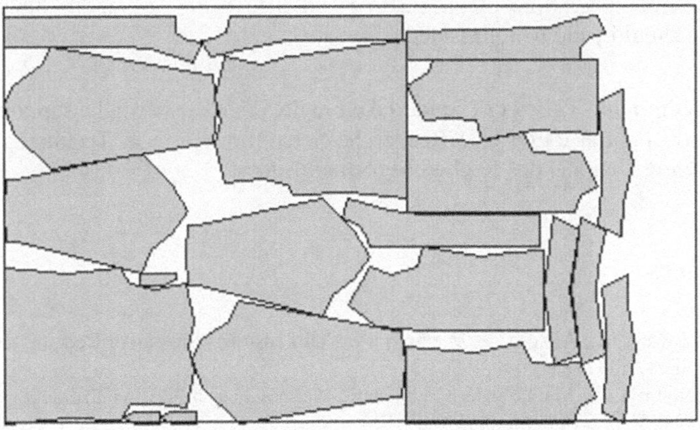

Fig. 4. Optimal layout of example 3 using GA

These results, the run times t in seconds, and the number of generations g needed to converge to l^* are summarized in Table 1. It is noteworthy that the run times include the input and output phases. They were obtained using a Pentium II 266 MHz.

In conclusion, GA converge very rapidly while yielding satisfactory results, comparable to those obtained by a human marker. The run times increase as the number of pieces increases and/or the shapes of the pieces become more complex. In addition, it is sensitive to the order and subsequently to the number of possible positions for each piece. For instance, the run time of a chromosome that starts with smaller pieces is longer than the run time of a chromosome starting with larger ones.

Table 1. Length of the layout

Example	l	l_0	l^*	$t(sec)$	g
1	60	70	60	7	2
2	1560	1425	1422	360	6
3	2017	2069	2017	6828	2

5 Conclusion

The optimal layout problem has been treated as assembling parts into positions, eliminating the need for lengthy geometric computations involved in detection of overlaps and/or definition of the minimal enclosure area. The proposed approach is very fast yielding good results; particularly when an intelligent ordering of the pieces is at hand. GA directs the search toward improving orderings. The meaningful chromosome representation adopted herein allows an efficient use of the crossover operator and reduces the computation time.

To further reduce the computation time, some of the human markers' techniques are currently being investigated in order to be integrated with GA. An interactive GA platform is under construction. The user will direct the selection procedure of GA during the first generations by eliminating and/or favoring certain combinations. This procedure should yield better results.

Acknowledgment. This work, undertaken at IRSIT, was partially supported by the Tunisian Secretariat d'Etat à la Recherche Scientifique et à la Technologie and the French Centre National des Recherches Scientifiques.

References

1. Adamowicz, M., Albano, A.: Nesting Two Dimensional Shapes in Rectangular Modules. Computer Aided Design **8** (1976) 27-33.
2. Bounsaythip, C., Maouche, S.: A Genetic Approach to a Nesting Problem. Proc. of the 2NWGA, Vaasa, Finland, (1996) 89-104.
3. Cheng, C. H., Feiring, B. R., Cheng, T. C. E.: The Cutting Stock Problem - A Survey. Int. J. of Prod. Econ. **36** (1994) 291-305.
4. Dighe, R., Jakiela, M. J.: Solving Pattern Nesting Problems with GA Employing Task Decomposition and Contact Detection. Evolutionary Computation **3** (1996) 239-266.
5. Dori, D., Ben-Bassat, M.: Circumscribing a Convex Polygon by a Polygon of Fewer Sides with Minimal Area Addition. Computer Vision, Graphics and Image Processing **24** (1983) 131-159.
6. Dowsland, K. A., Dowsland, W.: Solution Approaches to Irregular Nesting Problems. Eur. J. of Oper. Res. **84** (1995) 506-521.
7. Dyckhoff, H., Finke, U.: Cutting and Packing in Production and Distribution, a Typology and Bibliography. Physica Verlag, Wurzkurg (1992).
8. Fujita, K., Akagi, S., Hirokawa, N.: Hybrid Approach for Optimal Nesting Using a Genetic Algorithm and a Local Minimization Algorithm. Proceedings of the ASME Conferences on Advances in Design and Automation **65** (1993) 477-484.

9. Grinde, R.B.: Applying Minimal Enclosure Tools to the Pattern Layout Problem. Working paper, University of New Hampshire (1996).
10. Hopper, R., Turton, B. C. H.: An Empirical Investigation of Meta-heuristics and Heuristic Algorithms for a 2D Packing Problem. Eur. J. of Oper. Res., to appear.
11. Li, Z., Milenkovic, V.: Compaction and Separation Algorithms for Non-Convex Polygons and Their Applications. Eur. J. of Oper. Res. **84** (1995) 539-561.
12. Milenkovic, Z., Daniels, K., Li, Z.: Automatic Maker Making. Proc. of the 3rd Canadian Conf. on Comp. Geometry, Simon Fraser University, Vancouver, Shermer, T., Ed. (1991) 243-246.
13. Poshyanonda, P., Dagli, C. H.: A Hybrid Approach to Composite Stock Cutting: Neural Networks and Genetic Algorithms. In: Jamshidi, M., Lumia, R., Mullins, J., Shahinpoor, M. (eds.): Robotics and Manufacturing: Recent Trends in Research, Education, and Applications **4** (1992).

An Application of Genetic Algorithms to Course Scheduling at the United States Army War College

MAJ James J. Donlon

Knowledge Engineering Group
United States Army War College
650 Wright Avenue
Carlisle, PA 17013, USA
donlonj@csl.carlisle.army.mil

Abstract. Genetic algorithms can be applied with great success on a wide range of problems, including scheduling problems. This paper presents an application of genetic algorithms to a complex scheduling problem, wherein student demand for courses and scheduling constraints inform the production of a course schedule. The scheduler is currently in use in a decision support system at the U.S. Army War College, and has produced excellent results for two academic years. The problem domain and software solution are described, and the representations and algorithms used by the scheduler are presented. Empirical observations about the scheduler's performance and problem-solving characteristics are also presented.

1 Introduction

The United States Army War College (USAWC) is the Army's senior service college, which prepares senior military leaders to assume strategic leadership roles in military, national, and coalition operations. The USAWC Department of Academic Affairs produces schedules for a significant portion of the curriculum based on students' priority demands for courses. This introduces a scheduling challenge, which we have solved by creating a software component that employs genetic algorithms to generate course schedules. This software is a central problem-solving component in a decision support application currently in use for course scheduling and student assignments.

This paper presents our solution to the scheduling problem at USAWC. We first introduce the problem domain. Then we provide a brief overview of genetic algorithms. Next we present our specific application of the technique to the USAWC scheduling problem. Finally, we describe the results we obtained with this application and discuss the implications for further development and broader application.

L. Monostori, J. Váncza, and M. Ali (Eds.): IEA/AIE 2001, LNAI 2070, pp. 412-427, 2001.

2 Problem

A significant portion of the USAWC curriculum is made up of elective courses, which the students take during two terms (terms II and III) of an academic year (AY). The USAWC elective curriculum is not fixed, and the course offerings can change drastically from one academic year to the next. In addition, the interests of the student body can be expected to change from one year to the next, influencing the demand for courses. In order to provide the most accommodating elective course curriculum possible under these conditions, the college schedules courses immediately before an academic term begins, and after students have requested in priority the courses they would like to take. These variables made it difficult to produce a course schedule that adequately anticipates elective offerings and accommodates student demand.

Prior to each elective term, students indicate ten courses they would like to take in order of preference, and then the college generates student assignments based on that data. Our goal is to satisfy the students' demand for their highest course preferences such that at least 90% of the students receive their three or four assignments from their top five preferences. We refer to this goal as "student satisfaction". We approach this in two steps. First we generate a schedule that allocates courses (typically 82 to 93 in a given term) to time periods (typically 3 to 7 periods, depending on the term), based on scheduling constraints and student course preferences. The second step, assignment of students into courses, is accomplished subsequently as an optimization problem, which takes the schedule resulting from the first step as input. This paper describes our use of genetic algorithms to achieve the goal of the first step -- generate a schedule of elective courses that both reflects student preferences and conforms to scheduling constraints.

3 Brief Overview of Genetic Algorithms

A genetic algorithm (GA) is a stochastic search method that takes its inspiration from the Darwinian theory of natural selection. In biological evolution, better-adapted individuals thrive and reproduce, passing on their traits to future generations via their offspring. Less fit individuals do not thrive and contribute less to the gene pool of future generations. Over many generations, the overall quality of the population improves as the fitness levels of individuals generally improve.

More precisely, a GA draws from the properties of natural selection found in biological evolution to search for better solutions to complex problems. Populations of individuals "evolve" in the search for a very fit individual as the traits of selected individuals are combined to form individuals in successive generations. The overall fitness of the population improves in the course of the search. Eventually we stop evolving and select the fittest individual produced thus far as a solution. As in biological species, factors such as variation of individuals, selection from across the entire population, and random mutation prevent the search from prematurely stagnating at a local optimum.

GA techniques are particularly well suited for search spaces that are very large and/or difficult to construct ahead of time [5,7]. A predefined search space is not needed for GAs, and throughout the search helpful traits are encouraged and propagated to future generations, leading to the improvement of the population. The basic algorithm is straightforward to apply and can yield very good results on a variety of complex problems, including scheduling [2,8,11,12] and timetabling [1,3,6,9].

The following is a very general description of GA [10]:

```
Function: GENETIC-ALGORITHM(population, FITNESS-FN)
  returns: an individual
  inputs:  population, a set of individuals
           Fitness-Fn, a function that measures the fitness of an
             individual

  repeat
    parents = Selection(population, FITNESS-FN)
    population = Reproduction(parents)
  until some individual is fit enough
  return the best individual in population,
         according to FITNESS-FN
```

Our problem, the efficient arrangement of elective courses into class periods, is well suited for this technique. It is not practical to exhaustively evaluate all possible schedules because the number of possible arrangements of courses into periods is exponential in the number of courses. It is also not practical to construct a good schedule from first principles because we must also observe constraints on the schedule's suitability that vary from term to term and complicate schedule generation. However, we can devise a way to distinguish better schedules from worse ones. In addition, it is not necessary to find the optimal schedule in order to create suitable conditions to produce good assignment results. GAs do a very good job of finding a suitable solution in an acceptable amount of time under these conditions.

4 Implementation

While the basic algorithm is straightforward, applying GA to a specific problem requires selection of appropriate representations and relationships to the properties of natural selection (e.g., encoding of individuals and their traits). We must also devise methods to evaluate the fitness of individuals, select individuals for reproduction, produce offspring, and introduce random mutation in individuals.

Our goal in constructing a schedule is to determine an arrangement of courses in some number of periods so that we establish favorable conditions for the assignment of students into those courses. We judge schedules to be fit to the extent that they both minimize the degree to which courses that are requested together are scheduled together, and follow scheduling rules. Using this strategy, the scheduler spreads the highest demand courses throughout the schedule, while observing user-imposed constraints on schedule acceptability.

4.1 Representation

Each individual in a population represents a complete schedule (assignments of courses to periods). We use an integer representation for the individual. The schedule is encoded as an integer array, wherein the position in the array represents the course and the value in that position represents a period assignment. For example, the following individual represents the assignment of 93 different elective courses to a time period in a 7-period schedule (identified by the integers 1 through 7).

Position (course)	*1*	*2*	*3*	*4*	*5*	...	*93*
Integer value (period)	2	4	1	6	5	...	7

In this individual, the course identified by the first position in the array is assigned to the time period identified by the integer 2, the next course is assigned to the time period identified by the integer 4, and so on.

An interesting aspect of the representation used for this GA implementation is that it varies from one problem to the next. The size of the array used to represent an individual varies depending on the number of courses to be scheduled. The finite alphabet that is used to represent the traits of an individual (i.e., courses and periods) varies in that it will be the integers 1 through the number of periods in the desired schedule for periods, and 1 through the number of courses to be scheduled for courses.

A set of individuals constitutes a population, over which the GA procedures operate.

4.2 Algorithm

Prior to evolving, we perform problem setup, which includes initializing a new GA problem with the needed settings (e.g., population size, mutation rate), data (i.e., course offerings, student preferences, faculty assignments), and the scheduling constraints that restrict schedule acceptability. This information is passed to the component from the calling application (i.e., a user-interface in a decision support system). Through the user interface, the user can influence the GA's behavior and performance by changing parameters such as population size, mutation settings, crossover type, and selection probabilities.

During setup, the scheduler creates the initial population, and also constructs several important data structures, which are referenced throughout the solving process. One array is built to record the number of times courses are requested together on the same student preference sheet. We will describe later how this "conflict matrix" is used as a basis for evaluating schedules. A "rank scale" array, described below, is computed for use in the rank weighting method [7] of selection.

Following setup, a top-level loop runs the GA:

```
Function EVOLVE (theGA)
  returns: a GA problem object with its population evolved some number
           of generations
  inputs: theGA, an object that contains the GA's data, settings, and
          procedures

  repeat
    RUNGENERATION(theGA)
  until max generations or some individual is fit enough or time limit
        reached
End
```

Problem solving proceeds by invoking RUNGENERATION until the objective has been met, the maximum number of generations has been reached, or a time limit is reached.

```
Function RUNGENERATION (theGA)
  returns: theGA evolved one generation
  inputs: theGA

  Population(theGA)  = MAKENEXTGENERATION (Population(theGA),
      CrossoverType(theGA))
  APPLYMUTATION (Population(theGA), MutationRate(theGA),
     MutationDegree(theGA))
  EVALUATEPOPULATION (Population(theGA), ConflictMatrix(theGA),
     Constraints(theGA))
  ASSIGNSELECTIONPROBABILITIES (theGA)
End
```

The following sections detail the procedures used by RUNGENERATION to implement reproduction, mutation, evaluation, and selection.

Reproduction. RUNGENERATION begins by reproducing individuals from the current population into the next generation. Replacement is used as the reproduction scheme, in that offspring completely replace the parents in the following generation. The process of passing traits from parents to offspring during reproduction is commonly referred to as crossover. MAKENEXTGENERATION can use one of four different crossover schemes during reproduction – traditional single-point crossover, standard two-point crossover, variable two point crossover (wherein the section of genes to be exchanged is randomly chosen), and uniform crossover. (A basic familiarity with these crossover strategies is assumed. An accessible discussion can be found in Haupt and Haupt [7]). The single and two-point crossover strategies use randomly selected crossover points to encourage variation and avoid premature convergence on a local optimum.

```
Function MakeNextGeneration (Population, CrossoverType)
  returns: a new population of Individuals, constituting a new
           generation
  inputs: Current population, crossover type

 repeat

  Parent1 = SelectForBreeding (Population)
  repeat
    Parent2 = SelectForBreeding (Population)
  until TestForSiblings (Parent1, Parent2) = False

  Create NewPopulation
  Conduct Crossover of genes (course-period assignments) from Parent1
     and Parent2 according to selected CrossoverType to create Child1 and
     Child2

  Add Child1 and Child2 to NewPopulation

 until NewPopulation is full
End

Function SelectForBreeding (Population)
  returns: an individual
  inputs: Current population

   RANDOMIZE(n)
     So that (0 < n < 1)
   For p = 1 to Count(Population)
      If RankScale(p) ≥ n then
        Return Population(p)
End
```

We added the TestForSiblings check to further encourage variation in the population by preventing individuals with the same two parents from producing offspring into the following generation. Although crossover involves a degree of chance regarding which traits are inherited from which parent, and the rank style pairing in SelectForBreeding allows selection from the entire population, we found that premature convergence on local optima was further discouraged when we prevent this sort of "incest".

```
Function TestForSiblings (Ind1, Ind2)
  inputs: individuals: Ind1, Ind2
  returns:  True if the individuals were reproduced from common parents,
            False otherwise

  TestForSiblings =
        Parent1(Ind1) = Parent1(Ind2)
          Or Parent1(Ind1) Parent2(Ind2)
        And
        Parent2(Ind1) = Parent1(Ind2)
          Or Parent2(Ind1) = Parent2(Ind2)
End
```

Mutation. RUNGENERATION next applies mutation across the newly generated population, according to the mutation settings provided in problem setup. The probability that any offspring will undergo mutation is between 0 and 1, inclusive. The number of genes affected if mutation occurs can be predetermined or randomized. A controlled amount of mutation is another important source of variation needed to overcome convergence on local optima.

```
Function APPLYMUTATION (Population, MutationRate, MutationDegree)
  inputs: Population of Schedules
          MutationRate: probability that any individual will undergo
            mutation
          MutationDegree number of genes that will be affected if
            mutation occurs
  returns: Population with zero or more Individuals mutated, depending
            on degrees and probabilities played out

  If MutationRate = 0 then
        Return
  If MutationDegree = 0 then
    MutationDegree = RANDOMIZE(MutationDegree)
  For Each Schedule In Population
        RANDOMIZE(ChanceOfMutation)
          So that (0 < ChanceOfMutation < 1)
    If ChanceOfMutation <= MutationRate Then
      For i = 1 to MutationDegree
        RANDOMIZE(aCourse)
           So that aCourse is an integer that represents a course to be
           scheduled
        RANDOMIZE(aPeriod)
           So that aPeriod is an integer that represents a period in the
           schedule
        Assign aCourse to aPeriod
End
```

Evaluation. Next RUNGENERATION evaluates the individuals in the new population.

```
Procedure EVALUATEPOPULATION (Population, ConflictMatrix, Constraints)
  effects:  Each individual in Population is evaluated according to a
            fitness function and violated constraints are identified
            for each individual
  inputs: Population of Schedules
          ConflictMatrix, a 2-D array of the number of times courses are
            requested together
          Constraints, a collection of restrictions that a schedule must
            observe

  For Each Individual In Population
    EVALUATE (Individual, ConflictMatrix, Constraints)
End
```

For each individual, EVALUATE records the fitness score and flags all rules that are violated by that schedule. The fitness score determined by EVALUATE is conducted according to a fitness function, *f(S)*, where S is an individual, which represents a schedule. EVALUATE combines two important measures: the degree to which courses that are requested together are scheduled together, and how well the individual adheres to scheduling rules.

The first component of the fitness function, which we call the schedule's "conflict score", is a sum of the occurrences that two courses assigned to the same period in the schedule have both been requested by a single student. We find that schedules with lower conflict scores provide better conditions for the assignments model to assign students to the courses they request thereby increasing student satisfaction.

Each time courses that are scheduled in the same period are found to have been requested together by the same student, the "conflict score" for that period is incremented by one. The conflict in a schedule *S*, denoted S_c, is defined as:

$$S_c = \sum_{p=1}^{m} \sum_{i=2}^{n} \sum_{j=1}^{i-1} C_{ijp} \tag{1}$$

where

S_C is the conflict score for schedule S,
p is an integer that represents a period (a value the array that represents an individual, where $1 \leq p \leq m$),
m is the number of periods in the schedule,
C_{ijp} is the number of times course i and course j are requested by a single student, where both i and j are scheduled in p,
i is a position in the array which represents a course (where $1 < i \leq n$),
j is a position in the array which represents a course (where $1 \leq j < i$), and
n is the number of courses to be scheduled.

The conflict matrix, which is computed once during problem setup, is an upper-triangular two-dimensional array representing the number of times pairs of courses have been requested by the same student. References to this table facilitate conflict scoring.

The second component of the fitness function is the schedule's adherence to constraints. The scheduler accepts guidance on the acceptability of schedules in the form of scheduling rules, such as pairwise constraints between courses (i.e., $\texttt{Course}_{C1}$ must be/cannot be scheduled in the same period as $\texttt{Course}_{C2}$) and constraints between courses and periods (i.e., $\texttt{Course}_{C}$ must be/cannot be scheduled in $\texttt{Period}_{P}$). The user specifies some of these rules explicitly. In use during AY 1999-2000, some rules were installed to de-conflict courses requiring the same resources. Others ensured that select courses met in predetermined periods.

Another important source of constraints is faculty assignments to teach electives. The scheduler can automatically derive and install all pairwise constraints necessary to prevent courses that share at least one instructor from being scheduled in the same period. Thus the user only has to specify additional constraints by exception.

In addition, the scheduler automatically accounts for constraints that logically follow from others. For example, if it is asserted that $\texttt{Course}_{A}$ cannot be scheduled with $\texttt{Course}_{B}$ and it is already asserted that $\texttt{Course}_{B}$ cannot be scheduled with $\texttt{Course}_{C}$, then the component will infer and install the constraint that $\texttt{Course}_{A}$ cannot be scheduled with $\texttt{Course}_{C}$. The scheduler prevents duplication of rules, keeps track of violated constraints, and flags those that contradict other constraints.

The penalty for a schedule's violation of scheduling constraints is based on S_v, the number of restrictions that are violated in schedule S, defined as:

$$S_V = \sum_{t=1}^{q} r_t \tag{2}$$

where

r is a restriction (i.e., a scheduling rule),
q is the number of restrictions, and
r_t is a penalty factor for a restriction (where $1 \leq t \leq q$) defined as $\{r_t = 1$ if r is violated in S, 0 otherwise$\}$.

All rules are considered "hard" constraints in the sense that a schedule is not considered acceptable if it violates any one of them. To penalize schedule fitness for violating the rules, the final fitness function combines S_v with S_c to impose a penalty proportionate to the number of violations:

$$f(S) = S_C(1 + S_V) \tag{3}$$

Because we wish to minimize S_c and encourage S_v to be 0, the GA seeks to minimize $f(S)$.

Selection. Finally, RUNGENERATION sorts the new population according to fitness and determines whether a new best individual has been found.

```
Procedure ASSIGNSELECTIONPROBABILITIES (theGA)
  effects: Population is sorted with the most fit individual in position
           1, so that each individual's position in the sorted
           population corresponds to a position in the RankScale of
           selection probabilities, and the current most fit individual
           is identified
  inputs: theGA

  Population(theGA) = SORTPOPULATION (Population(theGA))
  CurrentBest = BestFoundThusFar(theGA)
  BestOfGeneration = Population(theGA)(1)

 If FITNESS(BestOfGeneration) < FITNESS(CurrentBest) Then
    BestFoundThusFar(theGA) = BestOfGeneration
End
```

This sorted population, together with the rank scale, is used in the next iteration of RUNGENERATION to perform selection.

We perform selection based on the relative fitness of individuals, rather than selecting proportionate to the fitness score. This allows us to control for undesirable effects that might be introduced by the use of S_c as a measure of schedule quality. It also prevents us from disproportionately disadvantaging schedules that violate scheduling rules (due to the magnitude of the penalty imposed by S_v), but might nonetheless have valuable traits to pass on to future generations.

Selection from the sorted population is informed by a rank scale, computed once in problem setup as previously described. The rank scale records the cumulative probabilities for selecting from any position in the sorted population, such that the probability of selecting the nth candidate is a seed probability, given that the n-1 candidates before it were not already selected. For example, using a seed probability of 0.10, the cumulative probabilities for selecting the first 10 individuals are:

Table 1. Selection probabilities for first ten individuals in a population using the rank scale method with a seed value of 0.10

Position	Cumulative probability	Selection probability
1	0.1	0.1
2	0.19	0.09
3	0.271	0.081
4	0.3439	0.0729
5	0.40951	0.06561
6	0.468559	0.059049
7	0.5217031	0.0531441
8	0.5695328	0.0478297
9	0.6125795	0.0430467
10	0.6513215	0.038742

So the most fit individual has a 0.1 chance to be selected during each pairing, while the individual ranked 10th has less than a .04 probability. The last individual is always selected if none of the previous individuals is selected.

In SELECTFORBREEDING, a random number between zero and one is generated. The first position in the rank scale (say, position n) with a cumulative probability greater than or equal to the random probability generated determines the candidate chosen from the sorted population (the nth).

The extent to which fitness is rewarded in selection is influenced by the "seed" probability (i.e., the probability that the most fit individual will be selected) and the size of the population to be ranked. The seed value 0.10 works well for populations of 50-100 in this problem.

The scheduler is now ready to evolve the population again through another iteration of RUNGENERATION. EVOLVE ends when max generations, a time limit, or an objective is reached.

5 Results

The GA application was developed for first use in AY 1999-2000 scheduling, and the results during that year were excellent. The power of the GA is provided to the end user through a graphical decision support system, so that the user can solve the problem with no knowledge of the problem-solving methodology. The user is free to focus on the data and user-defined constraints that bear on the problem. The user is also allowed to modify the GA's settings if necessary. We had great success in delivering the solution to technically untrained users. The ease of use and flexibility of the system that automates this GA component, combined with the scheduler's efficient setup and solution of the problem, allowed end users to easily create schedules in a matter of minutes. This replaced a process by which analysts painstakingly constructed and ran scheduling models over a period of days.

When the resulting schedules were used as input to the assignment of students to courses, the assignment model obtained student satisfaction rates (as defined in the problem description) of 90% and 96% in terms II and III respectively, under tightly constrained assignment conditions. During that process, administrators used this scheduler to compare alternative schedules in "what-if" analyses of curriculum decisions such as splitting courses into sections, dropping courses, and imposing or relaxing constraints. This improved the final outcome of the assignment process.

The scheduler continues in use at the USAWC, and has scheduled electives for AY 2000-2001 with equal success.

6 Discussion

Effective application of GAs to a practical problem such as this is an empirical endeavor in that it is difficult to predict in advance what combination of GA settings will produce the best results for the problem. We have observed the performance of this scheduler on available data for two academic years, and have examined a range of GA settings under these conditions. Our experiments have resulted in some observations about the most productive settings for this problem. The deployed decision support system takes advantage of those conditions by default, and also allows the user to modify these settings (e.g., population size, termination criteria, mutation, selection probability, and crossover strategy) to influence the performance of the scheduler.

Here we present findings about the performance of the scheduler, as well as the conditions that seem to yield the best results on this problem. We illustrate the results with trial runs from term III AY 1999-2000 scheduling, but consistent results have been repeated for all elective terms over two academic years.

6.1 Results of Evolution

The scheduler evolves generations at the rate of approximately 6 per second for populations of 100 individuals, running on a low-end (233mhz) Pentium-II desktop computer with 64 MB of RAM. This enables the solver to evolve 500 generations, normally more than enough to produce excellent results, in roughly a minute and a half. Fewer generations are needed in practice to produce satisfactory schedules – schedules produced during the first 100 generations of evolution are often found to contribute successfully to a quality assignments result. The chart in figure 1 shows the progress made in the first 100 generations of a trial run using the scheduling conditions encountered in term III AY 1999-2000 -- 71 courses, 7 periods, 66 scheduling constraints. The GA settings used in this trial were population of 100, mutation rate of 5%, number of course-period assignments affected by mutation = 1, rank scale probability = .1, and uniform crossover.

In this sample run, the fitness of the best individual in the first five generations ranged between 18,354 and 7504 due to constraint violations (not shown on the chart). At 100 generations the fitness of the best individual was 2181 (recall that lower fitness scores are better because we seek to minimize conflict). At the end of 5000 generations, fitness had improved to 2061. Typically, suitable schedules (in that they do not violate any scheduling rules, and they contribute to high student satisfaction in the assignments) are obtained within the first 100 generations.

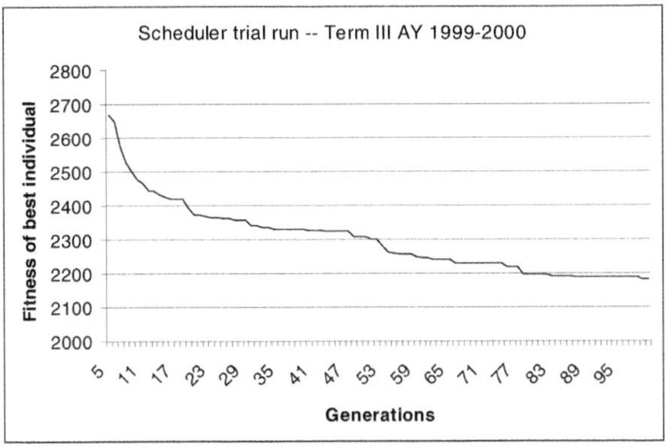

Fig. 1. Example scheduler results

Beyond 100 generations, progress is sporadic and much slower (as is the case at some point with any GA search). In our experience, schedules attained within the first 500-1000 generations consistently provide excellent conditions to enable the assignment model to achieve high satisfaction rates. Nonetheless, the user can attempt to improve the results of the assignments process by resuming the evolution process to further improve the schedule.

6.2 Impact of Crossover Strategy

The scheduler produces suitable schedules using any of the supported crossover strategies mentioned earlier. We found that uniform crossover performed best on our problem, as measured by progress toward more fit schedules. We demonstrated this by running trials under the same conditions as those in the preceding term III test. In each trial, the scheduler evolved 500 generations for each crossover strategy ten times and averaged the fitness scores of the best schedules found in each trial for each strategy. We performed ten rounds of these trials. The average performance of each crossover strategy in each round is plotted in figure 2.

From the scatter plot, it is clear that uniform crossover performed best in every round. This is consistent with the findings by DeJong and Spears [4] that uniform crossover outperforms less disruptive crossover strategies in that it helps smaller populations overcome inadequate sampling of the solution space. When the same test is repeated at population sizes of 500, 1000, and 5000, the advantage of uniform crossover is less clear; no one crossover strategy performed consistently better than the others at these populations sizes.

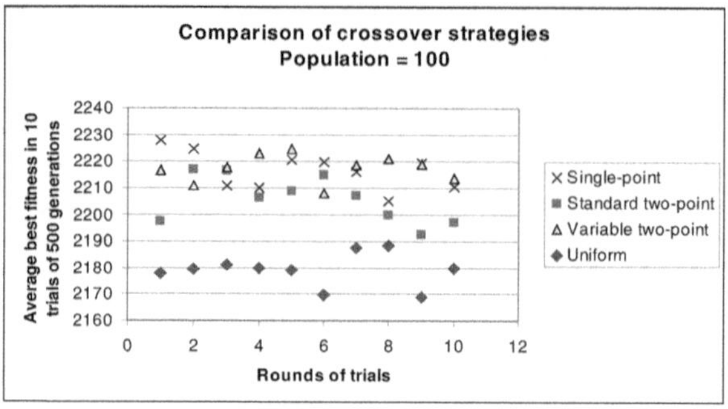

Fig. 2. Comparison of crossover strategies

6.3 Effect of Population Size

In a third experiment under the same conditions, we tested the impact of population size on the scheduler's performance. To do this we established the fitness objective at 2200 and ran trials with the population size varying from 50 to 3000 in increments of 10. We conducted 20 trials at each population increment and averaged the number of generations and time in seconds that the scheduler required to reach the goal for each population size.

Figure 3 illustrates the average performance over 20 trials under these conditions in terms of time required to solve. The best times were attained with populations between 100 and 150, taking on average 10.3 seconds to reach the goal. Populations below 100 appear to sample the possible schedules inadequately, requiring a greater number of generations and more time to reach the goal. As population size increases beyond 200, the time required to solve the problem increases linearly, and this continued to a population of 3000 (the extent of our testing).

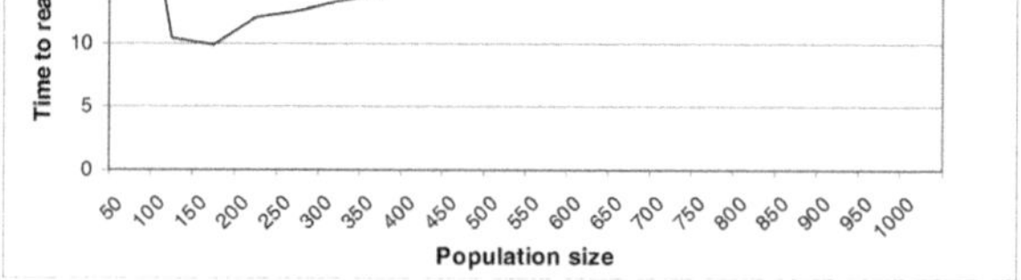

Fig. 3. Effect of population size on time required to reach goal

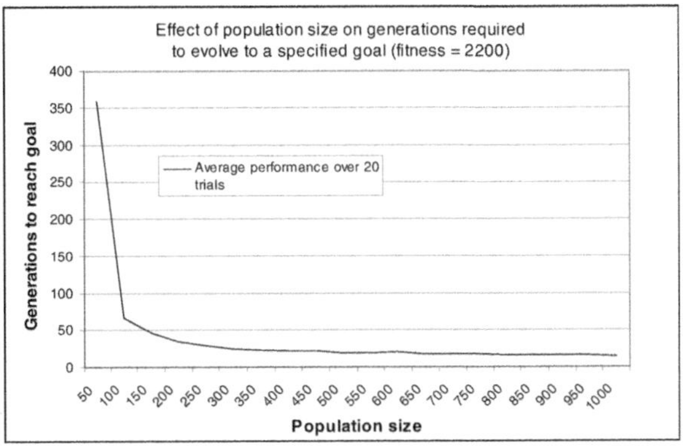

Fig. 4. Effect of population size on number of generations required to reach goal

As one would expect, the number of generations required to achieve the goal goes down as populations get larger, as shown in figure 4, but at the expense of time required to evolve generations of larger populations.

6.4 Mutation

Finally, we observed the effects of mutation by varying both the chance that mutation will occur in any individual *(Mut)*, and the number of course-period assignments affected if mutation does occur *(MutA)*. We tested combinations of these settings over a wide range for each parameter and found that rate of mutation is consistently effective in the range $.05 \leq Mut \leq .93$. Amount of mutation has a more pronounced effect on the scheduler's progress. *MutA* is most effective when it is kept to a small nonzero value ($1 \leq MutA \leq 3$), and consistently performed best at $MutA = 1$. Figure 5 shows the effect of mutation on average best fitness where *Mut* is varied between 0 and .05 in increments of .001, at several *MutA* settings. We ran 20 trials for each increment and averaged the best fitness scores attained. Other GA conditions were as previously described.

The results showed that higher values of *MutA* have a clear disruptive effect on the search. Average best fitness becomes steadily worse as *MutA* gets larger, until the scheduler's performance approaches that of random search at $MutA > 20$.

7 Conclusion

Our use of genetic algorithms proved to be a very effective technique for the USAWC, where course schedules are generated based on both traditional scheduling constraints, and on a measure of quality derived from student demand for courses. This domain-specific implementation produced excellent results on the practical problem of scheduling elective courses in support of a curriculum that sees a significant amount of yearly change in terms of both course offerings and student interest in the courses. The scheduler is deployed as part of a successful decision support system used by college administrators. Empirical testing of the component bears out the solution's effectiveness and consistency with current theoretical and applied work in genetic algorithms.

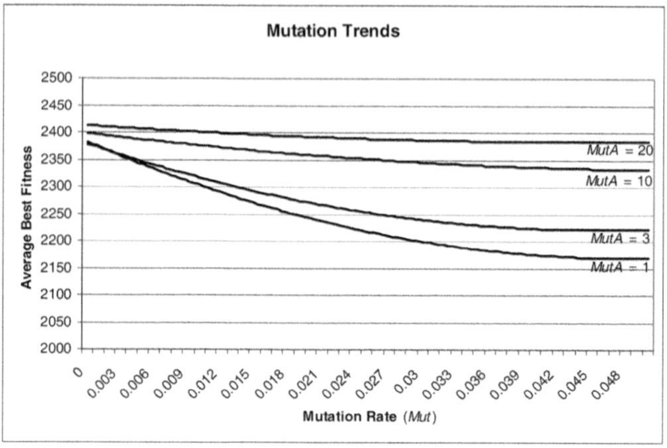

Fig. 5. Effect of mutation on scheduler progress

A next step for the development of this solver is to generalize the solution to be applied to other USAWC scheduling and partitioning problems. Potential applications include several scheduling tasks in support of strategic simulations, and the assignment of students to seminars.

Acknowledgements. I wish to acknowledge the contributions of former Knowledge Engineering Group members MAJ Kevin Giles and MAJ George Hluck, who initially devised the conflict matrix for fitness evaluation in the application of a commercial GA solver. I would also like to acknowledge the USAWC Department of Academic Affairs for providing the problem and user testing opportunities, and the Center for Strategic Leadership for support to the development effort.

References

1. Abramson, D. and Abela, J. 1991. A Parallel Genetic Algorithm for Solving the School Timetabling Problem, Technical report, Division of Information Technology, C.S.I.R.O.
2. Cartwright, H. 1994. Getting the Timing Right - The Use of Genetic Algorithms in Scheduling. In *Proceedings of Adaptive Computing and Information Processing Conference*, 393-411, Brunel, London: UNISYS.
3. Colorni, Alberto; Dorigo Marco; and Maniezzo, Vittorio 1990. Genetic Algorithms and Highly Constrained Problems: The Time-Table Case. In *Parallel Problem Solving from Nature*, 55-59. Springer-Verlag.
4. DeJong, K. and Spears, W.M. 1990. An Analysis of the Interacting Roles of Population Size and Crossover in Genetic Algorithms. In *Parallel Problem Solving from Nature*, 38-47. Springer-Verlag.

5. DeJong, K. and Spears, W.M. 1989. Using Genetic Algorithms to Solve NP-complete Problems. In *Proceedings of the Third International Conference on Genetic Algorithms*, 124-132. Morgan Kaufmann,
6. Erben, Wilhelm and Keppler, Jurgen 1995. A Genetic Algorithm Solving a Weekly Course-Timetabling Problem. In *Proceedings of the 1st International Conference on the Practice and Theory of Automated Timetabling (ICPTAT '95)*, 21-32. Napier University, Edinburgh.
7. Haupt, Randy L. and Haupt, Sue Ellen, eds. 1998. *Practical Genetic Algorithms.* New York, NY: John Wiley & Sons, Inc.
8. Husbands, P., Genetic Algorithms for Scheduling, *AISB Quarterly*, No. 89.
9. Levine, D. M. 1993. A Genetic Algorithm for the Set Partitioning Problem. In *Proceedings of the 5th International Conference on Genetic Algorithms*, 481-487. San Mateo, CA: Morgan Kaufmann Publishers.
10. Russell, Stuart J., and Norvig, Peter, eds 1995. *Artificial Intelligence: A Modern Approach*. Upper Saddle River, NJ: Prentice-Hall.
11. Shaw, K.J. and Fleming, P.J. 1997. Which Line is it Anyway? Use of Rules and Preferences for Schedule Builders in Genetic Algorithms Production Scheduling. In *Proceedings of the AISB '97 Workshop on Evolutionary Computation.*
12. Shaw, K.J. and Fleming, P.J. 1996. An Initial Study of Practical Multi-Objective Genetic Algorithms Production Scheduling using Genetic Algorithms. In *Proceedings of the International Conference on Control '96*. University of Exeter.

Separation Surfaces through Genetic Programming

José C. Riquelme, Raúl Giráldez, Jesús S. Aguilar, and Roberto Ruiz

Departamento de Lenguajes y Sistemas Informáticos.
Av. Reina Mercedes s/n 41012 Sevilla Spain
{riquelme,giraldez,aguilar,rruiz}@lsi.us.es

Abstract. The aim of this paper is to describe a study for the obtaining, symbolically, of the separation surfaces between clusters of a labelled database. A separation surface is an equation with the form $\phi\ (x)=0$, where ϕ is a function of $\Re^n \rightarrow \Re$. The calculation of function ϕ is begun by the development of the parametric regression by means of the use of the Genetic Programming. The symbolic regression consists in approximating an unknown function's equation, through knowledge of certain points' coordinates and the value that a function reaches with the same ones. This possibility was propose in [Koza92a] and its advantage in front of the classic statistical regressions is that it is not necessary previously to know the form the function. Once this surface is found, a classifier for the database could be obtained. The technique has been applied to different examples and the results have been very satisfactory.

Keywords: genetic programming, classification, dynamical systems.

1. Introduction: Problem Statement

The Evolutionary Algorithms (EA), according to [Goldberg89], are adaptive procedures for the search of solutions in complex spaces inspired by the biological evolution, through operation patterns based on the Darwin's theory about reproduction and survival of the individuals that better adapt to the surroundings where they live. In 1989, J. R. Koza, in [Koza89], introduced the paradigm of the genetic programming (GP), which was developed in his texts [Koza92b] and [Koza94] later.

The search space for the GP is the hyperspace of the valid trees, which can be recurrently created from the composition of possible functions and terminals. The initial information is made up by a database where each register is composed of two fields: a n-tuple of real values, that represent the coodinates of a point in a domain Ω_p, which we denominated *parameters* or *characteristics*, and of a *class* or *label* associate to that point, which takes values in a discreet finite space. Therefore, we have N points P_j (j=1..N) in $\Re^n$, each one with an assigned label. This is a typical problem of classification in supervised learning. Multiple approaches to the problem exist in bibliography: neuronal networks, decision trees, nearest neighbours, etc.

This simplification to limit itself two regions, which does not constitute a limitation to a more general classification problem, because if there exist more than two different regions, is enough with repeating the scheme for all the possible pairs. It is necessary to consider that to speak about a surface that separates three regions does not have sense, and to assume a connected region of the space is conformed by

L. Monostori, J. Váncza, and M. Ali (Eds.): IEA/AIE 2001, LNAI 2070, pp. 428-433, 2001.

points of some type. If the points of a same type did not conform an only connected region, we can calculate the connected regions ([Riquelme97] exposes an approach to this problem) and apply the algorithm these.

The evolutionary process will try to find a function f^* of $\Re^n$ in $\Re$, like optimal function to approximate to a function ϕ which theoretically defines the surface. Basically, the method consists of choosing the points of Ω_p for a training file, assigning to each point a value of function ϕ that we want to approximate. Thus each point of Ω_p becomes one tuple of a training file for the parametric regression. The training file is organised like N records with the coordinates of each P_j and the value of $\phi(P_j)$.

An evolutionary process like the GP applied to this file of training obtains that the parametric regression provides a function, which will tend to separate two subspaces constituted by two sets of points with different characteristics. This is thus because the function will have to take positive values for the points from a set and negatives for those of the other. So, the function ϕ $(x_0, x_1 ... x_n)=0$ will be a separation surface between the points of both types.

The advantages of the GP as opposed to other techniques of the classification would be the following ones: With regard to the trees of the decision, we not only can work with any type of separation surface, also with hyperplanes, which are used habitually by these techniques. With regard to the neuronal networks, the GP does not have to find the architecture of the network, nor a parametric equation for the surface, task that is not simple in a neuronal network. The main disadvantage is the time of computation, mainly with regard to using decision trees. Nevertheless, the classification problems usually do not need a learning in real time, although once this learning are done, its application yes must be immediate, and our technique fulfils this characteristic.

2. Proposed Solution

2.1 Representation of the Individuals of the Population

The tree structure will be, with arithmetic operators F={ +, -, *, \ } and operand T = { x_0, $x_1 ... x_n$ } which are coordinate of the space to classify, the chosen one for the representation of the individuals of the population. The operands will only appear in the terminal nodes, whereas the internal nodes will be labelled with the operators.

To generate each tree in the initial population is made through the random obtaining of a tree with the labelled nodes. It will be begun at random selecting one of the functions, which will be the root's label of the tree. We will restrict the election of this label to the set F because we want to generate a structure hierarchic, not a degenerated structure only composed of an only terminal.

Whenever a point of the tree is labelled with an operator of F we will generate two subtrees which will represent the parameters of this operator. Then, an element is selected randomly to label those new subtrees. If a function is chosen to be the label, then the generation process continues recurrently as we described previously. However, if a terminal is chosen to be the label in any point, that point becomes a leaf of the tree and the generation process finishes for that subtree.

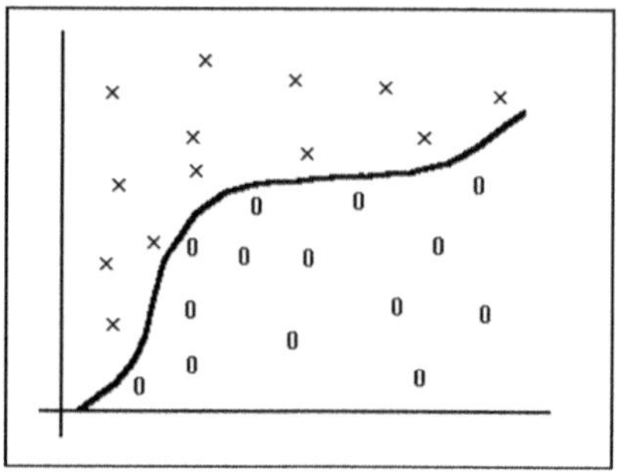

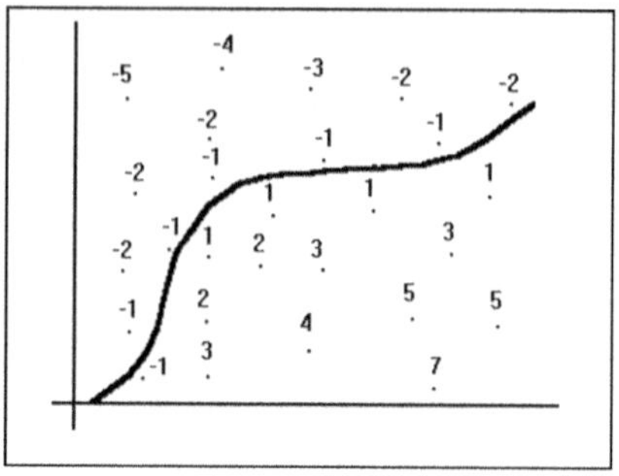

Fig. 1. and **Fig. 2.** Example: Assignment of values to the points of the training file.

2.2 Fitness Function

The notation in this section is as follows: the function ϕ is the searched ideal function, that is to say, the one that defines the separation surface. This function will be approximated by a set of individuals f_i during the evolutionary process. When this process has finished, an approach f^* will be obtained. And finally, the function φ is defined like the function that measures the error of approach of f_i to ϕ. In other words, φ is the function that must be minimised.

The function ϕ, in each point P of the training file, is defined as follows: If P is a point of the Region A, the nearest points to P (V_j j=1..Nv) are calculated, but only if these belong to B. Then the average value of the points V_j and P is assigned to the function ϕ in P. Otherwise, if P is a point of Region B, the operation previous is repeated with the class A neighbours, but the function ϕ take the value of the average distance but with negative sign. This allocation of values for the training file tries that the space of points is classified clearly in two subspaces of values (positive and negative) and where the transition of the points of a type to those of the other is made gradually (Fig. 1 and 2).

The adjusted function φ has to be optimise. This function is inversely proportional to the average of the errors of the individuals of a generation. This error can be calculated through two methods:

1. The error of an individual f_i in a point P_j in the training file can define itself as the absolute value of the difference between the functions f_i and ϕ for that point. If we added the error of each point P_j, we obtain a possible function of error that will try to approach the searched function of separation ϕ by means of f_i:

$$Error_1(f_i) = \sum_{j=1}^{N} \left| f_i(P_j) - \phi(P_j) \right|$$

2. Another possibility is to calculate the error of a function f_i based on the number of incorrectly classified points. If the aim is that the functions f_i come near to a function ϕ, which separates the points of class A of the B, an individual f_i commits an error in P_j if the value of its sign is not equal than the previously assigned sign. That is to say, if the P_j is of class A, then the values taken by ϕ are positives, and therefore, f_i is punished if it is negative in P_j. And if the P_j is of class B, the opposite happens. Formally:

$$Error_2(f_i)=\sum_{j=1}^{N} g(P_j) \quad where \quad g(P_j)=\begin{cases}0 & if\ P_j \in regionA \wedge f_i(P_j)>0\\ 0 & is\ P_j \in regionB \wedge f_i(P_j)<0\\ 1 & otherwise\end{cases}$$

After making diverse tests, we choose a linear combination of both possibilities: on the one hand, the number of incorrectly classified points which gave rise to the integer part of the error; on the other, the fractional part that had been formed by the sum of the differences between the approach *fi* and ϕ for each point P. This means that, definitively, the error of a function *fi* is

$$Error(f_i)=Error_2(f_i)+10^{-m} * Error_1(f_i)$$

where m>1 is selected so that the fractional part is smaller than 1.

2.3 Reproduction Model

We must solve how to produce the next generation of trees (functions) from the initial population, once well-known the convenience of the same ones. To make this task, we must choose a reproduction elitist model, is to say, the best individual of the present generation is duplicated and introduced in the next one. Besides a constant percentage of the new generation is obtained by means of copy of the selected individuals randomly in the previous generation with a probability based on its fitness. Finally, the remaining individuals of the new generation are obtained through crossovers between the individuals of the precedent generation.

The sizes of population are 100 and 200. We worked with initial heights from 4 to 5 and with maximum heights between 7 and 9. The passage by the generations 100, 200 and 400 will be analysed. With the percentage of the best individuals that pass directly from a generation to another one, we can regulate that the generations are more or less elitist. The values with which we work are 10%, 15%, and 20%.

3. Application

3.1 Iris File

A typical database example for classification problems is IRIS DATA since it was proposed in [Fisher 36]. This is a file of 150 registers with four parameters and three labels. The method has been applied for the obtaining of an approach to the surface that separates the different labels. The first approach consists of separating the first type of the other two. This is a easy exercise, because the classes are clearly separated. The simplest solution is p2-p3=0, that is to say, if p2>p3 then type 1 and if p3>p2 then type 2 or 3. This solution does not commit any error.

More difficult is to separate types 2 and 3. Nevertheless, the reached solution to separate these two types has 4 errors (Fig 3. left) or only two errors with a more complex solution (Fig. 3 right)

$$(p_1 p_4)(p_4 - p_1 + p_3) - p_4 = 0 \qquad (p_2 + p_3 p_4 + p_3 - 2p_1)(p_2 - p_3) + p_1 = 0$$

Fig. 3. Surfaces for IRIS data

3.2 Basins of Attraction of a Dynamical System

A more complex example of application is to obtain the surfaces that separate the basins of attraction of a dynamic system. The studied model is a predator-prey ecological system. The points to classify based on the obtained attractors are 500 with the following division: 317 points converge to a equilibrium points, 154 points are limit cycles and 15 points are indetermined attractors. The aim of this example is to try to find surface that separates the attraction basins, that is to say, the 317 equilibrium points from the 154 limit cycles. The figure 4 shows a projection of the types of attractors on coordinates y (axis of abscissa) and z (axis of ordinate) of the initial conditions, where the X represent balance points, the circles represent limit cycles and the crosses represent the undetermined points.

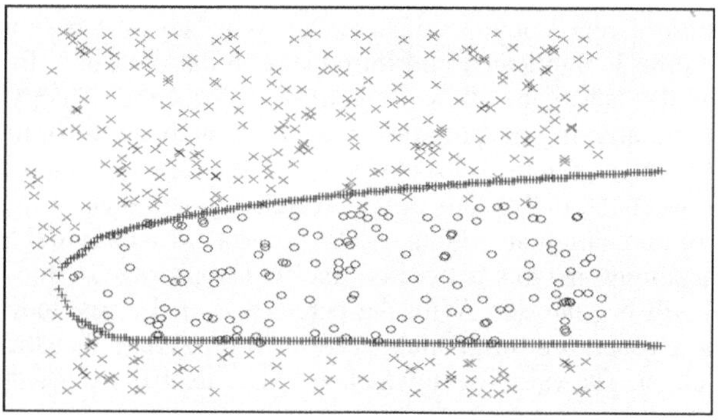

Fig. 4. Separation surface.

If we notice the figure 4, the limit cycles are concentrated in a strip determined by coordinate z and for almost all the values of the coordinate y (except for values very next to zero). This strip seems a parabola with the axis parallel to the axis of abscissas and with the almost parallel branches in the represented region. If it is tried to find an analytical approach to the surface, the found equation with smaller number of errors (3%) is as follows:

$$(3z^3 + 4y^2 - y - 3z)(4y^2 + 10yz) + y + 2z^6 - yz^2 = 0$$

A graphical approach of this function can be obtained. In the figure 4, these border points are shown by means of crosses.

4. Conclusions

An application of the genetic programming is shown to find the symbolic expression of a surface that separates two regions of points of different type. The symbolic parametric regression can be applied after assigning to a numerical value to each tuple of points in the space that we want to classify. This value has been chosen like the average distance of a point to the nearest points of the other type (for some it is positive and for others it is negative). Therefor, if we demand the continuity of the function, its value equal to zero provides us the searched surface and, in addition, a symbolic classifier for any database. The main disadvantage that we found is the time of computation, mainly if we related it to the decision trees. For example, the execution with the IRIS file can need about 15 minutes computation in a present PC. But the obtained error rates are very inferior and the classification is immediate once the surface is found.

Acknowledgements. This work has been supported by the Spanish Research Agency CICYT under grant TIC99-0351.

5. References

1. Fisher, R.: The use of multiple measurement in Taxonomic problems. Annals of Eugenics, nº 7, pp. 179-188, 1936.
2. Goldberg, D.E.: Genetic algorithms in search, optimization and machine learning. Addison-Wesley, 1989.
3. Koza, J.R.: Hierarchical genetic algorithms operating on populations of computer programs. Proc. of 11th Int. J. Conf. on A.I., I, pp 768-774, Morgan Kauffman,. 1989.
4. Koza, J.R.: The genetic programming paradigm: genetically breeding populations of computer programs to solve problems. Dynamic, Genetic and Chaotic Programming, Ed. Baranko Soucek e IRIS Group, pp 269-276. John Wiley & Sons. 1992.
5. Koza, J.R.: The genetic programming: on the programming of computers by means of natural selection. The MIT Press. 1992.
6. Koza, J.R.: Genetic Programming II. Automatic discovery of reusable programs. The MIT Press. 1994.
7. Riquelme, J. y M. Toro: Search and linguistic description of connected regions in quantitative data. Proc. of the IFAC Conference on the Control of Industrial Systems CIS-97, Vol. 3 pp. 310-316, Belfort (France), 1997.

Distributed Configuration as Distributed Dynamic Constraint Satisfaction

Alexander Felfernig, Gerhard Friedrich, Dietmar Jannach, and Markus Zanker

Institut für Wirtschaftsinformatik und Anwendungssysteme, Produktionsinformatik,
Universitätsstrasse 65-67, A-9020 Klagenfurt, Austria,
{felfernig,friedrich,jannach,zanker}@ifi.uni-klu.ac.at.

Abstract. Dynamic constraint satisfaction problem (DCSP) solving is one of the most important methods for solving various kinds of synthesis tasks, such as configuration. Todays configurators are standalone systems not supporting distributed configuration problem solving functionality. However, supply chain integration of configurable products requires the integration of configuration systems of different manufacturers, which jointly offer product solutions to their customers. As a consequence, we need problem solving methods that enable the computation of such configurations by several distributed configuration agents. Therefore, one possibility is the extension of the configuration problem from a dynamic constraint satisfaction representation to *distributed* dynamic constraint satisfaction (DDCSP). In this paper we will contribute to this challenge by formalizing the DDCSP and by presenting a complete and sound algorithm for solving distributed dynamic constraint satisfaction problems. This algorithm is based on asynchronous backtracking and enables strategies for exploiting conflicting requirements and design assumptions (i.e. learning additional constraints during search). The exploitation of these additional constraints is of particular interest for configuration because the generation and the exchange of conflicting design assumptions based on *nogoods* can be easily integrated in existing configuration systems.[1]

1 Introduction

Dynamic constraint satisfaction is a representation formalism suitable for representing and solving synthesis tasks, such as configuration [11], [13]. These tasks have a dynamic nature in the sense that the set of problem variables changes depending on the initial requirements and the decisions taken during the problem solving process resulting in a reduction of the search space to relevant problem variables. In this context the notion of activity constraints discussed in [11] is well suited for stating decision criteria on the activity state of problem variables.

There is an increasing demand for applications providing solutions for configuration tasks in various domains (e.g. telecommunications industry, computer industry, or automotive industry). This demand is boosted by the mass customization paradigm and e-business applications. Especially the integration of

[1] This work was partly funded by the EU commission under contract IST-1999-10688.

L. Monostori, J. Váncza, and M. Ali (Eds.): IEA/AIE 2001, LNAI 2070, pp. 434–444, 2001.

configurators in order to support cooperative configuration such as supply chain integration of customizable products is an open research issue. Current configurator approaches [3] , [7] are designed for solving local configuration problems, but there is still no problem solving method which considers variable activity state in the distributed case. Security and privacy concerns make it impossible to centralize problem solving in one centralized configurator.

As a consequence, we have to extend dynamic constraint satisfaction to *distributed* dynamic constraint satisfaction. Based on asynchronous backtracking [14] we propose an extension for standard distributed CSP formalisms by incorporating activity constraints in order to reason about the activity states of problem variables. In the sense of distributed constraint satisfaction we characterize a Distributed Dynamic Constraint Satisfaction Problem (DDCSP) as a cooperative distributed problem solving task. Activity constraints, compatibility constraints as well as variables are distributed among the problem solving agents. The goal is to find a variable instantiation which fulfills all local as well as inter-agent constraints. In this context each agent has a restricted view on the knowledge of another agent, but does not have complete access to the remote agents knowledge base.

Asynchronous backtracking offers the basis for bounded learning strategies which supports the reduction of search efforts. This is of particular interest for integrating configurators. Configurators send configuration requests to their solution providing partners. These partners eventually discover conflicting requirements (i.e. *nogoods*) which are communicated back to the requesting configurator thus supporting the efficient revision of requirements or design decisions. Based on asynchronous backtracking we provide a sound and complete algorithm for distributed dynamic constraint satisfaction where a very limited *nogood* recording is sufficient.

In the following we give a formal definition for a DDCSP *(Section 2)* and show how to employ this formalism for representing a distributed configuration problem. Following this formal definition we propose an algorithm for solving DDCSP *(Section 3)*. We analyze runtime and space complexity of this algorithm and show completeness and soundness. Finally we discuss related work followed by general conclusions.

2 Distributed Dynamic Constraint Satisfaction Task

Before giving a definition of a DDCSP we recall the definition of a distributed CSP. A set of agents must find a solution for a distributed set of finite domain variables. There exist n agents, where each agent a_i has m variables x_{ij}, $i \in \{1..n\}$, $j \in \{1..m\}$. Agent variables have a priority denoted as p_{ij}. Each variable x_{ij} is assigned to a domain $D_l \in Doms = \{D_1, D_2, ...\}$, where $Dom\,(\mathrm{x}_{ij})$ denotes the domain of the variable x_{ij}. Constraints are distributed among agents, where C_{ik} denotes constraint k of agent a_i. A distributed CSP is solved *iff* $\forall \mathrm{x}_{ij}$, $\forall \mathrm{C}_{ik}$: x_{ij} is instantiated with one $d \in Dom\,(\mathrm{x}_{ij})$, and C_{ik} is true under the assignment $\mathrm{x}_{ij}{=}d$.

In order to formulate constraints on the activity state of problem variables, [11] propose four major types of activity constraints as follows. Note, that $x_{ij} \notin \{x_{pq} \wedge x_{vw} \wedge \ldots\}$ must hold, where x_{ij}, x_{pq}, and x_{vw} are different agent variables.

1. *Require Variable* ($\overset{RV}{\Rightarrow}$): the activity state of a variable depends on the value assignment to a set of active variables, i.e. $P(x_{pq}, x_{vw}, \ldots) \overset{RV}{\Rightarrow} x_{ij}$. P denotes a predicate determining whether the variable x_{ij} must be active or not.
2. *Always Require* ($\overset{ARV}{\Rightarrow}$): the activity state of a variable depends on the activity state of a set of other variables, i.e. $(x_{pq} \wedge x_{vw} \wedge \ldots) \overset{ARV}{\Rightarrow} x_{ij}$.
3. *Require Not* ($\overset{RN}{\Rightarrow}$): a variable must not be active if a certain assignment of a set of variables is given, i.e. $P(x_{pq}, x_{vw}, \ldots) \overset{RN}{\Rightarrow} x_{ij}$.
4. *Always Require Not* ($\overset{ARN}{\Rightarrow}$): a variable must not be active if a set of variables is active, i.e. $(x_{pq} \wedge x_{vw} \wedge \ldots) \overset{ARN}{\Rightarrow} x_{ij}$.

Based on the above definition of a distributed CSP and the notion of activity constraints we give a formal definition of a DDCSP. In order to determine whether a variable x_{ij} is active or not we associate a state variable with each x_{ij} denoted as $x_{ijstatus}$, where $Dom(x_{ijstatus}) = \{active, inactive\}$. Additionally there are two different types of constraints, namely *compatibility constraints* (C_C), which restrict the compatibility of variable assignments, and *activity constraints* (C_A), which constrain the activity state of constraint variables.

Definition 1 *Distributed Dynamic CSP (DDCSP)*
Given:

- *n agents, where agent* $a_i \in \{a_1, a_2, \ldots, a_n\}$.
- *Each agent* a_i *knows a set of variables* $V_i = \{x_{i1}, x_{i2}, \ldots, x_{im}\}$, *where* $V_i \neq \emptyset$ *and each* x_{ij} *has a dedicated state variable denoted as* $x_{ijstatus}$[2].
- *Furthermore,* $V_{istart} \subseteq V_i$ *denotes the initial active variables of agent* a_i, *where* $V_{start} = \bigcup V_{istart}$ *and* $V_{start} \neq \emptyset$. *Additionally, the following condition must hold:* $\forall x_{ij}: (x_{ij} \in \{V_{istart}\}) \Rightarrow x_{ijstatus} = active$, *i.e.* $true \overset{ARV}{\Rightarrow} x_{ij}$.
- *A set of domains* $Doms = \{D_1, D_2, \ldots\}$, *where each variable* x_{ij} *is assigned to a domain* $D_l \in Doms$ *and* $Dom(x_{ijstatus}) = \{active, inactive\}$.
- *A set of constraints C distributed among agents, where* $C = C_C \cup C_A$ *and* C_{Cik} (C_{Aik}) *denotes compatibility (activity) constraint k of agent* a_i.

Find:
A solution Θ *representing an assignment to variables which meets the following criteria:*

1. *The variables and their assignments in* Θ *satisfy each constraint* $\in C$, *i.e.* Θ *is consistent with* $C_C \cup C_A$.
2. *All variables* $x_{ij} \in V_{start}$ *are active and instantiated.*
3. *There is no assignment* Θ' *satisfying 1. and 2., s.t.* $\Theta' \subset \Theta$.

[2] In the following we denote x_{ij} as content variable, $x_{ijstatus}$ as status variable.

Following this definition we give an example of representing a distributed configuration task as DDCSP *(Figure 1).* A car manufacturer (a_1), a chassis and motor supplier (a_2), and an electric equipment supplier (a_3) cooperatively solve a distributed configuration task. Shared knowledge is represented through variables belonging to common constraints. User requirements are provided as additional constraints, which are denoted as C_R= {(package=standard),(car-body=4door-limo)}, furthermore V_{1start} = {car-body, package}; V_{2start} = {transmission, motorization}; V_{3start} = {battery}. A solution for this configuration task is the following: {car-body= 4door-limo, package= standard, transmission= manual, motorization= 55bhp, battery= medium}. Note that the variables airbag, front-fog-lights, and electric-windows are not part of the above solution.

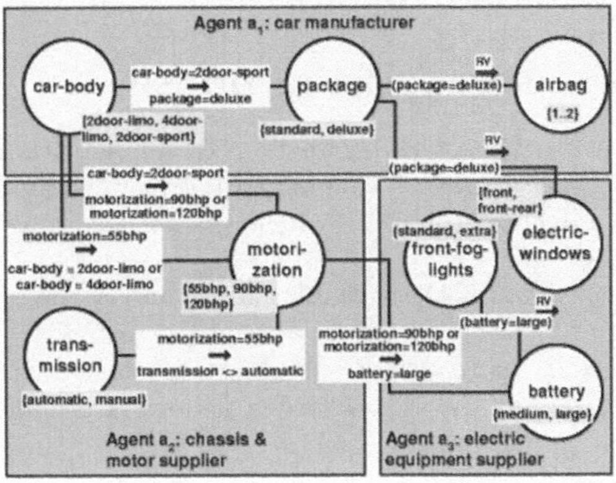

Fig. 1. Example: Distributed Configuration

3 Solving Distributed Dynamic Constraint Satisfaction Problems

In the following we discuss our extensions to *asynchronous backtracking* [14], which is a complete, asynchronous version of a standard backtracking algorithm for solving distributed CSPs. Problem variables are distributed among problem solving agents, where each agent a_i has exactly two variables (x_i and $x_{istatus}$)[3]. Each agent variable x_i has a unique priority p_i, furthermore x_i and $x_{istatus}$ always have the same priority[4]. We assume that constraints are binary, which is not limitating, because it is well known that any non-binary discrete CSP can be translated to an equivalent representation with binary constraints. For this

[3] The case of solving a distributed CSP with multiple local variables is discussed in [15]. In this case multiple virtual local agents (each working on a local variable) try to find a solution which satisfies all local constraints. The principles of asynchronous backtracking [14] remain the same for the case of multiple local variables.

[4] The lowest value represents the highest priority.

conversion two general methods are known: the dual graph method [6] and the hidden variable method [12]. We denote two agents whose variables participate in the same binary constraint as *connected.* Furthermore we can say that these links between variables are *directed*, because of the unique priority that is associated with each variable. The agent with the higher priority is sending the variable value (via *ok?* messages) after each change of his variable instantiation to the connected agents. The latter evaluate their local constraints and inform corresponding agents about local inconsistencies (via *nogood* messages). *Nogoods* represent conflicting variable instantiations which are calculated by applying resolution. Their generation is a potential source of inefficiency because of space complexity[5]. Variable assignments of value sending agents are stored as tuple $(j,(y_j,d))$ in the local *agent_view* of the connected constraint evaluating agent, where y_j can either represent a content variable or a state variable.

3.1 Asynchronous Backtracking for DDCSP

Based on asynchronous backtracking we propose an algorithm for solving DDCSPs (*Algorithm 1*). The messages exchanged between agents have the following signatures, where j denotes the index of the message sending agent a_j.

- *ok?*$(j,(y_j,d))$: y_j denotes the variable name, and d the actual instantiation of y_j *(Algorithm 1 (a)).*
- *nogood*$(j,nogood_j)$: $nogood_j$ is a set of inconsistent variable instantiations represented as $\{(k,(y_k,d)),...\}$, where k denotes the index of the agent a_k storing variable y_k with value d *(Algorithm 1 (b)).*

Both, *ok*?, and *nogood* messages can contain content information as well as state information about communicated variables, e.g. *ok?*$(1,(x_{1status},inactive))$ communicates activity information about variable x_1, *nogood*$(3,\{(1,(x_{1status},active)), (2,(x_2, 3))\})$ denotes the fact that either $x_{1status}$ must not be active or x_2 must not be instantiated with 3. If a tuple $(i,(x_i,d))$ (x_i is a content variable) is added to the *agent_view*, an additional tuple $(i,(x_{istatus},active))$ is added. If a tuple $(i,(x_{istatus},inactive)$ is added to the agent_view, the tuple $(i,(x_i,d))$ is deleted from the *agent_view.*

When the algorithm starts, all agents instantiate their active variables x_i, where $x_i \in V_{start}$, propagate their instantiations to connected agents and wait for messages. All other agents a_j propagate $x_{jstatus}=inactive$ to connected agents[6]. When an agent receives a message, it checks the consistency of its local *agent_view (Algorithm 1 (c)).* Similar to the ATMS-based approach discussed in [11] our algorithm contains *two* problem solving levels.

First, all local activity constraints are checked in order to determine the *Activity State Consistency.*

[5] In *Section 3.3* we show how space complexity can be significantly reduced.

[6] This initialization is not included in *Algorithm 1.*

Definition 2 *Activity State Consistency*
Activity State Consistency is given, iff $x_{selfstatus}$ is consistent with agent_view, i.e. all evaluated activity constraints are true under the value assignments of agent_view, and all communicated nogoods are incompatible with agent_view[7].

The variable $x_{selfstatus}$ represents the state variable of the local agent a_{self}[8]. The function *ASC (c.1)* checks the *Activity State Consistency*, tries to instantiate $x_{selfstatus}$ with a consistent value if needed, and returns *true* if *Activity State Consistency* is given, otherwise it returns *false*. If an inconsistent *Activity State* is detected, e.g. there is a contradiction between activity constraints, and $x_{selfstatus}$ can not be adapted consistently, *nogoods* are calculated including the domain constraints of $x_{selfstatus}$ and backtracking is done *(c.7)*. If *Activity State Consistency* is given and $x_{selfstatus}$ has been changed to inactive, an *ok?* message containing the new variable state is sent to the constraint evaluating agents *(c.6)*.

Second, if *Activity State Consistency* is given *(c.1)* and the local variable is active *(c.2)*, the algorithm checks the *Agent Consistency.*

Definition 3 *Agent Consistency*
Agent Consistency is given, iff the agent is in a Consistent Activity State and x_{self} is consistent with agent_view, i.e. all evaluated compatibility constraints are true under the value assignments of agent_view, and all communicated nogoods are incompatible with agent_view.

The variable x_{self} represents the content variable of the local agent a_{self}. The function *AC (c.3)* checks the *Agent Consistency*, tries to instantiate x_{self} with a consistent value if needed, and returns *true* if *Agent Consistency* given, otherwise it returns *false*. If no *Agent Consistency* is given and x_{self} can not be instantiated consistently, *nogoods* are calculated including the domain constraints of x_{self} and $x_{selfstatus}$, and backtracking is done *(c.5)*. Else, if the value of x_{self} has been changed, an *ok?* message is sent to the connected constraint evaluating agents of a_{self} *(c.4)*.

Algorithm 1 *Asynchronous Backtracking for DDCSP*[9]

```
(a) when received (ok?(j,(y_j,d))) do
       add {(j,(y_j,d))} to agent_view;
       x_selfstatusold ← x_selfstatus; x_selfold ← x_self;
       check_agent_view; end do;
(b) when received (nogood(j,nogood_j)) do
       add nogood_j to nogood_list[10];
       if ∃ (k,(x_k,d)) in nogood_j:
                       x_k ¬connected[11] then
```

[7] *Agent_view* is compatible with a *nogood*, *iff* all *nogood* variables have the same value as in *agent_view*, $x_{selfstatus}$, and x_{self}.

[8] *self* denotes the index of the local agent a_{self}.

[9] The algorithm does not include a stable-state detection. In order to solve this task, stable state detection algorithms like distributed snapshots [2] are needed.

[10] The *nogood_list* contains the locally stored *nogoods*.

[11] In order to check the *nogood*, all variables of connected agents part of the *nogood* must be represented in the *agent_view*.

```
          request a_k to add a link to self;
          add current {(k,(x_k,d))} to agent_view;
        end if;
        x_selfstatusold ← x_selfstatus; x_selfold ← x_self;
        check_agent_view;
        if x_selfold = x_self ∧
              x_selfstatusold = x_selfstatus then
          send (ok?,(self,(x_self,d_self))) to a_j;
        end if; end do;
(c) procedure check_agent_view;
(c.1) if ASC(agent_view, x_selfstatus) then
(c.2)     if x_selfstatus = active then
(c.3)       if AC(agent_view, x_self) then
              if x_self ≠ x_selfold ∨
                      x_selfstatus ≠ x_selfstatusold then
(c.4)           send (ok?(self,(x_self,d_self)))
                to connected constraint evaluating agents;
              end if;
(c.5)       else nogoods←{K_s|K_s ⊆ agent_view∧
             inconsistent(K_s,Dom(x_self),Dom
                 backtrack(nogoods);
            end if;
          elseif x_selfstatus ≠ x_selfstatusold then
(c.6)       send (ok?(self,(x_selfstatus,d_selfstatus)))
            to connected constraint evaluating agents;
          end if;
(c.7) else nogoods←{K_s|K_s ⊆ agent_view∧
        inconsistent(K_s,Dom(x_selfstatus))};
                 backtrack(nogoods);
        end if; end check_agent_view;
(d) procedure backtrack (nogoods);
        if ∅ ∈ nogoods then
          broadcast to other agents (¬∃ solution);
          terminate algorithm;
        end if;
        ∀ K_s ∈ nogoods do
          select a_k∈ agents(K_s):lowest priority (a_k);
          send (nogood(self,K_s)) to a_k;
          remove {(k,(x_k,d)),(k,(x_kstatus,d_status))}
                      from agent_view;
        end do; check_agent_view; end backtrack;
```

3.2 Example: Solving a DDCSP

In the following we give a simple example consisting of three agents a_1, a_2, and a_3 (see *Figure 2*). We define a set of variables $\{x_1,x_2,x_3\}$ belonging to the agents a_1, a_2, and a_3 where $Dom(x_1)=\{1,2\}$, $Dom(x_2)=\{3\}$, and $Dom(x_3)=\{2\}$.

We define sets of initially active variables: $V1_{start}=\{x_1\}$, $V2_{start}=\emptyset$, $V3_{start}=\emptyset$. In order to store the variable state of agent variables we define $\{x_{1status}, x_{2status}, x_{3status}\}$, where $Dom\ (x_{1status}) = Dom\ (x_{2status}) = Dom\ (x_{3status}) = \{active, inactive\}$. Finally, we introduce the following activity constraints: C_{A31}: $(x_1=1)\overset{RV}{\Rightarrow}x_3$, C_{A21}: $(x_1)\overset{ARV}{\Rightarrow}x_2$, and C_{A22}: $(x_3)\overset{ARN}{\Rightarrow}x_2$, where C_{Aik} denotes activity constraint k of a_i. *Figure 3* shows four snapshots of the solving process.

Agent a_1 locally instantiates its variables without regarding the instantiations of remote agents: $x_1=1$. Now a_1 sends its variable instantiation to the constraint evaluating agents a_2 and a_3 , i.e. *ok?(1,(x₁,1))* . Agents a_2 and a_3

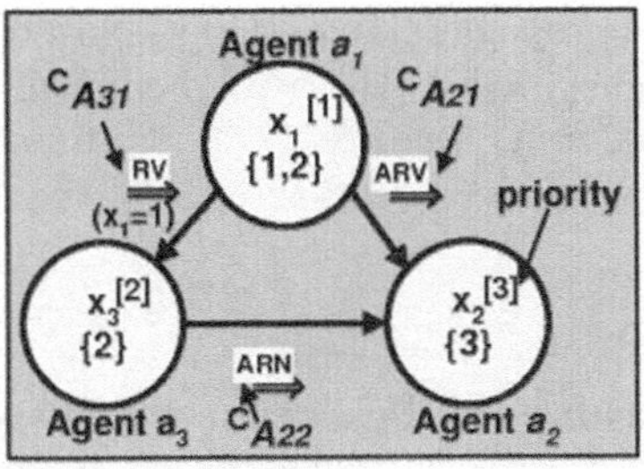

Fig. 2. Example: Distributed Dynamic CSP

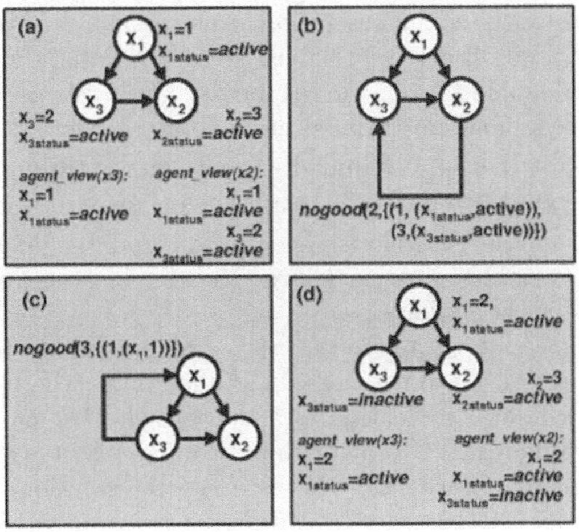

Fig. 3. Views on the solving process

store these values in their local *agent_view*. Both agent variables are activated, i.e. the state of x_2 and x_3 is changed to *active*. Now agent a_3 sends its variable instantiation to agent a_2, *i.e. ok?(3,*$(x_3,2)$*)*. The *view (a)* of *Figure 3* represents the situation after agent a_2 has stored the value change of x_3 in its *agent_view*. Agent a_2 detects an inconsistency while checking its *Activity State Consistency*, since the activity constraints C_{A21} and C_{A22} are incompatible, i.e. x_2 can neither be activated nor deactivated. Agent a_2 determines those variables of the *agent_view* responsible for the inconsistent *Activity State* and communicates *nogood(2,*$\{(1,(x_{1status},active)),\ (3,x_{3status},active))\}$*)* to a_3, which is the lowest priority agent in the calculated *nogood (view (b) of Figure 3)*. This *nogood* is stored in the *nogoods_list* of a_3. Agent a_3 detects an inconsistent *Activity State*, since no value of $x_{selfstatus}$ is consistent with the *agent_view* and C_{A31}. The *nogood* $\{(1,(x_1,1))\}$ is sent to a_1 *(view (c) of Figure 3)*. Note that $(x_1,1) \Rightarrow (x_{1status},active)$.

Agent a_1 is in a consistent *Activity State*, i.e. no activity constraints are violated. For achieving *Agent Consistency* the value of x_1 is changed, i.e. x_1=2.

The new instantiation is propagated to a_2 and a_3. Subsequently a_2 and a_3 enforce *Activity State Consistency.* x_3 is deactivated *and ok?(3,($x_{3status}$,inactive))* is communicated to a_2. Agent a_2 removes *(3,(x_3,2))* from its *agent_view (view (d) of Figure 3).*

3.3 Analysis

In order to show the soundness of *Algorithm 1* we must show that each generated solution (algorithm is in a stable state, i.e. all agents wait for incoming messages and no message is sent) satisfies the criteria stated in *Section 2. First*, the assignments satisfy each constraint, since each agent checks all local constraints after each value change in the local *agent_view. Second*, all variables $x_i \in V_{start}$ are active and instantiated in a solution, since $x_{istatus}$=*active* is a local constraint of agent a_i and all active variables are instantiated. Furthermore, x_i can not be deactivated, since $x_{istatus}$=*active* holds. *Third*, the minimality of the solution is guaranteed, since no variable has a solution relevant value, unless it is *active*. Each variable has well founded support either through $\overset{(A)RV}{\Rightarrow}$ constraints or through its membership in V_{start}. After each change in the local *agent_view*, the activity state of the variable is checked and updated. If no $\overset{(A)RV}{\Rightarrow}$ constraint is activated, the variables state is set to *inactive*, i.e. there is no further well founded support for the variable.

In order to show the completeness of the algorithm we must show that if a solution exists the algorithm reaches a stable state, otherwise the algorithm terminates with a failure indication (empty *nogood*). Let us first assume that the algorithm terminates. If this algorithm terminates by reaching a stable state then we have already shown that this is a correct solution. If this algorithm terminates by deducing the empty *nogood* then by applying resolution we detected that no consistent value assignment to the variables exists, i.e. no solution to the DDCSP exists. Finally we have to show that the algorithm terminates. Sources for infinite processing loops are cycles in message passing and subsequent searching of the same search space. Infinite processing loops are avoided because we require a total order of the agents. The *ok? (nogood)* messages are passed only from agents to connected agents with lower (higher) priority. *Nogoods* avoid subsequent searching of the same search space.

Dynamic constraint satisfaction is an NP-complete problem [13]. The worst-case time complexity of the presented algorithm is exponential in the number of variables. The worst-case space complexity depends on the strategy we employ to handle *nogoods.* The options range from unrestricted learning (e.g. storing all *nogoods*) to the case where *nogood* recording is limited as much as possible. For the agents in the presented algorithm it is sufficient to store only one *nogood* for each $d \in Dom(x_i)$. These *nogoods* are needed to avoid subsequent assignment of the same value for the same search space. In addition all *nogoods* can be deleted which contain a variable-value pair not appearing in the *agent_view.* Consequently the space-complexity for *nogood* recording is $O(n$ —D—), where n is the number of agents and —D— is the maximum cardinality of the domains. In addition the generation of *nogoods* is another source of high computational costs. Note, that in the presented algorithm it is sufficient to generate one *nogood.*

This *nogood* needs not be minimal, i.e. for the *nogood* generation in the procedure *backtrack* even the complete *agent_view* is an acceptable *nogood*. However, non-minimal *nogoods* lead to higher search efforts. The advantages and strategies for exploiting *nogoods* to limit the search activities are discussed in [1], [5].

4 Related Work

Different algorithms have been proposed for solving distributed CSPs. In [10] a distributed backtracking algorithm (DIBT) is presented which is based on the concept of graph based backjumping. The exploitation of *nogoods* is not supported. DIBT is especially powerful if combined with variable ordering techniques. Note that our presented algorithm can use any total ordering, which takes advantage of the actual problem structure and this algorithm also performs graph based backtracking. However, in practice variable ordering must take into account that sets of variables are assigned to one agent and that this assignment cannot be changed because of security or privacy concerns.

Asynchronous weak commitment search proposed by [14] employs a min-conflict heuristic, where a partial solution is extended by adding additional variables until a complete solution is found. In contrast to asynchronous backtracking all detected *nogoods* must be stored, in order to prevent infinite processing loops. In many configuration domains the problem size does not permit the storage of all generated *nogoods*, i.e. asynchronous backtracking is more applicable.

In [4] an agent architecture for solving distributed configuration-design problems employing an algorithm based on the concurrent engineering design paradigm is proposed. The whole problem is decomposed into sub-problems of manageable size which are solved by agents. The primary goal of this approach is efficient distributed design problem solving, whereas our concern is to provide effective support of distributed configuration problem solving, where knowledge is distributed between different agents having a restricted view on the whole configuration process.

5 Conclusions and Further Work

The integration of businesses by internet technologies boosts the demand for distributed problem solving. In particular in knowledge-based configuration we have to move from stand-alone configurators to distributed configuration. Dynamic constraint satisfaction is one of the most applied techniques in the configuration domain and therefore we have to extend this technique to distributed dynamic constraint satisfaction. In this paper we proposed a definition for distributed dynamic constraint satisfaction. Based on this definition we presented a complete and sound algorithm. This algorithm allows the exploitation of bounded learning algorithms. Configuration agents can exchange information about conflicting requirements (e.g. *nogoods*) thus reducing search efforts. The algorithm was implemented by using ILOG configuration and constraint solving libraries. The concepts presented in this paper are an essential part of an integrated environment for the development of cooperative configuration agents, where a conceptual model of configuration agents is automatically translated into an executable logic representation [8].

Further work will include additional applications of the presented algorithm to various configuration problems. These applications will help us to gain more insights in the nature of configuration problems thus providing the basis for further work on DDCSP strategies. E.g. applications in the telecommunication domain support the assumption that in configuration domains *nogoods* tend to be small in their arity. This suggests the application of constraint learning techniques to focus the search.

In addition we are investigating extensions of the basic dynamic CSP paradigm in order to include concepts such as disjunction or default negation as proposed by [13] and generative CSP representation [9].

References

1. R.J. Bayardo and D.P. Miranker. A complexity analysis of space-bounded learning algorithms for the constraint satisfaction problem. In *Proceedings AAAI*, pages 298-304, Portland, Oregon, 1996.
2. M. Chandy and L. Lamport. Distributed snapshots: determining global states of distributed systems. *ACM Trans. Comput. Syst.*, 3,1:63-75, 1985.
3. R. Weigel D. Sabin. Product Configuration Frameworks - A Survey. In E. Freuder B. Faltings, editor, *IEEE Intelligent Systems, Special Issue on Configuration*, volume 13,4, pages 50-58. 1998.
4. T.P. Darr and W.P. Birmingham. An Attribute-Space Representation and Algorithm for Concurrent Engineering. *AIEDAM*, 10,1:21-35, 1996.
5. R. Dechter. Enhancements schemes for constraint processing: backjumping, learning and cutset decomposition. *Artificial Intelligence*, 40,3:273-312, 1990.
6. R. Dechter and J. Pearl. Tree clustering for constraint networks. *Artificial Intelligence*, 38:353-366, 1989.
7. B. Faltings, E. Freuder, and G. Friedrich, editors. Workshop on Configuration. *AAAI Technical Report WS-99-05*, Orlando, Florida, 1999.
8. A. Felfernig, G. Friedrich, and D. Jannach. UML as domain specific language for the construction of knowledge-based configuration systems. In *11th International Conference on Software Engineering and Knowledge Engineering*, pages 337-345, Kaiserslautern, Germany, 1999.
9. G. Fleischanderl, G. Friedrich, A. Haselböck, H. Schreiner, and M. Stumptner. Configuring Large Systems Using Generative Constraint Satisfaction. In E. Freuder B. Faltings, editor, *IEEE Intelligent Systems, Special Issue on Configuration*, volume 13,4, pages 59-68. 1998.
10. Y. Hamadi, C. Bessiere, and J. Quinqueton. Backtracking in distributed Constraint Networks. In *Proceedings of ECAI* 1998, pages 219-223, Brighton, UK, 1998.
11. S. Mittal and B. Falkenhainer. Dynamic Constraint Satisfaction Problems. In *Proceedings of AAAI 1990*, pages 25-32, Boston, MA, 1990.
12. F. Rossi, C. Petrie, and V. Dhar. On the equivalence of constraint satisfaction problems. In *Proceedings of ECAI 1990*, Stockholm, Sweden, 1990.
13. T. Soininen, E. Gelle, and I. Niemelä. A Fixpoint Definition of Dynamic Constraint Satisfaction. In *5th International Conference on Principles and Practice of Constraint Programming - CP'99*, pages 419-433, Alexandria, USA, 1999.
14. M. Yokoo, E.H. Durfee, T. Ishida, and K. Kuwabara. The distributed constraint satisfaction problem. *IEEE Transactions on Knowledge and Data Engineering*, 10,5:673-685, 1998.
15. M. Yokoo and K. Hirayama. Distributed constraint satisfaction algorithm for complex local problems. *Proceedings of the 3rd International Conference on Multi-Agent Systems (ICMAS-98)*, Paris, pages 372-379, 1998.

Representation Choice Methods as the Tool for Solving Uncertainty in Distributed Temporal Database Systems with Indeterminate Valid Time

Ngoc Thanh Nguyen

Department of Information Systems, Wrocław University of Technology,
Wyb. St. Wyspianskiego 27, 50-370 Wrocław, Poland
thanh@pwr.wroc.pl

Abstract. Up to now in the field of temporal database systems there have been investigated 3 kinds of time: valid time, transaction time and indeterminate valid time. Indeterminate valid time serves to describe the timestamps and possibility event occurrences in the future. In this paper the author assumes that in distributed temporal database systems it often happens that for the same event the sites may associate different scenarios in their fragments. Thus after making the union of these fragments there may exist such inconsistency that the proper scenario for the event is not known. The author proposes solving of this kind of uncertainty by developing a representation of the tuples representing the scenarios of this event. For this purpose a distance function between tuples referring to the same event is defined, and the representation choice functions are proposed and analyzed. Next an algorithm is worked out and some of its properties are given.

1 Introduction

Up to the present there are two kinds of "time" well known in temporal database models: *valid time* and *transaction time*. Valid time is the time when an event has place in the reality. Valid time is independent from the system. Transaction time, however, is connected not only with events, but also with the database. Transaction time informs us what information at the present is up–to–date. If in given database an event has transaction time, it means that during this time the information about the event is current. So valid time is an objective parameter of information, while transaction time is a subjective one.

Notice that both kinds of time (valid time and transaction time) concern only the events, which took place in the reality. However we often need to keep in the database our plans referring to the future and to have the possibility to analyze them. The time, in which an event probably will take place, we call *indeterminate valid time.* Such kind of time is also an objective parameter of information like valid time. The similarity of valid time and indeterminate valid time is that they indicate the position of events in the time space, but the difference is that the position indicated by valid

L. Monostori, J. Váncza, and M. Ali (Eds.): IEA/AIE 2001, LNAI 2070, pp. 445-454, 2001.

time is in past and with probability 100%, while the position indicated by indeterminate time should have smaller probability. If we say „The paper will be published in this year" we indicate that event „publishing of the paper" will take place in this year, with consciousness that only with some probability.

The above consideration shows that it is natural to assign to an event which may take place in the future a time scenario and some probability for its occurrence. So the information in a database with indeterminate valid time should consist of 4 attributes: *scenario*, *event*, *time* and (optionally) *probability*. Attribute *scenario* refers to the resource from which the scenario of an event is given; attribute *event* consists of the description of the event; attribute *time* informs when the event will take place, and the value of *probability* is the degree of certainty of this statement. Notice that attributes *scenario*, *event*, and *time* may be complex. Models of temporal databases supporting valid time and transaction time are worked out by many authors, among others in [1],[2],[6],[9],[11],[12]. Indeterminacy of valid time has been investigated by Dyreson and Snodgrass, among others, in works [7],[8]. In [14] the authors defined the notion of modal time, they proposed a model of databases supporting modal time and extended SQL for operating this kind of information.

In this paper we deal with another aspect of indeterminate valid time. It sometime happens that in temporal distributed database systems the same event in different horizontal fragments [17] is associated with different scenarios, and when we make the union of these fragments we may obtain an inconsistent result because the proper scenario for given event is not known. This kind of situations may have various sources, here we mention some of them: Uncertainty in forecasting (the appointed time of some process is not known theoretically and it is possible to be determined only by observations or experimentation); uncertainty in planning (the dates of completion of some project are often inexactly specified); and missing of unanimity in diagnosing (a group of experts may have different opinions about the occurrence time of some events).

This paper presents an attempt of new approach to solving uncertainty in distributed systems, which refer to determining of proper scenarios of future events. We propose to solve an uncertain situation, in which an event is associated with several different scenarios, by determining their representation and treating it as the proper scenario of the event. Section 2 shows a motivating example. Section 3 presents the model of indeterminate valid time. In section 4 the method for representation choice is proposed and finally section 5 presents an algorithm for choice.

2 An Example

In a distributed weather–forecast system, which has local stations located in different places of the country, the information about the time of sunshine in next day in the towns given by the stations can be represented by horizontal fragments of a distributed database in Figure 1. The union of these fragments gives result relation named *Sunshine_for_tomorrow* (see Figure 2). In this relation we assume that the attribute

Station_Id corresponds to attribute *Scenario* (described in Introduction), and attributes *Town* and *State* to attribute *Event*. Notice also that in relation *Sunshine_for_tomorrow* there are 3 tuples which inform about the tomorrow sunshine state in Opole. These tuples differ from each other by the time periods. If now we assume that in the opinion of each station outside the given period there should not be sunshine, then the question is: *What is the sunshine time in Opole next day*? As we shall show below, this problem should be solved by determining the representation of these tuples.

Station s_1

Town	*Weather State*	*Time*
Wroclaw	Sunshine	9a.m. – 2p.m.
Opole	Sunshine	10a.m. – 11a.m.

Station s_2

Town	*Weather State*	*Time*
Czestochowa	Sunshine	9a.m. – 2p.m.
Opole	Sunshine	8a.m. – 4p.m.

Station s_3

Town	*Weather State*	*Time*
Katowice	Sunshine	9a.m. – 2p.m.
Opole	Sunshine	12a.m. – 5p.m.

Fig. 1. Horizontal fragments of weather–forecast database

Sunhine_for_tomorrow

Station_Id	*Town*	*Weather State*	*Time*
s_1	Wroclaw	Sunshine	9a.m. – 2p.m.
s_1	Opole	Sunshine	10a.m. – 11a.m.
s_2	Czestochowa	Sunshine	9a.m. – 2p.m.
s_2	Opole	Sunshine	8a.m. – 4p.m.
s_3	Katowice	Sunshine	9a.m. – 2p.m.
s_3	Opole	Sunshine	12a.m. – 5p.m.

Fig. 2. The union of horizontal fragments

3 Data Model Supporting Indeterminate Valid Time

In this section we present a data model supporting indeterminate valid time. This model should enable keeping and manipulation of data referring to events, which probably will take place in the future. The difference of this model from other temporal models is that it allows storing all the scenarios (often contradictory) of the same event and relationship between them.

3.1 Time Notion

Time is a dimension serving to chronological sorting events and their occurrences in the reality. The measurement of time is done by clocks or stopwatches, which have the smallest unit (for example a second). A time period should be measured by a number of units. To define absolute time we assume a begin of time, and every moment t of time is the number of time units from the begin to t. A point of time is a moment of time, and an interval $[t_1,t_2]$ of time, where $t_1 \le t_2$, is a set of all points t of time such that $t_1 \le t$ and $t \le t_2$ For implementation one should adopt the model of time–line presented in [7]. Time itself is a line segment (assuming a bounded universe). A point on the time–line is called an *instant.* The time–line segment is partitioned into a finite number of smaller *segments* called *chronons.* A chronon is the smallest amount of time that can be represented in the implementation. The chronons can be consecutively labeled with the integers 0,1,...,N, where N is the largest number of values that a timestamp can represent. Most often a chronon is identified by the indicator of time measure, for example "9a.m. July 22, 2000" (or 9a.m. if the day, month an year are known). Notice that in the set of chronon labels or indicators there may be defined relation "≥" and operations "+" and "–" as the same between integers. The time between 2 instants is called a time *period.* A time *period* is represented as a segment of time–line, which is denoted by lower and upper chronons. Thus time period p is an interval $p=[p_*,p^*]$ where $p^* \ge p_*$. A time period is then a contiguous set of chronons. In work [14] the authors denoted by symbol *NOW* an abstract chronon representing the current instant of time. Thus *NOW* is a point of time, which represents the current moment and should be identified by the system.

3.2 Kinds of Events

In this model we distinguish 3 following kinds of events:
– *Historical event:* it is an event whose valid time is included in interval $(-\infty, NOW)$. We say that the event took place and is finished.
– *Open event:* it is an event, which started in the past and is not finished yet. For such events only part of valid time is determined and included in $(-\infty, NOW]$. The second part (non–determined) of valid time called *indeterminate valid time* should be included in $(NOW,+\infty)$.
– *Supposed event:* it is an event, which has to take place in the future. Such an event often is assigned with some timestamp of its occurrence and some probability of this statement. In this paper we assume that the probability is the same for all events.

In a database based on the model there should be 2 segments of data:
– *Historical segment* containing historical events and historical parts of open events,
– *Modal segment* containing supposed events.

3.3 Historical Relation and Modal Relation

A temporal relational schema R consists of 2 schemas: historical schema and modal schema.

Definition 1. For given set of attributes $A = \{A_1,A_2,...,A_n,From,To\}$ and a set of attributes' functional dependencies F, pair $R_H=(A,F)$ is called a *historical schema* if all the values v of temporal attributes *From* and *To* fulfill condition $v \le NOW$. ♦

Definition 2. For given set of attributes $A = \{A_1, A_2, ..., A_n, Scen, Prob, From, To\}$ and set of attributes' functional dependencies F, pair $R_M=(A,F)$ is called a *modal schema* if all the values v of temporal attributes *From* and *To* fulfill condition $v>NOW$. ♦

Notice that in above definitions the attributes $A_1, A_2, ..., A_n$ should describe events, attributes *From* and *To* should represent time period in which an event occurs. Additionally in modal schema values of attribute *Scen* should identify the scenarios of events (in given example in section 2 scenarios are identified by values of attribute *Station_Id*), and values of attribute *Prob* are probabilities of such statements as, in period of time [*From*,*To*] scenario s will take place. In what follows we do not assume appearing of this attribute. More concrete assumptions were considered in work [14].

A relation is historical if it is an instance of historical schema and a relation is modal if it is an instance of modal schema. A database is modal if it contains at least one modal relation.

3.4 Scenarios of Events

A *scenario* of an event should be represented by one tuple in a modal relation. One event may have more than one scenario. To determine the relationship between scenarios we distinguish following groups of scenarios:

1. Scenarios, which exclude themselves: scenarios of this group have the property that occurring of one of them excludes occurring of others.
2. Scenarios that are alternative: these scenarios may (but do not have to) occur simultaneously.
3. Scenarios, which are dependent from others: occurring of one of them causes occurring of another one.

A language for scenario calculus was worked out in work [14]. In this paper we assume that a temporal relation supporting indeterminate valid time is a set of tuples t, each of them could be represented by the following form $t=(s,e,p)$, where s represents the scenario of event e and p is a time period, in which the event e probably will occur. In other words p is the time period to which the timestamp of event e probably belongs. We assume that if according to some scenario s event e will take place in period p then it should not take place outside this time period. Besides the timestamp should be the indeterminate valid time of e, so $p_* \geq NOW$ for $p=[p_*,p^*]$.

We also assume that in a modal relation to given event there may be associated more than one scenario, that is more than one timestamp.

The following definition specifies when a temporal relation supporting indeterminate valid time is consistent.

Definition 3. Temporal relation supporting indeterminate valid time $R=\{t \mid t=(s,e,p)\}$ is consistent if and only if for every 2 tuples $t_1=(s_1,e_1,p_1)$ and $t_2=(s_2,e_2,p_2)$ if e_1 and e_2 represent the same event then $p_1=p_2$. ♦

If the temporal relation is not consistent then one should choose the representation of all tuples referring to the same event, and take it as the proper scenario of the event.

4 Determining Representation Problem

4.1 General Representation Choice Problem

In this section we present the representation choice problem and a method for its solution. Let U_e be a finite set of objects representing potential scenarios of event e, and let U_{re} be the set of all non–empty, finite subsets with repetitions of set U_e. The calculus of sets with repetitions should be consistent with the one given by Lipski and Marek [13], below we present some examples of this calculus: Let $X=\{a,a,b,b\}=\{2*a,2*b\}$ and $Y=\{b,c,c\}=\{b,2*c\}$ be sets with repetitions, then $X\cup Y=\{2*a,3*b,2*c\}$, $X\cap Y=\{b\}$ and $X\backslash Y=\{2*a,b\}$.

Let set $X\in U_{re}$ be presented, the choice of representation of set X consists of determination of some subset Y of set U_e. If the choice is made in a determinate way then a *representation choice function* should be defined as R: $U_{re}\rightarrow 2^{U_e}$. An element of set $R(X)$ is called a *representation* of set X.

The representation choice problem as formulated above has been investigated for many structures of objects belonging to U_e [4],[5],[15],[16]. These methods are based on the assumption that the structures of objects are known, and on the basis of these structures the structure of U_e is defined. Here we assume that the structure of set U_e is known Let it be a distance function $d{:}U_e\times U_e\rightarrow[0,+\infty)$. Function d must satisfy the following conditions: for all $x,y\in U_e$ $d(x,y)\geq 0$, $d(x,y)=0$ iff $x=y$ and $d(x,y)=d(y,x)$.

Function d can also be interpreted as a similarity function among the objects belonging to set U_e.

By $\boldsymbol{R}$ we denote the space of all representation choice functions in space (U_e,d). We propose 5 axioms for representation choice function:

Let $X,X_1,X_2\in U_{re}$, for $x\in U_e$ let $d(x,X)=\sum_{y\in X}d(x,y)$. The axioms are following:

A1. $R(X)\neq\emptyset$.

A2. If $R(X_1)\cap R(X_2)\neq\emptyset$ then $R(X_1)\cap R(X_2)=R(X_1\cup X_2)$.

A3. For $x\in U_e$, $x\notin R(X)$ there exists a natural number n such that $x\in R(X\cup\{n*x\})$

A4. If $X_1\subseteq X_2$, $x\in R(X_1)$, $y\in R(X_2)$ then $d(x,X_1)\leq d(y,X_2)$.

A5. If $x\in R(X)$ then $d(x,X)=\min_{y\in U_e} d(y,X)$.

The above axioms are conditions for representation choice function. Although they are intuitive we try to give their interpretation. According to axiom A1 every non empty set X should have its (non empty) representation. Axiom A2 (Condorcet consistency) says that if some object x is simultaneously in representations of X_1 and X_2 then it should be in representation of their sum and only such object can be a representation of set $X_1\cup X_2$. For example, if a place is suitable for building a warehouse for markets' nets X_1 and X_2 then it should be suitable for the net being connection of X_1 and X_2. According to A3 if any element x does not belong to the representation of set X then it should belong to the representation of set X' containing X and n elements x for some large enough n. In example of expert solution choice, every expert solution has a chance to be chosen as the final solution of given problem if there exists a enough number of experts which proposed the same solution. According to axiom A4 if shops net X_1 is a subnet of shops net X_2, x and y are places for warehouses for X_1 and X_2 correspondingly, then the sum of distances from x to shops belonging to X_1 should not be larger than the sum of distances from y to shops of net X_2. Axiom A5 requires minimization of sum of distances from element of set representation to elements of this set. In other words, the representation should be nearest to the elements of set X.

Each of these axioms treated as a characteristic property of representation choice function would specify in space $\boldsymbol{R}$ a region (domain) denoted as $\boldsymbol{R}1$, $\boldsymbol{R}2$,..., and $\boldsymbol{R}5$ respectively. Below we will present some results of axioms analysis.

Theorem 1. $\boldsymbol{R}1\cap\boldsymbol{R}2\cap\boldsymbol{R}3\cap\boldsymbol{R}4\cap\boldsymbol{R}5\neq\emptyset$.

Proof. Let $X\in U_{re}$, we will show that the following representation choice function $R(X)=\{x\in U_e: d(x,X)= \min_{y\in U_e} d(y,X)\}$ belongs to all of these domains. It is obvious that R fulfils axioms A1,A2 and A5. For A3 let 's assume that $x\notin R(X)$ for some $x\in U_e$. Thus there exists $y\in U_e$, $y\neq x$ such that $d(y,x)=\min_{z\in U} d(z,x)$. Let n be a natural number where $n\geq(d(x,X)-d(y',X))/d(y,x)$ for $y'\in R(X)$, and let $X'=X\cup\{n*x\}$, then for each $z\in U_e$ we have $d(z,X') = d(z,X) + nd(z,x) \geq d(y',X)+nd(y,x) \geq d(y',X)+d(x,X)-d(y',X)=d(x,X)= =d(x,X')$, hence $x\in R(X')$. For axiom A4 if $X_1\subseteq X_2$, $x\in R(X_1)$, $y\in R(X_2)$, and $d(x,X_1)>d(y,X_2)$, then because $d(y,X_1)\geq d(y,X_2)$ so $d(y,X_1)<d(x,X_1)$. It is not possible because $x\in R(X_1)$, so there must be $d(x,X_1)\leq d(y,X_2)$. ♦

Theorem 2. $\boldsymbol{R}1\cap\boldsymbol{R}3\cap\boldsymbol{R}4=\boldsymbol{R}5\cap\boldsymbol{R}1$.

Proof. a) Let $R\in\boldsymbol{R}1\cap\boldsymbol{R}3\cap\boldsymbol{R}4$, we will prove that $R\in\boldsymbol{R}5\cap\boldsymbol{R}1$. Let $X\in U_{re}$, according to A1 we have $R(X)\neq\emptyset$. Let $x\in R(X)$, $y\in U_e$ and $y\neq x$ (assume that $|U_e|>1$ because for $|U_e|=1$ the proof is trivial), if $y\in R(X)$ then on the basis of A4 we have $d(x,X)=d(y,X)$ because $X\subseteq X$. If $y\notin R(X)$ then on the basis of A3 there exists number n such that $y\in R(X')$ where $X'=X\cup\{n*y\}$. Because $X\subseteq X'$, axiom A4 implies that $d(x,X)\leq d(y,X')=d(y,X)$, so for all $y\in U$ $d(x,X)\leq d(y,X)$, it means that $R\in\boldsymbol{R5}\cap\boldsymbol{R}1$.

b) Let $R\in\boldsymbol{R}5\cap\boldsymbol{R}1$, then it implies that $R\in\boldsymbol{R1}$. We shall show that $R\in\boldsymbol{R3}$ and $R\in\boldsymbol{R4}$. Let $x\notin R(X)$ for some $x\in U_e$. Then find $y\in U_e$, $y\neq x$ such that $d(y,x)= \min_{z\in U_e} d(z,x)$. Let n be a natural number where $n\geq(d(x,X)-d(y',X))/d(y,x)$ for $y'\in R(X)$. Let $X'=X\cup\{n*x\}$, $z\in U_e$ and $z\neq x$, we have the following: $d(z,X')-d(z,X)+(n+1)d(z,x)>d(y',X)+nd(y,x)\geq \geq d(y',X)+d(x,X)-d(y',X)=d(x,X)=d(x,X')$. It implies that $x\in R(X')$, more strongly $R(X')=\{x\}$, so $R\in\boldsymbol{R}3$. Similarly like in the proof of theorem 1 we can prove that $R\in\boldsymbol{R}4$. ♦

Theorems 1 and 2 imply the following conclusions:

1. $R(\{x,...,x\})=\{x\}$ for $x\in U_e$ and $R\in\boldsymbol{R}1\cap\boldsymbol{R}3\cap\boldsymbol{R}4$ (unanimity).
2. $\boldsymbol{R}1\cap\boldsymbol{R}2\cap\boldsymbol{R}3\cap\boldsymbol{R}4 \subseteq \boldsymbol{R}5\cap\boldsymbol{R}1$.

It has been shown that axioms A1, A2, A3 and A4 determine representation choice functions belonging to region $\boldsymbol{R}5\cap\boldsymbol{R}1$ which consists of non–empty functions satisfying axiom R5. The functions of this region are very often used in practice, and the axioms A1,...,A5 exactly show why.

4.2 Representation of Event Tuples

As mentioned above the temporal relation determined by the union operation on the horizontal fragments, may be inconsistent. The reason is that there may exit more than 1 tuple which represent the same event but are associated with different modal time periods. In such case the representation of these tuples should be determined. The theorems in section 4.1 show that the choice criterion specified by axiom R5 should be a good one because a representation satisfying this criterion satisfies also other axioms. Assume that there is given a set X_e of n tuples referring to the same event e, let $X_e=\{t_i \mid t_i=(s_i,e,p_i),\ i=1,2,...,n\}$ where p_i is a time period and $p_i=[p_{i*},p_i^*]$. Define the following set with repetitions $\tilde{X}_e=\{(e,p_i) \mid \exists s_i\ (s_i,e,p_i)\in X_e\}$. Let X_e^* be the set of all admissible tuples which may represent the event e, elements of this set consist of 2 values: e and p_i, of course $\tilde{X}_e\subseteq X_e^*$.

Definition 4. Distance between tuples from X_e^* is a function g: $X_e^*\times X_e^*\rightarrow R_+$, where $g(t_i,t_j)=|p_{i*}-p_{j*}|+|(p_i^*-p_{i*})-(p_j^*-p_{j*})|$ for all $t_i,t_j\in X_e^*$. ♦

The interpretation of the distance function is following: the first component $|p_{i*}-p_{j*}|$ determines the number of chronons which are needed for moving interval p_i to interval p_j so that their lower chronons are covered, and the second component $|(p_i^*-p_{i*})-(p_j^*-p_{j*})|$ determines the number of chronons needed for moving one upper chronon to cover the second. It is easy to show the following

Remark 1. Function g is a metric, that is: $g(t_i,t_j)= g(t_j,t_i)$; $g(t_i,t_j)=0$ iff $t_i=t_j$ and $g(t_i,t_j)+g(t_j,t_k) \geq g(t_i,t_k)$ for all $t_i,t_j,t_k\in X_e^*$. ♦

The metric property of function g motivates its using to measure the distances between the tuples from X_e^*. Of course, there may exit other (possibly metrics) functions for this aim, but their analysis is not the matter of this paper. Using now the general methods proposed in section 4.1 we have the following definition:

Definition 5. By the representation of set X_e we call a tuple $t=(e,p)\in X_e^*$ satisfying the following condition:

$$\sum_{t'\in \tilde{X}_e} g(t,t') = \min_{t'\in X_e^*} \sum_{t''\in \tilde{X}_e} g(t',t'') \qquad ♦$$

Notice that above definition specifies a choice function which satisfies axiom R5.

5 Algorithm for Event Tuples' Representation Choice

We now propose an algorithm for determining the representation of set X_e.

Algorithm: DC(X_e) – determining of representation for set X_e.

Data: Given set $X_e=\{t_i \mid t_i=(s_i,e,p_i),\ i=1,2,...,n\}$.

Result: An element α of X_e^* which satisfies the condition of definition 5.

Procedure:

```
BEGIN
  1. X̃e :={t'i=(e,pi) | i=1,2,...,n};
  2. If n=1 then  begin α:=t'1;goto END; end
            else
             begin
               s*:=min {pi* | i=1,2,...,n};
               s*:=max {pi* | i=1,2,...,n}; s:=[s*,s*];
             end;
  3. S:= Σ_{i=1}^{n} g(t'1,t'i);
  4. For u:=s* to s* do
     for v:=i to s* do
       begin
         a:=[u,v]; t:=(e,a);
         if S> Σ_{i=1}^{n} g(t,t'i) then begin S:= Σ_{i=1}^{n} g(t,t'i);α:=t end;
       end;
END.
```

From the above algorithm one can prove the following properties:

Remark 2. Algorithm DC(X_e) determines correctly the representation $t=(e,p)$ of set X_e satisfying condition specified in Definition 5. ♦

Remark 3. The computation complexity of DC(X_e) is $O(n*m^2)$ where n is the number of given tuples and m is the length of interval s defined in step 2 of the algorithm. ♦

For the example giving in section 2, we can determine the representation of 3 tuples representing event "*sunshine in Opole*" as the following:

Town	*State*	*Time*
Opole	Sun	10a.m. – 4p.m.

Thus the final sunshine forecast for town *Opole* for tomorrow should be "*from 10a.m. to 4p.m.*".

6 Conclusions

In this paper a method for solving problems which arise from missing of unanimity and certainty in generating of future events' scenarios has been proposed. This method should be applied in these situations where there are no tools to verify the credibility of diagnosing (forecasting) information that is supplied by sites of a distributed system. One can notice that the solution is presented here with the simplest assumptions. It can be extended by adding other assumptions, such that the weights of the sites which represent the credibility degrees of scenarios, or different probabilities of scenarios' occurrences. Representation choice methods could also be used in reconciling of user preferences in information retrieval [3], agent knowledge states in multiagent systems [10], or user activities in evaluations of information systems [18].

References

1. Allen, J.F.: Maintaining knowledge about temporal intervals. Commun. ACM **26** (1983) 832–843.
2. Ariav, G.: A temporally oriented data model. ACM Transaction on Database Systems **11** (1986) 499–527.
3. Danilowicz, C.: Modelling of user preferences and needs in Boolean retrieval systems. Information Processing and Management **30** (1994) 363–378.
4. Danilowicz, C., Nguyen, N.T.: Methods for choice of set ordered partitions and coverings representations. Monographs, Wroc•aw University of Technology Press (1992).
5. Danilowicz, C., Nguyen, N.T.: Consensus–based methods for restoring consistency of replicated data. In: M. Klopotek et al. (eds): Advances in Soft Computing, Proceedings of 9th International Conference on Intelligent Information Systems'2000. Springer–Verlag (2000) 325–336.
6. Dyreson, C.E., Soo, M., Snodgrass, R.T.: The data model for time. In Snodgrass, R.T. (ed.): The TSQL2 Temporal Query Language. Kluwer Academic Publish Hingham (1995) 327–346.
7. Dyreson, C.E., Snodgrass, R.T.: Supporting valid–time indeterminacy. ACM Transaction on Database Systems **23** (1998) 1–57.
8. Dyreson, C.E., Snodgrass, R.T.: Temporal indeterminacy. In R.T. Snodgrass (ed.): The TSQL2 Temporal Query Language. Kluwer Academic Publish Hingham (1995) 475–499.
9. Gadia, S.K.: A homogeneous relational model and query languages for temporal databases. ACM Transactions on Database Systems **13** (1983) 418–448.
10. Katarzyniak, R. Intentional models and BDI theories, an inquiry into a relational and logical method of modeling autonomous processes for possible worlds construction. In: Proc. of Int. ICSC Congress on Intelligent Systems & Applications ISA'2000. Wollongong University, Australia (2000) 885–896.
11. Knight, B., Ma, J.: General temporal theory. The Computer Journal **37** (1994) 114–123.
12. Knight, B., Ma, J.: An extended temporal system based on points and intervals. Information Systems **18** (1993) 111–120.
13. Lipski, W., Marek, W.: Combinatorial analysis. WTN Warsaw (1986).
14. Nguyen, N.T., Kisielewicz, K.: The model of temporal database with modal time. In Zupancic et al. (eds.): Evolution and challenges in systems development. Kluwer Academic Publish NY (1999) 261–269.
15. Nguyen, N.T.: Using consensus methods for determining the representation of expert information in distributed systems. Lecture Notes on Artificial Intelligence **1904** (2000) 11–20.
16. Nguyen, N.T.: Using consensus methods for solving conflicts of data in distributed systems. Lecture Notes on Computer Science **1963** (2000) 409–417.
17. Ozsu, T.M.: Principles of distributed database systems. Prentice–Hall, New Jersey (1991).
18. Zgrzywa A.: User's activity models for evaluation of the information system performance. In: M. Bazewicz (ed.), Proc. of ISAT'97. Wroclaw Univ. of Technology (1997), 168–175.

Checkpoint-Recovery for Mobile Intelligent Networks

Yoshinori Morita and Hiroaki Higaki

Department of Computers and Systems Engineering
Tokyo Denki University
{mine,hig}@higlab.k.dendai.ac.jp

Abstract. For supporting recent intelligent applications, high performance and intelligent networks is required to be developed. Here, fault-tolerance is one of the most important properties. In addition, a mobile computer network is an infrastructure for an intelligent network. This paper discusses a hybrid checkpoint protocol. In order to apply the protocol, mobile-to-mobile communication in wireless LAN protocols such as IEEE 802.11 and HIPERLAN has to be supported. This paper proposes a novel logging protocol which requires no additional messages.

1 Background and Objective

According to the advances of computer and communication technologies, many kinds of mobile stations like notebook computers and personal data assistants (PDAs) are widely available. Intelligent Transport Systems (ITS) with mobile communications are now being developed. A mobile computing system is composed of *fixed stations* and *mobile stations* interconnected by communication networks. A fixed station is located at a fixed location in the network. A mobile station moves from one location to another in the network. The mobile network is divided into multiple *wireless cells.* A mobile station moves from one wireless cell to another and sometimes out of any wireless cell. There is an *access point* (AP) in each cell. APs and fixed stations are interconnected by a high-speed wired network. A mobile station communicates with directly another mobile station in the same wireless cell. It communicates through an AP supporting it with a fixed station or a mobile station in another wireless cell. This is realized by using wireless LAN protocols such as IEEE 802.11 [5] and HIPERLAN [4].

In a distributed system, applications are realized by cooperation of multiple stations. Usually, stations and a network are developed by using a widely available products. Mission-critical applications cannot always be implemented in such a system. Hence, it is important to discuss how to make and keep the system so reliable and available. Checkpoint-restart [2,6,13,14] is one of the well-known methods to achieve reliable distributed systems. Each station s_i takes a local checkpoint c_i where local state information of s_i is stored in a stable storage. If some station fails, s_i restarts from c_i. A set of local checkpoints is required to be

L. Monostori, J. Váncza, and M. Ali (Eds.): IEA/AIE 2001, LNAI 2070, pp. 455–464, 2001.

consistent [2]. Fixed stations take consistent checkpoints by *synchronous* checkpoint protocols [2,6] with low synchronization overhead since they can communicate with each other through a high-speed wired network and they have enough amount of stable storages to store state information [3,7]. Some papers [8,10] discuss synchronous checkpoint protocols for mobile stations. However, it is difficult for mobile stations to take checkpoints by themselves since they have neither enough volume of stable storages nor so much battery capacity as to frequently access the stable storages [8]. Moreover, it gets more difficult for mobile and fixed stations to take checkpoints synchronously if wireless connections between mobile stations and APs are often disconnected. In a protocol in [8], mobile stations in a wireless cell take a consistent global checkpoint without communication by synchronized realtime clocks and state information is stored into a stable storage in a fixed station. However, it is difficult to achieve synchronized realtime clocks since message transmission delay among mobile stations are unpredicatable. Mobile stations may fail to take local checkpoints due to lack of battery capacity or movement to outside of any wireless cell. In a synchronous checkpoint protocol, every station has to give up to take a consistent global checkpoint if a certain mobile station fails to take a local checkpoint. Hence, asynchronous checkpoint protocols for mobile stations [1,9] have been proposed. However, in these protocols, each AP is required to take a local checkpoint for a mobile station each time a message is transmitted between them. Thus, high synchronization overhead is required.

In this paper, we newly propose a *hybrid checkpoint protocol* where local checkpoints are asynchronously taken by mobile stations while synchronously taken by fixed stations. Mobile stations take local checkpoints by storing state information into stable storages in APs. Here, local checkpoints of mobile stations are taken when they send a checkpoint request message to an AP. By combining synchronous and asynchronous checkpoint protocols, number of checkpoints is reduced. Hence, frequency of accesses to stable storages is also reduced. Thus, our hybrid checkpoint protocol makes mobile systems so reliable that mission-critical applications are implemented with less overhead.

2 System Model

A distributed system $\mathcal{S} = \langle \mathcal{V}, \mathcal{L} \rangle$ is composed of a set $\mathcal{V} = \{s_1, \ldots, s_n\}$ of stations and a set $\mathcal{L} \subseteq \mathcal{V}^2$ of communication channels. A *state* of s_i changes at each *event* in s_i. There are two kinds of events: *local events* and *communication events*. At a local event, s_i updates a state by local computation without exchanging a message. At a communication event, s_i communicates with another station by exchanging a message and updates a state. There are two kinds of communication events: a *message sending event* $s(m)$ and a *message receipt event* $r(m)$ for a message m.

In a mobile computing system, which is a kind of $\mathcal{S}$, there are three kinds of stations; *fixed stations* $F_1, \ldots, F_f$, *mobile stations* $M_1, \ldots, M_m$ and *access points* (APs) $A_1, \ldots, A_a$ as in Figure 1. M_i communicates with another station by a

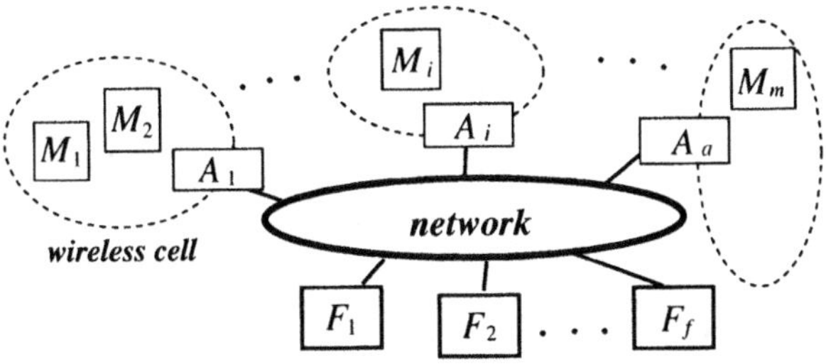

Fig. 1. Mobile computing system.

wireless LAN protocol like IEEE 802.11 [5]. Here, each M_i is included in a single wireless cell. A message exchanged between M_i and M_k in the same wireless cell is transmitted directly by using CSMA/CA (Carrier Sense Multiple Access with Collision Avoidance) protocol. Since a wireless LAN protocol is intrinsically broadcast-base, a message transmitted from M_i is received by all the stations including an AP in the same wireless cell. Messages exchanged between M_i and a mobile station in another wireless cell and between M_i and a fixed station are transmitted through an AP. These messages are also transmitted by broadcast-based communication protocol. M_i does not have enough computation power and storage capacity like disk storages. Hence, it is not easy for M_i to take a local checkpoint by itself.

3 Hybrid Checkpointing

Synchronous checkpoint protocols have an advantage that stations can restart from the most recent checkpoints without domino effect. However, it is difficult for multiple mobile stations to take local checkpoints synchronously. Hence, we propose *hybrid checkpointing* [Figure 2].

[Hybrid checkpointing]

- F_i takes c_{F_i} by a synchronous checkpoint protocol. A set $\tilde{C} = \{c_{F_1}, \ldots, c_{F_f}\}$ of local checkpoints taken by the fixed stations is referred to as a *coordinated checkpoint*.
- M_i takes c_{M_i} by an asynchronous checkpoint protocol. □

At c_{M_i}, state information of M_i is stored into a stable storage in an AP A_j. M_i fails to take c_{M_i} if a wireless connection between M_i and A_j is disconnected or battery power in M_i is exhausted. Thus, M_i takes c_{M_i} only if M_i does not move out of a wireless cell and has enough battery power for taking c_{M_i}. Therefore, M_i asynchronously takes c_{M_i}, i.e. independently of the other stations. M_i has to restart from a local state consistent with $\tilde{C}$. However, c_{M_i} is not always consistent with $\tilde{C}$ since M_i takes c_{M_i} independently of fixed stations taking $\tilde{C}$. Hence, a kind of log-based restart protocols [11, 12] is adopted [Figure 3]. Messages exchanged between M_i and other stations after c_{M_i} are stored into a stable storage in A_j. In recovery, M_i restores the state information at c_{M_i} and

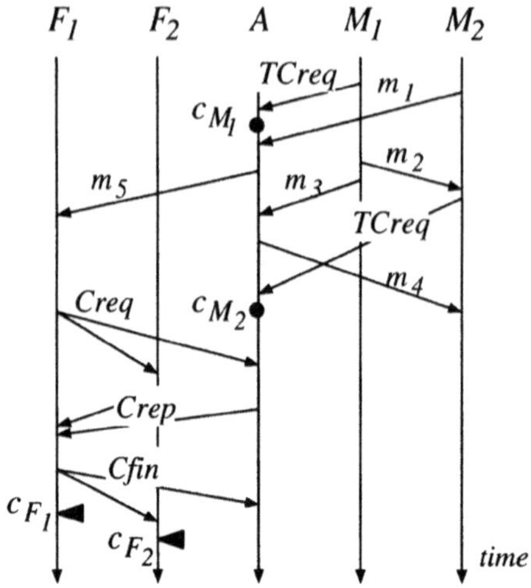

Fig. 2. Checkpoint in hybrid protocol.

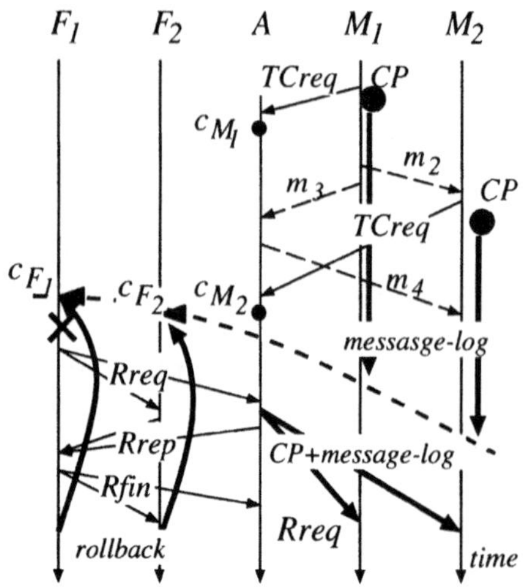

Fig. 3. Restart in hybrid protocol.

the messages from the stable storage in A_j. After replaying a sequence of events according to the messages, M_i gets a state consistent with $\tilde{C}$ and restarts. There is a *checkpoint agent process* p_{ij} for M_i in A_j. p_{ij} stores state information of M_i at c_{M_i} into a stable log sl_{ij}. p_{ij} also stores m into a message log ml_{ij} on behalf of M_i. Since every message m sent and received by M_i is transmitted by a broadcast-based wireless LAN protocol, all the mobile stations and A_j in the same wireless cell receive m. Thus, p_{ij} stores sufficient state information and messages to get a consistent local state with $\tilde{C}$ in recovery. Here, the order of events sending and receiving the stored messages in recovery is significant. Only by receiving messages broadcasted from M_i by a wireless LAN protocol, the order of events observed by A_j might be different from that really occurred in M_i.

4 Message logging in wireless LAN

Now, we consider the following two cases for achieving a consistent order of events in a mobile station M_i:

- A message m is transmitted between M_i in a wireless cell of an AP A_j and a mobile or fixed station out of the wireless cell [case 1].
- m is transmitted between two mobile stations M_i and M_k within a wireless cell of A_j [case 2].

[case 1] In A_j, there exists a checkpoint agent process p_{ij} for M_i. First, suppose that p_{ij} forwards two messages m and m' to M_i in this order as in Figure 4(a). Here, p_{ij} knows occurrences of $r(m)$ and $r(m')$ in M_i and stores m and m' into a message log for recovery. Since p_{ij} identifies an order of occurrences of $r(m)$ and

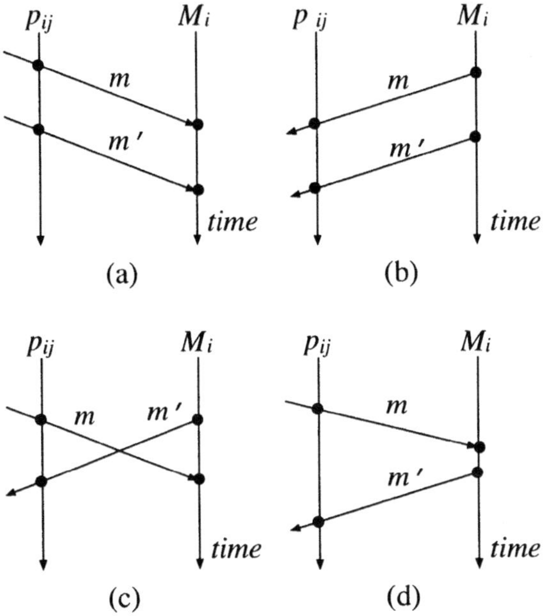

Fig. 4. Message Logging [case 1]

$r(m')$ in M_i, p_{ij} gets an ordered message log for recovery. Next, suppose that p_{ij} forwards two messages m and m' from M_i in this order as in Figure 4(b). Here, p_{ij} knows occurrences of $s(m)$ and $s(m')$ in M_i and stores m and m' into a message log for recovery. Since, p_{ij} identifies an order of occurrences of $s(m)$ and $s(m')$ in M_i, p_{ij} gets an ordered message log for recovery. Finally, suppose that p_{ij} forwards m to M_i and m' from M_i as in Figures 4(c) and 4(d). Here, p_{ij} knows occurrences of $r(m)$ and $s(m')$ in M_i and stores m and m' into a message log for recovery. However, p_{ij} does not identify an order of occurrences of $r(m)$ and $s(m')$ in M_i. □

[case 2] In A_j, there exist two checkpoint agent processes p_{ij} and p_{kj} for M_i and M_k, respectively. First, suppose that M_i sends a message m to M_k and p_{ij} forwards another message m' to M_i as in Figure 5(a). Here, since m is transmitted by a wireless LAN protocol, m is broadcasted in the wireless cell and A_j receives m. Hence, p_{ij} knows occurrence of $s(m)$ in M_i and stores m into a message log for recovery. However, p_{ij} does not identify an order of occurrences of $s(m)$ and $r(m')$ in M_i. Next, suppose that M_i sends a message m to M_k and p_{kj} forwards another message m' to M_k as in Figure 5(b). Here, since m is transmitted by a wireless LAN protocol, m is broadcasted in the wireless cell and A_j receives m. Hence, p_{kj} knows occurrence of $r(m)$ in M_k and stores m into a message log for recovery. However, p_{kj} does not identify an order of occurrences of $r(m)$ and $r(m')$ in M_k. Finally, suppose that M_i sends a message m to M_k and M_k sends another message m' to M_i as in Figure 5(c). Here, since m and m'

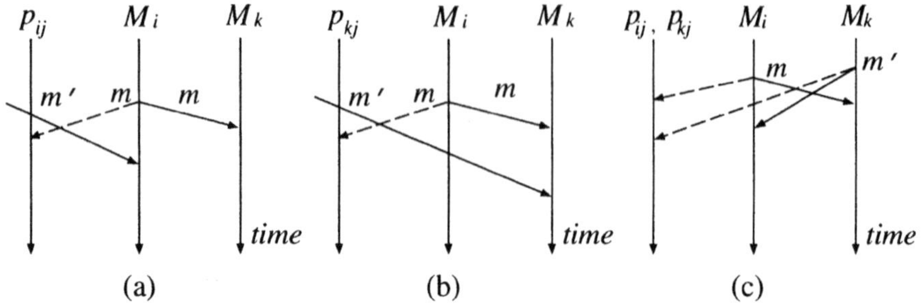

Fig. 5. Message Logging [case 2].

are transmitted by a wireless LAN protocol, m and m' are broadcasted in the wireless cell and A_j receives m and m'. Hence, p_{ij} knows occurrences of $s(m)$ and $r(m')$ in M_i and p_{kj} knows occurrences of $s(m')$ and $r(m)$ in M_k. Both p_{ij} and p_{kj} stores m and m' for recovery. However, p_{ij} does not identify an order of occurrences of $s(m)$ and $r(m')$ and p_{kj} does not identify an order of occurrences of $s(m')$ and $r(m)$. □

Though p_{ij} receives all the messages transmitted and received by M_i, it is impossible for p_{ij} to store messages into a message log in the same order as M_i transmits and receives them by only receiving them broadcasted by a wireless LAN protocol. One idea to get correctly ordered message log for M_i is that M_i stores messages into a storage temporarily and transmits them to p_{ij} for storing them into a stable storage. However, a mobile station does not always have enough capacity of storage to store the messages. Moreover, additional messages are required to be transmitted for carrying the messages from a mobile station to an AP. Thus, communication overhead is increased.

In order to solve this problem, we design a following protocol:

- A message transmitted in a wireless cell is stored into a message buffer $mbuf_i$ for M_i in an AP temporarily. Even if the message is transmitted between mobile stations in a wireless cell, an AP can receive the message due to broadcast property of a wireless LAN protocol.
- Order information of message sending and receipt events in M_i is piggied back to another message transmitted from M_i. Even if the message is transmitted between mobile stations within a wireless cell, an AP can get the order information due to broadcast property of a wireless LAN protocol.

As a consequence of separation of a message itself and its transmission and receipt order information, no additional message is transmitted to store the messages in a consistent order into a stable storage in an AP. In this protocol, a unique identifier is assumed to be assigned to each message. In addition, M_i has a variable $Rseq_i$ which holds a sequence of message identifiers. Initially, $Rseq_i = \phi$.

[Message logging in M_i]

- At a message receipt event $r(m)$ for a message m, a message identifier $id(m)$ of m is added to the end of $Rseq_i$. m is delivered to an application.

- At a message sending event $s(m)$ for m, $Rseq_i$ is piggied back to m. $Rseq_i = \phi$.

[Message logging in p_{ij}]

- If A_j receives m destined to M_i, p_{ij} stores a copy of m into $mbuf_i$. p_{ij} forwards m to M_i if m is from a station out of the wireless cell.
- If A_j receives m from M_i,
  1) p_{ij} takes messages, whose identifiers are included in $Rseq_i$ which is a sequence of message identifiers piggied back to m, out of $mbuf_i$.
  2) p_{ij} stores the messages into a message log according to the order of message identifiers in $Rseq_i$.
  3) p_{ij} stores m into a message log.
  4) p_{ij} forwards m to a destination station if m is destined to a station out of the wireless cell. □

[Example]
In Figure 6, there are three mobile stations M_i, M_j and M_k in a wireless cell of an AP A. First, M_i sends a message m_1 to M_j. Next, M_k sends another message m_2 to M_j. Since m_1 and m_2 are broadcasted, a checkpoint agent process p_j for M_j in A also receives a copy of m_1 and m_2. However, the orders of messages received in M_j and p_j might be different. Here, M_j receives m_1 before m_2 and p_j receives m_2 before m_1. Thus, p_j stores m_1 and m_2 in $mbuf_j$ without ordering them. When M_j sends another message m_3 to M_k, an order information $\langle\langle id(m_1), id(m_2)\rangle\rangle$ is piggied back to m_3. Since m_3 is also broadcasted, p_j receives this order information and stores m_1, m_2 and m_3 into a tentative message log tml_j according to the order. □

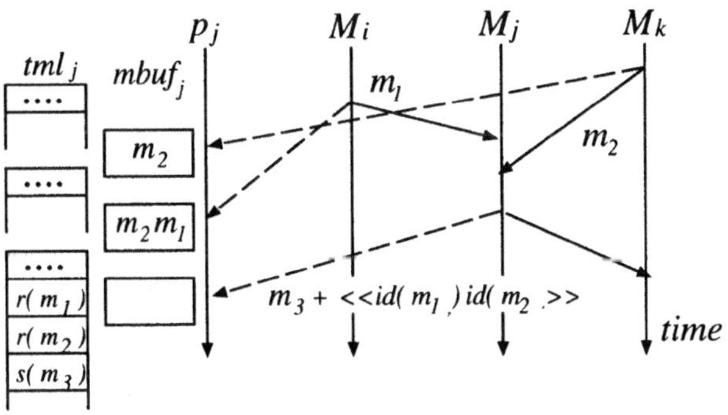

Fig. 6. Message logging.

5 Checkpoint protocol

In our hybrid checkpoint protocol, fixed stations $F_1, \ldots, F_f$ take a coordinated checkpoint $\tilde{C} = \{c_{F_1}, \ldots, c_{F_f}\}$ by a synchronous checkpoint protocol while mobile stations $M_1, \ldots, M_m$ take local checkpoints $c_{M_1}, \ldots, c_{M_m}$ by an asynchronous one. $F_1, \ldots, F_f$ take a consistent coordinated checkpoint $\tilde{C}$ by the following protocol:

[Coordinated checkpoint $\tilde{C}$]

1) A *coordinator station* CS sends a request message *Creq* to $F_1, \ldots, F_f$ and $A_1, \ldots, A_a$.
2) On receipt of *Creq*, each F_i takes a tentative local checkpoint tc_{F_i}.
3) Each F_i and A_j sends back a reply message *Crep* to CS.
4) If CS receives all the *Creps*, CS sends a final message *Cfin* to $F_1, \ldots, F_f$ and $A_1, \ldots, A_a$.
5) On receipt of *Cfin*, each F_i makes tc_{F_i} stable, i.e. takes c_{F_i}. □

In order to avoid orphan messages, each station suspends transmission of application messages while the station has a tentative checkpoint.

Next, we discuss how each mobile station M_i takes a local checkpoint c_{M_i}. Here, suppose that M_i is supported by an AP A_j. A checkpoint agent process p_{ij} in A_j takes a *tentative local checkpoint* tc_{M_i} independently of the other stations. State information required for M_i to restart from tc_{M_i} is carried by a tentative checkpoint request message *TCreq*. On receipt of *TCreq*, p_{ij} stores the state information of M_i into a *tentative state log* tsl_{ij} in a volatile storage of A_j.

[Tentative checkpoint tc_{M_i} in p_{ij}]

1) M_i sends *TCreq* to p_{ij}. *TCreq* carries state information of M_i.
2) On receipt of *TCreq*, p_{ij} takes tc_{M_i} of M_i by storing the state information into tsl_{ij}. □

Let $\langle p_i \rangle$ be a sequence of checkpoint agent processes $\langle p_i^1, \ldots, p_i^c \rangle$ supporting M_i where p_i^1 has tc_{M_i} and p_i^c is a current checkpoint agent process of M_i in an AP A_i^c. If A_i^c receives *Creq* for taking $\tilde{C}$, p_i^1 updates tc_{M_i} to a *stable local checkpoint* c_{M_i} by storing the state information in tsl_i^1 into a *stable state log* sl_i^1. Moreover, each p_i^k $(1 \leq k \leq c)$ stores the messages in a tentative message log tml_i^k into a *stable message log* ml_i^k. The stable logs are stored in a stable storage while the tentative logs are stored in a volatile storage.

[Stable checkpoint c_{M_i} in p_i^k]

- If A_i^1 with tc_{M_i} receives *Creq*, p_i^1 stores the state information in tsl_i^1 into sl_i^1 before sending back *Crep*. $tsl_i^1 = \phi$.
- If A_i^k $(1 \leq k \leq c)$ receives *Creq*, p_i^k stores the messages in tml_i^k into ml_i^k before sending back *Crep*. $tml_i^k = \phi$. □

The checkpoint protocol proposed here has the following properties:

[Property 1]

Each M_i has one stable checkpoint c_{M_i} for consistent recovery with $\tilde{C}$ most recently taken by fixed stations. □

[Property 2]
Each M_i has at most one tentative checkpoint tc_{M_i}. □
[Property 3]
Necessary and sufficient messages for a consistent local state of M_i with $\tilde{C}$ are stored into a stable message log in the same order as M_i exchanged. □

6 Evaluation

In this section, we show a brief evaluation of performance of our protocol compared with a conventional one proposed in [8]. In the conventional protocol, each time a mobile station communicates with another station, a message is stored into a message log in a stable storage to keep the system consistent. However, in the hybrid checkpoint protocol, only when a checkpoint agent process receives a *Creq* message, a set of state information and message log is stored into a stable storage. Otherwise, i.e. on receipt of a *TCreq* message or at a communication event, information is stored into a volatile storage with lower access overhead. Figure 7 shows numbers of accesses to a stable storage in these protocols. Here, in the conventional protocol, an average duration between two successive communication events in a mobile station is assumed 30 sec. On the other hand, in the hybrid checkpoint protocol, the number of communication events is the same as in the conventional protocol and a duration between two successive receipt of *Creq* messages is assumed 120 sec. According to this evaluation, our proposed protocol achieves fault-tolerance with less stable storage access overhead than the conventional one.

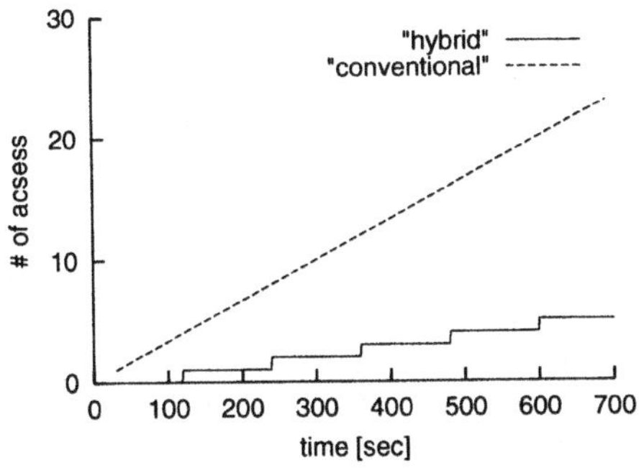

Fig. 7. Stable storage access overhead.

7 Concluding Remarks

It is significant to discuss how to make the system including mobile stations more reliable and available. This paper has discussed how the mobile stations and fixed ones take consistent checkpoints and restart from them. We have newly proposed the *hybrid checkpoint protocol* where mobile stations asynchronously and fixed ones synchronously take local checkpoints. In addition, mobile stations use message logs to get a consistent state. These logs are taken by APs even if mobile-to-mobile communication occurs in wireless LAN protocols like IEEE 802.11 and HIPERLAN. Here, by separating messages and order information, communication and synchronization overheads are reduced.

References

1. Acharya, A. and Badrinath, B.R., "Checkpointing Distributed Applications on Mobile Computers," The 3rd International Conference on Parallel and Distributed Information Systems, pp. 73–80 (1994).
2. Chandy, K.M. and Lamport L., "Distributed Snapshots: Determining Global States of Distributed Systems," ACM Trans. on Computer Systems, Vol. 3, No. 1, pp. 63–75 (1985).
3. Elozahy, E.N., Johnson, D.B. and Wang, Y.M., "A Survey of Rollback-Recovery Protocols in Message-Passing Systems," Technical Note of Carnegie Mellon University, CMU-CS-96-181 (1996).
4. "Radio Equipment and Systems(RES); HIPERLAN," ETSI Functional Specifications (1995).
5. "Wireless LAN Medium Access Control(MAC) and Physical Layer(PHY) Specifications," Standard IEEE802.11 (1997).
6. Koo, R. and Toueg, S., "Checkpointing and Rollback-Recovery for Distributed Systems," IEEE Trans. on Software Engineering, Vol. SE–13, No. 1, pp. 23–31 (1987).
7. Muller, G., Hue, M. and Peyrouz, N., "Performance of consistent checkpointing in a modular operating system: Result of the FTM experiment," Lecture Notes in Computer Science: Dependable Computing -EDCC-1, pp. 357–365 (1994).
8. Neves, N. and Fuchs, W.K., "Adaptive Recovery for Mobile Environments," Communications of the ACM, Vol. 40, No. 1, pp. 69–74 (1997).
9. Pradhan, D.K., Krishna, P.P. and Vaidya, N.H., "Recovery in Mobile Wireless Environment: Design and Trade-off Analysis," The 26th International Symposium on Fault-Tolerant Computing, pp. 16–25 (1996).
10. Prakash, R. and Singhal, M., "Low-Cost Checkpointing and Failure Recovery in Mobile Computing Systems," IEEE Trans. on Parallel and Distributed Systems, Vol. 7, No. 10, pp. 1035–1048 (1996).
11. Smith, S.W., Johnson, D.B and Tygar, J.D., "Completely asynchronous optimistic recovery with minimal rollbacks," The 25th International Symposium on Fault-Tolerant Computing, pp. 361–370 (1995).
12. Smith, S.W. and Johnson, D.B., "Minimizing timestamp size for completely asynchronous optimistic recovery with minimal rollback," The 15th IEEE Symposium on Reliable Distributed Systems, pp. 66–75 (1996).
13. Tsuruoka, K., Kaneko, A. and Nishihara, Y., "Dynamic recovery schemes for distributed processes," The 2nd IEEE Symposium on Reliability in Distributed Software and Database Systems, pp. 86–95 (1995).
14. Wang, Y.M., "The maximum and minimum consistent global checkpoints and their applications," The 14th IEEE Symposium on Reliable Distributed Systems, pp.86–95 (1995).

Automotive Product Documentation

Andreas Kaiser* and Wolfgang Küchlin

Symbolic Computation Group
Wilhelm-Schickard-Institut für Informatik
Universität Tübingen
72076 Tübingen, Germany
{kaiser, kuechlin}@informatik.uni-tuebingen.de
http://www-sr.informatik.uni-tuebingen.de/

Abstract. This paper discusses applications of AI methods in the context of electronic product data management in the automotive industry. It describes the main characteristics of the rule based legacy product documentation expert system currently employed by one of the major car and truck manufacturers in the world. As a basis for investigations of refinements and alternatives of the current documentation method, the product data centered business processes are analyzed.

1 Introduction

In the automotive industry the trend towards highly individualized products is unbroken [5]. Model class, design line, engine type and capacity, transmission type and interior are only a few of the most common categories within which a customer can choose. Even a relatively small number of options combines to a vast number of different car types. This is, e.g., illustrated by the Mercedes-Benz C-class limousines which in practice are ordered in tens of thousands of variations specified from a set of 1,151 options. Rising product value even increases the extent of individualization. E.g. barely any of the more than 80000 orders one of the DaimlerChrysler truck manufacturing plants processed in a one year cycle was produced identically for a second time. No car company can escape this development without loss of market share especially not in the segment of high priced vehicles [12].

However, new organizational challenges affecting all company units and even reaching beyond the single company boundaries have to be met to benefit from mass customization [11]. These challenges are mainly due to the need for an effective means to communicate about the set of products a company plans to offer, manufacture, sell and service in the future. During the engineering and selling phase the *exorbitant number of product variations* makes an explicit enumeration and processing of all potential product instances impractical. Not all theoretical combinations of options are feasible nor desirable as are not all assemblies of parts. *Various technical and legal limitations as well as restriction*

* Supported by debis Systemhaus Industry GmbH and DaimlerChrysler AG.

L. Monostori, J. Váncza, and M. Ali (Eds.): IEA/AIE 2001, LNAI 2070, pp. 465–475, 2001.

from the sales department complicate the separation between producible and not producible orders. While any constraint in its own local context appears to be intuitive and well justified it has the potential to interfere with any other constraint from a completely different domain. In a worst case scenario, every new option or part doubles the complexity of the documentation [10]. *Speed of innovation* is a key value to set a company apart from its competitors. Time for propagation of new product knowledge and quality convergence through refinement cycles is limited. Consequently the exact meaning and correctness of constraints should be obvious in the first place and inconsistencies should be detected automatically in the second place. Different individuals have in accordance with their intentions *differing views*, and a representational approach that seems to be adequate for one view makes knowledge handling unnecessarily difficult for another view. Philosophies in the four major organizational units of an automotive company, namely engineering, production, sales, and after sales, are so different that a product knowledge representation that is not able to adjust to their own special way of viewing products would hardly be accepted but rather forced into the intended view by expensive ad-hoc solutions. Therefore, efficient handling of customizable products throughout an automotive company will be crucial for its prosperity, and successful research in this area will lead to a considerable market advantage [14].

2 DaimlerChrysler's Product Documentation

Currently DaimlerChrysler[1] applies the product documentation system EDS-BCS/DIALOG for mass production of Mercedes passenger cars and trucks (cf. [5]). The system was originally modeled after the administrative processes that were used before the IT infrastructure was employed, and it evolved driven by user feedback and practical needs. It defines, from a functional as well as from a aggregational point of view, the complete set of products that can be manufactured and are released for sale. It allows for automated completion and correctness detection of functional specifications and supports automated mapping from functional to aggregational product descriptions. Finally it contains all relevant data about parts for production and after sales purposes and is the basis for the generation of sales catalogues and configurators. All data is stored in a conventional relational data base. Combinatorial information is enforced only due to adequate post processing.

2.1 Product Instance Description

DaimlerChrysler's product documentation system reflects different product views in that it knows a functional and an aggregational way of representing a product instance.

[1] To keep the text readable *DaimlerChrysler* is used instead of the more precise term *DaimlerChrysler, Stuttgart*.

Functional Description. From a functional point of view products are described in terms of *codes*, which are company wide standardized symbols for product characteristics. Generally, there is a one to one relation between codes and product properties appearing in sales language. For Mercedes-Benz passenger cars these codes can be categorized as model class, design line, engine type, cylinder capacity, steering wheel position, point of sale, color, interior decoration and supplementary equipment codes as illustrated in Figure 2.1. An *order* as it is internally processed consists of a selection of exactly one product characteristic in each of the first eight categories and an optional list of additional equipment codes. A *basic product type* is determined by a list of eight codes from the before mentioned categories whereas supplementary equipment codes specify modifications to this basic product type. For historical reasons there also exist symbols called *patterns* summarizing model class, design line, engine type, engine capacity and steering wheel position. Codes from these categories are also addressed as *pattern codes*. The mapping from patterns to the list of five pattern codes is defined by an explicit and complete enumeration.

Selection Category	Product Characteristics	Codes
Basic Product Type		
Product Pattern		
Model Class	A-Class	C1
	C-Class	C2
	...	...
Desgin Line	Limousine	D1
	agon	D2
	Convertible	D
	...	...
Engine Type	Fuel Injection	E1
	Diesel	E2
	...	...
Cylinder Capacity	2.0 l	M1
	2.8 l	M2
	.2 l	M
	...	...
Steering heel Position	left	L
	right	R
Mandatory Options		
Country	Germany	O1
	USA	O2
	Hungary	O
	...	...
Color	Red	L1
	hite	L2
	...	...
Interior	Fabric blue	I1
	Leather	I2
	...	...
Supplementary Equipment		
Upgrade	Elegance	U1
	Esprit	U2
	Sport	U
	...	...

Fig. 1. Codes and patterns

Aggregational Description. Information on how a product is composed from its parts is represented as a list of part-whole pairs specifying the set of parts from which to build the product, and for each part instance the location where the instance is to be fixed. Parts are uniquely determined by a part number and can themselves be aggregates. In general, instances of a part can appear in different locations. For passenger cars a location is uniquely described by a module number which decomposes to main module, basic module, and sub module, and a position number. Main module, basic module and sub module are organized in a three level hierarchy according to functional and geometric considerations. They form a company wide agreed on disposition of passenger car structure. A module can be part of the aggregational description of any product instance whereas not any module need to be present in such a description.

2.2 Product Overview

The *product overview* determines all products that have been released for sale after their technical feasibility has been verified. For planning purposes it serves as reference to sales, production and after sales departments while during customer order processing it provides the basis for automated order supplementation and constructibility checking. The instructions for supplementation of partial orders and for checking order correctness are stored as propositional formulas over codes. While in principle it is possible to interpret the product overview as a large, structured Boolean formula implicitly describing the complete set of feasible and released products, in practice the data base contains declarative instructions for order processing algorithms, e.g. algorithms scanning the data base one or several times to apply step by step each rule to an input code list.

Constructibility Checking. Two different types of instructions for constructibility checking can be distinguished: *model class dependent* and *model class independent instructions.* The latter ones associate a code with a rule, stating that independent of the model class specified in an order, it is constructible only if it satisfies the rules for all codes which are part of the order.

In contrast, model line dependent constructibility information consists of a model class, group, position, variant, design line, steering wheel position, code and rule specification. Model line and group form a hierarchical organization of positions. A code is uniquely determined by model class, group and position whereas within a model class and group there may be more than one position relating to the same code. Variants are used in connection with order completion to uniquely determine single constructibility rules. A constructibility checking instruction is derived from all lines with identical model class, group, position and code specifications. The instruction is considered only if model class and code are part of the processed order. An order is constructible only if it satisfies at least one of all those rules whose associated design line and steering wheel position codes matches the corresponding codes within the order. If due to the filtering effect of design line and steering wheel position no rules remain within a position the order is rejected. Likewise an order is rejected if it contains a code that is not mentioned in the data base in relation with the model class specified in the order.

Order Completion. For sales purposes, special equipment is often offered in packages like e.g. *elegance* or *luxury.* These imply various modifications to a

Model Class	Group	Position	Variant	Design Lilne	Steering Wheel Position	Code	Rule
C1	G1	P1	V1	L1	R	U1	-U2
C1	G1	P1	V2	L1	R	U1	M2+-O2
C1	G1	P1	V	L2	L	U1	M2/M
C1	G2	P2	V1	L	R	U2	I1+M1
C1	G	P2	V1	L	L	U2	L2+-O

Fig. 2. Product overview schema

basic product type. These kinds of implications are stored within completion rules, which are composed from the same information as model class dependent constructibility checking rules. As for model class dependent constructibility checking, for one model class, design line and steering wheel position there may be several rules associated with the same code. But in contrast to model class dependent constructibility checking, completion rules are interpreted completely independent of each other. However, during execution of supplementation steps not only the completion condition but also constructibility is checked in order to prevent order completion from undermining constructibility. Hence in addition to a completion rule for code c with group g, position p, variant v, a supplementation instruction considers the model class independent constructibility rule of code c and the model class dependent constructibility rule selected by group g, position p and variant v. Code c is only added if the order satisfies the supplementation rule and its extension by c complies with the respective constructibility rules.

The completion algorithm distinguishes model class and code related supplementation instructions. In contrast to the latter the completion rules of the first is empty and henceforth supplementation is only controlled by the associated constructibility rules. The completion algorithm scans completion rules three successive times, where during the first two passes only model class related supplementation is performed while in the third pass code related supplementation is executed.

2.3 Product Structure

The *product structure* lists for each model class the set of part-whole pairs that can appear in one of its instances and uniquely defines for each complete and constructible specification its aggregational structure. Hence it can be viewed as a mapping from functional to aggregational product descriptions.

The mapping is stored by model class and organized according to module and position. Within a model class for each module and position a list of parts which can possibly fill this position is given. With each part a key called variant, a design line, steering wheel position and a Boolean formula built over codes is associated. From those parts whose design line and steering wheel position are matching the corresponding order information the part for the respective position is selected. However for a part to be selected it is not enough if the order complies with the related rule. Rather an extended version of the rule which incorporates all rules of alternative parts needs to be satisfied. Basically the extended version states that the rule associated with the selected part needs to be satisfied and all rules of alternatives must be falsified. But it also accounts for the priority of parts in accordance with their ordering within a position.

Model Class	Module	Position	Variant	Design Lilne	Steering Wheel Position	Part	Rule
C1	040210	2000	100	L1	R	P1	-U2
C1	040210	2000	110	L2	L	P2	M2+-O2
C1	040210	2010	100	L1	L	P	M2/M
C1	0402 0	2010	100	L1	R	P1	I1+M1
C1	200470	1 20	100	L	L	P6	L2+-O

Fig. 3. Product structure schema

3 Product Data in the Automotive Business

Each of the engineering, production, sales, and after sales departments has its own characteristic view of a company's product line. A company wide product data management solution must be able to integrate their views with minimal data management effort providing maximal benefits.

3.1 Sales

The sales department shapes the customer's impression of a company. Therefore its requirements towards a product documentation system should be handled with highest priority. In any way the rules that constrain the set of products should be comprehensible to a sales person as well as to any kind of customer. During a product selection phase ideally they should only come in contact with those rules that are relevant to the considered specification. Similarly, details should only be visible as far as requested by the user. Some customers will be content with a predefined package, others have more precise conceptions or may request certain parts to be used. In some cases engineering tasks might be involved, if customers' wishes are beyond the anticipated specifications.

To be more precise, from a sales perspective the primary function of a product data system is to provide sales personnel and customers with a means to determine interactively, without the help of an expert, whether a specification is feasible, why a specification is not feasible, in which ways a specification can be extended, and some derivable attributes like price, or time to delivery.

3.2 Production

The manufacturing infrastructure forms the backbone of a car company. Any evidence for an order acceptance or rejection can be derived from its projected state at the time of production. This projection is by nature only a commitment statement and as such can only provide statistical assurance. On the one hand the production department is concerned with committing only to orders it certainly can produce. On the other hand it is pulling out all the stops to realize an order it committed to earlier. A description of all acceptable orders serves as a filter for incoming orders to guarantee a continuous production process as well as a basis for production planning. Clearly to avoid costly ad-hoc measures, customer dissatisfaction and a tarnished company image, a high quality, if not error free, product documentation is aspired.

Besides filtering and planning, a product documentation can support the generation of a detailed manufacturing program from a concrete product specification. This kind of mapping from product specification to production program represents one of the immediate cost benefits a product documentation system can provide. But to take advantage of it program correctness is at least as important as order correctness. In addition to constraints on the product structure logistic considerations constrain the practicability of a program and hence the successful processing of an order. These restrictions appear mainly as time latency on the availability of some intermediate product.

3.3 Engineering

A product database of the engineering department gives in the first place reference to the manufacturing units about the set of products that are scheduled for sales at a future time period. It guarantees for nothing more than the technical feasibility of the products based at most on prototype experiments or simulations. The product set is constrained in two ways. On the bottom the collection of parts bound the range of assemblies to those that can be obtained by arbitrary combination in accordance with their interface definition. From the top the overall functional product conception confines the variety of combinations.

The outermost limits of engineering activities are defined by the laws of geometry and physics. It evolves at the most with scientific progress e.g. with respect to product data at a rather slow pace. Engineering in its most general form explores the in this fashion given space of infinite possibilities. The direction of these kind of exploration activities are not random but controlled by conceptions. To reduce the costs of misdirections conceptions are refined in several steps and at each step reevaluated in order to backtrack to and modify a more abstract specification in case of failure. A product knowledge system can support this activity in several ways. Firstly with the help of systematic storage and retrieval functions reusage of old designs in a copy and modify manner can be supported. Secondly, designing a bundle of similar objects in analogy to parameterized programming could be a beneficial option.

Automated verification that a refinement or optimization complies with a given specification is another functionality to back product engineering. As illustrated above, engineering activities do not end with a concise description of all the products a company is willing to produce. Rather the set of products is translated to a manufacturing infrastructure and to programs that should allow for all the specified products to be manufactured. Hence from an enterprise wide perspective the final engineering task is not to design a collection of products but a set of processes. On this background a comparison with hardware design and an evaluation of some of the sophisticated methods employed there might be a promising field of research.

3.4 After Sales

From an after sales point of view information on production processes is completely irrelevant since product upgrades and failure driven modifications are too dispersed to be standardized and performed in a central location. Therefore, after manufacturing, process data is only of interest for analysis purposes or as a pattern for future process design activities, with the exemption of data about sources of supply for product parts. In contrast to process data, knowledge about products that have been offered in the past and all their variations remain relevant as long as service for these products is offered, even though certain variations of a product may not have been sold yet. What is more, product variations might grow although mass production has already been terminated. Thus, in case of alternatives, it must be precisely investigated if produced benefits still justify managing an product data base, which is growing in complexity. A clear negative answer must result in the deletion of the appropriate product data and its variations to keep the data base manageable. With respect to algorithms, product upgrading or modification is similar to sales configuration with the difference that a complete product specification serves as a starting point and additional restrictions might apply concerning the extent or simplicity of modifications.

3.5 Synchronization

Obviously there is a need for synchronization of the different departmental views on product knowledge. The various situations that can come up due to replicated data in the engineering, sales, production and after sales departments can be illustrated best along the development over time of a product set with time independent instances. Such a product set is identified by the time point or time interval where it is projected to become effective for production. A product instance is time independent if it is effective for the complete interval associated with a product set.

The *engineering phase* has the widest time horizon and lasts until for all instances of a product set service has been finished. Of course sort and frequencies of changes mutate over time. After committing the data as technically correct and providing it to the other departments clearly any modification needs to be propagated. The *production planning phase* sets in with product data release by the engineering department and ends with the exact predefinition of a production program. In addition to the engineering unit the production unit may commit its product data to the sales and after sales department to confirm that a product can not only be produced as prototype but also within the mass production process. The *selling phase* may already start in parallel to the engineering or

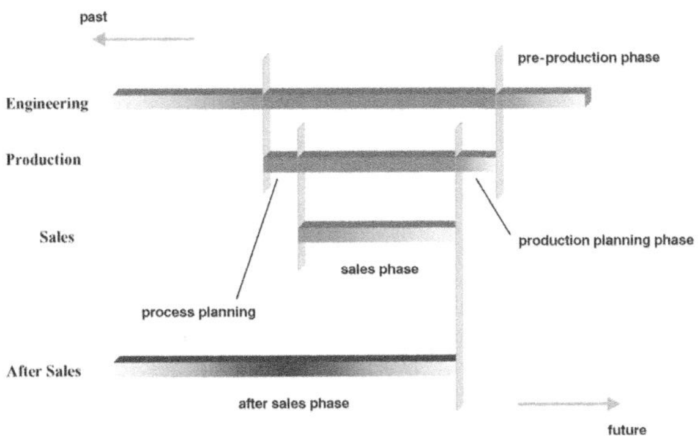

Fig. 4. Interdependencies of the departmental product data views

process planning activities but until engineering and production data has not been committed product data management efforts might be in vain. For the sales department product data is only of interest as long as the projected production and delivery time lies in the future. Hence the time associated with a product set is for sales coevally its expiration date. Generally the *after sales phase* spans the same time period as the engineering phase. But similar to the sales phase only with a commitment statement of the engineering department after sales product data receives its reliable basis. In contrast to the other departments the after sales product data knowledge for a time t consists not only of an extended and for its special needs modified product set at time t but of the sum of all product sets that have been offered in the past and are still serviced.

4 Conclusion

DaimlerChrysler's product documentation is a hybrid of relational database and rule-based expert system. Its characteristics with respect to knowledge organization are company wide standardization, hierarchies, propositional rules, time intervals and simple attributes. Daily usage in a high volume mass production process proves its indispensability. Data management efforts are substantial, though, and hence there is demand for further investigations directed towards improving the product data quality on the one hand while reducing management costs on the other hand. While these criteria are easy to measure for a running system as errors or costs per processed, delivered or offered products, to compare different documentation methods there is a need for an adequate translation. Another quality gauge that lacks a direct transformation to theory is simplicity – a crucial factor due to the sheer number of people without academic background that come into contact with such a system. Prerequisite for any method to be accepted in a production environment are guarantees on its statistically or even better deterministically low complexity.

Logic and AI have developed various knowledge representation methods spanning from propositional logic over first order logic to modal, temporal and higher order logics as well as semantic networks and frame languages. For a principal discussion of automotive product documentation these methods need to be evaluated with respect to their applicability for describing product sets from different points of view. Infinity, inherent incompleteness and default handling are aspects for which, at least in the automotive setting, an adequate answer must be found. Yet, not only product space representation languages, but also ways of synchronizing, combining, comparing, validating, and organizing product spaces are of importance. Particularly mapping a functional to an aggregational product space, integrating the geometric and technical information from construction plans, unifying, separating or comparing geometric, electric, legal and sales spaces, verifying production spaces, and investigating product space exploration and optimization strategies are some of the issues to mention here explicitly.

The fact that only the simplest knowledge representation methods are used within DaimlerChrysler's product documentation system leaves wide room for alternative solutions. But to improve a running system changes must integrate well without interfering negatively with the rest of the system. Here one of the more concrete starting points is the generalization from Boolean to finite domains. This would allow to eliminate the rules stating mutual exclusiveness of codes, which grow quadratical in the size with the number of items. Alternatively one might think of introducing number restrictions into the Boolean language. Another point are meta rules to extend the idea of model class independent rules to a more flexible scheme. Investigations on formalization and verification of the overall system represent another way for quality improvements [12]. But for such methods to be effective a completely declarative product data description is desirable. While huge parts of the documentation can indeed be interpreted in a declarative way, there still remain dozens of exceptions that are wrong with respect to a global formalization but are deliberately documented to handle some special cases whose correct specification would have been impossible or too work intensive. Also due to imperative documentation order completion can be a source of distraction. The order dependence with respect to interpretation makes its administration a sophisticated task and verification hard because of knowledge that is hidden within algorithms.

References

1. Brown, D. C. Defining configuring. *Artificial Intelligence for Engineering Design, Analysis and Manufacturing 12* (1998), 301–305.
2. Feigenbaum, E., Friedland, P. E., Johnson, B. B., Nii, H. P., Schorr, H., and Shrobe, H. Knowledge-based systems in Japan. Tech. Rep. PB93-170124, World Technology Division at Loyola College, May 1993.
3. Fleischanderl, G., Friedrich, G. E., Haselböck, Schreiner, H., and Stumptner, M. Configuring large systems using generative constraint satisfaction. *IEEE Intelligent Systems 13*, 4 (1998), 59–68.

4. HAAG, A. Sales configuration in business processes. *IEEE Intelligent Systems 13*, 4 (1998), 78–85.
5. KÜCHLIN, W., AND SINZ, C. Proving consistency assertions for automotive product data management. *Journal of Automated Reasoning 24*, 1–2 (2000), 145–163.
6. MAILHARRO, D. A classification and constraint-based framework for configuration. *Artificial Intelligence for Engineering Design, Analysis and Manufacturing 12* (1998), 383–397.
7. MCDERMOTT, J. R1: A rule-based configurer of computer systems. *Artificial Intelligence 19*, 1 (1982), 39–88.
8. MCGUINNESS, D. L., AND WRIGHT, J. R. Conceptual modelling for configuration: A description logic-based approach. *Artificial Intelligence for Engineering Design, Analysis and Manufacturing 12* (1998), 333–344.
9. MCGUINNESS, D. L., AND WRIGHT, J. R. An industrial-strength description logic-based configurator platform. *IEEE Intelligent Systems 13*, 4 (1998), 69–77.
10. MITTAL, S., AND FRAYMAN, F. Towards a generic model of configuration tasks. In *Proccedings of the 11th International Joint Conference on Artificial Intelligence* (1989), vol. 2, Morgan Kaufman Publishers, pp. 1395–1401.
11. SABIN, D., AND WEIGEL, R. Product configuration frameworks – a survey. *IEEE Intelligent Systems 13*, 4 (1998), 42–49.
12. SINZ, C., KAISER, A., AND KÜCHLIN, W. Detection of inconsistencies in complex product configuration data using extended propositional SAT-checking. In *Proceedings of the 14th International FLAIRS Conference* (2001), AAAI Press.
13. SOININEN, T., TIIHONEN, J., MÄNNISTÖ, T., AND SULONEN, R. Towards a general ontology of configuration. *Artificial Intelligence for Engineering Design, Analysis and Manufacturing 12* (1998), 357–372.
14. TIIHONEN, J., SOININEN, T., MÄNNISTÖ, T., AND SULONEN, R. State-of-the-practive in product configuration – a survey of 10 cases in the finnish industry. Tech. rep., IIA-Research Centre, Helsinki University of Technology, 1995.
15. TIMMERMANS, D. P. The business challenge of configuration. In *AAAI'99 Configuration Workshop Notes* (1999).
16. WIELINGA, B., AND SCHREIBER, G. Configuration-design problem solving. *IEEE Intelligent Systems 12*, 2 (1997), 49–55.

The Design and Implementation of a Traffic Accident Analysis System

Haiyi Zhang [1], Barbro Back[1], and WanLei Zhou[2]

[1] Turku Centre for Computer Science TUCS
Department of Information Systems, Abo Akademi University,
Lemminkinengatan 14 B, Fin-20520
Turku, Finland
{zhang.haiyi, Barbro.Back}@abo.fi
[2] School of Computing and Mathematics, Deakin University, Rusden,
Victoria 3168, Australia
wanlei@deakin.edu.au

Abstract. We designed and implemented a traffic accident analysis system (TAAS) in the paper. TAAS is the system faced traffic accident analysis, which uses the traffic rules (law) as knowledge sources to judge if the driver is responsible for a traffic accident. TAAS has characteristics of separating knowledge base and inference engine, using production rule and backward chaining. Besides, TAAS used predefined text and tracing program to realize explanation mechanism.

1 Introduction

Expert System itself is a technique for practicality. The production of the technique methods for expert system's knowledge representation, knowledge acquisition, and knowledge usage is strongly relying on practice backgrounds [4]. The new techniques and new methods, that are valuable and at high level, are produced only through practice. Without practices Expert System is no way to go. There is an experience in the international, that is, the more specific and narrow the practice problem is solved by the expert system, the easier and successful[1]. So, for the expert system technologies, first we strengthen the research of the basis and attach importance to the combination between an expert system and other new technology; secondly, we attach importance to the technologies, which are successfully applied to a real domain, practicable, valuable from the features of the real domain [3]. The research and development of Expert System Developing Tools provides an efficient and facile means for the construction of an expert system. It cannot only shorten developing cycle of an expert system and reduce its developing cost, but also improve its quality. Traffic accidents in our real life often happen. This is a special domain, which is narrow but practicable. Traffic accident analysis uses the traffic rules (law) as knowledge sources to judge if the driver is responsible for a traffic accident. In the paper we designed and implemented a traffic accident analysis system (TAAS) in order to provide a software tool for the user.

L. Monostori, J. Váncza, and M. Ali (Eds.): IEA/AIE 2001, LNAI 2070, pp. 476–481, 2001.

2 The System Design

TAAS mainly composed of two modules, which are judging responsibility module and system maintenance module. The system maintenance module is divided into three sub modules that are rule list maintaining, attribute-value list maintaining and context list maintaining.

2.1 The System Software Structure

The functions of the system software are described as follows: *Knowledge Base* It stores domain knowledge from experts. In the system the knowledge base consists of three parts: Rule list, Attribute-Value comparing list and Context list. *Database and management* Database is used to store the information provided by the users, the intermediate results and running information. In our system the database is used to store fact link list, matching rules, belief list and context list. The system dispatcher may complete to add, to delete, to modify and to search for data, which is in the database. *Explanation Mechanism* The explanation mechanism in our system may answer the question which is proposed by the user while running the system in order to enhance the system transparency and credit. It provides a WHY explanation and a HOW explanation. *Inference Engine* It is the thought mechanism of the system. It may apply the knowledge in the knowledge base and data in the database to produce the final conclusion following the special inference methods and control strategies. *System dispatcher* It is the director of the system. It may control the running order of modules. *System I/O* According to the command from the system dispatcher, the system I/O will complete to output the results, to accept keyboard interruption and to input some related information. *Judgement* It provides the service for judging responsibility *Maintenance* It is used to maintain for Knowledge base. It can be used to create any list in the database and it also has the functions such as seeking, inserting, modify, deleting, sorting, etc for the knowledge base.

2.2 The Partition of an Application Domain and Inference Technological Process

When we develop an expert system, if the application domain is complex, we should decompose the task according to the task content. After decomposing completely, the problem becomes several sub-tasks. Based on the analysis, we can draw a context tree for the problem. The context tree reflects one side of the domain. An inference flowchart reflects another side of the problem. TAAS is the system that judges if a driver is responsible for a traffic accident. So, the driver should be the root of the context tree. The sub-context of the driver is two locations in which a traffic accident possibly happens. They are respectively the road and the parking lot. In the road context we can decompose seven sub-contexts according to the behavior of the driver when the accident happened. These seven sub-contexts are "Crossing intersect with traffic signal", "Crossing intersect without traffic signal", "Enter or exit the road", "Running on the road", "Making turn" and "Parking aside". They are independent each other.

TAAS is the system that judges if a driver is responsible for a traffic accident. So, responsibility should be the goal. The responsibility has three attributes, which are judging ability, the speed reasonable and driving behavior reasonable. The speed reasonable is respectively relying on " the speed reasonable on the road" in the road context and " the speed reasonable on the parking lot" in the parking lot context. Driving behavior reasonable is respectively relying on " the driving behavior reasonable on the road" in the road context and " the driving behavior reasonable on the parking lot" in the parking lot context. The driving behavior reasonable on the road is relying on the attributes of child contexts in the road context. All the attributes are finally relying on the observed attributes.

2.3 The Design of Knowledge Base and Maintenance

2.3.1 The Design of the Knowledge Base

Knowledge base in TAAS consists of three parts: rule list, attribute-Value comparing list and context list. *1. Rule List* It consists of the rule clusters, which is a set of rules in which the same attribute and value can be deduced. Each rule cluster has two parameters: the context name and the rule cluster name. Here the rule cluster name is an attribute name of the attribute value which can be deduced by the rule cluster. It has the following form: Context name Rule cluster name Rule 1, Rule 2,....., Rule n. Here, we use production rule method to represent a rule, that is *Premise conclusion* Each rule has three parameters: Rule numbers, Premise operating relation (and / or), a credit of the conclusion. The credit of the conclusion is an integer between 0 and 100. It has the following form: Rule numbers, Premise operating relation, A credit of the conclusion Premise 1, Premise 2, ... Premise n, Conclusion. Each premise and conclusion is respectively a triple (context name, attribute name, value) The rule base is divided into the clusters because our system adopts backward chaining (that is goal-driven reasoning [2]). The system proposes a hypothesis in the backward chaining procedure at beginning. In order to verify the hypothesis, the system needs to find out the rules in the knowledge base and to match. These rules can deduce the attribute of the hypothesis. After classifying the rule base with the clusters, we can read the all rules that we need at one time. *2. Attribute-Value comparing List* An attribute can be obtained with three methods: asking for the user, deducing from other rules and calling a function. The rule itself does not have the character. In order to obtain the attributes for the system, we create an attribute-value comparing list. The list consists of nodes of attribute-value. Each node has following contents: Attribute name, explanation, obtaining a value method, query form, type of values, the number of values, value 1, value n. Here, the explanation is a predefined text for explanation mechanism. The query form is a predefined text for the user query. There are three types of values. That is Yes-No, input, and enumerable. Only when the value is enumerable type, the node has the numbers of values and the content of values. *3. Context*

List The context list is set in order to obtain the parameter value of the context. It consists of context nodes. Each context node contains a context name, a explanation, query 1, query n. Here, the context name is a searching index, query I is a predefined text for the user querying a parameter value, It is also the predefined text for a explanation. The explanation is a predefined text for explanation mechanism.

2.3.2 The Knowledge Base Maintenance

There are three knowledge base maintenance methods, that is, traditional logic way, the checking method based on Petri net, and TMS techniques[5]. Our system adopts the traditional logic way. The system realized to create rule base, to add a rule, to delete a rule and to modify a rule in the rule base. We adopt the interactive method to realize the functions. The output prompts the user for data parameters and read them after the user confirmed. The system illustrates if the functions are completed and the reasons if a function is not completed. It is convenience for the domain experts and knowledge engineers to create and to maintain.

2.4 The Design of Database and Management Mechanism

2.4.1 The Design of Database

The database in TAAS has four parts: Fact link list, credit list, Context list and the rule matched currently. *1. Fact link list* It consists of fact nodes. Each fact node is a 4-tuple (context name, attribute name, value, credit), The fact link list is used to keep the facts and intermediate results. *2. Credit list* It consists of credit nodes. Each credit node respectively keeps a credit of the premise in the rule matched currently and a credit of the premise in the rule matched successfully. It is used for determining a credit of a conclusion fact when activating a rule. *3.Context list* It consists of context nodes. Each node includes context name, explanation, parameter name 1, parameter value 1, parameter name n, parameter value n. It is used for producing a conclusion output text. . *4. The rule matched currently* It is a point which points a rule node. It is used for the explanation mechanism.

2.4.2 Management Mechanism of the Database

By the system dispatcher the management mechanism of the database may complete to initialize all the lists in the database, to propagate a list, to search a node and to add a node. It can cooperate with the inference engine and explanation mechanism.

3 The Design for Inference Mechanism of TAAS and its Implementation

Inference is one of the hot topics in AI research. Based on the existing conclusions and technologies, AI researchers are working on new inference methods. At present time, there are mainly non-resolution method (for example Bledson' s natural deduce method [3], Knuth' s rewrite rule method[2], Boyer and Carth's bonded reasoning, Reiter 's default reasoning, fuzzy reasoning, probability reasoning[5], time sequence reasoning[3], etc. An inference mechanism is main part of an expert system execution mechanism. It is constrained by the knowledge representation and knowledge base organization. It is also influenced by the commands that the user interface can accept. As in our system we use production rule method to represent knowledge, our inference mechanism is a rule inference execution programs.

As for TAAS the problem solving space is small, its goal is providing a reference opinion for judging responsibility in a traffic accident. So we adopt the backward chaining inference engine to implement. In this way the system can control the reasoning direction according to the user 's query. Here, the matched function for the premise node of a rule has following called form: Integer type function name (premise node *p). Its function is depicted as following: Propagating the fact link list in the database, checking if there is a fact node that has same context name and same attribute. If yes, comparing the value of the fact node to the value of the premise node, if equal (successful matched) return 2, if unequal (fail matched), return 1, if no, return 0. The matched function for the rule has following called form: Integer type function name (rule *p). Its function is depicted as following: there are two operation relations for the premises: *and* operation and *or* operation. 1. The operation relation for the premises is *and* operation Taking a premise of the rule, calling the matched function of premise node, if return value 0, then saving the premise and return 0. If return value 1, then return 1; if return value 2, taking the credit of the fact node and adding it to the credit list, taking next premise condition, calling the matched function of the premise node. If all the premises are matched successfully, return 2 (successfully matched). 2. The operation relation for the premises is *or* operation Taking a premise of the rule, calling the matched function of premise node, if return value 0, then saving the premise and return 0. if return value 2, taking the credit of the fact node and adding it to the credit list, return 2, If return value 1, taking next premise condition, calling the matched function of the premise node. If all the premises are matched unsuccessfully, return 1 (unsuccessfully matched). In the activating rule function, we use following algorithm to calculate a credit of a rule conclusion: (1) When each premise operation relation is *and* operation credit = integer part of (MIN (credit nodes in the credit list) * credit of the rule conclusion /100). (2) When each premise operation relation is *or* operation credit = integer part of (MAX (credit nodes in the credit list) * credit of the rule conclusion /100).

The system outputs the conclusion of the rule and prompts the user to input 0 for querying How to get the conclusion. The system also asks the user if you want to see the reason Why. The system successfully returns the information for the user: any contexts and parameters related to the inference procedure. From the context we can get if the driver is responsible for the accident and reasons.

4 The Explanation Mechanism of TAAS and its Implementation

The explanation mechanism in our system is realized with the path-tracing method and Predefined text combining the dictionary base [4]. The system provides a WHY explanation and a HOW explanation for the user.

5 Summaries and Conclusion

We designed and implemented a traffic accident analysis system (TAAS) in the paper. The structure and implemented technologies of TAAS are discussed in detail. TAAS adopts the production rule method to represent knowledge. It is natural and clearly to modulate. We use the rule cluster form to classify the rules. In this way it is convenience for managing the rule base. In our system we have paid attention to maintaining the rule base. TAAS has characteristics of separating knowledge base and inference engine, using production rule and backward chaining. Besides, TAAS used predefined text and tracing program to realize explanation mechanism. Finally we should point out that our system has some shortcomings, which is needed to improve. As each rule cluster and attribute-value comparing node is orderly stored in the file, the inference engine has to start from the beginning to search a rule. It takes too much time. While the system is executing some function, if the user inputs a error information, it can be modified in time. Only way the system can do is that after the function is completed, the error can be corrected, then can execute it again.

References

1. Randall Davis, Howard Shrobe, and Peter Szolovits. What Is a Knowledge Representation? AI Magazine.(1993)Vol.14,No.1:17-33
2. B. Hayes-Roth. An architecture for adaptive intelligent systems. Artificial Intelligence,(1995) 72:329-365.
3. E. Oliveira, R. Camacho. A Shell for cooperating expert systems. Expert System. May (1991)Vol.8,No.2:75-84
4. Hugh J. Watson and Robert I. Mann. Expert System: Past, Present, and Future. Journal of International System management. (1998) Vol. 5, No. 4:39-46.
5. H. Zhang, K. Wang, X. Sun "the design and implementation of an abductive inference system NJ-A" Harbin institute of technology Journal, China. No. 2(1995)

Decision Support System for Shadow Mask Development Using Rule and Case

Honggee Jin[1], Minsung Kim[1], Sabum Jung[1], Keymok Shon[1], Hyungtae Ha[2], Byungjin Ye[2], and Jiwon Jo[2]

[1] Knowledge Base Group, LG PRC, 19-1, Cheongho-Ri, Jinwuy-Myun, Pyungtaek-Si, Kyunggi-Do, 451-713, Korea
{jinhg, minsung, skk1991, shonkm}@lge.co.kr

[2] Development Team, Head Office, 2Plant, LG Micron, 624, Kupo-Dong, Kumi-Si, Kyoungsang buk-Do, 730-400, Korea
{lgmhht, lgmybj, bbm2001}@micron,lg.co.kr

Abstract. The knowledge-based system using rules and cases has been applied in many fields and studies. This paper introduces knowledge based system for design of the master pattern to manufacture a shadow mask(part of CRT). The System gives a useful information for design on the basis of rules and cases that are made from designer's know-how and past design pattern. We used pseudo-hybrid expert system (PHES) using rule-based reasoning (RBR) and case-based reasoning (CBR) appropriately. So, this system can perform its function by using a variety of useful knowledge acquisition.

1 Introduction

Recently, case-based reasoning(CBR) and rule-based reasoning(RBR) are used in various parts as a tool of knowledge acquisition[2],[3],[4],[8],[9]. CBR and RBR have been used separately. But there are some cases which apply two methods appropriately for reliability[5],[7].

Each of two reasonings(CBR, RBR) has its drawback. In CBR, various case data and rule evolution function must be prepared for reliable and accurate function[6]. Using RBR, it takes much time and efforts to learn and organize expert knowledge. So, it is desirable to use both methods appropriately in each case like hybrid type. This paper presents a pseudo-hybrid approach that uses RBR mainly and makes up for the weak point by CBR.

This research has been implemented to externalize and organize knowledge in development and design of shadow mask for color display tube(CDT).

2 Knowledge Based Decision Support System

2.1 Shadow Mask Configuration and Development

Electron gun shoots electronic beam to mark information on the screen. The electronic beam(red, green, blue color) is deflected by deflection yoke(DY). Shadow

L. Monostori, J. Váncza, and M. Ali (Eds.): IEA/AIE 2001, LNAI 2070, pp. 482–487, 2001.

Mask is a steel plate that screens and accelerates the beam to land at the exact phosphor position. There are two kinds of shadow mask. One is for color display tube(DSM) and the other is for color pictured tube(PSM).

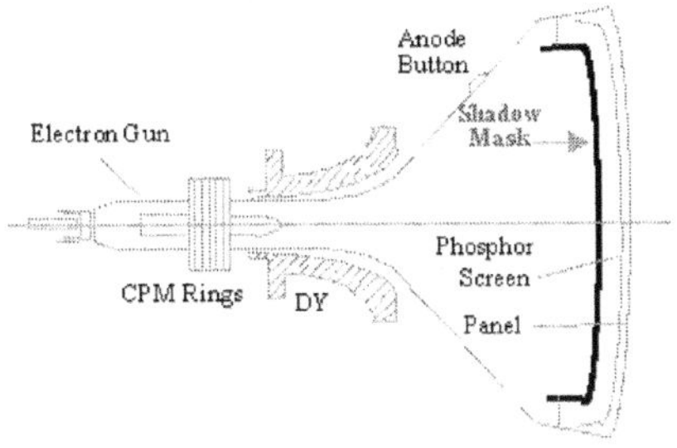

Fig. 1. CDT(Color Display Tube) configuration

Shadow mask has two sides(front side and rear side). Each side has a lot of holes. Front side has larger hole than rear side. The difference of both holes makes two tapers. The taper near center of shadow mask is inner taper(Ti). The opposite taper is outer taper(To). The size of Ti and To is same at the center. But the farther from the center, the larger difference of Ti and To size due to variant beam landing position caused by the deflection. So, Ti is smaller than To at the corner. The relation between taper and hole size is Formula 1 and 2.

$$D\Phi = \ d\phi + To + Ti \ . \tag{1}$$

$$Taper = To + Ti = D\Phi - d\phi \ . \tag{2}$$

Before shadow mask is developed, customer specification must be prepared. And then design process is begun considering production factors(etching performance, etching trend and so on). Master pattern(MP) is made by the design output. So, shadow mask design process is to decide the hole size printed on MP. Master pattern is copied at working pattern(WP) which is used for shadow mask. MP and WP are made of transparent glass which be able to transmit light. Because shadow mask has a negative shape, MP is a negative shape and WP is a positive one.

Shadow mask is produced through a clearing(removing dirt on WP glass), light exposure, developing(the shape of WP is copied at steel plate) and etching. So, it is important to know the production condition related to each process.

2.2 Production Line Knowledge Utilization

Shadow mask development is mainly dependent on production line knowledge. Etching performance is the most important thing among the design factors. So,

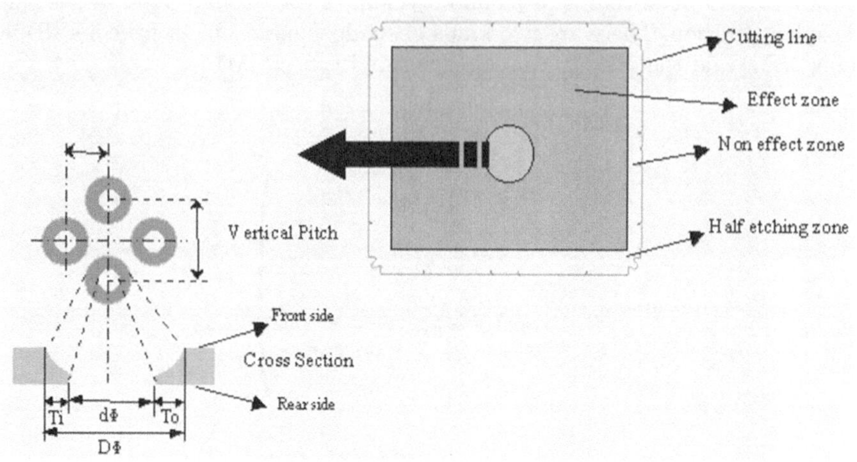

Fig. 2. DSM Shape

developer must know etching quantity along with steel material, size, thickness, customer specification, production line and so on. Cross section shape must be considered as main factor which is the main customer requirement. The cross section shape is various on the pattern hole size, type and production line condition.

The main factors of production line were classified into several production knowledge. The effect of the factors was analyzed on the basis of past data(for example, how much MP type has an effect on the hole). The parts which don't have enough data were estimated through experiment(for example, the relation of production condition and final hole shape).

Knowledge can be analyzed, externalized as qualitative or quantitative type. But the most difficult thing is to grasp and standardize each developers' knowledge, because shadow mask is mainly dependent on their tacit knowledge. So, knowledge acquisition was performed by interview with them. If there were discrepancy or uncertainty between developers, these were solved through consensus meeting.

2.3 Knowledge Based System Development

Shadow mask design is performed through effect side and non-effect side design. Developer decides pitch size, DΦ size, taper compensation quantity, etching quantity and MP size by customer requirements at the effect side design. At the non-effect side design, cutting line and half etching design are performed.

The design is done by the fixed design rule and similar case. Rule-based reasoning is mainly used because the rule is organized very well. So, case data are used as reference due to insufficiency. CBR may be very powerful when it has enough data to perform. But if there are not enough data for each model like this case, much more design data(material, thickness, inch, pitch and so on) must be prepared for CBR. In this case, it is desirable to use RBR. But CBR can be used as reference for decision making even though it can't be directly applied.

Developers don't use only rules. They modify the rough design by considering past experience(maybe, tacit knowledge) and current condition. In this process, cases are much more helpful for their decision making. So, knowledge-based system is required to perform multi-dimensional data analysis and retrieve appropriate similar cases.

Usually, CBR has a cycle(retrieval, evaluation, adaptation and learning). In this cycle, retrieval is the most important thing. The reuse of experience and the creation of new development concept are possible through retrieval of similar cases. The similarity can be measured by distance [1] between two cases.

The RMS(Root Means Square) method is used for similarity measure. And the number of similar cases is limited to three. The evaluation and adaptation are performed by the following formula 3. The retrieval process is performed through several stage.

1. Classify past data into several clusters.
2. Mark the cases by design values.
3. Calculate distance between current design model and past models.
4. Select appropriate cases.

$$(\hat{x},\hat{y}) = Min \sum_{i=1}^{3} \sqrt{(x-x_i)^2+(y-y_i)^2}\ . \tag{3}$$

$$x,y = New\ Problem(D\Phi, d\phi)\ . \tag{4}$$

$$x_i, y_i = Case(D\Phi_i, d\phi_i),\ where\ i = 1,2,3\ . \tag{5}$$

KDS(Knowledge based Development supporting System) has seven modules(customer specification input module, effect side design module, non-effect side design module, rule management module, case management module, user management module, line/material/inch code management module). KDS performs effect and non-effect side design by these modules.(Fig.3.)

2.4 System Evaluation

KDS evaluation is performed by two methods(design accuracy and pilot test). KDS design data is evaluated by qualified data at design accuracy test. In pilot test, developer's design and KDS design are applied on the same steel plate and produced. The test criteria are output quality(hole shape, conformity)

[1] $\sqrt{(x-x_i)^2+(y-y_i)^2}$

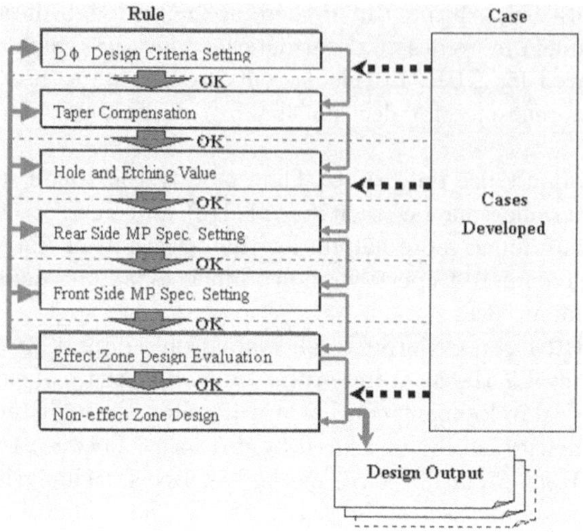

Fig. 3. Shadow Mask Development Process

In accuracy test, discrepancy is calculated by the absolute difference between two data. If the discrepancy is negligible, KDS design is accepted. If not, the one is rejected.

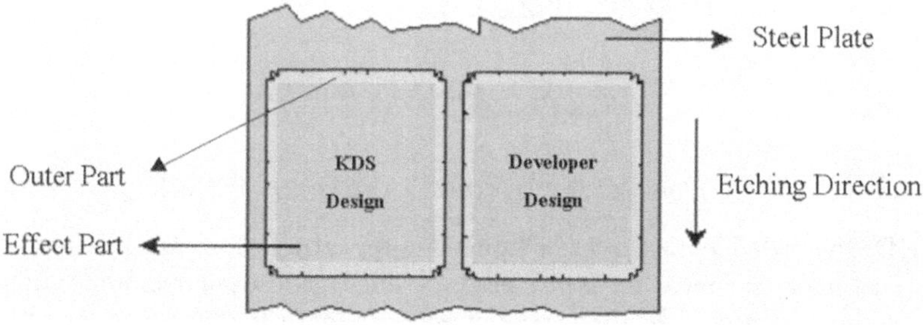

Fig. 4. KDS evaluation(Production test)

After design accuracy test, production test is performed. KDS and developer design is printed on a steel plate through light transmission. The quality of shadow mask is evaluated after etching under same condition. Total 25 models is tested. The number of models within 2 μ(negligible gap) are 23 for front side and 24 for rear side.

3 Conclusion

Evaluation result in section 2.4 shows that computer aided decision support system can be applied to production line. Before KDS was developed, there were only data about past development experience. So, it was difficult to externalize tacit knowledge from the data. Without knowledge sharing, developer did the same error that others had done.

KDS didn't only automate shadow mask design process but also make the tacit knowledge visible in applicable form. Developers could reduce fatal error and spend more time to another creative work by KDS. KDS could replace higher level work by RBR and CBR. It'll be also learning tool for the new member.

There are some complementary works to enhance KDS reliability in several parts.

- Reinforcing CBR with preparing enough case data
- Automating rule evolution
- Enhancing analysis ability(for rule elicitation) by knowledge visualization

Most of all, it is very important that a Knowledge sharing environment must be instilled among the developers and organization. And developers must be trained to document and share their experiences. Therefore others can use the knowledge. KDS is a just tool to help these kinds of works systematically.

References

1. David P., Shane S.: Human-centered knowledge acquisition: a structural learning theory approach, Int. J. Human-Computer Studies, Vol. 45. (1996) 381–396.
2. Ketler, K.: Case-Based Reasoning: An Introduction, Expert systems with Applications, Vol. 6 (1993) 3–8.
3. Kolodner, J.: Case-Based Reasoning, Morgan Kaufmann publishers, Inc. (1993)
4. Andrew R., Raul S.: Improving accuracy by combining rule-based and case-based reasoning, Artificial Intelligence (1996) 215–254.
5. Lundy L.: A Case-Based Reasoning Approach to the Management of Faults in Communications Networks, the IEEE Inforcom'93, Vol. 3 (1993), 1422–1429.
6. Shelesh-Nezhad K., Siores E.: An Intelligent System for Plastic Injection Molding Process Design, Journal of Materials Processing Technology (1997) 458–462.
7. H. Li, X. Wu: Learning Design Knowledge As Generation, Cybernetics and Systems: An International Journal, Vol. 29 (1998) 181–207.
8. B.U. Haque, R.A. Belecheanu, R.J. Barson, K.S. Pawar: Towards the application of case based reasoning to decision-making in concurrent product development(concurrent engineering), Knowledge-Based Systems, Vol. 13 (2000) 101–112.
9. J.L. Gordon: Creating knowledge maps by exploiting dependent relationships, Knowledge-Based Systems, Vol. 13 (2000) 71–79.

An Expert System for Ironmaking

Javier Tuya[1], Eugenia Díaz[1], Marta Hermida[1], José A.L. Brugos[1], Angel Neira[1], Alfredo Alguero[1], and Faustino Obeso[2]

[1] Computing Department. University of Oviedo. Campus de Viesques, 33271 Gijón, Spain
{tuya, eugenia, hermida}@lsi.uniovi.es

[2]Aceralia Corporación Siderúrgica S. A., Spain

Abstract. This paper describes an expert system for the on-line diagnosis of blast furnaces. The system analysis more than a hundred parameters in real time and shows the operator the status of the blast furnace and its behaviour. The system also gives suggestions and control set-points in order to achieve a better hot metal quality and aimed analysis, as well as to increase the production in the blast furnace. In addition to the information given by the furnace, the expert system also takes advantage of a theoretical model of behaviour of thermal status and permeability and apply the considerations given by the human experts in order to solve all the conflicts.

1 Introduction

A modern blast furnace is a complicated system with hundreds of variables that need to be controlled for its correct and economical running. Currently, the control of this large amount of variables is a human operation 8assisted by a mathematical model, but years of experience give rise to fundamental empirical knowledge in said operation. A new, more modern blast furnace in an iron and steel industry, or the modernisation of an old blast furnace means that all the knowledge accumulated in the scenarios of others furnaces becomes useless.

ACERALIA is an iron and steel industry situated in the outskirts of the town of Gijón, in the North of Spain. The majority shareholder is the ARBED group. Since 1997, there are two new, modern blast furnaces, where the problem of the old empirical knowledge of its operators has arisen. The requested task was to construct an expert system that collects the useful knowledge about the running of old furnaces, and the experience accumulated in the last one and half year by operators and technicians with respect to the new furnaces. This knowledge should be sufficiently coherent with the mathematical model that is used. At the same time, a user-friendly monitoring system of blast furnace control should be also put into effect. The task is not an easy one. It entails many problems: incoherent, poor or erroneous knowledge, a very harsh environment for software, suspicions on the part of operators due to the typical fear of the ghost of unemployment, etc. But, finally we were able to construct an expert system and an interface to control the two blast furnaces, in accordance with the imposed specifications, and whose main features shall be explained in this paper.

L. Monostori, J. Váncza, and M. Ali (Eds.): IEA/AIE 2001, LNAI 2070, pp. 488-493, 2001.

2 The Expert System Architecture

Most expert systems acquire knowledge about symptoms, faults and corrective actions through the usual process of codifying human expertise in rules or decision trees. Their problem is the existence of discrepancies between different operators in fault diagnosis and decision taking based on their empirical knowledge and perhaps with insufficient degrees of reliability. A possible solution to this discrepancies should be to use a model of the process to predict its behaviour or to check consistency among observed variables [5].

It isn't relevant to define a general model in the blast furnace, to describe the general behaviour, because of its complexity and the intrinsic interdependence of its performance variables, but rather, sub-models of particular aspects of the burning process and its performance [4] in which theoretical and empirical knowledge is integrated (Fig. 1).

2.1 Data Management Module

Since the expert system must work with a large number of variables, these variables were divided into different groups: variables used for making calculations of burden hangs, drops and slips; those used for displaying the calculated data; variables of the actions file for preventive actions and hangs; and other internal variables used in the control of slips and hangs. It is necessary to design a specific module called, in terms of the specific tool used, the data management workspace. This module makes the connection between the expert system and the "physical system". By means of this module, the parameters that define the behaviour of the furnace are periodically updated through its monitoring. All this data can optionally be used during the inference process by the expert system. Besides those previously referred to, the data management workspace also accomplishes the following functions:

- Collecting furnace input data and the maintenance operations carried out by technicians.
- Adapting the acquired data from the sensors to the expert system format (G2/Exad requirements through GFI objects).
- Making prior calculations to be used in future malfunction analysis.

2.2 Definition of the Theoretical Models for the Furnace

The monitoring system carries out general control functions in the following areas of analysis:

- Blast Furnace Thermal Status Control.
- Control of Burden Slips and Hangs.
- Control Variations in CO/CO_2 Analysis and Top Temperatures.

The first is now test-running, and is the object of this paper.

COMMON MODULES	THERMAL STATUS MODULE
HANGS AND SLIPS MODULE	GAS ANALYSIS AND THROAT-FURNACE TEMPERATURE MODULE

Fig. 1. Expert System Modules

Next, we shall present the theoretical construction for the Thermal Status. The corresponding models for Burden Slips and Hangs Control and CO/CO_2 Variations Control are analogous.

The implementation of these relationships implies a structured form of knowledge that permits its description in hierarchical forms [7]. To achieve this, a classical object network, in which the models are integrated, was defined. This net performs several essential functions:

- It specifies the variables of the furnace as a set of objects related at different levels of abstraction.
- It inserts the models within the objects that integrate the net.
- It establishes the analytical relationships that will define the behaviour of the models.
- It provides means of information interchange between the models and the furnace parameters.

2.2.1 Thermal Status of the Blast Furnace

The Thermal Status model simplifies the states space of the blast furnace, where each state depends on many variables. It is defined according to the most reliable data: the temperature of the hot metal and the percentage of silicon, due to there being a correlation between both. Then, each pair of values of the hot metal temperature and the percentage of silicon is identified with a point on the plane Temperature-Percentage of Silicon and this plane is divided by isothermal status lines into seven areas, one of which -Thermal Status ET(0)- is the best work area because it includes the targeted pair, hot metal temperature and percentage silicon.

The percentage of silicon is the result of the general function $Si = (T^a - K)/m$, which is the correlation between the hot metal temperature and % Si, for more than 35-40 heats, and for a targeted hot metal temperature. Thus, the typical error is lower when short periods of time (3 or 4 days) are taken than if you take months, due to the variations in basicity. Accordingly, the correlation is always calculated dynamically with the last three days data.

The influence of coke consumption on the % of silicon was estimated. At the same time, the influence of the hot metal temperature on the coke consumption was also estimated. Then, the transformation of the specific heat of the hot metal to the specific consumption of coke was calculated. ET will represent the increase in coke in Kg./Hmt. and will be called the thermal status.

$$ET = A(X,Y)(Y-Y_0) + B(X,Y)(X-X_0) \quad \textbf{(1)}$$

where X is the percentage of Si, Y is the temperature in °C, X_0, Y_0 is the targeted pair temperature-% silicon.

Then, the isothermal lines, one for each ET, are the following:

$$X=(222.5ET-20.517Y+34669.25)/(11125-0.445(Y-1500)) \quad (2)$$

Other considerations are made until obtaining the final equations for the isothermal lines (Fig. 2).

$$X=(ET-0.08770(Y-1500)+17.5)/(50.89326-0.000595Y) \quad (3)$$

In summary, once the targeted temperature and targeted percentage of silicon have been defined, the isothermal status lines are calculated dynamically. The parameters of the final functions are the targeted hot metal temperatures and the percentage of silicon that results from the correlation T^a / %Si. Moreover, we shall use the increments in the specific consumption of coke in Kg/Hmt. to indicate the different thermal statuses and we shall consider the level 0, ET(0), as the targeted temperature and percentage of silicon. From this level 0, we calculate the different thermal status increasing or decreasing the coke. A new thermal status area is defined every two kilograms.

3. Inference Engine

The following subsections present the inference mechanisms used to produce a diagnosis.

3.1. Detection of Discrepancies

The first stage in the inference process is the detection of discrepancies between the behaviour of the machine and the models. To achieve this, a specific set of rules is available. In premises of rules, the results from the sensors of the monitoring process are compared with the model outputs. The conclusions of these comparisons are incorporated into a list of abnormal working conditions. Since all the discrepancies between model outputs and the behaviour of the furnace must be found, the process consists of a classical forward chaining. During this phase, all the possible causes of failure are included in the list of abnormal working conditions. For instance, if it is considered that the thermal status of the blast furnace corresponding to the last heat and its values shows a large decrease of more than 8 units, regardless of the actual value of the thermal levels, it is necessary to act on the system.

3.2. Failure Identification

The knowledge used in failure identification is also structured in rules. Said rules are grouped together in workspaces that can be optionally related to one another. Each workspace comprises the knowledge of failures corresponding to a specific part of the furnace process. This modular conception of the knowledge base improves inference efficiency and facilitates the introduction of new knowledge.

The elements in the abnormal conditions list will trigger the inference process in the corresponding workspace. Considering the past example about the large decrease in the thermal status, here it is necessary to analyse the value of the last heat in a comparative manner with the others and to check if the tendencies are more or less inclined. Moreover, it is necessary to check whether the operator had acted to correct the problem in the system. With all this information, it is possible to decide about subsequent action, which may be that of correcting the steam level, the percentage of coal to be injected (PCI), the O_2 variation, the wind temperature or other combined actions. This will cause a series of actions that could restart the inference cycle. In general, rule evaluation can trigger the following actions:

- Adding a new hypothesis to the inference engine.
- Consulting the models again.
- Reading from the historical databases.
- Asking the user for additional data.

3.3. Maintenance Plan

During malfunction identification, all the testimonies obtained are stored to be used in the results output. The maintenance plan is carried out by means of a standard rule system. These rules were obtained from expert operators in conjunction with a statistical study of historical databases using techniques of machine learning [1], [2], [9].

Due to the different information sources used to construct the knowledge workspaces, it is essential to prove their consistency and completeness. To achieve this, it was necessary to identify redundant, unnecessary, conflicting, circular and subsumed rules, and which must also look for potential gaps, not referenced or illegal attribute values, unreachable conclusions and dead-end goals [8] . When a discrepancy is detected in the value tables or rules given by the experts with respect to the analytical models and machine learning induced rules, it is necessary to check the problem throughout the historical behaviour and to consider the actions performed there. Finally, of course, all the decisions must be contrasted by the current expert technicians.

The final output of the system consists of:

- The diagnosed malfunction.
- The evidence collected during the identification process.
- The recommendations derived from the maintenance rules.

4. Conclusions

The system proposed in this paper attempts to aid blast furnace operators in the following ways:

- It monitors more than a hundred variables in real time and produces a basic diagnosis of the furnace conditions.

- It presents an architecture in which traditional concepts of knowledge-based systems are fused with model-based diagnosis techniques. Thus, the possible inconsistency of the former and the complexity of the latter do not appear.
- It combines analytical models with expert rules and methods obtained in historical databases with machine learning algorithms.

Acknowledgements. This work forms part of a European Coal and Steel Community (ECSC) multi-partner multi-national research project on Intelligent Monitoring Systems for Ironmaking (INSI) Ref. 7210-PR-002/P3721 with British Steel (UK) as co-ordinator and the participation of the Centro Sviluppo Materiali (Italy), VDEh-BFI (Germany) and ACERALIA (Spain). The Informática Department of the University of Oviedo is working together with ACERALIA in the Intelligent Monitoring of the two new blast furnaces at the Gijón Factory.

References

1. Alguero, A. Algoritmos para el Tratamiento de Reglas Aprendidas a partir de Ejemplos. Doctoral Thesis (1996). University of Oviedo, Spain.
2. Alguero, A., Pérez-Llera, C. Alonso, J. Medical Data Mining with a new Inductive Learning Tool. ISAS'97 , Caracas Venezuela (1997).
3. Davis, Randall; Hamscher, Walter. Model based reasoning: Troubleshooting. In Model based diagnosis. Morgan Kaufman Publishers (1992).
4. De Kleer, Johan; Willians, Brian C. Diagnosis with behavioural models. In Model based diagnosis. Morgan Kaufman Publishers (1992)
5. Dvorak, Daniel; Kuipers, Benjamin. Process Monitoring and Diagnosis. A model based approach. IEEE Expert.June (1992)
6. Jovic, F. Expert Systems in Process Control. Chapman & Hall (1992)
7. Neira, A.; Otero, A.; Cabanas, M.; Sanz, M.A.; Gomez-Aleixandre, J. Electric motor on-line diagnosis. A model-based approach. Int. Conf. on Integrated Logistics & Concurrent Engineering ilce'95. Paris (1995)
8. Nguyen, Tin A.; Perkins, Walton A.; Laffey, Thomas J.; Pecora, Deanne. Knowledge Base Verification. In AI Magazine. Summer (1987).
9. Quinlan, R. C4.5: Programs for Machine Learning. Morgan Kaufmann, S (1993).

Short Circuit Detection on Printed Circuit Boards during the Manufacturing Process by Using an Analogic CNN Algorithm

Timót Hidvégi and Péter Szolgay

Analogic and Neural Computing Systems Laboratory, Computer and Automation Institute, Hungarian Academy of Sciences, P.O.B 63, H-1502, Budapest, Hungary
hidvegi@sztaki.hu

Abstract. One of the most critical errors is the short circuit in the manufacturing of printed circuit boards. In this contribution we extend the already existing solution to more general cases where the errors can be detected by checking two production layers. The algorithm was tested with software simulator and 64*64 CNN-UM chip of ALADDIN System.

1 Introduction

Short circuits are serious problems in Printed Circuit Board (PCB) production. Several algorithms were developed in connection with PCB quality control. [2], [3], [4], [5], [6], [7], [8] The algorithm is based on the Celluar Nonlinear Network (CNN) paradigm. [10a], [10b] Due to the local connectivity of the CNN cells, the local layout errors can detect the errors effectively [1]. Analogic CNN algorithms were developed to detect new types of layout errors. The CADETWin simulation environment, the CNN Chip Prototyping System (CCPS) [12], 64*64 CNN-UM [14], [15] and 176*144 CNN-UM [16], [17] were used in the development and test phases of our layout detection algorithm.

Here we analyze simultaneously two layers of Printed Circuit Boards. Naturally we can detect some errors with the help of the method on a single layer too. The analogic CNN algorithm proposed in this contribution can detect all types of short circuits generated in manufacturing process.

The basic idea of the algorithm is as follows. Two input images are the two production layers of the PCB production. Two objects are selected on the input images to test the proper isolation between them. On these images there are two pads of different equipotential areas. The reference image is the result of the logic OR of the two marker images. We will analyze these images with some waves starting from the selected black object, the pad. Based on number and size of the errors, the production of a given PCB sample may be continued or stopped.

An analogic CNN algorithm is shown in section 2, as a solution to the problem. The algorithm uses two input pictures: two production layer markers and reference

L. Monostori, J. Váncza, and M. Ali (Eds.): IEA/AIE 2001, LNAI 2070, pp. 494-501, 2001.

images. In the output image of the algorithm only two pads can be seen. In section 3 we can see an example where the algorithm runs on software simulator and on different types of CNN-UM chips. The size of the test image is 176*144 pixels. The limits of the method and concluding remarks can be found in section 4.

2 A Short Circuit Detection Analogic CNN Algorithm

The main steps of our short circuit detection analogic CNN algorithm can be seen in Figure 1.

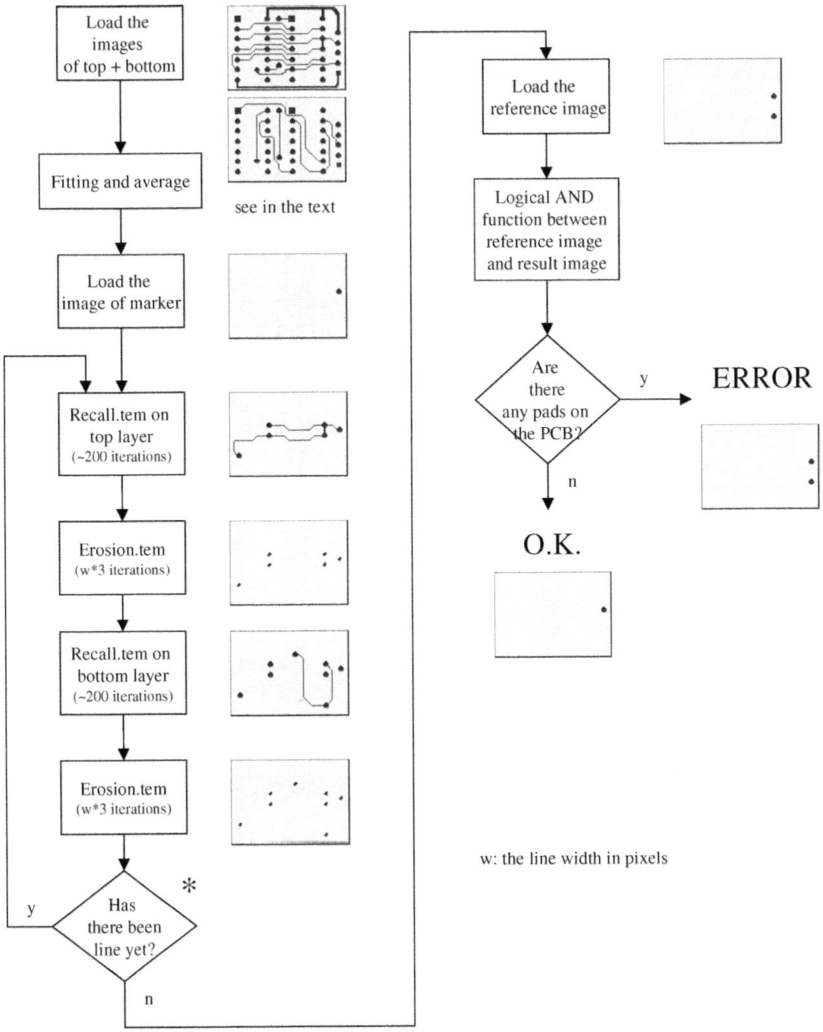

Fig. 1. The flowchart of the algorithm

The inputs of the analogic CNN algorithm are the two production layers of a PCB and the marker images to define the two objects belonging to two different equipotential nodes. We want to detect short circuits between the two equipotential areas. In the first step by the algorithm the images are converted into black & white ones. We start a wave from the marker image to reconstruct the layout elements belonging to this node. The tracks of the different signals can be found by a wave. The waves arise on the marker image but the form of the waves follows the tracks of the current production layer by using "recall.tem" (Figure 2.).

The input images are the marker and the production layer images. By using the recall template, we can build up the complete net defined on the marker image.

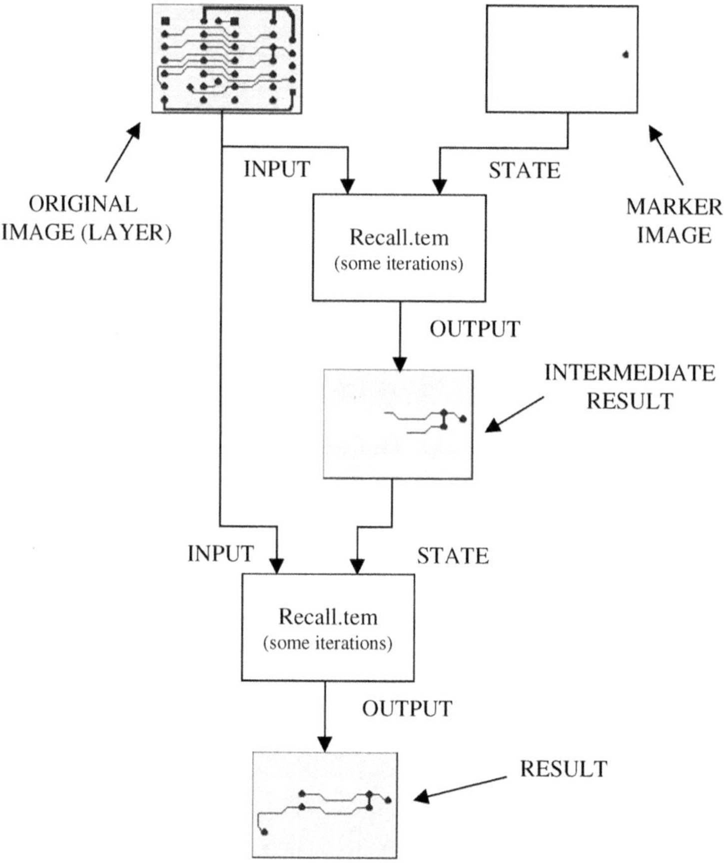

Fig. 2. The operation of the "recall.tem" template

In the 4*th* step the same algorithm is used for the other production image and the erosion template to remove the tracks from the reconstructed equipotential net. (Figure 5.). The number of the iterations is directly proportional to the linear size of the images.

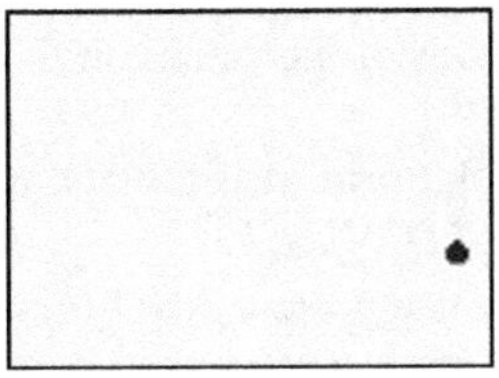

Fig. 3. The marker image

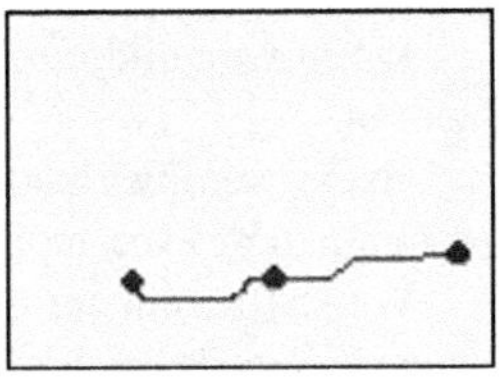

Fig. 4. The top layer

From the pads (Figure 5.) that we found on the top layer we start the waves on the bottom layer (Figure 6.).

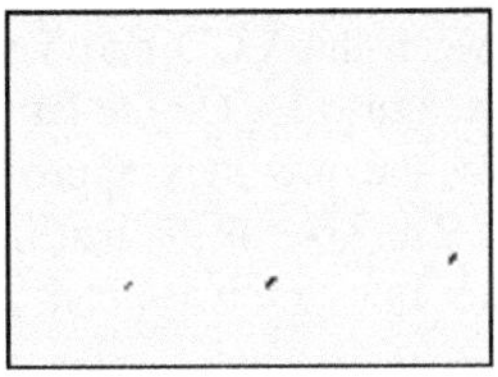

Fig. 5. The top layer after erosion

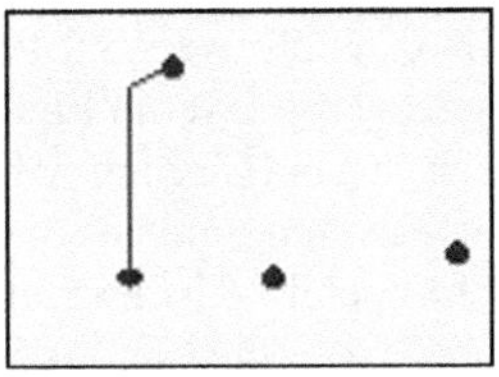

Fig. 6. The bottom layer

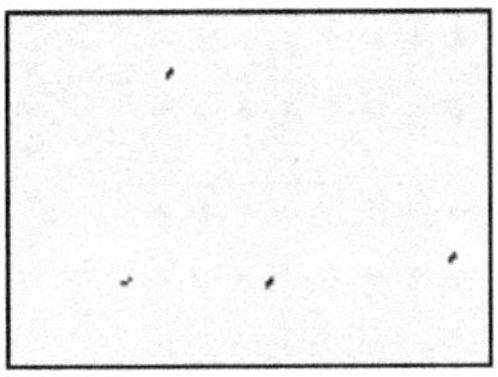

Fig. 7. The bottom layer after erosion

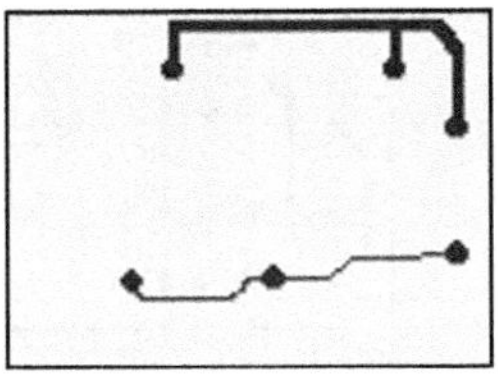

Fig. 8. The top layer

If we substract the image (n-1)*th* from the image n*th* and get a white image, then we do not have to run the wave generation (iteration) again (Figure 9.).

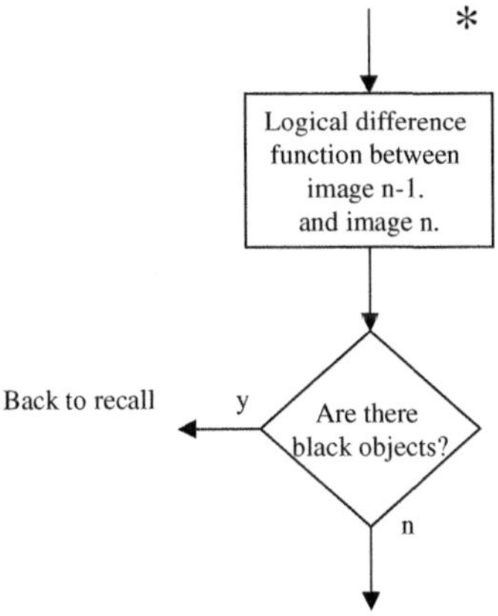

Fig. 9. Are the nth and (n-1)th images equal?

When we build up the selected signal, the total pads of the signal on the image can be seen.

Next we download the reference image into a platform. It is a black & white image and includes some pads of the different signals (VDD, VSS).

We shall compare the pads of the two images by using logic AND function. If we get several pads on the result image, it means that there is at least one short-circuit on one of the production layers.

3 Example

In this example we want to detect the short-circuit between the VDD and VSS. We can see the top layer in Figure 10 and the bottom layer in Figure 11. On the latter layer there is a short circuit which we would not detect by the previous approach [1] because even a correct connection may cause this error. The size of the test image is 176*144 pixels. The line width is one pixel and the thicker lines are two-pixel-wide.

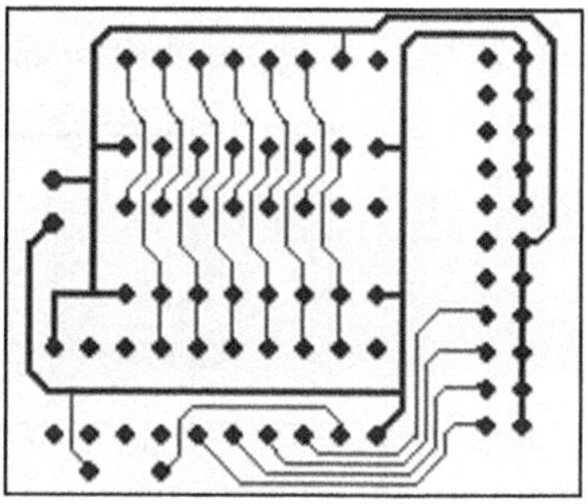

Fig. 10. Top layer

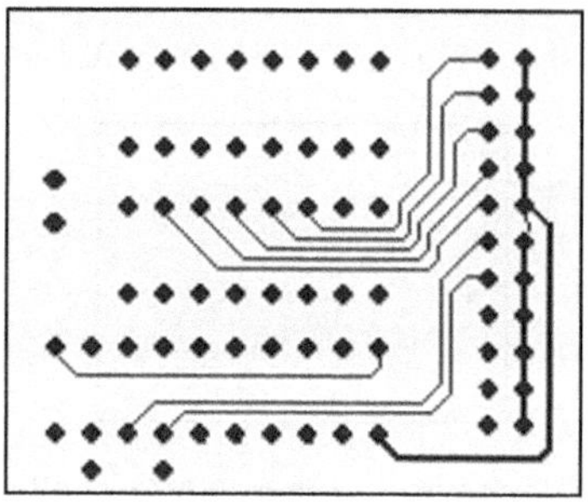

Fig. 11. Bottom layer

The marker image can be seen in Figure 12. The whole VDD signal is built up from the marker image on the TOP layer (Figure 13.).

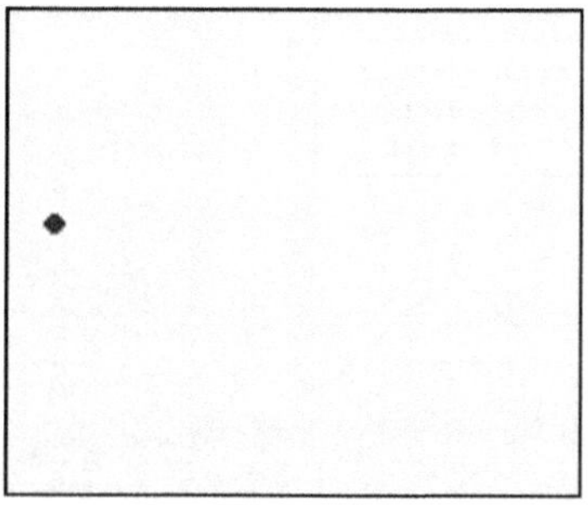

Fig. 12. Marker image

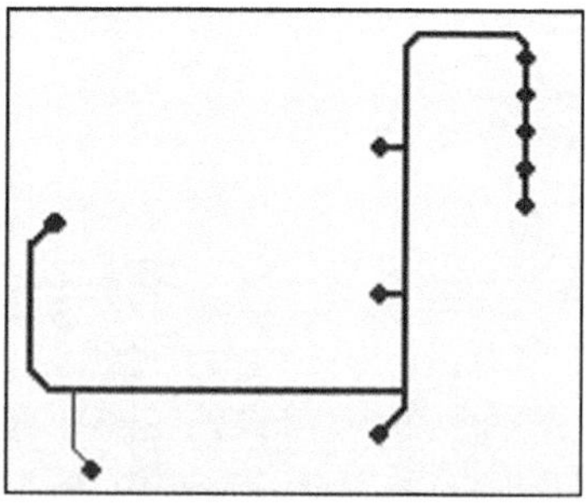

Fig. 13. The intermediate top layer after some iterations

From the pads of Figure 13 we start the waves on the bottom layer. With this step we get some additional pads from which we can start some waves (Figure 14). We can see the additional pads and the VDD signal on the top layer (Figure 15).

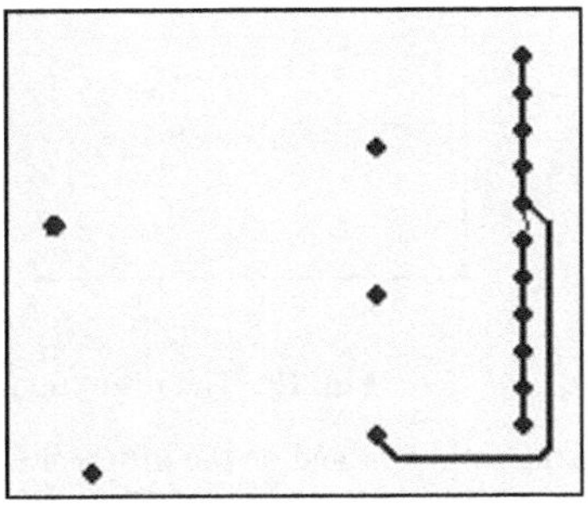

Fig. 14. The intermediate bottom layer

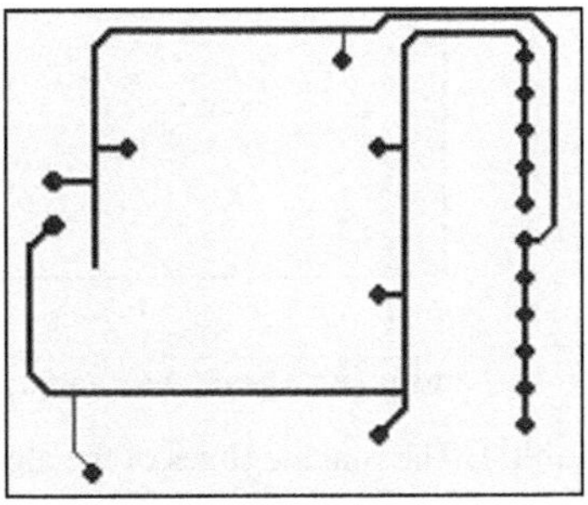

Fig. 15. The intermediate top layer after some iterations

In Figures 15 and16 we can see the VDD and VSS signals as well as the pads. (Figure 16).

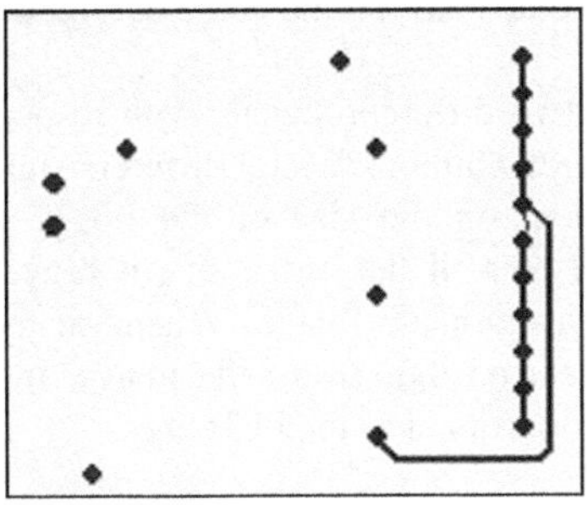

Fig. 16. The intermediate bottom layer

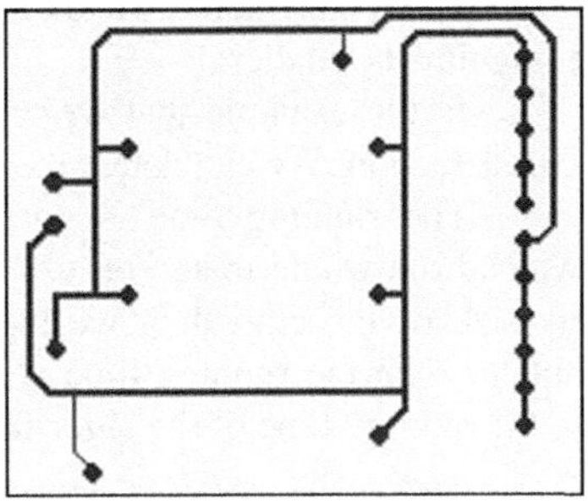

Fig. 17. The intermediate top layer after some iterations

The reference image can be seen in Figure 18. The reference image and the resulting image are compared by logic AND function. If there are some pads (at least 2) on the result image, then an error exists on one of the production layers (Figure 19.). It means that there is a short circuit between the VDD and VSS signals.

If there are more than two pads on the reference image, then we can detect the short-circuits among several signals.

4 Conclusions

The analogic CNN algorithm was implemented on software simulator and a 64*64 CNN-UM chip as well. The running time of our algorithm depends on the size of the image. The size of the test images is 176*144 pixels.

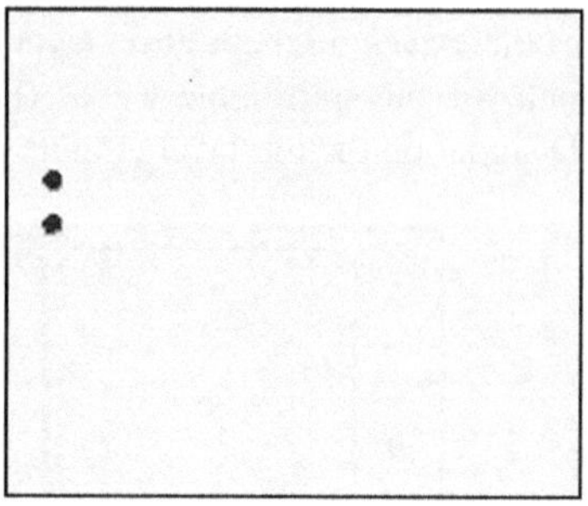

Fig. 18. The reference image

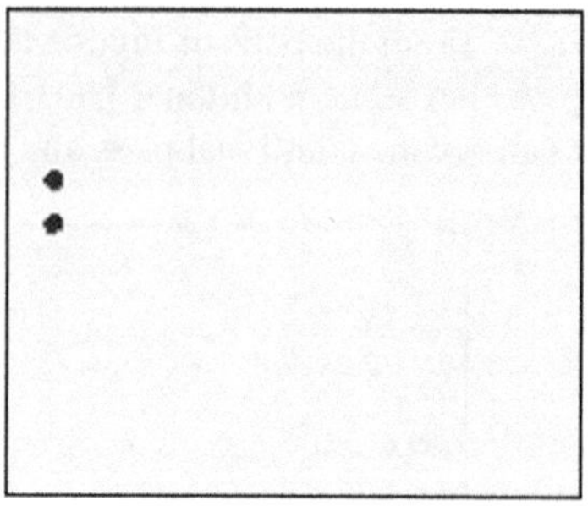

Fig. 19. The result image

Table 1. The running times of the algorithm on the simulator and on the different CNN-UM (* The running time of the algorithm's core is 30 msec by using 64*64 CNN-UM.)

Simulator on the PC	64*64 CNN-UM
105 sec	90 msec *

It is supposed that in the analogic CNN algorithm that the track width of a marked signal is smaller than the pad size of the selected signal.

If we start some waves from several pads of the selected signal, then the running time is smaller.

In the example that we analyzed two different signals with respect to short circuit detection. We can detect the short-circuit among several different signals too.

The running time is not dependent on the size of the image if we can download the whole image on a CNN-UM chip. If the image size is bigger than the array size of the chip then we have to partition the image. When we use a CNN simulator then the running time is dependent on the size of the image. In this latter case the running time of the algorithm is proportional to the PCB area.

Acknowledgements. The helpful comments of Prof. Tamás Roska, László Kék and Tamás Bezák are kindly acknowledged.

References

[1] P. Szolgay, K. Tömördi, "Analogic algorithms for optical detection of breaks and short circuits on the layouts of printed circuit boards using CNN" International Journal of Circuit Theory and Applications 27, pp. 103-116, 1999

[2] R. T. Chin, C. A. Harlow, "Automated Visual Inspection: A Survey", IEEE Trans. on Pattern Analysis and Machine Intelligence, Vol. PAMI-4, No. 6, pp. 557-573, (nov. 1982.)

[3] A. M. Darwish, A. K. Jain, " A Rule Based Approach for Visual Pattern Inspection", IEEE Trans. on Pattern Analysis and Machine Intelligence, Vol. PAMI-10, No. 1, pp. 56-68, (Jan. 1988.)

[4] Y. Hara, H. Doi, K. Karasaki, T. Iida, "a System for PCB Automated Inspection Using Flusorescent Light", IEEE Trans. on Pattern Analysis and Machine Intelligence, Vol. PAMI-10, No. 1, pp.69-78, (Jan. 1998.)

[5] E. B. D. Lees and P. D. Hensshaw, "Printed circuit board inspection - a novel approach", SPIE - Automatic Inspection Measurements, 1986.
[6] J. R. Mandeville, "Novel method for analysis of printed circuit images", IBM J. Res and Dev. Vol. 29, pp. 73-87, (1985.)
[7] M. Moganti, F. Ercal, C. H. Dagli and S. Tsunekawa, "Automatic PCB Inspection Algorithms: a Survey", Computer vision and Image Understanding, Vol. 63, No. 2. pp. 287-313 (March 1995.)
[8] M. Moganti, F. Ercal "A subpattern level inspection system for printed circuit boards", Computer vision and Image Understanding, Vol. 70, No. 1. pp. 51-62 (April 1998.)
[9] W. K. Pratt, "Digital Image", J. Wiley, New York, 1978.
[10.a] L.O.Chua and L.Yang, "Cellular neural networks: Theory", IEEE Trans. On Circuits and Systems, Vol.35, pp. 1257-1272, 1998.
[10.b] L.O.Chua and L.Yang, "Cellular neural networks: Applications", IEEE Trans. On Circuits and Systems, Vol.35, pp. 1273-1290, 1988
[11] T.Roska and L.O.Chua, "The CNN Universal Machine: an analogic array computer", IEEE Transactions on Circuits and Systems-II Vol.40, pp. 163-173, March, 1993
[12] T. Roska, P. Szolgay, Á. Zarándy, P. Venetianer, A. Radványi, T. Szirányi, "On a CNN chip-prototyping systems" Proc. of CNNA'94, Rome, pp. 375-380, 1994.
[13] R.Dominguez-Castro, S.Espejo, A.Rodriguez-Vazques, R.Carmona, P.Földesy, Á.Zarándy, P.Szolgay, T.Szirányi and T.Roska "A 0.8 μm CMOS 2-D programmable mixed-signal focal-plane arrayprocessor with on-chip binary imaging and instructions storage" Vision Chip with Local Logic and Image Memory, IEEE J. of Solid State Circuits 1997
[14] G. Linan, S.Espejo, R. Domínguez-Castro, A. Rodríguez-Vázquez "The CNNUC3: An Analog I/O 64*64 CNN Universal Machine Chip Prototype with 7-bit Analog Accuracy" Proc. of CNNA '2000, Catania, pp. 201-206, 2000
[15] G. Linan, S.Espejo, R. Domínguez-Castro, S. Espejo, A. Rodríguez-Vázquez "Design of a Large-Complexity Analog I/O CNNUC" Proc. of ECCTD '99, Stresa, pp. 42-57, 1999
[16] A. Paasio , J. Paakkulainen, J. Isoaho "A Compact Digital CNN Array for Video Segmentation System" Proc. of CNNA '2000, Catania, pp. 229-233, 2000
[17] A. Paasio, A. Kananen, V. Porra "A 176*144 processor binary I/O CNN-UM chip design" Proc. of ECCTD '99, Stresa, pp. 82-86, 1999
[18] "CNN Software Library" in CADETWin, T. Roska, L. Kék, L. Nemes, A. Zarándy, M. Brendel, and P. Szolgay, Eds. Budapest, Hungary: Hungarian Academy of Sciences, 1998. Processing"
[19] T. Hidvégi, P. Szolgay, Á. Zarándy „A New Type of Analogic CNN Algorithm for Printed Circuit Board Layout error Detection" Proc. of INES'99 IEEE, Stará Lesná, pp. 501-506
[20] T. Roska, "CNN chip set architecture and the Visual Mouse", Proc. of CNNA'96, pp. 369-374, Seville, 196.
[21] T. Roska, L. O. Chua and Á. Zarándy, "Language, compiler, and operating systems for the CNN supercomputer", Report UCB/ERL M93/34, University of California, Berkeley, 1993
[22] S. Zöld, "CNN Alpha Language and Compiler" Report DNS-10-1997, Computer and Automation Research Institute, Budapest, 1997
[23] P. Földesy, L. Kék, Á. Zarándy, T.Roska, G. Bártfai "Fault-Tolerant Design of Analogic CNN Templates and Algorithms-Part I: The Binary Output Case" IEEE Trans. On Circuits and Systems, Vol.46, pp. 312-322, 1999.

Application of Feature Transformation and Learning Methods in Phoneme Classification

András Kocsor, László Tóth, and László Felföldi

Research Group on Artificial Intelligence
of the Hungarian Academy of Sciences and of the University of Szeged
H-6720 Szeged, Aradi vértanúk tere 1., Hungary
{kocsor, tothl, lfelfold}@inf.u-szeged.hu
http://www.inf.u-szeged.hu/speech

Abstract. This paper examines the applicability of some learning techniques to the classification of phonemes. The methods tested were artificial neural nets (ANN), support vector machines (SVM) and Gaussian mixture modeling. We compare these methods with a traditional hidden Markov phoneme model (HMM) working with the linear prediction-based cepstral coefficient features (LPCC). We also tried to combine the learners with feature transformation methods, like linear discriminant analysis (LDA), principal component analysis (PCA) and independent component analysis (ICA). We found that the discriminative learners can attain the efficiency of the HMM, and after LDA they can attain practically the same score on only 27 features. PCA and ICA proved ineffective, apparently because of the discrete cosine transform inherent in LPCC.

1 Introduction

Automatic speech recognition is a special pattern classification problem which aims to mimick the perception and processing of speech in humans. For this reason it clearly belongs to the fields of machine learning (ML) and artificial intelligence (AI). For historical reasons, however, it is mostly ranked as a subfield of electrical engineering, with its own unique technologies, conferences and journals. In the last two decades the dominant method for speech recognition has been the hidden Markov modeling (HMM) approach. Meanwhile, the theory of machine learning has developed considerably and now has a wide variety of learning and classification algorithms for pattern recognition problems. The goal of this paper is to study the applicability of some of these methods to phoneme classification, making use of so-called feature-space transformation methods applied prior to learning to improve classification rates. We also present results with the application of such transformations. In essence this article deals with the neural network (ANN), support vector machine (SVM) and Gaussian Mixture modeling (GMM) learning methods and with the transformations linear discriminant analysis (LDA), principal component analysis (PCA) and independent component analysis (ICA). We compare the performance of the learners

L. Monostori, J. Váncza, and M. Ali (Eds.): IEA/AIE 2001, LNAI 2070, pp. 502–512, 2001.

with that of the HMM on the same feature set, namely the so-called linear prediction-based cepstral coefficients (LPCC).

The structure of the paper is as follows. First, we proveide a short review of the phoneme classification problem itself, and suggest some possible solutions. Then we briefly describe the acoustic features that were applied in the experiments and examine the feature transformation methods used. The final part of the paper discusses aspects of the experiments, especially the advantages and drawbacks of each learning method, the effectiveness of each transformation and of course the results obtained.

2 The Task of Phoneme Classification

Speech recognition is a pattern classification problem in which a continuously varying signal has to be mapped to a string of symbols (the phonetic transcription). Speech signals display so many variations that attempts to build knowledge-based speech recognizers have mostly been abandoned. Currently researchers tackle speech recognition only with statistical pattern recognition techniques. Here however, a couple of special problems arise that have to be dealt with. The first one is the question of the recognition unit. The basis of the statistical approach is the assumption that we have a finite set of units (in other words, classes), the distribution of which is modeled statistically from a large set of training examples. During recognition an unknown input is classified as one of these units, using some kind of similarity measure. Since the number of possible sentences or even words is potentially infinite, some sort of smaller recognition units have to be chosen in a general speech recognition task. The most commonly used unit of this kind is the phoneme, thus this paper deals with the classification problem of phonemes.

The other special problem is that the length of the units may vary, that is utterances can "warp" in time. The only known way of solving this is to perform a search in order to locate the most probable mapping between the signal and the possible transcriptions. Normally depth-first search is applied (implemented with dynamic programming), but breadth-first search with a good heuristic is also viable.

3 Generative and Discriminative Phoneme Modeling

Hidden Markov models (HMM). [10] synchronously handle both the problems mentioned above. The speech signal is given as a series of observation vectors $\mathbf{O} = \mathbf{o_1}...\mathbf{o_T}$, and one has one model for each unit of recognition C. These models eventually return a class-conditional likelihood $P(\mathbf{O}|C)$. The models are composed of states, and for each state we model the probability that a given observation vector belongs to ("was omitted by") this state. Time warping is handled by state transition probabilities, that is the probability that a certain state follows the given state. The final "global" probability is obtained as the product of the proper omission and state-transition probabilities.

When applied to phoneme recognition, the most common state topology is the three-state left-to-right model (see fig.1). We use three states because the first and last parts of a phoneme are usually different from the middle due to coarticulation. This means that in a sense we do not really model phonemes but rather phoneme thirds.

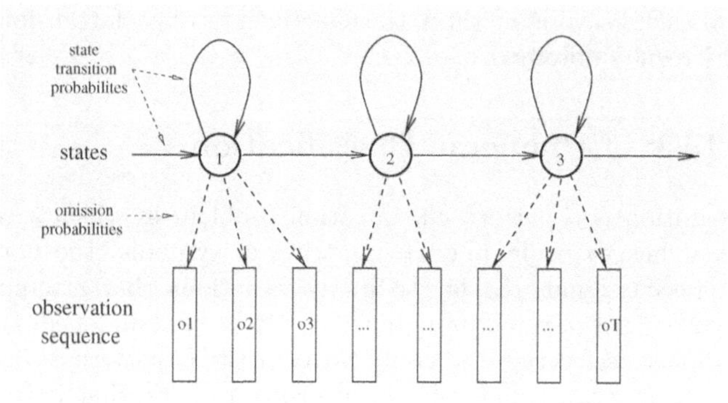

Fig. 1. The three-state left-to-right phoneme HMM.

Because the observation vectors usually have continuous values the state omission probabilities have to be modeled as multidimensional likelihoods. The usual procedure is to employ a mixture of weighted Gaussian distributions of the form

$$p(\mathbf{o}) = \sum_{i=1}^{k} c_i \mathcal{N}(\mathbf{o}, \mu_i, \mathbf{C_i}), \tag{1}$$

where $\mathcal{N}(\mathbf{o}, \mu_i, \mathbf{C_i})$ denotes the multidimensional normal distribution with mean μ_i and covariance matrix $\mathbf{C_i}$, k is the number of mixtures, and c_i are non-negative weighting factors which sum to 1.

In the following experiments we apply these **Gaussian mixture models (GMM)**[3] not only in HMMs but also in isolation, so as to model the conditional likelihood $P(\mathbf{X}|C)$ of a set of features $\mathbf{X}$ having been generated by a phoneme class C.

The final goal of classification is to find the most probable class C. We can compute the probabilities $P(C|\mathbf{X})$ from $P(\mathbf{X}|C)$ given by class-conditional or *generative models* like HMM and GMM making use of Bayes' law. Another aproach is to employ *discriminative learners* which model $P(C|\mathbf{X})$ directly. Instead of describing the distribution of the classes, these methods model the surfaces that separate the classes and usually perform slightly better than generative models. Their drawback in speech recognition tasks is that they cannot implicitly handle the "time-warping" characteristic os speech as HMM can, so on the word-level they have to be combined with some sort of search method.

From the family of discriminative learners we chose to experiment with the now traditional **artificial neural networks** (ANN)[11], and a relatively new technology called **support vector machines** (SVM). Rather than describing this method in detail here we refer the interested reader to an overview in [14].

4 Evaluation Domain

The feature space transformation and the classification techniques were compared using a relatively small corpus which consists of several speakers pronouncing Hungarian numbers. More precisely, 20 speakers were used for training and 6 for testing, and 52 utterances were recorded from each person. The ratio of male and female talkers was 50%-50% in both the training and testing sets. The recordings were made using a cheap commercial microphone in a reasonably quiet environment, at a sample rate of 22050 Hz. The whole corpus was manually segmented and labeled. Since the corpus contained only numbers we had samples of only 32 phones, which is approximately two thirds of the Hungarian phoneme set. Since some of these labels represented only allophonic variations of the same phoneme some labels were fused together, hence in practice we only worked with a set of 28 labels. The number of occurrences of the different labels in the training set was between 40 and 599.

5 Frame-Based and Segmental Features

There are numerous methods for obtaining representative feature vectors from speech data[10], but their common property is that they are all extracted from 20-30 ms chunks or "frames" of the signal in 5-10 ms time steps. The HMM system employed in our experiments was the FlexiVoice speech engine[12] trained and tested by Máté Szarvas at the Technical University of Budapest. In his tests he worked with the so-called lpc-based cepstral coefficients (LPCC)[10], so for comparison we conducted a series of experiments with this feature set. To be more precise, 17 LPCC coefficients (including the zeroth one) were extracted from 30 ms frames. The HMM system used the derivatives of these as well, so *a speech frame* was characterised by 34 features altogether.

All the other classifiers were tested within the framework of our speech recognizer called OASIS[8][13]. This is a segment-based recognizer which means that the frames are not evaluated separately and then combined as in the HMM, but certain segmental features are first calculated. The aim of using these segmental features is to model the evolution of the frame-based features in time. In our case the 17 LPCC coefficients were averaged over segment-thirds, and the differences of these were also calculated to model their dynamics. These derivative-like features were also extracted at the segment boundaries. We found that the so-called modulation spectrum[4] also facilitates the classification process. It was evaluated as the 4 Hz Fourier-coefficient of 250 ms sections of the LPCC trajectories.

Further segmental features were the variance of LPCC coefficients over the segment and the length of the segment. Thus altogether 154 features were used to describe *a complete phoneme.*

Having found earlier that LPCC is not the optimal representation for our system, we also report findings obtained via the bark-scaled filterbank log-energies (FBLE). This means that the signal is decomposed with a special filterbank and the energies in these filters are used to parameterize speech on a frame-by-frame basis. The filters were approximated from Fourier analysis with triangular weighting as described in[10]. The segmental features were calculated from FBLE in the same way as from LPCC.

6 Linear Feature Vector Transformations

Before executing a learning algorithm, additional vector space transformations may be applied on the extracted features. The role of these methods is twofold. Firstly they can improve classification performance, and secondly they can also reduce the dimensionality of the data.

Without loss of generality we will assume that the original data set lies in $\mathbb{R}^n$, and that we have l elements $\mathbf{x_1}, \ldots, \mathbf{x_l}$ in the training set and t elements $\mathbf{y_1}, \ldots, \mathbf{y_t}$ in the testing set. After applying a feature space transformation method, the new data set lies in $\mathbb{R}^m$ $(m \leq n)$, the transformed training and testing vectors being denoted by $\mathbf{x'_1}, \ldots, \mathbf{x'_l}$ and $\mathbf{y'_1}, \ldots, \mathbf{y'_t}$ respectively. With the linear feature space transformation methods, we search for an optimal (in some cases orthogonal) linear transformation $\mathbb{R}^n \to \mathbb{R}^m$ of the form $\mathbf{x'_i} = \mathbf{A}^\top \mathbf{x_i}$ $(\mathbf{y'_j} = \mathbf{A}^\top \mathbf{y_j})$, noting that the precise definition of optimality can vary from method to method. The column vectors $\mathbf{a_1}, \ldots, \mathbf{a_m}$ of the $n \times m$ matrix $\mathbf{A}$ are assumed normalized. These algorithms use various objective functions $\tau() : \mathbb{R}^n \to \mathbb{R}$ which serve as a measure for selecting one optimal direction (i.e. a new base vector). Usually linear feature space transformation methods search for m optimal directions. Although it is possible to define functions that measure the optimality of all the m directions *together*, we will find the directions of the optimal transformations *one-by-one*, employing the τ measure for each direction separately. One rather heuristic way of doing this is to look for unit vectors which form the stationary points of $\tau()$. Intuitively, if larger values of $\tau()$ indicate better directions and the chosen directions needs to be independent in some ways, then choosing stationary points that have large values is a reasonable strategy.

In the following subsections we describe three linear statistical methods. Principal component analysis (PCA), linear discriminant analysis (LDA) and independent component analysis (ICA), which will be dealt with in a unified way by defining a τ measure. Although some nonlinear extensions of these methods have been presented in recent years, in this paperwe restrict our investigations to their linear versions.

6.1 Principal Component Analysis

Principal component analysis[7] is a ubiquitous technique for data analysis and dimension reduction. Normally in PCA

$$\tau(\mathbf{a}) = \frac{\mathbf{a}^\top \mathbf{C}\mathbf{a}}{\mathbf{a}^\top \mathbf{a}}, \tag{2}$$

where $\mathbf{C}$ is the sample covariance matrix. Practically speaking, (2 defines $\tau(\mathbf{a})$ as the variance of the $\{\mathbf{x_1}, \dots, \mathbf{x_l}\}$ n-dimensional point-set projected onto vector $\mathbf{a}$. So this method prefers directions having a large variance. It can be shown that stationary points of (2 correspond to the right eigenvectors of the sample covariance matrix $\mathbf{C}$ where the eigenvalues form the corresponding optimum values. If we assume that the eigenpairs of $\mathbf{C}$ are $(\mathbf{c_1}, \lambda_1), \dots, (\mathbf{c_n}, \lambda_n)$ and $\lambda_1 \geq \dots \geq \lambda_n$, then the transformation matrix $\mathbf{A}$ will be $[\mathbf{c_1}, \dots, \mathbf{c_m}]$, i.e. the eigenvectors with the largest m eigenvalues. Notice that the new data represented in the new orthogonal basis is uncorrelated, i.e. its covariance matrix is $diag(\lambda_1, \dots, \lambda_m)$.

6.2 Linear Discriminant Analysis

The goal of linear discriminant analysis[1] is to find a new (not necessarily orthogonal) basis for the data that provides the optimal separation between groups of points (classes). The class label of each point is supposed to be known beforehand. Let us assume that we have k classes and an indicator function $f() : \{1, \dots, l\} \to \{1, \dots, k\}$, where $f(i)$ gives the class label of the point $\mathbf{x_i}$. Let l_j ($j \in \{1, \dots, k\}$, $l = l_1 + \ldots + l_k$) denote the number of vectors associated with label j in the data. The function $\tau(\mathbf{a})$ is similar to that employed in PCA:

$$\tau(\mathbf{a}) = \frac{\mathbf{a}^\top \mathbf{B}\mathbf{a}}{\mathbf{a}^\top \mathbf{W}\mathbf{a}}, \tag{3}$$

where $\mathbf{W}$ is the within-class scatter matrix, while $\mathbf{B}$ is the between-class scatter matrix. Here the within-class scatter matrix $\mathbf{W}$ shows the weighted average scatter of the covariance matrices $\mathbf{C_j}$ of the sample vectors having label j:

$$\mathbf{W} = \sum_{j=1}^{k} \frac{l_j}{l} \mathbf{C_j}, \tag{4}$$

$$\mathbf{C_j} = \frac{1}{l_j} \sum_{f(i)=j} (\mathbf{x_i} - \mu_\mathbf{j})(\mathbf{x_i} - \mu_\mathbf{j})^\top, \quad \mu_\mathbf{j} = \frac{1}{l_j} \sum_{f(i)=j} \mathbf{x_i} \tag{5}$$

and the between-class scatter matrix $\mathbf{B}$ represents the scatter of the class mean vectors, $\mu_\mathbf{j}$ around the overall mean vector μ:

$$\mathbf{B} = \sum_{j=1}^{k} \frac{l_j}{l} (\mu_\mathbf{j} - \mu)(\mu_\mathbf{j} - \mu)^\top. \tag{6}$$

The value of $\tau(\mathbf{a})$ is large when its nominator is large and its denominator is small. Therefore the within-class averages of the sample projected onto $\mathbf{a}$ are far from each other, while the variance is small in each of the classes. The larger the value of $\tau(\mathbf{a})$, the farther the classes are spaced out and the smaller their spreads will be.

Much like in the case of PCA it can be shown that stationary points of (3 correspond to the right eigenvectors of $\mathbf{W}^{-1}\mathbf{B}$, where the eigenvalues form the corresponding optimal values. As in PCA, we again select those m eigenvectors with the greatest real eigenvalues. Since $\mathbf{W}^{-1}\mathbf{B}$ is not necessarily symmetric, the number of the real eigenvalues can be less than n. In addition, the corresponding eigenvectors will not necessarily be orthogonal.

6.3 Independent Component Analysis

Independent component analysis [2] is a useful feature extraction technique, originally developed in connection with blind source separation. The goal of ICA is to find directions along which the distribution of the sample set is the least Gaussian. The reason for this is that along these directions the data is supposedly easier to classify. Several measures can be used to assess non-Gaussianity. We always choose from those ones which are non-negative and give zero for the Gaussian distribution. A useful measure of non-Gaussianity is negentropy, but obtaining this quantity via its definition is computationally very difficult. Fortunately, there exist some simpler, readily-computable approximations of the negentropy of a variable y with zero mean and unit variance, e.g.

$$\mathbf{J}(y) \approx \left(E\left[G(y)\right] - E\left[G(\nu)\right]\right)^2 \qquad (7)$$

where $G() : \mathbb{R} \rightarrow \mathbb{R}$ is an appropriate doubly-differentiable contrast function, $E()$ denotes the expected value and ν is a standardized Gaussian variable. Three conventionally used contrast functions are G_1, G_2 and G_3:

$$\begin{aligned} G_1(y) &= y^4 \\ G_2(y) &= \log(\cosh(y)) \\ G_3(y) &= -\exp(-\tfrac{1}{2}y^2) \end{aligned} \qquad (8)$$

It is worth noting that in (7) $E(G(\nu))$ is a constant, its value depending on the contrast function G. For instance in the case of $G_1()$ its value is 3.

Hyvärinen proposed a fast iterative algorithm called FastICA, which uses these contrast functions [5], [6]. This method defines the functional $\tau()$ used for the selection of the base vectors of the transformed space by replacing y with $\mathbf{a}^\top\mathbf{x}$ in the negentropy functions above:

$$\tau_G(\mathbf{a}) = \left(E(G(\mathbf{a}^\top\mathbf{x})) - E(G(\nu))\right)^2. \qquad (9)$$

Before running FastICA, however, some preprocessing steps need to be performed:

- **Centering:** An essential step is to shift the original sample set $\mathbf{x_1}, \ldots, \mathbf{x_l}$ with its mean μ so as to obtain a set $\tilde{\mathbf{x}}_1, \ldots, \tilde{\mathbf{x}}_\mathbf{l}$, with a mean of $\mathbf{0}$.
- **Whitening:** The goal of this step is to transform the $\tilde{\mathbf{x}}_1, \ldots, \tilde{\mathbf{x}}_\mathbf{l}$ samples via an orthogonal transformation $\mathbf{Q}$ into a space where the covariance matrix $\hat{\mathbf{C}}$ of the points $\hat{\mathbf{x}}_1 = \mathbf{Q}\tilde{\mathbf{x}}_1, \ldots, \hat{\mathbf{x}}_\mathbf{l} = \mathbf{Q}\tilde{\mathbf{x}}_\mathbf{l}$ is the unit matrix.
  With the PCA discussed earlier we can transform the covariance matrix into a diagonal form, the elements in the diagonal being the eigenvalues of the original covariance matrix. Thus it only remains to transform each diagonal element to 1. This can be done by dividing the normalized eigenvectors of the transformation matrix by the square root of the corresponding eigenvalue. Consequently, the whitening procedure with a dimension reduction($dim = m$) can be computed via:

$$\mathbf{Q} := \left[\tilde{\mathbf{c}}_1 \tilde{\lambda}_1^{-1/2}, \ldots, \tilde{\mathbf{c}}_\mathbf{m} \tilde{\lambda}_m^{-1/2}\right]^\top \tag{10}$$

  where the eigenpairs of the matrix

$$\tilde{\mathbf{C}} = \frac{1}{l} \sum_{i=1}^{l} \tilde{\mathbf{x}}_\mathbf{i} \tilde{\mathbf{x}}_\mathbf{i}^\top \tag{11}$$

  are $(\tilde{\mathbf{c}}_1, \tilde{\lambda}_1), \ldots, (\tilde{\mathbf{c}}_\mathbf{n}, \tilde{\lambda}_n)$.

After centering and whitening the following statements hold:

- Firstly, for any normalized $\mathbf{a}$ the mean of $\mathbf{a}^\top \hat{\mathbf{x}}_1, \ldots, \mathbf{a}^\top \hat{\mathbf{x}}_\mathbf{l}$ is 0, and its variance is 1. In fact we need this since (7) requires that y has a zero mean and variance of 1, and so because of the substitution $y = \mathbf{a}^\top \hat{\mathbf{x}}$, $\mathbf{a}^\top \hat{\mathbf{x}}$ must also have this property.
- Secondly, for any matrix $\mathbf{R}$ the covariance matrix $\hat{\mathbf{C}}_\mathbf{R}$ of the transformed points $\mathbf{R}\hat{\mathbf{x}}_1, \ldots, \mathbf{R}\hat{\mathbf{x}}_\mathbf{l}$ remains the unit matrix if and only if $\mathbf{R}$ is orthogonal, since

$$\hat{\mathbf{C}}_\mathbf{R} = \frac{1}{l} \sum \mathbf{R}\hat{\mathbf{x}}_1 (\mathbf{R}\hat{\mathbf{x}}_1)^\top = \mathbf{R} \left(\frac{1}{l} \sum \hat{\mathbf{x}}_1 \hat{\mathbf{x}}_1^\top \right) \mathbf{R}^\top = \mathbf{R}\mathbf{I}\mathbf{R}^\top = \mathbf{R}\mathbf{R}^\top \tag{12}$$

Actually FastICA is an approximate Newton iteration method which seeks such an orthogonal basis for the centered and whitened data, where the values of the non-Gaussianity measure $\tau_G()$ for the base vectors are large. Note that as the data remain whitened after an orthogonal transformation, ICA may be considered an extension of PCA.

7 Experiments

All the experiments were run on the LPCC and FBLE features described in section 5. As mentioned, HMM results were obtained only for the LPCC case. Overall, the exact parameters for the learners and the transformations were as follows.

Hidden Markov modeling (HMM). In the HMM experiments the phoneme models were of the three-state strictly left-to-right type, that is each state had one self transition and one transition to the next state. In each case the observations were modeled using a mixture of four Gaussians with diagonal covariance matrices. The models were trained using the Viterbi training algorithm.

Gaussian mixture modeling (GMM). Unfortunately there is no closed formula for getting the optimal parameters of the mixture model, so the expectation-maximization (EM) algorithm is normally used to find proper parameters, but it only guarantees a locally optimal solution. This iterative technique is very sensitive to initial parameter values, so we utilised k-means clustering [10] to find a good starting parameter set. Since k-means clustering again only guaranteed finding a local optimum, we ran it 15 times with random parameters and used the one with the highest log-likelihood to initialize the EM algorithm. After experimenting the best value for the number of mixtures k was found to be 2. In all cases the covariance matrices were forced to be diagonal.

Artificial neural networks (ANN). In the ANN experiments we used the most common feed-forward multilayer perceptron network with the backpropagation learning rule. The number of neurons in the hidden layer was set at 150 in all experiments except in the case of LDA where a value of 50 was found sufficient because of enormous dimension reduction (these values were chosen empirically based on preliminary experiments). Training was stopped when, for the last 20 iterations, the decrease in the error between two consecutive iteration steps stayed below a given threshold.

Support Vector Machine (SVM). In all experiments with SVM a third-order polynomial kernel function was applied.

As regards the transformations, in the case of LDA the original 154 dimensions were reduced to only 27, the number of classes minus one. In the case of PCA and ICA we kept the largest m components that retained 95% of the spectrum. In our case m turned out to be 93.

Naturally when we applied a certain transformation on the training set before learning, we applied the same transformation on the test data during testing.

8 Results and Discussion

Table 1 shows the recognition accuracies where the columns represent the feature sets (transformed/not-transformed) while the rows correspond to the applied learning methods. For the HMM we have only one score, as in this case no transformation could be applied.

Upon inspecting the results the first thing one notices is that the discriminative learners (ANN, SVM) always outperform the generative one (GMM). Hence there is a clear advantage of modeling the classes together rather than separately. Another important observation is that the HMM, in spite of being a generative model, has produced the second highest score. But one has to keep

Table 1. Recognition accuracies for the phoneme classification. The maximum is typeset in bold.

	none *variable*	none 154	LDA 27	PCA 93	ICA 93
ANN	-	**92.67**	91.12	90.89	88.29
GMM	-	89.83	91.08	84.57	80.56
SVM	-	92.11	92.37	88.12	88.07
HMM	92.53	-	-	-	-

in mind that the HMM uses many more features per phoneme (the exact number depending on the segment length), and also a quite different integration technique. Moreover, it can optimize the division of the observation into thirds (states), while our segmental feature calculation works with rigid phoneme segments. Actually, we consider the fact that we could attain practically the same score with our quite simple feature extraction method as proof that the HMM technology can be easily surpassed with a more sophisticated discriminative segmental phoneme model. We should aslo mention here that our segmental feature calculation method was invented with the FBLE preprocessing in mind and that it works much better with those features. Our current best result with FBLE is 95.55%, which shows that LPCC is definitely not an optimal choice for our system - but the goal of this paper was to compare HMM and the other learners *with the same preprocessing technique.*

As regards the transformations, one can see that after LDA the learners could produce the same or similar scores in spite of the drastic dimension reduction performed (154 features reduced to 27). In an earlier study[9] we found that PCA also retains the recognition accuracy after the dimension reduction. Here, however, one can see that PCA was definitely detrimental. We attribute this to the fact that LPCC inherently contains an orthogonal transformation (the discrete cosine transform), so PCA could not bring any additional gain. ICA was even slightly worse, which accords with our earlier findings, where we could find no could no real advantage of using ICA in the phoneme recognition task.

9 Conclusions and Future Work

The main goal of this paper was to test our classification and transformation methods on the LPCC feature set. In previous experiments we used the FBLE features and we clearly outperformed the HMM recognizer (which used LPCC). In contrast to these scores, we now found that we could only reach the same performance. We conclude that our segmental feature calculation method is quite sensitive to the frame-based features, and also that it requires further development. In addition, we plan to make further comparisons with the HMM, but using the same feature set.

As regards the transformations, we ascertained that LDA is the most useful one, while PCA and ICA are advantageous only under certain conditions. In the future we intend to study the *non-linearized* version of these transformations.

As regards the applicability of the classifiers in a continuous speech recognizer, with the application of the learners and transformations presented in this paper on the number recognition task we can attain results equivalent to those of the HMM. The interested reader can read about our full recognition system in [13].

Acknowledgments. The HMM system used in our experiments [12] was trained and tested by Máté Szarvas at the Department of Telecommunications and Telematics, Technical University of Budapest. We greatly appreciate his indispensable help in making this study complete.

References

1. Battle, E., Nadeu, C. and Fonollosa, J. A. R. Feature Decorrelation Methods in Speech Recognition. A Comparative Study. *Proceedings of ICSLP'98*, 1998.
2. Comon, P. Independent component analysis, A new concept? *Signal Processing,* 36:287-314, 1994.
3. Duda, R., Hart, P. Pattern Classification and Scene Analysis. *Wiley and Sons, New York, 1973.*.
4. Greenberg, S. and Kingsbury, B. E. D. The Modulation Spectrogram: In Pursuit of an Invariant Representation of Speech. *Proceedings of ICASSP'97, Munich, vol. 3., pp. 1647-1650*, 1998.
5. Hyvärinen, A. A family of fixed-point algorithms for independent component analysis *Proceedings of ICASSP*, Munich, Germany, 1997.
6. Hyvärinen, A. New Approximations of Differential Entropy for Independent Component Analysis and Projection Pursuit. In *Advances in Neural Information Processing Systems*, 10:273-279, MIT Press, 1998.
7. Jolliffe, I. J. *Principal Component Analysis,* Springer-Verlag, New York, 1986.
8. Kocsor, A., Kuba, A. Jr. and Tóth, L. An Overview of the OASIS speech recognition project, *In Proceedings of ICAI'99*, 1999.
9. Kocsor, A., Tóth, L., Kuba, A. Jr., Kovács, K., Jelasity, M., Gyimóthy, T. and Csirik, J., A Comparative Study of Several Feature Transformation and Learning Methods for Phoneme Classification, *Int. Journal of Speech Technology,* Vol. 3., No. 3/4, pp. 263-276, 2000.
10. Rabiner, L. and Juang, B.-H. *Fundamentals of Speech Recognition,* Prentice Hall, 1993.
11. Schürmann, J. *Pattern Classification, A Unified View of Statistical and Neural Approaches,* Wiley & Sons, 1996.
12. Szarvas, M., Mihajlik, P., Fegyó, T. and Tatai, P. Automatic Recognition of Hungarian: Theory and Practice, *Int. Journal of Speech Technology,* Vol 3., No. 3/4, pp. 237-252, 2000.
13. Toth, L., Kocsor, A., and Kovács, K., A Discriminative Segmental Speech Model and Its Application to Hungarian Number Recognition, In *Sojka, P. et al.(eds.):Text, Speech and Dialogue, Proceedings of TSD 2000,* Springer Verlag LNAI series, vol. 1902, pp. 307-313, 2000.
14. Vapnik, V. N., *Statistical Learning Theory,* John Wiley & Sons Inc., 1998.

A Smart Machine Vision System for PCB Inspection

Tie Qi Chen[1], Jianxin Zhang[1], Youning Zhou[2], and Yi Lu Murphey[1]

[1]Department of Electrical and Computer Engineering
University of Michigan - Dearborn, Dearborn, MI 48128, USA
yilu@umich.edu
[2]Jabil Circuit, Inc. 1700 Atlantic Boulevard, Auburn Hills, Michigan 48326, USA

Abstract. In this paper, we present a smart machine vision (SMV) system for printed circuit board (PCB) inspection. It has advantages over the traditional manual inspection by its higher efficiency and accuracy. This SMV system consists of two modules, LIF (Learning Inspection Features) and OLI (On-Line Inspection). The LIF module automatically learns inspection features from the CAD files of a PCB board. The OLI module runs on-line to inspect PCB boards using a high-resolution 2-D sensor and the knowledge provided by the LIF components. Key algorithms developed for SMV are presented in the paper. The SMV system can be deployed on a manufacturing line with a much more affordable price comparing to other commercial inspection systems.

1 Introduction

The PCB(Printed Circuit Board) industry continues to adopt increasingly higher levels of integration and achieving higher and higher levels of component density. As a consequence, the tolerances on PCB assembly become tighter and tighter. This causes an increased need for reliable and accurate visual inspection of PCB boards[1,2,3]. The manufacturing of PCB circuits uses the SMT (Surface Mount Technology). Placing a proper amount of solder paste on a pad is the key to prevent unwanted opens or shorts. Sometimes, it is possible to catch these unwanted opens or shorts using an in-circuit-test after all components are placed on the board, but most solder paste defects are impossible to catch after components are mounted.

The focus of this research is to develop a technology for inspection of solder paste on PCB's. Due to the development of the semiconductor technology, the electronic components are getting smaller and smaller, and more and more components can fit on one PCB board. A pad on a PCB can be as small as 0.01 inch. Machine vision inspection of solder paste on PCB's is a non-trivial task. In this paper we describe a smart machine vision (SMV) system for inspecting defects of solder paste on PCB's. SMV was developed using machine learning technology combined with advanced machine vision techniques. SMV has been deployed on a manufacturing line and been tested on more than 2000 PCB boards, the accuracy of detection has exceeded 97%.

L. Monostori, J. Váncza, and M. Ali (Eds.): IEA/AIE 2001, LNAI 2070, pp. 513-518, 2001.

2 Overview of SMV System

The objective of the SMV system is to detection whether there is a sufficient amount of solder paste on a pad, or if there is smear on a solder pasted pad. In theory, the bare pads and the solder pastes on a PCB should have different reflection rate under direct illuminating (see Fig. 1). The major challenging is the high density of PCB boards and low contrast bare pads and paste. Even with the highest resolution CCD cameras, images of high density PCBs typically have less than five pixels for a small pad and the paste on a small pad can be as small as one or two pixels. The SMV system was developed and tested using images of a variety of PCBs acquired by a high resolution 2K×2K Kodak camera. Fig. 2 gives an overall view of SMV system.

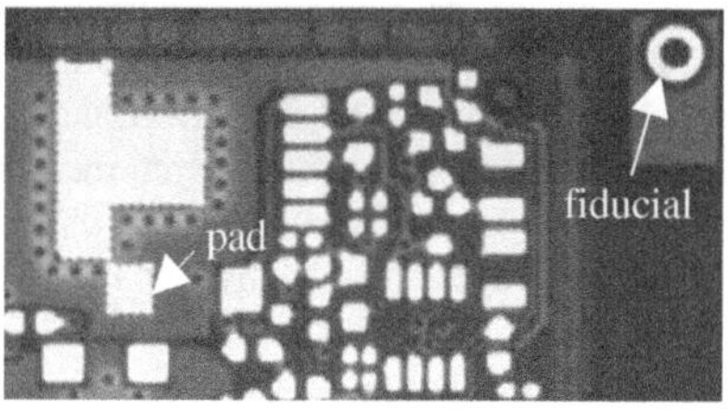

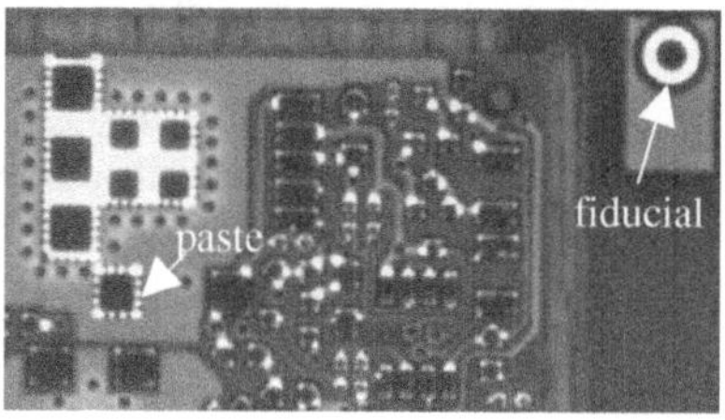

Fig. 1 a. The pads without solder paste. **b.** The pads with solder paste

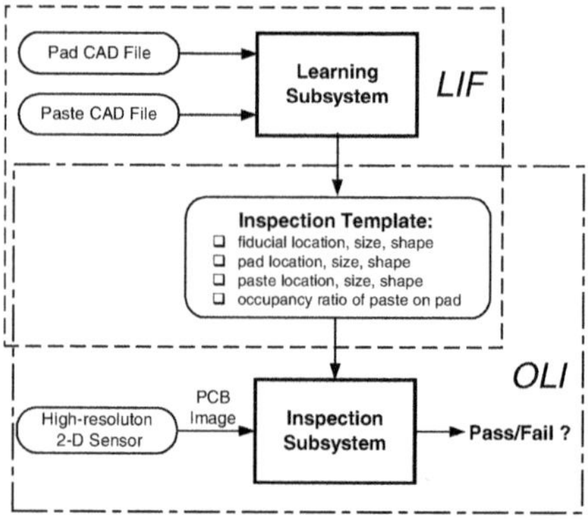

Fig. 2. The SMV system

The SMV is composed of two modules: LIF (Learning Inspection Features) and OLI (On-Line Inspection). The LIF module was developed to learn visual inspection features of a PCB from CAD design data, and the OLI module applies the knowledge learnt by LIF to on-line PCB inspection. The LIF module automatically learns the inspection features and outputs the knowledge in a template file to be used in the on-line inspection program, OLI, during the manufacturing process. The learning program consists of algorithms for extracting inspection features from the input, image processing, and computing statistics. The OLI program consists of algorithms for image registration, image processing, comparing the features of the input image with the learnt features from the LIF. The output from the OLI will indicate whether the product has failed or pass the test. The exact format of the output from the OLI can vary depending on the task specification.

3 Learning Inspection Feature (LIF) Module

The primary function of LIF is to learn the solder features of a PCB from its CAD design files. PCBs are designed using CAD tools and the design information is contained in a CAD file. A PCB CAD file contains a set of instructions that, when interpreted, enable a photoplotter or laser imager to produce an image of the PCB. The challenge of implementing these operators lies in the dynamics of these operators. For example, a number of operators may dynamically change the appearance of a line, the shape of the joint of two lines; and the target coordinates. In order to effectively inspecting PCB images, LIF module needs to learn the following features from the CAD file: number of pads on each array, location and shape of each pad, fill or no-fill status of each pad, and location of every fiducial point on the PCB image.

A learning algorithm has been developed for the LIF module and it has three major steps, detecting components, finding bounding boxes, and computing occupancy ratio. The occupancy ratio is a measurement to be used in the on-line inspection procedure and is critical to the result of inspection.

A component on a PCB is a region that can be a pad, a paste, or a fiducial. Fiducials (see Fig. 1) used to map CAD data to the images captured on line can be in any shape. A component in a CAD file typically has one or more closed paths, each of them consists of a number of strokes. A stroke can be as simple as a straight line, or as complicated as a part of Bézier curve. The information we are most interested in is the bounding box, which tells us the exact location of a component, and the occupancy ratio, which will be used in paste inspection in the OLI module.

The algorithm repeatedly searches for the bounding boxes of the strokes that are connected. The stroke bounding boxes are then merged to form the bounding boxes of the closed paths. Finally the bounding boxes of overlapped closed paths are merged to form the bounding box of a component.

The occupancy ratio is defined as the ratio of the solder paste area verses the bounding box of a pad. In this algorithm we represent complicated curves by straight-line segments, in which the area of a stroke is quite close to the area of its bounding box. The occupancy ratio is calculated by computing the sum of the areas of the bounding boxes of the strokes with the overlapping regions subtracted. The following outlines the computational steps used to compute occupancy ratio.

Let R be an array of N rectangles, A_n be the total area of $R[1]$, $R[2]$, …, $R[n]$, and B_n be the area of $R[n+1]$ subtracting the part where it overlaps with the first n rectangles. Thus we have,

$$A_N = A_{N-1} + B_{N-1} = \ldots = A_1 + \sum_{n=1}^{N-1} B_n \tag{1}$$

where A_1 is the area of $R[1]$, which is easy to calculate. In order to calculate B_n, we first compare $R[n+1]$ with $R[1]$. If they overlap, we split $R[n+1]$ into up to 4 rectangles denoted as r_1, r_2, r_3 and r_4 (see Fig. 3). Then we compare r_1, r_2, r_3 and r_4 with $R[2]$ one by one. They split if necessary. This procedure continues until $R[n]$ is split and its four rectangles are compared. B_n equals to the sum of the areas of the rectangles from final splitting. It is guaranteed that the rectangles from splitting after comparison with $R[i]$ do not overlap with any rectangle of $R[1]$, ..., $R[i]$, and they do not overlap with each other either of course.

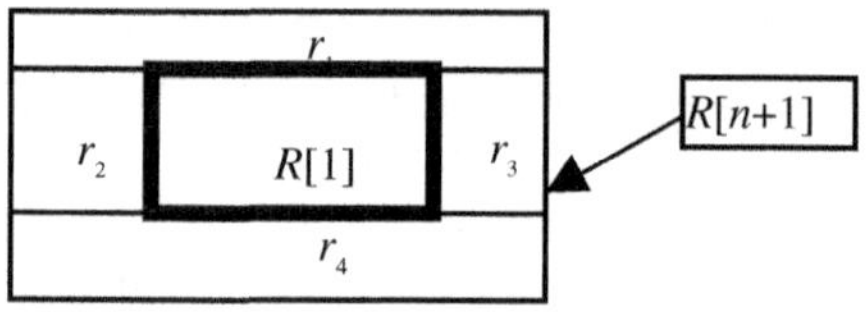

Fig. 3. $R[n+1]$ splits into up to 4 rectangles if $R[n+1]$ and $R[1]$ overlap

As the result of learning, LIF module stores the following attributes for every component on a PCB, component name, location, occupancy ration, and test threshold. The test threshold is determined by the size of the component. In addition, the location and size of each fiducial is detected for use in the inspection module. The file containing the knowledge of inspection features is referred to as a template file.

4 On-Line Inspection (OLI)

The OLI module inspects PCBs on a manufacturing line under the guidance of the inspection knowledge provided by the LIF module. The major processes within the OLI include:

1) Finding the fiducials in the image of a PCB
2) Binarizing the image;
3) Detecting the tilt angle and then correct the image;
4) Mapping components based on the information provided by LIF to the image;
5) Detecting the paste occupancy on each component in the image.

The accuracy of fiducial finding algorithm is critical to the inspection result, because the tilt angle and the mapping scale and the mapping offset all come from the fiducials. The fiducials are usually in symmetric shapes such as round shape.

According to the information from the template we can get the approximate locations of the fiducials on the image. Around these approximate locations we set searching areas for the fiducials. In each searching area, the least-square fitting method is applied to calculate the center of the round-shape fiducial.

The objective function of the least square fitting is defined as:

$$E(x_c, y_c, r) = \sum_{i=1}^{n}\left[\rho(x_i, y_i)\left(\sqrt{(x_i - x_c)^2 + (y_i - y_c)^2} - r\right)^2\right] = \min \qquad (2)$$

where the weight $\rho(x_i, y_i)$ is the intensity value of (x_i, y_i) on the original image.

In order to avoid using non-linear optimization method to solve Eq.(2), another objective function is defined:

$$E'(x_c, y_c, r) = \sum_{i=1}^{n}\left\{\rho(x_i, y_i)\left[(x_i - x_c)^2 + (y_i - y_c)^2 - r^2\right]^2\right\} = \min \tag{3}$$

Eq.(3) can be rewritten as:

$$E'(x_c, y_c, r) = \sum_{i=1}^{n}\left\{\left(\sqrt{(x_i - x_c)^2 + (y_i - y_c)^2} + r\right)^2 \cdot \left[\rho(x_i, y_i)\left(\sqrt{(x_i - x_c)^2 + (y_i - y_c)^2} - r\right)^2\right]\right\} = \min \tag{4}$$

From Eq.(4) we can see, Eq.(3) equals to Eq.(2) multiplied by a scale k.

$$k = \left(\sqrt{(x_i - x_c)^2 + (y_i - y_c)^2} + r\right)^2 \tag{5}$$

If k is a constant, the solution of Eq.(2) and that of Eq.(3) will be same. If k is not a constant, but we can get better approximate values for x_c, y_c and r, then Eq.(3) can be changed into:

$$E''(x_c, y_c, r) = \sum_{i=1}^{n}\frac{\rho(x_i, y_i)\left[(x_i - x_c)^2 + (y_i - y_c)^2 - r^2\right]^2}{\left(\sqrt{(x_i - x_0)^2 + (y_i - y_0)^2} + r_0\right)^2} = \min \tag{6}$$

An iteration algorithm has been developed for calculating x_c, y_c and r. First, we used Eq.(3) to obtain the original values for x_0, y_0 and r_0. Then we used Eq.(6) to calculate x_c, y_c and r, and replaced x_0, y_0 and r_0 by these new x_c, y_c and r in the next calculation of Eq.(6) until the difference between x_0, y_0, r_0 and x_c, y_c, r was very small.

After the fiducials are accurately located on the image, the global bounding box of the inspection area on the image is calculated, and an automatic binarization operation is applied on the image content within the global bounding box.

On a manufacturing line, a PCB is not always mounted perfectly on the test table. It may tilt in a small angle. But this small tilt angle may cause big errors while the template mapping on the image. So the PCB image has to be untilted first.

The least mean square method is used in estimating the tilt angle. Suppose there are n fiducials, their locations in the learning template are (X_i, Y_i), and their locations in the image are (x_i, y_i), where i=1, 2, ... n. Suppose the tilt angle of the image relative to the template is α, the scaling factor is k, and (x_0, y_0) are offset, then,

$$\begin{cases} x_i \approx k(X_i \cos\alpha - Y_i \sin\alpha) + x_0 \\ y_i \approx k(Y_i \cos\alpha + X_i \sin\alpha) + y_0 \end{cases} \quad (i=1, 2, \ldots, n) \tag{7}$$

Clearly, α, k and (x_0, y_0) can be determined by minimizing the objective function:

$$E(\alpha, k, x_0, y_0) = \frac{1}{n}\sum_{i=1}^{n}\left\{\left[k(X_i \cos\alpha - Y_i \sin\alpha) + x_0 - x_i\right]^2 + \left[k(Y_i \cos\alpha + X_i \sin\alpha) + y_0 - y_i\right]^2\right\} = \min \tag{8}$$

By letting $\frac{\partial E}{\partial \alpha} = \frac{\partial E}{\partial k} = \frac{\partial E}{\partial x_0} = \frac{\partial E}{\partial y_0} = 0$, we will get the following solution:

$$\begin{cases} \tan\alpha = \dfrac{\overline{xY - yX} - \left(\overline{x}\,\overline{Y} - \overline{y}\,\overline{X}\right)}{\overline{xX + yY} - \left(\overline{x}\,\overline{X} + \overline{y}\,\overline{Y}\right)} \\ k = \dfrac{\left[\overline{xX + yY} - \left(\overline{x}\,\overline{X} + \overline{y}\,\overline{Y}\right)\right]\cos\alpha - \left[\overline{xY - yX} - \left(\overline{x}\,\overline{Y} - \overline{y}\,\overline{X}\right)\right]\sin\alpha}{\overline{X^2 + Y^2} - \left(\overline{X}^2 + \overline{Y}^2\right)} \\ x_0 = \overline{x} - k\left(\overline{X}\cos\alpha - \overline{Y}\sin\alpha\right) \\ y_0 = \overline{y} - k\left(\overline{Y}\cos\alpha + \overline{X}\sin\alpha\right) \end{cases} \tag{9}$$

where $\bar{f} = \frac{1}{n}\sum_{i=1}^{n} f_i$ is the mean.

After the tilt angle is estimated, the image is untilted then the new locations of the fiducials in the modified image are re-calculated. The least mean square method is also used in mapping the learning template onto the image.

Finally, the occupancy ratio of paste on each pad is calculated. The occupancy ratios calculated at the LIF stage are the occupancy ratios of the pastes themselves. And it is the bare pads (not the pastes) that reflect the light while the CCD camera captures the image. Therefore, if the occupancy ratio of a component is above the test threshold, then it implies a missing or damaged paste.

For a 2K×2K image with more than 4000 components, the processing time of automatic inspection is about 6 seconds on a Pentium Pro computer.

5 Conclusions

We have presented an automatic solder paste inspection system, SMV (Smart Machine Vision), which relieves human test operators from a stressful and unrealistic inspection task. The SMV system has two modules, namely the LIF and the OLI. During the off-line learning process, the LIF learns from the CAD files of the PCB and generates an inspection template for every new type of PCB layout. The OLI module runs on the production line accurately and efficiently inspects PCBs. The key algorithms for supporting the SMV system are introduced. This automatic solder paste inspection system finds defects at the early stage on the production lines, which can significantly reduce the manufacturing cost. The whole system has been tested over 8000 boards on a manufacturing line and the detection accuracy was above 97%.

Acknowledgements. This work is supported in part by a contract from Jabil Circuit, Inc.

References

1. Langley, F. J.: Imaging Systems for PCB inspection. Circuit Mauf. 25(1) (1985) 50–54
2. Beck, M., Clark, D.: SMT Inspection Strategies: Maximizing Cost Effectiveness. Proc. of Technical Program: NEPCON West'91 (1991) 1075–1081
3. Taylor, B. R.: Automatic Inspection in Electronics Manufacturing., SPIE Autom. Opt. Inspection 6541 (1986) 157–159
4. Lu, Y.: Machine Vision Algorithms Using Interactive Learning for VFD Inspection. submitted to Journal of Applied Intelligence (2000)

Linguistic and Logical Tools for an Advanced Interactive Speech System in Spanish

Jordi Álvarez, Victoria Arranz, Núria Castell, and Montserrat Civit

TALP Research Centre, Universitat Politècnica de Catalunya,
Barcelona, Spain
{jalvarez,varranz,castell,civit}@talp.upc.es

Abstract. This paper focuses on the increasing need for a more natural and sophisticated human-machine interaction (HMI). The research here presented shows work on the development of a restricted-domain spontaneous speech dialogue system in Spanish. This human-machine interface is oriented towards a semantically restricted domain: Spanish railway information. The paper focuses on the description of the *understanding module*, which performs the language processing once the dialogue moves have been recognised and transcribed into text. Following the morphological, syntactic and semantic analysis, the module generates a structured representation with the content of the user's intervention. This representation is passed on to the *dialogue manager*, which generates the system's answer. The dialogue manager keeps the dialogue history and decides what the reaction of the system should be, expressed by a new structured representation. This is sent to the natural language generator, which then builds the sentence to be synthesised.

1 Introduction

The increasing need for telephone information systems allowing a communication that is as natural as possible for the user has boosted the interest and research on the topic. Work has already been done on the development of both application modules (cf. *TIDAISL* project [1]), or full applications for a specific functionality (cf. *IDAS* project [2]). At a higher level of elaboration and user-friendliness there are other systems that offer more interaction during the information exchange. Some examples of the latter systems, and also related to our domain of interest, are the following: *ARISE* (*Automatic Railway Information Systems for Europe*) [3], and *TRAINS* [4], both about railway information, and *ATIS* (*Air Travel Information System*) [5], about flights. Furthermore, the *TRINDI* (*Task-Oriented Instructional Dialogue*) [6] project should also be mentioned, which focuses on a more generic technology, i.e., multi-application and multi-language, for the creation of a dialogue movement engine.

The work described in this paper is part of the project "*Development of a Spontaneous Speech Dialogue System in a Semantically Restricted Domain*", which involves six research groups from several Spanish universities[1]. The main objective of

[1] Combining both Speech and NLP groups (cf. http://gps-tsc.upc.es/veu/basurde). This project is partially financed by the CICYT (TIC98-0423-C06) and by the CIRIT (1999SGR150).

L. Monostori, J. Váncza, and M. Ali (Eds.): IEA/AIE 2001, LNAI 2070, pp. 519-528, 2001.

this project is of a twofold nature: a) it aims at constructing a human-machine oral interface that allows the user obtain the necessary information about a train trip (and not only regarding timetables, as it happens in *ARISE*), while b) providing a relatively user-friendly communication exchange. The user should be capable of asking for a wide range of information, concerning both the data stored in the database (DB) or that within the dialogue history that has been created throughout the dialogue. Moreover, he should be able to correct any system's errors or demand for clarifications, always expressing himself by means of spontaneous natural language.

The paper has been structured as follows: section 2 describes the construction of the corpora to be used. Section 3 provides an overview of the whole system architecture, while sections 4 and 5 focus on the understanding module and dialogue manager, respectively.

2 Corpora Construction

The collection of dialogues in spontaneous speech from real users is an essential step towards the building of a spoken language dialogue system for real use [7]. When building this type of system, it is of major importance to study real user speech and language usage. Therefore, the data collected to build the corpus must comprise a set of examples which is representative enough of the type of queries to take place, as well as large enough to contain a rich variety of dialogue moves, turns, from both speakers. Further, the corpus must be built upon relatively simple sentences.

Given that there is no public corpus available of such characteristics for Spanish, its building has become an objective of the project in itself. In fact, the building of the corpus has consisted in the development of two different *corpora*: an initial *human-human* corpus [8], based on real conversations between users and personnel from a telephone railway information system; and a *human-machine* corpus [9] that has been obtained by means of the *Wizard of Oz* technique [10]. The former has been created as a reference for the initial study of the language involved in a dialogue system of this kind, and also as a guide to elaborate the scenarios upon which to base the latter. The latter is the corpus used for the main task of the research. Several instances have been created for every scenario type (based on a number of objectives and variants already defined). This has allowed us to establish a set of about 150 different situations. In addition, there is an open scenario that the informant specifies, thus obtaining 227 dialogues. Finally, this human-machine corpus is the one currently used as test bed for the understanding module and for the design of the dialogue manager.

3 System Architecture

In order to illustrate the system architecture, figure 1 shows its main components. As it can be observed, this architecture follows the standards of other such systems [7]. The initial stage is that of speech recognition, which translates the spoken utterance into a word sequence. In the present work, this is carried out by a speech recogniser that belongs to one of the project partners. However, despite its working rather well, the recogniser needs to incorporate the treatment of spontaneous-speech extra-linguistic phenomena, such as pauses, hesitations, coughs, background noise, etc.

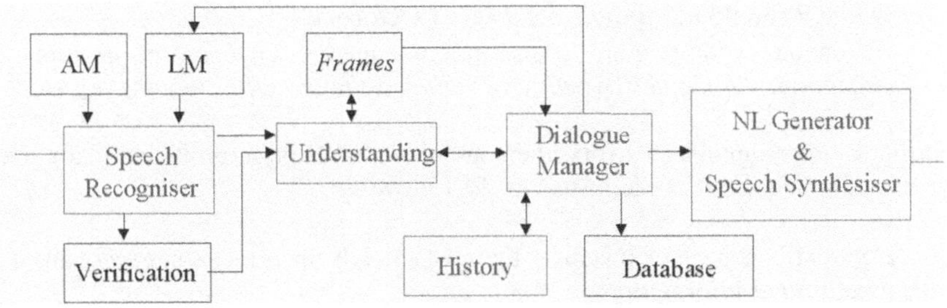

Fig. 1. System Architecture

Once the spoken utterance has been recognised and transcribed into written text, this is sent to the understanding module. This module is in charge of the linguistic processing of the text, its understanding and the generating of a formal representation (*frame*) with the extracted meaning that is to become the input of the dialogue manager module. The dialogue manager controls all the exchanges taking place within the dialogue, establishing, when necessary, the interactions with the dialogue history and the DB. Whatever information is extracted and has to be communicated to the user as the system's answer is passed on to the next module, the Natural Language (NL) generator, to be converted into sentences that the following and final module, the text-to-speech synthesiser, will produce as a spoken response for the user.

4 Understanding Module

This module performs the NLP tasks required to obtain the representation of the user's utterance. Figure 2 shows its architecture and below follows a detailed description.

4.1 Input to the Module

Ideally, the recogniser should provide the correct orthographic transcription for the user's utterances. Nevertheless, erroneous transcriptions also take place, which is something expected when working with spontaneous speech. The recogniser's errors the understanding module has to face can be basically classified into three types:

- Excess of information in the recognition, providing words that do not represent any part of the user's utterance. For example:
  - *user*: "sábado treinta de octubre" (Saturday 30 October).
  - *recogniser*: "**un tren que o** sábado treinta de octubre" (**a train that or**...).
- Erroneous recognition: recognised words do not match those uttered by the user, such as:
  - *user*: "gracias" (thank you).
  - *recogniser*: "sí pero ellos" (yes but they).

- Grammar errors in a broad sense, such as:
  - Lack of preposition+determiner contractions: "*de el*", instead of "*del*".
  - Misuse of the indefinite article instead of the cardinal: "***un** de octubre*", while it should be "***uno** de octubre*" (1 October).
  - Erroneous orthographic transcriptions causing changes in grammatical categories: "*qué/que*" (what/that), "*a/ha*" (to/has), "*e/he*" (and/have), etc.

Further to the recogniser's errors, there are also transcription problems that are due to the use of spontaneous speech, such as the following:

- Syntactic disfluencies: for instance, the syntactically incorrect sentence caused by the repetition of information:
  - *user*: "a ver los horarios de los trenes que van de Teruel a Barcelona **el este** próximo viernes y que vayan de Barcelona a Teruel **el próximo que vuelvan de Barcelona a Teruel el próximo** domingo".
- Other disfluencies: lexical variations, pauses, noises, etc.

As it can be expected, all these problems become added difficulties for the understanding module. The solutions adopted to deal with them, even if only partially, are mainly the following three:

- Adapting the recogniser to the task domain.
- Adapting, within their limitations, the understanding module components (cf. section 4.3) so as to increase their robustness when facing such problems.
- The possibility of closing the entry channel when the recogniser believes it relevant is also being considered.

Despite all these difficulties, the understanding module will have to be capable of providing a representation of the user's query, even if not a complete one.

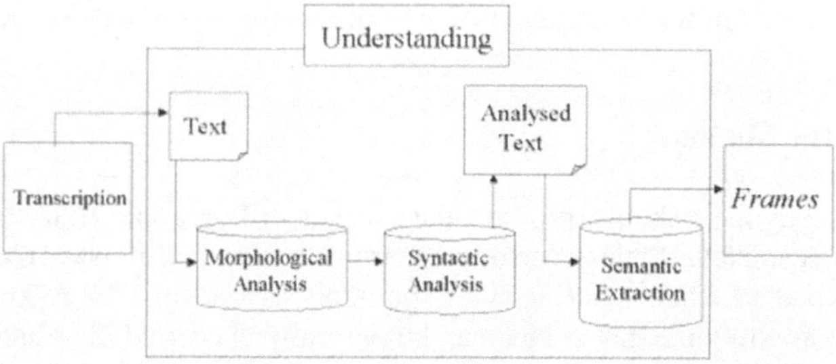

Fig. 2. Understanding Module

4.2 Morphological Processing

Once the recogniser's task is finished and thus having the utterance transcription, the morphological analysis of the text is performed. Then, its output undergoes a syntactic analysis (cf. section 4.3), which precedes the generation of semantic *frames* (cf. section 4.4) to be sent to the dialogue manager (cf. section 5).

The morphological analysis is carried out by means of MACO+ (*Morphological Analyzer Corpus Oriented* [11]), which has been adapted for the task domain. The linguistic knowledge employed by this tool is organised into classes and inflection paradigms. Further, forms are considered from an orthographic point of view. Adapting this tool to the domain allows to reduce partially the ambiguity that would be generated by a general language analyser. For example, eliminating verb *salgar*[2] from the lexicon allows the analyser to select, without any ambiguity, verb *salir* when encountering verb form *salgo*. In addition, the fact of working with a smaller lexicon (and with a restricted grammar within the syntactic analyser) does also help to reduce the system execution time, which is of major importance for a dialogue system of these characteristics.

The result of this morphological analyser is a set of possible morphological labels per word with their corresponding lemma. Therefore, a disambiguation process is required, which is performed by RELAX (*Relaxation Labelling Based Tagger* [12]), selecting the appropriate label among all those provided. The set of labels employed is based on the *EAGLES* guidelines [13]. Figure 3 shows the morphological (already disambiguated) analysis of the sample sentence: *Me gustaría información sobre trenes de Guadalajara a Cáceres para la primera semana de agosto*[3]:

me yo PP1CSO00	**Cáceres** cáceres NP000C0
gustaría gustar VMCP1S0	**para** para SPS00
información información NCFS000	**la** la TDFS0
sobre sobre SPS00	**primera** primero MOFS00
trenes tren NCMP000	**semana** semana NCFS000
de de SPS00	**de** de SPS00
Guadalajara guadalajara NP000C0	**agosto** agosto NCMS000
a a SPS00	**.** . Fp

Fig. 3. Morphological Analysis and Disambiguation

This particular application has required some slight tag adaptations. This has been done so as to identify within the tag itself some domain-specific terms referring to both *city* and *station* names. The adaptations have consisted in using digit #6 in the morphological label (that of semantic case) to mark them as "C" and "E"[4].

4.3 Syntactic Analysis

Further on the linguistic processing, the morphologically analysed and disambiguated sentence is then syntactically processed by the shallow parser TACAT [14]. TACAT's output is a series of phrasal groupings with no internal dependency made explicit.

---

2 *Salgar* means "give or put salt to/on" and it does not belong to the task domain, but it shares some basic conjugated verb forms with *salir* ("to leave/exit"), such as *salgo*.

3 I would like some information about trains from Guadalajara to Cáceres for the first week of August.

4 "C" stands for *ciudad* (city) and "E" for *estación* (station).

Generally, TACAT works with a context-free grammar for unrestricted domains. Here, though, it has been adapted so as to treat our domain. The adaptations applied have basically consisted in re-writing some grammar rules in order to incorporate lexical information. This avoids certain syntactic ambiguity and speeds up the process. The main rules affected are those referring to dates, timetables and proper names (covering both cities and stations). The rules for timetables are the following:

```
sn-h ==> j-fp, grup-nom-h.                                   %las doce horas
grup-nom-h ==> numer-fp, n-fp(horas).                        %doce horas
grup-nom-h ==> grup-nom-h, coord(y), grup-nom-m.             %doce horas y diez minutos
grup-nom-m ==> numer-mp, n-mp(minutos).                      %diez minutos
grup-nom-m ==> numer-mp, coord(y), numer-mp, n-mp(minutos).%treinta y cinco minutos
```

By means of these rules, the referred information is propagated towards the high nodes in the analysis tree. This helps the semantic searches performed with PRE+ (cf. section 4.4) to be more immediate and direct. Nevertheless, some rules covering structures that do not occur in this domain have been removed for this particular application. Figure 4 shows the syntactic analysis for the sample sentence above.

```
[ { pos=>S }
[ { pos=>patons } [ { pos=>pp1cso00 , forma=>"Me" , lema=>"yo" } ] ]
[ { pos=>grup-verb }
        [ { pos=>vmcp3s0 , forma=>"gustaría" , lema=>"gustar" } ] ]
[ { pos=>sn }
        [ { pos=>ncfs000 , forma=>"información" , lema=>"información" } ] ]
[ { pos=>grup-sp }
        [ { pos=>sps00 , forma=>"sobre" , lema=>"sobre" } ]
        [ { pos=>sn }
        [ { pos=>ncmp000 , forma=>"trenes" , lema=>"tren" } ] ] ]
[ { pos=>grup-sp }
        [ { pos=>sps00 , forma=>"de" , lema=>"de" } ]
        [ { pos=>sn }
        [ { pos=>np000c0 , forma=> "Guadalajara" , lema=> " Guadalajara" } ] ] ]
[ { pos=>grup-sp }
        [ { pos=>sps00 , forma=>"a" , lema=>"a" } ]
        [ { pos=>sn }
        [ { pos=>np000c0 , forma=>"Cáceres" , lema=> " Cáceres" } ] ] ]
[ { pos=>grup-sp }
        [ { pos=>sps00 , forma=>"para" , lema=>"para" } ]
        [ { pos=>sn }
        [ { pos=>tdfs0 , forma=>"la" , lema=>"la" } ]
        [ { pos=>mofs00 , forma=>"primera" , lema=>"primero" } ]
        [ { pos=>ncfs000 , forma=>"semana" , lema=>"semana" } ] ] ]
[ { pos=>grup-sp }
        [ { pos=>sps00 , forma=>"de" , lema=>"de" } ]
        [ { pos=>sn }
        [ { pos=>ncms000 , forma=>"agosto" , lema=>"agosto" } ] ] ]
[ { pos=>punto }
        [ { pos=>Fp , forma=>"." , lema=>"punt" } ] ] ]
```

Fig. 4. Syntactic Analisis

4.4 Semantic Extraction

Previous to the semantic extraction stage, a thorough study has been carried out of a representative part of the dialogue corpus. The aim of this study is to define the type of restricted information that should be considered. The semantic representation to be generated is based on the concept of *frame*, which can be easily translated as a query to the DB. The concept of *frame* has been previously used [15] and it functions as a summary of the dialogue turn. This implies that for every user turn that is sent to the understanding module a *frame* will be generated, i.e., a pattern holding all extracted semantic information. Moreover, a *frame* can have two different types of information:

1. *Concepts*: specific information the user is enquiring about.
2. *Cases*: restrictions applied to the concepts.

In order to clarify these classification concepts, figure 5 offers a specific *frame*. The sample sentence in section 4.2 becomes a concept (query) about a train departure time (*Hora-Salida*) and the restrictions applied are: 1) departure city (*case Ciudad-Origen*) is *Guadalajara*, 2) destination city (*case Ciudad-Destino*) is Cáceres, and 3) departure date interval (*case Intervalo-Fecha-Salida*) is the first week of August.

(HORA-SALIDA)

CIUDAD-ORIGEN: Guadalajara
CIUDAD-DESTINO: Cáceres
INTERVALO-FECHA-SALIDA: 31-7-2000/6-8-2000

Fig. 5. Example of *Frame*

Once this has been established, the going from syntax to semantic *frames* is performed by means of a semantic extraction system implemented in PRE+ [16]. PRE+ is a production rule environment that runs on PERL and allows us to declare rules for information extraction. The formalisation of these rules requires the morpho-syntactic representation of the text, together with the study of the *markers* (different ways) used to express a query, confirmation, correction, etc. Figure 6 shows an example of the diversity of expressions used to ask for information.

Querría saber...	Me gustaría saber...
Querría pedir...	Podría decirme...
Quisiera saber...	Me gustaría que me dijera...
Quisiera obtener...	Desearía saber...
Quería información...	Deseo información sobre...
Me gustaría información...	Llamaba para saber...

Fig. 6. Query Markers

PRE+ establishes conditions and actions. The former contain the syntactic patterns and lexical items to search for in the word strings. The latter represent the extraction method for each pattern. The way a specific PRE+ rule functions could be paraphrased as follows: "if in a syntactic tree there is a prepositional phrase, *grup-sp*, with a daughter node whose terminal item has lemma *de* (of/from) or *desde* (from), and another daughter node containing the name of a city, *np000c0* (cf. section 4.2), this proper name represents the *Ciudad-Origen case* (restriction) to be extracted for the query". Figure 7 shows the PRE+ rule used to extract such information.

```
(rule CiudadOrigen3
    ruleset CiudadOrigen
    priority 10
    score [0,_,1,0]
    control forever
    ending Postrule
    (InputSentence ^tree <+a>tree_matching(
        [{pos=>grup-sp}
            [{lema=> de|desde}]
            [{pos=> np000c0, forma=>?forma}]
        ]))
    ->
    (?_ := Print(CiudadOrigen,?forma))
    (?_ := REM(CiudadOrigen,X,+a)))
```

Fig. 7. Example of PRE+ Rule for *CiudadOrigen*

Further to the conditions and actions, this type of rules allow to establish explicitly the way in which they should be applied (in a static/dynamic manner, which priority and control should they have, etc.) and the location of the concept to be extracted within the domain hierarchy. Given both the speech recogniser's problems and those caused by spontaneous speech (cf. section 4.1), semantic information is approached as locally as possible. This implies a search for and extraction of information from the lowest nodes of the syntactic tree, by means of phrases and lexical items.

5 Dialogue Manager

This is one of the main components of the system since it directs the system behaviour. The interpretation and administration of the content in a user's utterance would not be possible without this module's supervision, and neither would the co-reference resolution. This module must decide which the system reaction is: inquiring about information in order to complete a query to the DB, asking for repetitions, offering information, etc.

The dialogue manager is implemented using YAYA [17], which is a terminological reasoning system. The dialogue manager strategy is expressed in a declarative manner by means of a set of axioms. The reasoning engine combines both a) the facts (*frames*) generated by the understanding module, and b) the facts that represent the dialogue history, with the axioms that represent the strategy, in order to generate the facts that represent the system reaction (this includes, if possible, access to the DB).

Below follows an example of a concept axiom, where the user has not specified the departure date for a trip and thus the system needs to enquire about this information:

```
(:and informacion-usuario (:not (:some fsalida :top)))  ≤
   (:some (:inv rdominio) (:and speech-act-usuario (:some rrespuesta pregunta-fecha-salida)))
```

The dialogue manager output is also based on the concept of *frame*. The NL generator receives a *frame* comprising all the information required to build the system answer. Then, the sentence is synthesised by the text-to-speech translator.

(CONFIRMACIÓN)

TIPO: implícita
CIUDAD-DESTINO: Valencia

(SOLICITUD)
CONCEPTO: FECHA-SALIDA

Fig. 8. Dialogue Manager Output *Frame*

For example, the NL generator can build the following system answers: "*¿Cuándo desea viajar a Valencia?*", *A Valencia, ¿cuándo desea viajar?*"[5] (cf. fig. 8), based on the *frames* received from the dialogue manager in a hypothetical situation where the date of travelling has not been specified by the user.

The dialogue manager will also inform the recogniser about the type of *speech act* that is expected in the next user turn. In order to generate such predictions, the dialogue manager has a speech act grammar at its disposal. This grammar has been designed by studying the available corpora and evaluating the possible types of speech act. The types of speech act already expected from the user are: *consulta* (with several subtypes depending on the aim of the query), *falta de comprensión, confirmación, afirmación, negación* and *cierre*[6].

6 Conclusions

This paper aims to present the work done on the development of a spontaneous-speech dialogue system for a semantically restricted domain, such as a railway information system for Spanish.

The present article focuses on the understanding and dialogue manager modules, although the remaining modules are also developed by now. However, no evaluation of the whole system can be provided for the time being since the system integration is currently taking place and its testing is planned within the next few months. In spite of this, and at a sub-module level, some conclusions have already been drawn: the morphosyntactic analysis tools (which already contain a lexicon and grammar adapted for the task) have already proved their efficiency during corpus analysis. Furthermore, the production rule environment PRE+ used for the semantic extraction has shown to be appropriate for the task and robust in an information extraction environment. In addition, the use of a declarative tool to implement the dialogue manager allows the development of the module prototype in a relatively short time and it also allows easy

[5] "When do you wish to travel to Valencia? ", "To Valencia, when do you wish to travel?"

[6] *Query, not understood, confirmation, affirmation, negation* and *closing*.

modifiability. Therefore, once the evaluation of the whole system has been done it will be decided whether its translation to a conventional tool is required.

Last but not least, the importance and cost of the corpora construction and analysis tasks should also be emphasised. In fact, one of the project objectives was the development of a Spanish speech corpus of such characteristics. Once tagged and standardised, this corpus can become a valuable resource for future work.

References

1. Ferreiros, J., Macías-Guarasa, J., Gallardo, A., Colás, J., Córdoba, R., Pardo, J.M., Villarrubia, L.: Recent Work on Preselection Module for Flexible Large Vocabulary Speech Recognition System in Telephone Environment. In *Proceedings of ICSLP'98*, Sidney (1998)
2. San-Segundo, R., Colás, J., Montero, J.M., Córdoba, R., Ferreiros, J., Macías-Guarasa, J., Gallardo, A., Gutiérrez, J.M., Pastor, J., Pardo, J.M.: Servidores Vocales Interactivos: Desarrollo de un Servicio de Páginas Blancas por Teléfono con Reconocimiento de Voz (Proyecto IDAS: Interactive Telephone-Based Directory Assistance Service). In *IX Jornadas Telecom I+D*, Barcelona-Madrid (1999)
3. Lamel, L., Rosset, S., Gauvain, J.L., Bennacef, S.: The Limsi Arise System for Train Travel Information. In *Proceedings of ICASSP'99* (1999)
4. Allen, J.F., Miller, B.W., Ringger, E.K., Sikorski, T.: A Robust System for Natural Spoken Dialogue. In *Proceedings of ACL'96* (1996)
5. Cohen, M., Rivlin, Z., Bratt, H.: Speech Recognition in the ATIS Domain Using Multiple Knowledge Sources. In *Proceedings of the ARPA Spoken Language Systems Technology Workshop*, Texas (1995)
6. *TRINDI* project: http://www.linglink.lu/le/projects/trindi.
7. Giachin, E., McGlashan, S.: Spoken Language Dialogue Systems. In: Young, S., Bloothooft, G. (eds.): *Corpus-Based Methods in Language and Speech Processing*. Kluwer Academic Publishers (1997)
8. Bonafonte, A., Mayol, N.: Documentación del corpus INFOTREN-PERSONA. Project Report BS14AV20, UPC, Barcelona (1999)
9. Sesma, A., Mariño, J.B., Esquerra, I., Padrell, J.: Estrategia del Mago de Oz. Project Report BS52AV22, UPC, Barcelona (1999)
10. Fraser, N.M., Gilbert, G.N.: Simulating Speech Systems. *Computer Speech and Language*, Vol. 5 (1) (1991)
11. Carmona, J., Cervell, S., Màrquez, L., Martí, M.A., Padró, L., Placer, R., Rodríguez, H., Taulé, M., Turmo, J.: An Environment for Morphosyntactic Processing of Unrestricted Spanish Text. In *Proceedings of LREC'98*, Granada (1998)
12. Padró, L.: *A Hybrid Environment for Syntax-Semantic Tagging*. PhD Thesis, UPC, Barcelona (1997)
13. *EAGLES* group: http://www.ilc.pi.cnr.it/EAGLES96/home.html.
14. Castellón, I., Civit, M., Atserias, J.: Syntactic Parsing of the Unrestricted Spanish Text. In *Proceedings of LREC'98*, Granada (1998)
15. Minker, W., Bennacef, S., Gauvain, J.L.: A Stochastic Case Frame for Natural Language Understanding. In *Proceedings of ICSLP'97* (1997)
16. Turmo, J.: PRE+: A Production Rule Environment. Working Report LSI-99-5-T, UPC, Barcelona (1999)
17. Alvarez, J.: The YAYA Description Logics System: Formal Definition and Implementation. Research Report LSI-00-40-R, UPC, Barcelona (2000)

Selecting a Relevant Set of Examples to Learn IE-Rules

J. Turmo and H. Rodríguez

Dept. Llenguatges i Sistemes Informàtics
Universitat Politècnica de Catalunya. Spain
{turmo,horacio}@lsi.upc.es

Abstract. The growing availability of online text has lead to an increase in the use of automatic knowledge acquisition approaches from textual data, as in Information Extraction (IE). Some IE systems use knowledge learned by single-concept learning systems, as sets of IE rules. Most of such systems need both sets of positive and negative examples. However, the manual selection of positive examples can be a very hard task for experts, while automatic methods for selecting negative examples can generate extremely large example sets, in spite of the fact that only a small subset of them is relevant to learn. This paper briefly describes a more portable multi-concept learning system and presents a methodology to select a relevant set of training examples.

1 Introduction

The growing availability of on-line text has lead to an increase in the use of automatic knowledge acquisition approaches from textual data as in Information Extraction (IE). The aim of an IE system consists in automatically extracting pieces of information relevant for a set of prescribed concepts (scenario).

One of the main drawbacks of applying IE systems is the high cost involved in manually adapting them to new domains and text styles. In recent years, the portability of IE systems to new domains has been improved by the use of a variety of Machine Learning techniques. In fact, learning systems like SRV [1], RAPIER [2], CRYSTAL [3] and WHISK [4], among others, have been used into IE systems to learn rules (IE-rules) for each concept in the scenario from a collection of training documents. However, some drawbacks remain in the portability:

– *Text style problem*: existing IE-rule learning systems depend on the supported text style (structured texts, semi-structured texts or free texts).
– *Combination problem*: IE-rule learning systems are mostly single-concept learning systems; consequently, an extractor (e.g. a set of IE-rules) is learned for each concept within the scenario in an independent manner. Moreover, the order of execution of the learners is set manually and so are the scheduling and way of combining the resulting extractors.

L. Monostori, J. Váncza, and M. Ali (Eds.): IEA/AIE 2001, LNAI 2070, pp. 529–538, 2001.

– *Training set size problem*: The size of the set of positive examples[1], $\mathcal{E}^+$, can be small to accurately learn an extractor for a concept within the scenario. This could be the case when dealing with some combinations of text style and domain.
– *Training set relevance problem*: The size of the negative example set[2], $\mathcal{E}^-$, if needed, can be extremely large to be tractable, while only a small subset is relevant to learn.

EVIUS is a multi-concept learning system to learn IE-rules from free text, that deals with such drawbacks. It has been incorporated to a multilingual IE system, M-TURBIO [5]. EVIUS strategies for the first two drawbacks are described in [7]. This paper shortly describes EVIUS and presents a method to deal with the *training set relevance* problem.

2 Test-Domain Model

Our methodology has been tested on the domain of mushrooms[3]. The reasons for choosing this domain are, basically, the difficulty of the documents, their lexical and grammatical richness, the frequent use of ellipsis and anaphora and the variety of information to be extracted. Furthermore, we can find fuzzy features, as in *olor algo dulce* (a rather sweet smell), multivaluated features, as in *se encuentran en prados o zonas soleadas* (found in pastures or sunny places) , features whose values can be expressed as intervals, as in *su color varía de rojo sangre a marrón ligeramente claro* (its colour ranges from blood red to slightly pale brown) and features that change values throughout a mushroom's life, as in *blanco constante que pasa a amarillo huevo con la edad* (permanent white changing to egg yellow with time). Figure 1 partially shows the scenario of extraction represented as hierarchy of frames.

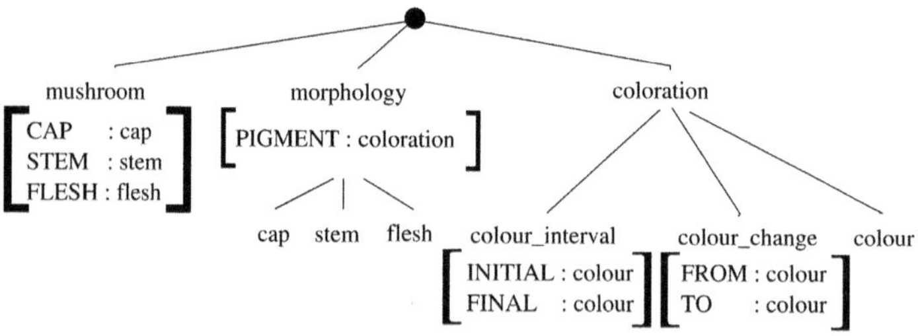

Fig. 1. Representation of part of the mycological scenario.

[1] This set is, in general, manually selected from the training corpus.
[2] This set is, in general, automatically selected from the training corpus.
[3] A set of documents (Catalan/Spanish) describing mycological specimens has been used for training and testing

In this paper, we will focus on the extraction of the feature PIGMENT in the scenario, since it presents the largest richness to express values. Generalization of results can be easily accomplished.

3 EVIUS Description

The input of EVIUS consists of 1) a set of preprocessed texts (POS-tagged, partially-parsed and semantically tagged[4]), as training corpus and, 2) a scenario of extraction $\mathcal{S}$. Using such information as background knowledge, EVIUS learns a set of extractors for the whole set of concepts within the scenario. In this process two kind of such concepts are distinguished: *fundamental concepts*, which are terminal concepts in the scenario hierarchy, concepts having neither by-default features nor inherited ones; and *complex concepts*, owning features, inherited or by default. Such concepts are learned as sets of rules in the form of conjunction of first-order predicates, which are predefined within a predicate model.

Definition of the predicate model. As a preprocess of EVIUS, the training corpus is translated into the following predicate model:

- Attributive predicates: pos_X(A), word_X(A), lemma_X(A), isa_X(A) and has_hypernym_X(A), where X is instantiated with categories related to node A of the parsed corpus.
- Relational meta-predicates: distance_le_X(A,B), stating that there are X terminal nodes, at most, between A and B.
- Relational predicates: ancestor(A,B), where B is the syntactic ancestor of A, and brother(A,B), where B is the right brother node of A sharing the syntactic ancestor.

Examples used to learn a concept c can be modeled as tuples $< a_1, \ldots, a_n >$, where each a_i is a terminal node within the input parse. On the one hand, if c is a fundamental concept, then $< a_1, a_2 >$ is defined as the pair of terminal nodes being delimiters of a textual instance of c. For instance, example *rojo algo claro* (slightly pale red) for concept *colour* is represented as $< a, b >$, where a and b are, respectively, the nodes corresponding to *rojo* and *claro*. On the other hand, if c is a complex concept, then a_i is the value of the i-th feature of an example. For instance, assuming the concept *colour* has been learned and added to the background knowledge, then example *vira de rojo algo claro a marrón* (changes from slightly pale red to brown) for concept *colour_change*, will be represented as $< a, b >$, where a and b are, respectively, terminal nodes corresponding to the value for the feature FROM (the first *colour*) and the value for the feature TO (the second *colour*).

[4] With EuroWordNet (EWN - http://www.hum.uva.nl/~ewn) synsets. No attempt has been made to sense disambiguate such tags.

The resulting rules can take the pattern $c(A_1, \ldots, A_n)$:- *<conjunction of predicates>*, where each A_i is a variable representing either the limits of possible textual instances for a fundamental concept, or values of i-th feature of possible instances for a complex one. For instance, one of the rules learned for the concept *colour* in our experiments is:

colour(A,B) :- has_hypernym_03464624n(A), ancestor(A,C)
has_hypernym_03464624n(B), ancestor(B,C).

which represents those expressions delimited by words that are achromatic colours (hyponyms of 03464624n) and share the same syntactic ancestor in the parsed sentence.

Learning a Concept. An initial extractor is learned with FOIL (First-order Induction Learning) [6] by manually selecting the set of positive examples, $\mathcal{E}^+$, and generating automatically the set of negative ones, $\mathcal{E}^-$. The task of selecting $\mathcal{E}^+$ can be very hard due to the complexity of some concepts in the scenario. In this sense, we can proceed by using a supervised *bootstrapping approach.* Initially, a small set of positive examples is selected by hand and an extractor is learned from them. The resulting set of rules can be applied to the training documents and extracted values can be manually classified as positive and negative examples. These new examples are added to the initial ones and the learning process is iterated until no further improvement is achieved. This approach is simpler for the human experts than selecting positive examples from the whole set of documents but, independently of whether it is used or not, $|\mathcal{E}^+|$ can be inadequate to accurately learn an extractor.

In order to improve the accuracy of such an initial extractor, EVIUS uses an active learning approach by 1) incrementally adding artificial examples to $\mathcal{E}^+$, 2) learning a new extractor from the new set of examples and 3) merging both extractors by appending unrepeated and non empirically subsumed[5] rules from the new extractor. Artificial examples are created by combining features from both the examples covered and uncovered by the current rules, as explained in [7]. Experiments demonstrate that using this technique the F value[6] improves in four points with only two iterations.

Learning the Whole Scenario. As a whole learning process, EVIUS learns a set of extractors for the set of concepts within in the scenario. This is done by using a multistrategy constructive learning (MCL) approach, which integrates: a)*closed-loop learning*, in which concepts to be learned at each step (as explained before) are determined, b) *deductive restructuring* [9], by adding a new set of

[5] A rule r_1 is empirically subsumed by another one, r_2, if examples covered by r_1 are also covered by r_2.

[6] This measure is defined in the MUC conferences (http://www.muc.saic.com) as a consensus between recall and precision.

examples being instances of the learned concept c and c) *constructive learning*, by adding new attributes isa_c(X) for each new generated example X. The set of new examples are used for further learning.

One of the drawbacks that appears when using FOIL to learn, as in EVIUS, is the training set relevance problem. In the next sections some methods for selecting a relevant set of negative examples, $\hat{\mathcal{E}}^-$, from the whole, $\mathcal{E}^-$, are compared.

4 The Training Set Relevance Problem

A common assumption in Machine Learning is to consider all non-positive examples as negative ones. This closed-world assumption can be used by FOIL only when dealing with small learning spaces. When the learning space consists of hundreds of predicates, as in our case, the resulting $\mathcal{E}^-$ becomes untractable in practice. Moreover, only a small subset is effectively relevant to learn the concept. Three strategies can be applied to select a set of relevant negatives, $\hat{\mathcal{E}}^-$:

- *Use of intuitive observations.* Sometimes, all positive examples share a set of properties. $\hat{\mathcal{E}}^-$ can be generated by selecting those non positive examples sharing these properties. For instance, taking strings of words as examples, Freitag [1] computes the minimum and the maximum lengths in words of the positive examples and takes as negative ones those other examples whose length is between these values. In [7], some experiments were done by using Freitag's strategy to learn an initial extractor for the concept *colour* in the mycological domain. In order to test them, 58 documents of the mycological domain were used (45 for training and 13 for testing), taking five different corpora with different sizes from the 45 training documents (5, 15, 25, 35 and 45 documents). Recall (R), precission (P) and F measure for our five different sizes of training corpus are presented, as baseline, in the last line, in table 3.
- *Use of a distance measure.* A more general approach consists in defining a distance measure between examples and selecting the closest negative ones to each positive. However, as a consequence of the extremely large size of $\mathcal{E}^-$, the bigger $\mathcal{E}^+$ is, the higher the cost to compute all distance values between positive and negative examples is, until becoming prohibitive.
- *Use of clustering techniques.* In order to reduce the cost in practice of the second strategy, we can take into account that some positive examples can be very similar to each others. Then, applying clustering techniques to $\mathcal{E}^+$, we can take the *medoids*[7] as the most representative positive examples to compute the distances explained in the second strategy.

The subsections above describe the distance measure, the clustering method used in the third strategy, and the method applied to select the negative examples that are closest to the positive ones.

[7] A medoid is an actual data point representing a cluster in a similar way to a *centroid*.

4.1 Distance Measure Definition

Bearing in mind the input partially-parsed semantically-tagged training corpus and the fact that examples in $\mathcal{E}^+ \cup \mathcal{E}^-$ follow pattern $e_i =< a_{i,1}, \ldots, a_{i,n} >$, we define a function $\mathcal{P}$ between the example space and an $n+4$ dimensional space, $\mathcal{P}(e_i) = (n_i, \delta_i, \mathcal{L}_i, \mathcal{W}_i, \mathcal{S}_{i,1}, \ldots, \mathcal{S}_{i,n})$, where n_i is the number of words between $a_{i,1}$ and $a_{i,n}$; δ_i is a number that codes the syntactic paths between nodes $a_{i,1}, \ldots, a_{i,n}$, as described in [5]; $\mathcal{L}_i$ is the set of lemmas involved between $a_{i,1}$ and $a_{i,n}$; $\mathcal{W}_i$ is the set of words between $a_{i,1}$ and $a_{i,n}$; and, $\mathcal{S}_{i,j}$ is the set of all possible senses for the lemma occurring in $a_{i,j}$, preserving ambiguities[8], or as names of concepts in the scenario[9].

Due to the different nature of these dimensions, an Heterogeneous Overlap-Euclidean Metric (HOEM) [10] has been used with the aim of measuring the difference between examples. It has been defined as the euclidean distance among the following $n+4$ distance values:

$$d_1(\mathcal{P}(e_i), \mathcal{P}(e_j)) = |n_i - n_j| \qquad d_2(\mathcal{P}(e_i), \mathcal{P}(e_j)) = \frac{max(\delta_i, \delta_j)}{min(\delta_i, \delta_j)}$$

$$d_3(\mathcal{P}(e_i), \mathcal{P}(e_qj)) = |\mathcal{L}_i \cup \mathcal{L}_j| - \frac{|\mathcal{L}_i \cap \mathcal{L}_j|}{|\mathcal{L}_i \cup \mathcal{L}_j|}$$

d_4 is the same formula as d_3, but substituting $\mathcal{L}$ with $\mathcal{W}$ [10]. And finally,

$$\forall k \in [5, n+4] : d_k(\mathcal{P}(e_i), \mathcal{P}(e_j)) = min_{s \in \mathcal{S}_{k,i},\ r \in \mathcal{S}_{k,j}} \{dc(s, r)\}$$

where $dc(s, r)$ is the conceptual distance between two synsets s and r in EWN as defined in [11].

4.2 Clustering $\mathcal{E}^+$

Set $\mathcal{E}^+$ can be partitioned into a set of clusters, $\mathrm{E} = \{< \mathcal{E}_i^+, m_i >\}$, being m_i the medoid of cluster $\mathcal{E}_i^+$. This can be done by adopting some clustering technique [12]. We have applied an agglomerative clustering technique based on medoids. The closest example to the others in a cluster, according to the distance average, will be selected as medoid. However, as the desired number of clusters is unknown, agglomerative techniques generate dendrograms and, as a consequence, a dendrite method has to be used in order to select the best set of clusters within the dendrogram. We propose the following simplification of the dendrite method explained in [13]. Being E_g the set of clusters in the level

[8] This is why $\mathcal{S}_{i,1}, \ldots, \mathcal{S}_{i,n})$ are not collapsed into a single set

[9] In our MCL approach, explained in section 3, new semantics are added as predicates isa_c and new labels c are linked as virtual synsets to EWN.

[10] These distances is defined from Jaccards' coefficient of similarity between sets, being the fraction between the cardinality of the intersection and the cardinality of the union

g of the dendrogram, and m the associated general medoid among individual clusters, we define,

$$\mathrm{B}_g = \sum_{i=1}^{|\mathrm{E}_g|} \left[|\mathcal{E}_i^+| \sum_{k=1}^{n+4} d_k(\mathcal{P}(m), \mathcal{P}(m_i))^2 \right]$$

$$\mathrm{W}_g = \sum_{i=1}^{|\mathrm{E}_g|} \left[\sum_{j=1}^{|\mathcal{E}_i^+|} \left(\sum_{k=1}^{n+4} d_k(\mathcal{P}(e_j), \mathcal{P}(m_i))^2 \right) \right]$$

and we redefine the Calinski value, which measures how different are both the clusters between themselves (B_g value) and the examples between themselves and within each cluster (W_g), as $c_g = \frac{B_g\,(n-g)}{W_g\,(g-1)}$. The E_g having the first local maximum value c_g^{max} is selected as the best set of clusters, E. As a consequence, the set of the most representative positive examples will be $\hat{\mathcal{E}}^+ = \{m_i \in \mathrm{E}\}$.

This strategy has been applied to the different corpus sizes described in section 3. We have obtained different $\hat{\mathcal{E}}^+$ sets, for each one of them. An average of 14.4% and a maximum of 21.9% of reduction, from $\mathcal{E}^+$ to $\hat{\mathcal{E}}^+$, was achieved.

Once obtained E, we classify all negative examples into such a set, generating sets $\mathcal{E}_i^-$ for each cluster $\mathcal{E}_i^+$, as follows: a negative example, e^-, belongs to $\mathcal{E}_i^-$ if $d(m_i, e^-)$ is the minimal one with respect to other clusters[11]. As a final step, set $\hat{\mathcal{E}}^-$ of relevant negative examples to learn the concept, will be selected from $\mathcal{E}_i^-$ sets. The subsection bellow describes a study of different approaches.

4.3 Selecting a Relevant Set of Negative Examples

At least two hypotheses could be applied to select $\hat{\mathcal{E}}^-$, when using $\mathcal{E}_i^-$ sets: a) the larger the size of a cluster $\mathcal{E}_i^+$ is, the larger is the number of negative examples from $\mathcal{E}_i^-$ to be selected, and b) the more similar the medoids are, the fewer negative examples have to be selected. From the first hypothesis, $E_i^-(\alpha) = \{e^- \in \mathcal{E}_i^- \mid d(e^-, m_i) \leq \alpha\}$ can be taken as relevant enough for the i-th cluster, where α is a distance value, being computed by taking into account the second hypothesis. The following six formulas have been experimented for such a computation, from which only 2 and 3 are dependent on the cluster:

$$\frac{\sum_{i,j \leq |\mathrm{E}|} d(m_i, m_j)}{|\mathrm{E}|} \tag{1}$$

$$max_{j \leq |\mathrm{E}|}\{d(m_i, m_j)\} \tag{2}$$

$$\frac{\sum_{j \leq |\mathrm{E}|} d(m_i, m_j)}{|\mathrm{E}| - 1} \tag{3}$$

$$min_{i \leq |\mathrm{E}|}\{max_{j \leq |\mathrm{E}|}\{d(m_i, m_j)\}\} \tag{4}$$

[11] A negative example can belong to more than one cluster.

$$max_{i \leq |\mathrm{E}|} \left\{ \frac{\sum_{j \leq |\mathrm{E}|} d(m_i, m_j)}{|\mathrm{E}| - 1} \right\} \quad (5)$$

$$\frac{\sum_{i \leq |\mathrm{E}|} \frac{\sum_{j \leq |\mathrm{E}|} d(m_i, m_j)}{|\mathrm{E}|-1}}{|\mathrm{E}|} \quad (6)$$

Taking into account these hypotheses, two approaches have been studied.

First approach. $\hat{\mathcal{E}}^-$ is generated as the union of sets $E_i^-(\alpha)$. Two different corpus sizes have been used here (5 and 25 documents). Table 1 shows that, for the 5-documents corpus and for all six α formulas, the recall and the F values outperform those using Freitag's method[12]. However, the second formula generates a bigger set $\hat{\mathcal{E}}^-$ (6088) than Freitag's method (2790) does. Moreover, the sizes of $\hat{\mathcal{E}}^-$ generated by the rest of the formulas when using 25 documents, always exceed the Freitag's method (13116). As a conclusion, this alternative cannot be used because extremely large sets $\hat{\mathcal{E}}^-$ are generated.

Table 1. Results from applying α formulas.

Formula	5 docs					25 docs	
	α	$\lvert\hat{\mathcal{E}}^-\rvert$	R	P	F	α	$\lvert\hat{\mathcal{E}}^-\rvert$
1 & 6	0.759	658	50.00	98.08	66.23	0.679	**37867**
2	-	**6088**	58.82	96.77	76.17		
3	-	1259	78.43	93.02	85.10	-	**38536**
4	1.362	2465	55.88	91.93	69.51	1.352	**66749**
5	1.415	2534	55.88	91.93	69.51	1.404	**67049**
Freitag's baseline		2790	43.14	97.78	59.87		13116

Second approach. For each cluster, a number of negatives N_i is computed according to the dimension of $\mathcal{E}_i^+$, as follows:

$$N_i = \beta \, |\mathcal{E}_i^+| \qquad \beta = \frac{\sum_{i \leq |\mathrm{E}|} |E_i^-(\alpha)|}{|\mathrm{E}|} \quad (7)$$

Then, $\hat{\mathcal{E}}^-$ is generated as the union of the N_i negative examples within each $\mathcal{E}_i^-$ being closest to the associated m_i. We have tested formula 7 combined with formulas 1, 4, 5 and 6 as α distance values[13] and using 5 documents. The results of our experiments are shown in table 2. We can see that using values from

[12] The - mark means that every cluster has a different α value, so they cannot be shown in practice.

[13] Formulas 2 and 3 cannot be used within β formula because they depend on the clusters.

formulas 4 and 5 as α, the results outperform those using Freitag's method taking only about half the number of negative examples. The use of formula 4 seems to generate a more restricted set $\hat{\mathcal{E}}^-$ without loosing accuracy. As a conclusion, we have adopted formula 7 combined with formula 4 as α value, in order to select set $\hat{\mathcal{E}}^-$.

Table 2. Results from applying different α values to β.

Formula	α	β	$\lvert\hat{\mathcal{E}}^-\rvert$	R	P	F
1 & 6	0.759	21	380	29.41	100	45.45
4	1.362	79	**1000**	**43.14**	**100**	**60.28**
5	1.415	81	1021	43.14	100	60.28
Freitag's baseline			2790	43.14	97.78	59.87

5 Final Experiments

We have applied the method for selecting $\hat{\mathcal{E}}^-$ (explained before) to the 5 different corpus sizes. The results are presented in table 3. Comparing them to those in table 3, a much smaller set $\hat{\mathcal{E}}^-$ is generated by using our method than using Freitag's one. Moreover, the resulting F values show that better extractors are learned when using small sizes of traning corpus. However, for bigger sizes (45 documents), F values resulting from applying the Freitag's method tend to be slightly better (0.15 points over), but a much bigger set of examples is taken. Finally, comparing the number of rules, the extractors learned by using our approach are slightly more compact than those learned by using the baseline method.

Table 3. Test results from both Freitag's baseline and 7.4 method.

Corpus Size	Freitag's baseline					7.4 method				
	$\lvert\hat{\mathcal{E}}^-\rvert$	R	P	F	Rules	$\lvert\hat{\mathcal{E}}^-\rvert$	R	P	F	Rules
5	2790	43.14	97.78	59.87	11	1021	43.14	100	60.28	9
15	7553	56.86	100	72.50	15	2784	59.80	100	74.84	14
25	13116	62.74	98.45	76.64	33	7621	72.55	97.37	83.15	30
35	18036	73.53	97.40	83.80	37	10640	73.53	97.40	83.80	35
45	29523	75.49	98.72	85.56	39	17479	74.51	100	85.39	37

6 Conclusions

This paper describes some of the remaining drawbacks of the existing IE-rule learning systems. EVIUS has been briefly described as a possible methodology to deal with the *combination problem*, *training set size problem* and the *training set relevance problem*.

We have presented a new method to deal with the later one. This method consists in selecting a calculated number of negative examples, being these the closest to the positive ones. Some experiments have been done in order to compare the new method to a baseline one. These comparisons prove that our method generates a much smaller set of relevant examples that is good enough to learn good extractors.

References

1. D. Freitag: Machine Learning for Information Extraction in Informal Domains. Ph.D. thesis, Computer Science Department. Carnegie Mellon University. (1998)
2. M.E. Califf and R. Mooney.: Relational learning of pattern-match rules for information extraction. In Workshop on Natural Language Learning, ACL (1997) 9–15.
3. S. Soderland, D. Fisher, J. Aseltine, and W. Lehnert.: Crystal: Inducing a conceptual dictionary. In proceedings of IJCAI (1995) 1314–1321.
4. S. Soderland.: Learning information extraction rules for semi-structured and free text. Machine Learning, 34, (1999) 233–272.
5. J. Turmo, N. Català, and H. Rodríguez.: An adaptable IE system to new domains. Applied Intelligence, 10(2/3) (1999) 225–246.
6. J. R. Quinlan.: Learning Logical Definitions from Relations. Machine Learning, 5(3) (1990) 239–266.
7. J. Turmo and H. Rodríguez.: Learning IE-rules for a Set of Related Concepts. In proceedings of CoNLL (2000) 115–118.
8. R.S. Michalski.: Towards a unified theory of learning: Multistrategy task-adaptive learning. In B.G. Buchanan and D. Wilkins, editors, Readings in Knowledge Acquisition and Learning. Morgan Kauffman. (1993)
9. H. Ko.: Empirical assembly sequence planning: A multistrategy constructive learning approach. In I. Bratko R. S. Michalsky and M. Kubat, editors, Machine Learning and Data Mining. John Wiley & Sons LTD. (1998)
10. D. Randall and T. Martínez.: Improved heterogeneous distance functions. Journal of Artificial Intelligence, 1. (1997)
11. Eneko Agirre and German Rigau.: A Proposal for Word Sense Disambiguation using Conceptual Distance. In Proceedings of RANLP, Tzigov Chark, Bulgaria (1997)
12. B. Everitt.: Cluster analysis. Edward Arnold, cop, 3. (1993)
13. T. Calinski and J. Harabasz.: A dendrite method for cluster analysis. Communications in Statistics, 3, (1974) 1–27.

An Environment for Formal Specification and Verification of Lingware

Bilel Gargouri, Mohamed Jmaiel, and Abdelmajid Ben Hamadou

LARIS Laboratory
FSEG-SFAX B.P. 1088 - 3018 TUNISIA
{Bilel.Gargouri,Abdelmajid.Benhamadou}@fsegs.rnu.tn
Mohamed.Jmaiel@enis.rnu.tn

Abstract. This paper presents an environment that supports formal specification and verification of lingware (applications related to Natural Language Processing :NLP). This environment provides interfaces enabling the specification of both linguistic knowledge and functional aspects of an application. Linguistic knowledge are specified with the usual grammatical formalisms, while functional aspects are specified with a suitable formal notation. Both descriptions will be integrated, after transformation, in a same framework in order to obtain complete requirements specification that can be refined towards an executable program.

1. Introduction

In spite of the fact that applications related to Natural Language Processing (NLP) are widely used in several industrial domains, such as marketing, safety systems, security systems, etc., their development is until now based on classical tools and use ad-hoc methods. Indeed, the lingware developers make use of their know-how and their domain master's. They use several programming languages (i.e., Prolog, C++, Lisp, etc.) and varied approaches (i.e., classic, object oriented, etc.). In a study of some NLP application developments at all levels (i.e., lexical, morphological, syntactic, semantics and pragmatic), we observed an almost total absence of methodologies that cover the whole software life cycle. The application of formal concepts is restricted, in most cases, to the linguistic knowledge representation. Generally, only algorithmic notation has been applied to describe functional aspects.

In the other hand, formal methods (i.e., VDM, Z, CSP, CCS, etc.) have made their evidences in specifying and developing several safety critical systems where reliability is indispensable, such as air-traffic control systems, safety systems of nuclear reactors and communication protocols. Nowadays, formal methods provide environments and tools enabling the development of provably correct software products.

Starting from these advantages, we investigated the application of formal methods in the lingware development process, in order to provide solutions for the general

L. Monostori, J. Váncza, and M. Ali (Eds.): IEA/AIE 2001, LNAI 2070, pp. 539-545, 2001.

problems indicated above. Our approach is based on a unified (or a pivot) specification language (a formal method notation) that supports the description of both linguistic knowledge and related treatments (for more details on the formal approach see [5]). In this paper, we concentrate on the design of an environment integrating a set of tools permitting several functionality relating to lingware engineering.

This paper is organised as follows. First, we present the development environment associated with this approach. We indicate, for all components of the environment, the role, the set of the related tools and our overview of the functional aspects. Second, we give a parallel between our environment and previous works in the lingware engineering area.

2. An Environment for Lingware Formal Specification

2.1. General Presentation

The main purpose of our environment is to assist lingware engineers especially at the first steps of development. This environment proposes to construct the design specification of a lingware parting from its requirements' specifications. Accordingly, our environment provides a user-friendly interface enabling the description of the both aspects (linguistic knowledge and related treatments) separately. In our environment, functional aspect is described directly in the pivot notation, while knowledge aspect description is made by usual grammars formalisms. In this way we release the user from mastering a formal language (i.e., VDM-SL), particularly for describing linguistic knowledge. Moreover, in order to favour reusability of verified specifications, our environment manages a dynamic library. This library includes, among others, verified specifications of standard linguistic routines (i.e., generation, analysis, etc.) and linguistic knowledge.

Additionally, the user of the presented environment can benefit from a platform of linguistic formalism evaluation that we developed separately. This platform applies a formal process based on the unified representation of the different formalisms and on a certain number of evaluation criteria [6]. This helps the user in the choice of an appropriate formalism for developing a lingware.

It should be noted that we use, as pivot or unified notation, VDM-SL [3] which is the specification language of the formal method VDM [1].

2.2. Components of the Environment

The presented environment is composed of the following four units corresponding to a provided functionality:

- Linguistic knowledge specification;
- Processing modules specification;
- Generation of the requirements' specification;
- Refinement and formal validation.

These units would be described in detail in the following sections.

2.2.1. Specification of Linguistic Knowledge

This unit provides the necessary tools for generating a verified requirement VDM specification of the needed linguistic knowledge for the desired application. It includes the following components:

- Set of graphical interfaces;
- Set of syntactic and lexical checkers;
- Transformation tools.

The following figure explains how the present unit operates:

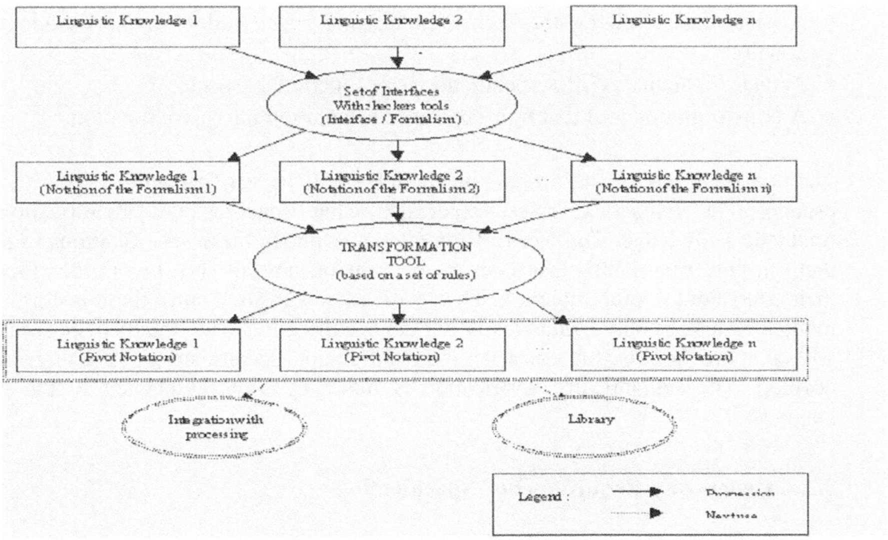

Fig. 1. Acquisition and transformation of linguistic knowledge specification.

The linguistic knowledge would be introduced using the appropriate formalisms. For each formalism we provide a suitable interface. The given descriptions will be lexically and semantically analysed until validation. Thereafter, they will be transformed in the pivot language using of a specific tool based on a set of rules. This transformation guarantees the equivalence between the initial descriptions and the final ones. The resulted specification will be integrated into the processing specification of the lingware to develop. The verified final specification may be added to the library for a possible reuse.

It should be noted that the present unit is already implemented for several formalisms (i.e., Formal Grammars, Unification Grammars, Augmented Transition Networks, etc.). Also, it is open for extensions since it is always possible to consider new formalisms by integrating tools handling them.

2.2.2. Processing Modules Specification

This unit concerns the specification of the functional part of a lingware. Such a specification operates on the data types describing the linguistic knowledge. At this level, functional specifications are made in a pseudo-pivot notation. This notation is a slightly modified version of the pivot notation. Indeed, it is based on VDM-SL, but it uses usual grammatical notations, when handling linguistic data. In order to obtain the pure pivot specification we need to make links between the VDM-SL and the used grammatical notations. Such a pseudo-pivot language facilitates the user task, since he does not need to master the notation of the pivot language (for linguistic data).

This unit is composed of the following modules :

- An interface allowing the formal processing specification in the pseudo-pivot notation;
- A syntactical analyser for specifications of functional aspects;
- A transformation tool that translates pseudo-notation into pivot notation.

The specifications of the processing modules will be verified with respect to the pseudo-pivot syntactical rules, especially what concerns the identification of linguistic knowledge. This verification allows to purify these specifications to make them in pure pivot. This task consists of transforming all "not pivot" identifiers to their equivalent in pivot notation. The verification is insured since the transformation module generates only syntactically correct specification. The obtained specification will be, thereafter, used to construct the requirements specification of the lingware to develop. The semantically verification is made by tools associated to the pivot language.

2.2.3. Generating Requirements' Specification

The role of this unit is to construct verified complete requirements' specification of a lingware by integrating, in the unique description, the functional modules and related linguistic knowledge.
This unit is composed of the following tools (see Figure 2) :

- A library of verified specifications (linguistic knowledge, routines processing, requirements);
- An integration tool;
- A validation tool (for requirements specification).

The following figure explains the process of constructing the proved correct requirements' specification of a lingware:

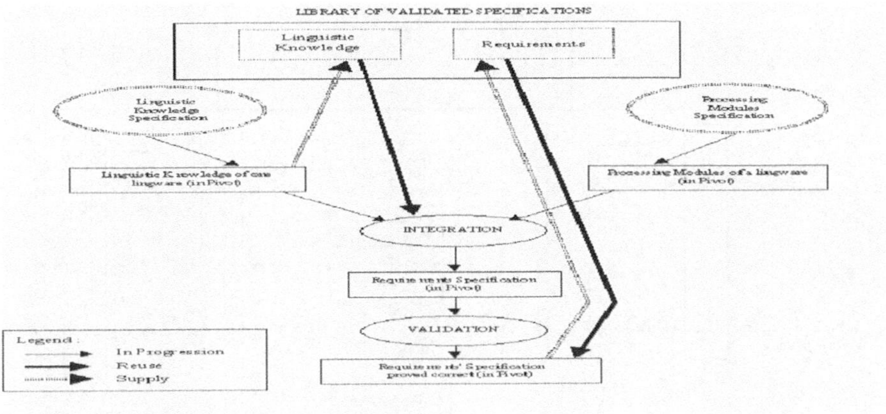

Fig. 2. Construction of the requirements' specification (proved correct) of a lingware.

The resulted requirements' specifications will be verified (i.e., syntactically and semantically) using specific tools associated to the used formal method. The requirements' specification, stored in the library, can be imported (reused) and added to the current specification, in order to obtain a complete one.

2.2.4. Refinement and Formal Validation

The aim of this unit is to generate a design specification which satisfies the requirements one. Currently, we make use of tools, associated to the retained formal method (i.e., SpecBox, VDMTools), which allow to ensure the refinement and the validation of specifications.

2.3. Architecture of the Environment

The following figure presents the interaction of the different units presented above. It gives the global architecture of the proposed environment for lingware specification.

In this figure, the unit3 (generating requirements' specification) links all the environment's units. Indeed, it uses (integrates) the two kind of specifications obtained from the unit1 (specification of linguistic knowledge) and the unit2 (processing modules specification). Moreover, the output of the unit3, constitutes the input of the unit4 (Refinement and formal validation).

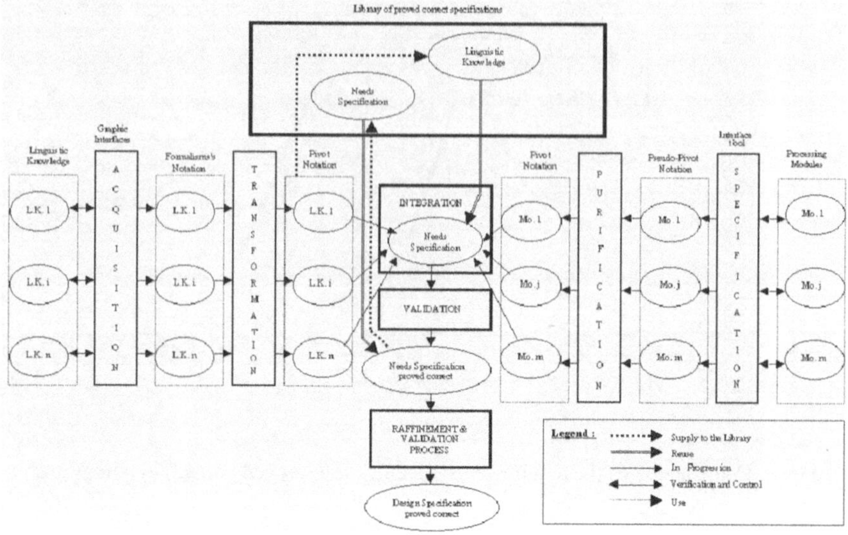

Fig. 3. Architecture of the lingware specification environment.

3. Related Works

Several environments and platforms related to the lingware engineering area already exist. These environments can be classified according to their objectives. Indeed, we indicate in this section three kind of environments. First, we distinguish some environments that are interested only in the manipulation of linguistic formalisms and consequently of grammars. Among this kind of environments, we can quote D-PATR [9] and HPSG-PL [11]. Second, we make out the environments that deal with the development of specific lingware such that TIPSTER [7] and ALEP [10]. Finally, the third kind of environments concerns the normalised development of lingware. We can tell that these last are relatively recent. Indeed, some of them have just coming to be proposed in a first version such that PLNLP [8],GATE[2] and EAGLES[4].

These environments manipulate, in general, a particular family of formalisms for linguistic knowledge description (i.e., formalisms based on the unification) which limit the possibility to consider others types of knowledge. Furthermore, some of these environments allow the integration of data and processing using, in general, the object oriented approach, but they do not perform a formal correctness proofs. The effort is rather put on the reuse. These environments propose, generally, their proper languages for the linguistic knowledge description and processing.
Compared with the environments indicated above, our formal development environment finds its originality in the following points :

- The use of a formal method that covers all the lingware life cycle;
- The pivot representation for the majority of description formalisms of linguistic knowledge while keeping, for simplicity, the later as interfaces with users;
- The integration of data-processing in a unified framework;
- The reuse of provably correct and complete specifications.

4. Conclusion

In this paper, we presented a formal development environment of lingware based on a specific approach using formal methods. This approach presents solutions to the majority of the lingware engineering problems. Also, it offers a methodology that guides the user at all steps of the development process.

Currently, we try to achieve and finalise the implementation of the development environment. We note that a first version is already implemented in windows using visual C++. Also, it should be noted that we are carrying out an experimentation of specifying two real applications (a morphologic and a syntactical analysers) using our formal approach and profiting from the available tools.

References

1. Cliff B. J., Systematic software development using VDM. Prentice Hall International, 1986.
2. Cunningham, H., & al., A General Architecture for Text Engineering (GATE): a new approach to language Engineering R&D. Technical report, University of Shiffield.
3. Dawes J., The VDM-SL reference guide. Pitman publishing, 1991.
4. Erbach J.D., Manandhar S. & Uszkoreit H., A report on the draft EAGLES encoding standard for HPSG. Actes de TALN'96, 1996, Marseille, France.
5. Gargouri B., Jmaiel M. & Ben Hamadou A., A formal approach to lingware development, IEA/AIE'99, May 31 - June 03, 1999,Cairo, EGYPT (LNCS, Springer-Verlag n°1611).
6. Gargouri B., Jmaiel M. & Ben Hamadou A., Using a formal approach to evaluate grammars, LREC'2000, 31 May - 02 June 2000, Athenes, Greece.
7. Grishman R., TIPSTER Architecture Design Document Version 2.2. Technical report, DARPA., Available at http://www.tipster.org/.
8. Jensen K., Heidorn G. E. & Richardson S. D., Natural Language Processing :The PLNLP Approach. Kulwer academic publishers, 1993.
9. Karttunen L., D-PATR : A development environment for unification based grammars, COLING-ACL'86, Bonn, Germany, Auguste 1986.
10. Myelemans P., ALEP-Arriving at the next platform. ELSNews, 1994, 3(2):4-5.
11. Popowich F., Available at ftp://sfu.ca/pub/cs/nl/HPSG-PL/manual.ps.Z/.

Sentence Analysis by Case-Based Reasoning

Fairouz Chakkour and Yannick Toussaint

LORIA - INRIA Lorraine 615 rue du Jardin Botanique
F-54602 Villers-les-Nancy Cedex
France
{chakkour, yannick}@loria.fr

Abstract. In this paper we propose a sentence analysis which relies on case-based reasoning principles. Our approach provides a semantic interpretation of a sentence in natural language, which can be used in a textual data mining process. This analysis is based on several types of knowledge: a thesaurus, a case base and a hierarchy of index. We adopt a case-based reasoning model founded on the classification principles and paths of similarity in order to guarantee the adaptability.

1 Introduction

We aim at conceiving a system which produces an interpretation of a natural language utterance by using Case-based Reasoning (CBR). We think that a CBR approach mixing syntactic information and semantic types should perform a conceptual indexing on scientific or technical texts. This indexing should feed a text mining process based on a symbolic method. Conceptual indexing should be viewed as the step beyond the term indexing. At present, text mining or information retrieval processes are based upon term cooccurrences. The idea we want to develop is that we can relate these terms using predicate structures, usually expressed by verbs. We will consider that the input of our system is sentences parsed using a robust parser. In this article, we present the very first step of our experiment which consists of defining the global architecture of the system and discribing the different steps of our process. We are currently setting an experiment on real scientific texts.

2 From Syntactic to Conceptual Analysis

The utterance interpretation consists of identifing the agent and the object in an utterance, the role it plays in this utterance and also the relation that the verb establishes between them or the event it expresses. Consequently, the utterance interpretation adds an abstraction level to the syntax. Thus, in the utterance *Mary has a computer*, knowing that the relation between Mary and the computer is a relation of POSSESSION is more informative than the simple syntactic decompositon according to which *Mary* is the subject of the verb *to have* and the *computer* is its object. Similary, in the utterence *John has a brain*, the relation between *John* and *brain* is a relation of composition, named here PART-OF,

L. Monostori, J. Váncza, and M. Ali (Eds.): IEA/AIE 2001, LNAI 2070, pp. 546–551, 2001.

expressing the fact that *brain* is a part of *John*. We take as initial input an utterance tagged and segmented in nominal and verbal chunks, as proposed by [3] and [1].Thus, the utterance `ph`: *John has a brain* is associated with the following syntactic structure, which represents the input of the system:

Representation: rep(ph)

```
John: nominal chunck (NC) / subj:v to have
has: verbal chunck (VC)
a brain: nominal chunck (NC) / obj.:v to have
```

The interpretation of this utterance, which is the output of the system, will be represented by a structure which we call `concept`, as follows:

Interpretation: Int(ph)

```
1. C - to have - part-of
2. relation: part-of
3. agent: lex: John                7. object: lex: a brain
4. agent: rsyntax: subject         8. object: rsyntax: obj
5. agent: role: composedobj        9. object: role: component
6. agent: type: animatedobj        10. object: type: organ
```

`C - to have - part-of` show the fact that the utterance contains the verb *to have* as principal verb (1.). This verb express a relation of composition, called `part-of`, between the agent and the object (2.). In this concept, "John" forms the lexical facet, `lex`, of the agent (3.). Its syntactic role, `rsyntax`, is the subject of the verb. Semantically, the agent is a composed object, `composedobj`, and its class in the thesaurus is `animatedobj`. In the same way, the object is represented by these four facets: a brain, obj., component, organ. This structure is inspired by the works in the field of information extraction, particularly the work of G. Lapalme [4] and E. Riloff [8]. They use similar structures in the process of information extraction. The interpretation of the sentence preserves fields of syntactic nature, which come from the input, like the syntactic roles. The fields 2., 5., and 9. come from the semantic representation, produced by the system.

We chose to start with the analysis of utterances formed by simple sentences before approaching more complex situations. Consequently, the sentences chosen to be treated in this paper have an elementary syntactic structure. All the presented examples are based on artificial sentences constitued with the intention of making our approach more comprehensible. We mention that this work is still beginning. Nevertheless, we look to extend our work to utterances with real meaning of the term.

3 The System Using Case-Based Reasoning

Some approaches in case-based reasoning were interested in the exploitation of the CBR principles for the natural language processing (NLP) and textual data mining [7], [9], [5],[2]. In our approach, the analysis of sentences relies mainly on examples already analysed, which constitute a knowledge base named case base (Sec.3.1). This approach is called **case-based sentence analysis**. Given a sentence called target sentence, `targetph`, the task of a case-based system is to use the case base to give an interpretation for the target sentence, `Int(targetph)`. This reasoning is carried out in two phases: the CASE RETRIEVAL and the CASE ADAPTATION. The CASE RETRIEVAL aims to search, in the case base, for a source sentence, **`srceph`**, similar to the target sentence, **`targetph`**. The task of the CASE ADAPTATION is to build an interpretation for the target sentence, `Int(targetph)`, using the interpretation of the source sentence, `Int(srceph)`, and another knowledge types which will be presented in the next section.

3.1 Exploited Knowledge

In this section we will present the types of knowledge that are used for the analysis of utterances, a case base, a thesaurus and a hierarchy of index.

Case Base. A case base is a set of source cases. Each source case , `srce-case`, is associated to a source sentence and defined as a pair, `srce-case = (rep(srceph), Int(srceph))`, where `rep(srceph)` is the **syntactic representation** of the sentence `srceph`, and `Int(srceph)` is its **interpretation**. The **representation** of the sentence `srceph` contains the string of the words of the sentence, the tags of these words, and also the segmentation of this sentence in chunks. The **interpretation** of the sentence `srceph` is the `concept` corresponding to this sentence (Sec.2).

The Thesaurus. The thesaurus is used to represent a source knowledge by the means of a hierarchy of terms. In such a hierarchy each node represents a specialisation of the term represented by its parent node. This thesaurus helps us to find a similarity between the nouns. Closer the nouns are in the hierarchy, more similar they are. Given two nouns N_1 and N_2, the distance between them, noted $dis(N_1, N_2)$, is the cost of the path between these two nouns. This cost is the sum of the costs of the arcs traversed in the thesaurus to go from N_1 to N_2. This cost cannot be fixed independently of the verb and the domain. The costs of the arcs as well as the heuristics of the calculation of the distance are points which we will explore in the near future.

The Hierarchy of Index. As we have shown earlier, the source cases are specific sentences, and they correspond to a low level of generality. Consequently, to facilitate the access to a source case in the case-base, we need to index them. We associate each source case `srce-case = (rep(srceph), Int(srceph))` with an index `ind(srceph)` which is a sentence more general than the sentence `srce`. The index of the cases are organized in a hierarchy of index, (fig.1), following an organization from generic to most specific. The root in this hierarchy is the generic sentence, the classes of the first level of the hierarchy correspond to the various possible verbs. The classes of the second level of the hierarchy are built according to the syntactic structure of the sentence. That is illustrated in the hierarchy of index (Fig.1).
Given a target sentence in input, **`targetph`**, to look for the source sentence,

sourceph, which is similar to it, we search for the index of srceph in the hierarchy of index. That will be accomplished by the CLASSIFICATION. The CLASSIFICATION is the process which allows the search of the closer index to the target sentence, targetph, in the hierarchy of index [6].

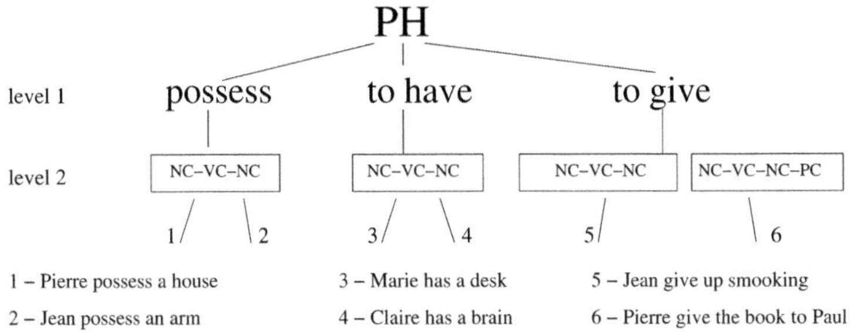

Fig. 1. The hierarchy of index

3.2 Similarity: Paths of Similarity and Transformations

To produce the conceptual representation of a sentence, we adopt a model of case-based reasoning founded on hierarchic classification and paths of similarity. This model is presented and detailed in the PHD. thesis of J.Lieber [6]. In this model the similarity is linked to the adaptation since "srceph is similar to targetph " means that the source case is adaptable to the target one. Adaptation knowledge is used in the case retrieval process in the objective to guarantee the adaptability of the retrieved case to the target sentence. That is based on the use of *paths of similarity*. A path of similarity from srceph to targetph is built from the *relations of transformation*. A transformation is a relation connecting two sentences ph1 and ph2. The idea is that two sentences in natural language, ph1 and ph2, are similar if ph1 can be transformed in ph2 by the application of sequences of transformations. We will consider in our approach the transformations on the syntax level, and the transformations on the verbal chunks whose consequences are of semantic nature.

Similarity and Adaptation. A path of similarity sim(srceph, targetph) from srceph to targetph clarify in what srceph is *similar* to targetph. In other words, such a path must guarantee the adaptability of srce-case to targetph. For that we suppose that to each *relation of transformation* is associated a *specific function of adaptation*. We take as example, the relation of transformation between passive voice and active voice of the sentence, $tr_{(p-a)}$. A specific function of adaptation $A_{tr_{(p-a)}}$ is associated with this relation of transformation,

$tr_{(p-a)}$. This function of adaptation contains information on the modification of the interpretation of the source sentence `Int(srceph)` so that it becomes an interpretation of the target sentence `Int(targetph)`.

4 Case Retrieval

The case retrieval is a function which takes in input a target sentence, `targetph`, and return a pair `(srce-case, sim(srceph, targetph))` where `srce-case` is a case from the case base and `sim(srceph, targetph)` is a path of similarity from `srceph` to `targetph`. This function must carry out two tasks: a task of *choice* - to choose the `srce-case` from the case base - and a task of *construction* - to build a path of similarity from `srceph` to `targetph`. The construction method relies on the use of the *transformations*. In order to choose the most similar `srce-case` from the case base, the general algorithm of case retrieval accomplishs a classification task which search, in the hierarchy of the index, for the closer index to the targer sentence and if necessarly computes the distance between the target sentence, `targetph`, and each sentence in the case base with the same syntactic structure and the same verb as `targetph` . The algorithm choose the closer source case, which minimizes the distance dis_{NC}(`targetph`, `srce-case`).

Example 1. Let us suppose that the case base contains the following sentences:
1. `Pierre possess a house.`
2. `Jean possess an arm.`
3. `Marie has a desk.`
4. `Claire has a brain.`
5. `Jean give up smooking.`
6. `Pierre give the book.`

who are indexed and organised in the hierarchy of index (Fig.1).
Given the target sentence, `targetph`, *The report is given by Jacques*, the case retrieval algorithm will choose the sentence 6.*Pierre give the book* from the case base as the most similar sentence to the target sentence. Similarly, given the target sentence *Pierre has a heart*, the case retrieval algorithm will choose the sentence 4.*Claire has a brain* as the most similar sentence to the target sentence.

5 Case Adaptation

The case adaptation is a function which provides the interpretation of the `targetph` sentence using the closer `case-srce`, and the path of similarity `sim(phsrce, targetph)` associated. The case adaptation of `case-srce` to `targetph` according to `sim(phsrce, targetph)` is to achieve the adaptation step by step by using the adaptation functions associated with the transformations.

Example 2. The case retrieval algorithm have chosen in the last example the `srceph` sentence, 6.*Pierre give the book*, from the case base as closer source sentence to the `targetph` sentence, *The report is given by Jacques*. The CASE ADAPTATION process adapts the interpretation of the sentence `srceph` according

to `sim(srceph, targetph)` to build the interpretation of the sentence `targetph` to give the information that the event communicates by the verb is `donation`, the `donor` is `Jacques` who is the object of the verb and the `gift` is `the book` which is the subject of the verb.
Similarly, the CASE ADAPTATION process adapts the interpretation of the sentence 4.*Claire has a brain* to build the interpretation of the sentence `targetph` *Pierre has a heart*. It accomplishs that by a substitution of the `relation`, the `agent role` and the `object role`.

6 Conclusion

We propose in this article the architecture of a CBR system to perform a sentence analysis task to be used for conceptual indexing of scientific texts. The complexity of the linguistics phenomena we have to deal with leads us to start our analysis using very simple sentences written on purpose. The architecture we defined reflects the different levels of analysis we need to create an indexing concept starting from the real sentence. The knowledge base is used both to type semantically the linguistic entities as well as defining a distance. This distance enables us to rank several analysis from the best one to the worst. The next step is to simplify real texts in order to get simple sentences that could be treated by our system. We will then be able to test the system we designed.

References

1. S. Aït-Mokhtar and J.-P. Chanod. Incremental finite-state parsing. In *Proceedings of ANLP'97*, pages pp.72-79, Washington, March 31st to April 3rd 1997.
2. C. Cardie. *Domain-specific knowledge acquisition for conceptual sentence analysis.* PhD thesis, University of Massachusetts Amherst, 1994.
3. Gregory Grefenstette. Light parsing as finite-state filtering. In *ECAI'96 workshop on "Extended finite state models of language"*, Budapest, Hungary, Aug. 11-12 1996.
4. L. Kosseim and G. Lapalme. Exibum: Un système expérimental d'extraction d'information bilingue. In *Proceedings of RIFRA-98*, Sfax, Tunisie.
5. M. Lenz, A. Hubner, and M. Kunze. *Case-Based Reasoning Technology*, chapter 5, Textual CBR. Springer, 1998.
6. Jean Lieber. *Raisonnement à partir de cas et classification hiérarchique.* PhD thesis, Université Henri Poincaré - Nancy 1, 10 octobre 1997.
7. C.K. Riesbeck and R.C. Schank. *Inside Case-Based Reasoning*, chaptor 10, Case Based Parsing. Lawrence Erlbaum Associates, 1989.
8. E.M. Riloff. *Information Extraction as a Basis for Portable Text Classification Systems.* PhD thesis, Graduate School of the University of Massachusetts Amherst, 1994.
9. S. Sato and M. Nagao. Example-based translation of technical terms. In *Proceedings of TMI-93*, pages 58-68, Koyoto, 1993.

Topic Detection Using Lexical Chains

Yllias Chali

Department of Mathematics and Computer Science
University of Lethbridge
4401 University Drive
Lethbridge, AB T1K 3M4
E-mail: chali@cs.uleth.ca

Abstract. This paper describes an algorithm for identifying the topic of unrestricted texts. The algorithm takes as input segments of text that represent grouping of contiguous portions of the text, and discovers lexical chains as indicator of their topics. Two implementation, based on public domain resources, are presented: one based on WordNet and the second one based on Roget's thesaurus. The evaluation of the algorithm shows that lexical chains are acceptable as topic indicator with 45% of precision and 65% of recall.

1 Motivation

Dividing documents into topically-coherent units and discovering their topic might have many uses:

- In information retrieval, documents in many collections likely address multiple topics and various aspects of the primary topic. Indexing and clustering these documents based on topical words, instead of frequent phrases, can be exploited to improve the accuracy of an information retrieval system.
- In text summarization, the primary problem is detecting the relevant portions of texts. Characterizing those portions by their topic will improve the summarization task, especially when the purpose of the summary is user-focused (Mani and Maybury, 1999).
- In text understanding, the scope of several phenomena is intersentential, the topic can take account of such a scope and hence can help in their resolution, e.g., in resolving anaphora and ellipsis (Kozima, 1993).
- In structuring text with regard to its discourse hierarchy (Halliday and Hasan, 1976, Hahn, 1990, Morris and Hirst 1991).
- In improving document navigation and hypertext links (Green, 1997, Hearst, 1999).

2 Related Work

Much research has been devoted to the task of structuring text - that is dividing texts into units based on information within the text. Existing work falls roughly

L. Monostori, J. Váncza, and M. Ali (Eds.): IEA/AIE 2001, LNAI 2070, pp. 552–558, 2001.

into one of the two categories: linear text segmentation aims to discover the topic boundaries, and discourse segmentation focuses on identifying relations between utterances. Methods for finding the topic boundaries include word repetition within a sliding window (Hearst, 1997), lexical cohesion based on word similarity (Morris and Hirst, 1991, Kozima, 1993), entity repetition with regard to its position within the paragraph (Kan et al., 1998), word frequency algorithm and maximum entropy model (Reynar, 1999), context vectors (Kaufmann, 1999), feature induction model (Beeferman et al., 1999), divisive clustering (Choi, 2000). On the other hand, discourse segmentation is fined-grained, (Litman and Passonneau, 1995) combine multiple knowledge sources for discourse segmentation using decision trees, and (Marcu, 1997b) uses rhetorical parsing (Marcu, 1997a) and decision tree (Marcu, 1999) to build up the discourse structure based on relations.

The systems for understanding "what the text is about" are based on world knowledge. DeJong (1982) developed a system based on templates that organize its world knowledge in order to skim newspaper stories and extract the main details. Radev and McKeown (1998) developed a system that takes template outputs of information extraction systems developed for the MUC conference and generates summaries of multiple news articles. Those systems rely on prior knowledge of their domains. However, to acquire such prior knowledge is labor-intensive and time-consuming. In order to reduce the knowledge engineering bottleneck, Riloff and Lorenzen (1999) present a system that generates extraction patterns and learns lexical constraints automatically from preclassified texts. Lin and Hovy (2000) present a procedure to automatically acquire topic signatures from preclassified documents of specific topics which are then used to identify the presence of the learned topics in previously unseen documents. However, learning extraction patterns from corpora makes those systems domain-specific. We present a method based on common available resources such as WordNet, and which can be applicable for unrestricted texts.

The approach that we are proposing to pursue below is a step further to the approaches intending to identify the boundaries between paragraphs in a text where the text changes topic. We present a system that proceeds in two steps: (1) the input text is segmented at places where there is a probable topic shift using one of the following public domain segmenters: *TextTiling* system (Hearst, 1997), *Segmenter* system (Kan et al., 1998), or Choi's system (2000), (2) lexical chains are extracted from each segment, using either WordNet or Roget's thesaurus, as indicators of its topic. In the remainder of the paper, we will present each of these steps, then we will evaluate the whole system.

3 Text Segmenting

The linear segmentation task is motivated by the observation that comprehension of longer texts benefits from automatic chunking of cohesive sections. This task involves breaking input text into segments that represent some meaningful grouping of contiguous portions of the text. The input text is divided into a linear sequence of adjacent segments and segment boundaries are found at various paragraph separations which identify one or more subtopical shifts.

Multi-paragraph subtopic segmentation should be useful for many text analysis tasks, including information retrieval and summarization, especially, text segmentation is interesting for the following purposes:

- Segmentation is intended to identify the boundaries between paragraphs in a text where the text changes topic. Thus, a text can comprise merely a single segment, or perhaps several different segments, when it touches on several different topics.
- It helps in processing the user needs when they are specified as terms in the sense that only segments that are relevant to the terms specified by the user are chosen (Reynar, 1999, Chali et al., 1999).

We are using three public domain segmenters *TextTiling* system (Hearst, 1997), *Segmenter* system (Kan et al., 1998), and Choi's system (2000).

Segmentation is followed by the characterization of the segment in terms of lexical chains as clues of the segment topic.

4 Lexical Chaining

Structural theories of text are concerned with identifying units of text that are about the "same thing". When this happens, there is a strong tendency for semantically related words to be used within that unit. The notion of cohesion, introduced by Halliday and Hasan (1976), is a device for "sticking together" different parts of the text to function as a whole. It is achieved through the use of *grammatical cohesion*, i.e. reference, substitution, ellipsis and conjunction, and *lexical cohesion*, i.e. semantically related words. Lexical cohesion occurs not only between two terms, but among sequences of related words, called *lexical chains* (Morris and Hirst, 1991). Lexical chains (1) provide an easy-to-determine context to aid in the resolution of ambiguity and in the narrowing to specific meaning of a word, (2) tend to delineate portions of text that have a strong unity of meaning. We investigate how lexical chains can be used as an indicator of the text segment topic. The step of the algorithm of the lexical chain computation are as follows:

1. We select the set of candidate words. To this end, we run a part-of-speech tagger (Brill, 1992) on a text segment, and only the open class words that function as noun phrases or proper names are chosen.
2. The set of the candidate words are exploded into senses, the senses are given by the thesaurus in use, at this step all the senses of the same word are considered. In the actual implementation, we are using two different thesauri: Roget's thesaurus (1988) and WordNet thesaurus (Miller et al., 1993). From this step each word sense is represented by distinct sets (see *Figure 1*) considered as levels, the first one constitutes the set of synonyms and antonyms, the second one constitutes the set of first hypernyms/hyponyms and their variations (i.e. meronyms/holonyms, etc.), and so on.

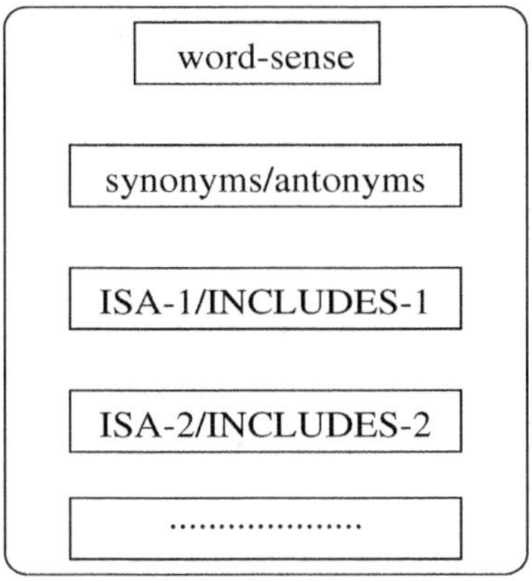

Fig. 1. Word sense representation

3. We find the semantic relatedness among the set of senses according to their representations. A semantic relationship exists between two word senses if comparing two sense representations of two distinct words, a matching exists, i.e., a non-empty intersection exists between the sets of words. To each semantic relatedness is associated a measure which indicates the length of the path taken in the matching with respect to the levels of the two compared sets.
4. We build up chains which are sets such as

$$
\begin{array}{l}
\{\ (word_1[sense_{11}, sense_{12}, \ldots]),\\
\{\ (word_2[sense_{21}, sense_{22}, \ldots]),\\
\{\ \ldots\}
\end{array}
$$

in which $word_i$-$sense_{ix}$ is semantically related to $word_j$-$sense_{jy}$ for $i \neq j$

5. We retain longest chains relying on the following preference criterion:

$$
\begin{array}{l}
word\ repetition\ \gg\\
\quad synonym/antonym\ \gg\\
\qquad ISA-1/INCLUDE-1\ \gg\\
\qquad\quad ISA-2/INCLUDE-2\ \gg\\
\qquad\qquad \ldots
\end{array}
$$

We will show the output of the lexical chaining on a fragment of text (1). (2) and (3) are the lexical chains computed using respectively WordNet and Roget's thesauri[1].

(1) With its distant orbit - 50 percent farther from the sun than the earth - and slim atmospheric blanket, Mars experiences frigid weather conditions. Surface temperatures typically average about -60 degrees Celsius (-76 degrees Fahrenheit) at the equator and can dip to -123 degrees Celsius near

[1] The number in parenthesis are the word occurrence positions within the text.

the poles. Only the midday sun at tropical latitudes is warm enough to thaw ice on occasion, but any liquid water formed in this way should evaporate almost instantly because of the low atmospheric pressure.

(2) a. { orbit (4), degree (31 34 44), latitude (55) }
b. { degree (31 34 44), occasion (63) }
c. { degree (31 34 44), way (71) }
d. { sun (11 52), earth (14), mars (20) }
e. { weather (23), ice (61), water (67) }

(3) a. { orbit (4), sun (11 52), earth (14), weather (23), equator (38) }

Lexical chains are computed for each text segment.

5 Evaluation

We conducted an evaluation of the whole system (i.e., segmenter + lexical chainer). We selected randomly three texts from the Brown corpus as test corpus, we segmented them using Choi's segmenter because it is more precise than the two others (cf. (Choi, 2000)), this gave us a sample of 34 text segments, then we computed the lexical chains for each of these segments using both of the thesauri, and we presented them to five judges. We asked all the judges (1) to read the text segment, then (2) to read each lexical chain and answer the following question: "Is the chain's topic present in the segment?", (3) After reading all the lexical chains corresponding to one segment and answering the previous question, we asked them to answer the following question: "Is the segment's topic covered by all its chains?"

We considered the answer as *yes* or *no* given the majority of the judges. Related to the information retrieval measures, the answers to the first question correspond to precision (i.e., how many lexical chains are good among all the possible lexical chains), the answers to the second question correspond to recall (i.e., how much of the segment's topic is contained in the lexical chains). The results are as follow: using WordNet, we got a precision of 45% and a recall of 65%, compared to Roget's thesaurus where we got a precision of 38% and a recall of 56%.

6 Discussion and Future Work

This experiment shows that the whole system is more accurate using WordNet than Roget. This is due on one hand to the number of entries in the thesaurus (i.e., 99,642 synsets and 121,962 unique words in WordNet as of version 1.6 compare to Roget's thesaurus 1035 categories and 46,500 unique words as of version 7.1). On another hand, the classification into categories in Roget are more general abstraction compared to the organization into synsets defined in WordNet. Indeed, WordNet represents the largest publically available lexical resource to date.

Lexical chains have been proposed by Morris and Hirst (1991) as indicator of the structure of text. Barzilay and Elhadad (1997) investigate the production of summaries based on lexical chaining. The summaries are built using scoring which is based on chain length and the extraction of significant sentences is based on heuristics using chain distribution, for example, choose the sentence that contains the first appearance of a chain member in the text. In this paper, we investigate the production of lexical chains to account for the text segment topic.

The results reported in this paper suggest that we should refine the process of lexical chaining. Instead of choosing any content word tagged as noun or proper noun as candidate for the computation of the chains, it seems that restricting the set of candidate words will improve the precision of the chains as in the present system most of the chains are judged inaccurate because of the broad coverage of the lexical resource. This work is in progress.

Acknowledgments

This work was supported by the Natural Sciences and Engineering Research Council (NSERC) research grant and the Alberta Heritage Foundation for Science and Engineering Research under the Research Excellence Envelope funding.

References

Barzilay, Regina and Michael Elhadad. (1997) Using lexical chains for text summarization. In *ACL/EACL Workshop on Intelligent Scalable Text Summarization*, pages 10–17, Madrid.

Beeferman, Doug, Adam Berger, and John Lafferty. (1999). Statistical models for text segmentation. *Machine Learning, Special Issue on Natural Language Processing*, 34(1 – 3):177 – 210.

Brill, Eric. (1992). A simple rule-based part of speech tagger. In *Proceedings of the Third Conference on Applied Natural Language Processing, ACL*, pages 152–155, Trento.

Chali, Yllias, Stan Matwin, and Stan Szpakowicz. (1999). Query-biased text summarization as a question-answering technique. In *Proceedings of AAAI Symposium on Question-Answering Systems*, Massachusetts.

Choi, Freddy Y. Y. (2000). Advances in domain independent linear text segmentation. In *Proceedings of the 1st North American Chapter of the Association for Computational Linguistics*, pages 26 – 33, Seattle, Washington.

DeJong, Gerald. (1982). An overview of the frump system. In Wendy G. Lehnert amd Martin H. Ringle, editor, *Strategies for natural language processing*. Lawrence Erlbaum Associates, pages pages 76–49.

Green, Stephen J. (1997). *Automatically Generating Hypertext by Computing Semantic Similarity*. Ph.D. thesis, Department of Computer Science, University of Toronto.

Hahn, Udo. (1990). Topic parsing: Accounting for text macrostructures in full text analysis. *Information Processing and Management*, 26:135 – 170.

Halliday, Michael and Ruqaiya Hasan. (1976). *Cohesion in English*. Longman, London.

Hearst, Marti A. (1997). TextTiling: Segmenting text into multi-paragraph subtopic passages. *Computational Linguistics*, 23(1):33–64.

Kan, Min-Yen, Kathleen R. McKeown, and Judith L. Klavans. (1998). Linear segmentation and segment relevance. In *Proceedings of 6th International Workshop of Very Large Corpora (WVLC-6)*, pages 197–205, Montréal.

Kaufmann, Stefan. (1999). Cohesion and collocation: Using context vectors in text segmentation. In *Proceedings of the 37th Annual Meeting of the Association for Computational Linguistics (Students Session)*, pages 591 – 595, College Park, Maryland.

Kozima, Hideki. (1993). Text segmentation based on similarity between words. In *Proceedings of the 31th Annual Meeting of the Association for Computational Linguistics*, pages 286–288.

Lin, Chin-Yew and Eduard Hovy. (2000). The automated acquisition of topic signatures for text summarization. In *18th International Conference in Computational Linguistics*, Saarbrücken, Germany.

Litman, Diane J. and Rebecca J. Passonneau. (1995). Combining multiple knowledge sources for discourse segmentation. In *Proceedings of the 33rd Annual Meeting of the Association for Computational Linguistics*, pages 108 – 115, Cambridge, Massachusetts.

Mani, Inderjeet and Mark T. Maybury. (1999). *Advances in Automatic Text Summarization.* MIT Press.

Marcu, Daniel. (1997)a. The rhetorical parsing of natural language texts. In *Proceedings of the 35th Annual Meeting of the Association for Computational Linguistics and the European Chapter of the Association for Computational Linguistics*, pages 96–103, Madrid, Spain.

Marcu, Daniel. (1997)b. *The Rhetorical Parsing, Summarization, and Generation of Natural Language Texts.* Ph.D. thesis, Department of Computer Science, University of Toronto.

Marcu, Daniel. (1999). A decision-based approach to rhetorical parsing. In *Proceedings of The 37th Annual Meeting of the Association for Computational Linguistics*, pages 365 – 372, College Park, Maryland.

Miller, George A., Richard Beckwith, Christiane Fellbaum, Derek Gross, and Katherine Miller. (1993). Five papers on wordnet. CSL Report 43, Cognitive Science Laboratory, Princeton University.

Morris, Jane and Graeme Hirst. (1991). Lexical cohesion computed by thesaural relations as an indicator of the structure of text. *Computational Linguistics*, 17(1):21–48.

Pratt, Wand, Marti A. Hearst, and Lawrence M. Fagan. (1999). A knowledge-based approach to organizing retrieved documents. In *Proceedings of the Sixteenth National Conference on Artificial Intelligence*, Orlando, Florida.

Radev, Dragomir R. and Kathleen R. McKeown. (1998). Generating natural language summaries from multiple on-line sources. *Computational Linguistics*, 24(3):469–500.

Reynar, Jeffrey C. (1999). Statistical models for topic segmentation. In *Proceedings of the 37th Annual Meeting of the Association for Computational Linguistics*, pages 357 – 364, College Park, Maryland.

Riloff, Ellen and Jeffrey Lorenzen, (1999). *Generating domain-specific role relationships automatically*, chapter Natural Language Information Retrieval, editor Tomek Strzalkowski. Kluwer Academic Publishers.

Roget. (1988). *Roget's Thesaurus.* Longman, London.

A Mixed Closure-CSP Method to Solve Scheduling Problems

María Isabel Alfonso Galipienso[1] and Federico Barber Sanchís[2]

[1] Universidad de Alicante, Depto. Ciencia de la Computación e Inteligencia Artificial, Ap. Correos 99, E-03080, Alicante, Spain
eli@dccia.ua.es

[2] Universidad Politécnica de Valencia, Depto. de Sistemas Informáticos y Computación,
Ap. Correos 22012, E-46020 Valencia, Spain
fbarber@dsic.upv.es

Abstract. Scheduling problems can be seen as a set of temporal metric and disjunctive constraints. So, they can be formulated in terms of CSPs techniques. In the literature, there are CSP-based methods which interleave (sequentially) searching efforts with the application of consistency enforcing mechanisms and variable/value ordering heuristics. Alternatively, in this paper, we propose a new method that integrates effectively the CSP process into a limited closure process. Such integration allows us to define better informed heuristics. They are used to limit the complete closure process applied, with a number of disjunctive constraints, and so reduce their complexity, while reducing the search space. Moreover, we can maintain more time open disjunctive solutions in the CSP process, limiting the number of backtrackings realized. We show preliminary results obtained from several instances of scheduling problems.

1 Introduction

The scheduling problem is a NP-complete problem [11] and it is usually solved by CSP (Constraint Satisfaction Problem) techniques. One approximation is based on backtracking search methods by using variable and value ordering heuristics [15], in order to bound the search. In the worst case, a backtracking algorithm takes an exponential amount of time to obtain a feasible solution (schedule). In spite of the worst case estimate, we can speed up a backtracking algorithm by interleaving search with the application of consistency enforcing mechanisms [5]. One feature of CSP based methods is that they assume that the overall constraint set is known beforehand. However, there are particular problem domains in which this is not possible, because constraints are known dynamically, i.e. dynamic scheduling [1], integrated planning-scheduling processes [12], and so on. In these cases, the scheduler should have an incremental character. This implies that it should maintain open a set of possible solutions at each new input constraint. Therefore, pure CSP based methods are not appropriate in this cases, because they would obtain unique solutions (variable assignments) at each new constraint is asserted.

L. Monostori, J. Váncza, and M. Ali (Eds.): IEA/AIE 2001, LNAI 2070, pp. 559–570, 2001.

On the other hand, closure (or path consistency) algorithms [4] prune efficiently the search space and can maintain several solutions at a time, but this leads to a very computationally expensive process. These techniques proceeds by eliminating successively local inconsistencies that cannot participate in a global solution [13]. More precisely, if the closure is complete, it obtains a minimal consistent network, i.e. it removes all inconsistent values to variable domains [8]. However, in the worst case, such techniques take, probably, an exponential time, with the number of variables [10]. Our idea is to propose a new method that integrates the CSP techniques into a limited complete closure method in order to achieve the following features:

- handling a set of metric and disjunctive based temporal point constraints, which represent the scheduling problem constraints,
- minimizing the domains of variables, and maintaining open disjunctive solutions, and thus avoiding a lot of backtrackings. The number of open disjunctive solutions can be parameterized,
- using to more informed heuristics, due to clausure process, which prune more efficiently the search space. The heuristics used can also be parameterized.

The rest of the paper are organized as follows: first, we define the scheduling problem as a set of metric and disjunctive-based temporal point constraints. Next, we explain the total closure process used in order to handle metric and disjunctive-based labelled temporal point constraints. In the next section we show the integrated process closure-CSP proposed. Next, we review some heuristics used in traditional CSP processes, and introduce some new ones. Finally, we show our experimental results and we present our conclusions.

2 The Scheduling Problem as CSP and Closure Processes

A scheduling problem requires a set of jobs $J = \{j_i\}, i = 1..n$,which uses a set of physical resources $M = \{m_j\}, j = 1..m$. Each job j_i consists of a set of m operations $O = \{o_{ij}\}$ to be scheduled according to a routing process that specifies a partial ordering among these operations (precedence constraints). When this routing process is the same for each job, we have a flow-shop problem. On the other hand, when each job has a particular routing process, then this problem is named job-shop. A resource m_j can process only an operation o_{ij} at a time (which implies manage disjunctive constraints). Each operation o_{ij} has a fixed duration dur_{ij}. Furthermore, each job j_i has a release date rt_i and a due date (or deadline) dt_i. We can obtain either a feasible solution (an instantiation of values of each variable which satisfies all constraints), or an optimal solution (an instantiation that minimizes the *makespan*, which is defined as the time by which all jobs have been completely processed).
We consider the constraints outlined above, as a set of metric and disjunctive-based temporal point constraints. And the scheduling problem as the problem of finding solutions for the set of these constraints.

The sintaxis for a constraint is: $(t_i \ \{[d_1 D_1], [d_2 D_2], ...[d_n D_n]\} \ t_j)$, with $d_i \leq D_i$, which means: $(t_j - t_i \leq [d_1 D_1]) \vee (t_j - t_i \leq [d_2 D_2]) \vee \ldots \vee (t_j - t_i \leq [d_n D_n])$.

So, the form of a non disjunctive constraint is $(t_i \ \{[d_1 D_1]\} \ t_j)$. And the form of a disjunctive constraint is $(t_i \ \{[d_1 D_1], [d_2 D_2]\} \ t_j)$. We will use the notation $(o_i \longrightarrow o_j)$ to mean that o_i precedes o_j. So, we indicate the previous disjunctive constraint as $(o_i \longrightarrow o_j) \vee (o_j \longrightarrow o_i)$.

Moreover, we use two special temporal points *T0* and *TF* to identify the initial and final point of scheduling, respectively.

We represent the set of constraints outlined above as a constraint network. And we process it with a method that realizes a total closure process of metric and disjunctive constraints, like the one defined in [3]. This method infers new constraints from those explicitly asserted, and it obtains always a minimal LTCN (Labeled Temporal Constraint Network), from one LTCN minimal previous. This process is able to find by itself any solution, if it exists, by successively instantiating variables. Then, no backtracking is needed.

The advantages provided by the closure process are mitigated by the disjunctive constraints imposed by the scheduling problem. This results in an expensive computational cost. In order to reduce such complexity, we limit the number of disjunctive constraints maintained in the network using a set of heuristics which we will explain later.

On the other hand, in traditional CSP based methods, search is improved by the use of several heuristics in order to guide the search efficiently and minimize the need of backtracking, [14], [15], [7], [2], [16]. Generally, the goodness of CSP process, is strongly conditioned by knowing from the start every constraint-set for a particular problem. And the order in which constraints are added to the scheduler influences the number of backtrackings needed to obtain a solution. Moreover, the methods outlined above carry out successive instantiations to variables (they do not maintain any open solutions, as occurs in closure processes). Therefore, successive known constraints can not be adapted to a partial solution that has being already proved.

Usually the approaches that sequentially apply closure and CSP, have the disadvantages of both of them: they obtain only one solution, the closure process removes only partially the inconsistent values, and so the heuristics applied are not sufficient to avoid a large number of backtrackings.

The method proposed here integrates the CSP techniques into a limited total closure process, in order to exploit the advantages of both of them. So, we can obtain a set of minimal solutions, maintaining several disjunctive constraints at a time in the search tree. In order to decrease the complexity of a total closure process, we limit the number of disjunctive constraints, k, that can exist at a time in the search tree. As an additional advantage the set of disjunctive constraints maintained is not fixed (we fix the maximal number k, but not which constraint is considered). Then, as we have more information, we decide one of the alternatives of a disjunctive constraint, reducing the number of backtrackings. Next, we explain the algorithm proposed.

3 Integrating Closure and CSP Processes

We have combined a closure process with a CSP process in a integrated form. This is a new approximation that differs from the traditional point of view: apply first closure and next CSP. Moreover, the method proposed can act as a total closure process, or as a completely CSP process depending of number of disjunctive constraints that we decide to maintain in the network at the same time.

Using the temporal constraints set as input, our algorithm combines the advantages of both processes. It is a iterative algorithm, in which we add a new constraint each time. It results in a flexible model that can be parametrized by:

- the maximum number of indecisions. If it takes a 0 value, this means that none disjunctive constraint is present in the network. The greater is this number, the higher is the computational cost of inserting a new disjunctive constraint, but the lower is the number of backtrackings needed to obtain a solution,
- the set of heuristics to apply. We can use several combinations of heuristics in order to obtain better results depending of the particular features of a scheduling problem. The corresponding parameters are *hvariables* for variable ordering heuristics, and *hvalues* for value ordering heuristics.

The method is somehow similar to the based-CBA processes [16], but the fundamental difference is that CBA processes do not maintain disjunctive constraints in the network. When they choose a disjunctive constraint, they take a decision based in some heuristic criteria. In our method, when we add a disjunctive constraint, we can maintain both orderings, and leave (delay) the decision for later, if we consider that the information supplied by the heuristics it is not sufficient to decide.

Before a disjunctive constraint is propagated, each possible ordering between these two operations (not yet scheduled) have a label associated that identifies it. For example, suppose that we have added the three following constraints: $\{(t1\ \{([-\infty - 20], \{Ra\}), ([10\ \infty], \{Rb\})\}\ t2), (t1\ \{([(-\infty - 15], \{Rc\}), ([10\ \infty], \{Rd\})\}\ t4), (t2\ \{([(-\infty\ 15], \{Re\}), ([20\ \infty], \{Rf\})\}\ t4)\}$, corresponding to three disjunctive constraints on non simultaneous use of resources.

Suppose that *t1*, *t2*, and *t4*, are the start points of operations o_1, o_2, and o_4, respectively. Then the label *Ra*, corresponds to the ordering $o_2 \rightarrow o_1$, *Rb* to $o_1 \rightarrow o_2$, and so on.

Therefore, after propagation, if we obtain the constraint $\{(t3\{([40\,47],\{Ra,Rc,Rf\})\ t6)\}$, we know that it corresponds to the combination of orderings associated to *Ra*, *Rc*, and *Rf*. This means that the resulting ordering is o_2, o_1 and o_4. The complete algorithm is illustrated in Fig. 1.

First, we select the non-disjunctive constraints and use *add_constraints* in order to propagate them and detect inconsistent values early. As a result of this process we always obtain a minimal network. Then, we perform a loop in which we choose the next disjunctive constraint to add.

algorithm **Scheduler** (indecisions, hvariables, hvalues)

$C \leftarrow$ create_constraint_set /* $C = \{(t_i\ c_ij\ t_j)\}$ */
$S \leftarrow \{c_ij\} \mid c_ij \in C \wedge \mid c_ij \mid = 1$
$C \leftarrow$ add_constraints(C, S)
While $C \neq \emptyset$ **do**
non_disj ← detect_non_disjunctives(C) /* value heur. */
result ← add_constraints (C, non_disj)
next_constraint ← apply_h (hvariables) /*var. heur. */
result ← closure (next_constraint)
If not result **then** backtracking **end-if**
decision ← apply_h (hvalues)
decision ← validate_decision (decision, C)/*value heur.*/
decision ← revise_pending_decis (decision)
If | decision | > indecisions **then**
decision ← any_decision (decision) **end-if**
If decision $\neq \emptyset$ **then**
result ← add_constraints (C,decision) **end-if**
end-while

end scheduler

Fig. 1. The scheduler process.

Depending of the next propagated disjunctive constraint, the disjunctive network (before the propagation),would convert it in to another non-disjunctive network after the propagation. For example, suppose we have the constraint $(t_i\{([10\ 40], \{RaRb\}), ([50\ 80], \{RcRd\})\}t_j)$ in the network (the cardinality of the disjunctive constraints is 2). And we consider the disjunctive constraint $(t_i\{([10\ 20], \{Rc\}), ([90\ 200], \{Rd\})t_j)$ to add. After the propagation it will be transformed into $(t_i\{([10\ 20], \{RaRbRc\})\}t_j)$. Then the cardinality of the constraints in the network will be 1. This is the purpose of the process named *detect_non_disjunctives.*

Next, we apply the variable heuristic value indicated by the parameter *hvariables*, in order to select the next disjunctive constraint to propagate, named *next_constraint.*

After *next_constraint* is propagated, we have to decide which ordering apply, (even or don't take a decision yet). The value heuristic to apply is indicated by the *hvalues* parameter, and the result is named decision. Before propagating the decision value, we must first, validate it. This is performed by *validate_decision*: i.e. suppose that decision takes the value $\{(t_i\{[10\ 40]\}t_j)$. Suppose also that among the disjunctive constraints that still have not been added, we find $(t_i\{([-\infty\ 9], [50\ \infty])\}t_j)$. In this case we have to change the decision value because it will produce an inconsistency later.

We can not decide at all (if the resultant cardinality of disjunctive constraints is minor or equal to *indecisions* parameter). In this case, we record that we have a pending ordering decision, that can be decided later.

The next step is to revise the pending ordering decisions from previous iterations, done by *revise_pending_decis*. We modify the decision value eliminating possible remaining ordering decisions, that now can be decided. This is possible because we have more information due to new constraints added in previous iterations. As a result, the computational cost of the propagation process will be lower. Moreover, we can maintain during a certain chosen time an indecision in the network, by fixing a limited number of iterations in order to reduce the propagation cost.

We iterate until all disjunctive constraints have added (propagated) to the network (C has no elements). When the propagation process detect inconsistent values, then we perform a backtracking process, as we explain in the next subsection.

3.1 Backtracking

When a decision (o_i, o_j) is taken after the addition of a disjunctive constraint, we record the alternative ordering (o_j, o_i). Later, if we detect any inconsistent value, we will return to the alternative rejected previously (o_j, o_i) and explore the other branch in the search tree. In this case, we have used a simple chronological backtracking, good enough to obtain good experimental results.

If we record all rejected alternatives our spatial cost is too high, due to network size. The solution adopted is to record one alternative each (decisions maintained. The value α= 10 has been fixed in the experiments realized.

4 New Variable and Value Heuristics

4.1 Slack and Edge-Finding Based Heuristics

First, we explain the modifications realized over slack based heuristics, in order that they can be applied to a set of labelled temporal interval-based constraints. Moreover, we modify this in that we can not decide any ordering. Then we record it, to revise it later (*revise_pending_decis* procedure).

In our model, an operation o_j, has a number of k possible values of earliest start times/latest finish times, being k the number of labelled intervals at each constraint.

We define the disjunctive earliest start time and the latest finish time *(estD, lftD)*, of an operation o_j as the set of his k earliest start/latest finish times, respectively
$estD(o_j) = \{(est_z(o_i)\}, z = 1..k; lftD(o_j) = \{(lft_z(o_i)\}, z = 1..k;$

So, for each pair of operations o_i, o_j, that requires the same resource, we have k possible values of temporal slack remaining after sequencing o_i before o_j, defined as:
$slack_z(o_i, o_j) = lft_z(o_j) - (est_z(o_i) - (dur(o_i) + dur(o_j))$
with $est_z(o_i) \in estD(o_i), and\ lft_z(o_j) \in lftD(o_j)$.

Next, we define the disjunctive temporal slack of sequencing o_i before o_j, as the set of k slack values corresponding to the labelled intervals of constraints: $slackD(o_i, o_j) = \{slack_z(o_i, o_j)\}, z = 1..k,$
Given these new measures of temporal slack, we define a variable ordering heuristic (*min_slackD*), that selects the ordering decision with the overall minimum slack, as the decision ordering (o_i, o_j) for which:
$min\{slack_z(o_i, o_j), slack_z(o_j, o_i)\} = min_{p,q}\{min\{slack_z(o_p, o_q), slack_z(o_q, o_p)\}$,
with $slack_z(o_p, o_q) \in (slackD(o_p, o_q), slack_z(o_q, o_p) \in (slackD(o_q, o_p)$, for all unassigned ordering (o_p, o_q).

A value ordering heuristic is used (named *max_slackD*), that selects the sequencing constraint (o_i, o_j) if $max(slackD_z(o_i, o_j)) > max(slackD_z(o_j, o_i)), z = 1..k$, the sequencing constraint (o_j, o_i) if $max(slackD_z(o_i, o_j)) < max(slackD_z(o_j, o_i)), z = 1..k$, and we can not choose any ordering if they have the same value (we maintain several solutions open at the same time).

Second, we explain the modifications on *edge-finding* based heuristics, used in [7]. We pretend to choose those pairs of non yet scheduled operations (o_i, o_j), as both could be first/last operations out of the set of task intervals. We have m task intervals (one per machine). Each one is formed at each moment with the operations already scheduled.

For a task interval $S = [o_i, o_j]$, we define the disjunctive latest finish time of S, as $lftD(S) = max(lft_z(o_p)), z = 1..k, \forall o_p \in S$. We also define the disjunctive earliest start time of S, $estD(S)$, as $estD(S) = min(est_z(o_p)), z = 1..k, \forall o_p \in S$. The duration of S is $dur(S) = \sum dur(o_p), \forall o_p \in S$.

Done a pair of operations not yet scheduled (o_i, o_j), then we apply her the following rules:
(a) $\exists z, z = 1..k, (lftD_z(S) - (estD(o_x) - dur_z(S)) \geq 0$
(b) $\exists z, z = 1..k, (lftD_z(o_x) - (estD(S) - dur_z(S)) \geq 0$

If (a) is true, then o_x can be the first operation in S. If (b) is true, then o_x can be the last operation in S. So, we construct two sets with the operations that can be the first/last operations in S, named respectively, *PRIM(i)* and *ULT(i)*, (*i* =*1..m*, m is the number of resources),
$PRIM(i) = \{(o_x, o_y) \mid (1)$ is true for o_x and $o_y\}$
$ULT(i) = \{(o_x, o_y) \mid (2)$ is true for o_x and $o_y\}$
We define the most critical resource M_i, as that with a minor cardinality of sets $PRIM(i)$ and $ULT(i)$. And we select a pair on non yet scheduled operations (o_x, o_y) that pertain both to $PRIM(i)$ or $ULT(i)$.

If there are several candidate pairs, we choose one of them. This is a simplified version of variable heuristic used in [7].

Moreover, we apply the exclusion rules defined in [7], as a value heuristic, in that it adds redundant constraints that force an ordering between two operations. The result is that a disjunctive constraint is eliminated, and the corresponding ordering is propagated. We apply this rules only when the constraints in the network have one interval.

4.2 Makespan-Based Heuristic

After the propagation process of each new constraint, all the constraints between each pair of points are deduced. Due to this fact, we can know the makespan achieved by retrieving the resultant constraint between the special temporal points *T0* and *TF*.

We define a new value ordering heuristic consisting of choosing the labelled interval with a minor left value. The labels associated with this interval indicate the operations ordering preferred. We denote by $makespan_z$ the left value of the *zth* interval of the constraint existing between the temporal points *T0* and *TF*. Similarly, we denote $set\_labels(makespan_z)$ as the set of labels associated with the $makespan_z$ value. Therefore, we select the decision orderings indicated by: $min\_makespan = set\_labels(min(makespan_z)), z = 1..k$
Suppose that we have the constraint: $(t1\{([(-\infty\ 20], \{Ra\}), ([10\ \infty], \{Rb\})\}t2)$. The *label_set* $\{Ra\}$ corresponds to ordering $(o_x \rightarrow o_y)$, and the *label_set* $\{Rb\}$ to the ordering $(o_j \rightarrow o_i)$. After the process propagation, we obtain the constraint: $(T0\ \{([12\ \infty],\{Ra\}),\ ([25\ \infty],\{Rb\})\}\ TF)$,
This means that with the ordering $(o_x \rightarrow o_y)$ we obtain a minimum makespan of 12 units, and 25 units if the order preferred is $(o_x \rightarrow o_y)$. Therefore, we prefer the first ordering, where we obtain a minimum makespan-value. And the result we obtain is $\{Ra\}$.

4.3 Mixed CSP-Closure Heuristics

In order to achieve better results we define a new value and variable heuristics. The first ones combine the makespan (provides global information) and slack value-based heuristic (provides local information). That allows us take more informed value ordering decisions.

We have named the new value heuristic *makespan_slack*. We apply the *min_makespan* and *max_slackD* heuristics. If one of them, not take a decision, then we consider that we need more information, and not decide at all. If both heuristics take a decision, then we consider the intersection of both results.

We also define a new mixed variable heuristic that combines the slack and edge-finding based variable heuristics. We named this heuristic *edge_slack*. First we calculate the S_i task intervals (one for each resource) and the *slackRD* of each resource i defined as: $slackRD(S_i) = \{(lftD_z(S_i) - estD_z(S_i) - (dur_z(S_i)\}$, $z{=}1..m$
Next we calculate the cardinality of *PRIM(i)*, and *ULT(i)* for each resource Mi, we named this value crit(i) Finally, we select the next pair or unordered operations (o_x, o_y) from the resource that have the maximum product value: $slackRD(S_i) \times crit(i)$. The operations of the pair (o_x, o_y) selected belongs either to *PRIM(i)* or to *ULT(i)*.

Other combinations are also possible. But these have demonstrated be adequate to solve the instances used in the experiments that we have performed and that are showed in the next section.

5 Empirical Evaluation

We have performed our experiments over a set of instances of a benchmark scheduling problem, that can be obtained at ftp://ftp.mscmga.ms.ic.ac.uk/pub/. The files are named as jobshop1.txt (with several job shop problems) and flowwhop1.txt (with several flow shop problems).

First, we analyze the number of backtrackings avoided by of our model. As we have already mentioned, it depends fundamentally on the number of pending decisions maintained. In Table 1, we have annotated the results obtained varying the number of maximal pending decisions (varying from 0 to 2). The first three instances: ft06, la01, and la02 are job shop, while the last two: car1 and car2 are instances flow shop. We observe that the greater is this number, the greater is the number of backtrackings avoided. This is calculated comparing the decision that we would have taken, (when we maintain the disjunction), and the decision that we will take later. Note that the 0 value indicates that given a pair of unordered operations (o_i, o_j), we always select one of two possible orders $(o_i \rightarrow o_j)$, or , $(o_j \rightarrow o_i)$. The 2 value means that the cardinality of network constraints have a maximal value of 4.

Table 1. Backtrackings avoided versus pending decisions.

instance	indecis	solution	b.realiz	b.avoid
ft06 (6x6)	0	55/55	0	0
la01 (10x5)	0	741/666	0	0
	1	700/666	0	17
	2	666/666	0	25
la02 (10x5)	0	734/655	0	0
	1	677/655	0	20
	2	655/655	0	22
car1 (11x5)	0	7894/7038	0	0
	1	7326/7038	0	32
	2	7038/7038	5	34
car2 (13x4)	0	7632/7166	0	0
	1	7166/7166	0	50

Table 2. Global versus local heuristics. Indecisions=0.

instance	indecis	solution	b.realiz
ft06 (6x6)	Local	56/55	0
	Global	56/55	0
	Glob+Loc	55/55	0
la01 (10x5)	Local	757/666	0
	Global	753/666	0
	Glob+Loc	741/666	0
la02 (10x5)	Local	734/655	0
	Global	677/655	0
	Glob+Loc	655/655	0
car1 (11x5)	Local	7910/7038	0
	Global	7899/7038	0
	Glob+Loc	7894/7038	5
car2 (13x4)	Local	7650/7166	0
	Global	7646/7166	0
	Glob+Loc	7632/7166	0

In the other hand, the obtained solution is close to the optimum (or reaches this optimum) when we increment the number of pending decisions (we use the notation x/y, in which x is the obtained solution, and y the optimal solution). Also note that, due to closure processes, no backtracking is needed in most of the cases.

In some cases, we obtain the optimal solution, as a consequence of the effective use of combined closure-heuristic processes. In this case, we have used the *makespan_slack* and *edge_slack* heuristics.

Secondly, we analyze the impact of global/local heuristics in the obtained solution and in the number of backtrackings avoided. The local heuristic that we have used is *max_slackD* to value ordering, and *min_makespan* as global heuristic. We have applied the two mixed heuristics as in Table 1. We can note out of Table 2 that the global heuristics, when used by themselves, allow better results than when we use uniquely local heuristics. When we use both types of heuristics, we obtain a solution closer to optimal. This fact is due to the greater information obtained when we combine the two types of heuristics (in comparison with the amount of information dealt when we apply them by separate).

In Table 3, we show the results using local or global heuristics, when two indecisions are permitted. We reach the optimum values when we combine both types of heuristics.

Table 3. Global versus local heuristics. Indecisions=2.

instance	indecis	solution	b.realiz	b.avoid
ft06 (6x6)	Local	55/55	0	0
	Global	55/55	0	0
	Glob+Loc	55/55	0	0
la01 (10x5)	Local	671/666	0	20
	Global	668/666	0	20
	Glob+Loc	666/666	0	25
la02 (10x5)	Local	652/655	0	21
	Global	650/655	0	20
	Glob+Loc	655/655	0	22
car1 (11x5)	Local	7070/7038	0	27
	Global	7057/7038	0	30
	Glob+Loc	7038/7038	5	34
car2 (13x4)	Local	7170/7166	0	38
	Global	7189/7166	0	41
	Glob+Loc	7166/7166	0	50

Table 4. Impact of several heuristic set. Indecisions=2.

instance	C1	C2	C3	C4	sol.opt.
ft06	55	55	55	55	55
la01	668	666	666	666	666
la02	659	675	655	655	655
car1	7038	7038	7044	7038	7038
car2	7182	7173	7170	7166	7166

Finally, we have used several combinations of heuristics in order to see how they affect in the solution obtained. In Table 4 we show the results: C1, corresponds to the use of the variable heuristic and the value heuristic based in slack; C2 is the combination edge-finding based variable heuristic plus slack based value heuristic; C3 uses the slack based heuristic variables and the *min_makespan* value heuristic; finally C4 combines edge-finding based variable heuristic with the mixed value heuristic *makespan_slack*.

We can observe that, in general, the best results are obtained with the combination C4, this is due to the fact that the value ordering heuristic use more information and in consequence we can take better decisions.

We have not showed the seconds of CPU used to solve each instance because we have focused on reducing the complexity of the process. However, using Common Lisp with a Pentium II computer, the car2 instance with the combination C4 of Table 4, takes 15 secs. to complete.

These are preliminary results. We are preparing more experiments with instances randomly generated. Moreover, we are currently investigating new mixed heuristics, in order to obtain better results.

6 Conclusions

We have proposed a new approximation to deal with the scheduling problem, considered as a temporal constraint satisfaction problem. It specifically handles a set of metric and disjunctive based temporal point constraints.

Our method combines a closure process with CSP techniques in order to achieve the following features:

- it allows the use of local and global heuristics, due to major information inferred by the closure process (in previous approximations, global heuristics are not applicable),
- it permits delaying the ordering decision among operations that use the same resource. Therefore maintains a limited number of solutions versus previous approximations that maintain just an unique solution,
- it reduces the number of backtracking needed on the expense of a complex closure process,
- We obtain a parameterizable process in which we can decide the maximal number of disjunctive constraints that will remain active in the network at the same time. The disjunctive constraints in the network vary dynamically as more information is obtained due to closure process,

Finally we would like to remark that this system is adequate both for an independent scheduling process (all constraints are known from the start) or an integrated process of planning-scheduling (due to the fact to maintain a certain number of open solutions).

References

1. Albers, S., and Leonardi S.: Online algorithms. ACM Computing surveys, 31(3es) (1999)
2. Baptiste, P., Le Pape, C., and Nuijten, W.: Constraint-Based Optimization and Approximation for Job-Shop Scheduling. Paper presented at the IJCAI-95 Workshop on Intelligent Manufacturing Systems, August, Montreal, Canada. 22–25 (1995)
3. Barber, F.: Reasoning on Interval and Point- Based Disjunctive Metric Constraints in Temporal Contexts. Journal of Artificial Intelligence Research 12, (2000) 35–86.
4. Beek, Peter Van.: The design and experimental analysis of algorithms for temporal reasoning. Journal of Artificial Intelligence Research 4, (1996) 1–18.
5. Beck, J.C., and Fox, M.S.: A generic framework for constraint-directed search and scheduling. Artificial Intelligence Magazine (1998) 101–129.
6. Caseau Y., and Laburthe, F.: Disjunctive Scheduling with Task Intervals. In Proceedings of the Eleventh International Conference on Logic Programming:MIT Press (1994).
7. Caseau Y., and Laburthe, F.: Improving Branch and Bound for Job-Shop Scheduling with Constraint Propagation. In Proceedings of the Eighth Franco-Japanesse Conference. Brest, France (1995).
8. Dechter, R.: Studies in the use and generation of heuristics. Ph.D. Thesis.UCLA. Los Angeles, CA. (1985).
9. Dechter, R., Meiri, I., and Pearl, J.: Temporal Constraint Networks Artificial Intelligence Journal 49 (1991) 61–95.

10. Dechter, R.: From local to global consistency Artificial Intelligence 55 (1992) 87–107.
11. Garey, M.R., and Johnson, D.S.: Computers and intractability: a guide to the theory of NP-completeness. New York: Freeman (1979).
12. Garrido, A., M. A. Salido, and Barber, F.: Scheduling in a planning environment. Proceedings of ECAI 2000 Workshop on New Results in planning, scheduling and design, Berlin: (2000) 36–43.
13. Mackworth, A.K., and Freuder, E.: The complexity of some polynomial network-consistency algorithms for constraint-satisfaction problems. Artificial Intelligence 25 (1985) 65–74.
14. Sadeh N.: Look-ahead techniques for micro-opportunistic job shop scheduling. PhD thesis, Dept. of Computer Science, CMU-CS-91-102, Carnegie Mellon University (1991).
15. Sadeh, N. M., and Fox, M. S.: Variable and Value Ordering Heuristics for the Job-Shop Scheduling. Constraint Satisfaction Problem. Artificial Intelligence Journal 86 1 (1996) 1–41.
16. Smith, S. F., and Cheng, C.: Slack-based heuristics for constraint satisfactions scheduling. Proceedings of the eleventh National Conference on Artificial Intelligence, Washington DC. (1993) 139–144.

Decentralized Autonomous FMS Control by Hypothetical Reasoning Including Discrete Simulator

Hidehiko Yamamoto[1] and Etsuo Marui[2]

Gifu University, Faculty of Engineering, Dept. of Mechanical and Systems Engineering, 1-1, Yanagido, Gifu-shi, 501-1193, JAPAN
[1] yam-h@cc.gifu-u.ac.jp
[2] marui@mech.gifu-u.ac.jp

Abstract. This paper describes the method to decide AGVs' action planning in decentralized autonomous FMS operations. The method is to use information from each agent and to foresee the future operation situations of FMS in advance by guessing a few steps of the next actions that AGV can take. The method is called RAF(Future Reasoning to Anticipate the Future). RAF consists of a hypothetical reasoning to consider the next actions that AGV can take as competitive hypotheses and a discrete simulator to foresee the future. Because of RAF, the pre-scheduling of AGV movements and input parts orders is useless. RAF was applied to decentralized autonomous FMSs and executed virtual productions.

1. Introduction

With the development of network technology and information communication technology, the basic technology of a new production system has been developed. One of the directions it can take is a decentralized autonomous Flexible Manufacturing System (FMS). The decentralized autonomous FMS aims at high production efficiency by giving self-control or decentralizing the plan, design and operation of FMS. This paper discusses the basic research necessary for realizing a decentralized autonomous FMS with Automatic Guided Vehicles (AGVs) and Machining Centers (MCs). AGVs automatically move on to MCs to load or unload parts. MCs are NC machine tools that have several kinds of tools and automatically change the tools to machine many parts.

In general, if it is possible to make plans by considering near future trends and information, it is considered wiser than acting blindly. As the AGV actions' decision, this idea is introduced. This research develops a real-time decision method for AGV actions based on the predictions that foresee not only current production situations but also anticipate future ones. Also, the developed decision method is applied to a decentralized autonomous FMS. Because of the results, it can be seen that multi-production that keeps the target production ratio is possible even though neither AGV actions' plans nor parts input schedules are given beforehand. Especially, it can be shown that the method will operate a FMS without influencing the production ratio even when unpredicted troubles happen, which is often seen in an actual factory.

There are few researches for a decentralized autonomous FMS [1][2]. They do not consider what will happen in FMS. This research's characteristic is to foresee the near future situations of FMS. In this point, the research is different from the ordinal researches.

L. Monostori, J. Váncza, and M. Ali (Eds.): IEA/AIE 2001, LNAI 2070, pp. 571-581, 2001.

2. Hypothetical Reasoning and Discrete Simulator

2.1 Decentralized Autonomous FMS and Its Control

The construction of a decentralized autonomous FMS that this paper deals with is shown as Fig. 1. It shows a Parts Warehouse that supplies parts for a factory, a Products Warehouse for finished parts from MCs, some AGVs that carry parts and some MCs are arranged. Each AGV carries one part. AGVs move on the dotted lines of the figure at a uniform velocity. MCs can work several kinds of parts and each of the parts has decided manufacturing processes and manufacturing time. Some MCs do the same kinds of work processes. The set of the same type MC is called a Group MC and is distinguished by describing subscripts, for example, ${}_gMC_1$, ${}_gMC_2$, ··· . Each MC in the same Group MC is distinguished by attaching a hyphen and figures after the name of Group MC, for example, $MC_{1\text{-}1}$, $MC_{1\text{-}2}$, ···.

Note that later sentences uses the term " parts ". The parts meaning is not limited to the same variety but includes different varieties.

The contents of information exchanges and cooperative actions between each agent in a decentralized autonomous FMS is basically the following. The Parts Warehouse sends the information on the names of parts that are in the Parts Warehouse. The AGV sends both the information on the name of the part that the AGV currently has and the information on its next destination. The MC sends both the information on the name of the part it is currently manufacturing and the information about the remaining manufacturing time. When necessary, an agent uses the received information to make the agent movement decisions.

One of FMS's characteristics is to realize efficient production by jointly sharing manufacturing operations among the MCs in a Group MC that has the same manufacturing processes. The parts delivers by AGVs are responsible for the sharing operation. Because the AGV moving distance and time and the waiting time in front of each MC bay are inexplicably linked with FMS operating efficiency. According to which parts the AGV will deliver to which MC and which part the AGV will take, the FMS operating efficiency can change much.

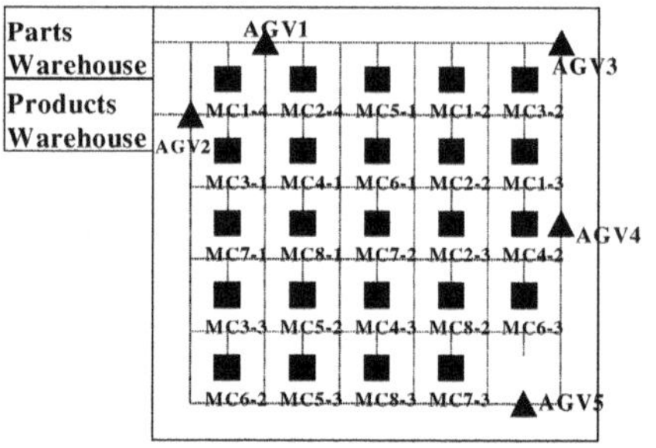

Fig. 1. FMS model

With the predetermined scheduling for AGVs' movement, which is the ordinary method, it is difficult to deal with unpredicted troubles such as manufacturing delay and machine breakdown. If the ordinary method is used, once this kind of unpredicted trouble occurs, re-consideration of the production schedule must be necessary. Moreover, in a FMS that uses many AGVs and MCs, it is difficult to make a predetermined schedule for efficient AGV movement order and parts delivering order.

In order to solve the problems, this research adopts the following process procedure: ① use each agent information, ② foresee several future steps of probable

AGV actions, ③ foresee probable FMS operating situations. ***R****easoning to* ***A****nticipate* ***F****uture* (**RAF**) to control the AGV's next actions based on the prediction results of ③ is proposed and solves the above mentioned problems. RAF resembles a chess strategy that moves a piece after anticipating the several alternatives for one move. The controls by RAF are both where the AGV moves next and which part it carries next. In this way, predetermined parts delivering schedule is not needed.

The probable action (**Next Action**) that an AGV will take next is not decided as a single action but as many actions because there are some MCs that are doing the same manufacturing process jointly. Hypothetically, if an AGV chooses one of the above actions, in an actual FMS, each agent in the FMS keeps doing its chosen operation. When an AGV needs the choice of Next Action again, it chooses a single Next Action from among the possible choices again. In this way, the operating situation of a FMS is expressed as the choice process of unending cycle of AGV Next Actions. That is, it is expressed as a tree construction which includes nodes corresponding to possible AGVs Next Actions. The tree construction can be extended infinitely. The strategy of RAF considers the possible Next Actions that the AGV will be able to take locally a few steps ahead as a foreseeable range, as well as globally foreseeing phenomena happening in the FMS in a near future and, then going back to the present, decides which choice should be chosen at present. In order to do RAF, by the hypothetical reasoning which considers the choices that the AGV will be able to take as competitive hypotheses and the discrete simulator, the reasoning process is controlled.

2.2 Competitive Hypotheses and Discrete Simulator

Hypothetical reasoning regards events that can happen simultaneously as competitive hypotheses, classifies each hypothesis among them into a true hypothesis and the rest false hypotheses, then hypothetically continues to reason with the true hypothesis and follows the true hypothesis till a contradiction occurs [3][4].

Based on hypothetical reasoning, RAF tentatively decides AGV Next Actions a few steps ahead locally and foresees FMS operating situations globally. In this situation, what are established as competitive hypotheses strongly depends upon RAF executions. This research establishes competitive hypotheses in the following way.

Considering the Next Action that an AGV will be able to take from a standpoint of the AGV, two kinds of actions are possible, ① where it will move next, ② which part it will take next. This classification is reflected in the two kinds of competitive : competitive hypotheses for moving places (**C-hypotheses-move**) and competitive hypotheses for parts (**C-hypotheses-parts**). C-hypotheses-move may be analyzed into three types : (1) move to MC bay to exchange parts, (2) move to the Parts Warehouse to input new parts , (3) move to the Products Warehouse to deposit parts when all manufacturing processes are finished. As the elements of C-hypotheses-move, each MC ($MC_{1\text{-}1}$, $MC_{1\text{-}2}$,···), the Parts Warehouse and the Products Warehouse are established. As the elements of C-hypotheses-parts, each part (P_1,P_2,P_3,···) is established.

Now, the functions of RAF will be described. When an actual FMS is operating, RAF beforehand foresees near future FMS operating situations. This means the thinking process called RAF begins just before an AGV in the actual world has to choose its Next Action. When RAF begins, the first step is to search all possible next actions that the AGV could take. The actions are called **Next Action Set** . The next step is to choose a single Next Action from among Next Action Set. The third step is to simulate with all agents what would happen if the Next Action is chosen as the AGV's next action till a certain AGV needs to choose a Next Action. This discrete simulation is called **Simulation in Hypotheses (SiH)**. In carrying out SiH, the situation comes that an optional AGV in the simulation searches Next Action Set. At this time, the Next Action Set is re-searched, one Next Action is chosen from among the Next Action Set and SiH is carried out again. By the results of the SiH that is followed by the choice of a Next Action, FMS future operating situations can be seen again. That is, RAF can be shown as tree construction where the three layers repeatedly lie one upon another : ① the action choice that an AGV in the actual world took last, ② the Next Action Set of the AGV in the actual world, ③ Next Action Set of an AGV in SiH, as shown in Fig. 2.

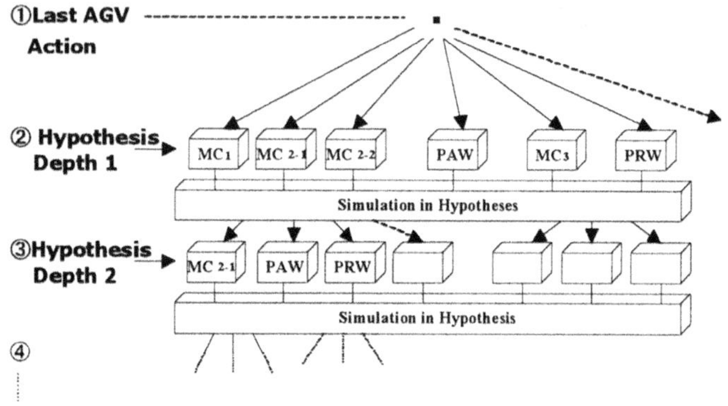

Fig. 2. RAF tree construction

In Fig. 2, the layer corresponding to one depth from the root of the tree construction is called one step hypotheses depth (D_{hy}=1), the node set belonging to hypotheses depth is called foreseeing actions one step ahead (Foresee[1]). Foreseeing actions located below each node of the foreseeing actions of one step ahead corresponds to hypotheses depth 2 (D_{hy}=2) and are called as foreseeing action of two step ahead (Foresee[2]). In the same way, foreseeing actions corresponding to hypotheses depth are expressed as three step ahead, four step ahead, ··· . Then, RAF considers foreseeable actions an optional n step ahead, Foresee[n], as a foreseeable range, regards foreseeable actions in each layer as competitive hypotheses and carries out the reasoning control by regarding one optional foreseeable action among each layer of competitive hypotheses as a true hypothesis and the remaining foreseeable actions as false hypotheses. By judging FMS operating situations n steps ahead, the actual AGV Next Action is decided.

The algorithm to carry out RAF is described as below. First, the terms used in the algorithm are defined.

[Definition] Standard to Judge True and False: Standard to judge the contradictions in hypothetical reasoning with the results of FMS total operating efficiency gained by the executions of SiH. The standard has ***s*** kinds of standards' range. If the standard is not satisfied, it is judged that a contradiction occurs. Some concrete examples are :

- ***if*** FMS total operating efficiency is over ***e***(1)%, it is true,; ***if*** under, false.
- ***if*** FMS total operating efficiency is over ***e***(2)%, it is true,; ***if*** under, false.
- ***if*** FMS total operating efficiency is over ***e***(3)%, it is true,; ***if*** under, false.

...

- ***if*** FMS total operating efficiency is over ***e***(***s***)%, it is true,; ***if*** under, false.

as $e(1) > e(2) > e(3) > \cdots > e(s)$

[Definition] Group MC Selection Priority Value, *Fm*: The values indicates the aim how long each Group MC will operate and is expressed as Equation (1).

$$Fm(gMc.N) = \sum_{Pn=1}^{Pn=Pn'} gMc.process.time(Pn) \times \left\{ \frac{production.rate(Pn)}{100} - \left(\frac{finished.parts.N(Pn) + \frac{inprocess.parts.N(Pn)}{2}}{all.finished.parts.N + \frac{all.inprocess.parts.N}{2}} \right) \right\} \quad (1)$$

gMc: name of Group MC, (*Pn*:parts variety *Pn*=1~*Pn*)
gMc.process.time(*Pn*): time that Group MC needs to manufacture parts *Pn*
production.rate(*Pn*): target production ratio (%) of parts *Pn*
finished.parts.N(*Pn*): number of parts *Pn* when all processes are finished (number of parts *Pn* in Products Warehouse)
inprocess.parts.N(*Pn*): number of parts *Pn* that are in process or in being transferred (number of parts *Pn* that AGV or MC has)
all.finished.parts.N: number of all parts where all processes are finished (number of all parts in Product Warehouse)
all.inprocess.parts.N: number of all parts that are in process or being transferred (number of all parts that AGV or MC has)

The Group MC that has the large Priority Value is considered to have many jobs left and the priority ranking that is selected as a true hypothesis is given a high ranking .

[Definition] Parts Warehouse Selection Priority Value, *Fp*: The value indicates how many parts are in process or in being transferred and is expressed as Equation (2). This value becomes the priority ranking for competitive hypotheses. The value is an integer after being rounded off.

$$Fp = \left(1 - \frac{\max.parts.N - all.inprocess.parts.N}{\max.parts.N} \right) \times destinatio\,n.N \quad (2)$$

max.parts.N : possible maximum parts input number (sum of AGVs and MCs)
destination.N : number of parts destinations (sum of AGVs, MCs, Parts Warehouse, and Products Warehouse)

[Definition] Products Warehouse Selection Priority Value, F_f: The value indicates the parts condition of the Products Warehouse and is expressed as Equation (3). The value corresponds to the priority ranking in competitive hypotheses.

$$Ff = destination.N - Fp \quad (3)$$

$$V(Pn) = all.process.time(Pn) \times \left\{ \frac{production.rate(Pn)}{100} - \left(\frac{finished.parts.N(Pn) + \frac{inprocess.parts.N(Pn)}{2}}{all.finished.parts.N + \frac{all.inprocess.parts.N}{2}} \right) \right\} \quad (4)$$

all.process.time(*Pn*); total manufacturing time for parts *Pn*

[Definition] Parts Selection Priority Value, *V(Pn)*: The value indicates how many parts are still waiting to be input into the production line and is expressed as Equation (4). The part that has a large Priority Value has a high rank order of priority that is taken from the Parts Warehouse by AGVs and is input into the production line.

[Definition] Job Variance Value, F_d(MC.N): In the case of a Group MC that has the same type MC, it is necessary to keep the job equality among MCs, that is, each MC should be doing an equal amount of work. In order to do this, the Job Variance Value F_d(MC.N) expressed with Equation (5) is adopted. The equation is based on MC operating efficiency. The MC whose operating efficiency is low becomes a large Job Variance Value and this MC is likely to be chosen for work.

$$Fd(Mc.N) = \frac{100}{Mc.efficiency} \quad (5),$$ *Mc.efficiency* ; operating efficiency of Mc.N (%)

[Algorithm of RAF]

Step1: Establish hypotheses depth D_{hy}=1 and the Standard to Judge True and False ***s*** =1.

Step2: Search all Next Actions (Foresee[D_{hy}]) that can be foreseen and classify them into competitive hypotheses elements of C-hypotheses-move and C-hypotheses-parts, as shown in Equations (6) and (7). The elements are established so that the left side element in the parentheses has a high priority. At this stage, the ranking is tentative.

C-hypotheses-move = {PartsWarehouse, ProductsWarehouse, $MC_{1\text{-}1}$, $MC_{2\text{-}1}$··· } (6)
C-hypotheses-parts = {P_1, P_2, P_3···· } (7)

Step3: Confirm the current position of an AGV that needs to decide its next action and carry out the following rule.

If { the AGV location is in the Parts Warehouse and the AGV does not have parts}
Then{Go to Step5}, ***Else***{Go to Step4}

Step4: Carry out Hypothetical Reasoning for Moving Decisions from Step4-1~Step4-9.

Step4-1: Replace MC, the element among competitive hypotheses C-hypotheses-move, with Group MC that the MC belongs to, as shown in Equation (8). At this time, repeated Group MCs are integrated into one Group MC. The resulting Group MC is called a **Competitive Group MC**.

$$\text{C-hypotheses-move} = \{\text{PartsWarehouse}\square\text{ProductsWarehouse}\ {}_gMC_1,\ {}_gMC_2,\ {}_gMC_3\cdots\} \quad (8)$$

Step4-2: Find Group MC Selection Priority Value *Fm* for each Competitive Group MC among competitive hypotheses C-hypotheses-move and renew the elements' row of competitive hypotheses C-hypotheses-move by changing the Group MC row with the highest Group MC Selection Priority Value *Fm* first.

Step4-3: Find Parts Warehouse Selection Priority Value, *Fp* and Products Warehouse Selection Priority, F_f and renew the elements' row of competitive hypotheses C-hypotheses-move by inserting Parts Warehouse and Products Warehouse in the priority ranking positions among competitive hypotheses C-hypotheses-move, whose positions correspond to acquired Parts Warehouse Selection Priority Value, *Fp* and Products Warehouse Selection Priority, F_f .

Step4-4: Randomly Select an optional competitive Group MC, ${}_gMC_\alpha$ from among competitive hypotheses C-hypotheses-move.

Step4-4-1: Search all MCs belonging to ${}_gMC_\alpha$, call it $MC_{\alpha\text{-}\beta}$ and find their MC's Job Variance Values, $F_d(MC_{\alpha\text{-}\beta})$.

Step4-4-2: Compare each value of Job Variance Values, $F_d(MC_{\alpha\text{-}\beta})$ and make a list called MC_α-List such that MCs form a queue according to the Job Variance Value with the highest value first, like Equation (9).

$$MC_\alpha\text{-List} = \{MC_{\alpha\text{-}1}, MC_{\alpha\text{-}2}, MC_{\alpha\text{-}3}\cdots\} \quad (9)$$
$$\text{as } F_d(MC_{\alpha\text{-}1})\ \ F_d(MC_{\alpha\text{-}2}) \geq F_d(MC_{\alpha\text{-}3}) \geq\cdots$$

Step4-4-3: Renew the elements of competitive hypotheses by replacing ${}_gMC_\square$ with MC_α-List.

Step4-4-4: Renew the elements of competitive hypotheses C-hypotheses-move by giving the remaining competitive Group MC the repeated processes from *Step4-4-1* to *Step4-4-3* .

Step4-5: Select the action whose priority ranking is No.1 from among the elements of competitive hypotheses C-hypotheses-move, corresponding to the left end element, establish it as a true hypothesis and establish the remaining elements as false hypotheses.

Step4-6: By using a true hypothesis, carry out SiH till an AGV must make its Next Action choice and calculate FMS total operating efficiency ***E*** at the time when SiH stops.

Step4-7: Perform the following rule.

If{ e(s)≤*E* }, **Then**{ Go to Step6}

Else{ Admit that a contradiction has occurred and go to Step4-8}

Step4-8: Perform the following rule.

If { An element that has not been chosen as a true hypothesis among the competitive hypotheses C-hypotheses-move still exists }

Then { Replace a true hypothesis with a false hypothesis, select the next priority ranking element among competitive hypotheses C-hypotheses-move as a true hypothesis and return to step4-6 }, **Else** {Go to Step4-9}

Step4-9: Perform the following rule.

If { Hypothesis depth D_{hy}=1} **Then** { Establish s$\leftarrow\geq$s+1 and return to Step2}

Else{ Backtrack after establishing $D_{hy} \leftarrow D_{hy}-1$ and select the next priority ranking hypothesis element among competitive hypotheses of the layer D_{hy} as a true hypothesis.

If the selected hypothesis belongs to C-hypotheses-move, return to Step4-6. If not, go to Step5.}

Step 5: Carry out Hypothetical Reasoning for Parts Decisions from Step5-1 to Step5-6.

Step5-1: Calculate Parts Selection Priority Value *V(Pn)* for ***n*** kinds of parts *Pn* among competitive hypotheses C-hypotheses-parts and renew the elements in competitive hypotheses C-hypotheses-parts by changing the parts row with a large Parts Selection Priority Value *V(Pn)* .

Step5-2: Select the part whose priority ranking is No.1 from among the elements of competitive hypotheses C-hypotheses-parts, corresponding to the left end element, establish it as a true hypothesis and establish the remaining elements as false hypotheses.

Step5-3: By using that true hypothesis, carry out Simulation in Hypotheses till the AGV is forced to make its Next Action choice and calculate FMS total operating efficiency ***E*** at the time when Simulation in Hypotheses stops.

Step5-4: Perform the following rule.

If { $e(s) \leq E$ }, **Then**{ Go to Step6}

Else { Admit that a contradiction occurs and go to Step5-5}

Step5-5: Perform the following rule.

If { An element that has not been chosen as a true hypothesis among competitive hypotheses C-hypotheses-parts still exists }

Then { Replace a true hypothesis with a false hypothesis, select the next priority ranking element among competitive hypotheses C-hypotheses-parts as a true hypothesis and return to step5-3 }, **Else** {Go to Step5-6}

Step5-6: Perform the following rule.

If { Hypothesis depth D_{hy}=1}, **Then** { Establish s$\leftarrow$s+1 and return to Step2}

Else{ Carry out backtracking after establishing $D_{hy} \leftarrow D_{hy}-1$ and select the next priority ranking hypothesis element among competitive hypotheses of the layer D_{hy} as a true hypothesis. If the selected hypothesis belongs to C-hypotheses-move, return to *Step4-6*. If not, go to Step5.}

Step6: Perform the following rule.

If { $D_{hy} < n$}, **Then** { Establish s$\leftarrow$s+1 and return to Step2}, **Else** {Go to Step7}

Step7: Select a true hypothesis in hypotheses depth D_{hy}=1 as the next action of an actual FMS and execute the actual FMS. □

3. Application Examples

The RAF by a hypothetical reasoning and a discrete simulator, proposed in **Chapter** 2, is applied to the operations of a decentralized autonomous FMS. As there is no actual FMS production system, nine kinds of decentralized autonomous FMSs are constructed in a computer and some numerical experiments are carried out. The nine FMSs are the production systems whose number of parts subject to manufacturing, MCs, Group MCs and AGVs are different. That is, **<Type 1>** parts number 3, Group MC number 3, MC number for each Group MC 1 and AGV number 3, **<Type 2>** parts number 3, Group MC number 3, MC number for each Group MC 1,2,1 and AGV number 3, **<Type 3>** parts number 3, Group MC number 3, MC number for each Group MC 2 and AGV number 3, **<Type 4>** parts number 6, Group MC number 6, MC number for each Group MC 1 and AGV number 5, **<Type 5>** parts number 6, Group MC number 6, MC number for each Group MC 2 and AGV number 5, **<Type 6>** parts number 6, Group MC number 6, MC number for each Group MC 3 and AGV number 5, **<Type 7>** parts number 9, Group MC number 8, MC number for each Group MC 1 and AGV number 5, **<Type 8>** parts number 9, Group MC number 8, MC number for each Group MC 2 and AGV number 5 and **<Type 9>** parts number 9, Group MC number 8, MC number for each Group MC 3 and AGV number 5. The factory layout of Type9 is shown in ***Fig.1***. Other Types' layouts are the ones that MCs disappear according to MCs number. The manufacturing time for each part is different. For example, in a case where Type 1, the manufacturing time of parts P_1,P_2 and P_3 are established as ***Table 1***. The target production ratios for each of the parts are also different as follows. They are : P_1:P_2:P_3 =5:6:2 from Type 1 to Type 3 ; P_1:P_2:P_3:P_4:P_5:P_6 =5:6:3:3:2:1from Type 4 to Type 6 ; P_1:P_2:P_3:P_4:P_5:P_6:P_7:P_8:P_9 = 5:6:3:3:2:1:4:5:2 from Type 7 to Type 9.

Allowing for unpredicted troubles that happen where an actual FMS operating, the numerical experiments adopt four operating conditions: **<Condition 1>** there are not any unpredicted troubles : **<Condition 2>** each AGV randomly breakdowns three times a day (24 hours) and is break-down time is five minutes :**<Condition 3>** parts manufacturing time at each MC is randomly extended 10 % : **<Condition 4>** both unpredicted troubles of Condition 2 and Condition 3 happen. In Condition 2, Condition 3 and Condition 4, ten kinds of happening time for manufacturing time extensions and breakdowns are established as unpredicted troubles' random conditions by adopting ten random series. As a result, Type 1 executed one numerical experiment under Condition 1 and executed ten numerical experiments under each other Condition. A numerical experiment time 24 hours is adopted and n of foreseeable actions range (Foresee[n]) in hypothetical reasoning is established as 3.

Table 1. Examples of machining time

Parts	P1	P2	P3
Machining Time (seconds)	gMC1 180	gMC2 120	gMC3 180
	gMC2 120	gMC1 60	gMC2 150
	gMC3 120		

One result of the numerical experiments is shown in Table 2. Table 2 indicates the production outputs for each of the four Conditions in Type 5. As a comparison, the numerical experiment of the case that n of foreseeable actions range (Foresee[n]) is 1 was carried out. Judging from the result, the outputs of the case n=3 were bigger than that of the case n=1 under every Condition. In other Types, the same results were obtained. Fig.3 shows the output ratio for each of the parts of Type 5. All four Conditions could get the ratio very close to the target production ratio, $P_1{:}P_2{:}P_3{:}P_4{:}P_5{:}P_6=5{:}6{:}3{:}3{:}2{:}1$ even though a conventional prior parts input scheduling system was not used. In other Types, the same results were also obtained. For example, the production ratio of Condition 4 in Type 9 is 5.049: 6.028:3.049:3.049:2.042:1.000: 4.049:5.092:2.049 and its target ratio is $P_1{:}P_2{:}P_3{:}P_4{:}P_5{:}P_6{:}\ P_7{:}P_8{:}P_9 = 5{:}6{:}3{:}3{:}2{:}1{:}\ 4{:}5{:}2$.

In consequence, it was ascertained that the decentralized autonomous FMS using RAF can keep a target production ratio even if unpredicted troubles happen.

4. Conclusions

This research dealt with the method to control an AGV action plan to operate a decentralized autonomous FMS and developed RAF to anticipate the FMS operating situations happening in the near future by using information from each agent and forecasting several steps ahead of AGV's practicable next actions. RAF consists of a hypothetical reasoning that regards practicable AGV next actions as competitive hypotheses and a discrete simulator that simulates the future alternative possibilities. Because of the reasoning, AGV next moving destinations and which part is transferred next are decided and both a prior AGV moving plan and a prior parts input schedule are unnecessary. The numerical experiments were executed by applying the developed RAF for a decentralized autonomous FMS that exists on a computer. As a result, it was ascertained that the FMS can have the product ratio very close to the target production ratio even when a prior parts input schedule is not used. Compared with the result of the case that looked just one step ahead as a foreseeable action range, it was also ascertained that the developed reasoning method to foresee several steps ahead could get the better outputs.

Table 2. Simulation results

A \ B	Condition1	Condition2	Condition3	Condition4
1		573 (550)	562 (551)	566 (538)
2		572 (550)	556 (552)	543 (545)
3		576 (558)	556 (550)	564 (537)
4		574 (560)	554 (546)	560 (552)
5		580 (557)	560 (547)	558 (543)
6		575 (555)	568 (545)	568 (544)
7		576 (550)	561 (555)	559 (546)
8		574 (558)	565 (550)	556 (556)
9		565 (553)	566 (545)	559 (546)
10		573 (558)	563 (555)	553 (541)
Average	578 (559)	573.8 (554.9)	561.1 (549.6)	558.6 (544.8)

A: Random Numbers B: Conditions

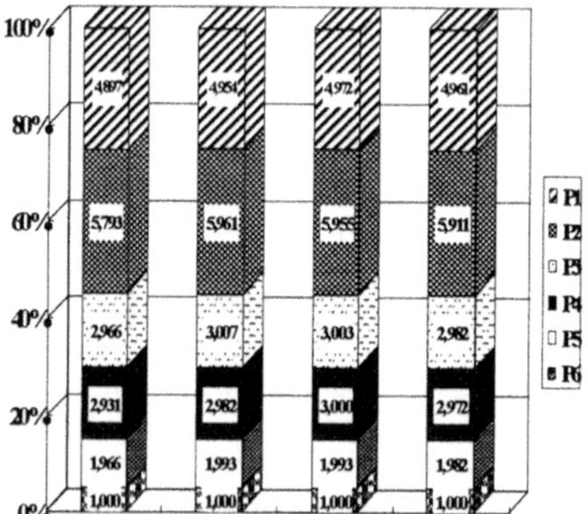

Fig. 3. Production ratio of Type 5

The research started as a basic research to decide the AGV actions plan of a decentralized autonomous FMS with the idea to look several steps ahead. Although there are still some problems left, such as how many steps to foresee is optimal and how closer to the target production ratio is achieved, it was ascertained that the idea to foresee the future in order to control the productions of a decentralized autonomous FMS is one of the available methods.

References

1. Duffie, N.A. and Kaltjob, P.O., Dynamics of real-time distributed scheduling in multiple-machine heterarchical manufacturing systems, CIRP Annals, Vol.47,No.1, (1998)pp. 415.
2. Ueda, K. et al., Reinforcement learning approaches to biological manufacturing systems, CIRP Annals, Vol. 49, No.1,(2000),pp. 343.
3. Doyle J., A Truth Maintenance System, Artificial Intelligence, (1979).
4. Reiter,R. and de Kleer, J., Foundations of Assumption-based Truth Maintenance System, Proc. of AAA1-87, (1987)pp.183,.

Distributed Learning and Control for Manufacturing Systems Scheduling

Joonki Hong and Vittal Prabhu

Department of Industrial and Manufacturing Engineering, The Pennsylvania State University, University Park, PA 16802, USA
{jxh183@psu.edu, prabhu@engr.psu.edu}

Abstract. A new distributed learning and control (DLC) approach is presented in this paper which integrates part-driven distributed arrival time control (DATC) and machine-driven distributed reinforcement learning control. This approach is suitable for just-in-time (JIT) production for multi-objective scheduling problem in dynamically changing shop floor environment. While part controllers are adjusting their associated parts' arrival time to minimize due-date deviation, machine controllers equipped with learning components are searching for optimal dispatching policies. The machines' control problem is modeled as Semi Markov Decision Process (SMDP) and solved using one-step Q-learning. The DLC algorithms are evaluated for minimizing the sum of due-date deviation cost and setup cost using simulation. Results show that DLC algorithms achieve significant performance improvement over usual dispatching rules in complex real-time shop floor control problems for JIT production.

1 Introduction

During the last two decades, JIT scheduling has drawn increasing attention from scheduling community [1]. Most of these works belong to traditional static scheduling methods such as mathematical programming, branch and bound, and heuristics. However, today's manufacturing systems are subject to great deal of uncertainties such as machine breakdowns, unexpected arrivals of hot jobs, and so on. Under this dynamic environment, static shop floor control based on traditional optimization based scheduling methods cannot keep up with the up-to-date shop floor status and thus often become ineffective. There is a need to develop adaptive scheduling methods that are not only suitable for JIT-oriented production environment but also adaptive to dynamically changing shop floor conditions.

2 Reinforcement Learning

Reinforcement Learning (RL) is a model of an agent that learns behavior through trial-and-error interactions with a dynamic environment [2]. RL has its mathematical

L. Monostori, J. Váncza, and M. Ali (Eds.): IEA/AIE 2001, LNAI 2070, pp. 582-591, 2001.

foundation on dynamic programming and closely related to optimal control theory. Recently, RL has drawn increasing attention from manufacturing community. Yih and Thesen [3] formulated a real-time scheduling problem with SMDP and used Q-learning to maximize throughput. One key feature of their approach is that they explicitly reduced the large search space by observing and analyzing the decisions made by an experienced scheduler. Mahadevan et al. [4] modeled switching policy and machine repair policy by SMDP and solved using R-learning. They assumed key parameters required for modeling with probability distributions. McDonnell [5] used game theory and reinforcement learning to solve setup decision problems for distributed manufacturing system. He modeled machines' setup decisions as Normal Form game and solved it using both a heuristic approach and a reinforcement learning based approach. Also, utilizing the concept of RL, several researchers proposed dynamic rule selection approach [6, 7].

There are several differences between the previous research and this paper. First, most of previous research assumes some form of probability distributions for service times and arrival times and usually deals with long term performance of the system. In contrast, in our case no assumption is made in service times and arrival times and short term performance is the objective. With one exception McDonnell [5] no approach minimizes due-date deviation. Finally, none of the previous approaches explicitly controls the arrival time of parts at the shop. Instead they adjust dispatching decisions to improve a certain performance measure. In other words, parts are treated as passive resources that machines process. In this respect, these approaches can be considered as 'machine-driven scheduling'. The approach taken this work is integration of 'part-driven scheduling' and 'machine-driven scheduling' where parts and machines are autonomous control entities actively participating in the scheduling. A key distinction of our approach is a significantly higher level of distribution in control and intelligence throughout the manufacturing shop floor.

2.1 DATC: A Part-Driven Scheduling Algorithm

Distributed Arrival Time Control (DATC) is a closed-loop distributed control algorithm for manufacturing shop floor in which each part controller uses only its local information to minimize deviation from its part's due-date. The objective of DATC is minimizing Mean Squared Deviation (MSD), which is defined as

$$\mathrm{MSD} = \sqrt{\sum_{i=1}^{n} (d_i - c_i)^2 / n}\,, \tag{1}$$

where d_i is the due-date and c_i the completion time of Part i and n is the total number of parts.

Figure 1 shows the closed-loop control structure of DATC. Deterministic simulations that run orders of magnitude faster can be used to provide completion times feedback [8]. These simulations can be run continuously and concurrently with the real system. The best schedule found during this process is used for releasing parts into the real shop floor. The system frequently reevaluates the best schedule to ensure that the schedule remains effective. The resultant system is a highly decentralized and can handle unexpected disturbances such as rush orders, machine failures, tool breakage in real-time with minimal global information.

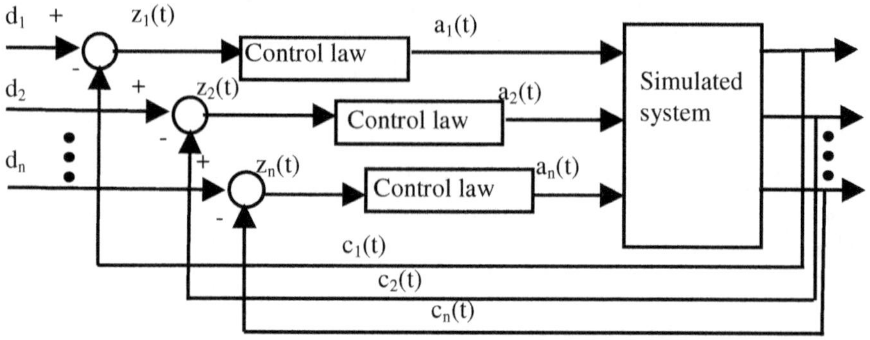

Fig. 1. DATC algorithm forms multivariable control structure and changes a discrete event scheduling problem to continuous variable dynamical problem

DATC consists of autonomous part controllers that use only local feedback information to meet its own due-date. If there are n-parts, the resulting system will be an n-dimensional multivariable control system where due-date, completion time, due-date deviation, and arrival times are n-dimensional vectors which act as the command, output, error and manipulated vectors respectively. In Prabhu and Duffie [8] the following integral control law has been used:

$$a_j(t) = k_j \int_0^t (d_j - c_j(\tau))d\tau + a_j(0), \tag{2}$$

where k_j is the controller gain for the jth part in the system and $a_j(0)$ is an arbitrary initial condition, d_j is the due-date, $c_j(t)$ is the predicted completion time and $z_j(t) = d_j - c_j(t)$ is the due-date deviation.

When due-dates of the parts cannot be met simultaneously, all arrival times of the coupled parts converge to an equal value in a region called the discontinuity region. As a result, the processing sequence of the parts could change at every iteration while their arrival times remain in the infinitesimal neighborhood of the discontinuity region. This causes the completion times to oscillate between possible processing sequences. Due to this discontinuous dynamics, an implicit search is performed without direct cooperation among part controllers. This system is considered to have reached steady-state when z(t) of every part is balanced such that no significant change of arrival time occurs.

It has been shown that a unique steady-state exists in single machine case and the steady-state arrival time can be predicted exactly using discontinuous differential equation theory [8]. For more general cases such as flow shop, sequence dependent setup, and parallel machines case, the steady-state arrival time is not necessarily unique and a method has been developed that can approximate the steady-state arrival time closely in most cases [9]. The performance of DATC in several manufacturing systems has been investigated and the results show considerable performance improvement over usual dispatching rules. These results demonstrate the stability, predictability, and effectiveness of DATC for a broad class of manufacturing systems.

3 Distributed Learning and Control

DATC uses deterministic simulation for providing feedback to part controllers. During these simulations, considerable amount of information is generated such as waiting time of the parts in the queue, machine utilization, and flow time. This information can be useful for machine controllers to improve their dispatching policy.

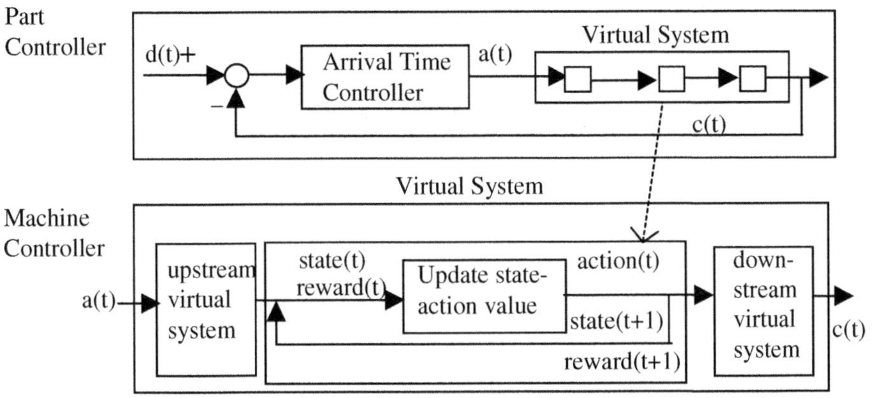

Fig. 2. This diagram shows the structure of DLC. Here, DATC is controlling the part arrival times while machine controllers are learning to improve their own objectives

For this work, DLC is applied to a family setup flow shop manufacturing system. There is a setup cost when part family is changed from one to another. Each part has its associated due-date. The objective is to minimize the sum of mean squared due-date deviation (MSD) and setup cost.

Scheduling with sequence dependent setup began in the late 1980's. However, so far only one approach deals with family setup problems with early tardy penalty [10]. The problem is different from ours in that they allow varying processing time within the family and the method works only for the common due-date single machine sequence independent setup problems.

3.1 Reinforcement Learning Formulation

SMDP generalizes MDP by allowing, or requiring, the decision maker to choose actions whenever the system state changes, modeling the system evolution in continuous time, and allowing the time spent in a particular state to follow an arbitrary probability distribution. SMDP is combination of two processes: a natural process and a SMDP. In DLC, natural process corresponds to the part arrivals and SMDP corresponds to the machine's decision-making process. The states, actions, and reward used for this SMDP are defined as follows:

States

Number of parts in the queue can be an ideal candidate for state. Also, since setup is sequence dependent, the previous part family processed is added to the state representation. Finally, to differentiate identical queue patterns which occurs when idle times occur within the scheduling horizon, the number of parts processed from the beginning of the horizon up until a decision epoch is included. Thus a state vector is {number of parts processed so far, number of part family1 in the queue, number of part family 2 in the queue, ..., number of part family f in the queue, previous part family} where f is the number of different part families.

Actions

It is assumed that if only one part is available when machine is idle, the machine will process it. Thus, up to f actions are available corresponding to selecting one among f families of parts waiting in the machine's queue.

Reward

The reward is the sum of squared waiting time of parts in the queues. This reward is to encourage fair service and reduce overall waiting time. If setup time is chosen as the reward, it only can make the machine agent prefer minimal setup, potentially causing unfair service to some part families and decreasing global performance.

3.2 Q-Learning for SMDP

Q-learning [11] with tabular method is chosen to solve SMDP. Q-learning is guaranteed to asymptotically converge to the optimal discounted policy for a finite MDP. Q-learning also converges for undiscounted cases when zero reward is received at the absorbing state s_a which is reachable under all policies, and the state-action value $Q_t(s_a,act) = 0$ for all actions and time t. The optimality is only valid when all Q-values are stored and updated in a table.

Q-learning uses the following updating rule:

$$Q(s_t, act_t) \leftarrow Q(s_t, act_t) + \alpha[rw_{t+1} + \min_{act} Q(s_{t+1}, act) - Q(s_t, act_t)]\,. \quad (3)$$

The learning agent learns to estimate the reward rate from the natural process. Combined with the immediate reward, this provides the value estimate for each state-action pair. Q-learning has been shown to find an optimal policy long before the Q-values converge. This characteristic can be effective on real-time adaptive scheduling for dynamic environment.

In DLC, the system will always reach the absorbing state when there are no more parts to process. Also, zero reward is received at the absorbing state, and $Qt(s_a, act) = 0$ for all actions and time t. The only requirement for optimality is that the starting states are stochastically chosen so that all possible states can be visited infinitely often. DATC does not exclude any possible sequences from starting state and thus theoretically the optimality condition is not violated. In practice the search space has to be restricted in order to achieve real-time learning. If the state space becomes large, then filling the entire table of Q-values takes long time, making real-time implementation infeasible. However, the number of actual trajectories the machine controller goes through are quite limited and more importantly the trajectories are partly constrained by DATC. Thus they already possess good due-date deviation performance, which is a major component of our objective function. This is similar to the idea of on-line RL [2] where the agent puts more effort into learning to make good decisions for frequently encountered states at the expense of less effort for infrequently encountered states.

In Equation (3), to track non-stationary environment, a fixed step size, α, is be used. In this case, Q-values never completely converge but continue to vary in response to the most recently received rewards. This is actually desirable in a non-stationary environment. Also, to encourage exploration of unvisited states, ε-greedy policy is used. This ε-greedy policy is a simple way of encouraging exploration for non-stationary problems [2].

3.3 Dynamics of DLC System

An example, a single machine 6-parts 2-family case, is used to explain the dynamics of DLC. Configuration for the example is shown in Table 1.

Table 1. Example problem configuration

Part Family	parts/part family	Processing Time (p(i))	Setup Time (s(i,j))	(Part ID, Due-date)
1	3	20	50	(1,1110), (2, 1020), (3, 1045)
2	3	30	50	(4,1090), (5, 1025), (6, 1035)

Figure 3 shows the arrival time trajectories of DLC. Figure 4 shows the learning curves of Q-values of the state-action pair (4,2,1,1,1) and (4,2,1,1,2). The graph shows after about 1100 iteration the Q-value of (4,2,1,1,1) converges to the correct value while that of (4,2,1,1,2) still increases. The state transition diagram under the steady-state arrival time pattern is shown in Figure 5. Because not all parts arrived at the first decision epoch, there are several transitions when new part arrivals occurred because of the natural process (DATC) not by the chosen action. These transitions are denoted by dotted arrows and corresponding part arrivals are shown ('f1' denotes a part which belongs Family 1 arrives in between two decision epochs). The nodes denoted by solid circles are where transition occurs stochastically because of the natural process. Thus the learning agent has to estimate this transition probability as well as the reward accumulated during the transitions with Q-learning. It has been found that the machine agent successfully learned an optimal policy in this case. The optimal paths found are denoted by thick arrows in Figure 5.

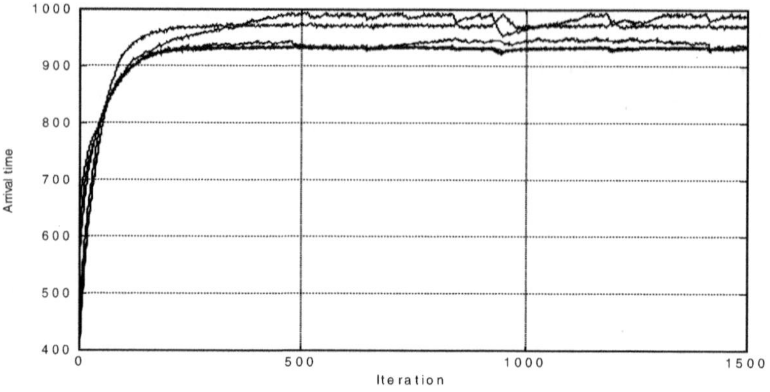

Fig. 3. The graph shows the arrival time trajectories generated from applying DLC algorithm to the example problem. After about 300 iteration the system reaches a steady-state

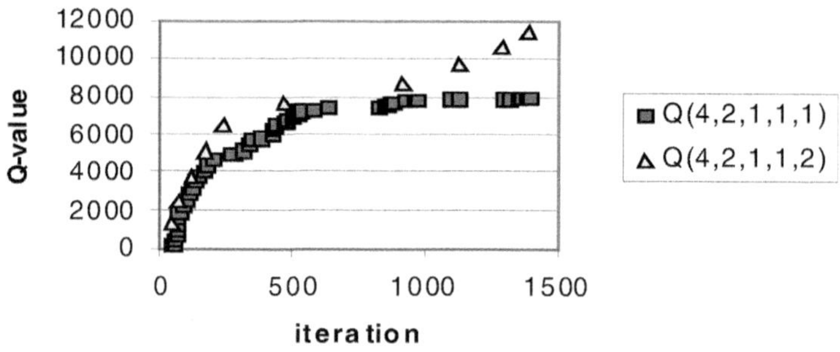

Fig. 4. The learning curve of two Q-values for the example problem. With ε-greedy policy, the agent occasionally chooses action with less reward

4 Performance Evaluation

There is no known solution procedure for minimizing MSD, or the sum of MSD and setup cost in distinct due-dates sequence dependent setup problems. Here, the result of DLC is compared with two common dispatching rules, earliest due-date (EDD) and minimum slack time (MST) rules, as well as with DATC. A problem set that has significant setup times with different tightness of due-dates and different setup matrix was tested. Two different number of part families (2, 3) and two different number of parts in a family (20, 30) are used. Step size (α) of 0.1and exploration factor (ε) of 0.1

are used for all tests. For testing the effect of increasing tightness of the due-dates, ten different due-date distributions are used. Each test consists of 10 replications. Figure 6 shows the performance test results.

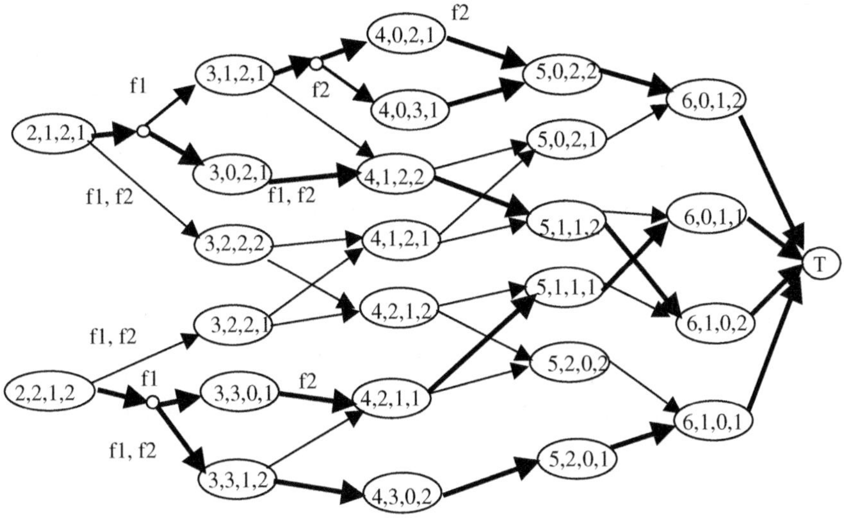

Fig. 5. State transition diagram of the example problem. The dotted arrows denote the transition because of part arrivals and the thick arrows denote the optimal paths

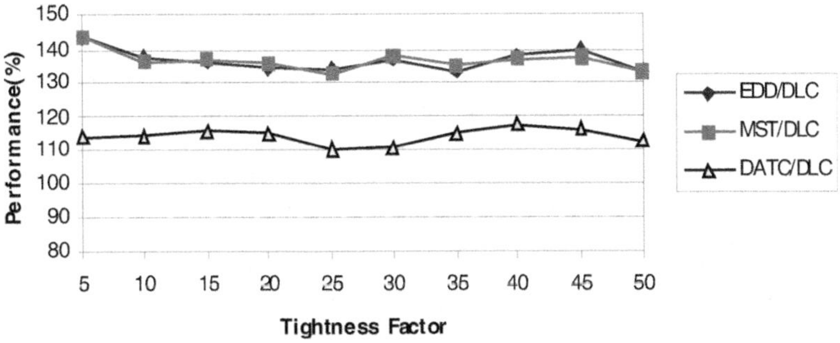

Fig. 6. Performance test results of DLC with DATC EDD, and MST in single stage case. DLC performs better in all tested cases

Only the MSD performance results are discussed since that of the overall objective turned out to be very similar except for 3 to 5 % increment of performance when setup time is considered as the setup cost. The test result shows that DLC outperforms the others significantly in all cases. The overall average improvement is 36.5%. One important issue is whether learning prevents DATC from visiting better MSD sequences and degrades the combined objective. However, since learning components maintain constant exploration factor, no search space is completely removed at any time. Although this constant exploration is for machine controllers to search for optimal policy, this can also make DATC move away from repeatedly visiting a pattern of sequences in the steady-state. This provides DATC an opportunity to potentially visit better sequences. The test result shows that DLC outperforms DATC in average 14.1% for MSD. It has been observed that it takes more iterations for DLC to improve the performance over that of DATC when due-dates are looser than when they are tighter. This is because as due-dates become looser, the system becomes more non-stationary and needs more iterations for effective learning.

For multiple stages, two problem configurations, two and three family 2-stage problems, were tested. Each consists of part families with processing time of 35 and setup time of 30. With 11 different due-date tightness factor, 10 replications are performed for each case. The average performance improvement over DATC is 15.6%. WIP of the second stage was also measured. Average improvement over DATC is 6.1% and over EDD is 7.0 %. Similar result is obtained for three family problems. It can be concluded that both MSD performance and WIP performance are improved using the learning components.

5 Conclusion

In this work, an integrated shop floor control algorithm of part-driven distributed arrival time control and machine-driven RL based control for just-in-time (JIT) production, Distributed Learning and Control (DLC), has been developed. It has been shown that with DLC the machines' control problem can be modeled as SMDP. Since the natural process is not known, Q-learning, a model-free learning method that can deal with large state space, is used to solve this SMDP. Simulation results show that DLC can be effective for multi-objective problems where there is a trade-off between conflicting objectives.

The contribution of the current work is that it shows the feasibility of incorporating real-time RL agents in highly complex manufacturing systems. This differs from many existing works of RL in manufacturing systems where agents are trained off-line. The key of this approach is effective search space reduction by DATC, which provides RL agents opportunity to learn on-line. Interesting future research issues includes applying multi-agent RL [7], scaling up to parallel machines and large families utilizing function approximation [12] as well as other objectives, such as real-time load balancing and batch sizing to maximize machine utilization.

References

1. Baker, K.R., Scudder, G.D.: Sequencing with Earliness and Tardiness Penalties: A Review, Operations Research, Vol. 38. No. 1 (1990) 22-36
2. Barto, A.G., Bradtke, S.J., Singh, S.P.: Learning to act using Real-time dynamic Programming. Artificial Intelligence, Vol. 72 (1995) 81-138
3. Yih, Y., Thesen, A.: Semi-Markov Decision Models for Realtime Scheduling, International Journal of Production Research, Vol.29. No.11 (1991) 2331-2346
4. Mahadevan S., Marchalleck N., Das, T.K., Gosavi, A.: Self-Improving Factory Simulation using Continuous-time Average Reward Reinforcement Learning. Proceedings of the 14th International Conference on Machine Learning, Nashville, TN, July (1997) 202-210
5. McDonnell, P.: Resource Reconfiguration Decisions for Distributed Manufacturing Systems: A Game Theoretic Approach. Ph.D. Thesis, Industrial Engineering, Pennsylvania State University (1998)
6. Rabelo, L.C., Jones, A., Yih, Y.: Development of a Real-Time Learning Scheduler using Reinforcement Learning Concept. IEEE International Symposium on Intelligent Control, Columbus, Ohio (1994) 291-296
7. Brauer, W., Weiss, G.: Multi-machine scheduling-a multi-agent learning approach. Proceedings. International Conference on Multi Agent Systems (1998) 42-48
8. Prabhu, V.V., Duffie, N.A.: Distributed Simulation Approach for Enabling Cooperation Between Entities in Heterarchical Manufacturing Systems. In: Lumia, R. (eds.): Modeling, Simulation, and Control Technologies for Manufacturing. SIPE Proceedings, Vol. 2596 (1995) 234-242
9. Hong, J., Prabhu, V.V.: Steady-State Properties of Distributed Arrival Time Control with Parallel Machines, PSU IME Working Paper Series 98-117 (1998)
10. Azizoglu, M., Webster S.: Scheduling Job Families about an Unrestricted Common Due Date on a Single Machine, International Journal of Production Research, Vol. 35, No. 5 (1997) 1321-1330
11. Waktins, C.J.C.H.: Learning from Delayed Rewards. Ph. D. Thesis, Cambridge University, Cambridge, England (1989)
12. Bertsekas, D. P., Tsitsiklis, J.N.: Neuro-Dynamic Programming, Athena Scientific, Belmont, MA (1996)

An Agent for Providing the Optimum Cycle Length Value in Urban Traffic Areas Constrained by Soft Temporal Deadlines

L.A. García and F. Toledo

Departamento de Ingeniería y Ciencia de los Computadores
Universitat Jaume I, 12071, Castellón, Spain
{garcial, toledo}@icc.uji.es

Abstract. This paper puts forward a method for calculating the optimum duration for every group of intersection controllers working on the same cycle. It uses a process of deep reasoning to deal with problems related to uncertainty and unavailability of sensor data. Furthermore, this process is constrained by soft temporal deadlines. Its execution can be disturbed by interactions of other agents or by external control actions performed by the human operator. The method is implemented as the primary task of an agent which collaborates with other agents to deal with various open problems concerning urban traffic. This paper shows that its execution, in isolation or together with other agents, is stable and provides suitable results.

1 Introduction

Urban Traffic Control Systems (UTCS) generally arrange intersection controllers in groups. Each group, known as CCI (*Identical Cycle Controllers*),works on the same cycle length value (the number of seconds needed to perform a complete succession of green lights for every direction at the intersection). One of the main tasks performed by UTCSs is to calculate the optimum value cycle length for every CCI under control associated with the current urban traffic situation. However, this task is usually related to one of the most critical aspects of UTCSs: predictive behavior. This means that UTCSs must prevent traffic-jams before they appear. Given the inherent uncontrollability of the urban traffic problem, there is no algorithmic method which eliminates traffic-jams when they appear.

In this paper we show how an agent can be integrated in a UTCS, which calculates the optimal value for the length of the cycle, subject to two conditions that are present in almost every UTCS currently in use. The first condition is that there is a small number of traffic detectors. The second condition establishes that the data provided from these detectors is only available at periodic time intervals.

L. Monostori, J. Váncza, and M. Ali (Eds.): IEA/AIE 2001, LNAI 2070, pp. 592–601, 2001.

2 Techniques Applied

Current UTCSs can only have a limited number of sensors due to operational and economic restrictions, so there are segments in the area under control from which UTCSs receive no information. Moreover, the UTCS usually has different types of sensors (loop detectors, TV cameras, infra-red detectors and so on). Each one of them produces data with different formats related to the same or a different measurable feature. It is essential for the UTCS to collate all this data since the control decisions taken by the system depend on their reliability [1].

In addition to these sensor data problems there are other open problems related to the different functional levels that can be defined in a UTCS. These are mainly concerned with the selection of the best control action to execute and the monitoring and prediction of the urban traffic situation, as shown in [2]. These problems are usually classified in layers [1] [3].

2.1 A Deep Knowledge Model

The complexity of these open problems has led several authors [1] [2] [4] [5] to include deep knowledge based systems inside the UTCS architectures. This knowledge, to be really useful, should integrate reasoning structures, generally known as application domain theories: knowledge of the inner structure, behavior and/or composition of the studied objects. Therefore, knowledge should be structured on two levels: knowledge which explains system behavior (application knowledge), and knowledge on how to find the solution to a given problem (control knowledge).

Application knowledge is developed in this agent by qualitative simulation: prediction of possible behaviors, consistent with incomplete knowledge of the structure of the current urban traffic situation. The main idea behind this qualitative simulator is to model the spatio-temporal fluctuations in traffic levels by defining a discrete qualitative state in which the density of traffic is given a value. The spatio-temporal limit common to two adjacent regions, each one with constant density, is represented by a straight line. The vertexes of each qualitative region are called *events* as they represent changes in the dynamics of the system: the appearance or disappearance of qualitative regions, traffic light changes and so on. In this way, it is possible to achieve entities with cognitive meaning due to the selection of events as primitive ones that represent the evolution of the system. The urban traffic network is modeled with a set of objects (segments, intersections, traffic-lights, inputs, outputs, etc.) that have associated parameters whose evolutions are restricted by means of uni- or bi-dimensional constraints. This qualitative simulator is broadly explained in [4] [6].

Current urban traffic behavior is calculated by using both the qualitative simulator and pre-processed data from sensors. Both are necessary, as the current traffic situation cannot be obtained from sensors alone for two main reasons. Firstly, sensors usually integrate in periods, so current information from sensors is not always available. Secondly, sensors usually give only a small part of the information necessary to reconstruct the current traffic situation. The approach chosen is to generate the current state of the system by qualitative simulation from the previous state, instead of using a direct analysis from the sensor data. The qualitative simulation from the previous state will give a complete image of the state of the system assuming that the previous state is correct, the simulation process is correct, and that no incidents have happened during the simulation. When the sensor data arrives, the current traffic situation is calculated by reconstructing all the events produced during the last temporal interval without real sensor data. The process of matching these new calculated events with the old ones, produced during the previous temporal interval without real sensor data, is used to detect possible urban traffic incidents [7]. The time overhead of this matching process is small for two reasons. Firstly, the time complexity of the simulator is small (quadratic on the number of intersections, segments and the length of the simulation interval in the urban network, i.e., the simulator runs much faster than real time). Secondly, the length of the temporal interval without real sensor data, $t_{integration}$, is also small (usually five minutes).

2.2 Description of the Primary Task

The agent for calculating the optimum cycle length uses this qualitative model intensively. The basic idea is to simulate what the urban traffic behavior will be, the number and kind of bad regulation problems that appear, when the cycle length of every CCI in the system is modified. Current UTCS usually apply lengths around 80, 100 and 120 seconds. These are values empirically obtained from traffic engineering techniques related to the characteristics of urban traffic flow and driver behavior.

The study of these bad traffic regulation problems is carried out by means of an analysis of the events generated by the qualitative simulator. This analysis arranges the problems detected in a hierarchical and layered classification. The problems belonging to a particular level are detected as a consequence of problems from the level immediately below. The problems arranged in the higher levels are more critical than the ones belonging to lower levels [6] [8].

This agent, known as *cci length agent*, simulates $t_{integration}$ seconds with every possible value for the cci length. Thus, if CCIs in the urban traffic network are defined as N, there are 3^N simulations to evaluate, each one associated with a tuple that arranges a different value of cycle length for every CCI.

From the evaluation of each simulation, a value is calculated which summarizes its goodness. This value, known as the *urban traffic congestion value (utcv)*, it is obtained from two intrinsically related measures:

- IP: this represents the temporal evolution of the detected problems in every instant for every intersection during every cycle that belongs to the actual temporal interval of simulation. If this value increases then there is an increase in the traffic congestion. If it decreases then the traffic congestion is lower.
- NP: this represents the accumulation of the evolution of the current detected problems weighted by their presence time, $NP = \sum_{event}(t_{start}(event) - t_{end}(event)) * IP_{end}$.

In this way, a method for selecting the optimum cycle length is to run every possible simulation. When they are finished, the agent must communicate the solution with the best *utcv*. However, this method has a major disadvantage: the time spent on running all the simulations is limited by the time taken to receive the data from the sensors, $t_{integration}$. So, this time might not be long enough if the urban traffic network is large and too many CCIs are defined.

Therefore, a collection of heuristics is needed to select the next set of values for the CCIS to simulate. This agent implements the following ones:

- Minimum changes: Its execution involves arranging the tuple set in reverse order to the number of modifications for the current value of every CCI. Therefore, the simulations associated with the fewest changes to the current values of every CCI are executed first.
- Neighbor values: Its execution involves the preference for executing the tuples that represent neighbor modifications to the current value of every CCI.

The definition of these heuristics is related to the normal functioning of conventional UTCS. The execution of a change in the duration of a CCI is an operation that involves a long term stabilization time (it usually takes five minutes in currently used UTCSs). This is because it must be executed gradually to try to avoid a major disturbance of the traffic flow. Therefore, this operation is not very often executed. This is why values next to the current ones are prioritized over those differing significantly.

However, the application of these heuristics is not enough on its own. Application domains with a large number of CCIs and large urban traffic network will need more time than $t_{integration}$ to perform all simulations. Therefore the agent integrates a bounding method in the execution of the simulations. This method works as follows. First, it chooses the first tuple from the list of tuples sorted by using *minimum changes* and *neighbor values* heuristics. Its associated execution provides the first value of the *utcv*. The following simulations are performed by applying the best value obtained from the *utcv* and an estimation of the remaining time to reach $t_{integration}$ seconds pounded by the remaining number of tuples to be simulated.

The selection of the temporal instants in which the calculus of this estimation is to be performed must be subject to the following conditions:

- It must not be too frequent because present severe congestion levels might be bound that may later improve.
- It must not be too infrequent because time might be spent on simulations that cannot improve on the best congestion value calculated.

The option chosen is to divide the $t_{integration}$ time into slices of length t_{cycle} seconds. The value of t_{cycle} must be a divisor of $t_{integration}$. Moreover, the t_{cycle} value must be related to one of the possible lengths for the CCIs since in this way, the simulator has enough time to evaluate the traffic situation at a moment close to the end of a cycle. Therefore, the value of t_{cycle} must be close to 80, 100 or 120 seconds.

Every time a simulation reaches a multiple of t_{cycle} then it estimates what the *utcv* could be at the end of the simulation. If this value is worse than the best one previously obtained, the current simulation is bound. Thus, the agent chooses the next simulation to carry out and the same method is applied.

Let an example be put forward. Suppose that there are two CCIs in the urban traffic network, cci_1 and cci_2. There are 9 tuples of possible values for these CCIs. Let $t_{integration}$ be 300 seconds (five minutes). Therefore, a good t_{cycle} value will be 100 seconds (100 is a divisor of 300 and it is a valid value for the length of a CCI). Fig. 1 shows a possible execution of this method.

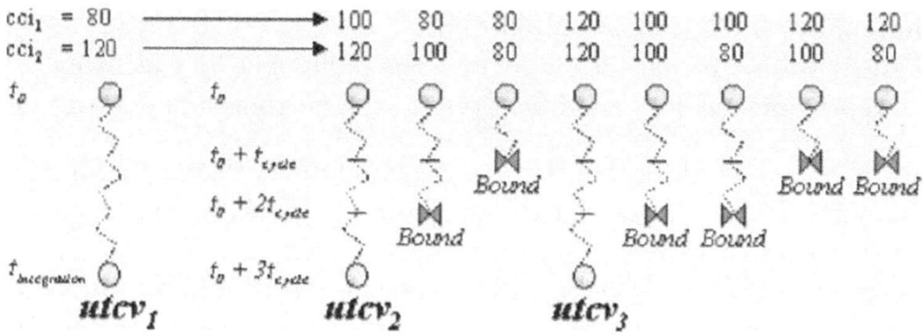

Fig. 1. Bound process around a maximum time for execution of 300 seconds. Only three complete simulations are done. The first is always done because it provides the first value of the *urban traffic congestive value*, $utcv_1$. The other two are calculated only when it is estimated that $utcv_2$ and $utcv_3$ can be lower than $uctv_1$

The first simulation is associated with the current values of each CCI defined on the urban traffic network. This simulation provides the current value of the *utcv* assuming that no incidents appear during $t_{integration}$ seconds. In the example shown there are 8 more simulations to perform, each one related to the modification of the length of every CCI. These modifications are sorted by using the *minimum changes* and *behavior values* heuristics. Each one of these modifications is then simulated. Every time the simulated time reaches a multiple of t_{cycle}, the final value of the *utcv* is estimated. If the estimated value is lower than the best value previously obtained the simulation continues until the next multiple of t_{cycle}. If it is greater, then this simulation is bounded and the next tuple of modifications is selected for execution. At the end of every complete simulation the best *utcv* is compared with the newly calculated one. The system adopts the lowest of them as the best *utcv*.

This is the usual execution of the primary task of this agent. But this task can be interrupted by external control actions executed by the operator of the UTCS. The operator can decide to change the way intersections are working (changing the green times of their addresses, their coordination values or the length of a CCI). These external control actions can be executed at any time.

Hence, once executed, there are important changes in the development of the traffic flow in the urban traffic network that the process of simulation must apply.

Therefore, the execution of this agent is interrupted and it starts a process of adopting the changes made in the data related to the simulation. When this process is finished, the agent runs the primary task again. The time available for performing this primary task has been reduced. Hence, in this new execution the simulations that can not provide a much better *utcv* than the current best are bounded.

The primary task of this agent calculates the best *utcv* within the temporal interval $[t_{start}, t_{start} + t_{integration}]$ by applying the following algorithm:

ALGORITHM *BestLength* (IN $ccis, t_{start}, t_{integration}$; OUT $best_{tuple}, best_{utcv}$)
BEGIN
  $Deadline(t_{start} + t_{integration})$; {maximum running time allowed}
  $Simulation(t_{start}, t_{start} + t_{integration}, best_{utcv}, msg_{rec})$;
  $best_{tuple} \leftarrow first(ccis)$
  IF not(msg_{rec}) THEN
    $Sort(ccis, tuple\_list, minimum, neighbor)$
    WHILE (not$(empty(tuple_list))$ and not(msg_{rec})) DO
      $tuple \leftarrow first(tuple\_list)$;
      $tuple\_list \leftarrow tail(tuple\_list)$;
      $Prepare\_simulation(tuple)$;
      $t_0 \leftarrow t_{start}$;
      $t_{finish} \leftarrow t_{start} + t_{cycle}$;
      $ok \leftarrow true$
      WHILE $(t_{finish} \leq t_{start} + t_{integration})$ and *ok* DO
        $Simulation(t_0, t_{finish}, utcv_{aux}, msg_{rec})$;
        $ok \leftarrow Estimation(utcv_{aux}, best_{utcv}, t_{integration}, tuple\_list)$;
        $ok \leftarrow ok$ and not(msg_{rec});
        $t_0 \leftarrow t_{finish}$;
        $t_{finish} \leftarrow t_{finish} + t_{cycle}$
      ENDWHILE
      IF *ok* THEN
        $best_{utcv} \leftarrow utcv_{aux}$;
        $best_{tuple} \leftarrow tuple$
      ENDIF
    ENDWHILE
  ENDIF
END.

In this task the action $Simulation(t_{begin}, t_{end}, utcv, msg_{rec})$ carries out the qualitative simulation associated with the temporal interval $[t_{begin}, t_{end}]$. It returns the calculated *utcv*, and a boolean value, msg_{rec}, representing the reception of messages from other agents that cancel the current execution of this primary task. The action $Estimation(utcv, best_{utcv}, t_{integration}, tuple\_list)$ returns true if it is estimated that the current simulation being executed can provide a better value for the *utcv* that the current best one constrained to the $t_{integration}$ and *tuple_list* values. The updating of the knowledge base for the performance of the next simulation related to the new values of every CCI, which are stored in the parameter *tuple*, is performed by the action $Prepare\_simulation(tuple)$. The maximum time spent on the execution of this task is bounded by $t_{start} + t_{integration}$ real seconds. This is done by the daemon executed by the action $Deadline(t_{start} + t_{integration})$.

2.3 Secondary Tasks

In addition to the primary task puts forward (which represents the specialization of the agent), this agent performs tasks related to inner (coherence maintenance of its data) and outer administrative work (data coherence that represent the belief of other agents on the UTCS state, synchronicity or the analyses of alerts). These tasks are called secondary. The task *start_up_agent* prepares the agent to be included in the set of active agents in the multi-agent system. Consequently, there is another task, *cease_agent*, which prepares the agent to be erased from the set of active agents. The human operator can execute external control actions on the UTCS. Thus, there is a task, *external_action*, to deal with this situation. The task *chg_mode* establishes the way the results are communicated to other agents. The last task to describe is known as *monitor*. It measures the main behavior characteristics of the execution of this agent. These measures are stored and communicated to other agents when they are required.

3 Implementation Environment

The *cci length agent* is a component of the MASHGREEN DM (a MultiAgent System for HelpinG uRban traffic dEcision takEN with Distributed Memory) prototype. This prototype is made up of a collection of agents that carry out the following tasks: sensor data pre-processing, monitoring, problem detection and diagnosis, traffic prediction, generation of automatic control actions and communication with the human operator. Each agent has the same architecture: communication, methods, workspace and control. Each agent is executed in a different computer. Data on the dynamic behavior of the urban traffic is distributed among the agents and every agent knows this distribution. So, the agents interchange messages to look for information they need or to provide results. The system also implements several primitives to perform synchronicity tasks subject to soft real time deadlines and to maintain a common temporal reference for every agent of the prototype.

The MASHGREEN DM prototype is implemented in a high performance computational architecture, a *Beowulf* computer system made up of of 1 server, 32 workers and 2 interconnection networks (a Fast Ethernet with $100 Mbits/s$ and a high performance one with $1.2 Gb/s$).

4 Implementation Results

The *cci length agent* was executed in laboratory tests and evaluated in two different situations: in isolation from other agents and as a component of the MASHGREEN DM prototype.

Table 1. Results obtained from isolated execution of the *cci length agent*. The value D_iT_j shows that the data set used was D_i and the length of the temporal interval of simulation was j seconds

Cycle Length	80/100/120	80/100/120	80/100/120	80/100/120
	$\mathbf{D_1T_{100}}$	$\mathbf{D_2T_{100}}$	$\mathbf{D_3T_{100}}$	$\mathbf{D_4T_{100}}$
Prepare_simulation	17/17/17	18/50/20	17/17/17	17/48/19
80	130-2	920-11	121-1	1003-10
utcv 100	162-2	1040-13	140-2	941-9
120	143-2	996-10	152-1	862-8
80	4542	4939	3933	5010
Execution Time 100	4148	5201	3705	4251
120	3737	4562	3583	4004
	$\mathbf{D_1T_{200}}$	$\mathbf{D_2T_{200}}$	$\mathbf{D_3T_{200}}$	$\mathbf{D_4T_{200}}$
Prepare_simulation	21/21/21	21/24/26	20/21/20	21/24/24
80	643-7	2403-14	388-2	2311-12
utcv 100	850-8	2391-17	829-7	2267-12
120	396-2	2533-10	457-4	2778-15
80	8738	8838	7995	9196
Execution Time 100	7696	8463	7060	7727
120	6934	7768	6685	7446
	$\mathbf{D_1T_{300}}$	$\mathbf{D_2T_{300}}$	$\mathbf{D_3T_{300}}$	$\mathbf{D_4T_{300}}$
Prepare_simulation	26/22/24	21/24/26	20/21/20	21/24/24
80	1667-7	3769-11	1164-6	4008-14
utcv 100	1840-9	4155-19	1764-9	3926-14
120	1507-7	4353-17	1718-9	4577-18
80	13969	13614	12955	13984
Execution Time 100	12203	12576	11216	12085
120	10905	11551	10478	11690

The isolated analysis was done using four starting data sets. These data sets are the result of the combination of two different initial conditions for the urban traffic status (previous to congested and free flow status) with two different coordination values for the intersection of the urban traffic network. The system was applied to the town of *Castellón de la Plana*, whose real urban traffic network has only one defined cci. Therefore, the evaluation of this agent was directed to measure the suitability of every performed simulation related to this specific real urban traffic network.

The results were obtained by measuring three parameters: time spent in preparing each qualitative simulation executed (in ms), better cost obtained -

utcv, in the form $NP - IP$ (section 2.2)- and time spent in executing each qualitative simulation (in ms). Table 1 shows these results.

These results show that for data set representing lightly congested traffic (data sets D_2 and D_4) the best cost calculated is worse than the best cost calculated for data set representing free flow traffic (data sets D_1 and D_3). Moreover, the analyses of the best cost obtained also shows that for lightly congested traffic it is better to choose a short cycle length and that for free flow traffic is better to choose a long cycle length. The time spent on preparing every simulation is more or less stable regardless of the data set used and the length of the temporal interval of simulation. Another fact from these results is that the greater the value for the length of the cycle, the shorter the time needed for simulation. This is easy to understand as the greater the value for the length of the cycle, the fewer times the color of traffic lights alternate. Thus, the qualitative simulator produces fewer events.

The behavior of the *cci length agent* in the execution of the MASHGREEN DM prototype was analyzed by monitoring some of the main components of its primary task. The first action this agent makes when it is going to execute its primary task is to send a message to the *pre-processing agent* to obtain the starting data related to the new temporal interval of execution without current sensor data. Once received, data is prepared to perform all the simulations that it can execute until the data integration time is held. The time spent on this task is insignificant compared to the time spent on the execution of other components of its primary task. If external control actions are executed in the prototype, the *cci length agent* cancels the process of searching for the best length, and it waits until the execution of this external control action is finished. It then requests the new updated data from the *pre-processing agent* and it starts the execution of its primary task again.

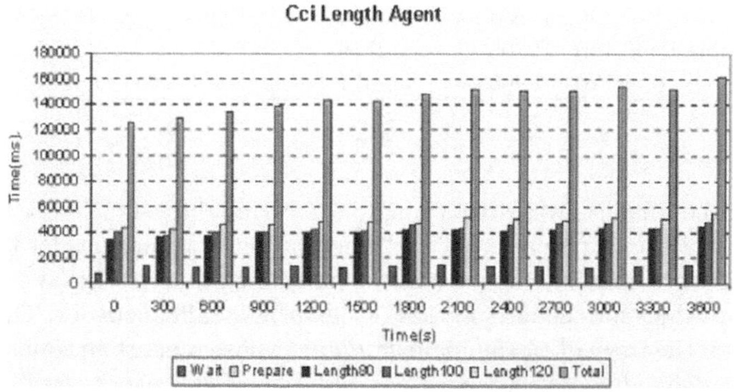

Fig. 2. Behavior of the cci length agent as a component of the MASHGREEN DM prototype when its primary task is executed. The data integration time is 300 seconds. During this execution external control actions were not executed

Fig. 2 shows that with a cci with three different lengths, the execution of the primary task finishes before the data integration time is held. This analysis shows that, in contrast to the isolated execution, the time needed for executing each simulation in the same period increases slightly. This is because there is extra work related to the data maintenance cost for every simulation.

5 Conclusion

The deep reasoning mechanism puts forward in this article integrates current data from sensors and a process for qualitative reasoning. This mechanism is used to calculate the best value of the length for every cci in an urban traffic network. The suitability of this approach has been evaluated by implementing the *cci length agent* into it, a component of the MASHGREEN DM prototype. Its execution execution in laboratory tests shows that its results are reasonably related to the data representing the starting data flow. The best length calculated is sent to the *pre-processing agent*, which decides, together with the human operator, what to do with this value.

Acknowledgements. This work is partly supported by the Spanish CICYT project TAP1999-0590-c02-02 and Fundacio Caixa Castello project P1A98-11.

References

1. García L.A., Toledo F.: A Deep Knowledge Expert System for Urban Traffic Control. Submitted for publication in Computational Intelligence Techniques in Traffic Control, L.C. Jain (ed), CRC Press.
2. U.S. Department of Transportation, FHWA: Workshop in Models in Support Advanced Traffic Management Systems (ATMS). Florida, may, 1999.
3. Ambrosino G., Bielli M., Boero M.: Application of Artificial Intelligence and Expert Systems to Traffic Control. In: Advance Vehicles and Infrastructure Systems. John Willey & Sons, 1997.
4. Moreno S., Toledo F., Rosich F., and Martín G.: Qualitative Simulation for Temporal Reasoning in Urban Traffic Control. In: Qualitative Reasoning and Decision Technologies. N.Piera Carreté and M.G. Singh (eds), CIMNE, Barcelona, 1993.
5. Bell M.C., Scenama G. and Ibbetson L.J.: CLAIRE: An Expert System for Congestion Management. In: Advance Telematics in Road Transport. Proc. of the DRIVE Conference. ELSEVIER pp 596-614, Brussels, 1991.
6. Toledo F., Moreno S., Bonet E., Martín G.: Using Constraint Technology for Predictive Control of Urban Traffic Based on Qualitative and Temporal Reasoning. Proc. of the Ninth International Conference IEA/AIE-96, Fukuoka, Japan, June, 1996.
7. García L.A., Toledo, F.: Urban Traffic Incident Detection using Qualitative Data and Temporal Intervals. Proc of IC-AI'2000, Las Vegas, USA, June, 2000.
8. García L.A., Toledo, F.: Space-Temporal Urban Traffic Problem Identification using Qualitative Data over Temporal Intervals. Proc of the IC-AI'2000, Las Vegas, Nevada, USA, June, 2000.

Interactive Modeling for Batch Simulation of Engineering Systems: A Constraint Satisfaction Problem

Debasis Mitra

Jackson State University
Department of Computer Science, P.O. Box 18839
Jackson, Mississippi 39217, USA
dmitra@ccaix.jsums.edu

Abstract. We have presented here an algorithm CPRAO for doing constraint processing using relational algebraic operators. Van Beek and others have investigated such constraint processing in the relational algebraic framework, for quite some time, producing some unique results. Apart from providing new theoretical angles, the framework also provides the opportunity to use the existing efficient implementations of relational database management systems as the underlying data structures for any relevant algorithm. Our algorithm here enhances that framework. The algorithm is quite general in its current form. Weak heuristics (like forward checking) developed within the CSP area could be plugged in this algorithm. The algorithm is developed here is targeted toward a component-oriented modeling problem that we are currently working on, namely, the problem of interactive modeling for batch-simulation of engineering systems (IMBSES). However, it could be adopted for many other CSP problems as well. The article here discusses the algorithm and many aspects of the problem we are addressing.

Keywords: Intelligent interfaces, AI application to design, Planning and scheduling, Interactive Planning, Constraint-based reasoning, Modeling for simulation, Component-oriented programming, Intelligent software engineering.

1 Introduction

We have encountered a constraint satisfaction problem in the context of developing an intelligent interface to a numerical simulation package for some engineering systems. User of the system develops a model to be simulated using some components. In general, more than one subroutines are available in the package for each of the components. The choice of a subroutine for a component in the model under development (a graph, an example in Figure 1) depends on the choice of the other subroutines for the adjacent components/nodes in the model/graph. The input parameters needed by a subroutine must be supplied by those adjacent subroutines in the model. The user typically starts with a conceptual model - developed out of the components, and represents the model as a graph. However, he/she needs to know a great deal about the

L. Monostori, J. Váncza, and M. Ali (Eds.): IEA/AIE 2001, LNAI 2070, pp. 602-611, 2001.

subroutines corresponding to those components, as available in the library, in order to instantiate the model elements (components) with acceptable subroutines. This is where our intelligent interface is designed to provide assistance. Our framework would allow the user to concentrate on the modeling activity at a higher level, hiding the detailed constraints between the underlying software modules from him/her. This type of expert systems for the purpose of modeling is addressed before in the literature (Dijk et al, 1991, Pos et al, 1996).

This problem has a flavor of graph coloring problem, but it is an n-ary (n>2) constraint satisfaction problem. In our current set up we expect the instantiation of a component (with a corresponding subroutine) to be done by the user. Hence, in this article we are not concerned with the heuristics behind such a choice.

We have proposed here an algorithm for the purpose of doing constraint propagation in our problem IMBSES. The output of the algorithm is a globally consistent solution, as a graph with all its nodes being instantiated. A novelty in our approach is to deploy the relational operators in the algorithm. For some time van Beek and Dechter (van Beek, 1995, Dechter, 1997) have been investigating the issues in such a multidisciplinary approach. Their results include some new concepts of consistency, e.g., relational consistency. Our work enhances the field from that angle by providing a concrete algorithm. Although the algorithm presented here is targeted to our problem in engineering simulations, it could easily be modified for handling other constraint satisfaction problems (CSP) as well. Enhancing the algorithm with weak heuristics (like forward checking, backjumping, etc.) is also feasible and is a future direction of our work.

We have discussed the background and the essence of the algorithm in the next section. The algorithm CPRAO ("constraint processing with relational algebraic operators") itself is presented next, followed by some of its implementation issues. The problem has a strong flavor of AI planning. Those aspects are discussed next, followed by a simplified version of the problem, namely the linear modeling, which may have many real-life applications. We have concluded the article with some discussions and future directions.

Background

The problem domain contains a set of generic class of modules $M = \{M_1, M_2, \dots M_m\}$ corresponding to some physical components or processes of the targeted engineering system, e.g., pipe, valve, volume, etc. that the user uses to identify the domains of nodes in his/her model-graph. Once again, each of these modules is a variable with its own domain of values, $M_i = \{v_1, v_2, \dots v_k\}$, e.g., the domain for pipe could be {pipe01, pipe02, pipe03, pipe04}, which corresponds to the subroutines available in the library for that component/process. Each of these domain values in reality is a software module or a subroutine. As far as we are concerned, each such module is defined by its name (v_j) and two sets: its input parameters (I_{vj}) and its output parameters (O_{vj}). All these three types of information: (1) the generic classes, (2) corresponding domain values, and (3) the input and output parameters list for each module, form the background for any problem instance. They could be stored in appropriate files or in a simple database.

The user typically draws a graph G = (V, E) for the conceptual model, where the nodes (V) are chosen from the generic classes M (Figure 1). Note that two different nodes of the graph can be of the same class, i.e., mapped onto the same domain. Then, the user chooses a domain value interactively for each of his/her nodes in the graph, until all the nodes are instantiated with a domain value or no consistent instantiation is found for the graph. As mentioned before, we call this problem "interactive modeling for batch-simulation of engineering systems" or IMBSES. The word "interactive modeling" comes from the fact that the algorithm interacts with the user rather than working in an automated mode. The word "batch simulation" comes from the nature of the actual simulation activities here (after the model is developed interactively), which is done in a batch-processing mode, rather than on a real-time interactive mode.

Every time the user instantiates a node v with its domain value (say, v_1) all its adjacent nodes are constrained, so that, together they supply all the input parameters needed by the subroutine v_1. (This is because in a simulation problem the sequence may be repeated in a loop for several times and the parameter passing is not uni-directional as the physical connections between the components in a model actually are.) Hence a set of (n+1)-aried tuples (T_v) will be created, for n adjacent nodes to the node v - including the node v itself, which are consistent with the value chosen on v.

It is possible that some of the adjacent nodes to v might have been already constrained before v is attempted. In that case they already exist in other constraining tuples in tables in the "database" (collection of all the tables). In such a situation, the set of tuples T_v needs to be joined with all such tuples to propagate the constraints. Thus, although the target of our constraint propagation is local (only between adjacent nodes) the process spreads as more and more nodes get constrained, eventually achieving a global solution (Figure 3). We find natural join operation in relational algebra particularly suitable for such multi-aried constraint propagation, as noted in the past in the CSP literature (Dechter and van Beek, 1997). The RDBMS systems may also provide efficient implementation for doing such joins that we can take advantage of.

The algorithm will start with all nodes in the graph being represented as a set of single-column tables (initial database, an example in Figure 2). Each such table T_i has rows for all the domain values corresponding to the generic class (M_k) chosen by the user for the respective node n_i. As the constraint propagation progresses, by the user choosing domain values for the nodes - one by one, the tables get joined with other tables corresponding to the constrained adjacent nodes. Eventually a consistent instantiation is developed as a single row table for all the nodes of the graph (example in

Figure 3). At that point the algorithm stops. However, it is possible that the algorithm may stop detecting an inconsistency also.

The user may have to backtrack over the domain values chosen in case of an inconsistency (when no tuple is generated on a join operation, or no consistent domain values are available for the adjacent nodes). The backtracking may have to be performed over the nodes also, when no available value is acceptable on the current node. Note that we are leaving the responsibility of backtracking to the user. However, with some problem-related heuristics a user could be guided on this regard also. A natural candidate seems to be the dependency directed back-jumping heuristics.

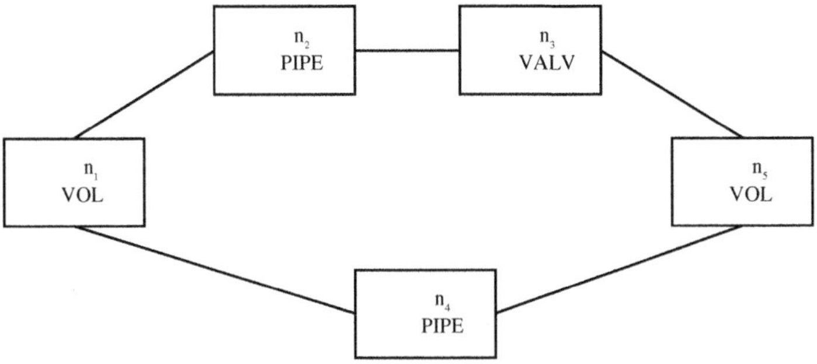

Fig. 1.

T_1	T_2	T_3	T_4	T_5
n_1	n_2	n_3	n_4	n_5
VOLM01	PIPE01	VALV03	PIPE03	VOLM02
VOLM05	PIPE02	VALV01	PIPE06	VOLM07
VOLM04	PIPE05		PIPE07	VOLM03
	PIPE04		PIPE08	VOLM08

Fig. 2. T at the beginning

n_1	n_2 n_3	n_4	n_5	
VOLM01	PIPE04	VALV03	PIPE06	VOLM03

Fig. 3. T at the end

The Constraint Propagation Algorithm

Input: (1) A graph G=(V, E), V is the set of nodes to be instantiated with software modules, and E is the set of arcs indicating physical connections between pair of components/nodes. The graph may be originally directed for physical connections between components of the designed system. However, the directions are unimportant for our problem. Arcs here indicate the parameter-passing connections between modules.
(2) A set of tables (or a "database") D = $\{T_1, T_2, \ldots, T_{|V|}\}$, T_i corresponds to the node n_i in V, initialized with domain values (or all available subroutines) for the chosen class of modules on n_i. Thus, each T_i is a column-table (Fig 1).

Output: Updated D = $T_{12\ldots|V|}$, a row table containing a consistent set of instantiations for each node in G; OR, detected *inconsistency*.

Constraint: Any instantiation v_1 (a software module) on a node v in V must have all its required input parameters being supplied by the output parameters of the instantiations on all the adjacent nodes to v put together (not necessarily by any one of them).

Algorithm CPRAO

```
(1)     v = pick_up_node(V);  // picked up initial node
(2)     L = {v}; U = V - {v};  //list of instantiated and uninstantiated nodes resp.
(3)     D_v = D;  D_c = D;  // initialize back-up database for v and current database
(4)     do until (L == empty  or  U == empty)        // no more values for node v
(5)       if ( (v_1 = pick_up_next_value (v, D_c) )  ==  null)   then
(6)             L = L -{v};   U = U + {v};
                      // move v from instantiated to uninstantiated
(7)             if  (L  =/= null) then
(8)                v = pick_up_node(L);   //  backtrack over some old node
(10)               D_c = D_v ;         // current database reverted to the corresponding
old one
(11)            else      goto  20;  // return inconsistency
                endif;
          else
(12)            D_c  =  Update_DB (D_c ,  v=v_1);
                      // propagate constraint with v_1 on v
(13)            if  (D_c   ==  null)   then
(14)               goto  5;                    // try a different value on v
                else
(16)               v  =  pick_up_node(U);   // move forward for next instantiation
(17)               L = L + {v};    U = U - {v};    // move v off from uninstantiataed
(18)               D_v = D_c ;
                      // backup database for node v prior to its instantiation
                endif;
          endif;
        enddo;
```

```
(19)    if ( U == empty) then  return D_c ;
(20)    if ( L == empty) then  return INCONSISTENCY;
EndAlgorithm CPRAO.
```

The actual constraint propagation takes place within the following sub-algorithm.

```
Algorithm Update_DB (D, v=v_1)  // returns a database or "null" on inconsistency
(1)     D_c = D;  // create a local copy
(2)     ∀ T_i ∈ D_c  if ( v ∈ schema(T_i)) then
(3)       T_i = select (v=v_1, T_i );
        endfor;
(4)     if (T_i == null) then  return null; // v=v_1 is not there in the database

(5)     T' = BuildTable (v=v_1);  // initialize building the table

(6)     for every adjacent node n to v in G do
(7)        ∀ T_c ∈ D_c  if ( n ∈ schema(T_c)) then
(8)              for each value n1 for n in T_c do  // projecting T_c on n
(9)                T' = T' ⊗ (n=n1);                  // cross product
                 endfor;
          endfor;
        endfor;

(10)    for each tuple t in T' do
(11)       O = output_parameters_list_of (t - {v});
(12)       I = input_parameters_list_of (v_1);
(13)       if ( not (O ⊇ I) ) then                 // constraint checking
(14)             T' = T' - t;        // eliminate tuple t from the table T'
          endif;
        endfor;
(15)    if (T' == null) then  return null;  // no consistent solution for v=v1
(16)    ∀ T_c ∈ D_c  if ( (schema(T_c) • schema(T')) =/= null ) then
(17)       T' = T' ⋈ T_c ;          // natural join to propagate constraints
(18)       if (T' == null) return null;
(19)       D_c = D_c - T_c ;
        endfor;
(20)    D_c = D_c ∪ T' ;
(21)    return D_c ;
EndAlgorithm Update_DB.
```

The following functions are being used in the above algorithms.

pick_up_node(S): returns a node from the list of node S. We presume this to be done by the user, but some heuristic like back-jumping could be used here either for automated pick up or for providing help to the user.

pick_up_next_value(v, D): same as above, any search heuristics could be encapsulated in these two functions.
schema(T): returns a set of attributes in the table T
select ($v=v_1$, T): relational algebraic select operation on table T, for an attribute v with value v_1.
BuildTable ($v=v_1$): returns a table with one attribute v and its value v1.
T $\otimes$ ($n=n_1$): a binary operation, it returns a table that is a cross product of table T and BuildTable(n=n1).
output_parameters_list_of (t): returns a union of all output parameters of the software modules in the tuple t.
input_parameters_list_of (v_1): returns the input parameters needed by the software module v_1.
T' $\bowtie$ T_c : the relational natural join operation between two tables (Connolly, 1999).

One has to be careful with the semantics of the tables as they are updated. A row in a table does not mean that the elements/modules there are consistent with respect to each other. It only means that they satisfy the constraints for the instantiated variables/columns on that row.

Implementation Aspects

We expect the two sets of input available as the background information for the problem domain: the module names and their input/output parameter lists, and the generic class name and their domain values (the subroutine names). They should be on some permanent storage, and updated only by the software module-developers. The front-end is expected to be a graphical user interface, on which the user would "draw" the conceptual model as a problem instance, and interactively instantiate the nodes/variables on his/her graph-cum-model by running the algorithm. The algorithm would parse the constraints as described in this article, restricting user's choice of modules on the nodes. Our algorithm uses a database system as its dynamic data structure. An important challenge there is to efficiently copy databases for creating backup that may be needed for backtracking, as in Line 18 of CPRAO. The algorithm may have to be adopted in order to do this efficiently. For example, it may not be necessary to "undo" all tables (as in line 10 of CPRAO), rather only those tables affected by the backtracking may have to be replaced by the corresponding older tables, while unaffected tables remain same. It is also feasible to keep track of the "nogood" tuples that violate constraints and utilize them to improve efficiency in future iterations, or in future runs of the algorithm on different problem instances.

Modeling as a Planning Problem

The whole problem of developing a model (IMBSES), as described here, could be viewed as a simple case of *planning* as defined within the Artificial Intelligence (Russell and Norvig, 1995) area. Here the input and output parameters of a subroutine are akin to the "preconditions" and "effects" of an "operator" in a planning problem respectively. The domain values or the subroutines themselves resemble the operators. An advantage in our problem is that a plan-schema is available as input to the problem - in the form of the graph G. From that angle it is akin to the abstraction hierarchy of operators where a node is initially mapped onto a fixed set of operator instances (the domain). The problem is to find a consistent set of instantiation. The input graph resembles a partially ordered plan.

A significant difference here compared to the planning approach is that any of the adjacent nodes to a node V in the graph can satisfy the input parameters list needed by V (that are equivalent to the preconditions of the operators). As opposed to that, in a regular planning problem a chronological ordering of operators is expected, thus, making the arcs as directed ones. Also, in planning the preconditions of an operator O in the plan graph could be satisfied by any other operator temporally ordered before O in the graph, whereas in our problem the input parameters of a module on a node must be supplied by its adjacent nodes only.

From a very generalized point of view, many component-oriented programming problems other than the batch-simulation problems addressed here could also be viewed as planning problems. In such a framework one should be able to group the software components (within the library) into a finite set of generic classes so that a node in a user developed graph is chosen from those generic classes. With some adaptation our algorithm then would be able to provide intelligent help to a user in developing a "program" using those pre-stored components.

Linear Modeling

A simpler version of the problem would be where the input graph G is a linear order rather than a partial order. Although in most of the engineering systems such a linear order may not be useful, there are many applications where the latter may be a norm. For example, constructing a GIF animation from a sequence of pictures based on some criteria (similar to the input/output parameters in our case, or the preconditions and effects in regular AI planning), or making a musical piece by ordering a sequence of audio clips based on some criteria, may be formulated as the problem discussed here with some simplifications for working with linear orders rather than partial orders. A semi-automated mode of developing models, as is being addressed here, may be helpful in those situations also. A future direction of our work is to adapt our algorithm for a better efficiency in the case of linear modeling.

Conclusion

In this article we have proposed an algorithm for doing constraint propagation using the relational algebraic operators. This approach would make it feasible to use efficient implementations of relational database systems commercially available in the market. This approach also leads to new ideas about consistency as have been proposed before (Dechter and van Beek et al, 1997). Our algorithm targets for achieving a globally consistent solution. It could be easily modified to generate all globally consistent solutions.

Many constraint propagation domains could be attacked using the proposed approach. We have addressed a specific problem here related to a software development environment that we have encountered in the domain of numerical simulation of some engineering systems. Our algorithm is targeted toward such component-oriented programming applications. The practical objective here is to provide interactive help at the user interface level while the user is trying to develop a model of a system to be simulated by using a given software package. It is done by instantiating the components with the corresponding program modules available in the given software package. Such component-oriented approach could be useful in GUI test case generation-problems also (Memon et al, 2000). The algorithm is easily adaptable for many other constraint propagation problems, like N-queens problem.

Apart from implementing the algorithm we are currently working towards seeking heuristics from the AI planning area to improve the efficiency of the algorithm. The relation between the addressed constraint satisfaction problem here and the planning problem (as defined within the AI) is quite apparent and is discussed in a section in this article. Our algorithm should be considered as a shell in which weak or strong heuristics could be added.

Acknowledgement. This work is primarily supported by the NASA Glenn Research Center (NAG3-2277). Partial support is also provided by a grant from the NSF (IIS-9733018). We are indebted to Joseph A. Hemminger and Barabara Sakowski of NASA Glenn Research Center for numerous discussions. Ajai Thomas has helped in preparing the figures.

References

1. Van Beek, P., and Dechter, R.: On the minimality and global consistency row-convex constraint network. Journal of the ACM (1995) 42:543-561

2. Connolly, T., Begg, C., and Strachan, A.: Database Systems: A Practical Approach to Design, Implementation, and Management. Addison Wesley Longman Limited, Edinburgh Gate, England (1999)
3. Dechter, R., and van Beek, P.: Local and global relational consistency. Theoretical Computer Science journal (1997) 173:283-308
4. Dijk, J. van, and Breedveld, P.C.: Automated mechatronic system modeling. Proceedings of the Thirteenth IMACS World Congress (1991)
5. Memon, A. M., Pollack, M. E., and Soffa, M. L.: Proceedings of the Fifth International Conference on Artificial Intelligence Planning and Scheduling, Eds. Chien, S., Kambhampati, S., and Knoblock, C. A., AAAI Publishers (2000)
6. Pos, A., Borst, P., Top, J, and Akkermans, H.: Reusability of simulation models. Knowledge-Based Systems journal (1996) 9:119-125
7. Russell, S., and Norvig, P.: Artificial Intelligence: A Modern Approach. Prentice Hall, Inc., Engelwood Cliffs, New Jersey (1995)

Approaches to Increase the Performance of Agent-Based Production Systems

Botond Kádár and László Monostori

Computer and Automation Research Institute, Hungarian Academy of Sciences
Kende u. 13-17, Budapest, POB 63, H-1518, Hungary
Phone: (36 1) 2096-990, Fax: (36 1) 4667-503,
{kadar, laszlo.monostori}@sztaki.hu

Abstract. The paper outlines two attempts to enhance the performance of agent-based manufacturing systems using adaptation/learning techniques. Some agent-level parameters are introduced, by which the system behavior can be tuned. The research was carried out with the help of a simulation framework for agent-based manufacturing architectures developed by the authors earlier. A short description of the framework, including the agents' structure, communication and cooperation techniques, is also given. The paper briefly introduces the main DAI approaches supporting the realization of distributed manufacturing structures, such as agent-based and holonic manufacturing systems. Some main results of this field are also enumerated.

1 Introduction

Nowadays an essential role is assigned to the manufacturing and engineering industry that faces a very dynamic and continuously changing environment. Today's and future production systems must not only function effectively with small costs but at the same time they must respond rapidly to market changes in a flexible way, producing environmentally friendly. Moreover, *growing complexity* is one of the most significant characteristics of today's manufacturing, which is manifested not only in manufacturing systems, but also in the products to be manufactured, in the processes and the company structures [1].

During the past decade several approaches have been emerged to formulate the structural and procedural features of future manufacturing systems and the term *Intelligent Manufacturing Systems (IMSs)* has been used world-wide to classify the new manufacturing systems of 21st century. In a landmark paper of J. Hatvany in 1983, *IMSs* were outlined as the next generation of manufacturing systems. In this context, they were expected to solve, within certain limits, unprecedented, unforeseen problems based on even incomplete and imprecise information by utilizing the results of *artificial intelligence (AI)* research [2]. The *World-wide IMS Programme* initiated by H. Yoshikawa in 1992 has a much broader perspective: here the foundation of manufacturing science and technology for the next century is put in the center [3].

L. Monostori, J. Váncza, and M. Ali (Eds.): IEA/AIE 2001, LNAI 2070, pp. 612-621, 2001.

1.1 New Manufacturing System Paradigms and DAI

The effective operation of automated manufacturing systems requires efficient control structures. In [4] the main steps in the development of manufacturing control approaches are described including their application possibilities, benefits and drawbacks. Fig. 1 illustrates the fundamental manufacturing control structures in the sequence of their appearance.

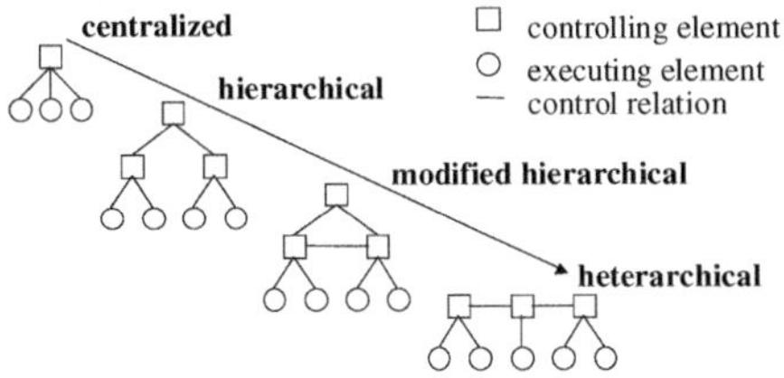

Fig. 1. Evolution of control architectures [4]

The topic addressed in the paper relates to heterarchical architectures. Several new manufacturing paradigms have been proposed in the past years that are more or less connected to the heterarchical control concept. Some of these are *Holonic Manufacturing Systems (HMSs)* [5], [6], *Fractal Factory* [7], *Random Manufacturing Systems* [8], *Bionic Manufacturing Systems* [9], *market based control of manufacturing systems* [10]. *Distributed Artificial Intelligence (DAI)* provides the supporting technologies for the development of such systems.

Parallel to the evolution of AI the implementation of computer networks has catalyzed the organization of computers in communicative "societies". *DAI* is a sub-field of *AI* and researchers in this domain are investigating *communication* and *co-operation techniques*, as well as knowledge models that computational nodes participating in a network might need to take part in *"societies"* composed of computers and people [11]. Two main, sometimes overlapping areas of research can be distinguished in DAI: *distributed problem solving* and *multi-agent systems* [12]. Distributed problem solving considers how different tasks or problems can be divided among a number of nodes that co-operate in dividing and sharing knowledge about the problem and its solutions. Research in *multi-agent systems (MAS)* considers the behavior of a collection of autonomous nodes aiming at solving a given problem.

2 Agent-Based Manufacturing Systems

Methods developed in the field of multi-agent systems are suitable for realizing the heterarchical control concept[1]. In the eighties, the DAI community paid only limited attention to manufacturing. It mainly focused on problems where agents contended for

[1] Naturally, techniques developed and applied in MAS are not exclusively preserved for heterarchical control, they can be successfully utilized in other control architectures as well.

computational resources. Since factories are inherently distributed, the need for distributed decision making arose quite naturally. The recent developments in *multi-agent systems* and the rapid progress in IT brought new and interesting possibilities in using *DAI* techniques in the field of manufacturing.

Agent-based manufacturing systems, as one of the new paradigms of manufacturing, consist of autonomous, intelligent, flexible and co-operative agents. They offer an architecture that decreases the centralization and rigidity, and on the other hand increases the flexibility of the plant. They support production systems that are decentralized rather than centralized and concurrent rather than sequential. The multi-agent structure replaces the centralized data base and control system with a network of agents with local data bases and advanced communication capabilities. The overall system performance is not globally planned, but develops through the dynamic interactions of agents in real time.

A number of researchers have attempted to apply agent technology to manufacturing enterprise integration, supply chain management, manufacturing planning, scheduling and control, materials handling and holonic manufacturing systems [13]. In [14] a distributed scheduling algorithm is presented, where a group of agents share knowledge about bottleneck machines and rush orders, in order to co-operate to achieve global optimization. In [15] a review of possible multi-agent manufacturing structures is given. One of the first applications of agent-based modeling and co-ordination techniques to manufacturing control was the prototype factory control system *Yet Another Manufacturing System (YAMS)* presented in [16]. In [17] a dynamic scheduling method for cellular manufacturing systems is described that employs a network-wide bidding mechanism for dynamic task assignment and a knowledge based scheduler for cell level scheduling. A fully distributed scheduling method for heterarchical manufacturing systems is introduced in [18].

Though, numerous research projects dealt with the problems of multi-agent manufacturing systems, several issues still have to be resolved [19]. These questions can be answered by extensive simulation only. D In the following space the main features of the *object-oriented framework* for the evaluation of distributed manufacturing architectures [19] developed at the Computer and Automation Research Institute, are summarized. The research presented in the second part of the paper concentrates on the further improvement of agent's capabilities used in the framework.

3 Simulation Framework for Agent-Based Manufacturing

The object-oriented framework for the development and evaluation of distributed manufacturing architectures described in [19] provides a root model that represents a plant and can contain different agents. The object library incorporates two main agent types*: resource agent* and *order agent.* A plant in the model will contain only one order agent that is responsible for order processing, job announcements and job dispatching. A model may incorporate several resource agents functioning as manufacturing service providers With the help of developed objects, distributed manufacturing architectures with different layouts can be built in a comfortable way. Detailed structure of the presented agents, their processes and the operation of the whole system can be found in [19], [20].

3.1 The Basic Inter-agent Architecture

The agents used in a manufacturing system can be classified in two fundamental groups according to their basic structure. The first group includes agents that have only information processing parts while the second group contains agents with information processing and physical processing parts as well. A generic manufacturing agent architecture was proposed that served as the root concept of the agents in the developed system (Fig. 2). Since the *autonomy* and *co-operation* are the most important features of the agents, they always must include a communication module. This unit is responsible for the accurate communication through which the agent can participate in a negotiation.

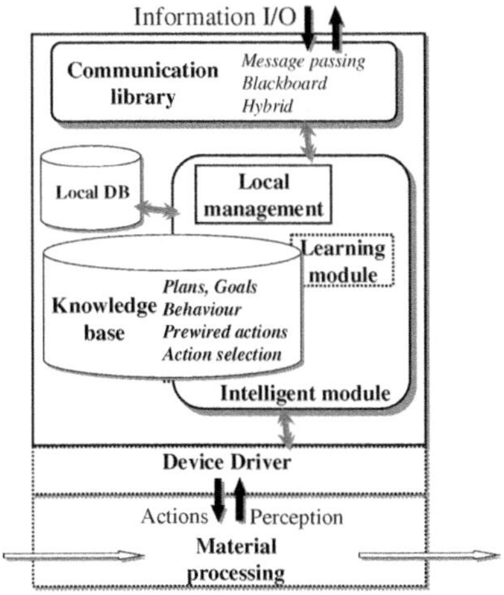

Fig. 2. Generic architecture of manufacturing agents

The intelligent module, which represents the brain and control center of the agent, is connected to the communication library through which it receives information from the environment. The local management part of the intelligent module provides with the necessary functionality to insert the agent in agent community. The intelligent module contains a *knowledge base* that includes the plans and goals of the agent, behavior patterns and strategies, rules for changing its actions based on environmental changes and it contains algorithms for specific situations called pre-wired actions. Naturally, not all of these elements are needed simultaneously, depending on the complexity of the functions provided by the agent, only one or some of the enumerated components are required. Connected to the knowledge base with dashed line, the presence of the learning module is optional.

The intra-agent architecture presented in Fig. 2 offers a flexible structure for implementing agents in a manufacturing environment. Behavior of agents built on the base of this architecture can range from minor functional reaction to planning, learning and sophisticated decision making abilities. The structure of the agent objects in the developed framework is based on the presented intra-agent architecture.

4 Approaches to Enhance the Performance of Agents

Heterarchical architectures have a number of inherent advantages, such as modularity, reconfigurability, adaptability, fault tolerance, extensibility, etc. The elements of such architectures, however, are distributed, usually have no access to global information and, therefore, global optima cannot be guaranteed. Empowering the agents with learning skills creates the opportunity to improve the performance of the system. Learning denotes changes in the system that is adaptive in the sense that learning techniques enable the system to do the same or similar task more effectively next time. Taking the complexity of manufacturing systems and the dynamically changing environment into account, adaptation and learning is one of the most important features of agent based manufacturing systems.

In the following space, two different attempts for improving the performance of the manufacturing system are introduced by expanding the adaptive characteristics of the agents. The investigations were made by further developing and using the simulation framework presented in the previous section.

The derived models apply a *fully heterarchical system architecture.* If it was possible, central information handling was omitted and all the modifications have been striven for permitting maximum local decision power. In this distributed environment global state variables such as overall system load, bottleneck resources are not available for local decision making, consequently the agents cannot always behave to guide the system towards a global interest. Research aimed at the enhancement of system performance through the improvement of agent's adaptive behavior.

4.1 Cost Factor Adaptation on Resource Agent Level

In this concept, a purely local adaptation scheme is proposed. In the former system each resource included a cost factor, which was used for all the tasks performed on that particular resource and the cost of the resource was calculated with this resource-specific cost factor. In the new scheme, keeping the processing time of each task constant, the cost factor became an *adjustable variable for each operation.* Considering the resource objectives, the resource agents can adjust their cost factors according to their local state variables and previous observations. For these procedures the local knowledge base of the agents were enlarged with a rule base, in which different rules are triggered according to actual agent states.

It is assumed that the goal of the agents is to maximize their profit and the evaluation of the bids is done on cost basis. Each agent incorporates a rule base with which it can locally decide on the cost factor to be applied for an announced task. The preconditions of these rules are the utilization of the resource and the ratio between the won and lost bids. The data about the bidding history are stored locally for each agent in the table of machine abilities and history (Fig. 3)

Choosing appropriate rules for dynamically changing the service prices, global objectives can be achieved. With the help of the local rule-based price-adjusting mecha-

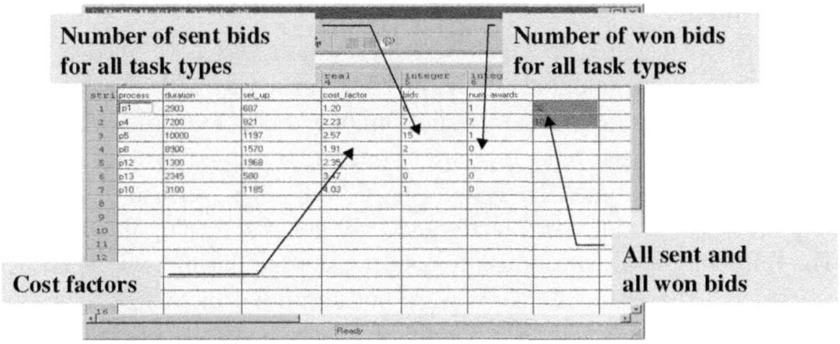

Fig. 3. The table including the bidding "history" of an agent

nism the system quickly reacts to changes in the system load. On the one hand, decreasing the cost factor, a lightly utilized resource can attract tasks from other resources, on the other, the high prices of heavily utilized resources are not attractive for the order agent while evaluating the bids. Through this scheme, a balanced utilization of the overall system can be achieved. The adaptation of the cost factor is performed when the resource sends a bid for an announced task. Before the calculation of the overall cost, on the base of local observations the resource tries to modify its cost variable for maximizing its profit. A possible adaptation rule of the cost-factor can be as follows:

```
IF resource utilization <= resource_util_min_limit
AND
IF (the number of awarded bids for the same task)/(the number
of all bids for the same task) <= task_won_bid_limit
AND
the cost factor of the task > profitable_cost_factor_limit
THEN
decrease the cost factor by a%
```

The preconditions of the above rule are the low utilization of the resource and the relative small number of won bids from all the bids sent for the specific task. This means that the resource employs probably a high cost factor for that particular task. Other rules, which enable the increase of the cost factor, are also implemented. If for example, during a bid preparation procedure, a resource identifies that its utilization extends a predefined threshold (it is highly utilized) and the just announced task was awarded to the given resource relatively many times (it is probably cheaper than the others) the resource can increase its task specific cost factor. Increasing the cost in this manner, however, enhances the chances of other resources to win and by this way the system will be directed to a more balanced utilization.

It should be underlined that the right adjustment of the thresholds and the decrease and/or increase factors depends on the modeled manufacturing system and its actual loads. The proper policy can be derived by using simulation runs and fine-tuning the specific limits during operation.

4.1.1 Experiments

A small model of a job shop manufacturing system was developed for testing purposes. The test system integrates four different resources with overlapping capabilities, but there is no complete substitution among them. Four different types of jobs were used in the analysed model, each of which represented by a linear process plan. 80 orders dynamically enter the system in 76 hours. The release times of the orders and the corresponding due dates were randomly generated using the uniform distribution. The following table illustrates the results recorded during two experimental runs. In the first case, the resource agents were not permitted to change their cost factors, while in the second case they were entitled to do so. In the second experiment the precondition limits for the low and high level utilization were set to 40% and 80% respectively, while the resource agents were permitted to change their cost factor with 10% in each modification stage.

Table 1. Comparison of two simulation runs. Some performance measures of the system are enumerated in the first column. The second column illustrates the results without cost factor adaptation, while the third column shows the results achieved with cost factor adaptation.

	Constant cost factors	*Adapting cost factors*
Mean. Flowtime	2:22:07:01	2:07:31:55
Min. Flowtime	5:22:12	4:37:33
Max. Flowtime	5:20:54:00	4:13:37:32
Mean. Tardiness	1:19:59:23	21:43:49
Max. Tardiness	4:17:36:23	3:08:11:59
Min. Lateness	-1:10:33:36	-1:02:59:46
Num. of Tardy Jobs	68	53
Utilization res1	28%	59%
Utilization res2	89%	81%
Utilization res3	35%	52%
Utilization res4	75%	66%
Makespan	9:21:44:55	8:18:11:55
Total cost	3277829	3282259

4.2 Adaptation of Task Announcement Parameters by the Order Agent

The second attempt concerns the task announcement procedure initiated by the order agent. In the former system, the first task of each order is announced exactly when the particular order enters the system. By using this task allocation procedure, resource capabilities will be occupied without any information on later orders. It can be expected that better performance can be reached by postponing the task allocation procedure in an appropriate way, taking the system state into consideration. To resolve this problem, and to keep some free capacity for further and more urgent orders, the order agent was empowered with the capability of deciding on the time of the first task announcement. On the base of the previous processing times of different tasks, the order agent calculates a *mean completion period* for order j, marked with ΔT_{MCj}.

Knowing the due date (d_j) of the order j and assuming that the order could be completed in the ΔT_{MCj} period, the remaining "free" time period for this order is: $\Delta T_{Rj} = d_j - \Delta T_{MCj} - r_j$, where r_j denotes the release time of order j. Let us introduce the threshold parameter α and a simple rule referring to this parameter in the following way:

IF ΔT_{Rj} / ΔT_{MCj} > α THEN postpone the first task announcement

For the calculation of the admitted delay parameter β was introduced with the following formula: $T_{Aj} - r_j = \beta * \Delta T_{MCj}$, where T_{Aj} denotes the planned announcement time of the first task from order j (Fig. 4).

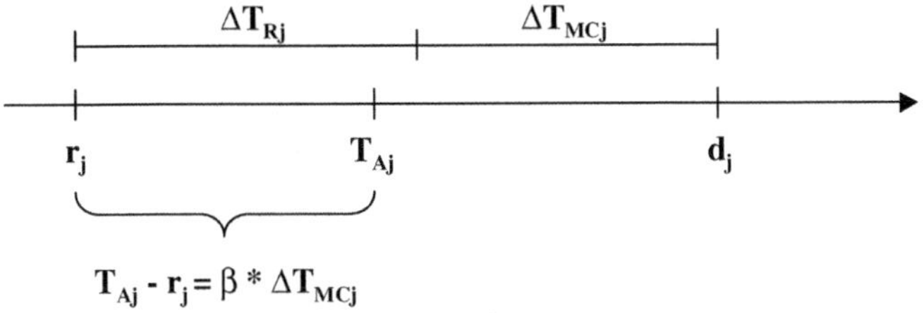

Fig. 4. Dynamic determination of announcement time through the β parameter

According to the above notations, the rule is changed in the following way:

IF ΔT_{Rj} / ΔT_{MCj} > α THEN announce the first task at $r_j + \beta * \Delta T_{MCj}$

Assuming that he objective is to minimize the makespan a dynamic order pattern, it is expected that the order agent can adjust its α and β parameters to achieve its goal(s). To provide the knowledge for the order agent regarding the adjustment of these parameters a large number of simulations have to be performed.

4.2.1 Experiments

The same test environment was used for the experiments conducted to evaluate the behavior of the order agent. As mentioned above, the goal of the order agent, as a system level component, is to minimize the makespan. Supposing a preliminary knowledge about the parameters α and β, they were randomly generated. As shown in Fig. 5 the makespans calculated during the simulation runs are different using different α and β parameters. Naturally, other system level parameters can be tested as well.

5 Conclusions

The paper presented two different attempts for improving the performance of distributed manufacturing systems by expanding the adaptive characteristics of the participating agents. A *resource level learning and adaptation* is presented in section 4.1. The results of this approach showed that within certain limits system level goals can be achieved by adaptation of resource parameters in the possession of exclusively local knowledge. New parameters were introduced in a *system level learning and adaptation* scheme presented in section 4.2. The investigations demonstrated that adaptation of simple time-based parameters could contribute to a significant improvement in the performance of the whole system.

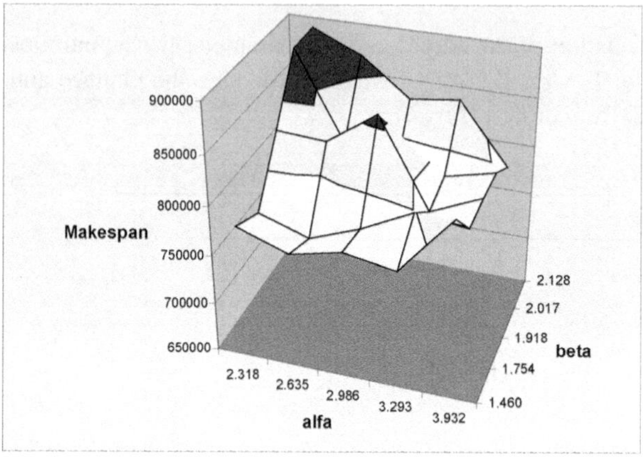

Fig. 5. Makespan of the system plotted against α and β parameters. It should be mentioned that the makespan values are always discrete points in the search space. The surface was fitted on these points only for illustration purposes.

Further research activities has been initiated:

- to find other system and agent level parameters, by which the performance measures of the system can be influenced in a flexible way,
- to investigate machine learning approaches applicable for tuning these parameters in a distributed setting.

Acknowledgements. This work was partially supported by the *National Research Foundation, Hungary,* Grant Nos. T 026486 and T034632. Botond Kádár greatly acknowledges the support of Bolyai János Scholarship of Hungarian Academy of Sciences that significantly eased the contribution.

References

1. Wiendahl, H.-P.; Scholtissek, P.: Management and control of complexity in manufacturing, CIRP Annals, Vol 43, No. 2, (1994) 533-540.
2. Hatvany, J.: The efficient use of deficient information, CIRP Annals, Vol. 32, No. 1, (1983) 423-425.
3. Yoshikawa, H.: Intelligent Manufacturing Systems Program (IMS), Technical Cooperation that Transcends Cultural Differences, University of Tokyo, Japan (1992).
4. Dilts, D.M., N.P. Boyd, H.H. Whorms: The Evolution of Control Architectures for Automated Manufacturing Systems, J. of Manufacturing Systems, Vol.10, No.1. (1991) 79-93.

5. Bongaerts, L.; Monostori, L.; McFarlane, D.; Kádár, B.: Hierarchy in distributed shop floor control, Computers in Industry, Elsevier, Special Issue on Intelligent Manufacturing Systems, Vol. 43, No. 2, (2000), 123-137.
6. Van Brussel, H., Wyns, J., Valckenaers, P., Bongaerts, L., Peeters, P.: Reference architecture for holonic manufacturing systems, Computers in Industry, Special Issue on Intelligent Manufacturing Systems 37/3 (1998) 255-276.
7. Warnecke, H.J.: Revolution der Unternehmenskultur - Das fraktale Unternehmen, Springer Verlag, Berlin, Germany, (1993).
8. Iwata, K., Onosato M., Koike, M.: Random manufacturing system: a new concept of manufacturing systems for production to order, CIRP Annals, V.43, N.1, (1994) 379-383.
9. Ueda, K., Ohkura, K.: A biological approach to complexity in manufacturing systems, Proc. of the 27th CIRP Int. Seminar on Manufacturing Systems, Design, Control and Analysis of Manufacturing Systems, (1995) 69-78.
10. Márkus, A., Kis, T., Váncza, J., Monostori, L.: A market approach to holonic manufacturing, CIRP Annals, Vol. 45/1, (1996) 433-436.
11. Moulin, B.; Chaib-Draa, B.: An overview of distributed artificial intelligence, In: Foundations of distributed artificial intelligence, Morgan-Kaufmann, (1996) 3-56.
12. Bond, A. H.; Gasser, L. (Eds.). Readings in DAI, Morgan-Kaufmann (1988).
13. Shen, W., Norrie, D.H.: Agent-Based Systems for Intelligent Manufacturing: A state-of-the-art survey, Knowledge and Information Systems, Int. J., Vol. 1, No. 2 (1999) 129-156.
14. Sycara, K. P.; Roth, S.; Sadeh, N.; Fox, M.: Resource allocation in distributed factory scheduling, IEEE Expert, February, (1991) 29-40.
15. Baker, A.D.: A Syrvey of Factory Control Algorithms that Can Be implemented in a Multi-Agent Heterarchy: Dispatching, Scheduling and Pull, Journal of Manufacturing System Vol. 17, No. 4, (1998) 297-320.
16. Van Dyke Parunak, H.: Manufacturing Experience with the Contract Net, In: Distributed Artificial Intelligence, Morgan-Kaufmann, Pitman, London, (1987) 285-310
17. Shaw, M.J.: Dynamic Scheduling in Cellular Manufacturing Systems: A Framework for Networked Decision Making, Journal of Manuf. Systems, Vol. 7, No. 2, (1988) 83-93.
18. Duffie, N. A.; Prabhu, V. V.: Real-time distributed scheduling of heterarchical manufacturing systems, Journal of Manufacturing Systems, Vol. 13, No .2, (1994) 94-107.
19. Kádár, B., Monostori, L., Szelke, E.: An object oriented framework for developing distributed manufacturing architectures, J. of Intelligent Manufacturing, Vol. 9, No. 2, April 1998, Special Issue on Agent Based Manufacturing, Chapman & Hall, (1997) 173-179.
20. Kádár B., Monostori, L.: Agent based control of novel and traditional production systems, Proceedings of ICME98, CIRP International Seminar on Intelligent Computation in Manufacturing Engineering, July 1-3, Capri, Italy, (1998) 31 - 38. (key-note paper)

Scheduling of Production Using the Multi-agent Approach by Hierarchical Structure

B. Frankovic and T.T. Dang

Institute of Control Theory and Robotics
Slovak Academy of Sciences
842 37 Bratislava, Dubravská cesta 9, utrrfran@, utrrtung@savba.sk.

Abstract. In this paper we present one of numerous possible applications multi-agent systems – using them to resolve scheduling problem of production systems. We consider a large problem, which can be decomposed to smaller sub-problems and every individual one may be resolved as more efficiently as whole initial problem. We implement also several mechanisms to decomposition and coordination between agents in one level or between themselves in whole system. Our experiments analyze a relation between performances of multi-agent systems to achieve a feasible result and agents' methods coordination or even a type of agent we have considered.

Keywords: Agent, scheduling, decomposition, coordination, control.

1. Introduction

The main objective of the flexible manufacturing systems (FMS), flexible production lines (FPL) and workshop is the optimal scheduling of system resources. The recommendations for the solution of this problem are the application of intelligent agent technology. The result of the solution may be a management network in which is wanted to understand the following factors:

- how to build the agent based network and management system,
- what types of management problems are suited to agent solution,
- how to integrate the agent technology with conventional technology.

Many publications are concerned to the solution of such problem. The paper [5] deals with the application of Distributed Artificial Intelligence (DAI) techniques on system automation, such as flexible production line. Ideas from DAI are becoming important to research fields such as distributed decision making and multi machine scheduling. The paper [1] deals with the problem of optimal scheduling of n parts-types in a machine manufacturing system. In [6] is to point out the influence of machine failures on the performances of a scheduling strategy in a job-shop system. The paper [2] deals with the economical basis of the scheduling problem. In next part the basic formulation of Multi-Agent System (MAS) approach for scheduling of production in the system with hierarchical structure is introduced.

L. Monostori, J. Váncza, and M. Ali (Eds.): IEA/AIE 2001, LNAI 2070, pp. 622-631, 2001.

2. MAS Formulation in General

Collins [3] defines MAS as a "set of possible organized agents, which interact in a common environment". In [4] MAS is defined as a "loosely coupled network of problem solvers that work together to solver problem that are beyond the individual capabilities or knowledge of each problem solver. These problem solvers-agents are autonomous and may be heterogeneous in nature". The characteristics of MAS are:

- each agent has incomplete information or capabilities for solving the problem, thus each agent has a limited viewpoint.
- there is global system control.
- data is decentralized.
- computation is asynchronous.

In general MAS is a heterogeneous set of agents where the concrete relations and frames among agents are defined. Each agent has some means to disposition in order to obtain the given goal with consideration of required constraints.

A possible architecture of agents may be explicated as follows: Let assume that the state of agent's environment is characterized as a set $S=\{s_1, s_2, ...\}$ of *environment states* and at any given instant the agent is assumed to be in one of these states. Capabilities of an agent effect to environment can be modeled a set of actions $A=\{a_1, a_2, ...\}$. The realization of an agent action viewed as a function F expressed as follows:

$$s_{i+1} = f_{a_i}(s_i) \equiv \exists (s_i, a_i, s_{i+1}) \in F \tag{1}$$

which takes the current state of the environment $s \in S$ and action $a \in A$ (performed by the agent), and maps them to a set of environment states-those that could result from performing action a in state s. Then the goal of the agents in MAS from the scheduling aspect is to find the optimal sequences of actions $\{a_1, a_2, ...\} \subset A$ and states $\{s_1, s_2, ...\} \subset S$. Generally in same time is possible to realize different types of agent performance, but in finite step only one performance (sequence of action) is realized. If all the sets in the range of environment are all singletons, then the environment is deterministic and its behavior can be accurately predicted. For one agent, the interaction of agent and environment can represent as a history H, which is a sequence:

$$H : s_0 \xrightarrow{a_0} s_1 \xrightarrow{a_1} s_2 \xrightarrow{a_2} \text{.........} \xrightarrow{a_{k-1}} s_k \xrightarrow{a_k} \ldots \tag{2}$$

The history (2) can be expressed as the trajectory of the dynamics in state space of the variables with which the due agent works.

In the MAS a performing any action by one agent can affect to environment other agents. It is assumed all agents of MAS are in same environment, at any instant one agent takes and executes any action and consequently comes to next state. From point of view of another agent the environment at this instant is changed and in a choosing the action to be executed each other agent must reason this change. While considering affect of action to environment it is assumed only one action is executed at any moment. Generally I_i is indicated as an influence *i-th* agent on the environment, that the chosen action to be executed of any agent can be defined as follows:

$$s_{i+1} = f_{a_i}\left(s_i, \bigcup_{j \neq i} I_j \right) \equiv \exists(s_{i+1}, a_i, s_i) \in F \tag{3}$$

when is paid a condition $I_1 \cup I_2 .. \cup I_{i-1} \cup I_{i+1} ....$

$\bigcup_{j \neq i} I_j$ is specified as all influences of neighboring agents on *i-th* agent. Similar as above it may be define history *H* of MAS as:

$$H : \vec{s}_0 \xrightarrow{a_0} \vec{s}_1 \xrightarrow{a_1} \vec{s}_2 \xrightarrow{a_2} .... \xrightarrow{a_{k-1}} \vec{s}_k \xrightarrow{a_k} ... \tag{4}$$

when $\vec{s} = \{s_1, s_2, ...\}$is a vector of state of all agents in any time and $\vec{a} = \{a_1, a_2, ...\}$is a vector of action of all agents, which are executed in this time.

In the hierarchical structure of MAS each agent in a higher level not only reason about influence of neighboring agents in the same level but also must reason all changes in its environment caused by execution of all agents in lower levels. Let E_k is defined to be environment in the *k-th* level that the chosen action of the agent in the k_0 level at any moment can be defined as follows:

$$s_{i+1}^{k_0} = f_{a_i}\left(s_i^{k_0}, \bigcup_{j \neq i} I_j, \bigcup_{k > k_0} E_k \right) \equiv \exists(s_{i+1}^{k_0}, a_i, s_i^{k_0}) \in F \tag{5}$$

when is paid a condition $\bigcup_{j \neq i} I_j$ and $\bigcup_{k > k_0} E_k$

$\bigcup_{k > k_0} E_k$ is specified as all influences of lower levels on environment k_0-*th* level.

3. Agent Based Network and Management System

Let be such agents dispose of inputs, algorithms for problem solution and outputs. According to the level or properties of used algorithms, it considers in FPL mainly with the autonomous, adaptive, intelligent and interactive agents. The autonomous agent is characterized by certain independence from external control and it can operate without external invocation and intervention. Autonomy has two independent aspects: dynamic autonomy and unpredictable autonomy. Agents are dynamic because they can exercise some degree of activity and react not only to specific method invocation but to observable events within the environment, as well. Adaptive agent is capable of responding to other agents and/or its environment to some degrees. The intelligent agent is created on the basis of expert system. Then it is able to work in changing and uncertain situations, and after executing the solution may to extend the own databases, too. It is the case of learning process of fuzzy decision, which is established in the form of neural network where the agent has training and improving phase. In the basis of this property, the agent reacts to unknown situation that happens in its area very flexible. The interactive agent ensures the communications in agent-based network.

The creation of agent-based network in the case of resources scheduling in FPL requires the decomposition of production process to such elements, which work a one of defined agents. The decomposition may be done on the technological or dynamical basis. The technological decomposition considers with the production sequences and the dynamic decomposition the production time, which may be expressed by the following definition:

- **decomposition according to given order** of production process (PS), when one PS needs output result of other, therefore terminated order of every PS is important for whole process. For example: if $Time\_End_1 < Time\_End_2 < \ldots < Time\_End_n$, where $Time\_End_i$ is the deadline for the PS_i. The decomposition may be made as: the n PS are divided to k groups with same quantity, the first group involves n/k elements PS_1, PS_2, ..., $PS_{n/k}$ and the second group involves the next n/k of remained PS, etc. The last group involves the last $PS_{n(k-1)/k}, \ldots, PS_n$.
- **decomposition according to duration** of every PS, when in a situation what the time condition must be hardly kept, therefore the PS with the longest duration may be serviced as first.
  For example: if $\sum_j T_{1,j} > \sum_j T_{2,j} > \ldots\ldots > \sum_j T_{n,j}$, where $\sum_j T_{i,j}$ is sum of all operations' duration of PS_i and it equals the minimal time necessary to terminate this PS_i. The decomposition of these PS to k groups may be made similar as above: the first group involves n/k products PS_1, PS_2,..., $PS_{n/k}$ etc., and the last group involves n/k last remained PS.
- **decomposition according to worthiness** of every PS, when two above mentioned conditions (terminated order and time condition) are less important than economic condition, then the PS with the biggest worthiness may be executed as first.
  For example: if every PS has certain worthiness (WO), which may be reached after the PS is terminated. For some conveniences it is possible to sort all PS according to their WO and separating these PS to individual group is made similar as above depicted.

The decomposition also may be made in many levels and in every level it can be made according to various criteria.

In the Figure 1 is depicted a method of decomposition, which will be applied in illustrative example. There are 6 products consisted from a set of operations, every product can be considered as one PS with given parameters as deadline, cost, worthiness, etc. The whole process is decomposed in 3 levels. The first level is decomposition these products to single groups, the second is decomposition to single groups machines (agents) and the third is decomposition to individual the machine in the group.

4. General Knowledge

In the example as mentioned above the technological process, which has that many parameters and various modules, such technological process may be considered as large system and it is defined as system, which is specified on performance a lot of tasks of various types and is constructed from various types of mutually related individual units or groups of units. For resolving these tasks of the large system it is assumed:

- The possibility of decompositions to single groups for performance the given tasks and requirements.

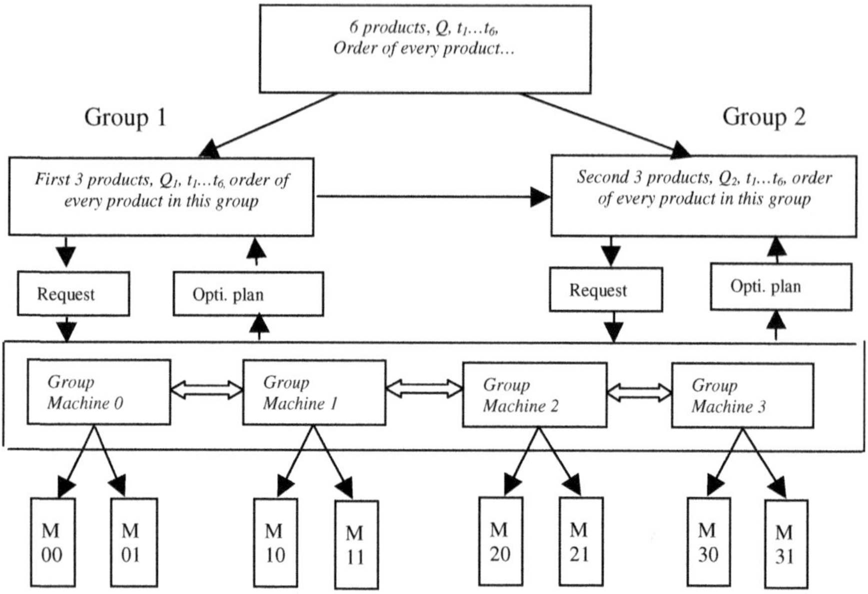

Fig. 1. Agent based network created by the decomposition

- In the stage of planning it is possible to consider with inverse progress, i.e. combination the single units to the group.

In both cases it is assumed knowledge of characteristic of given systems are implemented to individual units.

- Knowledge of technological process.
  For example: In the system excite two equivalent machines 0, two equivalent machines 1.... with various parameters.
- Requirements of production: deadline, order of product, limit of capacities,..
  $Time\_End_i < t_i$, i is a index of product and t_i is given deadline for i-th product.
  $Time\_End_1 < Time\_End_2 < \ldots\ldots < Time\_End_n < \ldots$
- Global criterion function:

$$Q = T + N \tag{6}$$

where T is global function of idle time, and it equals a sum of all idle time in each machine and it is defined as follows:

$$T = \sum_k T_{idle}^k \tag{7}$$

where T^k_{idle} is sum of all idle intervals of k-th machine, or equals distinction between all flow time in each machine and all working time in them too,

$$T = \sum_k T^k_{max} - \sum_{\forall i,j} T_{i,j} = \sum_k [T^k_{max} - \sum_{\forall i,j} T_{i,j,k}] \qquad (8)$$

T^k_{max} is time of k-th machine after performance the last operation assigned for it, $T_{i,j}$ is duration of i-th operation of j-th product ($O_{i,j}$), $T_{i,j,k}$ is time when $O_{i,j}$ spends in k-th machine and it equals $T_{i,j}$ if $O_{i,j}$ is assigned for k-th machine and equals 0 if the $O_{i,j}$ is not assigned for other machine.

N is performance's cost function of all products. It is consisted from 2 functions when these machines work and when they are idle.

$$N = N_{idle} + N_{work} \qquad (9)$$

where N_{idle} and N_{work} are cost function of all machines when these machines are in a idle state or when they are working respectively. These functions are defined as following:

$$N_{idle} = \sum_k T^k_{idle} * c_k = \sum_k [T^k_{max} - \sum_{i,j} T_{i,j,k}] * c_k \qquad (10)$$

$$N_{idle} = \sum_k T^k_{idle} * c_k = \sum_k [T^k_{max} - \sum_{i,j} T_{i,j,k}] * c_k \qquad (11)$$

k is a number of the machine, where $O_{i,j}$ is produced,
c_k is a const and is cost per unit time when k-th machine is idle,
α_k is given const and it is cost per unit time when k-th machine works.

- Time of the scheduling (T_{sche}) is defined as maximum of all T^k ,

$$T_{sche} = \max_k \{T^k_{max}\} \qquad (12)$$

5. Decomposition Criterion Functions

The whole technological process is decomposed to respective groups as described in the section 3 and after decomposition all constrains need to be kept (deadlines, order of every product, capacities...). Despite the decomposition, the global criterion function as showed in the section 4 also needs to be decomposed to partial functions, where every of them is as sub-criterion function for this sub-problem.

Decomposition global criterion function Q to sub-criterion functions, it depends on approach of decomposition requirements initiated above,

$$Q = \sum_r Q_r = \sum_r [T(G_r) + N(G_r)] \qquad (13)$$

where Q_r is criterion function for *r-th* group of products, it is defined similar as Q and G_r is an *r-th* set of products after decomposition. The functions T and N are also decomposed to single functions and they are defined as following:

$$T(G_r) = \sum_k [T_{\max}^k - \sum_{\forall j \in G_r, i} T_{i,j,k}] \tag{14}$$

it is function of idle time for these products belong to set of G_r.

$$N(G_r) = N_{idle}(G_r) + N_{work}(G_r) \tag{15}$$

it is cost function for these products belong to set of G_r and it equals:

$$N(G_r) = \sum_k [T_{\max}^k - \sum_{\forall j \in G_r, i} T_{i,j,k}] * c_k + \sum_k \sum_{\forall j \in G_r, i} T_{i,j,k} * \alpha_k$$
$$= \sum_{\forall j \in G_r} \{ \sum_k [T_{\max}^k - \sum_i T_{i,j,k}] * c_k + \sum_k \sum_i T_{i,j,k} * \alpha_k \} \tag{16}$$

6. Scheduling and Some Results

In our concrete example is considered a technological process with 6 products and every of them request a queue of operations:

P1: 0 1 2 3 0 1 3	P2: 0 2 3 2 0 1 3
P3: 1 3 2 0 1 3 0	P4: 1 2 3 0 2 3 1
P5: 0 3 2 1 0 3 1	P6: 0 1 2 1 3 1 0

where 0,1,2,3 note a type of the operation. Each type of the operation must be executed in one certain group machine. These group machines work individually and have a common goal to achieve the best performance, but each of them can be considered as one agent with all properties as mentioned above in section 2.

The first the process begins by decomposing all products to smaller groups according to introduced mechanism as in the section 3. In the next step the process begins schedule all products in every group to individual machine, with respecting all given constrains and characteristics of every machine.

In every group of machine (one agent) the designated operations are also divided to single equivalent machine in this group (agent in lower level) according to following methods.

- Every machine (autonomous agent) may work independently without communication or knowledge about another machine in its group and executes this operations sent down from higher level first-come first-serve (version 1).
- In one group every machine exchanges information with another and they negotiate among themselves and choose the best plan, which minimize the sub-criterion function (version 2).
- Every group of machine exchanges information with another and in one group every machine communicates with another. The message, which these groups of machine exchange between themselves, involves all information of every own machine (version 3).

- Similar as version 3, but in a basis of all information received from another groups, every group of machine tries to predict the plan of another groups and improves own plan before sending it to all groups (version 4).

In the last level all machines (agent in the last level) try to compose such scheduling, which may minimize the all sub-criterion function (14) and (16) in each group, and finally as most as possible minimize global criterion function defined in (6).

Complex program for simulation was made in language C under LINUX, where the system is divided to 5 agents: agent CE and 4 agents MA1, MA2, MA3, MA4. Four agents MA1-MA4 present 4 group machines and behaviour of all equivalent machines in each group (agent in lower level) are involved in their inside.

- Agent CE is intelligent agent, it holds all requirements and initial constrains. Agent CE has these tasks:
  - decomposition whole initial problem to sub-problems according to above presented principles with respecting of all given constrains.
  - sending successively every sub-problem to lower level and waits for a result.
  - if the result satisfies all given constrains and sub-optimal conditions the program finishes, else tries again to make decomposition.
- Every agent of MA1, MA2, MA3, and MA4 is adaptive agent, and it includes 2 autonomous agents (2 equivalent machines), their behaviour is according to these introduced versions above (version 1 to 4). These agents have tasks: manipulate these requests from agent CE, try to search a scheduling, which minimizes the sub-criterion function.

Because agents MA1-MA4 are in a same environment and they have a common goal to achieve a good scheduling for all products, each choosing plan of one agent certainly influences to choosing other one in next step, therefore their behaviour is precisely according to a equal (3) and (4).

The agent CE is a master of all agents MA1-MA4, it makes all agents in lower level (MA1-MA4) satisfy its aim and in a case negative response it must select a new aim in a basis of a results what it received from lower level.

Table 1. $T_{i,j,1}$ Duration of operations if all first machines of every group are used.

Number of operation	*1*	*2*	*3*	*4*	*5*	*6*	*7*
Pro. 1	2	2	3	2	2	5	1
Pro. 2	1	3	1	2	2	4	2
Pro. 3	1	2	2	1	4	2	5
Pro. 4	2	1	5	3	1	1	2
Pro. 5	2	2	1	1	4	4	2
Pro. 6	1	4	2	2	4	4	2

Table 1

Table 2. $T_{i,j,2}$ Duration of operations if all second machines of every group are used.

1	*2*	*3*	*4*	*5*	*6*	*7*
1	1	3	2	2	5	2
1	2	2	1	3	5	2
2	3	2	2	4	4	5
2	2	6	4	2	1	2
2	3	2	2	2	2	4
2	4	4	2	4	5	1

Table 2

Each new aim agent CE is a result of choosing combined of its own knowledge, its historic (historical aims) and the results received from lower levels, its behaviour is therefore precisely according to a equal (5) described in section 2.For our example we chose $\alpha_k = c_k = 1$ for all indexes k and the result from this choice is the minimizing criterion function in (6) is equivalently with minimizing $T^k_{\max}$ for all k. In table 3 are presented the results when agents' behaviour is successively according to version 1,2,3. $T^k_{\max}$ is expressed in unit time.

Table 3. Results of the simulation agent's behaviours.

	T^{00}_{max}	T^{01}_{max}	T^{10}_{max}	T^{11}_{max}	T^{20}_{max}	T^{21}_{max}	T^{30}_{max}	T^{31}_{max}	T_{sche}
Ver. 1	22	26	25	27	15	11	29	25	**29**
Ver. 2	21	14	21	22	12	6	24	14	**24**
Ver. 3	21	21	21	19	14	6	18	18	**21**

In the basis of obtained results it may be affirm that the best result gave version 3, but the agents had to exchange a lot of information between themselves, it might cause overload a net and slow an execution. The version 1 executed the fastest but to feasible result it needed to run several steps more than another version. The version 2 gave a meanly good result, but the result very depends on the method of decomposition. In the suitable decomposition it could give such good result as version 3 after a few steps. In figure 2 is shown the illustrative result of applying version 3 to agent's behaviours.

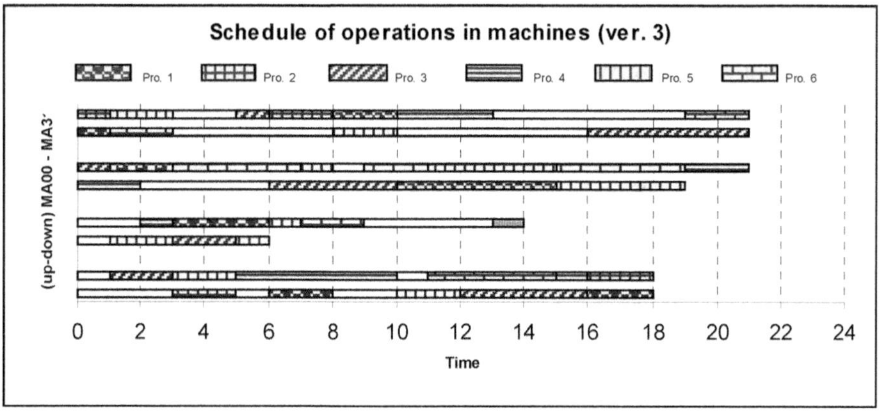

Fig. 2. The schedule of operations in machines- Version 3

For another value α_k and c_k this problem is more complicated, it is similar as *min-max* problem when a force to minimize the function T causes a increasing value of cost function N. The function of flow time T and the cost function N one another influences, the effect is to find optimal plan, which minimizes global criterion function Q, it is necessary to try a more variants decomposition or add more utilities to every agent's belief. In following part are presented some results what we have tried with concrete value α_k, value c_k we have omitted (c_k=0 cost when the machine is in idle state). A more details associated with this problem we will show in future work. In our experiment the version 3 showed soon same results, expressive different results were obtained by changing method of decomposition, for example by changing order of one product with other, but this mechanism is not built in any firm algorithm and it claimed a patiently temptation and more experiences.

Table 4. α_k , cost when a machine works per unit time.

Machine's number	0	1	2	3
α_0 (unit)	3	4	5	3
α_1 (unit)	2	2	4	1

Table 5. Results of using ver.1

T_{sche} (unit)	24	25	28	34
N (unit)	295	282	290	286

Table 6. Results of using ver.2

21	22	25	26
288	278	262	259

Generally the presented problem can be resolved as simple centralized *NP*-problem, but with the decomposition we can decrease a time of a computation, despite it the reached result may be considered as optimal (as in our case we searched all possible variants and the best solution only gives a result as version 3) or near optimal.

7. Discussion

In this paper has been presented one mechanism – using MAS – that can compute optimal or near optimal solution to the distributed scheduling problem in a computationally efficient manner. However it cannot guarantee the global optimal solution for given problem, but using MAS can offer feasible sub-optimal solution and many abilities to flexible react on dynamic change in the system. The results showed in this paper by applying MAS mechanism are surely good but some points of that problem also may be extended and explored a more as example for various values α_k and c_k, the problem to find optimal Q becomes to solve min-max problem with N and T. Some features we have omitted in this paper and will continue in future works as problem of decomposition, coordination between agents or the method of agent's prediction.

References

1. Montgomery, T. and Durfee, E.: A hierarchical protocol for coordinating multi-agent behaviours. In *Proceeding of the Eighth National Conference on AI, 1990.*
2. Rauber, T. and Runger, G.: Compiler support for task scheduling in hierarchical execution models. In *Journal of Systems Architecture 45, 483-503,1998.*
3. Collins, P. and Shepherdson, J.: Process management using intelligent workflow systems.
4. Wooldrige, M. and Jennings, N. R.: Intelligent agents: Theory and practice. *The knowledge engineering review, 10; 115-152,1995.*
5. Chaib, B., Draa, Moulin, B.: Trends in distributed Artificial Intelligence; *Artificial Intelligence review, Vol. 6, No. 1, 1992, p 35-66.*
6. Geneste, L. and Domenech, J.: Evalution of job-shop scheduling heuristic in workshop subject to disturbances. *In Proc. CIMAT 96, ENSIEG-INPG, France 1996, p. 9-13.*

Optimization of Disassembly Sequences for Recycling of End-of-Life Products by Using a Colony of Ant-Like Agents

F. Failli and G. Dini

DIMNP - Department of Mechanical, Nuclear and Production Engineering,
University of Pisa, Via Bonanno Pisano 25b,
56126 Pisa, Italy
{failli, dini}@ing.unipi.it

Abstract. In this paper the problem of recycling of end-of-life goods is approached using a computer-aided technique named Ant Colony Optimization system. The need of disassembly for recycling and the opportunity of using computer-aided techniques, AI tools in particular, are discussed. The basic concepts of Ant Colony Optimization systems are also introduced. The main topics related to a future application of this methodology to a software system able to support the designer in choosing the best disassembly sequences of products are discussed.

1. Introduction

In these last years the need to optimize the use of energy and raw materials has been often stressed in political and technical areas of interest.

The idea of a sustainable growth of the life quality is now well known and deeply diffused in all industrialized countries. So, the time has come to study very deeply all the problems related to the recycling of discarded goods, mainly for basic commodities as household appliances, cars, motorcycles and so on.

Recycling is not an easy problem to approach. Since the aim of this procedure is the minimization of the environmental impact of the human production activities, it is very important to detect procedures able to recover materials and energy with respect to the standard production processes using raw materials. Furthermore, for each process using recycled materials, it is crucial to establish if its pollution rate is higher or lower than traditional production procedures.

The need of taking into account all these issues forces the researchers to use increasingly powerful tools to approach the problems related to recycling. Starting from these considerations, new branches of technology have been opened, e.g. life cycle analysis techniques.

In this scenario, one of the problems to be solved is the detection of the optimum way to disassembly a discarded good in order to recover its materials and/or some of

L. Monostori, J. Váncza, and M. Ali (Eds.): IEA/AIE 2001, LNAI 2070, pp. 632-639, 2001.

its components. This problem is known as *sequencing* because the final goal is the best sequence to adopt for disassembling the product. Usually the term "best sequence" means, in this context, "most profitable sequence".

2. Software Methodologies in Disassembly Planning

Disassembly planning is a typical combinatorial problem. In usual products, in fact, a huge number of different ways (sequences) to separate the components can be performed, but only a limited number of these ones are economically convenient from the point of view of recovering and recycling parts and materials. Therefore, the problem can be split into 2 sub-problems:

- *generating feasible disassembly sequences*, taking into consideration geometrical and technological constraints of the product (e.g.: contact relationships among components, kinds of connections, etc.);
- *detecting the best sequences*, taking into consideration a balance between disassembly and disposal costs, and revenues deriving from recovering parts and materials.

The first sub-problem has been deeply investigated by many researchers, considering also the related area of assembly planning, and can be efficiently approached and solved by traditional methods using:

- connection or disassembly graphs [9], [7], allowing an easy representation of relationships among components;
- so called "recyclinggraphs", needed to include in such models further information concerning materials, weight, etc. [6];
- contact and connection matrices, as representative model of the product for an easy generation of all the possible sequences [2].

The second sub-problem apparently seems to be a simple problem. Typically, for each disassembly step, the profit achievable from recycling has to be calculated [7]. A further method consists in evaluating a "disassembly difficulty"; this approach is used when information about values of materials, disposal costs, etc. are not available or are not exactly known [10].

Difficulties arise in detecting best sequences when a combinatorial explosion of sequences to be analyzed takes place. In this situation, which often occurs also in low or medium-complex products, the huge number of feasible sequences for which the profit has to be calculated, leads very often to unacceptable computing times.

The objective is therefore to reduce this time by searching best disassembly sequences without analyzing all the possible alternatives, but approaching the final goal through a step-by-step procedure. This way of searching is well represented by *Genetic Algorithms* (GAs). The basic idea of GAs is quite simple: a population of individuals is created in a computer; this population evolves, accordingly to the biological principles of selection and inheritance, and converges toward structures representing optimal or sub-optimal solutions to the problem. Examples of this technique applied to the similar problem of assembly planning can be found in [8], [1].

In the present paper another approach to the problem of disassembly for recycling, derived from the AI world, is proposed. It is based on previous experiences of the authors in the field of assembly planning [4], [5] and uses a technique named *Ant Colony Optimization* (ACO) developed from the biological researches focused to the behavior of real ants.

3. Overall Description of the Proposed System

At the Department of Mechanical, Nuclear and Production Engineering of the University of Pisa, a software tool aimed to support the designer in detecting the best disassembly sequence has been developed.

The system, named DIRECT (DIsassembly for RECycling Tool), is formed by the following modules (Fig.1):

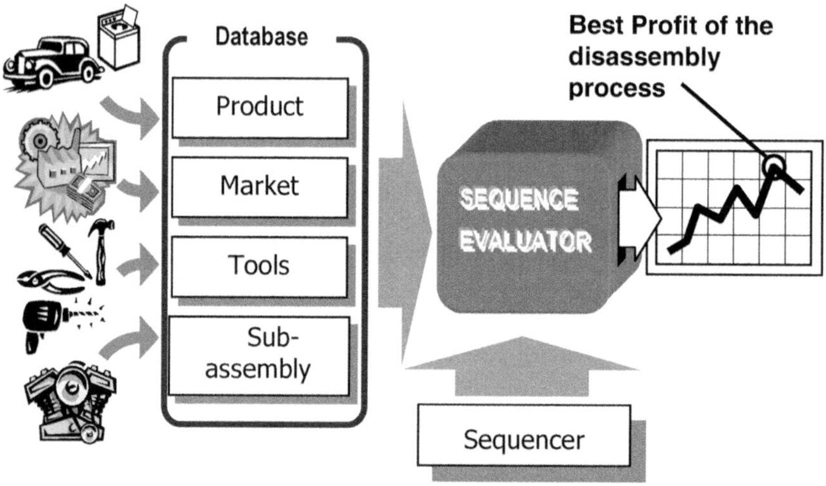

Fig. 1. Schematic overview of DIRECT system.

- *product database*, containing all the needed information about the product: number of the components, weights and materials, connections between the components, geometrical relationships, etc.;
- *market database*, containing information about the market: labor costs, energy costs, disposal costs, market values of recycled materials, etc.;
- *tool database*, containing information about the tools to be used for the disassembly of the components. Each component is related to the tool suitable for its disassembly. Only one tool can be considered for the disassembly of a single component;
- *subassembly database*, containing information about the valuable subassemblies included in the product. In this context a subassembly is a group of connected ele-

ments suitable for re-using and having a market value (e.g. an electric engine, a compressor in a home appliance, etc.);

- *sequencer*, able to automatically detect all the possible disassembly sequences starting from the geometrical and technological relationships among components;
- *sequence evaluator*, able to assign to each disassembly sequence its profit in terms of recovered materials and components.

In its first version, DIRECT detected best disassembly sequences by means of an exhaustive method. All the disassembly sequences were automatically generated by the *sequencer* through a simulated extraction of each component. After each extraction, numerical matrices (representing the relationship model of the product) were automatically updated to the new configuration, repeating the process until the disassembly was completed. The *evaluator* assessed each sequence calculating, for each disassembly step, the total profit P through the following expression:

$$P = R_1 + R_2 - (C_1 + C_2) \tag{1}$$

being R_l the revenue obtained from the disassembled components or materials, R_2 the revenue obtained from the remaining part of the product (not yet dismounted), C_l the total disassembly costs and C_2 the disposal costs for unrecoverable components.

As also remarked in the previous section, this way of running led to very high computing times, also for relatively simple products having less than 50 components. This fact stimulated the authors to seek alternative methods more oriented to combinatorial problems and advantageously applicable in disassembly planning systems. One of these methods seems to be the ACO system.

4. Implementation of Ant Colony Optimization

4.1 What Is an ACO System ?

In the field of AI tools, one of the new entries is represented by the Ant Colony Optimization systems. This original name derives from the studies performed on the behavior of the ants in the real world. Many researchers noticed that, during the collection of the food, the real ants always use the shorter trail between the food and the nest. This fact occurs also when the food is very far from the nest, and no visual landmark is present.

After many studies it emerged that this capacity is related to the use of a substance named "pheromone" secreted by the ants during their searching for the food.

The key of the ant behavior is their bent to follow a trail where a quantity of pheromone is already deposited, rather than a completely new one. Furthermore, the higher is the pheromone quantity on a trail, the stronger is the bent of the ants to follow that trail.

When lots of ants are searching for food around the nest and one of them finds something interesting, e.g. a dead insect too big to bring it to the nest, a "coming and going" starts between the food and the nest.

The shorter is the trail between the nest and the food, the higher is the number of times that a single ant can cover that trail in the time unit. Therefore the concentration of pheromone, at first randomly distributed on the ground, will increase on the shortest trail and this trend will be quickly reinforced by the bent of the ants to follow the trail with the highest concentration of pheromone. Because the pheromone evaporates, after some time only the shortest trail remains (Fig.2).

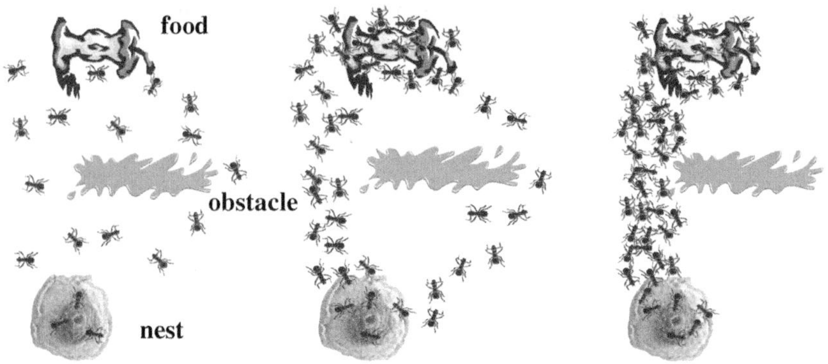

Fig. 2. Real ant behavior in searching food: (a) random searching, (b) detecting the shortest trail, (c) moving on the best trail.

It has to be stressed that the shortest way rarely is a straight line. In fact very often many obstacles are present between the food and the nest. But the power of the ant behavior is just its independence from the shape of the trail.

Using the described system, the ants are able to optimize (in this case, to minimize) the length of the trail to cover between the food and the nest. But transforming the real ants into mathematical agents, the described process becomes a powerful tool to face general optimization and combinatorial problems.

4.2 Basic Expressions for ACO Application in Disassembly Planning

The concepts described above are undoubtedly charming, but are they exploitable to solve "human" technical problems? Many researchers tried to answer this question and, at the end, the response was positive. Now there are many works applying these concepts to the solution of typical optimization problems, such as Traveling Salesman Problem [3].

The main question to face for making possible the use of the ACO technique in a new application field is the modeling of the problem. In fact to solve an optimization problem using ACO, its rearrangement in terms of trails and pheromone deposition is necessary.

In general, the main decisions to be taken involve the following topics:
- *definition of trails* for the specific problem to be solved;
- best way to model the *pheromone deposition* and evaporation phenomena;
- best way to model the *ant choice* to follow a particular trail.

4.2.1 Definition of Trails

In ACO systems, the aspect to be optimized determines the trail structure. Thus, for the disassembly planning problem, the trail becomes the sequence of the disassembly operations. The best trail is the best way to "connect" the different disassembly operations, i.e. the most profitable disassembly sequence. The problem is quite similar to the TSP problem, where there is a sequence of cities to be connected by the shortest path. In that case is necessary to minimize the distance to cover, whereas in the case of disassembly planning is necessary to maximize the total profit.

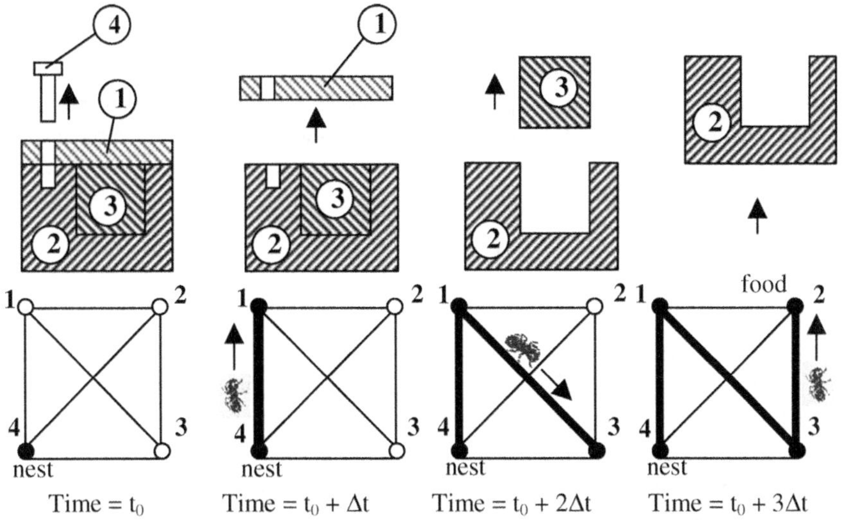

Fig. 3. Example of step-by-step procedure of product disassembly with associated graph representing ant trails.

4.2.2 Pheromone Deposition

In real world each ant releases on trails always the same rate of pheromone. In virtual world different techniques can be more advantageous. The quantity of pheromone on trails can be updated by a step-by-step procedure measured by the time interval Δt (Fig.3). The following relation is usually applied:

$$\tau_{i,j}(t+\Delta t) = \rho\tau_{i,j}(t) + \Delta\tau_{i,j}(t) \tag{2}$$

where $\tau_{i,j}(t)$ represents the amount of pheromone deposited at the time t on the part of the trail linking the ith element and the jth element; ρ is the evaporation coefficient and $\Delta\tau_{i,j}(t)$ is the amount of pheromone released in the current disassembly operation by the ant. The evaluation of $\Delta\tau_{i,j}(t)$ depends on the function to be optimized and, in the case proposed in this paper, on the profit P (evaluated through the expression (1)) to be maximized. A first tentative expression could be:

$$\Delta\tau_{i,j}(t) = kf(P) \tag{3}$$

where k is a non negative number weighing the contribution of $\Delta\tau_{i,j}(t)$ to the formula (2) and $f(P)$ is a non negative function of P.

In this way each disassembly operation belonging to a good sequence receives a higher quantity of pheromone, that allows a successive ant chooses it again. At the end of the process, the best chain of disassembly operations is therefore generated. But how can a virtual ant choose a trail instead of another one? This will be described in the next paragraph.

4.2.3 Ant Choice

The pheromone rate on a trail determines the probability that an ant chooses to move on that trail. The stronger is the pheromone track on a trail, the higher is the probability that ants follow that trail. Thus, it is possible to model the ant choice by calculating a probability:

$$p_{i,j}(t) = \frac{[\tau_{i,j}(t)]^{\alpha}[\eta_{i,j}]^{\beta}}{\sum_{k=1}^{N}[\tau_{i,k}(t)]^{\alpha}[\eta_{i,k}]^{\beta}} \tag{4}$$

where $\tau_{i,j}(t)$ is the rate of pheromone laying on the section i-j of the trail at the time t; $\eta_{i,j}$ contains an arbitrary value necessary to allow a choice when the pheromone is not yet deposited on the trail; α and β are non-negative numbers measuring the weight of $\tau_{i,j}(t)$ and $\eta_{i,j}$; N is the total number of possible choices.

The terms $\eta_{i,j}$ play an important role in the initial phase of trail searching. For this reason, these terms have to be set to proper values, known *a priori*, in order to force the selection of profitable disassembly operations (e.g. separation of high value materials or components).

5. Future Work

The ideas expressed in the system DIRECT together with the potential of the Ant Colony Optimization seem to be a promising way to solve the difficulties of the disassembly and recycling process planning. The future work will be the implementation of this AI technique in order to test its performance in finding the best way of disassembling an end-of-life product in order to recycle its materials and components. Several difficulties and peculiar problems have to be faced and solved in this application: dismounting by cutting, destruction of single parts of the product, use of customized tools allowing faster disassembly processes, etc. These aspects may be identified as "obstacles" on the way toward the detection of the most profitable disassembly process, exactly as pebbles and puddles are obstacles to be avoided by ants to find the shortest trail to the food.

References

1. Dini, G., Failli, F., Lazzerini, B., Marcelloni, F., 1999, Generation of optimized assembly sequences using genetic algorithms, Annals of the CIRP, Vol.48/1/1999, pp: 17-20.
2. Dini, G., Failli, F., Santochi, M. 2001, A disassembly planning software system for the optimization of recycling processes, Production Planning and Control, (to be published).
3. Dorigo, M., Gambardella, L.M., 1997, Ant colony system: A cooperative learning approach to the traveling salesman problem, IEEE Transactions on Evolutionary Computation v 1 n 1 Apr 1997. pp. 53-66.
4. Failli, F., Dini, G., 1999, Searching optimized assembly sequences by ant colony systems, Proc. of 4th AITEM Congress, Brescia (Italy), Sept. 13-15, pp. 87-94.
5. Failli, F., Dini, G., 2000, Ant colony systems in assembly planning: a new approach to sequence detection and optimization, Proc. of ICME 2000, Capri (Italy), June 21-23, pp 227-232.
6. Feldmann, K., Scheller, H., 1994, Design for recyclability and economic planning of disassembly based on the recyclinggraph tool, Proceedings of 2nd. International Seminar on Life Cycle Engineering, pp.76 90.
7. Lambert, A.J.D., de Ron A.J., Splinter M.A.M., 1996, Optimal disassembly, Proceedings of 3rd. International Seminar on Life Cycle Engineering, pp.203 210.
8. Sebaaly, M.F., Fujimoto, H., 1996, A Genetic Planner for Assembly Automation, IEEE Conf. on Evolutionary Computation, Nagoya, May 20-22, pp. 401-406.
9. Spath, D., 1994, Utilization of hypermedia-based information systems for developing recyclable products and for disassembly planning, CIRP Annals, 43, (1), pp.153 156
10. Zussman, E., Krivet, A., Seliger, G., 1994, Disassembly-oriented assessment methodology to support design for recycling, Annals of the CIRP, 43, (1), pp.9 14.

Sound and Visual Tracking for Humanoid Robot

Hiroshi G. Okuno[1,2], Kazuhiro Nakadai[1], Tino Lourens[1], and Hiroaki Kitano[1,3]

[1] Kitano Symbiotic Systems Project, ERATO, Japan Science and Technolog Corp.
Mansion 31 Suite 6A, 6-31-15 Jingumae, Shibuya, Tokyo 150-0001 Japan
{okuno, nakadai, tino, kitano}@symbio.jst.go.jp
[2] Science University of Tokyo, Noda Chiba 278-8510, Japan
[3] Sony Computer Science Laboratories, Inc., Shinagawa, Tokyo 141-0022

Abstract. Mobile robots with auditory perception usually adopt "*stop-perceive-act*" principle to avoid sounds made during moving due to motor noises or bumpy roads. Although this principle reduces the complexity of the problems involved auditory processing for mobile robots, it restricts their capabilities of auditory processing. In this paper, sound and visual tracking is investigated to attain robust object tracking by compensating each drawbacks in tracking objects. Visual tracking may be difficult in case of occlusion, while sound tracking may be ambiguous in localization due to the nature of auditory processing. For this purpose, we present an active audition system for a humanoid robot. The audition system of the intelligent humanoid requires localization of sound sources and identification of meanings of the sound in the auditory scene. The active audition reported in this paper focuses on improved sound source tracking by integrating audition, vision, and motor movements. Given the multiple sound sources in the auditory scene, *SIG the humanoid* actively moves its head to improve localization by aligning microphones orthogonal to the sound source and by capturing the possible sound sources by vision. The system adaptively cancels motor noise using motor control signals. The experimental result demonstrates the effectiveness and robustness of sound and visual tracking.

1 Introduction

Mobile robots with auditory perception usually adopt "*stop-perceive-act*" principle to avoid sounds made during moving due to motor and mechanical noises or uneven grounds [1,2,3]. Although this principle reduces the complexity of the problems involved in auditory processing for mobile robots, it restricts their capabilities of auditory processing and thus limits the application areas. In this paper, sound and visual tracking is investigated to attain robust object tracking by compensating each drawbacks in tracking objects. Visual tracking may be difficult in case of occlusion, while sound tracking may be ambiguous in localization due to the nature of auditory processing.

The goal of the research reported in this paper is to establish a technique of multi-modal integration for a robust object tracking. We use an upper-torso humanoid robot as a platform of the research, because we believe that a sensori-motor system is essential to simulate intelligent behavior. This paper focuses

L. Monostori, J. Váncza, and M. Ali (Eds.): IEA/AIE 2001, LNAI 2070, pp. 640–650, 2001.

on integration of audition, vision, and motor control at the level of directional information.

Since a mobile robot produces various sounds and is able to "understand" many kinds of sounds, auditory scene analysis is the process of simulating useful intelligent behavior, and even required when objects are invisible. While traditionally, auditory research has been focusing on human speech understanding, understanding auditory scenes in general is receiving increasing attention. Computational Auditory Scene Analysis (CASA) studies a general framework of sound processing and understanding [4,5,6,7]. Its goal is to understand an arbitrary sound mixture including speech, non-speech sounds, and music in various acoustic environment. It requires not only understanding of the meaning of a specific sound, but also identifies the spatial relationship of sound sources, so that sound landscapes of the environment can be recognized. This leads to the need of active audition that has capability of dynamically focusing on a specific sound in a mixture of sounds, and actively controlling motor systems to obtain further information using audition, vision, and other perceptions [8].

The main problems with humanoid audition during motion includes understanding general sounds, sensor fusion, active audition, and internal sound suppression.

1. **General sound understanding** — Since a robot hears a mixture of sounds, sound stream separation is essential for CASA [7].
2. **Sensor fusion for sound stream separation** — Sound stream separation performs better with binaural input (a kind of stereo sounds) than monaural input. In addition, integrating a stereo input with vision processing may improve the performance of sound stream separation.
3. **Active audition** — A humanoid should be active in the sense that it tries to do some activity to improve perceptual processing. Such activity includes to change the position of cameras (active vision) and microphones (active audition) by motor control, and object tracking.
4. **Internal sound suppression** — Since active perception causes sounds by the movement of various movable parts, internal sound suppression is critical to enhance external sounds. A cover of the humanoid body reduces sounds of motors emitted to the external world by separating internal and external world of the robot.

The error in sound source direction obtained by using harmonic structures of binaural sounds is about $\pm 10°$ [9], which is similar to $\pm 8°$, that of a human [10]. However, this is too coarse to separate sound streams from a mixture of sounds. Nakagawa et al. [11] improved the accuracy of the sound source direction by using the direction extracted by image processing. By using an accurate direction, each sound stream is extracted by using a *direction-pass filter*. In fact, by integrating visual and auditory information, they succeeded to separate three sound sources from a mixture of sounds by two microphones. They also reported how the accuracy of sound stream separation measured by automatic speech recognition is improved by *adding more modalities*, from monaural input, binaural input, and binaural input with visual information.

A cover affects the spectrum of sounds like a dummy head in which a pair of dummy headphones are embedded. This spectral effect is known as the *HRTF* (*Head-Related Transfer Function*). The HRTF plays an important role in localizing (calculating the position of) a sound source. To localize sound sources with two microphones, a set of peaks are extracted for left and right channels, respectively. Then, the same or similar peaks of left and right channels are identified as a pair and each pair is used to calculate the *interaural phase difference* (*IPD*) and the *interaural intensity difference* (*IID*). The IPD and IID for a particular direction are calculated by the HRTF.

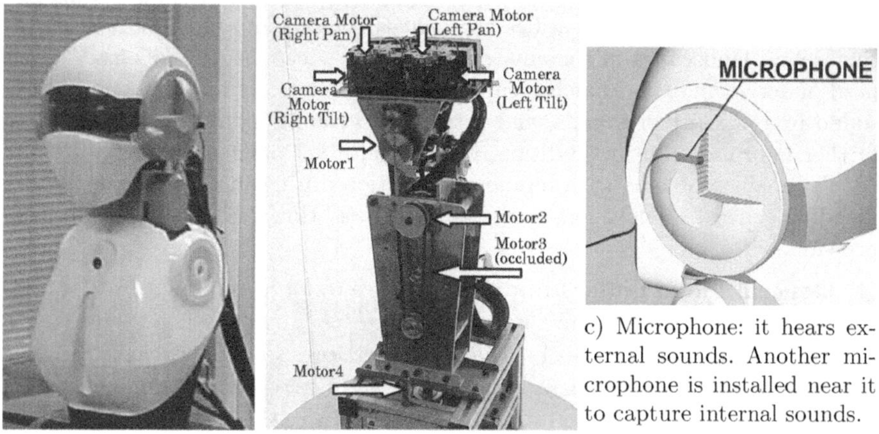

c) Microphone: it hears external sounds. Another microphone is installed near it to capture internal sounds.

a) Cover made of FRP b) Mechanical structure

Fig. 1. The Upper-Torso Humanoid *SIG*

The HRTF is obtained by measuring an impulse response for each spatial position, which is timeconsuming. In addition, the HRTF should be re-measured for a different environment, since it depends on the shape and objects in the room and so on. Therefore, we adopt the localization algorithm based on the auditory epipolar geometry proposed by Nakadai *et al* [8] to dispense with the HRTF.

2 Sound and Visual Tracking System

As a testbed for integration of perceptual information to control motor of high *Degree of Freedom* (*DOF*), we use the upper-torso humanoid robot *SIG* [12]. The cover of the body (Figure 1a) reduces sounds to be emitted to external environments, which is expected to reduce the complexity of sound processing. *SIG* has 4 DOFs of body, driven by each DC motor. Its mechanical structure is shown in Figure 1b. Each DC motor is controlled by a potentiometer. *SIG* has a pair of CCD cameras of Sony EVI-G20 for visual stereo processing. Each camera has 3 DOFs. It has two pairs of omni-directional microphones (Sony ECM-77S); one pair are installed at the ear position of the head to gather sounds from the external world (Figure 1c). Each microphone is shielded by the cover to prevent from capturing internal noises. The other pair of microphones are installed very close to the corresponding microphone to capture sounds from the internal world.

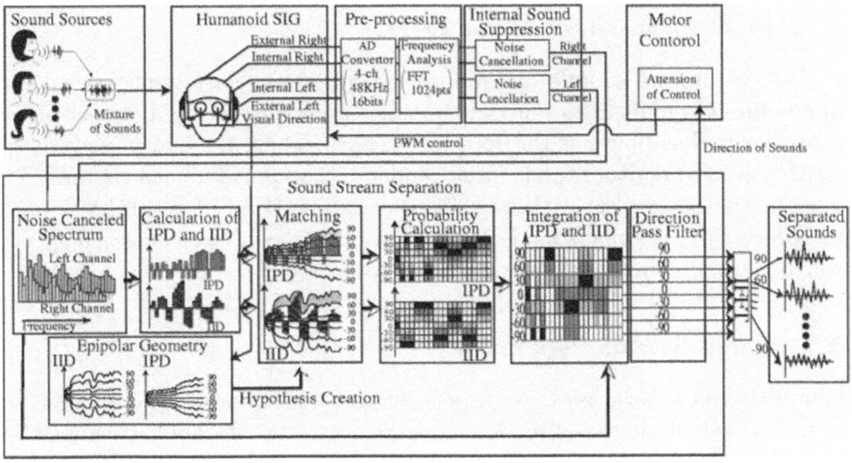

Fig. 2. Sound and Visual Tracking System for Humanoid *SIG*

The sound and visual tracking system for *SIG* consists of two main subsystems; internal sound suppression, and sound stream separation (Figure 2).

2.1 Internal Sound Suppression by Adaptive Filter

Internal sounds of *SIG* are caused mainly by camera and body motors. A standby sound of a camera motor is about 3.7 db, but its moving sound is quiet enough to ignore. A standby and moving sound of a body motor are about 5.6 dB and 23 dB, respectively.

Since a burst noise causes most trouble in auditory processing, sound tracking, in particular, the adaptive filter is designed to suppress burst noises. Such burst noises include a thump at stoppers, a click by friction between cable and body, a creak at joints of cover parts may occur. Therefore, *"heuristics about internal microphones"* is used to specify the conditions to cut off burst noises mainly caused by motors [13].

First, burst noises are collected by moving various motors repeatedly. The noise data of each motor is stored as a power spectrum of the averaged measured noises. Next, the stored data is used as templates to judge burst noises. When the motors and body make a burst noise, the intensity of the noise is quite stronger because microphones location is relatively near the motor. Therefore if the spectrum and intensity of captured noises is similar to those of a noise template, the captured noise is regarded as a burst noise. Specifically, the subband is canceled if the following conditions hold:

1. Intensity difference between external and internal microphones is similar to one of stored motor noise intensity differences.
2. Intensity and pattern of the spectrum are similar to one of stored motor noise frequency responses.
3. A motor command is being processed.

Before internal sounds are suppressed, pre-processing is performed on the input. Input sounds from four microphones are captured by a four-channel AD converter and sampled at the speed of 48 KHz. Then, frequency analysis transforms captured digital sounds into sound spectrograms for each channel. This is done by the Discrete Fast Fourier Transformation (FFT) for 1,024 points. After pre-processing, internal sound suppression generates a noise canceled spectrum, which is used as input of sound stream separation.

2.2 Sound Stream Separation

Sound stream separation takes a noise canceled spectrum, localizes each sound source by calculating its direction, and extracts a set of sound streams. The key idea of localization is associating auditory, visual and motor directions [8].

The direction by stereo visual processing is obtained by using a corner detection algorithm [14]. It extracts a set of corners and edges then constructs a pair of graphs. A matching algorithm is used to find corresponding left and right image to obtain depth.

The head direction is obtained from potentiometers in the servo-motor system. It is quite accurate by the servo-motor control mechanism. Since only the horizontal rotation motor is used, horizontal direction of the head is obtained accurately, about $\pm 1°$. By combining visual localization of an object and the head direction, *SIG* determines its direction in the world coordinates.

Sound Source Localization by Auditory Processing. To localize sound sources with two microphones, first a set of peaks are extracted for left and right channels, respectively. Then, the same or similar peaks of left and right channels are identified as a pair. The IPD and IID for each subband (47 Hz) of a pair are calculated. The IPD is not calculated for subbbands of more than 1,500 Hz, because the IPD becomes ambiguous in modulo 2π due to the length of the baseline of the two microphones.

Auditory, visual, and head directions are associated in terms of IID and IPD. Visual and head direction are combined to calculate the relative direction of each sound source. Then, the IPD and IID for every $5°$ direction are calculated by auditory epipolar geometry, and are used as IPD and IID hypotheses of the direction. Then the probability of each IPD hypothesis is calculated by matching the IPD obtained by auditory processing with the IPD hypotheses. The probability of each IID hypothesis is also calculated similarly. Then, the belief factors of the IPD and IID for each direction are combined by Dempster-Shafer theory. Finally, the direction with the most plausible combined belief factor is determined.

Direction-Pass Filter by Epipolar Geometry. Sound streams are extracted by the direction-pass filter from a mixture of sounds. As explained above, the IPD and IID are calculated by auditory epipolar geometry for a specific direction. The direction-pass filter selects a subband whose IPD and IID match those of the specified direction, respectively. The detailed algorithm is described as follows:

1. For each subband (47 Hz), the IID, $\triangle\mathcal{I}$, and IPD, $\triangle\varphi$, for the specified direction, θ, are calculated by auditory epipolar geometry.
2. From the subband of the input, peaks are extracted and the IPD, $\triangle\varphi'$ and IID, $\triangle\mathcal{I}'$, are calculated.
3. If the IPD and IID satisfy the condition, namely, $|\triangle\varphi' - \triangle\varphi| < C_P$, and $|\triangle\mathcal{I}' - \triangle\mathcal{I}| < C_I$, then collect the subband.
4. Construct a wave consisting of collected subbands by Inverse FFT.

Sensori-Motor Control. The direction of each sensor is given to the motor control system. First, attention of control system selects one sound source. Focus of attention and action selection modules are described in [14]. As a rule of thumb, the current implementation adopts a very simple rule of focus of attention: *the newer, the more attention.* In other words, *SIG* changes the focus of attention to a newly appeared sound sources. Once the focus of attention, or a sound source is selected, the motor control generates PWM (Pulse Width Modulation) motor commands to *SIG*. Of course, during executing PWM commands, *SIG* tracks all the sound streams simultaneous by canceling motor movement noises.

3 Experiments of Sound and Visual Tracking

In this section, we will demonstrate how vision, audition and motor control compensate each missing information to localize sound sources while *SIG* is rotating to see an unknown object.

3.1 Conditions of Experiments

There are two sound sources: two small loud speakers located in a room of 10 square meters as is shown in Figure 3. One loud speaker, **A**, is located at 58° from the rightmost position, and the other one, **B**, at 127°. **A** plays a pure-tone sound of 500 Hz. After 3 seconds, **B** plays a pure-tone sound of 600 Hz. In tracking of sound sources, that is, loud speakers, *SIG* cannot see any loud speakers during rotation, since the visual field of the camera is only 45°. Figure 3b shows this situation. Therefore, visual tracking may fail in tracking of sound sources due to its out of sight situation.

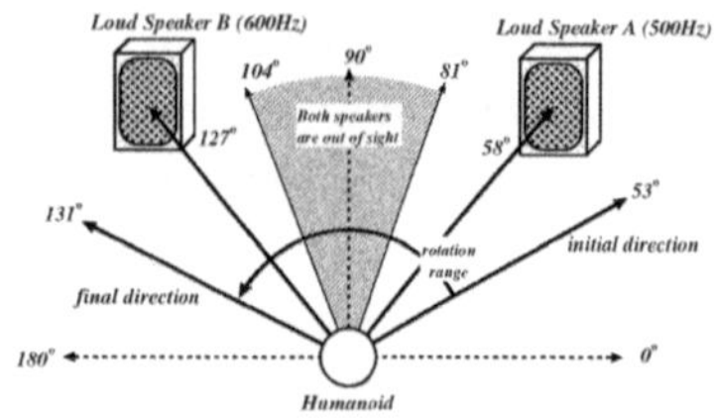

a) Image from *SIG* at 53° b) at 90° c) at 131°

Fig. 3. Experiment: sound and visual tracking of sound sources while *SIG* moves.

Two kinds of sound source tracking are examined; *fast* (68.8 degree/sec) and *slow* (14.9 degree/sec) rotations of *SIG*. The signal ratio of a pure-tone sound to standby motor noises is about 0 dB, that is, almost the same power. Spectrograms of input sounds for slow and fast rotations are shown in Figure 4a and 4c, respectively. In these spectrograms, burst noises are observed as vertical dark sharp lines. In particular, burst noises are quite strong during fast rotation. Due to these strong burst noises, sound tracking fails in tracking and separating sound sources, since the current noise reduction technology cannot be applied to such a loud burst noise.

The initial position of *SIG* is at 53°. Sound and visual tracking system will be evaluated from the viewpoint of how it can track two sound sources (loud speakers) by integrating vision, audition, and motion position information.

3.2 Results of Experiments

The results of sound source tracking by the sound and visual tracking system are shown in Figure 4b and 4d. The direction of a sound source obtained by vision, auditon, and/or motor control is depicted by a line in the figures. The direction is represented in the ego-centric polar coordinate where 0° is the direction dead front of the head, minus is right of the head direction.

In the fast rotation as is shown in Figure 4b, **A** is tracked well by vision up to 81°, i.e., 2.7 sec. During rotation, the head direction by motor control is dominant over the other information, the direction line is more stable than during stopping. **B** comes into sight at 104°, i.e., 3.4 sec., its direction is adjusted by using visual information as is shown by the dotted line. In the slow rotation as is own in Figure 4d, The phenomenon of out-of-sight situation is observed well.

The behavior that *SIG* took is summarized below in tempral order:

1. *SIG* looks at **A** at 5° left to the initial head direction. It associates the visual object with the auditory one, because their extracted directions are almost the same.
2. When **B** plays a sound, *SIG* knows that it is outside of its visual field according to the direction of **B** obtained by audition.
3. *SIG* turns toward the direction of the unseen sound source **B** in order to associate it with visual information. Its direction is maintained by auditory processing and motor control.

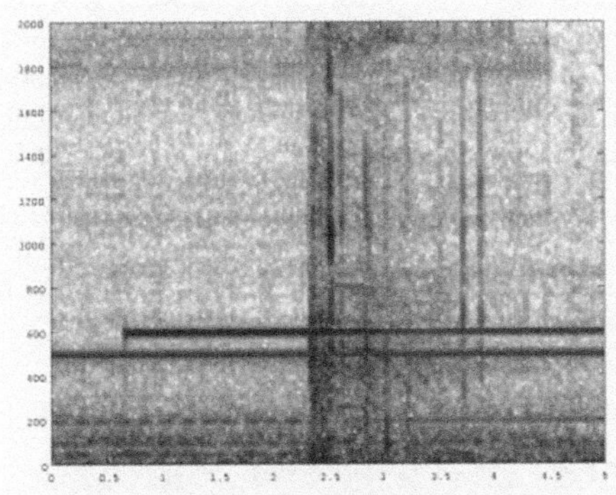

a) Spectrogram of *fast rotation*

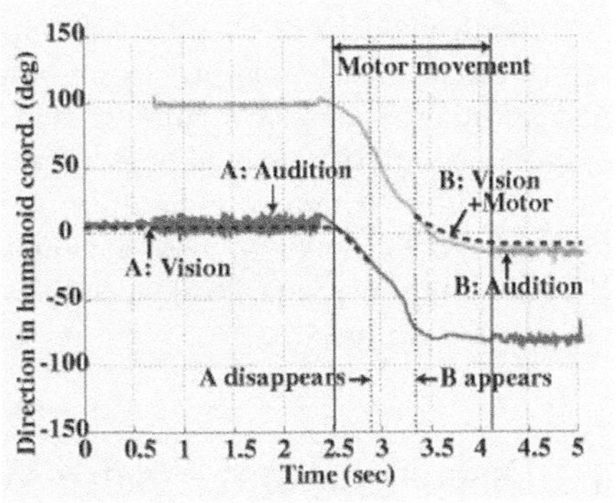

b) Direction of separated sound sources

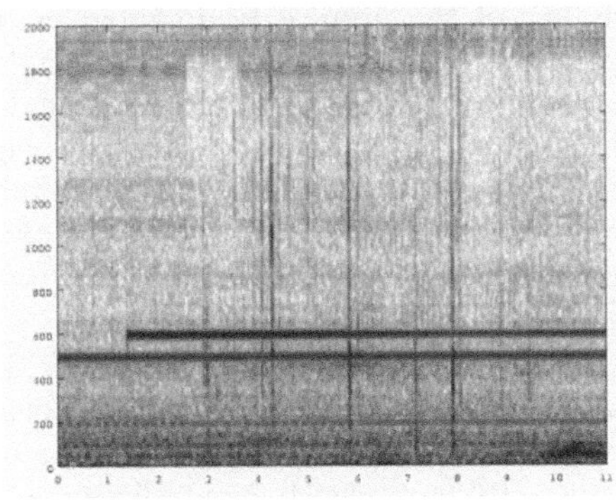

c) Spectrogram of *slow rotation*

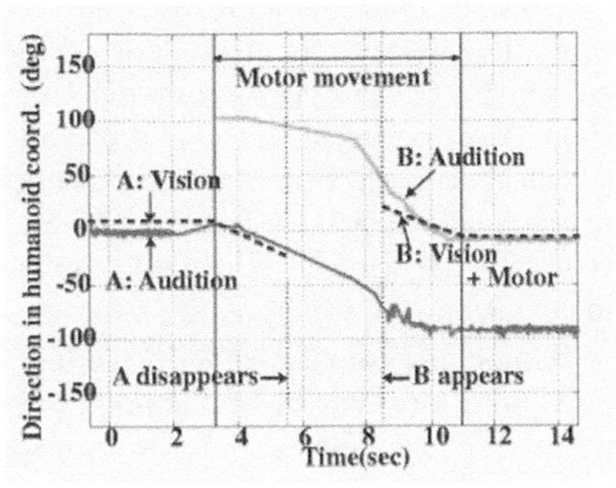

d) Direction of separated sound sources

Fig. 4. Results of sound and visual tracking of sound sources

4. When *SIG* finds a new object **B**, it associates the visual object with the auditory one.

3.3 Observation of Results of Experiments

Results of the experiment are very promising in applying auditory processing in real-world applications. Integration of visual and auditory directions provides a robust sound source tracking. Without integration, such robustness in sound source tracking is difficult to attain, since visual or auditory direction are not always available and accurate.

Accurate sound source localization is accomplished by using auditory epipolar geometry not but using the HRTF. Epipolar geometry based method locates approximate direction of sound sources well. For example, its effectiveness is demonstrated by the temporal data of localization for initial 2 seconds in Figure 4b and 4d.

The effect of internal noise suppression is clearly shown; for example, temporal data of auditory localization during rotation in Figure 4b and 4d proves that burst noises are effectively reduced.

The drawbacks of the current implementation of sound and visual tracking are the lack of real-time processing and multi-layered association. Neither visual nor auditory processing runs in real-time. Auditory processing with auditory epipolar geometry runs almost in real-time, while visual processing based on early vision mechanism runs quite slowly, which is the bottleneck for real-time processing. The current association is based on the belief factor of IPD and IID, that is, only one level of assoication. For a complex task, more levels of association are needed.

4 Discussion and Future Work

The experiment demonstrates the feasibility of the proposed humanoid audition in real-world environments. Since there are a lot of non-desired sounds, caused by traffic, people outside the test-room, and of course internal sounds, the CASA assumption that input sounds consist of a mixture of sounds is essential in real-world environments. Similar work by Nakagawa et al. [11] was done in a simulated acoustic environment, but it may fail in localization and sound stream separation in real-world environments. Most robots capable of auditory localization developed so far assume a single sound source.

Epipolar geometry gives a means to unify visual and auditory processing, in particular localization and sound stream separation. This approach can dispense with HRTF. As far as we know, no other systems can do it. Most robots capable of auditory localization developed so far use HRTF explicitly or implicitly, and may fail in identifying some spatial directions or tracking moving sound sources.

The cover of the humanoid is very important to separate its internal and external worlds. However, we've realized that resonance within a cover is not negligible. Therefore, its inside material design is important.

Social interaction realized by utilizing body movements extensively makes auditory processing more difficult. The Cog Project focuses on social interaction, but this influence on auditory processing has not been mentioned [15]. A cover of the humanoid will play an important role in reducing sounds caused by motor movements emitted toward outside the body as well as in giving a friendly outlook.

As future work, active perception needs self recognition. The problem of acquiring the concept of itself recognition in robotics has been pointed out by many people. For audition, handling of internal sounds made by itself is a research area of modeling of self. The concept of itself is also important in designing the attention control and action selection. Other future work includes more tests for feasibility and robustness, real-time processing of vision and auditory processing, internal sound suppression by independent component analysis, addition of more sensor information, and applications. We are working on real-time processing and recent achievements in real-time processing with additional layers of association will be reported as a separate paper [16].

5 Conclusion

In this paper, we present a sound and visual tracking system for a humanoid which includes internal sound suppression, a new method for auditory localization, and a new method for separating sound sources from a mixture of sounds. The key idea is to use epipolar geometry to calculate the sound source direction and to integrate vision and audition in localization and sound stream separation. This method does not use the HRTF (Head-Related Transfer Function) which is a main obstacle in applying auditory processing to real-world environments. We demonstrate the feasibility of motion tracking by integrating vision, audition and motion information. The important research topic now is to explore possible interaction of multiple sensory inputs which affects quality (accuracy, computational costs, etc) of the process, and to identify fundamental principles for intelligence.

Acknowledgments. We thank our colleagues of Symbiotic Intelligence Group, Kitano Symbiotic Systems Project; Yukiko Nakagawa, Tatsuya Matsui, and Dr. Iris Fermin (currently with Aston University) for their discussions. We thank Prof. Hiroshi Ishiguruo of Wakayama University for his help in active vision and integration of visual and auditory processing.

References

1. J. Huang, N. Ohnishi, and N. Sugie: Building ears for robots: sound localization and separation, *Artificial Life and Robotics*, Vol. 1, No. 4 (1997) 157–163.
2. Y. Matsusaka, T. Tojo, S. Kuota, K. Furukawa, D. Tamiya, K. Hayata, Y. Nakano, and T. Kobayashi: Multi-person conversation via multi-modal interface — a robot who communicates with multi-user, *Proceedings of 6th European Conference on Speech Communication Technology (EUROSPEECH-99)*, 1723–1726, ESCA, 1999.
3. A. Takanishi, S. Masukawa, Y. Mori, and T. Ogawa: Development of an anthropomorphic auditory robot that localizes a sound direction (*in japanese*), *Bulletin of the Centre for Informatics*, Vol. 20 (1995) 24–32.
4. G. J. Brown: *Computational auditory scene analysis: A representational approach.* University of Sheffield, 1992.
5. M. P. Cooke, G. J. Brown, M. Crawford, and P. Green: Computational auditory scene analysis: Listening to several things at once, *Endeavour*, Vol. 17, No. 4 (1993) 186–190.
6. T. Nakatani, H. G. Okuno, and T. Kawabata: Auditory stream segregation in auditory scene analysis with a multi-agent system, *Proceedings of 12th National Conference on Artificial Intelligence (AAAI-94)*, 100–107, AAAI, 1994.
7. D. Rosenthal and H. G. Okuno (eds.): *Computational Auditory Scene Analysis.* Mahwah, New Jersey: Lawrence Erlbaum Associates, 1998.
8. K. Nakadai, T. Lourens, H. G. Okuno, and H. Kitano: Active audition for humanoid, *Proceedings of 17th National Conference on Artificial Intelligence (AAAI-2000)*, 832–839, AAAI, 2000.
9. T. Nakatani, H. G. Okuno, and T. Kawabata: Residue-driven architecture for computational auditory scene analysis, *Proceedings of 14th International Joint Conference on Artificial Intelligence (IJCAI-95)*, vol. 1, 165–172, AAAI, 1995.

10. S. Cavaco and J. Hallam: A biologically plausible acoustic azimuth estimation system, *Proceedings of IJCAI-99 Workshop on Computational Auditory Scene Analysis (CASA'99)*, 78–87, IJCAI, 1999.
11. Y. Nakagawa, H. G. Okuno, and H. Kitano: Using vision to improve sound source separation, *Proceedings of 16th National Conference on Artificial Intelligence (AAAI-99)*, 768–775, AAAI, 1999.
12. H. Kitano, H. G. Okuno, K. Nakadai, I. Fermin, T. Sabish, Y. Nakagawa, and T. Matsui: Designing a humanoid head for robocup challenge, *Proceedings of the Fourth International Conference on Autonomous Agents (Agents 2000)*, ACM, 2000.
13. K. Nakadai, T. Lourens, H. G. Okuno, and H. Kitano: Humanoid active audition system improved by the cover acoustics, *PRICAI-2000 Topics in Artificial Intelligence (Sixth Pacific Rim International Conference on Artificial Intelligence)*, Lecture Notes in Computer Science, No.1886, 544–554, Springer Verlag, 2000.
14. T. Lourens, K. Nakadai, H. G. Okuno, and H. Kitano: Selective attention by integration of vision and audition, *Proceedings of First IEEE-RAS International Conference on Humanoid Robot (Humanoid-2000)*, IEEE/RSJ, 2000.
15. R. Brooks, C. Breazeal, M. Marjanovie, B. Scassellati, and M. Williamson: The cog project: Building a humanoid robot, *Computation for metaphors, analogy, and agents* (C. Nehaniv, ed.), 52–87, Spriver-Verlag, 1999.
16. K. Nakadai, K. Hidai, H. Mizoguchi, H. G. Okuno, and H. Kitano: Real-time auditory and visual multiple-object tracking for robots, *submitted*, 2001.

Developing a Mobile Robot Control Application with CommonKADS-RT

M. Henao[1], J. Soler[2], and V. Botti[2]

Department of Informatics Systems and Computation
[1]Universidad EAFIT, Medellín – Colombia
mhenao@sigma.eafit.edu.co
[2]Universidad Politécnica de Valencia, Spain
jsoler@dsic.upv.es vbotti@dsic.upv.es

Abstract. The advances achieved in Real-Time Artificial Intelligence (RTAI) allow us to apply techniques to build large applications. However, developing such applications require having a methodology that defines the techniques, tools and processes to allow for modeling their characteristics. There are several important lines of research in RTAI, such as architectures, languages, methods and methodologies. All of them provide the necessary information and knowledge to be able to build computer systems based on real-world problems. This paper describes CommonKADS-RT, a method to develop Real Time Intelligent Systems. This method is based on CommonKADS with the addition of necessary elements to model real time restrictions. We also present an application of this approach to the control of an autonomous mobile robot.

1. Introduction

Currently many types of systems are being developed that, in general, are identified with some of the research areas of computing science. Some researchers have been interested in creating systems that manage the domain knowledge and others researches are interested in systems where time is one of the most important variables in carrying out their tasks. Therefore, intelligent systems and real-time system areas are becoming of increasing importance.

Important advances have been achieved in each one of these areas, but the point has been reached where the techniques of one can serve the other. This has generated the area of the Real-Time Artificial Intelligence Systems - RTAIS to solve complex problems, which require intelligence and real time responses. In this new area, there are three possible ways to integrate them [17], [11]: a) Integrate intelligent system in real-time systems. This is based on applying Artificial Intelligence - AI techniques in real-time systems. b) Integrate real-time systems in intelligent systems where the intelligent system has tasks with temporal restrictions. c) Systems where a real-time component and an intelligent component work in a cooperative way.

One of the lines of research in RTAI has been to build large applications or architectures that embody real-time concerns in many components. Almost all the

L. Monostori, J. Váncza, and M. Ali (Eds.): IEA/AIE 2001, LNAI 2070, pp. 651-660, 2001.

architectures are designed for soft real-time systems (without critical temporal restrictions).

To develop each one of these types of systems, it is important to have methodologies that define the techniques, tools and more importantly to have processes to carry out the project construction in a successful manner. These methodologies should not be ad hoc but widespread in order to be able to guarantee certain necessary standards to assure the project's success and the quality of the software system.

The objective of this paper is to present CommonKADS-RT, based on the CommonKADS methodology and based on RT-UML to develop real-time intelligent systems - RTIS, including intelligent agents and temporary-task or time-restriction modeling.

The second section of the article presents some aspects that are related to this proposal, the models included in the methodology and their application to an autonomous physical agent, a mobile robot application based on CommonKADS-RT. The third section shows some application results. The fourth section present our conclusions. Next there are acknowledgements and finally the references are showed.

2. Modeling a Mobile Robot Control Application with CommonKADS-RT

CommonKADS [13] is a methodology that gathers a set of methods, techniques and tools to develop Knowledge Based Systems - KBS. It is based on the fact that building a knowledge-based system is essentially a modeling activity. From this point of view, the system is an operational model that exhibits the wanted behaviors that have been specified or observed in the real world. The methodology reflects some methods of structured analysis and design, some of the object paradigm and some management theories such as strategic planning and reengineering, among others.

CommonKADS offers a structured approach reflecting the knowledge engineering process and bringing to the knowledge engineer a series of worksheets or templates to make the system development easier. These worksheets contain some of the most important factors to be considered when the knowledge engineer has to model knowledge-based systems.

This methodology is currently one of the most widely used for the development of knowledge-based systems. It has even been taken as the European standard to develop systems of this type. It has been used in numerous universities and European companies such as banks and different industries. Also, Carlos Iglesias [9] defined MAS-CommonKADS to develop multiagent systems, integrating other models that allow the characterization of intelligent agents and their communication.
CommonKADS-RT [2] is based on these methodologies because they are strong and incorporate the most important software engineering concepts following the object-

oriented and agent-oriented paradigms. Obviously, this implies making some changes to CommonKADS, especially on the models that must consider temporal conditions, reactive responses and the handling of physical devices like sensors and/or actuators. We believe that all of these can be used to specify and to model systems of this kind.

To model the real time features, we selected RT-UML [5], [6] because it has a tool set to apply on the real-time analysis and even on knowledge-based systems in real time. RT-UML is an object analysis and design methodology to develop hard real-time systems. It uses UML to model real-time tasks, including temporal constrains.

First of all, we have distinguished between how the task is handled in real-time and how it is handled in knowledge engineering areas. The CommonKADS task is a complex function that is a relevant part of a business process and it has a method for doing task. The task is formed by other tasks, inferences or transfer functions. In contrast, in Real-Time Systems a task is associated with a temporal execution process. It is in the low-level architecture, so it is imperative to distinguish between these task concepts. We propose the High Level Task – HLT for the complex functions (high level) and a Real-Time Task – RTT for the low-level process [14]. For HLT it is necessary to include CommonKADS task considerations such as the task process description, its components, the agents involved, among other things. At the same time, for RTT it is important to determine its periodic behavior, a deadline and the worst execution time [16]. CommonKADS-RT includes the following models (Fig.1) that allow us to explain why, what and how solve a problem with a RTIS.

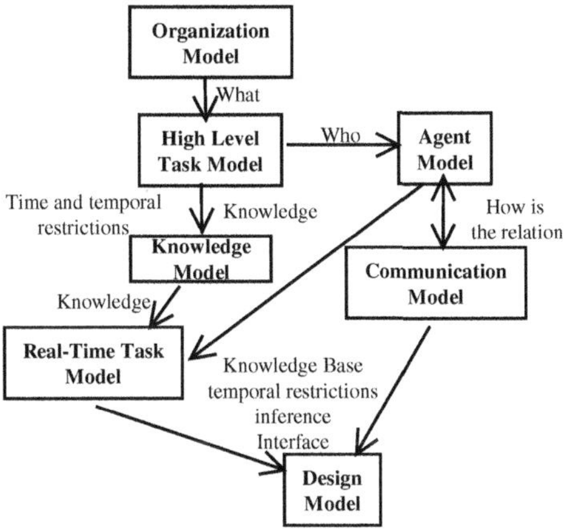

Fig. 1. The CommonKADS RT models. They allow to obtain a different view of the problem and the solution. This shows the artifacts produced into the models.

2.1 Organization Model (OM)

Apart from including every CommonKADS point, this model describes the organization in which the system will be used, including some issues such as the following: The priority that is associated with a process, the average time of the computation process, the slack time (if it is allowed, especially for considerations of soft temporary restrictions), the specifications of specialized equipment for data acquisition like sensors or sonars, whether the process is periodic or not, etc.

We will present some parts of the models, which were developed in the case to construct a mobile robot control application.

Preliminary conditions: The robot is in a closed room, a micro world with walls. Each wall has a hole with a geometric shape. It is in a known fixed initial position. The environment is also known. There is a set of objects with a geometric shape. In the room, one of the objects is in an established place, which is defined in random way. The object should be found by the robot, pushed and placed in the appropriate hole that has the same geometric shape.

Goal: In the micro world, the robot has to find the object and push it into the appropriate hole. The geometric shapes are a rectangle, a triangle, and a half-circle.

Robot characteristics: This physical agent has been developed for the mobile robot "Mobile Pioneer 2". The robot contains all the basic components for sensing and navigation in a real-world environment, including battery power, drive motors and wheels, position/speed encoders and integrated sensors and accessories. They are managed via onboard micro controller and mobile-robot server software. The robot has a ring of 16 sonars. The sonar positions are fixed in two arrays (front and rear): one on each side and six facing outward at 20-degree intervals providing more than 180 degrees of nearly seamless sensing, and all-around sensing when using both forward and rear arrays. The server software has an internal localization mechanism, which provides an approximate estimation of its location. All this information is sent through the RS-232 serial port. The control application is executed in a notebook over the RT-Linux operating system. The notebook has a radio Ethernet that allows the connection to the request senders.

Process: Initially, the robot has to activate and check its state through the readings of its sensors and battery. When the robot is o.k., it must start to look for the object in the micro world (see the specification below). Then, when the object is found, the robot has to identify it based on the shapes that it recognizes. The robot must also plan how to move the object around the micro world to put it in the respective wall. To make the proof easier, we defined that there are only four walls with a fixed hole (the hole will always be in the same wall).
Furthermore, there is only one hole on the wall and it must be different from the others. Next, the robot has to move the object to the appropriate hole and, finally, the process ends when the object is in its hole.

The robot's global behavior has been modeled into a high-level task set. That process could be considered as a HLT that has been divided to better structure it and to know every detail about the activities realized by the robot. With the OM-3 template (Description of the High Level Task that make up the process), we can observe the HLT specifications:

Table 1. OM-3 HLT for the Robot application.

HLT ident.	HLT name	Knowledge intensive?	Knowledge asset	Significance
ActRobot	Active robot	No	Start, protocol, Check states	It is the first HLT to begin the process.
LookObj	Look for object	Yes	Planning action, interpret micro world, verifying trajectory	It would be done with a planner and a scheduling.
IdObj	Identify object	Yes	Knowledge about the object shapes, pla-nning trajectory, inter- pretation, verification	The clue is knowing the differences between the shapes.
MoveObj	Move object	Yes	Defining wall target, planning trajectory and the object movement, interpreta-tion, verification	It is necessary to have a planner and knowledge about how is the best way to move the object

And, if the task is described or divided in more tasks it is necessary to show it again with a similar graphic. For example, the task *ActionExecuting* is possible to divide in *ExecutingCommand* and *VerifyingEnvironment*, and so on with every HLT or RTT.

2.2 High Level Task Model (HLTM)

This model describes the processes assigned to the system and those related to the organization. For this reason, some of the UML diagrams of [5] and [6] are taken as a reference, specifically the different scenarios of the domain, the sequence diagrams and the transition state diagrams. Of course, the templates have to include the factors refer to, previously. It is important to say that, in an organizational process, it is possible to have HLT with temporal restrictions. In this case, the analyst has to determine and must define these factors from the beginning.

The *LookObj* HLT must include activities with temporal restrictions to control some of the robot actions. For example, we have define in the *ActionPlanning* a 100 milliseconds period, meaning that this task has to be repeated each 100 milliseconds. The same happens with *ReadSensor*, a leaf task that has defined 2 milliseconds for the worst computer execution time. It will be show in the Model Knowledge, later.

2.3 Agent Model (AM)

In CommonKADS, an agent is the entity that executes a task in the organizational process. It can be a human or an information system. This model is used as a link between the Task Model, the Communication Model and the Knowledge Model. Its objective is to reflect the agent capabilities and restrictions involved in the task solution. CommonKADS-RT uses the same idea of this Model taking into account temporal restrictions. The use case is used to model the human agents and an external event list contains the environmental event and the expected system response. It is possible to define an agent with temporal restrictions, especially when it has to reply under temporal restrictions. The robot is a especial case because there is not an agent associated with its knowledge intensive task, only there is an agent to activate it. Therefore, in this paper we do not present the agent model details.

2.4 Communication Model (CM)

It describes the interaction among the agents working on the process, while they carry out their HLT. Iglesias [9] proposed having an additional model to express the special communication between intelligent agents called the Collaboration Model. Our research group is currently studying this topic because it is very important to not only include it in CommonKADS-RT methodology, but also to include it in the architecture and tools developed [1], [8], [3]. For the moment, we do not need it because we have only one agent. This model is not defined to this robot application, similar to the previous section 2.2.

2.5 Knowledge Model (KM)

This model shows the knowledge used by the system to solve its HLT, including real-time specifications. The Knowledge Model is developed with a Conceptual Modeling Language – CML2 [4] and is divided into three important components: a) the domain knowledge composed of static structures of the domain. b) The inference knowledge that describes how the static structures can be used to do the reasoning. c) The task high level knowledge to define the goals that we are trying to reach by applying the knowledge. It has to involve the real-time variables. A plan should be made – scheduling - in which the order of execution of the tasks and the important variables of time are determined. First, it is necessary to define the concepts in which the temporary properties of the class are specified (the execution period, the computational time, the ending time, the answer time, deadline, etc.). Therefore, it would be necessary to add or change CML2. For example, the real-time task and a new primitive type called **time**, which represents an absolute time (determined by the pulses of a clock) or a relative time (the partial order strictly imposed on the groups of all transaction occurrences) [7] is added.

primitive-type : := **number** | **integer** | **natural** | **real** | **string** | **boolean** | **universal** | **date** | **text** | **absolute-time** | **relative-time**

2.6 Real-Time Task Model (RTTM)

The Real-Time Task Model describes the real-time tasks. It is based on the ARTIS architecture [8]. In the next section, we will show the structure syntactic of a real-time task example. Although ARTIS has a language to define entities, we use CML2 to describe the real-time tasks. This model can be considered as part of the Design Model, but the reason for establishing it separately is to emphasize the aspects of real-time. The HLTs can have RTT associated to them. Examples of this situation are the following fig. 2.

```
real-time-task ActionPlanning;
  rt-task-type: periodic;
  from: LookObj;
  relative-time: Yes;
  deadline: 8; /* milliseconds*/
  period: 100; /* milliseconds */
  wcet: ; /* milliseconds */
  real-time-task-before: EnvironmentPerception;
  formed-by-others: Yes;
end real-time-task ActionPlanning;
```

```
real-time-task ReadSensor;
  rt-task-type: periodic;
  from: ActionPlanning;
  relative-time: Yes;
  deadline:; /* milliseconds */
  period:; /* milliseconds */
  wcet: 2; /* milliseconds */
  real-time-task-before: none;
  formed-by-others: No;
end real-time-task ReadSensor;
```

Fig. 2. Description of the *ActionPlanning* RTT and the *ReadSensor* RTT.

2.7 Design Model (DM)

This model describes the architecture and the detailed functionality of the RTIS to be implemented. The most important thing to consider in this model is the software (including the operational system and the language) and hardware characteristics (the computer architecture like the memory capacity, the processor speed, etc). It must be kept in mind to develop a real time system, it is necessary to have an off-line planning to prove the system integrity and the logical correctness and robustness. We used the ARTIS agent architecture [1] to develop the RTTM and the DM. ARTIS is an extension of the blackboard model [12], which has been adapted to work in hard real-time environments. According to the usual classification of the agent architectures, the ARTIS Agent architecture could be labeled as a hybrid architecture [10]. This architecture provides a hierarchy of abstractions, which organize the knowledge in order to solve the global problem, in a modular and gradual way. The ARTIS Taxonomy is: Each one of the modules that makes up an AA corresponds with one of the former entities in the hierarchy of abstractions. Therefore, the ARTIS Agent (AA) is the root of the hierarchy, which is the highest level of abstraction. The AA models the system and its interaction with the environment through sensors and effectors. Applying this to the robot control application explained above, we have the following structure (Fig. 3). Therefore, the following different entities can be distinguished:

- ARTIS Agent (AA) represents the physical agent, which is also autonomous, reactive, and proactive and has temporal continuity. It is made up of a set of sensors and effectors, a control module (which is responsible for the real-time execution of every AA component), an intelligent server (which is used for higher quality answer if there is enough time).
- An Internal Agent (in-agent) is an internal entity that has the necessary knowledge to solve a particular problem (this knowledge can incorporate AI techniques that provide "intelligence" for solving the problem). This entity periodically performs a specific task (which may or may not be complex).
- A Multiple Knowledge Source (MKS) implements the concept of anytime algorithm and multiple methods, providing different solutions to the same problem with different computation times and different levels of quality.
- Knowledge Source (KS) represents the knowledge (either procedural or rule-based) to solve some part of a problem.

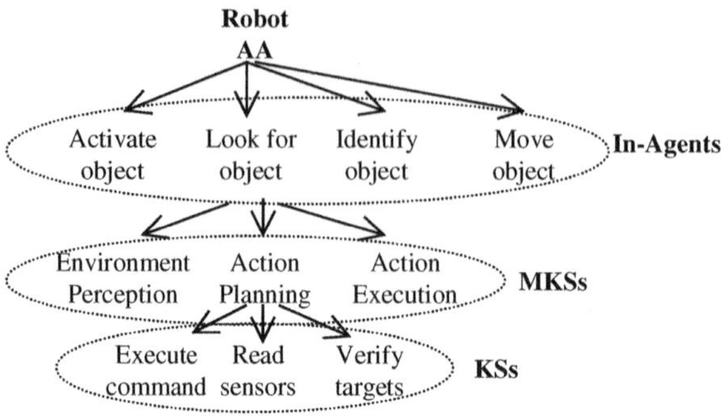

Fig. 3. The robot knowledge in the ARTIS taxonomy.

In our research group, we have developed a visual toolkit to make agent-oriented implementation and management for ARTIS agents, called INSIDE [15]. By means of this toolkit an user can build a prototype of an ARTIS Agent directly executable. Inside allows extremely rapid development of agents. It has been developed in Java, therefore Inside can be executed on a wide variety of computer platforms and operating systems. The Inside main characteristics are: 1) Provides sophisticated graphical tools for development.2) Ease of use, for its visual feature. 3) Debugging environment during the specification process. 4) Simulates the critical part of the real-time system, this option allows the user to detect fails in the specification.

Just like CommonKADS, the methodology that we are proposing is based on the spiral model of the life cycle that is widely used in Software Engineering. This paradigm provides a structure for the development of a computational system, dividing it in a group of phases with a predetermined execution order. Inside each phase, a group of different activities should be carried out. At the end of each phase one or more tangible products must be delivered (documents, reports, designs, etc.) usually as input to other phases. In several phases of the life cycle, there are milestones where decisions are made.

3. Application Results

We have built a simulation of the robot behavior and actually we are implemented it with ARTIS. Due to the limits of this paper, we obviously can not show every consideration explained in this section, but we will illustrate some relevant aspects, figure 4. Finally, in figure 5 is possible appreciate the robot used in this project.

a) 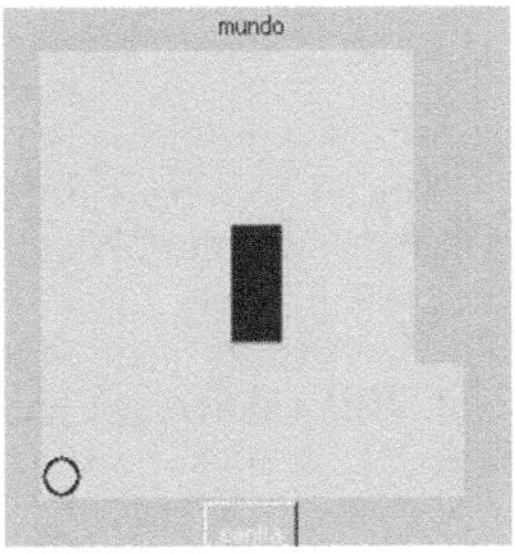

b) 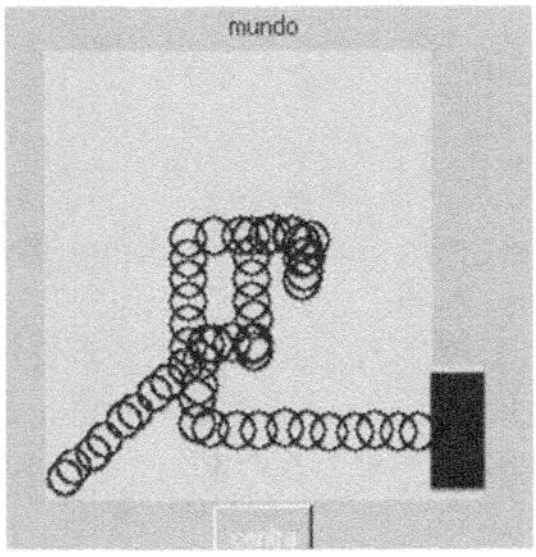

Fig. 4. a) Initial state of micro world and Final state of micro world. The first one shows the robot in an initial position. The object that the robot has to find is a rectangle in the middle of the room, and it should be moved and located at the bottom of the wall on the right. b) The final state shows the final situation when the robot has just located the object in the appropriate place. It is also possible to see the trajectory followed to achieve the final goal.

Fig. 5. The Pioneer 2 in front of an object with a rectangular shape.

4. Conclusions

We have used CommonKADS-RT to develop this control application and we have proved the functionality of this method for modeling systems based on one intelligent agent. Now we are working to add new features to CommonKADS-RT to support multi-agent system modeling. In this paper we have presented some of the CommonKADS-RT characteristics through an intelligent control application. The application was designed, simulated and implemented using its own architecture called ARTIS.

Acknowledgements. Thanks to the Comisión Interministerial de Ciencia y Tecnología, Spain, because they have sponsored the project "ARTIS: Herramienta para el desarrollo de sistemas inteligentes en tiempo real estricto". TAP98-0333-C03-01

References

1. Botti, V., Carrascosa, C., Julian, V., Soler, J. Modelling Agents in Hard Real-Time Environments. Proceedings of the MAAMAW'99. Lecture Notes In Computer Science, vol. 1647. Springer - Verlag Valencia 1999, 63-76.
2. Botti, V., Henao, M., Soler, J. Un Método de Análisis para Modelar Sistemas Basados en el Conocimiento en Tiempo Real. VIII Conferencia de la Asociación Española de Inteligencia Artificial, CAEPIA'99. Murcia, Spain. 1999, 17-25. (Spanish).
3. Carrascosa, C., Julian, V. J., García-Fornes, A., Espinosa, A. Un lenguaje para el desarrollo y prototipado rápido de sistemas de tiempo real inteligentes. Conferencia de la Asociación Española de Inteligencia Artificial, CAEPIA´97, Málaga, España. 1997, 685-694. (Spanish).
4. CML2 and KADS22 Documentation. http://www.commonkads.uva.nl/
5. Douglass, B. P. Real-Time UML. Addison-Wesley, United States of America. 1998, 365.
6. Douglass, B. P. Doing Hard Time; Developing Real-Time Systems with UML, Objects, Frameworks, and Patterns. Addison-Wesley, United States of America. 1999, 749.
7. Falkenberg, E., Hesse, W., Lindgreen, P., et to the one. FRISCO, To Framework of Information System Concepts. The IFIP WG 8.1 Task Group FRISCO. 1996, 221.
8. García-Fornes, A., Terrasa, A., Botti, V., Crespo, A.: Analyzing the Schedulability of Hard Real-Time Artificial Intelligence Systems. Engineering Applications of Artificial Intelligence. Pregamon Press Ltd. 1997, 369-377.
9. Iglesias, C. Una Metodología para Desarrollar Sistemas Multiagentes. Tesis de Doctorado, Universidad Politécnica de Madrid, España. 1998, 294. (Spanish).
10. Muller, J. P.: A conceptual model for agent interaction. In Deen, S. M. Editor, Proceedings of the second International Working Conference on Cooperating Knowledge Base Systems, DAKE Centre, University of Keel. 1994, 213-234.
11. Musliner, D., Hendler, J., Agrawala, A., et al. The Challenges of Real-Time AI. Computer. January 1995, 58-66.
12. Nii, H.P., "Blackboard Systems: The blackboard model of problem solving," Part I AI Magazine. 1986, 38-53.
13. Schreiber, G., Akkermans, H., Anjewierden, A., et al. Knowledge Engineering and Management: The CommonKADS Methodology. The MIT Press, United States of America. 2000, 455.
14. Soler, J., Henao, M., Botti, V. A Mobile Robot Application with an Analysis Method based on CommonKADS. Proceedings of the IASTED International Conference: Intelligent Systems and Control (ISC 2000). Hawaii. 2000, 299-303.
15. Soler, J. Julian, V. Carrasco, C., et al. Applying the ARTIS Agent Architecture to Mobile Robot Control. Iberamia, Nov., 2000. Atibaia, Brazil.
16. Stankovic, J. Misconceptions About Real-Time Computing. IEEE Computer, Vol. 21 N. 10, Oct. 1988, 10-19.
17. Vivancos, E, Hernández L., V. Botti. Construcción y Análisis Temporal de Sistemas Basados en Reglas para Entornos de Tiempo Real. VII Conferencia de la Asociación Española de Inteligencia Artificial, CAEPIA´97, Málaga, España. 1998, 675-68. (Spanish).

Intelligent Control of Mobile Robot during Autonomous Inspection of Welding Damage Based on Genetic Algorithm

Dong-Ying Ju[1,2] and Satoshi Kushida[2]

[1] Department of Mechanical Engineering, Saitama Institute of Technology Fusaiji 1690, Okabe, Saitama 369-0293, Japan. ju@sit.ac.jp

[2] Department of Materials Science and Engineering, Saitama Institute of Technology, Fusaiji 1690, Okabe, Saitama 369-0293, Japan. mat98004@sit.ac.jp

Abstract. In this paper, an intelligent control of a mobile robot in order to inspect damage in welding joint of various steel structures is presented. In the mobile robot, a drive method with caterpillar of equipped stronger magnet coil is employed to navigate on wall of a welding structure. And, a few of photo sensors and a CCD camera are equipped in the robot for recognizing joint line of welding and inspecting welding surface. Here, a genetic algorithm for predicting damage information in the joint line of welding is proposed, and it is possible that recognized map and photograph on the joint line of welding be reproduced on the screen for remote control. Depending on the experiments, reliability of the genetic algorithm is confirmed in the reality of the welding.

1 Introduction

In prediction and inspection of damage in welding joint of the building, bridge and lager-scale structures, the flaw detector by ultrasonic wave often is used into the inspection of structural damage in engineering. However, in order to raise inspecting efficiency, it is necessary to develop a mobile robot for autonomous inspection. The ability to guarantee the feasibility of a mobile robot during autonomous navigation for inspection on a joint line of welding is important to propose an intelligent controller or algorithm. Especially, when the inspection is completed to follow the local recognition of a welding line for the task of autonomous navigation, the safe position of the mobile robot has to be satisfied, while the orientation can be arbitrary. On the other hand, with an autonomous navigation and inspection on welding joint, an intelligent control is important exactly to recognize its own position for the robot and to utilize the inspection and on-line control on the welding joint line. Recently, a lot of studies for proposing intelligent control combined with fuzzy and genetic algorithms are carried out, for example references [1]-[6]. However, them applications in engineering problems remain to be solved. In this connection, an intelligent control of a mobile robot in

L. Monostori, J. Váncza, and M. Ali (Eds.): IEA/AIE 2001, LNAI 2070, pp. 661-669, 2001.

order to inspect damage in welding joint of various steel structures is presented in this paper. In development of the mobile robot, a drive method with caterpillar of equipped stronger magnet coil is employed to navigate on wall of a welding structure. And, a few of photo sensors and a CCD camera are equipped in the robot for recognizing joint line of welding and inspecting welding surface. Here, a genetic algorithm for predicting damage information in the joint line of welding is proposed, and it is possible that recognized map and photograph on the joint line of welding are reproduced on the screen for remote control. Depending on the experiments, reliability of the genetic algorithm is confirmed in the reality of the welding.

2 System of Mobile Robot

In the research work, a mobile robot (only with A4 size of a paper) developed by ASPECT Corporation is improved to inspect the surface of welding line. The robot is provided with two caterpillars in which equipped stronger magnet coil for navigation on vertical wall of a welding structure. And, equipped five photo sensors are used to recognize line of welding joint.

As improvement of the robot shown in Fig.1, a CCD camera is equipped in the robot for inspecting welding surface. On the other hand, in order to increase ability of control and utilize intelligent algorithm, a Z80 CPU board in original system of the robot is replaced to a V25 CPU board. The CPU board is employed to control navigation of the mobile robot and to judge position of welding joint line depending on the optical sensors. The ultrasonic sensor of the robot is jointed to a flaw detector by ultrasonic wave. The CCD camera is jointed to other PC computer for inspecting the damage on surface of the welding joint.

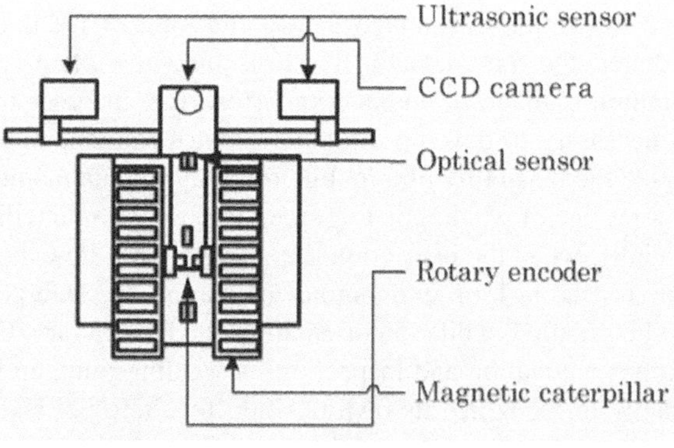

(a) System of inspection robot

(b) Photogragh of the robot

Fig. 1. Synoptic representation of the inspecting robot.

3 Autonomous Navigation Based on Genetic Algorithm

In autonomous inspecting of welding joint, the ability to guarantee the feasibility of the mobile robot during autonomous navigation for inspection on a joint line of welding is very important to propose an intelligent controller or algorithm. In order to utilize the objects, a genetic algorithm is applied into navigation of the mobile robot.

3.1 Genetic Encoding and Evolving of Gene

In design and proposal of the genetic algorithm, the count number in which optical sensors recognize a white tape along a side of the welding joint is defined as a generated gene. However, we deal with the counter number recognized from the two sensors at front and back of the robot as deference gene individuals BL and FL, respectively. On the other hand, when left (or right) sensor at front and right (or left) sensor at back of the robot at the same time recognize the welding joint, the gene for describing round of the robot is defined by TL. Table 1 shows a sample of gene group. Here, the number in Table 1 denotes the information of these genes, so that evolving of the genes due to crossover can be obtained. However, when the number is five, the present control condition will be remained to variation of information at next crossover step as a present control level PCL.

Table 1. Group of gene

BL	FL	TL
9	9	1
7	7	3
6	6	**PCL=5**
PCL=5	**PCL=5**	6
3	3	7
1	1	9

3.2 Evaluation for the Robotic Navigation

In order to reflect randomness of the fitness λ_f and λ_b in selected gene individual, a scaling method of index type is introduced into the algorithm, i.e., the fitness at front and back of the robot can be expressed as follows as

$$\lambda_f = (BL - PCL) + (PCL - TL) \tag{1}$$

$$\lambda_b = (FL - PCL) + (PCL - TL) \tag{2}$$

Here, the gene individual with large probability will be selected to next step for crossover operation. In the paper, random crossover based on one-point method[6]-[7] is used as shown in Fig. 2.

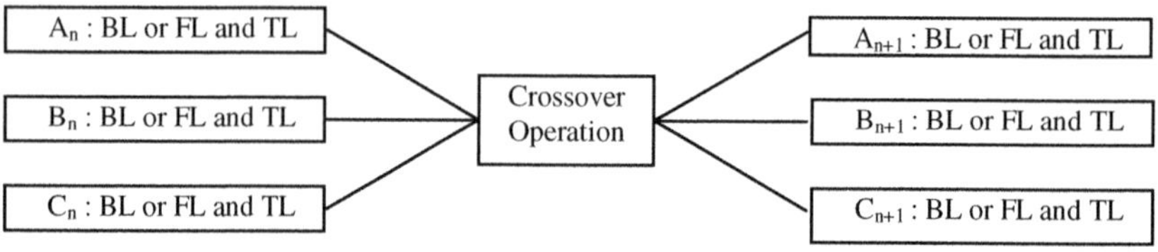

Fig. 2. Crossover of gene group.

3.3 Selection

Depending on computed fitness, we can select optimum gene group to decide the control parameter for next step of navigation. The selection algorithm is given by

$$S(0) = 0 \tag{3}$$

and

$$S(i) = \sum_{j=1}^{i} \lambda(X_j) \qquad i = 1,2,\cdots,p \tag{4}$$

where p is the population-size.

3.4 GA Operation

We propose a special framework shown in Fig.3 to integrate the intelligent algorithm as a control method for inspecting damage on welding surface by using autonomous navigation. Depending on the flowchart, we can decide increase of distance and direction in navigation of the mobile robot.

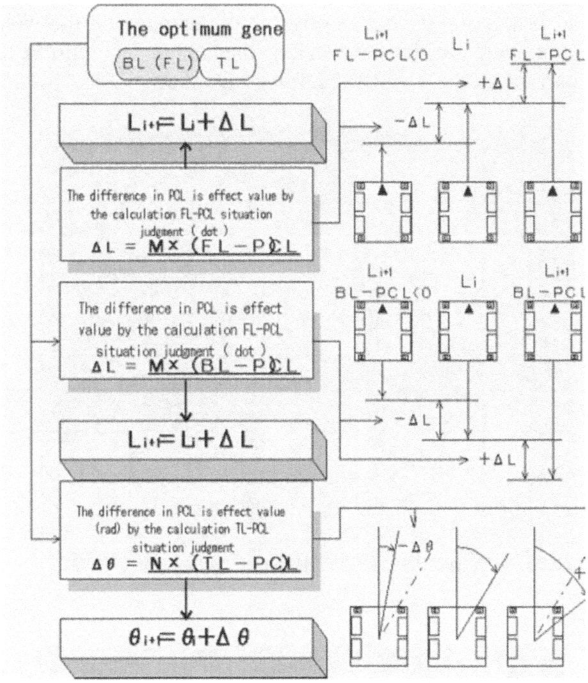

Fig. 3. Flow chart based on genetic algorithm.

In the genetic algorithm processing reflected for controlling value in which it will come by next calculation the highest fitness optimum so. The sum of present turning angle θ_i and effect value N by the situation judgment ΔL and $\Delta\theta$ in which are multiplied TL-PCL. By the similar method L_{i+1} of advance and regression distance request and actual control value of the independence travel survey robot the latency of advance and regression distance it handles handle. As turning angle θ_{i+1} after it reflects the gene this turning angle actual control value of the micro mouse the latency of the turning angle it handles handle. Effect value N,M used by this calculation fluctuates by the situation judgment rule pattern.

4 Results and Discussions

4.1 Inspecting Results of Welding Damage

In the study, an inspecting experiment depending on the developed robot is carried out. Here, the CCD the welding surface based on image recognition. camera on the robot is used to inspect image on welding surface. The obtained pictures are sent to a host computer by ATM network. And also, these picture can be turn to a web server computer, so that inspecting users can observe the damage on the welding surface by using a client computer. On the other hand, the image recognition of the inspected picture also be carried out by a general software Dr.View.

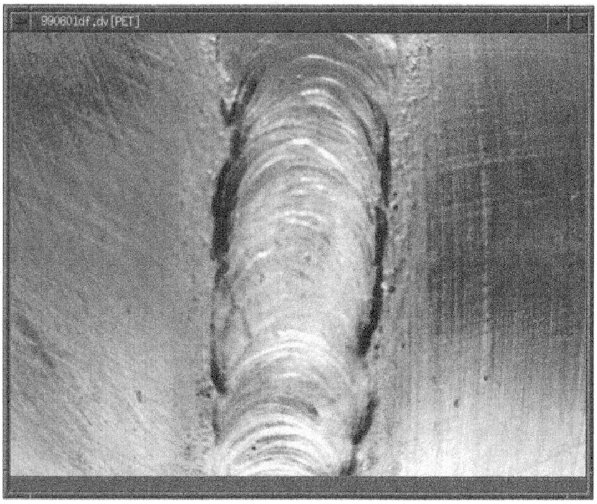

(a)

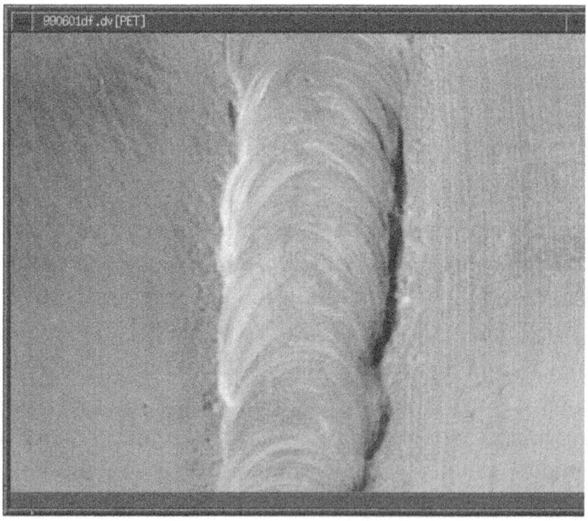

(b)

Fig. 4. Shows the inspected image on the welding plate.

4.2 Results during an Intelligent Control of Robot Navigation

In order to verify effectiveness of the genetic algorithm (GA) in the navigation, the inspecting experiment along welding line on a steel plate is carried out. In the inspecting, two cases of welding line are employed. A white tape is stick on a side of welding line in order to recognize the coordinate position of course by four light sensors. The count number of left or right light sensors recognized on the white line is used as the gene component in each genetic group. Advances of round angle of the robot incorporate with the calculated results as a local leaning method of GA. When coordinate position of the sensor of the autonomous travel survey robot is different from course of the welding line, the coordinate will be send to a host computer for presenting the navigated orbit of the robot by using network. The calculation for making the GA processing can decide advanced straight and whirl moving during inspection of welding line. On the other hand, we can keep watch on moving of the robot using by a CCD camera set on the robot, so that we also can give a manual control from the host, when robot separate the welding line. Therefore, the navigation and inspecting of the robot along welding line is not only to consider autonomous control based on GA processing, and also have cooperation between human-machine.

As case 1 of the inspecting experiment, we mainly consider that the robot only be navigate along a straight line and a smooth curve. So, the situation judgment factor is renewed, when non-perception of the sensor followed the navigation course in which the uniformly space and loop was done as results of local leaning by GA. Figure 5(a) shows the navigated orbit in inspecting along the welding line as case 1. The central coordinate of the robot in detecting by white line and both light sensors is save as a travel data of the untreated. The parameter is turning angle during navigation process with the initial stage, when the initial stage advance regression distance in the initial stage. In the case 2 of navigation sample, we gave a complex welding line in order to verify effective moving based on GA processing. Figure 5(b) shows the result of carrying out the navigation presented from host computer, and give that the robot moving along the welding line as limited advanced angle. The count number in order to require sake and optimum situation judgment factor which deviate from the course, when the navigation of the mobile robot runs at to some extent angle on the course, and carried out leaning process of the navigation. However, in the case, when the robot navigate to point A, the robot separate out the welding line as failure of autonomous navigation. In this time, we gave a manual control to the robot so its navigation to back to the side of the welding line.

From the above experimental results, we can know that the control methods based on GA and cooperation of human-machine can are applied into navigation for inspecting welding damage.

5 Conclusions

In this paper, we develop an autonomous robot system for inspecting damage in welding joint in which imitates intelligent learning. As control tasks of robot become ever more demanding, more intelligent controller are needed. As the autonomous method with leaning ability, genetic algorithm is offered to utilize optimization of control parameters in navigation of the robot. Our research work developed a new technique for GA involving with a local learning method. Based on some successful performances of navigation and experiment, we know the proposed method can be applied to inspection of welding joint and autonomous navigation in the inspection.

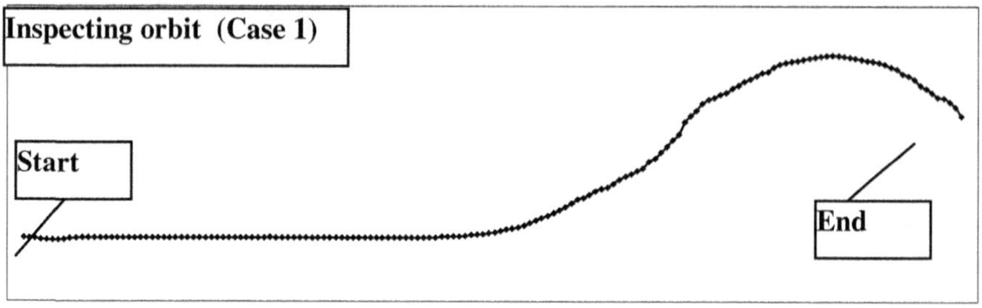

(a) Result of robot navigation (Case 1)

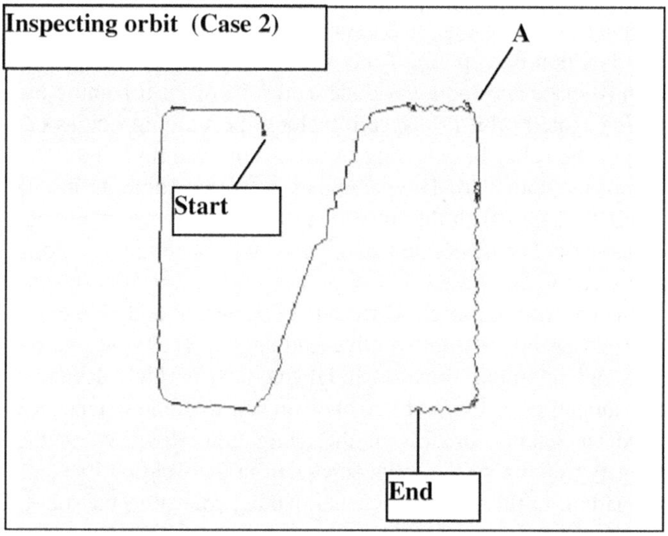

(b) Result of navigation (Case 2)

Fig. 5. Performance of navigation

Acknowledgments. The support provided by the high technological research center of Saitama Institute of Technology in carrying out this work is gratefully acknowledged.

References

[1] Floreano, D. and Mondada, F.: Evolution of homing and navigation in a real robot, Transactions on Systems, Man and Cybernetics, Vol.26, No.3, (1996) 396-407

[2] Brooks, R.D.: A Robust Layered Control System for a Mobile Robot, IEEE Journal of Robotics and Automation, Vol. RA-2, No. 1, (1986) 14-23

[3] Mahadevan, S. and Connell, J.:Automatic Programming of Behavior-based Robots using Reinforcement Learning, Aritifial Intelligence, Vol. 55, (1991)311-365

[4] Ju, D.Y, Toyota, K., Nemoto M. and Iwata, T.:Integration of Fazzy System and Genetic Algorithm and Its Application to the Autonoumous Navigation of Mobile Robot, *Journal of Bejing Mathematics*, Vol.4, No.2, (1998)16-25

[5] Varsek, A., Urbancic, T. and Filipic, B.: Genetic Algorithms in Controller Design and Tuning, IEEE Transaction on Systems, Man, and Cybernetics, Vol. 23,No.5, (1993)1330-1339

[6] Montana, D.: Strongly Typed Genetic Programming, Evolutionary Computation, Vol. 3, No. 2, (1995) 199-230

[7] Holland, John L.(ed.):Genetic Algorithms, Scientific American(1992)

Machine Learning for Car Navigation

Dejan Mitrovic

University of Canterbury, New Zealand
dmi24@cosc.canterbury.ac.nz

Abstract. In this paper we present the usage of neural networks and hidden markov models for learning driving patterns. We used neural networks for short-term prediction of lateral and longitudinal vehicle acceleration. For long-time prediction, hidden markov models provide recognition of individual driving events. The experiments performed showed that both techniques are very reliable. Recognition rate for driving events is above 98% and prediction error for events in the near future is very low. Predicted events will be used to support drivers in solving guidance navigation tasks.

1 Introduction

Fast development of motor vehicles during the twentieth century enabled quick replacement of the animal powered vehicles, which have been used during many previous centuries. Motor vehicles influence all aspects of human life, providing much greater mobility for people and products, and thus enabling advances in many other areas. However, road infrastructure and human driving capabilities could not follow this fast development.

We believe patterns in someone's driving could be easily identified and learned, and could be used to support the driver in fulfilling a range of different driving navigational tasks, particularly guidance tasks. A guidance driving task involves the maintenance of safe speed and a proper path relative to the road and traffic elements; for example, following the road and maintaining a safe path in response to the road and traffic conditions. Learning from previous driving experiences has many advantages over conventional systems. It allows adaptation to particular environment or a driver's habits. For example, a set of driving patterns for the same road could be very different in the morning from during the night, and for some purposes these should be treated as two different driving experiences. On the other hand, two segments of a driving route on different geographic locations can be very similar from the driving perspective, and for some navigational purposes could be regarded as the same route. Systems that are not based on learning techniques cannot identify and use such similarities.

In this paper we will present two popular machine learning techniques and results of our experiments in their application to some guidance navigation tasks. In the first section, short introduction to neural networks is given and results of short term vehicle motion prediction. In the next section, basic concepts of hidden markov models are presented and results of experiments in driving event recognition.

L. Monostori, J. Váncza, and M. Ali (Eds.): IEA/AIE 2001, LNAI 2070, pp. 670-675, 2001.

2 Neural Networks for Vehicle Control

An artificial neural network is a computational model that tries to mimic information processing in the human brain. The basic information processing of both brain and neural networks is the neuron, a simple processing element consisting of number of input and one output connection. Complex operations are possible by the existence of a large number of highly interconnected neurons operating in parallel.

The most common computational model for neuron is known as the perceptron [1]. Output signal in perceptron is calculated by applying activation function on the weighted sum of input signals. Connection weights are learning parameters which are changed during the training phase in order to find the best mapping between input signals and desired outputs.

Networks of neurons are created by connecting outputs of one neuron to the inputs of the other neurons. There are two major types of neural network architectures: *feedforward*, where neurons are generally organized into layers and the outputs from the neurons in one layer are brought to the inputs of the neurons in the next consecutive layer; and *recurrent*, where output of one neuron could be also connected to the inputs of the neurons in the same layer or in the previous layers. Artificial neural networks found many different applications in the last decade, ranging from pattern recognition tasks to optimization and scheduling. A number of neural network applications in various vehicle systems have been reported in [2].

The main goal of our experiments described in this section was to investigate neural network capabilities for reliable prediction of vehicle motion in the near future using only the simplest navigational sensors - accelerometers. Due to advances in micro-machined electronics, accelerometers have become inexpensive and could be found in most of the new cars. Neural network applications for vehicle lateral and longitudinal control has been previously reported, however presented systems required large number of sensors [3].

In our experiments we used Analog Devices ADXL05 accelerometers, which are set to measure longitudinal and lateral vehicle acceleration. A Trimble Placer 400 global positioning system (GPS) receiver is used as a simple velocity sensor and positions provided by the GPS are also collected to serve as a reference during data analysis. Data from accelerometers are collected at 50 ms intervals. Actual data reading from AD converters is done at a much higher rate and data are averaged to increase the signal to noise ratio. The second order normalized low pass Butterworth digital filter is used to eliminate noise. The data are further normalized to range [0-1] in order to simplify neural network training.

For neural network experiments, we selected a data set consisting of longitudinal and lateral acceleration data for approximately 10 minutes drive. Data was selected to provide the right balance of driving events and to avoid long periods of uniform data, which could lead to training problems. The selected data set was split into training and testing subsets. We chose to start experiments by using standard three layer feedforward network commonly refereed to as a Multi-Layer Perceptron (MLP)

In the first experiment, we tested the capabilities of a three layer MLP for acceleration prediction for a different number of time epochs in advance. The MLP neural networks used in our experiments had an input layer with 2 neurons, a hidden layer with 4 neurons and an output layer with 2 neurons. The neurons in the hidden and output layer use a sigmoid transfer function. Standard backpropagation learning algorithm with momentum learning rule and batch weight update was used. As expected, the neural network prediction capabilities decrease sharply with the increasing number of time epochs. However, prediction capabilities of MLP networks for short period of time in the future (250ms) are very good and could be used to support decision-making in lower-level navigation tasks.

The other important goal of our experiments with neural networks was to compare the prediction capabilities of MLP in this application with the capabilities of architectures that are usually recommended for time series predictions. Time-delay neural networks (TDNN) are commonly used to represent time in neural networks. A TDNN is a multilayer feedforward network whose input and hidden neurons are replicated across time. This way, information about previous input values is preserved in a network, and should improve prediction capabilities of the network. The price for increased information content is in increased network complexity and computing power required. In our experiments we used TDNNs with two different numbers of replicated nodes, 5 and 20, to better explore the influence of data history on prediction.

Recurrent neural networks differ from feedforward in having at least one feedback loop. A feedback loop is a synaptic connection from one neuron to itself or to neurons in the same or in the previous network layer. Feedback loops provide memory capabilities for neural networks, providing an opportunity for the current neuron state to influence output in a many following time epochs. The network used here has one hidden layer with 6 Gamma neurons, which provide a recursive memory of the input signal and behave as leaky integrators.

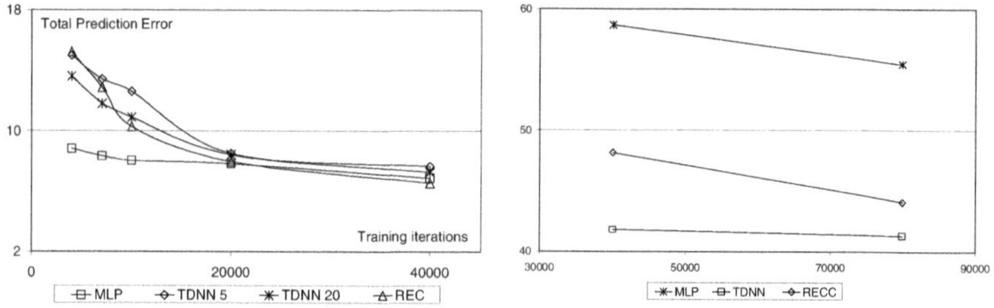

Fig. 1. Short-term Prediction Error for 5 (left) and 20 (right) time epochs.

Figure 1 presents the results of experiments for predicting accelerations for 5 and 20 time epochs in advance. The total prediction error for each architecture is represented as a function of the number of training iterations. In a shorter-term prediction case, a plain MLP network compares well to other architectures. It is obvious that more complex architectures need more learning iterations than MLP in order to reach better performances. As we could expect, a TDNN with larger number of replicated nodes gives better results. However, the difference in results between various architectures is very small and does not favor the use of more complex architectures over MLP. In the case of predicting for a longer period of time in advance, as expected, the performance of TDNN and recurrent networks becomes better than MLP performances. However, total prediction error for long term prediction by neural networks is too large for practical use [4].

3 Driving Event Recognition by Hidden Markov Models

The hidden markov models are probabilistic tools for studying time series data. They attract great attention in the pattern recognition research community due to their success in a range of applications, notably in speech recognition [5]. The foundation for the hidden markov model (HMM) is a stochastic Markov process consisting of a number of states and the transitions between them. At discrete time intervals, the Markov process moves from one state to another according to the transition probabilities. State changes in the underlying Markov process are not observable (hence name "hidden"). However, the user can observe process changes through a sequence of observations that are produced at each state change. Observations could be continuous signals or discrete symbols from the finite alphabet. More formally, a discrete hidden markov model λ can be specified as $\lambda = (N, M, A, B, \pi)$, where N is the number of states in the model, M is the size of the alphabet, A is the state transition probability matrix, B is the observation symbol probability matrix and π is initial probability vector. The probability that an observation sequence O is generated by the model λ is denoted as $P(O|\lambda)$. Left-to-right models always start at the first ("leftmost") state, and transitions are allowed only toward later ("right") states or to the same state. It has been shown that the left-to-right model is better than the general model at capturing dynamic characteristics of data, by imposing a temporal order to the model. For this reason we use left-to-right models in our experiments. For training we used the popular Baum-Welch re-estimation method [6]. Due to its re-estimation nature, in our experiments we repeat it many times with different initial model parameters. The model with the highest probability was chosen as the training result.

We use the term driving event to refer to any major change in vehicle attitude or speed, such as a left or right turn, a stop, making a U-turn and so on. From the decision-making point of view, driving events are demanding as they require the driver to act on vehicle controls while, at the same time, the relationship between the vehicle and the environment (road infrastructure) is far more complex than in periods between events. In these circumstances driving safety margins are very small, and even a minor disturbance can cause an accident. Accordingly, driving events have a very significant role in guidance navigation and driving safety.

As common driving events last for a few seconds, a large quantity of data is produced by the data acquisition system. In order to reduce the amount of data and simplify pattern recognition, we use a waveform segmentation technique. Normalized acceleration and speed data are split into segments (frames) of predefined length. Frames overlap each other in order to emphasize the influence of the global trend in the collected data. The least squares method for linear data approximation is used to calculate frame parameters: average (mean) value and slope (change in values). As a result, each frame is represented by five parameters: average speed, average lateral acceleration, average longitudinal acceleration, lateral acceleration slope, and longitudinal acceleration slope. Segmentation preserves all important waveform features, while the number of required data values has been significantly reduced.

In order to use discrete HMMs, we need to translate continuous frame parameters into symbols from a small predefined set. We use vector quantization for joint quantization of a set of continuos-amplitude signals into one of the codebook (discrete-amplitude) values. Vector quantization is widely used in data compression, telecommunication and speech coding. The design of the codebook is a process of determining the set of vectors that will minimize the quantization error for a given data set. We use a well-known iterative clustering algorithm known as the K-Means algorithm. As the K-Means algorithm is known to converge to the local minimum of the quantization error, we repeat it many times with different initial values in order to find the best possible solution. Input into the vector quantifier are vectors consisting of five parameters describing each frame, while output is a stream of codebook indexes which represent observation symbols for HMMs. The codebook size of 16 was selected.

For our experiments with hidden markov models we used data from 22 test drives. We tried to incorporate a variety of urban road features which could be found in medium-sized New Zealand towns. Some of the routes, or parts of routes, are repeated in order to provide data for our later experiments with driving event prediction. Training and testing data for experiments were manually selected from test drive data. A program has been developed for manual selection of data representing a driving event and marking it as particular type of event. We selected and marked 263 events. We used only seven of the most common types of driving events for our experiments: driving a vehicle along left and right curves, turning a vehicle left and right on intersections, with and without roundabouts (rotary intersections), and driving straight across an intersection with a roundabout.

We constructed seven HMM models - one for each type of driving event we try to recognize. Small preliminary tests with various model sizes (from five to eight states) were made in order to find an optimal model for each driving event. Data for our HMM experiments consist of a number of short observation sequences (5 to 30 observations per sequence) which are grouped according to the type of driving event they represent. A small number of observations in the training set, and an observation probability distribution that is far from uniform, lead to typical numerical problems encountered in HMM implementations. In order to prevent these, probabilities are scaled after each iteration.

In the beginning we evaluated each trained model separately by calculating the probability for each observation sequence in all test data sets. Firstly, we calculated probabilities for observations from the data set for the event type for which the model was trained. We used the resulting probabilities to determine the threshold value. All probability values above the threshold are marked as recognized events of this type. Recognition by an isolated HMM is the simplest approach in pattern recognition by HMM, but results obtained by experiments show that, in most cases, driving event recognition was accurate. Isolated HMMs almost always correctly recognized events of the type for which they were trained. Number of false acceptances, except for four pairs of events, is zero, which confirms that the HMM very reliably differentiated between events of these types.

In order to improve the recognition performance, we tested parallel evaluation of observation sequences by multiple HMMs. For each observation sequence, we computed the probabilities for all models. The highest of these probabilities determines the driving event type to which a sequence belongs. Using this approach, the models successfully recognized all events except four cases (of 56, or 7.1%) of left curve events recognized as right curve events. We suspect that the above problem is caused by the coarse vector quantization grid, which does not discriminate well between small lateral acceleration on the left and right sides. Furthermore, in 29 cases (of 79, or 36.7%) the models could not distinguish between left turns and left turns on a roundabout. However, the geometry of intersections, and traffic rules for left turns on intersections, with or without roundabouts are the same, so this result is expected and we believe that these two event types should be regarded as one.

If we exclude the above problem, we can conclude that, even with a very limited set of sensors, the system correctly recognized 234 of 238 (or 98.3%) driving events. This proved that the presented model for driving event recognition is very accurate, reliable and robust. It could be expected that an increase in the number of training sequences could further improve the recognition rate of the method by providing a greater variety of training data for each driving event.

4 Conclusion

The goal of our research is to prove that patterns in someone's driving could be easily identified and learned. We believe that patterns could be used to support the driver in fulfilling different navigational, particularly guidance tasks. We tested the prediction capabilities of Multi-Layer Perceptron and compared them with the prediction capabilities of time-delay and recurrent neural networks. Our experiments proved that short-term prediction for all architectures, including MLP is very good. The advantages of the more complex architectures become more obvious when predicting events further into future. However, in such cases, the total prediction error increases and predictions become less usable.

Hidden markov models are popular probabilistic tools for various temporal pattern recognition applications. Here we used HMM to recognize driving events from lateral and longitudinal acceleration and velocity data. The experiments proved that even isolated recognition of driving events managed to recognize proper events very often and that the false acceptance rate is larger only for a few particular pairs of events. Improving decision system to use parallel evaluation of all models for the same observation, made the recognition rate very high - 98.7%. The results proved that driving events could be reliably recognized even by using a very limited set of sensors.

Research described in this paper is supported by the Road Safety Trust New Zealand.

References

1. Rosenblatt, F.: The Perceptron: a Probabilistic Model for Information Storage and Organization in the Brain. Psych. Rev. 6 (1958) 386-408
2. Ghazi Zadeh A., Fahim A., El-Gindy M.: Neural network and fuzzy logic application to vehicle systems: literature survey. Int. J. of Vehicle Design. 2 (1997) 132-193
3. Kraiss, K.P., and Kuttelwesch, H.: Identification and application of neural operator models in a car driving situation. IFAC Symposia Series 5, Pergamon Press Inc, Tarrytown, NY, USA (1993) 121-126
4. Mitrovic D.: Experiments in Subsymbolic Driving Pattern Prediction. Proc. of the 6th International Conference on Neural Information Processing. (1999) 673-678
5. Rabiner L.R.: A Tutorial on Hidden Markov Models and Selected Applications in Speech Recognition. Proceedings of the IEEE. 2 (1989) 257-286
6. Baum L.E., Petrie T.: Statistical interference for probabilistic functions of finate state Markov chains. Annals of Mathematical. Statistics, 30 (1966) 1554-1563

Implementing Agent Management Using Conversation Patterns and Role Theory

Christos Stergiou[1] and Geert Arys[2]

[1]Imperial College, Dept. of Elec. & Electronic Eng., Exhibition Road, London SW7 2BT
c.stergiou@ieee.org
[2]Free University of Brussels, Pleinlaan 2, 1050 Brussels, Belgium
geert.arys@chello.be

Abstract. In this paper we provide a framework for building management services for software agents using conversation patterns. These patterns classify agent interaction, using the principles of Object Oriented software design patterns, encapsulating pure communication requirements and responsibilities. All services, including management services, interact with their clients using the same conversation patterns as defined in this paper. Any conversation is started in three steps: requesting a service, negotiating a pattern and establishing pattern roles. Role theory and reusable policy specifications regulate the way agents participate, providing a rich source of information for conversation management. The methodology promotes platform independence and fits the needs of a modular, distributed environment; enabling services use the powerful plug-and-play concept. Co-operation patterns are built upon conversation patterns, but also describe the 'social' relationships between agents based on beliefs, desires and intentions.

1. Introduction

In this paper, we propose a technique for organising agent communication in a way to be more easily manageable and to better fit the specific needs of agent technology. The progress in another software domain has greatly influenced our way of thinking and approach on this subject. A remarkable trend in software applications is currently that of the e-business world, which is booming at an exponential rate. In the wake of these events we observe the birth of developing standards like Java and XML. At present, e-business is young. But soon the e-business community shall shift its focus from fancy web pages or mere data exchange over the Internet to truly inter-operating systems. Companies will want to integrate their software with their partners, clients and/or suppliers. Autonomous agents in a Multi-Agent System will emerge as the paradigm for designing this kind of complex software system. We predict that the *golden age* of commercial interest in agents will start within the next five years due to developments in the Internet business.

E-business development will bring along a heritage of more-or-less established standards, by which the agent community has to abide in order to prosper. While the use of Java, HTML and XML are obvious examples, one has to be aware of more elaborate emergent technologies and standards in the domain of Internet-enabled component technology. For example, Enterprise Java Bean (EJB) containers with Java Messaging Service (JMS) offer facilities that are similar to those offered by pure agent platforms like DECAF, FIPA-OS and ZEUS to name a few. These facilities

L. Monostori, J. Váncza, and M. Ali (Eds.): IEA/AIE 2001, LNAI 2070, pp. 676-686, 2001.

include directory services (yellow pages), security, messaging layers, etc. On top of that, compared to agent platforms, EJB containers have paid more attention to some important aspects like concurrency, distributed management, persistence, Internet integration, but most of all *openness* (software platform independence). All these facilities are a direct result of the nature and requirements of an application server for the Internet. The requirements *must* be met by any other e-business technology in order for it to survive and be successful.

On the other hand, almost every multi-agent system project that we have encountered has devoted significant resources to implementing such an infrastructure from scratch. During this implementation stage, valuable time and resources are often spent implementing libraries and software tools for simply exchanging KQML-like messages across a network. In contrast, we take the features of an Internet-based Application Server as a basis on which to build our agents. The advantage is that from then on we can concentrate on the specific needs for agent management in such an environment and at a later stage integrate the strong points and features of existing true agent platforms as well.

Yet one does not successfully adapt a technology by simply *using* it. One has to adapt also the design *philosophy* behind it. The research in application servers is strongly akin to building quality components, including layered design, defining co-operation contracts, the use of design patterns and so on. In other words, we have to design an independent *service* with a well-defined interface. In short, we propose a technique to manage agent communication -based on their specific needs- in a separate service/layer, which can be used in both true agent-oriented platforms and in other application servers.

2. Conversation Patterns

The work described later on constitutes a method to provide distributed Agent services with out the need of a centralised agent platform. The agent services (security, visualisation, agent mobility, yellow pages, quality of service) are provided and controlled through Manager agents. Manager agents are modelled using role theory where as the services are modelled through a policy based framework. The agents and the manager agents communicate with each other and between themselves using conversation patterns. In sections 2.1 and 2.2 we introduce some background technology that lead to the creation of our Conversation patterns.

2.1 Middle-Agents

Middle-agents are a special class of agents designed to perform various useful communication services, by relieving its clients from some of their responsibilities. For the sake of simplicity, we will use the KQML-facilitators[1] as an example of a communication framework based on middle-agents. When we examine the facilitator object (F) more closely, we recognise three different types of communication agreements:

Firstly, the "client" agent (A) knows a basic "command" to initiate some technique of communication (recruit, broker, subscribe, recommend). Using the shopping analogy, this is choosing self-service or the old-fashioned counter.

Secondly, the agents know how the rest of the conversation will take place: who is going to tell(X), what, to whom? In the shop example, once clients choose self-service, they should be aware that one has to fill a shopping cart and then go to the cashier.
Thirdly, the agents A and B know about what they ask and what they tell. This is called 'domain knowledge'. The facilitator does not have a clue. In the shop example, when a client buys a lamp, they will have an idea how many Watts they desire, whether they need a halogen lamp, etc, while the cashier at the supermarket can be ignorant of all these details.

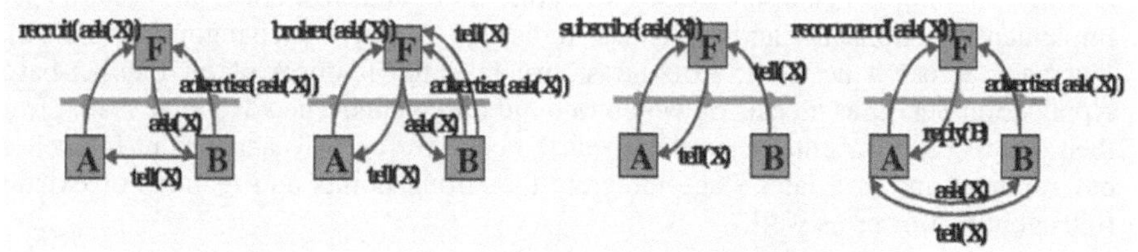

Fig. 1. KQML communication facilitation services

As with the contract-net protocol, the value of these services is the frequency with which they occur in different applications[2]. Beside the advantage of reuse, we recognise some other advantages from the management point of view:

- They show predictable communication behaviour. For example, we can identify the objects that have advertised but don't respond to ask(X) messages anymore. From the Object-Oriented point of view, one could define *co-operation contracts* for the facilitators.
- This model separates the communication service from the domain logic. Separation of services in layers is a prerequisite for manageability.

Given these strong points as a start, conversation patterns, as described later, will improve upon this technique:

- By finding more general "facilitators", useable not only in the case of an ask/tell situation, but also, for example, for task delegation or for technical services like protocol translation.
- By clearly defining the co-operation contracts in terms of obligations and allowed actions based on roles.
- By allowing the type of facilitator to be negotiated between the participating agents.
- By trying to propose a standard, useable not only by one platform (i.e. Zeus uses KQML where as JADE uses FIPA-ACL), but on any platform. Especially, also *between* different platforms, possibly non-agent based too.
- By not coupling the co-operation contract to the use of a specialized agent. A middle-agent is useful in many cases, but it will not fully relieve the participants from all their pure communication responsibilities. The communication between client and middle-agent follows a contract itself.

Basically, the technique we aim to use for managing multi-agent dynamics is to direct (or restrict) the way agents interact for as many situations as possible by proposing a set of generic roles that can be played. Thus, either very simple co-operation protocols or well-defined generic co-operation patterns are preferable according to our experience. However, before we explain *conversation patterns*, we will first describe the *design patterns* that form their basis.

2.2 Design Patterns

Design patterns are a very popular software engineering technique, which can best be described in the words of the famous "Gang of Four"[4]:
"*A design pattern systematically names, motivates, and explains a general design that addresses a recurring design problem in object-oriented systems. It describes the problem, the solution, when to apply the solution, and its consequences.*"
Those patterns represent the experience of designers in tackling some common problems. Following their advice will render the developer a better designer. However, from the point of view of managing agent conversation we discover some interesting features:

- A design pattern will assign roles to the objects involved and impose the way these objects will communicate with each other; (just as we mentioned earlier on, this makes KQML facilitators easier to manage).
- A design pattern is generic and will indicate in general terms when it is applicable (the first improvement we wanted to make to facilitators).
- A design pattern describes only a part of a participating object's responsibility, not imposing anything on the domain knowledge.
- Design patterns are programming language independent and their vocabulary has become a generally accepted standard (the last improvement we wanted to make to facilitators).

Clearly, the conversation patterns will stay close to their design pattern counterparts. However, we will have to adapt their vocabulary and their definition, which differs in some very important aspects. Conversation patterns are i) *implemented* in an agent system, they are not purely design constructs, ii) are based on the way agents interact with true messages, not on procedure-call type object messages and iii) use Authorisation and Obligation Policies as a formalisation technique for management purposes by other manager agents.
The following design patterns show great potential for use in an agent communication environment. Here we describe some patterns, mentioning the definition given by the Gang of Four[4], and also how agents could make use of them.

Proxy: "Provide a surrogate or placeholder for another object to control access to it." Handles some requests from a client locally, while some are passed to a remote agent. The proxy can receive the answer and, maybe after some filtering, pass it to its client. Proxies should not change the message contents, as decorators would. The "subscription" facilitator can be solved with a proxy.

Façade: "Provide a unified interface to a set of interfaces in a subsystem. Facade defines a higher-level interface that makes the subsystem easier to use." This is an agent that acts as a representative of a complex system of agents, in order to make the underlying system look more simple or coherent.

Mediator: "Define an object that encapsulates how a set of objects interact. Mediator promotes loose coupling by keeping objects from referring to each other explicitly, and it lets the developer vary their interaction independently." This is a conversation leader, which prevents requests from being sent in an un-orderly fashion by taking requests and sending them to the right agent(s). It acts like the chairman in a meeting. The "broker" and "recruit" facilitators can be solved by using this pattern.

Observer: "Define a one-to-many dependency between objects so that when one object changes state, all its dependants are notified and updated automatically." The

Zeus agent platform (developed at BT Labs, UK) obliges every agent subscribed in the platform to forward all its messages to the visualiser agent or to any other management service agent. These agents are observers.

2.3 From Middle Agents & Design Patterns to Conversation Patterns

Conversation patterns are the combination of the principles used by the facilitators and those of the design patterns. They are a set of roles, with policies that define a "standard" conversation. Any agent that wishes to be able to participate in the pattern in any given role must implement the policies for that particular role.
The example below informally describes a simple conversation pattern. In section 0, we propose a way to formalize them. For the moment, we use only the following convention: **A+** means "allowed to", **A-** means "is not allowed to" and **O+** means "has the obligation to".

The Conversation Observer
Description:
This conversation pattern allows *the observer* to see the envelope of all messages sent and received by *the observed client.*
Use:
Allow an object to give limited support regarding message traffic, without allowing any interference.
Examples:
Visualisation of message traffic, Automated address books.
Roles:
Observer, Observed client.
Observed client role:
O+whenever a message is sent to a third party within a conversation, send the envelope[1] of the message to the observer
O+whenever a message is received within a conversation, send the envelope of the message to the observer
Observer role:
A+see the envelope[1] of the messages between the observed and a third party.
A- see the contents of the messages between the observed client and a third party.[2]
A- forward the messages received by the client without authorisation.
A+reply to any message forwarded by the client.
Variants:
Expand the O+ to all conversations (Messaging Traffic Observer).

A conversation pattern should be simple and generic, leaving no room for confusion. Note that the authorisation policies of the roles are formalised just enough for clear understanding. They can be even more formalised using techniques described in the Ponder specification language[6], in order to make a cross-platform communication possible and, at the same time manageable.

Whenever an agent offers a service that requires an interchange of messages, the agent can "offer" one or more conversation patterns to his client. When they agree on a certain pattern to be used, they assume the roles and start the communication.

---

[1] The envelope of a message includes the receiver (main and secondary), the sender, the sending date and the subject (including the conversation id).

[2] Describing what the observer may and may not see, seems superfluous, given the obligation of the client to only send the envelope to the observer. However, from these role specifications, an agent must determine if a certain pattern is useable or not for its intended purpose during pattern negotiation.

The Distributing Mediator
Description:
This conversation pattern makes *the client* send message in a conversation to the *mediator*. The mediator can forward this message to any third party in the name of the client (called recipients), informing the client which recipients were selected. The client can specify some required destinations. Any replies on this message from the recipients should be sent to the client, possibly enriched by extra information.
Use:
Allow an object to decide upon suitable recipients of a message sent by the client.
Examples:
Implementation of the KQML Broker.
Roles:
Mediator, client.
Client role:
O+send all message in a conversation to the mediator
A+indicate required set of destinations for this initial message.
Mediator role:
A+see the messages in a conversation sent by the observed client.
O+forward this message to the required destinations.
A+forward this message to another third party.
O+forward a list of thus contacted third parties to the client.
A+see envelope of any reply to this message by third parties.
O+forward these replies to the client.
A- see -or change- the contents of these replies.
A+add extra information to the replies.
Variants:
Remove the O+ of the mediator role regarding forwarding received messages to the client.
Make a formal agreement about the type of message in a message header. The mediator need then not have access to the entire message.
Allow the mediator to see the replied message and change it in any way it sees fit.

2.4 Co-operation Patterns

Conversation patterns are limited to the description of the roles in terms of messaging concepts. Co-operation patterns extend conversation patterns by including role specifications based on beliefs, desires and intentions, or, on AI-type goals and facts. A co-operation pattern can thus include concepts as delegation of tasks and joining forces to reach a goal. The relationship the agents assume in the pattern follows one of the types of relationship defined in[5]: control, peer, benevolence, dependency or ownership. In other words, they encapsulate also the 'social' relationship between roles. *Co-operation patterns* mimic human interaction behaviour. Therefore, the specific strengths of agents are used. Manager agents will now be able to measure a new aspect in agent interaction: quality of work delivered (how set goals are met and to what extent). The simplest of co-operation patterns, the Delegate Mediator, is described below.

The Delegate Mediator
Description:
This simple co-operation pattern allows *the client* to delegate a task by transferring a task and additional information. After this task is concluded, the mediator will relay its findings to the client.
The task given by the client consists of a set of goals and desires, the additional information and the findings of the mediator, are sets of facts, maybe also beliefs and intentions.
The pattern also allows also the transfer of credentials from the client to the mediator. It is thus a dependency relationship.
Use:
Allow the delegation of goal-oriented tasks from an agent to another agent.
Examples:
Different types of purchase advisors, Intelligent brokers
Roles:
Client, Mediator.

Client role:
O+transfer a set of goals, desires to the mediator
A+accompany this with facts, beliefs and intentions
A+specify a time limit or another kind of abortion constraints
A+relay a set of credentials
Mediator role:
O+transfer a result set upon reaching the set goals or after meeting an abortion constraint
A- pose as its client
A+use the given credentials in order to reach the given goal
Variants:
Restrict further delegation of the task, in order to protect the facts and beliefs transferred.

Conversation patterns use standard messaging semantics and thus require only a small number of new formalisms. The definition of co-operation patterns, on the other hand, has to rely also on conventions for transferring goals, facts, beliefs, desires and intentions from one agent to another. We strongly believe that research focused on such communication, in contrast to mere request/response communication, will earn the agent community a distinct place in the e-business market, where agents should be 'sent out' to collect information or to carry out any other task in the 'world wide web'.
As in humans, agents will never reach true intelligent behaviour without true intelligent communication. Co-operation patterns, once standardised, could provide a basis of 'polite' behaviour necessary for fluent relationships with others, just what humans find important when talking to others, especially to 'strangers'. The techniques used in the conversation patterns provide a solid basis for building co-operation patterns. In this paper, we will focus on the first kind of customised agent patterns.

3. A Formal Model for the Conversation Patterns

In this section we will propose a way to formalise the conversation patterns. To do this we have to start by describing the responsibilities of each role. Several authors have already tackled the problem of formalisation of agents. We will choose the "policy based design" model developed for managing distributed objects from the computing department of Imperial College [3] and show how it should be applied to patterns in order to manage agents. A simple policy rule defines a set of policy actions that are carried out when a set of conditions becomes true. Many others like the IETF Policy Group, provide a policy-based methodology, for quality of service management and configuration within a network (http://www.ietf.org/draft-ietf-policy-req-01.txt) valuable for our purpose. We have chosen one that explicitly differentiates authorisation and obligation policies, which is of great use when describing responsibilities.
We start by introducing Roles, which are defined as a set of policies applying to the same subject domain. While policies may be used to specify the rights and duties for groups of agents in the organisation, they are also used to specify the behaviour expected from manager agents assigned to particular organisational positions. Agents can then be assigned to or removed from a role without re-specifying the role's policies.
Policies[3] establish a relationship between the service manager agents and domains of agents, which are targets of the agents' activities. Domains[3][6] are essentially a means of grouping software agents, or other domains; they are used to partition the

enterprise scope according to geographical boundaries, administrative departments, agent service type, agent societies and so on.

An agent policy applying to a domain propagates to all the agents in that domain, including sub-domains and their members, thus making it possible to specify policies for large numbers of agents in a hierarchical structure. Since policies are used in order to specify the rights and duties of the organisational agents, we distinguish between authorisation and obligation policies.

Authorisation Policies define what activities a set of subjects (agents) can perform on a set of target agents. The notation below is borrowed from[6]. The positive authorisation policy: $S \rightarrow T.A$? C, states that all members of the subject set S (in our case, one or more role names) are authorised to invoke action A on any member of the target set T if constraint C is satisfied. The policy can also be read from the point of view of the target i.e., that all members of the target set T are authorised to accept action A from any member of the subject set S if constrained C is satisfied. As far as the negative authorisation is concerned, the formula is similar: $S \rightarrow| T.A$? C, states that no member of the subject set S is authorised to invoke action A on any member of the target set, when constraint C is satisfied.

Obligation Policies define what activities an agent must or must not perform on a set of target objects/agents. Positive obligation policies are triggered by events and constraints can be specified to limit the applicability of the policy based on time or attributes of the objects to which the policy refers. In contrast to other basic policy types -which are essentially access-control policies- obligation policies are event-triggered methods that carry out management tasks. An obligation policy: $E, S \rightarrow M$? C states that all members of the subject set S are obliged to execute method M each time that event E occurs provided that constraint C is satisfied. Below in Tables 1 and 2, we carry on by providing a formal reference implementation model for one of the patterns we have implemented; the Observer Pattern through the use of policies (obligations and authorisations) defining two roles: the Manager role and the Client role.

Table 1. Reference implementation model for the Client agent role

1	O+ Client-agent.send (msg, A_2), Client-agent
2	→ forward (msg.envelope, Observer)
3	? DONE [Observer.subscribe(Client-Agent, "observation")]
1'	Each time the Client Agent sends a message (msg) to Agent 2, the Client Agent has the Obligation
2'	to call method "Forward" for the envelope of the message to the Observer
3'	If Client Agent has done a subscribe to the Observer for a service "observation"
4	O+ Client-agent.receive (msg, A_2) , Client-agent
5	→ forward (msg.envelope, Observer)
6	? DONE [Observer.subscribe(Client-agent, "observation")]
4'	Each time the Client Agent receives a message (msg) from Agent 2, the Client Agent has the Obligation to
5'	Call method "Forward" for the message envelope to the Observer,
6'	If Client Agent has done a subscribe to the Observer for a service "observation"

Table 2. Reference implementation model for the Observer manager role

1	A+ Observer → msg.envelope.READ
2	? DONE [Observer.subscribe(A_1, "Observation") && A_1.send(msg, Observer)]
A	Observer has a positive Authorisation → To invoke a Read message action on any Agent 1 message (msg) envelope,
B	If Agent 1 has done a subscribe to the observer manager for a service "observation" and Agent 1 has sent already a message (msg) to the Observer
3	A- Observer → I msg.content.READ
4	? DONE [Observer.subscribe(A_1, "observation") && A_1.send(msg, Observer)]
C	Observer has a negative Authorisation, → To invoke a Read message action on any Agent 1 message (msg) content,
D	If Agent 1 has done a subscribe to the observer manager for a service "observation" and Agent 1 has sent already a message (msg) to the Observer
5	A- Observer →I msg.forward (X)
6	? DONE [Observer.subscribe(A_1, "observation") && A_1.send(msg, Observer)]
E	Observer has a negative Authorisation → To invoke a Forward message action on any Agent 1 message,
F	If Agent 1 has done a subscribe to the observer manager for a service "observation" and Agent 1 has sent already a message (msg) to the Observer
7	A+ Observer → msg.reply (msg_r)
8	? DONE [Observer.subscribe(A_1, "observation") && A_1.send(msg, Observer)]
G	Observer has a positive Authorisation → To invoke a Reply message (msg_r) action on any Agent 1 message,
H	If Agent 1 has done a subscribe to the observer manager for a service "observation" and Agent 1 has sent already a message (msg) to the Observer

4. Agent Management, Software Patterns, and Role Theory

The use of roles in services allow to group policies with the same subject. This subject can be dynamically assigned or removed without having to change the policies of that role. As shown in the diagram below, the *Service Role* concept holds all policies specific to a service (possibly a management service). The *Service Position Domain* can be vacant or occupied with any agent that satisfies the pre-specified authorisations and obligations towards the client. Thus, policy roles are an implementation (and platform) independent way to describe the responsibilities attached to a service.

Conversation pattern roles relieve the service role of conversation specific requirements. They too describe responsibilities in an implementation (and platform) independent manner. But in contrast, they are typically independent of the provided service and can be chosen to suit the needs of the client, as long as they do not contradict the rules set by the service role. They also encapsulate all conversation requirements imposed on the *client* of the service. Standardising this has great advantages:

- Openness and distribution: 'alien' platforms and agents need only to implement a few conventions to play along;
- Plug-and-play: any new service can use the patterns for their conversations. Any additional requirements imposed on the client are rare and specific to the service itself.

- Reuse: it saves a lot of time and effort for the agent developer, if the conversation scenario is already dealt with. Additionally, management services built upon a set of patterns are available to all agents using them.

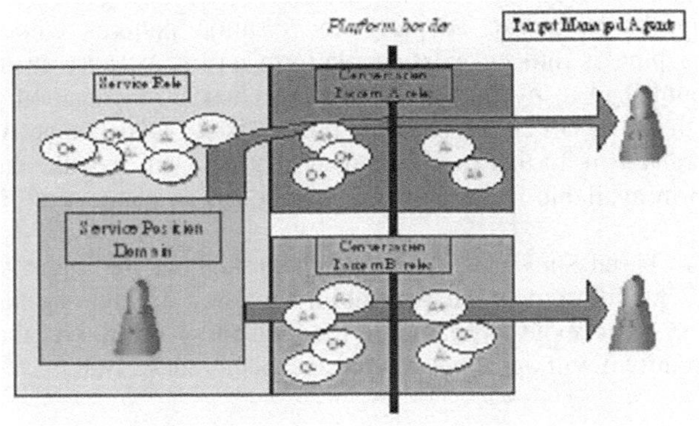

Fig. 2. Agent management using a policy based framework

Co-operation patterns will expand the horizon from mere client-service relationships, typical to Object Orientation, to more complex social behavior, more suited to agents like for example goal sharing, delegation and leadership.

As a service, agent management uses conversation patterns on two levels: Firstly, the management modules can use the patterns to communicate with the other agents. In other words, it is the hook into the system they manage. Secondly, patterns contain extra information on how the communication between agents works. Management modules can use this to enforce policies, measure response time to obligation triggering events, agent visualisation, 'law' enforcement police agents and so on. In other words, any interaction between agents can be established in an infinite number of ways. In order to standardise some of them without constraining or limiting the capabilities of the software agent at all, we use a set of pre-defined software design patterns. This creates also a more visible system to manage.

5. Conclusions

We believe that this novel approach to agent management, which consists of the combination -in a new manner- of already known technologies of neighbouring fields, will benefit the agent community substantially. These technologies include: a) Some of the principles and vocabulary of software design patterns from the Object Oriented world are applied to agent communication and co-operation needs; b) The policy based framework used in managing objects in distributed systems is adapted in a way to suit our purpose of managing agents; c) Role theory is used to formalise our management services (see table 1 and 2).

Also, we still rely on the established agent-based techniques, like conversation management. We think this approach will benefit the Agent community because it focuses on some of the specific management and communication needs of agent in any advanced environment, agent-based or not. This unique combination also enables us to structure agent services in an open and fully distributed way.

It constitutes a different approach than the one used by the conventional Agent Platforms (like Jade, Zeus from BT and Fipa-os from Nortel). There, the management is centralised and the services have specific interfaces. Using conversation patterns, all services can be distributed. Moreover, all services, management or otherwise, use the same mechanisms. So, adopting conversation patterns empowers an agent developer to plug it into an existing platform easily, because his communication needs are published using the policies of the chosen conversation patterns. In the mean time, the new service is backed with the existing management services through the same mechanism. In theory, a non-agent platform can provide agents to any true agent platform available in the network, simply by implementing the conversation patterns.

When pattern-based standards are accepted throughout the agent community, our novel approach will promote inter-operability amongst different agent platforms, akin to the open systems about to emerge in the e-business world over the coming years. More importantly it will open the way for agents *into* these systems.

6. References

[1] C. Stergiou, J. Pitt, F. Guerin, Protocols and Intentional Specifications for Multi Party Agent Conversations for Brokerage and Auctions., in the Proceedings of Autonomous Agents 2000 Conference.

[2] C. Stergiou, J. Pitt, F. Guerin, A. Artikis, Implementing Multi Party agent Conversations, in the Proceedings of the 13th IEA/AIE-2000 conference, New Orleans, USA.

[3] E. Lupu and M. Sloman, "Towards a Role-Based Framework for Distributed Systems Management". Plenum Press Journal of Network and Systems Management, 5(1):5-30, 1997.

[4] E. Gamma, R. Helm, R. Johnson and J. Vlissides, Design Patterns, Elements of Reusable Object-Oriented Software. Addison-Wesley Publishing Company, 1995.

[5] F. Zamborelli, N.R. Jennings, M. Woolridge, Organisational Abstractions for the Analysis and Design of Multi-Agent Systems.

[6] N.Dulay, E.Lupu, M.Sloman, N.Damianou, Towards a Runtime Object Model for the Ponder Policy Language. To be published in DSOM 2000 conference.

An Approach to Coalition Formation Using Argumentation-Based Negotiation in Multi-agent Systems

Hiromitsu Hattori, Takayuki Ito, Tadachika Ozono, and Toramatsu Shintani

Department of Intelligence and Computer Science, Nagoya Institute of Technology
Gokiso, Syowa-ku, Nagoya, 466-8555, Japan
{hatto, itota, ozono, tora}@ics.nitech.ac.jp

Abstract. In this paper, we propose an argumentation-based negotiation method for coalition formation. In existing argumentation method, it is difficult for an agent to calculate the effectiveness of each proposal, since agents are constructed based only on a logical framework. In our method, agents can calculate the effectiveness using a mechanism which can evaluate arguments. In order to evaluate the arguments, we prepare certain functions, so we employ the AHP. During the negotiation, agents can create the most effective proposal and change a negotiation strategy autonomously. An advantage of our method is that agents can reach an agreement reflecting user's multiple valuations, and the negotiation among agents is completed quickly. Another advantage is that if agents have no need to create proposals, each user's private data is not opened to others during the negotiation.

1 Introduction

In the field of AI (*Artificial Intelligence*), software agents have been investigated very actively [11]. Software agents can act autonomously in a network and carry out various task on behalf of users. In multiagent systems, each agent has different goals and interacts with the others in order to reach an agreement. The interaction between agents for reaching an agreement is called a negotiation. Agent negotiation is one of the most important research topic in the domain of multiagent systems.

In recent years, multiagent systems have been applied practically. For example, in the field of EC (*Electronic Commerce*) some prototype systems based on multiagent systems have been implemented [1,3]. In these systems, an agent negotiates on behalf of its user in order to achieve a reasonable transaction. Therefore, it is necessary to reflect the relevant user's preferences and knowledge effectively during negotiation. The Contract Net Protocol [10] is one of typical negotiation protocols. This protocol is effective when agents solve a task allocation problem. However, there are few opportunities for interaction among agents, so users' preferences and knowledge are not reflected sufficiently during negotiation.

L. Monostori, J. Váncza, and M. Ali (Eds.): IEA/AIE 2001, LNAI 2070, pp. 687–696, 2001.

Interest in argumentation-based negotiation among agents [6,7,9] has been growing. Argumentation-based negotiation is a promising approach to resolving conflicts and reflecting preferences. In argumentation-based negotiation, agents exchange proposals and counter-proposals in order to reach an agreement. Proposals and counter-proposals consist of a claim and arguments which justify it. Various researches on argumentation-based negotiation have been made. However most of these researches are theoretical studies [5,7], and practical applications have not been implemented. In existing argumentation methods, agents are constructed based only on a logical framework, so a proposal is expressed by using the logical expressions. Therefore it is difficult to evaluate a proposal itself, that is, an agent cannot calculate the effectiveness of each proposal. Currently, we are trying to develop an argumentation method which can evaluate proposals, for use in our multiagent system which helps agents make a reasonable choice from alternatives.

The purpose of our research is to develop a new argumentation method which combines a logical framework and an argument evaluation mechanism. In this paper, we focus on an argument evaluation mechanism and propose an argumentation method which is not based on a logical framework. We define an agent's knowledge as the user's valuations of alternatives. Agents create a proposal by using a part of the user's valuations in order to reflect the user's preferences in an agreement. Agents evaluate all declared proposals, so they can decide the most preferable alternative. Agents can evaluate the proposals since they have an user's valuations which are quantified by using an appropriate quantification method. In addition, agents can change a negotiation strategy autonomously in order to reach an agreement which is more preferable for its user.

An advantage of our method is that agents can reach an agreement reflecting multiple valuations, and the negotiation among agents is completed quickly. Another advantage is that user's private data is not opened to others except when agent has to attack the opponent's claim.

This paper consists of five sections. In Section 2, we show the architecture of our system, and a quantification method for users' preferences. Moreover, we present an argumentation method between two agents. In Section 3, we show the procedure for coalition formation in a multiagent environment. In Section 4, we show an example of our prototype system. In Section 5, we conclude and summarize.

2 Coalition Formation Based on Argumentation

2.1 System Architecture

Figure 1 shows the architecture of our system. Our system consists of multiple "User Agents" and one "Mediator Agent." User Agent has two kinds of knowledge bases. The first is a set of user's valuations of alternatives with respect to several criteria. User Agent uses these valuations as the private data of its user, and it does not revise the valuations because the agent always refers to

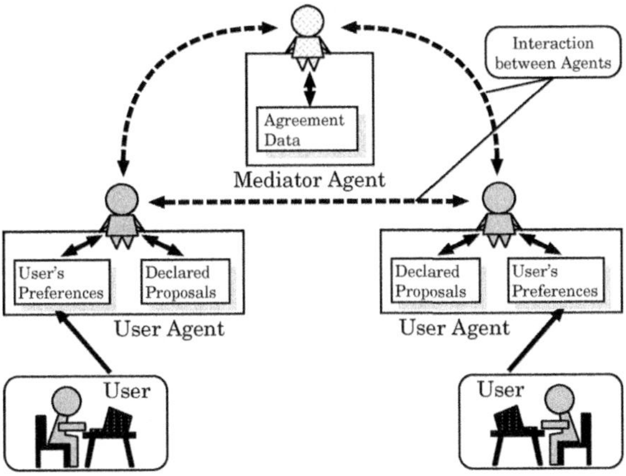

Fig. 1. Architecture of our System.

them during negotiation to decide a negotiation strategy. The user's valuation is quantified by the Analytic Hierarchy Process (AHP) [8]. The other knowledge base is a set of arguments which are declared during the negotiation. User Agent evaluates these arguments synthetically, i.e., it decides the current most preferable alternative and whether it can create a new proposal.

The Mediator Agent facilitates reaching an agreement in the negotiation. It has preference data which consist of the most preferable alternative of each agent. During the negotiation, the Mediator Agent encourages appropriate User Agents to join in, based on these data in order to facilitate reaching an agreement. When all User Agents reach an agreement after the negotiation, the Mediator Agent broadcasts negotiation results to all User Agents, and then stops the system.

2.2 Quantification of User's Preferences

In our system, each agent creates a proposal based on the corresponding user's valuation of alternatives. In general, a user evaluates alternatives considering several criteria. Multi-Attribute Utility Theory (MAUT) [4] handles this by characterizing outcomes by two or more attributes. In MAUT, for an alternative denoted C_i, there are n attributes denoted by $X_1, X_2, ..., X_n$, and their values $x_1(C_i), x_2(C_i), ..., x_n(C_i)$. We can represent the utility $u(C_i)$ for the alternative C_i:

$$u(C_i) = f(f_1(x_1(C_i)), ..., f_n(x_n(C_i)))$$

where f is a certain function. We can select several options with respect to f according to the application area. In this paper, we employ the Analytic Hierarchy Process(AHP) [8] for quantifying user's utility, that is, this is user's valuations. AHP is an effective quantification method for measuring the subjective judgements of users.

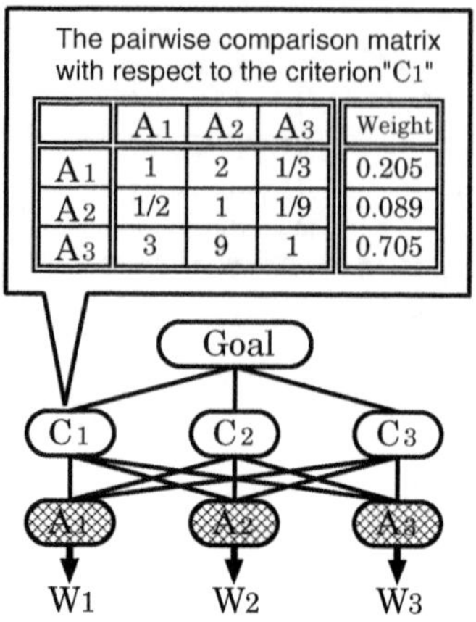

Fig. 2. Analytic Hierarchy Process.

In the AHP, users decompose a problem into a hierarchy that consists of a goal, criteria, and alternatives. In the hierarchy, a judgement of pairwise comparisons between factors (in Figure 2, alternatives A_1, A_2 and A_3) on a certain level is made with respect to the criterion that is a factor (in Figure 2, the criterion C_1) on the upper level. The weights of factors are calculated analytically by making a matrix of values of judgements (top of Figure 2). To be concrete, we can get weights of each factor as an eigen-vector for a maximum eigen-value of a pairwise comparison matrix. For example, in Figure 2 the most preferable alternative with respect to C_1 is A_3. As a whole hierarchy, the weights of alternatives can be calculated by composing weights of criteria. In Figure 2, the weights of A_1, A_2, and A_3 are W_1, W_2, and W_3, respectively.

Based on the weights of alternatives, the user's preference order of alternatives is defined as follows.

$$W_i > W_j \Leftrightarrow A_i \succ A_j$$
$$W_i = W_j \Leftrightarrow A_i \sim A_j$$

$A_i \succ A_j$ means that a user prefers A_i to A_j. $A_i \sim A_j$ means that a user is indifferent between A_i and A_j.

2.3 Argumentation-Based Negotiation

In this section, we present argumentation-based negotiation between two agents.

Firstly, we define the final agreement among agents as follows: the final agreement is the most preferable alternative when there are no agents which can create a new proposal. Thus, the purpose of each agent is to make its own current most preferable alternative become the final agreement. Therefore, at some point, if

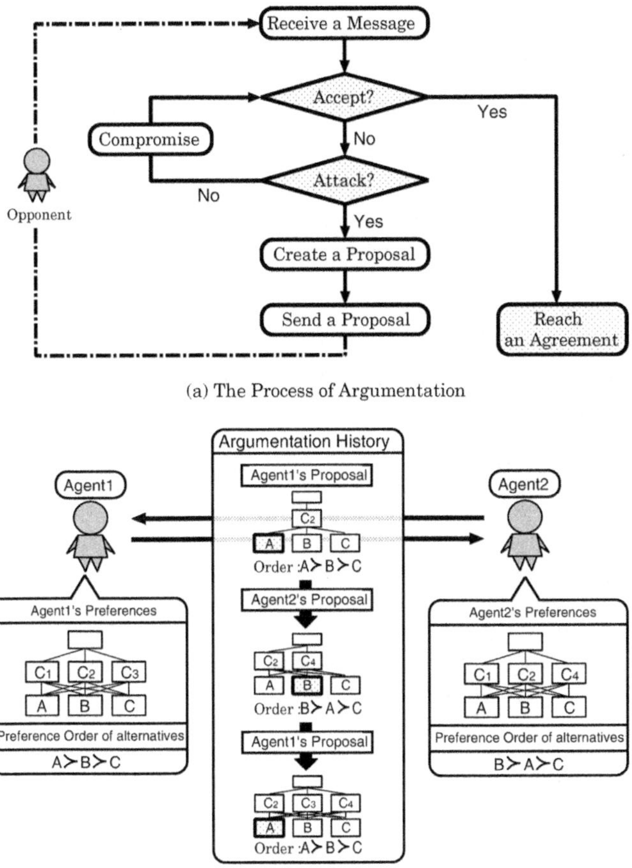

(a) The Process of Argumentation

(b) An Example of Argumentation

Fig. 3. The Argumentation between Two Agents.

the most preferable alternative is different among two agents, they must negotiate in order to resolve conflicts.

Secondly, we define the form of a proposal created by agents. Here, we assume that there are m alternatives denoted by $A_1, A_2, ..., A_m$ and n criteria denoted by $C_1, C_2, ..., C_n$. A certain agent creates a proposal P. A proposal P claims that alternative A_i is the most preferable alternative. Besides, P includes arguments V which justify the claim. Arguments V consist of one criteria C_j and a set of values of each alternative $\{v(A_1), v(A_2), ..., v(A_m)\}$ with respect to C_j. A proposal P is defined as follows.

$$P = (A_i, V)$$
$$V = (C_j, f(v(A_1)), f(v(A_2)), ..., f(v(A_m)))$$

where f is a certain function. We can select several options with respect to f according to the application area. As I mentioned before, we employ the AHP. $P = (A_i, \phi)$ means that the agent accepts a proposal $P = (A_i, V)$.

We present a process of argumentation-based negotiation between two agents (see Figure 3 (a)).

Step 1: When the agent receives a message, the agent checks whether it accepts a proposal. If an alternative claimed in the proposal is the same as the agent's own most preferable alternative, it accepts the proposal, so two agents reach an agreement. If the agent does not accept the proposal, the process advances to the next step.

Step 2: If the agent does not accept the proposal, it judges whether it is possible to create a counter-proposal to attack the opponent's claim.
In order to judge, the agent evaluates all declared proposals and a potential proposal together. Actually, the agent combines all proposals to construct a hierarchy in AHP and then evaluates it. If the most preferable alternative in the constructed hierarchy is the same as its own most preferable alternative, the agent sends a counter-proposal.
To put it precisely, the counter-proposal claims that the agent's own most preferable alternative is appropriate as an agreement. If the agent cannot create a counter-proposal, it must compromise. To put it concretely, the agent changes its most preferable alternative to another alternative which is the next most preferable of alternatives. Then it restarts the process from Step 1.

Step 3: The agent creates a new proposal. The proposal claims that the agent's own most preferable alternative is appropriate as an agreement. If there are several arguments, the agent selects the most appropriate argument. The degree of effectiveness of each argument can be decided based on the weight of alternatives in AHP. Namely, the agent selects the argument which gives the highest weight to the most preferable alternative.

Step 4: The agent sends a new proposal. The negotiation is continued until either agent accepts a proposal.

Figure 3 (b) shows a simple example of argumentation between Agent1 and Agent2. Agent1 and Agent2 have valuations of alternatives with respect to three criteria, C_1, C_2, C_3 and C_1, C_2, C_4, respectively. Agent1's order of preferences is $A \succ B \succ C$, and Agent2's order of alternatives preferences is $B \succ A \succ C$. Accordingly, Agent1's primary purpose is to effect an agreement supporting alternative A. Agent2's primary purpose is to effect an agreement supporting alternative B.

As a beginning, in this example, Agent1 sends the first proposal. The proposal claims that alternative A is the most appropriate alternative, and includes valuations of alternatives with respect to criterion C_2 as an argument. So the temporal agreement is alternative A. Then, Agent2 judges that it is possible to create a counter-proposal. Agent2 creates and sends a proposal that claims that alternative B is the most appropriate. This proposal includes valuations of alternatives with respect to criterion C_4 as an argument. Subsequently, Agent1

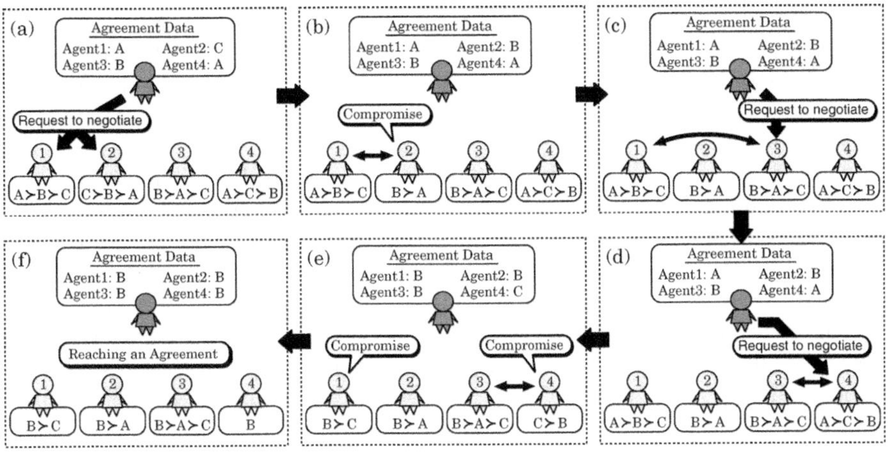

Fig. 4. The Process of Multiagent Argumentation.

creates and sends a counter-proposal that includes an argument which consists of criterion C_3 and valuations with respect to C_3. At this point, Agent2 cannot attack Agent1's claim, so Agent2 must compromise. Thus Agent2's purpose is to reach an agreement on alternative A because alternative A is the next most preferable of Agent2's preferences. Therefore, Agent2 accepts Agent1's proposal, so Agent1 and Agent2 agree to alternative A.

3 The Negotiation Process among Agents

In this section, we show the procedure for coalition formation among agents by using the method discussed in Section 2.3. In our system, the Mediator Agent selects two agents from all agents, and makes them negotiate. The Mediator Agent works according to the following two mediation policies.

Policy 1: If the most preferable alternative is mutual to both agents, the Mediator Agent considers them a cooperative group. Accordingly, if the agent cannot create a proposal and it is a member of such a group, the Mediator Agent requests another member to join the negotiation. When a Mediator Agent makes requests, it sends all declared proposals in order to tell the negotiation status.
If one of the group members makes an opponent compromise (that is to say, wins in negotiation), it is unnecessary for all members to compromise. On the other hand, if there are no agents in the group which can win in negotiation, all member must compromise.
According to this policy, User Agents join negotiation sequentially, as a result, they can reach an agreement efficiently.

Policy 2: The Mediator Agent selects one agent from the largest group, and another from the smallest group. According to Policy 1, the more group members, the more advantageous in negotiation. Hence the Mediator Agent can facilitate reaching an agreement.

Figure 4 shows an example of coalition formation based on our method. In this example, there are four agents. Each agent's order of preferences is $A \succ B \succ C$, $C \succ B \succ A$, $B \succ A \succ C$, and $A \succ C \succ B$, respectively. In the initial state (Figure 4 (a)), a larger number of agents prefers alternative A. Thus, the Mediator Agent requests Agent1 and Agent2 to join in negotiation. In this negotiation, Agent2 compromises, and then changes negotiation strategy to prefer alternative B (Figure 4 (b)). In Figure 4 (c), Agent2 can not create a proposal again. Accordingly, the Mediator Agent requests Agent3 to join in negotiation instead of Agent2. Similarly, in Figure 4 (d), Agent4 is requested to join in negotiation instead of Agent1. Consequently, Agent1 and Agent4 are made to compromise (Figure 4 (e)). Agent1 reaches an agreement supporting alternative B. However Agent4 changes a negotiation strategy to prefer alternative C. Finally Agent4 is made to compromise again, and all agents reach an agreement supporting alternative B (Figure 4 (f)).

4 An Example and Experimental Result

In this section, we show an example of our system, using MiLog (a mobile agent framework for implementing intelligent agents with logic programming) [2], which is written in Java language.

Figure 5 (a) shows AHP interface windows. A user enters his/her preferences using these windows. The ① in Figure 5 shows the hierarchy in AHP. A user can create new criteria and check the alternatives. The ② in Figure 5 shows the pairwise comparison matrix. A user can check the result of pairwise comparisons. The ③ in Figure 5 is opened when a user clicks a cell in ②. A user judges

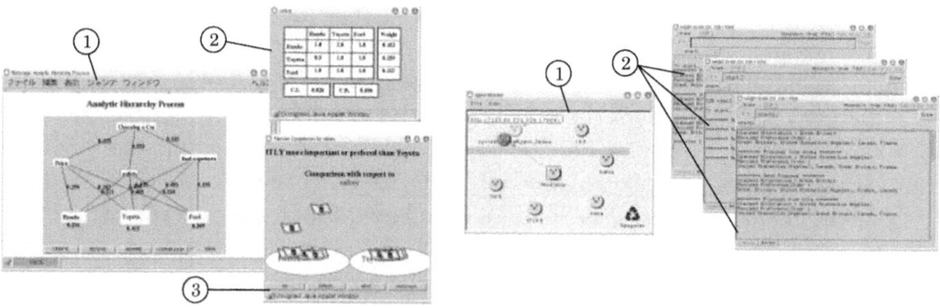

(a) AHP Interface (b) Agent Communication Viewer

Fig. 5. System Examples.

pairwise comparisons individually by using ③ window. A user can enter his/her preferences only by using the mouse.

Figure 5 (b) shows the windows for monitoring agents. The ① presents the interface for monitoring agent communication status. We call this monitoring tool the "Agent Monitor." The ② shows each agent interface. A user can check the argumentation status by using these tools.

We evaluated the performance of our argumentation-based negotiation method. Our preliminary set of experiments involved 15 agents with 6 alternatives. Each agent's valuation of alternatives was given at random. The utility was given according to "Borda Count", which is suitable for deciding the acceptable winner.

Figure 6 shows the experimental result. "Best" is the highest possible utility in each trial. "Worst" is the lowest possible utility. Our method produces moderate utility. Namely, our method is not dependent on both a majority opinion and a minority opinion. Moreover, when worst utility is very low, our method can avoid selecting such an alternative.

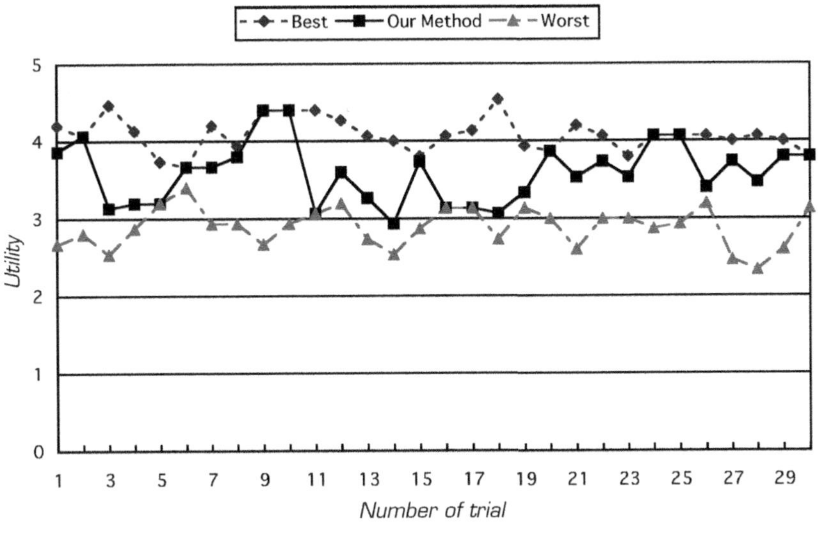

Fig. 6. Comparison on Utility.

5 Conclusion

In this paper, we proposed an argumentation-based negotiation method for coalition formation. We focused on a mechanism which can evaluate arguments. In order to evaluate the arguments, we prepare certain functions, so we employ the AHP.

In this paper, we defined the procedure for argumentation-based negotiation between two agents. During the negotiation, agents can create the most effective proposal and change a negotiation strategy autonomously because they can calculate the effectiveness of potential proposals. Moreover, we presented the procedure for coalition formation in a multiagent environment using our argumentation method. An advantage of our method is that agents can reach an agreement reflecting multiple valuations, and the negotiation among agents is completed quickly. Another advantage is that if agents have no need to create proposals, each user's private data is not opened to others during the negotiation. The experimental result shows that an agreement is not dependent on both a majority opinion and a minority opinion. This indicates that agents examine potential proposals autonomously by using our method.

Our future work is to develop a more flexible mechanism. Currently, we are trying to combine a logical argumentation framework and a more appropriate evaluation mechanism.

References

1. Chavez, A., and Maes, P., : Kasbah: An Agent Marketplace for Buying and Selling Goods, Proceedings of First International Conference and Exhibition on The Practical Application of Intelligent Agents and Multi-Agents (PAAM-96), pp.75–90, 1996.
2. Fukuta, N., Ito, T., and Shintani, T., : MiLog:A Mobile Agent Framework for Implementing Intelligent Information Agents with Logic Programming, Proceedings of the First Pacific Rim International Workshop on Intelligent Information Agents(PRIIA2000), pp.113–123, 2000.
3. Guttman, R. H., and Maes, P., : Agent-mediated Integrative Negotiation for Retail Electronic Commerce, Proceedings of the Workshop on Agent Mediated Electronic Trading(AMET-98), 1998.
4. Keeney, R. L., and Raiffa, H., : Decisions with Multiple Objectives : Preference and Value Tradeoffs, Cambridge Univ. Press, 1993.
5. Kraus, S., Sycara, K., and Evenchik, A., : Reaching agreements through argumentation: a logical model and implementation, Artificial Intelligence, 104:1-70,1998.
6. Parsons, S., Sierra, C., and Jennings, N. R., : Agents that reason and negotiate by arguing, Journal of Logic and Computation, Vol. 8, No. 3, pp.261–292, 1998.
7. Prakken, H., and Sartor, G., : Argument-based extended logic programming with defeasible priorities, Journal of Applied Non-Classical Logics, Vol. 7, No. 1-2, pp.25-75, 1997.
8. Saaty, T., : The analytic hierarchy process, McGraw Hill, 1980.
9. Sierra, C., Jennings, N. R., Noriega, P., and Parsons, S., : A framework for argumentation-based negotiation, Proceedings of the Fourth International Workshop on Agent Theories,Architectures and Languages(ATAL-97), pp.167–182, 1997.
10. Smith, R. G., : The contract net protocol: High-level communication and control in a distributed problem solver, IEEE Transactions on Computers, Vol. 29, No. 12, pp.1104–1113, 1980.
11. Weiss, G., : Multiagent systems: a modern approach to distributed artificial intelligence, The MIT Press, 1999.

A Negotiation Model to Support Material Selection in Concurrent Design

Robin Barker[1], Leigh Holloway[2], and Anthony Meehan[3]

[1] Bartec Systems, Barnsley, UK

[2] University of Sheffield, Environmental Business Network,
5 Palmerston Road, Sheffield S10 2TE, UK;

[3] Sheffield Hallam University, Pond Street, Sheffield S1 1WB, UK.
a.s.meehan@shu.ac.uk

Abstract. Based upon empirical studies, this paper describes a negotiation model to support materials selection by design teams using concurrent design methodologies. The model is realised in a tool that supports designers in this task. Given a list of materials currently proposed, similar alternatives are offered to individual designers based upon both shared and private representations. Fuzzy measures of similarity are used to identify possible counter proposals. A fuzzy measure of value is used to rank these. Conventional negotiation protocols from economics or game theory did not correspond well to the negotiation behaviour of designers. Currently, the human user remains responsible for the communication of any proposal he or she wishes to make, and for the supporting argumentation.

1 Introduction

We are engaged in the development of knowledge-based approaches to supporting design engineers using concurrent design methodologies. We are particularly interested in supporting design teams in optimising designs over the whole life cycle of a product: from conception, through manufacture, use, maintenance, reuse, recycling and disposal.

The successful deployment of knowledge-based systems in design is relatively limited. A number of explanations are offered. Landauer [1] observes that knowledge models underpinning the systems developed do not align with the motivation and cognition of the individuals concerned. Smithers [2] suggests that, in the field of design, the computational techniques that have been used focus on what machines can achieve and do not reflect how people actually reason and behave. This observation can be extended to include systems that support or implement negotiation. Researchers have drawn extensively upon game theory and decision science but the extent to which these economic approaches can be connected to human-oriented negotiation is very much an open question [3].

L. Monostori, J. Váncza, and M. Ali (Eds.): IEA/AIE 2001, LNAI 2070, pp. 697-707, 2001.

In response to the above situation, we have developed knowledge models which better reflect the cognition of the designers, facilitate (some of) the normal dynamics of the design process, and examine ways in which these might be computationally achieved [4], [5]. This paper reports on that part of a design support system, which assists a concurrent design team in negotiation during the materials selection stage of design. It seeks to identify ways in which designers may be supported in identifying alternative materials, the choice of which would improve the design from their perspective, and which are more likely to be acceptable to partners in negotiation.

The paper first describes the nature of the concurrent design problem; looks at how designers view the artefacts about which they negotiate; and considers computational support for negotiation. The paper then describes an agent-based architecture that supports the design team in negotiation during materials selection. Finally, it discusses the resulting system and outlines related work in progress.

2 The Concurrent Design Problem

Design can be considered as consisting of two distinct tasks: the *analysis* task generates a formal design specification from an informal problem description; the *synthesis* task entails the generation of a design solution from the formal specification [6]. Concurrent design is a specialisation of this model and is distinctive in the degree to which it incorporates a large number of different life-cycle perspectives at the very earliest stages of product design [7]. Perspectives that may be considered include design for market, manufacture, assembly, transportation, maintenance, energy efficiency, reusability (of components), recycling and disposal.

Concurrent design is characterised by an iterative process of 'propose-critique-negotiate' [8]. Iteration occurs both at the stage where a (revised) conceptual design is arrived at during *analysis*, and in the detailing of that conceptual design during *synthesis* (Figure 1).

In previous work with product designers we have developed a knowledge model to guide the development of design support systems. This involved using a technique to re-represent the designers' linguistic representation of their knowledge, behaviour and their organisational context in a semi-formalism based upon the CommonKADS model set [9]. The methodology is described more fully elsewhere [4].

In the research above, negotiation emerged as a significant (socio-political) experience in the product design domain. Our studies revealed the need to deploy computational techniques that aspire to allow systems to facilitate and maintain at least some of the dynamics which characterise human interaction in concurrent design. To achieve this we have already proposed an agent-based approach which features human/agent interaction in which the autonomy of the agent may be determined by the designer it represents at any stage [10], [5].

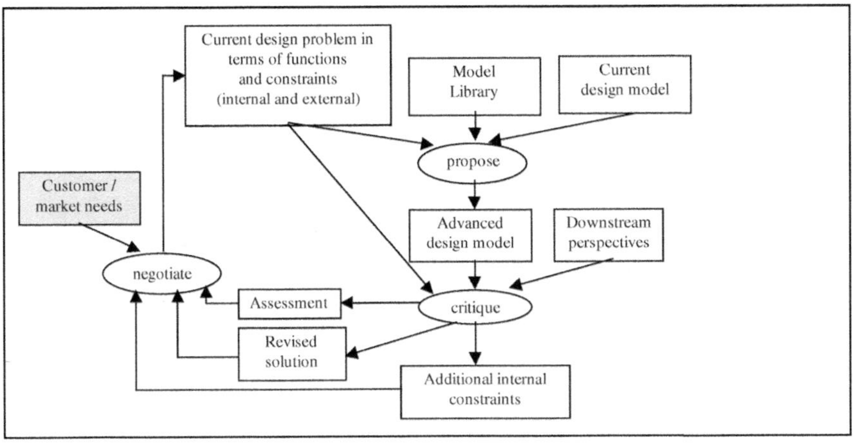

Fig. 1. Concurrent designers iterate through a cycle of 'propose-critique-negotiate'. The contributions from different design perspectives vary over this cycle. There are 3 knowledge intensive reasoning steps: propose, critique and negotiate. The negotiation step is the stage when the differing assessments of the designers are resolved to the extent that another iteration is initiated, or an acceptable solution, is agreed (Barker, Meehan and Tranter, 1999)

3 Representing Designers

We support designers with computational agents, which share each designer's own viewpoint on a design artefact. Holloway [11] has detailed attributes of materials used by concurrent designers. Designers' viewpoints appear to be partially shared with other members of the team (e.g. some attributes have a shared 'label'). Table 1 records some of the attributes of materials considered from three different concurrent design perspectives. It reveals both those attributes for which designers have shared labels and those attributes that are not shared (or are not reported as such).

In some cases, it is possible to have considerable confidence that the 'understanding' of the attribute is genuinely shared. The shared concept 'specific heat' provides such an example in the context of materials selection. Air Pollution Index (API) and Water Pollution Index (WPI) [11], [12]. are examples of concepts that are constructed deliberately in order to facilitate shared meaning. Some shared 'labels' may be far from agreed between designers (e.g. 'toughness', 'suitability').

Table 1. Concurrent designers represent materials in an attribute space. For many attributes, designers share labels (if not meanings) and this facilitates dialogue and argumentation in negotiation. Many attributes belong to just one perspective on the concurrent design process

Material Property (for HDPE)	**Materials Analyst**	**Mech. Analyst**	**Disposal Analyst**
API/WPI	✔	✔	✔
Applications	✔	✔	
Chemical Resistance	✔	✔	
Chloride Ions	✔	✔	
CO/CO2	✔		✔
Corrosion Resistance	✔	✔	
Cost	✔		✔
Density	✔	✔	
Durability		✔	
Dust	✔		✔
Electrical Conductivity	✔	✔	
Hardness	✔	✔	
Hydrocarbons	✔		
Incineration Waste			✔
Lubricants		✔	
NO/NO2			✔
Organics	✔		
Permeability	✔	✔	
Recovered Energy			✔
SO/SO2			✔
Specific Heat	✔	✔	
Strength	✔	✔	
Temperature Range		✔	
Thermal Conductivity	✔	✔	
Toughness	✔	✔	
Transparency	✔	✔	
H2O Absorption	✔	✔	

Even if attribute meanings are shared, the values they take may not (e.g. when comparing 'high' and 'low' for the concept 'durability').

When designers recognise that certain attributes/concepts appear to be shared, these may feature explicitly in the decision making process. Designers who perceive they share common concepts are able to conduct a dialogue in which proposals and counter proposals are made, along with supporting argument that uses these concepts. A dialogue (in the context of the design of a drink container) illustrates this:

Designer 1. *"Can we consider HDPE instead of PET: I think we can live with the loss in strength and we will achieve a significant reduction in WPI."*

Designer 2. *"I'm happy to look at that but I think the permeability of the HDPE will be too great."*

Designer 1. *"Not if we reduce the gas pressure, or perhaps the shelf life."*

The materials mentioned in the dialogue (HDPE, PET) are the highest level of shared concept (without shared terminology at this level, there can be no negotiation). The attributes of these materials that the designers appear to share include 'strength', 'WPI' and 'permeability'. The values these take in the dialogue are qualitative and have an implied order e.g. 'too great'. (Negotiators do not always propose new values in an explicit sense. Rather, these are implied by the offer and argumentation often relies on higher order terms which imply how the values should change e.g. there should be a 'loss' or 'a significant reduction'.)

When designers do not share labels/concepts, they tend (or perhaps learn) not to feature these in dialogues. These concepts may be important to the individual concerned, and a high priority may be attached to optimising them in a negotiation, but, they do not naturally form the basis of argumentation. This implies that a computational agent representing a specific designer should distinguish between the (apparently) shared representation and a private representation of any artefact.

4 Computational Support for Negotiation

Computational approaches to negotiation may be characterised in a number of ways. For example, negotiating agents may be co-operative or competitive, or may be constrained to tell the truth or to honour contracts. In terms of human interaction during agent-mediated negotiation, it does not significantly misrepresent the current situation to assert that there is a largely bimodal distribution of computational approaches to negotiation. There are systems that seek to facilitate efficient and effective human negotiation, which leave members of a (distributed) process team firmly in control of their associated communication agents [13]. Sometimes this strategy is adopted from a philosophical point of view: at other times it is legitimated as pragmatic. Other systems aim to implement more fully autonomous, agent-based negotiation [14], [15], [16], [17], [18], [19]. Our review of the literature suggests that the majority of recent work in the field of computational models for agent-based negotiation is designed to achieve autonomous negotiation with minimal human involvement (e.g. in the context of e-commerce and communications systems).

A useful framework for understanding agent-based negotiation is provided by Zlotkin and Rosenschein [17], [18]. As valuable as this framework is, it seems to us that the assumptions underlying these techniques are overly restrictive. Typical assumptions are that agents agree to be truthful, to adhere to agreements, to share goals. Other assumptions commonly made are that the agents share vocabulary, meaning and viewpoint. These assumptions do not always (or even commonly) characterise human negotiation in design. Thus, in seeking to realise more flexible, agent-based approaches which support negotiation we have been led to exclude many computational approaches which, whilst valuable in many other contexts, do not allow us to support negotiation dynamics as we have witnessed them. However, we have identified some approaches that contribute to a way forward. We have combined and extended these to develop a prototype system which supports negotiation in the context of materials selection for product design.

5 Negotiation Model

Drawing upon a template provided by Faratin et al. [19], we examine negotiation between members of the design team and identify features of the situation which inform the choice of a negotiation model.

1. **Co-operation**. Although designers in a concurrent design team may be perceived to share a common goal and thus be expected to act co-operatively, this is not, in general, the case. Even if the final goal is shared, the designers often pursue their own objectives within a project; not least because they have different perspective on the design artefact. Thus, the negotiation model cannot assume co-operative behaviour during the design cycle.

2. **Information sharing.** Similarly, the model cannot assume information sharing in the sense required were the negotiation to be a process of identifying an optimal resolution (usually Pareto optimal). If designers have different representations of an evolving artefact, then of necessity, some information is non-sharable. (Thus, the question of whether they might withhold information in order to seek an advantage is academic in this context.)

3. **Proposal Evaluation.** The degree to which agents' models are public depends upon the extent of the shared perception of the object of negotiation and upon willingness to share that representation. However, in evaluating a proposal, the agents will, in general, rely upon a private evaluation function, not least because some perceived dimensions of the proposal are private.

4. **Time constraints.** Time constraints do exist for designers and do feature in the dynamics of negotiation. Outcomes are frequently the best solution given the time available for consideration. We have not studied the effect of time on negotiation behaviour in material selection and so do not explore it further in this paper. (We do not feel that the introduction of time will fundamentally change the *process* of negotiation. It will influence the outcome in the sense that the continued evolution of the design artefact is curtailed.)

5. **Resource Constraints.** Resource constraints are an issue in design negotiation. Interestingly, they do not always feature as attributes of the design artefact itself though they may do so for some members of the concurrent design team, e.g. in production planning or processes. They feature in reasoning about proposed changes to a design; e.g. change may imply additional costs. Resource costs can be incorporated into the concept of 'utility', which is a function of the value attributed to a proposal by an agent and the cost to that agent of agreeing to the proposal (e.g. the additional work required to bring about the change).

6. **Tactics.** Negotiation can be viewed as search for agreement. The tactics of the negotiators determines the character of the negotiation. It is possible to discern a spectrum of tactics. At one end of this spectrum is the monotonic concession protocol (Zlotkin and Rosenschein, 1996b; see also Huns and Stephens, 1999). Negotiators make stepwise minimal concessions from individually maximal positions and hope to converge towards agreement. At the other end of the spectrum is an approach, more akin to collaborative hill climbing, in which offers and counter-offers are intended to be perceived as similar to the current proposal but which have added-value for one, more, and possibly all of the negotiators. To facilitate human negotiation, it is necessary to allow both of these protocols (and many in between).

In seeking to realise a flexible, agent-based approach to support negotiation among designers, the above characterisation necessitates the exclusion of many negotiation protocols. However, it is important that it should not be proscriptive in respect of tactics allowed to the users. The analysis implies the need for a similarity measure that can be used to compare proposals. For any individual, it should be applicable to what they perceive to be a shared representation or to their private representation. It also implies the need for a measure of value that can be applied to distinguish between similar proposals.

5.1 Similarity

From the perspective of any one member of the design team, the materials under consideration share a set of attributes or properties. The values attributed to each property will vary between individual materials. Given two materials (m,n) from a set of materials, M, under consideration, the similarity of these materials over a set of properties, P, associated with the materials may be given by:

$$Sim(m, n) = \Sigma_{p\in P}\, w_p Sim_p(m, n)\ . \qquad (1)$$

where w_p is a normalised weight associated with a property, p, by the designer ($\Sigma_{p\in P}\, w_p=1$); and Sim_p is the similarity function for property, p [19].

The values associated with some properties vary continuously (subject to natural limits or constraints). For other properties, discrete values only may be found: the values of a property may be explicitly ordered but sometimes an order results from the perceptions of the designer (see dialogue above). In such circumstances, it is appropriate to choose a fuzzy measure of similarity.

Valverde [20] offers a definition of an appropriate similarity function:

$$Sim_p(m, n) = Inf_{1 \leq i \leq m} (h_i(m) \leftrightarrow h_i(n)) . \quad (2)$$

where *Inf* is the *infimum* and $h_i(m) \leftrightarrow h_i(n)$ is a fuzzy equivalence relation induced by the ith criteria or comparison function, h_i: common examples include:

$$h(m) \leftrightarrow h(n) = 1 - | h(m) - h(n) | . \quad (3)$$

and

$$h(m) \leftrightarrow h(n) = min(h(m)/h(n), h(n)/h(m)) . \quad (4)$$

5.2 Value and Utility

Designers commonly evaluate similar materials. In choosing a function that seeks to capture the evaluation of a given designer, the concept of 'value' is an attempt to condense the motivation(s) of the designer into a single discriminant term. Given some material, *m*, with a set of properties, *P*, a measure of the value which a designer attaches to the material, in some context, is:

$$Score(m) = \Sigma_{p \in P}\, w_p Score_p(m(p)) . \quad (5)$$

again, w_p is a normalised weight ($\Sigma_{p \in P}\ w_p = 1$) associated with a property, *p*, by the designer: these weights are not, in general, the same as those used in the similarity function. $Score_p$ is the score assigned to a material property, *p*, arising from its value, *m*(*p*). For each property, a scoring function mapping to [0,1] is chosen.

Both *Sim* and *Score* produce values in the range [0,1] as this is believed to help designers in evaluating proposals and counter proposals.

Utility is related to the value of a proposal but makes explicit any cost associated with its acceptance. A suitable expression is:

$$Utility(m,n) = (Score(m) \text{-} Score(n)) - c(m,n) . (6)$$

where (*Score*(*m*)-*Score*(*n*)) is the difference in value between choices *m* and *n* and *c*(*m,n*) is the cost associated with making the change, if agreed. In general, explicit representations of these costs are not available, mainly because they tend to be highly volatile. Accordingly, it is not usually practicable to incorporate these costs in to the computational support system. In many cases, it is possible to view these costs as contributing to the weights in (5).

It is necessary to determine various weights for the above expressions. It is possible to use machine learning to determine such weights. However, an approach, which gives more control to the user, is to derive the weights from user preferences at the time of use. In addition, as observed above, the weights are often volatile and many machine learning approaches may not be suited.

The easiest way to express preferences is by ranking. If normalised weights are required [21], they can also be obtained directly from the ranking. If a simple ordering does not adequately express the preference weightings, they would have to be obtained more directly. It is easy to take account of the relative 'distances' between ranked objects if desired.

6 A Negotiation Support Tool

The negotiation support tool for material selection is specified as follows. We use a distributed agent architecture supporting negotiation between human members of concurrent design teams. Agents share the same architecture but differ in their domain specialism i.e. they represent domain objects (materials in this case) in different spaces (see description above and Table 1). Holloway [11], [12] documents the materials related knowledge of the system and the sources of the data.

A design team comprises individuals who contribute a variety of perspectives to the emerging artefact. In some teams there will be one member representing each perspective. In other teams there may be a many: many mapping between perspectives and people. In some circumstances, an individual designer seeks to represent many or all of the perspectives for themselves. In practice, the mapping from perspectives to people may vary over the product design lifetime. The system is designed for use in all these modalities. The mapping of people to agents is left as an issue to be determined when the system is actually used.

Each member of the team may rank materials, viewed from their own perspective, using a graphical interface in which sub-trees and leaves of a class/instance hierarchy of materials related concepts can be ordered. They can also rank the properties associated with materials (although these seem less prone to change with time and context). These rankings enable the various weights in the similarity and value functions to be obtained.

Given a list of materials currently proposed for the design, similar alternatives are offered to individual designers based upon both shared and private representations. The system uses expressions (1), (2) and (3) to determine similarities. It does this for each agent and gives two similarity values, one over all (private) properties, the other using what are perceived by the user to be the shared concepts. Expression (5) is used to evaluate similar materials. The human user remains responsible for the communication of any proposal he or she wishes to make, and for the supporting argumentation.

7 Discussion

The system described above is intended as a step towards a materials selection support tool for concurrent designers. Negotiation, is a key sub-task in the design process: designers evaluate proposals from their peers; consider alternatives based upon their preferences and choose a counter proposal in the event of non-acceptance. This paper offers a model for that process and suggests computational means to support designers which are sensitive to the designers' changing preferences and criteria. The systems described is intended for use by individual members of the design team but could be used by smaller teams, even individual designers, interested in accessing other design perspectives.

Future work on this project has a number of different objectives. The system does not yet provide direct support for argumentation in relation to counter proposals (though the basis for this is clearly present). We are developing extensions to the system which assist in the selection of counter proposals by attempting to model other members of the team in respect of shared representations but also in respect of the consistency with which they are perceived to pursue particular goals and sub-goals. A significant empirical trial of the system is needed to verify (or otherwise) the extent to which it succeeds in supporting the negotiation dynamics that are observed in design teams as this is seen as crucial to successful adoption of the technology.

As currently specified, initiative in negotiation lies very much with the human user. More flexible/adjustable agent autonomy would seem to offer increased likelihood of adoption of design support systems, more scope for reproducing the dynamics of collaborative design and increased cost effectiveness.

References

1. Landauer, T.K.; The trouble with computers. Academic Press, Cambridge Ma. (1995)
2. Smithers, T.; On knowledge level theories of the design process. in Artificial Intelligence in Design. Gero, J.S., Sudweeks, F. (eds.) Kluwer Academic Publishers. (1996) 561-579.
3. Huns, M.N. and Stephens, L.M.; *Multiagent Systems and Societies of Agents* in Multiagent Systems: A Modern Approach to Distributed Artificial Intelligence. Weiss, G. (ed.), MIT Press. (1999) 79-120
4. Barker, R., Meehan, A., Tranter, I.; A Knowledge-level Model for Concurrent Design. Applied Intelligence, 10: (1999) 113-122

5. Barker, R., Holloway, L., Mardell, J. and Meehan, A.; Supporting Knowledge-based processes using flexible intelligent agents. AAAI Spring Symposium 2000, Stanford, Ca., USA (2000).
6. Bernaras, A. and Van de Velde, W.; *Design*. in Breuker, J., Van de Velde, W. (eds.) CommonKADS library for expertise modelling: reusable problem solving components. IOS Press, (1995) Chapter 8.
7. Shiva Kumar, Suresh, S., Krishnamoorthy, C.S., Fenves, S.J.. Rajeev, S.; GENCRIT: a tool for knowledge-based critiquing in engineering design. Artificial Intelligence for Engineering Design, Analysis and Manufacturing, vol. 8, Cambridge University Press, 1994.) 239-259.
8. Barker, R., Tranter, I. and Meehan, A.; *Towards a knowledge-level model of concurrent design*. In IEA-AIE'98, Proceedings of 11th International Conference on Engineering Applications of AI and Expert Systems, Mira, J, del Pobil, A.P., Moonis Ali (eds), Lecture Notes in Artificial Intelligence 1415; Springer-Verlag, (1998) 57-67.
9. de Hoog, R., Martil, R., Wielinga, B. et al.; The CommonKADS Model Set, ESPRIT Project P5248: Document Id. KADS-II/WP I-II/RR/UvA/018/4.0, University of Amsterdam (1992)
10. Barker, R. and Meehan, A.; Supporting Concurrent Design Teams with Adjustably Autonomous Agents, AAAI Spring Symposium 1999, Stanford, Ca., USA (1999)
11. Holloway, L.; A methodology and support tool for environmentally conscious design and manufacture. PhD Thesis, Sheffield Hallam University, Sheffield S1 1WB, UK. (1997)
12. Holloway, L.; Materials selection for optimal environmental impact in mechanical design. Materials & Design 19; Elsevier Science Ltd. (1998) 133-143
13. Wong, S.T.C.; Preference-based decision making for co-operative knowledge-based systems. ACM Trans on Information Systems, 12:4 (1994) 407-435.
14. Sycara, K., Lewis, C.; Modelling group decision making and negotiation in concurrent product design. International Journal of Systems Automation 1:217-238.
15. Ephrati, E. and Rosenschien J.S., 1996. Deriving concensus in multiagent systems. Artificial Intelligence 87 (1991) 21-74
16. Kraus, S. Sycara, K., Evenchick, A.; Reaching agreement through argumentation: a logical model and implementation. Artificial Intelligence 104 (1998) 1-69.
17. Zlotkin, G., Rosenschein, J.S.; Mechanisms for automated negotiation in state oriented domains. Journal of Artificial Intelligence Research 5 (1996) 163-238.
18. Zlotkin, G., Rosenschein, J.S.; Mechanism design for automated negotiation and its application to task oriented domains. Artificial Intelligence 86 (1996) 195-244.
19. Faratin, P., Sierra, C., Jennings, N.R.; Negotiation Decision Functions for Autonomous Agents. Int. J. of Robotics and Autonomous Systems 24 (3-4) (1997) 159-182.
20. Valverde, L.; On the structure of F-indistinguishability. Fuzzy Sets and Systems 17 (1985) 313-328 (cited in Sierra, et al 1999.)
21. Sierra, C., Faratin, P. and Jennings, N.R.; Deliberative Automated Negotiators Using Fuzzy Similarities. Proc EUSFLAT-ESTYLF Joint Conference on Fuzzy Logic, Palma de Mallorca, Spain, (1997) 155-158

An XML-Based Language for Coordination Protocol Description in Multi-agent System

Mao Weiliang, Sheng Huanye, and Dingpeng

Room 2025, ICHI Lab Dept. of Computer S&E
Shanghai Jiao Tong University, Shanghai, 200030
P.R. China
Wlmao816@mail1.sjtu.edu.cn

Abstract: In this paper, we present a new high-level descriptive language for coordination protocol description in multi-agent system. Our language is both programmer and non-programmer oriented. We construct our language underlying XML under the consideration that XML is not only easily understandable by people who do not have a complete understanding of XML, but also facilitates the developing and maintaining parsers, and also facilities our language easily to integrate with WWW-world. In order to enable our language to describe complex coordination protocol, on one hand, we use interaction-oriented model as the design model for our language, which enables our language to easily describe a coordination protocol, where each interaction agent is indicated as a role. On the other hand, our language enables calling outer functions/methods written in general programming language to implement complex computation. We also enable our language to support multi-role description and the inheritance mechanism among coordination protocols. Its capability is demonstrated by giving out an example on the Vickrey auction.

1 Introduction

Agents usually interact with each other to deal with affairs in some multi-agent environment. In order to make such interactions take place, the environments will provide a computational infrastructure, i.e. coordination mechanism, which will include protocols for agents to communicate and coordination protocols for agents to interact. The communication protocol specifies the classes of messages that can be exchanged among agents and the coordination protocol specifies and governs the exchange of those messages, i.e. the conversation, among agents.

In the field of distributed artificial intelligence, some coordination protocols have been proposed for the interaction of the agents. For examples, the contract net protocol [1] is used for task allocation; the unified negotiation protocol [2] for exchanging tasks among agents that are heterogeneous and self-motivated; TRACONET [3] is used for bounded rational, self-interested agents to make announcing, bidding and awarding decisions; and so on.

L. Monostori, J. Váncza, and M. Ali (Eds.): IEA/AIE 2001, LNAI 2070, pp. 708-717, 2001.

However, different coordination protocols are suited for different applications and usage scenarios. For example, there would be the protocols for electronic commerce, travel applications, student registration, and so on. That means while constructing a multi-agent system that allows users to freely define various applications, only having a set of standard or predefined coordination protocols is not enough and impossible. The tools, mainly the languages, for supporting defining and customizing protocols are demanded.

In this paper, we present a new high-level descriptive language, which is both programmer and non-programmer oriented. We construct our language underlying XML under the consideration that XML is not only easily understandable by people who do not have a complete understanding of XML, but also facilitates the developing and maintaining parsers, and also facilities our language easily to integrate with WWW-world. In order to enable our language to describe complex coordination protocol, on one hand, we use interaction-oriented model (see section 2) as the design model for our language, which enables our language to easily describe a coordination protocol, where each interaction agent is indicated as a role. On the other hand, our language enables calling outer functions/methods written in general programming language to implement complex computation. And also, our language supports multi-role description and the inheritance mechanism among coordination protocols.

2 Our Agent Interaction Model

2.1 Basic Conceptual Model for Agent

Fundamentally, an agent is an active object with the ability to perceive, reason and act. In our agent interaction model, agent perceives by receiving message from other agents. Agent reasons according to communication protocol, interaction protocol and the message it received. The actions of agent will include the sending of the messages and other actions defined by agent users.

Interaction-Oriented Idea: In order to simplify the design of our agent interaction model, we take interaction-oriented idea [9] into consideration where commitments are the key element that is viewed as pledges to undertake a specified course of action. By having commitments, agents become easier to deal with. Also, the desired commitments serve as a sort of requirements on construction of an agent.

Therefore, in our interaction model, from the point of the view of the interaction-oriented idea, in the interaction every agent adopts the different commitments regulated by communication and interaction protocol. And by that, in the interaction, different agent plays their respective role. More exactly, in our interaction model, where agent perceives by receiving messages, we could understand the commitments of the opposing interaction agents are the messages should be replied.

Formulating Model: Below we give out a formal description on our agent interaction model.

- Interaction agent set-- $AG=\{ag_1,ag_2,\ldots ag_h\}$, this also denotes an interaction including h agents.
- Sending message sets for an agent-- $M_S=\{m_{s1},m_{s2},\ldots m_{si}\}$, $|M_S|>=0$;
- Receiving message sets for an agent-- $M_R=\{m_{r1},m_{r2},\ldots m_{rj}\}$, $|M_R|>=0$;
- User-defined action sets for an agent-- $A_U=\{a_1,a_2,\ldots a_k\}$, $|A_U|>=0$;
- The parameter set of a message--$P(m_i)=\{p_{i1}, p_{i2},\ldots, p_{il}\}$, $|P(m_i)|>=0$;
- The parameter set of an action--$P(a_i)=\{p_{i1}, p_{i2},\ldots, p_{in}\}$, $|P(a_i)|>=0$;
- Interaction database of an agent--L.

From the interaction-oriented perspective, M_S reflects the commitments of this agent to other agents. And accordingly, M_R reflects the commitments from other agents. These two sets construct the role that an agent will play. Au reflects the right of users to control the interaction, and we could understand that every a_i denotes the user's control strategy in the interaction. So, to an agent, its actions set A should be $A=M_S \cup A_U$. As to $P(m_i)$, we could say it reflects the definition of the communication protocol which defines the message exchanged among agents. Interaction database L is used to record the messages sent and received before and also record the current state of the agent. L will be used in the reasoning process of an agent. To be notable, in our model, interaction database records the information only of one ongoing interaction because currently we assume each interaction process is independent of each other.

According to the above definitions, we could describe out the model of an agent with the tuple $ag=<E, M_S, M_R, A_U, L>$ where symbol E denotes agent engine of an agent, which will mainly include three parts, i.e. one for perceiving, one for reasoning and one for action. Agent engine E reflects the process model of an agent.

- Agent ag_i perceiving-- M_R'=ag_i.receiveMessagesFrom(AG-{ ag_i })
  M_R' denotes the messages that ag_i received from other agents. AG-{ ag_i } denotes the set of other agents in an interaction AG. Apparently M_R' should be the subset of M_R of ag_i.
- Agent ag_i Reasoning--A'=ag_i.reasonBasedMessages(M_R', L)

A' denotes the result after agent ag_i reasoning on the received message set M_R'. And there is $A'= M_S' \cup A_U'$ where respectively, M_S' and A_U' are the subset of M_S and A_U. To be notable, reasoning process involves dealing with the parameters of the message and actions. That is to say, reasoning process is not the simply mapping from M_R to A' and possibly complex computation will be involved for determining the parameters values for any $m_i \in M_S'$ or $a_i \in A_U'$. So the more detailed reasoning representation could be:

$$M_R', P(m_1), P(m_2),\ldots P(m_{|MR'|}), L \text{ where } m_i \in M_R'$$

$$\overset{ag_i.reasonBasedMessages}{====>} \begin{array}{l} 1)\ M_S', P(m_1), P(m_2),\ldots P(m_{|MR'|}) \text{ where } m_i \in M_S' \\ 2)\ A_U', P(a_1), P(a_2),\ldots P(a_{|A_U'|}) \text{ where } a_i \in A_U' \end{array}$$

We have ever said that every a_i denotes the user's control strategy in the interaction. Exactly, every a_i only reflects the outer behaviors of user's strategy, and the true strategy settings should be in this reasoning process. Similarly, although M_S represents the commitments of an agent to other agents, how to controlling and managing commitments should also be set in this reasoning process. It is Ms and reasoning process ag_i.*reasonBasedMessages* that construct the whole interaction protocol.

- Agent ag_i acting: L'=ag$_i$.doActions(A')
  ag_i will send the messages $m_i \in M_S'$ and execute the user-defined actions $a_i \in A_U'$. And new interaction database L' will be formed by updating L.

2.2 Our XML-Based Markup Language

-Functionality of Our Language. From our interaction model in the section 2, we know the model of an agent could be simply represented as a tuple, i.e. $ag=<E, M_S, M_R, A_U, L>$, which underlies the functionality of our description language for coordination protocol.

In our language, we take the form of rule set R to enable users to describe the reasoning process ag_i.*reasonBasedMessages* of agent engine E. For M_S, M_R and A_U, they can be described in our language. $m_I \in M_S$ could be set, which denotes the initiative message an agent sends out at the beginning of the interaction process. User-defined action set A_U consists of two types, i.e. the internal functions F_{IN} our language itself provides and the outer methods F_{OUT} in outer Java classes, For interaction database L, our language enables users to define and operate variable set V freely that may be used to record the state of an interaction process. In an interaction process, our language interpreter will be responsible for recording the history messages M_H in interaction database L. Therefore, our language don't provide functionality to describe the structure of history messages database, however, they exist objectively. Thus, access to M_H is provided for users.

If we call *script* as the description on the coordination process under some protocol in our language, an *script SC* for an agent will be, $SC=<R, M_S, m_I, M_R, F_{IN}, F_{OUT}, V>$.

-Representing Sending Message. We enable user to define message without strong limitation by providing a simple framework where a message is composed of two parts, i.e. common attributes part and the free parameters part, shown as below:

<message MsgLabel="*labelname*"OwnerName="*ownername*" MsgName="*msgname*" Priority="*priorityvalue*" MsgType="*messagetype*">
<para Name="*paraname*" Type="*typename*"><paraee>...</paraee></para>...</message>

-Representing Receiving Message The following framework shows the receiving messages that are the commitments from other agents in an interaction.

<inputmessage Name="*inputmsgname*" Owner="*/*ownername*">
<para Name="*paraname* " Type="*typename*"> </para>... </inputmessage>

-Representing User-Defined Action. Our interaction model requires us to enable users to define their actions. In order for that, our language provides two ways. One is by the functions the language itself provides. Another is by the interface with procedural language (here we mean Java) the language provides.

So far, the functions our language itself provides are limited, which include assignment statement, some basic arithmetic functions such as 'add', 'sub', 'div', 'mul', 'sin', 'cos', and so on. The below shows the framework of using function in our language.

<functionname>< functionnameee>…</functionnameee>…</functionname>
The following framework shows the interface with general programming language Java, by that, user could specify the outer class name and method name, conceptually which denotes the action user defined.

<method ClassName=" *classname*" MethodName="*methodname*">
<para Name="*paraname*" Type="*type*"> </paraee>… </paraee> </para>… </method>

-Representing Interaction Database. In our interaction model, interaction database of an agent is used to save the related data in one interaction. We divide the related data into two categories, that is, message that an agent received and the variables that user defined for recording the temporary or the final result in an interaction.
Representation of receiving message is shown in the previous section "Representing Receiving Message".

For the definition of the variables, so far, in our language, we provide two types of variable. One is 'STRING' that is the default type, and the other is 'LIST'. The following framework shows the definition of the variables.

<variables><var Name="*varname*" Type="STRING" Value="*initvalue*"></var>
<var Name="*listvarname*" Type="LIST" >
<value>*initvalue* </value> … <value>*initvalue* </value> </var> …</variables>

For messages in the interaction database of an agent, it is quite possible that messages are from different owners, with different classes and received at different time. As a result, in order to visit a message, exactly the parameters of one specified message, in our language, we have the following framework.

<*xxx*ee Type="MSGVAR" MsgOwner="*ownername*" MsgName="*msgname*" ParaName="*paraname*" >
<indexee>*indexvalue*</indexee></*xxx*ee>

*The tag '*xxx*ee' generally denotes a parameter variable object, for examples, '<paraee>'.
* <indexee>*indexvalue*</indexee> defines the sequence number of this class of message.

Accordingly, we provide two ways to access the history variables. For the variable with type "STRING", we have the following framework:

<*xxx*ee Type="USERVAR" VarName="*varname*"/>
For the "LIST" type one, there is the similar framework as for the parameters of message:
<*xxx*ee Type="USERVAR" VarName="*varname*"><indexee>*indexvalue*</indexee>
</*xxx*ee>

-Representing Reasoning Process. The basic form of a rule is conditions in the LHS and actions in the RHS. According to our reasoning model in the section 2, further we could see that conditions should be the result of a computing process to M_R', $P(m_1)$, $P(m_2)$,… $P(m_{|MR'|})$ and L. The actions should be the corresponding messages to be sent, i.e. M_S', $P(m_1)$, $P(m_2)$,… $P(m_{|MR'|})$ and the actions user defined, i.e. A_U', $P(a_1)$, $P(a_2)$,… $P(a_{|A_U'|})$. For simplicity, we assume the general situation. That is in an interaction, every time when an agent does actions, it sends out at most one message or the copies of one same message (in the case of broadcast). Under this assumption, we provide the framework for rule representation as below:

<message MsgLabel="*msglabel*", OwnerName="*ownername*" MsgName="*msgname*" Priority="*priorityvalue*">
<para Name="*paraname*" Type="*typename*"><paraee>... </paraee> </para>...
<condition> <and><andee>...</andee>... </and> </condition></message>

3 Improvement

3.1 Necessities

In the previous sections, we have presented our XML-based markup language for defining and describing coordination protocol. However, that language is not very strong from the two points below.

Single role support: From our agent interaction model, there is $ag=<E, M_S, M_R, A_U, L>$. Ms and M_R construct the role an agent plays in an interaction process. However, generally, in an interaction process, agent will play several different roles.

No inheritance: Inheritance is very useful for incrementally designing new protocols based on the existing protocols. In our language above, there is no such mechanism.

3.2 Improving Agent Interaction Model

In order to support multi-role playing of an agent in an interaction process and inheritance mechanism, we redefine our agent interaction model recursively:

1). On the top-level, we change the agent model definition into $ag=<E, Rs, A_U, L>$, where Rs denotes the role set that an agent plays in an interaction process. That is, $Rs=\{r_0,r_1,r_2,...r_N\}$. We call r_I a sub-role used by ag. Conversely, ag is the parent-role of role r_I.
At the same time, because of the involvement of the multi-role, some corresponding actions such as start, stop, suspend, resume, etc., here that is denoted as set A_R, supporting scheduling roles should also be added, that is to say, $A_U=A_U \cup A_R$. E and L have the same definition as in the previous sections.

2). We define $r_0=\{M_S,M_R,P\}$, which denotes the true role agent plays. We add item P to denote from which the definition of sub-role r_0 inherits. When P is *null,* that indicates the role definition has no inheritance.
To be notable, the concept P is different from the concept of parent-role P' of sub-role r_0. The former reflects the static attribute of sub-role r_0 and the latter reflects the dynamic relationship in an interaction process, i.e. on "runtime". On the top-level, P' must be null and P is not.

3). We define r_I $(I>0)$ as another tuple $<E_I, R_{IS}, A_{IU}, L_I>$. E_I, R_{IS}, A_{IU}, and L_I have the same definitions in 1) on the next level. Besides, we allow that sub-role r_I is able to refer to the variables in L of its parent role.

From the definition, we could see that the definition is recursive and leveled. The definition of *ag* implies the definition of a top-level role. That indicates new definition is compatible with our original definition ag=$<E, M_{S,}, M_{R,}, A_{U,} L>$, because that actually in the improved definitions is ag=$<E,\{r_0\},A_{U,} L>$ where $r_0=\{M_{S,},M_{R,},null\}$.

Now accordingly, we could give out the new *script* definition that is also recursive. That is $SC=<R, SCs, F_{IN}, F_{O,}, V>$ where $SC_S=\{ sc_0, sc_1, sc_2,\ldots sc_N\}$, $sc_0=\{ M_S, m_I , M_R, sc_P\}$ and $sc_I =\{ R_I, SC_{IS},F_{IN} ,F_{IOUT}, V_I \}$ $(I>0)$. SC_{IS} has the same definition as SC_S. It is clear that sc_I denotes the *script* for sub-role r_I . script sc_0 of sub-role r_I has the inheritance from sc_P. Additionally, F_{IN} now includes the set A_R that denotes the set of the operating roles.

-Representing Multi-role Supporting. From our improved agent interaction model, there is *script* $SC =<R, SCs, F_{IN}, F_{OUT}, V>$, so in our language, firstly, we provide the framework below for representing SCs-$\{sc_0\}$ in one script.

```
<outerole> <outerolee Name="outerolename" Location="scriptlocation">
   <rolevariables> <var Name="varname" Type="STRING" Value="initvalue"></var>
   <var Name="listvarname" Type="LIST" ><value>initvalue </value>... </var>...
</rolevariables></outerolee>...</outerole>
```

All possible sub-roles used in this script should be defined in-between the tag pair <outerole></outerole>. The tag pair <outerolee Name="*outerolename*" Location="*scriptlocation*"></ outerolee> is used to represent the reference to some sub-role with the script located at "*scriptlocation*" that is the form of URL. "*outerolename*" is the role-name assigned by user that acts as the identity of this sub-role in this script The tag pair <rolevariables> </rolevariables> represents re-initializing the user-defined variables defined in the script of sub-role (refer to section 2, representing interaction database).

After the definition on the sub-roles to be used in this script, the operations in set F_{IN} on those sub-roles could be made. In current version of our language, we provide four kinds of operations, which are starting a sub-role, stopping a sub-role, suspending a sub-role and resuming a sub-role. The following example shows stopping the sub-role "register":

```
<para Name="%STOPROLE%" Type="%PROCEDURE%">
  <paraee><stop><stopee>register</stopee></stop></paraee></para>
```

-Representing Inheritance Mechanism. In order to represent the inheritance relationship of some script for some role, the tag pair shown below is provided:

```
<role Name="rolename" Interaction="interactionname" ParentRole="parentrolename"
Location=" scriptlocation "/>
```

If in the terminology of Object-Oriented, the attribute "Name" denotes the role class name defined by some script including such tag pair. The attribute "ParentRole" denotes the parent role class from which current role class inherits. That is, the attribute "ParentRole" is the representation of P in $r_0=\{M_{S,},M_{R,},P\}$. The attribute "Location" specifies where the script of "ParentRole" is, which is the form of URL. The attribute "Interaction" specifies the interaction class that maybe the role will take part in.

4 Experiment

In the previous sections, we have outlined the framework of our XML-based markup language for coordination protocol. In order to verify that our language has enough functions, we show an example about Vickrey auction .

In our experiment, we have three classes of agents. One is auctioneer who will sell something; the other is bidder who will buy something from the auctioneer; the last one is mediator agent who will be responsible for organizing the auction activity. The auction activity consists three phases:

Registration phase-every auctioneer wanting to make auction should make registration to mediator agent, so should do every bidder wanting to bid. *Waiting phase*-auctioneer and bidders wait for the notification from the mediator agent for beginning auction *Auction phase*-auctioneer makes announce and bidders bid. Auctioneer computes the auction winner.

Therefore, both auctioneer and bidder agent will play two classes of roles besides their top-level role. For the former, those are "Registrar" and "Auctioneer". For the latter, those are "Registrar" and "Bidder".

Because of the limited paper space, here we just show the most important messages and actions settings for role Top-level Auctioneer and Auctioneer. The other related documents and full implementation will be put on our website http://www.ichi.sjtu.edu.cn in near future.

Table 1. Related Messages Setting in our Experiment

Role	Sending Messages	Receiving Messages	Actions
Top-level Auctioneer	S:StartRegister () V S:StopRegister () V S:StartAuctioneer() V S:StopAuctioneer()V L: local Message V: Virtual Message *:Broadcast Message	R:RegisterOK(Owner) R:RegisterFail(Owner) R:AuctionOK(Owner) R.AuctionFail(Owner) R:Notification(Owner)	StartRole("Registrar") StopRole("Registrar") StartRole("maoauctioneer") StopRole("maoauctioneer") PrintInfo**(Variable Registerfailreason) PrintInfo(Variable Auctionfailreason) PrintInfo(Variable,Auctionresult)
Auctioneer	S:Announce(Owner) * S: AuctionOK(Owner)L S: AuctionFail(Owner)L S: WaitBid (Owner)L	R:Bid(Owner, Price, Email) R:TimeEvent(Eventname)	SaveBidInfo **(R:bid.owner,price,email) ComputingResult**() Set (variable auctionresult with value from action ComputingResult) Set(Bidflag with value 1)

: Those actions are methods in outer Java class. **PrintInfo has the function to show information in a dialog. **SaveBidInfo** has the function to saving bid price from each bidder. **ComputingResult** has the function to get the winner of the auction according to Vickey auction rule.

The following accordingly shows the reasoning rule set:

Table 2. Related Rule Sets in our Experiment

Role	Rule Set
Top-level Auctioneer	1) (start)=>startRole(Registrar), S:StartRegister (V) 2) (R:RegisterOK) and (R:RegisterOK.owner=='mao') =>stopRole(Registrar), S:StopRegister (V) 3) (R:RegisterFail) and (R:RegisterOK.owner=='mao') =>stopRole(Registrar), S:StopRegister (V), PrintInfo(registerfailreason) 4) (R:AuctionOK) and (R:AuctionOK.owner=='mao') =>stopRole(Auctioneer), S:StopAuctioneer (V) PrintInfo(auctionresult) 5) (R:AuctionFail) and (R:AuctionFail.owner=='mao') =>stopRole(Auctioneer), S:StopAuctioneer (V) PrintInfo(auctionfailreason) 6) (R:Notification) and (R:Notification.owner=='mediatoragent') =>startRole(Auctioneer), S:StartAuctioneer (V)
Auctioneer	1) (start)=>S: Announce(*) 2) (R:Bid) => S: WaitBid(V), SaveBidInfo(R:Bid.owner, R:Bid.price, R:Bid.Email), set(bidflag) 3) (R:timeout) and (bidflag==1) => S: AuctionOk(L), ComputeResult(), set(auctionresult) 4) (R:timeout) and (bidflag==0) => S: AuctionFailure(L), set(auctionfailreason)

5 Conclusions and Future Work

The main contribution of this paper is an XML-based Markup Language for describing coordination protocols. In such field, at present, there have been some related research projects. For example, COOL [4] is based on KQML messages, describes the protocol with state transition rules. CooL [5] describes coordination protocols based on a multi-agent plan, which consists of procedures agents to follow and communication primitives. AgenTalk [6] incorporates an inheritance mechanism for supporting defining new protocols based on the existing protocols or customizing existing protocols.

Compared with those languages, our language will have the following several advantages combined with the those brought from XML-based approach: 1) Both Non-programmer and Programmer oriented;2) Directly Rule-based Idea; 3)Agent 'Memory'-enabled;4) Facilitating Agent Mobility;5)Facilitating Script Sharing in the Internet

Our language is being developed and we have developed the interpreter by using IBM parser XML4J for its preliminary version in Java. We also have developed some experimental applications in our language, such as agent bargain and auction, with the IBM Aglet Environment in order to verify the ability of our language.

We design our language for constructing mobile-agent based services for digital city [8], and the functionality of current version of our language will be further extended. For example, we will include the mobilizing control actions into our language, which will be used to describe the behavior related to agent mobility. We also think of developing the more easy-to-use interface for our language users, though in XML field, XML document editors are available.

References

1. R.G.Smith:"The Contract Net Protocol:High-leveral Communication and Control in a Distributed Problem Solver", IEEE Trans. Comput.,Vol.29, No.12, pp.1104-1113
2. J.S.Rosenschein and G.Zlotkin:"Designing Conventions for Automated Negotiation ", in M.N.Huhns,M.P.Singh (Eds) Readings in Agents,Morgan Kaufuman Publishers Inc, San FranCisco, California, USA,1998
3. T.W.Sandholm: "An Implementation of the contract net protocol based on marginal cost calculations", in Proceeding of 11th National Conference on Artificial Intelligence (AAAI-93), July, 1993
4. M.Barbuceanu and M.S.Fox: "COOL: A language for describing Coordination in Multi Agent Systems", Proceedings of first International Conference on Multi-Agent Systems(ICMAS'95), pp.17-24(1995)
5. M.Kolb: "A Cooperation Language", Proceedings of first International Conference on Multi-Agent Systems (ICMAS'95), pp.233-238 (1995)
6. K.Kuwabara, T.Ishida and N. Osato: "Agent Talk: Coordination Protocol Description for Multi-agent Systems", Proceedings of first International Conference on Multi-Agent Systems (ICMAS'95), pp.455 (1995)
7. Charles F.Goldfarb and Paul Prescod: "The XML Hand book ", Prentice Hall PTR, Prentice-Hall, inc, Upper Saddle River, NJ, 07458, ISBN 0-13-081152-1,1998
8. Mao Weiliang, Dingpeng, Shanehuanye: "Sketching Agent-Based Information Services for Digital City", In Proceedings of International ICSC Symposium on Multi-Agents and Mobile Agents in Virtual Organizations and E-Commerce (MAMA'2000), ICSC Press, Canada.
9. M.N. Huhns, M.P. Singh:"Agents and Multiagent Systems:Themes, approaches, and Challenges" in M.N. Huhns, and M.P. Singh(Eds.): Readings in Agent. Morgan Kaufmann, San Francisco, 1998.

A Distributed Multi-agent Model for Value Nets

Chad Dodd and Soundar R.T. Kumara

Department of Industrial and Manufacturing Engineering
The Pennsylvania State University
310 Leonhard Building
University Park, PA 16802 U.S.A.
{cid102, skumara}@psu.edu

Abstract. In this paper, we discuss an agent based solution strategy to the new customer centric economy created by the Internet. This solution strategy includes changing the current supply chain model into a value net model that is driven by the customer and coordinated by a complex multi-agent network. To coordinate all activity within the multi-agent value net a new agent based communication language based on the Extensible Markup Language (XML) is proposed.

1 Introduction

Over the past few years' enormous technological advances have changed the way many organizations conduct business. During the digital age, companies are expected to be agile, flexible, and customer oriented. They're required to provide cost quotes, delivery times, delivery tracking, and production updates to the customer in real time. In response, organizations are reengineering and streamlining various processes and business practices to improve customer relations and productivity. One process that has improved customer relations, productivity, and efficiency during the digital age is the supply chain.

The supply chain is a process that spans the entire enterprise integrating processes based on flawless delivery of basic and customized services. Therefore the objective of Supply Chain Management is to optimize information and product flow from the receipt of the order to the purchase of raw materials, to delivery and consumption of the finished product [Fox et al, 1993]. For the supply chain to operate efficiently during the digital era, all the functions and processes must be integrated within a network providing a rapid and quality response to any demand or informational request from the customer. Therefore the supply chain becomes a digitalized and dynamic, high performance network of customer/supplier partnerships and information flows. This new model of the supply chain is known as a value net [Bovet and Martha, 2000].

The value net model creates an informational infrastructure that facilitates the distribution of information from a customer to the various manufacturing sites and suppliers. Therefore the purpose of the value net model is to fulfill the customer order with high quality products meeting delivery requirements while minimizing the cost of the parts, manufacturing, and transportation. To make these decision-making processes efficient and hence construct a reliable

L. Monostori, J. Váncza, and M. Ali (Eds.): IEA/AIE 2001, LNAI 2070, pp. 718–727, 2001.

net reliable, it is imperative that we integrate and automate all the decision-making processes to solve the various value net problems. Within the old supply chain model, decisions were made by humans with the aid of computer processes such as Enterprise Resource Planning (ERP). However the customer centric value net model requires organizations to make decisions and pass information to suppliers, distributors, and customers in real time. Agent based systems by virtue of their adaptability, autonomy, and social ability make them a viable technology to be used in implementing real time decisions and communication. Each agent within the value net would represent a part of the decision making process. Hence creating an agile network of decision makers that react to the customer in real time as opposed to a rigid process flow that is decided before the customer places an order.

To make the multi-agent value net efficient, reliable, and practical a multi-agent communication language to send messages across the Internet needs to be developed. This language will connect the customer to all the decision-making agents within the value net making one complete interactive, and seamless network.

2 Problem Definition

The current supply chain problem within many organizations is two fold. The first problem concerns the way orders are proposed by the customer, quoted by the manufacturer, and agreed upon by both the customer and the manufacturer. The second problem concerns the actual decision processes and methodology used from the time an order is placed to the delivery of the final product to the customer. Though these two problems may seem to be different, both deal with integrating information from different sources. This similarity leads to the generation of a common solution strategy. In this paper we look at an agent based framework for implementing such a solution strategy.

The first part of the current supply chain problem lies within the company organization and process flow. The typical manufacturing organization has many different facilities, customers and suppliers that are all interconnected by a supply chain system in which many companies use an Enterprise Resource Planning (ERP) system to help with the decision making process. This type of ERP system begins with a demand forecast, which goes to the manufacturing facility, and finally to finished goods distribution where the customer can select the final product. Therefore the product is pushed through the system from the supplier to the customer as seen in Figure 1. With the aid of ERP systems most of the information is passed via Electronic Data Interchange (EDI).

Smaller organizations have the same supply chain model, however they utilize more archaic and manual methods to make the necessary decisions. These types of supply chains are slow, inefficient, and often, but not always, conform to a fixed product line. Therefore a multi-agent value net needs to be implemented, so that all information given to the company and driven by the customer will be distributed to the network of departments and suppliers in real time as in Figure 2.

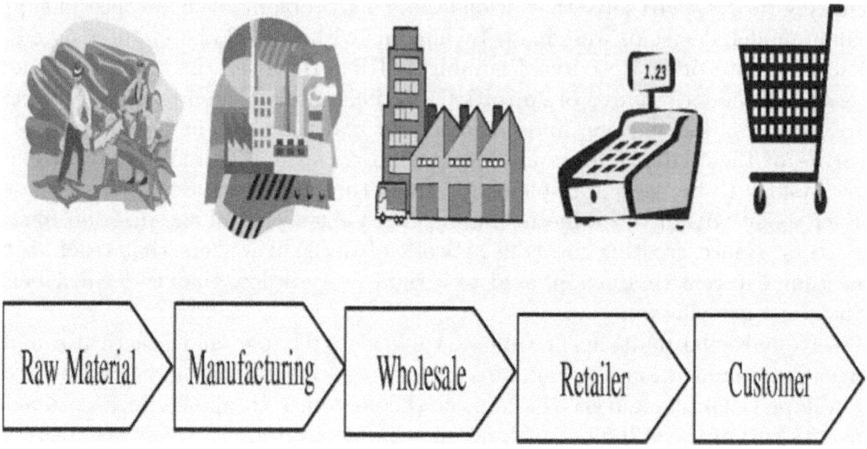

Fig. 1. The Supply Chain

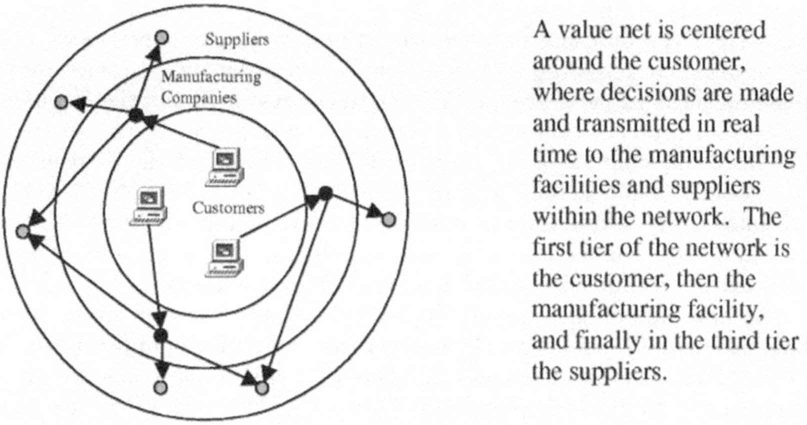

Fig. 2. Value Net [Bovet and Martha, 2000]

The other problem of the current supply chain model involves the decision-making processes. This problem is particularly complex since the input to one manufacturing facility is the output from another facility within the network. Thus each facility must make decisions based upon their suppliers' decisions and consequently making the value net as strong as the decision-making abilities of each facility. Therefore, a facility needs to make accurate decisions in real time concerning their inventory levels, manufacturing schedule, and total cost and then relay that information to their respective customers. This flow of information and decisions will then originate from the customer and be passed through the value net to the raw material supplier, the intermediary supplier, the manufacturer, and then returned to the end customer in real time.

Presently, automation of the supply chain model has been researched using intelligent agents, however a technology based value net using multi-agents has not been investigated. Agent-based approaches have been applied for enterprise integration, manufacturing production planning, scheduling and process control, and material handling within the past decade, but few models incorporate Internet based networks and communication languages. Most of the models created for these applications utilize KQML for communication, and ignore the Internet as a promising networking medium. Thus the current multi-agent models designed for the supply chain have many limitations when compared to the requirements of a customer centric value net. These limitations are as follows:

a) A customer centric value net requires a communication language that can directly communicate, interact, and pass data with clients, or other intelligent agents (digital decision support) that are located globally. Therefore the value net must be digitalized and Internet enabled. The Internet will provide for the most diverse and location independent network, and digitalization will provide for easy manipulation and decision support. KQML and the respective deviations do not support Internet processing and distribution.
b) The assimilation of digital support within business processes requires the integration of heterogeneous systems (databases, independent departmental software, and individual companies). For a true seamless value net, the intelligent agents have to communicate with every aspect of the business and current Agent Communication Languages (ACL) are not designed nor created for these heterogeneous systems. However the Extensible Markup Language (XML), is designed for data communication within heterogeneous systems and is supported by the Internet.
c) The multi-agent value net will have to stretch across many different businesses and sectors of industry. Therefore the strength of the communication language will be the ability to manipulate the language to fit every sector or industry standard. The Extensible Markup Language allows for each industry to change, add, or delete the actual markup without changing the structure of the platform or communication process. This will allow for the multi-agent value net to be utilized within any sector of industry.
d) The final limitation of current multi-agent supply chain models is the future limitations. These supply chain models cannot be easily scalable or manipulated for wireless interactions. The future of the value net relies on its ability to receive wireless data from multiple intelligent machines around the world. [Bovet and Martha, 2000]. For example, the office copier will let the supplier know that it is low on toner and paper before running out. Robots will send and receive wireless messages to suppliers pertaining to the inventory levels as they browse the line side inventory. Finally, an intelligent computer chip inside a car timing belt will send a wireless message to the owner and the manufacturer of the vehicle concerning the status of the belt. These are only a few of the possibilities, however the strength of these implementations resides within the value net platform.

Current supply chain models and multi-agent supply chain models have many limitations that prevent a customer centric value net. The customer will drive future orders, and the decisions within the value net, and therefore the decisions will have to be made instantly and accurately. Hence to make any organization truly efficient, agile, and customized a technology-based multi-agent value net must be implemented. We therefore propose in a multi-agent system to implement a customer centric value net.

3 Background Work

To our knowledge we feel that there are no Internet based value net implementations. However considerable work is reported on agent based implementation of supply chains and the coordination/communication within a multi-agent supply chain. In this section we briefly review the literature relevant to both of these subjects within a multi-agent supply chain.

Various multi-agent systems have been researched and created in order to generate models, however Mark Fox was probably the first to propose organizing the supply chain as a network of intelligent agents. In the work by Fox, Chionglo, and Barbuceanu in 1993 a multi-agent system was proposed that had two types of agents, functional and informational [Fox, M.S. et al, 1993]. The functional agents performed the control activities such as logistics, order acquisitions, transportation, resource management, scheduling, and dispatching. The informational agents were used to provide for the information and communication services. This design created a multi-agent model where each agent performs one or more supply chain functions. This specific model used KQML-based communication with user driven decision-making processes. Then in 1996 Barbuceanu and Fox created another "communication component that implements an extended version of the KQML language" for multi-agent supply chain models [Barbuceanu and Fox, 1996]. They stated that their commutation language within this model will communicate through various forms of messages in order to change the state of an agent or to perform actions. Nevertheless this language and architecture does not take the communication between the customer and the system nor between the system and current departmental software and databases into consideration.

In 1996, Swaminathan created a supply chain model through simulation with structural elements and control elements [Swaminathan, et al, 1996]. Structural elements include the production (retailers, distribution centers, plants, suppliers) and transportation elements and both of these elements are modeled as agents. The control elements (inventory, demand, supply, etc) are used to coordinate flow of products. In this work they also propose a message based communication system, where a set of message classes define the interaction between agents.

In 1996 Kalakota, Stallaert, and Whinston generated a model that created more generalized agents; agents that represented the distribution centers, manufacturing facilities, inventory, and the loading dock [Kalakota, et al, 1996]. Therefore only the flow of material through the supply chain was modeled in this multi-agent design. The real time supply chain optimization system generated by this team utilized the Internet and EDI to transfer information. In addition, the work by Hinkkanen in 1997 has suggested various distributed decision support systems for real time supply chain management systems that are completely managed by agents. They suggest that an agent can be modeled as a human and thus agents can drive the supply chain [Hinkkanen et al, 1997]. Like the work completed by Kalakota, Stallaert, and Whinston, this proposal suggests using EDI as the medium to exchange information. Although EDI connects multiple companies through data exchange, EDI does require a stringent standard for all companies within a network to comply and limits the accessibility of information to the customer; therefore preventing a customer driven value net. In addition, global organizational implementation would be limited.

Yung and Yang [Yung and Yang, 1999] proposed another multi-agent supply chain model. This model was designed to solve the constraint satisfaction problem within the supply chain and therefore consisted of three types of agents; propagation, interface, and control agents. The propagation agents perform the needed algorithms according to the problem distributed to them. The interface agents worked with the manager in the supply chain concerning orders, errors, or miscellaneous information and the control agent stored all the necessary information for the supply chain [Yung and Yang, 1999]. This model utilizes KQML, JDBC, and Socket/HTTP to coordinate all communication within the system and between suppliers. This approach enhances the communication process from previous work, however does not simplify the entire process by directly accessing (i.e. without passing through a database agent) current legacy systems, departmental software, databases, and customers across the Internet.

4 Value Net Implementation: A Multi-agent Approach

The multi-agent approach to value nets is composed of two componenets: the multi-agent system architecture and the communication component within the architecture. The design aspects of these components will fulfill the efficiency, agility, and customer centricity of a value net.

4.1 Multi-agent Value Net Architecture

The multi-agent value net model is created using agents that represent different aspects of the manufacturing organization within the value net (i.e. Logistics, Scheduling, Resources, Purchasing, and Accounting). This design is hierarchical in structure and imitates the physical organization of an industry (Figure 3). This organization naturally results in a master-slave agent configuration with a coordinating agent interfacing with the customer. This type of structure will force the entire value net to be responsive and driven by the end customer across the Internet and not by the manufacturing floor or a set of suppliers across a supply chain.

In addition, the hierarchical structure of this multi-agent system will allow for different agents to work in parallel to solve a customer order proposal or problem in real time. Since each agent has a unique domain and the associated knowledge base, they will all represent different departmental viewpoints and their combined knowledge will answer any customer proposal or response. Thus, each departmental agent will provide required answers to a coordinator who makes the final decisions and communicates them directly to the customer. After receiving the information regarding a customer proposal or problem from the respective agents, the coordinator will make a decision and either give a response to the customer across the Internet or confer with the slave (departmental) agents for further information. Once the customer and the coordinating agent agree on a final order, the coordinating agent then distributes the appropriate tasks to each agent in order to fulfill the order and therefore complete the customer driven value net. To make this multi-agent system function appropriately all communication with the customer must be in real time and across the Internet.

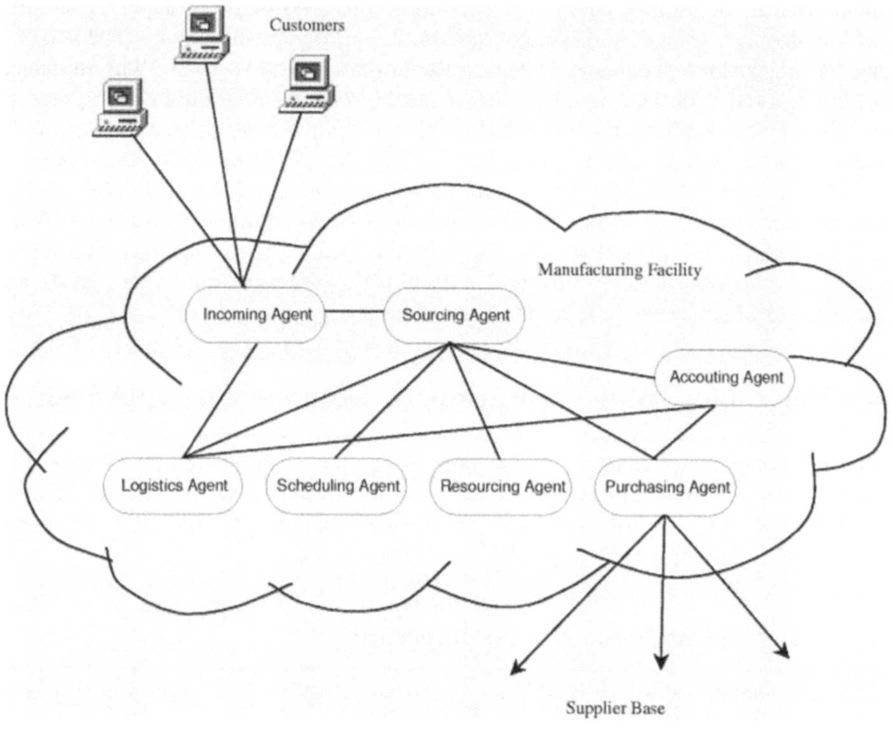

Fig. 3. Multi-Agent Value Net

4.2 Multi-agent Value Net Communication Language

To create the above architecture such that all communication and needed decisions within the value net are in real time and across the Internet, we propose an agent communication language that utilizes a combination of the Extensible Markup Language (XML), Java and HTTP.

This agent communication language will be message based and hence each agent will respond to an event that is generated by a message from another agent or the end customer. All messages within the multi-agent system will be associated with a class and the class will define the intent of the message and the type of response required.

```
Example:   Message Type -       Ask
           Speaker Intent -     The listener will assert the truth
                                based on their algorithms,
                                experiences, and knowledge base.
           Response Message -   Inform message with the assertion
                                as the content.
```

The content of the message will contain the destination agent name, the sending agent name, and the information being asserted or queried. Therefore a message can either initiate a new activity within the receiving agent or continue a dialog about a current activity. All messages created within the system will conform to a standard document type definition (DTD) created by the developer and poised by XML. These common DTD's will allow for easy parsing and composing capabilities using a simple Java program. This will allow one message to have information for many different agents, but each agent will only be able to view their appropriate assertion or query and thus creating one data source with many different views.

The combination of decision making agents and a real time communication language that can communicate with customers across the Internet, will make any value net agile, flexible, efficient, and customer oriented. This type of platform will be able to conform to various types of industries and value nets, therefore creating a company solution to current customer demands.

5 Conclusions

As companies begin to reengineer their supply chain process using information technology capabilities, their supply chain will begin to form into a value net. This value net will be agile, fast and customer driven. Therefore the customer will determine the product to be produced and the supplier that creates the resources. In order for companies to create this agile value net, they will need to generate a platform of autonomous agents that can respond to the customer in real time. These autonomous agents will represent the various departments within the manufacturing organization and will be able to efficiently communicate with each other, suppliers, and the end customer. The solution to this communication process lies within XML and Java messages. The purpose of this research is to investigate and develop an efficient communication process and ontology using XML within the value net organization.

Acknowledgements. This work is partially supported by NSF Grant DMI-0075584 and the authors gratefully acknowledge NSF for their support.

References

Barbuceanu, M., and M. S. Fox: Coordinating Multiple Agents in the Supply Chain. Proceedings of WET ICE, (1996).

Barbuceanu, M., and M. S. Fox: The architecture of an agent based infrastructure for agile manufacturing. http://www.eil.utoronto.ca/, Department of Industrial Engineering, University of Toronto, Toronto, Ontario, Canada.

Berry, N.M.: Reagere: A Hybrid Multi-Agent Architecture for Manufacturing. Doctoral Thesis, Department of Industrial and Manufacturing Engineering,Pennsylvania State University (1997).

Bovet, D., and J. Martha: Value Nets: Breaking the supply chain to unlock hidden profits. John Wiley and Sons, Inc: New York, New York (2000).

Carlson, D.: Component Interoperability with XML. Component Strategies, October, (1998).

Ferber, J.: Multi-Agent systems an introduction to distributed artificial intelligence. Addison-Wesley, Harlow, England, (1999).

Fox, M.S., J.F. Chionglo, and M. Barbuceanu. The integrated supply chain management system. http://www.eil.utoronto.ca/ Department of Industrial Engineering, University of Toronto, Toronto, Ontario, Canada, (1993).

Gerhard, W. ed.: Multiagent Systems A Modern Approach to Distributed Artificial Intelligence. Cambridge: The MIT Press (1999).

Gmytrasiewicz, P., and M.N. Huhns: The Emergence of Language Among Autonomous Agents. IEEE Internet Computing, July-August, 90-92 (2000).

Hinkkanen, R. Kalakota, P. Saengcharoenrat, J. Stalaert, A. B. Whinston: Distributed Decision Support Systems for Real Time Supply Chain Management using Agent Technologies. Working Paper, (1997).

Jennings, N. H., K. Sycara, and M. Wooldridge: A Roadmap of Agent Research and Developement. Autonomous Agents and Multi-Agent Systems, 1, 7-38 (1998).

Kalakota, R., J. Stallaert, A.B. Whinston: Implementing real-time supply chain optimization systems. http://crec.bus.utexas.edu/jan/sc_imp.html (1996).

Kulkarni, V. G., and N. Gautam: Intelligent software supply chain agents using ADE. Proceedings of AI and Manufacturing Research Planning Workshop, Albuquerque, NM (1998).

Lin, Y.: An Agent-Based Framework for Business Process Integration with Application to Complex Order Management. Master of Science Thesis, Department of Industrial and Manufacturing Engineering, Pennsylvania State University, University Park, PA (1997).

Navarro, A., C. White, and L. Burman: Mastering XML. Sybex, San Francisco, CA, (2000).

Mehra, A., and M. Nissen: Case Study: intelligent software supply chain agents Using ADE. AAAI Workshop on Software Tools for Developing Agents (1998).

Satapathy, G., and S.R.T. Kumara: Object oriented design based agent modeling. In Fourth International Conference on Practical Applications of Agents and Multiagents (PAAM99), London, UK, April 1999.

Satapathy, G., and S.R.T. Kumara: Semantics of KQML Messages based on illocutionary acts and BDI model of an agent. Working Paper Series, Department of Industrial and Manufacturing Engineering, Pennsylvania State University, University Park, PA (1999).

Shen, W., and D. H. Norrie: Agent-Based Systems for Intelligent Manufacturing: A State of-the-Art Survey. Knowledge and Information Systems, an International Journal, 1(2), 129-156, (1999).

Stader, J., and P. Jarvis: Intelligent support for enterprise modeling. Submitted to The 13th biennial European Conference on Artificial Intelligence (ECAI-98)), Brighton Centre, Brighton, UK, 23-28 (1998).

Swaminathan, J.M., et al.: Modeling Supply Chain Dynamics: A Multiagent Approach, Decision Sciences, 29(3): 607-632 (1998).

Wooldridge, M. and N.R. Jennings: Intelligent Agents: Theory and Practice. Knowledge Engineering Review, January (1995).

Yung, S.K., and C. C. Yang, A new approach to solve supply chain management problem by integrating multi-agent technology and constraint network. Proceedings of the 32nd Hawaii International Conference on System Sciences (ICSS) March, (1999).

Norms for DLP Agents Working in a Warehouse Scenario

Ioan Alfred Letia[1], Florin Craciun[1], and Zoltan Köpe[1]

Technical University of Cluj-Napoca,
Department of Computer Science
Baritiu 28, RO-3400 Cluj-Napoca, Romania
{letia,florin,kzoltan}@cs-gw.utcluj.ro

Abstract. We have studied the development of multi-agents that must collaborate within their working environment according to a set of norms. The agents used are defined and implemented in dynamic logic programming (DLP), using the LUPS knowledge updating system developed in XSB. The aim of this study is to experimentally find out how norms imposed on agents can lead to an acceptable and robust collective behavior. Such a normative generated behavior is more natural in an open environment where new agents may enter the world with expectation of social acceptance. The experiments carried out have shown where we have flaws in the initial definition of the norms. We have been able to learn how to modify the norms in order to improve the social behavior of the group of agents in the warehouse scenario.

Keywords: autonomous agents, KBS methodologies, distributed problem solving, knowledge representation, norms, social constraints

1 Introduction

Various coordination approaches have been developed for multi-agent systems, but quite often autonomy is required in open environments where agents have considerable autonomy [2]. However, autonomy comes with a price, materialized by norms or rules, if some reasonable and robust cooperation is expected from the society of agents [7]. Socially sophisticated BDI agents [4] have also been introduced by including norms and obligations in a BDI interpreter, with the the declared claim "to increase the efficiency of agent reasoning".

In the research reported in this paper we have used the extended logic programming for the general definition of the agents in the style of [5,6]. To describe agent behavior we have used, whenever convenient, the dynamic logic programming (DLP) paradigm [3], with its "Language of UPdateS" (LUPS) [1] that describes transitions between consecutive knowledge states.

Next we succinctly present the main DLP and LUPS ideas used in the agent model. Then the simulation framework with its warehouse scenario environment and implemented agent are described. Afterwards the experimental results are shown and discussed.

L. Monostori, J. Váncza, and M. Ali (Eds.): IEA/AIE 2001, LNAI 2070, pp. 728–733, 2001.

2 Dynamic Logic Programming Agent

The agent cycle is a variant of that proposed in [5]: (i) **observe** inputs, (ii) **think**, (iii) **select** one or more actions to perform, (iv) **act**. The main body of this cycle is defined in extended logic programming. Changes in the knowledge of the agent have been represented in *dynamic logic programming (DLP)*, where knowledge is conveyed by a set of theories, encoded as generalized logic programs. Propositional variables of the form *not* A are called *default atoms.* Propositional variables whose names do not begin with *not* are called *objective atoms.* A *generalized rule* has the form:

$$L_0 \leftarrow L_1, \ldots, L_n \tag{1}$$

where every L_i is an objective or default atom.

The language LUPS[1] has a precise declarative and procedural semantics. Various commands can be used to specify updates of knowledge. To specify a "persistent update command" we can use:

$$always\ [event]\ (L \leftarrow L_1, \ldots, L_n)\ when\ (L_{k+1}, \ldots, L_{k+n}) \tag{2}$$

that is the knowledge of the agent is updated with the given generalized rule $L \leftarrow L_1, \ldots, L_n$ when the *event* takes place and the condition specified by $L_{k+1}, \ldots, L_{k+n}$ is fulfilled. The commands available in LUPS allow us to very conveniently specify changes in the knowledge of agents. We can also express reasoning of agents regarding actions that they might have interest to undertake. Communication between agents, although not considered in this paper, is also facilitated by expressions of knowledge updating.

3 Simulation Framework

The agent has been implemented in XSB[2] and LUPS. The environment has been completely implemented in XSB. Swarm[3] has been used to control and visualize the experiments.

3.1 Warehouse Scenario

Our warehouse scenario consists of various zones with objects. Every object is defined by a utility value and a lifespan time. When the lifespan expires the object disappears, unless it has been picked up in the meantime by an agent. Each agent has the capability to execute the actions: moveLeft, moveRight, moveUp, moveDown, popLeft, popRight, push.

[1] LUPS is available from http://centria.di.fct.unl.pt/˜jja/updates/lups.p

[2] XSB home page http://xsb.sourceforge.net/

[3] Swarm home page http://www.santafe.edu/projects/swarm/

All agents have the duty to carry the object in an embarking zone. An agent can carry just one object at a time. When the agent succeeds in carrying the object to the embarking zone, it gains a value one utility.

The behavior of agents has been constrained by various norms (rules), like: (i) between object columns agents can move downwards just on the "down" column;(ii) between object columns agents can move upwards just on the "up" column. Prohibitions (restrictions) have been introduced like: (i) no two entities (agent or object) are allowed simultaneously on the same square;(ii) an agent can carry just one object;(iii) an agent cannot walk on zones for objects;(iv) an agent can pick up just an object adjacent to its square;(v) an agent can leave an object just on a square adjacent to its own position.

The map and the norms for agent moves among the zones of objects are illustrated in figure 1 (a). The change in the map after a few steps are shown in figure 1 (b). Agents carrying objects are shown in a darker grey, while the objects are shown in black, and the "warehouse" zone is pictured by a vertical lines texture.

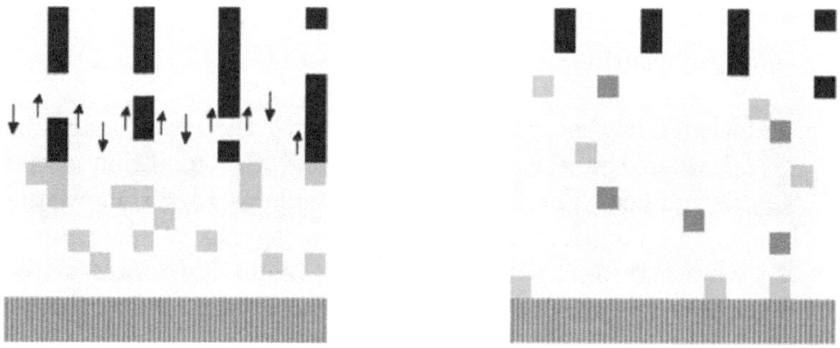

Fig. 1. (a) Scenario map representing the norms for agent moves among zones of objects. (b) Change in scenario after a few steps.

3.2 Implemented Agent

A cycle of the implemented agent is described by the pseudo-code below.

initialize currentWorldModel, currentGoals, mostPreferGoal, . . .;
while ¬member(finalState,currentStates) ∧ ¬expire(deliberationLimit)
  nextStates := successors(currentStates,capabilities);
  currentStates := filter(nextStates,norms,prohibitions);
endwhile
if member(finalState,curentStates)
then action := takeAction(finalState);
else mostUtilState := select(utilityCriterion,currentStates);
    action := takeAction(mostUtilState);
endif

We illustrate the usage of LUPS in the generation of the decision tree. The operators that generate the new state are declared as "persistent update commands". These operators, representing the capabilities of the agent, have been coded in an abstract space to ensure independence from agent position. For instance, moveUp is represented as "move(-1,0)", meaning that the agent can move on a square within the same column and the line is decremented by 1, while popLeft is "pop(0,-1)" meaning that the agent picks up an object on the same line with the agent and the column decremented by 1. Similarly push is "push(1,0)", that is the agent places the object on a location on the same column and the line incremented by 1.

```
always state(NewX,Y,HasObj,[move(-1,0)|ActionList],NewUtil)
when state(X,Y,HasObj,ActionList,Util),
     prolog((NewX is X - 1,evalState(NewX,Y,HasObj,NewUtil)),
     canDo(X,Y,HasObj,move(-1,0)), not stop.
```

Besides the generation of the new state an "update" of the "WorldModel" also takes place. The states are filtered by applications of norms and prohibitions imposed in the scenario on the "current updated WorldModels".

```
always canDo(X,Y,HasObj, move(-1,0)) <-
       prolog((NewX is X - 1, isOnMap(NewX,Y), isPosFree(NewX,Y),
       not(isOnDown(NewX,Y)))).
```

The selection of the action to fulfill the current goal is performed by the rule:

```
always selectAction(Goal) <- state(X,Y,HasObj,ActionList,Util),
       prolog((isPerformed(Goal, state(X,Y,HasObj,ActionList,Util)),
       extract(FirstAction,ActionList)).
```

The generation of the tree is finished when a state is found with the goal satisfied relative to the "current updated WorldModel". When the procedure terminates before "stop" becomes true, the action is chosen based on the utility of each state, in our scenario the number of objects that can be picked up before disappearing.

4 Experimental Results

Several experiments have been carried out to test the robustness of the architecture. The parameters used to control the experiments are: (i) *worldXSize and worldYSize* map dimension; (ii) *numberAgent* represents the the number of agents; (iii) *objColumn* length of object zones; (iv) *dimWarehouse*height of warehouse; (v) *maxObjVal* maximum utility value assigned to an object; (vi) *maxObjPersist* maximum life span of an object. The placement of entities on the map is random for each experiment. Deliberation has been limited by the parameter *deliberationLimit* on the depth of the decision tree. The maximum value used in our experiments for *deliberationLimit* was 4. The utility accumulated by agents, the number of objects carried to the warehouse and the objects lost (due to the fact that their life span expired) have been monitored. The parameters *objColumn* and *dimWarehouse* have been used to enlarge/decrease the space between objects and warehouse to see the behavior of agents in areas without prescribed norms.

The number of waisted objects is dependent on the parameters *numberAgent* and *maxObjPersist*. Increasing the life span of objects allows agents to pick up more objects, regardless of how weak their reasoning is. Increasing the number of agents leads to an overpopulation of the space available and to an increase in the number of conflicts.

The agents use a utility criterion to partially order the states in the decision tree. The action chosen is the one leading to a state with highest utility. In this version conflicts appear when two agents intend to move to the same position. Another conflict that appears is when two agents intend to pick up the same object. New norms have to be introduced that consider mutual behavior of agents.

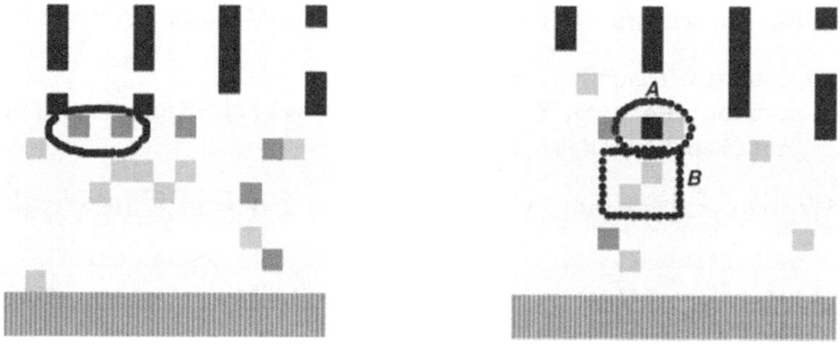

Fig. 2. (I) Conflict between two agents carrying objects and intending to move to the same position on the "down" column. (II) (A) Conflict between two agents without objects, intending to pick up the same object, (B) Conflict between two agents without objects intending to move to the same square

From several experiments we have found various conflicts occurring between agents: (i) two agents that carry objects intend to move at the same time on the "down" column to get the objects to the warehouse, figure 2 (I), (ii) two agents without objects intend to pick up at the same time the same object, part A in figure 2 (II), (iii) conflict between two agents without objects that intend to move to the same position in the zone between objects and warehouse, part B in figure 2 (II).

The simulation framework does not allow two or more agents to act on the same location. If the agents try to do it the environment forces them to stay on their position (their action is not executed).

Experiments have shown that conflicts in areas with existing norms are more persistent than conflicts in areas without norms. One conclusion would be that norms with higher degree of generality should be provided with exceptions for specific situations. For example, in figure 2 (I) the two agents carrying objects intend to go to the warehouse. Their only solution due to the norms imposed on them is to walk to the warehouse on the "down" column. Since their position does not allow both of them to do it at the same time, conflict resolution could be realized in two ways: (i) by adding a new norm "priority for the right side" as in traffic rules;(ii) by adding an exception to the norm saying that an agent is allowed to go down on the "up" column if the following three positions are free (a kind of overtaking in the traffic rules).

5 Conclusions

We have carried the concept of normative agent development a step further by experimenting with a multi-agent system defined using norms. We have used extended logic programming and dynamic logic programming to generate the desired behavior. This step is important for applications where nonmonotonic reasoning is imperative and change of agent knowledge is expected. This approach is also useful if we want to move towards a methodology that enables development of agent technology with normative facilities. Further work will include studying how general mechanisms conceived for policy management could be captured by norms. Run-time selection of coordination mechanisms in multi-agent systems should also be important to import into normative agents.

References

1. J. J. Alferes, L. M. Pereira, H. Przymusinska, and T. C. Przymusinski. LUPS - a language for updating logic programs. In M. Gelfond, N. Leone, and G. Pfeifer, editors, *5th International Conference on Logic Programming and Nonmonotonic Reasoning*, LNAI, vol 1730, pages 162–176. Springer-Verlag, 1999.
2. C. Castelfranchi, F. Dignum, C. M. Jonker, and J. Treur. Deliberative normative agents: Principles and architecture. In N.R. Jennings and Y. Lesperance, editors, *Intelligent Agents VI*, LNAI, vol 1757. Springer-Verlag, 1999.
3. P. Dell'Acqua, J. A. Leite, and L. M. Pereira. Evolving multi-agent viewpoints – an architecture. 2000. submitted.
4. F. Dignum, D. Morley, E. A. Sonenberg, and L. Cavedon. Towards socially sophisticated BDI agents. In *Proceedings of the 4th International Conference on Multi-Agent Systems (ICMAS-2000)*, pages 111–118, Boston, MA, 2000.
5. Robert Kowalski and Fariba Sadri. From logic programming towards multi-agent systems. *Annals of Mathematics and Artificial Intelligence*, 25:391–419, 1999.
6. L. M. Pereira and P. Quaresma. Modelling agent interaction in logic programming. In O. Barenstein, editor, *The 11th International Conference on Applications of Prolog*, pages 150–156, Tokyo, Japan, September 1998.
7. Sudhir K. Rustogi and Munindar P. Singh. Be patient and tolerate imprecision: How autonomous agents can coordinate effectively. In *Proceedings of the 16th International Joint Conference on Artificial Intelligence (IJCAI-99)*, pages 512–517, Stockholm, Sweden, 1999.

A Methodology for Reliable Systems Design

Jaime Solano-Soto[1] and Luis Enrique Sucar[2]

[1]Centro de Investigaciones en Computación
Escuela de Computación, Instituto Tecnológico de Costa Rica
A.P. TEC 159-7050, Cartago, Costa Rica
[2]Departamento de Computación,
ITESM – Campus Cuernavaca, A.P. 99-C, 62589 Cuernavaca, Morelos, México
esucar@campus.mor.itesm.mx

Abstract. A novel configuration method for systems design has been developed, that considers, at the same time, system reliability and cost. This method helps to maximize the reliability, minimize the cost and obtain the best possible configuration for the system to be designed. To accomplish this, a combination of Bayesian networks and heuristic search are used so to help the designer find the optimum configuration in the immense search space available. The method has as entry parameters: the minimal reliability requirement or maximum cost of the computer system to be designed, the function of the system as a reliability block diagram and a description of each component. From this input, the methodology transforms automatically the reliability block diagram to Bayesian network equivalent, from which the reliability of the system is obtained through probability propagation. Starting form the initial block diagram, a set of heuristic operators is used to generate new configurations. The "best" configurations are obtained using beam search with some heuristics to improve the search efficiency. There are 3 alternatives for defining the best configurations: (i) minimize cost with a reliability restriction, (ii) maximize reliability with a cost restriction, and (iii) make a compromise between reliability and cost (Pareto set). The methodology is applied to the design of a distributed control system with promising results.

1 Introduction

The design of critical systems has two fundamental stages. In the first stage, the reliability requirements are specified, the system components and its interconnection (architecture) are defined and a mathematical model for the reliability estimate is established. In the second stage, the form of implanting fault tolerance is specified [6].

Usually, the designers of high reliability systems receive three parameters. The first is the function that the system must accomplish to satisfy the user's requirements. The second parameter is the reliability degree that the design must fulfill. And the third, is the behavioral information of each one of the components that will be used. When the designer has all these information, he/she proceeds to generate a first system version with the indispensable minimal components. Since the system fails if some of these components fail, it is considered as a serial system from a reliability point of view. Given this initial configuration, the reliability of the system is estimated based on the individual components' reliability and standard analysis techniques. Some commonly used techniques are reliability block diagrams, fault trees and Markov models [1].

L. Monostori, J. Váncza, and M. Ali (Eds.): IEA/AIE 2001, LNAI 2070, pp. 734-745, 2001.

Once the reliability parameter from the first system version is obtained, an iterative cycle is entered and the designer proceeds to do several trials of the system design, until the required reliability is obtained. In each trial the initial system configuration is changed. Furthermore, the cost factor is generally not taken into account. The design process is generally *ad-hoc*. Therefore, a general configuration methodology is required, that considers the following two parameters: reliability and cost.

In this paper we present a new method for "rational" configuration of high reliability systems through the combination of Bayesian networks and heuristic search. The adjective *rational* means that a balance between the system reliability and its cost is sought. The method helps to select the best configuration, according to the user's needs. The methodology covers three alternative:

- Based on a reliability restriction, obtain the "best" possible system configuration, according to the cost.
- Based on a cost restriction, obtain the "best" possible system configuration, according to its reliability.
- Obtain a balance between reliability and cost to produce the best possible configuration, so that reliability is maximized and the cost is minimized.

The rest of the paper is divided in five parts: antecedents, reliability analysis with Bayesian networks, methodology, and conclusions and future work.

2 Antecedents

The methodology is based on reliability concepts and Bayesian networks.

2.1 System Reliability

Of the inherent characteristics in the concept of quality, reliability is probably the most important. The reliability expresses the probability that an equipment operates without defects in a period of time, in an environment which it was designed for. It refers to how well does the system fulfils the user's requirements [3]. The reliability of a complex system depends on the reliability of its components, so that it can be defined as a mathematical relationship between the reliability of the parts and that of the system.

The failure frequency is known as the failure rate. This is used as a parameter for the reliability mathematical formulation. The failure rate is measured in number of failures by operating time. Its reciprocal value is called mid time between failures (MTBF) and it is generally measured in hours between failures. A system reliability block diagram (RBD) tool is used in system reliability analysis. It represents the effect of the subsystem's failures on the reliability of the system. It is a form of black boxes for analysis that requires that a system is splitted into components or subsystems. It is assumed that each black box will be in one of two states: successful or with defect [2]. Given the failure probability of each component, the failure probability of the system can be evaluated based on the topology of the RBD. Basically, the probabilities are combined according to the structure of the RBD: for serial components (AND) the probabilities are multiplied, and for parallel components (OR) the complement (probability of success) is obtained by multiplying the success probability of the components.

2.2 Bayesian Networks

For reliability analysis we use Bayesian networks. Bayesian networks (BNs) are directed acyclic graphs (DAG) in which each node represents a random variable or proposition. The arcs between nodes represent dependencies or direct causal influences between the bound propositions. The force of these dependencies is quantified by conditional probabilities [5].

A Bayesian network (BN) contains the necessary information to answer probabilistic queries about its variables. These queries can be to interpret specific entry data or to recommend the better action course to be followed. This requires the instantiation of a set of variables corresponding to the entry data, propagation to calculate their impact on the probabilities of the other variables, and finally to obtain the posterior marginal probabilities of the unknowns.
The propagation procedure is based on Bayes' theorem and on the dependency structure of the net. For single connected networks, it is implemented through the communication between neighboring nodes by means of local operations, through the messages sent between nodes connected in the net [5]. This permits to update the probability of any variable by means of the evidence that comes form its parents and children. The posterior probability of a variable is obtained by Bayes' theorem. There are alternative methods for probability propagation in multiconnected networks [5].
BNs techniques offer some advantages with respect to the other techniques used in reliability analysis. BNs are an alternative to include the condition of event dependency in the conventional fault tree models. They have the property of probability propagation in both ways (causal and evidential), while the others techniques are only for analysis.

3 Reliability Analysis with Bayesian Networks

A method for reliability analysis based in BN is established. A RBD is transformed to a BN and reliability calculations are done through probability propagation [7]. Fault trees are a subset of BNs, so this technique has a wide potential of application in reliability analysis. In addition, it permits to represent aspects as dependencies between failures and the combination of sources of information.We first present the simple cases of serial and parallel systems using BN, and then a general method to transform any RBD to a BN equivalent.

3.1 Serial Systems

It is said that the system components are in series, from a reliability point of view, if they should work all so that the system is successful, and it is enough that one fails for the system to fail. The representation by means of a RBD of a serial system is shown in figure 1.b and its BN equivalent in figure 1.a.

A conditional probability matrix is defined, that represents the system arrangement and it permits to obtain ist joint probability distribution, through the following expression:

$$P(X/A,B) = \begin{matrix} & ab & a'b & ab' & a'b' \\ x & 1 & 0 & 0 & 0 \\ \bar{x} & 0 & 1 & 1 & 1 \end{matrix}$$

Where the elements of the conditional probability matrix columns, *P*(*X*/*A*,*B*), are the combination of the parent nodes states: *A*,*B* are operating, *A* has failed and *B* is operating, *A* is operating and *B* has failed, and both fail. For a serial arrangement, the first line represents the success probability of the system given *A* and *B*, it is one when *A* and *B* operate and zero when any fails. The second line represents the failure probability and it is inverse to the first line. This matrix is equivalent to an AND gate [7].

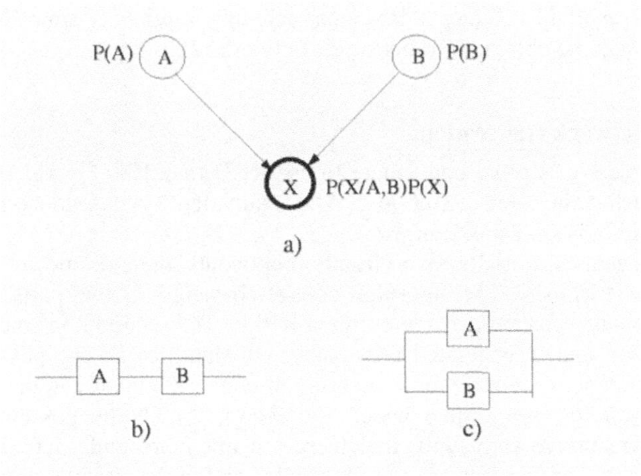

Fig. 1. RBD for basic serial and parallel systems and Bayesian network equivalent. a) Bayesian network for both cases. b) RBD for Serial System. c) RBD for Parallel System.

3.2 Parallel Systems

It is said that the system components are in parallel, from a reliability viewpoint, if only one is needed to work so that the system is successful, and the system only fails if all of its components fail. For a parallel arrangement as that of figure 1.c, a BN is obtained as shown in figure 1.a. The BN structure is the same for series and parallel configurations, but the conditional probability matrix, *P*(*X*/*A*,*B*), is different in each case. In this case only the conditional probability matrix is modified, such matrix is equivalent to an OR gate [7], and it is the following:

$$P(X/A,B) = \begin{bmatrix} 1 & 1 & 1 & 0 \\ 0 & 0 & 0 & 1 \end{bmatrix}$$

The generalization for multiple components is immediate. For instance, for a 3 component system which requires two components functioning, the probability matrix is:

$$P(X/A,B,C) = \begin{bmatrix} 1 & 1 & 1 & 1 & 0 & 0 & 0 & 0 \\ 0 & 0 & 0 & 0 & 1 & 1 & 1 & 1 \end{bmatrix}$$

3.3 Complex Combination of Serial-Parallel Systems

For complex systems, which combine subsystems in series-parallel the previous equations in recursive form are applied. There are combinations of components that are not in series or parallel in a strictest sense. For example, consider the arrangement which is known as a *bridge type system*. This system functions if at least one of the 4 possible paths is available. Using a BN approach the solution is simplified so the system reliability can be obtained from a single network [7].

3.4 Bayesian Network Generation

For system designers it is more convenient to use RBD than BN. So we developed a method for transforming any RBD to a BN equivalent. A pseudocode for the conversion algorithm is shown in figure 2.

The algorithm generates, initially, two virtual components, the extremes of the RBD, called "Start", and "Finish". The algorithm consists basically of two parts. The first generates an adjacency matrix that represents a RBD. The second constructs the BN from the adjacency matrix generated previously. It identifies all the possible paths from the first component ("Start") until the last component ("Finish") in the adjacency matrix. Each path forms a virtual node. The search for all the possible paths is accomplished in recursive form until that there are not more paths left. In the BN structure, the system components are the root nodes and each possible path is a node virtual (intermediate nodes), and there is a node leaf that represents the system. Each virtual node that corresponds to each path has a series (AND) probability matrix. The leaf node that represents the complete system has a parallel (OR) probability matrix.

4 Design Methodology

The proposed methodology has as main objective to define a "rational" method for configuration of high reliability systems that makes a compromise between cost and reliability. This method must help to maximize the reliability, minimize the cost and obtain the "best" possible system configuration. Figure 3 summarizes the algorithm for the proposed methodology.

```
Convert RBD to BN
begin
   Generate adjacency matrix
   Generate paths
end Converts of RBD to BN
Generate Adjacency Matrix
begin
   For each element of the connections' vector make
     To obtain the corresponding object to the
     component origin
     If this is not entry in Adjacency Matrix
       Adjacency Matrix ← to add that component
       as entry
     End If
     To obtain the corresponding object to the
     destination component
     Adjacency Matrix ← to add that component as
     output
   End For each
end Generates Adjacency Matrix
Generate Paths
begin
   For each output of the "Start" component of the
   Adjacency Matrix
     Make PathSearch (Start, output-i)
   End For each
end Generate Paths
PathSearch (Row, Column)
begin
   PathMatrix ← Adjacency Matrix [Row, Column]
   For each output-i of Adjacency Matrix [Row,
   Column]
     If output-number > 1
       PathMatrix[i+1] ← PathMatrix[i]
     End If
     PathSearch (Row, output-i)
   End For each
end PathSearch
```

Fig. 2. Pseudocode for the RBD to BN conversion algorithm.

The configuration system requires as input the following:

1. Configuration type, which can be one of the following:
   - Minimize cost given a reliability restriction.
   - Maximize reliability given a cost restriction.
   - Obtain configurations that make a balance between reliability and cost.
2. Cost of adding a redundant component.
3. Initial RBD. It is the graph with the minimal components so that the system accomplishes the required function.

4. For each component, the following data is required:
   4.1. Type of component: identifies component's family.
   4.2. Code of the component: identifies the component within others similar of the same type.
   4.3. Description.
   4.4. Reliability.
   4.5. Cost.
   4.6. Maximum number of components of this type that can operate in parallel.

1. Obtain, from the user, an initial RBD, with the minimal elements so that the system operates. This initial configuration corresponds to a RBD in which all the elements are connected serially.
2. Generate a first BN from RBD obtained in 1. With this model, the first value for system reliability and cost are obtained.
3. Iterate until finding the best configurations:
   3.1 Generate configurations selecting them based on heuristics to select the "best" configurations
   3.2. Evaluate its cost.
   3.3. Evaluate the configuration reliability through BNs.

Fig. 3. Methodology for reliable systems design.

There are 3 basic cases that that the user can select, which we denominate as *configuration type*:

a) Obtain the configurations with maximum reliability given a cost restrictions.
b) Obtain the configurations with minimum cost given a reliability restriction.
c) Obtain the configurations that at the same time maximize reliability and minimize cost. These are called non-dominated solutions (Pareto).

The output of the system is a set of configurations (the user can specify the number) according to the configuration type selected. For each configuration generated by the system, it evaluates its reliability and cost. The reliability is obtained by the method based on BN described on the previous section. For the cost calculation, we use a simple cost function. The cost of the system is obtained based on the cost of each component multiplied by the number of components, plus an additional cost for each redundancy. It is obtained using the following equation:

$$SystCost = (\#CR * \$GR) + \sum_{k=1}^{n} \#C_k * \$C_k$$

where $\#CR$ is the total number of redundant components, $\$GR$ is the general cost of adding any component in parallel, $\#C_K$ is the number of components of the type K, $\$C_K$ is cost of each type K component, n is the total number of types of components used in the system. The "best" configurations are obtained using a heuristic search procedure that is described in the next section.

4.1 Search Procedure

A search process starting from the initial (serial) configuration obtains the "best" configurations. The search for the best configuration is a kind of *beam* (*W*) search aided with heuristics. The criteria for the beam is based on the configuration type. The system returns the first *M* configurations with:

- Lower cost that have a reliability equal or above the specified limit (*Rmin*), or
- Maximum reliability that have a cost limit specified (Cmax), or
- Lower cost and maximum reliability (Pareto set).

The search procedure is based on the algorithm shown in figure 4. The parameters *W* and *M* are adjusted according to the specific application. The operators for generating new configurations are split into three groups, according to the configuration type:

Case 1: reliability restriction and minimize cost

1. Change low reliability components by similar components of higher reliability if they exist.
2. Add redundancy at the component level. The maximum number of parallel components should be observed.

Case 2: cost restriction and maximize reliability

1. If the maximum cost is surpassed, change high cost components for cheaper ones. If the maximum cost is not surpassed, change low reliability components for similar components of high reliability.
2. If the maximum cost is surpassed, eliminate redundancy. If the maximum cost is not surpassed, add redundancy at the component level. The maximum number of components in parallel should be observed.
3. Add redundancy at the subsystem level and system level, provided that the maximum cost is not surpassed.

Case 3: reliability and cost balance

1. Change low reliability components by similar components of higher reliability if they exist.
2. Add redundancy at the component level. The maximum number of parallel components should be observed.

The heuristics that are taken into account in order to reduce the complexity of the search procedure in the configuration process are the following:

1. First change the smaller reliability components for similar components (same type) of greater reliability.
2. First add redundancy at the component level and as second option add redundancy at the subsystems level.
3. Do not put many components in parallel, since as after putting 2 components in parallel, the marginal profit on the reliability of the system is minimal and the increase in the cost is at least linear.

```
Beam search
Obtain the reliability and cost of the initial (serial) configuration
If reliability > Rmin or cost > Cmax, terminate
Obtain the configuration number to evaluate (w)
Iterate until finding M configurations:
    For n system components do:
        Generate new configurations by changing low reliability components by an
            equivalent with higher reliability
    For n system components do:
        Generate new configurations by adding redundancy at the component level
    Obtain the cost and reliability of each configuration generated
    If Case1:
        Order the configurations by cost, in order ascendant
        Select the configurations that satisfy Rmin and put them in the optimum list
        If the number of configurations in the optimum list >= M terminate
    Otherwise If Case2:
        Order the configurations by reliability, in order descendent
        Select the configurations that satisfy Cmax and put them in the optimum list
        If the number of configurations in the optimum list >= M terminate
    Otherwise If Case3:
        Order the configurations by reliability, in order descendent
        Select the configurations non dominate and put them in the optimum list
End Beam search
```

Fig. 4. Pseudocode for the search algorithm.

The methodology is illustrated with a real example in the next section.

4.2 An Example

In order to illustrate the procedure, this was applied to a Programmable Logic Control System (PLC) for controlling thermoelectric plant burners, whose initial RBD is shown in figure 5. For simplifying the example, only five controllers are included.

a)

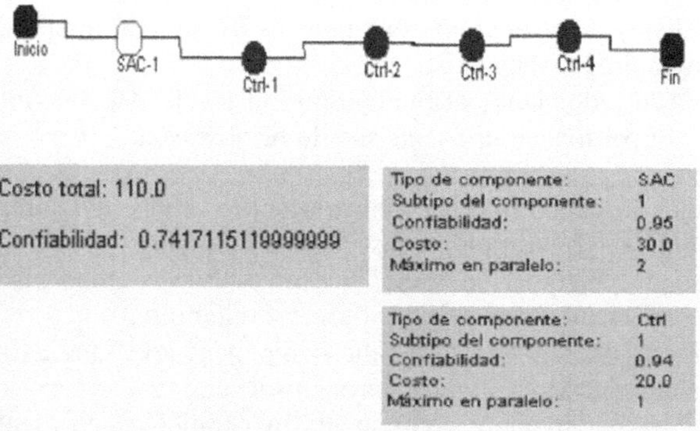

b) c)

Fig. 5. Programmable Logic Control System (PLC). (a) Initial RBD, (b) Cost and reliability results, and (c) Component's description.

The input parameters are the following:

- SAC has a reliability of 95% and costs \$30.
- Burner controller (C1 to C4) has a reliability of 94% and costs \$20.
- Alternative burner controller has a reliability of 96% and costs \$25.
- For reliability restriction case, the PLC system needs to have a reliability of 98%.
- For cost restriction case, the user has a \$250 as maximum cost.

Case 1: Reliability restriction

In the case in which we have as restriction to comply with a given reliability, we proceed to configure the previous system to try to obtain the reliability of 98%. For this, the following is done:

1. Receive as entry a first version from a RBD without redundancy, to solve the problem in question. According to the given formulation, the initial system cost is \$110.
2. From the initial RBD, a BN equivalent of the system is generated. This is shown in figure 9. From the reliability of each system component and propagation, a 0.7417 system reliability is obtained.
3. Since the reliability restriction has not been satisfied, an iterative process is entered generating different configurations, until a configuration with the required reliability is obtained. In this example, after applying the operator 1 we have as a result a 0.8069 for the system reliability.
4. The search process is continued until configurations that satisfy the reliability requirement are obtained. One of these is a redundant configuration (each component duplicated), with a reliability of 0.9832 and a cost of \$220.

Case 2: Cost restriction

In the case in which we have as restriction to comply with a given maximum cost (e. g. \$250), we proceed to configure the previous system to try to obtain the configurations with higher reliability. For this, the following is done:

1. The cost and reliability of the initial (serial) configuration is obtained: 0.7417 and \$110, respectively.
2. Although the cost restriction is satisfied, an iterative process is entered generating different configurations, until the W configurations with highest reliability are obtained
3. The search process obtains several configuration with higher reliability that satisfy the cost restriction. One of them is the same as the one obtained in case 1.

Case 3: Cost and Reliability restrictions

In the case in which we have to obtain the configurations that they comply with a given maximum cost and reliability minimum, that is, a the configurations that make a balance between reliability and cost. In this case, we consider a maximum cost of \$200 and a minimum reliability of 0.8. For this, the following is done:

1. Similar to cases 1 and 2, we receive as entry a first version from a RBD without redundancy, to solve the problem in question. According to the given formulation, the initial system cost is $110 and reliability of 0.7417.
2. Since the cost and reliability restrictions have not been satisfied, an iterative process is entered generating different configurations, until a set of non-dominated configurations (Pareto) are obtained.
3. After the search process, as set of Pareto solutions are obtained. Three of the non-dominated configurations are shown in figure 6.

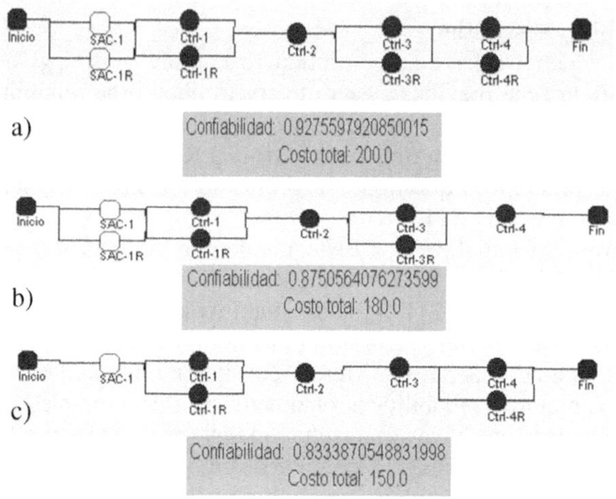

Fig. 6. Three of the final configurations for case 3.

5 Conclusions and Future Work

Reliability is one of the primary elements that must be taken into account in systems quality. We detected the need of having a methodology that supports systems designers in reliable systems configuration and that considers a reliability requirement and cost. Through the combination of BNs and heuristic search, a method for rational systems design was developed. This method helps to optimize the reliability, minimize cost and obtain the best system configuration. This methodology helps the designer to obtain the best configuration, so that an optimum balance between reliability and its cost is obtained. The methodology was applied to the design of a distributed control system.

As future work we plan to explore the possibility of bottom-up propagation in the BN model of the system. We think that this could help to find the optimal configurations more efficiently by discarding configurations that can not have the desired reliability.

References

1. ANSI-IEEE. *IEEE Guide for General Principles of Reliability Analysis of Nuclear Power Generating Station Safety Systems.* USA: American National Standards Institute, 1985.
2. Kapur, K., Lamberson, L. *Reliability in Engineering Design.* USA: John Wiley & Sons Inc., 1977.
3. Musa, John, Iannino, Anthony, Okumoto, Kazuhira. *Software Reliability: Measurement, Prediction and Application.* Singapore: McGraw-Hill International Editions, 1987.
4. Neapolitan, Richard. *Probabilistic Reasoning in Expert Systems: Theory and Algorithms.* USA: John Wiley & Sons, Inc., 1990.
5. Pearl, Judea. *Probabilistic Reasoning in Intelligent Systems: Network of Plausible Inference.* USA: Morgan Kaufmann Publisher, Inc., 1988.
6. Ramírez V., Carlos. "*Tolerancia a faltas: conceptos y aplicaciones del departamento de Instrumentación y Control*"; Boletín IEE. Morelos, México. (Jul 1996): p. 182-188.
7. Torres, José, Sucar, L.Enrique. "*Bayesian Networks for Reliability Analysis of Complex Systems*" Iberamia 1998. Portugal: 1998.

Intelligent Support for Interactive Configuration of Mass-Customized Products

A. Felfernig, G. Friedrich, D. Jannach, and M. Zanker

Computer Science and Manufacturing, University Klagenfurt, A 9020 Klagenfurt
{felfernig,friedrich,jannach,zanker}@ifit.uni-klu.ac.at

Abstract. Mass customization of configurable products made knowledge-based (and web-based) product configuration systems an important tool to support the sales engineer or end user when configuring systems according to the customer's needs. Configuration problems are often modeled as Constraint Satisfaction Problems, where the configuration process is an interactive search process. During this search process, the user may encounter situations, where a path in the search tree is reached, where no solution can be found. In this paper we show how model-based diagnosis techniques can be employed to assist the user to recover from such situations by calculating adequate (or optimal) reconfiguration or recovery actions. [1]

Keywords: Intelligent interfaces, Automated Problem Solving.

1 Introduction

Following the paradigm of mass-customization [4], products are offered to the customer in many variants. Knowledge-based configuration systems (configurators) are a successful application of AI technology and can assist the technical engineer, the sales representative, or even the customer to configure the products according both to technical restrictions and the customer's needs. An interactive configuration application has therefore to provide adequate support to guide the user through the problem solving process to come to a working solution. Modeling configuration problems as Constraint Satisfaction Problems (CSP) - as well as extensions like Dynamic CSPs [16] and Generative CSPs [9] - has shown to be applicable to a broad range of configuration problems due to the advantages of comprehensible declarative knowledge representation and effective computability. In a Constraint Satisfaction Problem, the configurable features of the product correspond to constrained problem variables with a predefined range of selectable values. In addition, constraints restrict allowed combinations of value assignments, i.e., legal product constellations. A solution (configuration) is found, if all the problem variables are assigned a value and no constraint is violated. In an interactive configuration session, the user is presented the choices and incrementally enters selections according to his/her specific requirements. During the interactive search for solutions there may be situations where after

[1] This work was partly funded by the EU commission under contract IST-1999-10688.

L. Monostori, J. Váncza, and M. Ali (Eds.): IEA/AIE 2001, LNAI 2070, pp. 746–756, 2001.

a sequence of selections no more solution can be found or a certain value is no longer selectable. The question arises which of these choices have to be taken back to recover from this situation. In another situation, after having already made some selections, the user decides to revise some of the prior choices. The problem then is to reconfigure the system in a way, that most of the other choices can be reused and do not have to be entered again. Note, that the calculations for reconfiguration may be done according to some optimality criterion, i.e., where the number of problem variables to be changed is minimized or some overall costs are minimized.

In this paper we present an approach to interactive reconfiguration where configuration problems are represented as CSPs with n-ary constraints and a model-based diagnostic algorithm is utilized to calculate recovery actions. The search for *suitable* alternative configurations given complete or partial configurations can be done without additional modeling efforts for repair actions. Furthermore the search for repairs can be guided by a domain dependent heuristic which takes change costs for the prior user inputs into account.

After giving an example we define the notion of reconfiguration (repair) of interactive configuration problems. After that we sketch an algorithm for the computation of such reconfiguration alternatives (with repair instructions). In the final sections we compare our work to previous work and end with conclusions.

2 Motivating Example

For demonstration purposes we show a small example from the domain of configurable personal computers, where the user can interactively make selections on certain features. The user selections for the *CSP* are unary constraints on the problem variables. During the session the user wants to revise one of the prior choices and select a feature which is inconsistent with the other choices. Let us assume, our PC has the following configurable features.

model = {*basic, pro, luxury*}. *case*={*desktop, minitower, tower*}.
cd-drive = {*none, 36-speed,48-speed*}. *dvd-drive* = {*no, yes*}.
cd-writer = {*no, yes*}. *scsi-unit* = {*none,10GB, 20GB*}.
ide-unit = {*none, 5GB, 12GB*}. *cpu* = {*PII, PIII, AMD*}.

In addition, certain constraints have to hold on correct configurations, e.g.,
(cd-writer =yes) ⇒ *(scsi-unit* ≠ *none)*.
(cd-writer = *yes)* ∧ *(dvd-drive* = *yes)* ∧ *(cd-drive =yes)* ⇒ *(case* ≠ *desktop)*.
(ide-unit ≠ *none)* ⇒ *(scsi-unit* = *none)*.
(scsi-unit = *none)* ⇒ *(ide-unit* ≠ *none)*.
(model = *basic)* ⟺ *(case* = *desktop)*.

Let us assume the user has already consistently configured some parts of the PC interactively and stated some requirements (R1 ... R7):
(R1) model = *basic, (R2) case* = *desktop, (R3) cd-drive* = *36-speed,*
(R4) dvd-drive = *yes, (R5) cd-writer* = *no, (R6) cpu* = *PII, (R7) ide-unit* = *5GB*.

At this moment, the user decides that he/she wants to have a CD-writer within the configuration. The configurator detects that this choice is not compatible with the prior choices, e.g., the CD-writer will require an SCSI-unit. In addition, not all of the three CD devices will fit into the small desktop case. Therefore, the selection of the CD-writer will not be possible. In addition, typical commercial systems (and online configurators) do not provide adequate support to explain the situation or to help the user to recover from it. In another situation the user may try to revise the decision on the case, where in commercial systems often all decision that were made afterwards will have to be re-entered. Finally, it may be better for the customer to revise his/her decision on the model and select the "pro" model where a mini-tower case is already included and will be cheaper than taking the "base" model where any case other than the desktop causes additional costs. This notion of optimality is also not present in nowadays systems.
It is the goal of our approach to calculate suitable configurations which retain most of the prior decisions or follows some other objective function like a minimal prize. Typically not all user decisions have to be revised and there will be several alternatives. In this context we assume that some part of the user requirements, is fixed and is regarded as a "must". In the example, the requirement "need CD-writer" should definitely not be revised. Possible "good" alternative solutions (S1 ... S4) and repair instructions are therefore, e.g.,
("change cd-drive and IDE-Unit selections" {R3,R7})
S1:(model=basic, case=desktop, cd-drive=none, cd-writer=yes, dvd-writer=yes, scsi-unit=5GB, ide-unit=none, cpu=PII).
("change dvd-drive and IDE-Unit selections" {R4,R7})
S2:(model=basic, case=desktop, cd-drive=36-speed, cd-writer= yes, dvd-writer=none, scsi-unit=5GB, ide-unit=none, cpu = PII).
("change case and IDE-Unit selections" {R2,R7})
S3:(model=basic, case=minitower, cd-drive=36-speed, cd-writer=yes, dvd-writer=yes, scsi-unit=5GB, ide-unit=none, cpu = PII).
("change model, case and IDE-Unit selections" {R1,R2,R7})
S4:(model=pro, case=minitower, cd-drive=36-speed, cd-writer= yes, dvd-writer=yes, scsi-unit=5GB, ide-unit=none, cpu = PII).

In all reconfiguration solutions, an SCSI-unit has to be installed. In addition, in reconfiguration solutions S1 and S2 we give up one of the other CD devices. In S3 we change the case and in S4 the case and the basic model (which already includes the minitower) are changed. The user decision on the CPU type does not necessarily be changed (although it would be possible to configure a completely different system). As a result, the user is prompted a set of possible repair actions (reconfigurations) where the user can select the alternative which matches his preferences best (assuming that we do not want the system to change values without notifying the user). In the following sections we will show how we can calculate a suitable set of reconfiguration solutions using a consistency-based diagnosis approach ([12], [17]) with extensions for our domain. Note, that in general we are not interested in the calculation of all possible other solutions and explanations as there may be too many for larger configuration problems. Our aim is to focus on alternatives where the suggested solutions are minimal with respect to the number of affected variables (user decisions) or some cost function (e.g., price of the components). Note, that if the number and size of these alternatives is too large, this will not help the user too much. The outcome of the diagnostic calculation will be one or more sets of variables (i.e., user decisions) that have to be changed. In addition, possible values for those variables are computed during the search. The affected variables and the value proposals correspond to actions that have to be taken for repair.

In the following section we will treat this model of interactive reconfiguration of constraint-based configuration problems more formally.

3 Defining Reconfiguration for Constraint-Based Configuration Problems

In terms of model-based diagnosis (MBD) a system is a pair $(SD, COMPS)$ where SD is the system description (describing the correct behavior of the components and $COMPS$ are the components of an actual system. Given a set OBS of observations that conflicts with SD and $COMPS$ the goal is to find an explanation (diagnosis), i.e., to find a subset $D \subseteq COMPS$ of components which - if considered faulty - explain the unexpected behavior, i.e. make $SD \cup OBS \cup \{COMPS - D\}$ satisfiable. Both the system and the observations are expressed in terms of logical sentences. We will now match the concepts of MBD with the problem sketched in Section 2.

Definition 1 *Constraint Satisfaction Problem: A Constraint Satisfaction Problem (CSP) is defined as a triplet* $< X, D, C >$, *where*

- $X = \{X1, ..., Xn\}$ *is a finite set of variables,*
- *each* X_i *can take its value from a finite domain* D_{Xi}, *where* $D = \{D_{X1} \cup ... \cup D_{Xn}\}$, *and*
- *a set* C *of constraints restricting the combination of values that variables can take.*

A solution to a CSP is an assignment of a value from its domain to every variable from X, *in such a way that every constraint from* C *is satisfied.* $\sqcap$

The configuration problem (expressed as CSP) corresponds to SD and any solution to the CSP is a valid configuration. During the interactive session, the *user requirements (UR)* are added to the CSP as unary constraints, e.g., *cd-writer=yes* from the example. If there are user constraints on all problem variables, we call UR *complete* and *partial* otherwise.

Definition 2 *User Requirements (UR):* UR *is a set of unary constraints for* $CSP < X, D, C >$ *of the form* $(X_i = V)$, *where* $X_i \in X$, V *is an element of the*

Domain D_{Xi} *and each* X_i *appears at most once in a constraint from* UR. UR *is called "complete" if for every* $x \in X$ *there is an unary constraint* $(x = V)$ *in* UR*; else* UR *is called "partial".* □

The user requirements are divided in two categories: *revisable* requirements RR (corresponding to $COMPS$) and *non-revisable* ones which must not be changed (corresponding to OBS) denoted as NR.

Definition 3 *Reconfiguration Problem: A Reconfiguration Problem (RCP) is a triple* $(< X, D, C >, NR, RR)$ *where* $< X, D, C >$ *is a CSP and* $UR = RR \cup NR$ *are user requirements.* □

A reconfiguration problem arises, if the $CSP < X, D, C \cup UR >$ is unsatisfiable. Our aim is to calculate a (minimal) subset S (diagnosis) of elements from RR, which have to be relaxed, such that the remaining problem is satisfiable.

Definition 4 *Reconfiguration Diagnosis: A Reconfiguration Diagnosis (S) for a Reconfiguration Problem* $(< X, D, C >, NR, RR)$ *is a set* $S \subseteq RR$ *such that the* $CSP < X, D, C \cup NR \cup (RR - S) >$ *is satisfiable.* □

Definition 5 *Minimal Reconfiguration Diagnosis: A Reconfiguration Diagnosis* S *for a RCP* $(< X, D, C >, NR, RR)$ *is said to be minimal iff there exists no* $S' \subset S$ *such that* S' *is a diagnosis for* $(< X, D, C >, NR, RR)$. □

Following a diagnose-and-repair approach we can calculate reconfiguration solutions in the context of a diagnosis:

Definition 6 *Reconfiguration Solution: Given a Reconfiguration Diagnosis* S *for*
$RCP(< X, D, C >, NR, RR)$, *every solution to the* $CSP < X, D, C \cup NR \cup (RR - S) >$ *is a reconfiguration solution for* RCP. □

Note that, if the $CSP < X, D, C \cup NR >$ is satisfiable, a reconfiguration solution will always exist, since in the worst case the Reconfiguration Diagnosis S will contain all elements of RR.

With the definitions so far, all solutions to the original CSP joined with the unrevisable user requirements are therefore legal reconfiguration alternatives. As a result, it is important to have a discrimination criterion for these alternatives, i.e., a preference function describing the "fit" or optimality has to be defined. One possibility to do this, is to assign each constraint from RR a corresponding value (weight), expressing e.g., the costs of changing the value or some user preference. In our example, changing the case of the PC could be undesirable for the user (expressed through preferences/weights). Consequently, a "good" reconfiguration solution would avoid relaxing this requirement. The fit of a reconfiguration solution could therefore be defined as the sum of the weights of the constraints from RR. If the constant value "1" is assigned to each of this constraints, the best reconfiguration solution will be the one, which minimizes the number of constraints in S.

Definition 7 *Optimal Reconfiguration Diagnosis:*
Let $RCP(< X, D, C >, NR, RR)$ be a Reconfiguration Problem and Π be a function assigning each constraint from RR a value w, $w > 0$. Given a Reconfiguration Diagnosis S for RCP, let $\Phi(S) = \Sigma_{e \in S} \Pi(e)$. An Optimal Reconfiguration Diagnosis for RCP is a reconfiguration diagnosis S such that there is no other reconfiguration diagnosis S' such that $\Phi(S') < \Phi(S)$. □

Note, that other optimality functions are possible, which take preferences for individual values for the variables into account.

4 Computing Reconfigurations

Having mapped the reconfiguration problem to a consistency-based diagnosis problem, we can use the standard hitting set algorithm ([17],[12]) for the calculation of diagnoses.

The approach is based on the notion of *conflict sets* and on the algorithm to solve overconstrained CSPs from [3]. In addition we adapt the algorithm for the reconfiguration problem and prune the search tree through the usage of an evaluation function for optimal reconfiguration diagnoses.

Definition 8 *Conflict Set: Given a reconfiguration problem $RCP(< X, D, C >, NR, RR)$, a conflict set is defined as a set $CS \subseteq RR$ such that the $CSP(< X, D, C \cup NR \cup CS >)$ is unsatisfiable.* □

Informally speaking, a conflict set is a subset of the constraints of the revisable user requirements which definitely violate a constraint from the original constraint satisfaction problem with the unrevisable requirements (or makes it at least impossible to get to a solution). We construct a directed acyclic graph (DAG) for the computation of minimal hitting sets according to [17] for the reconfiguration problem $RCP(< X, D, C >, NR, RR)$. The DAG is generated in breadth-first manner, since we are interested in diagnoses of minimal cardinality. The nodes are labeled with conflict sets for the reconfiguration problem, edges leading away are labeled with elements from these conflicts. The path from the root node to a node is denoted as $H(n)$. During the construction of the HS-DAG we make a call to the "theorem prover" (which is a constraint solver in our case) $TP(< X, D, C \cup NR >, RR - H(n) >)$ at each node which returns true and a solution if the $CSP(< X, D, C \cup NR \cup (RR - H(n)) >)$ can be solved. Otherwise, a conflict set for RCP is returned. When calculating solutions we can either compute all possible remaining solutions for that diagnosis, can optimize the solution according to some criterion, or can simply return an arbitrary solution (whereby this solution search can be guided by an additional heuristic).

Additional Closing of Nodes

In addition to the techniques for pruning and closing of nodes from the basic algorithm we can introduce an additional rule to reduce the size of the HS-DAG: If a new node n with $H(n)$ is to be generated, we can calculate $\Phi(H(n))$ which will be the reconfiguration costs for that new node. If there is already another node n' containing a diagnosis S in the tree where $\Phi(S) < \Phi(H(n))$ then node n can be closed, because there cannot be a better reconfiguration (according to the optimality criterion) under that node.

5 Experimental Results

We implemented a prototype environment for the proposed approach, where we support interactive reconfiguration. To allow for web-based interactive configuration we used a Java-based constraint solver library (JSolver [5]). With this extensible set of Java-classes one can solve n-ary constraint satisfaction problems using a forward propagation and backtracking search algorithm efficiently. The implementation of the HS-DAG calculation and the extensions for reconfiguration was also done as a set of Java classes, whereby the HS-DAG algorithm can also be employed for other application scenarios of model-based diagnosis [7]. When building an interactive configuration system, the constraint satisfaction problem has to be defined using the JSolver libraries. This configurator is then incorporated into a graphical user interface, where the user interactively makes his selections. In a situation when no more solutions can be found or some values are no longer selectable, the choices so far are handed over to the diagnostic engine, which calculates reconfiguration alternatives. Finally, the system can present a number n of best reconfiguration alternatives to the user to choose from in order to recover from the current situation. Given our simplified example from the domain of configurable PCs, these results can be computed instantaneously on a standard P-II computer. In our application scenario, both the configurator with the knowledge base, i.e., the selectable features and the allowed combinations of values, and the reconfiguration libraries, are integrated into an applet and can be viewed within the user's browser. So the communication costs with constraint checking/solving at the server side can be avoided. The reconfiguration alternatives can not only be presented to the user to choose from but the values of the selected alternative can also be changed automatically. Our experiments showed the applicability of our approach to real-world sized problems for interactive (online-)configuration with a number of about 30 user inputs. Note, that the coniguration problem itself contains possibly hundreds of variables, but these variables will not affect the computation time for diagnosis, because only the user inputs are revisable. However we found that diagnoses of higher cardinality (more than 7) will not help the user much because the alternatives are too complex. Therefore, the search depth can be limited to a certain level.

For diagnosis of larger problems the **exploitation of structural abstractions** in the system (knowledge base) has shown to be a promising approach ([2],[8]). The idea is to diagnose the system on different levels of abstraction, where several components of the system are grouped together and treated as one. This reduces the number of diagnosable components on the more abstract levels and the search space. The results of diagnosis on this abstract levels can be used to focus the diagnostic process on the next level. For our application domain this notion of grouping of components (in our case the user inputs) is intuitive, because typically the configurable system is decomposed into several parts and for each part there may be several user inputs which can be grouped. When searching for diagnoses we test the system on the more abstract level where always these groups of user inputs are relaxed for one consistency check. Note, that nearly no additional modeling effort for the different abstraction levels is needed (as e.g., described in [2]) because no abstract "behavior" is needed. (For detailed information on the hierarchical approach in another application domain which is implemented in the prototype, see [8].)

6 Related Work

Rich and Sidner [18] present an approach using a collaborative agent based on shared plans supporting the user to cooperatively solve a (e.g., travel planning) problem. The agent guides the user through the interactive process to find a solution. The system records previous user actions and supports the user to recover from situations where the user is lost or stuck in some stage of the process. The system then presents a suggestion to reduce some constraints to come to a solution. This is where our approach can be incorporated to efficiently find a suitable set of recovery actions for configuration problems. The approach of using a collaborative agent can be an interesting for the configuration domain. However, the generation of discourses (maybe using natural language) is beyond the scope of this paper, although the configuration domain can be an application domain for intelligent collaborative agents.

Mannistö et al. [14] describe a general framework for reconfiguration based on a given configuration and reconfiguration language. They assume the explicit existence of reconfiguration rules/operations which can be applied to an existing configuration. The optimality criterion can be expressed through a valuation function for the individual operations. They present a study on current practices of reconfiguration in industry showing the need for more automated support for reconfiguration. Our framework however does not require the existence of explicit reconfiguration rules, whereby the formulation of this knowledge causes additional knowledge acquisition and maintenance efforts. Using their notion of reconfiguration, the main focus lies in reconfiguration of an already installed system, whereas in our approach the interactive setting is of importance (although our approach can also be applied to reconfiguration of existing systems).

Crow and Rushby [6] extend Reiter's [17] framework for model-based diagnosis for fault detection, identification and reconfiguration. They introduce an additional predicate $rcfg$ (similarly to the ab predicate in model-based Diagnosis) on components of the system to be diagnosed. They describe a framework for reconfiguration merging model-based diagnosis with repair, and claiming that automated repair should be the consequence of the diagnostic process. However, in their approach, the reconfiguration knowledge (which comprises a model of "spare" components) has to be modeled explicitly. In addition, integration of optimality criteria is only considered to a small amount, whereas we think that the notion of "good" or "optimal" reconfigurations is an intrinsic feature of reconfiguration.

Bakker et al. [3] show an algorithm for diagnosing over-constrained Constraint Satisfaction Problems using a model-based diagnosis algorithm. This work strongly correlates with ours from the viewpoint of computation and algorithms. However, they focus on general CSPs and not on (interactive) configuration problems with their specific characteristics of constrainedness. In addition, in their algorithm, any of the given constraints of the knowledge base can be revised, whereas we only relax user decisions, i.e., the unary constraints. Therefore the size of the knowledge base, i.e., the number of constraints, does not affect the size of the HS-DAG, which is a limiting factor for efficient diagnosis. In our approach, only the user-selectable variables (resp. only the already given inputs) are taken into account making the resulting HS-DAG smaller in size.

The notion that solving a configuration problem by repairing an existing (and inconsistent) configuration can be more effective than solving the problem from scratch has been brought up already in one of the first configuration design problem solvers [13]. In this system, based on the VT elevator domain, a propose-and-revise strategy problem solving method was described using fixes when parts of the configuration (design) are inconsistent. A heuristic method of repairing a special inconsistent Constraint Satisfaction Problem (n-queens) was presented in [15]. They argue, that for this problem it is more effective to repair an existing setting (configuration) based on the min-conflicts heuristic than building a solution from scratch. Their approach uses a hill-climbing algorithm (with or without backtracking) where one starts with a situation which is "near" to a solution and incrementally changes parts of the configuration. At each step, a slight improvement of the overall situation is achieved. This can be related to our approach, where we start from a "good" situation (the user requirements which can be a complete configuration) and try to reduce conflicts and do not calculate solutions from scratch. Compared to our approach, this repair approach and other (local repair algorithms) only return one single reconfiguration without regarding any optimality criterions and without showing different alternatives.

Freuder et al. [11] describe an approach to solve overconstrained Constraint Satisfaction Problems, where we have a situation, where no solution exists (which can be compared to our reconfiguration situation where the unary user constraints make the problem overconstrained). In their approach, the goal is therefore not to find a "maximal" solution, where all constraints are satisfied (which is not possible) but rather find a solution where a maximal number of constraints is satisfied. During the search process, a search path does not fail when a single inconsistency is encountered but rather when enough inconsistencies (at a certain cut-off number) have been encountered, which can be compared to some extent with the additional tree pruning in our diagnostic algorithm. However, in the reconfiguration setting only the unary user constraints can be relaxed but not the constraints from the original CSP like in Freuder's approach.

Amilhastre et al. [1] present an approach to handle interactivity during the search for solutions for a constraint based configuration problem. They deal with situations during an interactive configuration session, when no solution can be found or features are no more selectable at a certain stage. They propose the construction of a finite automaton based on all possible solutions of the CSP in a preprocessing step before the configuration system is employed. At run time, corresponding answers or explanations (i.e., repair possibilities) for the user questions mentioned above can be calculated. This interactive setting can also be handled with our approach for small-sized problems, whereby immediate response times cannot be guaranteed. In a larger reconfiguration setting, the applicability of constructing an automaton describing all possible solutions to the original CSP may be limited since the graph operations are still exponential in the size of revisable user choices.

7 Conclusions

More and more configurable products are offered to the customer and made interactive configuration systems a valuable tool to support the customer in assembling a functioning system according to his specific needs. The complexity of the interactive configuration process creates new demands on the user interface, because the configuration process is an interactive search process in constraint-based systems. In nowadays systems, only little support is given to guide the user in cases no adequate solution can be found after the user entered some choices. In this paper we present an approach for an intelligent support for interactive configuration of constraint-based configuration problems. Reconfiguration (repair) alternatives can be presented to the user in cases the search process has reached a dead end. We described a framework for computing (optimal) reconfiguration solutions based on a standard algorithm for model-based diagnosis using conflicts for focusing purposes and extensions for our domain. In our approach, the reconfiguration knowledge (repair actions) does not have to be modeled explicitly but is inherently given in the basic underlying CSP model. Our approach is capable of providing reconfiguration solutions for CSPs (and also Dynamic Constraint Satisfaction problems) with n-ary constraints given partial or complete initial configurations. An extensible prototype environment was built to test the applicability of the approach in an interactive setting, whereby the implemented libraries can be incorporated into a system with additional user support.

References

1. J. Amilhastre, H. Fargier: Handling interactivity in a constraint-based approach of configuration, ECAI'2000 Workshop on Configuration, Berlin, 2000.
2. K. Autio, R. Reiter: Structural abstraction in Model-based Diagnosis, Proc. ECAI'98, Brighton, UK, 1998.
3. R.R. Bakker and F. Dikker and F. Tempelman and P.M. Wognum. Diagnosing and solving over-determined constraint satisfaction problems. Proc: IJCAI'93, p. 276-281, Chambery, Morgan Kaufmann, 1993.
4. D. Brady, K. Kerwin, D. Welch et al.: Customizing for the masses, Business Week, No. 3673, March 2000.

5. Hon Wai Chun , Constraint Programming in Java with JSolver, Proc. PACLP'99, London, UK, 1999.
6. J. Crow, J. M. Rushby: Model-Based Reconfiguration: Toward an Integration with Diagnosis, AAAI'91, California, 1991.
7. A. Felfernig, G.Friedrich, D. Jannach, and M. Stumptner, Consistency based diagnosis of configuration knowledge-bases. Proceedings ECAI 2000, Berlin, 2000.
8. A. Felfernig, G.Friedrich, D. Jannach, and M. Stumptner: Exploiting structural abstraction for consistency-based diagnosis of configurator knowlegde bases. ECAI Workshop on Configuration, Berlin, 2000.
9. G. Fleischanderl, G. Friedrich, A. Haselboeck, H. Schreiner and M. Stumptner, Configuring Large Systems Using Generative Constraint Satisfaction, IEEE Intelligent Systems, July/August, 1998.
10. G. Friedrich, W. Nejdl: Choosing Observations and Actions in Model-Based Diagnosis/Repair Systems, Proc. KR'92, Massachusetts, 1992.
11. E. Freuder, R. J. Wallace: Partial Constraint Satisfaction, Artificial Intelligence (58), 1992.
12. R. Greiner, B.A. Smith, and R.W. Wilkerson: A correction to the algorithm in Reiter's theory of diagnosis. Artificial Intelligence, 41(1), 1989.
13. S. Marco, J. Stout, and J. McDermott: VT: An expert elevator designer that uses knowledge-based backtracking. AI Magazine, 9(2), 1988.
14. T. Mannistö., T. Soininen, J. Tiihonen and R. Sulonen. Framework and Conceptual Model for Reconfiguration. AAAI'99 Workshop on Configuration, Orlando, Florida, 1999.
15. S. Minton, M. D. Johnston, A. Philips, P. Laird, Minimizing conflicts: a heuristic repair method for constraint satisfaction problems, Artificial Intelligence 58, p. 161-205, 1992.
16. S. Mittal, B. Falkenhainer: Dynamic Constraint Satisfaction Problems, In Proc. AAAI'90, August 1990.
17. R. Reiter: A theory of diagnosis from first principles. Artificial Intelligence, 32(1), 1987.
18. C. Rich and C.L. Sidner, Adding a collaborative agent to graphical user interfaces, Proc. ACM Symposium on User Interface Software and Technology, Seattle, 1996.

Knowledge Decomposition for Conceptual Product Design: An Approach to Develop Specific Domain Expert Systems for Supporting Concurrent Engineering Projects

Rodrigo Hermes de Araújo[1,2], Osmar Possamai[2], and Luiz Dalla Valentina[3]

[1] Multibras S.A. Eletrodomesticos (Whirlpool Corporation), Rua Dona Francisca, 7200, Joinville – SC - Brazil – 89219-900
rodrigo_h_araujo@multibras.com.br

[2] Universidade Federal de Santa Catarina-UFSC, Departamento de Engenharia de Produção, Campus Universitário, Trindade, Florianópolis - SC – Brazil – 88040-900
possamai@eps.ufsc.br

[3] Universidade do Estado de Santa Catarina – UDESC, Departamento de Engenharia Mecânica, Campus Universitário, Bom Retiro, Caixa Postal 631, Joinville – SC - Brazil – 89223-100
dem2ldv@joinville.udesc.br.

Abstract. The conceptual product design is highly dependent on people's experience, creativity, tacit knowledge and their availability. The proposed methodology guides the product design knowledge decomposition and acquisition, including information about consumers, product and manufacturing process required at the conceptual design stage. The methodology also proposes a framework for building up an expert system to support concurrent engineering teams early in the design by simulating the design process. The expert system, using object oriented programming structure, has the objective of detailing the product components from specific product requirements. A case study was developed in an appliance company to validate the proposed methodology. Several cases were ran comparing the simulated results with real projects. The speed in generating and evaluating product concept alternatives, the framework for knowledge construction and the transformation of tacit (company technology) into explicit knowledge (that can be manageable) were identified as the main benefits.

1 Introduction

Launching new products in the market place has became a fundamental factor for improving a company's competitiveness. But to achieve success, these products must be launched in the right time, that means, as fast as possible because competition has the same goals. So there is a huge pressure on product design teams to develop better products in the shortest time. Management and engineering systems have been developed for improving the design process but their application depends on people's experience, creativity, specific knowledge and availability (Chen & Occeña [5] and Yassine [18]). Conceptual product design is a crucial area in the design process and, besides this, it is highly dependent on people and on their tacit knowledge.

As more and more companies are developing products in families and platforms (Keane [10]; Pulkkinen [15]; Tichem [17]), there is an opportunity for using

L. Monostori, J. Váncza, and M. Ali (Eds.): IEA/AIE 2001, LNAI 2070, pp. 757-766, 2001.

artificial intelligence techniques to speed up the knowledge transfer process between concurrent engineering team members in the design process. Nowadays knowledge is becoming a competitive advantage (Frank [7]) and there is a need to make tacit knowledge an explicit one (Handenhoven [8]).

In available literature, the only knowledge acquisition techniques presented are generic ones such as interviews, protocol analysis and book reading (Durkin [6] and Sriram [16]). These generic methods do not work well to structure knowledge acquisition because they focus on contacting experts and their efficiency greatly depends on the experience and ability of the knowledge engineer rather than on experts' experiences. Some authors proposed techniques for helping this process but they do not direct address the problem of knowledge acquisition (Liu & Brown [12] and Myint & Tabucanon [13]).

In this paper we present a formal methodology which handles knowledge decomposition, knowledge acquisition and expert system construction for supporting concurrent engineering teams (Araujo [2]). The methodology focus on extracting and acquiring all knowledge about market, product and process required in the conceptual design stage and on structuring an expert system, that can simulate the product design process in this stage.. It is also discussed that an advantage of this methodology is to make tacit knowledge an explicit one and to help improving the overall knowledge of team members, thus enhancing their satisfaction.

2 Design Classification

Several authors have classified design tasks (Brown & Chandrasekaran [4], Goel [9], Pahl & Beitz [14]) according to different points of views. These classifications cover only 3 categories and they have in common that category 3 designs must use known knowledge. That does not mean that category 3 designs are easy, only that no innovations are required. Indeed, evolution design, parametric design, and modular design are the most common types of designs applied by companies all around the world because the required knowledge is available and easier to manage. The methodology to be discussed is specifically applied to design processes that fall into category 3 design.

3 The Methodology

The aim of this methodology is to give a tool to concurrent engineering teams for helping the task of developing and analyzing product concepts in the design concept stage as well as providing the team an important tool for structuring knowledge acquisition and knowledge representation in product design. The methodology is divided in 5 stages (Figure 1): (1) Problem definition; (2) Knowledge base conceptualization; (3) Knowledge base representation; (4) System development and testing; and (5) Knowledge and system documentation. As it will be shown, the first 3 stages are related to knowledge acquisition (involves product as well as artificial intelligence knowledge) and represents the planning stage in a PDCA (Plan-Do-Check-Act) cycle. The 4th is related to system construction (involves artificial intelligence as well as programming knowledge) and represents the execution and checking stage. The last one is a standardization stage for ensuring that all knowledge will be kept within the team and available to be used in future improvements.

3.1 Stage 1 - Problem Definition

At the first stage the product and its decomposition level are defined and resources and time schedule are assigned. It is compulsory to have experts on product design, marketing, manufacturing process and artificial intelligence. These experts will need to work together as a team in brainstorming sessions and technical meetings.

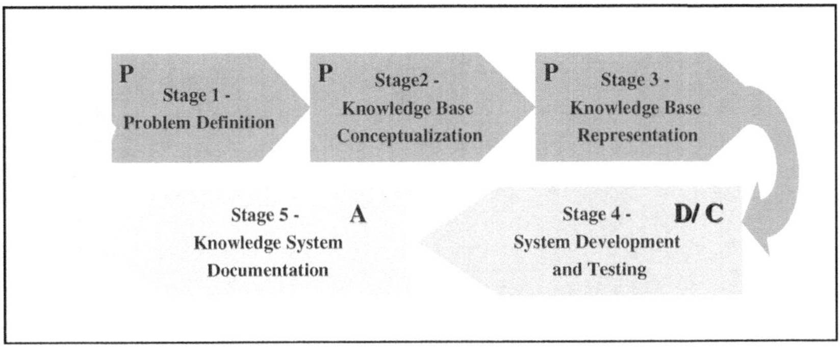

Fig. 1. Methodology Stages and the PDCA Process.

3.2 Stage 2 - Knowledge Base Conceptualization

The second stage has the important and critical goal of acquiring product, design process and manufacturing process knowledge. It provides the team a structured path for achieving the goal. For easing of explanation, it is divided in seven steps, as seen in Fig. 2 and Fig. 3. Figure 2 shows steps 1 to 5, from product planning to parts decomposition, and Fig. 3 shows steps 6 and 7 (process information and knowledge modeling).

In the Product Planning Matrix (Step 1- Engineering requirements) engineering requirements are identified (Y1, ..., Yk, ..., Yn, where $1 \leq k \leq n$) for product definition and correlated against each other; this data must be represented in a matrix (Akao [1], ASI [3]). For each engineering requirement (EngR) the set of values in which it is valid must be identified. All engineering requirements (Yk) will be input data for product design.

The next step is the engineering requirements modeling (Step 2), where algorithmic and heuristics rules must be developed for each previously identified correlation of EngR. The aim is to get $Yi = f(Yp, Yk)$, where $p,k \neq i$. In parallel (Step 3- Product Architecture), the product architecture must be deployed from the product concept and made explicit in a top-down decomposition showing how each part is related to other. All parts interfaces must be shown.

The Step 4 – Product Map requires that previous steps be completed and its goal is to get all critical part attributes (x_i , i integer). Critical part attributes are part specification although engineering requirements are product specification. Critical part attributes must be found by deploying a specific engineering requirement from product level to part level, using the product architecture and expert knowledge. One must identify if any specific usability or environmental characteristic can also affect the specific EngR. For each part attribute, the set of values or a standard value valid for the product must be identified.

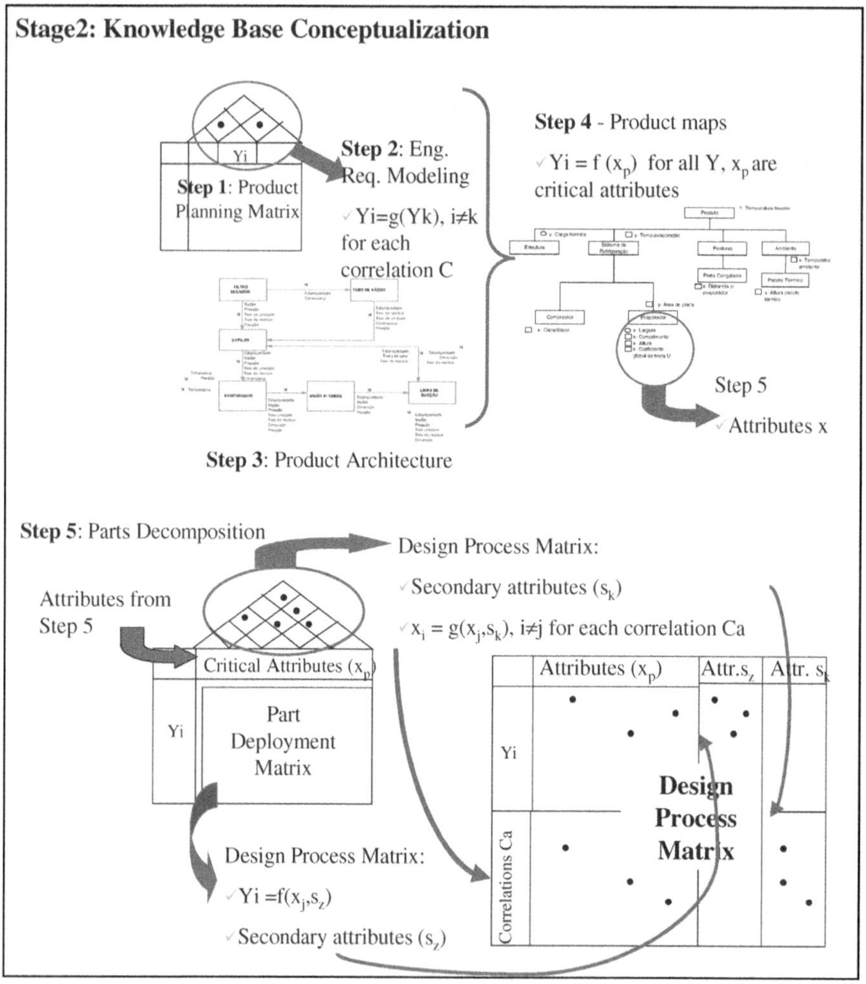

Fig. 2. Knowledge Base Conceptualization Framework – Steps 1 to 5. This figure shows how is the information flow between steps. Arrows indicate information transfer without transformation.

At next step (Step 5 – Parts Decomposition) the goal is to correlate all attributes found to each engineering requirement by using a matrix (Part Deployment Matrix). From this matrix, it is identified where there is a relation between two attributes. Using the Incidence Matrix concept (Kusiak & Larson [11]), each attribute correlation is now considered a design constraint. The attribute correlation must be added to the engineering requirements axis in the Part Deployment Matrix and then the Design Process Matrix is created. For each engineering requirement and each attribute correlation, algorithmic and heuristics rules must be developed showing the relation Yi = function $f(x_j)$ or x_i = function $g(x_j, i \neq j)$. To make these rules explicit, new attributes may be required – these attributes will be called secondary attributes. All secondary attributes must be placed in the critical attributes axis in the Design Process Matrix.

The new matrix clearly identifies which attributes are required for solving the engineering requirements and also identifies how these attributes are related to each other due to the product concept. But it is not a complete matrix because it does not have any process information.

The manufacturing process flowchart (Step 6) is required for identifying where the process puts constraints on product design, that means, how part attributes have their set of values limited. The manufacturing process flowchart must have the complete sequence of activities for manufacturing the final product. For each activity one must identify the required attribute inputs and the required resource (equipment, tooling or technology). If any required resource is restricting a part attribute set of values, it must be made explicit by rules. This new set of values (rule) must be understood as a constraint in the design process and therefore it must be added in the engineering requirements and attribute correlation axis of the Design Process Matrix, as seen in Fig. 3.

The Design Process Matrix now contains knowledge about product design and process, but it does not show how the design process itself starts. So, the remaining step (Step 7 – Knowledge modeling) is to make explicit the design process. The design process should be deployed in sequence of design tasks and represented in a flowchart. To each task the required part attributes must be associated as inputs and outputs, and if it is the case, the required engineering requirements as inputs. These part attributes must be classified according to the origin of its generation: (i) user must give it; (ii) data to be stored in database and retrieved when required; (iii) result of inference engine from initial data. The part attributes must be reorganized in the Design Process Matrix in the same order as required in the design process. As seen in Step 5, expressions have already been found to explicit part attributes relations. Each part attribute that is a result of inference engine must be solved by using engineering requirements, and other part attributes previously solved or known by developing expressions like x_i = function $g(Y_k, x_n, i \neq n)$ and all x_n must be known.

The completion of Stage 2 consolidates the knowledge acquisition in a systematic way and makes it explicit for the whole company. The next stage is to guide the acquired knowledge representation.

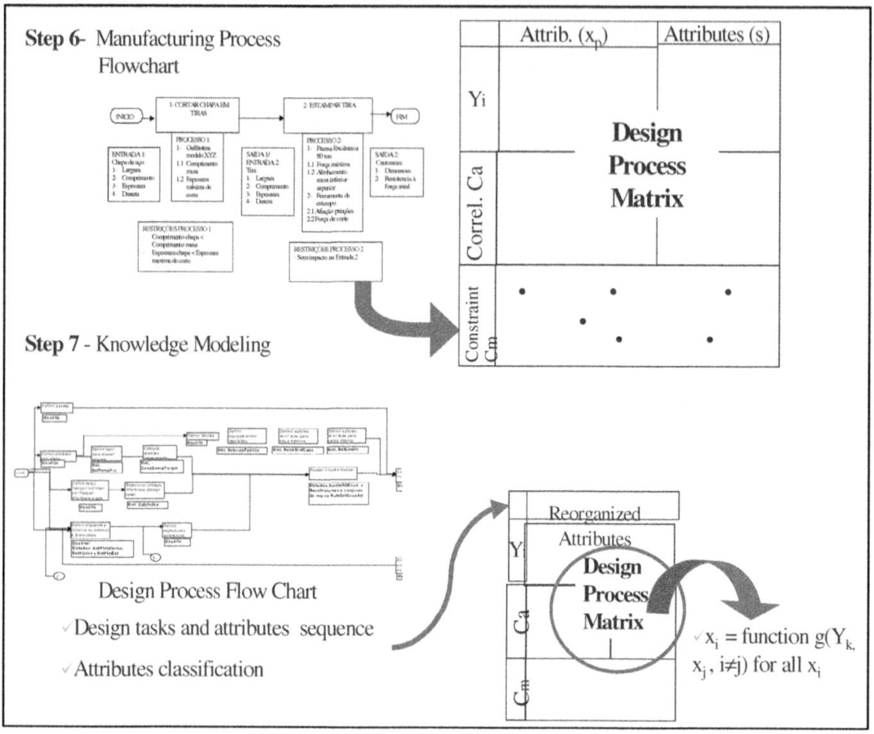

Fig. 3. Knowledge Base Conceptualization Framework – Steps 6 and 7. This figure shows how new information is added to the Design Process Matrix and its benefits.

3.3 Stage 3 - Knowledge Base Representation

Several representation techniques are available in the literature, but there is not a methodology for easing its application in product design. Stage 3 (Knowledge base representation) proposes a method for encoding the knowledge acquired in the previous stage using object oriented programming by guiding the development of object-attribute structures, rules, frames and the design process logic.

All information about manufacturing process must be represented in a specific class. Each kind of equipment must be represented in a specific subclass, such as roll formers subclass, cutters subclass, etc. A specific equipment will be an instance of the respective subclass. Each part attributes restriction is represented by the slots of these subclasses which must contain the allowed set of limits.

Each expression x_i = function g(Y_k, x_n , i≠n) must be represented by methods inside classes or subclasses or by production rules if it is not an algorithmic expression and they must be associated to the design task in which this information is generated or required.

3.4 Stage 4 - System Development and Testing

This stage requires a team member with programming skills. All objects, their slots, production rules and methods within frames must be coded. System interfaces must be developed for enabling the user to provide information whenever required (as identified in stage 2) and also to present the results. Specific functions for sending messages to objects must be developed for ensuring that the design process logic will be followed. The system must be checked for consistency by experts.

3.5 Stage 5 - Knowledge and System Documentation

The purpose of this stage is to ensure that all work done is registered. The knowledge documentation enables the experts tacit knowledge to become explicit for the whole company and it contains all matrixes, the product architecture, all product maps and the design process flowchart. The system documentation is required for helping inexperienced users to use the system.

4 A Case Study and Results

An appliance company with worldwide presence was selected for applying and validating the methodology. This company was selected because it uses concurrent engineering for developing products and because of the high number of Class 3 projects it develops. The methodology was applied by a concurrent engineering team and the system developed, called SEAPP, was validated with real data and by users.

4.1 The Application

The methodology was followed and all steps were executed in Stage 2. The main outcomes were that 9 product maps were done and 54 critical part attributes were identified. The Part Deployment Matrix was completed and critical parts that affect several requirements were selected. For completing the Design Process Matrix, 89 secondary attributes were identified. So, this means that it was required 89 secondary attributes for supporting the existence of 54 critical attributes. The manufacturing process analysis showed that 21 constraints were found related to 4 equipment (roll formers, door formers, wrapper assembly line and product assembly line). The design process flow was agreed and all tasks were identified.

The key factors that enabled a successful knowledge acquisition were the experts dedication and their knowledge about the product, the usage of known tools and the systematic approach. The team identified that the fact that knowledge was not homogeneous within the team, and the excessive number of attributes dealt with, were hurdles in applying the methodology; but at the same time they recognized that at the end the team was abler and much more knowledgeable about the product. Other benefits are that tacit knowledge was made explicit, critical attributes were identified and manufacturing constraints in product design became clear to the design team.

For representing knowledge, the object hierarchical structure was finished with 68 object classes and subclasses and 121 instances. A class to store historical data about former products was created for taking advantage of case-based reasoning techniques. The design tasks in which knowledge must be generated as a result of inference engine from initial data were represented by 26 production rules and 41 methods (inside frames).

The object communication strategy was based in the design process flow. It was a clear path used in evaluating the system. For user visualization and control, 5 graphical windows were created: 3 for setting initial data (project objectives) and 2 for presenting results. Besides this, a written report is also available to the user. The time spent in encoding the knowledge, creating the interfaces and testing each module in an isolated way was 35% of the total time used for finishing the expert system. The others 65% were spent to test the whole system, correct typing mistakes and adjust logic between modules. These results show that encoding the whole knowledge, as a coherent system is the second critical bottleneck after knowledge acquisition.

4.2 The Validation of SEAPP

The SEAPP system was tested and validated by 2 criteria: (i) Efficiency in detailing a product concept; (ii) Importance in supporting concurrent engineering teams.

The efficiency in detailing a product concept was measured by using data of past projects and comparing the parts specifications given by the system with real parts specifications. The system was ran for 4 projects and all data was collected and compared. The difference between the real data and the simulated one was calculated for each part attribute in percentage (attribute deviation-DA). For the same project, the average of all DA in module gave the project average absolute deviation – DMP, considering that all part attributes have the same importance. With similar thought, we also calculated the attribute average absolute deviation (DMA) within the 4 projects. The partial results are seen in table 1.

Table 1. System efficiency. It shows calculated deviations for each simulation run.

Project	Model 1	Model 2	Model 3	Model 4	
Variables	DA %	DA%	DA %	DA %	Attribute average absolute dev. (DMA)
External height	-0,8%	-1,4%	0,7%	-0,4%	0,8%
Internal height	-1,3%	-2,0%	0,7%	0,9%	1,2%
Evaporator height	0,0%	0,0%	0,0%	0,0%	0,0%
Evaporator width	0,4%	0,4%	-5,9%	0,4%	1,8%
Evaporator length	-1,6%	-1,6%	1,1%	0,8%	1,3%
Suction line length	-3,4%	5,3%	3,8%	5,7%	4,6%
Mettalic sides weight	5,1%	5,1%			5,1%
Heat exchange area	10,5%	-4,7%	11,6%	-12,5%	9,8%
Heat loop length				3,4%	3,4%
Compressor model	0,0%	0,0%	0,0%	0,0%	0,0%
Polyurethane weight	-2,0%	-4,3%	4,9%	-8,3%	4,9%
Product average absolute dev. (DMP)	2,5%	2,5%	3,2%	3,2%	

The users considered the calculated DMP low, especially because SEAPP is aimed to be used at the product concept stage in the product design process. The calculated DMA were considered negligible for almost all attributes, except one –

heat exchange area. Further analysis showed that the heat exchange area was not matching well because real products were deviating from the recommended standards.

The importance in supporting concurrent engineering teams was measured by applying a questionnaire to users after their trials with SEAPP system. They pointed out that the system can reduce product design concept time, optimize resources usage, turn tacit in explicit knowledge and be used as a training tool. They evaluated the efficiency as good (as measured before) and did not think that the system was difficult for using, but they did think that the users must be slightly knowledgeable about the product.

5 Conclusions

The results seen in the case study showed that the methodology has several important points and it also has broadened the area of knowledge acquisition techniques. The benefits can be found in 3 domains: (i) product design process; (ii) knowledge acquisition and decomposition and (iii) team motivation and learning.

In the knowledge acquisition and decomposition domain an important contribution was the development of a procedure to acquire knowledge about product design in a systematic approach and its decomposition into an easy structure for knowledge representation. In the product design process domain the main benefits are: the speed in generating and evaluating product concept alternatives, increased capability in decision making by enlarging the number of simulated alternatives, the setting up of an information system about technical requirements unfeasibility, effectiveness in part specification, and understanding of manufacturing constraints in design. In the team motivation and learning domain the advantages lie in the transformation of tacit into explicit knowledge and in increased team members satisfaction due to incremental knowledge gains about product design, as well as in their ability to understand and handle the concept design factors.

Acknowledgements. The support of Whirlpool Corporation, mainly the Product Development Center in Joinville- Brazil, is gratefully appreciated.

References

1. AKAO, Y.: Quality Function Deployment - Integrating Customer Requirements into Product Design. Cambridge MA: Productivity Press, (1990)
2. ARAÚJO, R.H.: Decomposição de Conhecimento para Projeto de Produto- Abordagem para Estruturar Sistema Especialista como Sistema Auxiliar de Informações em Projetos de Engenharia Simultânea. Master Degree Thesis at Production Engineering Dept – Federal University of Santa Catarina (Universidade Federal de Santa Catarina-UFSC). Brazil. (2000)
3. ASI - American Supplier Institute.: Quality Function Deployment - Implementation Manual for Three Day QFD Workshop. Version 3.4. Michigan - USA, (1989)
4. BROWN, D.C. & CHANDRASEKARAN, B.: **Design Problem Solving: Knowledge Structures and Control Strategies**. Pitman. London. (1989)

5. CHEN, C. & OCCEÑA, L.G.: *Knowledge Decomposition for a Product Design Blackboard Expert System*. **Artificial Intelligence in Engineering**, 14, (2000) 71–82
6. DURKIN, J.: **Expert System - Design and Development**. Prentice Hall: New Jersey - USA, (1994)
7. FRANK, D.: *The Importance of Knowledge Management for BMW*. **International Conference on Engineering Design (ICED)**, Vol. 1, Munich, August, (1999) 33-40
8. HANDENHOVEN, E.V. & TRASSAERT, P.: *Design Knowledge and Design Skills*. **International Conference on Engineering Design (ICED)**, Vol. 1, Munich, August, (1999) 153-158
9. GOEL, A K.: *Design, Analogy and Creativity*. **IEEE Expert**, May-June (1997) 62-70
10. KEANE, A J.: **Case for Support for an Investigation into Flexible Engineering Design Methods Using Knowledge Based CAD Systems and Evolutionary Search Methods**. http:// www.soton.ac.uk/~ajk/indemand.txt, (1998)
11. KUSIAK, A. & LARSON, N.: *Decomposition and Representation Methods in Mechanical Design. Journal of Mechanical Design* - **Transactions of the ASME**, Vol 117B, June (1995) 17-24
12. LIU, J. & BROWN, D.C.: *Generating Design Decomposition Knowledge for Parametric Design Problems*. In J.S. Gero and F. Sudweeks (eds.), **Artificial Intelligence in Design 1994**, Netherlands. (1994) 661-678
13. MYINT, S. & TABUCANON, M.T.: *The Framework for an Expert System to Generate Alternative Products in Concurrent Engineering Design*. **Computers in Industry**. Volume 37, Issue 2, September (1998) 125-134
14. PAHL, G. & BEITZ, W.: **Engineering Design: A Systematic Approach**. Springer Verlag, (1988)
15. PULKKINEN, A., LEHTONEN, T. & RIITAHUHTA, A.: *Design for Configuration – Methodology for Product Family Development*. **International Conference on Engineering Design (ICED)**, Vol. 3. Munich, August, (1999) 1495-1500
16. SRIRAM ,R. D.: **Intelligent Systems for Engineering: a Knowledge-Based Approach**. Springer-Verlag London Limited. Great Britain. (1997)
17. TICHEM, M., ANDREASEN, M.M. & RIITAHUHTA, A.:*Design of Product Families*. **International Conference on Engineering Design (ICED)**, Vol. 2. Munich, August, (1999) 1039-1042
18. YASSINE, A A., CHELST, K.R. & FALKENBURG, D.R.: *A Decision Analytic Framework for Evaluating Concurrent Engineering*. **IEEE Transactions on Engineering Management**, vol.46, n.2, May (1999) 144-157

Intelligent Control Synthesis of Manufacturing Systems*

František Čapkovič[1] and Peter Čapkovič[2]

[1] Institute of Control Theory and Robotics, Slovak Academy of Sciences
Dúbravská cesta 9, 842 37 Bratislava, Slovak Republic,
utrrcapk@nic.savba.sk,
http://www.savba.sk/~utrrcapk/capkhome.htm
[2] Department of Informatics, Faculty of Electrical Engineering and Information Technology, Slovak University of Technology,
Ilkovičova 3, 812 19 Bratislava, Slovak Republic

Abstract. An alternative approach to the synthesis of the intelligent control of manufacturing systems understood to be the discrete-event dynamic systems (DEDS) is presented in this paper. The Petri nets (PN) are used to express analytically both the model of DEDS to be controlled and to represent knowledge about the control task specifications expressing goal criteria of control, constraints and further external conditions. Both the DEDS model and the knowledge base (KB) are simultaneously used in the procedure of the control system synthesis. The elementary control possibilities are generated (by means of the model) in any step of the procedure and tested with respect to existence conditions. When there are several control possibilities satisfying the conditions the most suitable one is chosen by means of the KB.

1 Introduction

DEDS are large-scale, asynchronouos, complex systems with concurrency or/and parallelism among subsystem activities, e.g. manufacturing systems, transport systems, communications systems. Their behaviour is influenced by the occurrency of discrete events that start or stop the activities of the subsystems. The problem of the successful automatic control of them is very actual. The main aim of this paper is to point out a simple alternative approach to dealing with the problem of the knowledge-based intelligent control synthesis. On that way the PN-based based model of the system to be controlled as well as the rule-based representation of knowledge about the control task specifications are utilized. The presented approach is built on base of [2]-[5] with utilizing the results of [6].

* Partially supported by the Slovak Grant Agency for Science (VEGA) under grants # 2/4036/97-99 and # 2/7145/20

L. Monostori, J. Váncza, and M. Ali (Eds.): IEA/AIE 2001, LNAI 2070, pp. 767–776, 2001.

2 The PN-Based Model of DEDS

PN-based models [13] are used very frequently. An analogy with the ordinary PN (OPN) is used also here, in order to build the mathematical model of the DEDS to be controlled. It is the analogy between the DEDS subprocesses or activities and the OPN positions as well as the analogy between the DEDS discrete events and the OPN transitions. The OPN are understood here (as to their structure) to be the directed bipartite graphs

$$\langle P, T, F, G \rangle; \quad P \cap T = \emptyset; \quad F \cap G = \emptyset \tag{1}$$

where $P = \{p_1, ..., p_n\}$ is a finite set of the OPN positions with $p_i\,,\, i = 1, n$, being the elementary positions; $T = \{t_1, ..., t_m\}$ is a finite set of the OPN transitions with $t_j\,,\, j = 1, m$, being the elementary transitions; $F \subseteq P \times T$ is a set of the oriented arcs entering the transitions. The corresponding arcs incidence matrix $\mathbf{F} = \{f_{ij}\}\,,\, f_{ij} \in \{0, 1\}\,,\, i = 1, n\,;\, j = 1, m$. The element f_{ij} represents the absence (when 0) or presence (when 1) of the arc oriented from the position p_i to its output transition t_j; $G \subseteq T \times P$ is a set of the oriented arcs emerging from the transitions. The arcs incidence matrix $\mathbf{G} = \{g_{ij}\}\,,\, g_{ij} \in \{0, 1\}\,,\, i = 1, m\,;\, j = 1, n$. The element g_{ij} represents the occurrence of the arc oriented from the transition t_i to its output position p_j; $\emptyset$ is an empty set.

However, PN have also their dynamics - marking of their positions and its dynamic development. The simplest form of the OPN-based model of the DEDS dynamics in analytical terms is the following linear discrete system

$$\mathbf{x}_{k+1} = \mathbf{x}_k + \mathbf{B}.\mathbf{u}_k \quad , \quad k = 0, N \tag{2}$$

$$\mathbf{B} = \mathbf{G}^T - \mathbf{F} \tag{3}$$

$$\mathbf{F}.\mathbf{u}_k \leq \mathbf{x}_k \tag{4}$$

where k is the discrete step of the dynamics development; $\mathbf{x}_k = (\sigma^k_{p_1}, ..., \sigma^k_{p_n})^T$ is the n-dimensional state vector of the system in the step k. The elements $\sigma^k_{p_i} \in \{0, c_{p_i}\}$, $i = 1, n$ express the states of the DEDS elementary subprocesses or operations. The passivity is expressed by $\sigma_{p_i} = 0$ and the activity is expressed by $0 < \sigma^k_{p_i} \leq c_{p_i}$ where c_{p_i} is the capacity of the PN position p_i as to its marking. In the so called safety PN the $c_{p_i} = 1$; $\mathbf{u}_k = (\gamma^k_{t_1}, ..., \gamma^k_{t_m})^T$ is the m-dimensional control vector of the system in the step k. The elements $\gamma^k_{t_j} \in \{0, 1\}$, $j = 1, m$ represent occurring of the DEDS elementary discrete events (1 - presence, 0 - absence), e.g. starting or ending elementary subprocesses, other activities, failures, etc.; $\mathbf{B}$, $\mathbf{F}$, $\mathbf{G}$ are, respectively, $(n \times m)$, $(n \times m)$ and $(m \times n)$ structural matrices of constant elements. $\mathbf{F} = \{f_{ij}\}\,;\, i = 1,\, n\,,\, j = 1,\, m$; $f_{ij} \in \{0, M_{f_{ij}}\}$ expresses the causal relations among the DEDS states (the causes) and the discrete events (the consequences) where 0 expresses the nonexistence and $M_{f_{ij}} > 0$ the existence and multiplicity of the corresponding causal relations. $\mathbf{G} = \{g_{ij}\}\,;\, i = 1,\, m\,,\, j = 1,\, n$; $g_{ij} \in \{0, M_{g_{ij}}\}$ expresses analogically the causal relation among the discrete events (the causes) and the DEDS states (the consequences). Both of these matrices are the arcs incidence matrices; $(.)^T$ symbolizes the matrix or vector transposition.

3 The Control Synthesis Problem

The control synthesis problem is that of finding a sequence of the control vectors $\mathbf{u}_k$, $k = 0, N$ that is able to transfer the controlled system from the given initial state $\mathbf{x}_0$ to a prescribed terminal state $\mathbf{x}_t$. However as a rule, the DEDS control policy cannot be expressed in analytical terms. Knowledge concerning the control task specifications (like constraints, criteria, etc.) is usually expressed only verbally. Consequently, the proper knowledge representation (e.g. the rule-based one) is needed in the form of a domain oriented KB. KB is utilized at the choice of the most suitable control vector $\mathbf{u}_k$ in any step k when there are several possibilities how to proceed to the next step (in order to avoid any ambiguity as to the further development of the DEDS dynamics).

In order to find the suitable control vector $\mathbf{u}_k$ able to transfer the system from the existing state $\mathbf{x}_k$ into a following state $\mathbf{x}_{k+1}$ the simple procedure can be used. It can be concisely described as follows:

START

- $k = 0$ i.e. $\mathbf{x}_k = \mathbf{x}_0$; $\mathbf{x}_0$ is an initial state; $\mathbf{x}_t$ is a terminal state

LABEL:

- generation of the control base $\mathbf{w}_k$
- generation of the possible control vectors $\{\mathbf{u}_k\} \in \mathbf{w}_k$
- generation of the corresponding model responses $\{\mathbf{x}_{k+1}\}$
- consideration of the possibilities in the **KB** (built on IF-THEN rules)
- choice of the most suitable control possibility
- *if* (the $\mathbf{x}_t$ or another stable state was found) *then (goto* END) *else (begin* $k = k + 1$; *goto* LABEL; *end*)

END

This procedure is schematically illustrated on Fig. 1. To express the control base generation in analytical terms let us write

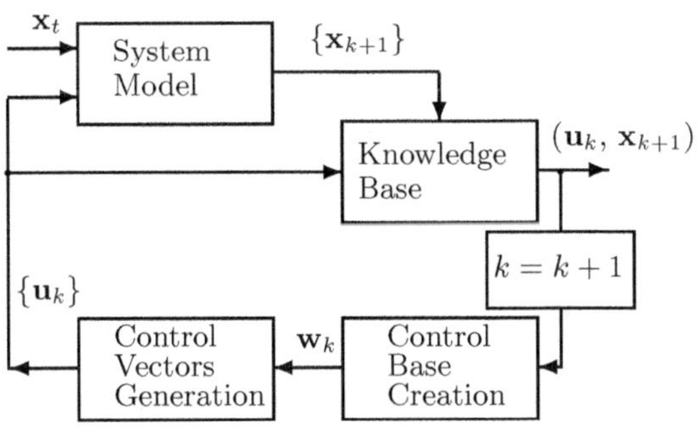

Fig. 1. The principial procedure of the control synthesis

$$\mathbf{x}_k = ({x_1}^k, ..., {x_n}^k)^T \tag{5}$$

$$\mathbf{y}_k = ({y_1}^k, ..., {y_n}^k)^T, \quad {y_i}^k = \begin{cases} 1 \text{ if } {x_i}^k > 0 \\ 0 \text{ otherwise} \end{cases} \; ; \; i = 1, n \tag{6}$$

$$\overline{\mathbf{y}}_k = \underline{neg}\, \mathbf{y}_k = \mathbf{1}_n - \mathbf{y}_k \tag{7}$$

$$\mathbf{v}_k = \mathbf{F}^T.\overline{\mathbf{y}}_k \, , \quad \mathbf{v}_k = ({v_1}^k, ..., {v_m}^k)^T \tag{8}$$

$$\mathbf{z}_k = ({z_1}^k, ..., {z_m}^k)^T, \quad {z_j}^k = \begin{cases} 1 \text{ if } {v_j}^k > 0 \\ 0 \text{ otherwise} \end{cases} \; ; \; j = 1, m \tag{9}$$

$$\mathbf{w}_k = \underline{neg}\, \mathbf{z}_k = \mathbf{1}_m - \mathbf{z}_k \, , \quad \mathbf{w}_k = ({w_1}^k, ..., {w_m}^k)^T \tag{10}$$

where $\underline{neg}$ is the operator of logical negation; $\mathbf{1}_n$ is the n-dimensional constant vector with all of its elements equalled to the integer 1; $\mathbf{y}_k$ is n-dimensional auxiliary binary vector; $\mathbf{v}_k$, $\mathbf{z}_k$ are, respectively, m-dimensional auxiliary vector and m-dimensional auxiliary binary vector; $\mathbf{w}_k$ is m-dimensional vector of the base for the control vector choice.

The vector $\mathbf{w}_k$ represents the control base because it expresses the possible candidates for generating the control vector $\{\mathbf{u}_k\}$ in the step k. Its nonzero components point out the enabled transitions (when the PN analogy is used) in the step k, i.e. the possible discrete events which could occur in the system in the step k and which could be utilized in order to transfer the system from the present state $\mathbf{x}_k$ into another state $\mathbf{x}_{k+1}$. When only one of the $\mathbf{w}_k$ components is different from zero, $\mathbf{w}_k$ can be used (when (4) is met) to be the control vector, i.e. $\mathbf{u}_k = \mathbf{w}_k$. When there are several components of the $\mathbf{w}_k$ different from zero, the control vector $\mathbf{u}_k$ has to be chosen on base of additional information about the actual control task. The choice of the control vector can be made either by a human operator or automatically on base of a corresponding domain oriented knowledge representation built in the form of the rules (e.g. IF-THEN ones) predefined by an expert in the corresponding domain. Such a KB consists of a suitable expression of the constraints imposed upon the task in question, criteria, and further particulars concerning the control task or the controlled object.

To obtain the elementary control vectors $\{\mathbf{u}_k\} \in \mathbf{w}_k$ the following generation procedure is necessary:

$$\mathbf{u}_k \subseteq \mathbf{w}_k \, , \quad \mathbf{u}_k = ({u_1}^k, \, ..., \, {u_m}^k)^T, \quad {u_j}^k = \begin{cases} {w_j}^k & \text{if chosen} \\ 0 & \text{otherwise} \end{cases} \; ; \; j = 1, m$$

Theoretically (i.e. from the combinatorics point of view) there exist

$$ {N_p}^k = \sum_{i=1}^{{N_t}^k} \binom{{N_t}^k}{i} = 2^{{N_t}^k} - 1 \quad , \quad {N_t}^k = \sum_{j=1}^{m} {w_j}^k . \tag{11}$$

possibilities of the control vector choice in the step k. There are the control vectors containing single nonzero elements of the base vector $\mathbf{w}_k$, the control vectors containing pairs of its nonzero elements, triples, quadruplets of its nonzero elements, etc. (until the vector containing all of the nonzero elements of the base vector $\mathbf{w}_k$).

4 Knowledge Representation

A suitable form of the knowledge representation is needed in the control synthesis procedure to decide which control possibility should be actually chosen in any step k when there exist more than one of the realizable possibilities. The rule-based knowledge representation is usual in practice to construct a suitable KB. To express the KB, even in analytical terms, the PN-based approach is used here. However, it is supported by the logical PN (LPN) or/and fuzzylogical PN (FPN) defined in [11], [12]. Some pieces of knowledge (e.g. some statements) are expresed by means of the PN positions and the rules are expressed by means of the PN transitions (taken together with their input and output positions). The mutual causality interconnections among the statements and rules are expressed by means of the analogy with the oriented arcs among the PN positions and transitions - see Fig. 2. More details about such an approach are given in [2]-[5].

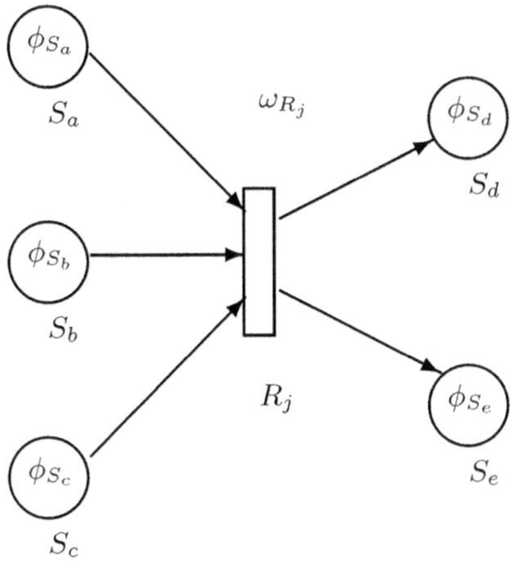

Fig. 2. The rule R_j with input and output statements

The KB structure can be formally expressed as

$$\langle S, R, \Psi, \Gamma \rangle; \quad S \cap R = \emptyset; \quad \Psi \cap \Gamma = \emptyset \tag{12}$$

where $S = \{S_1, ..., S_{n_1}\}$ is a finite set of the statements; S_i , $i = 1, n_1$, are the pieces of knowledge (the elementary statements); $R = \{R_1, ..., R_{m_1}\}$ is a finite set of the rules; R_j , $j = 1, m_1$, are the rules either in the form of implications: R_j : $(S_a \, and \, S_b \, and \ldots and \, S_c) \Rightarrow (S_d \, and \, S_e)$ or in the form of IF-THEN structures: R_j : IF $(S_a \, and \, S_b \, and \ldots and \, S_c)$ THEN $(S_d \, and \, S_e)$, where S_a, S_b, ..., S_c are the input statements of the rule R_j, and the S_d, S_e are the output statements of the rule; $\Psi \subseteq S \times R$ is a set of the causal interconnections among the statements entering the rules and the rules themselves. It can be expressed by means of the incidence matrix $\mathbf{\Psi} = \{\psi_{ij}\}\,,\, i = 1, n_1\,;\, j = 1, m_1$, where $\psi_{ij} \in \{0, 1\}$ in case of the LPN and $\psi_{ij} \in < 0, 1 >$ in case of the FPN. In other words the element ψ_{ij} represents the absence (when 0), presence (when 1) or a fuzzy measure of existence (when its real value is between these boundary values) of the causal relation between the input statement S_i and the rule R_j; $\Gamma \subseteq R \times S$ is a set of the causal interconnections among the rules and the statements emerging from them. It can be expressed by means of the incidence matrix $\mathbf{\Gamma} = \{\gamma_{ij}\}\,,\, i = 1, m_1\,;\, j = 1, n_1$, where $\gamma_{ij} \in \{0, 1\}$ in case of the LPN or $\gamma_{ij} \in < 0, 1 >$ in case of the FPN. γ_{ij} expresses the occurrence of the causal relation between the rule R_i and its output statement S_j.

The KB "dynamics" development (i.e. the statements truth propagation) can be formally expressed as follows

$$\mathbf{\Phi}_{K+1} = \mathbf{\Phi}_K \,\underline{or}\, \mathbf{\Delta} \,\underline{and}\, \mathbf{\Omega}_K\,, \quad K = 0, N_1 \tag{13}$$

$$\mathbf{\Delta} = \mathbf{\Gamma}^T \,\underline{or}\, \mathbf{\Psi} \tag{14}$$

$$\mathbf{\Psi} \,\underline{and}\, \mathbf{\Omega}_K \leq \mathbf{\Phi}_K \tag{15}$$

where $\mathbf{\Phi}_K = (\phi^K_{S_1}, ..., \phi^K_{S_{n_1}})^T\,,\, K = 0, N_1$, is the elementary state vector of the KB (i.e. the state of the statements truth propagation) in the step K; K is the discrete step of the KB dynamics development; N_1 is an integer (the number of different situations); $\phi^K_{S_i}\,,\, i = 1, n_1$ is the state of the truth of the elementary statement S_i in the step K. The statement is false (when 0), true (when 1) or true with a fuzzy measure (when $\phi^K_{S_i}$ acquires its value from the real interval $< 0,\ 1 >$); $\mathbf{\Omega}_K = (\omega^K_{R_1}, ..., \omega^K_{R_{m_1}})^T\,,\, K = 0, N_1$ is the "control" vector of the KB (i.e. the state of the rules evaluability) in the step K; $\omega^K_{R_j}\,,\, j = 1, m_1$ is the state of the rule R_j evaluability in the step K. The rule is not able to be evaluated (when 0), able to be evaluated (when 1) or able to be evaluated with a fuzzy measure (when $\omega^K_{R_j}$ is from the real interval $< 0,\ 1 >$); $\underline{and}$ is the operator of logical multiplying in general. For both the bivalued logic and the fuzzy one it can be defined to be the minimum of its scalar operands - e.g. $a \,\underline{and}\, b = c = min\,\{a, b\}$; $\underline{or}$ is the operator of logical additioning in general. For both the bivalued logic and the fuzzy one it can be defined to be the maximum of its scalar operands - e.g. $a \,\underline{or}\, b = d = max\,\{a, b\}$.

The knowledge inference procedure is analogical to that generating the above introduced control base vector $\mathbf{w}_K$. It is the following

$$\overline{\mathbf{\Phi}}_K = \underline{neg}\, \mathbf{\Phi}_K = \mathbf{1}_{n_1} - \mathbf{\Phi}_K \tag{16}$$

$$\mathbf{v}_K = \mathbf{\Psi}^T \underline{and}\, \overline{\mathbf{\Phi}}_K \tag{17}$$

$$\mathbf{\Omega}_K = \underline{neg}\, \mathbf{v}_K = \mathbf{1}_{m_1} - \mathbf{v}_K = \underline{neg}(\mathbf{\Psi}^T \,\underline{and}\, (\underline{neg}\, \mathbf{\Phi}_K)) \tag{18}$$

where the meaning of quantities is also very analogical to those utilized at the vector $\mathbf{w}_k$ deriving. Hence, $\mathbf{v}_K$ is the m_1-dimensional auxiliary vector pointing out (by its nonzero elements) the rules that cannot be evaluated, because there is at least one false (of course in the LPN analogy) statement among its input statements; $\mathbf{\Omega}_K$ is the m_1-dimensional "control" vector pointing out the rules that have all their input statements true and, consequently, they can be evaluated in the step K of the KB dynamics development. This vector is a base of the inference, because it contains information about the rules that can contribute to obtaining the new knowledge - i.e. to transfer the KB from the state $\mathbf{\Phi}_K$ of the truth propagation into another state $\mathbf{\Phi}_{K+1}$. These rules correspond to the nonzero elements of the vector $\mathbf{\Omega}_K$; $\underline{neg}$ is the operator of logical negation in general. For both the bivalued logic and the fuzzy one it can be defined to be the complement of its scalar operand - e.g. $\underline{neg}\, a = b = 1 - a$.

5 The Program Realization

To automatize the control synthesis process as well as to bridge the OPN-based model with the LPN/FPN-based KB the program system was created in [6]. Two files can be opened in the system: `'model.pnt'` created by the graphical editor of OPN [10] and `'kb.pnt'` created by the same editor extended for LPN/FPN in [1] and time/timed PN in [9]. Three windows are screened if KB operates (i.e. if the button KB is switched on). In the left window the OPN-based model or its verbal description can be alternatively seen while in the rihgt window the LPN/FPN model of the KB or the I/O interface between OPN model and the KB. The I/O interface yields (at the beginning) the empty skeleton. It can be fulfilled by the operator in order to define desirable relations between the OPN-based model and the LPN/FPN-based KB. In case of the KB with one rule (two input and one output statements) the skeleton is the following:

```
input {
            P1 {
                return F
            } end
            P2 {
                return F
            } end
   } end
   output {
   // output place:
   // P3,
            return F
   } end
```

The third window (the state one) is situated in the down part of the screen and it contains the actual state of the system as well as information about the enabled transitions of the OPN model. After finishing the control synthesis process the final sequence of the control interferences for the real DEDS can be obtained from this window. When KB is switched off, further small window appears in the center of the screen - see Fig. 3. It offers to the user the actual control possibilities and yields him the possibility to choose manually the most suitable one (from his subjective point of view). The detail description of the program system is given in the user handbook [7].

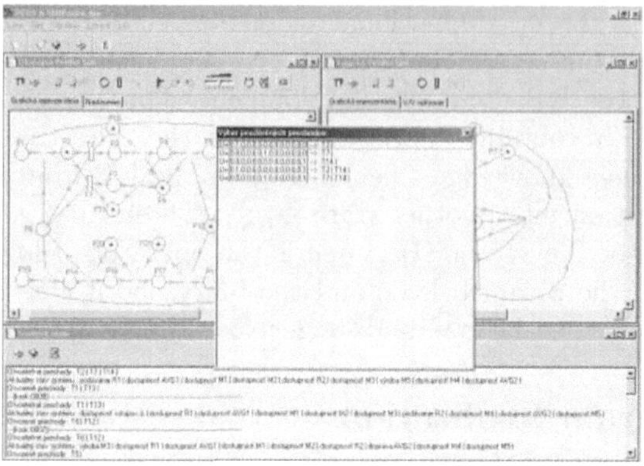

Fig. 3. A view on the screen when the button KB is switched off.

6 The Illustrative Example

To illustrate the above introduced approach consider the FMS given on the Fig. 4. It consists of two robots R1, R2 serving five machine tools M1-M5, two automatic guided vehicles (AGVs), two entries (raw materials A and B, respectively), and two exits (final A-parts and B-parts, respectively). M1, M2 produce the same intermediate A-parts and M4 produces the intermediate B-parts. M3, M5 produce the final A-parts and B-parts, respectively. Using above mentioned analogy the OPN-based model can be obtained - see Fig. 5. It can be knitted e.g. by means of the method [8]. Meaning the OPN positions is the following: P1 - availability of A-raw material, P2 - loading by R1, P3 - machining by M1, P4 - delivering via AGV1, P5 - loading by R2, P6 - machining by M3, P7 - machining by M2, P8 - availability of R1, P9 - availability of AGV1, P10 - availability of M1, P11 - availability of M2, P12 - availability of R2, P13 - availability of M3, P14 - loading by R1, P15 - loading by R2, P16 - machining by M4, P17 - delivering via AGV2, P18 - machining by M5, P19 - availability of B-raw material, P20 - availability of M4, P21 - availability of AGV2, P22 - availability of M5. The transitions T1 - T14 represent the starting or/and ending the corresponding operations. The nonzero elements of the structural matrices of the OPN-based model are in case of the $\mathbf{F}$: $\{f_{11}, f_{22}, f_{27}, f_{33}, f_{44}, f_{55}, f_{66}, f_{78}, f_{81}, f_{89}, f_{93}, f_{98}, f_{10,2}, f_{11,7}, f_{12,4}, f_{12,12}, f_{13,5}, f_{14,10}, f_{15,13}, f_{16,11}, f_{17,12}, f_{18,14}, f_{19,9}, f_{20,10}, f_{21,11}, f_{22,13}\}$ and in case of the $\mathbf{G}$: $\{g_{12}, g_{23}, g_{28}, g_{34}, g_{3,10}, g_{45}, g_{49}, g_{56}, g_{5,12}, g_{61}, g_{6,13}, g_{77}, g_{78}, g_{84}, g_{8,11}, g_{9,14}, g_{10,8}, g_{10,16}, g_{11,17}, g_{11,20}, g_{12,15}, g_{12,21}, g_{13,18}, g_{13,12}, g_{14,19}, g_{14,22}\}$. Starting from the initial state vector $\mathbf{x}_0$ of the system

$$\mathbf{x}_0 = (1\,0\,0\,0\,0\,0\,0\,1\,1\,1\,1\,1\,1\,0\,0\,0\,0\,0\,1\,1\,1\,1)^T \; ; \; \mathbf{v}_0 = (0\,1\,1\,1\,1\,1\,1\,1\,0\,1\,1\,1\,1\,1)^T$$
$$\mathbf{w}_0 = (1\,0\,0\,0\,0\,0\,0\,0\,1\,0\,0\,0\,0\,0)^T \; ; \; \mathbf{u}_0^1 = (1\,0\,0\,0\,0\,0\,0\,0\,0\,0\,0\,0\,0\,0)^T$$
$$\mathbf{u}_0^2 = (0\,0\,0\,0\,0\,0\,0\,0\,1\,0\,0\,0\,0\,0)^T \; ; \; \mathbf{u}_0^3 = (1\,0\,0\,0\,0\,0\,0\,0\,1\,0\,0\,0\,0\,0)^T$$

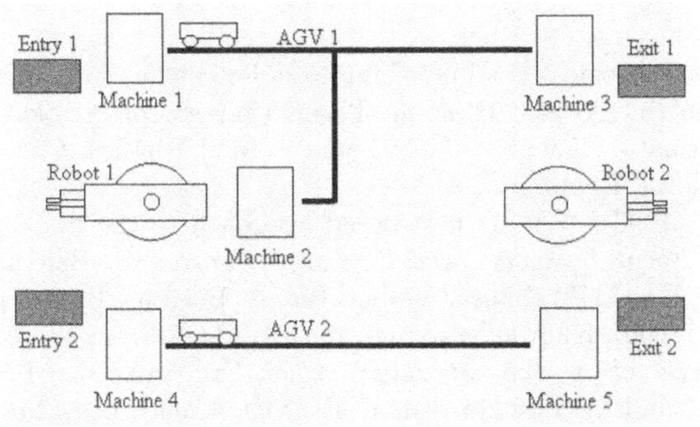

Fig. 4. The flexible manufacturing system.

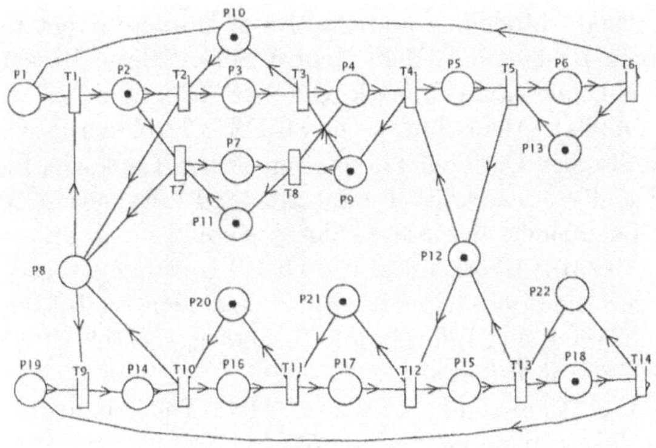

Fig. 5. The Petri nets-based model of the FMS.

While $\mathbf{u}_0^3$ does not satisfy the existence condition (4), $\mathbf{u}_0^1$, $\mathbf{u}_0^2$ are admissible, however, not simultaneously because of the conflict between the enabled transitions T1 and T9 (R1 can take either A or B raw material). It has to be solved by the KB. When the maximal parallelizm is used and the number of the final A-parts has the priority with respect to the number of the final B-parts, the following table presents the final sequence of the control interferences into the real DEDS found automatically by the proposed program system.

step k	0	1	2	3	4	5	6	7	8	...
transitions	t_1	t_2	t_3 & t_9	t_4 & t_{10}	t_5 & t_{11}	t_6 & t_{12}	t_1 & t_{13}	t_2 & t_{14}	t_3 & t_9	...

References

1. Bugár, Z. (1998). Logical Petri nets and fuzzy Petri nets as the means of knowledge representation (in Slovak). Diploma Thesis (Supervisor: Čapkovič, F.). Department of Informatics, Faculty of Mathematics and Physics, Comenius University, Bratislava, Slovak Republic.
2. Čapkovič, F. (1993). A Petri nets-based approach to the maze problem solving. In: *Discrete Event Systems: Modelling and Control* (S. Balemi, P. Kozák and R. Smedinga, Eds.). Birkhäuser Verlag. Basel - Boston - Berlin. pp. 173–179.
3. Čapkovič, F. (1996). Knowledge-based control of DEDS. In: *Proceedings of the 13th IFAC World Congress, June 30-July 5, 1996, San Francisco, USA.* (J.J. Gertler, J.B. Cruz, Jr. and M. Peshkin, Eds.). Elsevier Science Ltd., Pergamon. London. Vol. J. pp. 347–352.
4. Čapkovič, F. (1998). Representation of fuzzy knowledge about control task specifications. In: *IT & KNOWS Information Technologies and Knowledge Systems. Proceedings of XV. IFIP World Computer Congress, August 31-September 4, 1998, Vienna and Budapest* (J. Cuena, Ed.). Riegelnik. Vienna. pp. 215–228.
5. Čapkovič, F. (2000). Modelling and Control of Discrete Event Dynamic Systems. Research Report RS-00-26, BRICS Report Series, Basic Research in Computer Science, Aarhus University, Denmark, October 2000, 58 pages.
6. Čapkovič, P. (1999a). Algorithm of the DEDS control synthesis and its program realization (in Slovak). Diploma Thesis (Supervisor: Čapkovič, F.). Department of Informatics, Faculty of Electrical Engineering and Information Technology, Slovak University of Technology, Bratislava, Slovak Republic.
7. Čapkovič, P. (1999b). Algorithm of the DEDS control synthesis and its program realization. User Handbook (in Slovak). Department of Informatics, Faculty of Electrical Engineering and Information Technology, Slovak University of Technology, Bratislava, Slovak Republic.
8. Chao, D. Y., M. C. Zhou and D. T. Wang (1994). The knitting technique and Petri nets synthesis. *The Computer Journal,* **37**, 67–76.
9. Csontos, M. (2000). Timed and time Petri nets in modelling discrete event dynamic systems (in Slovak). Diploma Thesis (Supervisor: Čapkovič, F.). Department of Informatics, Faculty of Mathematics and Physics, Comenius University, Bratislava, Slovak Republic.
10. Nemes, C. (1997). Graphical editor for the Petri nets creation (in Slovak). Diploma Thesis (Supervisor: Čapkovič, F.). Department of Informatics, Faculty of Mathematics and Physics, Comenius University, Bratislava, Slovak Republic.
11. Looney, C.G., Alfize, A.A. (1987). Logical controls via boolean rule matrix transformations. *IEEE Trans. on Syst. Man and Cybern.*, **SMC-17**, No 6, 1077–1081.
12. Looney, C.G. (1988). Fuzzy Petri nets for rule-based decisionmaking. *IEEE Trans. Syst. Man Cybern.*, **SMC-18**, No 1, 178–183.
13. Peterson, J.L. (1981). *Petri Net Theory and Modeling the Systems.* Prentice Hall, New York.

A Knowledge Based System for the Maintenance of Chemical Plants and Its Implementation Using OPTRANS

Giovani Pieri[1], Michel R. Klein[2] , and Mario Milanese[3]

[1]ROI Softwell, via Bolati 4
28100 Novara, Italy
pierig@msoft.it
[2]HEC Group, Dept. Système d'Information et d'Aide à la Décision
78350 Jouy-en-Josas, France
kleinm@hec.fr
Fax: (33) 1.39.56.57.42
[3]Politecnico di Torino
Departimento di Automatica e Informatica, via Duca degli Abruzzi,24
Torino 10129 Italy

Abstract. This paper presents MAIC a knowledge-based decision support system for the maintenance of chemical plant equipment. The main functions of the system are:
- The management of information concerning the components of pieces of equipment together with the corresponding corrosion agents and critical factors for this component.
- A case based reasoning and retrieval function to search the corrosion case database for similar cases.
- Several knowledge-based functions to support the economic assessment of a technically feasible solution.

The last part of the paper describes the conceptual framework of the OPTRANS development environment which was used to develop MAIC and which gives it many of its interesting features.

Keyword: chemical plant construction & maintenance, case-base reasoning, expert-system, knowledge based DSS, coupling case-base and deductive reasoning

1 Introduction to the Problem

1.1 Description of the Engineering and Maintenance Decision Process

The study and choice of construction material for chemical plant equipment is a task performed by process and maintenance engineers. This task has both technical and economical aspects which are described in Pieri et als [16]. Very often lack of time and budget constraint compels the process engineer to take his decision with only a limited amount of information. Not only corrosion tests and accurate economical analysis are not performed, but even in-house information is hardly accessible. In these conditions the only resource available is personal experience, which very often tends

L. Monostori, J. Váncza, and M. Ali (Eds.): IEA/AIE 2001, LNAI 2070, pp. 777-790, 2001.

to suggest reiterating some previous choice. However a process engineer only rarely meets two identical decision situations, and so he may run the risk of unexpected failures or excessive costs due to an unnecessarily conservative choice of materials. Consequently the problem is to design a system which will speed up and improve the decision process of the engineer by giving him the opportunity to learn from previous cases. The ideal system should guide the engineer to gather information on costs and possible failures from a database of cases and help him to generate alternatives and evaluate them. Ideally the database should include cases originating from in-house experience as well as cases from outside sources such as the Corrosion Protection Institute. Both the difficulty and the interest of designing a DSS application to support such a kind of decision process comes from the need to combine analogical reasoning on a large data base of cases with deductive reasoning to support the selection of the right material (during plant design) or the right protection measure (during maintenance). This problem is made even more complex by the fact that the selection of material implies a mixture of both technical and economic computation with reasoning based on chemical as well as economic knowledge.

1.2 Survey of Literature Concerning This Problem

Several systems have been described in the literature to help solve part of this problem. Since the main cause of chemical plant shut-down or malfunction is due to corrosion problems [20] it is not surprising that nearly all of these systems concentrate on providing advice on selecting the right material and maintenance procedure to prevent corrosion. CORIS by Gerven et als [7] was designed to support the decision of selecting a material to avoid pitting corrosion. The Donegani antiCorrosione Expert System (DOCES) by Farina et als [6] was designed to diagnose corrosion phenomena in boilers and to assist the operating personnel in identifying the cause of boiler failure. The expert system described by Christaldi et als [3] assists the process engineer in the task of selecting suitable materials during industrial plant design. The above mentioned systems rely on technical knowledge only. They do not take costs into consideration and as a consequence can lead to misleading decision when the economical aspect have to be taken into account. To provide expert advice mixing chemical knowledge and economic knowledge implies the coupling of numerical simulation (or computation) and reasoning. A survey of the literature on this coupling problem can be found in Boudis [2]. With respect to coupling case base and rule based system see Stuchlik [18]. It should be also pointed out that the adoption of the system by the process engineer is dependent on the ease with which it can be upgraded according to needs. To reach this goal the conceptual framework and knowledge representation formalism used must remain as clear as possible so that the process engineers can understand it easily and eventually involve themselve in the development of the application. Recent papers have emphasised the need to manage and computerise maintenance knowledge to develop a Maintenance Management Information System [19].

1.3 Approach Proposed by MAIC

In the present paper a different approach is proposed: MAIC (Materialy per Apparecchiature di Impianti Chimici.) is designed to support the tasks described in §1.1 by:

- allowing engineers to search a data base of maintenance cases, simulating reasoning by analogy to provide a small sample of solutions which have already been applied in similar situations and that the engineer can study.
- forecasting possible failure using a description of the case at hand and deductive reasoning in conjunction with corrosion knowledge.
- proposing protection measures to prevent corrosion using deductive reasoning and corrosion knowledge, the final choice being left to the engineer.
- providing maintenance support for, not only a large spectrum of corrosion types, but also for a large set of materials and for all phases of corrosion protection.

The approach we propose enables the maintenance and process engineer to take economic variables into consideration for his investment decisions in equipment over the life time of the plant. Not only are the cost criteria always taken into consideration when comparing alternatives but the system also provide advice on how to avoid failure, shut-down and damage during construction and production of the plant. If this advice implies costly maintenance measures such as periodical control and tests, their cost will be taken into account by the system when comparing alternatives. MAIC is implemented using a knowledge based DSS development environment, using formalism very close to the formalism natural to the users. Before providing some insights concerning the structure of MAIC we shall describe the system from the user point of view. For more details the user is refered to Pieri[16].

2 Description of the System

2.1 Nature of Data Used

MAIC uses a file management system and three databases:

User files	Contains corrosion cases created by the user, including the original data and the results of MAIC knowledge based advice. It takes the form of files created by the user.
Corrosion DataBase:	Contains cases from the company Donegani Anticorrosione, organised in a database which cannot be modified by the user but which is accessible for retrieval.
Material DataBase:	Contains unit costs, physical properties and mechanical characteristics of materials which can be updated.
Cost DataBase:	Contains all the factors necessary to compute the total investment cost which can be updated by the user.

2.2 Functions Provided by the System

MAIC provides five main functions. They help the user to make the main steps of the analysis by allowing him to study similar cases, by generating suitable material alternatives, rating them according to their performance and estimating the economic impact of each alternative, until a final choice is made.

File:	Activates a menu to manage user data.
Input:	Activates a menu to input user data
Dbase:	Activates a menu to search and display analogous cases from the Donegani Antocorrosione database.
Material choice:	Activates the expert assistant (KBS) which will provide the user with alternative materials and maintenance rules for the case under review.
Economics:	Generate the economic parameters necessary to make a final decision.

User data describing cases are recorded in files. Each record of a file contains the description of a single case. That is to say the set of input data and, possibly, the results obtained by analysing the data of this single component with MAIC.

Functions for data capture and user data management. All the standard functions for file managment are provided. A function **Find** facilitates retrieval of cases containing a given string, a function **Filter** filters the cases which satisfy a set of conditions. An input form allows the user to enter data (see fig.1) on a new case or to modify an existing one.

Searching the data base and simulation of analogical reasoning. Both the user case and the data base cases are specified by standard variables, a subset of which are listed and explained in table 1. Variables can be considered as attributes of the case

Table 1. A sample of the variables describing a case.

Variable	Description	Type	Interval or number of possible values
Temperature		real	0-1000°C
Pressure		real	0-200Kg/cm2
PH	Measure of acidity	real	0-14
Velocity		real	0-50 m/s
Component		qualitative	35
Equipment		qualitative	26
Duty	fluid contacting the component	qualitative	25
Physical state		qualitative	7
Corrosive agent	Corrosive present in duty	qualitative	65
Critical factors	Non chemical factors affecting corrosion	qualitative	10
Material		qualitative	59
Failures		Qualitative	63
Remedies		Qualitative	85

and interpreted as co-ordinates which set the position of a case in a multi-dimensional attribute space. In table 1 physical variables (type real number) refer to the fluid in contact with the component subject to corrosion. This fluid is called "duty". In table 1 two different kinds of variables are used:
-in the first group of variables the values are real numbers defined within an interval - in the second group are included qualitative variables whose values are elements of a specific list.
This information can be used to calculate a dissimilarity factor between the user case and each of the data base cases. The variables, which identify each case, are grouped as shown on table 1. The simulation of reasoning by analogy implies that a measure of resemblance **r** (or similarity or association coefficient) between two cases is made available to the user and that such a measure can be modified easily if needed. If **E** is a set of cases, the coefficient **r** is defined by a function which assigns to each pair of cases X, Y∈ **E** a real number.
A resemblance coefficient must be symetric:

$$\mathbf{r}(X,Y) = \mathbf{r}(Y,X)$$

and must be so that either $\mathbf{r}(X,X) <= \mathbf{r}(X,Y)$ or $\mathbf{r}(X,X) >= \mathbf{r}(X,Y)$ holds
Resemblances usually have the property:

$$\mathbf{r}(X,X) = \mathbf{r}^*$$

In this case a new resemblance measure **d**: $\mathbf{d}(X,Y) = \mathbf{r}(X,Y) - \mathbf{r}^*$ can be defined which is order equivalent to **r**.
This resemblance measure called **dissimilarity** coefficient has several properties:

R1 $\mathbf{d}(X,Y)>=0$

R2 $\mathbf{d}(X,X) = 0$

R3 $\mathbf{d}(X,Y) = \mathbf{d}(Y,X)$

If the coefficient **d** has the following additional properties:

R5 $\mathbf{d}(X,Y)=0 => X=Y$

R6 $\mathbf{d}(X,Y) <= \mathbf{d}(X,Z) + \mathbf{d}(Z,X)$

d is called a **distance**.
For an interesting comparison of resemblance measures the reader is refered to Gatagelj and Bren [1]. Such resemblance measures have been defined for variables associated with cases. In the present situation the variables describing each case are a mix of quantitative and qualitative variables. This type of situation has been analysed by J.C. Gover [8]. In MAIC a distance measure has been computed according to the following basic principle:

a) In the case of quantitative variables a simple absolute difference is computed: $r_i - | a_i - b_i|/R_i$ where a_i and b_i are the values of the user case and the data base case and R_i is the range of the variable.

b) In the case of qualitative variables the list of variables can be arranged in a similarity/dissimilarity tree. In this tree the number of nodes to be crossed to connect two of the terminal nodes using the shortest path along the tree computes the dissimilarity coefficient. In this case the function r_i is computed: $r_i= n_i/N_i$. where n_i is the number of nodes crossed by the ith variable and N_i is the maximum number possible for that qualitative variable. In this way for each variable i a real number is computed with range [0,1]. For the second case let's take the physical state as an example. Seven possibilities are supplied in MAIC they appear as terminal nodes of branches in the tree of table 2.

From table 2 some examples of dissimilarity coefficients, measured by the number of crossed nodes can be put in evidence. Having calculated the previously described dissimilarity for each variable the final total distance between two cases D is computed: $D = \sum r_{i..}$ r_i being positive by definition, D is itself positive and the previous construction rule for the distance is equivalent to the well known city-bloc method. D is a distance in the sense that it complies with rules R1 to R6.

MAIC contains an algorithm to calculate D which use matrices of distance for each variable. For physical state, the matrix is as shown on table 3. The same method is used for the other variables. In some cases (material, corrosive agent, failure, remedies) the corresponding matrices are fairly large and therefore trees are complicated. For instance for remedies the matrix becomes very large since the list has 85 members and thematrix has 7225 elements. Taking into account that the matrix is symetrical and the diagonal elements vanish by definition of the distance, the number of elements to be memorised is reduced to 3570. MAIC will provide a list of cases sorted according to the distance computed as explained above. The engineer can then browse this list of cases or apply the distance computation to a subset of the case base to apply the analogous reasoning to a restricted list of cases selected according to a given criterion.

Table 2. Tree structure to compute dissimilarity for physical state.

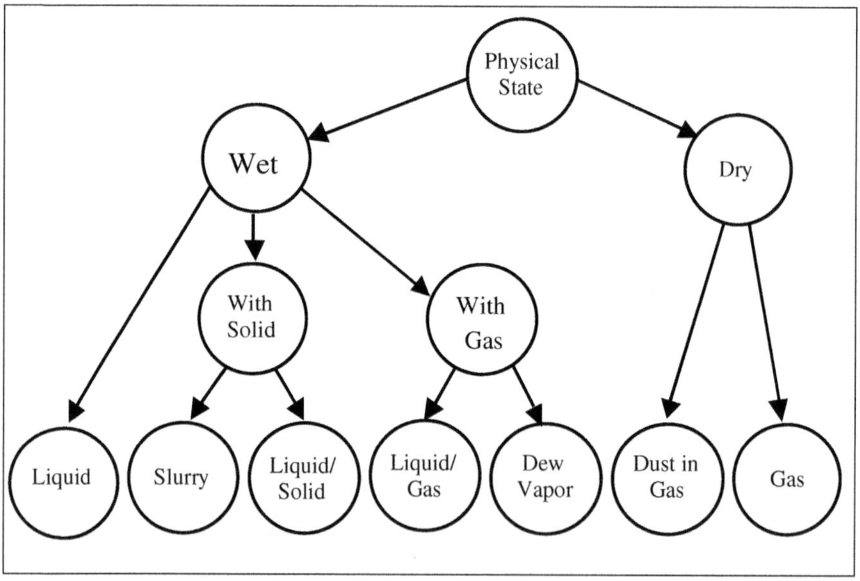

Functions to support the choice of material for a component. As shown on fig 2 three main functions are provided by the material choice option to: choose material, forecast failures, propose protection measures.

Table 3. Number of crossed nodes between physical states.

	Gas	Dust in gas	Dew vapor	Liquid/ gas	Liquid/ solid	Slurry	liquid
Gas	0	1	4	4	4	4	3
Dust in Gas	1	0	4	4	4	4	3
Dew vapor	4	4	0	1	3	3	2
Liquid/gas	4	4	1	0	3	3	2
Liquid/solid	4	4	3	3	0	1	2
Slurry	4	4	3	3	1	0	2
Liquid	3	3	2	2	2	2	0

The "Material Choice" button runs the inference engine which makes a choice within a list of more than 50 material types (metallic and non metallic) which are stored in the system cost data base, and assigns to each material a score on a scale from -100 to +100. This score measures the suitability of the material for the component under study and the planned conditions of use. The user can set a threshold to reject all the materials with a score lower than the threshold.

The "Failure Forecast" button runs the inference engine which uses a knowlege base which examines a list of possible failures (the system contains a predetermined list of over 40 items or components) and sets a certainty factor (CF) for each one. This failure "expert assistant" takes into account problem data and the specific material used in the case. The "expert assistant" has to be run for each alternative generated by the material choice expert assistant. The certainty factor is measured on a scale between –100 and 100, and expresses the degree of belief with which this particular failure is likely to occur.

The "Protection measure" button runs the inference engine which uses a knowlege base, which suggests protection and maintenance procedures (remedies) for the failure as forecasted by the "Failure Forecast" expert assistant. More than 60 possible protection measures are available in the system and each one is given a score (between –100 and +100). This score shows the degree of efficiency of the protection measure .

The method of certainty factor to update expert beliefs was used not only because it was provided by the inference engine but also for other reasons. No two chemical plants are identical and since this is also true for functioning conditions, the sample of nearly identical cases, to compute a statistical frequency of failure or reliability measure for components is very small or inexistant. The clearest treatment, in our opinion, of the two main methods of updating non probabilistic measures of belief: certainty factor and the Dempster-Shafer method, is made by Mark Stefik [17]

Supporting economic analysis of possible alternative. Economic analysis of alternatives is provided by the system. It uses several models which are described in Pieri [16]

Cost models: The cost of the alternative is computed according to the component geometry and the quantity of material used to construct the component. The simplest model computes cost using the component weight and the more sophisticated one calculates the cost using the component thickness according to pressure.

Investment cost: this model computes the investment costs, taking into account the expected life of the plant.

Multicriterium choice: this model compares cases concerning the same component but built with different materials over the expected life of the plant.

2.3 Example of the Use of MAIC

Input and data management. Let us assume that the user wants to choose a material for tubing of a superheater (of a bank heat exchanger type) in a process boiler that works in the following conditions:

Temperature	390 °C
Pressure	80 bar (gauge)

The input form of this case is shown in fig 1. The window contains three input zones: Project number, Project name, Item (identifier of equipment). These identifiers are for easy retrieval and identification of the case, they will appear in all outputs of MAIC. All the other problem data, are inputed in the appropriate zone. All the variables are useful to guide the choice of a material, but only two of them are required to obtain realistic results: temperature and "duty" (see §2.2). These two variables qualify physico-chemical conditions of corrosion and no prediction of material performance can be made if they are not known.

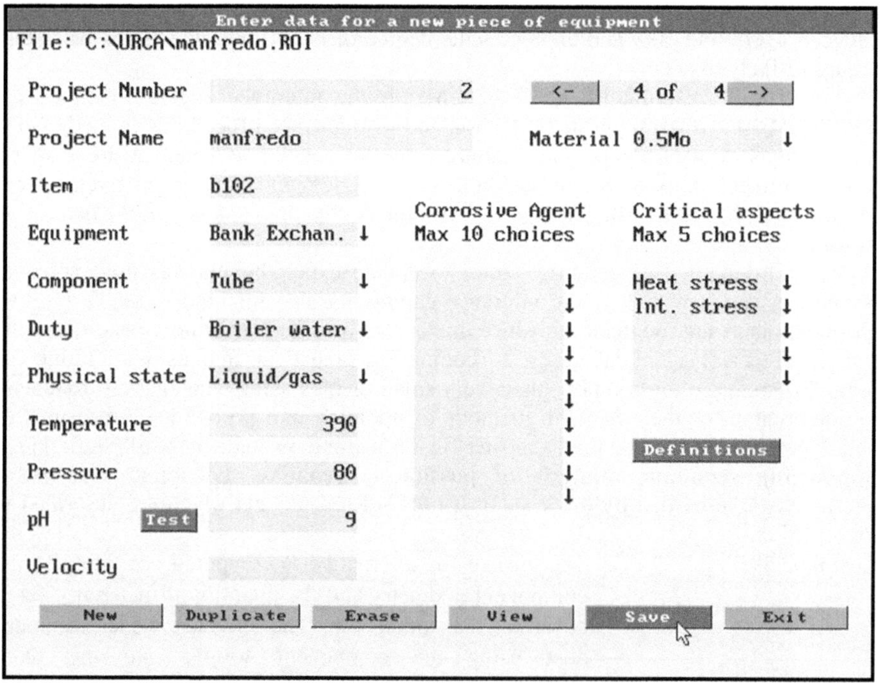

Fig. 1. Input form for the data concerning a component (the case describes a tube).

All the other variables (physical state, pressure, pH, velocity, corrosive agent and critical aspects) are optional. The system will work even if they are not specified, and will still give usable results. This does not mean that there is no effect if additional variables are specified. The more information is supplied, the better will be the proposed material choice. For instance, pressure is necessary if MAIC is required to indicate not only the choice of material, but also the component thickness (without pressure no thickness calculation is possible). Velocity is also an optional variable. However the user should keep in mind that if he is investigating a case with possible erosion, the specification of velocity will make the choice of material more accurate.

As shown in fig 1 under the title "corrosive agent" the user can specify the corrosive environment by specifying a set of corrosive agents. Specifying the corrosive agent is optional but it qualifies the role of "duty" much better and, if it is known to the user, it is strongly recommended that it be fed into the system.

pH is a special variable. It is optional, and where it is not pertinent (gas phase), MAIC simply ignores it. However pH greatly affects the corrosion behaviour of materials. A pH value can be estimated by the system using a specific knowledge base, using other variables, mainly duty and corrosive agents.

Search for similar cases. Informations in the Corrosion DataBase are stored in a plan (table) of the multi-dimmensional data base. The parameters used to describe the cases are more or less the same as the parameters for the material choice assistant. Some parameters can be added, for instance the year of the creation of the original maintenance report and the type and duration of service of the equipment. If the user wishes to find in the Corrosion DataBase a case analogous to the example of Fig 1, a stepwise search is started by finding cases with the string "**exch**" (exchanger) in the column Equipment followed by other searches (component = tube, temperature >350 °C, equipment use as superheater).

Out of the last 5 cases remaining after the search in the Corrosion DataBase, case 9 appears to be interesting. It refers to a primary superheater of an auxiliary boiler working at 454°C and 100 bar (gauge) The material used is Alloy Steel 1.25 Cr 0.5 Mo. The case was described because a tube had burst. An example of a report of the complete case is presented in Pieri [16]

Supporting material choice. Fig.2 represents the material choice display window. The diagnosis concerning material choice is obtained using the "Material choice" option of the main window.This window is structured in three columns. In the left column all the input data of the user case are displayed for reference including critical factors: in this case heat stress and internal stress.

In the top part of the central column the results concerning material choice for similar case found in the Donegani data base are displayed. In the example, Carbon Steel (CS R510) and Alloy steel (1.25 Cr 0.5 Mo) are suggested by the system with respectively 65 and 60 as measures of likelyhood for their use in such a situation .

The CS R510 material has been tested also for failure forecast and protection measures (remedies). The results provides by MAIC are shown in the top right column of the window. The types of failures observed for similar cases in the Donegani data base as well as remedies (none in this case) are displayed with their likelyhood. Fig 2 shows the number of occurrence (2) for the marerial choice given a threshold of 60.

The number of occurrences (5) for these types of failures given a threshold of 60 is also displayed, etc…

Economic analysis. The multi-criteria comparison of alternatives created by the choice of material expert function is done using all the relevant comparison elements, coming both from economical and corrosion analysis. A description of this analysis and the way the results are presented to the user is made in Pieri [16]

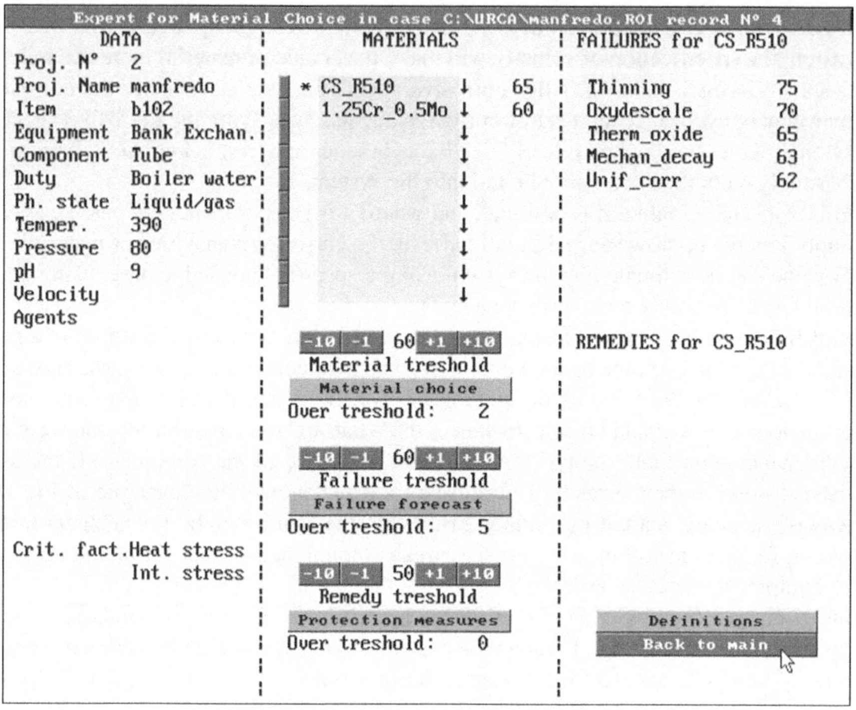

Fig. 2. Window for material choice.

3 Development Environment Used

The MAIC application was developped using the OPTRANS Object knowledge based DSS development environment.

3.1 The OPTRANS Object Development Environment

OPTRANS Object is the result of a research effort undertaken to solve some of the problems of the first generation KB-DSS development environment cf. Klein [13] The basic hypotheses taken in OPTRANS is that the development environment should be defined as a tool to formalise different kinds of knowledge needed to implement a solution. For a brief description of the system the reader is refered to Klein, Methlie[09]and Klein [10][12][14]. In OPTRANS an application is built from seven main objects classes or resources (Fig 3):

-the *application* (in its technical sense): The instructions of the application define the user interface and the global logic of the application .(scheduling of resources)
- the application common *data structure*
- the *models* which are used to formalise quantitative relations between variables.
- the *data base models* which are used to formalise computation procedure at the multi-dimensional data base level.
- the *reports* which are used to define the presentation of information
- the *knowledge bases* which are used to formalise knowledge as rules.
- the *multi-dimensional data bases* which are used to define and query more complex data which will be used by the application.

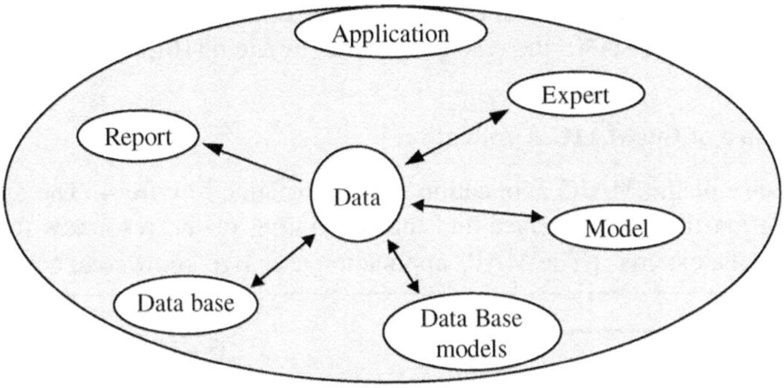

Fig. 3. Main components of a KB-DSS application designed with OPTRANS.

This approach which is based on a limited number of objects classes leads to the design of *structured* applications. It also provides applications were data capture, computation and presentation of information are to a large extent *independent*. This is the key to easy changes in the application according to the engineers' need.

3.2 Communication Mechanism between Objects and Rule Structure

The fundamental characteristic of OPTRANS is presented symbolicaly on fig 4. All sources of knowledge: database, models, statistical programs, experts, reports can exchange information through the common data structure of the application which plays the role of a *blackboard* under the control of the application which plays the role of a *scheduler*. This architecture presents several advantages described by Engelmore and Morgan in [4]. In OPTRANS a variable of a model can be used in the condition part of any rule. For example after running a numerical simulation the application can run an inference engine which will start reasoning using rules, the condition part of which contains expression using variables of the models. The conclusion of reasoning can be stored in a variable and then used by another expert. In the material choice knowledge base, the rules are regrouped in 13 rules subsets concerning: Duty, Agent, pH, criticity, component, temperature, velocity,...In OPTRANS the syntax of a rule is as follows :

```
If <Condition>
(Concluded_Fact        <Fact 1> is <Val1>
                       <Fact 2> is <Val2>
                       ...
```

```
                              <variable1> = <Val1>
                              <variable2> = <val2>
                           ...)
(Execute <Label>)
(Rule_Subset <Rule_Subset_Name> (<Priority>)
(Message <Text_of_Message>)
(Comment <Text_of_Comment>)
End_of_Rule
```

The **execute** key word allows the rule to send back the control to the application which can then open and run **a model** and then go on with the inferencing. For a brief description with an exemple of communication between the model and knowledge based system in OPTRANS the reader is refered to Klein [10][11],[14]

3.3 Structure of the MAIC Application

The structure of the MAIC application is best explained by fig 4. The application is used to define the user interface and the scheduling of the resources (calls to Data Bases, models, experts).The MAIC application uses five knowledge bases (KB):

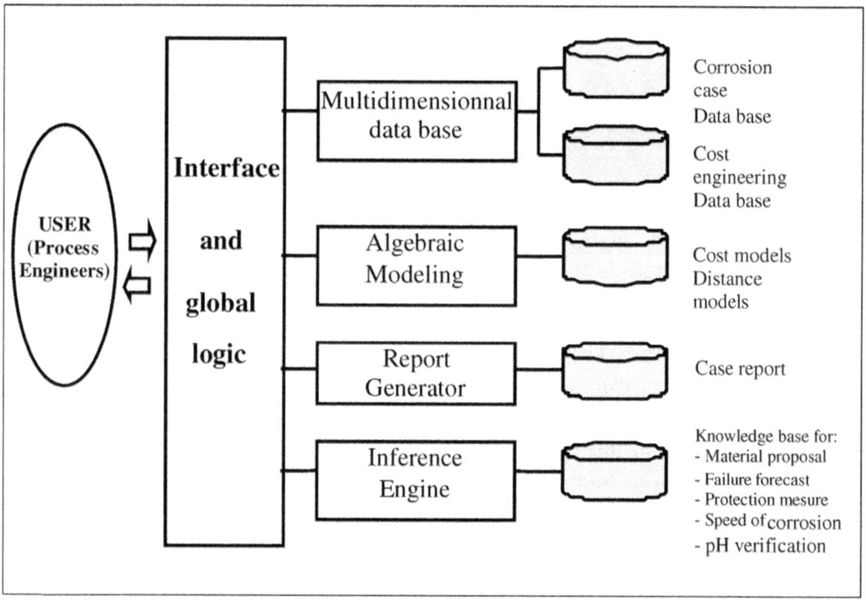

Fig. 4. Structure of the MAIC application a designer view.

-a KB to help select the right material component (702 rules)
-a KB to help forecast failure (500 rules)
- a KB to propose protection measures (600 rules)
-a KB to estimate the speed of corrosion (200 rules)
-a KB to check the pH value (150 rules)

These KB have been defined using knowledge from experts as well as theoretical knowledge. The knowledge concerning range of acceptable temperature for certain materials comes from the specialised literature. 30 cases out of the 450 cases of the Case Base have been use to develop the first version of the KB. Several months were spend testing the conclusion of the knowledge bases on other cases of the Donegani Case Base to validate the rules.

4 Conclusion and Future Research

This work has demonstrated the possibility of using OPTRANS object a knowledge based DSS tool to implement an application which integrates analogical reasoning, deductive reasoning and economic models to support better the work of process engineers when designing or maintening a chemical plant.. The system was written entirely by specialists in the domain with only methodological help from the OPTRANS designers and without using any algorithmic progamming. The system has now been in use for a year and some first conclusions can be made. The first request of users is to widen the knowledge base for the selection of material by extending it to more materials and to more chemical processes and by adding better images of corroded parts. This work demonstrate that the combination of rule based and case base reasoning together with formal models was successful in supporting better the work of the process and maintenance engineers when the engineers use knowledge which can be explicitely writen (or was explicitely writen in books) and when they can also learn from experience based on previous cases. Similar conclusions were drawn by Krogel and Stuchlik [18] in manufacturing planning.
With respect to the simulation of analogical reasoning, more work has to be done to test different measures of dissimilarities and compare their efficiency. A second direction is to improve the capacity of MAIC to support the bidding activity. Adding a database containing data on previous offers will then be needed. A third direction is to explore how automatic learning mechanism could be implemented to improve the quality of the diagnosis as new cases are observed.

Aknowledgements. We would like to thank the company Donegani for providing the case base that was used for testing the system. The company KTI for providing the opportunity to develop the MAIC application. Mr.Farina from Donegani for useful comments on case analysis. C.Danes from Decision Systems Research. V.Hargreaves for stylistic advice.

References

[1] Batagelj V. Bren M., Comparing Resemblance Measures, Journal of Classification 12:73-90, 1995
[2] Boudis M., Simulation et Systèmes à Base de connaissances, Thesis, Université Pierre Mendés-France, Grenoble, 11 march 1997.
[3] Cristaldi L. Orsini G., Sistema Esperto Materiali, Metallurgica Italiana Vol 84 n° 3 Mar 1992, p.249-254

[4] Engelmore R.S., Morgan A.J. Conclusion, in Blackboard Systems, Engelmore and Morgan (Eds) Addison Wesley, 1988.
[5] Farina C.A. Felicioli G., Grassini U., Salvà, D., Verzotto F., Corrosion Control Software and Non Destructive Testing, International Conference Corrosion in Natural and Industrial Environments, NACE Grado, Italy, May 1995
[6] Farina C. Mininni S., DOCES: an expert system for material damage in boilers, Proceedings of the 11th International Corrosion Congress, Florence 1990,vol. 3
[7] Gerven T, Gurnia H., Schlagner W., Wissenbasiertes System zur Lochkorrosion, Werkstoffe und Korrosion, vol 44, 10 Oct 1993, p426-430.
[8] Gover J.G. A General Coefficient of Similarity and some of its Properties, Biometrics, 27,857-74, December 1971.
[9] Klein Michel, Methlie Leif, Knowledge Based DSS, John Wiley 1995,
[10] Klein Michel, OPTRANS Object, Manuel d'introduction Decision Systems Research, 4 rue de la Libération, 78350 Jouy-en-Josas, France.1997
[11] Klein Michel, Using OPTRANS Objet: a Knowledge Based DSS development Environment to design KB-DSS applications, Proceedings Information Systems Architecture and Technology (ISAT'97), octo. 1997 Wroclaw Techn. University.
[12] Klein Michel, Traunmüller Rolland, User Interface of knowledge based DSS Development Environment, Some Further Developments in Data Base and Expert Systems Applications, Proceedings 4 th International Conference, DEXA, 1993, V. Marik, J. Lazansky, R.Wagner, (Eds), Springer Verlag, Lecture Notes in Computer Science, 1993
[13] Klein Michel, Research Issues for Second Generation knowledge based DSS in Decision Support Systems, Proceedings NATO Advanced Studies Institute, (Holsapple & Winston,eds) Springer,Computer and System Science n°101, 1993
[14] Klein M. OPTRANS Object a knowledge based DSS development environment, proceedings of the conference "Futures in Information Systems and Software Engineering Research", Bernd G. Lundberg (Ed), Dept of Computer and System Science Stockholm University and Royal Institute of Technology , April 1999.
[15] Klein M, Grubström R., Using Optrans as a tool to implement DSS for production management, European Journal of Operational Research, 1998.
[16] Pieri G, Klein M, et als, Knowledge-Based Maintenance of Chemical Plants, communication. 11 th Seminar on Production Economics, Igls, Austria, 2000.
[17] Stefik Marc, Introduction to Knowledge Systems, Morgan Kaufman, 1995.
[18] Stuchlik, Mixed Paradigm reasoning in a knowledgte based System for Manufacturing Planning, in Proceedings Information Systems Architecture and Technology, ISAT 94 Bazewicz, (Eds), Technical University of Wroclaw 1994
[19] Waeyenbergh G., Pintelon L., Knowledge Based Maintenance, paper presented at the 11 th International Working Seminar on Production Economics, Igls/Innsbruck, Austria, February 21-25, 2000
[20] William, G.P., Sawyer, J.G. What causes ammonia plant Shut-down ?, CEP, Vol, 70, N°2, 1974

Different Kinds of Neural Networks in Control and Monitoring of Hot Rolling Mill

L. Cser[1], J. Gulyás[2], L. Szűcs[3], A. Horváth[3], L. Árvai[1], and B. Baross[1]

[1]Bay Zoltán Foundation for Applied Research, H-1116 Budapest, Fehérvári út 130, Hungary,
[2]University of Miskolc, H3515 Miskolc-Egyetemvaros, Hungary,
[3]Dunaferr Steel Works, Dunaujvaros, Hungary

Abstract. Cutting the costs and increasing the added value of steel products using new production methods and advanced control systems are the key factors in competitiveness of the European steel producers. In order to meet the challenge of the steadily growing pressure to improve the product quality, rolling mills employ extensive automation and sophisticated on-line data sampling techniques. Since the number of factors involved in the processes is very large, it takes time to discover and analyse their quantified influence. The paper gives a survey about the knowledge processing, using neural networks in rolling. The two main streamlines are shown by exemplary case studies: Self Organizing Maps as Data Mining tool for discovering the hidden dependencies among the influencing factors, finding the relevant and irrelevant factors, as well as application of different types of neural networks for optimisation of the draft schedule.

1 Introduction

The knowledge processing, using methods of artificial intelligence opened new ways in "efficient use of deficient knowledge" [1] in rolling. A survey of knowledge-based methods in metal forming in 1992 [2] contained less than 200 papers. The growing interest toward these methods though is shown in a paper [3], which contains 50 reference items only about artificial neural networks in rolling. The mathematical models either describe only a very small part of the production process (e.g. in the rolling, stresses and strains in the billet in roll gap, using 3D FEM models), or simplify the entire process so, that it cannot be estimated, how big is the error introduced by the simplifications.

Every technological operation can influence the product quality. Technology affects the material properties that further influence the geometry that determines the design of the technology. Disciplines of mechanics and kinetics cannot easily handle the problems of friction, wear, fracture, and precipitation in metals, heat evolution, and distribution. Modelling such sophisticated phenomena needs new approaches. For process planning, measured and predicted data and their steady comparison are necessary.

L. Monostori, J. Váncza, and M. Ali (Eds.): IEA/AIE 2001, LNAI 2070, pp. 791-796, 2001.

The introduced on-line measurement systems in modern mills can register only the local changes, and control e.g. some stands in finishing mill in order to compensate the errors in the flatness, but can not estimate the reasons of the defect, because it is outside of the scope of measuring system, sometimes in the furnace, or in the transport line.

2 Different Types of Neural Networks in Hot Rolling

The use of Artificial Neural Networks (ANN) in rolling started in the beginning of 1990's, but the number of published works is growing rapidly. Prediction of process variables using measurements from previous process phases has been most common way of utilising ANNs in industrial applications. Metallurgical processes have also been extensively investigated and modelled using ANNs (e.g. blast furnace processes have been modelled with measured process data, as well as ANN based solution for temperature control in continuous steel strip annealing furnace, etc.).

Although the number of papers still remained small, the applications of neural networks in rolling cover a wide field of applications ranging from flatness control to the prediction of mechanical properties of the rolled material. In addition, in rolling the most effective way of applying neural networks may not be the global ANN model but a combination of a neural network and the classical mathematical model (e.g. [4]).

The greatest benefit of the ANN is the quick *interpolation ability*. Usually ANNs are used as correction factors in the physically based rolling models that take into account the features responsible for the variations in the process, like changes in alloying element compositions. These hybrid models give a solution in overcoming the difficulties of mapping between inputs and outputs, by leaving only unknown dependencies for ANN to solve.

Another field of ANN applications is to use them for developing fast models from numerically simulated data in order to avoiding the long computations in real-time environment. By using simulated data it is possible to overcome the common problem of unevenly distributed data associated with logged process data.

In the automation and control of the strip flatness and the determination of mill settings needed for an incoming strip before the strip actually enters the mill ANNs, based on both measured and simulated data are used. An efficient process model should be able to predict rolling forces, torque, material properties etc. It is sufficient accurate, reliable and can be updated fast. By using ANNs these goals can be reached provided, that sufficient amount of process data is available. In addition, taking post-calculation into account, which means compensating the pre-calculation error by continuously adapting the models to the real time process. The neural networks are able to do both modelling and adaptation and perform them equally well.

For control task a reasonable task sharing between the mathematical modelling and neural network based correction is necessary:

- the on-line computations should be performed by neural networks, but
- possibilities of the mechanically correct mathematical modelling should be utilised.

Traditional tasks solved by ANN are, as follows:

- prediction of the width in finishing mill,
- correction of the strip or plate temperature calculated by analytical models.

Fig. 1. Neural networks in control of rolling mill [5].

Networks used in rolling mill control can be divided into two groups, as networks trained off-line in development laboratories, and built into the control, and networks with "training on the job". Recently the ANN is an efficient method used in many rolling mills, as it can be seen in Fig. 1 [5].

3 Knowledge Discovery Based on Self Organizing Maps

Self Organising Maps (SOM), developed originally for speech recognition, are especially suitable in analysing the very complex processes, e.g. hot rolling. Unlike supervised learning methods, the SOM can be used for clustering data without knowing the class memberships of the input data.

Application of SOM helps to discover hidden dependencies influencing the quality parameters, such as flatness, profile, thickness and width deviation as well as wedge and surface quality. First steps of the SOM based Data Mining is the Data Warehousing; collection of data from different computers in the different hierarchical levels of computer control in the rolling mill, and transforming the data into the same format. The next step is data preparation (data cleansing), filtering out the noise of measurement units, as well as the idle states.

In order to find the relevant and irrelevant factors from ca. 40 different on-line measurements as well as from the ca. 100 statistically pre-processed (mean, standard deviation, average deviation, min. and max. deviation etc.) technological parameters, beginning from the chemical content, the casting and re-heating parameters by the coiling speed and temperature. SOM analysis enabled the estimation of main measured values that are closely connected with the change of quality parameters. As quality parameters, geometric accuracy, grain size, mechanical and magnetic properties can be chosen. Results have been published in e.g. [6]. The projection on the component planes shown in Fig. 2 can be interpreted, as slicing the n-dimensional model vectors of the map into component planes. The SOM component planes give the clustering of each component separately.

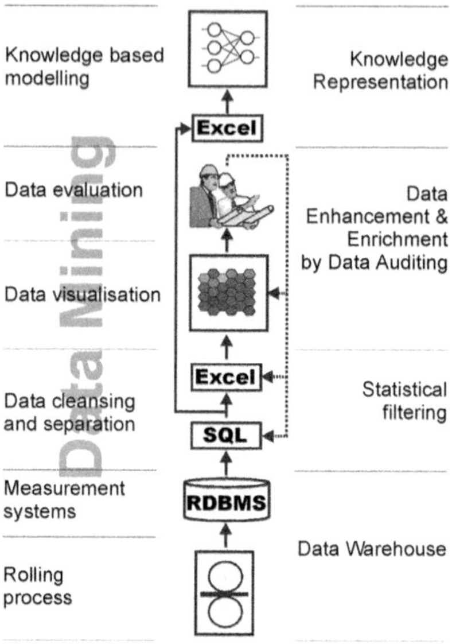

Fig. 2. Process of Data Mining.

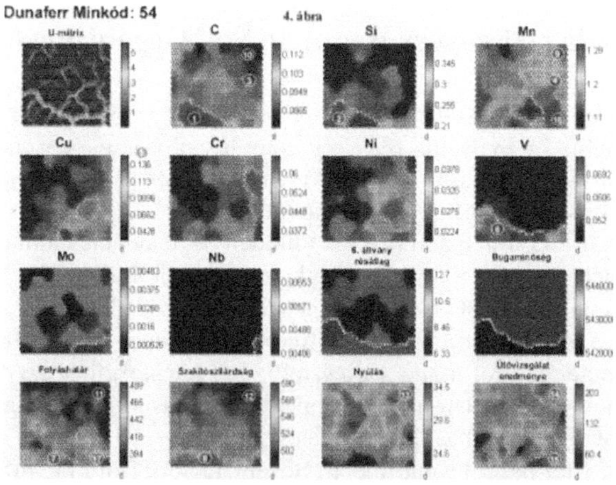

Fig. 3. Typical maps made by processing of 16.000 strips, showing the changes in some alloying elements, roll gaps, yield stress, maximum tensile stress, elongation, and ultimate tensile ratio.

Component planes can also be used for correlation hunting: discovering hidden *co-incidences*. Correlation between components can be seen as similar patterns in identical positions of component planes. Using component planes in correlation hunting is easy, selecting the "suspicious" component combinations for further investigations. However, the similar patterns do not mean a causal connection. Detailed analysis of the physical process is necessary to decide, whether the factor should be included into the neural network for draft scheduling, or not.

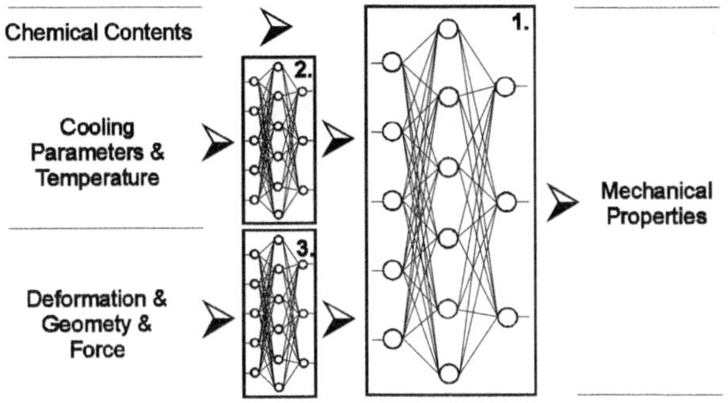

Fig. 4. Two level neural network model used for modifying the draft schedule in order to achieve the prescribed mechanical properties.

4 ANN Based Draft Schedule

Based on the results of the Data Mining a two level ANN model has been developed (Fig. 4). After having measured the transfer bar temperature, the ANN model suggests to modify the draft schedule, as well, as the cooling, and the rolling speed in order to achieve the necessary mechanical properties, as well as balanced currents of the stand drives. The user interface can be seen in the Fig.5.

5 Conclusions

- Self-Organising Maps represent an effective method for discovering the hidden dependencies among the technological parameters in the environment of the full automation.
- Neural networks are effectively used in rolling industry, both for prediction of the quality and for the control of equipment.
- In the framework of co-operation between Dunaferr Steel Works and Bay Zoltán Institute for Logistics and Production Systems a special program has been developed modifying the existing automatic control in order to achieve the same mechanical properties of the strips with different transfer bar temperature.

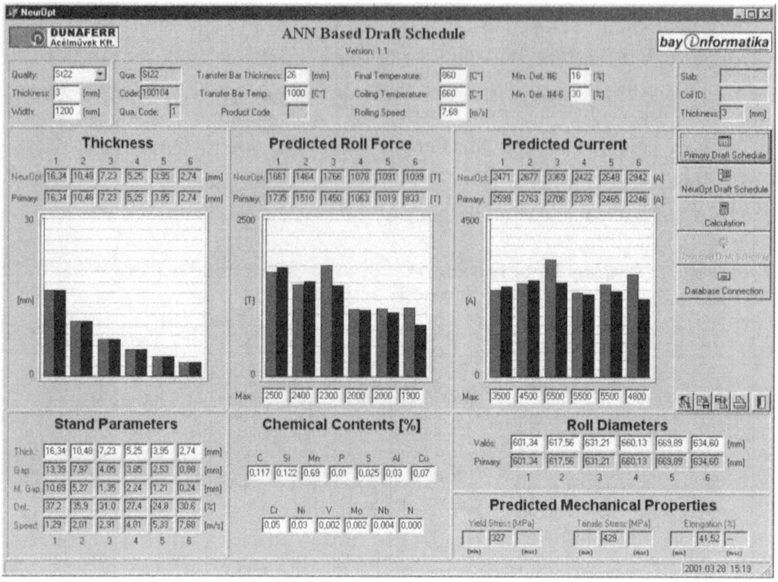

Fig. 5. User interface of the program, used on workshop level in the hot rolling mill.

Acknowledgements. The authors would like to thank the Committee for Technical Development (OMFB), Hungary, for the financial support of the research.

References

1 Hatvany, J.Efficient Use of Deficient Knowledge, Annals of the CIRP, 1983,Vol. 32/1, pp. 423-425.

2 L.Cser: Stand der Anwendung von Expertensystemen in der Umformtechnik, Umformtechnik 25 (1991) 4, pp.77-83, Umformtechnik 25 (1992) 1, pp.51-60, Meisenbach Verlag,

3 Larkiola, et al., (1995), Proc. of Materials Processing in the Computer Age II, 209-220, February, Las Vegas, Nevada, USA.

4 L.Cser, A.S. Korhonen, O. Simula, J. Larkiola, P. Myllykoski, J.Ahola: Knowledge Based Methods in Modelling of Rolling of Steel Strip (Keynote), Proc. of the CIRP International Seminar on Intelligent Computation in Manufacturing Engineering, ICME 98 (Ed. by R. Teti), Capri (Naples), Italy, July 1-3, 1998, 265-272.

5 Gramckow,O., Jansen,M., Feldkeller, B.: Anwendung Neuronaler Netze für die Prozeßsteuerung, Tagungsband MEFORM 98, 25-27 Februar 1998, pp. 1-23

6 L.Cser, A.S.Korhonen, J.Gulyás, P.Mäntylä, O. Simula, Gy. Reiss, P.Ruha:Data Mining and State Monitoring in Hot Rolling (Keynote), IPMM'99, The 2nd International Conference on Intelligent Processing and Manufacturing of Materials, Honolulu, Hawaii, July 10/15, 1999, IEEE, Proc. 529-536

Non-linear Prediction of Vibration Series for Turbogenerator Unit

Zhi-Hua Ge, Zhong-He Han, and Chang-Fu Ding

Thermal Power Engineering Department
Postbox 27, North China Electric Power University
Baoding 071003, P. R. CHINA
ge-zh@263.net

Abstract. A model for predicting vibration series of turbogenerator unit is proposed by combining ANNs techniques with non-linear phase space reconstruction. Such established model doesn't make any hypothesis to history data, but reproduces the dynamic specific of attractor by phase space reconstruction. ANNs architecture to which the prediction model applys is discussed. The influences of embedding dimension m and time delay τ on prediction accuracy are also discussed in detail. Fairly well agreement can be acquired between the predictions of model and actual vibration series of unit.

1 Introduction

As the development of technology, in order to realize optimal and effective management of turbogenerator unit, surely the fault diagnosis and preventive maintenance will be replaced by predictive maintenance, among which, prediction of future behaviors of machinery is of great importance. At present, time series predictions of vibration have two approach denotes as model with parameters and model without any parameters [1,2]. Based on the first method, hypothesis must be given for the history data. Prediction results are acquired by anticipating the parameters of the model. However, neglecting any other information which might be available may lead to lower prediction accuracy. It can be concluded as a linear method.

Vibration of turbogenerator unit is a characteristics non-linear behavior, thus any attempts to applying linear method to anticipate its future behavior will neglect much valuable non-linear characteristics. On the other hand, due to the complexity of vibration phenomena, exact mathematical model is still unavailable, or cannot be solved because of insufficient initial parameters.

In the past few decades, time series prediciton problem are approached to its close-to-exact results in many fields by employing chaotic prediction theorem, such as the attempts to predict electric power consumption, the tendency of stock market and sloar macula[3~6]. Based on non-linear theorem, manifold from the time series originated can be used to construct another space, which could reappears the complete characteristics of original system completely. Besides, the artificial neural network models are powerful enough to realize time series prediction by applying manifold reconstruction. A prediction model based on ANN technology is the method of non-parameter, that is to say, ANN techniques for time series prediction with respect to time series history doesn't require any hypothesis for the studied system to build a

L. Monostori, J. Váncza, and M. Ali (Eds.): IEA/AIE 2001, LNAI 2070, pp. 797-803, 2001.

reliable model. Many nonlinear systems can be described fairly well by such ANNs model.

It is the concern of the present study to explore the method of prediction of vibration series for turbogenerator unit by combining ANNs techniques with non-linear phase space reconstruction. In this paper, the proposed prediction model is verified by real vibration signals.

2 Non-linear Prediction Approach for Vibration of Turbogenerator

Two processes are necessary for non-linear prediction models, which are reconstruction of phase space and approximation of non-linear function.

2.1 Reconstruction of Phase Space

Real turbogenerator system is undoubtedly multi-dimension. However, only one or several variables for describling complicated phenomena can be deserved, such as amplitude, phase et al. For a system space of m-dimension, the instantaneous state of vibration system behaves a condition point in vibration curve. If the vibration characteistics can be summerized to a group of determined laws, it can be used to describe the continuous process of the system. According to chaotic theory, this indicates that all factors affect the vibration behavior will concentrate to one subclass of phase space named attractor. The attractor contains all specific of the current vibration system.

Expressing the outcomes of vibration phenomena over time form a vibration series as $\{x_i(t)\}$ (i=0, 1, ..., N-1), the information about current state can be then expressed as m-dimension time delay vector. The vectors that are reconstructed from the time series are as follows:

$$\tilde{x}_1 = \{x_1, x_{\tau+1}, x_{2\tau+1}, \ldots, x_{(m-1)\tau+1}\}$$

$$\tilde{x}_2 = \{x_{p+1}, x_{p+\tau+1}, x_{p+2\tau+1}, \ldots, x_{p+(m-1)\tau+1}\}$$

$$\vdots$$

$$\tilde{x}_N = \{x_{Np+1}, x_{Np+\tau+1}, x_{Np+2\tau+1}, \ldots, x_{Np+(m-1)\tau+1}\} \qquad (1)$$

where p is the inter-vector delay and τ is delay time, m stands for embedding dimension, N is the number of vectors reconstructed from the vibration series. The selection of these parameters can refer to literature [7].

According to Takens's theorem [7], if the dimension of attactor of the vibration series is estimated as d_G, the phase space of dynamic system can be embedded in a manifold of dimension $m \geq 2d_G + 1$. In such condition, the specific of system attactor will be contained in these series, which means that the history behavior contains the current information of the system. So phase space reconstructed by (1) can be taken as the differential homeomorphism of original space□and also, there exists a smooth mapping F: $R^m \rightarrow R$ between these two space. The mapping is with the conditions of

$$x(t+\tau) = F(x(t)) \tag{2}$$

expanded as:

$$x(t+\tau) = f\{x(t), x(t-\tau), \ldots, x(t-(m-1)\tau)\} \tag{3}$$

where f is mapping from m-dimensional space to one-dimensional real space. The essence of prediction of vibration state is that using known N dada to approximate functions f, or get the approximate mapping $\tilde{f}$.

2.2 Approximations of Non-linear Functions

Theoretical work shows that, in addition to their powerful ability to uniformly approximate almost any arbitrary continuous function on a compact domain, ANNs can also effectively construct approximations for unknown complex nonlinear functions by learning from examples (only known outcomes of the function) [8]. This ability to approximate unknown complex input-output mapping makes them attractive in practical applications where traditional computational structures have performed poorly, such as those with ambiguous data or large contextual influence.

3 ANNs Prediction Model

3.1 Architecture of Neural Network

As shown in Fig.1, a three-layer BP network is employed to construct a vibration prediction model. Three different layer types can be distinguished: input layer (the layer $[X] = \{x_1, x_2, \ldots x_n)$ that known series of measured signals at time *t-1*, *t-2*,..., *t-n* are applied to), output layer (the layer $[Y]$ that outputs result of predictive value at time t) and one hidden layer between input and output layer. The model doesn't need any assumptions to analytical signals, but trains the networks with original samples directly. The acquired non-linear function $\tilde{f}$ is saved by weights. The network considered here are either feedforward, in which the signal flow is from input layer towards output layer by activation function, or recurrent, in which the feedforward signal flow is supplemented with feedback error flow.

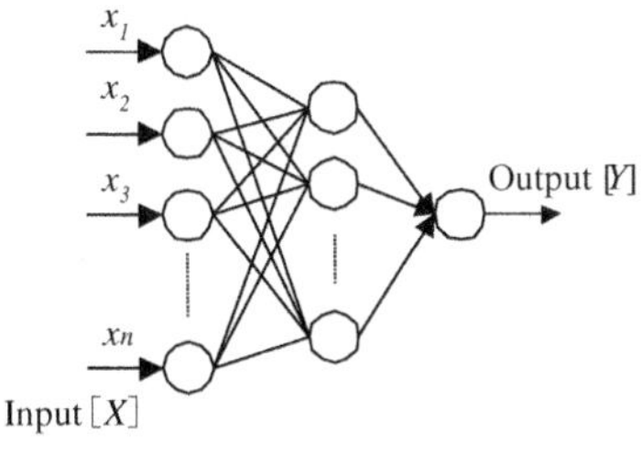

Fig. 1. ANNs architecture

3.2 Vibration Prediction Process

Step 1 The collected vibration signals are preprocessed by filtering the noise and possibly stationarization, and form the vibration curve with respect to continuous times. Then reconstruct the vectors [*X*] from the vibration series. The known vibration series are divided into two regions: training zone and verification zone, of which the former is about two times of the later. Here we define "window" of width n as region formed by n nodes with equal time interval on vibration series. Applying these n nodes to input layer of training NNs, the target output is the neighbour vibration value of the last node. Again according to Taken' theorem, the width of training window n must not be smaller than the embedding dimension m of the studied vibrations series in order to save as much inherent characteristics of dynamic system as possible. Of course, enough training windows should be includes providing more samples to NNs.

Step 2 In training region, n nodes in window are applied to input layer of NNs successively to obtain output result. The output is compared with target output, and the weights and output, as well as the number of the hidden layer neurons are modified by the gradient decent error minimization technique until the output values have fulfilled the tolerance requirement. Iterate this process by moving the window to obtain new input nodes and traget output until the window has been slided through the whole training region.

Step 3 Predicting the series value at verification region by the acquired NNs samples. Compare the output result with actual value in this zone and record every error. Iterate the process until the input window has been slided through the whole verification region.

3.3 Selection of Embedding Dimension m and Time Delay τ

For the vectors [*X*] reconstructed from the vibration series, the selection of embedding dimension m and time delay τ is of the most important effect on specific of the recontructed phase space. Too small time delay will lead to information redundancy, the vector may lose its independence. On the other hand, large time delay will weaken the correlation between neighbour signals.

As for embedding dimension, although Takens gave the principle $m>=2d+1$, the dimension d of dynamic system is unkown in most cases, so the selection of m is still a problem. However, it can be sure that a larger embedding dimension m will be more beneficial to some extent. But too large embedding dimension can also reduce the reliability of the model due to the improving complexity.

The most current methods of embedding dimension selection still have some randomicity[9]. In present paper, we use gradual approximation method to acquire embedding dimension and time delay by judging whether the accuracy of prediciton can converge as gradually increasing these two parameters respectively. A certain dynamic system can usually converge to a low-dimension space, which means a regular embedding dimension m. Furthermore, the later results will illustrate that, as increasing embedding dimension to a extent, the prediction accuracy will no longer improve.

Having selected the optimal window width n by the determined m and τ, we can conduct the above three steps in 3.2. The ANNs model such established can then be used to forecast the future development of vibration series of turbogenerator.

3.4 Prediction

Sliding the input window to the last *n* nodes of the known series and applying them into prediction networks, the output is the predictive value of vibration series on next step. Iterating the process continuously can obtain the future bahavior of vibration.

Self-adaptive ability is endued to the ANNs model by modifing input window with updated data during prediciton process.

4 Results with Discussion

Prediction of vibration state have been realized in condition monitor and fault diagnosis system of 100MW turbogenerator unit at the first power plant of Tianjin. Two vibration series were selected here for analyzing. Data sampling rate is defined 32 point per period while data sampling interval is defined as Δt, and time delay $\tau = k*\Delta t$ (*k* is integer).

Applying the parameter r^2 to express the accuracy of prediction model:

$$r^2 = 1 - \frac{1/n\sum(x_i - \hat{x}_i)^2}{1/n\sum(x_i - \bar{x})^2} \tag{4}$$

where, $x_i, \hat{x}_i$ denote actual and predicted vibration values respectively, while $\bar{x}$ denotes the mean of the actual data.

The coefficient r^2 is a function of the mean squared error normalized by the variance of the actual data. For a prefect prediction model, the coefficient of determination r^2 should be 1. r^2 closes to zero means that the prediction model cannot work.

For actual vibration signals, the influence of time delay τ on prediction accuracy r^2 is shown in Fig.2. While τ is selected a small value, the coefficient of determination r^2 is rather low, indicates a poor prediction result. As rising τ near to $4*\Delta t$, r^2 approximate to its greatest value. However, as τ is greater than $6*\Delta t$, the prediction accuracy r^2 begins to decrease. This may be concluded that the best value of time delay τ is about within $(4\sim6)*\Delta t$, among which Δt is data sampling interval.

Fig.3 shows the influence of embedding dimension *m* on prediction accuracy r^2. As far as embedding dimension *m* rises r^2 will increase. While embedding dimension $m>8$, the accuracy of prediction don't change obviously longer, r^2 will maintain a constant value.

The sample acquired by VDAX and computer from X direction of shaft vibration of bearing No.1 in a certain period is divided into two regions. The former one is used to establish prediction model for vibration series. The later one is employed to verify the model by comparing the prediction data with measured data. The comparison is illustrated by Fig. 4. Fig. 5 shows the results of another vibration series.

It can be shown from Fig.4 that the prediciton accuracy r^2 is as high as 0.925. Fig. 5 indicates that prediction accuracy of 0.874 is achieved, which may indicate that the predictions of model agree well with actual vibration series.

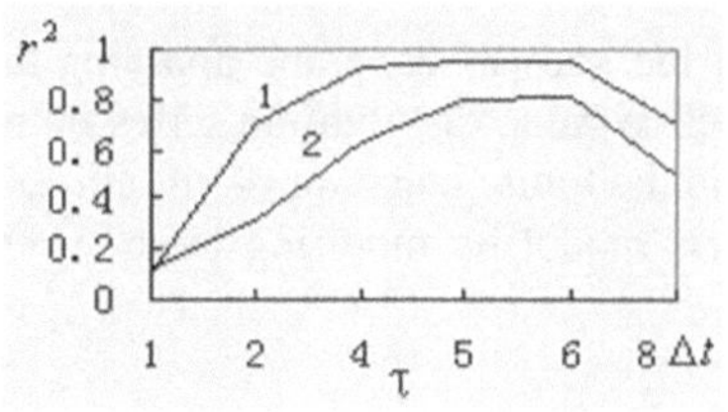

Fig. 2. Influence of time delay τ on $r^2$1: series 1; 2: series 2

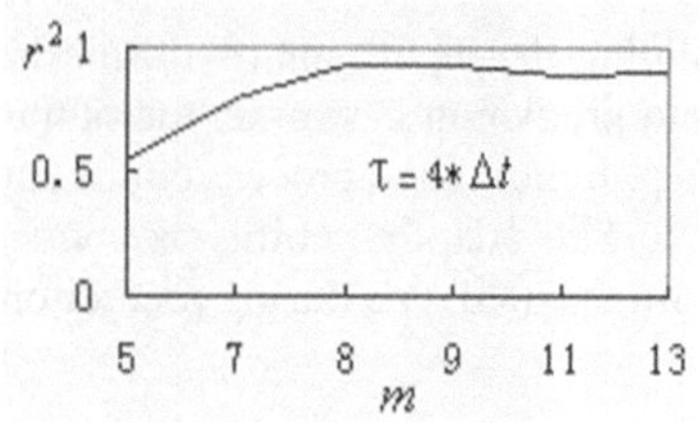

Fig. 3. Influence of m on r^2

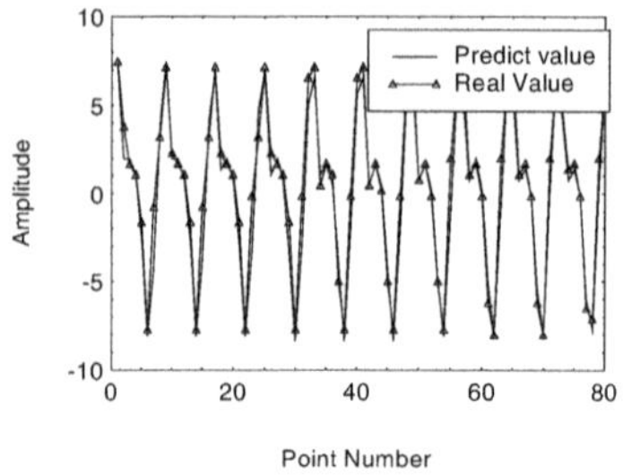

Fig. 4. The prediction result of X direction of bearing No.1

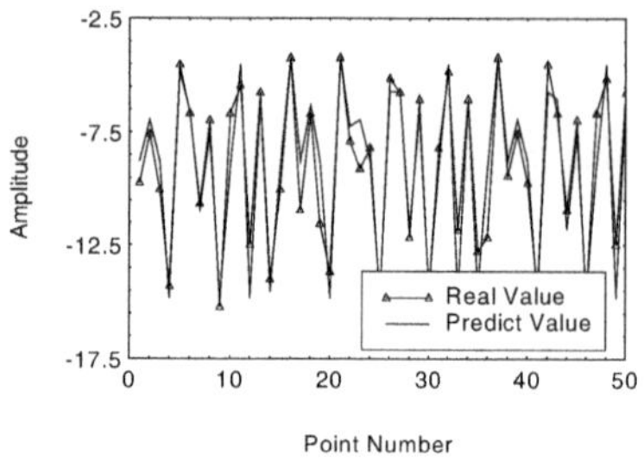

Fig. 5. The prediction result of Y direction of bearing No.1

5 Concluding Remarks

ANNs techniques is combined with non-linear phase space reconstruction to predict vibration behaviors for turbogenerator unit. The proposed prediction model doesn't make any hypothesis to history data, but reproduces the dynamic specific of attractor by phase space reconstruction according to embedding theorem. Proper ANNs model selected provides the basis to achive the reconstruction of attractor and conducts the prediction processes. A method of gradual approximation is employed to determine embedding dimension m and time delay τ, which have important influence on predictive accuracy. More effective method for determining m and τ should be explored further. Moreover, prediction accuracy can obviously depend on the dimensions of signal itself, which should be paid more attention in furture.

References

1. Najim K, Youlal H, Praly L, Najim M. Direct adaptive control of a pulsed liquid-liquid extraction column. Int J of Adaptive Control and Signal Processing, 1988, **2**(3): 181~191
2. Slock D T M, Kailath T. Fast transversal filter for adaptive linear phase filtering. Left bracket? Right bracket. Int J of Adaptive Control and Signal Processing, 1988, **2**(3): 157~179
3. Drossu R, Obradovic Z. Rapid design os neural networks for time series prediction. IEEE Computational Science & Engineering, 1996, (2): 77~88

4. Casdagli M. Nonlinear modeling of chaotic time series: series and application. In: Kim J H, Stringer J eds, Applied Chaos, New York: John Wiley & Sons, 1992
5. Chow T W S, Leung C T. Neural networks short-term load forecasting weather compensation. IEEE Trans on Power System, 1996, **11**(4): 1736~1742
6. Drossu R, Obradovic Z. Rapid design of neural networks for times series prediction. IEEE Computational Science and Engineering, 1996, 3(3): 78-89
7. Takens F. Detecting strange attractors in turbulence□in: Rand D A and Yang L S eds, Dynamical Systems and Turbulence. Berlin: Springer-Verlag, 1981
8. Funhashi K. On the approximate realization of continuous mapping by neural networks. Neural Networks, 1989, (2): 183~192
9. Kenel M B, Brown R, Abarbanel H D I. Determining embedding dimension for phase-space reconstruction using a geometrical construction. Phys Rev A, 1992, **45**: 3403~3411

Autonomous Agents Architecture to Supervise and Control a Wastewater Treatment Plant

David Riaño[1], Miquel Sànchez-Marrè[2], and Ignasi R.-Roda[3]

[1] Enginyeria Informàtica i Matemàtiques, Universitat Rovira i Virgili
Carretera de Salou s/n, 43006 Tarragona, Catalonia, Spain
drianyo@etse.urv.es

[2] Llenguatges i Sistemes Informàtics, Universitat Politècnica de Catalunya
Edifici C5, Jordi Girona 1-3, 08034 Barcelona, Catalonia, Spain
miquel@lsi.upc.es

[3] Laboratori d'Enginyeria Química i Ambiental, Universitat de Girona
Campus de Montilivi, 17071 Girona, Catalonia, Spain
ignasi@lequia.udg.es

Abstract. Intelligent agents and multiagent societies are becoming a recurrent solution to complex distributed artificial intelligence problems. Some of the agent properties determine the sort of problems that they can solve efficiently. Here, we describe a complex environmental process, Wastewater Treatment Plant, which is difficult to control. An agent-based architecture is proposed, which improves some previous works on Intelligent Systems which are not based on agents. The proposed architecture is described and several specific-purpose agents are designed for that problem and their interactions explicated.

1 Introduction

Intelligent agents [4][5] have become a common approach to solve an increasing number of problems which require artificial intelligence treatments. Some of the agent properties as autonomy, social behavior, reactivity, and initiative [2] are guidelines towards the sort of problems that agents can solve efficiently. These properties also indicate that agents are not isolate elements but elements which interact within a multiagent system (MAS) whose final purpose is to supply an intelligent global performance.

Environmental systems are usually described [9] as dynamic, spatially distributed, complex, random, periodic, and heterogeneous systems. Therefore, any Environmental Decision Support System (EDSS) [1] used to manage a particular environmental domain must be designed to satisfy all these features.

In the Wastewater Treatment Plant (WWTP) domain, the complexity of the process -composed by several operational units- makes the implementation of an automatic process control difficult. Different mathematical models have been put forward to describe them [3][11] though they cannot deal with all kind of WWTP deata as qualitative, uncertain and approximate knowledge, off-line and

L. Monostori, J. Váncza, and M. Ali (Eds.): IEA/AIE 2001, LNAI 2070, pp. 804–811, 2001.

subjective information, dynamic conditions, and constraints to keep the outflow under the environmental law limits and minimizing the environmental effects.

All these features reveal that WWTP supervision and control can only be treated in a multi-disciplinary way, that includes: monitoring, modeling, quality and cost control, qualitative information, expert knowledge and experiential knowledge. So, the management of a whole WWTP (system evaluation, diagnosis, supervision, actuation, etc.) seems appropriate for a multiagent distributed AI architecture [4].

In this paper we study the requirements of a WWTP control and supervision system. In section 2 we describe the WWTP domain. In section 3 we show some specific agents that work together in order to control and supervise a WWTP. Conclusions are in section 4.

2 Waste-Water Treatment Plants

Wastewater treatment processes [15] are usually called pre-treatment, primary and secondary. *Pre-treatment* includes simple screening to remove large floating objects and grit. *Primary treatment* uses sedimentation and coagulation-flocculation to settle most of the suspended solids from wastewater. Although pre-treatment and primary remove about 35% of the Biological Oxygen Demand (BOD) -a global organic measure-, and 60% of the Suspended Solids (SS), water still has both enough organic matter to cause dissolved oxygen depletion problems and also enough nutrients to accelerate eutrophisation in the rivers.

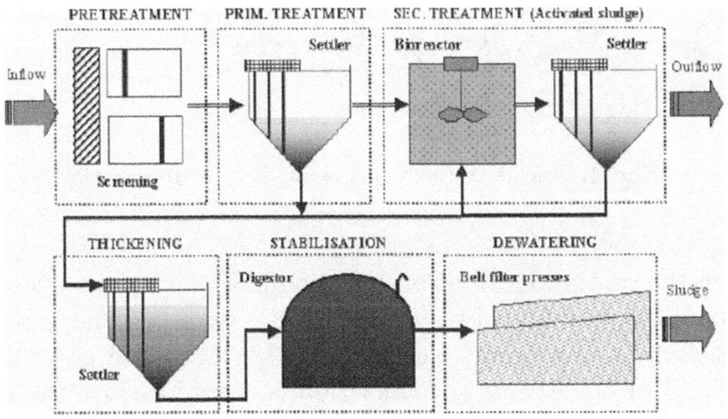

Fig. 1. Flowsheet of a conventional Wastewater Treatment Plant.

A *secondary treatment* involving the microbial oxidation of wastes is usually required to meet discharge permits. Such biological treatment mimics nature by using micro-organisms to oxidize biodegradable organic into stabilized, low-energy compounds. See arrows in figure 1. The most frequent secondary treatment is *activated sludge process*, where oxidation is carried out in a bioreactor.

Then, a settler is used to separate micro-organisms from the wastewater. Secondary treatment removes about 90% BOD and 90% SS. The process produces a large amount of a subproduct called sludge that must be treated before it is discharged to the environment. The sludge treatment involves a new set of units as thickening, stabilization and dewatering.

3 An Agent Architecture for WWTP Supervision and Control

Intelligent agents can be used to build a system for supervising and controlling a WWTP. Two alternatives to construct the system arise [9]:the *spatial distribution criterion* that studies the WWTP process units and assigns an agent to each unit in order to look after the unit behavior, and the *funtionality distribution criterion* that analyses the control actions that take place in the plant, groups these actions which are related to a same concept, and assigns an agent to each concept so that it is responsible of carrying out the control actions related.

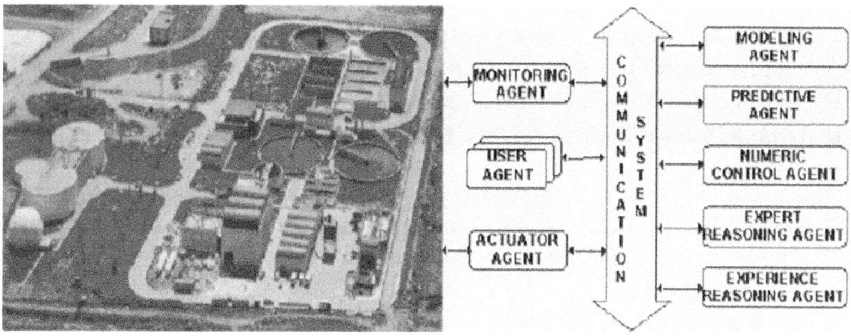

Fig. 2. The WWTP Multiagent System Interaction.

Although the spatial distribution criterion has been used to develop a previous agent-based system [11], two are the main criticisms: the autonomy of the units is not assured, and agents perform complex tasks that go in the detriment of their specialization. Agents specialization is desirable since the more specific an agent is, the more intelligent behavior it can have.

The main drawback of the functionality distribution criterion lies in the amount of experience required to select a correct set of WWTP basic actions. Nevertheless, agents under this option are autonomous, social, reactive, and they have initiative in the sense that they have their own vision of the WWTP, they know the functionality that they are supplying and they work to achieve it. Each agent has to decide what to do on the basis of an internal state and its perception of the WWTP. Moreover, it plans the course of action and it is engaged in a conversation with external agents whenever that is useful for its purposes.

Here we propose a WWTP supervision and control system which is the result of applying the functionality distribution criterion. The specific-purpose agents created are decided according to our experience in designing and implementing WWTP intelligent systems [10,12,13]. Figure 2 shows the architecture of the MAS conceived. There we can distinguish the WWTP, the communication system, and eight sort of agents.

3.1 The Monitoring Agent

The monitoring agent (MA) is responsible of the direct actions on the WWTP data income. Figure 3 represents it as a chart. It interacts with both the plant and the communication system. MA takes the information about the WWTP by means of sensors that supply continuous on-line information about the state of the plant at different places. A second source of information comes from both the laboratory and the operators. MA accepts the sensors inputs, decides which data to store and to ignore, and supplies a quick access memory organization. This organization is under continuous adaptation so that access is always efficient (dynamic indexing) [8]. The filtering block reduces the input noise. Then, data is evaluated and analyzed. Whilst superfluous, defective, or useless information is rejected, the rest of information is used to detect incoherent data. Coherent data is incorporated to the evolutive Data Base.

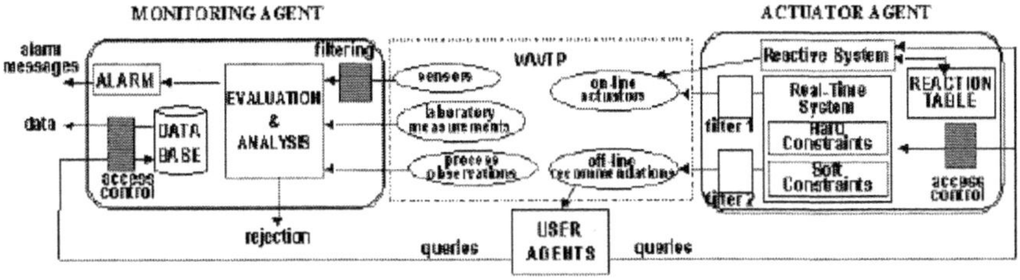

Fig. 3. The Monitoring Agent and the Actuator Agent.

MA accepts global and partial accesses to the data stored. All the queries are used to analyze how frequent these questions are and which organization of the data base warranties an efficient access. This organization involves the data fractionating [8], the use of indexes or hash files, sorting processes, etc.

MA can be used remotely to display functions that represent the temporal evolution of the data. Moreover, MA incorporates some basic alarm capabilities, e.g. if some sensor is out of the range of normality, an alarm is raised. This alarm will be captured by the actuator agent or a user agent that treats it.

The basic interactions of MA are the following: it supplies information on past situations, permits a continuous display of data or expressions, supplies a basic alarm system, and captures some data from the WWTP.

3.2 The Actuator Agent

This agent is responsible of interacting with the on-line actuators and sending the recommended actions to the operator (off-line actuation). The actuator agent (AA) acts over some parameters of the WWTP. In the activated sludge process, these parameters are the dissolved oxygen concentration (DO), the sludge purge flow (SPF) and the sludge recirculation flow (SRF).

Figure 3 depicts AA. On-line actions are the result of some alarm situation or user order. These actions are attended by a *reactive* system that acts on the actuators directly. The reaction table contains the situations on which the system must react. On-line *hard-constrained* actions affect the actuators but they have a filtering mechanism in order to control which of them must be really done. Finally, *soft-constrained* actions produce recommendations that goes to the WWTP laboratory.

The interactions of AA could be summarized in: it suggests orders, asks for checking in drastic actions, accepts direct orders over on-line actuators of the WWTP, processes alarms and reacts to solve them.

3.3 User Agents

The WWTP intelligent system must be carefully defined to meet the requirements of all the particular type of end users that work in the plant. EDSS are used by three user categories [9]: the environmental scientist that wants to develop models and experimentally test them, the environmental manager or operator that uses the models generated by the scientist, and the environmental stakeholder or head of the plant that wants access to understanding about the responses of different parts of the system under proposed management decisions.

We have already identified two more users which are the developer or knowledge engineer and the installer or computer scientist.

The basic interactions of the user agents (UA) are: they accept orders and transform them into MAS goals, receive and display information and suggestions, and supply justifications to certain actions.

3.4 The Modeling Agent

Mechanistic or numerical modeling of the WWTP contributes to have a global description of the plant to be used in the control process. There are many mechanistic models and classical control engineering methods [11]. They are based on a numeric model which is useful to control the plant in a stationary situation but which cannot work properly when there are either abnormal or unforeseen situations. The modeling agent (MO) integrates several numeric and qualitative models which are used whenever an agent requires a specific control or simulation of the WWTP.

The interactions of MO could be summarized in: it accepts a selection of simulation and control models, enables and disables the simulation and automatic control of the WWTP, asks for input data to perform simulation and control, and suggests control actions.

3.5 The Predictive Agent

Predictions are based on the WWTP models and they could be made by MO. However, prediction ia as an important feature of hard-real time control systema that it requires a special attention in WWTP. This is why we devote an agent (PA) to predict tasks exclusively. PA is in charge of selecting the best simulation model among the ones available from MO, interpreting the results of simulations and broadcasting them.

The interactions of PA could be summarized in: it studies hypothetical situations, informs about abnormal situations before they happen, admits user decisions on the simulation model, enables and disables simulation models, and decides the current best model.

3.6 The Numerical Control Agent

Whenever the operation of the WWTP is normal, numerical control algorithms are suitable to control the basic parameters of the process: DO, SPF, SRF, and other inputs to some automatic machines in the WWTP, such as the cleaning grid at the pretreatment, etc.

The numerical control agent (NC) is in charge of selecting the best control algorithm among the ones available from MO. The control algorithms can be predictive, optimal, adaptive, feedback or feedforward control schemes among others.

The interactions of NC could be summarized in: it accepts orders to activate or maintain the automatic control, accepts orders to deactivate the automatic control, admits user decisions on the control algorithm to apply, and analyzes the input data to decide the best control algorithm.

3.7 The Expert Reasoning Agent

Each WWTP has its own supervisor, regardless of it is a person or a team. This supervisor is expert the fields that are involved in the plant's daily activity: chemistry, biology, electricity, mechanics, etc. The expert reasoning agent (EX) is used to contain all the expert knowledge available. EX offers some knowledge engineering capabilities as knowledge acquisition methodologies [12], diagnosis techniques [14], and knowledge evaluation procedures. It also supplies an interface with the internet which is used to obtain information about other WWTPs.

EX is implemented as an expert system with a modular knowledge-base specialized in the different process units of the plant. From the current data available at the WWTP, EX diagnoses the state of the plant according to its rule-based knowledge, and proposes an actuation plan. EX can also act as a tutor system that explains what is happening in the plant.

The interactions of EX could be summarized in: it incorporates user knowledge, interacts with the Internet to have an updated knowledge-base, makes a rule-based diagnosis of the operating situation of the plant and justifies it, accepts data and incorporates it if the data is recurrent, asks for advise on knowledge before accepting it, explains why a new knowledge is rejected or accepted, and answers the actuator and the user agents questions.

3.8 The Experience Reasoning Agent

This agent makes an experiential-based diagnosis and solution plan, by means of case-based reasoning. The experiential knowledge about practical problem solving is represented by means of cases or experiences that include the description of situations. A case library contains information about previous situations and the solutions given to them as well as a measure of their efficiency.

Whenever a new problem is solved, the experience reasoning agent (EA) learns new experiences provided by an expert or another source of knowledge.

The interactions of EA could be summarized in: it learns about the success or failure of past solved practical knowledge, makes a case-based diagnosis of the WWTP operating situation and a case-based proposal of an actuation plan, forgets some cases if the feedback of their use is not good, explains why a new knowledge is rejected or accepted, and answers actuator or user agents questions.

4 Conclusions and Work in Process

Our work followed two lines: analyze the WWTP domain and select the developing tool. The analysis of a WWTP has been twofold. On the one hand, we have applied several AI methodologies to solve some aspects of the supervision and control of a WWTP [6][11][13]. On the other hand, we analyzed how a MAS could improve the supervision and control of a real WWTP [7]. Also, we have been working to find a tool for agent development that could satisfy all the requirements that the experts recommend in a system that has to supervise and control a WWTP. This tool is Jade[1].

Here, a new MAS architecture has been given to supervise and control a WWTP. Eight different types of specific-purpose autonomous agents have been identified, their role described, and their structure proposed. Now, we are working to implement and integrate all the methodologies to the final MAS system. Copious information is also being stored in order to have a feasible test bed for local executions of the agents.

Acknowledgements. This work has been supported by the Spanish CICyT projects BIO96-1229, TIC96-878, TIC96-1038-04, TIC2000-1011, and AMB97-889, the CIRIT SGR 177 (1997) of the Generalitat de Catalunya as a "Grup de Recerca Consolidat", and ACCES99-15.

[1] `http://sharon.cselt.it/project/jade`

References

1. Cortés U., Sànchez-Marrè M., Ceccaroni L., and Roda I. Environmental Decision Support Systems and Artificial Intelligence. Applied Intelligence, 13(1) (2000) 77-91.
2. Goodwin R., Formalizing properties of agents. Technical Report CMU-CS93-159. School of CS, Carnegie-Melon University. Pittsburgh, PA (1993).
3. Gujer, W., Henze, M., Takashi, M., van Loosdrecht, M. - IAWQ Task Group on Mathematical Modeling for Design and Operation of biological wastewater treatment. Fourth Kollekolle seminar on Activated Sludge Modeling: Modeling and Microbiology of activated sludge processes. Denmark, (1998).
4. Jennings N. R., Sycara K., Wooldridge M., A Roadmap of Agent Research and Development, Autonomous Agents and Multi-agents Systems **1** (1998) 275-306.
5. O'Hare G. M. P. and Jennings N. R. Foundations of Distributed Artificial Intelligence. John Wiley (1996).
6. Riaño D., On the process of making descriptive rules, Julian A. Padget (Ed.) Lecture Notes in AI **1624**, Springer-Verlag (1999).
7. Riaño D., Sànchez-Marrè M., Roda I. A Wastewater Treatment Plant Multiagent System. 3rd World Multiconference on Systemics, Cybernetics and Informatics (SCI'99), Orlando, USA (1999) 586-591.
8. Riaño D., Gramajo J., Automatic Extraction of Data Structure. Technical Report DEIM-RR-00-004. Departament d'Enginyeria Informàtica, URV, Tarragona, Spain (2000).
9. Rizzoli A. E., Young W. J., Delivering environmental decision support systems: software tools and techniques. Journal of Environmental Modelling & Software, **12**(2/3) (1997) 237-249.
10. Roda I. R., Comas J., Colprim J., Baeza J., Sànchez-Marrè M. and Cortés U. A Multi-paradigm Decision Support System to Improve Wastewater Treatment Plant Operation. In AAAI'99 Workshop on Environmental Decision Support Systems and Artificial Intelligence. AAAI 1999 National Conference on Artificial Intelligence. Orlando, FL, (1999).
11. Sànchez-Marrè M., Cortés U., Lafuente J., Roda I. R., Poch M., DAI-DEPUR: an integrated and distributed architecture for wastewater treatment plants supervision. Artificial Intelligence in Engineering **10** (1996) 275-285.
12. Sànchez-Marrè M., Cortés U., Béjar J., De Gràcia J., Lafuente J. and Poch M. Concept Formation in WWTP by means of Classification Techniques: a Compared Study. Applied Intelligence **7**(2) (1997) 147-166.
13. Sànchez-Marrè M., Cortés U., R-Roda I., Poch M., and Lafuente J.. Learning and Adaptation in WWTP through Case-Based Reasoning. Special issue on Machine Learning of Microcomputers in Civil Engineering **12**(4) (1997) 251-266.
14. Serra P., Sànchez-Marrè M., Lafuente J., Cortés U. and Poch M. ISCWAP: a knowledge-based system for supervising activated sludge processes. Computers Chem. Engng., **21**(2) (1997) 211-221.
15. WPCF. Operation of Municipal Wastewater Treatment Plants. Manual of Practice No. 11, Water Pollution Control Federation, Alexandria, (1994).

Agent-Based Support for Handling Environmental and Life-Cycle Issues

Elisabeta Zudor and László Monostori

Computer and Automation Research Institute, Hungarian Academy of Sciences
Kende u. 13-17, Budapest, POB 63, H-1518, Hungary
Phone: (36 1) 2096-990, Fax: (36 1) 4667-503,
ilie@sztaki.hu, laszlo.monostori@sztaki.hu

Abstract. The paper attempts to illustrate the positive interference of life cycle assessment techniques of products and production facilities, on the one hand, and of agent-based approaches applicable within their life cycles, on the other. In the approach proposed in the paper, not only the cost problems, but also the environmental impacts of processes and operations are considered during a resource allocation process relying on market principles. A hierarchical rule structure called Priority Rules System is introduced.

1 Introduction

Due to the numerous changes on the world market in the past decades, the key selling points for manufacturers have changed. In order to remain competitive, manufacturers had to extend their practices guided just by economic criteria like efficiency, productivity, profitability with new ones like health and environmental impacts, resource and energy conservation, waste management and social aspects. Therefore, a society must find a compromise between being internationally competitive and having a healthy environment, between productivity of labour and socially healthy workplaces, and other similar apparently contradictory matters.

The increasing product variety, together with demands for better quality, shorter throughput times and lower stock volumes, have called for an improved reaction to perturbations in the external environment, changes in the manufacturing systems and uncertainties of manufacturing processes.

In our view, the problem of the continuously growing complexity of manufacturing processes and the necessity of considering the environmental issues in the manufacturing, can be advantageous addressed by using agent-based approaches.

The paper gives a short overview of life cycle assessment techniques of products and production facilities, on the one hand, and of agent-based approaches applicable within their life cycles, on the other, in order to illustrate their positive interference.

Furthermore, an approach that incorporates environmental aspects in agent-based dynamic production control is presented. This includes the a.) Presentation of the functional structure of the agents in the model, b.) Description of the mechanism of resource allocation process, c.) Visualisation of information exchange.

L. Monostori, J. Váncza, and M. Ali (Eds.): IEA/AIE 2001, LNAI 2070, pp. 812-820, 2001.

2 Environmental Issues in the Life Cycle of Products and Production Facilities

The environmental focus must be shifted from the production to the products themselves covering all life cycle phases, i.e. material acquisition, production, distribution, use, and disposal [8]. In other words, Product stewardship is emphasized, which is an intrinsic part of any *environmental management system (EMS)* action plan, in that the responsibility of the company goes beyond its operations to include the responsibility for their products' environmental performance throughout the product life cycle [8].

Life cycle engineering is the art of designing the product life cycle through choices about product concept, structure, materials and processes, and *life cycle assessment (LCA)* is the tool that visualizes the environmental and resource consequences of these choices. And finally, *life cycle analysis* makes quantifying the environmental impacts possible [8].

In the designing or redesigning process for reduction of environmental effects, usually, the following *EcoDesign strategies* are applied. Try to

- find a product (service) that is more environmentally friendly than the present one used,
- select low impact materials,
- reduce weight and volume,
- choose clean production techniques,
- select a clean form of distribution,
- reduce energy and supply consumption during use,
- use a product as long as possible,
- make products easy to repair or manufacture,
- limit the size of toxic items,
- design with monomaterials,
- integrate parts that need to be disassembled.

During *life cycle costing (LCC)*, the costs of production, installation, usage and disposal are analyzed and allocated, aiming at minimizing the total costs. One important area of future activity is the internationalization of environmental externalities in cost calculations [12].

As an illustration for treating production facilities as products themselves, [13] presents a methodology for incorporating health and environmental hazard information into manufacturing systems planning through the use of process mechanics models, and system workflow modeling. Implementation examples included simulation of hazard impacts due to process parameter selection, catalyst selection and resource allocation (waterjet deburring versus mechanical deburring). Product life cycle costing is applied to manufacturing systems in [14].

As to process planning, a hierarchical part planning strategy for evaluating the energy, mass and environmental impact of machined parts is presented in [15]. The described strategy incorporates both micro planning (optimization at the feature level) and macro planning (determination of feature sequence through the analysis of geometric and process interaction). The allowable level of environmental data uncertainty for a given planning decision is also described.

3 Agent-Based Approaches within the Life Cycle of Products and Systems

Over the past years significant research efforts have been devoted to the development and use of *Distributed Artificial Intelligence (DAI)* techniques (e.g. [16]). An *agent* is a real or virtual entity able to act on itself and on the surrounding world, generally populated by other agents. Its behavior is based on its observations, knowledge and interactions with the world of other agents. An agent has capabilities of perception and a partial representation of the environment, can communicate with other agents, can reproduce child agents, and has own objectives and an autonomous behavior [17]. *A multi-agent system (MAS)* is an artificial system composed of a population of autonomous agents, which co-operate with each other to reach common goals, while simultaneously pursuing individual objectives [17].

The life cycle of products is made up of a series of stages: requirement analysis, design, implementation and deployment, operation, logistics and maintenance and decommissioning. Agents can be used in every phase of generic life cycle [18]:

- Requirements definition (definition of a set of needs or requirements that are to be satisfied)
- Positioning (relationship to other products in the enterprise).
- Specification (functions that the product will support).
- Design (mapping the functions to implementation strategies).
- Implementation (the phase of the life cycle in which the product is constructed).
- Commissioning (the product is put to use).
- Operation (maintaining the product in regular productive use).
- Decommissioning.

Without the aim at completeness, some main application fields are as follows:

3.1 Agents in Product Design

Design becomes increasingly decentralised (team of designers in different locations, working for different companies, dealing with the design the components and subsystems of a complex product, using many different analysis tools). A short survey of design systems working according to the agent principles is given in 18. Remaining at the main categories only, agents can be catalogs of pre-defined parts, pre-existing design tools or the designers themselves representing components and subsystems of the product.

3.2 Agents in Planning and Scheduling

Holonic manufacturing systems (HMSs), as one of the new paradigms in manufacturing, consist of autonomous, intelligent, flexible, distributed, co-operative agents or *holons* [19], [20].

Three types of basic holons, namely resource holons, product holons and order holons, together with the main information flows between them are defined in the reference architecture in [21]. These basic entities are structured by using object-oriented concepts such as aggregation or specialization. Staff holons are also foreseen to assist the basic holons in performing their work. Other authors refer only to two types of basic building blocks, e.g. order and machine agents in [2], job and resource agents in [22], order and machine (resource) holons in [6].

A common feature of these approaches is that the functions of the order and product holons are somehow integrated in one basic type. One of the most promising features of the holonic approach is that it represents a transition between fully hierarchical and heterarchical systems [19], [23].

3.3 Agents in Real-Time Control

Co-ordinated proactive objects in process control systems can usefully be viewed as agent-based systems. Among other examples, the control of transfer line type manufacturing system is described in [18].

Though many promising research results and a number of successful industrial applications are known, only a limited number of sources couple agent-based principles and environmental issues. In the next Section, an attempt is described for incorporating environmental issues in holonic production control.

4 Incorporating Environmental Aspects in Agent-Based Dynamic Production Control

The approach proposed is an agent-based one, more accurately, a holonic-based approach. The term of holon, introduced by the manufacturing community, represents an agent with or without manufacturing capabilities. The model is built on the principles of holonic manufacturing systems (HMSs)[19], [24], [21], [25].

4.1 The Functional Structure of the Agents in the Model

As part of the resource allocation mechanism, the model presented includes as information flow agent an element called Task Master (TM), and the resource holons as information and material flow agents.

The Task Master is responsible for job orders, including job decomposition into tasks, task announcement and assignment, monitoring and record keeping.

As part of the TM, the following units can be found (Fig.1.):

- the Task Decomposition unit,
- the Task Announcement unit,
- the Booking System,
- the Monitoring unit,
- the Record Keeping unit,
- the Task Assignment unit.

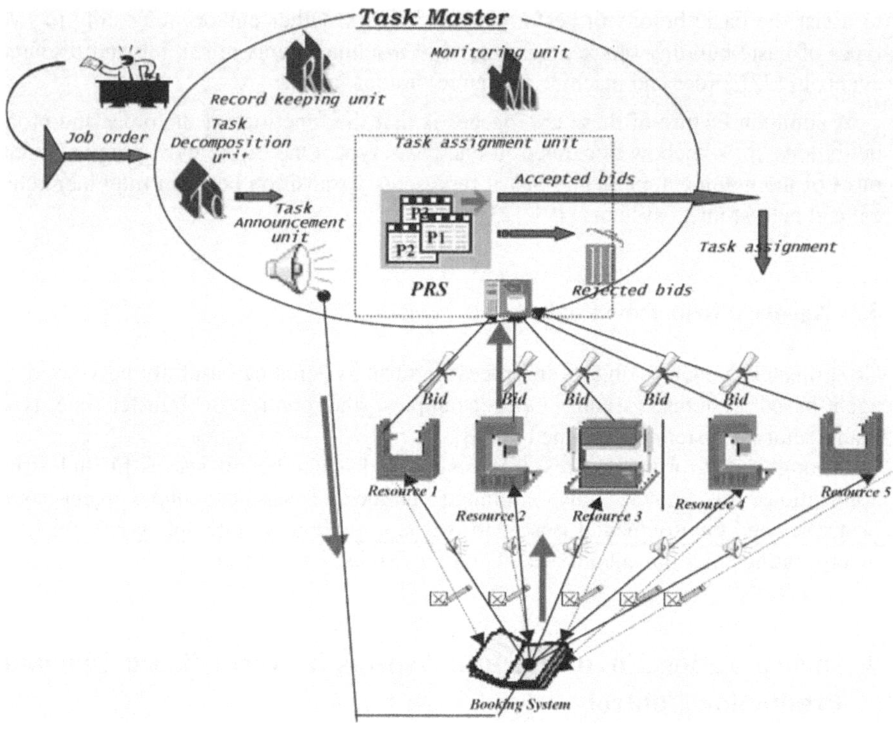

Fig. 1. The communication flow in the system when a job that has to be performed is announced

The task assignment unit comprises the bid gathering unit (where the resource holons send their offers for the task accomplishment), the Priority Rules System (system of rules for evaluating the bids), a temporary holder of rejected bids (rejected bids are temporary stored for the case of reevaluation), a task assignment unit (accepted bids are communicated to the winner resources).

The Booking System (BS) gathers the data about the abilities (the tasks that they are able to perform) of resources on the shop floor. All resources are expected to report towards the Booking System, in their own interest.

Resource holons communicate the status (started, paused, finished) of the task they are performing to the TM, which stores the information in the Record keeping unit.

A resource holon should include the following components:

- a communication interface for incoming and outgoing messages (bids, status etc),
- control mechanism for coordinating its actions and events,
- knowledge about itself (abilities, price, environmental effects, etc),
- knowledge about its environment (knowledge about other agents as TM, etc),
- reasoning mechanism for using the acquired knowledge,
- learning mechanism for updating the acquired knowledge,
- record keeping mechanism, which allows to learn from history.

4.2 The Mechanism of Resource Allocation

When a job order enters the system, after the decomposition of jobs into tasks, the TM starts the task assigning process by checking in the BS which resources could be able to perform the task in question. These resources will receive a *task announcement* containing the following information: the task description, the earliest time to start, the latest time to finish and the bidding window time (the time interval that is at its disposal for reacting to the task announcement).

The resource holons will respond to task announcements by sending bids, which will be evaluated by the TM by using its multi-level system of rules named *Priority Rules System (PRS)*. In the model presented, both the economic criteria and the environmental impacts of processes and operations are taken into account in the rules.

To go into details let J be the job needed to be processed on the shop floor, and T_j, $j=1 \ldots n$, the number of tasks comprising it. In this basic model the PRS is a three-level rule system. The number of levels can be increased if required. Let S be the set of rules in the PRS, and $R_1, R_2 \ldots R_t$ the rules. Then, $S=\{R_i\}$, and $R_i = \{N_i, O, U_i, P_i\}$, where N_i is the name given to the rule i, and U_i the utility of the rule. O represents the objective function for the rules having the same level of priority.

Based on the values of these types of variables, the TM is going to make the decision whether to select a certain bid or not. P_i denotes the priority of the rule. A rule with priority 1 is considered eliminatory. So, if these rule terms are not satisfied by the bid, it will not be taken into consideration further. The rules with P=3, e.g., are considered only in the case of equal results for bids previously analyzed by rules with P=2. Every decision variable will be multiplied by the corresponding utility value.

4.3 Visualization of Information Exchange with the Help of an Object Oriented Program

With the help of the SIMPLE++ production and logistics simulation package, the communication between agents on a shop floor was simulated. The mathematical model, which takes the PRS into consideration, was transposed in the SimTalk programming language.

In order to illustrate the functioning of the model, let incorporate 5 resources in the simulated system, each of them able to perform multiple operations. The job to be processed consists of 3 tasks, so $J = \{T_1, T_2, T_3\}$. The first task announced could be performed by the first and the fifth resource, the second task by all the resources and the third task by the second, forth and the fifth resource.

The PRS comprises 6 rules, so $S = \{R_1, R_2, R_3, R_4, R_5, R_6)$. These rules are on the first three levels of the priority system. The utility of the rules can be changed according to the actual goals of the given factory. The six rules are N_1 = Due date rule, N_2 = Bidding time rule, N_3 = Cost rule, N_4 = Environmental effect rule, N_5 = Breaks rule, and N_6 = Tool usage rule.

The Due date rule concerns the available interval of time for performing the task. If the time obtained by adding the processing time to the starting time of the task exceeds the requested latest time to finish (and found in the task announcement), then the bid is rejected.

The Bidding time rule concerns the time interval when the bids can be sent. If a resource sends a bid after the interval of time specified by the TM, that one is not going to be included in the competition.

The Cost rule concerns the cost of processing the task.

The Environmental effect rule concerns the value of the negative effects of operation on the environment. In this example the effects are measured in MET (Materials, Energy, Toxicity) point values 10.

The Breaks rule refers to the number of unplanned breaks in the past 2 years. The number of unplanned breaks influences the possibility of not being able to complete the task in time.

The Tool usage rule concerns the usage of the tools applied while accomplishing the job. It represents the percentage of the total lifetime until the tool reaches its end-of-life. Different rules for tool usage can be defined. The tool with sufficiently enough time left to the end-life is going to be chosen, as in the example, the safety of having completed the task in time is considered to be primary.

The priority for R_1, and R_2 is 1, for R_3, R_4, R_5 is 2, and for R_6 is 3.

The utility of rules R_1 and R_2 is not important, since they are eliminatory (P=1) rules and both have to be satisfied at the same time. However, the utility is important in the case of P=2. The result of the corresponding computation is going to be the weight of the bid according to the rule.

The total weight of the bid (BW) is the sum of the weights according to rules. The objective function is to minimise this weight. Then,

$$BW = U_c{*}C + U_e{*}EnvEf + U_b{*}B \qquad (1),$$

where C is the cost variable, U_c the utility assigned to the cost rule, EnvEf is the environmental effect variable and U_e the utility assigned to the environmental effect rule, B represents the unplanned breaks variable and U_b the utility assigned to the Breaks rule.

In this example the cost and environmental issues are of the same importance, therefore, the rules taking these two matters into consideration must have the same utility value. The objective function is to minimize the weight of the bid.

The bid to be chosen must have the smallest values for cost, environmental effect and unplanned breaks according to their utility, in this case 40, 40 and 20%. It means that for the TM, the cost and the environmental effects are of the same importance and more important than the unplanned breaks.

A more detailed description of the approach, together with a more comprehensive example can be found in [26].

5 Conclusion

The paper gave a short overview of life cycle assessment techniques of products and production facilities, on the one hand, and of agent-based approaches applicable within their life cycles, on the other.

In order to illustrate their positive interference, as an example, an approach was presented that incorporates environmental aspects in agent-based dynamic production control.

A more detailed elaboration of the proposed ideas is addressed in future research, and a more thorough series of experiments is foreseen.

Acknowledgements. This work was partially supported by the National Research Foundation, Hungary, Grant Nos. T026486 and T034632.

References

1. Henry, J., G., Heinke, G.W.: Environmental Science and Engineering, Prentice-Hall, Inc., U.S.A (1996)
2. Wiendahl, H.-P., Ahrens, V. : Agent-based control of self-organised production systems, Annals of the CIRP, 46/1 (1997) 365-368
3. Wiendahl, H.-P., Scholtissek, P.: Management and control of complexity in manufacturing, Annals of the CIRP, 43/2 (1994) 533-540
4. Hatvany, J.: Intelligence and co-operation in heterarchic manufacturing systems, Robotics & CIM, 2/2 (1985) 101-104.
5. Rabelo, R.J., and L.M. Camarinha-Matos: Negotiation in multi-agent based dynamic scheduling, Robotics & Computer-Integrated Manufacturing, 11/4 (1994) 303-309
6. Kádár, B., Monostori, L., Szelke, E.: An object oriented framework for developing distributed manufacturing architectures, Proc. of the Second World Congress on Intelligent Manufacturing Processes and Systems, June 10-13, Budapest, Hungary (1997) 548-554
7. Kádár B., Monostori, L.: Agent based control of novel and traditional production systems, Proc. of ICME98, CIRP International Seminar on Intelligent Computation in Manufacturing Engineering, July 1-3, Capri, Italy, (1998) 31 - 38 (key-note paper)
8. Alting, L.: Life cycle engineering and design, Annals of the CIRP, 44/2 (1995) 569-580

9. Hauschild, M., Wenzel, H., Alting, L.: Life cycle design - a route to the sustainable industrial culture?, Annals of the CIRP, 48/1 (1999) 393-396
10. Boothroyd & Dewhurst Inc. & TNO's: Design for Environment, Wakefield, U.S.A. (1996)
11. Ilie-Zudor, E., Mihálcz, I.: Environmental analysis of a robot hand driven by SMA wires, Int. Conf. on Inf. Techn. and Computer Science, MicroCAD '99, Febr. 23-25, Miskolc, Hungary, Section G (1999) 167-171.
12. Tipnis, V.A.: Product life cycle economic models - Towards a comprehensive framework for evaluation of environmental impact and competitive advantage, Annals of the CIRP, 40/1 (1991) 463-466
13. Sheng, P., Bennet, D., Thurwachter, S.: Environmental-based systems planning for machining, Annals of the CIRP, 47/1 (1998) 409-414
14. Westkämper, E., Osten-Sacken, D.: Product life cycle costing applied to manufacturing systems,, Annals of the CIRP, 47/1 (1998) 353-356
15. Sheng, P., Sinivasan, M.: Hierarchical part planning strategy for environmentally conscious machining, Annals of the CIRP, 45/1 (1996) 455-460
16. Bond, A.H., Gasser, L. (Eds.): Readings in DAI, Morgan-Kaufmann (1988)
17. Koussis, K., Pierreval, H., Mebarki, N.: Using multi-agent architecture in FMS for dynamic scheduling, J. of Intelligent Manufacturing, 16/8 (1997) 41-47
18. Parunak, H.D. Industrial and practical applications of DAI, in: Multiagent systems: a modern approach to distributed artificial intelligence (ed.: Weiss, G.), MIT Press (1999) 377-421
19. Valckenaers, P., Bonneville, F., Van Brussel, H., Bongaerts, L., Wyns, J.: Results of the holonic system benchmark at KULeuven, Proc. of the Fourth Int. Conf. on CIM and Automation Techn., Oct. 10-12, New York (1994) 128-133
20. Van Brussel, H., Valckenaers, P., Wyns, J., Bongaerts, L., Detand, J.: Holonic manufacturing systems and IiM. In: IT and Manufacturing Partnerships, Conf. on Integration in Manufact., Galway, Ireland (1996) 185-196
21. Van Brussel, H., Wyns, J., Valckenaers, P., Bongaerts, L., Peeters, P.: Reference architecture for holonic manufacturing systems, Computers in Industry, 37/3 (1998) 255-276
22. Tseng, M. M, Lei, M., Su, C.: A collaborative control system for mass customisation manufacturing, Annals of the CIRP, 46/1 (1997) 373-376
23. Bongaerts, L., Monostori, L., Kádár, B.: Hierarchy in distributed shop floor control, Computers in Industry, Elsevier, Special Issue on Intelligent Manufacturing Systems, Vol. 43, No. 2 (2000) 123-137
24. Márkus, A., Kis, T., Váncza, J., Monostori, L.: A market approach to holonic manufacturing, Annals of the CIRP, 45/1 (1996) 433-436
25. Monostori, L., Kádár, B., Hornyák, J.: Approaches to manage changes and uncertainties in manufacturing, Annals of the CIRP, 47/1 (1998) 365 - 368
26. Ilie-Zudor, E.; Monostori, L.: An environmentally benign approach to agent-based manufacturing, Preprints of the 1st IFAC Workshop on Multi-Agent-Systems in Production, December 2-4, Vienna, Austria (1999) 191-195

Fractal Businesses in an E-Business World

Dr.-Ing., Dipl.-Wirtsch. Ing. Wilfried Sihn and Dipl.-Ing. Joachim Klink

Fraunhofer Institute for Manufacturing Engineering and Automation (IPA), Stuttgart/ Germany

Abstract. The modern corporate management is still in a state of permanent change, whose dynamics of development is rather increasing than decreasing. This change takes place especially in a linking up of value added activities (that occurs more and more in a cross-company way) and the computerisation of business processes. It occurs under various approaches and keywords (e-business, supply chain management, virtual business, e-procurement,..). This change on the one hand includes a successive adjustment to known trends, and on the other hand it includes new challenges for corporate management. In this paper, the change in corporate management is discussed using the concept of the 'fractal business' as an example. Solutions for the future are sketched, too.

1 Changes in Management – Management of Change

For ten years, we have been living in a time that has been called a 'time of change' everywhere. Markets, products, and technologies are changing at an unprecedented speed. Since the beginning of the 90ies, when Europe was in the worst economic crisis of the post-war era, businesses have tried to keep up with that change. Market shares are being regained with various approaches, concepts, and strategies, as well as a reduction of costs and processing time and– last bust not least – the ability to react to changes quickly is being increased. It is interesting to watch how management concepts have developed during the past years.

Among all of the consultants', research institutes', and practical persons' trends, three fundamental developments can be extracted:

1. The development of 'adaptable' businesses
2. The development of business networks
3. The computerisation of added value (e-business)

When looking at these developments on an abstract level, the conclusion can be drawn that it is the development in the same state, seen from different perspectives. The first case is about transforming a rigid, centralistically organised structure into a dynamic shape with decentralised organisation units. In the second case, an attempt is made to co-ordinate and optimise several legally autonomous businesses together. In the third case, a technology revolutionises the possibilities of interaction between business and customer ("business to customer", B2C) and between business and busi

L. Monostori, J. Váncza, and M. Ali (Eds.): IEA/AIE 2001, LNAI 2070, pp. 821-826, 2001.

ness ("business to business", B2B). All of the three developments have a common objective: an added value, produced together and co-operatively with making full use of high degrees of freedom and the single added value partner's ability to react. Obviously, modern top-level organisations are a composite of extensively autonomous organisation units with common objectives and defined rules of co-operation. It is a form of co-operation we have propagated in the form of the 'fractal business' concept for nearly ten years and which has by now been practised in many businesses.

2 The Fractal Company – Origin of a Trend Reversal!?

In 1992, we published the book "The Fractal Company: A revolution in corporate culture". Connected to this book is a turn in the thinking of modern business management. The concept of the 'fractal business', as it has been called since the transmission to non-industrial branches, stands for a break with the paradigms that could then be found in theory and practice. New approaches, methods, and concepts have been developed and introduced in companies. For many, the 'fractal business' has become the 'European answer to lean production'. The management trends that were set then are today more relevant than ever. The direction in which we have been heading proved to be successful and is a signpost for modern corporate management. The features of fractal units of organisation are established in many businesses as a model.

3 Features of Fractal Units of Organisation

"A fractal is an autonomous unit whose objectives and performance can be described unambiguously" [1]. This is how the fractal was defined originally. With that, nothing is said about a fractal's size or organisational structure. A fractal is generally a unit of a business which has objectives, achieves results and acts autonomously. In this context, the description of objectives and achievements for business units is important. This was new at that time. What was new was that these objectives and achievements were not only fixed on financial scales. In contrast to the so-called Center-concepts, which generally include financial objectives, the objectives of a fractal are orientated on its contribution in the entire added value of an enterprise. This does not necessarily have to be a financial contribution.

3.1 Self-Similarity

A fractal has objectives, achieves results, can be described through connections (both within the fractal and with other fractals), elements, and qualities. Therefore, from the single employee to the entire business, everything can be described in fractals. Using systems theory, a fractal can be thought of as an open system which itself includes (subordinate) fractals and is also part of a superordinate fractal. All units of organisation are businesses within businesses; employees are entrepreneurs in their company.

3.2 Self-Organisation

Fractals run by self-organisation. They are allowed a defined amount of autonomy to reach their objectives and accomplish their results. Efficiency requires the ability to act. Fractals are able to act because they can command their resources which are necessary for the supply of performance on their own authority and own adequate freedom for acting and making decisions. Self-organisation also means market economy principles within a company. The fractals organise themselves and are not controlled from outside. The fractal's limits (see above) describe how far this self-organisation stretches, which scope of development it has. The rules of the game between fractals are set by their relationships.

3.3 Self-Optimisation

Fractals do not persist on their status quo, but are part of the change. They revise their objectives, performance, and qualities permanently and adjust them accordingly to the market's requirements. In this, there are evolutionary changes, e.g. through adaptation of qualities, relationships, etc. However, revolutionary changes, e.g. in the form of a partition, separation, or even dissolution of fractals are possible.

3.4 Dynamics, Vitality, Adaptability

The features described above allow fractals not only to adapt to changes, but to act anticipatingly and on their own initiative. Fractals are, to a certain extent, "autonomously viable". For an extensive definition of the term "adaptability" we refer to the works of the Sonderforschungsbereich "Wandlungsfähige Produktionssysteme" (special research field "adaptive production systems")1. For a better understanding of what is described by adaptability, the following sentences may suffice: Adaptability is the ability to reach lasting changes out of one's own strength. These changes lead to conditions that were unknown before the changes occurred. Entirety – The Six Level Concept

The fractal business sees itself as a holistic concept. It is based on the insight that a company is only fully efficient as a whole, as a unit. Local or one-sided optimisations are not very helpful; the unit is as weak as its weakest part. The approaches of cost accounting, of compensation and of PPC must fit, the entire philosophy must be harmonious, and the concept must be consistent. A fractal (and with it, the entire company) is described using the levels 'culture', 'strategy', 'finances', 'socio-informational level', 'information', and 'material flow and process level'.

---

[1] Westkämper, E.; Zahn, E.; Balve, P.; Zilebein, M.: Ansätze zur Wandlungsfähigkeit von Produktionsunternehmen – ein Bezugsrahmen für die Unternehmensentwicklung im turbulenten Umfeld. In wt Werkstattechnik 89 (1999) 9

4 New Developments, New Business Environments, New Challenges

Since the original development of the 'fractal company' concept, several influential factors and business environments which are relevant for business management have evolved or changed. These changes are manifold; they concern among other things:

- A new generation of businesses and entrepreneurs. Along with the buzzword "new economy" an unprecedented founding wave can be noticed which questions many "laws of success" that were valid until now.
- New business models, new markets. The term "new business models" stands for innovative ways to achieving economic success. The added value itself changes. Many businesses make money by producing "traffic" and creating a "community".
- A change in the understanding of what a product is. Whereas in the past the term "product" usually meant a physical product, today the virtual share of a product has increased. Instead of buying a car, you merely purchase mobility or the sensation that is combined with the brand's image.
- New technologies. Especially in the information and communication technology sector massive changes take place with a noteworthy influence on industrial products and production.
- New methods and procedures. The industrial added value is more and more supported by efficient methods and is realised both better and faster.

New forms and models of organisation. The developments and new models of organisation focus on cross-company organisation. Be that in the form of virtual enterprises, business networks, or supply chains – the added value that is linked up across companies is established step by step.

Despite these multifaceted changes of the past years, no fundamental break concerning the basic orientation for successful business management can be noticed. Rather, the significant paradigms of a "fractal company"(the "turbulent environment", adaptive business structures and processes, holistic management,...) have been confirmed and applied in various concepts. Especially the mega-trend of "linked-up added value" with its many specific characteristics follows the basic philosophy of fractal organisation – the common added value of extensively autonomous performance units with the objective to react very flexibly and quickly to the market's requirements.

These modified but still valid business environments offer the modern business management freedom to act. They are a reason for testing the validity and potentials of the fractal company concept. Also, new adaptations and further developments should be identified. An extension of the fractal model accordingly to the latest market developments – namely the trend towards linked-up added value and "e-business" – is at issue. Those two developments are currently the most prominent drivers for concepts and methods of business management.

5 "Fraktal+" – Adaptation and Further Development of a Successful Concept

The fractal company concept is generally practical for taking up the developments sketched and for offering suitable solutions. As mentioned in the beginning, the basic principles within a fractal company can be compared to those of a business network or a virtual enterprise. The linked-up added value is in this case achieved through legally autonomous fractals, i.e. the companies involved. The self-similarity principle thus makes the mapping of this linked-up added value possible and thereby offers an approach to view this form of added value in the framework of the known theory. The definition "A fractal is a business unit that acts autonomously" must simply be modified to that effect that the company itself and systems comprising several companies are to be regarded as fractals, too. It could be something like "A Fraktal+ is an autonomous performance or business unit consisting of parts of companies, the company itself, or several companies,...".

However, the adaptation of the fractal company concept is slightly more difficult regarding the e-business phenomenon, which is marked by changes in the business model area. Yet, at second view, it becomes clear that the generic fractal model offers adequate application possibilities. A fractal is, among other things, described through its objectives and accomplishments. These objectives can, as mentioned above, be manifold; they are not restricted to the financial dimension. Neither are the achievements restricted to producing material goods, but they comprise any form of producing performance. Thus, the models for describing the performance of so-called "not directly productive fractals" (as, e.g. in a personnel or quality department) are, at least in principle, conferrable to the "new economy" business models. Here, too, we find performance units (the start-ups) which do not (yet) generate any financial yield, but are appreciated (in the capital market) because of other performance features ("community" size, degree of being known,...).

The general applicability of the "fractal company" concept, however, must not lead us to ignore that the concrete solutions and concepts to be developed are new. Yet, this fact does not pose a real problem, as each fractal company is unique. It is just the individual specifications of fractals – depending on the context of the entire economic unit and their contribution to the entire added value – that make this concept so multifaceted and thereby efficient.

As a conclusion, you should bear in mind that the general approaches of the fractal business will be valid in the future and will offer the business management sufficient potentials. Furthermore, there are enough challenges and questions to be answered in this modified environment. We are looking forward to meeting these challenges.

References

1. Warnecke, Hans-Jürgen: Revolution der Unternehmenskultur: Das Fraktale Unternehmen. 2. Aufl. Berlin u. a.: Springer, (1993).
2. Warnecke, Hans-Jürgen: Aufbruch zum Fraktalen Unternehmen: Praxisbeispiele für neues Denken und Han-deln. Berlin u.a.: Springer, (1995).
3. Westkämper, Engelbert u.a.: Ansätze zur Wandlungsfähigkeit von Produktionsunternehmen: Ein Bezugsrahmen für die Unternehmensentwicklung im turbulenten Umfeld. In: Wt Werkstattstechnik 90 (2000) 1/2, S. 22-26
4. Sihn, Wilfried: Service aus Kundensicht. In: Westkämper, Engelbert (Hrsg.); Schraft, Rolf Dieter (Hrsg.); Fraunhofer-Institut für Produktionstechnik und Automatisierung IPA: Neue Servicekonzepte im 21. Jahr hundert: Fraunhofer IPA Seminar F52, 11. und 12. Mai (2000).
5. Sihn, Wilfried; Hägele, Thomas: Innovative company networks – Organization, technology and successful examples. In: National Defense Industrial Association (Hrsg.): CALS Expo International & 21st Century Commerce 1998: Global Business Solutions for the New Millenium, Long Beach/California, Arlington/Virginia 1998 26.-29.
6. Sihn, Wilfried; Klink, Joachim: Added Value in Production Networks In: Roller, Dieter (Hrsg.): Advances in Automotive and Transportation Technology and Practice for the 21st Century - Abstracts: Complete Symposium Abstract Vol. 32nd ISATA, 14th-18th June Vienna, Austria (1999) 128
7. Sihn, Wilfried; Hägele, Thomas; Deutsch, Oliver: Competitive production networks through software-based reengineering and added value networks. In: Mertins, Kai (Hrsg.); Krause, Oliver (Hrsg.); Schallock, Burkhard (Hrsg.); IFIP WG5.7: Global Production Management: IFIP WG5.7 International Conference on Advances in Production Management Systems, Berlin, 6.-10. September 1999. Dordrecht u.a.: Kluwer, (International Federation for Information Processing (IFIP), (1999), 432-439
8. Warnecke, H.-J.; Braun, J.: Vom Fraktal zum Produktionsnetzwerk; Berlin u.a.; Springer (1999).

Optimisation of Process Chains and Production Plants by Using a Hybrid-, AI-, and Simulation-Based Approach

Z.J. Viharos and L. Monostori

Computer and Automation Research Institute, Hungarian Academy of Sciences, POB 63, H-1518, Budapest, Hungary
viharos@sztaki.hu

Abstract. Based on the previous results of the authors, the paper highlights a novel approach for generating multipurpose models of machining operations, combining machine learning and search techniques. A block-oriented framework for modelling and optimisation of process chains is introduced and its applicability is shown by the results of the optimisation of cutting processes. The paper illustrates how the framework can support the simulation-based optimisation of whole production plants. The applicability of the proposed solution is demonstrated by the results of an industrial project where the task was to optimise the size spectrum of the ordered raw material at a plant producing one- and multi-layered printed wires.

1 Introduction

Reliable process models are extremely important in different fields of computer integrated manufacturing [5]. On the base of the applied knowledge, fundamental, heuristic and empirical models can be distinguished.

Model-based simulation is usually an efficient technique to make difficult problems more tractable. It can contribute to elaborating new algorithms, supporting decision makers, decreasing the risk in investments, and running the systems exposed to changes and disturbances more efficiently.

From simulation point of view, one can distinguish knowledge-based hybrid systems (KBHSs) if simulation and some kind of intelligent techniques, e.g. expert systems (ESs), artificial neural networks (ANNs), fuzzy systems or their combination are used together [8], [9].

Learning denotes changes in the system that is adaptive in the sense that learning techniques enable the system to do the same or similar task more effectively next time [3], [7]. Obviously, machine learning (ML) techniques can enhance the performance of any KBHS architecture, i.e. embedded, parallel, co-operative, intelligent front-end [8], [9]. From another point of view, simulation can be used for generating training examples for learning.

L. Monostori, J. Váncza, and M. Ali (Eds.): IEA/AIE 2001, LNAI 2070, pp. 827-835, 2001.

The paper illustrates the benefits of combining AI, ML and simulation techniques in the optimisation of:

- manufacturing processes,
- process chains, and
- production plants.

2 Multipurpose Modelling of Manufacturing Processes

Difficulties in modelling manufacturing processes are manifold: the great number of different machining operations, multidimensional, non-linear, stochastic nature of machining, partially understood relations between parameters, lack of reliable data, etc. A number of reasons back the required models: the design, optimisation, control and simulation of processes and the design of equipment [1], [4], [12].

Artificial neural networks (ANNs) are general, multivariable, non-linear estimators. This soft computing technique can offer viable solutions especially for problems where abilities for real-time functioning, uncertainty handling, sensor integration, and learning are essential features [7]. Successful applications in manufacturing were reported on in the literature [6], [10], [14]. The assignments to be performed determined the I/O configurations of the models, i.e. which parameters are to be considered as inputs and which ones as outputs. This predetermination, however, results in models, which do not necessarily realise the best mapping between the considered quantities.

2.1 Generation of Multipurpose ANN-Based Process Models with Automatic I/O Configuration

In the following space an approach based on back propagation ANN-learning and heuristic search for generating multipurpose models is described, which are expected to work with the required accuracy in different assignments. It consists of the following phases:

- Determining the (maximum) number of output parameters (N_o) from the available N parameters which can be estimated by using the remaining $N_i = N - N_o$ input parameters within the prescribed accuracy.
- Ordering the available parameters into input and output parameter sets having N_i and N_o elements, respectively.
- Training the network whose input-output configuration has been determined in the preceding steps.

The above phases are performed parallel, using the speed of the learning process as an indicator for the appropriateness of the ANN architecture in question to realise the required mapping. The selection of the right I/O configuration is especially important in the case of noninvertible dependencies. In order to accelerate the search for the ANN configuration, which complies with the accuracy requirements with the minimum number of input parameters, the sequential forward search (SFS) technique

[2] is used. As result, the algorithm gives a general model of the given system incorporating all of the connections among considered quantities but without any regards to any possible assignment related to the given system. A more detailed description of the algorithm can be found in [13].

2.2 Application of the Multipurpose Models in Various Assignments

Because of the general nature of the multipurpose models, almost in every application only some of the model parameters are known and the task is to determine the unknown parameters while satisfying some constraints. In a general case it means that a part of the model input and a part of the model output parameters are known while all of the other parameters have to be determined independently if they are on the input or on the output side of the model. To build up a method able to handling such general cases, a simulated annealing based search technique was developed. The method applies the general model that realises the dependencies among system parameters built up according to the algorithm described in the previous paragraph. As a result, this search algorithm gives one solution for a given assignment of the user. To generate a larger number of solutions the search has to be repeated. A more detailed description of the algorithm can be found in [13].

3 Optimisation of Machining Processes by Using the Multipurpose Model

Optimisations can be realised to satisfy some constrains or goals where there are several solutions of a given assignment. There are different approaches to optimise a given process or process chain [4], [11]. The final part of the paper deals with the problem of modelling and optimisation of process chains through the extension of the modelling and search techniques introduced for single processes. At the Computer and Automation Research Institute a block-oriented software was developed named *"ProcessManager"* to optimise operations and/or production chains form various points of view at the same time. The *"ProcessManager"* block-oriented framework for modeling and optimisation of manufacturing processes and process chains referred above incorporates (Fig. 1.):

- definition of the elements of the chain,
- determination of the process models by integrating analytical equations, expert knowledge and example-based learning,
- connecting the single models into a process chain by coupling input-output model parameters not limited to models of successive processes in the chain,
- definition of eligible intervals or limits for the process parameters and monitoring indices,
- definition of a cost function to be optimised, etc.

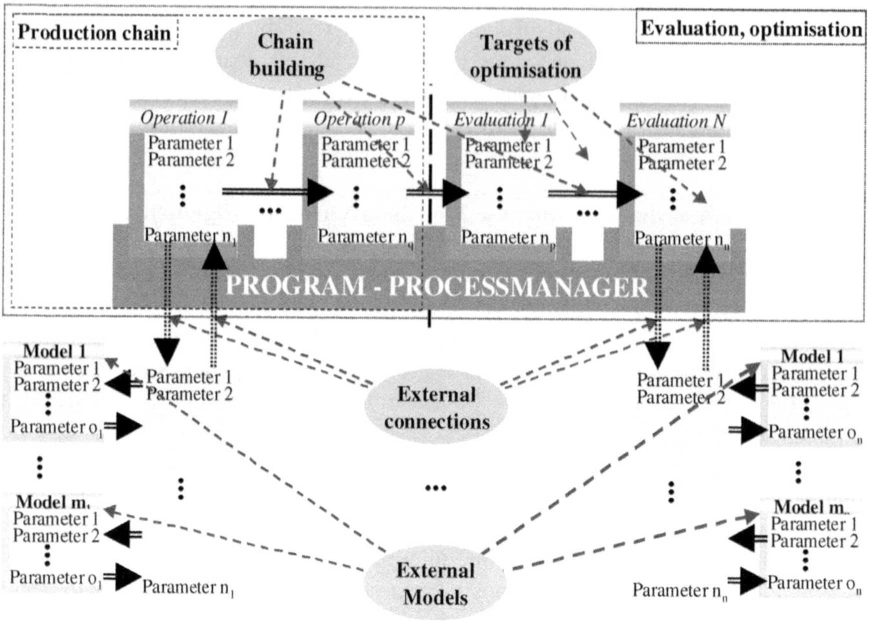

Fig. 1. The framework called *"ProcessManager"*.

Fig. 2. illustrates the application of *"ProcessManager"* for the threefold optimisation of the viewpoints of the customer (minimisation of the surface roughness), owner of the company (profit/productivity maximisation) and the employed engineer (maximisation of process stability through minimisation of the 'a/f' ratio).

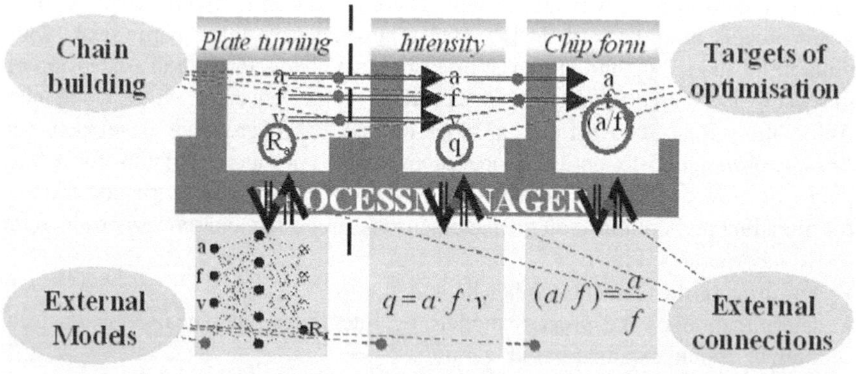

Fig. 2. Chain model for optimisation of the plate turning operation with optimisation criteria.

The figure shows the building up phase of *"ProcessManager"*, where the model of the plate turning is realised by an ANN and the other variables to be optimised, e.g. cutting intensity 'q' and 'a/f' for stability, are given by equations. Parameters resulted by the optimisation of the plate turning operation are illustrated by 3D-plots in Fig. 3.

Ratios of the weighting factors of the three variables to be optimised are represented along the axes.

The "surfaces' are to be used together, i.e. the moving along the plane marked by 'R_a' and 'a/f' occurs on each of the diagrams at the same time. The corner marked by 'q' indicates the position, where the viewpoint of the company owner is the most important and by moving along the axes 'R_a' and 'a/f' represents that the viewpoints of the customer and the engineer become more and more important with respect to 'q'. The determined surfaces show the possible compromises among different viewpoints.

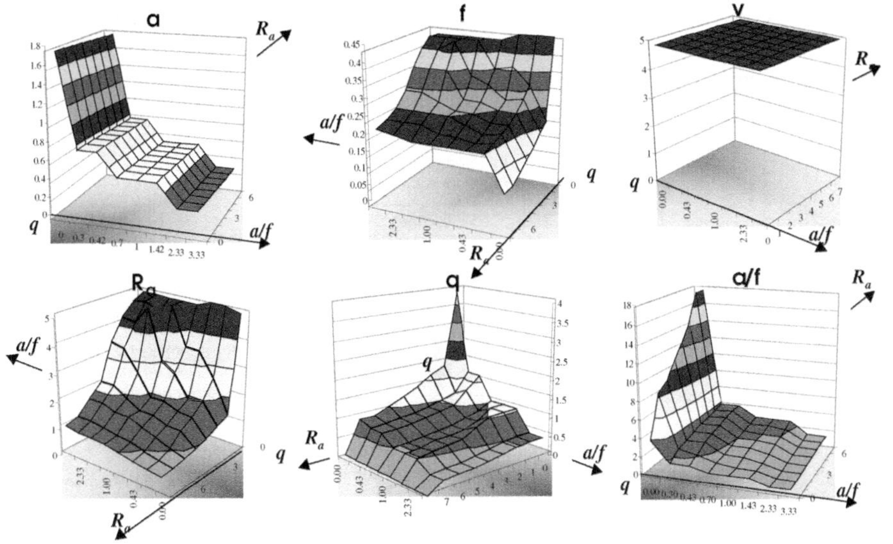

Fig. 3. Parameters resulted by the threefold optimisation of the plate turning operation.

4 Hybrid, AI-, ML-, and Simulation-Supported Optimisation of Production Plants

Simulation techniques can be advantageously used in the design of new production plants. However, their application is usually extremely time-consuming. Some preliminary results of an iterative procedure for the design of manufacturing systems (resource requirements) employing ANNs in conjunction with simulation were presented in [1]. The aim of the ANN was to learn the inverse of the simulation function. Given desired performance measure levels (e.g. mean job tardiness, mean job flow time, mean resource utilisation and the completion time of all tasks), the network should output appropriate values for the system parameters (e.g. the number of resources for each work centre of a job shop). The approach was regarded as a valuable tool for the manufacturing system design problem, guiding the highly iterative design process and hence reducing the required number of simulations by a simple and automatic training procedure.

Now, it will be shown how the modelling and optimisation approach and the developed framework described in the previous sections can be used for the optimisation of whole production plants where the simulation function cannot be inverted, therefore, a search process is required. The concept is illustrated in Fig. 4.. According to this concept, the production plant is represented as a chain of processes where the most important part (parts) is (are) simulated by appropriate (in most cases discrete event) simulation packages. In the case of plant optimisation, most of the parameters are fixed and - satisfying some constraints - the values of other parameters are to be determined in order to reach some performance measures. Naturally, some constraints have to be satisfied at the same time.

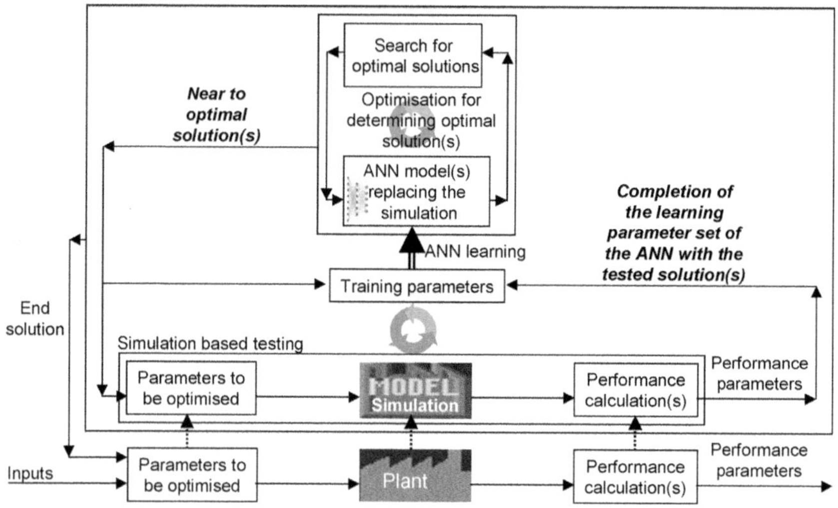

Fig. 4. Concept of the hybrid, AI-, ML- and simulation-supported optimisation of production plants.

It is appropriate to replace the time consuming simulation with ANN-based models initially trained by patterns generated by the plant or - in most cases – by the simulation. An optimisation framework as the *"ProcessManager"* described above, can search for solutions by using the ANN model(s). Whether a found solution is appropriate, i.e., it is within the region appropriately realised by the ANN model(s), is to be checked by simulation. If this run indicates unexplored region, the related patterns are added to the training set(s) of the ANN(s) and after training, a new optimisation step is started. If the simulation provides with reinforcement, the found solutions are used for the determination of the system parameters searched for.

4.1 Industrial Application

The above concept was applied for the optimisation of the production plant of a Hungarian firm producing one- and multi-layered printed wires. In a previous project the task was to analyse the production plant by using the SIMPLE++ simulation package and to initiate business-process reengineering measures if needed. The subject of optimisation in the project to be reported on here was to determine the geometrical (height and width) parameters of a given number of boards serving as raw material for the production. The aim was to maximise the average surface utilisation and to minimise the mean flow time.

The parameters to be determined influence the whole production, i.e., the machines used, their scheduling, part routing, etc. Moreover, the mapping between these parameters and the performance parameters of the plant is not invertable, consequently, in order to obtain the required results, the use of the previously developed simulation model of the plant was straightforward. Production orders were generated randomly based on the statistical data of a month, which could be considered as characteristic. A new algorithm was developed for placing the printed wires on the boards. Substituting the simulation for an appropriate neural network trained by the back propagation technique an acceleration of the optimisation with a factor of about 6000 was experienced. The average surface utilisation of the raw material was increased by about 20%, with the additional benefits of using only some, this way standardised boards as raw material, i.e. lower purchase prices, lower storage costs and better quality of the end products.

Some proposals for further improvement of the production were also given as some supplementary results of the project:

- introduction of a more flexible working time,
- modification of the production information system,
- pointing out the bottlenecks in the production,
- warehousing of some frequently ordered products,
- introduction of new operations in the production,
- extension of the simulation for the order processing and some preparatory phases of the production.

The success of the project indicates the applicability of the concept presented in this section, i.e., the hybrid, AI-, ML- and simulation-supported production optimisation.

5 Summary

The paper presented a novel approach for generating multipurpose models of machining operations, which combines machine learning and search techniques. Simulated annealing search was used for finding the unknown parameters of the multipurpose model in certain applications. A block oriented framework for modelling and optimisation of process chains was introduced and its applicability was illustrated by the results of the optimisation of cutting processes. The concept of the hybrid, AI-,

ML- and simulation-supported optimisation of production plants was also outlined. Some results of an industrial project demonstrated the applicability of the concept where the task was to optimise the size spectrum of the ordered raw material at a plant producing one- and multi-layered printed wires. Further industrial applications of the concept and the developed modelling and optimisation framework are in the preparation phase.

Acknowledgements. This work was partially supported by the National Research Foundation, Hungary, Grant Nos. F026326, T026486 and T034632.

References

1. Chryssolouris, G., Lee, M., Pierce, J., Domroese, M.: Use of neural networks for the design of manufacturing systems, Manufacturing Review, Vol. 3, No. 3, (1990) 57-63.
2. Devijver, P.A., Kittler, J.: Pattern recognition, a statistical approach, Prentice-Hall Inc., London (1982).
3. Hatvany, J.; The efficient use of deficient knowledge; Annals of the CIRP, Vol. 32/1, (1983) 423-425.
4. Horváth, M; Somló, J: Optimisation and adaptive control of cutting processes (In Hungarian). Technical Press (1979).
5. Merchant, M.E.: An interpretive look at 20th century research on modeling of machining, Inaugural Address, Proc. of the CIRP International Workshop on Modeling of Machining Operations, Atlanta, Georgia, USA, May 19 (1998) 27-31.
6. Monostori, L.: A step towards intelligent manufacturing: Modeling and monitoring of manufacturing processes through artificial neural networks, Annals of the CIRP, 42/1 (1993) 485-488.
7. Monostori, L., Márkus, A., Van Brussel, H., Westkämper, E.: Machine learning approaches to manufacturing, Annals of the CIRP, 45/2 (1996) 675-712.
8. Monostori, L.; Egresits Cs.; Kádár B.: Hybrid AI solutions and their application in manufacturing, Proc. of IEA/AIE-96, The Ninth Int. Conf. on Industrial & Engineering Applications of Artificial Intelligence & Expert Systems, June 4-7, 1996, Fukuoka, Japan, Gordon and Breach Publishers, (1996) 469-478.
9. Monostori, L; Egresits, Cs; Hornyák, J; Viharos, Zs. J.: Soft computing and hybrid AI approaches to intelligent manufacturing. Proc. of 11th International Conference on Industrial & Engineering Applications of Artificial Intelligence & Expert Systems, Castellon, (1998), 763-774.
10. Rangwala, S.S., Dornfeld, D.A.: Learning and optimisation of machining operations using computing abilities of neural networks, IEEE Trans. on SMC, 19/2, March/April (1989) 299-314.
11. Tóth, T., Erdélyi, F.: The inner structure of computer aided process planning having regard to concurrent engineering, 2nd International Workshop on Learning in Intelligent Manufacturing Systems, April 20-21, Budapest, Hungary, (1995) 142-167.
12. Van Luttervelt, C.A. Childs, T.H.C., Jawahir, I.S., Klocke, F., Venuvinod, P.K.: Present situation and future trends in modeling of machining operations, Annals of the CIRP, 47/2 (1998) 587-626.

13. Viharos, Zs. J.; Monostori, L.: Automatic input-output configuration of ANN-based process models and its application in machining, Book: Lecture Notes of Artificial Intelligence - Multiple Approaches to Intelligent Systems, Conference, Cairo, Egypt, May 31-June 3, Springer Computer Science Book, Springer-Verlag Heidelberg, (1999) 569-668.
14. Warnecke, G., Kluge, R.: Control of tolerances in turning by predictive control with neural networks, Journal of Intelligent Manufacturing, 9/4 (1998) 281-287.
15. Westkämper, E.: Supervision of quality in process chains by means of learning process models, Proc. of the Second Int. Workshop on Learning in IMSs, Budapest, Hungary, April 20-21 (1995) 566-590.
16. Viharos, Zs. J., Monostori, L., Markos, S.: Selection of input and output variables of ANN-based modeling of cutting processes, Proc of the X. International Workshop on Supervising and Diagnostics of Machining Systems, Innovative and Integrated Manufacturing, Karpacz, Poland, March 21-26, (1999) 121-131.

A Multi-Agent Fuzzy Cognitive Tool For Reengineering Manufacturing Systems

Julio Macedo[1]
[1]Institut Strategies Industrielles, 229 Forest, Pincourt, P.Q., J7V8E8, Canada

Abstract. Discrete simulation models are suggested as tools to support reengineering. However, these models cannot identify the nature of the improvements. Furthermore, they are tedious to build when they must be detailed enough to produce accurate evaluations of the improvements impacts. A new system for reengineering that supports the identification of the improvements using benchmarking implemented with fuzzy cognitive maps is presented. This system uses qualitative optimal control models to evaluate the impacts of the improvements and behavior-based learning to reach analysts' agreement. The new system is applied to reengineer a filling line of pharmaceuticals and the results are compared to the ones obtained by optimizing a discrete simulation model of this same line.

1 Introduction

The operations required in making a product constitute a process. The latter marks the product with managerial characteristics like production delay, rate of defective products, poor quality cost and product variety. In serial production, the observed managerial characteristics often differ from the ones desired by the target market so that it is necessary to reengineer the process. Reengineering consists of modifying the designs of the manufacturing system's components so that they become integrated into a form such that the managerial characteristics of the products satisfy the values desired by the target market. Literature surveys of reengineering indicate that simulation models of manufacturing systems are used to support the identification of the improvements and the evaluation of their impacts [1]. However, simulation models present two weaknesses. First, they are not aware of the improvements introduced by the top-performing firms in the industry. Second, their construction is long when they are made detailed enough in order to produce accurate evaluations of the improvements impacts.

This paper presents a new system to support process reengineering named MC-ENREMOS (Multi-agent Cognitive Expert-Neural Reference Model System). It includes fuzzy cognitive maps (named reference models) that support the identification of the manufacturing system improvements from the ones introduced by top-performing firms in the industry. In addition, MC-ENREMOS includes qualitative optimal control models (named calibration models) that calculate the economic sizes of the improvements.

2 Literature Position

An agent is a computational procedure that is capable of autonomous intelligent reaction to its environment in order to meet its design objectives [7]. In addition, an agent has its own model of the environment that surrounds it and can exchange information with other agents in order

L. Monostori, J. Váncza, and M. Ali (Eds.): IEA/AIE 2001, LNAI 2070, pp. 836–845, 2001.

to meet its design objectives. In practice, automation agents are used to automate real-time decisions and design-support agents to provide assistance to designers [6]. MC-ENREMOS uses design-support agents named reference models [3] that help the analysts identify the design improvements during a reengineering exercise. MC-ENREMOS includes reference models that cover one of the following topics: Product structure, set-up operations, production flow, human factor and production planning. However, each reference model includes variables related to different components of the manufacturing system so that it is an integrative model. At this point note that MC-ENREMOS is applied by a group of analysts that converge to common sizes and physical realizations for new designs of the manufacturing system components without negotiation as in classic multi-agent systems [7], but using an adaptation of behavior-based learning [2].

3 MC-ENREMOS System

The application of MC-ENREMOS starts by the selection of a typical product portfolio and the description using storyboards and multi-agent diagrams of how the products use the manufacturing system's components during production. The descriptions are directed to delimit the process that should be reengineered and to identify the attributes of the manufacturing system's components that correspond to the control variables of the reference models.

MC-ENREMOS consists of two procedures directed to redesign the current physical realizations of the manufacturing system components [3]. The first one supports the design of the target physical realizations using the knowledge of the top-performing firms in the industry and disregarding the current constraints of the problematic firm (Fig. 1). The second one supports the design of the physical realizations of the economic sizes of the manufacturing system components (Fig. 2). The economic sizes are the ones that minimize the sum of the poor quality costs (those appear because the current managerial characteristics of the product portfolio deviate from the ones desired by the target market) and improvement investments, and respect the firm constraints to implement new designs. At this point note that application of procedures in Fig. 1 and 2 requires establishing correspondences between the attributes of the manufacturing system components (objects), which are at a physical level, and the reference model variables, which are at the conceptual level. In addition, it is necessary to transform the values of the attribute objects from real units (physical level) to 0-1 scales (conceptual level), because the reference and calibration models work with 0-1 scales to avoid the huge problem of converting units that belong to different domains.

As indicated in Fig. 1, the procedure for conceiving the target physical realizations of the manufacturing system's components consists of the following steps. First, select one topic for reengineering the manufacturing system so that the reference model variables related to this topic are displayed. Second, introduce approximate values for the cause-effect forces of the reference model and for the managerial characteristics desired by the target market. Third, MC-ENREMOS matches the introduced values to a reference model of the chosen topic (when this matching is not possible MC-ENREMOS displays a reference model to be used as a qualitative simulator) and solves it producing zeroes and ones for its control variables. In addition, MC-ENREMOS displays implementation examples of the control variables in the industry. Fourth, guided by the examples displayed and the control variable values (a value of one indicates to increase the current value of the corresponding object attribute and a value of zero to decrease it), the group of analysts designs the target physical realizations of the manufacturing system components. The divergences of the analysts are solved by negotiation.

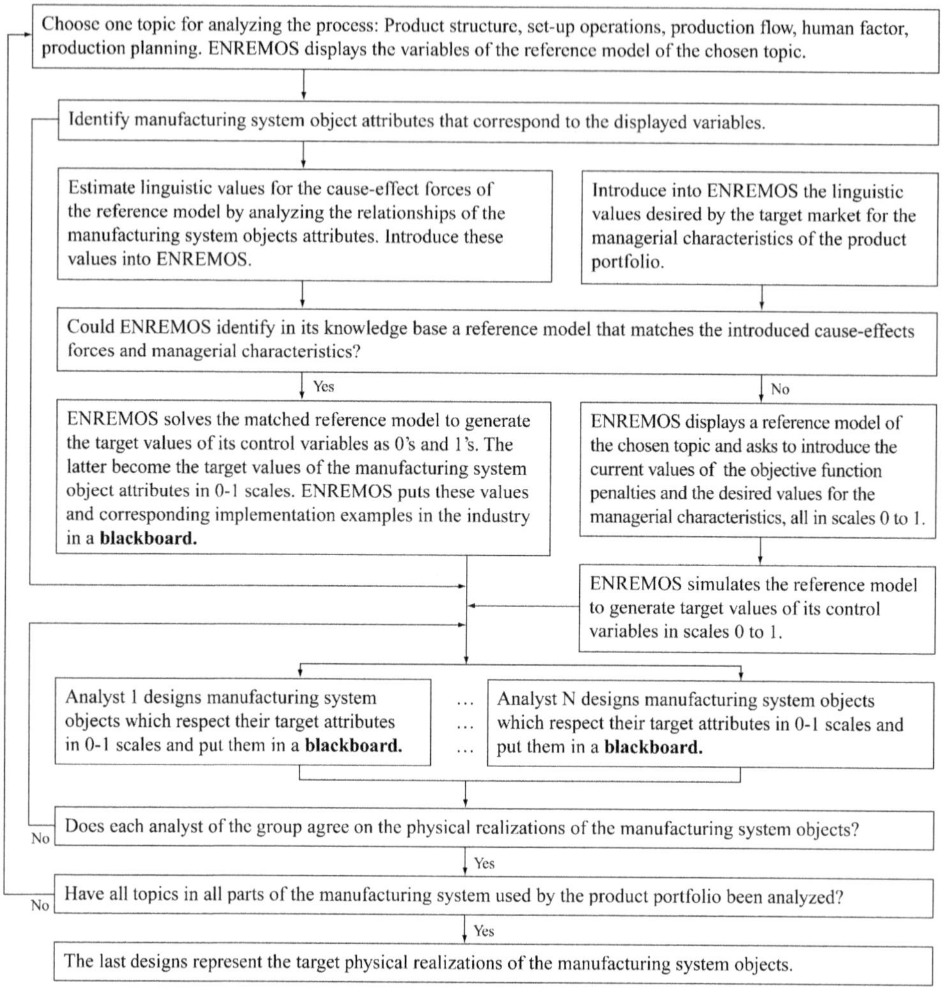

Fig. 1. MC-ENREMOS procedure to design the target physical realizations of the components (objects) of a manufacturing system.

The procedure for designing the physical realizations of the economic sizes of the manufacturing system objects (Fig. 2) is supported by calibration models. The latter are optimal control models that include the variables and state equations of the corresponding reference model, the firm constraints to implement the design changes and an objective function that minimizes the poor quality costs and investments to implement these changes. As indicated in Fig. 2, this procedure consists of two main parts. The first one (upper part of Fig. 2) is the feeding of MC-ENREMOS with data that remains unchanged during the iterations of the procedure. The second one (middle of Fig. 2) is a behavior-based learning that allows the group of analysts to reach an agreement on the sizes and physical realizations of the redesigned manufacturing system components.

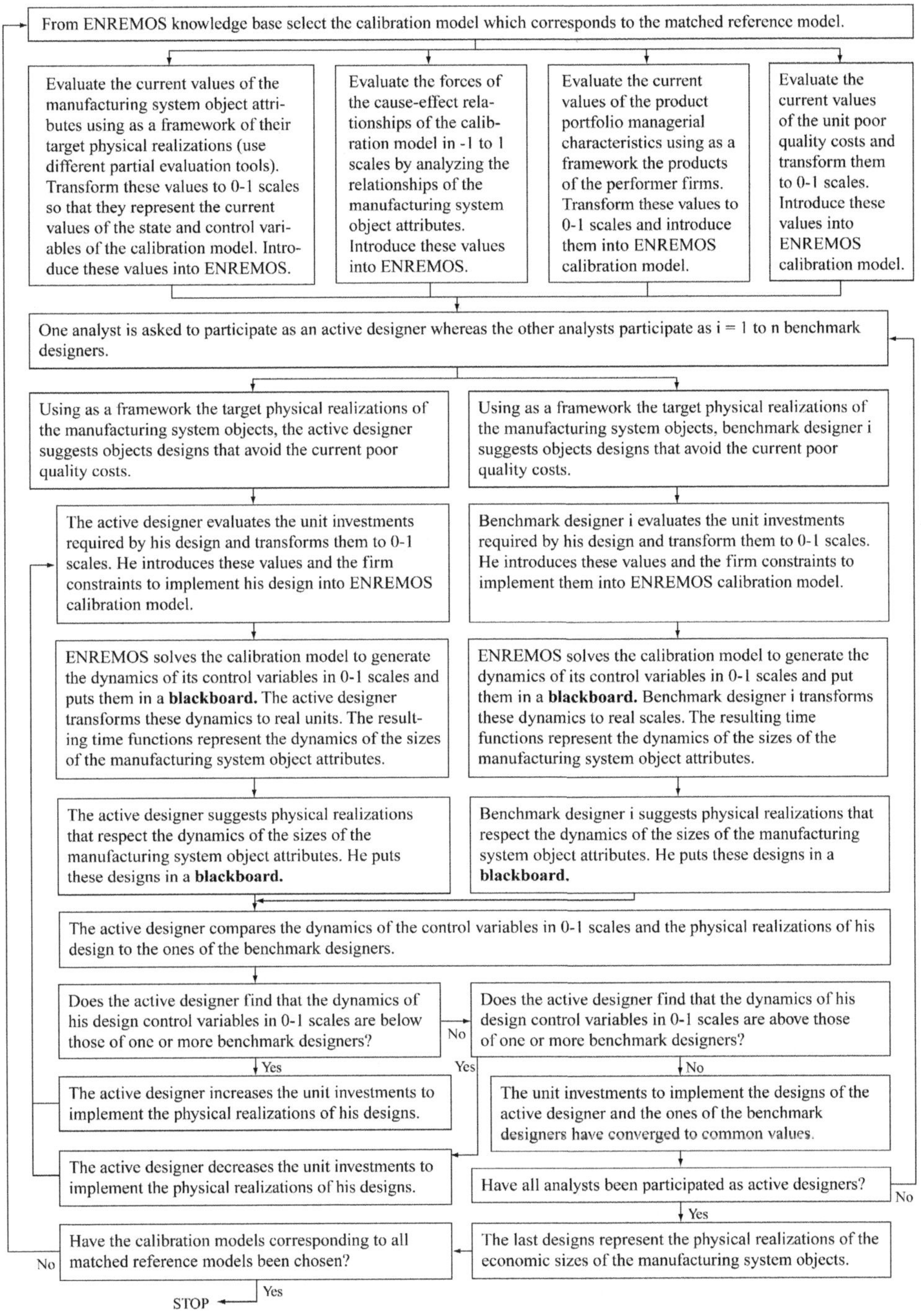

Fig. 2. MC-ENREMOS procedure to design the physical realizations of the economic sizes of the manufacturing system components (objects).

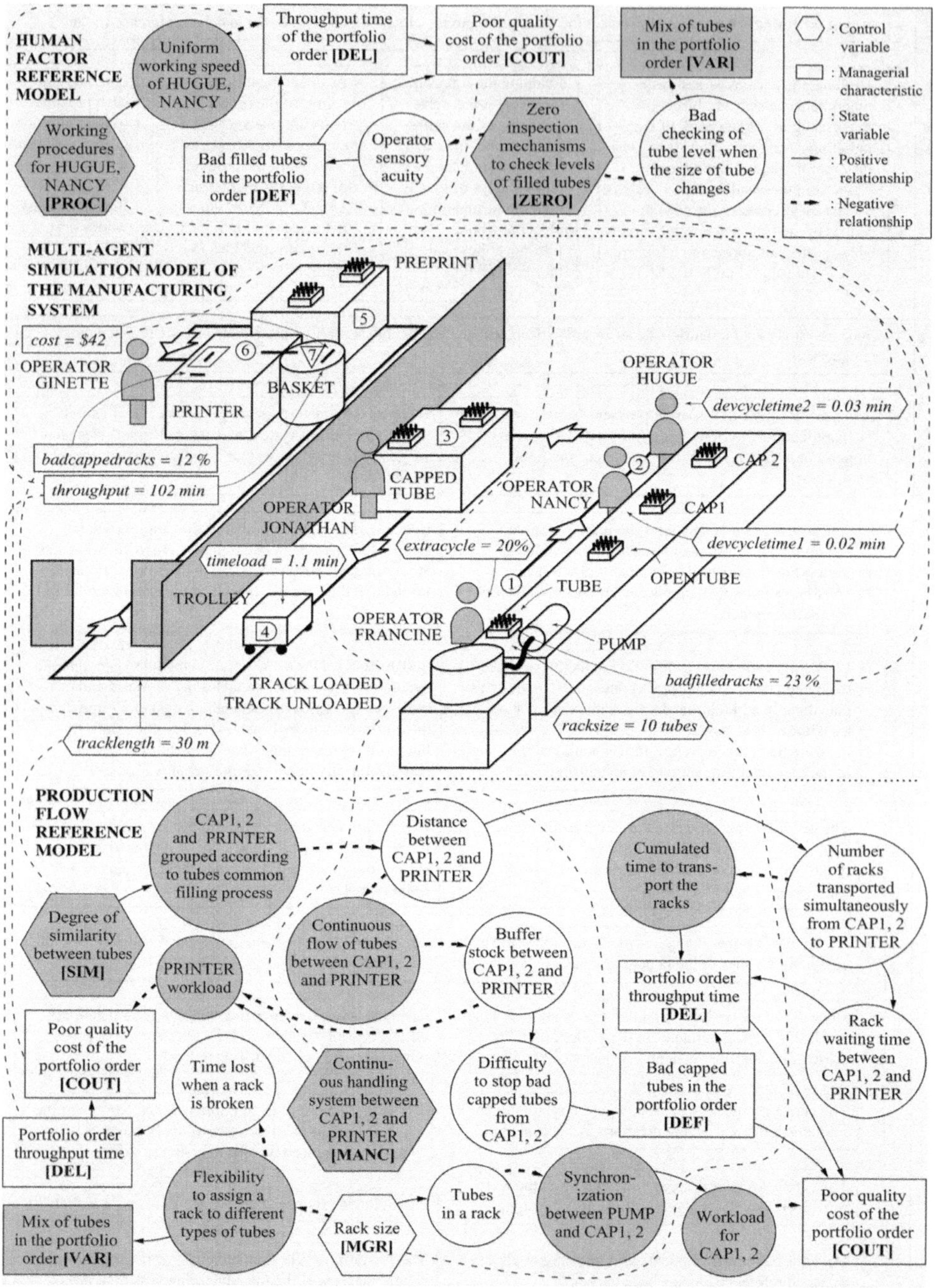

Fig. 3. Correspondence between the attributes (italic) of the simulation model objects (capital letters) and the variables of the reference models (bold). The solutions of the reference models are indicated by the shaded (means 1) and unshaded (means 0) shapes. Only partial views of the reference models are illustrated.

As indicated in the upper part of Fig. 2, the feeding of MC-ENREMOS consists of the following steps. First, introduce into MC-ENREMOS the current values of the product portfolio managerial characteristics and those of the state and control variables of the calibration model. The latter are obtained by evaluating the attributes of the manufacturing system objects related to the variables of the calibration model and transforming the results to 0-1 scales. This evaluation is done with different partial evaluation tools that use as benchmarks the target physical realizations previously designed. Second, evaluate and introduce into MC-ENREMOS the values of the cause-effect forces of the calibration model.

As indicated in the middle of Fig. 2, the behavior-based learning procedure consists of the following steps. First, one analyst of the reengineering group is chosen as an active designer while the other analysts participate as benchmark designers (which means that they do not communicate with the active designer but put their designs on a blackboard so that the active designer can evaluate his suggested design by comparison). Second, each analyst suggests a tentative design for the manufacturing system components and estimates the unit investment required to implement it in 0-1 scale; finally, he introduces this unit investment and the firm constraints to implement his suggested design into the calibration model. Third, MC-ENREMOS solves the calibration model producing time functions for the sizes of its state and control variables in scales of 0-1. Fourth, the analysts transform the preceding sizes to real units of the corresponding attributes of the manufacturing system objects and put them on the blackboard. Fifth, using the displayed sizes, the analysts redesign the physical realizations of the manufacturing system components and put them on the blackboard. Sixth, the active designer compares the current sizes and physical realizations of the components on the blackboard to the ones of his design and takes one of two actions in order to agree with the benchmark designers: If the size of his current design is below (above) the ones of one or more designs in the blackboard, he increases (decreases) his current unit investment to implement a new design and increases (decreases) the sizes of the attributes of his current design. Then, the active designer goes to step two above (the tentative design step) until he is satisfied with his design; at this point, another analyst is chosen as an active designer. The procedure stops when the group of analysts converges to common unit investments, sizes (named economic sizes) and physical realizations for the redesigned manufacturing system components.

4 Application

MC-ENREMOS was successfully applied to reengineer a real production line that fills pharmaceuticals in tubes. However, in order to facilitate experimentation, this application is reported using an agent simulation model of the current filling line.

The agent simulation model of the current filling line is a high nonlinear 3D virtual reality model represented in the middle of Fig. 3. The agents (capital letters) are modeled as objects that include structural attributes (some of them are in italic in Fig. 3) and plans to act depending on the information or the resource received. These agents exchange resources and messages between them so that a typical portfolio of pharmaceuticals is filled according to the following process: First, a number of tubes arrives at the line in racks of size *racksize* so that operator FRANCINE takes one tube at a time, fills it with a pharmaceutical using a manual PUMP, checks the level of the pharmaceutical in the tube (the number of racks containing tubes with wrong levels of pharmaceutical is PUMP's attribute *badfilledracks*) and puts it back in the rack. When the same type of tubes to fill is less than two, FRANCINE's cycle time increases of a percentage *extracycle* (FRANCINE's attribute). Second, the racks of filled tubes wait in the buffer OPENTUBE until operator NANCY or HUGUE pulls one rack at a time and caps the tubes manually in workstations CAP1 or CAP2. These operators have cycle times that vary according to a normal distribution with standard deviations *devcycletime1* and *devcycletime2*, respectively; in addition, the probability that at least one tube is badly capped increases with the number of capped tubes. Third, NANCY or HUGUE transfer the racks of capped tubes to the CAPPED TUBE buffer so that operator JONATHAN takes one tube at a time, tightens the tube cap and puts it back in the rack. Fourth, when 4 or more racks are waiting in CAPPED TUBE, operator JONATHAN puts a number of these racks in a vehicle TROLLEY in *timeload* minutes (TROLLEY's attribute) and drives it to another room where he unloads the racks to buffer PREPRINT. The TROLLEY currently transports 20 racks per trip because CAPPED TUBE buffer is at least *tracklength* meters from the PREPRINT buffer. Fifth, operator GINETTE takes one tube at a time from the racks waiting in buffer PREPRINT, prints it using machine PRINTER and puts it in a BASKET. When the tubes are not properly capped by NANCY or HUGUE (the number of racks with one or more bad capped tubes is *badcappedracks*), GINETTE recaps the tubes, but this increases her cycle time. At this point note that the total time to execute the five steps above on a number of tubes arriving in racks of size *racksize* is *throughput* and the total poor quality cost is *cost*.

According to the procedure in Fig. 1, the reference models of production flow [5] and human factor [4] were chosen and their variables (shown in brackets in Fig. 3) were matched to the attributes (in italic in Fig. 3) of the simulation model objects. Then, these reference models were solved generating the target values for their control variables in the fourth column of Table 1. For example, MANC=1 means, at a conceptual level, to increase the continuous handling between workstations CAP1, CAP2 and PRINTER machine so that, at the physical level, the

Table 1. Convergent solutions of some variables of production flow and human factor reference models and corresponding calibration models.

Control variable	Initial value	Reference model		Calibration model
	(t = 0)	(t = 4)	(t = 40)	(t = 4)
Production flow				
SIM	0.2	0.93	1	0.89
MANC	0.2	0.93	1	0.91
MGR	0.7	0.05	0	0.43
Human factor				
PROC	0.2	0.93	1	0.39
ZERO	0.2	0.94	1	0.80

Table 2. Transformation of unit poor quality costs from real scales to 0-1 scales.

Managerial characteristics (object attributes)	Managerial characteristics values: Value at t = 0		Value at t = 40		Unit poor quality cost	
	Real units	0-1 scale	Real units	0-1 scale	Real units	0-1 scale*
DEL (throughput)	102 min.	0.70	86.63 min	0	$2.57/min	$0.5657/0.01 gap
DEF (badcappedracks)	5 boxes	0.12	0 boxes	0	$0.576/box	$0.17/0.01 gap
DEF (badfilledracks)	12 boxes	0.23	0 boxes	0	$0.19/box	$0.17/0.01 gap
COUT (cost)	$42.3	0.07	$2	1	—	—

* Calculated by interpolation from the other values in the table.

Table 3. Unit investments in 0-1 scales to implement the object designs.

Control variables (object attributes)	**Degree of implementation of the improvement**				**Unit improvement investment**	
	Real units	%	Real units	%	Real units	0-1 scale*
Production flow						
SIM (tracklength)	30 m	0%	22.23 m	100%	\$8.10/m	\$0.63
MANC (timeload)	1.1 min	0%	0.99 min	100%	\$201.8/min	\$0.22
MGR (racksize)	10 tubes	0%	1 tube	100%	\$0.35/tube	\$0.0316
Human factor						
PROC (devcycletime1)	0.02 min	0%	0 min	100%	\$150/min	\$0.03
PROC (devcycletime2)	0.03 min	0%	0 min	100%	\$100/min	\$0.03
ZERO (extracycle)	20 %	0%	0	100%	\$2.74/1%	\$0.5477

* Per 1% of implementation (calculated by interpolation from the other values in the table.)

Table 4. Convergent objective functions of the calibration models corresponding to production flow and human factor reference models.

Production flow

$$\text{Min}\int_0^{40} 0.2236^2\,[BAL(t) - BAL(t)^*]^2 + 0.22^2\,[MANC(t) - MANC(t)^*]^2 + 0.0316^2\,[MGR(t) - MGR(t)^*]^2 + 0.3162^2\,[MMOB(t) - MMOB(t)^*]^2 + 0.6325^2\,[SIM(t) - SIM(t)^*]^2 + 0.10^2\,[SURA(t) - SURA(t)^*]^2 + 0.173^2\,[DEF(t) - DEF(t)^*]^2 + 0.5657^2\,[DEL(t) - DEL(t)^*]^2\,dt$$

Human factor

$$\text{Min}\int_0^{40} 0.7521^2\,[ELOI(t) - ELOI(t)^*]^2 + 1.82^2\,[MAIN(t) - MAIN(t)^*]^2 + 0.752^2\,[METH(t) - METH(t)^*]^2 + 0^2\,[NAUTO(t) - NAUTO(t)^*]^2 + 0.7521^2\,[PAL(t) - PAL(t)^*]^2 + 0^2\,[POS(t) - POS(t)^*]^2 + 0.03^2\,[PROC(t) - PROC(t)^*]^2 + 0.7036^2\,[SIG(t) - SIG(t)^*]^2 + 0.5477^2\,[ZERO(t) - ZERO(t)^*]^2 + 0.7036^2\,[PROP(t) - PROP(t)^*]^2 + 0.7521^2\,[NSUP(t) - NSUP(t)^*]^2 + 0.7036^2\,[ERG(t) - ERG(t)^*]^2 + 0.7521^2\,[DPDE(t) - DPDE(t)^*]^2 + 1.4071^2\,[EQUI(t) - EQUI(t)^*]^2 + 0^2\,[DIF(t) - DIF(t)^*]^2 + 0^2\,[EXC(t) - EXC(t)^*]^2 + 0.173^2\,[DEF(t) - DEF(t)^*]^2 + 0.5657^2\,[DEL(t) - DEL\,(t)^*]^2\,dt$$

Table 5. Calibration model solutions in real scales at the last iteration of the procedure to design the economic sizes of the manufacturing system objects.

Control variables (object attributes)	**Current value (t = 0)**		**Target value (t = 40)**		**Economic size (t = 4)**	
	Real units	0-1 scale	Real units	0-1 scale	0-1 scale	Real units*
Production flow						
SIM (throughput)	30 m	0.2	22.23 m	1	0.89	23.3 m
MANC (timeload)	1.1 min	0.2	0.99 min	1	0.91	1 min
MGR (racksize)	10 tubes	0.7	1 tube	0	0.43	7 tubes
Human factor						
PROC (devcycletime1)	0.02 min	0.2	0 min	1	0.39	0.015 min
PROC (devcycletime2)	0.03 min	0.2	0 min	1	0.39	0.02 min
ZERO (extracycle)	0.2	0.2	0	1	0.80	0.05

* Calculated by interpolation from the other values in the table.

attribute corresponding to MANC, namely *timeload* attribute of TROLLEY, should be decreased from its current value 1.1min. Guided by these values and implementation examples, the group of analysts designed the target physical realization of the filling line in Fig. 3 as a high-speed machine that automatically fills and caps one tube at a time.

Using as a benchmark the automatic machine above, the procedure of Fig. 2 was applied to design the physical realizations of the economic sizes of the manufacturing system objects. Tables 2 to 5 illustrate some key calculations done during the last iteration of this procedure. For example, the last column of Table 2 shows the unit poor quality costs in 0-1 scales per 1% of deviation from the targeted managerial characteristics; these values were calculated from the known current (with the filling line of Fig. 3) and targeted values of the managerial characteristics (with the automatic filling machine), and the known unit poor quality costs in real units. Another example is the last column of Table 3, that shows the unit investments in 0-1 scales per 1% of improvement implementation; these values were calculated using the known current and targeted values of the object attributes, and the known unit investments in real units. The poor quality costs and unit investments in 0-1 scales above were the parameters of the objective functions of the last calibration models (Table 4; from [2]). These models were solved producing values of the control variables in 0-1 scales (last column but one of Table 5) that were transformed to real units (last column

Table 6. Results obtained by solving the agent simulation model fed with the economic sizes of the attributes of the manufacturing system objects.

Simulation model inputs and outputs	Initial values (t = 0)	With the attributes economic sizes generated by the calibration models at t = 4			Simulation model optimization*
		Production flow	Human factor	Poduction flow + Human factor	
Input: Object attributes					
tracklength	30 m	23.3 m	30 m	23.3 m	22 m
timeload	1.1 min	1 min	1.1 min	1 min	1 min
racksize	10 tubes	7 tubes	10 tubes	7 tubes	4 tubes
devcycletime1	0.02 min	0.02 min	0.015 min	0.015 min	0.01 min
devcycletime2	0.03 min	0.03 min	0.02 min	0.02 min	0.01 min
extracycle	0.2	0.2	0.05	0.05	0
totalfilledtubes	400 tubes	420 tubes	400 tubes	420 tubes	400 tubes
Input: Unit investments					
unitinvtracklength	0	8.10	0	8.10	8.10
unitinvtimeload	0	201.8	0	201.8	201.8
unitinvracksize	0	0.35	0	0.35	0.35
unitinvdevcycletime1	0	0	150	150	150
unitinvdevcycletime2	0	0	100	100	100
unitinvextracycle	0	0	2.74	2.74	2.74
Output: Managerial characteristics					
throughput	102.4 min	95.5 min	101.2 min	94.7 min	82.8 min
throughput/tube	0.26 min	0.23 min	0.25 min	0.23 min	0.24 min
badfilledracks	23%	8%	23%	16%	0%
badcappedracks	13%	8%	13.1%	8%	7%
Square poor quality cost	$1793	$603	$1529	$510	$84.3
Square investment	$0	$84	$9	$93	$11.9
Total square cost	$1793	$687	$1538	$603	$96.2
Squ. poor qual. cost/tube	$4.48	$1.44	$3.82	$1.21	$0.2
Square investment/tube	$0	$0.2	$0.02	$0.22	$0.03
Square cost/tube	$4.48	$1.64	$3.85	$1.44	$0.24

*: Minimize total square cost = square poor quality cost + square investment

$$\text{Square poor quality cost} = \sum_{i=1}^{i=\text{total tubes made}} \text{unitcostbadcappedracks}^2 (\text{badcappedracks}_i - 0)^2 + \text{unitcostbadfilledracks}^2 (\text{badfilledracks}_i - 0)^2 + \text{unitcostthroughput}^2 (\text{throughput}_i - 86)^2$$

$$\text{Square investment} = \sum_{i=1}^{i=\text{total tubes made}} \text{unitinvdevcycletime1}^2 (\text{devcycletime1}_i - 0)^2 + \text{unitinvdevcycletime2}^2 (\text{devcycletime2}_i - 0)^2 + \text{unitinvextracycle}^2 (\text{extracycle}_i - 0)^2 + \text{unitinvtracklength}^2 (\text{tracklength}_i - 22.23)^2 + \text{unitinvtimeload}^2 (\text{timeload}_i - 0.99)^2 + \text{unitinvracksize}^2 (\text{racksize}_i - 1)^2$$

$20 \le \text{tracklength}_i \le 30$ for all i	$0 \le \text{devcycletime1}_i \le 0.03$ for all i	unitcostbadcappedracks = \$0.576
$1 \le \text{timeload}_i \le 2$ for all i	$0 \le \text{devcycletime2}_i \le 0.03$ for all i	unitcostbadfilledracks = \$0.19
$2 \le \text{racksize}_i \le 10$ for all i	$0 \le \text{extracycle}_i \le 0.3$ for all i	unitcostthroughput = \$2.57

of Table 5). The latter are the economic sizes of the object attributes and served to design the physical realization of the reengineered filling line: An easy-loading conveyor (respects *timeload*=1 minute) between workstations CAP1, CAP2 and PRINTER machine (respects *tracklength*=23.3 m), racks of size 7 tubes (respects *racksize*=7) and a trained operator FRANCINE who does not lengthen her cycle time significantly when the type of tube to fill changes (she respects *extracycle*=5%).

A last point is to investigate how close are the economic sizes generated by MC-ENREMOS to the ones obtained by optimizing the agent-oriented simulation model of Fig. 3. Hence, this model was optimized producing the results in the last column of Table 6. The last column but one of this Table includes also the results of solving the simulation model fed with the solutions of MC-ENREMOS calibration models. As noted, the optimal solution produces a global cost of 0.24\$/tube and MC-ENREMOS a cost of 1.44\$/tube instead of the original 4.48\$/tube. In addition, the solutions of MC-ENREMOS calibration models are highly correlated to the ones of the optimal solution. Hence, in spite of using a qualitative approach and with the implementation of only 20% of the total number of control variables in two reference models, MC-ENREMOS produces acceptable results.

References

1. Kettinger, W., Teng, J., Guha, S.: Business Process Change: A Study of Methodologies, Techniques and Tools. MIS Quarterly **March** (1997) 55-80.
2. Macedo, J.: A Multi-agent Based System for Manufacturing System Reengineering. In Urban, Ch. (ed.): Agent Based Simulation. The Society for Computer Simulation International Press, Ghent, Belgium (2000) 93-98.
3. Macedo, J.: A Generative System for Reengineering Manufacturing System Organization. International Journal of Production Research **37** (1999) 2639-2664.
4. Macedo, J.: Intelligent Reference Models for Designing Virtual Factories. In: Kocaoglu, D. (ed): Managing Virtual Enterprises: A Convergence of Communications, Computing and Energy Technologies. IEMC96 Proceedings. IEEE Press, Piscataway NJ (1996) 346-350.
5. Macedo, J.: (1994): Reference Model Recognition System for Designing the Manufacturing System Organization. In: Kopacek P. (ed.): Intelligent Manufacturing Systems. Pergamon Press, Oxford UK (1994) 205-210.
6. Nwana, H.: Software Agents: An Overview. Knowledge Engineering Review **II** (1996) 1-40.
7. Weiss, G.: Multi-Agent Systems, MIT Press, Cambridge MA (1999).

Product Line Design with Customer Preferences

András Márkus and József Váncza

Computer and Automation Research Institute, Hungarian Academy of Sciences
1518 Budapest, P.O.B. 63
{markus ; vancza@sztaki.hu}

Abstract. When customizing their product lines, manufacturers attempt to fulfill the requirements of the customers within the technical and economical constraints of the manufacturing environment. Product line design is a recurrent process that aims at finding the proper balance between the exploration of new product alternatives and the exploitation of the known selling potential of the available variants. This paper offers a framework where, driven by the interaction of customer preferences and the reallocation of manufacturing resources, product families emerge from technically feasible product alternatives.

1 Introduction

In order to decrease the development, manufacturing and marketing costs of their products, manufacturers usually prefer to develop, produce and sell several product versions in parallel. Treating such a group of product variants, a so-called *product line* (PL) as a single, integrated unit promises advantages at all stages of the products' life cycle. However, the unqualified commitment toward a *group* of products may produce adverse effects. In the short range, it is cost effective to apply a single, well-established technical solution or to focus just at some specific needs of the customers—however, such an attachment may be disastrous when new technologies or new requirements emerge. On the other hand, keeping too many product variants alive is expensive for the manufacturer, since he offers capabilities that are not actually exploited by the customers.

The paper outlines novel methods applicable in various stages of the design of PLs: the aim is to find a subset of the technically feasible product variants that—in order to achieve maximal profit—should be offered to the customers. Although the actual technical and organizational details may be transposed to various stages of PL design, the methods will be explained here with concepts fitted to a specific situation: when the products actually meet the customers. As for another example: usually, a large number of technical options should be evaluated at the design of a specific detail of an artifact. Since working out the details of all these variants would be too expensive, the design office has to select a subset of the alternatives.

The paper is organized as follows: Sect. 2 refers to related work; Sect. 3 discusses our basic assumptions on products, producers and customers. Sect. 4 presents our approach where the clarification of the customers' preferences is interwoven with an incremental PL design process. Sect. 5 concludes the paper.

L. Monostori, J. Váncza, and M. Ali (Eds.): IEA/AIE 2001, LNAI 2070, pp. 846–855, 2001.

2 Related Work

The design of product lines (sometimes called *product positioning*) is on the crossroads of engineering and economical research, however, neither the practitioners nor the academic circles pay due attention to the results of the other community. Below the views of both parties are summarized, with additional emphasis on findings that urge for developing novel methods.

Analytical and Heuristic Methods. From the management and marketing science point of view, product positioning aims to determine which combination of products should be offered to the customers, and on what prices, so as to maximize the expected, long-term total profit of the firm. Classical economical theory postulates that the full satisfaction of the customers' *demand for variety* could not be supplied because of increasing production costs [3]. Intuitive explanations and formal analytical approaches agree on the causes for this phenomena of the mutual segmentation of offer and demand: upper segments of the market should be prevented from switching to lower priced products by providing less than ideal products for the lower segments [8].

Most present-day models are equipped with detailed cost and selection schemes and combine the customers' strive for maximum *welfare* with the producers' intent to earn maximal *profit* by selecting a subset from the technically feasible product variants and by setting their prices. Most of such settings lead to non-linear, mixed integer mathematical programming formulations [2] and call for the application of heuristic optimization methods. Elsewhere, products in the line are generated by combining promising attribute values of *partially defined* products [6]. Relevant *perceptual attributes* of the products are selected for guiding the sequential elimination of product candidates in [5]. These methods operate at moderate problem sizes and suffer from lack of real-world data and from verification problems: hence, approaches with less formal rigor should be taken into consideration, too.

Evolutionary Approaches. This line of research postulates that product selection is too difficult to be treated as a straightforward optimization process: they call for dynamic and path-dependent models that allow for randomness, where success depends on cycles of *reorientation and convergence*, and where the internal environment is affected by the selection pressures from outside [1].

Strategies of *local adaptation and system-wide coordination* have to be evaluated over long time periods: it may turn out that learning had taught outdated lessons and decreased the ability to compete with *new* rivals.

The *local search* nature of innovation has been attributed to the limiting role of *organizational routines* that generate similar responses to similar stimuli. Since the accumulation of competitive advantage can be self reinforcing, nonlinear effects may occur and lessons of chaos theory may be relevant [4]: long term planning is essentially impossible, short term forecasting *is* possible, and best strategies might achieve goals indirectly and even appear counter-intuitive. The important skills arc in anticipating the *shape* of the future [7].

3 Problem Setting

The inherent drawback of the usual cost/price base models of product lines is that each product should be evaluated by each customer to obtain a filled-in matrix of product evaluations; small changes of these values may cause discontinuities in the customers' behavior and, indirectly, in the final results. In order to overcome this difficulty of data acquisition, in our model the producer's and the customers' knowledge of each other comes from two sources: (a) they have a mutual understanding what the key characteristics of the products are, and, (b) in the course of their repeated encounters, the producer learns the preferences of her customers. (With a convention borrowed from the theory of games, one of the sides, in our case the producer, is distinguished as called *she*.) Starting with (a) type knowledge, the producer strives to collect further, (b) type knowledge and exploits her knowledge to update the product offer.

The Product Model. Our basic assumptions on the products are as follows:

- The products belong to the same product line, so they are comparable with each other and may (partially) substitute each other at the customers.
- The products can be delivered in several variants that influence both production cost and the product's value for the customer.
- The product is purchased at a single action. The usage, maintenance and disposal aspects can be judged at the time of purchase.

In other words, this model can not be applied to products that are either (1) frequently bought (short term effects of advertising and variety seeking nature of the customers are not considered here); or (2) purchased by a sequence of events, by adding/replacing some modules of the products.

Each product is described as a vector of *attribute* = *value* pairs. The values of each attribute are discrete. There is a set of distinguished attributes that are directly used both for product selection by the customers and in product positioning by the producer: these are called the *perceptual dimensions* (PD-s) of the product. The value of each PD should be explicitly given or derivable from other attributes of the product.

A key novelty of our approach is that the values of each PD form a partially ordered set (i.e., a preference graph). Obviously, these partial orders include the usual types of the perceptual dimensions, i.e., the nominal values and the totally ordered values. The price of the product has no distinguished role in the model; it may be one of the perceptual dimensions.

The Producer. She intends to maximize her profit from the PL; competition with other manufacturers is captured by giving the customers the option of not to buy from her products.

The producer has limited resources for developing, manufacturing and selling products; her main concern is how to use the limited resources in the most profitable way. We assume that there exists a large set of technically feasible product variants, but only a small fraction of these variants will be exposed to *further* processing. Considering the design office example, further processing means detailed design here; considering the situation of selling a variety of ready-made products, focusing further processing means that only a small set of the product variants will be actually presented to the customers. The running example is the situation of selling ready-made products to customers; the limited resource is the showcase where the producer exhibits some products from her product offer. Increasing the capacity of the showcase requires additional investment, so the producer should prefer to show an offer of limited size.

The producer faces two problems: The static one is whether she has to offer a small set of generally acceptable products—but, perhaps, not the most preferred ones—for the typical customers *or* to offer the most preferred products for some—perhaps, smaller—subset of the customers. The dynamic problem is whether she has to introduce new products in order to explore their selling potential, *or* to avoid the risk with new products that may turn out unsuccessful.

The Customers. Each *customer entity* represents an amount of needs toward the products in the PL, generated by a number of individual (but, for us, indistinguishable) customers. The word *customer* is used for this aggregated entity. While each customer is homogeneous in his relation to the products, there is no further feature available to characterize a customer: the existence of the customer is limited to his buying demand and behavior.

Our customer model assumes that his decisions are based on his specific *preference structure*. Two individual customers are represented by the same (abstract) customer if and only if they have the same preference structure:

- For each customer, the preferences form a directed, acyclic graph (a partial order): nodes represent products, an edge goes from node p to q if and only if product p is more preferred than q ($p \succ q$). In presence of a more preferred product others are not selected.
- Nodes of the graph that can not be reached from each other (the incomparable elements of the partial order), are considered as products of incomparable values. The customer's selection among such elements is random.
- The preference graphs do not change in time.
- The producer does not know the preference graphs *a priori*, she has to explore them by observing the buying behavior of the customers.

Such preference graphs are derivable from the more usual models: First, from *spatial product evaluation schemes* where one kind of points represent the offered products, and another kind of points represent the best products of the customers. These points are scattered in the same multidimensional space of perceptual dimensions. Vectors from product to customer points are considered: whenever, for a specific customer, one vector is "much better" than another, this constellation creates a preference edge between these two products. Second, our preference structures may come from an additive *part-worth model* where customer-specific weights are attached to the product attributes, and scores are derived for each level of each attribute: the preferences should be based on the differences of the part-worth values. Although the above-mentioned models have rich numerical structure and attractive geometric connotations, it remains doubtful whether conclusions drawn from such models are based on firm grounds: the acquisition of the coordinates and weights has to be free from subjective bias and other (e.g., sampling) errors. As usual in such geometrically inspired approaches, small changes in the numerical values may cause large differences in the qualitative decisions.

Before discussing how should the producer explore the preference graphs, we have to define a reasonable *product selection protocol* that each customer is assumed to follow. Let us define the *front* of a preference graph as the set of its non-dominated elements. Elements of the front are the *best products*, incomparable between each other. The *k-th front* is given by a recursive definition by removing the $k-1$-th front.

While the preference graph is defined over the whole set of products, the customer's selection is limited to the offer he actually meets. The protocol of product selection from the actual offer is as follows:

(1) Selection of a best element: If some elements of the front are present in the actual offer, one of these products is selected with equal probabilities, and the purchase action terminates.
(2) Extension of the range of acceptable elements: If no element from the front is available in the current offer, then with probability p the customer extends the range of the acceptable products to the next front and acts as in *(1)*. With probability $(1-p)$ the action is finished without purchasing anything.

In this protocol, the selection is wholly deterministic with respect to a pair of comparable elements: whenever a product has been selected, the producer may be sure that, *for that specific customer*, no other element in the offer is definitely better than the selected product.

4 Incremental Methods of Preference Based PL Design

In order to optimize her PL, the producer has to solve several subproblems: first, she should create an initial offer, then the offer should be refined via exploring the customers' preferences. The next sections outline solutions to the consecutive subproblems.

4.1 Preference from Perceptual Dimensions

Let us assume a known, fixed set of perceptual dimensions of the products (called Δ) and their values. (Obviously, price may be one of these PDs.) Supposing that the values of the PDs are known, a straightforward way of generating a single preference graph is to take the Cartesian product of all the PDs and define the preference graph so that product p with perceptual values $(a_1, \ldots, a_k)$, $k \in \Delta$ is preferred over q with perceptual values $(b_1, \ldots, b_k)$ if and only if all a_k values are preferred over or equal to b_k.

With this definition the producer creates a preference graph that captures her reasonable default assumptions at product modeling: (1) all the PDs are indeed relevant, and the partial order of the values is the most she can know of a single dimension. Having built the preference graph, it is obvious that the producer should make her offer with using front elements. If there are not enough places in the showcase to include some element(s) of the fronts of each customer, then she has to select an offer that includes products that are "not too bad for most customers"—this problem will be discussed later.

4.2 Preference from Customers' Choice

Here we assume that the producer observes which products are being selected, and builds the preference graph(s) of the elements in her offer. Whenever the observed preferences generate a cycle-free graph, there is nothing to do. Unfortunately, this hardly ever happens, since conflicts of the observations arise, due to two reasons:

Ambiguity in the observation of preferences: First assume that a single customer repeatedly selects products from a fixed offer. Whenever he selects product p, any other product q in the offer may be either (1) less preferred than p (the selection of p over q was deterministic), or (2) q may be incomparable to p (the selection was random). The producer is unable to distinguish between the above alternatives. Therefore, the producer has to assume that all the selections were deterministic. However, as soon as (over the same offer) the customer makes two different selections, a conflict arises among the observed preferences.

Mixed observations from several customers: In case of several customers, conflicts of the observations arise from the fact that the producer does not know the identity of her customers. Accordingly, based on all observations she has made, she should either (1) build a single "best" preference graph for the observed mixture of customers, or (2) create more than one preference graphs to represent the different customers.

These two problems can be solved in the same framework: let nodes n_i represent products ($i \in I$) and edges e_{ij} ($i, j \in I$) represent observed preferences. Weights of the edges $w_{ij} = 1, 2, \ldots$ represent the multiplicity of the observations. The set of observations is conflicting if and only if there are cycles in this graph. As an explanation of the observations, the producer has to find a cycle-free subgraph by removing some edges. By removing no more than a minimal set of edges, she takes into account the maximal summed-up worth of the observations.

Generating all the cycles of a directed graph is an easy enumeration exercise with depth-first search. The computational cost of finding the best cutting edge set can be relaxed by using a decreasing threshold: observations below the threshold are to be discarded immediately. After this preprocessing the cycle cutting problem can be formulated as a linear program with 0/1 variables for deleting/keeping edges, a constraint for each cycle to formulate that the cycle has to be cut, and with an objective function that minimizes the total weight of deleted edges.

This way the producer obtains a maximal explanation of her observations on the behavior of a *single* customer. However, if the observations came from different customers, only those products will belong to the front that are preferred by a majority of the customers. Different customers can be discriminated in the following way: First, let us suppose that there are two customers, called

here *Green* and *Red*, both with their own preference graphs. The observations of the producer came from a superpositition of these graphs, *colors removed.* Restricted to equal edge weights, the problem can be formulated as follows:
g_{ij} 0/1 variable, becomes 1 iff e_{ij} is to be deleted from the *green* graph
r_{ij} 0/1 variable, becomes 1 iff e_{ij} is to be deleted from the *red* graph.

Since the edge e_{ij} is discarded (the observation is disregarded) iff both g_{ij} and r_{ij} are set to 1, the objective is to minimize:

$$\sum_{i \in I\, j \in I} g_{ij} \cdot r_{ij}$$

so that each cycle of the graph has some cutting element(s), both in the *green* and *red* versions of the graph:

$$\left.\begin{array}{l} \sum_{g_{ij} \in C} g_{ij} \geq 1 \\ \\ \sum_{r_{ij} \in C} r_{ij} \geq 1 \end{array}\right\} \quad \forall C \in \text{cycles of the graph}$$

This formulation can be developed into a recursion of segmentation steps with feeding back the disregarded *red* edges into the *green* graph which will be further segmented.

4.3 Finding the Relevant Perceptual Dimensions

Here we consider first a single customer's product selection from a given product offer: what kind of conclusions the producer can draw on the *unknown* relevance of the particular perceptual dimensions for a single customer. Let Δ be the overall set of PDs; its subsets will be called *styles*; our aim now is to find out the style in which the customer is *in fact* interested.

Let us assume that the customer with his (unknown) style Ψ selected a product p, but in the offer there exists another product q, so that q is definitely better with respect to some style χ (denoted as $p \prec_\chi q$). There are two explanations: (1) he is interested in some dimension not in χ and the good value in that dimension makes the chosen product *for him* incomparable with q; or (2) he is not interested in a dimension in χ, i.e., the good value there is irrelevant for him. Obviously, the above explanations may refer to more than one dimensions, and both may be valid. In this way, taking into consideration against p all the non-chosen products, the producer can collect upper and lower estimates for the unknown style Ψ of the customer.

With this construction the producer exploits all information available in a single product selection step and now she should look at the *stream* of purchase actions (over an offer that may be changing as well). In this step, a minimal explanation for the product selections made by a set of customers is needed: for each customer we have a number of styles that explain his choice, and we are looking for a minimal set of (simple) styles that explains all the selections. Again, this can be formulated as a 0/1 linear programming problem, but we do not go into details here.

4.4 Estimating the Weights of the Customer Styles

At this point of PL design, the producer, having collected selling data of her offer, would like to know what are the relative weights of the different customer styles. Below such a method will be outlined by an example.

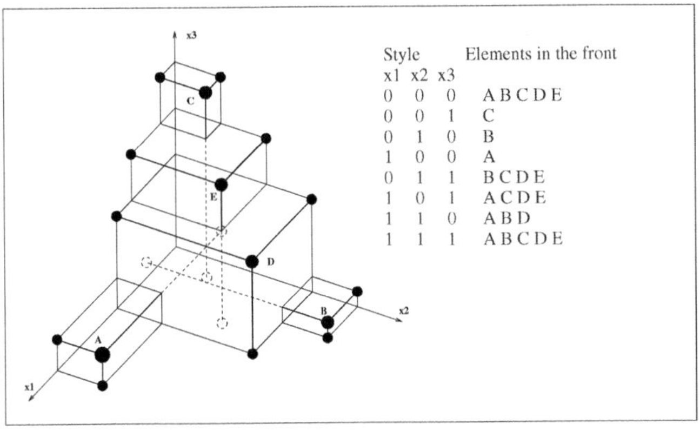

Fig. 1. Product line with three perceptual dimensions

We consider three perceptual dimensions (x_1, x_2 and x_3) and five products (A, B, C, D and E); their relative positions and the front products are as shown on Fig. 3. The observed buying frequencies of the products are $f_A, f_B, \ldots, f_E$. The producer would like to know the most plausible frequency distribution $p_i \geq 0,\ i = 1, 2, \ldots, 8$ of the eight customer styles.

The first five rows of the matrix below represent the five products, and the last row ensures that the p_i values are indeed a frequency distribution. The columns of the matrix represent the eight styles. The equal fractions in each column express the assumption of random choice from among the products of the front.

$$\begin{bmatrix} 1/5 & 1 & 0 & 0 & 0 & 1/4 & 1/3 & 1/5 \\ 1/5 & 0 & 1 & 0 & 1/4 & 0 & 1/3 & 1/5 \\ 1/5 & 0 & 0 & 1 & 1/4 & 1/4 & 0 & 1/5 \\ 1/5 & 0 & 0 & 0 & 1/4 & 1/4 & 1/3 & 1/5 \\ 1/5 & 0 & 0 & 0 & 1/4 & 1/4 & 0 & 1/5 \\ 1 & 1 & 1 & 1 & 1 & 1 & 1 & 1 \end{bmatrix} \star \begin{bmatrix} p_1 \\ p_2 \\ p_3 \\ p_4 \\ p_5 \\ p_6 \\ p_7 \\ p_8 \end{bmatrix} = \begin{bmatrix} f_A \\ f_B \\ f_C \\ f_D \\ f_E \\ 1 \end{bmatrix}$$

As for finding the most plausible explanation, an appropriate objective function is the quadratic sum of the p_is: it is symmetric as entropy and finding its minimum is a routine optimization problem.

4.5 Positioning of the Product Offer

Now, the producer has a preference graph for each customer and weights expressing their relative importance. The aim is to find the best offer, i.e. that subset of the available products that gives the maximal chance of satisfying the customers' needs. The offer has to satisfy constraints: first of all the constraint of the limited size of the offer.

If the allowed size of the offer is as high as the number of perceptual dimensions, it might be enough to offer a product from the front of each one-dimensional style, and these products will do for the customers with more-dimensional styles as well. However, such an offer may be poor since it is made solely of products with good values in one of the dimensions, while they are (perhaps) pure in the other dimensions. Obviously, a product with good values in each dimension might be good for anybody—but such a product, due to the conflicting nature of the dimensions, may be either technically unfeasible, or too expensive (or both).

If the allowed size of the offer is less than the number of PDs, then some customers may not find their best products in the offer. In such cases, elements shared by the 2nd and deeper fronts of several styles may be selected, *as a compromise*, by several customers (with some probability, as described in the customer model): in such a case the presence of *generally acceptable substitutes* may increase the selling power of the offer.

Within the framework of our preferential model, we can cope with the above factors as well. Elements in the front of a preference graph are incomparable: one of them is better in *some* dimension(s) and worse in *some other* dimension(s). When jumping to another product for improvement along one dimension, values in some other dimension(s) decrease (otherwise the later product would dominate the first). Accordingly, one can define a *distance* of any two products, where $ind_d(p)$ is the rank of element p along dimension d:

$$dist(p,q) \stackrel{def}{=} \sum_{d\in\Delta} |ind_d(p) - ind_d(q)|$$

This product distance can be refined to include factors for the weights of the customer styles and with probabilities of the customers extending their selection range behind the front. With using this distance, the problem of finding a good offer can be formalized as a variant of the so-called *P-median* problem.

5 Conclusion

Product positioning aims at finding a proper balance between the exploration of new product alternatives and the exploitation of the selling potential of the available variants. Key assumptions of our model are that (1) the products can be described in terms of perceptual dimensions, (2) the customers' behavior is driven by their preferences between the products offered, and (3) they behave rationally by selecting a most preferred item from the offer.

Departing solely from the choices of customers, we have given methods for the producer (1) to anticipate the relevant perceptual dimensions – so-called styles – for her customers, (2) to reconstruct the customers' preferences, and (3) to estimate the relative weight of different customer styles. These information are the inputs of the producer's product positioning decision. When making this decision she attempts to offer product variants that may maximally meet the needs of the customers. By using the above methods repeatedly, the producer can better and better anticipate the demand and refine her offer.

Our model poses a series of *qualitative decision problems*. Research reported here strives to help incremental PL design with the help of ideas widely used in Artificial Intelligence (such as conflict resolution or explanations), in Operations Research (such as the formulation of the optimization models) and in Decision Support (such as preference based methods). We hope that the integration of these techniques, with proper assumptions on the artifacts and the participants will open up new ways of PL design. Missing links and further details will be discussed in a forthcoming paper.

Acknowledgments. Work carried out by A. Márkus has been supported by the "Methodology for Emergent Synthesis" project in the "Research for the Future" Program of the Japan Society for the Promotion of Science. Work carried out by J. Váncza has been supported by the research grant OTKA T023305 of the Hungarian NSF.

References

1. W. P. Barnett and R. A. Burgelman. Evolutionary perspectives on strategy. *Strat. Management J.*, 17:5-19, 1996.
2. G. Dobson and C. A. Yano. Product line and technology selection with shared manufacturing and engineering design resources. Technical report, Simon Graduate School of Business Administration, Univ. of Rochester, 1995. OP 95-01 WP.
3. K. Lancaster. The economics of product variety: A survey. *Marketing Sci.*, 9(3): 189-206, 1990.
4. D. Levy. Chaos theory and strategy: Theory, application and managerial implications. *Strat. Management J.*, 15:167-178, 1994.
5. A. K. Manrai. Mathematical models of brand choice behavior. *Eur. J. of Oper.* Res., 82:1-17, 1995.
6. S. K. Nair, L. S. Thakur, and K.-W. Wen. Near optimal solutions for product line design and selection: Beam search heuristics. *Management Sci.*, 41(5):767-785, 1995.
7. H. A. Simon. Strategy and organizational evolution. *Strat. Management J.*, 14:131-142, 1993.
8. J. Tirole. *The Theory of Industrial Organization*. MIT Press, 1995.

Applying Logic of Information Flow and Situation Theory to Model Agents That Simulate the Stock Market Behaviour

Sueli Bandeira Teixeira Mendes, Ph. D. and
Oscar Luiz Monteiro de Farias, D. Sc.

Universidade do Estado do Rio de Janeiro - Centro de Tecnologia e Ciências - Faculdade de Engenharia, Departamento de Engenharia de Sistemas e Computação, tel.: (+55) (21) 587-7442, fax.: (+55) (21) 587-7374
{smendes, oscar}@eng.uerj.br

Abstract. Logic of Information Flow (LIF) and Situation Theory (ST) are formal systems that furnish a rich source of models for formalisation of several types of computational systems. In this paper, both LIF and ST provide us the tools needed for formalising a multi-agent system that simulate the stock market behaviour.

Keywords: Agents, Theory of Situation, Logic of Information Flow, Stock Market

1 Introduction

First of all we have to agree that there isn't a common acceptable definition for *agent.* Consider a pragmatic approach, and we'll pick up, in the several existing definitions , what appear to us be a common ground about what an *agent* really is. In the intersection of several definitions we could find that *agents* are software components that perceive, reason, communicate and act in someone's favour, influencing its environment. One of the keys characteristics attributed to *agent* is that they are capable of reasoning, infer and extrapolate on bases of current experience and knowledge, in a rational manner, and in a way that can be reproduced . They also must have an adaptable behaviour, that is, they must be capable of analysing the external environment and act (or react), according to previous successful actions took under similar conditions, and to adapt these actions in order to meet their goals [5]. Others, like Bates [4] even consider that *agents* have feelings or emotional characteristics. So, what we perceived of the several definitions on *Agents* is that, on a certain sense, what people really want, is that *agents* behave like human beings.

Of course, when saying "perceive", "reason", "communicate", and "act in someone favour" we are using anthropomorphic concepts, but we here do not compromise ourselves on a philosophical or psychological discussion, that will take us astray of our main goal. The pragmatic view that we adoptis that *agents* are pieces of software. Being so, they are successful on the imitation of human behaviour, depending on someone's ability to program them to some specific task that mimic that behaviour .

L. Monostori, J. Váncza, and M. Ali (Eds.): IEA/AIE 2001, LNAI 2070, pp. 856-867, 2001.

An important question then raises. Given a specific behaviour of an *agent* is it satisfactory or not? The answer probably involves the comparisons between *agents* and human beings submitted to the same conditions. In case of simple tasks, like buying a given book for the best price, the comparison is straightforward and very favourable to *agents*, that is, they can do these kind of repetitive tasks even better than human beings. But, when we deal with complex systems the answer is very difficult, indeed, even more if our simulation of the system behaviour comprises several *agents* acting together, and with goals that conflict among them. In the case of the stock market, the problem raises another important question related to rationality or irrationality of the stock market itself. So, if the investors (human beings) behaviour are not rational themselves, how could we represent these behaviour by *agents*? Whichever *agent* behaviour would be admitted, on the basis of the irrationality of the stock market? This would lead us to a situation analogous to the proposition $p \Rightarrow q$ of First Order Logic. The truth table of this formula say us that if p is false, then the implication $p \Rightarrow q$ would be true anyway. In this basis, any behaviour would be accepted for a given *agent*[7].

Any psychologist will say at that point that if we don't know how a human being behaves, what is a measure of success of a *software agent*? Considering that what we are trying in this paper is a formalisation process of real world behaviour, we know of no case where this process led to all original questions being answered, nor do we know of any case where it has not led to greater understanding of the original phenomena than was previously possible. At least we try putting as a criteria of understanding the ability of predicting, controlling, or manifesting features of the stock market behaviour to our own advantage. Considering that what we want is a simple definition of a rational *agent*, this definition will only say that being rational is never behave against your own well being, being aware of this.

Anyway, we will simplify the question here considering the aim of this paper. Viewed from the standpoint of the use of *agents* within LIF and ST framework, our present enterprise may be thought of as an attempt to use and develop tools from LIF and ST viewpoint, in order to capture the complexity of real stock market behaviour.

So, we decided to make an experiment to enable us observe the behaviour of *agents* vis-à-vis human beings in a complex system, and calculate how much the behaviour of *agents* deviate from the behaviour of human beings. In this experiment we follow the track of the system when submitted only to interactions with human beings – this is the real world, that traces a specific path. Then we compute the evolution of the system when submitted only to interactions with *agents*. This give us another trajectory, a virtual one, perhaps very different from the real one. If our *agents* replicate the behaviour of human beings in a suitable manner, then we'll find that the two paths – the real one and the virtual one - will be very close. Then we can say that our *agents* model the behaviour of humans well, perhaps with all the limitations and even wrong decisions inherent to humans, perhaps incorporating also elements of irrationality.

The complex system we chose to make this experiment was the stock market behaviour. The state of the stock market on a given day can be thought of as the stocks value (overture, minimum, maximum, mean, closed), the volume negotiated for each stock, the number of negotiations, the total value negotiated in the market, and the value of an index like IBOVESPA, IBV, NASDAQ, DOW JONES, NIKEI etc, that is directly associated to a particular bourse. The stock market evolves from its state today, to a new state tomorrow, based mainly, on several orders to buy or sell specific stocks, given to brokers by investors. These investors fundament their decisions on various new facts about the world, usually brought to people trough the media: TV, radio, newspapers, magazines, Internet, etc.

We simulate the behaviour of this complex system through several *agents,* that represent the investors in real life [9]. These *agents* are modelled in a way such that they mimic different kinds of investors. These *agents* face some trends in the stock market, trends which are determined in a broad sense in a analogous way the news about the world are interpreted by the investors in real life. Different kinds of *agents* (those that search to realise the profit in short term, medium term and long term, that are more aggressive, in a sense that take more risks, those more conservative take less risks, etc) will analyse the overall trends in the stock market and will act (buying or selling stocks) based on their profile. The ensemble of the actions performed by all these *agents* will give us the behaviour of our virtual market. A comparison of the paths along the time of an index like the DOW JONES, with the corresponding path of a virtual equivalent index in our model, will give us a measure of the degree of adherence of our model to the real world. That is, if our model simulates well enough the stock market behaviour or not. If $f(x)$ is the index trajectory in real life, and if $g(x)$ is the index trajectory in our model, we could say that

$$\int |f(x) - g(x)|$$

give us a measure of the absolute error presented in our model.

We'll use *Logic of Information Flow (LIF)* [3] *and Situation Theory (ST)* [6] to model the different process, entities, information flow, and decisions related to the stock market behaviour. In that way, will present now a brief overview of these systems. After this short explanation, we'll present our model and we'll say something about its implementation.

2 Introduction to Logic of Information Flow (LIF) and Situation Theory (ST)

Situation Theory was presented in the way we use it here by Barwise and Perry [1]and Devlin [6]. Barwise and Perry presented ST mainly as a way of knowledge representation, intended to representing semantics of Natural Language. Later on, Devlin considered ST as means of presenting a new approach to a Science of Information (SI). Barwise et all [3] considered that the results of their paper were directly related to Barwise [2]. Here, in this paper, we choose to maintain Barwise [2] formalism, specially because in his paper Barwise uses parallel channels, solution that we consider the most appropriated to our model.

[6] consider that, even so we do not possess a complete formal system for SI, its development is possible, the same way Arithmetic was studied and developed, in spite of, in its beginning, we did not have a formal concept of number. The same could be

said about the field of *Physics of Particles* with the elementary particles like electrons and protons, that can be viewed as the fundamentals of a whole science like Physics. So, [6] elected the so called - *infon* – as the angular stone of his theory. The *infon* is to be considered as an unit of information. It has the form:

<R(a_1, a_2, ..., a_n, l, t), i)>, where:

i. a_1, a_2, ..., a_n are the arguments of R and can be any individual carved out of the world as contents of possible propositions. These arguments may be objects of everyday experience, like, tables, chairs, etc, or more formal objects like numbers and classes of mathematical knowledge, the truth values of Propositional Calculus, *infon*s themselves, and situations (as we explain below).
ii. **R** is a **n+2** place relation.
iii. **i** is a polarity. It can assume the values **0** or **1**, depending on it affirms or negates the relation **R**.
iv. **l** and **t** are special arguments for location and time, respectively.

An *infon* is an object, so it cannot be *true* or *false*.

Now we try first to explain what a situation is. A situation can be viewed as a chunk of the world, as perceived by a cognitive agent. A cognitive agent can be a robot, a piece of software or a human being. In a formal way we will define a situation as a set of *infons*.

In ST there is a way of saying that a situation either supports or not an *infon*. If

$$s \models \tau,$$

where s is a situation and τ is an *infon* then we say that s supports τ.
If

$$s \;|\!\neq\; \tau$$

We say that s does not support τ.
The relation "support" defines a situation, since it can be defined by the set of *infons* it "supports".

ST is a typified system [6]. In ST we have the basic types:

i) *Tim:* the type of a temporal location; *LOC*: ii) the type of a spatial location; iii) *IND:* the type of an individual; iv) *REL***:* the type of a n place relation; v) *SIT:* the type of a situation; vi) *INF:* the type of an *infon*; vii) *TYP:* the type of a type; viii) *PAR:* the type of a parameter; ix) *POL:* the type of a polarity (i.e. the "truth values" 0 e 1).

For instance, if *l* is a location, then it is of type *LOC* and the *infon* <of-type, l, *LOC*, 1> is a fact, i.e., there is a situation that supports it. A proposition in ST always has the form:

x:T

saying that x is of type T. Being a proposition it can be true or false, i.e., it says that an *infon* may have or not, a situation that supports it. So, another way of representing a proposition is:

$$s \models \tau$$

that is the same as we said above.

An *infon*, a situation, or even a proposition can be an argument of an *infon.* So, ST is not a first order theory. By the way it is defined, ST raises the problem of well-foundness. In another paper [10] one of the authors discusses this problem and proves that a particular application is well-founded.

We said before, our model is applied to the stock market behaviour, so we use both LIF and ST. Now, we try to explain, in a very concise way, the basic ideas of LIF. LIF is presented by Barwise [2] as a way of formalising the Information Flow. In this system we have basically two entities: sites and channels. Sites are the locations where the information is located. Channels are the paths that permit information flow. Sites and channels are defined by its types. Types can be thought as uniformities of a high order than sites and channels. LIF is proved by Barwise to be a generalisation of several formal systems, in particular First Order Predicate Calculus (FOPC) and Situation Theory. For both the proof is reasonably simple.

In the case of FOPC we say that sites are the collection of propositions, premises for instance, and inference rules are channels. In this case, since propositions and inference rules use the same language, we might say that C⊆S, where C is the set of channels and S the set of inference rules. Inference rules are a particular form of constraints. Constraints are the way we, human beings, organise the world. Constraints may be physical, logical, moral or even conventional laws. A conventional law may be for instance, being on time for a meeting.

Below we have an example of *sites* and *channels* in the Classical Logic context:

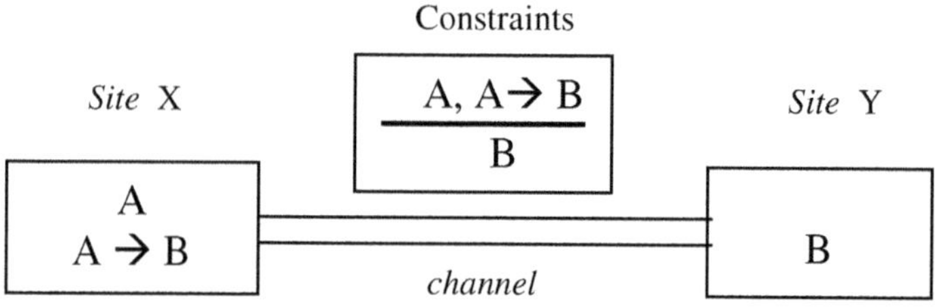

Fig. 1.

3 A LIF and ST Based Stock Market Model

The basic elements of our model are only *sites* and *channels.* Intuitively we can say that *sites* are places or situations where information are. *Channels* are pathways that link different *sites.* Information flows from one *site* to another one through a *channel.* Then *sites* are a set of sentences describing a given situation, and *channels* are constraints that, when applied, make it possible to go from one situation to another one. In our model, the news originated after the end of a daily stock market operation (trading day) and before the market opening of next day, will, given a specific world situation or world configuration, determine some trends in the stock market, affect the prices specific shares, etc. These trends could be mapped on a graduated scale in order to facilitate the implementation of our model. Figure I give us a illustration of this process.

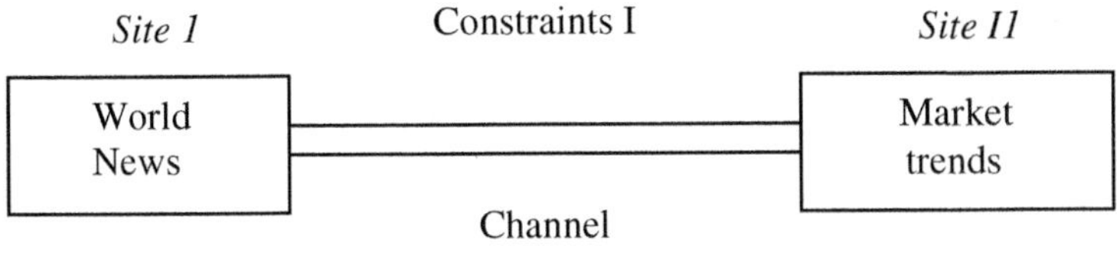

Fig. 2.

Exemplifying, the news could be sentences like that, first shown in English form, then, in ST notation:

- NASDAQ index rise (or fall) x%; <<Rise (index, NASDAQ, t, x%), 1 >>
- Rise of y% in the FED interest rate; <<Rise (interest rate, Fed, t, y%), 1 >>
- An optimistic speech of Dr. Greenspan; <<Speech (Greespan, optimistic, t), 1 >>
- Rise of z% in the economic activity in last quarter; <<Rise (economic activity, l, t, z%), 1 >>
- Microsoft will be split in two or more companies; <<Split (Microsoft, n^0 of companies, t), 1 >>

Constraints are cause and effect relationships from the news, relative to the state of the stock market on the last trading day, and their impact on the stock market. Examples of these are: first shown in English form, then, in ST notation:

- (Dow Jones index at day t = A) AND (NIKEI index at day t = -B) → (Dow Jones index at day t+1 = A - C); <<index (Dow Jones, t, A), 1>> ∧ <<index (NIKEI, t, -B), 1>> → <<index(Dow Jones, t+1, A-B),1>>
- (Russia's president today is capitalist) AND (elections) AND (projections indicate that Russia's today president is K% ahead of his competitors) AND (Moscow's bourse index yesterday = A) → (Moscow's bourse index today = A + B);
- <<capitalist(Russia's president, t), 1>> ∧ <<election(t), 1>> ∧ <<projections (election, Russia's president, t, k% ahead competitors), 1>> ∧ <<index(Moscow Bourse index, t, X),1>> → <<index(Moscow Bourse index, Moscow, t+1, A+B), 1>>

The *agents,* in our model (see Fig. 3), will act different from each other, based on their investor's *profile* and by: i) market trends - a scale well graduated to show the net effect of the world news submitted to the constraints shown at Figure I; ii) daily share price - a table showing the prices and volume negotiated for each specific share, like the ones that we see at the economic sections of newspapers; iii) The particular *agent* situation, that is: kinds and quantities of shares held by the *agent*, and the amount of money owned by the *agent.* "i", "ii", and "iii" are *sites*, and the *agent investor profile* is a *channel*, in the sense that, depending on this profile, the shares will find another equilibrium point ('ii') and the *agent situation* ("iii") will change, because the *agent* will sell or buy some shares at given prices. All of this can be illustrated by Figure II. In reality we have an intermediary *site* where the *agents* register their intention of buying or selling some specific share at a given price. These intermediary site provides for realisation of the investors *(agents)* orders.

Constraints represent the *agents profile*, which mimic the investors profile in real life. An example of these kind of constraints could be:

- (the NASDAQ index has a trend of rise (or fall) x%) AND (the *agent* bought the share at a price w% less than today's price) AND (the *agent* subjective evaluation of the market behaviour is of fall at medium run) → (the *agent* sells the share);

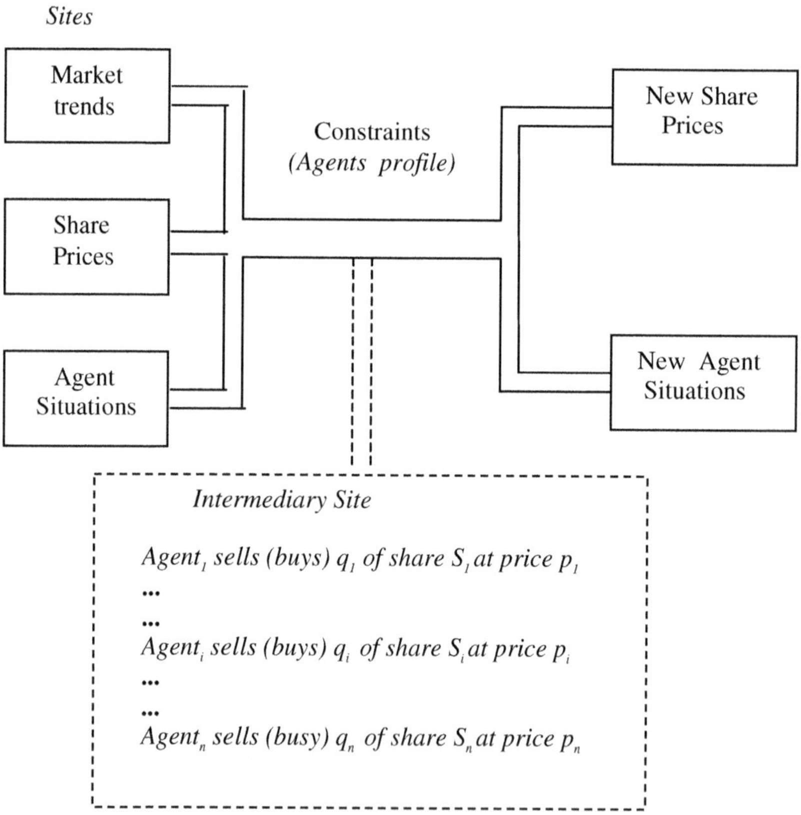

Fig. 3.

An *agent* will order to buy or sell an amount of shares without taking in account whether there are any *agent* with shares to sell or money to buy shares. In this case there is a no operation. It is similar to several other cases in modelling, where we say that there is no change, i.e., the state s_i is identical to state s_{i+1}.

In our analysis what are *sites* and *channels*? We said above that our task was to simulate the stock market behaviour, based on rational multi-agents. We know, by everyday experience, that world news have a strong influence on stock market behaviour. For instance, a President of Federal Reserve's declaration may determine an up or down stock market tendency. Actually, this change happens because of investor's behaviour, influenced, of course, by FED's President declaration. But, in our first analysis, we are treating market behaviour and investor's behaviour as two separated phenomena. As in [2] *sites* are locations for information and *channels* are paths for information flow. In our case, world news, stock market trends, and *agent's* status (amount of money and number and type of shares it owns) are *sites.* They are described in ST as sets of *infons.* These sets define *site types. Software agents,* implemented by human beings, are *channels.* These *channels* also have a type. These. *agents* or *channels* are classified on different *types*, depending on some *constraints*, that reflect the *agents profile.* These profiles mimics types of investor's profile in real life

In [2], Barwise explicits a necessary relation among specific situations, i.e., *tokens* and relation among type of situations. As an example we may use a relation between *tokens*, such as:

{<<index (Bovespa, 03/05/2000, X), 1)} → {<<sells (agent , shares, amount_A, share_T, price_B), 1>>}

But the relation between

{<<index (Bovespa, up), 1>>} → {<<buy (stock, price / X, amount [Y), 1>>}

is a relation between types of situation. For him, this distinction supports the following inference

$$\varphi \to \psi, \qquad h \mapsto t, \qquad h \models \varphi \Rightarrow t \models \psi,$$

where $\to$ is a relation between *types of situations*, and $\mapsto$ a relation between *situation tokens.* Here, an infomation *channel* means one of these relations between situations. Barwise, in the same paper [2], explicits the following basic notions:

i. *Sites* and *channels* are objects of his theory. *Channels* may be or not a subset of *sites.*
ii. There is a *three place relation*

$$s_1 \overset{c}{\longmapsto} s_2$$

that holds between *channels* and *site tokens.*

iii. There is another object:

$$\varphi \rightarrow \psi$$

called a *constraint channel* that holds between types of situation.
Barwise affirms that the Axiom of Soundness there is: The *channel* ***c*** is of type

$$c : \varphi \rightarrow \psi$$

iff for all sites

$$s_1, s_2, \quad \mathit{iff} \quad s_1 \overset{c}{|\!\longrightarrow} s_2 \quad \mathit{and}\ s_1 : \varphi \quad \mathit{then} \quad s_2 : \psi \quad \mathit{holds}.$$

According to Barwise [2], we may have a parallel composition of *channels* meaning: c_1

$$s_1 \overset{c}{|\!\longrightarrow} s_2 \quad \mathit{iff} \quad s_1 \overset{c_1}{|\!\longrightarrow} s_2 \quad \mathit{and} \quad s_1 \overset{c_2}{|\!\longrightarrow} s_2 \ \mathit{and} \quad c = c_1 \parallel c_2.$$

and c_2 will form a parallel composition provided that for all *sites* s_1, s_2 such that:

Parallel *channels* are represented by $c_1 \parallel c_2$.
We particularly need parallel *channels* in our model, because our *software agents* will be implemented using constructions like that:

> If condition 1, condition 2, . . . , condition N, then buy,
> and
> If condition 1, condition 2, . . . , condition N, then sell,

depending on the *agent's* profile.

We have said before that *agents* are like *channels*. This is precisely what happens here. Each *agent* is implemented essentially by saying that such and such conditions will make the *agent* buy (sell) a given amount of a specific share at a pre-determined price, depending on the *agent's* money, its amount of shares, and on its profile.

On reality Figure II above is a simplification of Figure III below. In Figure III, for matter of simplification, we show only two *agents* realising buy/sell operations, but we analyse in more detail these operations.

In the case of fig. 4, we see an example where constraints $q_{j,k} \geq q_{i,k}$ and $p_{i,k} \geq p_{j,k}$ obtained, and *sites* New Share Prices and New Agent Situation are really different of the old ones. That is not always the case, as we said above.

4 Implementation Aspects / System Architecture

The implementation of our model - *Virtual Stock Market based on LIF, ST, and Mobile Agents* – will be based in a previous application already implemented:

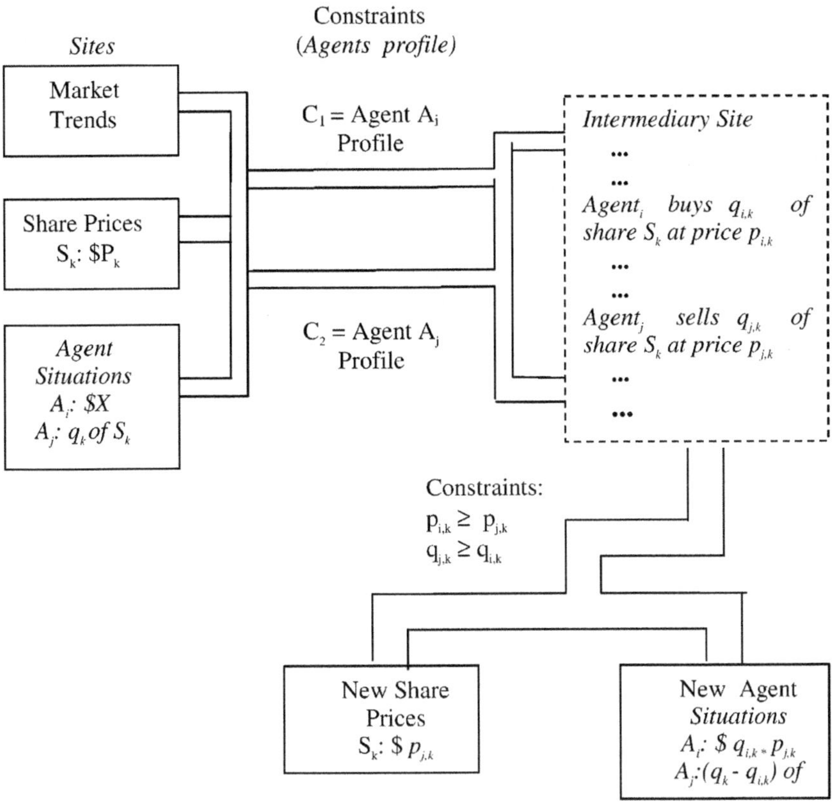

Fig. 4.

Mercado Eletrônico Baseado em Agentes Móveis – MEBAN ("Electronic Market Based on Mobile Agents") [11]. This system implemented an electronic market on an Internet host machine with a given and known IP address, in which *mobile agents* trade among them, sometimes acting as vendors, sometimes acting as buyers, on behalf of their masters, human beings that logged on at remote machines, created their *agents*, and gave them specific instructions to buy or sell some products, books in that case. Implementing *MEBAN* [11] we built all the basic framework needed to implement our simulation of the stock market described here.

Likewise the implementation of *MEBAN* system, our *Virtual Stock Market* will use the *Aglets* framework. We will not use a specific *agents standard*, but as the *Aglets* framework follows the *MASIF (Mobile Agent System Interoperability Facility)* in its own implementation, we will indirectly do the same. Using the *Aglets* framework will give us some advantage, because we will not have to disperse efforts building an infra-structure to support the use of *agent* technology. The *Aglet* API is a development kit for building mobile *agents,* written completely in Java. An *aglet* is merely an instance of a class in the *Aglet* API, that implements the functionality

needed to a mobile *agent*. An *aglet* integrates itself with all the infra-structure put at disposal by the others components of the framework, such that: servers execution environments, mechanisms to support code migration between different Internet hosts, support to actions of the type: suspend and resume execution of an *agent*, *agent* intercommunication through messages, clone making, *agent* search, etc... [8], [11]. So, in using the *Aglet* framework we'll concentrate all our attention in programming only the specific aspects of our application.
The system architecture of our *Virtual Stock Market* is as follows: i) at remote hosts (base agencies), users will make instances of their *agents*, based on investors profile, giving them specific orders to buy or sell determined shares at given quantities and prices; These agents then, will travel to an Internet specific host - the *Virtual Stock Market*, a machine with a known IP address ; ii) There, all *agents* sent by other Internet hosts, will evaluate market trends, analyze share prices, their own situations (amount of money, and types an quantities of shares owned), and then, decide to sell or buy determined shares at given prices and quantities; iii) Then the agents will travel back to their source hosts to inform the users the result of their actions. This architecture is very similar to that adopted in the *MEBAN* system.

5 Conclusions

The most important improvement we obtained in the present paper was that, through modelling using LIF and ST, it was possible to represent clearly agent profiles and stock market situations. In that way, we can easily compare virtual stock markets with real ones. Our main goal is to make the difference between real and virtual markets, measured by the integral of the difference between the two index curves as small as possible. Here we have not tried to maximise the profit of a particular virtual *agent*. Our objective is to represent a complex system through the use of several agents acting together, even if they have goals that enter in conflict. But , in real life, what people really want are *agents* that do something useful, and to make money is certainly a very useful thing. So, we are developing a special *agent* whose aim is to make money in the stock market. This *agent* will buy or sell shares in a real stock market, depending on information obtained on the sites News and Market Trends. All variables like shares price, quantities of shares bought and/or sold, volume negotiated, bourse index, etc. will assume the same values we find in the real market. Our assumption is that the operations realised by this *agent* will be very small compared with the total operations realised in the market, so that its own operations will not influence prices in the market. This experiment, when applied in a time interval, will show us if our *agent* is capable or not of making money in the stock market.

References

1. Barwise, J. & Perry, J. Situations and Attitudes, Cambridge, MA: MIT Press, 1983.
2. Barwise, J. Constraints, Channels and Flow of Information, in *Situation Theory and Its Applications*. Vol. 3. Aczel, Israel, Katagiri and Peters (eds), 1993, CSLI, Stanford University, 3-27.
3. Barwise, J & Gabbay, D & Hartonas, C. On the Logic of Information Flow, in *Bulletin of IGPL*, vol. 3, n.1, 7-50, 1995.

4. Bates, J. The Role of Emotion in Believable Characters. Communications of the ACM, 37, N^0 7, pp122-125 (1994).
5. Bradshaw, J. M. An Introduction to Software Agents, in *Software Agents*. AAAI Press / The MIT Press. 1997
6. Devlin, K., Logic and Information. Cambridge University Press, 1991.
7. Goel, Vinog & Grafman, John. Are the Frontal Lobes Implicated in "Planning" Functions? Interpreting Data from the Tower of Hanoi. Neuropsychologia, vol. 33, N^0 5, pp. 632-642, 1995. Elsevier Science Ltd.
8. Lange, D. B.; Oshima M.; Programming and Deploying Java Mobile Agents with Aglets. Addison Wesley, 1998.
9. Maes, P., Guttman, R. H., Moukas, A. G. Agents that Buy and Sell: Transforming Commerce as we Know It. Submitted to the Communications of the ACM, March 1999 Issue.
10. Mendes, S. B. T. & Motta, C. L. R. Modelling the Cooperative Information Filtering Problem. Relatório Técnico NCE – 12/99, Núcleo de Computação Eletrônica, Universidade Federal do Rio de Janeiro, 1999.
11. Sugar, Márcio Henrique Carrilho. Mercado Eletrônico Baseado em Agentes Móveis. Monografia. Universidade do Estado do Rio de Janeiro, Departamento de Engenharia de Sistemas e Computação, 1999, Rio de Janeiro.

GAs and Financial Analysis

Matty Leus [1], Dwight Deugo [2], Franz Oppacher[2], and Rob Cattral[2]

Carleton University, School of Computer Science, 613-5200-4333,
Ottawa, Ontario, Canada, K1S 5B6

[1]matthew.leus@sympatico.ca
[2]{deugo,oppacher,rcattral}@scs.carleton.ca

Abstract. Technical analysis provides an alternative, and in some ways simpler, method of predicting stock movement. The majority of existing genetic algorithm approaches in the financial area look at fundamental stock characteristics to determine trading rules. Our hypothesis is that one can develop a genetic algorithm that simultaneously considers many different technical rather than fundamental characteristics to develop rules that indicate attractive buying opportunities and signal that it is time to sell specific stocks.

1 Introduction

Genetic Algorithms (GAs) [5] have been used in several different ways in the financial area. For example, Colin described a GA [3] for discovering trading rules for buying and selling that maximize profits while minimizing draw downs. His chromosome model included four periods of moving averages that make up two price oscillators and a percentage stop-loss. Rabatin [6] described a GA for trading multicurrency trading portfolios. Chen and Lee [2] described a GA for determining prices of European call options. Bauer [1] constructed a GA that selected series combinations that showed high correlations with stock returns of the recent past, regressing the various macroeconomic time series and changes in them, over the 1984-1988 time period. A select subset of other real and potential applications is available in [4].

The majority of these approaches are considered stock fundamental approaches. That is, each looks at fundamental stock characteristics, such a low debt level, to determine rules. An alternative approach examines technical characteristics of stocks, for example patterns in a stock price's trading or volume. Colin's approach falls into this category. However, it only considers moving averages.

Our hypothesis is that one can develop a GA that simultaneously considers many different technical characteristics to develop rules that indicate attractive buying opportunities and signal that it is time to sell specific stocks.

Our goal is to use technical indicators that rely on the recent past to predict the future. However, not only do we want to produce rules that turn a good profit, we want to generate rules that will decrease the risk involved with being in the market.

L. Monostori, J. Váncza, and M. Ali (Eds.): IEA/AIE 2001, LNAI 2070, pp. 868-873, 2001.

In section 2, we briefly describes the technical indicators our GA uses and section 3 outlines the structure of our GA. Section 4 describes the results of using our approach and section 5 summarizes.

2 The Indicators

Some indicators work well with equities that oscillate at a great rate. Others do well with stocks that don't fluctuate that much at all. For this reason, we use a combination of different indicators to represent the stock movement for all types of equities.

Moving Average: serves to flatten out the sometimes-rampant daily fluctuations of a stock, in a sense filtering out the noise and de-emphasizing the daily distortion due to erratic upward and downward movements.

Money Flow RSI Breakout (MFSRI): a moving average indicator that measures the flow of money into or out of a stock and relates it to the volume change.

Bollinger Band Crossover: an example of a moving average indicator. Crossovers work by placing two "bands" around the moving average of the stock, thus outlining the normal trading range of the equity.

Volume Accumulation Percent (VAP): a volume indicator that uses the amount of shares traded during a time period to indicate the amount of buying and selling that goes on for a particular stock.

Candlestick Patterns: formed buy looking at the open, close, high and low for the time period, usually the previous day or two. If the stock closes higher than it opened the body of the candle is white. If the stock closes lower than the open the body is black.

Oscillator Indicators: Oscillators focus on the fact that a given equity will oscillate between an overbought state and an oversold state.

Williams Peaks: After choosing a period P, we calculate the Williams peak as follows:

WP = (High in Period – Today's close)/(High in Period – Low in Period)

After choosing an upper and lower signal line, it will indicate a buy whenever the WP moves below the lower signal line, forming a valley. A sell will be generated when the WP moves above the upper signal line, peaking.

3 GA Structure

GA's are a form of evolutionary computing modeled after nature's inherent mechanisms to induce diversity and maintain a healthy gene pool. They begin with an encoding of what possible solutions to the problem at hand would look like. In our case, the encoding is in the form of a rule. The rule is comprised of the possible outputs from the twelve technical indicators, namely a 's' for sell, 'b' for buy, 'c' for stay in cash and a '#' for don't care what this value is. Therefore, a possible rule is:

('c','#', '#', '#', '#', '#','b', '#', 's', '#', '#', '#')

Now, say the VAP indicator represents the first index, MFRSI the seventh and Candle Doji Star the ninth. This would mean that this rule would be triggered if, for a given day for a given equity, the VAP told us to stay in cash, the MFRSI told us to buy and the Candle Doji said to sell.

3.1 Mutation, Crossover, Selection Schemes

For our experiments, we used simple mutation, single point crossover, and tournament selection [5]. The probability of mutation was set at 0.07 to encourage slight changes over many generations and the probability of crossover was set at 0.8. We chose tournament selection because it is less prone to premature convergence than other types of selection, such as rank or roulette wheel selection, and because it was more efficient. Tournament selection employs the fitness function at most once for every member of the population, assuming that no chromosome is chosen more than once to compete. Since it is unlikely that a given chromosome will only compete once, this results is in fewer calls to the fitness function. If the fitness function is computationally intensive, this results in superior performance.

3.2 Fitness

To determine a rule's fitness, the process begins by attaining data on a given equity dating back to Jan 1999. This date was chosen in order to provide a training period in excess of one year along with an extra quarter to validate the best rules. Considering the forces that drive the market, the older data is, the less relevant it becomes. One may suggest this period isn't long enough to properly train the rule set. However, rules that worked well two years ago are most likely obsolete to trade with today. For this reason, the periods we're dealing with here are a couple of weeks at most, not years.

Once the data is attained, it's broken into two chunks. One chunk is for the last 66 days and represents the quarter that the rule will trade in after it has evolved from the system. We use the remaining data as a training set to determine rule fitness. The initial population consists of a configured set of chromosomes and a randomly generated set of chromosomes. The configured set consists of rules in which only a single indicator is set and the rest are "#"'s. This was done because it is quite possible that one indicator works very well for a given equity. It is also desirable to produce general rules. Single set chromosomes serve as a means of maintaining this notion, since when you cross two single set chromosomes the child will only have two genes set. The remainder of the population consists of randomly generated chromosomes.

The historical data is fed through the technical indicators, which in turn produce results for every day in the trial period under consideration. More precisely, once an indicator is given the proper data, it outputs an action to take – either buy, sell or stay in cash. The outputs from the indicators, taken together, form a "rule" which the chromosomes in the population are matched against. For example, say the output from the indicators produce the following actions:

('b','b','s','s','s','c','c','c','b','c','s','c')

The chromosomes that are in competition for selection would then be compared to this pattern. For instance, this chromosome would trigger:

('#",'#",'#",'s', '#",'#",'c', '#",'#",'#",'#",'#")

In this case, the rule would create a 'sell' transaction with the closing price on that day as the sell price. The rule would then stay "in the market" as long as the rule was triggered. When the day comes that the rule doesn't match, and hence does not trigger, a "buy" transaction is generated with the opening price of the next day. The process continues throughout the entire training period, roughly one and a half years worth of daily data, accumulating transactions along the way.

During the process, the rule keeps track of how many days it was in the market for. After it processed the historical data and generated the appropriate transactions, the transactions are evaluated and the percentage change is calculated along with the number of trades that made money and the number of trades that lost money. Once this has completed, the rule is ready to determine its fitness.

Our goal was not to solely produce rules that turn a good profit. We want to generate rules that will decrease the risk involved with being in the market. One way of doing this is to minimize the number of days one is actually in the market, the idea being that if you're not in the market you cannot lose money. Another way of accomplishing this is to minimize the number of negative gain trades and maximize the number of positive trade gains. This notion was implemented using exponential functions that greatly benefit the rules that performed well in these areas, and to punish the rules that didn't perform according to the plan. The idea behind this is that a rule that makes numerous bad trades should be punished exponentially more than rules that only made a few bad trades. This theory applies also to percentage gains.

To begin with, if the rule loses money, it received a fitness of zero. It doesn't make sense to reward a rule that lost you money. If the rule made money, the following formula was used:

$$\text{UaFitness} = (10)^{\text{percentageGain}} * (20)^{\text{goodBadRatio}}$$

The benefit of this method is that rules that made profitable trades were rewarded generously, since a good to bad ratio of 2:1 vs. 3:1 will produce extremely different results, rewarding the 3:1 ratio far more than the 2:1 and thus encouraging good trades. The same applies to the percentage gain but to a lesser extent, since the focus was on positive trading habits over profit grabbing.

The unadjusted fitness is sent to a function to adjust it based on the number of days it spent in the market. The longer you're in, the riskier it is. Therefore, the fitness value was adjusted as follows. If a rule was in the market for less than 15 days, the fitness remained the same. If it was in the market between 15 and 25 days, it lost 10% of its fitness, otherwise it lost 25% of its fitness.

Now we have a newly adjusted fitness to reflect the number of days it was trading for. At this point the new adjusted fitness gets altered once again, this time based on how many genes were set and how many were '#''s. Rules that are more general are less dependent and therefore more desirable and should be rewarded. Therefore, if the rule had 2 or less indicators set, the fitness remained unchanged. If it had between 2 and 4 set, it lost 50%, and more than four lost it 75%. We also did this because rules that have many indicators set will rarely fire since the number of genes that must match is greater.

This cycle of crossover, mutation, selection was repeated with a population size of 200 initial rules and repeated for 300 generations. This was more as a result of the running time of higher populations and more numerous generations than anything else since, at the time, having the system run for days on end was not feasible.

4 Results

Our experiments produced some extremely profitable and stable rules for given stocks on the Toronto Stock Exchange (TSE) in the first quarter of 2000 – an extremely volatile environment given the high-tech meltdown in March, 2000. The following tables show sample results including the stock, the indicators that were set in the best rule produced for that stock, the percentage gain the rule produced, and the number of days the rule was in the market.

Table 1. Rule Application to the Markey

Stock	**Indicator**	**Action**	**%**	**Days in Market**
Entrust	Candle Dojji Star	Cash	107	60
Aspen Resources Group	Bollinger MFRSI Breakout	Cash Buy	46	13
Corel Corp	CandlePiercingLine Williampeaks MFRBreakout	Cash Buy Sell	9	23
Loewen Group	CandleDojjiStar	Cash	47.5	64

In all, we found that our market timing was good and the number of days in the market was particularly good. Some issues to consider are the fact that some of the rules that lost money were run on stocks that were steadily increasing over the period in question, a very treacherous time to be short selling. Others incurred a loss due to being forced out of the market at the end of the training period.

5 Conclusion

We live in a very different market today than we did even five years ago. Equities can soar or sink based on rumors circulating around financial chat sites. With such uncertain, baseless and erratic behavior, one seeks a method of interpreting and predicting such actions. Enter technical analysis. It is because of these new and often unforeseen forces that technical indicators have something to contribute to market analysis. Much of the market behavior is induced on a day-to-day basis, so the fundamentalist approach will often go awry with the short-term investor. By the time the information has been accounted for, the market will have swayed already.

Overall our approach was a success, producing some extremely profitable and stable rules. Our GA provides good coverage of the different types of indicators and movements that a stock may engage in, thus enabling us, by combining the indicators together, to produce rules that will act on equities that behave differently. However, a combination of more or perhaps different indicators could be even more beneficial.

References

1. Bauer, R.J.: Genetic Algorithms and Investment Strategies. John Wiley & Sons, Inc., New York (1994).
2. Chen, S. and Lee, W.: Option Pricing with Genetic Algorithms: The Case Of European-Style Options, Morgann Kaufmann, San Francisco, CA, (1997), 704-711.
3. Colin, A.M.: Genetic Algorithms for Financial Modeling. In: Deboeck, G. J. (ed.): Trading on the Edge. John Wiley & Sons, Inc., New York (1994) 148–173.
4. Davis, L.: Genetic Algorithms and Financial Applications. In: Deboeck, G. J. (ed.): Trading on the Edge. John Wiley & Sons, Inc., New York (1994) 133–147.
5. Goldberg, D.E., Genetic Algorithms in Search Optimization, and Machine Learning. Reading, MA, Addison Wesley (1989).
6. Rabatin A.: Adaptive Portfolio Trading. In: Chambers, L. D. (ed.): Practical Handbook of Genetic Algorithms. CRC Press, New York (1999) 433-457.

Semi-structured Knowledge Representation for the Automated Financial Advisor

Boris Galitsky

iAskWeb, Inc.
261 Main Str #1B Waltham MA 02451
bgalitsky@iaskweb.com

Abstract. In this paper, we describe the natural language (NL) question-answering system for financial domains. Technique of semantic headers is applied to represent the semi-structured and logically complex data in the form of textual answers by matching the semantic representation of a query with the ones of the answers. Multiagent architecture of financial advising is suggested, where each agent represents the specific domain coverage and viewpoint. We analyze the customer experience and knowledge engineering process for the Tax domain, which is rather sophisticated on one hand and requires rather precise answers on the other hand.

1. Introduction

Due to a recent explosion of information available online, question-answering (Q/A) systems are becoming an attractive means for finding relevant information, particularly in the business domains. Attracting new customers and keeping them surfing the web site of a financial services portal is essential to establish the competitive advantage of the financial and investment companies.

In this paper, we present the case study of the Q/A applications, where the customers receive advices on a variety of business-related topics. We have developed the suite of financial domains including tax, mortgages, insurance, real estate, investments, retirement planning, etc. Because of the complicated nature of financial questions, these Q/A domains must satisfy the requirements of both logical complexity and high accuracy. Representation of business, financial and legal knowledge, oriented to the general audience, is much less structured than that of the geographical domain and requires much richer set of entities than the mental states domain, explored earlier [5]. Furthermore, the structure of semantic links between these entities is significantly more complex in the financial domains.

Several current NLP-based statistical technologies are able to provide a framework that approximates the complex problem of answering questions from large collections of texts [1-3], based in particular on machine learning. However, legal and financial domains require rather deterministic technique to provide the accurate answers[7]. It was experimentally verified that just producing the portion of related information,

L. Monostori, J. Váncza, and M. Ali (Eds.): IEA/AIE 2001, LNAI 2070, pp. 874-879, 2001.

such that a customer needs an additional step to select the actually relevant portion, is unsatisfactory in the legal and financial domains. Because of the complicated nature of the questions, our Q/A domain has to satisfy the requirements of rather large-scale vertical domain capability, with both logical complexity and high accuracy (Table 1).

Table 1. The samples question of *mortgage* domain. NLP system needs to handle up to four entities to perform Q/A in financial domains. Neither keyword search – based nor statistical nor syntactic match can provide satisfactory advising in vertical domains.

How much lower is an adjustable rate mortgage compared to a fixed rate loan?
Does the "start" rate quoted by lenders on a loan stay in effect for the term of the mortgage?
How can I avoid negative amortization on an adjustable rate mortgage?
How risky is a 125 percent loan to value second mortgage?

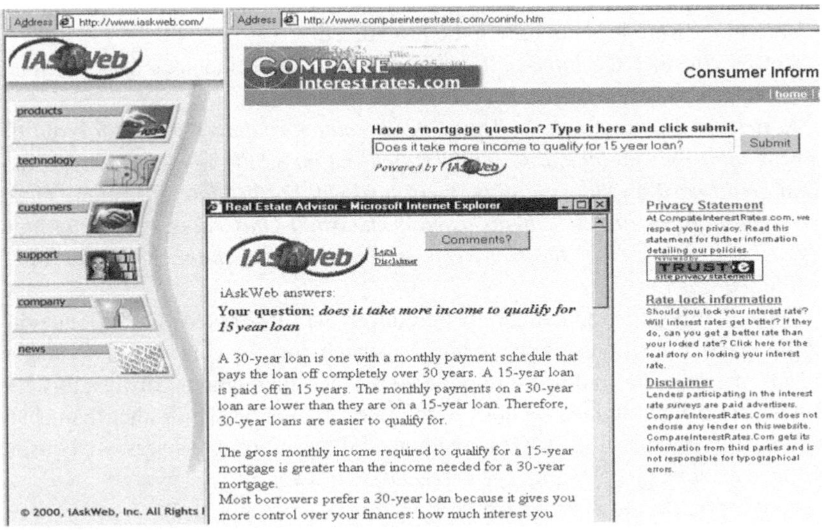

Fig. 1. Mortgage advisor, deployed by compareinterestrates.com. Customers are encouraged to ask a question about mortgage and provide an answer quality feedback. The log of question and answers will then be processed by domain expert and incorporated in a new version of the mortgage advisor by knowledge engineers. See Table 1 for the list of sample questions.

2. Technique of Semantic Headers for Question-Answering

The technique of semantic headers (SH) is intended to resolve the problem of converting an abstract textual document into a Q/A form. There are two opposite approaches to this problem with respect to the optimal degree of formalization. The first one assumes that complete formal representation of any textual document is possible

[4,8,9], and the second one assumes that the textual information is too tightly linked to NL and it cannot be satisfactorily represented without it.

The first approach brings the advantage of understanding based on full-range reasoning capabilities, but it sacrifices the necessity of NL generation, which introduces additional deviation from the answer semantic. Attempts to provide an exact answer, inherent to the full formalization approach, reduces the overlap between a potential query and existing answers. (Query understanding is posed as a recognition problem [10]: how to find the most relevant answer for a given query, even if there is no direct answer). The second series of approach (from the primitive syntactic match to the full-range morphological and syntactic parsing), which does not require answer formalization, is not sufficiently precise for the financial domains and does not allow proper disambiguation of common-usage terms.

Evidently, knowledge of the semantic model of the whole domain is required to build the set of semantic headers for a given paragraph. Only the data, which can be explicitly mentioned in a potential query, occurs in semantic headers. The rest of the information, which would be unlikely to occur in a question but can potentially form the relevant answer, does not have to be formalized.

Let us consider the *Internet Auction* domain, which includes the description of bidding rules and various types of auctions.

"*Restricted-Access Auctions. This separate category makes it easy for you to find or avoid adult-only merchandise. To view and bid on adult-only items, buyers need to have a credit card on file with eBay. Your card will not be charged. Sellers must also have credit card verification. Items listed in the Adult-Only category are not included in the New Items page or the Hot Items section, and currently, are not available by any title search.* "

What is this paragraph about? It introduces the "Restricted-Access" auction as a specific class of auctions, explains how to search for or avoid selected category of products, presents the credit card rules and describes the relations between this class of auctions and the highlighted sections of the Internet auction site. Rather than changing the paragraph in order to adjust it to the potential questions it answers, we consider all possible questions this paragraph can serve as an answer to:

1. *What is the restricted-access auction?*
2. *What kind of auctions sells adult-only items? How do I avoid adult-rated products for my son? How do you sell adult items?*
3. *When does a buyer need a credit card on file? Who needs to have a credit card on file? Why does a seller need credit card verification?*

Below is the list of semantic headers (formal representations for the canonical questions above). These semantic headers are assigned to the answer.

auction(restricted_access,_):-restrictedAuction.
product(adult,_):-restrictedAuction.
seller(credit_card(verification,_),_):-restrictedAuction.
credit_card(verification,_)):-restrictedAuction.
sell(credit_card(reject(_,_),_),_):-restrictedAuction.
bidder(credit_card(_,_),_):-restrictedAuction.
seller(credit_card(_,_),_):-restrictedAuction.
what_is(auction(restricted_access,_),_):-restrictedAuction.

Then the call to *restrictedAuction* will add the paragraph above to the current answer, which may consists from the multiple pre-prepared ones.

We conclude the section by the final definition what semantic headers for the semi-structured domains are [6]. *Semantic headers of an answer are the formal generalized representation of potential questions, taking into account the set of other semantically close answers and relevant semantically close questions.* Therefore, natural language understanding problem is posed as a recognition of a question and relating it to a fixed set of answers.

The totality of semantic headers forms the axiomatic environment serves as a basis to produce the inference link to the query. Those semantic headers involved in the resultant link are considered to be associated to the relevant answers. Matching the translation formula (formal query representation) with SHs is therefore the central operation [6], which follows NLP for semi-structured domains [5].

3. Multiagent Q/A Architecture

Advising in the domains with semi-structured knowledge representation requires the distribution of knowledge between the Q/A agents. Any real-world domain is some combination of central topics (principle domains) and accompanying domains, helping to answer questions involving information not directly related to the central topics. The set of principle and accompanying domains is called meta-domain. Particularly, in the meta-domain *family law* we have the principle domains *family & college, marriage & divorce, wills &trusts*. However, some questions to this meta-domain can be of rather psychological or financial nature; therefore it is necessary to use accompanying psychological and financial domains. For example, the query "how to file tax return after divorce", addressed to the *family law* meta-domain, must involve tax knowledge as well. It seems reasonable to include some relevant tax knowledge into the *divorce* domain, but using the *tax* domain itself is still required for some questions. It is very inefficient in terms of information redundancy, design reusability and knowledge update viewpoints to incorporate complete "foreign" knowledge into each domain.

We choose the multiagent architecture to resolve the issue of answering inter-domain issues. Each domain is associated with the agent, providing Q/A in this domain and cooperating with the other agents in the sense of sharing the degree of confidence this agent actually understood the question and found it relevant. It is worth illustrating the Q/A architecture using the analogy with the human agent. To get an advice, it is reasonable to consult multiple persons. It is even better to allow these "human Q/A agents" to have a discussion between each other to exchange their advices, taking into account their respective confidence of the answer relevancy.

Multiagent architecture delivers better domain coverage, as well as optimizes the knowledge distribution between domains, than a single-agent advisor. To decrease the conflicts between ambiguous entities when a set of accompanying domains grows in size, knowledge is distributed between Q/A agents. These agents have the common domain environment (set of predicates and values for their semantic types), but the domain information is addressed from the various prospective. For the *tax* domain (Table 2), the first agent knows the general data about taxes based on the "TeleTax" information, the second agent knows how to file forms, and the third agent provides longer answers for more specific topics [7]). The distributed architecture allows us to generate better coverage of the domain, though the same information can be stored from two different viewpoints. Therefore, we improve the domain coverage, without increasing the total amount of data. The customer gets the first answer from the agent that has obtained a more specific (usually, a single) answer. The other agents may be initiated upon request. Distributed architecture helps the customers to obtain more complete answers without a loss of accuracy.

Table 2. Agents for the *tax* domain. For each meta-domain, it is possible to include the agents as the script parameters to provide Q/A for a particular customer.

Three-character code	Agent name	Domain source	Domain size (#questions/#answers)
IRS	Main individual tax domain	TeleTax topics	2200/400
FRM	Individual tax forms	IRS references on how to fill forms	1700/300
TIP	Taxpayer's tips	E-mails with tax questions, submitted to Tax-Logic, Inc.	400/100
SMB	Small business tax	Small-business tax (IRS CD)	2000/250
HRB	Tax Topics, not addressed by the agents above	E-mails with tax questions, submitted to H&R Block, Inc.	400/100
http://www.iaskweb.ru/scripts/demo2.pl?name=irs,frm,tip,smb,hrb			

Multiagent architecture allows imitating Q/A in horizontal domain by means of detailed NLP, inherent to the vertical domains. Usually, Q/A system is either very robust but performs a shallow processing for a horizontal domain, or implements the detailed processing of a limited amount of data. Combining multiple agents, we derive a horizontal domain, having as complex Q/A as would be expected for vertical domains.

4. Developing and Using Question-Answering Domains

The Tax Adviser was subject to evaluation by about 6 thousand users per month during the 1999 tax-filing season. The customers were attracted to iaskweb.com site by the articles in "Boston Globe" newspaper and "Mass HighTech" magazine, describing the Q/A system as an alternative to the traditional way of tax counseling. Currently, simplified Tax Advisor is available from the web site of hrblock.com, the major provider of tax services in US with more than 100 million web site visitors annually (www.hrblock.com/taxes/fast_facts/tax_search.html).

In accordance to the opinions of a series of tax return assisting, investment, mortgage (see Fig.1), insurance and financial companies, which have employed iAskWeb's advisors, they can replace human agents, automatically answering financial questions in more than 50% of cases. We log all transactions; customers have the options to provide feedback to the system concerning a particular answer if they are dissatisfied (too long, non-relevant, partially relevant, etc.). Though the length of answers usually does not exceed a page of text (rather short and specific), the customers had more than 90% satisfaction with the system. Human agents intervene Q/A process in case of failure of automatic system. With the answer size not to exceed 6 paragraphs, the system correctly answers more than 70% of all queries, in accordance to the analysis of the Q/A log by the experts. Even with 70% accuracy, which is relatively low for traditional pattern recognition systems, over 95% of customers and quality assurance personnel agreed that the automated financial adviser is the preferable way of accessing information for non-professional users. Using the natural language Q/A system for advising is the fastest way to receive a reasonable advice, compare to Internet keyword search or human customer support.

Desired accuracy can be achieved only by thorough domain adjustment in accordance to the query logs, processed by the domain experts. In the financial domains, the accuracy of an agent just alpha-released by a knowledge engineer frequently lies below 40 %. In each of the financial agents, desired accuracy is achieved after more than a month of the adjustment, carried out by a knowledge engineer and an expert.

References

1. Katz, B., Using English for Indexing and Retrieving, In P. H. Winston and S. A. Shellard, editors, *Artificial Intelligence at MIT: Expanding Frontiers*, volume 1, MIT Press, Cambridge, MA (1990).
2. McCallum, A., Nigam, K., Text Classification by Bootstrapping with Keywords, EM and Shrinkage. *Technical Report, Just Research* http://www.cs.cmu.edu/~mccallum. (1999).
3. Gey, F.C., Chen, A. Phrase Discovery for English and Cross-language Retrieval at TREC-6, *Text Retrieval Conf,* NIST Special Publication (1998).
4. Tarau,P. De Boschere, K., Dahl,V., and Rochefort, S. LogiMOO: an Extensible Multi-User Virtual World with Natural Language Control. Journal of Logic Programming, 38(3) (1999) 331-353 .
5. Galitsky, B. Natural Language Understanding with the Generality Feedback. *DIMACS Tech. Report 99-32*, Rutgers University (1999).
6. Galitsky, B. Technique of semantic headers: a manual for knowledge engineers *DIMACS Tech. Report #2000-29*, Rutgers University (2000).
7. Galitsky, B. Technique of semantic headers for answering questions in tax domain. *IASTED Intl Conf on Law & Technology,* San Francisco, CA (2000) 117.
8. Antoniou, G. Nonmonotonic reasoning. Chapter 14. MIT Press Cambridge, MA London England (1997).
9. Dahl, V. The logic of language, in *The Logic Programming Paradigm,* Apt, Marek, Truszczynski, Warrens, eds, Springer-Verlag (1999).
10. Fain, V.S. and Rubanov, L.I. Activity and Understanding *World Scientific Publishing* (1996).

Improving Space, Time, and Termination in Rewriting-Based Programming

Nadia Nedjah and Luiza de Macedo Mourelle

Department of Systems Engineering and Computation, Faculty of Engineering, State University of Rio de Janeiro.
(nadia, ldmm)@eng.uerj.br

Abstract. Pattern-matching is a fundamental feature in many applications such as logic programming [5,13], theorem proving [4], term rewriting and rule-based expert systems[3]. Usually, patterns size is not constrained and ambiguous patterns are allowed. This generality leads to a clear and concise programming style. However, it yields challenging problems in the compilation of such programming languages. In this work, we deal with such problems in order to improve time and space requirements of pattern-matching as well as termination properties of term evaluation.

1 Introduction

Pattern-matching automata have been studied for over a decade. Pattern-matching can be achieved as in lexical analysis by using a finite automaton [2,7,8,11,14]. Gräf [7] and Christian [2] construct deterministic matching automata for unambiguous patterns based on the left-to-right traversal order. In functional programming, Augustsson [1] describes matching techniques that are also based on left-to right traversal of terms but allow prioritised overlapping patterns. Although these methods are economical in terms of space usage, they may re-examine symbols in the input term. In the worst case, they can degenerate to the naive method of checking the subject term against each pattern individually. In contrast, Christian's [2] and Gräf's [7] methods avoid symbol re-examination at the cost of increased space requirements. In order to avoid backtracking over symbols already examined, like Gräf's our method introduces new patterns. These correspond to overlaps in the scanned prefixes of original patterns. When patterns overlap, some of the added patterns may be irrelevant to the matching process. The method proposed here improves Gräf's in the sense that it introduces only a subset of the patterns that his method adds. This improves both space and time requirements as we will show later. Sekar [14] uses the notion of irrelevant patterns to compute traversal orders of pattern-matching. His algorithm eliminates a pattern π whenever a match for π implies a match for a pattern of higher priority than π. In contrast with Sekar's method, we do not introduce irrelevant patterns at once.

The pattern-matching order in lazy evaluation may affect the size of the matching automaton, the matching time and in the worst case, the termination properties of term evaluations [16]. The adaptive strategy is the top-down left-to-right lazy strategy used in most lazy functional languages [14]. It selects the leftmost-outermost redex but may force the reduction of a subterm if the root symbol of that subterm fails to

L. Monostori, J. Váncza, and M. Ali (Eds.): IEA/AIE 2001, LNAI 2070, pp. 880-890, 2001.

match a function symbol in the patterns. So, the order of such reductions coincides with that of pattern-matching. Using left-to-right pattern matching, a subject term evaluation may fail to terminate only because of forcing reductions of subterms when it is unnecessary before declaring a match. For the left-to-right traversal order, such unnecessary reductions are required to ensure that no backtracking is needed when pattern-matching fails.

First, we introduce from [11] a method for generating a deterministic tree matching automaton for a given pattern set. Although the generated automaton is efficient since it avoids symbol re-examination, it may contain unnecessary branches. The main reason for this is the presence of ambiguous patterns with more general patterns having higher priority. Here, we modify that method so that only relevant patterns are added. A smaller and more efficient automaton is thereby obtained.

Then, we investigate strategies to select a traversal order that should normally improve space requirements and/or matching times. *Indexes* for a pattern are positions whose inspection is necessary to declare a match. Inspecting them first for patterns which are not essentially strongly sequential allows us to engineer adaptive traversal orders that should improve space usage and matching times as shown in [10,14]. When no index can be found for a pattern set, we show that a position which is an index for a maximal number of high priority patterns can always be identified. Selecting such a position attempts to improve matching times for terms that match patterns of high priority. We conclude the paper by proposing a *good* traversal order.

We will use some notation and concepts defined as follows: symbols in a *term* are either function or variable symbols; the non-empty set of function symbols F is *ranked* i.e., every function symbol f in F has an *arity* which is the number of its arguments and is denoted $\#f$; a term is either a constant, a variable or has the form $ft_1 t_2 \ldots t_{\#f}$ where each t_i, $1 \leq i \leq \#f$, is itself a term. Terms are represented by their corresponding abstract tree. We abbreviate terms by removing the usual parentheses and commas. Variable occurrences are replaced by ω. A term containing no variables is said to be a *ground* term. We generally assume that patterns are linear terms, i.e. each variable symbol can occur at most once in them. A term t is said to be an *instance* of a (linear) pattern π if t can be obtained from π by replacing the variables of π by corresponding subterms of t.

2 Deterministic Left to Right Matching Automata

In this section, we briefly recall from [11] a practical method to construct a deterministic tree matching automaton for a prioritised ambiguous pattern set. Throughout Sections 3 and 4, left-to-right traversal order is used. We first define *LR-matching items* and *LR-matching sets*.

Definition 2.1. An *LR-matching item* is a triple $r{:}\alpha\bullet\beta$ where $\alpha\beta$ is a term and r is a *rule label*. The label identifies the origin of the term $\alpha\beta$ and hence, in a term rewriting system, the rewrite rule which has to be applied when $\alpha\beta$ is matched. The label is not written explicitly below except where necessary. The meta-symbol $\bullet$ is called the *LR-matching dot*, α and β are called the *prefix* and *suffix* respectively. A *final* LR-matching item is one of the form $\alpha\bullet$.

So the LR-matching item $\bullet\beta$ represents the initial state prior to matching the pattern β. In general, the matching item $\alpha\bullet\beta$ denotes that the symbols in α have been matched and those in β have not yet been recognised. Finally, the LR-matching item $\alpha\bullet$ is reached on successfully matching the whole pattern α.

Definition 2.2. A set of LR-matching items in which all the items have the same prefix is called a *LR-matching* set. An LR-matching set in which all the items have an empty prefix is called an *initial* LR-matching set whereas an LR-matching set in which all the items have an empty suffix is called a *final* LR-matching set.

The automaton is represented by the 4-tuple $\langle S_0, S, Q, \delta\rangle$ where S is the state set, $S_0 \in S$ is the initial state, $Q \subseteq S$ is the final state set and δ is the state transition function. The states are labelled by matching sets which consist of original patterns whose prefixes match the current input prefix, together with extra instances of the patterns which are added to avoid backtracking in reading the input. In particular, the matching set for S_0 contains the initial matching items formed from the original patterns and labelled by the rules associated with them. Transitions are considered according to the symbol at the *matching position*, i.e. that immediately after the matching dot. For each symbol $s \in F \cup \{\omega\}$ and state with matching set M, a new state with matching set $\delta(M,s)$ is derived using the composition of the functions *accept* and *close* defined in Fig. 2.3.

$accept(M, s)$	$= \{r{:}\alpha s\bullet\beta \mid r{:}\alpha\bullet s\beta \in M\}$
$close(M)$	$= M \cup \{r{:}\alpha\bullet f\omega^{\#f}\mu \mid r{:}\alpha\bullet\omega\mu \in M \text{ and } \exists\, q{:}\alpha\bullet f\lambda \in M$ for some suffix λ and $f \in F\}$
$\delta(M, s)$	$= close(\ accept(M, s)\ )$

Fig. 2.3. Previous Automata Transition Function.

The items obtained by recognising the symbols in those patterns of M where s is the next symbol form the set $accept(M,s)$ which is called the *kernel* of $\delta(M,s)$. However, the set $\delta(M,s)$ may contain more items. The presence of two items $\alpha\bullet\omega\mu$ and $\alpha\bullet f\lambda$ in M creates a non-deterministic situation since the variable ω could be matched by a term having f as head symbol. The item $\alpha\bullet f\omega^{\#f}\mu$ is added to remove this non-determinism and avoid backtracking. The transition function thus implements simply the main step in the closure operation described by Gräf [6] and set out in the previous section. The item labels simply keep account of the originating pattern for when a successful match is achieved. As we deal here with root-matching, every failure transition ends up in a single global *failure state.*

Definition 2.4. A pattern set L is *ambiguous* if there is a ground term that is an instance of at least two distinct patterns in L. Otherwise, L is *non-ambiguous*.

Definition 2.5. A *priority rule* is a partial ordering on patterns such that if π_1 and π_2 are distinct ambiguous patterns then either π_1 has *higher* priority than π_2 or π_2 has *higher* priority than π_1. In the latter case, we write $\pi_1 \prec \pi_2$

When a final state is reached, if several patterns have been successfully matched, then the priority rule is engaged to select the one of highest priority. An example is the *textual* priority rule which is used in the majority of functional languages [1,9,10,15]. Among the matched patterns, the rule chooses the pattern that appears first in the text. Whatever rule is used, we will apply the word *match* only to the pattern of highest priority which is matched:

Definition 2.6. For a prioritised pattern set L and pattern $\pi \in L$, the term t is said to *match* π *in* L if, and only if, t is an instance of π but not instance of any other pattern in L of higher priority than π.

3 Fast and Concise Automaton for Ambiguous Patterns

Now, we observe that the *close* function of Fig. 2.3 may add more items than it need when the patterns are ambiguous. We start by developing several definitions.

A *position* in a term is a path specification which identifies a node in the abstract tree of the term. Positions are specified here using a list of positive integers. The empty list Λ denotes the position of the root of the abstract tree and the position $p.k$ ($k \geq 1$) denotes the root of the kth argument of the function symbol at position p. For a term t and a position p in this term, we denote by $t[p]$ the symbol at position p in t.

Definition 3.1. A term t is said to be *more general than a term* t' *at the position* p if, and only if, the symbol $t[p]$ is ω, $t'[p]$ is a function symbol and the prefixes of t and t' ending immediately before (i.e., in the linear representation of t) p are the same. Without too much confusion, we hope, we will also say t is *initially more general than* t' if t is more general than t' at the first position for which the symbols of t and t' differ.

The function *close* adds new patterns to which the priority rule of the original rule set must be extended. The following definition enables us to select a unique item amongst all those which pattern-match a given term: if there is a unique pattern-matched item whose rule has highest priority then that is chosen; otherwise, when there are several pattern-matched items associated with rules of maximal priority, those items must all derive from the same original pattern and we can select the initially most general. (Any other uniquely defined choice would also be acceptable, but this is the most convenient in what follows.)

Definition 3.2. Item $r{:}\alpha{\bullet}\beta$ has *higher priority* than item $r'{:}\alpha'{\bullet}\beta'$ if the original pattern of r has higher priority than that of r' or $r = r'$ and $\alpha\beta$ is initially more general than $\alpha'\beta'$. For a matching set M and item $r{:}\alpha{\bullet}\beta \in M$, the term t is said to *match* $r{:}\alpha{\bullet}\beta$ *in* M if, and only if, t is an instance of $\alpha\beta$ but not an instance of any other item in M of higher priority.

Although the pattern $\alpha\beta$ of the item $r{:}\alpha{\bullet}\beta$ will always match the pattern of rule r, it may match a pattern of higher priority. This could have been used in defining a priority rule on all terms and hence on items, but is computationally more expensive, and unnecessary here. It is now possible to determine which patterns are useful for *close* to include. Indeed, we can start by considering the usefulness of each pattern in the initial pattern set:

Definition 3.3. Suppose $L \cup \{\pi\}$ is a prioritised pattern set. Then π is said to be *relevant for L* if there is a term that matches π in $L \cup \{\pi\}$ in the sense of Definition 2.6. Otherwise, π is *irrelevant for L*. Similarly, an item π is *relevant for (the matching set) M* if there is a term that *deterministically* matches π in $M \cup \{\pi\}$ in the sense of Definition 3.2.

Clearly, any term that matches an element of a pattern set, respectively item of a matching set, will still have that property even when an irrelevant pattern, resp. item, is removed. We can therefore immediately prune irrelevant patterns one by one from the initial pattern set until every remaining pattern is relevant to the remaining pattern set, and do the same for each matching set generated by close.

The function close of Fig. 2.3 may certainly supply items that are irrelevant for subsequent matching. This may happen when the original pattern set contains ambiguous patterns with more general ones having lower priorities.

Since the relevance of items may depend on the order in which items are added to a matching set M to form *close*(M), we need to be careful about re-defining close to exclude irrelevant items; the result may depend on this order. The new, improved function is *close*′ defined (non-uniquely) from the initial *close* by Fig. 3.4. It seems best to consider items for inclusion using an ordering which preserves decreasing priorities. So, highest priority items will be added first. This ensures that items added to the partially created *close*′(M) never subsequently become irrelevant.

close′(M)	=	any maximal subset S of *close*(M) such that if $\pi \in$ *close*(M)$\backslash S$ then π is irrelevant for S.

Fig. 3.4. Closure function which supplies only relevant items.

Finally, we consider a special case where the revised specification for *close* can be computed more easily. For this new definition, we assume that there is at least one function symbol in F which does not occur in any original pattern. This definition is given in Fig. 3.5 where the first line duplicates the conditions of the initial *close* and the subsequent lines add an extra condition to exclude some irrelevant items. Roughly speaking, this condition says that any potentially added item $\alpha \bullet f\omega^{\#f}\beta$ must contribute new terms which are not already covered by patterns in M with higher priority. However, in the general case when *close* is computed iteratively, an added item may actually be covered by a previously added item, superseded by a subsequent item of higher priority or even covered by a number of more specific items.

$$
\begin{aligned}
close''(M) = M \cup \{\, r:\alpha \bullet f\omega^{\#f}\beta \mid\; & r:\alpha \bullet \omega\beta \in M \text{ and } \exists r', f, \beta' (r':\alpha \bullet f\beta' \in M) \wedge \\
& \forall r'':\alpha \bullet f\beta'' \in M \;(\text{if } r:\alpha \bullet \omega\beta \prec r'':\alpha \bullet f\beta'' \\
& \quad \text{then } \alpha f\omega^{\#f}\beta \not\trianglelefteq \alpha f\beta'' \\
& \quad \text{else } \beta \neq \omega \ldots \omega\;) \,\}
\end{aligned}
$$

Fig. 3.5. Closure function which may supply only relevant items.

Theorem 3.6. Assuming that there is at least one function symbol which does not occur in any pattern, then all items supplied by the function close″ are relevant.

Proof. The proof is straightforward. It suffices to proceed by induction on matching sets. ■

4 Adaptive Pattern-Matching Automata

States of adaptive automata are computed using *matching items* and *matching sets*. Since here the traversal order is not fixed a priori (i.e., it will be computed during the automaton construction procedure), the symbols in the patterns may be accepted in any order. When the adaptive order coincides with the left-to-right order, matching items and matching sets coincide with LR-matching items and LR-matching set respectively (Definition 2.1 and Definition 2.2 respectively).

Definition 4.1. A *matching item* is a pattern in which all the symbols already matched are now *ticked* i.e., they have the *check-mark* √. Moreover, it contains the hollow *matching dot* ° which only designates the *matching symbol* i.e., the symbol to be accepted next. The position of the matching symbol is called the *matching position.* A *final* matching item, namely one of the form π°, has the *final* matching position which we write ∞. Final matching item may contain unchecked positions. These positions are irrelevant for announcing a match and so must be labelled with the symbol ω.

The term obtained from a given item by replacing all the terms with an *unticked* root symbol by the placeholder _ is called the *context* of the items. In fact, no symbol will be checked until all its parents are all checked. So, the positions of the placeholders in the context of an item are the positions of the subterms that have not been checked yet. The set of such positions for an item i is denoted by $up(i)$ (short for unchecked positions).

Definition 4.2. A *matching set* is a set of matching items that have the same context and a common matching position. The *initial* matching set contains items of the form $\circ\pi$ because we recognise the root symbol (which occurs first) first whereas, *final* matching sets contain items of the form $\pi\circ$, where π is a pattern. For initial matching sets, no symbol is ticked. A final matching set must contain a final matching item i.e., in which all the unticked symbols are ωs. Furthermore, the rule associated with that item must be of highest priority amongst the items in the matching set.

Since the items in a matching set M have a common context, they all share a common list of unchecked positions and we can safely write $up(M)$. The only unchecked position for an initial matching set is clearly the empty position Λ.

Constructing adaptive automata. We describe adaptive automata by a 4-tuple $\langle S_0, S, Q, \delta\rangle$. S is the state set, $S_0 \in S$ is the initial state, $Q \subseteq S$ is the set of final states and δ is the state transition function. The transition function δ of an adaptive automaton is defined using three functions namely, *accept*, *choose*, and *close*. The function *accept* and *close* are similar to those of the same name in [3], and *choose* picks the next matching position. For each of these functions, we give an informal description followed by a formal definition, except for *choose* for which we present an informal description. Its formal definition will be discussed in detail in the next section.

accept: for a matching set and an unchecked position, this function accepts and ticks the symbol immediately after the matching dot in the items of the matching set and inserts the matching dot immediately before the symbol at the given unchecked position. Let t be a term in which some symbols are ticked. We denote by $t_{\circ_p}$ the matching item which is t with the matching dot inserted immediately before the symbol $t[p]$. then the definition of *accept* is as in Fig. 4.3:

$$accept(M, s, p) = \{\, (\alpha s^{\surd}\beta)_{\circ_p} \mid \alpha^{\circ} s\beta \in M \,\}$$

Fig. 4.3. Function accept for adaptive automata.

choose: this function selects a position among those that are unchecked for the matching set obtained after accepting the symbol given. For a matching set M and a symbol s, the *choose* function selects the position which should be inspected next. The function may also return the final position ∞. In general, the set of such positions is denoted by $\overline{up}(M, s)$. It represents the unchecked positions of $\delta(M, s)$, and consists of $up(M)$ with the position of the symbol s removed. Moreover, if the arity of s is positive then there are $\#s$ additional unchecked terms in the items of the set $\delta(M, s)$, assuming that ωs are of arity 0. Therefore, the positions of these terms are added. Recall that if a function symbol f is at position p in a term, then the arguments of f occur at positions $p.1, p.2, \ldots, p.\#f$. We can now formulate a definition for the set of unchecked positions $up(\delta(M, s)) = \overline{up}(M, s)$ as in Fig. 4.4, wherein p_s is the position of s which is also the matching position of M.

$$\overline{up}(M, s) = \begin{cases} up(M) \setminus \{p_s\} & if\ \#s = 0 \\ (up(M) \setminus \{p_s\}) \cup \{p_s.1, \ldots, p_s.\#s\} & otherwise \end{cases}$$

Fig. 4.4. Set of unchecked positions.

For the construction procedure of the left-to-right matching automaton, the *choose* function is not required because the leftmost unchecked position, if it exists, is always selected. Otherwise, the final position is used.

close: given a matching set, this function computes its closure in the same way as for the left-to-right matching automaton. As it is shown in Fig. 4.5, the function adds an item $\alpha\circ f\omega^{\#f}\beta$ to the given matching set M whenever an item $\alpha\circ\omega\beta$ is in M together with at least one item of the form $\alpha\circ f\beta'$.

$$\begin{aligned} close(M) = M \cup \{\, r{:}\ \alpha\circ f\omega^{\#f}\beta \mid\ & r{:}\ \alpha\circ\omega\beta \in M \text{ and } \exists\beta' \text{ s.t. } r'{:}\ \alpha\circ f\beta' \in M \\ & \text{and } \forall\beta'' \text{ If } r''{:}\ \alpha\circ f\beta'' \in M \text{ and } \alpha\omega\beta \prec \alpha f\beta'' \\ & \text{Then } \neg(\alpha f\omega^{\#f}\beta \lhd \alpha f\beta'')\,\} \end{aligned}$$

Fig. 4.5. Function close for adaptive automata.

The definition of function *close* above allows us to avoid introducing irrelevant items [4] wherein $\prec$ and $\lhd$ express the priority rule and the instantiation relation between patterns respectively.

For a matching set M and a symbol $s \in F \cup \{\omega\}$, the transition function for an adaptive automaton can now be formally defined by the composition of the three functions accept, choose and close is $\delta(M, s) = close\ (\ accept\ (M, s, choose\ (M, s)\ )\ )$. This function proceeds by first computing the list of unchecked positions of the expected set $\delta(M, s)$, then selecting an unchecked position p in $\overline{up}(M, s)$ and computing the matching set $N = accept(M, s, p)$ and finally computing the closure of N i.e., $\delta(M, s) = close(N)$. The set $accept(M, s, p)$ is called the *kernel* of $\delta(M, s)$.

5 Position Selection Strategy

In this section, we show how to design selection strategies to choose positions that need to be inspected. This is done using kernels of matching sets as the patterns added by *close* do not affect the choice. First, we define positions, called *indexes* whose inspection certainly improves matching time and termination of term evaluation. Then, we define *partial indexes*, whose inspection attempts to improve matching times for patterns of high priority. We conclude by prescribing a *good* traversal order for patterns that are not essentially strongly sequential.

5.1 Inspecting Indexes First

Knowing that a placeholder can match any term, a context u of a term t is a term containing placeholders such that t is an instance of u. Indexes for a context u with respect to a pattern set L are placeholder positions in u that must be inspected to announce a match for any pattern in L that unifies with u. Therefore, in any matching automaton, indexes for a context u must occur in every branch with final state recognising a pattern which is an instance of u.

Definition 5.1. Let $i = \alpha \circ s\beta$. A position $p \in \overline{up}(\{i\}, s)$ is an *index* for i if, and only if, for every term t that matches $\alpha s\beta$, $t[p]$ is a function symbol. For a matching set M and a symbol s, position $p \in up(M, s)$ is said to be an *index* for M if, and only if, p is an index for every item in M with matching symbol s.

The normalisation of subterms occurring at indexes is necessary. So, *safer* adaptive automaton (w.r.t. termination properties) can be obtained by selecting indexes first whenever such positions exist and using one of the heuristics otherwise. Furthermore, adaptive automata that choose indexes first have a smaller (or the same) size than those that do not [10].

5.2 Selecting Partial Indexes

Here, we assume, as for most functional languages that deal with overlapping patterns, that the priority rule is a total order for the pattern set. That is, for every pair of patterns π_1 and π_2 in the pattern set, there exists a priority relationship between them. Example of such priority rule include textual priority rule which is used in most functional languages.

For equational programs that are not strongly sequential [3], there are some matching sets with no index. When no index can be identified for a matching set, a heuristic that consists of selecting a *partial indexes* can be de used. A partial index is an index for a maximal number of consecutive items in a matching set with respect to pattern priorities. Partial indexes can be defined as follows:

Definition 5.2. Let $M = \{\alpha_1 \circ s\beta_1, \ldots, \alpha_k \circ s\beta_k, \ldots, \alpha_n \circ s\beta_n\}$ be a matching set ordered according to pattern priorities. Then a position $p \in up(M.s)$ is a *partial index* for M if, and only if, p is an index for $\alpha_1 \circ s\beta_1, \ldots, \alpha_k \circ s\beta_k$, p is not an index for $\alpha_{k+1} \circ s\beta_{k+1}$, and no position p' is an index for $\alpha_1 \circ s\beta_1, \ldots, \alpha_{k+1} \circ s\beta_{k+1}$.

Of course, there are other possible ways of defining partial indexes. For example, one may choose to define a partial index for a matching set as the position which is an index for a maximal number of items in the matching set. Another way consists of associating a weight to each pattern and another to each position in the patterns. A pattern weight represents the probability of the pattern being matched whilst a position weight is the sum of the probability of the argument rooted at that position leading to a non-terminating reduction sequence. Let L be a pattern set and p a position in the patterns of L. At run-time, the sum of the products of the weight of each pattern and the weight of position p determines the probability of having a non-terminating sequence at p. One may consider to minimise such a sum for partial indexes to improve termination. However, pattern and position weights may be difficult to obtain. Choosing partial indexes defined an in Definition 5.2 attempts to improve the matching times for terms that match patterns of high priority among overlapping ones. It may also reduce the breadth of the matching automaton as the closure operation adds only few patterns. Except for final matching sets which have no partial indexes, such a position can always be found. The motivation behind choosing such partial indexes is that we believe patterns of high priority are of some interest to the programmer.

5.3 A Good Traversal Order

It is clear that a *good* traversal order selects indexes first whenever possible. If a matching set has more than one index then the index with a minimal number of distinct symbols must be chosen. Doing so allows us to reduce the breadth of the automaton but does not affect the height of any branch in the subautomaton yielded by the matching set. This because all the positions are indexes and so must occur in every branch of the subautomaton. Now, if there is more than one index with a minimal number of distinct symbols then either of them can be selected as the choice affects neither the height nor the breadth of the automaton.

When no index can be found for a matching set, a partial index can be selected. If more than one partial index is available then some heuristics can be used to discriminate between them.

6 Index and Partial Index Computation

In unambiguous pattern sets, the indexes for an item i are exactly those placeholder positions in the context of i wherein i has a function symbol. However, with prioritised ambiguous pattern sets, a variable position p in the item i may be an index too. This may happen if i unifies with another item i' in the same matching set which has higher priority and i' has a function symbol at p.

The following Theorem 6.1 provides an algorithm to compute indexes for an item $i = \alpha \circ s\beta$ with respect to the matching set M in which it occurs. A position $p \in up(M.s)$ is an index for $\alpha \circ s\beta$ if either i has a function symbol at position p or (i.e., i has an ω at p) there is an item i' in M such that i' has higher (or the same) priority that i, and p is the only position to instantiate in i to announce a match for i'. Notice that the empty position Λ is always an index for an initial matching set as it is labelled with a function symbol in every item of the set.

Theorem 6.1. Let M be a matching set and $\alpha \circ s\beta$ be an item of M. The position $p \in up(M, s)$ is an index for $\alpha \circ s\beta$ with respect to M if, and only if, the following predicate holds:

$Index(\alpha\circ s\beta, M, p) = (\alpha s\beta[p]\in F)$ or $(\exists\beta'(\alpha\circ s\beta'\in M$ and $\alpha s\beta \prec s\beta'$ and $\alpha s\beta'[p]\in F$ and If $\alpha s\beta'[p]=f$ Then $\alpha s\beta[p\leftarrow f\omega^{\#}] \lhd \alpha s\beta'))$

Proof. ($\Rightarrow$) Let M be a matching set, $\alpha\circ s\beta$ an item of M and p a position in $\overline{up}(M.s)$. We need to show that if $Index(\alpha\circ s\beta, M, p)$ holds then every term t that matches $\alpha s\beta$ must have a function symbol at p (see Definition 5.1). This is clear when $\alpha s\beta[p]$ is a function symbol. Otherwise, i.e., $\alpha s\beta[p] = \omega$, there must be an item $\alpha\circ s\beta'$ in M such that $\alpha s\beta'$ has higher priority than $\alpha s\beta$. $\alpha\circ s\beta'$ must have a function symbol f at position p, such that $\alpha s\beta[p\leftarrow f\omega^{\#}]$ is an instance of $\alpha s\beta'$. Moreover, by definition of unification, t matches $\alpha s\beta$ means that i is an instance of $\alpha s\beta$ and t does not unify with $\alpha s\beta'$. This happens only when t/p does not unify with $\alpha s\beta'/p$. So, $t[p]$ is a function symbol but distinct from f.

($\Leftarrow$) Here, we need to prove that if $Index(\alpha\circ s\beta, M, p)$ does not hold then there is a term t that matches $\alpha s\beta$ yet $t/p = \omega$. Let t be the instance of $\alpha s\beta$ which is obtained by replacing all ωs in $\alpha s\beta$, except that of position p, with a symbol that does not occur in any original pattern leaving $t/p = \omega$. $Index(\alpha\circ s\beta, M, p)$ does not hold means that $\alpha s\beta[p] = \omega$ and there is no item $\alpha\circ s\beta'$ in M that meets the requirements needed in the predicate for this case. Three cases may occur:

1. If there is no item $\alpha\circ s\beta'$ in M of higher priority than $\alpha^\circ s\beta$ then t will clearly match $\alpha\circ s\beta$;
2. Suppose there is an item $\alpha\circ s\beta'$ in M of higher priority than $\alpha\circ s\beta$ such that $\alpha\circ s\beta'$ has a function symbol f at position p. Then $\alpha s\beta[p\leftarrow f\omega^{\#}]$ must not be an instance of $\alpha s\beta'$ since the predicate does not hold. So, there is a non-variable position q such that the symbol s' in $\alpha s\beta[p\leftarrow f\omega^{\#}]$ at q is different from the function symbol $\alpha s\beta'[q]$. This means s' is either ω or a function symbol distinct from $\alpha s\beta'[q]$. The latter case is impossible because $\alpha s\beta'$ and $\alpha s\beta$ are overlapping. In the former case, t will not unify with $\alpha\circ s\beta'$ because $t[q] \neq \alpha s\beta'[q]$. then t will match $\alpha s\beta$;
3. Suppose there is an item $\alpha\circ s\beta'$ in M of higher priority than $\alpha\circ s\beta$ such that $\alpha\circ s\beta'$ has a variable symbol at position p. If $\alpha s\beta$ is not an instance of $\alpha s\beta'$ then using the same argument as in the second case, t would not unify with $\alpha s\beta'$ and therefore would match $\alpha s\beta$. Otherwise, suppose that $\alpha s\beta$ is an instance of $\alpha s\beta'$, t would then match $\alpha s\beta'$ and so $\alpha s\beta$ will never be matched. This means that $\alpha s\beta$ is an irrelevant item for M. This is a contradiction since all original patterns are relevant and the *close* function adds relevant items only (see [3]). ■

7 Conclusion

In the main body of the paper, Then, we devised a new closure operation that still yields a deterministic matching automaton but recognises and avoids such irrelevant instances and hence improves space and time requirements for such an automaton. We presented an example that shows clearly how the matching automaton obtained using the devised closure operation can improve both the space and time requirements. We also focused on traversal orders of terms during patter-matching. We first generalised the method of constructing left-to-right matching automata described in [3], [4], [5], [6], [7] to build adaptive automata. Then, we proposed an adaptive traversal order of terms that improves the termination properties for term evaluations as we look at positions that must be inspected before announcing a match first. These positions are indexes and partial indexes.

References

[1] A. Augustsson, *A Compiler for Lazy ML*, Proc. ACM Conference on Lisp and Functional Programming, ACM, pp. 218-227, 1984.

[2] J. Christian, *Flatterms, Discrimination Nets and Fast Term Rewriting*, Journal of Automated Reasoning, vol. 10, pp. 95-113, 1993.

[3] D. Cooper and N. Wogrin, *Rule-Based Programming with OPS5*, Morgan Kaufmann, San Francisco, 1988.

[4] N. Dershowitz and J.P. Jouannaud, *Rewrite Systems*, Handbook of Theoretical Computer Science, vol. 2, chap. 6, Elsevier Science Publishers, 1990.

[5] A.J. Field and P.G. Harrison, *Functional Programming*, International Computer Science Series, 1988.

[6] J.A Goguen and T. Winkler, *Introducing OBJ3*, Technical report SRI-CSL-88-9, Computer Science Laboratory, SRI International, 1998.

[7] A. Gräf, *Left-to-Right Tree Pattern-Matching*, Proc. Conference on Rewriting Techniques and Applications, Lecture Notes in Computer Science, vol. 488, pp. 323-334, 1991.

[8] C.M. Hoffman and M.J. O'Donnell, *Pattern-Matching in Trees*, Journal of ACM, vol. 29, n° 1, pp. 68-95, 1982.

[9] P. Hudak and al., *Report on the Programming Language Haskell: a Non-Strict, Purely Functional Language*, Sigplan Notices, Section S, May 1992.

[10] A. Laville, *Comparison of Priority Rules in Pattern Matching and Term Rewriting*, Journal of Symbolic Computation, n° 11, pp. 321-347, 1991.

[11] N. Nedjah, C.D. Walter and S.E. Eldridge, *Optimal Left-to-Right Pattern-Matching Automata*, Proc. Conference on Algebraic and Logic Programming, Southampton, UK, Lecture Notes in Computer Science, Springer-Verlag, vol. 1298, pp. 273-285, 1997.

[12] N. Nedjah, C.D. Walter and S.E. Eldridge, *Efficient Automata-Driven Pattern-Matching for Equational programs*, Software-Practice and Experience, John Wiley Eds., vol. 29, n° 9, pp. 793-813, 1999.

[13] M.J. O'Donnell, *Equational Logic as Programming Language*, MIT Press, 1985.

[14] R.C. Sekar, R. Ramesh and I.V. Ramakrishnan, *Adaptive Pattern-Matching*, SIAM Journal, vol. 24, n° 5, pp. 1207-1234, 1995.

[15] D.A. Turner, *Miranda: a Non Strict Functional Language with Plymorphic Types*, Proc. Conference on Lisp and Functional Languages, ACM, pp. 1-16, 1985.

[16] P. Wadler, *Efficient Compilation of Pattern-Matching* , In „The Implementation of Functional Programming Languages", S.L. Peyton-Jones, Prentice-Hall International, pp. 78-103, 1987.

Knowledge Intensive Case-Based Assistance for Framework Reuse*

Mercedes Gómez-Albarrán and Pedro A. González-Calero

Dep. Sistemas Informáticos y Programación, U. Complutense de Madrid
28040 Madrid, Spain
{albarran, pedro}@sip.ucm.es

Abstract. Our knowledge intensive Case-Based Reasoning approach faces the reuse of frameworks using cases that correspond to framework usage experiences. Knowledge about the framework design, code and domain complements the cases. The case retrieval, adaptation and learning mechanisms developed distinguish our work from others in the framework reuse literature. An authoring tool that helps in the implementation of the approach is sketched. A prototype tool that helps in the reuse of a framework in the graphical user interface domain illustrates the approach.

1 Introduction

An object-oriented framework provides a reusable and extensible high level design for (sub)systems in a specific domain, together with an incomplete implementation that consists of a set of interdependent abstract and concrete classes. Frameworks constitute an important contribution to attain the improvements in software quality and productivity that software reuse promise. However, they are quite difficult to understand and master and the documentation provided with them used to be inappropriate. Thus, the framework-based development becomes a hard and time-consuming task, taking several months to become a productive developer [8]. The information needs of framework-based application developers are [2]: first, prescriptive information that guides in framework use, and second, descriptive information that helps in framework understanding.

Following these guides, we propose a knowledge intensive Case-Based Reasoning (CBR) approach to the framework reuse problem. We present CBR as a plausible approach to profit from the experience acquired in the use of frameworks. When developing applications from a framework, the user needs to know how to use/extend the framework to implement domain actions and (s)he profits from the way in which similar domain actions were previously implemented. Therefore, past framework usage experiences are interesting pieces of information from the reuse point of view, by acting as a prescriptive guide for the use of the framework. And we propose to develop a CBR system on them.

* This work is supported by the Spanish Committee of Science & Technology (CICYT TIC98-0733).

L. Monostori, J. Váncza, and M. Ali (Eds.): IEA/AIE 2001, LNAI 2070, pp. 891–900, 2001.

The case base collecting past usage experiences is complemented with descriptive knowledge about the framework design and implementation along with a formalization of the domain terminology. The user can inspect this knowledge in order to overcome the cognitive gap (s)he faces. Apart from this, it is useful in the processes of the CBR cycle.

The main contributions of our work in the framework reuse area are:

- Providing an intelligent mechanism to retrieve framework usage experiences similar to a new problem (the query).
- Providing a mechanism that helps the user to modify the retrieved usage experiences according to the new problems. This mechanism helps in the knowledge discovery process, the nontrivial extraction of potentially useful knowledge (in the form of new usage experiences) implicit in previous experiences and descriptive knowledge.
- Providing a learning mechanism that lets the user enrich the experience base. That way, a dynamic approach to knowledge acquisition is obtained, what reduces the initial acquisition effort: a set of seed cases is provided and we trust in the user to make this set grow.

An important feature of our approach is the use of Loom, a knowledge representation system based on Description Logic (DL) and descendant of the KL-ONE system [3]. We have chosen Loom because of: (a) its richness and expressiveness, which let us build structured representations for the cases and the descriptive knowledge; and (b) the existence of mechanisms like the automatic classification of structured descriptions –concepts– with respect to a taxonomy of other concepts, the completion that enriches the definition of instances of concepts –individuals– and the incoherence detection. These mechanisms facilitate the organization of the information, the construction of the case index scheme and the development of similarity-based retrieval.

OoFRA (Object-Oriented Framework Reuse Assistant), a prototype tool that helps in the reuse of a framework to develop applications with Graphical User Interface (GUI) in the VisualWorks environment, exemplifies our approach.

The paper is organized as follows. Section 2 presents the descriptive knowledge represented. The contents of the case base, the implementation of the case-based processes and the authoring support are described in Section 3. Related work, conclusions and future work appear in last section.

2 Descriptive Knowledge

Two types of descriptive knowledge are represented: domain knowledge, and framework code and design information. Due to the use of Loom, the descriptive knowledge base is implemented as a frame network. Every node represents a structured description (a concept in the DL terminology). Slots, defined in terms of relations, restrict concepts and connect them to other concepts in the network. The terminological component (concept and relation definitions) serves as lexicon for assertions about objects (represented as individuals) in the world described. The work in [6] deeply describes the descriptive knowledge represented and the access modes to it. Here an abstract is presented.

2.1 Domain Knowledge

It is organized in two types of elements: entities of the domain and actions performed by/on these entities. The result is a taxonomy of concepts representing a terminological categorization of the domain and individuals representing the domain terminology.

Domain action definitions result from analyzing the operations that GUI entities can perform, or the operations that can be performed on GUI entities. A domain action is defined as a generic action (i.e., update, access) plus a number of attributes that modify it. Generic actions are organized in a taxonomy where, for instance, "add", "remove" and "replace" are below "update". Once generic actions are identified, the attributes that modify them and the restrictions that apply on these attributes are determined. The attributes can be specific to a generic action or shared by different ones. The entity that is object of the action (i.e., list box, input field) and the entity feature affected by the action (i.e., activity setting, appearance setting, data managed) are attributes common to the generic actions "update" and "access".

The domain terminology represented acts as a language with which case indexes are built and the user builds the query. In this sense, the concept attribute restrictions that are included in the domain model help to maintain the consistency of the knowledge base when new cases are included, and assist in the query construction process (see Section 3). Besides, CBR systems need similarity knowledge. When retrieving cases that solve problems similar to the query, the system compares descriptions built from the domain terminology. Thus, we need similarity knowledge among the domain terms. This knowledge is implicitly represented in the taxonomy organization. Individuals are classified as instances of concepts. The more similar two individuals are, the nearer they will be classified. Therefore, the individuals most similar to a new individual I, instance of C, are other instances of C. The next individuals in decreasing order of similarity are the instances of the direct superconcepts of C, and so on. So, the domain taxonomy is of double use: it defines a conceptual framework of the representation and it implicitly includes similarity information.

2.2 Framework Implementation and Design Knowledge

Framework implementation knowledge consists of a structured representation of the framework class and method information. The information of a class consists of its superclass, its comment, the methods it implements and the variables it defines. The information of a method consists of its comment, its code and the messages sent in its code. Once the concepts representing the class and method information structure are defined, the information about specific framework elements is automatically extracted from the framework environment and gathered by individuals that are instances of these concepts.

The framework design knowledge consists of:

- The specialization restrictions of the framework classes. It is useful when extending the framework in order to preserve its consistency.

- The class collaborations. Domain entities are not modeled by one framework class, but by a group of classes. A class collaboration connects the information of the classes that collaborate in order to model a domain entity with the entity modeled.
- The operation description of the methods. This information is automatically extracted from the method names, and when two methods are similar their operation descriptions are close in the corresponding taxonomy. This similarity information is used in the adaptation process.

3 A Case Base of Framework Usage Experiences

In our approach, a case is a usage experience that explains, by means of a set of steps, how to implement a domain action –the problem– using specific pieces of the framework code. We distinguish three parts in a case: description, solution and additional information.

The description are the case features related to the problem it solves. It consists of a natural language description of the problem, for presentation purposes, and the terminological description of the problem, an individual from the knowledge base that defines a domain action and acts as the case index.

The solution consists of a natural language description of the case steps, for presentation purposes, and a formal representation of these steps, in order to reason about them in the adaptation process. This formal representation is the sequence of Object-Oriented Programming (OOP) actions to which the natural language steps correspond. We have defined concepts that represent classes of common OOP actions (i.e., sending a message, instantiating a class, redefining a method). For instance, the attributes of the action "sending a message" are the class of the recipient object and the method corresponding to the message. Once concepts corresponding to the OOP classes are defined, the OOP actions that formalize each case solution are instances of these concepts and are described in terms of the framework classes and methods used in the solution.

The additional information consists of cases that solve related problems and information that is used in the adaptation task to identify which OOP actions need to be modified in the solution. The adaptation information consists of: on which items of the problem terminological description the OOP actions of the solution depend, and on which previous OOP actions in the solution later OOP actions depend.

Next, we describe the processes of the CBR cycle exemplified by an interaction with OoFRA (technical details can be found in [5]). So, let's assume that a user is implementing an application from the framework in the VisualWorks environment and (s)he needs to know how to implement a specific domain action: accessing the information about the selected item in a list box. The section finishes presenting the authoring tool used to develop OoFRA.

3.1 Retrieving Cases

A query formulation process lets the user build a terminological description of the problem using the domain terminology represented. The user selects one of the

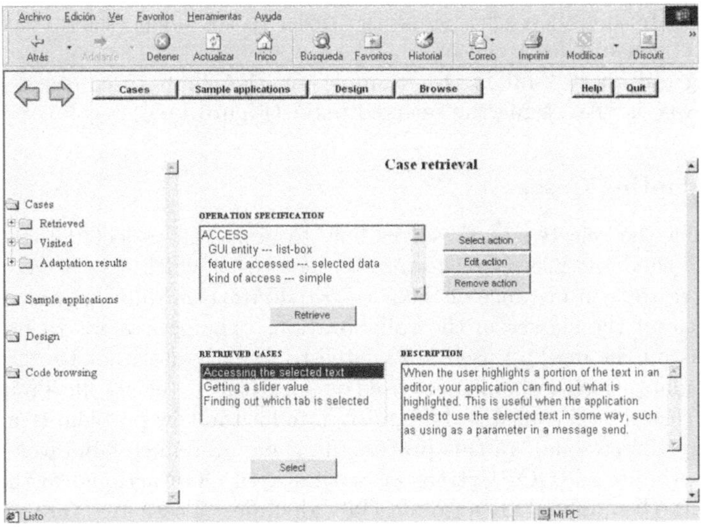

Fig. 1. OoFRA query formulation and retrieval page.

generic actions in the knowledge base and specializes it. The system guides the user in the specification of action modifiers and in the use of values appropriate for these modifiers. Modifiers and values are dynamically obtained from the definitions of the generic action specializations existing in the knowledge base.

Figure 1 depicts the page for query formulation and retrieval in OoFRA. It shows the results of our sample retrieval process. The user selects the generic action "access". The query formulation mechanism builds an instance of the corresponding concept and suggests three modifiers to specialize the action: the GUI entity that is the object of the action, the accessed feature of this entity and the kind of access. And the earliest values suggested for the modifier "Kind of access" are "multiple", "simple", "all" and "partial".

On selecting "list box" as value for the modifier "GUI entity", a new assertion is made upon the individual representing the query and this individual is automatically classified. The completion mechamism infers then that the only value appropriate for the third modifier is "simple"; "all" and "partial" are values valid for widgets that display text and a list box does not allow a multiple selection. Thus, the use of the completion mechanism lets the domain knowledge assist in the query formulation process.

Once the query construction finishes, relevant cases are found through a two-step process. First, a number of candidate cases are located: those, if any exists, whose index is an instance of the most specific concept the query is an instance of. The rationale of this process is, as outlined before, that the most similar individuals to the query must have been classified in its surroundings. If no case exists satisfying the condition mentioned, more and more abstract concepts of which the query is an instance are used. In a second step, the cases located are ranked by non-increasing similarity order to the query using the numerical similarity measure described in [7].

Using the query built in the example, OoFRA finds three cases. The most relevant one is "Accessing the selected text" (Figure 1).

3.2 Adapting Cases

"Accessing the selected text" solves how to access the selected text in a text editor: to send the message *selection* to the object which acts as controller for the text editor –an instance of the class *TextEditorController.* (Controller is the role of one of the classes in the collaboration.) The case needs to be adapted: the class and the method used are related to a text editor, not to a list box.

The adaptation mechanism is based on substitution (each solution item of the selected case that is considered inappropriate for the new problem is substituted by a more correct one). In this process, user and system collaborate.

First, the items (OOP actions or attributes of OOP actions) in the solution that need to be adapted are automatically identified. These items are those which depend on a feature of the case index which has a different value in the query, and those others that depend on a solution item that also needs to be adapted. In our example, the query and the selected case index differ in the value of the object of the action: a list box and a text editor, respectively. (The selected text in the case is equivalent to the selected data in the query.) The class in the solution depends on that case index feature. The method depends on the class. So, the class and the method should be adapted.

In a second step, every item that needs to be adapted is substituted by a proper new one. First, those that only depend on features of the case index; then, those that depend on other items of the solution that have already been adapted. This process assumes that when *A* depends on *B*, *A* and *B* are related in the domain model.

Substitution-based adaptation mechanisms keep the structure of the solution and replace elements of it with more appropriate ones. So, these new elements must fit the solution structure. Let's suppose that a solution item *A* depends on an item *B* and *B* has already been substituted by another item *B'*. Then, a substitute *A'* for *A* has to be found. In order to fit the solution structure, *A'* has to conform to two conditions:

- It must have characteristics similar to the item it replaces. In other words, it must be an element in the surroundings of *A*.
- It must be an element that, in the resulting solution, allows maintaining dependencies similar to the corresponding ones in the source case. In other words, it must be related to *B'* in a similar way than *A* is related to *B*.

Initially, the system looks for those items which are the most similar to *A* and depend on *B'* in exactly the same way as *A* depends on *B*. The user is responsible for selecting the best substitute among the ones suggested, profiting from the code and design knowledge represented. If none of the candidates is acceptable, or there are no candidates, the user can relax the location of substitutes. Backtracking processes can be also made in order to find new substitutes for items that have already been substituted. This ability is of interest specially when it is difficult to find appropriate substitutes for items depending on these that have been substituted. The abstract idea is to try using a substitute *B"* for *B* that allows to find a more suitable substitute *A"* for *A* than *A'* is.

Let's exemplify the sketched substitution process by means of the adaptation process of the case "Accessing the selected text". The first item that has to be substituted is the class *TextEditorController*. The most similar class to *TextEditorController* which is related to a list box in exactly the same way as *TextEditorController* is related to a text editor, is *SequenceController*: the class that acts as the controller for the list box. The user accepts *SequenceController* as substitute for *TextEditorController* and the search of a substitute for the method *selection* begins. *dispatchMenuSelection:*, a method of *SequenceController*, is proposed as substitute. But, after inspecting the method code and comment, the user rejects it: the method functionality is to interpret the selected option in the menu of actions related to the middle button in a three-button mouse. The user decides to relax the conditions of the search and the method *changeRequest* is proposed (the actions *select* and *request* are close in the knowledge base). But this method does not implement the functionality needed: it is the method that an application sends to itself when the user close the application.

So, the most obvious adaptation (changing the text editor controller by the list box controller, and the method of the first one by a similar one of the second) does not seem to be adequate. The user decides then to start a backtracking process: trying to find a less obvious substitute for the class that, in its turn, allows finding a method with a suitable functionality.

The restrictions to find a new class are relaxed. Then, four classes related with the list box are found: *SequenceController* (which is not suggested to the user because it was rejected before the backtracking process), *SequenceView*, *SelectionInList* and *SpecWrapper*. These four classes collaborate to model the domain entity "list box". The user has to select one among the last three. And the comment and the design information of the classes do not help in this task. The user starts then a trial-and-error process: (s)he selects a class and asks the system for substitutes for the second item, the method. The user will finally decide which are the best substitutes with regard to the method *goodness*. If the user selects *SequenceView*, the method *strokedSelection* is suggested. This method lets update the way elements in a list box are highlighted when selected. Therefore, it is not useful. However, if the user selects *SelectionInList*, the system finds two methods, *selection* and *selectionIndex*, whose comments are "Get the selected element from the underlying collection" and "Answer the index of the current selection in the list", respectively. So, the first one implements the required functionality. And the user selects the class *SelectionInList* and its method *selection* as the definitive substitutes.

3.3 Learning Cases

The user has a fundamental role in case learning: (s)he proposes which adaptation results to include as new cases. Although we are aware of the need of a mechanism to control the quality of the knowledge learnt, specially in collaborative uses of the tool, for the moment, we are confident of a responsible use of the learning mechanism.

The user has to provide the natural language description of the problem and the solution, together with the related cases. The system will provide the skeleton for this information from the adapted case. The case index (the terminological description of the problem) is the individual representing the query used to retrieve the source case. The formal representation of the solution and the adaptation information are automatically built from the corresponding ones in the source case, replacing the original items by the new ones. This is possible because, as stated before, the structure of the solution in the new case (the one that results after the adaptation process) coincides with the structure of the solution in the source case. In the example, the solution in the source case is formally represented by an instance of the concept corresponding to the OOP action "sending a message". And the values of the two attributes of this OOP action (class of the recipient object and method corresponding to the message) has been substituted: *SelectionInList* instead of *TextEditorController* and the method *selection* of *SelectionInList* instead of the method *selection* of *TextEditorController*. Thus, an individual which is an instance of the concept representing the OOP action "sending a message" is automatically built and the values of its attributes are the individuals that represent the class *SelectionInList* and its method *selection*.

3.4 Author Support

The information representation process required to develop tools similar to OoFRA is supported by DocumentationAuthor, an authoring tool which has two main subsystems:

- JCopernico, a graphic tool for the edition and visualization of knowledge bases implemented in Loom. JCopernico is the Java version of a previous tool implemented in Lisp, Copernico [1]. JCopernico is used to build the descriptive knowledge base. It helps in the definition of concepts, relations and individuals, diminishing the complexity of the knowledge representation language and controlling the consistency of the definitions. It also depicts the information included in the knowledge base in an intuitive manner, properly presenting the different relations among the elements already defined.
- CaseAuthor, which features an advanced GUI to populate the case base. CaseAuthor lets introduce plain text description of the case problem and solution, and build the formal representations of these two case parts and the additional information. Let's sketch how the formal representation of a case solution is built using CaseAuthor. When the developer describes an OOP action in a case solution, CaseAuthor presents the different kinds of OOP actions defined and the developer selects one. Let's suppose that the OOP action is "sending a message", which has two attributes: the class of the recipient object and the method corresponding to the message sent. CaseAuthor lets the developer inspect the classes and methods previously represented in order to select the attribute values. Once the formal representation of the

solution and the case index are represented, CaseAuthor visualizes them and lets the developer establish the dependencies that conform the adaptation information.

4 Related Work, Conclusions, and Future Work

Several efforts in the literature face the framework reuse problem gathering prescriptive information in the so-called cookbooks. The work in [4] presents the *hooks*, a means of documenting frameworks similar to cookbook recipes.

Cookbooks and similar approaches have two major drawbacks. The first one is that they rely on a kind of table of contents, and the manual selection of one of its entries, as the basic way to access information. This results in sequential searches, very inefficient in a real context. We face the sequential search drawback by means of an approximate retrieval mechanism that allows locating the usage experience most adequate to the query. The query construction mechanism that we have developed helps to build coherent descriptions, profiting from the domain knowledge represented and the completion mechanism of the DLs.

The second drawback of cookbooks is that they are insufficient to describe every use of the framework. It is impossible to anticipate all the different questions asked by the users and even the framework designers do not know all the frameworks uses. Some works face this drawback also gathering descriptive framework knowledge and allowing the user to inspect it. An example of this mixed strategy is the work of Meusel *et al.* [10].

Providing access to descriptive information lets undoubtedly cover a wider spectrum of user necessities, but the user has to face the nontrivial process of discovering new uses from the information represented. We have represented deep knowledge about the framework and developed an interactive adaptation mechanism which, using that knowledge, helps the user to modify the usage experiences according to the new problems. Thus, not only the access to the descriptive knowledge is allowed, so that the user may look it up to understand the framework and modify herself/himself the cases. This knowledge is directly used by the system in order to help the user to obtain new experiences. Besides, a learning mechanism allows including the adaptation process results as new cases. Thus, the user helps in generating new framework documentation.

Knowledge intensive approaches suffer from the so-called knowledge acquisition bottleneck. The reasoning mechanisms of the DLs, such as the automatic classification of concepts and the completion of individuals, reduce the cost of organizing the initial knowledge and the inclusion of new one as a result of the case learning process. Thus, DLs are considered an extremely appropriate technology to develop information systems and CBR systems [9].

In order to prove the feasibility of our approach, we have developed OoFRA, a prototype tool. Apart from people involved in the project, OoFRA has been used by some of our post-graduate computer science students, what offers us confidence about its robustness and usability.

Nowadays, we are involved in the development of a comprehensive case-based approach to framework user training. Apart from the current cases, this training approach will include cases in the form of sample applications.

References

1. Blanco, J. Fernández-Manjón, B., González-Calero, P., Fernández-Chamizo, C.: Copernico: una herramienta de ayuda para la construcción de bases de conocimiento. Procs. Conf. Española Para la Inteligencia Artificial (1995) 269-278
2. Butler, G., Dénommée, P.: Documenting Frameworks. In: Fayad, M., Schmidt, D., Johnson, R. (eds.): Building Application Frameworks, Object-Oriented Foundations of Framework Design, John Wiley & Sons (1999) 495-503
3. Brachman, R.J., Schmolze, J.G.: An overview of the KL-ONE knowledge representation system. Cognitive Science 9(2) (1985) 171-216
4. Froelich, G., Hoover, H.J., Liu, L., Sorenson, P.: Hooking into Object-Oriented Application Frameworks. Procs. International Conference on Software Engineering (1997) 491-501
5. Gómez-Albarrán, M., González-Calero, P., Díaz-Agudo, B., Fernández-Conde, C.: Modelling the CBR Life Cycle Using Description Logics. In: Althoff, K-D., Bergmann, R., Branting, L.K. (eds.): Case-Based Reasoning Research and Development. Lecture Notes in Artificial Intelligence, Vol. 1650. Springer Verlag (1999) 148-161
6. Gómez-Albarrán, M., González-Calero, P., Fernández-Chamizo, C.: Framework Understanding Through Explicit Knowledge Representation. Procs. Iberoamerican Conference on Artificial Intelligence (1998) 17-28
7. González-Calero, P., Díaz-Agudo, B., Gómez-Albarrán, M.: Applying DLs for Retrieval in Case-Based Reasoning. Procs. Int. Workshop on Description Logics (1999) 51-55
8. Johnson, R.E.: How frameworks compare to other object-oriented reuse techniques. Frameworks = Components + Patterns. Comm. of the ACM 40 (10) (1997) 39-42
9. Kamp, G.: Using Description Logics for Knowledge Intensive Case-Based Reasoning. In: Smith, I., Faltings, B. (ed.): Advances in Case-Based Reasoning. Lecture Notes in Artificial Intelligence, Vol. 1168. Springer Verlag (1996) 204-218
10. Meusel, M., Czarnecki, K., Kopf, W.: A model for Structuring User Documentation of Object-Oriented Frameworks Using Patterns and Hypertext. Procs. European Conference on Object-Oriented Programming (1997) 496-510

Deciding on a Pattern

Jonathan C. McPhail[1] and Dwight Deugo[2]

Carleton University, School of Computer Science, 613-5200-4333,
Ottawa, Ontario, Canada, K1S 5B6

[1]mcphail@mondenet.com
[2]deugo@scs.carleton.ca

Abstract. Object-oriented software patterns account for knowledge regarding a solution to a programming problem in a context. Software patterns are increasingly popular and consequently their numbers are growing. Under these circumstances, it is a challenge for the pattern user to decide on which patterns to incorporate into their design. In this paper, we describe a pattern decision analysis approach that provides pragmatic support to making this design decision.

1 Introduction

Based on an individual's programming experience, an object-oriented software pattern accounts for knowledge regarding a solution to a problem in a context. With the increased popularity of developing reusable object-oriented patterns, a wealth of patterns is emerging from different origins. In some cases, there is the potential for candidate patterns to address similar design issues or problems. Under these circumstances, the designer or team of an object-oriented design is faced with a dilemma, „Which pattern is more appropriate for incorporation into the target design?" Conducting comparisons of patterns to answer this question has never been explicitly considered. The general problem examined in this paper is providing pragmatic support to making this design decision: the *pattern decision problem.*

The concept of articulating patterns, as originally envisaged by Christopher Alexander [1], is to develop a pattern language through which a complete structure may be constructed by applying interrelated patterns. Given a single coherent pattern language, Alexander offered a straightforward procedure for choosing relevant patterns to be compressed into the decision maker's particular design [1]. With the adaptation of the pattern to object-oriented software design and given the yearly deliberations to introduce new patterns [4] the number and diversity of patterns available to the designer continues to grow. Hence, it is no longer practical to scan and choose from among a list of pattern titles as originally suggested by Alexander.

The implication is that the pattern user must scrutinize the contents of each pattern before make a decision to apply it. Pattern writers tend to discuss the benefits and liabilities of applying their pattern, which are identified as *consequences* in some pat-

L. Monostori, J. Váncza, and M. Ali (Eds.): IEA/AIE 2001, LNAI 2070, pp. 901-910, 2001.

tern formats. By reading the consequences, the pattern user can determine, by subjectively trading off the consequences of those patterns under consideration, to select the pattern with more perceived merit [2]. Again, with the number of possible candidate patterns vying for the pattern user's attention, this approach can become impractical. The challenge of refining the number of candidate patterns to a practical number for the pattern user's final decision forms the prime motivation to this paper.

The overall goal of this paper is as follows: to describe an approach that facilitates the comparison of candidate Object-Oriented Software Patterns with the intent to establish those patterns more appropriate for use in a target design. To meet this goal, we will include discussions on the following objectives:

- Develop a *pattern decision analysis* approach suitable for comparing candidate object-oriented software patterns. This endeavour will entail tailoring the identified decision analysis approach to deal with pattern specific criteria and metrics that distinguish one pattern from another.
- Identify distinguishable features that make patterns comparable

The remainder of the paper is organized as follows. Section 2 describes the important ingredients of any approach attacking the pattern decision analysis problem. Section 3 describes our approach in detail, breaking it down into three stages: input, applying the method, and output. Section 4 concludes with some brief closing statements.

2 Making a Decision

Before a designer can attempt to understand and apply a particular pattern to their own context, they must first decide on the appropriate pattern. Given this challenge, important ingredients to any approach solving this problem are a description of the decision, the decision maker, the decision procedure and decision analysis.

The Decision

The decision is comprised of a set of candidates. The candidates in question are those pattern alternatives that have been selected, by the decision maker, for further consideration. Candidates are described by a set of properties that distinguish them from the other candidates [9].

The Decision Maker

The decision maker is described by the manner in which they react when two candidates, *a* and *b*, are presented to them. In principle, the decision maker will exhibit one of the following [9]:

- Preference. The decision maker prefers one at the exclusion of the other. The strength of this preference can be further qualified
- Indifference. The decision maker is indifferent between the two candidates
- Incomparability. The decision maker is unable or refuses to compare them

The Decision Procedure

The aim of any decision procedure is to place more emphasis on those candidates that will enhance the decision maker's *total satisfaction* with the recommended results [3]. This overarching objective will tie together the conflicting objectives typical of the pattern decision problem.

Decision Analysis

The intent of decision analysis, that has been adopted here, is not to dictate the selection of a particular solution, but rather organize the candidate solutions while leaving the final selection to the decision maker [8,9]. Although comparison is considered an important application of object-oriented software design measurement, this subject has received little attention [10].

The microcosm of designs collected by object-oriented design patterns provides a suitable proving ground for approaches to decision-making within the context of object-oriented software design. The environment of the decision being made here is very specific. In particular:

- **The decision maker** is isolated to the pattern user who is likely to be a software designer, investigating a set of particular candidate patterns to be applied within the scope of a larger design.
- **The point in time** a decision is expected is during initial design activities where the design begins to take form. It is possible that decisions concerning patterns may take place later in the design, development or maintenance activities, but it is presumed that they will not be as frequent as the initial design.

3 Approach

Initially, the **EL**imination **E**t **C**hoix **T**raduisant la **RE**alitė II (ELECTRE II) emerged as the selected decision analysis method due to the limited amount of user input. Another consideration in favour of ELECTRE II is that it can be extended to account for specific decision problem properties [7]. A particular challenge facing the pattern decision problem is that many criteria may be applied to compare different candidates. Given this number, there exists a useful extension to ELECTRE II, which further reduces the input requirement with a view to enhance the decision reliability [6].

Depending on the description of criteria related to patterns, the number has the potential to be quite extensive. This number will likely detract from the feasibility of developing a pattern decision aid if the decision maker must assign a preference to each of the criteria. This difficulty has been examined and it has been previously postulated elsewhere that an increasing number of decision criteria impacts negatively on the reliability of an associated decision result [7]. Accompanying this assertion are options to remedy the challenge. The option applied in this paper entails establishing a *hierarchy of criteria*, where many criteria can be categorized or generalized. The decision maker then assigns weights at the highest level in the hierarchy. This new alternative was selected over conducting a multivariate or interdependence analysis between criteria to reduce the numbers. Such analysis among object-oriented design metrics is a field of study possessing its own merits.

The remainder of this section outlines our new extension to conducting ELECTRE II of applying a hierarchy of criteria. It should be noted that the proposed pattern decision analysis adapts the extension offered in [7], and is tailored to deal with the specific pattern decision problem, and to address perceived shortcomings in the presented extension. In addition, the original extension [6] attempted to simplify ELECTRE II. In essence, this simplification entails removing the application of the ELECTRE II decision rules and does not make use of the concordance and discordance thresholds. Pattern decision analysis re-examines these specific issues.

3.1 The Pattern Decision Analysis Approach

In the pattern world there are typically two potential actors implicated in patterns: the pattern writer and the pattern user. With the pattern user in mind, it is presumed that their total satisfaction is dominated by software quality factors. Hence, Figure 1 represents the pattern user's hierarchy of values, in our case forces such as performance, rooted on total satisfaction. We leverage this hierarchy in pattern decision analysis.

3.2 Pattern Decision Analysis Input

The specific input for this method includes:

- **The Candidates.** The candidates are those patterns to be evaluated during the decision analysis method. Each pattern must have specific values assigned to its forces indicting how well the pattern supports those forces.
- **The Criteria.** In the context of the pattern decision problem, the criteria are analogous to the forces that have been organized into a hierarchy, as shown in Figure 1, rooted on total satisfaction.
- **The Decision Maker's Preference.** The pattern user will assign preference to the highest level of forces in the related hierarchy. For the purposes here, this level is represented by Performance, Maintainability, Reliability, and Utility.
- **Concordance Thresholds.** Defined in terms consistent with the original ELECTRE II method, two concordance (the agreement that candidate *a* outranks candidate *b*) thresholds $\hat{c}_1$ and $\hat{c}_2$ are required.
- **Discordance Threshold.** Likewise, a discordance (the refusal that candidate *a* outranks candidate *b*.) threshold $\hat{d}$ is required.

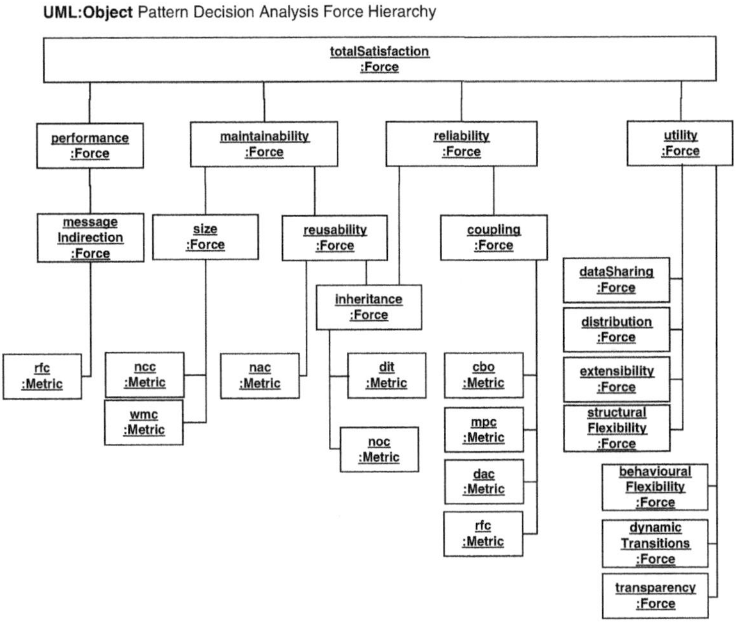

Fig. 1. Pattern Force Hierarchy

3.3 Pattern Decision Analysis Method

The pattern decision analysis method contains two stages:

1. Comparing the candidates
2. Analyzing the comparison results

The two stages are repeated, beginning with the deepest forces of the force hierarchy and moving up until the results have been generated from comparison against the highest level of forces with the candidate patterns.

Stage 1: Comparing the Candidates
This stage contains three steps:

1. Normalizing the criteria
2. Calculating pairwise concordance and discordance indices
3. Calculating candidate concordance indices

Comparing the Candidates Step 1.1: Normalizing the criteria
Beginning with the metrics in the force hierarchy, metric values are normalized. Criteria values are normalized to avoid calculations with criteria representing different quantitative units or qualitative indices. An assumption regarding normalization made in the original extension [6] and applied to our approach, is that a particular criteria value can be divided by a norm aligned to a desired criteria value. In this regard, the normalized values are oriented towards the desirable criteria value [7].

$$h_{ji} = 1 - \frac{g_j^{\max} - g_{ji}}{g_j^{\max} - g_j^{\min}}$$

Normalizing Benefit Criteria **(1)**

- **Benefit Criteria.** The desired value is the maximum value. Given the value, g_{ji} for criteria *j*, candidate (pattern) *i*, the associated benefit normalization, h_{ji}, bounded by $0 \leq h_{ji} \leq 1$, is included in equation 1; and
- **Cost Criteria.** The desired value is the minimum value. The calculation for nomalizing cost criteria, h_{ji}, bounded by $0 \leq h_{ji} \leq 1$, is calculated according to Equation 2.

$$h_{ji} = 1 - \frac{g_{ji} - g_j^{\min}}{g_j^{\max} - g_j^{\min}}$$

Normalizing Cost Criteria **(2)**

As the comparison proceeds up the force hierarchy, the number of candidates a particular candidate outranks will be normalized. This latter calculation is dealt with in Stage 2.2. In the case of the number of outranks, it will always be treated as a benefit criteria.

Comparing the Candidates Step 1.2: Calculating pairwise concordance and discordance indices
It is at this step that pattern decision analysis diverts from the extension to ELECTRE II and introduces our new extension to ELECTRE II to accommodate a hierarchy of criteria. The pairwise concordance and discordance indices are calculated consistent with the original ELECTRE II.

- **Pairwise Concordance Index.** Given the preference weights from the user for the forces and the representation of candidates by the values related to the multiple criteria, a *pairwise concordance index,* $c(a,b)$, is calculated by pairwise comparison of the candidates *a* to *b*.

$$c_k(a,b) = \begin{cases} \dfrac{m_{k+1}}{n_{k+1}} & \textit{given: } \begin{array}{l} \textit{a force in hierarchy level } k \geq 1; \\ G_{k+1}, \textit{ set of sub-criteria;} \\ j : g_j \in G_{k+1} \\ m_{k+1} = \left| g_j(a) \geq g_j(b) \right| \\ n_{k+1} = \left| G_{k+1} \right| \end{array} \\ \dfrac{\sum\limits_{\substack{j:g_j \in G_1 \\ g_j(a) \geq g_j(b)}} p_j}{\sum\limits_{j:g_j \in G_1} p_j} & \textit{given: } \begin{array}{l} k = 0; \\ \textit{preference weight, } p_j, \textit{ for criteria } j \end{array} \end{cases}$$

Pairwise Concordance Index **(3)**

- **Pairwise Discordance Index.** The pairwise discordance index is the maximum difference of criteria values within a particular comparison, normalized by the maximum difference, δ, among all such differences. An interesting side effect of using normalized criteria values entails the maximum separation, δ, which will always be 1. Thus, the calculating of a pairwise discordance index, transforms into a search for the maximum disagreement that candidate *a* outranks candidate *b*.

$$d_k(a,b) = \begin{cases} 0 : \forall j (g_j(a) \geq g_j(b)) \\ \textit{otherwise} : \max\limits_j [g_j(b) - g_j(a) \end{cases}$$

given:

a force in hierarchy level k • 1;
G_{k+1}, *set of sub-criteria;*
$j : g_j \in G_{k+1}$

Pattern Pairwise Discordance Index **(4)**

Comparing the Candidates Step 1.3: Calculating candidate concordance indices
The original ELECTRE II was interested in conditions where the strong and weak outranking of candidate *a* over candidate *b* could be established. With a view to accommodate incomparable candidates, the calculation of candidate concordance indices

is amended to reintroduce the decision rules of the original ELECTRE II method. In so doing, the net flow of preference between two candidates can be qualified by the strength of that preference.

The notion of a preference out-flow and in-flow has been used in the exploitation of other outranking methods [9]. Consequently a precedent is not being established herein. For the purposes of pattern decision analysis, calculating four candidate concordance indices will be of interest, distinguishing between strong and weak flows and whether it is an in-flow or out-flow.

strong out-flow
$$c_{ki}^{so} = \sum_{\substack{i,b \in C \\ b \neq i \\ c_k(i,b) \geq \hat{c}_1 \\ c_k(i,b) - c_k(b,i) \geq 0 \\ d_k(i,b) < \hat{d}}}^{C} c_k(i,b) - c_k(b,i)$$

weak out-flow
$$c_{ki}^{wo} = \sum_{\substack{i,b \in C \\ b \neq i \\ \hat{c}_2 \leq c_k(i,b) < \hat{c}_1 \\ c_k(i,b) - c_k(b,i) \geq 0 \\ d_k(i,b) < \hat{d}}}^{C} c_k(i,b) - c_k(b,i)$$

strong in-flow
$$c_{ki}^{si} = \sum_{\substack{i,b \in C \\ b \neq i \\ c_k(b,i) \geq \hat{c}_1 \\ c_k(b,i) - c_k(i,b) \geq 0 \\ d_k(b,i) < \hat{d}}}^{C} c_k(b,i) - c_k(i,b)$$

weak in-flow
$$c_{ki}^{wi} = \sum_{\substack{i,b \in C \\ b \neq i \\ \hat{c}_2 \leq c_k(b,i) < \hat{c}_1 \\ c_k(b,i) - c_k(i,b) \geq 0 \\ d_k(b,i) < \hat{d}}}^{C} c_k(b,i) - c_k(i,b)$$

Pattern Decision Analysis Candidate Concordance Indices **(5)**

With the calculation of these candidate concordance indices, the comparison stage for particular forces is completed. Although psychologically complex, the intent is not for a person to have to carry out the calculations. Rather the distributed decision aid will handle all related calculations while deriving the final ordering of pattern candidates. With the candidate concordance indices calculated, the following analysis stage will entail considering the associated preference flows similar to the analysis accompanying the original ELECTRE II explanation.

Stage 2: Analyzing the Comparison Results
This stage is comprised of one step that is repeated as each level in the force hierarchy. This stage marks the completion of the method with the calculation of the number of outranks. The step is entitled:

- Determine the number of other candidates a particular candidate outranks.

Stage 2.1: Determine the number of other candidates a particular candidate outranks
As explained previously, the original ELECTRE II derived its final ranking by treating each candidate as a vertex in a directed graph and considered the strong out-degree and in-degree of each candidate vertex. The respective weak degrees were considered to break ties. In the pattern decision analysis, a particular visit to a force node in the force hierarchy is completed by generating the *number of outranks* a candidate possesses which indicates that the candidate in question has a more dominant strong outflow and lower strong in-flow than the other candidates. Similarly weak out-flow and in-flow is used to break ties. This number of outranks forms the relative position of preference for the force in question and in turn forms the basis for normalization in the subsequent visit to a higher-level force in the force hierarchy.

3.4 Pattern Decision Analysis Output

When the number of outranks is generated at the Total Satisfaction level in hierarchy the number of outranks for each candidate is normalized one last time. This final normalized value represents the relative order of candidates from highest to lowest, with preferred candidates having a normalized value of 1.00. It must be stressed that this final value is not indicative of the amount that one candidate is better than another, but is useful to generate a final ordering of candidates. That is, if candidate a has a final value of 1.00 and candidate b has a value of 0.75. This does not imply that candidate a is 25% better than candidate b. The only inference suggested is that based on the input preference weights it is concluded that candidate a will be preferred to candidate b by the decision

4 Conclusion

The proposed pattern decision analysis, facilitates the comparison of candidate object-oriented software patterns with the intent to establish those patterns more suitable for use in a design. By applying this approach in independent tests [5], results confirm the suitability of the proposed approach to the pattern decision problem, although limited space prevents us from reporting them here. Acknowledging that issues exist, pertaining to the composition of a force hierarchy around which a pattern decision must be formed, we presents a legitimate starting point upon which further examination of comparing object-oriented software patterns can be based. With the suitability of the approach confirmed and by accommodating the evolution of the force hierarchy and object-oriented metrics, a design for a pattern decision aid has been formed.

References

1. Alexander,C., Ishikawa,S., Silverstein, M.: A Pattern Language, Oxford University Press, NY, (1977)
2. Buschmann, F., Meunier, R., Ronhert, H., Sommerlad, P., Stal, M.: Pattern – Oriented Software Architecture, A System of Patterns, John Wiley & Sons Ltd., (1996)
3. Golub, D.L.: Decision Analysis An Integrated Approach, John Wiley & Sons, Inc, (1997)
4. Harrison, N., Foote, B., Rohnert, H.: Patterns Languages of Program Design, Vol. 4, Addison Wesley, (1999)
5. McPhail, J. C.: Deciding on a Pattern: Towards a distributed decision aid that supports the selection of an Object-Oriented Software Pattern, Carleton University, (2000)
6. Nijkamp, P.: Stochastic Quantitative and Qualitative Multicriteria Analysis for Environmental Design. Papers of the Regional Science Association, Regional Science Association, Vol. 38, (1977), 175-199
7. Nijkamp, P., van Delft: A., Multi-Criteria Analysis and Regional Decision Making., H.E. Stenfert Kroesė B.V., Leiden, (1977)
8. Simpson, L.: Do Decision Makers Know What They Prefer?: MAVT and ELECTRE II, Journal of the Operational Research Society, Vol. 47, No. 7, (1996), 919-929
9. Vincke, P.: Multicriteria Decision-aid, John Wiley & Sons Ltd, Chichester, UK, (1992)
10. Whitmire, S.A.: Object-oriented Design Measurement, John Wiley & Sons, Inc, (1997)

Program Modeling for Fault Definition Based Static Analysis

Thomas Illgen

University of Paderborn, 33095 Paderborn, Germany,
tho@adt.upb.de

Abstract. Generating effective test data to show that a faulty structure could produce a failure poses many complexity problems. Code reviews are known as an effective method for detecting potential critical program structures. But detecting this structures in a code review takes a lot of effort and is error prone.
This paper presents a method to detect potential faulty structures by program modeling. Therefore we build a database containing informations about classified faults. For analyzing the program we generate a first order predicate logic model implemented in horn clauses. We show how to detect the fault structures defined in the database and how to reduce the effort for the code review by slicing the relevant parts of the program.

1 Introduction

Detecting potential critical structures in a program is a difficult but important part in software development and re-engineering. To show that a critical part of a program can produce failures in some cases poses a lot of complexity problems, because in most cases we have to find test cases which generate a marginal value for a variable at specific program points. On the other hand most of these potential critical structures are well known and understood. This is the first step to reveal them. A formal definition of these potential faulty structures is useful and enables the automation of program analysis.

In industrial practice code reviews, inspections and walkthroughs are effective methods for detecting potential faulty program structures. Unfortunately the effort of these methods is very high and the support of automation fells short. On the other hand, if we have defined these critical structures formally human static analysis of a program could be partial automated. Therefore we need an adequate representation of the program. First order predicate logic implemented in horn clauses seems to be a very good representation for this analysis. A first order predicate logic model for the program under test could be generated by a parser. The parser builds the well defined interface between the program and the model.

The method presented in this paper detects a critical program point depending on a potential faulty structure and generates a static slice. The structure of the potential fault is defined in a knowledge-base and has the character of

L. Monostori, J. Váncza, and M. Ali (Eds.): IEA/AIE 2001, LNAI 2070, pp. 911–918, 2001.

a fault specification. If the critical part contains only constants we can fix the potential fault directly. If the critical program part contains variables we have to build a static slice including all program paths effecting each variable of the critical program part. The slice reduces the program complexity and narrows the focus of attention to the relevant parts of a program during the test process. Depending on the defined knowledge about the fault structure it is possible to generate a checklist that tells the tester which parts of the program are critical and what to analyze.

2 Background

We use first order predicate logic to define the potential fault structures and to model the program under test. Implementing these definitions in horn clauses represented in PROLOG makes the definitions executable. The declarative model enables an easy analysis of the program. It enables the detection of critical program structures and static slicing of this parts. In this section we give an overview to the used methods for modeling the program, complexity reduction using slicing techniques and fault classification.

2.1 Horn Clauses

We use PROLOG as modeling language and for the definition of potential faults. PROLOG is a logic programming language consisting of a set of Horn clauses. Horn clauses are universal quantified disjunctive clauses with at most one positive literal. These are classified in three types called *fact*, *rule* and *goal*. Definite clauses, or program clauses are facts and rules. A rule has a head A and a body $B_1, ..., B_n$. As usual, we denote Horn clauses by

$$\begin{array}{ll} A, & (fact) \\ A \leftarrow B_1, ..., B_n, & (rule) \\ \leftarrow B_1, ..., B_n. & (goal) \end{array}$$

A fact states something which is true, a rule has the meaning that its head A is true provided that the conjunction of its body literals $B_1, ..., B_n$ is true. A goal is used to activate a logic program P, i.e., it is a question if the conjunction of the literals $B_1, ..., B_n$ follows from P [1]. The representation in PROLOG-clauses enables execution of the program model and the call of the specified potential faults as goal. The goal is a call of a PROLOG-rule that specifies the fault to be detected in the program. The call of a fault specification initiates the program analysis.

2.2 Slicing

The definition of a program slice differs lightly in different papers. There are two main classes of slicing criteria; static Slicing and dynamic slicing. The difference between static and dynamic slicing is that dynamic slicing assumes fixed input for a program, whereas static slicing does not make any assumptions regarding the input. In this paper we use static slicing to reduce the complexity of the program. Therefore we use the static slicing definition of Weiser [9], e. g. we build executable static slices. Therefore it is important, that the static slice contains the critical path, e. g. all parts of the program effecting the critical structure defined in the fault knowledge-base.

In Weiser's approach, slices are computed by computing consecutive sets of transitively relevant statements, according to data flow and control flow dependences. Only statically available information are used to compute slices [9,8]. Weiser defines a static slice as an executable subset of statements of a program. The static slicing criteria could be further break down in two types [5]:

- The static slicing criterion $C = (p, v)$ requires the computation of a static slice with respect to a program point p and a variable v, which is not necessarily used or defined at p [9,3].
- The static slicing criterion $C = (p, v)$ requires the computation of a static slice with respect to a program point p and a variable v, which is used or defined at p [6]

The computation of static slices is shown as a reachability problem in a program dependence graph [4], i. e. data dependence and control dependence. Weiser computes slices with respect to a set of data flow equations [9].

2.3 Fault Classification

The definition and classification of faults is a fundamental requirement for their systematic and analytic detection. The set of faults classified in their characteristics depends on the requirements of the analysis. Our requirement is to define fault classes for an effective static analysis. Therefore it is useful to build a set of fault definitions with common characteristics. These definition is the knowledge base for detecting them in our program model. We initiate the analysis by an inquiry to the system. Therefore we build a search tree containing a set of fault definitions in their nodes. The edges in the tree couple the nodes in a logical AND.

3 Program Modeling and Analysis

In this section we summarize the terminology to be used in the paper, without being complete and formal in order to brief our analysis and modeling approach. We model the program in three types of facts.

- Facts to describe the data flow.
- Facts to describe the control flow.
- Facts to describe the program instructions and to couple the data flow with the control flow.

The facts to describe the data flow are outlined in the typical manner of variable use, e.g. d-use for the definition of a variable, c-use for the computational use of a variable and p-use for the predicative use of a variable [7,2]. The data flow of the program is modeled in the following PROLOG-facts:

- d_use(<variable name>,<line number>,<operation>).
- c_use(<variable name>,<line number>).
- p_use(<variable name>,<line number>,<operation>).

The variable name defines the specifier of the variables data-flow. The line number specifies the line in which the variable is used. The operation declares the manipulation or use of the variable. The program under test is expressed by the parser to instrument the program (adding of line numbers, write each instruction in a new line) for identification of the variable use by line numbers.

The possible control flow of the program is modeled in directed edges without respect to conditions:

edge(<line number>,<line number>).

The first line number identifies the start line of the edge, the second line number identifies the end line.

The third type of PROLOG-facts generated describes the program instructions. Examples are:

Statements: state(<line number>,<list of data-flow predicates>).
Decisions: decision(<line number>,<if, else, switch>).
Loops: loop(<kind of loop>,<line of loop condition>,
<list of data-flow predicates>).
The third argument in for-loops contains a list of the three arguments defining the data flow n the loops head.
End of block: end(<line number>, <kind of structure>,<line of structure>).

The line number specifies the line of the instrumented file to locate the instruction presently under work. The list of data-flow predicates contains the names of the variables which are manipulated or used by the specified command. They close the connection between data flow and control flow. Inputs could also be seen as a definition use of the variable but they have the character of a start-node. Thus, it is useful to model them separately.

In the first step we have to model the program in the presented manner. The model is oriented on the lines of the statements. To unify a statement exactly with a program line we first have to expand the program, especially the loop. The loop contains three statements in its head. Between this statements exists a defined control-flow to be modeled. To be able to identify the statement at the code line we have to write them in separate lines. In the first parse the program in figure 1 is generated.

The parser generates the following facts for the data flow on the left side and for the control flow on the right side.

```
1 main()
2 {
3   int
4     i,
5     x,
6     y,
7     a;
8   scanf("%i %i", &x, &y);
9   a = -3;
10  FOR
11    (
12       i = a;
13       i = i + 1 <= x;
14       i = i + 1;
15    )
16    {
17       y = y + i;
18       i = i * 2;
19    }
20  printf("%i", y);
21 }
```

Fig. 1. Expanded example-program containing some potential faults

```
declaration(4, int, i).
declaration(5, int, x).
declaration(6, int, y).
declaration(7, int, a).
d_use(x, 8, scanf).
d_use(y, 8, scanf).
d_use(a, 9, a = -3).
d_use(i, 12, i = a).
d_use(i, 13, i = i + 1).
d_use(i, 14, i = i + 1).
d_use(y, 17, y = y + i).
d_use(i, 18, i = i * 2).
c_use(a, 12).
c_use(i, 13).
c_use(i, 14).
c_use(y, 17).
c_use(i, 17).
c_use(i, 18).
p_use(i, 13, i = i + 1 <= x).
p_use(x, 13, i = i + 1 <= x).
```

```
edge(1,2).   edge(2,3).
edge(3,4).   edge(4,5).
edge(5,6).   edge(6,7).
edge(7,8).   edge(8,9).
edge(9,10).  edge(10,11).
edge(11,12). edge(12,13).
edge(13,15). edge(13,14).
edge(13,19). edge(14,15).
edge(15,16). edge(16,17).
edge(17,18). edge(18,13).
edge(19,20). edge(20,21).
```

The third type of clauses, adopting the data flow with the control flow and representing the program instructions are for the example outlined in the following PROLOG-notation.

```
func(1, main).
func(8, scanf).
loop(FOR, 10, [[d_use(i, 12, i = a),c_use(a, 12)],
  [p_use(i, 13, i = i + 1 <= x),p_use(x, 13, i = i + 1 <= x),c_use(i, 13)],
  [d_use(i, 14, i = i + 1),c_use(i, 14)]]).
state(9, [d_use(a)]).
state(12, [d_use(i), c_use(a)]).
state(14, [d_use(i), c_use(i)]).
state(17, [d_use(y), c_use(y), c_use(i)]).
state(18, [d_use(i), c_use(i)]).
state(20, [output]).
output(20, [["%i", y]]).
end(15, loop_condition, 10).
end(19, loop, 10).
end(21, func, 1).
```

The method we introduce is a static analysis of the program code. The analysis process will be carried out in following steps.

1. Define potential faults as knowledge base for the static analysis.
2. Expand the program (Each statement in separated lines).
3. Generate a model of the program under test.
4. Detect critical structures in the program under test by an inquiry to the fault database. This initiates the analysis process.
5. Build static slices containing all dependencies of the variable v at location l for a given fault definition *Def.*

The analysis is initiated by an inquiry to the system. The program in figure 1 contains two potential critical points. The first one is a potential error in line 13. Depending on the compiler the relation $1 <= x$ could be evaluated before the calculation $i = i + 1$. In this case the loop will not terminate. The detection is not difficult. It is a *depth one fault.* That means, the search tree has only a search depth of one. The fault is classified as priority fault. To detect it we have to expand the relation in the third term of all p_use-facts and control if one term in the relation is calculated. If one term is calculated, the next step is to find out, if it is enclosed in brakes. We can throw a message that the tester obviously means $(i = i + 1) <= x$ instead of $i = i + 1 <= x$. This fault is not very critical, because it occurs in every test-run that involves this loop and could be detected by a code coverage.

The second potential fault is much more critical. It depends on the test-cases to detect it with conventional test methods. Consider the example in figure 1. i is initiated in the loop by a. a is defined with the value -3. In the loop-head i is increased with one and in the loop-body multiplied with 2. Because the multiplication manipulates the value of i faster then the term in the loops head, i will decrease in every run of the loop. The other variable used in the termination conditions of the loop x is not manipulated in the loop. So this situation causes a not terminating loop.

Let us now see how we could detect this fault. First we have to detect the loop condition. It is described in the clause `loop(FOR, 10, [p_use(...`. After that we have to find all d_uses in the loop for the variables used in the loop condition. This terms are also described in the rule above. We find $i = i + 1$ in the relation of the condition, $i = i + 1$ in the third argument of the loop and $i = i * 2$ in the loops body. The last term is described in the `d_use(i, 18, i = i * 2)` clause. This clause must be in the loops body, because the loop starts in line 10 and ends in line 19 (clause `end(19, loop, 10)`). With this knowledge we can create a list of manipulations for the loop index i. In the example we could solve the problem with the result (critical for $x >= 0$) because the initial value of i has a defined value of a. This is not possible at all. If we don't know the initial value of i or it is calculated in the program the problem is to complex to solve. In this case we have to add the checkpoint (critical for $i <= 0$) in the analysis report. That means, the automation of the analysis depends on the number defined variables in the critical structure. If all used variables are constant we could defintly detect a fault. In presence of variables in this structures we could give some checkpoints for a further manual analysis like described above. The exactness of this checkpoints depends on the number of variables and on the knowledge about the faulty structure defined in the fault classification.

To reduce the complexity of the program for further manual analysis we generate a static slice. Therefore we have to consider all dependencies of the critical path, e. g. each statement which influences i in the loop condition and the loop body up to line 13. In the example the lines 6, 17 and 20 could be removed.

4 Conclusion

We have presented a method for a fault classification based static analysis to detect potential critical program structures. Therefore we build a model of the program implemented in horn clauses. Most of these faulty structures are dependent on the data flow of variables. Thus we could definitely detect a fault, if all variables are defined, e. g. they are constant. If some variables are not constant in the critical program path, we generate a static slice containing all program paths which influence the not defined variables in the critical path to reduce the complexity for a further inspection. In the analysis report we outline checkpoints for these inspection based on our knowledge about the fault structure.

References

1. O. Jack F. Belli. A test coverage notation for logic programming. *Proceedings of the Sixth International Symposium on Sofiware Reliability Engineering*, pages 133-142, 1995.
2. John H. R. May Hong Zhu, Patrick A. V. Hall. Software unit test coverage and adequacy. *ACM Computer Surveys*, 29:366-427, December 1997.
3. M. Weiser J. R. Lyle. Automateic program bug location by program slicing. *IEEE Symposium on Computers and Applications*, pages 877-883, 1987.
4. L. M. Ottenstein K. J. Ottenstein. The program dependence graph in a software developement environment . *ACM Sigsoft/Sigplan Software Engineering Symposium on Practical Software Development Environments*, 19(5):177-184, 1984.

5. Mariam Kamkar. An overview and comparative classification of program slicing techniques. *J. Systems Software*, 31:197-214, 1995.
6. D. Binkley S. Horwitz, T. Reps. Interprocedural slicing using dependence graphs. *ACM Trans. Progr. Lang. Syst.*, 12:26-61, 1990.
7. E. J. Weyuker S. Rapps. Selecting Software test data using data flow information. IEEE *Transactions on Sofiware Engineering*, pages 367-375, 1985.
8. Frank Tip. A Survey of program slicing techniques. *Journal of Programming Languages*, 3:121-189, 1995.
9. M. Weiser. Program slicing. *IEEE Transactions on Software Engineering*, 10:352-357, 1984.

Goal-Driven, Scalable Generation of Complete Interaction Sequences for Testing Graphical User Interfaces

Fevzi Belli

University of Paderborn
Germany
(belli@upd.de)

Abstract. Short Paper; Topics: Verification/Validation, Planning

Graphical User Interfaces (GUIs) are very popular and common in computer-based systems. Testing GUIs is, on the other hand, a difficult and challenging task for many reasons: First, the input space possesses a great, potentially indefinite number of combinations of inputs and events as system outputs and external events may interact with these inputs. Second, even simple GUIs possess an enormous number of states which are also due to interact with the inputs. Last but not least, many complex dependencies may hold between the states of the GUI system, and/or between its states and -inputs.

Nevertheless, most Human-Computer-Interfaces (HCI) will be designed and implemented via GUI nowadays. There exist a vast amount of research work for specification of HCI, there has been, however, little well-known systematic study in this field, resulting an effective testing strategy which is not only easy to apply, but also scalable in sense of stepwise increasing the number of test cases, thus also increasing the test costs in accordance with the test budget of the project.

Test cases generally require the determination of meaningful test *inputs* and expected system *outputs* for this inputs. To generate test cases for GUI, one has to identify the test objects and test objectives. The *test objects* are the instruments for the input, e.g. screens, windows, icons, menus, commands, function keys, alphanumerical keys, etc. The *objective* of a test is to generate the expected system behaviour *(desired event)* by means of well-defined test inputs. Robust systems possess a good exception handling mechanism, i.e. they are responsive not in terms of behaving properly in case of correct, expected inputs, but also by behaving good-natured in case of illegal inputs, generating constructive warnings, or tentative correction trials, etc. helping to navigate the user in the right direction. In order to validate such robust behaviour, one needs systematically generated erroneous inputs which would usually entail *undesired events,* e.g. system crash.

Test inputs of GUI represent usually sequences of GUI objects activations and/or selections that will operate interactively with the objects *(Interaction Sequences - IS).*

L. Monostori, J. Váncza, and M. Ali (Eds.): IEA/AIE 2001, LNAI 2070, pp. 919-920, 2001.

Such an interactive sequence is *complete (CIS),* if it eventually invokes the desired system responsibility. From AI point of the view, the testing of GUI represents a typical *planning* problem that can be solved goal-driven: Given a set of operators, an initial state and a goal state, the planner is expected to produce a sequence of operators that will change the initial state to the goal state. For the GUI test problem described above, this means we have to construct the test sequences in dependency of both the desired events and the undesired events.

The paper will summarize our research work that have also been used in real projects. The favorized methods concentrate on state diagrams and regular events, for systematically, scalable generating test sequences. Predicate Logic-based methods will be introduced for test case selection to reduce the test costs, resulting in better test process efficiency.

Planning Agents in a Multi-agents Intelligent Tutoring System

Roger Nkambou[1] and Froduald Kabanza[2]

[1]Département d' Informatique
Université du Québec à Montréal, Montréal (QC) Canada
nkambou.roger@uqam.ca
[2]School of Computer Science
University of Windsor, Windsor (ON) Canada
kabanza@cs.uwindsor.ca

Abstract. Most recent architectures of intelligent tutoring system (ITS) focussed on the tutor or the curriculum components, but with little attention being paid to planning. Therefore, some works identified two main planning process in ITS: content planning and delivery planning. In this paper, we propose a new ITS architecture that involves sophisticated planning agent at four different levels of the ITS processing. The first planning level (course planning) and the second one (Lesson planning) are derived from the traditional content planning. The third and fourth planning levels come from a decomposition of the tutor module into two different components, one specialized in the tutorial actions planning and the other tailored for the generation of multimedia presentations. After a brief presentation of the new architecture, the paper mainly focussed on the first level planning using SIMPLAN. This planning oriented achitecture takes advantages of previous ITS architecture and provides a uniform view of ITS components that can facilitate collaboration between them.

1. Introduction

Over the last ten years, intensive research has been conducted on Intelligent Tutoring Systems (ITS), several of them focusing on architectural issues. The first proposed ITS architectures and included four main components (Burn and Caps, 1988): a curriculum module, a student model, a tutor (pedagogic model), and an interface between the student and the system. This basic architecture has since been extended by many researchers, including Bass, 1998; Titter and Blessing 1998; Frasson et al. 1996, Nkambou, Gauthier and Lefebvre, 1997; Both the architectures designed by Ritter and Blessing and Frasson et al. are focused on the tutor. Bass architecture mainly improves the interface. Nkambou et al. mostly focus on the curriculum component.

One problem with those architecture is the heterogeneity of the components. This makes it difficult to design the communication between components because one has

L. Monostori, J. Váncza, and M. Ali (Eds.): IEA/AIE 2001, LNAI 2070, pp. 921-930, 2001.

to deal with different data representations in different components. This problem is addressed in our new architecture by observing that the curriculum, the planner and the tutor are all concerned in a manner or another with the planning problem, that is, the problem of deciding in advance actions that will be executed in expected future situations in order to achieve a particular goal. Hence, each component can be considered basically as a planning process, although each process operate at its own level of abstraction.

Another problem with the above ITS architecture is that planning tasks are currently done in an ad-hoc and scruffy way. The underlying planning algorithm is not bolstered by a clear model upon which one could rely to prove the correctness or optimality of generated plans. Furthermore, currently used planning approaches in ITS do not reason about temporal constraints associated with the learning process or timing constraints in the synchronization of different medias used to present a course. Rather, such constraints are dealt with heuristically outside the planning processes. Note that these limitations not only apply to the above architecture, but also to most existing ITS architectures.

A great deal of these planning limitations can be overcome by using well-known planning algorithms in the area of artificial intelligence (e.g., see Dean et al. 1995; Kabanza, Barbeau and St-Denis, 1997). These algorithms rely on well defined semantics that allow to prove the correctness and optimality of generated plans. On the other hand, AI planning research has been addressing various issues that are relevant to planning in ITS such as handling temporal constraints and reasoning about uncertain information. Some of this research has been applied to the automatic generation of multimedia presentations (André and Rist, 1996). As part of the tutor may consist in producing presentation, this last application is very relevant to tutor planning.

It is surprising that AI planning techniques have been so under-exploited in ITS, despite the acknowledged importance of planning in ITS. Our new architecture fills in this gap. It is not designed as a mere plug-in of AI planning algorithms into an existing ITS system. In fact, it also involves innovative ideas on the coordination between different planning processes.

Our new ITS architecture hinges on a multi-layer planning system in which several planning agents run concurrently, collaborating in order to prepare lessons and teach them to the learners. Since planning agents play an important role in our new architecture, it helps to pursue immediately with some general background on planning agents in artificial intelligence. Then, we will outline the new architecture by focusing only on its main components, leaving aside the details on how each component actually behave. Finally, we will describe one of the components with more details. Due to space limitations, the other components will not be detailed in this paper.

2. Planning Agents

We are interested in the design and implementation of agents that are processes capable of accomplishing autonomously various tasks on behalf of users or other processes, sometimes with various intelligent competencies, such as the ability to plan courses at different level of abstraction, or to learn from previous student and ITS interactions, and to plan multimedia presentation from raw media materials.

Planning agents will play three main roles in our new ITS architecture. Firstly, the ITS will be able to accomplish tasks or deal with events for which it has not been explicitly programmed, by planning on-line decision rules that coordinate more basic ITS processes so that they react correctly. Secondly, since planning agents yield decision rules that are constructively proven correct and optimal, the ITS reliability will become increased.

Basic algorithms for planning agents can be defined using explicit exploration of tree of possible ITS and student actions, the dynamic programming of Markov decision processes (e.g., see (Dean et al. 1995)) or control theoretical techniques (e.g., see (Kabanza, Barbeau and St-Denis, 1997)). All these approaches explore a search space to compute decision rules. The search space may, however, be differently structured, depending on formalisms used to model actions, goals, and environments, and search techniques. Since different formalisms and search techniques yield incomparable performances or expressiveness, this justifies research on hybrid approaches.

SIMPLAN (Simulation Based Planner) is a recently developed planning system that combines model checking and Markov decision theoretic techniques (Kabanza, 1999). It will be used as the basic planning system in our architecture. Although we opted for this particular planning system in order to fix a concrete development framework, the architecture of our ITS is open so that the planning algorithm underlying a particular planning agent may be replaced without jeopardizing the correct functioning of the system as a whole.

3. An ITS Architecture Based on Collaborative Planning Agents

The new architecture (figure 1) is articulated around four planning agents, each of them is in charge of a particular aspect of the ITS. Different planning agents may be implemented by the same planning algorithm, but with different input knowledge.

By "planning process", we mean any process that decide what action to do and when in order to achieve a particular goal. A set of decision rules for accomplishing a given goal is also called plan in the sense that decisions are computed by anticipating future interactions between the processes composing the system and its environment. In the case of the curriculum, the task is to plan individualized course. A basic action is to achieve a particular instructional objective; the goal is to mastery a set of concepts at a given levels. The individualized course planner agent *(IC-Planner agent)* responsibility is to generate a course graph (plan) that fit to the current student group and according to a given goal that is expressed as set of capabilities to be acquire by the student (learning requirement). The Lesson planner agent (*LE-Planner*) based on the course plan, dynamically create the next concept the system has to focus on and recommends general context of its achievement in the current session. A basic action is to include an introduction statement, or a reminder statement; the goal is to have a lesson plan that can permit to mastery a specific concept at a given level. As the learning actions are based on student abilities, the TA-Planner agent plans the sequence of basics activities for the student and the way those activities will be presented to the student. A basic action is "choosing a learning strategy" to sustain the activity delivery; the goal is to have the sequences of resources that will be activated in order to realize lessons goals.

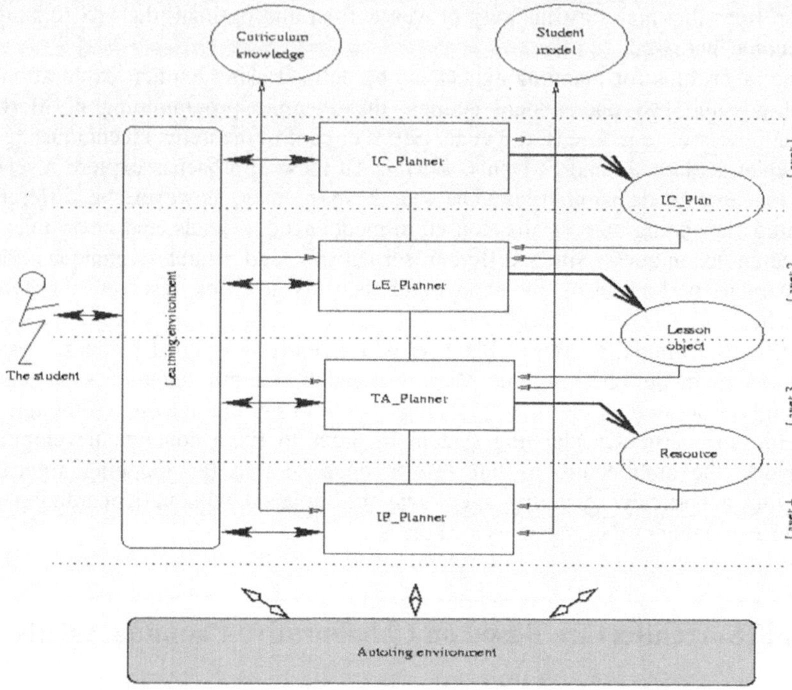

Fig. 1. The new architecture

The IP-Planner is in charge of the presentation of the activity by planning the sequence of basic actions the student deals with. Any planning agent can communicate with the student through a learning interface.

In the next sections, we focus only on the planning strategy in IC-Planner.

4. Using SIMPLAN as the Foundation of Planning Processes in ITS

For our initial implementation, we have decided to use the SIMPLAN planning system (Kabanza, 1999). Reactive plans such as those produced by SIMPLAN are finite state machine. They specify the actions to be executed by an agent depending on the current agent's state and current environment situation. This contrast with sequential plans often produced by other planning systems in which produced plans are just sequences of actions without any additional pre-condition or context under which actions in the plan are applicable. In fact, sequential plans are appropriate for predictable environments in which a planned sequence of actions is always expected to provide the anticipated outcome. On the other hand, reactive plans such as those produced by SIMPLAN are suitable for unpredictable environments in which the agent has no control on events generated by the environment. Hence the agent cannot anticipate the outcome of its own actions and this is why a conditional plan that map agent actions to sets of expected situations is necessary. This is the case in ITS planning because the IC-Planning agent for example cannot anticipate choices made by the student when following a course.

The IC-Planning agent relies on *Curriculum Knowledge Transition Network (CKTN)* for representing planning knowledge (Nkambou, Frasson and Gauthier, 1998). However, although SIMPLAN accepts different planning knowledge representations, none of them coincides with CKTN. The closest one is the *Action Description Language (ADL)* frequently encountered in the artificial intelligence planning field. So we begin with a brief reminder of CKTN description. Then we explain how this knowledge is translated into an ADL representation acceptable for SIMPLAN. This should demonstrate that SIMPLAN effectively fits the new architecture, at least as far as IC-Planning is concerned.

4.1. IC-Planning: The Actual Process

The Curriculum and its Transition Network. By using CREAM modeling approach, curriculum knowledge are represented as a network of domain knowledge, of instructional objectives and of learning materials. Thoses networks contains special links from instructional objectives to domain knowledge, which denote the contribution of an instructional objectives to the acquisition of a domain knowledge, or the fact that a domain knowledge is prerequisite to an instructional objective. Learning materials are attached to instructional objective as resources that support its achievement. Instructional objective with the attached learning materials constitute a special node called "transition". The resulting network is called CKTN (Curriculum-knowledge-transition network). An example of CKTN is shown in figure 2. The CKTN is central in the old planning process in ITS. The core of the system reasoning during planning process is based on this network.

The Target Group Knowledge. We define a target group (TG) as a group of students' state of knowledge of various capabilities which may be part of several curriculums. For instance, the knowledge of a novice nurse on the handling of the Baxter pump will not be the same as that of an advanced nurse. Therefore, a course on this topic should not include the same transitions for the former as for the latter. The advanced nurse would waste her time learning things that she already knows. Thus, these two groups of nurses constitute two different student target groups and the planner should build a course well-suited to each one.

The Training Requirement. Training requirement is expressed either as a set of objectives that the course should reach, or as a set of capabilities to be acquired by the student. It is also possible to mix these two approaches.

The old IC_Planning Process. The generation is performed by going through the CKTN. But before that, the TG state of knowledge is assigned to the capability nodes and the links which constitute the CKTN. The resulting graph is called a dynamic CKTN (DynCKTN) and we call this operation the marking of CKTN. More precisely, it consists firstly in attributing to each prerequisite link a value in the list: {*acquired, partially acquired, not acquired*} indicating whether the minimum acquisition level on this link has been reached according to the target group state of knowledge; and secondly, to each domain knowledge (capability) a value in {*possessed, partially possessed, not possessed*} representing the acquisition level of the target public and calculated from the levels assigned to the links.

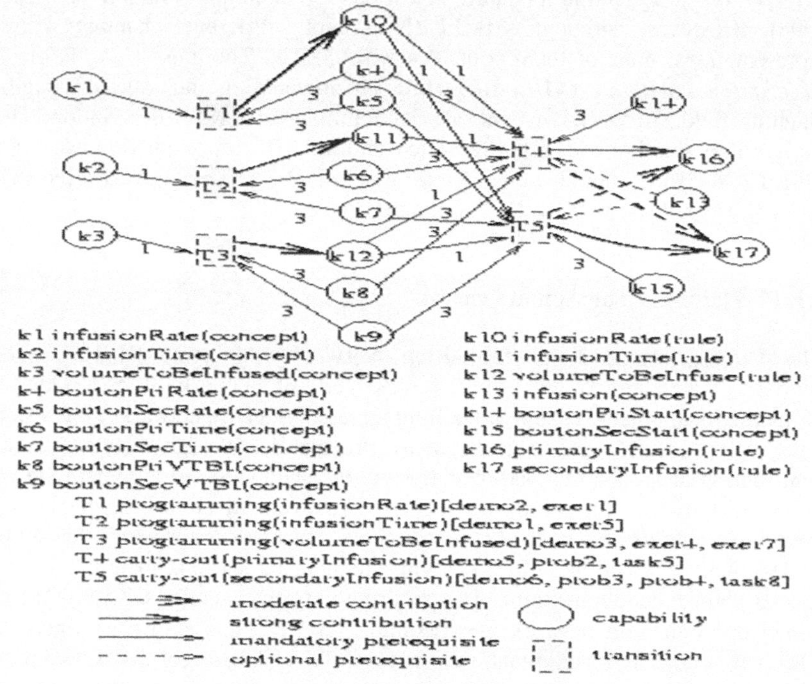

Fig. 2. Part of CKTN on the Baxter Pump

After the marking process, the generation algorithm traverses the resulting DynCKTN to determine which transition have to be included in the course in order to permit the acquisition of the knowledge specified in the requirement, a backward chaining traversal of the sub-graph rooted at the capability in order to choose the transition judged as necessary for the acquisition of that capability. We first evaluate the immediate transition that contribute to the capability and then, since some transitions possess mandatory prerequisite knowledge which in turn has contributing transition, we have to trace the sub-graph back until we reach a transition without any pre-requisite or a capability already mastered by the student (as specified in the training requirement or seen by the marking).

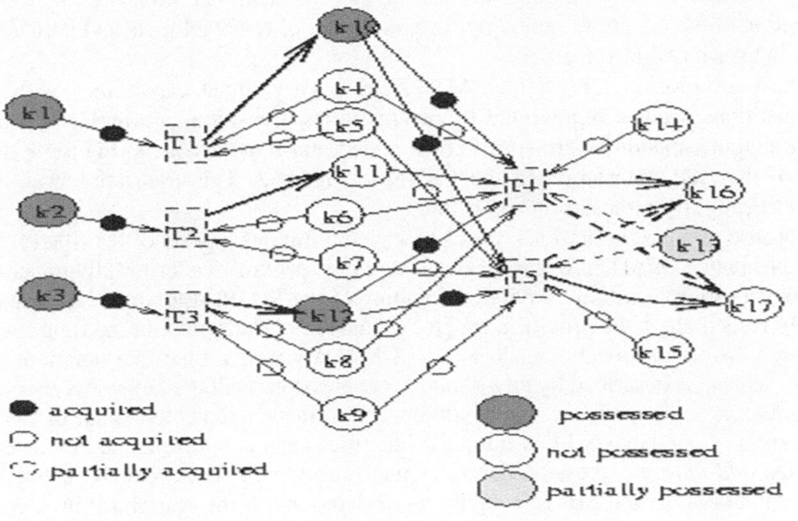

Fig. 3. DynCKTN from the CKTN in figure 2

The choice of relevant transition is carried out by applying heuristic rules introduced into the system and which consider several parameters: the links between capabilities and transitions (prerequisite or contribution), the knowledge in the training requirement and also the DynCKTN. As the output of this process, a course graph is generated. Figure 3 shows the DynCKTN derived from the CKTN in figure 2 after the marking process. If the teaching goal is to make student acquire the concept k16 at a strong level, then one possible generated course graph will includes transitions T1, T3, T4 and T5.

4.2. From CKTN to ADL

ADL specifies an agent's action in terms of *precondition*, *a set of removed facts*, and *a set of added facts*. Roughly, the *precondition* is a logical formula expressing facts that must be true in a state for the action to be meaningful in that state. In other words, if the precondition is true, then we are in a state where the agent *can* accomplish that action. Whether the agent *will* indeed accomplish the action or not, this will depend on whether or not the agent's plan specifies that action for that state. In fact, in every state, there may be several actions that the agent can execute. However, an agent can execute only one action at a time, so it must decide upon which action to execute. This is why it needs a plan that tells which action to execute in the current state. The *set of removed facts* specifies facts that are true in the current state become false after the action is executed, while the *set of added facts* specifies facts that are not true in the current state but becomes true after the execution of the action. Both the set of removed and added facts form the *effects* or *postconditions* of the action. Hence, given a description of a current state in term of facts true and an ADL description of an agent's action, a planning system can predict the state that would result from the execution of the action by removing facts in the set of removed facts and then adding facts in the set of added facts.

The translation of CKTN into ADL is quite easy. Input capabilities with their preconditions become represented by preconditions, transitions are replaced actions, while output capabilities are specified as added and removed facts. Figure 4 shows part of the ADL translation of the CKTN in Figure 3. This translation was made automatically, by a translation algorithm.

Because of space limitations, we cannot give a full description of the SIMPLAN's implementation of ADL. Accordingly, we do not expect the reader to fully understand the above example without a previous reading of the SIMPLAN's manual (Kabanza, 1999). Nonetheless, we provide a rough explanation of the syntax in the figure which allows a coarse understanding. Roughly, SIMPLAN uses a Lisp-like notation. Each action schema is described by an *adl-add-op* expression, with the keywords *:pre*, *:add* and *:del* for, respectively, the precondition, added facts and deleted facts. In addition we have a *:name* keyword that uniquely identifies each action schema. For instance, the first *add-adl-op* expression describes the transition *T1* in the CKTN of Figure 3. The expression *:var-gens* is roughly a declaration of the variables involved in description of the action together with some information on how the variable will get instantiated. The *:form* keyword describes a logical formula that must hold for the precondition to be true, for a literal to be deleted (in the *:add* component) or to be deleted (in the *:delete* component).

```
(add-adl-op
  :name '(T1)
  :pre (adl-pre :var-gens '((?x1) (k1 ?x1) (?x4) (k4 ?x4)
                            (?x5) (k5 ?x5))
  :form  '(and (>= ?x1 1) (>= ?x4 3) (>= ?x5 3)))
  :add (adl-add (adl-cond :form '(not (exists (?x) (k10 ?x)
                                   (>= ?x 10)))
  :lit '(k10 10)))
  :del (adl-del  (adl-cond :var-gens '((?x) (k10 ?x))
  :form '(< ?x 10)
  :lit '(k10 ?x))))
```

Fig. 4. Part of the ADL corresponding to the CKTN in figure 2.

4.2. SIMPLAN Planning with CKTN

Once we have a translation of CKTN into ADL it becomes easy to generate plans. The training goal is easily expressed as a *goal* for SIMPLAN while the student's profile corresponds to *the initial state* for SIMPLAN. Figure 5 shows a trace generated by SIMPLAN from a goal and initial state corresponding respectively to the target knowledge and student's profile highlighted in the CKTN of Figure 2, and with the ADL actions (part of this is shown at Figure 4) which are translated from the CKTN of Figure 2. The plan is at the end of the trace.

More explanations on the representation of plans by SIMPLAN are needed in order to better understand the plan in Figure 5. A plan is an automaton with states identified by numbers (ID) and labeled with sets of propositions true. To each state corresponds the action to be executed by the agent and a set of expected resulting states. More specifically, because of nondeterminism resulting from uncontrollable events, it may be the case the outcome of an action is uncertain. In this case, we have a set of successor states, which means that when the action is effectively executed, we cannot predict beforehand the outcome, but the resulting state is expected to be one among the set of successors. For instance, the first two lines of the reactive plan in Figure 5 specify that state with ID 0 has the attached set of proposition true. Whenever these conditions hold, the planning agent must perform transition T3 and the expected resulting state is the one with ID 1. In this particular example, all actions are deterministic so that we always have only one successor state. We can see that, the state with ID 5 contains the goal (K16, 5) that is why the planner stops.

```
SimPlan 1.0
Init state: ((K15 5) (K14 5) (K9 4) (K8 4) (K7 4) (K6 4) (K5 3) (K4 3)
            (K3 2) (K2 1) (K1 2))
Goal: (EVENTUALLY (K16 5))
Reactive Plan:
[ID 0 state ((k15 5) (k14 5) (k9 4) (k8 4) (k7 4) (k6 4) (k5 3) (k4 3)
         (k3 2) (k2 1) (k1 2)) ACTION ((T3) 1)]
[ID 1 state ((k15 5) (k14 5) (k12 7) (k9 4) (k8 4) (k7 4) (k6 4) (k5 3)
         (k4 3) (k3 2) (k2 1) (k1 2)) ACTION ((T2) 2)]
[ID 2 state ((k15 5) (k14 5) (k12 7) (k11 10) (k9 4) (k8 4) (k7 4)
         (k6 4) (k5 3) (k4 3) (k3 2) (k2 1) (k1 2)) ACTION ((T1) 3)]
[ID 3 state ((k15 5) (k14 5) (k12 7) (k11 10) (k10 10) (k9 4) (k8 4)
         (k7 4) (k6 4) (k5 3) (k4 3) (k3 2) (k2 1)
         (k1 2)) ACTION ((T5) 4)]
[ID 4 state ((k17 10) (k16 5) (k15 5) (k14 5) (k12 7) (k11 10) (k10 10)
         (k9 4) (k8 4) (k7 4) (k6 4) (k5 3) (k4 3) (k3 2) (k2 1)
         (k1 2)) ACTION ((T5) 5)]
[ID 5 state ((k17 10) (k16 5) (k15 5) (k14 5) (k12 7) (k11 10) (k10 10)
         (k9 4) (k8 4) (k7 4) (k6 4) (k5 3) (k4 3) (k3 2) (k2 1)
         (k1 2)) ACTION ((w 1) 5)]
```

Fig. 5. SIMPLAN generated plan from ADL of figure 4

Conclusion

We have presented a multi-agent ITS architecture that includes four planning agents. In this architecture, planning agents collaborate in order to make the learning process more adapted to the student. The planning process is supported by SIMPLAN, a recently developed planning system that combines model checking and Markov decision theoretic techniques. Reactive plans produced by SIMPLAN specifies the actions to be executed by an agent depending on the current agent's state and current environment situation (student knowledge, learning goals ...). By considering teaching/learning process in an ITS as a multi-layer planning task, we lead to a uniform view of ITS processes from one layer to another. What change is the semantic of the planning process. Thus communication between ITS component is made more easy due to the homogeneity of the components. Also, generic planning agent view of ITS components make it easy to re-use the same technology in many application domain. This represent a major contribution in component-based ITS which is the current focus of several ITS researches (Ritter, Brusilovski and Medvedeva, 1998; Devedzic, Radovic, and Jerinic, 1998). Our future works will concentrate on the collaboration between planning agents and more experimentation in real word applications.

References

André, E. and Rist, T. Coping with temporal constraints in multimedia presentation planning.In *Proc. of 13th National Conference on Artificial Intelligence*, pp 142-147. AAAI Press, 1996.

Bass, E.J. Towards an Intelligent Tutoring System for Situation Awarwness Training in Complex, Dynamic Environments. In proceedings of the 4th International Conference on ITS., pp..26-35. Springer-Verlag, Berlin, 1998.

Burn and Caps. *Intelligent Tutoring Systems.* Lawrence Erlbaum Ass., Hillsdale, NJ., 1988.

Dean, T., Kaelbling L.P., Kerman, J. and Nicholson, A. Planning under time constraints in stochastic domains. *Artificial Intelligence*, 76(1--2):35-74, 1995. Elsevier.

Devedzic, V., Radovic, D. and Jerinic, L. On the notion of components for intelligent tutoring systems. In: Proceedings of the 4th International Conference on ITS., pp..504-513. Springer-Verlag, Berlin, 1998.

Frasson, C., Mengelle, T., Aïmeur, E. and Gouardères, G. An Actor-Based Architecture for Intelligent Tutoring Systems. In proceedings of the 3rd International Conference on ITS., pp 57-65. Springer-Verlag, Berlin, 1996.

Kabanza, F. SimPlan's Manual. 1999. The manual is part of the system which can be downloade from the site http://www.dmi.usherb.ca/~kabanza/simplan.

Kabanza, F., Barbeau, M. and St-Denis, R. Planning control rules for reactive agents. *Artificial Intelligence*, 5(1):67--113, 1997. Elsevier.

Klausmeier, H.J. Conceptualizing. In: B.F. Jones and L. Idol (Eds). Dimensions of thinking and cognitive instruction, pp. 93-138. NJ:LEA, 1990.

Nkambou, R., Gauthier, G. et Lefebvre, B.. Un modèle d'architecture de STI pour l'enseignement à grande échelle. *Dans Environnement interactif d'apprentissage avec ordinateur*, pp. 236-249. HERMES, Paris, 1997.

Nkambou, R., Frasson, C. and Gauthier, G. "A New approach to course authoring for Intelligent Tutoring System: The authoring environment". Computer in Education: an international journal, Vol. 31, No. 1, pp. 105-130, Elsevier Science, London, 1998.

Ritter, S., Brusilovsky, P. and Medvedeva, O. Creating more versatile intelligent. Learning environments with a component-based architecture. In: Proceedings of the 4th International Conference on ITS., pp. 554-563. Springer-Verlag, Berlin, 1998.

Constraint-Based Tutors: A Success Story

Antonija Mitrovic, Michael Mayo, Pramuditha Suraweera, and Brent Martin

Intelligent Computer Tutoring Group
Department of Computer Science, University of Canterbury
Private Bag 4800, Christchurch, New Zealand
{tanja,mmayo,psu16,brent}@cosc.canterbury.ac.nz

Abstract. Student modeling (SM) is recognized as one of the central problems in the area of Intelligent Tutoring Systems. Numerous SM approaches have been proposed and used with more or less success. Constraint-based modeling is a new approach, which has been used successfully in three tutors developed in our group. The approach is extremely efficient, and it overcomes many problems that other student modelling approaches suffer from. We present the advantages of CBM over other similar approaches, describe three constraint-based tutors and present our future research plans.

1 Introduction

It is well known that one-on-one human tutoring is much more effective than traditional classroom instruction, providing an increase of two standard deviations in learning performance [4]. The goal of the research in the area of Intelligent Tutoring Systems (ITS) is to build computer-based tutors that achieve the effects of learning individually with a human tutor. It is a very ambitious goal, and currently available systems are not near achieving it, although there are ITSs that provide an increase of one standard deviation over a longer time period [3].

Student modeling is widely accepted as one of the central problems in ITSs. If a system is to be effective, it must reason about student's knowledge and adapt its actions to the needs and abilities of each individual student. Many SM approaches have been suggested over the years. Some of them are suited to a particular domain, or a teaching strategy. The research presented here focuses on effective and computationally tractable student modeling. We adopted Constraint-Based Modeling, a student modeling approach recently proposed by Ohlsson [15], and have had extremely good experiences with it. We have developed three constraint-based tutors. Our focus is on student models; they should be precise enough to guide instruction, and computationally tractable at the same time. In the next section we present CBM briefly, and then turn to the three implemented systems in the following section. The final section presents conclusions and directions for future work.

L. Monostori, J. Váncza, and M. Ali (Eds.): IEA/AIE 2001, LNAI 2070, pp. 931-940, 2001.

2 Constraint-Based Modeling

Student modeling can be defined as the process of gathering relevant information in order to identify the knowledge state of a student. In an ideal case, the model of a student should illustrate his/her knowledge, preferred learning strategies, areas of interest besides that of instruction, preferred presentation style, and so on. Several techniques for student modeling have been developed for particular domains, the generality of which is yet to be determined. The survey of SM approaches is outside the scope of such a paper and the interested reader is referred to [7].

The task of building a student model is extremely difficult and laborious, due to huge search spaces involved. Several researchers have pointed to the inherent intractability of the task [8, 15, 16]. Self [16, 17] recommends such design of the interactions that information necessary for building a student model is provided by the student, and not inferred by the system. If the goal is to model student's knowledge completely and precisely, student modeling is bound to be intractable. However, a student model can be useful even if it is not complete and accurate [15, 17, 18]. Even simple and constrained modeling is sufficient for instruction purposes, and this claim is supported by findings that human teachers also use very loose models of their learners, and yet are highly effective in what they do [8, 17]. Anderson [2] also points out that informative error messages are much more beneficial to students than being told about the sources of their misconceptions

One of the SM approaches that focus on reducing the complexity of the task is Constraint-Based Modeling (CBM) [15]. CBM is based on Ohlsson's theory of learning from performance errors [14]. CBM focuses on faulty knowledge, realizing that it is not sufficient to describe what the student knows correctly. The basic assumption is that diagnostic information is not hidden in the sequence of student's actions, but in the problem state the student arrived at. This assumption is supported by the fact that there can be no correct solution of a problem that traverses a problem state, which violates fundamental ideas, or concepts of the domain.

Because the space of false knowledge is vast, much more so than the space of correct knowledge, Ohlsson suggest the use of an abstraction mechanism realized in the form of state constraints. A state constraint is an ordered pair (C_r, C_s), where C_r is the relevance condition and C_s is the satisfaction condition. C_r is used to identify the equivalence class, or the class of problem states in which C_r is relevant. C_s identifies the class of relevant states in which C_s is satisfied. Each constraint specifies the property of the domain that is shared by all correct paths. In other words, if C_r is satisfied in a problem state, in order for that problem state to be a correct one, it must also satisfy C_s. Conditions may be any kinds of logical formulas, hence may be constructed from various tests on the problem state in question.

In such a way, CBM represents domain knowledge as a set of state constraints. Constraints define sets of equivalent problem states. An equivalence class triggers the same instructional action; hence the states in an equivalence class are pedagogically equivalent. All correct problem solutions do not violate any of the constraints. A violated constraint signals the error, caused by incomplete and incorrect knowledge.

CBM does not require a runnable expert module, as many other SM approaches do. This is a very important advantage of CBM, because in many domains it can be very difficult to build the problem solver. CBM-based computerized tutors are able to generate instructional actions even without being able to solve problems on their own, by focusing on violated constraints. Of course, CBM does not prevent an ITS from having a domain module. On the contrary, the existence of a domain module can be very beneficial to the student, as it can provide the answer to student's questions such as ''What do I do next?". However, the constraint set, if appropriately represented, might also form the knowledge base of a runnable domain module, because it contains rich information about the domain. We have developed a constraint representation for this purpose, and are currently evaluating its potential [9].

Another advantage of CBM is its computational simplicity. Instead of using complex reasoning required by other diagnostic approaches, CBM reduces student modeling to pattern matching. Conditions are combinations of patterns, and can therefore be represented in compiled forms, su as RETE networks [6]. In the first step all relevance patterns are matched against the problem state. In the second step, the satisfaction components of relevant constraints are matched. If a satisfaction pattern matches the state, then the constraint is satisfied. In the opposite case, the constraint is violated. The student model consists of all violated constraints. This technique can be used for both on- and off-line student modeling.

Furthermore, CBM does not require extensive studies of student bugs as in enumerative modeling [1]. Another deficiency of many SM approaches that CBM is not sensitive to is the *radical strategy variability phenomenon*. Namely, some approaches assume that a student systematically uses a single procedure for the task at hand. However, Ohlsson shows [15] that each student knows several procedures at the same time and that he or she can switch between them on different problems. CBM allows students to be inconsistent; it ignores the particular strategy the student applied, since different strategies may result in the same constraint broken.

3 SQL-Tutor

SQL-Tutor is an intelligent educational system, which helps university-level students to learn SQL. The architecture of the stand-alone version of the system is illustrated in Figure 1. For a detailed discussion of the system, see [10, 11, 12, 13]; here we present only some of its features. SQL-Tutor consists of an interface, a pedagogical module, which determines the timing and content of pedagogical actions, and a student modeller (CBM), which analyzes student answers. The system contains definitions of several databases, and a set of problems and the ideal solutions to them. SQL-Tutor contains no domain module. In order to check the correctness of the student's solution, SQL-Tutor compares it to the correct solution, using domain knowledge represented in the form of more than 500 constraints.

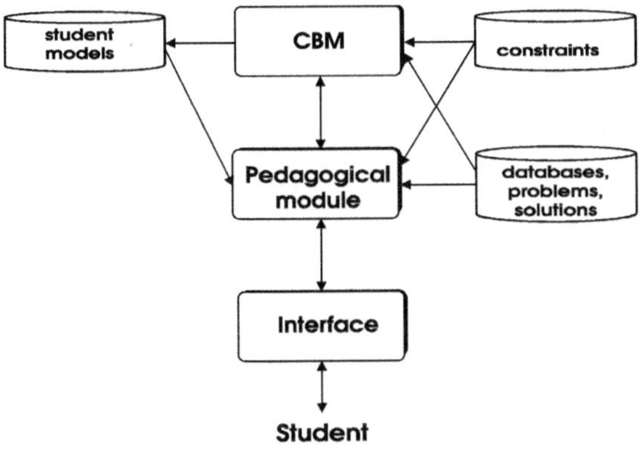

Fig. 1. Architecture of SQL-Tutor

At the beginning of a session, SQL-Tutor selects a problem for the student to work on. When the student submits a solution, the pedagogical module sends it to the student modeller, which analyzes the solution, identifies mistakes (if there are any) and updates the student model appropriately. On the basis of the student model, the pedagogical module generates an appropriate pedagogical action (i.e. feedback). When the current problem is solved, or the student requires a new problem to work on, the pedagogical module selects an appropriate problem on the basis of the student model.

The interface of the Web-enabled version of SQLT-Tutor [11], illustrated in Figure 2, has been designed to be robust, flexible, and easy to use. It reduces the memory load by displaying the database schema and the text of a problem, by providing the basic structure of the query, and also by providing explanations of the elements of SQL. The main page is divided into three areas. The upper part displays the text of the problem being solved and students can remind themselves easily of the elements requested in queries. The middle part contains the clauses of the SQL SELECT statement, thus visualizing the goal structure. Students need not remember the exact keywords used and the relative order of clauses. The lowest part displays the schema of the currently chosen database. Schema visualization is very important; all database users are painfully aware of the constant need to remember table and attribute names and the corresponding semantics as well. Students can get the descriptions of databases, tables or attributes, as well as the descriptions of SQL constructs. The motivation here is to remove from the student some of the cognitive load required for checking the low-level syntax, and to enable the student to focus on

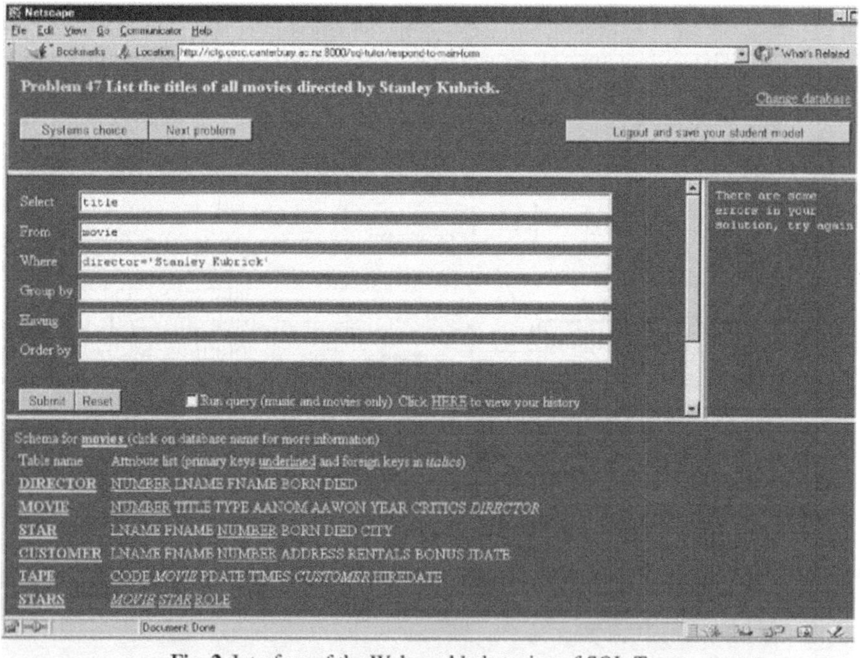

Fig. 2. Interface of the Web-enabled version of SQL-Tutor

higher-level, query definition problems. We have also implemented an animated pedagogical agent, which had a very positive motivational effect on the students [13].

Students have several ways of selecting problems in SQL-Tutor. They may work their way through a series of problems for each database, ordered by their complexity, by clicking on the *Next Problem* button. The other option is a system-selected problem (the *System's choice* button), when the system selects an appropriate problem for the student on the basis of his/her student model. We have also implemented a problem-selection strategy based on Bayesian networks [10].

SQL-Tutor was evaluated in four evaluation studies during 1998-2000, which proved that students who learnt with the system achieved significantly higher results than those who did not use the system. An improvement of nearly one standard deviation was achieved after a single, two-hour long session [12]. All the studies showed that CBM has sound psychological foundations and that students acquire constraints at a high rate [12].

4 CAPIT: A Punctuation Tutor

CAPIT (Capitalisation And Punctuation Intelligent Tutor) is a constraint-based tutor designed for, and evaluated with, school children in the 10-11 year old age group. The system teaches a subset of the basic rules of English capitalisation and punctuation, and currently contains 46 problems and 25 constraints. The problems are relevant to the constraints in roughly equal proportions, although a small number of constraints (such as capitalisation of sentences) are relevant to all the problems. The constraints cover the following parts of the domain: capitalisation of sentences and the names of both people and places, ending sentences with periods, contracting *is* and *not* using apostrophes, denoting ownership using apostrophes, separating clauses using commas, separating list items using commas, denoting direct speech with quotation marks and the correct punctuation of the possessive pronoun *its*.

In CAPIT the student must punctuate and capitalise a fully lowercase, unpunctuated piece of text. If the child makes a mistake, an error message is displayed. For example, Figure 3(a) depicts one of the shorter problems in the ITS. Figure 3(b) shows an incorrect solution submitted by a student, with two errors: the direct speech does not start with a capital letter, and the period is outside the quotation marks. The system displays only one error message at a time, and the student is expected to correct the error and resubmit the problem before any more feedback is displayed. A feedback message would be displayed if the student submitted this solution. Error messages are typically short and relate to only a single mistake, but more detailed information is available on request.

(a) the teacher said open your books
(b) The teacher said, "open your books".
(c) The teacher said, "Open your books."

Fig. 3. (a). A problem, (b). a student's incorrect solution, and (c). the correct solution.

The user interface was designed with the target age group of 10-11 year olds in mind. Before starting the exercises, a short tutorial is given to all new users of the system. A child can review the tutorial at any time by clicking the help button. The main interface is then displayed, as depicted in Figure 4. Brief instructions relevant to the current problem are clearly displayed at the top of the main interface. This reduces the cognitive load by enabling the child to focus on the current goals without needing to remember them. Immediately below the instructions is the current problem. In this area, the child interacts with the system by moving the cursor, capitalising letters, and inserting punctuation marks.

Motivation is provided in two forms. Firstly, children accrue points every time they submit a correct solution. Secondly, when a correct solution is submitted, a simple animation is displayed as a reward. We have found this to be adequate motivation for 10-11 year olds.

The architecture of CAPIT comprises databases of constraints, problems and student models, the user interface, the student modeller, and the pedagogical module. When the student submits a solution, it is passed to the student modeller. The student modeller determines firstly which constraints are relevant to the current solution, and secondly, which constraints are satisfied. The violated constraints are then passed to the pedagogical module so that an error message can be selected.

The pedagogical module solves two key decision tasks: it selects the next problem when the child clicks *Pick Another Problem*, and it selects a single error message for display when the child submits an incorrect solution. A probabilistic student model is used for these decisions. Initially, a student model is set to a population student model, which is later individualized after each student's action. The system uses Bayesian networks and decision theory to decide what problem or feedback to give to the student.

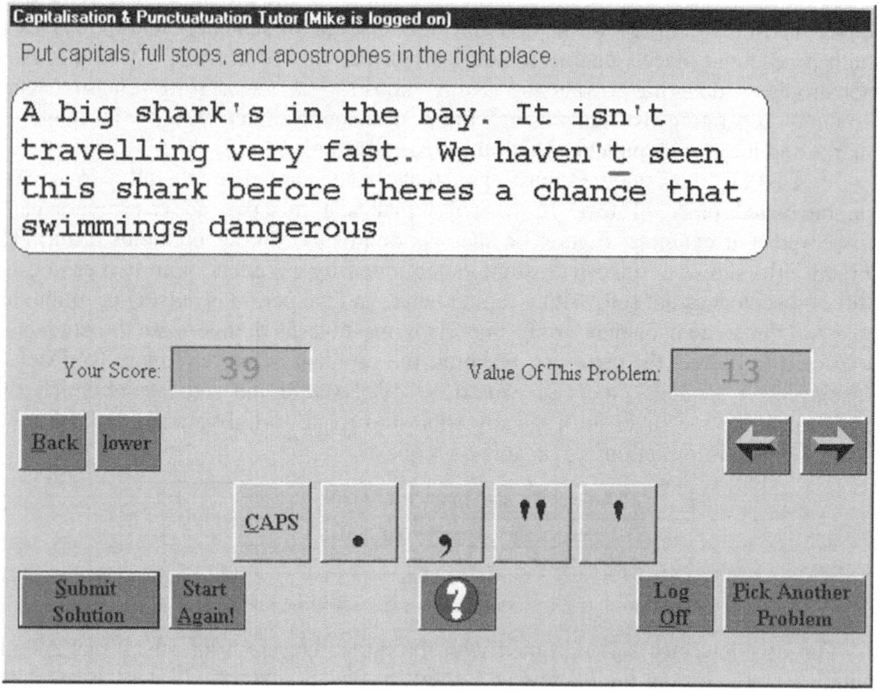

Fig. 4. The tutor's main user interface

CAPIT was evaluated with three classes of 9-10 year olds at an elementary school in Christchurch, New Zealand, over four-weeks. The first class (Group A) did not use CAPIT. The second class (Group B) used the version of the tutor with randomised problem and error message selection, and the third class (Group C) used the full version of the tutor with the adaptive Bayesian student model. Groups B and C had one 45-minute session per week. Every student attempt and tutor decision was logged. All groups were administered the same pre- and post-tests. No statistically significant differences were found between the results of the pre-test for the three groups, indicating that the groups were all of comparable ability to start with.

The pre- and post-tests were comparable and consisted of eight exercises similar to those presented by CAPIT. The mean scores and standard deviations are shown in Table 1. Group A, the class that did not use the tutor, regressed. Groups B and C improved significantly (one-tailed paired difference for group B, $\alpha = 0.05$, $t = 1.86$; for group C, $\alpha = 0.01$, $t = 3.4$). The improvement is thus much more significant for Group C, which used the full version of the tutor.

Table 1. Mean pre- and post-test scores.

Group	Pre-test (%)	Post-test (%)
A	54.5	47.8
B	58.1	62.7
C	51.0	61.3

Figure 5 shows how the students learned the constraints. We looked at the proportion of violated constraints following the *n*th attempt, averaged across all students and all constraints. Just over half of the students were still using the tutor by the 55th attempt, so the data analysis was concluded at this point. Very similar behaviour was observed in SQL-Tutor [12]. Such a smooth learning curve is a proof of psychologically good foundations of CBM.

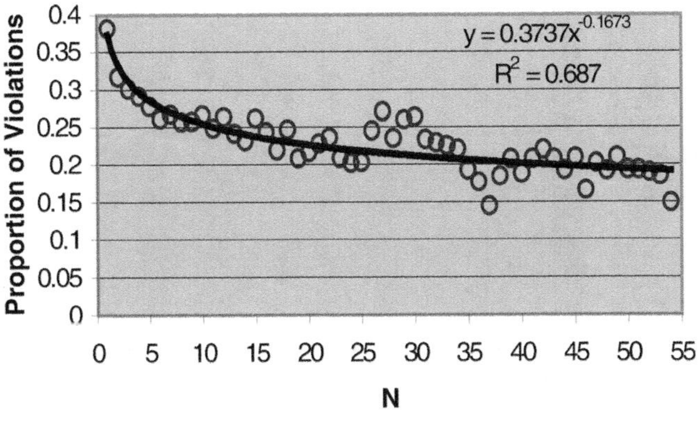

Fig. 5. Mean proportion of constraints that were violated on *n*th attempt.

5 KERMIT: An ITS for Database Design

Database (DB) modelling is a complicated task, which requires significant amounts of practice to achieve expertise. DB modelling is traditionally taught in a classroom environment where concepts and solutions to typical databases are explained. Our experiences point to the need of providing students with individualized feedback, as students' solutions differ enormously between each other. We have developed KERMIT, an ITS for ER modelling, a popular high-level conceptual data model.

KERMIT is implemented in Microsoft Visual Basic, and supports the entity relationship data model as defined in [5]. The workspace of KERMIT is implemented

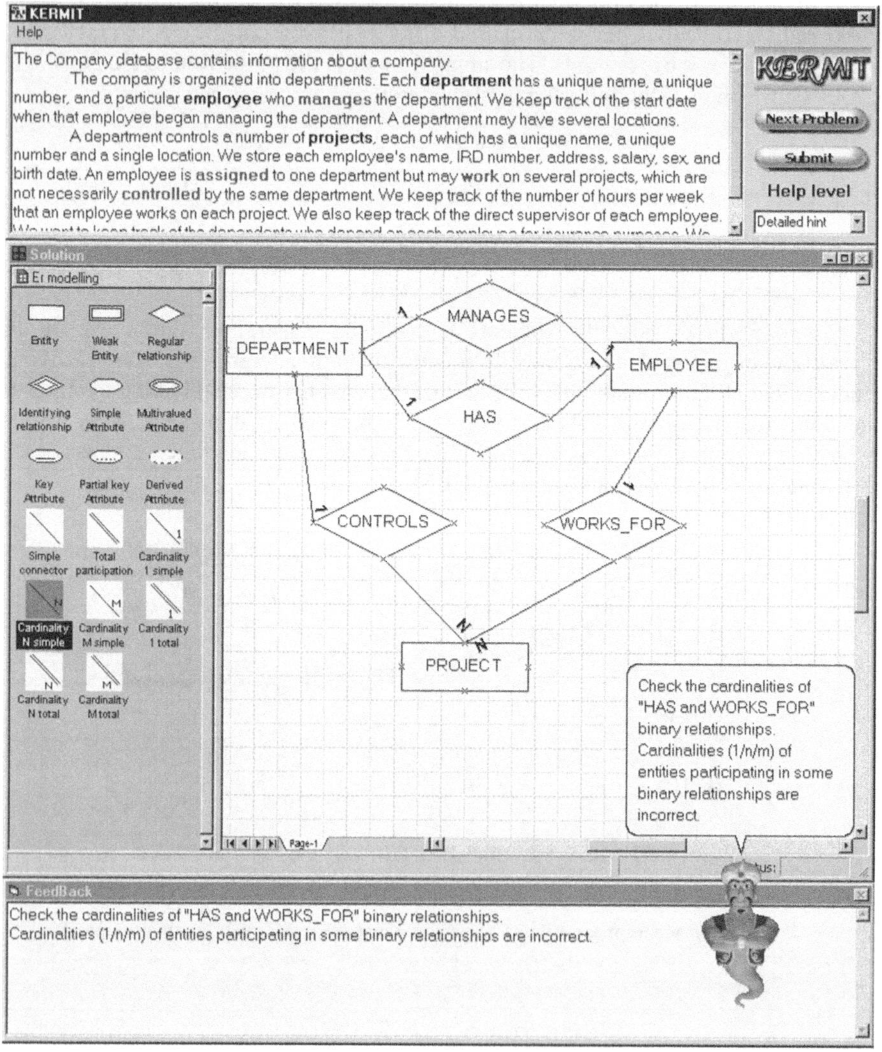

Fig. 6. User interface of KERMIT

using Microsoft Visio. KERMIT consists of a user interface, a student modeller and a pedagogical module. The interface of KERMIT, illustrated in Figure 6, consists of three separate windows. The top window is used to display the problem to the student. It also has a drop down list for students to choose their desired level of feedback. The middle window is the workspace, containing a stencil developed for ER modelling,. Students can drag and drop constructs onto their workspace to construct their ER model. The feedback window displays textual pedagogical messages, whereas the animated agent communicates them verbally.

When the student has composed their solution to the given problem, the student modeller evaluates it, and after that the PM would generate appropriate feedback depending on the errors. When the current problem is solved the PM selects the next problem that best suits the student model.

The feedback is grouped into six levels in an increasing amount of information: "Correct", "Error flag", "Hint", "Detailed hint", "All errors" and "Solution". The first level of feedback simply indicates whether the submitted solution is correct or not. The "Error flag" indicates the type of construct (e.g. entity, relationship, etc.) that is incorrect. "Hint" and "detailed hint" offer instructions on the most important error. "Hint" is a general message, whereas "detailed hint" provides a more specific message. Feedback on all violated constraints is displayed at the "all errors" level. The complete solution is presented as an image in the final level.

At the current stage, KERMIT's constraint base consists of 90 constraints. These deal with both syntactic and semantic errors. The syntactic constraints vary from simple constraints such as "an entity name should be in upper case", to more complex constraints such as "the weak entity participating in an identifying relationship should have a total participation". The syntactic constraints only concentrate on the student's solution and are independent of the ideal solution. The semantic constraints compare the student's solution to the system's solution. "The student's solution should consist of all the entities present in the ideal solution" is an example of a semantic constraint. The evaluation of KERMIT is planned for early 2001.

6 Conclusions

This paper presented three intelligent tutoring systems that implement Constraint–based Modeling. CBM is a promising new student modeling approach that resolves many of the difficulties present in other diagnostic approaches. It does not require a runnable expert module, which may be difficult or even impossible to develop for some domains. Furthermore, CBM does not require extensive studies of typical errors made by students (i.e. bug libraries), and it does not require complex reasoning about possible origins of student errors. CBM is also advantageous over probabilistic methods, such as Bayes networks, which require estimates of prior probabilities. All that CBM requires is a description of the basic principles and concepts in a domain. From our experiences, CBM is extremely effective and efficient. It may be used in various kinds of domain, such as highly structured procedural tasks and open-ended tasks. CBM does not dictate any pedagogical approach, it equally well supports online and off-line learning, immediate and delayed feedback.

We presented three constraint-based tutors: a system that teaches the SQL database language, a system that teaches punctuation and capitalization rules, and a system for database design. The domains for which these systems are developed are very different, and range from a fairly small set of punctuation rules, which are almost always deterministic, to an open task such as database modeling. SQL-Tutor and CAPIT were evaluated in real classrooms, and the results show students learn better with these systems. Furthermore, the analysis of how constraints are learned shows that CBM has a sound psychological foundation.

Current work at ICTG includes enhancements of the presented systems and the development of new constraint-based tutors. We have started developing a generic language tutor. Language learning is a task of very different nature to those we have developed tutors for so far. We have also started work on an authoring system based on CBM, which will make the development of new tutors much easier.

Acknowledgements. The work presented here was supported by the University of Canterbury research grants U6242 and U6430.

References

1. Anderson, J.R., Jeffries, R.: Novice LISP Errors: Undetected Losses of Information from Working Memory. *Human--Computer Interaction.* 22, 403-423, 1985.
2. Anderson, J.R.: *Rules of the Mind.* Hillsdale, NJ: Lawrence Erlbaum Associates, 1993.
3. Anderson, J.R, Corbett, A.T., Koedinger, K.R., Pelletier, R.: Cognitive Tutors: Lessons Learned. *The Journal of the Learning Sciences*, 4(2), 167-207, 1995.
4. Bloom, B.: The 2 sigma problem: The search for methods of group instruction as effective as one-to-one tutoring. *Educational Researcher*, 13, 3-16, 1984.
5. Elmasri, R., Navathe, S.: *Fundamentals of Database Systems.* Addison Wesley, 1994.
6. Forgy, C.L.: Rete: a fast algorithm for the many pattern/many object pattern match problem. *Artificial Intelligence*, 19, 17-37, 1982.
7. Greer, J.E., McCalla, G.I. (eds.): *Student Modeling: the Key to Individualized Knowledge--based Instruction.* Berlin: Springer-Verlag, NATO ASI Series, 1994.
8. Holt, P., Dubs, S., Jones, M., Greer, J.E.: 1994, 'The State of Student Modelling. In: J.E. Greer and G.I. McCalla (eds.): *Student Modeling: the Key to Individualized Knowledge--based Instruction.* Berlin: Springer-Verlag, NATO ASI Series, 3-35, 1994.
9. Martin, B., Mitrovic, A. *Tailoring Feedback by Correcting Student Answers.* Proc. ITS'2000, G. Gauthier, C. Frasson and K. VanLehn (eds), Springer, pp. 383-392, 2000.
10. Mayo, M., Mitrovic, A.: Using a Probabilistic Student Model to Control Problem Difficulty. In: Gauthier G., Frasson C., and VanLehn K. (eds): *Proc. 5th Int. Conf. ITS'2000*, Springer-Verlag, 524-533, 2000.
11. Mitrovic, A., Hausler, K.: Porting SQL-Tutor to the Web. Proc. ITS'2000 workshop on *Adaptive and Intelligent Web-based Education Systems*, 37-44, 2000.
12. Mitrovic, A., Ohlsson, S.: Evaluation of a Constraint-based Tutor for a Database Language. *Int. J. on Artificial Intelligence in Education*, 10(3-4), 238-256, 1999.
13. Mitrovic, A., Suraweera, P.: An Animated Pedagogical Agent. In: Gauthier G., Frasson C., and VanLehn K. (eds): *Proc. 5th Int. Conf. ITS'2000*, Springer-Verlag, (2000) 73-82.
14. Ohlsson, S: Learning from Performance Errors. *Psychological Review.* 103 (2), 241—262, 1996.
15. Ohlsson, S.: Constraint-based student modeling. In: Greer, J.E., McCalla, G (eds): *Student modeling: the key to individualized knowledge-based instruction*, 167-189, 1994.
16. Self, J. A.: Bypassing the intractable problem of student modeling. In: C. Frasson and G. Gauthier (eds.), *Intelligent Tutoring Systems: at the Crossroads of Artificial Intelligence and Education.* Norwood: Ablex, 107-12 3, 1990.

Applying Collision Avoidance Expert System to Navigation Training Systems as an Intelligent Tutor

Chunsheng Yang[1], Sieu Phan[1], Pikuei Kuo[2], and Fuhua Oscar Lin[3]

[1] National Research Council, Ottawa, ON, Canada
{Chunsheng.Yang, Sieu.Phan}@iit.nrc.ca
[2] National Taiwan Ocean University, Keelung, Taiwan, Republic of China
pkkuo@mail.ntou.edu.tw
[3] Athabasca University, Athabasca AB, Canada
oscarl@athabascau.ca

Abstract. To enhance the skills of captains and improve the existing training technologies, it is very important and urgent to research and develop an intelligent navigation training system. Therefore we propose to incorporate a collision avoidance expert system into real-time ship handling simulator to provide intelligent decision-making support for navigation training. The intelligent tutor aims to assist the trainee to master necessary skills for handling ship in complex navigating environments such as open sea, restricted waterway, and rough sea conditions by sharing multiple captains' experience. In this paper, the developed collision avoidance expert system will be outlined, then the proposed intelligent decision-making support for navigation training will be presented in details.

1 Introduction

The recent huge maritime casualties and their environmental impacts, especially the stranding of EXXON tanker in Alaska, showed that human error in ship navigation is one of the primary causes leading to accidents. In order to reduce maritime accidents and human errors in ship navigation, it is very important and urgent to improve the skills of navigators and develop advanced navigation support system for ship operations. A considerable amount of effort has been paid to the development of advanced navigation support systems. For example, an integrated navigation system (INS)[4] which is considered as a next generation navigation system was developed at Hiroshima University in Japan. This INS incorporates the developed Collision Avoidance Expert System (CAES) [2][3] as an intelligent decision-making support function to assist the operator to avoid collision during ship navigation. T. Tran et al [1] proposed to use a collision avoidance system to improve the efficiency and safety of marine transport, namely Marine Avoidance Navigation, Totally Integrated System (MANTIS). Furthermore, the most recent Canada's newest hi-tech ships collision incidents warn us that only making hi-tech ships alone is not sufficient for improving ship navigation safety. It is important for the captains be adequately trained to handle the hi-tech ships in different complicated waterways. At present, much effort is focusing on developing 3-D visualized ship-handling simulators, which can simulate real-time navigating environments and ship handling scenarios. In such an environment the navigators could have the real feeling and learn how to

L. Monostori, J. Váncza, and M. Ali (Eds.): IEA/AIE 2001, LNAI 2070, pp. 941-947, 2001.

operate ships. There have been a lot of achievements using ship-handling simulators to train seafarers and to investigate the navigation safety [5][6][7]. Although existing ship-handling simulators can be a useful means for training navigators, it does not provide decision-making support to trainees nor advise the trainee how to handle a ship in complicated situations. It remains that training is carried out under the instructions of a trainer. Trainees operate the ship following the trainer's instructions. To alleviate these shortcomings, we proposed to incorporate collision avoidance expert system into existing ship-handling simulator as an intelligent decision-making support system for navigation training, particularly for collision avoidance, in order to effectively train the navigators and improve their skills. In this paper, the developed collision avoidance expert system is first outlined in Section 2; then the proposed intelligent decision-making support for navigation training will be presented in Section3. Conclusions and future work are given in the last section.

2 Collision Avoidance Expert System

Collision Avoidance Expert System [2] was developed to assist ship navigators in their decision-making process to avoid collision. It is a rule-based knowledge base system. It was designed based on hierarchical architecture and modularized knowledge structure as shown in Figure 1. The top layer in the system is the inference control, which is responsible for the control of the inference procedure. The second layer is the main knowledge bases, which include the classification of target ships, the prediction of target ships' action, the identification of the method of collision avoidance, and the establishment of course-line way-points. The third layer contains knowledge modules of every knowledge base. The fourth layer includes the preliminary knowledge modules such as traffic regulation, identification of target ships, and so on. The system consists of the following main inference sequences:

(1) Prediction of target ship's scheduled action

First, the system uses a knowledge base to classify the navigation environment into one of three categories: open sea, coastal, or route navigation. The prediction of the target ship's scheduled action depends on this classification. In the case of open sea or coastal navigation the target will maintain its current course and speed, and in the case of the route navigation, it will follow the navigating route.

(2) Classification of target ships

After the computation of collision risk of target ships, the target ships are classified as the most dangerous, the dangerous, the restricting, or the indifferent ship depending on their risk of collision. A dangerous ship is defined as a ship having risk of collision that exceeds the safe level when both ships maintain their scheduled course lines. In the case of several dangerous ships, the most dangerous ship has the highest risk among dangerous ships. A restricting ship is defined as a ship that will cause no danger if own ship and target ship maintain their scheduled course lines, but it will frustrate the action of own ship if it takes the collision avoidance action for a dangerous ship. The target ship that lies outside the maneuvering space of the own ship is defined as the indifferent ship.

(3) Prediction of target ship's collision avoidance action according to the classification of the ship

For the dangerous ships and restricting ships, their collision avoidance actions are predicted by using the same approach and knowledge base as that of the own ship. The predicted actions of collision avoidance of target ships will be incorporated into the procedure when own ship's action of collision avoidance is formulated.

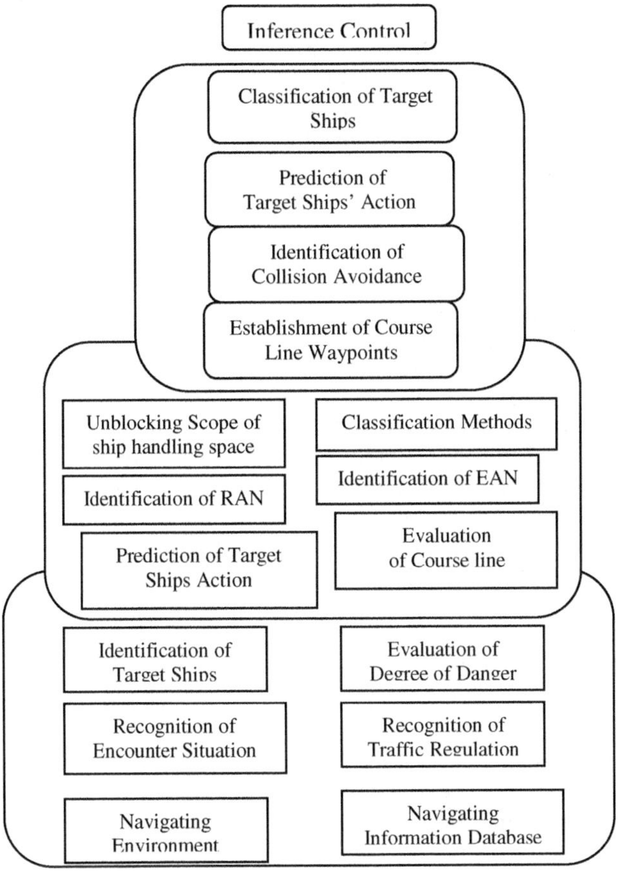

Fig. 1. The Architecture of the Collision Avoidance Exert System

(4) Establishment of the course line way-point as collision avoidance action

The action of collision avoidance of own ship is formulated basically against the most dangerous ship. The action in the own ship maneuvering space is evaluated considering the prediction of the action of the dangerous ships and the restricting ships. As a result, the most efficient and feasible action is selected.

3 Intelligent Decision-Making Support for Navigation Training

3.1 Weakness of Existing Navigation Training Systems

Existing navigation training systems such as ship-handling simulator are used to help the trainees to master basic navigation skills and traffic regulations before they go to practice on broad. The training is carried by providing realistic navigation environment and ship encounter situations under the instruction of experienced navigator. However, existing training systems do not provide automatic decision-making support for handling complex encounter situations. The trainee can't share the multiple captains' navigation experiences for handling ship in complicated situations, and the decision for collision avoidance is still made by instructor or trainee.

To overcome such shortcomings, we apply the developed collision avoidance expert system to existing navigation training systems, ship-handling simulator, to provide intelligent decision-making support for collision avoidance as an intelligent tutor. Such decision-making support is capable of automatically solving the problems in ship navigation for different encountered situations and complicated waterways. It is able to instruct the trainees how to take a collision avoidance action, and how to handle ship to execute the recommended actions for collision avoidance. It also shows the trainees the supporting information such as the application of traffic regulations, the encounter situation, the risk level of own ship or other ships. Such supporting information that will explain the current situation can assist trainees to understand collision regulations and marine safety regulations, and help trainees to master the basic navigation skills. It will make it possible for trainees to easily learn different captains' experience obtained in their navigation career.

3.2 Intelligent Decision-Making Support for Navigation Training

With the developed collision avoidance expert system, the navigation training systems could provide effective decision-making support information and recommend a proper action for collision avoidance. The decision-making support information includes target ship classification, encounter situation on the scheduled course line, the risk distribution around scheduled course line, and so on.

(1) Target ship classification

Each target ship is classified into dangerous ship, restricting ship and indifferent ship in terms of its risk to own ship. The dangerous ship is one that potentially causes the collision if both ships maintain their current speed and course; the restricting ship is one that prevents own ship from performing action for collision avoidance; and the indifferent one has no threat whatever alteration of course own ship makes.

(2) Encounter situation on the scheduled course line

This support information indicates the encounter type between dangerous or restricting ship and own ship, e.g., own ship overtaking, and so on. Using such supporting information, the trainee may easily classify the encounter relation between two ships at instant looking at the CRT.

(3) Risk distribution around the scheduled course line

This support information is aiming at helping trainee to analyze the risk situation around scheduled course line. In the real navigation, the ship has destination and scheduled plan. The captain hopes to keep the ship following the scheduled plan and not deviating so far from it. Figure 2 shows such support information.

(4) Recommendation of collision avoidance action

Using the above support information is useful for trainee to master and analyze the risk situation around scheduled course line. However, the final action for collision avoidance needs to be decided by trainee or instructor. It is desirable for the training system to be able to recommend a proper maneuvering action for collision avoidance in order to instruct the trainee how to determine the effective action in case of potential collision. Using CAES, it is possible for training system to recommend a proper action for collision avoidance to trainee. Figure 3 shows an example of the recommended collision avoidance route and risk distribution around the scheduled course line. The risk distribution information helps to explain the reason of the recommended collision avoidance action.

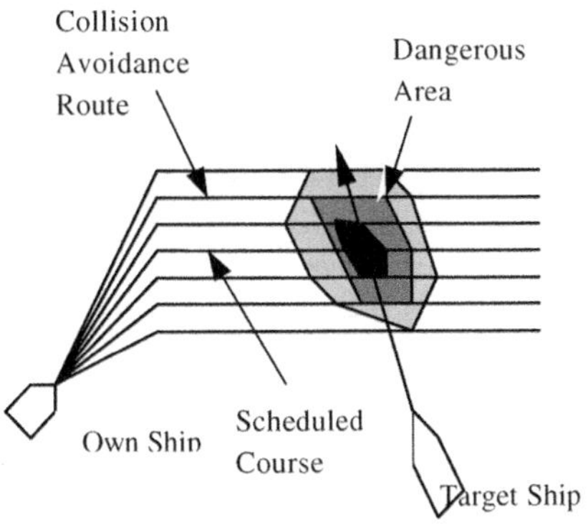

Fig. 2. Risk Distribution around Planed Route

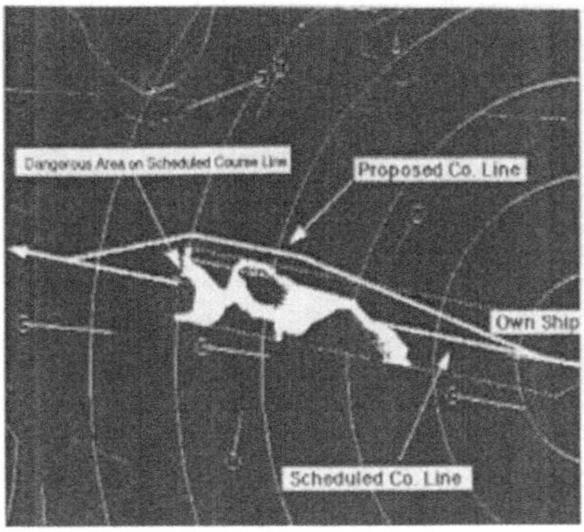

Fig. 3. Example of Recommended Course Line

3.3 Intelligent Navigation Training System Archtecture

The system architecture is designed based on a multi-tired distributed system. As shown in Figure 4, the system consists of three tires: decision-making support graphic user interface and information display layer, knowledge-based system for collision avoidance layer, and ship-handling simulator layer. The software components in different layer are connected with TCP/IP network. The graphic user interface provides all interactive operation for trainee to get the necessary information. The knowledge-based system for collision avoidance is the core of CAES, which provides all decision-making procedure and monitors current own ship status in terms of navigation environment and encounter situations. Ship-handling simulator is used to provide realistic navigation environment and ship-handling scenario. It provides the necessary realistic navigating date for CAES to make decision.

4 Future Work and Conclusions

In this paper, the authors proposed to incorporate a collision avoidance expert system into a real-time ship-handling simulator in order to provide intelligent decision-making support for navigation training, as an intelligent tutor. Using the developed CAES and ship-handling simulator, we implement the proposed intelligent navigation tutoring system. From the training operation, it can be pointed that CAES is effective to provide the necessary decision-making support to help trainee to master navigation skills and learn how to handle ship in complex encounter situation. According to authors' experience, it is necessary for navigation training system to be able to provide information of underwater environment. To this end, we are investigating the application of marine geographical information system (MGIS) to the navigation training system. Therefore the future work is to apply MGIS to the navigation training system and provide the underwater information in order to instruct the trainee how to handle more complex navigation situation. Another important task for future work is to provide safety-evaluation function for on-line evaluation of ship-handling action.

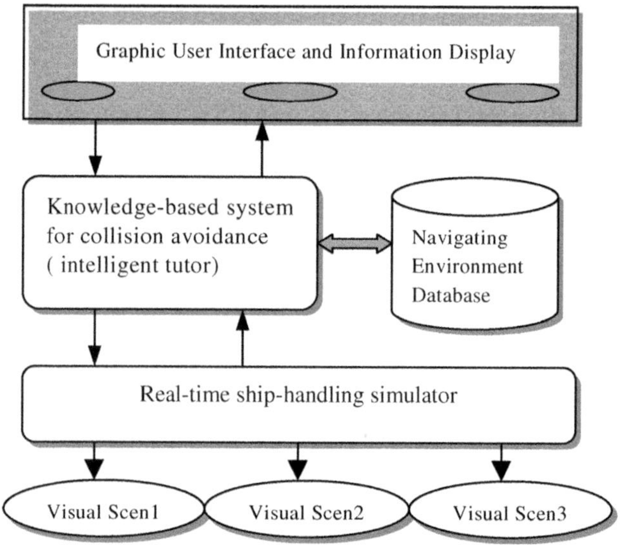

Fig. 4. Architecture of Navigation Training System

References

1. T. Tran, C. J. Harris, and P. A. Wilson, *Maritime Avoidance Navihation, Totally integrated System (MANTIS)*, Proceedings of IEA/AIE 13th International Conference, New Orleans, June, 2000
2. K. Kose and C. Yang, *A Collision Avoidance Expert System for Integrated Navigation System and Its Brush-up*, Journal of the Society of Naval architects of Japan. Vol. 177, 1995

3. C. Yang, *An Expert System for Collision Avoidance and Its Application,* Ph.D. Thesis, 1995
4. K. Kose, Y. Ishioka, and C. Yang, *A study on a Collision Avoidance Expert System for Decision-making Support in Integrated Navigation System,* Journal of The Society of Naval Architects of Japan. Vol.178, 1996
5. K. Kose, *On an Intellegent Harbor Maneuvering Simulator and Its Application*, MARSIM & ICSM 90, 1990
6. The bussiness profile, *The Center for Marine Simulation*, edited by Marine Institute of Memorial University of Newfoundland, 1999
7. *System Description Manual ---Shiphandling Simulator System*, SHIP ANALYTICS INC. USA, 98-U-150, June 2000.

Author Index

Lecture Notes in Artificial Intelligence (LNAI)

Vol. 1861: J. Lloyd, V. Dahl, U. Furbach, M. Kerber, K.-K. Lau, C. Palamidessi, L. Moniz Pereira, Y. Sagiv, P.J. Stuckey (Eds.), Computational Logic – CL 2000. Proceedings, 2000. XIX, 1379 pages.

Vol. 1864: B. Y. Choueiry, T. Walsh (Eds.), Abstraction, Reformulation, and Approximation. Proceedings, 2000. XI, 333 pages. 2000.

Vol. 1865: K.R. Apt, A.C. Kakas, E. Monfroy, F. Rossi (Eds.), New Trends Constraints. Proceedings, 1999. X, 339 pages. 2000.

Vol. 1866: J. Cussens, A. Frisch (Eds.), Inductive Logic Programming. Proceedings, 2000. X, 265 pages. 2000.

Vol. 1867: B. Ganter, G.W. Mineau (Eds.), Conceptual Structures: Logical, Linguistic, and Computational Issues. Proceedings, 2000. XI, 569 pages. 2000.

Vol. 1881: C. Zhang, V.-W. Soo (Eds.), Design and Applications of Intelligent Agents. Proceedings, 2000. X, 183 pages. 2000.

Vol. 1886: R. Mizoguchi, J. Slaney (Eds.), PRICAI 2000: Topics in Artificial Intelligence. Proceedings, 2000. XX, 835 pages. 2000.

Vol. 1898: E. Blanzieri, L. Portinale (Eds.), Advances in Case-Based Reasoning. Proceedings, 2000. XII, 530 pages. 2000.

Vol. 1889: M. Anderson, P. Cheng, V. Haarslev (Eds.), Theory and Application of Diagrams. Proceedings, 2000. XII, 504 pages. 2000.

Vol. 1891: A.L. Oliveira (Ed.), Grammatical Inference: Algorithms and Applications. Proceedings, 2000. VIII, 313 pages. 2000.

Vol. 1902: P. Sojka, I. Kopeček, K. Pala (Eds.), Text, Speech and Dialogue. Proceedings, 2000. XIII, 463 pages. 2000.

Vol. 1904: S.A. Cerri, D. Dochev (Eds.), Artificial Intelligence: Methodology, Systems, and Applications. Proceedings, 2000. XII, 366 pages. 2000.

Vol. 1910: D.A. Zighed, J. Komorowski, J. Żytkow (Eds.), Principles of Data Mining and Knowledge Discovery. Proceedings, 2000. XV, 701 pages. 2000.

Vol. 1916: F. Dignum, M. Greaves (Eds.), Issues in Agent Communication. X, 351 pages. 2000.

Vol. 1919: M. Ojeda-Aciego, I.P. de Guzman, G. Brewka, L. Moniz Pereira (Eds.), Logics in Artificial Intelligence. Proceedings, 2000. XI, 407 pages. 2000.

Vol. 1925: J. Cussens, S. Džeroski (Eds.), Learning Language in Logic. X, 301 pages 2000.

Vol. 1930: J.A. Campbell, E. Roanes-Lozano (Eds.), Artificial Intelligence and Symbolic Computation. Proceedings, 2000. X, 253 pages. 2001.

Vol. 1932: Z.W. Raś, S. Ohsuga (Eds.), Foundations of Intelligent Systems. Proceedings, 2000. XII, 646 pages.

Vol. 1934: J.S. White (Ed.), Envisioning Machuine Translation in the Information Future. Proceedings, 2000. XV, 254 pages. 2000.

Vol. 1937: R. Dieng, O. Corby (Eds.), Knowledge Engineering and Knowledge Management. Proceedings, 2000. XIII, 457 pages. 2000.

Vol. 1952: M.C. Monard, J. Simão Sichman (Eds.), Advances in Artificial Intelligence. Proceedings, 2000. XV, 498 pages. 2000.

Vol. 1955: M. Parigot, A. Voronkov (Eds.), Logic for Programming and Automated Reasoning. Proceedings, 2000. XIII, 487 pages. 2000.

Vol. 1967: S. Arikawa, S. Morishita (Eds.), Discovery Science. Proceedings, 2000. XII, 332 pages. 2000.

Vol. 1968: H. Arimura, S. Jain, A. Sharma (Eds.), Algorithmic Learning Theory. Proceedings, 2000. XI, 335 pages. 2000.

Vol. 1972: A. Omicini, R. Tolksdorf, F. Zambonelli (Eds.), Engineering Societies in the Agents World. Proceedings, 2000. IX, 143 pages. 2000.

Vol. 1979: S. Moss, P. Davidsson (Eds.), Multi-Agent-Based Simulation. Proceedings, 2000. VIII, 267 pages. 2001.

Vol. 1991: F. Dignum, C. Sierra (Eds.), Agent Mediated Electronic Commerce. VIII, 241 pages. 2001.

Vol. 1994: J. Lind, Iterative Software Engineering for Multiagent Systems. XVII, 286 pages. 2001.

Vol. 2003: F. Dignum, U. Cortés (Eds.), Agent-Mediated Electronic Commerce III. XII, 193 pages. 2001.

Vol. 2007: J.F. Roddick, K. Hornsby (Eds.), Temporal, Spatial, and Spatio-Temporal Data Mining. Proceedings, 2000. VII, 165 pages. 2001.

Vol. 2019: P. Stone, T. Balch, G. Kraetzschmar (Eds.), RoboCup 2000: Robot Soccer World Cup IV. XVII, 658 pages. 2001.

Vol. 2033: J. Liu, Y. Ye (Eds.), E-Commerce Agents. VI, 347 pages. 2001.

Vol. 2035: D. Cheung, G.J. Williams, Q. Li (Eds.), Advances in Knowledge Discovery and Data Mining – PAKDD 2001. Proceedings, 2001. XVIII, 596 pages. 2001.

Vol. 2039: M. Schumacher, Objective Coordination in Multi-Agent System Engineering. XIV, 149 pages. 2001.

Vol. 2056: E. Stroulia, S. Matwin (Eds.), Advances in Artificial Intelligence. Proceedings, 2001. XII, 366 pages. 2001.

Vol. 2070: L. Monostori, J. Váncza, M. Ali (Eds.), Engineering of Intelligent Systems. Proceedings, 2001. XVIII, 951 pages. 2001.

Lecture Notes in Computer Science